Colour Key

 Tundra

 Glacier

 Coniferous forest

 Mixed forest

 Deciduous forest

 Tropical rain forest

 Chacos

 Arable land

 Grassland, pasture

 Savanna

 Steppe, semi-desert

 Sand desert

 Other desert

 Mountain

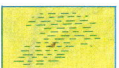 Marshland

 Salt lake

 Intermittent lake

 Salt desert, salt pan, dry lake

British Isles

Scale 1:1 250 000

LONDON — More than 1 000 000 inhabitants

Birmingham — 500 000 – 1 000 000 inhabitants

Leeds — 250 000 – 500 000 inhabitants

Bolton — 50 000 – 250 000 inhabitants

• Windsor — 10 000 – 50 000 inhabitants

○ Newhaven — Less than 10 000 inhabitants

LONDON — National capital

— Motorway

— Main road

— Other road

—+—+— Railway

— — — Train ferry

········ Car ferry

▨▨▨ International boundary

▭▭▭ National boundary

━━━ County boundary

•1344 Height above sea-level in metres

•159 Depth in metres

⊕ Airport

˙Stonehenge Prehistoric remains

⊢▷ Dam

⊨⊨ Canal

 Mountain

 Moorland, unimproved grassland

 Improved grassland

 Arable land

 Woodland

GEOGRAPHIA ATLAS OF THE WORLD

GEOGRAPHIA

ENCYCLOPEDIA OF THE EARTH

Visualisation	Lidman Production AB	Photographs	AAA photo
			Air France
Direction	Sven Lidman		Ragnar Andersson/TIOFOTO
			AP/Pressens bild
Text	Lars Bergquist		Bildarkiver/Ellbergs bilder
			Camera Press/IBL
Art Director	Sten Pettersson		Bo Dahlin/Bildhuset
Translator	Alan Tapsell		J. Arthur Dixon
			DPA/ Pressens bild
Consultants	Bertil Hedenstierna		ESA
	Ralph Mårtenson		Börje Försäter/Hallandsbild
Illustrators	Bob Chapman		J. Gaumy/Magnum
	David Cook		Claes Grundsten/Naturfotograferna
	John Flynn		Gunnar Gustafson
	Tony Gibbon		Mats Halling
	Rob Hillier		Bengt Hedberg/Naturbild
	John Potter		IBL
	Les Smith		Páll Imsland
	David West		Kjell Johansson/Bildhuset
	Maurice Wilson		Sture Karlsson/TIOFOTO
			Kungliga biblioteket
Photo research	Per Axel Nordfeldt		Frank W. Lane
			Örnulf Lautitzen
			J. Berry/Magnum
			Mount Wilson and Las Campanas observatories
			Norman Myers/TIOFOTO
			Ralph Mårtensson
			NASA
			Pål-Nils Nilsson/TIOFOTO
			Lars Olsson/Pressens bild
			G. Rodger/Magnum
			Ann Ronan
			SAS
			Per-Olle Stackman/TIOFOTO
			UPI/Pressens bild
			ZEFA
			Östasiatiska museet

THE WORLD IN MAPS
✸ ESSELTE MAP SERVICE

Geographia Ltd
17–21 Conway Street
London W1P 6JD

First published in 1984

Copyright © Esselte Map Service, Stockholm.

All rights reserved. No part of this publication may be reproduced, stored in a retrieval system, or transmitted, in any form or by any means, electronic, mechanical, photocopying, recording, or otherwise, without the prior permission of Geographia Ltd., and Esselte Map Serivce.

British Library Cataloguing in Publication Data

Geographia atlas of the world
  1. Atlases, British
  912   G1020
  ISBN 0-09-202840-3

Printed in Sweden

FOREWORD

Our understanding of the planet on which we live had, until fairly recently, been developed and sustained by a traditional approach to geographical concepts. Geography tuition presented a litany of facts to be learned by heart – populations, and places, crops, and countries, the highest mountain and the longest river.

Over the past two decades, however, Geography has developed into a multi-faceted science which acknowledges the complex and often delicate inter-relationships that exist between the different landscapes, climates and lifeforms of Earth and the impact that mankind has made upon all of these.

This new planetary geography demands new aids to understanding. The typical world atlas, the most fundamental learning medium in the study of Geography, has changed little over the years and, until now, remained firmly rooted in tradition. The Geographia Atlas of the World breaks with that tradition in representing the Earth as a series of inter-related environments, each environment being depicted on the maps by a particular colour. Hill shading, settlement patterns, communications and administrative divisions are overlaid to create a complete two-dimensional picture of every part of the Earth's surface.

The innovative collection of maps, together with the encyclopedia of the Earth in the first section, give a unique insight into our planet and the problems which beset it. The views of Earth from space, which have been seen by millions through the eye of a camera, emphasise the loneliness and remoteness of our globe in the void as well as its great beauty and fragility. The survival of mankind and the other species of Earth will depend ultimately upon understanding and enlightenment and upon our ability to maintain the delicately balanced environments which we presently call our own.

ENCYCLOPEDIA OF THE EARTH

Air	2–3

Air – the Earth's shield   4–5
The atmosphere and its different layers. Chemical and physical properties. Protection from dangerous radiation from outer space.

A matter of life and death   6–7
The air we breathe – the oxygen and carbon cycles. Interaction of the atmosphere with animals and green plants.

Airconditioning the Earth   8–9
Large scale air circulation. Earth's heat balance. Local and regional winds. Wind energy.

Among the clouds   10–11
Vertical circulation of the atmosphere. Fronts, clouds and precipitation. Thunder and lightning.

Seasons and climates   12–13
Climatic differences and seasonal variations. Climates of the world.

Signs in the sky   14–15
Pre-scientific weather forecasting. Weather data from meteorological balloons and satellites. Computerised forecasting.

Life in the air   16–17
Adaptations to aerial existence – from the flying saurians of the Mesozoic era to today's birds, bats and insects.

Man takes to the air   18–19
Man's dream of conquering the air, from Icarus and Leonardo da Vinci to the Wright brothers and Concorde.

Air routes   20–21
The modest beginnings of commercial air traffic and its expansion. Air lanes, traffic control, airports.

The leap into space   22–23
Early concepts of space and space travel. From primitive, naked eye astronomy to radio telescopes and space flights.

Man's impact on the atmosphere   24–25
Global air pollution. Acid rain over European forests. The burning of fossil fuels.

Water   26–27

Water, the prerequisite of life   28–29
The necessity of water for living organisms, including man, and its unique physical and chemical properties.

The water cycle   30–31
The circulation of water, from the seas through the atmosphere to the ground and back to the sea. Salt and fresh water. Irrigation.

The realm of ice   32–33
Ice Ages in history. The polar ice caps. Glaciers and glaciated landscapes. Winter – the annual Ice Age.

The oceans   34–35
The seas, their physical geography and characteristics. Oceans and marginal seas. Salinity.

The powerful sea   36–37
The energy of the sea. Waves, currents and tides. Beach processes. Harnessing power from the sea.

Aquatic life   38–39
The distribution of life in the sea. Adaptations for life in water. Ecological food chains.

Food from the deep   40–41
Sea and freshwater fisheries. Overfishing and international management of fisheries.

The conquest of the seas   42–43
The ages of discovery. Navigation. Exploration of the ocean depths.

Sea routes   44–45
Seafaring and navigation. Sea transport, different kinds of cargo.

Man's impact on the hydrosphere   46–47
Man's pollution of the oceans, and mismanagement of water resources. Mining the sea floor. Marine economic zones.

Earth 48–49

The crust 50–51
Alfred Wegener and the theory of plate tectonics. Types of bedrock and their origin. Vertical displacements in the crust.

The restless Earth 52–53
Plate tectonics – the crust in constant motion. The creation of mid-ocean ridges, mountain ranges and island chains. Earthquakes.

Weathering 54–55
Types of weathering. Weathering in cold, warm and humid climates and in limestone areas.

Erosion 56–57
Erosion processes, slope degradation and transportation. Denudation and the shaping of the landscape.

Life on land 58–59
The conquest of dry land by plants and animals and their adaptation to terrestrial life. Evolution of species into new ecological niches.

Tropical forests 60–61
Rain forests and deciduous monsoon forests, their flora and fauna and their climatic associations.

The grasslands 62–63
Savanna and steppe. The annual cycle of grasslands. Climatic control of vegetation and animal life. Effects of man's activities.

Deserts 64–65
Classification of deserts. Life in the deserts and the adaptation of animals and plants to heat and to lack of water. The spread of deserts worldwide.

Temperate forests 66–67
Deciduous, coniferous and mixed forests. Flora, fauna, silviculture and forestry.

The tundras 68–69
Environment and characteristics. How frost modifies the soil. Flora and fauna.

Mountain environments 70–71
Formation of mountains. Their physical setting in different parts of the world. Animal life, vegetation and land use.

Living off the land 72–73
Man's livelihood from the soil. Types of agriculture. Historical agriculture and distribution of agricultural systems.

Urbanization 74–75
Historical development of urbanized areas, from the small farming village through medieval towns to the modern conurbation.

Treasures underground 76–77
Mineral resources in the Earth's crust. Mining and metallurgy.

The ravaged Earth 78–79
Man's destruction of his own environment and the battle for survival.

Man's impact on the Earth's crust 80–81
Man as a geological force, remodelling the face of the planet.

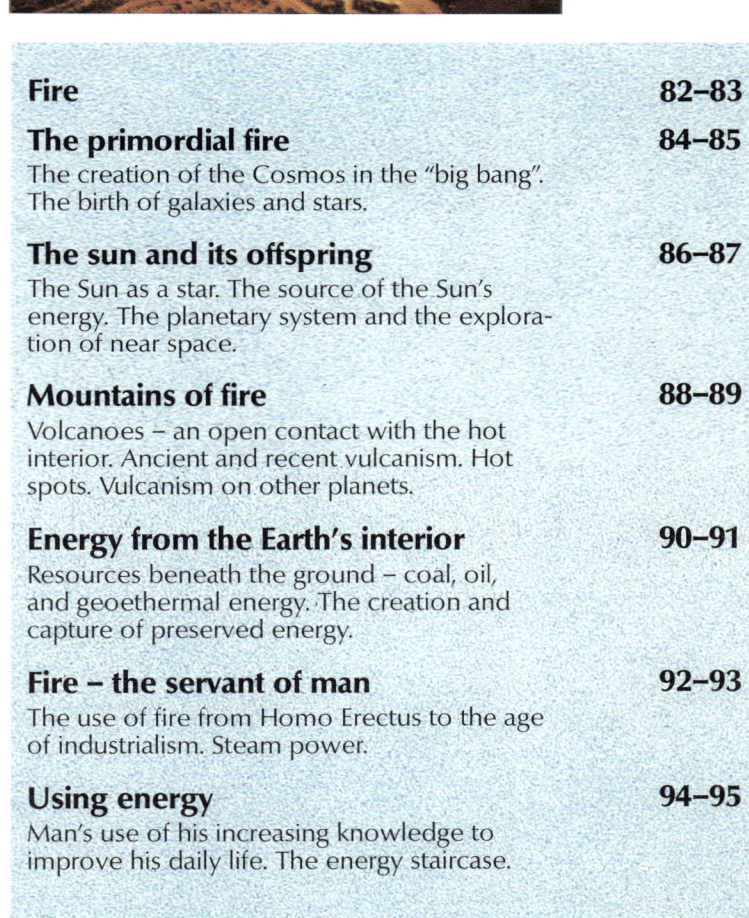

Fire 82–83

The primordial fire 84–85
The creation of the Cosmos in the "big bang". The birth of galaxies and stars.

The sun and its offspring 86–87
The Sun as a star. The source of the Sun's energy. The planetary system and the exploration of near space.

Mountains of fire 88–89
Volcanoes – an open contact with the hot interior. Ancient and recent vulcanism. Hot spots. Vulcanism on other planets.

Energy from the Earth's interior 90–91
Resources beneath the ground – coal, oil, and geothermal energy. The creation and capture of preserved energy.

Fire – the servant of man 92–93
The use of fire from Homo Erectus to the age of industrialism. Steam power.

Using energy 94–95
Man's use of his increasing knowledge to improve his daily life. The energy staircase.

THE WORLD IN MAPS

UNITED KINGDOM

Scotland   98–99
Environment

Northern England and Northern Ireland   100–101
Environment

Wales, Central and Southern England   102–103
Environment

United Kingdom   104
Population

United Kingdom   105
Industrial employment and energy

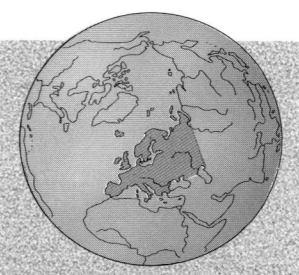

EUROPE

Europe   106–107
Population, political divisions, environment

Europe   108–109
Organic and inorganic production, climate, soils

The British Isles and Central Europe   110–111
Belgium, Czechoslovakia, Federal Republic of Germany, German Democratic Republic, Luxembourg, The Netherlands, Poland

Northern Europe   112–113
Denmark, Finland, Iceland, Norway, Sweden

South-West Europe   114–115
Austria, France, Italy, Liechtenstein, Portugal, Spain, Switzerland, Yugoslavia

The Balkans   116–117
Bulgaria, Cyprus, Greece, Hungary, Romania, Turkey

Western Soviet Union   118–119
European USSR, Western Siberia

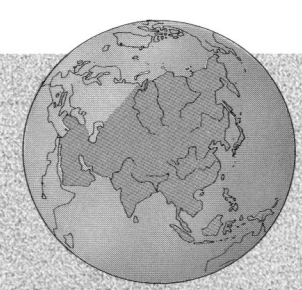

ASIA

Northern Asia   120–121
environment

Southern Asia   122–123
environment

Asia   124–125
organic and inorganic production, climate, soils

Asia   126–127
physical, precipitation, temperature, population, political divisions

The Middle East   128–129
Afghanistan, Iran, Pakistan

Eastern Soviet Union   130–131
Eastern Siberia, Mongolia

China and Japan   132–133
incl. Mongolia, North Korea, South Korea, Taiwan

India and South-East Asia   134–135
incl. Bangladesh, Bhutan, Burma, Kampuchea, Laos, Nepal, Sri Lanka, Thailand, Vietnam

The East Indies   136–137
Brunei, Indonesia, Malaysia, Philippines

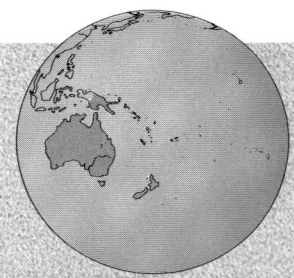

AUSTRALIA

Australasia   138–139
Population, political divisions, environment

Australasia   140–141
Organic and inorganic production, climate, soils

Australia   142–143

New Guinea and New Zealand   144–145

Oceania   146–147
Melanesia, Micronesia, Polynesia

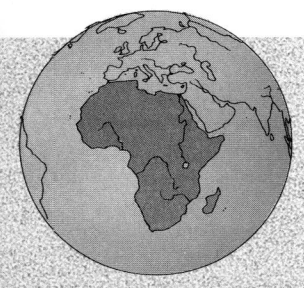

AFRICA

Africa 148–149
Population, political divisions, environment

Africa 150–151
Organic and inorganic production, climate, soils

North-West Africa 152–153
Algeria, Libya, Morocco, Mauretania, Niger, Tunisia

The Nile Valley and Arabia 154–155
Bahrain, Egypt, Iraq, Israel, Jordan, Kuwait, Lebanon, Oman, Qatar, Saudi-Arabia, Southern Yemen, Sudan, Syria, United Arab Emirates, Yemen

West Africa 156–157
Benin, Cameroon, Chad, Congo, Equatorial Guinea, Gabon, The Gambia, Ghana, Guinea, Guinea-Bissau, Ivory Coast, Liberia, Mali, Niger, Nigeria, Sao Tomé and Principe, Senegal, Sierra Leone, Togo, Upper Volta

East Africa 158–159
Central Africa, Ethiopia, Kenya, Sudan, Tanzania, Uganda, Zaire

Central and Southern Africa 160–161
Angola, Botswana, Comoros, Madagascar, Malawi, Mauritius, Mozambique, Namibia, Lesotho, South Africa, Swaziland, Zambia, Zimbabwe

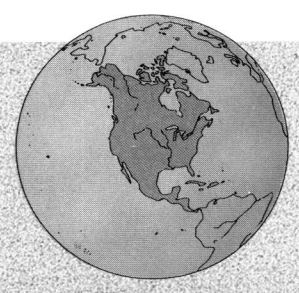

NORTH AMERICA

North America 162–163
Population, political divisions, environment

North America 164–165
Organic and inorganic production, climate, soils

Alaska and Western Canada 166–167
incl. the Aleutian Islands

Eastern Canada 168–169

The United States 170–171
incl. Mexico

Central America and the West Indies 172–173
Belize, The Caribbean Archipelago, Costa Rica, Cuba, El Salvador, Guatemala, Honduras, Mexico, Nicaragua

SOUTH AMERICA

South America 174–175
Population, political divisions, environment

South America 176–177
Organic and inorganic production, climate, soils

South America, north 178–179
Brazil, Colombia, Ecuador, Guyana, Panama, Peru, Surinam, Venezuela

South America, central 180–181
Bolivia, Brazil, Chile, Peru

South America, south 182–183
Argentina, Bolivia, Brazil, Chile, Paraguay, Uruguay

THE ARCTIC AND ANTARCTIC

The Arctic 184
Environment

Antarctica 185
Environment

THE WORLD

The World 186–187
Environment

The World 188–189
Climate

The World 190–191
Geology

The World 192–193
Oceans and the ocean floor

The World 194–195
Population

The World 196–197
Political divisions

The World 198–199
Energy

The World 200
Languages, religions, time zones

Glossary, Index 201–296

ENCYCLOPEDIA of the Earth

Research undertaken during the past few decades has resulted in a dramatic increase in scientific knowledge. In the fields of biology and the earth sciences, discoveries have led to a growing awareness of the inter-relationships between areas of knowledge which were previously regarded as totally separate disciplines. From mineralogy to micro-biology and from botany to bathymetry the pieces are fitting together like an immense jig-saw puzzle in which gaps remain but are fewer with each passing decade.

As knowledge expands, it becomes increasingly difficult to present a brief scientific account of the Earth as a whole since a systemised treatment with subjects grouped in distinct categories is no longer the ideal choice. The Encyclopedia of the Earth in this volume has turned to the pattern of the philosophical elements – air, water, fire and earth – to provide a basic framework within which a more free-ranging presentation can be achieved. It is said that a picture is worth a thousand words. Too often in books the pictures add nothing to the information in the text. In the following pages the co-ordination of words and pictures encompasses infinitely more in 96 pages than would have been possible with words alone.

Air

Of all the elements air is the most elusive and the most mystical. Among Greek thinkers of the 6th century BC Anaximenes of Miletus was the greatest philosopher on the subject of air. He elaborated upon the ancient concept that breath is the spirit of life in believing that air is the fundamental element of the earth: "Just as our soul, which is air, holds the body together so wind and air encompass our whole world." All the other elements, claimed Anaximenes, originated from densified or rarified air.

It was not until the 17th century, however, that scientists like the Frenchman Pascal and the Italian Torricelli discovered how to measure air pressure and so transformed the Greek philosopher's mystical, fundamental element into a tangible physical substance. A century later chemists discovered that air is a mixture of gases and identified its primary elements as nitrogen and oxygen.

The science of meteorology was developed in the 19th century and gradually replaced the old rules of thumb of peasant and seaman with more dependable weather forecasts. The meteorologists of the present century have studied the outer strata of the atmosphere in detail. This is a part of geophysics, the science of the Earth as a planet.

The Earth's atmosphere, in the depths of which we dwell, protects us against deadly radiation from outer space and provides us with the oxygen that our life processes depend upon. It evens out what would otherwise be unendurable extremes of heat and cold and transports moisture from the oceans across the continents in a never ending global circulation system.

Oxygen is a product of living green plants and hence was absent from the primeval atmosphere. A precondition for the development of life on Earth was that no free oxygen existed to oxidize and so break down the first unprotected living molecules. It took billions of years to build up the present oxygen content of our atmosphere.

The type of atmosphere that will surround our world in the future is a vital consideration and one that is dependent largely upon man himself. Only if we halt the destruction of the continents' forests and the poisoning of the oceans' plankton and cease using the air as a sort of universal sewer, can higher organisms hope to survive on our planet.

Air – the Earth's shield

At sea level the atmospheric pressure is about 1,000 millibars (mb). The measurement for this pressure was formerly expressed as 760 mm. mercury (mm Hg).

At ground level the atmosphere contains not only nitrogen but also oxygen and carbon dioxide, vital substances for plants and animals alike. It protects us from violent alternations between hot and cold and against being bombarded by charged particles—cosmic radiation—and meteorites.

The atmosphere also functions as an immense energy transport system between the hot tropical and cold polar regions. The efficiency of the atmosphere as a heat carrier depends on its humidity. Part of this moisture content is discernible as cloud, mist or haze. It is the capacity of water to retain heat when vaporized and then release it during condensation which evens out the climate on Earth and makes both tropics and polar regions habitable.

It is only the lower 80 km. of our atmosphere, however, which is of the same chemical composition as the air at ground level and even within this zone conditions vary so greatly that we usually divide it into three distinct strata. The lowest is the *troposphere* extending 10–18 km. upward from the ground. Practically all our weather is contained within this stratum and only the very highest tropical storm clouds reach up to the lower limit of the *stratosphere*. Here ultra-violet light from the sun forms a layer of ozone, triatomic oxygen, which absorbs the deadly radiation from outer space. The *mesosphere* is a transitional stratum where the air pressure falls to a mere 10,000th part of what it is at sea-level.

The uppermost region of the mesosphere is the threshold to outer space. Because of the intense solar radiation the upper atmosphere is ionized and electrically conductive. This stratum is known as the *ionosphere*. Charged particles from the sun—electrons, protons and heavier atomic nuclei—moving within the rarefied gas produce the aurora, a discharge phenomenon similar to that in a fluorescent tube. The outermost stratum from about 400 km. outward might best be described as condensed outer space. Here there exists practically nothing but hydrogen and helium, the thin gas between the stars.

Satellites launched by man orbit the Earth at altitudes ranging from 300–400 km. up to c. 36,000 km. in the case of the geostationary communication satellites.

The aurora often appears at altitudes of up to 1,000 km. where the blast of electrically charged particles from the sun encounters the Earth's atmosphere.

X-rays and short wave ultra-violet radiation from the sun is largely absorbed by the atmosphere. Certain wavelengths of electromagnetic radiation reach the ground however. Our eyes have evolved to utilize this radiation alone, which is why we call it "visible light".

Cosmic radiation consists of high energy particles from both the sun and from radiation sources far away in the universe. When such a particle encounters one of our atmosphere's atoms it gives rise to a shower of secondary particles.

Military satellites for reconnaissance often fly relatively low so as to be able to detect objects as small as possible on the ground. Air resistance at such low altitudes reduces the lifespan of these satellites.

Probe rockets are used for the scientific study of the upper regions of the atmosphere.

Meteors become extremely hot and gasify through friction on entering the atmosphere. These "falling stars" are caused by particles no larger than sand grains. Only the largest meteors reach the ground.

Charged layers in the ionosphere reflect radio short waves which can rebound several times around the Earth.

The lowest aurora can occur as far down as the ionosphere.

Noctilucent clouds are the only clouds above the troposphere. These are the subject of intensive study.

The ozone layer in the atmosphere halts most of the ultra-violet radiation.

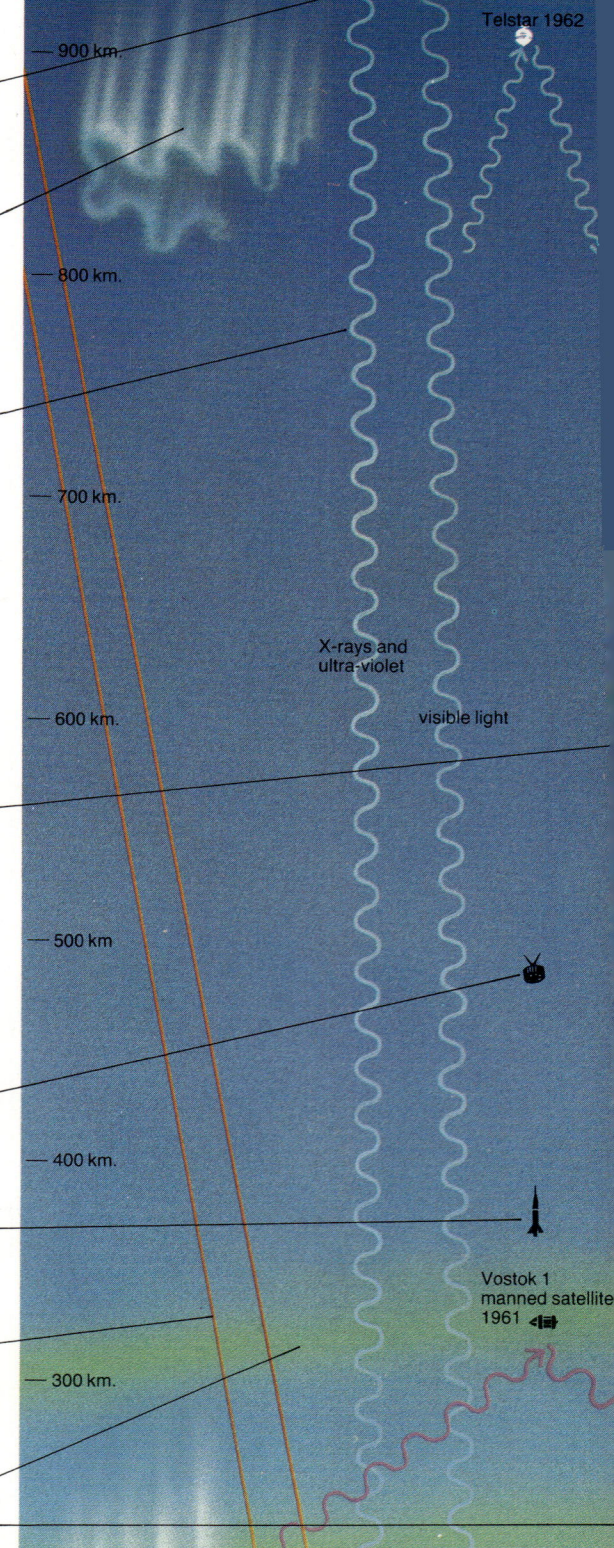

The lower atmosphere

Balloons filled with helium carried man to an altitude of 20 km. as early as the 1930's.

The air pressure in the lower stratosphere is one tenth of what it is at sea level.

Jet aircraft with pressurized cabins operate routinely at altitudes of 10 km. and more. The absence of weather changes up here makes flying safer.

Tropical thunder clouds rise to the limit between troposphere and stratosphere: the tropopause.

The highest mountains rise more than eight km. above sea level. But even at four km. most people have difficulty in breathing because of the rarefied air.

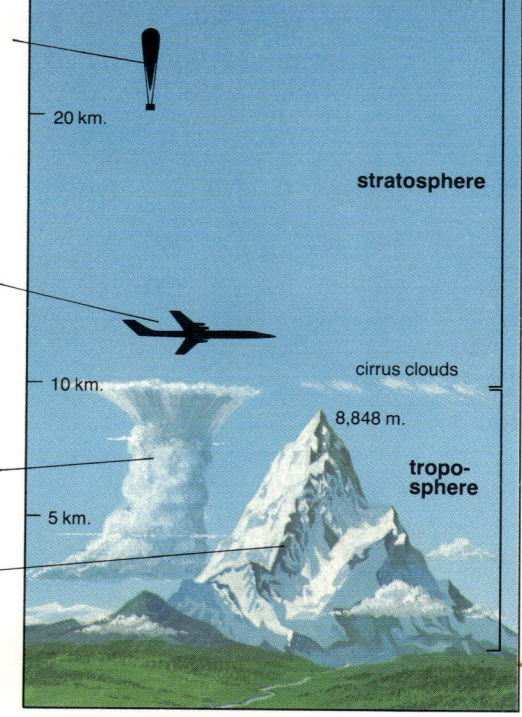

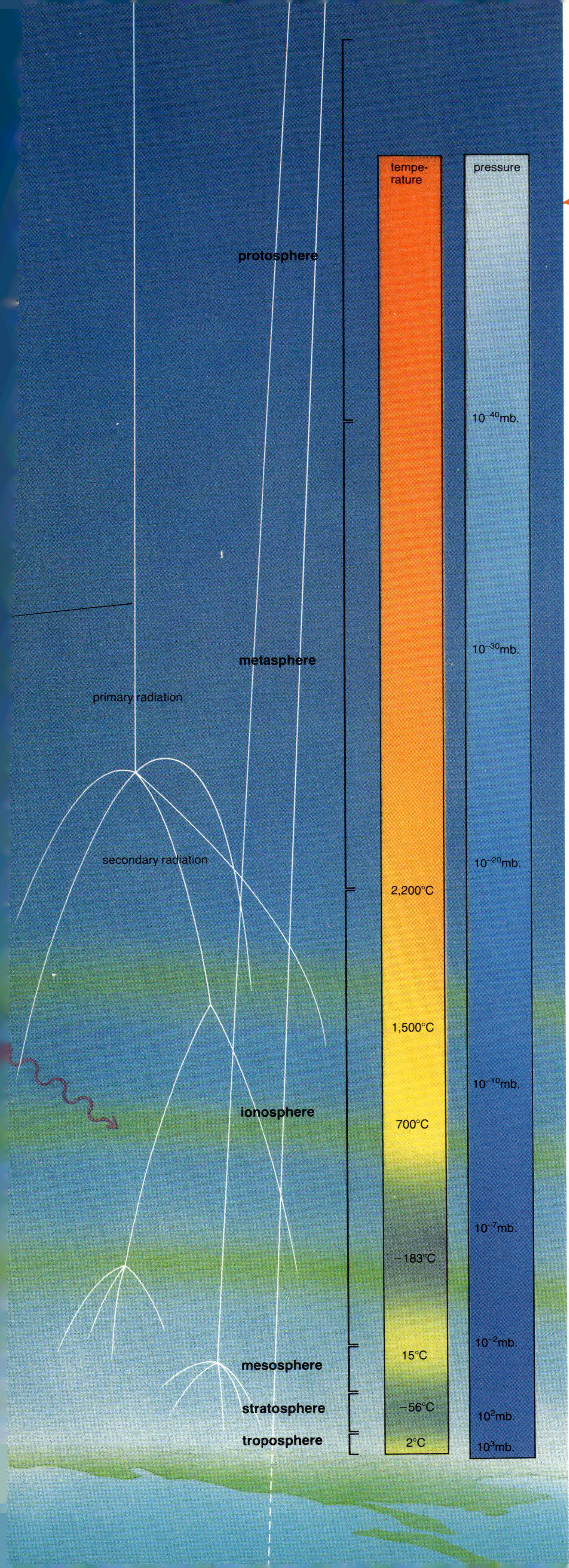

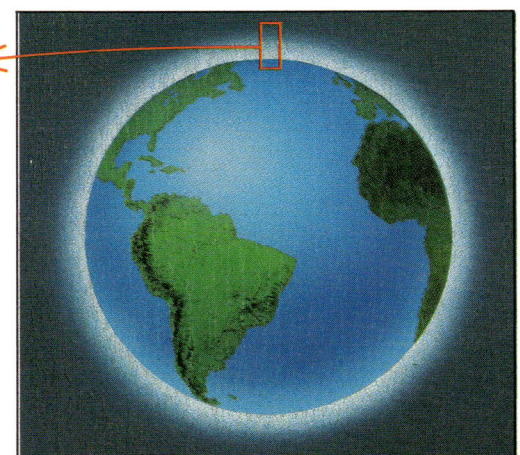

The atmosphere from outside
The 1,000 km. of the large diagram is shown (left) in correct proportion to the Earth. It is only the innermost 10–18 km., the troposphere, that has sufficient water vapour and dust for it to be visible to the naked eye. Beyond that is the blackness of space (photo below). Clouds seem to hang immediately above the ground.

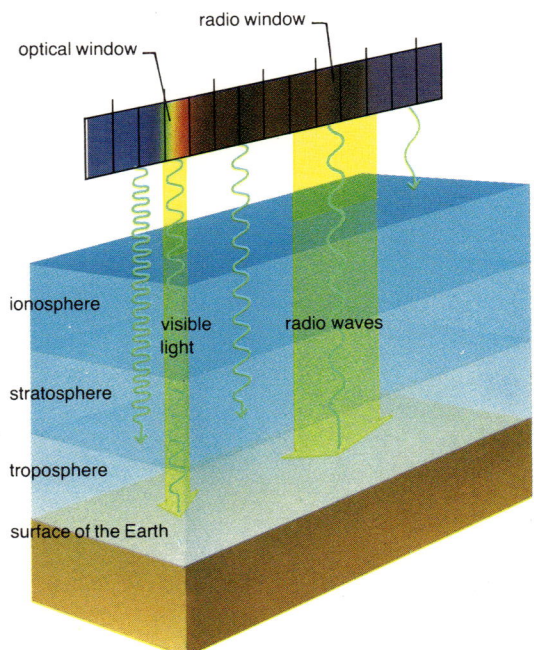

Two "windows"
The atmosphere is impenetrable for most types of electro-magnetic radiation. Only two "windows" admit radiation with distinctly limited wavelengths. The "optical window" is open for visible light and the adjoining parts of the ultraviolet and infrared areas; the "radio window" admits certain radio wavelengths. Short radio waves which normally pass through the atmosphere without hindrance can, however, sometimes bounce off charged layers in the ionosphere (see large diagram).

5

A matter of life and death

The Earth's atmosphere is associated with the life processes by two vital cycles: oxygen and carbon.

Oxygen is a decisive factor in the energy systems of nearly all plants and animals. These living organisms liberate energy by oxidizing large organic molecules, obtaining the oxygen through respiration. This oxygen consumption is compensated for by a corresponding process: photosynthesis or assimilation, whereby green plants build up their energy-abundant substance as they grow. This fundamental process, without which life on Earth would be impossible, is driven by solar energy and takes, as raw materials, hydrogen from water and carbon from carbon dioxide. Oxygen is the most important by-product of photosynthesis. Most living creatures have evolved complex defences against what is, to the delicate organic substances within their cells, a corrosive poisonous gas. Only in hot springs in the depths of the oceans, in seabed mud and in a few other extremely oxygen–deficient environments do there exist anaerobic bacteria, i.e. bacteria which are not dependent upon oxygen and which can survive without protection.

Carbon is the fundamental component in all organic compounds. It is the primary element of life. There is only a limited supply of carbon, however, and consequently it must be constantly re-cycled. The carbon in the biosphere—the Earth's thin film of life circulates continuously through death, living matter and death again. Carbon in the atmosphere is fixed by green plants, the autotrophs. It thus becomes part of the biomass of both these and the heterotrophs—all of us from fungi to mankind who are not endowed with chlorophyll but must sustain ourselves by consuming organic matter that the autotrophs have synthesized.

Our respiration process and likewise the decomposers, which dispose of our waste products and ultimately of our bodies, restore the carbon to the atmosphere in the form of carbon dioxide. The very fact that the carbon in the air is in the form of carbon dioxide means that the oxygen and carbon cycles are closely interwoven with each other.

These two cycles are connected in turn with cycles on a larger geological scale. Ultra-violet radiation dissociates water into hydrogen and oxygen in the outer atmosphere and some oxygen is fixed by the oxidizing of certain minerals. The carbon cycle is more closed, but carbon is fixed as calcium carbonate, in the form of limestone and chalk. In this part of the carbon cycle the duration is reckoned in millions of years.

Leaves absorb solar energy through a photo-chemical process conducted by the green substance chlorophyll.

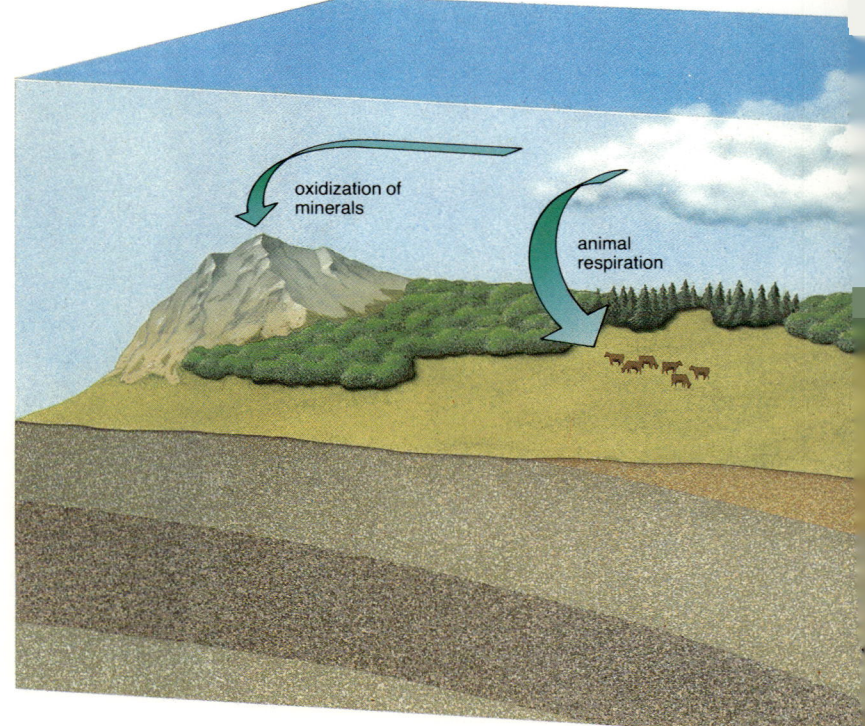

The oxygen cycle

The air contains about 21 % oxygen and this concentration is the result of millions of years of green plant photosynthesis. Such oxygen as may have existed in the primeval atmosphere has long since leaked away into outer space. Forests and plankton produce the greater part of the oxygen content in the atmosphere. Deforestation and oceanic pollution can thus have dangerous consequences by reducing the production of the oxygen that we breathe. In their turn the respiratory processes of animals and plants fix the oxygen, which is subsequently released as a component of carbon dioxide—a cycle analyzed in the panorama below.

The carbon cycle

Carbon dioxide is a common component in the atmosphere of the planets and is present, for example, around both Venus and Mars. The average CO_2 content of the Earth's atmosphere is only 0.033%. The free oxygen content of the air is over 600 times greater. The total quantity of carbon in the atmosphere is in fact no more than about one and half times that which is fixed in the living organisms. In other words carbon is in short supply and must be recycled much more rapidly than oxygen. Enormous quantities of carbon dioxide are dissolved in the oceans, but this carbon is not directly available to the 90 % (reckoned as per biomass) of all living organisms which are on land. The carbon cycle is complex but amounts mainly to carbon being fixed in green plant photosynthesis and liberated through breathing.

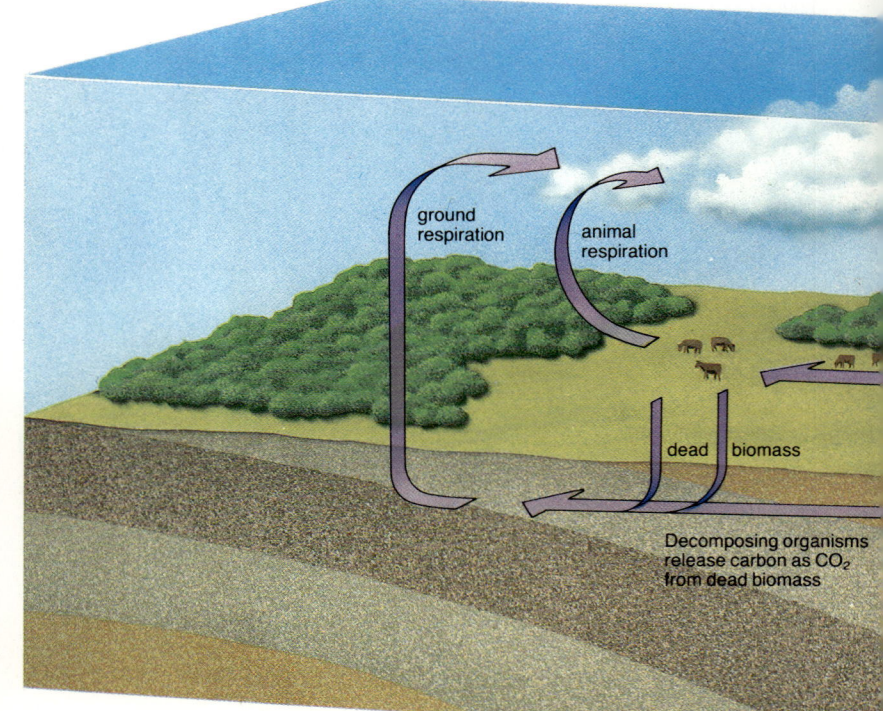

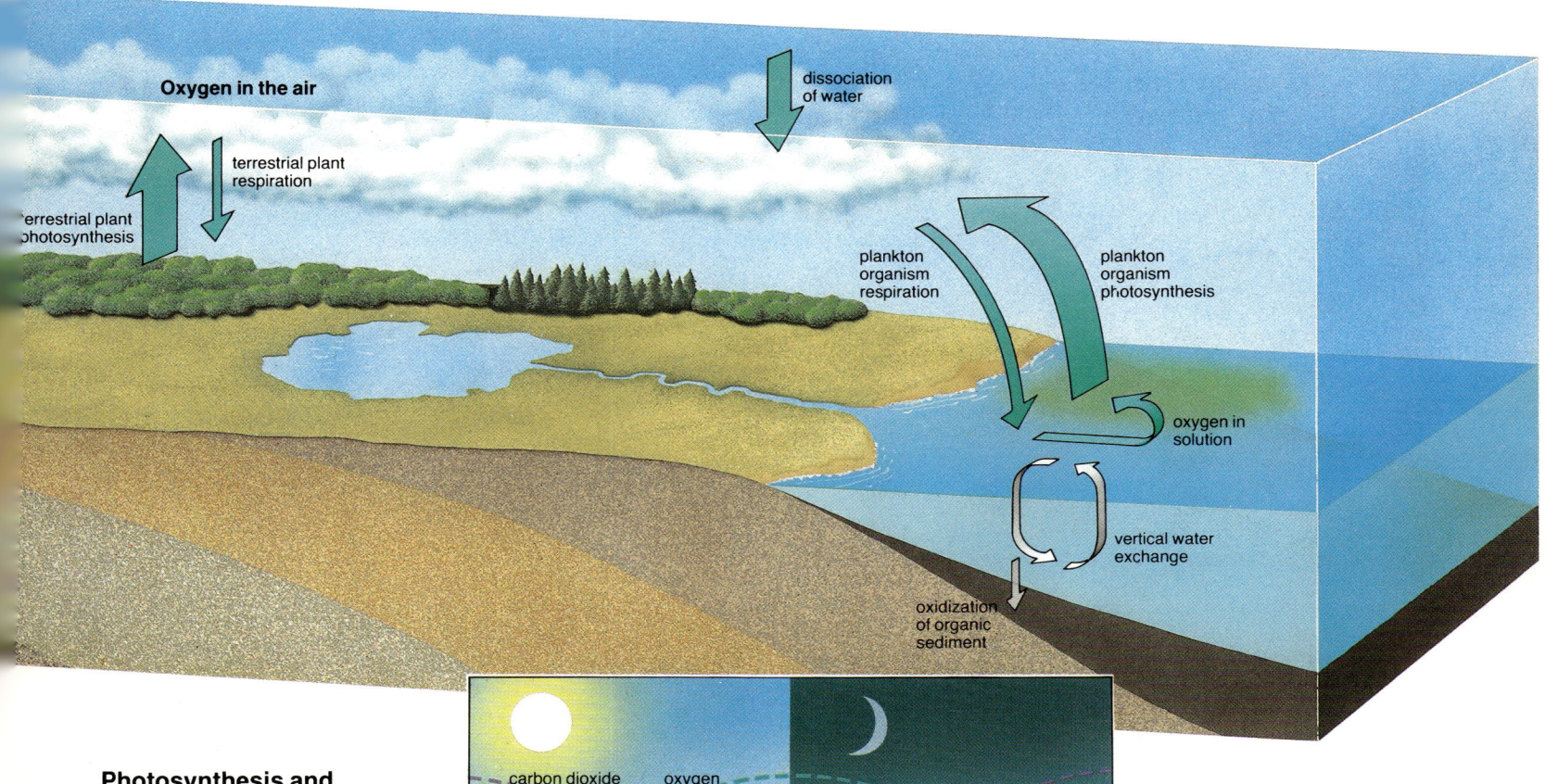

Photosynthesis and respiration

Photosynthesis extracts carbon from the atmosphere and the respiration of the green plants liberates carbon. The carbon dioxide content of the atmosphere is thus determined by a tug of war between these two processes. The life processes of animals have not affected the outcome to any great extent, since more than 90 % of all the living biomass is in plant-life. Only now with his combustion of coal and oil is man threatening to disrupt this equilibrium.

The forest respires around the clock
Photosynthesis takes place in daylight, increasing the oxygen level of the atmosphere and decreasing the CO_2 content. After dark photosynthesis ceases but respiration continues. The CO_2 level rises, reaching a peak around dawn when it can be more than 20 % higher than average.

Where is the carbon?

There may be some 40,000 billion tons of carbon available in the biosphere for the life processes. This is distributed approximately as follows (all figures are in billions of tons):

Atmosphere	700
Dissolved in the oceans	35,000
Living biomass: on land	450
in the sea	<5
Dead biomass	3,700

Airconditioning the Earth

The circulation of air in the atmosphere is activated by convection, the transference of heat resulting from the fact that warm gases or fluids rise while cold gases or fluids sink. For example: if one wall of a room is heated whilst the opposite wall is cooled, air will rise against the warm wall and flow across the ceiling to the cold wall before descending to flow back across the floor to the warm wall again.

The real atmosphere, however, is like a very long room with a very low ceiling. The distance from equator to pole is 10,000 km. while the "ceiling height" to the tropopause is only about 10 km. The air therefore splits up into a number of smaller loops or "convection cells". Between the equator and each pole there are three such cells and within these the circulation is mainly north-south.

Large-scale air conditioning
The result of this circulation is a flow of heat energy towards the poles and a levelling out of the climate so that both equatorial and polar regions are habitable. The atmosphere generally retains its state of equilibrium as every north-going air current is counter-balanced by a south-going one. In the same way depressions at lower levels in the troposphere are counter-balanced by areas of high pressure in the upper levels, and vice versa. The atmospheric transference of heat is closely associated with the movement of moisture between sea and continent and between different latitudes. Moist air can transport much greater quantities of energy than dry air.

Because the belts of convection cells run east to west, both climate and weather vary according to latitude. In the equatorial convergence zone (the doldrums), and around the Tropic of Cancer and Tropic of Capricorn known as "horse latitudes", sailing ships could drift for weeks unable to steer, while the "roaring forties" of the South Atlantic (40°–50°S) were notorious among mariners for their terrible winds. Climatic zones are particularly distinguishable at sea where there are no land masses to disturb the pattern.

Man and the winds
For thousands of years mankind has been dependent upon the winds: they brought rain to the land and carried ships across the seas. Thus the westerly wind belts, the trade winds and the monsoon winds of the global circulation system, have been known to us for many centuries. As recently as the present century Arab ships sailed on the south-west monsoon winds from East Africa to India and back again on the north-east monsoon winds, without need of a compass. The winds alone were sufficient.

It was not until the development of the balloon at the end of the 18th century, however, that it became possible to study meteorological conditions at high altitudes. The balloon is still a significant research device although today it carries a radar reflector or a set of instruments and a radio transmitter, rather than the scientists themselves. Nowadays high-flying aircraft and satellites are also important aids to meteorology. Through them we have discovered the west to east jet stream. This blows at speeds of up to 500 km/h at altitudes of 9,000–10,000 m. along the border between the Arctic and temperate zone convection belts.

Weather fronts
The circulation within the different convection cells is greater than the exchange of air between them and therefore the temperature in two cells that are close to each other can differ greatly. Consequently the borders between the different convection cells are areas in which warm and cold air masses oppose each other, advancing and withdrawing. In the northern hemisphere the dividing line between the Arctic and temperate convection zones is the polar front, and it is this which determines the weather in northern Europe and North America. This front is unstable, weaving sometimes northward, sometimes southward, of an average latitude of 60°N. Depressions become trapped within the deep concavities of this front and these subsequently move eastward along it with areas of rain and snowfall. In this way global air circulation determines not only the long-term climate but also the immediate weather.

Global circulation
The large-scale circulation of air takes place through convection. Warm air rises at the equator and then flows north or south, while corresponding flows of cold air move from the poles towards the equator. Each hemisphere has three belts of convection cells and the circulation within each belt is greater than it is between them.

If the Earth did not rotate, the winds would blow largely in a north/south direction. The earth's rotation causes them to veer off course (oblique arrows). The model above is schematic and presupposes a planet totally covered by sea. The continents create local wind systems.

At ground level, air streams towards the equator from both hemispheres. An equatorial convergence zone runs along the equator and seafarers of the past sought to avoid this because of its feeble and undependable winds. The exchange of air between the northern and southern hemispheres is a fairly slow process.

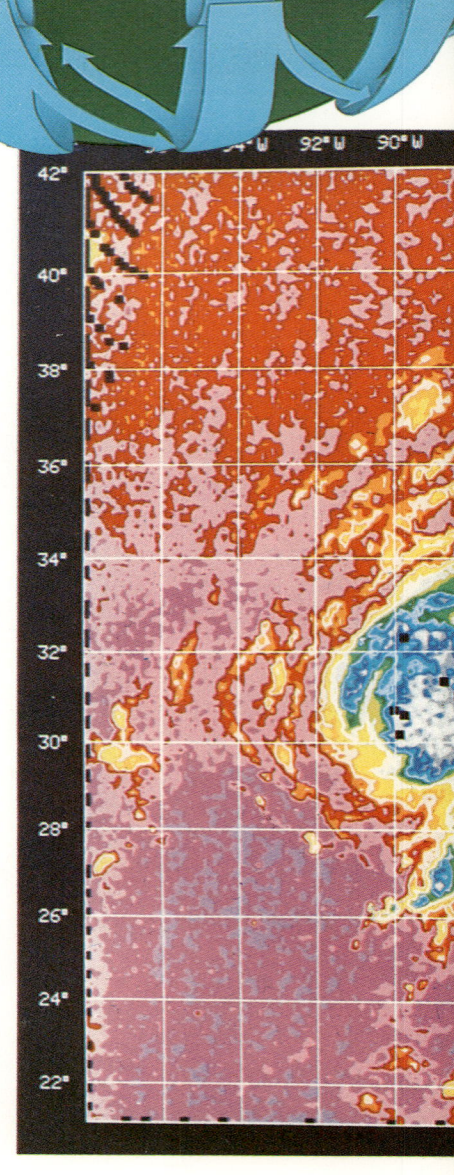

A tropical cyclone
A hurricane in the Gulf of Mexico heading towards the US coast is kept under surveillance by temperature sensing instruments in a weather satellite. At the ground station, numeric data is converted into a chart (right). The nucleus of the hurricane is a small but very intense depression and the spiral of air on its way into this "eye" is clearly visible.

The colours are produced by the computer which constructs the picture and these indicate the temperatures in the upper troposphere at about 10,000 m. The colour scale, far right, is graduated in Kelvins. One Kelvin (K) equates to 1°C., but the scale's zero is absolute zero, −273.2°C.

Utilizing the wind

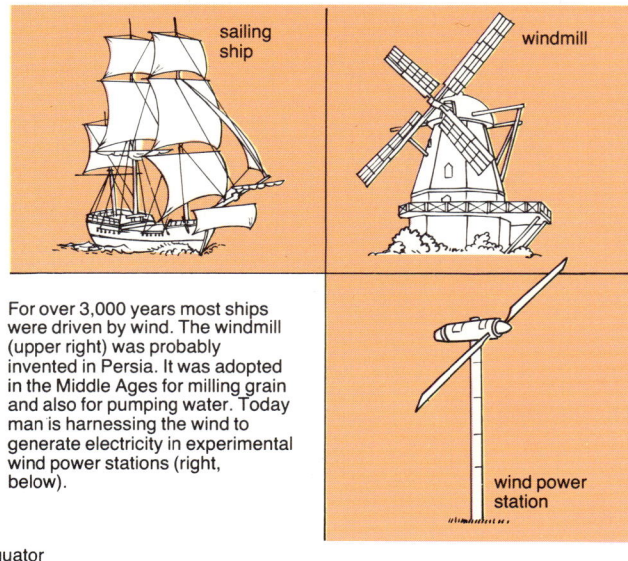

For over 3,000 years most ships were driven by wind. The windmill (upper right) was probably invented in Persia. It was adopted in the Middle Ages for milling grain and also for pumping water. Today man is harnessing the wind to generate electricity in experimental wind power stations (right, below).

Local circulation

In the northern hemisphere the Earth's rotation deflects the winds so that they blow in a clockwise direction around a high pressure area (an anticyclone) but counterclockwise around a depression (a cyclone). These directions are reversed in the southern hemisphere.

high pressure — low pressure

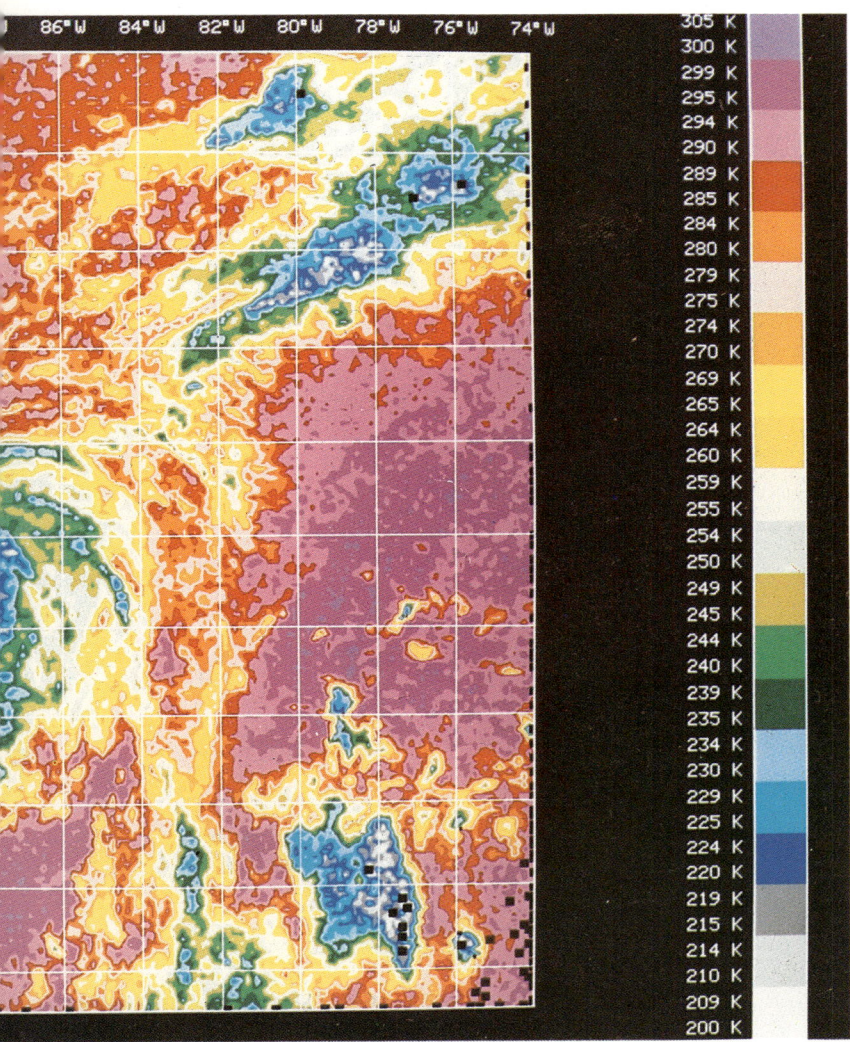

Mountains, winds and rain

When a mountain range lies right across the direction of the prevailing wind the upward moving air on the windward side of the range is cooled down and the moisture precipitates as rain. It is for this reason that the hills in Assam get as much as 250 cm. rain in one month during the south-west monsoon. The terrain on the leeward side is in the "rain-shadow" and has a dry climate.

Diurnal winds

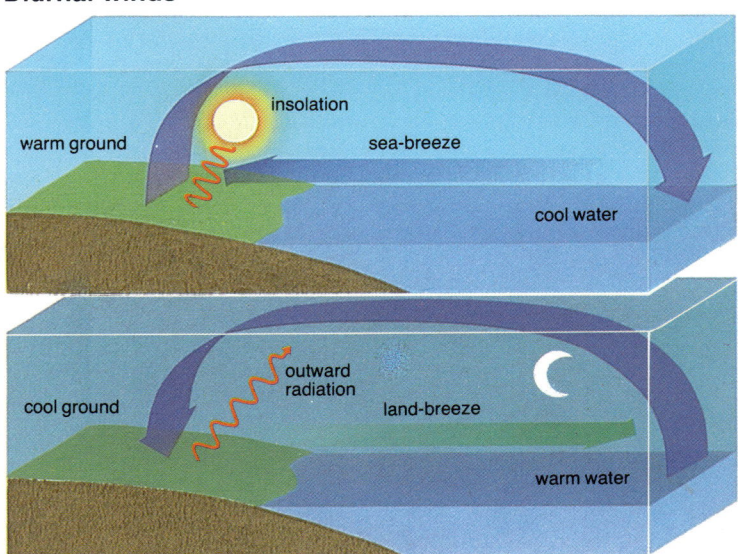

During the day the land is warmed more rapidly than the sea and the air over the land rises. Its place is taken by cooler air from over the water, creating a sea-breeze. At night the grounds cools off quickly while the water retains its warmth. The air then rises over the sea instead, causing a land-breeze. At higher altitudes these directions are reversed, unless larger scale wind systems upset the pattern.

Seasonal winds

The monsoons are large scale sea- and land-breezes, activated by annual rather than daily temperature changes. They give rise to rainy and dry periods in south and east Asia.

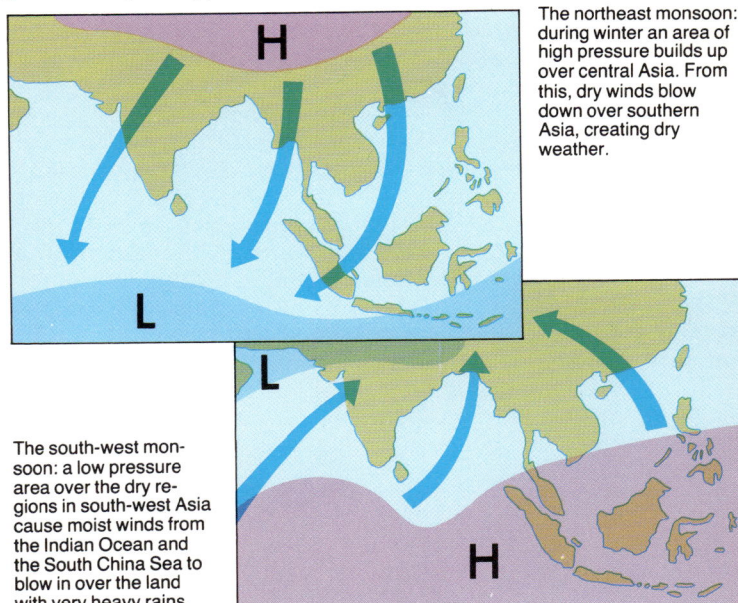

The northeast monsoon: during winter an area of high pressure builds up over central Asia. From this, dry winds blow down over southern Asia, creating dry weather.

The south-west monsoon: a low pressure area over the dry regions in south-west Asia cause moist winds from the Indian Ocean and the South China Sea to blow in over the land with very heavy rains.

9

Among the clouds

The solar energy which heats the Earth's atmosphere is not only responsible for the global circulation system, it also causes local air circulation. The global circulation takes place mainly in a horizontal direction, moving warm air from the tropics to the polar regions and cold air in the opposite direction. Local circulation on the other hand functions mainly vertically, giving rise to upwinds and fall winds. We cannot see these vertical winds and neither do we feel them—except in an aircraft when turbulence can produce uncomfortably "bumpy" intervals. Every day we see a by-product of the vertical winds: the clouds above our heads. Some well-known local winds, such as the mistral and the sirocco, are mainly "horizontal" winds.

Air and water
The air in the troposphere always contains a certain amount of water vapour. The actual quantity depends upon evaporation: over the sea the humidity is high, over the desert it is very low. There is also a maximum quantity and that is related to the temperature. At 20°C. a cubic metre of air can contain as much as 17.3 g. of water. If the temperature is reduced to zero the same air volume can only retain 4.9 g. of water, the rest precipitating in the form of microscopically small droplets. These droplets form around condensation nuclei which can either be dust particles or small salt crystals from the surface of the sea. When this takes place at ground level it is called mist, while at higher altitudes it produces clouds. These droplets are so tiny that they can remain suspended almost indefinitely on even the slightest upwinds. If they merge into larger drops then they fall as rain.

Mountains, fronts and thermals
How can a warm air mass be cooled down rapidly? In certain instances this heat loss can occur through thermal conduction when it passes over cold ground or an icy sea, or through radiation at night. But a swifter means is to force the air mass upward so that it expands because of the reduced pressure around it. This sort of adiabatic expansion (expansion without more heat being added) is always followed by a fall in temperature.

A mountain range right across the direction of the wind can, naturally, compel the air to rise. In this way rain clouds are often formed on the windward side of mountains or hills while the lee side is in a "rain shadow". For example, the Himalayas cause the moist monsoon winds to release most of the rain over northern India while the Tibetan plateau remains dry. Fronts function like moving mountain ranges: along a cold front air wedges its way in beneath a warm air mass, forcing the latter upward, often with violent rain and thunder storms. A warm front occurs when warm air moves upward over a cold air mass and displaces it.

Thermal upwinds, known simply as "thermals" by glider pilots, derive from local heating of the ground and the air above it by the sun. The warm air rises because of its temperature and humidity in relation to the surrounding air mass. When the air reaches a certain altitude, the "cloud base", the water vapour condenses. Billowy cumulus is thus formed over this level.

The thunder storm
Strong upwinds, either of a thermal nature or deriving from the passage of a cold front, are often followed by thunder storms. The circulating water droplets in the cloud develop different electrical charges and enormous voltage differences build up in various parts of the cloud until these are finally discharged as lightning. The interior of a thundercloud is a complex environment, however, and we are still not entirely sure how the positive and negative charges are separated and conveyed to different parts of the cloud. The total energy of an electrical storm can be of the same magnitude as in a nuclear explosion. Only a small proportion of this energy is released in the lightning flashes. Though the voltage is high the amperage is low; so their power is only modest.

Cold and warm fronts determine the changes in the weather in the temperate latitudes. When cold air (left) pushes its way in beneath warm air it often results in a severe storm. A warm front (right) occurs when warm, usually moist air moves in over the cold air. The result is then steady rain rather than heavy showers. The cold front is always steeper than the warm front; the slope angles are approx. 5° and 2.5°, respectively. The different fronts are heralded by typical cloud forms.

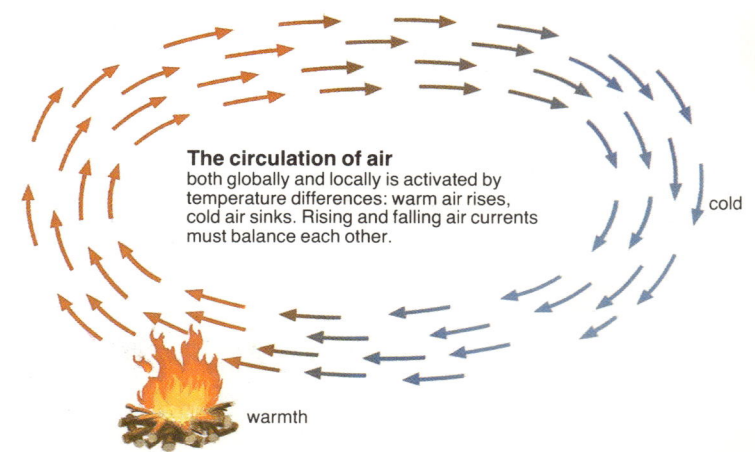

The circulation of air both globally and locally is activated by temperature differences: warm air rises, cold air sinks. Rising and falling air currents must balance each other.

Precipitation

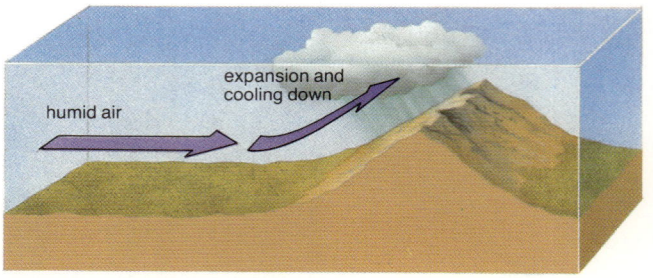

Mountains and rain
When moist winds are forced upward by mountains in their path, the resultant reduction in pressure at higher altitudes causes a fall in temperature and the formation of cloud. In this way places south of the Himalayas can get 250 cm. of rain in a month.

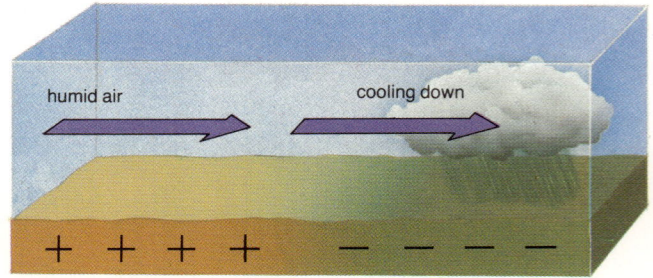

Cold and rain
A cooling process can also occur as a result of thermal conduction to the cold ground or cold water, or through radiation. This process also produces mist, i.e. cloud at ground level.

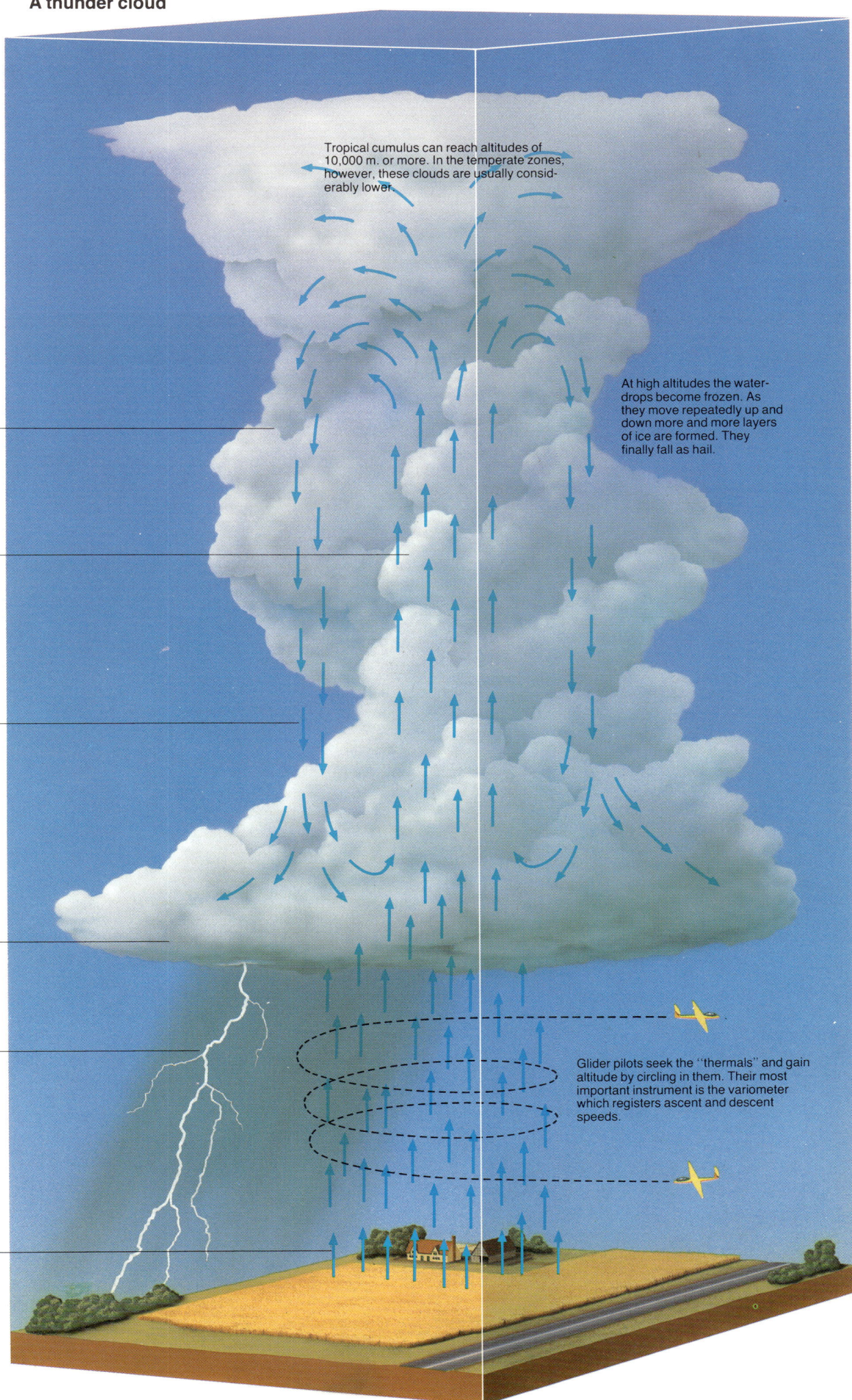

A thunder cloud

Cumulus is not only fine weather cloud. It can turn into thunder cloud (Cumulonimbus or Cumulus tonans) and sometimes the cloud assumes an "anvil" shape (Cumulonimbus incus, right).

The upper part of the cloud often consists of ice crystals. The level at which the waterdrops freeze depends on the temperature.

Upwinds sometimes attaining gale force blow inside the cloud. They are strongest immediately above the cloud base, as condensation releases heat, increasing the "buoyancy" of the air.

Fall winds are not as strong as the upwinds but can be quite violent. Fall and upwinds give rise to turbulence which has been known to break the wings of light aircraft.

The cloud base is that level at which the temperature allows condensation to commence.

Thunder storms occur in clouds with violent circulation. Air currents form a gigantic electrostatic generator.

Warm air gathers over warm ground until it loses contact with the surface and ascends like a hot-air balloon. It is then replaced by cool air which in its turn becomes warmer.

Tropical cumulus can reach altitudes of 10,000 m. or more. In the temperate zones, however, these clouds are usually considerably lower.

At high altitudes the waterdrops become frozen. As they move repeatedly up and down more and more layers of ice are formed. They finally fall as hail.

Glider pilots seek the "thermals" and gain altitude by circling in them. Their most important instrument is the variometer which registers ascent and descent speeds.

11

Seasons and climates

The Earth orbits the sun along an elliptical path and the sun, the central body in our planetary system, is at one of the focal points of this ellipse. In astronomical terms the distance between Earth and the sun does not vary greatly. The average distance is a little less than 150 million km. The Earth orbits the sun in just over 365 days 6 hours, the odd hours making up a leap day once every four years.

It is easy enough to comprehend that the seasonal variations are not a result of the Earth's varying distance from the sun—if that were the case then both northern and southern hemispheres would have summer at the same time. Seasonal variations in temperature and in hours of day and night derive from the Earth's oblique axis which leans one hemisphere and then the other towards the sun. If the Earth lacked an atmosphere and a hydrosphere then this oblique axis would be of no particular consequence. Our sister planet, the moon, has nothing in the way of seasons. On Earth, however, the movements of both air and sea are activated in a daily or annual cycle by differences in the distribution of incoming solar energy over the Earth's surface. Winds, waves and currents, the humid warmth of the rain forests and the bitter cold of the tundra; all these arise from local and periodic variations. The consequences extend even further: Climate determines vegetation type and the fauna that derives its nourishment from the plants. Every type of climate has its own particular ecological system.

Climate is the mean value of weather. Climatologists calculate this average over a 30-year period so as to produce representative figures upon which to base their classifications. In the 1910's the Austrian Köppen drew up a classification of the world's climates founded on only two variables: temperature and precipitation. This is still generally used and is the basis for the climate chart shown here. Other variables can be used: the balance between precipitation and evaporation, the number of hours of sunshine, elevation above sea-level, the balance between inward and outward radiation, and so on. The radiation balance, in particular, is of fundamental significance. The hot days and cold nights of the Sahara, for example, result from the fact that the dry atmosphere in no way hinders either the daytime inward radiation or the outward radiation at night.

The coldness of winter is intensified when white snow and ice reflect back a large proportion of the incoming solar heat. Distance from the sea causes the difference between a continental and a maritime climate. The continental climate tends to be dry with great differences between summer and winter temperatures, while the maritime climate is more humid and has a more even temperature. At Verkhoyansk on the Siberian tundra, the difference between the mean temperatures of the warmest and coldest months of the year is 68°C. In Godthåb on the west coast of Greenland it is only 17°C.

Scientists are attempting to learn something about the Earth's climate during past geological eras—the palaeo-climate. Geology itself provides certain keys. There are rock types in England, for example, which were formed during a desert climate. Study of the annual growth rings in living and fossil trees—dendrochronology—enables us to look several thousand years into the past. Quotients between different oxygen isotopes in Greenland's inland ice and between samples of deepsea ooze give us some insight into past climatic changes. But this is a complex subject and it is by no means easy to correlate the different results.

Climates and the biosphere
Water is the universal solvent and it is of vital significance to all organisms. Sunlight is the energy source of plants and hence in the final analysis of animals too. The temperature also determines whether water shall be available as liquid or ice. Precipitation (the blue graph lines in the small diagrams) and the temperature (red lines) determine between them the vegetation (large illustrations). Apart from these principal types there are many other variants as a result of local conditions, for example a mountain massif or irregularities in wind direction, etc.

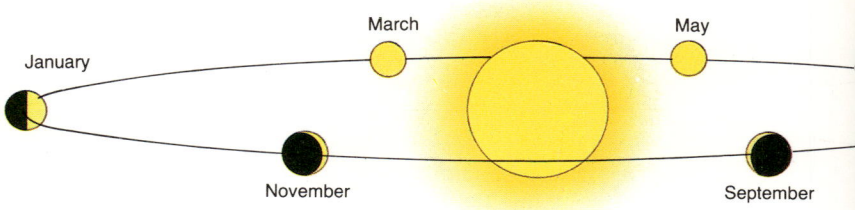

Around the sun
During the course of a year the Earth makes one complete orbit around the sun. This orbit, c. 940 million km., is elliptical but this is of no importance in relation to the seasonal changes. In fact the Earth is closest to the sun in January. The seasons are caused instead by the angle of the Earth's axis.

The seasons
The Earth's axis from North Pole to South Pole leans at 23°27' in relation to the plane of its orbit, the ecliptic. Like the axis of the gyroscope or the spinning top, the Earth's axis always points in the same direction, despite the fact that the planet circles the sun. This is why the two hemispheres alternately face the sun, creating summer and winter respectively.

Summer in the northern hemisphere
Arctic Circle 66°33' N.
Equator

Heat, humidity and vegetation

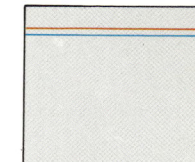

Equatorial lowland rain forest: high, steady temperature and humidity all the year round.

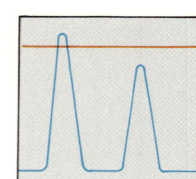

Savanna: high steady temperature but rainfall is unevenly distributed with often two rain periods a year.

Latitude and light

If the Earth's axis had no inclination then all the days would be the same length: 12 hours, irrespective of latitude or time of year. The daily height of the sun in the sky would be determined by latitude only. Because of the inclination, however, the height of the sun at noon and the number of hours of daylight vary from summer to winter, the differences being greater the closer one comes to the poles. Along the equator the day is always the same length and the sun's altitude varies at midday between the zenith and 66°33′ above the horizon.

The world's climates

are dictated, generally speaking, by two variables only: the temperature with its seasonal changes, and the quantity and distribution of precipitation over the year. The temperature depends upon the strength of the sun's rays and thus upon latitude, but it is modified by the global air circulation. The latter distributes humidity over the face of the Earth. The Earth's climatic zones (map) are thus related to latitude, though as a result of winds and elevation the limits of these zones do not exactly follow the parallels of latitude.

- Tropical climates
- Dry climates
- Warm temperate climates
- Snow climates
- Ice climates
- Various highland climates

Polar summer
The sun is low all the time but the days are long—a full 24 hours at midsummer at the Arctic Circle, six months daylight at the pole itself.

Polar winter
In winter the sun never rises over the horizon beyond the polar circles and at the poles there is six months of night.

Middle latitude summer
The sun is relatively high in the sky at midday. The days are longer than the nights—longest at the summer solstice.

Middle latitude winter
The sun is low over the horizon even in the middle of the day, and night is considerably longer than day.

Tropical "summer" and "winter"
The sun is always high around noon, sometimes at the zenith. Day and night are equally long and night falls rapidly. There are insufficient variations in the height of the sun and the length of the day to give rise to noticeable seasonal variations.

Winter in the northern hemisphere

Tropical lowland steppe: one, sometimes two rain periods. High, steady temperature results in a distinctively dry environment. Excessive evaporation.

Desert: no rain at all. Heat and drought cause a total absence of vegetation in extreme desert environments.

Temperate zone forest climates: high, steady humidity, temperatures vary characteristically between winter and summer.

Continental tundra: a dry, cold environment where the temperature rises above zero for only a month or two in summertime. Where this does not happen, an extreme ice climate results.

13

Signs in the sky

Meteorological folklore

Mariners' meteorology
"Rain before wind, bring your mainsail in. Wind before rain, set your mainsail again." In the past, seamen and farmers were always dependent upon being able to foresee changes in the weather. In time their experience produced a wealth of lore expressed in rhyme and doggerel. A lot of this made sense, but there was no real understanding of the causal relationship between "signs in the sky" and the next few hours' weather before the development of modern meteorological science (three examples, right).

Old signs—new science

Cirrus clouds form high up on the forward edge of a warm front. At ground level, the front is still a long way off though it will eventually bring a change in the weather, probably rain.

Haloes occur when a front forces a mass of air to rise to an altitude where ice crystals form. This also is a sign of a change in the weather—a warm front is on the way.

"Red sky at night, shepherd's delight. Red sky in the morning, shepherd's warning." A red sky is caused by light refraction in moist air, normal after a warm day. A red sunrise on the other hand indicates that the atmosphere is exceptionally humid, which can result in rain and gusty winds.

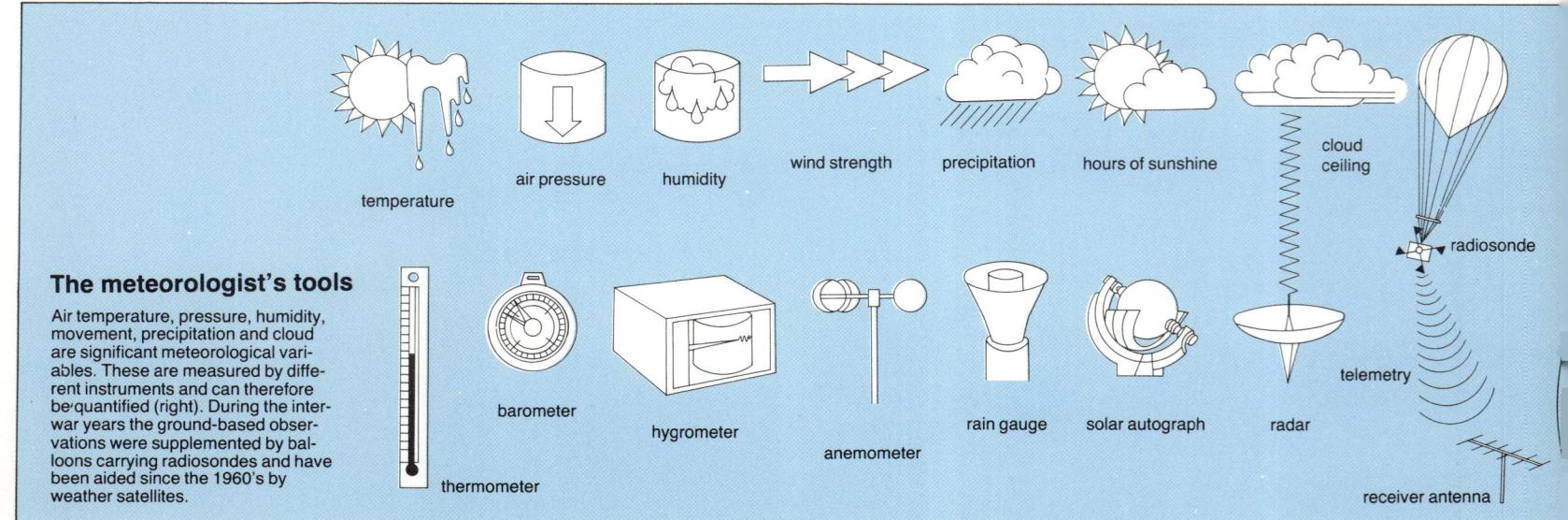

The meteorologist's tools
Air temperature, pressure, humidity, movement, precipitation and cloud are significant meteorological variables. These are measured by different instruments and can therefore be quantified (right). During the interwar years the ground-based observations were supplemented by balloons carrying radiosondes and have been aided since the 1960's by weather satellites.

14

The science of meteorology owes much to the development of telegraphic communication. Previously the meteorologist could work only with what he actually saw. Other information beyond his field of vision was no longer of any significance by the time it reached him. The telegraph, however, made it possible to assemble simultaneous observations from a wide area, thereby enabling the scientists to produce a synoptic picture of current weather conditions and to begin the analysis of atmospheric phenomena.

This capacity for swiftly collecting and processing data is of fundamental importance to the work of the meteorologist. Temperature, air pressure, wind, precipitation and cloud reports are continuously being received from weather stations, unmanned instruments and satellites.

Meteorologists could be overwhelmed by this never-ending flow of information, but the data is necessary. The recording of precise values allows scientists to subject different phenomena to mathematical analysis and thereby make meteorology an exact science. Since the beginning of this century simple equations have been known which can be applied to predict the behaviour of air masses. If these are to be used to produce practical forecasts, then the atmosphere has to be divided up into a large number of relatively small "air cubes" with sides of perhaps only two kms. When each such cube has been analyzed individually the results are adjusted in relation to what has happened in the adjoining spaces. This process has to be repeated several times over. This, of course, requires an enormous calculating capability. Before this capability existed the meteorologist, engrossed in his synoptic charts, had to predict the course of the weather on the strength of rules of thumb and personal experience. The duration of the forecast was never greater than 24 hours and, furthermore, it was often inaccurate.

Now for the first time modern high speed computers enable meteorologists to work out these complex equations within a reasonable time. The forecasts drawn up by the computers are no longer qualitative but quantitative, expressed in degrees, metres per second, millibars and millimetres of precipitation. Predictions have become more reliable. The forecast durations have increased during the 1970's from 24 hours to five days. Forecasts extending over much longer periods, weeks and even months, are also being made on an experimental basis, and although these are not yet adequately accurate they are likely to become so in the not too distant future. New super-computers of even greater capacity will most likely make possible dependable long-range forecasts before the close of the 1980's. In addition, meteorologists are receiving more and more information upon which to base their forecasts. Modern satellites register not only cloud conditions but also temperatures in the upper atmosphere and at ground and sea level. They record snow cover and sea ice. All this data is of the utmost importance to long-range meteorological predictions.

Many of our economically important activities are dependent upon the weather and this makes meteorology a science of great practical value. Farming, shipping and aviation rely heavily on correct forecasts as do many different industries. Thus, despite the high costs, weather satellites and super-computers are well worth the expense.

The making of a forecast
A depression over the North Sea is moving eastward (photo, left, and map). Ground observations are combined with satellite pictures and the weather situation is visualized on a synoptic chart showing high and low pressures, isobars, precipitation, cloud and winds. The real forecast is produced, however, by inserting the observations into a "numerical model" of the atmosphere and then processing this in a powerful computer. It is the predictions of the computer which the weathermen finally report to the public.

Both the satellite picture at the top and the synoptic chart show the weather at the same time on October 10th 1983. In addition to isobars showing air pressure in millibars the chart indicates showers (triangles) and drizzle (commas).

Life in the air

From reptile to bird
The evolution from crawling reptiles to flying birds took place between 230 and 140 million years ago. An intermediate developement was a group of small dinosaurs.

Early Triassic period: a small, fairly primitive lizard begins specializing in capturing insects and other agile prey.

Mid-Triassic: the reptile is still a reptile but has now become more nimble and sometimes rises up on to its hindlegs.

Late Triassic—early Jurassic: animals now walking on their hindlegs. These begin to become birdlike with elongated metatarsal bones—an adaptation for running. But long-distance running demands warm-blooded metabolism.

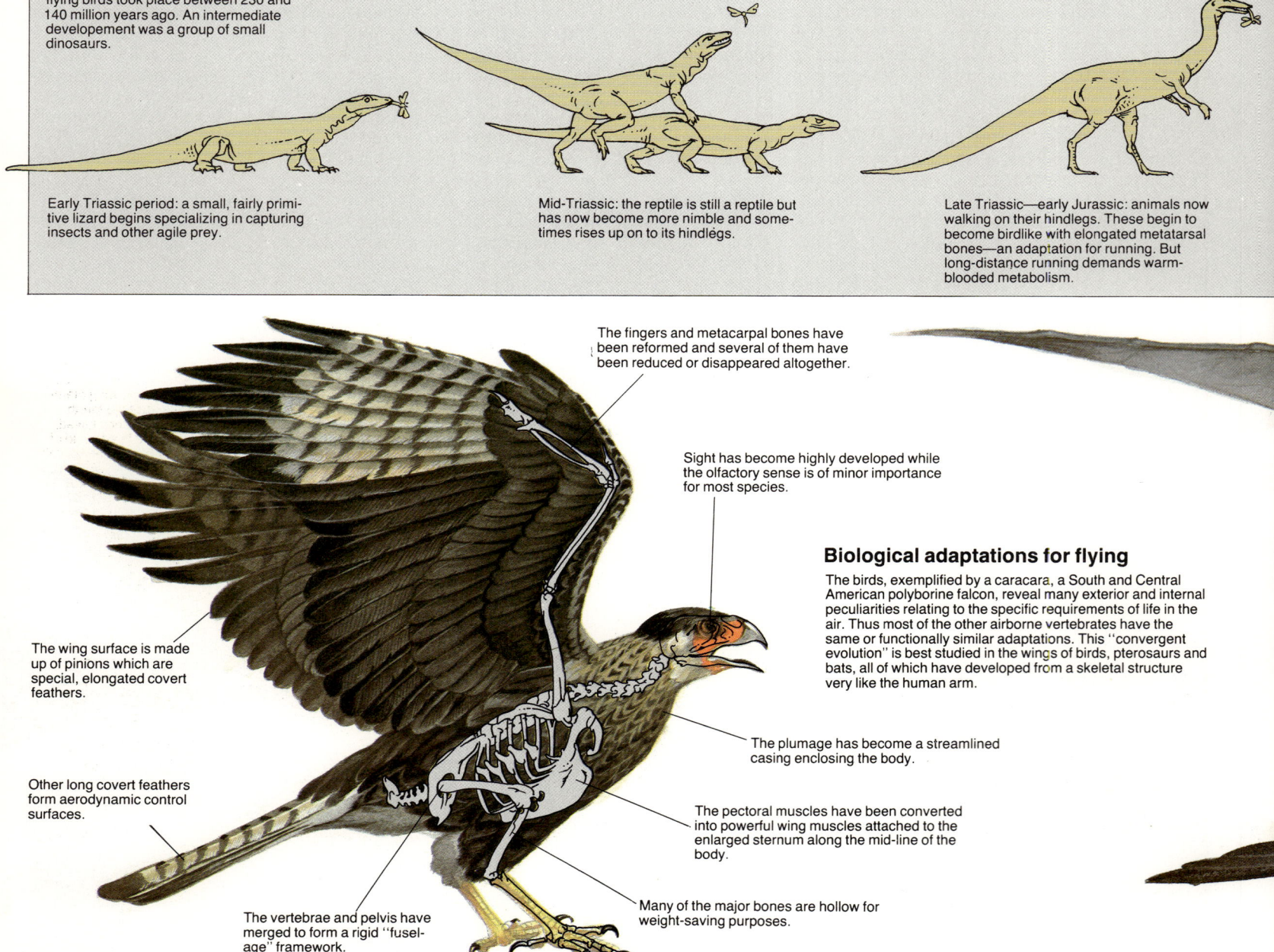

The fingers and metacarpal bones have been reformed and several of them have been reduced or disappeared altogether.

Sight has become highly developed while the olfactory sense is of minor importance for most species.

Biological adaptations for flying
The birds, exemplified by a caracara, a South and Central American polyborine falcon, reveal many exterior and internal peculiarities relating to the specific requirements of life in the air. Thus most of the other airborne vertebrates have the same or functionally similar adaptations. This "convergent evolution" is best studied in the wings of birds, pterosaurs and bats, all of which have developed from a skeletal structure very like the human arm.

The wing surface is made up of pinions which are special, elongated covert feathers.

Other long covert feathers form aerodynamic control surfaces.

The plumage has become a streamlined casing enclosing the body.

The pectoral muscles have been converted into powerful wing muscles attached to the enlarged sternum along the mid-line of the body.

Many of the major bones are hollow for weight-saving purposes.

The vertebrae and pelvis have merged to form a rigid "fuselage" framework.

The ability to fly is one of the most curious of all the biological adaptations. It is also very difficult to attain. Among other things it necessitates a restructuring of the body and once this has taken place it is irreversible. But in the struggle for survival flying is so advantageous that this adaptation has occurred not merely once but four times in the history of evolution: among insects, pterosaurs, birds and mammals.

The insects are a special case. The enormous success of the flying insects is attributable to their small size. An animal's weight varies according to volume but muscle power depends upon the cross-sectional area of the muscle. If an animal is scaled down to half its size then its weight diminishes to one eighth, but the muscle power is only reduced to one quarter. Thus at one stroke the power-to-weight ratio becomes twice as favourable. Moreover in minute quantities air behaves more like a fluid than a thin gas. Insects can thus generate lift by entirely different processes than birds.

Insects took to the air during the Carboniferous period about 300 million years ago. The pterosaurs evolved in the Triassic period some 200 million years ago. These were not really "flying reptiles". Reptiles are unable to fly; no cold-blooded animal is capable of prolonged muscular effort. The inner structure of the bones reveal that the pterosaurs were warm-blooded like birds and mammals and we know now from fossil finds that at least the smaller species grew an insulating fur. Some pterosaurs were no larger than sparrows while others had a wingspan of more than 10 metres.

Birds first appeared during the Jurassic period about 150 million years ago. They inherited their warm blood and insulating plumage from their ancestors, the small predatory dinosaurs. The birds displaced the pterosaurs, probably because they were more robust. A bird which loses some of its pinions can manage until new ones grow, but those incredible living sails, the pterosaurs, were doomed if their wing membrane was torn. They were helpless on the ground.

Today birds dominate our airspace so effectively that bats, the only flying mammals, are compelled to live a largely nocturnal life. Man flies too of course, but his flight technology is mechanical rather than biological.

Early Jurassic period: the lizard has become a coelurosaur; a warm-blooded dinosaur the size of a cat. The higher body temperature requires insulation—the scales become plumage.

Mid-Jurassic: longer feathers create control surfaces which facilitate manoeuverability. This is archaeopteryx, not the oldest bird, but one of its flightless ancestors.

Late Jurassic period: aerial leaps merge into sustained flight and the birds begin their conquest of the air.

Lords of the air
The pteranodon was one of the larger pterosaurs with a wingspan of up to seven metres. It is believed to have fed on fish like the albatross of our day.

Pterosaurs
Towards the close of their evolution these could be as big as a light aeroplane, though most of them were small. The wing membrane was kept stretched by the fourth finger, the others being free and clawed. The hindlegs were reduced in size and of little use for locomotion. Pteranodons probably rested on rock ledges since there can scarcely have been trees large enough for them to land in. It is not known what purpose the outgrowth on the head served and some pteranodon fossils lack this altogether.

Bats
have wing membranes like the pterosaurs had, but their forearm and finger skeletons are not the same. Most bats prey on small insects and they are all nocturnal.

The wandering albatross has a wingspan of up to 3.5 metres. By utilizing differences in wind velocity between lower and higher air strata this bird can soar out over the oceans for weeks at a time.

hummingbird

Birds vary in size
from the albatross and condor down to certain hummingbirds which are no larger than many flying insects. Generally speaking, however, the birds have occupied all the ecological niches for large, flying diurnal animals, and also most of the niches for nocturnal fliers. There are two phases to the flight of a large bird (photograph): the wing-beat which moves it forward and upward and the glide when it "rests on its oars". Smaller species do not have to economize with their energy to the same extent as the larger birds.

The flying technique of insects
is difficult to study because of the very high wing-beat rate and it was not until the introduction of high speed cameras in recent years that we were able to gain some insight into this. The drawings below are based on a series of photographs. The insect (here a wasp species) has a rotating wing-beat which is only superficially similar to that of birds. The aerodynamic process here is quite different.

Man takes to the air

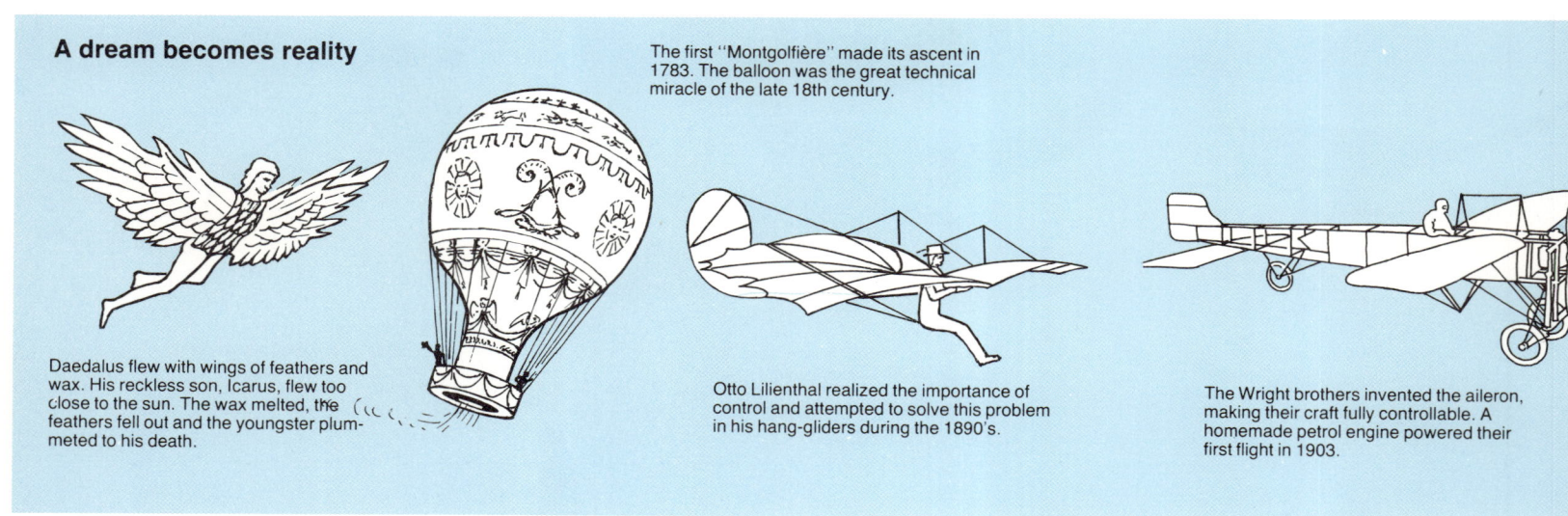

A dream becomes reality

Daedalus flew with wings of feathers and wax. His reckless son, Icarus, flew too close to the sun. The wax melted, the feathers fell out and the youngster plummeted to his death.

The first "Montgolfière" made its ascent in 1783. The balloon was the great technical miracle of the late 18th century.

Otto Lilienthal realized the importance of control and attempted to solve this problem in his hang-gliders during the 1890's.

The Wright brothers invented the aileron, making their craft fully controllable. A homemade petrol engine powered their first flight in 1903.

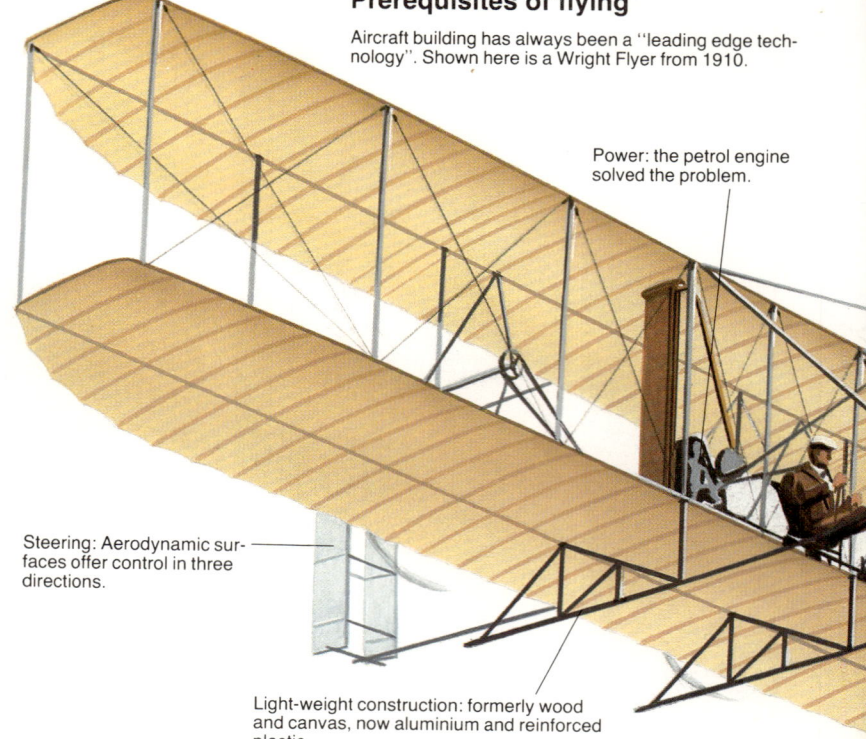

Prerequisites of flying
Aircraft building has always been a "leading edge technology". Shown here is a Wright Flyer from 1910.

Power: the petrol engine solved the problem.

Steering: Aerodynamic surfaces offer control in three directions.

Light-weight construction: formerly wood and canvas, now aluminium and reinforced plastic.

As long as he has been capable of contemplating the birds circling above his head, man has yearned to be liberated from his bondage under the force of gravity. In myths and legends human beings had no difficulty in flying. The Greeks described how Daedalus and Icarus took to the air to escape King Minos of Crete, and Völund too, the accomplished blacksmith of the Germanic sagas, had mastered the art of flying. In reality, however, it was not until the present century that man realized his dreams.

It would have been quite possible in Leonardo da Vinci's day to have built an operable hang-glider of the type in use today, but no-one did so. The apparent simplicity of the hang-glider is in fact deceptive. Three problems must be overcome in order to fly properly: lift, motive power and steering.

The first of these was solved after a fashion in 1783 when the Montgolfier brothers sent their first hot-air ballon up over Paris and this was followed soon afterwards by a hydrogen balloon. The balloon was widely used in the 19th century as a research device, as a moored observation platform and for sport. It was never a real flying machine however for the winds took it wherever they blew. Even when it was equipped with engines it nevertheless proved too frail to cope with wind squalls, not to mention the danger of conflagration.

It was realized early that aerodynamic lift could be attained by means of cambered wing profiles. The principle is simple enough. Air flows more swiftly over the curved, longer upper wing surface than along the straight, shorter under wing surface. In other words there is less pressure on the wing's upper side, and this difference in pressure produces lift. This requires that the aircraft moves forward through the air. Not until the close of the last century could an engine be built that was light and powerful enough to propel an aircraft. Many valiant attempts were made to get airborne but the short hops invariably ended in a crash. It was not sufficient simply to hurl a flying machine up into the air: once up there it had to be steered.

The German pioneer Lilienthal realized this. He was unable to control his hang-glider properly, however, and was killed in 1896. The Wright brothers experimented extensively with gliders before they made their first powered flight in 1903. This was the advent of aviation.

Since then the technique of flying has developed rapidly. Aircraft built of light metals, radio, jet engines and new navigational methods have increased the safety, speed, range and transport capabilities. The decisive step forward however was made by men like Otto Lilienthal and Orville and Wilbur Wright who first recognized the three problems—lift, motive power and control—and who prepared the way for dealing with these barriers.

Highly technological flying
For the uninitiated the cockpit of the Concorde is a bewildering array af dials and buttons. But in the days of piston engines there were even more instruments and gauges to keep check on. The jet engine has produced considerable technical simplification, while on the other hand communication and navigation equipment now plays a more prominent part than during the airscrew era.

18

The US F-15 is a typical example of the modern combat aircraft.

The Sopwith "Camel" was a famous World War I fighter. During the years 1914–18 flying moved on from being a challenging attainment to become a routine procedure.

The "Spitfire", the most renowned fighter aircraft in World War II.

The Douglas DC-3, the classical military and civil workhorse of the 1940's and '50's.

The Boeing 747 "Jumbo Jet" is a giant machine which in certain versions can carry almost 500 passengers. The take-off weight is over 370 tons, the fuselage is more than 70 m. in length and the tailfin is as high as a 6-storey building.

The dream lives on
The dream of flying like a bird has encouraged many enthusiasts to "start from the beginning" with hang-gliders (photo) and powered ultra-light aeroplanes.

Lift: the cambered wing profile creates negative pressure on the upper surface and thereby lifts the aircraft.

From walking to supersonic speed
The Concorde, built through co-operation between the British and French aircraft industries, flies across the Atlantic at twice the speed of sound and at an altitude of 20,000 m. It is incomparably larger and faster than the Wright brothers' primitive little flying machine. The development of aeronautical technology has been exceptionally rapid.

Air routes

Flying then and now

The history of commercial aviation begins in the 1920's and this "air taxi" from 1928 gives some indication of how primitive things were at that time. Fares were nevertheless high. Flying was a mode of travel—or rather an adventure—for the privileged few.

In less than sixty years, aviation has developed into one of the most important means of communication, recruiting its passengers from every walk of life. Below, holidaymakers board a DC-9 at a small airport in central Sweden.

Commercial aviation did not really appear until the period immediately after World War I. It was then that bold fliers in open machines first began flying sacks of mail between the larger European and North American cities. Sometimes they would take a passenger as well, thoroughly wrapped up against the cold air. It was not long, however, before the aircraft designers, utilizing their wartime experience, began building proper passenger planes. A network of air routes developed in Europe, extending to the British Empire's outposts in the east, and likewise connecting the east and west coasts of the United States.

Before World War II flying remained, nevertheless, a secondary form of travel. The services were irregular and the planes flew contact; in other words, they kept in sight of the ground and were thus dependent upon good weather conditions. World War II produced improved meteorological services, extended radio communications, radar, more airfields and, particularly, the jet engine. Thus the 1950's and '60's were the real turning point for commercial airlines.

The great advantage of flying is its speed. All types of goods which have to be delivered in a hurry and are valuable are potential air freight, everything from electronic chips to circus elephants. The man in the street has most contact, of course, with passenger aircraft (regular or charter) but for the airline the passenger is little more than an exceptionally demanding consignment of goods.

There are two types of air routes, one connecting big cities and crossing the oceans and the other consisting of feeder lines. Different types of aircraft are used on each and on the shortest feeder lines propeller aircraft are still a competitive alternative. Commercial aviation has not really kept abreast of the military trend towards increasingly high speeds. Cruising speeds of 850–900 km/h. are most economical and the Anglo-French Concorde is the only supersonic passenger aircraft operating today. Modern navigation systems are electronic, incorporating radio beacons and similar equipment. Transoceanic airliners employ inertial navigation with a complex system of gyroscopes, accelerometers and computers.

Airfields have also developed, from idyllic green pastures into vast industrial concerns. At the beginning of the 1980's the busiest airport in the world was Chicago's O'Hare, with a daily average of nearly 2,000 arrivals and departures and more than 120,000 passengers. London's Heathrow was the largest in Europe with over 1,000 arrivals and departures a day.

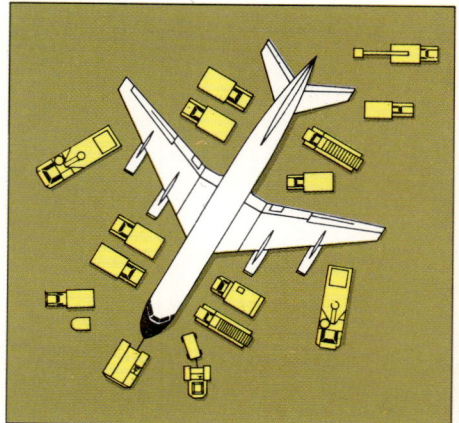

Ground service
Once on the ground the aircraft becomes surrounded by service vehicles—towing tractors, tank trucks, fire-engines and various vehicles for technical maintenance and catering. All this servicing has to be done quickly; it costs a lot to let an aircraft stand idle.

Airways and airports

Traffic in the air is carefully regulated. Each airport (right) is surrounded by a meticulously supervised terminal area within which incoming aircraft are "stacked" at different altitudes while awaiting their turn to land. These terminal areas are connected by airways through which aircraft fly at different altitudes in different directions. All traffic is watched over by radar and controlled by radio from traffic control towers. An airport (below) has several kms. of runways with lights and instrument landing systems. There are taxi strips so that aircraft moving on the ground do not interfere with take-offs and landings. The aircraft are assembled on the ramp; grouped around this are buildings for flight control, passengers and freight, technical services and administration.

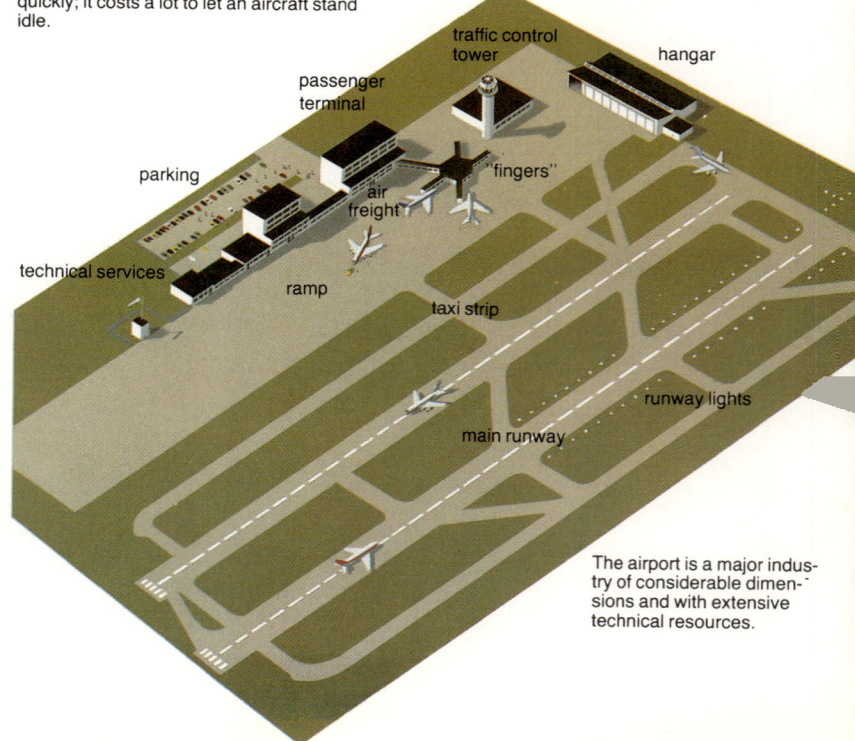

The airport is a major industry of considerable dimensions and with extensive technical resources.

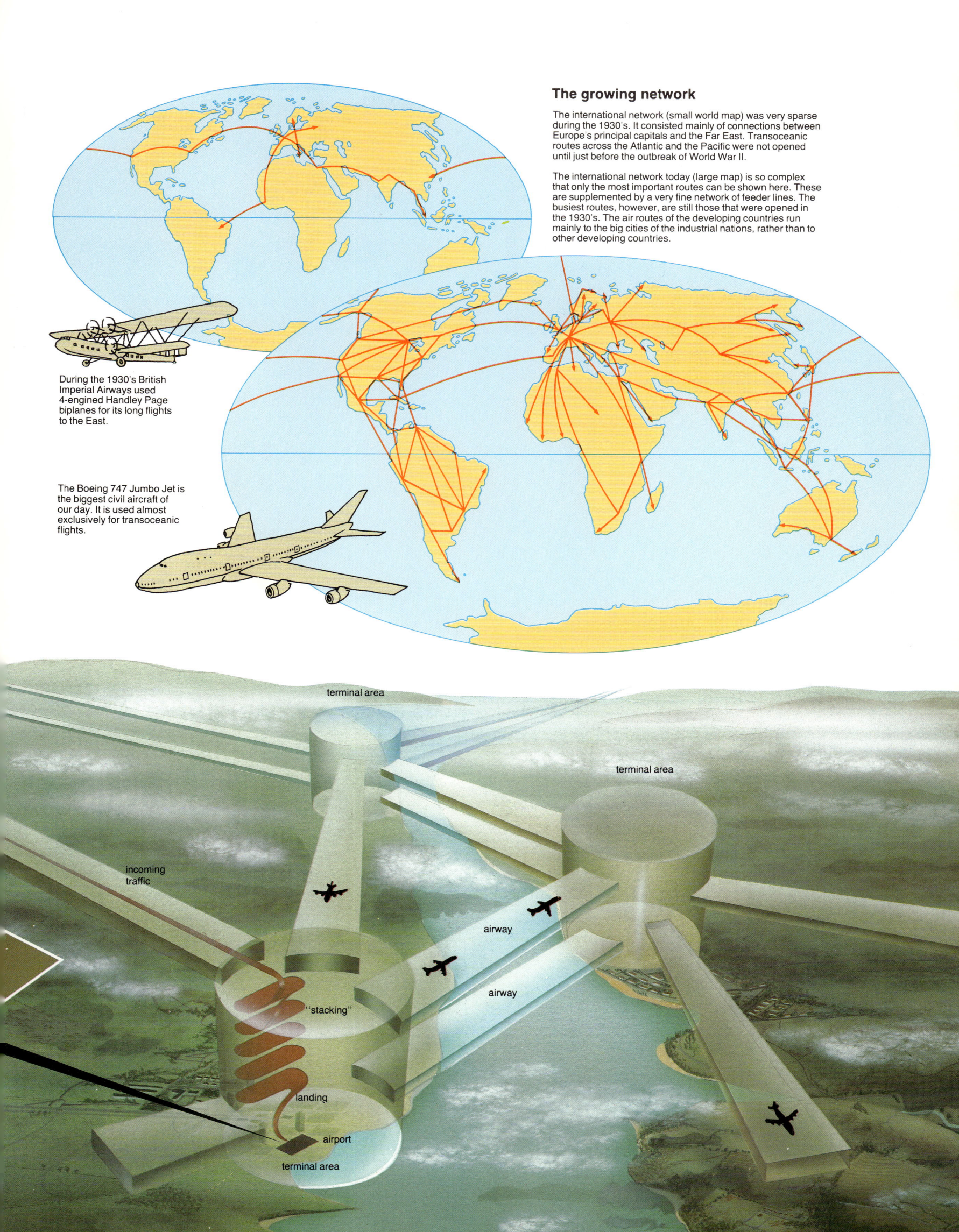

The growing network

The international network (small world map) was very sparse during the 1930's. It consisted mainly of connections between Europe's principal capitals and the Far East. Transoceanic routes across the Atlantic and the Pacific were not opened until just before the outbreak of World War II.

The international network today (large map) is so complex that only the most important routes can be shown here. These are supplemented by a very fine network of feeder lines. The busiest routes, however, are still those that were opened in the 1930's. The air routes of the developing countries run mainly to the big cities of the industrial nations, rather than to other developing countries.

During the 1930's British Imperial Airways used 4-engined Handley Page biplanes for its long flights to the East.

The Boeing 747 Jumbo Jet is the biggest civil aircraft of our day. It is used almost exclusively for transoceanic flights.

The leap into space

Looking out into space

Since time immemorial the stars have served man as both clock and signpost. Most "primitive" peoples have a better practical knowledge of astronomical time and celestial navigation than the average modern urban citizen.

Before the invention of the telescope astronomical instruments had to be made very large in order to attain sufficient accuracy. Sometimes such instruments grew into entire buildings (right).

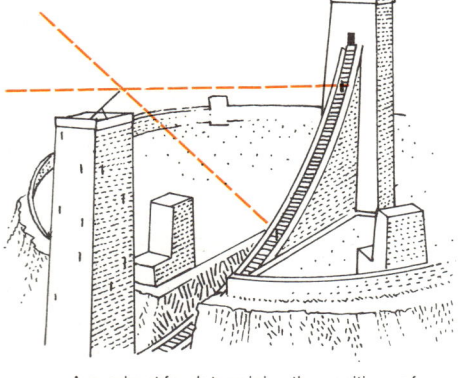

A quadrant for determining the positions of the stars, in Ulugh Begh's observatory in Samarkand, built in the 1440's.

Galileo constructed the first telescope (the idea as such was Dutch, however) and immediately directed this instrument at the stars. This brought about a scientific revolution, for now man could see farther out into space and distinguish the planets as celestial bodies instead of mere points of light. Galileo discovered the moons of Jupiter and the rings around Saturn.

Galileo's first telescope, made in 1609.

All radiation carries information about its source. Modern astronomers use radio telescopes (below) and register images by means of ultra-violet and infra-red light and X-rays.

A dream becomes reality

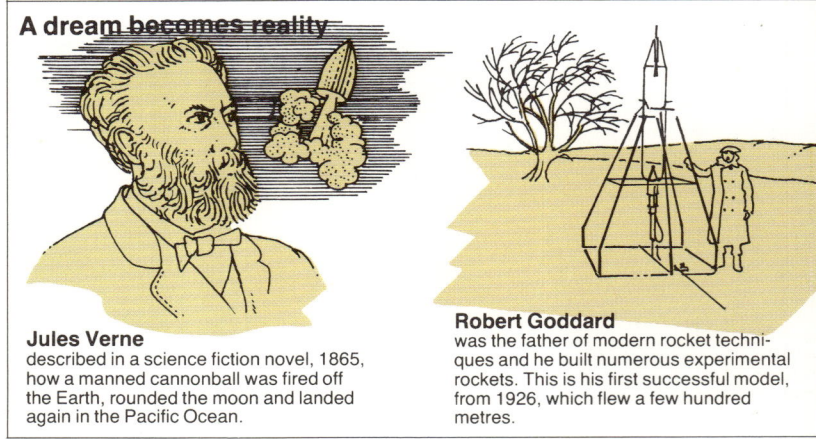

Jules Verne described in a science fiction novel, 1865, how a manned cannonball was fired off the Earth, rounded the moon and landed again in the Pacific Ocean.

Robert Goddard was the father of modern rocket techniques and he built numerous experimental rockets. This is his first successful model, from 1926, which flew a few hundred metres.

Mankind's departure into space began one April day in 1961 when the Soviet test pilot Yuri Gagarin orbited the Earth in one hour and forty-eight minutes in a space capsule. Man is now on his way out into an entirely new environment which makes new demands on him but also opens entirely new prospects.

We have only been aware of the existence of outer space for about 300 years. Though Copernicus in the 1500's made deductions about our planetary system it was the new physics of Galileo and Newton which replaced the mediaeval concepts of the universe. Newton would have been well able to understand how a rocket could continue to function in the vacuum of space. Ejecting combustion gases backward at high velocity increases the forward impulse in accordance with the laws of motion which Newton himself formulated. He would also have understood the artificial satellites of our day. Like the moon—whose orbit Newton was the first to calculate—these satellites fall constantly towards the Earth. Their orbital velocity is so high (3–8 km/sec) that their trajectory remains parallel with the Earth's surface. Consequently the satellites do not crash to the ground but continue orbiting for years.

Travelling and surviving in space requires advanced technical aids. Human beings need oxygen to breathe and protection against radiation and extreme temperatures. Prolonged weightlessness sometimes leads to mental confusion, deteriorating blood counts and skeletal decalcification. Keeping man alive in space calls for fundamental research and new, life-sustaining technology. If man is not merely to survive but also to work there then the technological requirements will become even greater.

Today some 300 active satellites are orbiting the Earth and permanent space stations are already on the drawing-board. Space exploration and research will give our civilization new dimensions. New knowledge awaits us, knowledge relating to the origins, history and ultimate fate of the planetary system and the universe. It is to be hoped that such knowledge will also lead to a clearer understanding of mankind's place in the infinity of the cosmos.

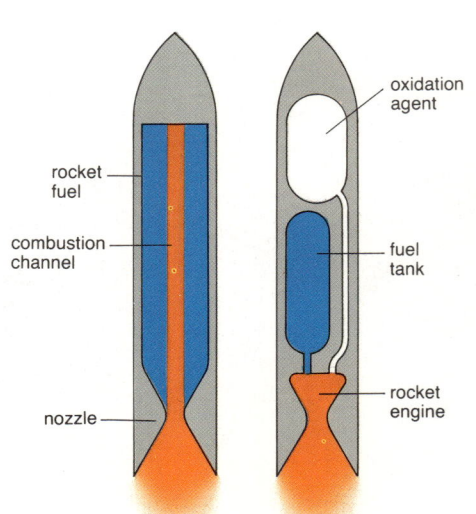

Solid and liquid fuel
The solid propellant rocket (left) is a sophisticated version of the popular firework rocket. The fuel—usually synthetic rubber mixed with an oxidation agent—has a combustion channel through the middle and the gases are emitted through a nozzle. The liquid fuel rocket (right) has separate tanks for fuel and oxidation agent. A vehicle with such an engine can thus be refuelled and used again, while the solid propellant rocket can normally only be used once.

Wernher von Braun
developed the V2 rocket at the German Peenemünde base during World War II. He subsequently worked on ballistic missiles and satellite projects in the USA.

Sputnik 1
was the first man-made satellite. The Soviet Union put this into orbit in 1957, thereby beginning the space race with the USA which is still going on.

The lunar voyages
in the late 1960's and early 70's rounded off an epoch in the history of space travel. Since then the emphasis has been more on practical applications and scientific results than on prestigious feats.

The space shuttle
was developed by the USA and made its first flight in 1982. This recoverable space vehicle has greatly reduced the cost of placing small satellites in orbit and of conducting scientific experiments in a weightless state or in the vacuum of space.

photo satellite   communications satellite   navigation satellite

Satellites with an altitude of 36,000 km. have an orbital period of 24 hours and thus remain stationary at the same point over the Earth. These are "geosynchronous" satellites.

Uses of space
Today there is intensive activity in our "immediate space". Meteorological, resource and reconnaissance satellites are constantly photographing our planet and studying its surface with different instruments. Satellites have revolutionized international telecommunications and navigation satellites are already in use. But man will not really be established in space until he has installed proper space stations—as envisaged for the next century (panorama below). Such stations will probably rotate so as to create an artificial sense of weight for the people manning them.

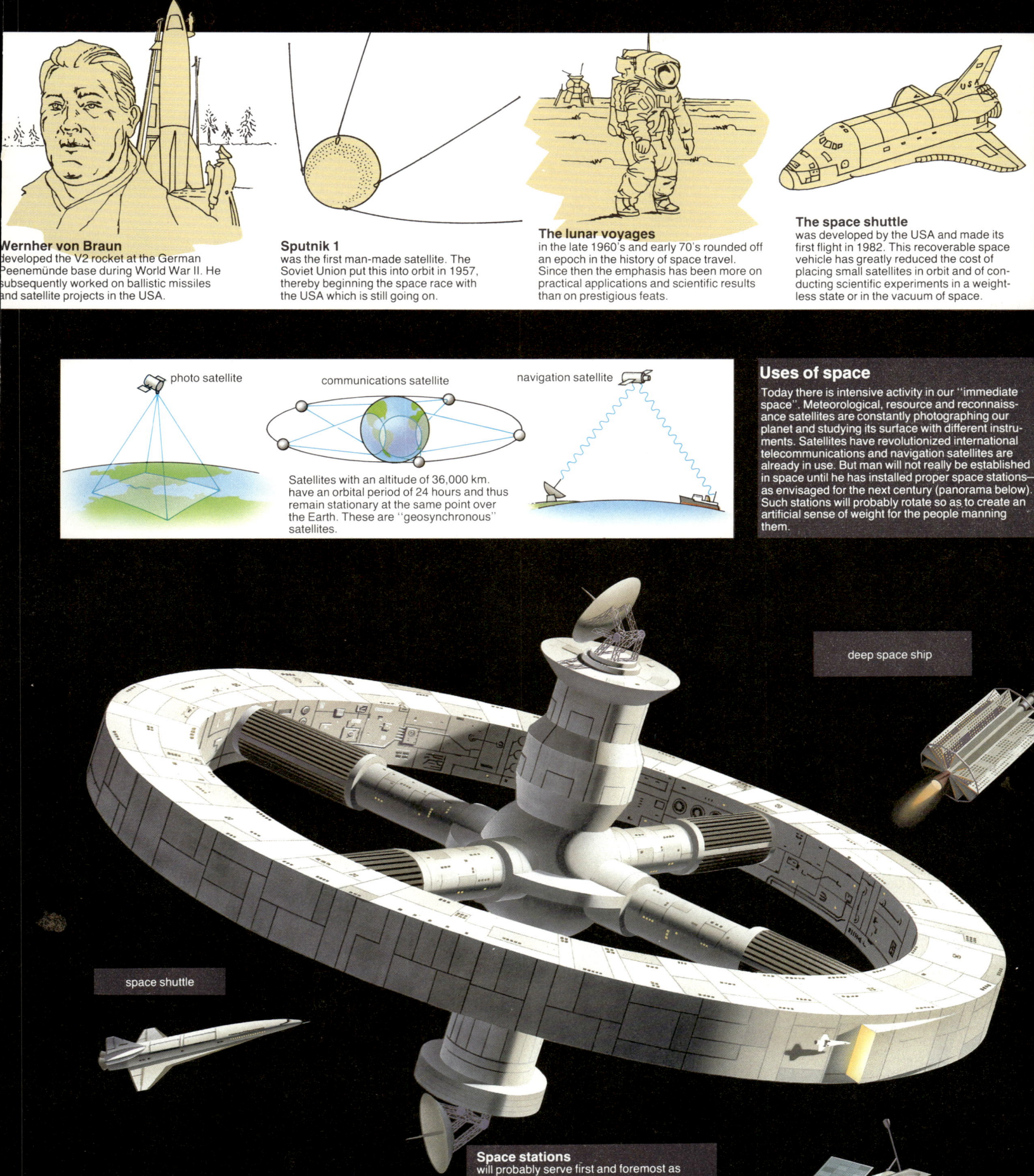

deep space ship

space shuttle

Space stations
will probably serve first and foremost as scientific outposts. One important area of research is physiology: we still do not know everything about the physical demands upon man which can arise from prolonged sojourns in space.

satellite with solar cells

Man's impact on the atmosphere

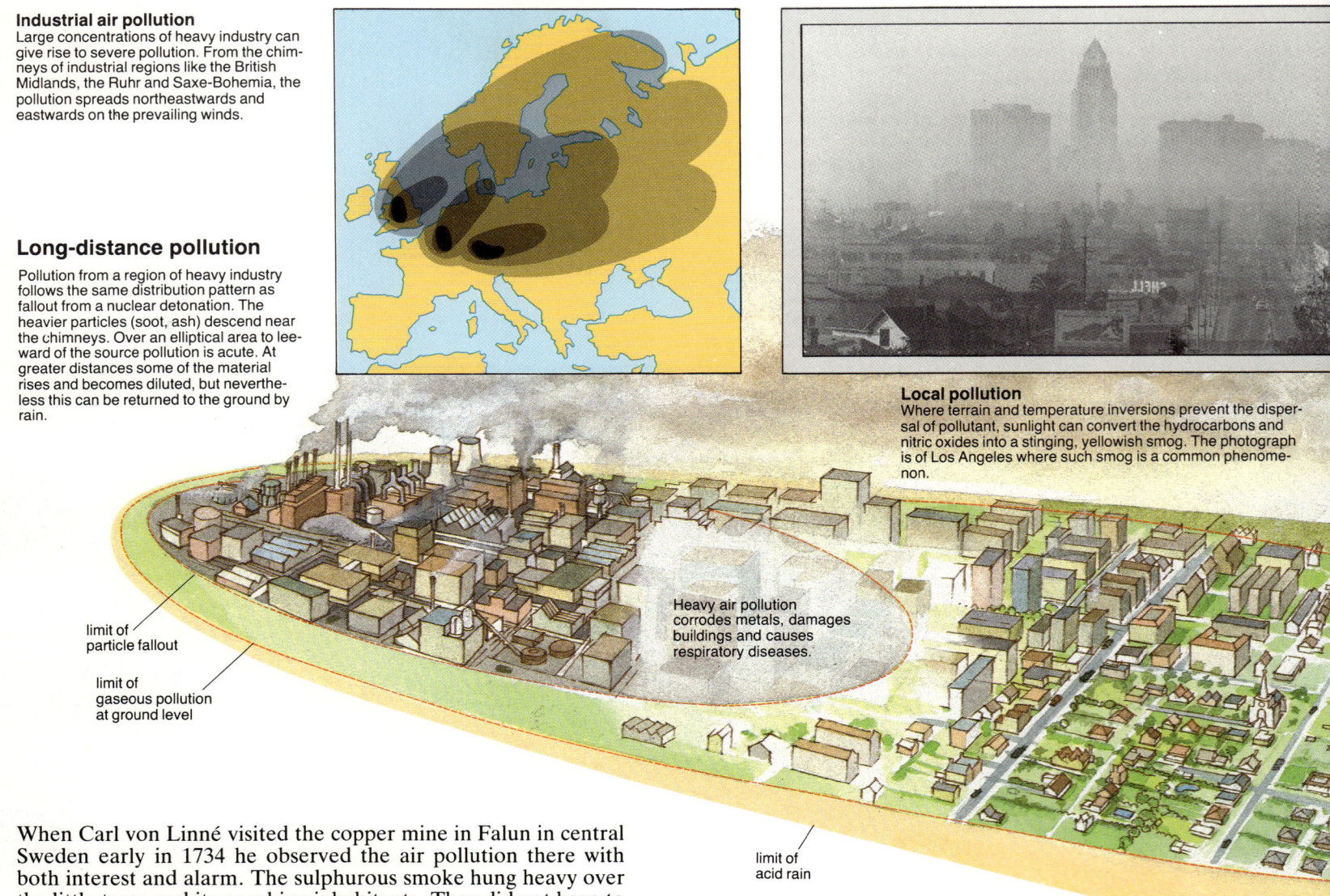

Industrial air pollution
Large concentrations of heavy industry can give rise to severe pollution. From the chimneys of industrial regions like the British Midlands, the Ruhr and Saxe-Bohemia, the pollution spreads northeastwards and eastwards on the prevailing winds.

Long-distance pollution
Pollution from a region of heavy industry follows the same distribution pattern as fallout from a nuclear detonation. The heavier particles (soot, ash) descend near the chimneys. Over an elliptical area to leeward of the source pollution is acute. At greater distances some of the material rises and becomes diluted, but nevertheless this can be returned to the ground by rain.

Local pollution
Where terrain and temperature inversions prevent the dispersal of pollutant, sunlight can convert the hydrocarbons and nitric oxides into a stinging, yellowish smog. The photograph is of Los Angeles where such smog is a common phenomenon.

Heavy air pollution corrodes metals, damages buildings and causes respiratory diseases.

limit of particle fallout
limit of gaseous pollution at ground level
limit of acid rain

When Carl von Linné visited the copper mine in Falun in central Sweden early in 1734 he observed the air pollution there with both interest and alarm. The sulphurous smoke hung heavy over the little town and its coughing inhabitants. They did not have to go far to find fresh air, however, for the pollution was localised.

Modern industry is not located in remote mining communities but within large cities. Consequently more and more people are being afflicted by air pollution. The growing discharge of fumes and airborne poisons is becoming more than the atmosphere's circulation system can cope with, and the capacity of vegetation to purify the air also diminishes as the plants themselves become poisoned.

Air pollution is caused mainly by the combustion of oil and coal. The burning of these substances releases heavy metals which have been fixed in the Earth's crust for millions of years. The most serious problem of all is created by sulphur. This is discharged into the atmosphere as sulphur dioxide (SO_2) but in contact with water it is converted into sulphurous acid (H_2SO_3) and ultimately into sulphuric acid (H_2SO_4). This acid corrodes machinery and metal components and damages stone buildings, the Acropolis in Athens being a good example. Even more seriously it engenders respiratory and lung diseases in millions of people.

For many years people refused to accept that this problem extended beyond the industrial centres themselves. But acids can be carried great distances on the wind, from the Ruhr to Scandinavia and from USA to Canada, before falling as acid rain. In both Scandinavia and Canada the bedrock has a low lime content and the ground thus lacks a protective alkaline reserve to neutralise the acid. The damage quickly becomes visible. Forest growth is disrupted and the debilitated trees become prone to disease and parasitic attack. Today, the forests of central Europe are beginning to die as the alkaline reserves in the bedrock become exhausted. In lakes and waterways all life ceases when the pH value falls below about 4. Many lakes in Scandinavia are already devoid of all organic life.

Scientists are worried about two long-term problems. One concerns the atmosphere's stratum of ozone, triatomic oxygen, which absorbs most of the sun's ultraviolet radiation. If this stratum disappears or deteriorates the Earth's vegetation will be severely damaged. One of the results of a nuclear war would be the destruction of the ozone stratum. The release of freon gas from spray containers and air conditioners and the exhaust of jet aircraft in the stratosphere can also damage the protective stratum.

The second problem is created by carbon dioxide. If the combustion of coal and oil further increases the carbon dioxide content in the atmosphere, then the presence of this gas could diminish the radiation of heat from Earth into space. Such an upset in the planet's radiation balance would have major effects on our climate which are only partly understood. The carbon dioxide content in the air has certainly increased during this century, but it has not been established that the Earth's mean temperature has also risen, The destruction of the forests also discharges large quantities of carbon dioxide into the atmosphere from burned and decomposed biomass creating a threat to our oxygen supplies.

These problems are not insurmountable. Industry can adopt cleaner processes. The problem of car exhaust can be overcome by better purification devices and/or other types of engines and fuels. Ruthless deforestation can be halted. Swift measures and co-operation between nations can secure clean air for future generations to breathe.

Temperature inversion
In some instances the atmosphere can be stratified in such a way that the temperature at a certain altitude can begin to rise again instead of falling. Such a temperature inversion keeps the pollution in place as though under a lid and in a short time it can reach a dangerous level of concentration.

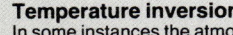

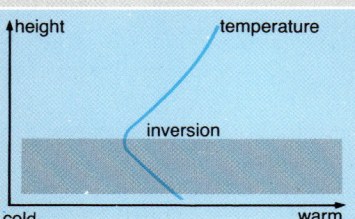

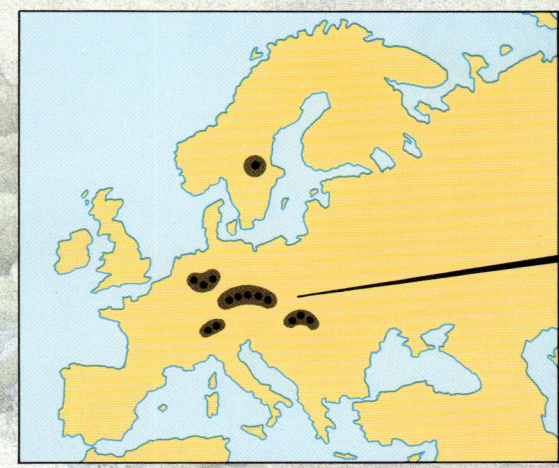

Air pollution in the past
Air pollution existed in the 16th century before industrialisation. It occured mainly in the mining districts where sulphide ores were processed (map). This was on such a small scale, however, that the air pollution was limited to very small areas.

16th century metallurgy
was primitive. The furnaces were inefficient and the sulphide ores were often processed on open hearths giving off an enormous volume of smoke. The release of sulphur dioxide in this way frequently destroyed the vegetation in the surrounding area.

Toxic substances in the air can enter food plants, reaching dangerous levels. The plants' own growth can also be seriously disturbed.

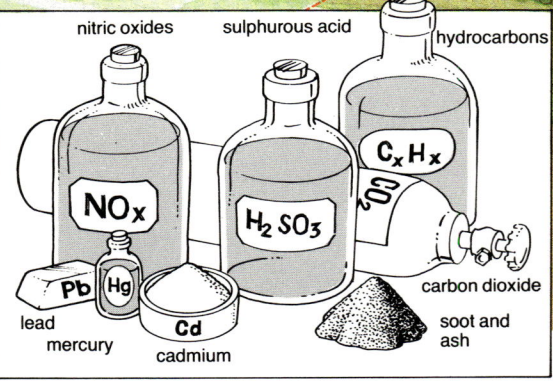

The air we breathe
often contains foreign substances (above, some examples). These are derived from different sources such as industry, vehicle exhaust, heating and refuse burning.

Long-term threats

Nuclear detonations and high flying jet aircraft can destroy the ozone stratum which protects us from the sun's dangerous ultraviolet radiation.

Carbon dioxide from coal and oil combustion could be a hindrance to the outward radiation of heat (greenhouse effect) and thereby change the world's climate.

Forests fix carbon dioxide through photosynthesis and emit it through respiration. Cleared areas can only emit carbon dioxide, never fix it.

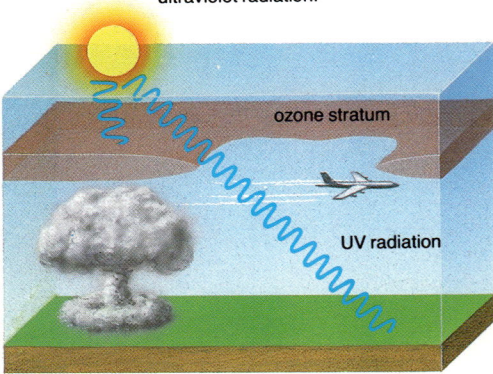
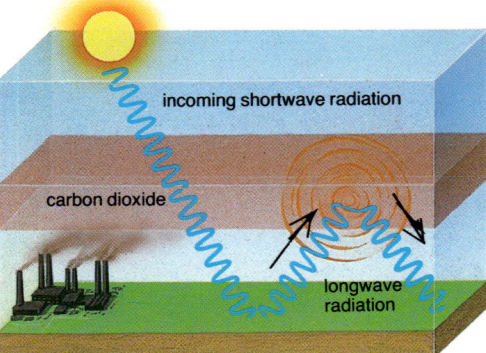
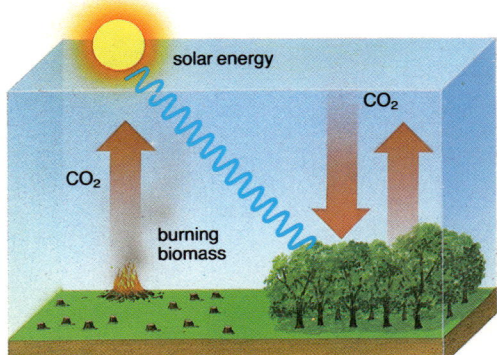

25

Water

The seafarers of ancient Greece thought of the Earth as a flat disk encircled by a great outer sea, – Oceanus. The first of all the Greek philosophers, Thales, who lived c. 600 BC, believed that water was the origin of the world.

When 18th century chemists demonstrated that water was a compound of hydrogen and oxygen it was deprived of its status as a primary element. But hardly had water suffered this setback when the dawning science of physiology discovered its fundamental importance to the processes of life, in that it is an excellent solvent for carbon compounds which are themselves the chemical building blocks of life. Scientists now believe that life first evolved in water, probably in a sheltered tidal water basin along the shore of the primeval sea.

Throughout mankind's cultural development water has always been an influence. Early man avoided arid deserts and impenetrable rain forests. The first advanced civilizations emerged where the great rivers—the Euphrates and Tigris, the Nile, the Indus and the Huang He—permitted man to irrigate his fields. Finally man also put sails on his still primitive ships and sailed forth across the oceans.

Today access to water is still a vital factor in our lives. It is not only in the parched regions of the Near East and south-western USA that diminishing water supplies have become a threat to the future. In central Europe, too, shortage of water is becoming an increasing obstacle to the expansion of towns and industries.

Our constant interest in water has resulted in the emergence of a whole group of "water sciences". Meteorology is one of these since it is closely concerned with the water cycle. Hydrology embraces studies of the surface- and sub-surface water, while limnology is the science of fresh water biology. Probably the most fascinating of all to the general public, however, are oceanography and marine biology. It was not until the last century that the ocean depths were sounded and their organisms studied and classified. In our day we have descended to the uttermost depths of the seas and found life there. All this has made us more conscious of the significance of water and of the folly of polluting it. The threatened extinction of some of its species is also constraining us to take worldwide measures to save them.

Water, the prerequisite of life

Reproduction in and out of water

Fishes have external fertilization: the male and female empty their milt and roe simultaneously into the water. They mingle and sperm-cell and ovum merge. The ovum hatches very swiftly and the fry emerge at an early stage of development.

Amphibians have taken their first step onto land but the reproductive system is still the same as that of the fish. However the mating position in which the male attaches itself to the female is a step towards copulation and internal fertilization.

Reptiles present two innovations. Copulation makes fertilization possible out of the water. The protective eggshell means that the egg can be laid on land and the embryo can develop at higher temperatures than would be possible in water.

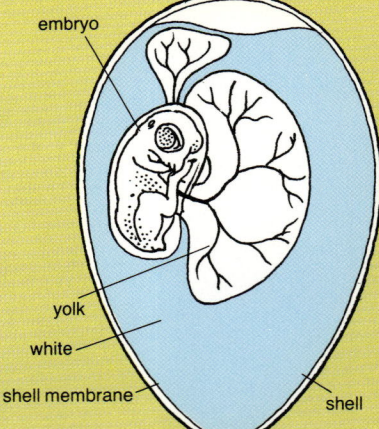

The bird's egg has a rigid shell with a sealing membrane inside. The mammal's foetus (right) develops in a similar fashion to that of the bird embryo, though this development takes place in the mammal's uterus.

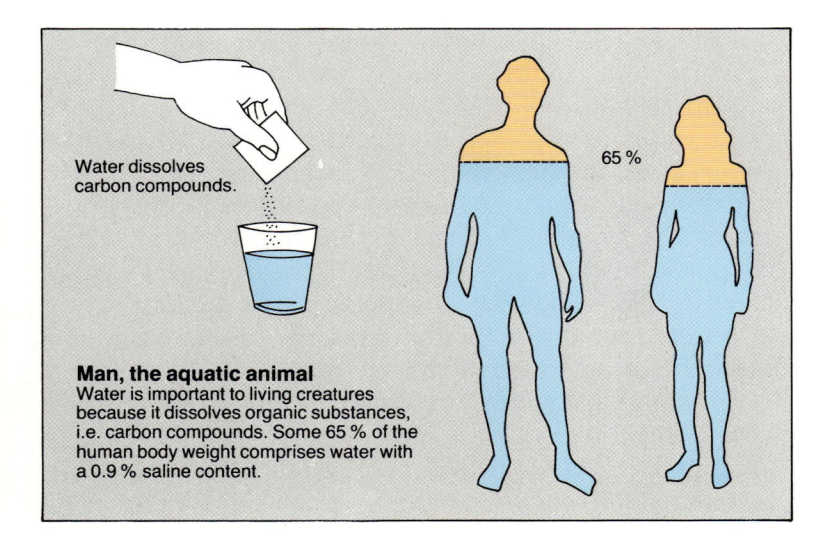

Man, the aquatic animal
Water is important to living creatures because it dissolves organic substances, i.e. carbon compounds. Some 65% of the human body weight comprises water with a 0.9% saline content.

Water is a simple compound of hydrogen and oxygen. A chemist encountering this substance for the first time would refer to it as dihydrogen oxide. Such a term, however, would lack the pleasant associations which the word "water" affords us: the clear, pure liquid that quenches our thirst, cools us, cleanses us, sustains the woodland verdure and the golden cornfields. Water has engendered all these associations because it truly is a vital substance; the prerequisite of life.

What are the unique qualities which make water so important to all living things?

Physical properties
The mean temperature of the Earth's surface is about +2°C and the air temperature normally keeps within 40°C above and below this. The freezing point of water is therefore just below the Earth's mean temperature, while its boiling point is 98° higher. This means that water can exist in liquid form for at least part of the year over most of the face of the Earth. Nowhere, however, does it get so hot that the water becomes gasified—a state which would be incompatible with life as we know it.

On our planet water exists in all three of its physical states: ice, water and vapour. Water can be present simultaneously in the atmosphere, in the hydrosphere, in the Earth's crust and in the living organisms—fulfilling vital functions.

Water has a high specific heat: a great deal of energy is needed to vaporize one litre of water. This heat can then be transported long distances as latent heat in atmospheric humidity and released again as heat in the air when moisture condenses into cloud, rain or snow. In this way water performs an important role in the levelling out of temperature differences.

Water and life
Water is important to living organisms because it is an effective and generally available solvent for carbon compounds. Most biochemical reactions can take place only in water solutions. This means that water can transport dissolved substances between different parts of the body, for example in the blood, the serum of which is water-based. The functions of water in the organism have their equivalents outside it. The water we drink and wash ourselves with is a solvent but water is also used to carry away our waste.

Life originated in water. For aquatic organisms the fluid environment is much the same outside and inside the cell and embryo. On land however fertilization and foetal development demand different mechanisms. The eggs of reptiles and birds are like miniature pools of water inside a protective shell which retains the liquid but admits oxygen. The mammalion foetus is suspended in an inner sea of fluid which supports and protects it. Water is important at all stages of development. An adult requires between 2½ and 3 litres a day for his or her physiological processes. We get some of this water through our food, the rest we simply drink.

Water and mankind
Because of his dependence upon water man has always sought to live close to it, even if this were merely a waterhole in the desert. He would usually invent mystical protective rituals for his water source and would react fiercely and even irrationally to any threat to his supply. In the Middle Ages massacres of the Jews were justified on the grounds that they were supposed to have generated the Black Death by poisoning the wells. In the industrial countries, the village pump has been replaced by pipes which bring in domestic water and carry away waste, often over considerable distances.

Practically all our water problems arise simply because the two prime functions of water are not properly separated: dirty water becomes mixed with pure. Diseases transmitted by water spread mainly where there are dense populations combined with poor standards of technology. Today most of the peoples of the world lack a sufficient supply of pure water, even though it is man's most fundamental need.

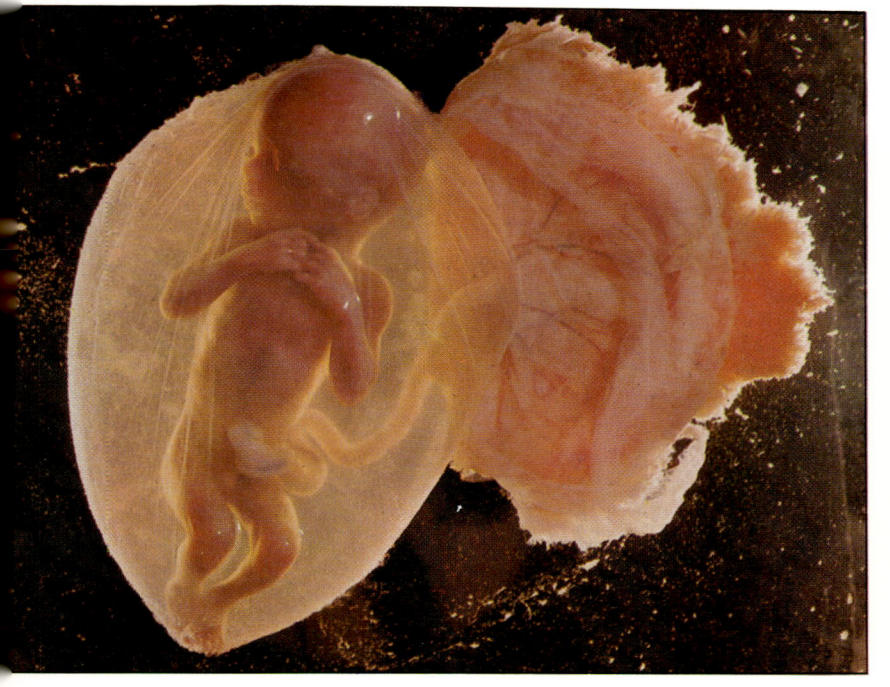

Our daily water
An adult human being needs about 3 litres of water a day to survive, excluding household water. Women in the rural districts of poor nations spend a large part of their working day hauling water from wells and rivers—water which is often insanitary.

The vital fluid

Vascular plants (exemplified by the tree, above) were the first organisms to adapt themselves completely to life on land. A complex fluid transport system raises the water from the roots of the tree up to its crown which may be 20–30 m. above the ground. In this manner the cells in the trunk and leaves acquire the moisture they need. This is a one-way system, however: the tree transpires through its foliage as much moisture as it absorbs through its roots.

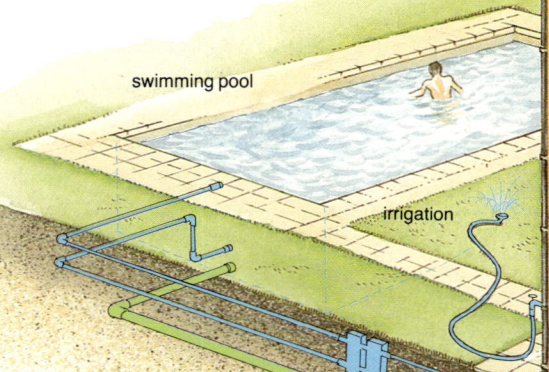

Man's water consumption

Apart from the body's internal requirements water is essential to man in many other ways. It is used for cleaning and bathing, in cooking and for drinking, in central heating systems and, ultimately, for washing away our waste products. A modern building has separate systems for the different functions. In the illustration hot and cold running water is shown in red and blue respectively, the water in the central heating system in orange and the drainage in green.

Man's water consumption has increased enormously during the last hundred years. The UN recommends 75 litres per 24 hours per person as the minimum limit for an acceptable water standard, but the industrial countries use 300–500 litres a day per capita. The greater part of this is not domestic but industrial water consumption.

29

The water cycle

To the best of our knowledge the Earth is the only place in the solar system where water exists in all three of its forms: gaseous (water vapour), liquid, and solid (ice). Closer to the sun or farther away from it, temperatures are either too hot or too cold for water to exist in liquid form. It is now believed that the Earth's waters were not part of the primeval atmosphere, but were expelled from the planet's interior when radio-active decay heated the cold minerals.

Water is essential to all forms of life and access to water is a limiting factor for many types of vegetation. During the course of one summer day a birch tree consumes 200–300 litres of water and many tropical trees require even more than this. The moisture is returned to the atmosphere through transpiration from the leaf surfaces. At the same time, however, vegetation is important to the hydrological cycle. Vegetation reduces evaporation from the ground and also protects the ground against run-off erosion. Surface roots and dense ground vegetation form innumerable barriers that slow down running water. Dead vegetation absorbs moisture like blotting paper. An unbroken covering of plantlife, especially forest, evens out the flow of surface water and hence the amount of water in the rivers and lakes. It also helps to increase the infiltration of water into the subsoil.

Most of the water on Earth is salt. The salt is believed to derive from the weathering of continental rocks. Fresh water can be equally unfit for plants and animals because of excessive

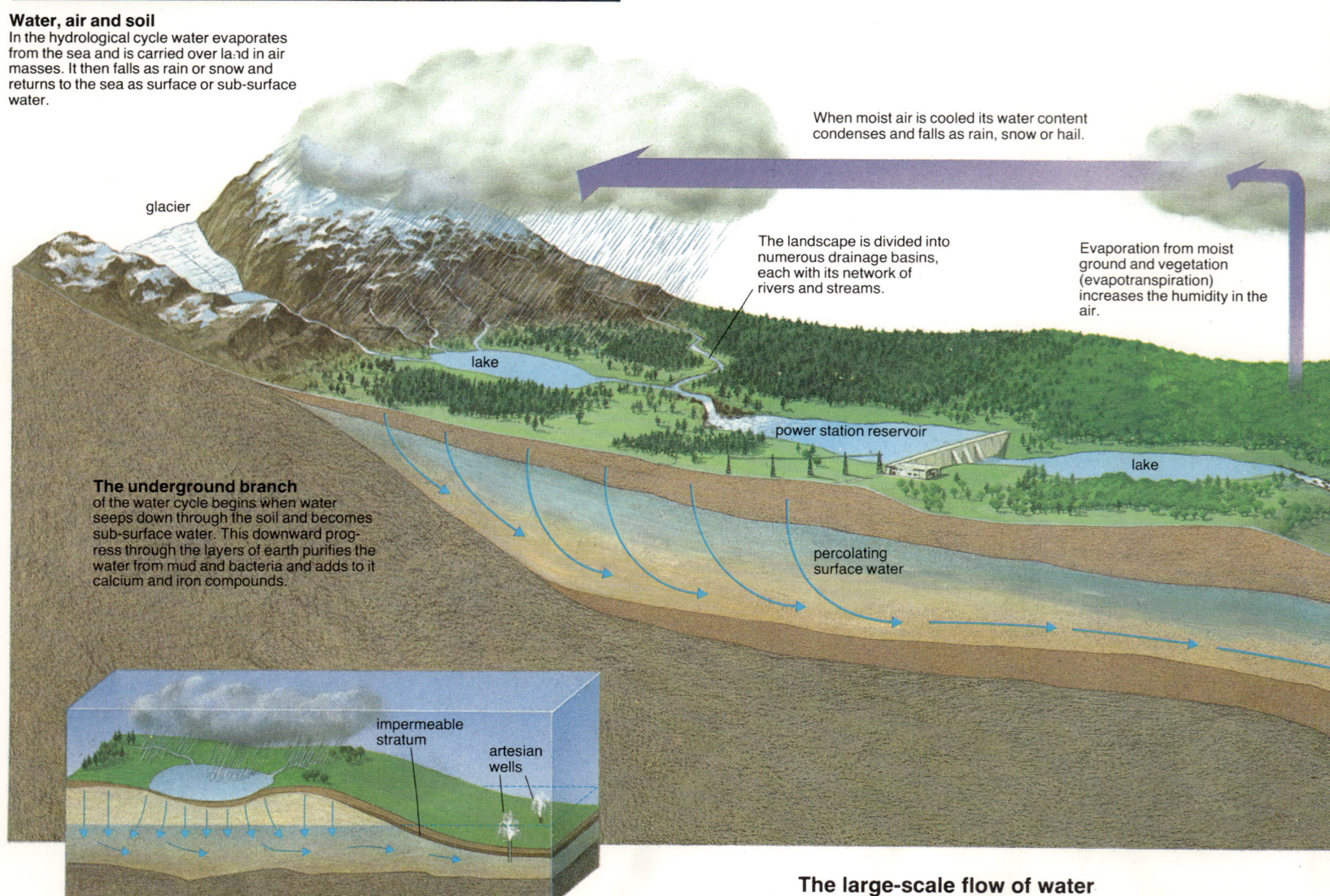

Water, air and soil
In the hydrological cycle water evaporates from the sea and is carried over land in air masses. It then falls as rain or snow and returns to the sea as surface or sub-surface water.

When moist air is cooled its water content condenses and falls as rain, snow or hail.

The landscape is divided into numerous drainage basins, each with its network of rivers and streams.

Evaporation from moist ground and vegetation (evapotranspiration) increases the humidity in the air.

The underground branch
of the water cycle begins when water seeps down through the soil and becomes sub-surface water. This downward progress through the layers of earth purifies the water from mud and bacteria and adds to it calcium and iron compounds.

Sub-surface water
(arrows) saturates the ground up to the level of the water table. Impermeable rocks above the water-bearing strata create pressure when the ground surface is below the natural water table (dotted line). If a hole is drilled through the impermeable strata the water spouts up, forming an artesian well.

The large-scale flow of water
The hydrological cycle unites the atmosphere, the hydrosphere and the Earth's crust. In the atmospheric sector of this cycle the water is present mainly in the form of water vapour. In the terrestrial sector there are two important branches: the surface water's course along streams, rivers and lakes, and the slow progress of sub-surface water through the aquifers, the water-bearing strata. Both of these normally terminate in the sea.

mud content and other impurities. Consequently, pure water can be a very valuable commodity. For the greater part of the year not a drop of water from the Colorado river reaches the Pacific Ocean. It is all used for irrigation and industrial purposes—distributed according to a water rights system that keeps teams of lawyers constantly employed.

The rivers' alluvial deposits created fertile river plains where the earliest civilizations emerged: in Mesopotamia and Egypt, along the Indus and in China. The Huang He, which in its upper reaches runs through loess country, moves about 10 % of all the alluvial silt in the world and its flow looks more like liquid mud than water. In the lower reaches this silt is deposited in the river bed, thereby raising it. This has many times caused the Huang He to burst its embankments, resulting in devastating floods. The silt which is not deposited but reaches the coast has given the Yellow Sea its name.

Nearly all fresh water is sub-surface water and the greater part of the total fresh water flow from rain pools to the sea probably also takes place underground. The normal cycle of sub-surface water can be reckoned in years or at the most in a few centuries. Beneath the Sahara, however, there is a layer of "fossil" water, which has been there since the rains of the last glaciation and which has been on its way towards the sea for tens of thousands of years. It was not until recently that man first discovered the presence of this vast reservoir and began to utilize it.

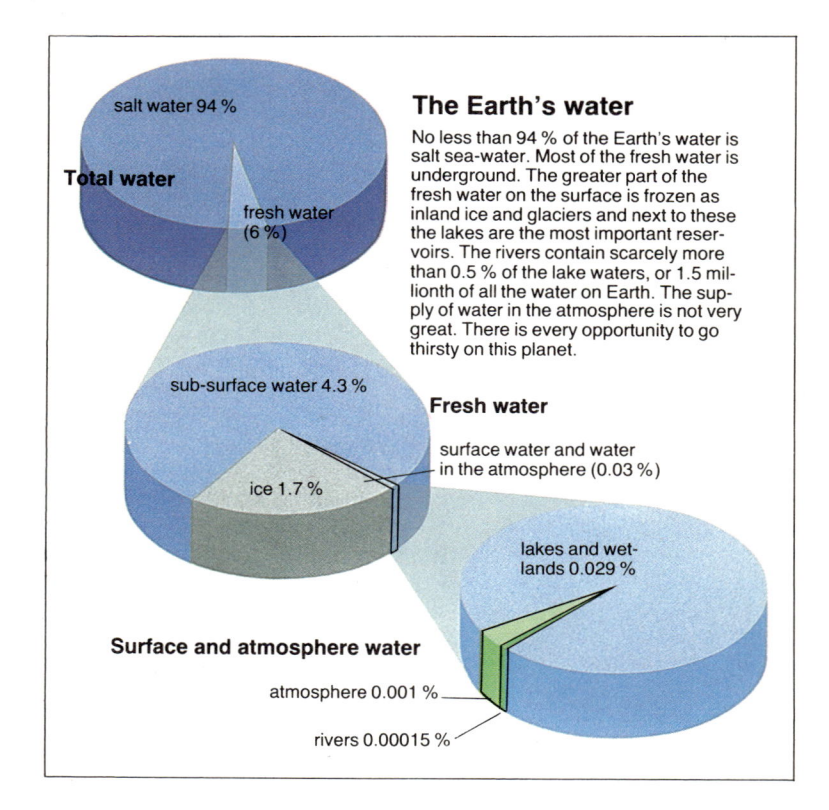

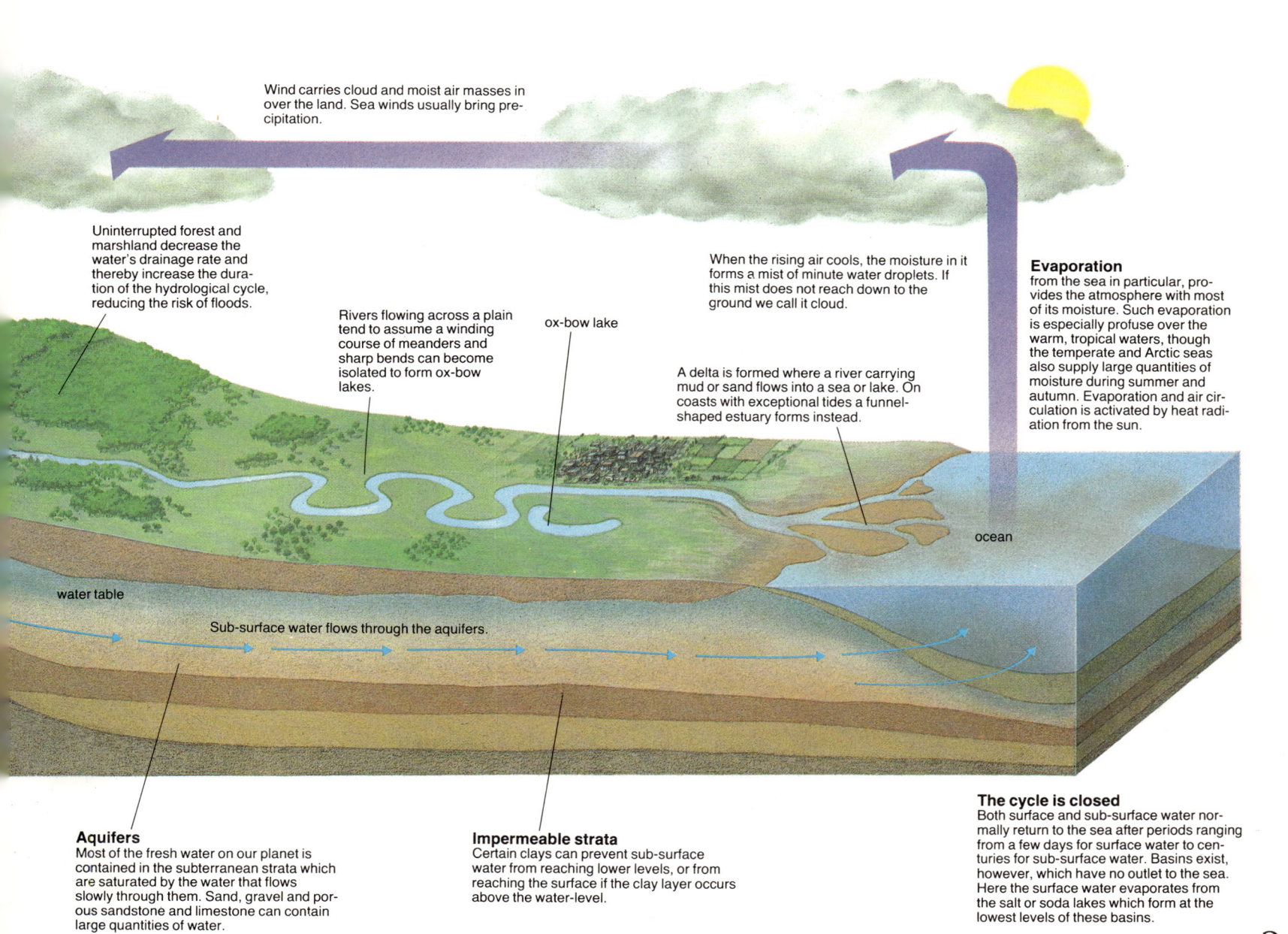

The Earth's water

No less than 94 % of the Earth's water is salt sea-water. Most of the fresh water is underground. The greater part of the fresh water on the surface is frozen as inland ice and glaciers and next to these the lakes are the most important reservoirs. The rivers contain scarcely more than 0.5 % of the lake waters, or 1.5 millionth of all the water on Earth. The supply of water in the atmosphere is not very great. There is every opportunity to go thirsty on this planet.

Total water
- salt water 94 %
- fresh water (6 %)

Fresh water
- sub-surface water 4.3 %
- ice 1.7 %
- surface water and water in the atmosphere (0.03 %)

Surface and atmosphere water
- lakes and wetlands 0.029 %
- atmosphere 0.001 %
- rivers 0.00015 %

Wind carries cloud and moist air masses in over the land. Sea winds usually bring precipitation.

Uninterrupted forest and marshland decrease the water's drainage rate and thereby increase the duration of the hydrological cycle, reducing the risk of floods.

Rivers flowing across a plain tend to assume a winding course of meanders and sharp bends can become isolated to form ox-bow lakes.

When the rising air cools, the moisture in it forms a mist of minute water droplets. If this mist does not reach down to the ground we call it cloud.

A delta is formed where a river carrying mud or sand flows into a sea or lake. On coasts with exceptional tides a funnel-shaped estuary forms instead.

Evaporation from the sea in particular, provides the atmosphere with most of its moisture. Such evaporation is especially profuse over the warm, tropical waters, though the temperate and Arctic seas also supply large quantities of moisture during summer and autumn. Evaporation and air circulation is activated by heat radiation from the sun.

ox-bow lake

ocean

water table

Sub-surface water flows through the aquifers.

Aquifers
Most of the fresh water on our planet is contained in the subterranean strata which are saturated by the water that flows slowly through them. Sand, gravel and porous sandstone and limestone can contain large quantities of water.

Impermeable strata
Certain clays can prevent sub-surface water from reaching lower levels, or from reaching the surface if the clay layer occurs above the water-level.

The cycle is closed
Both surface and sub-surface water normally return to the sea after periods ranging from a few days for surface water to centuries for sub-surface water. Basins exist, however, which have no outlet to the sea. Here the surface water evaporates from the salt or soda lakes which form at the lowest levels of these basins.

The realm of ice

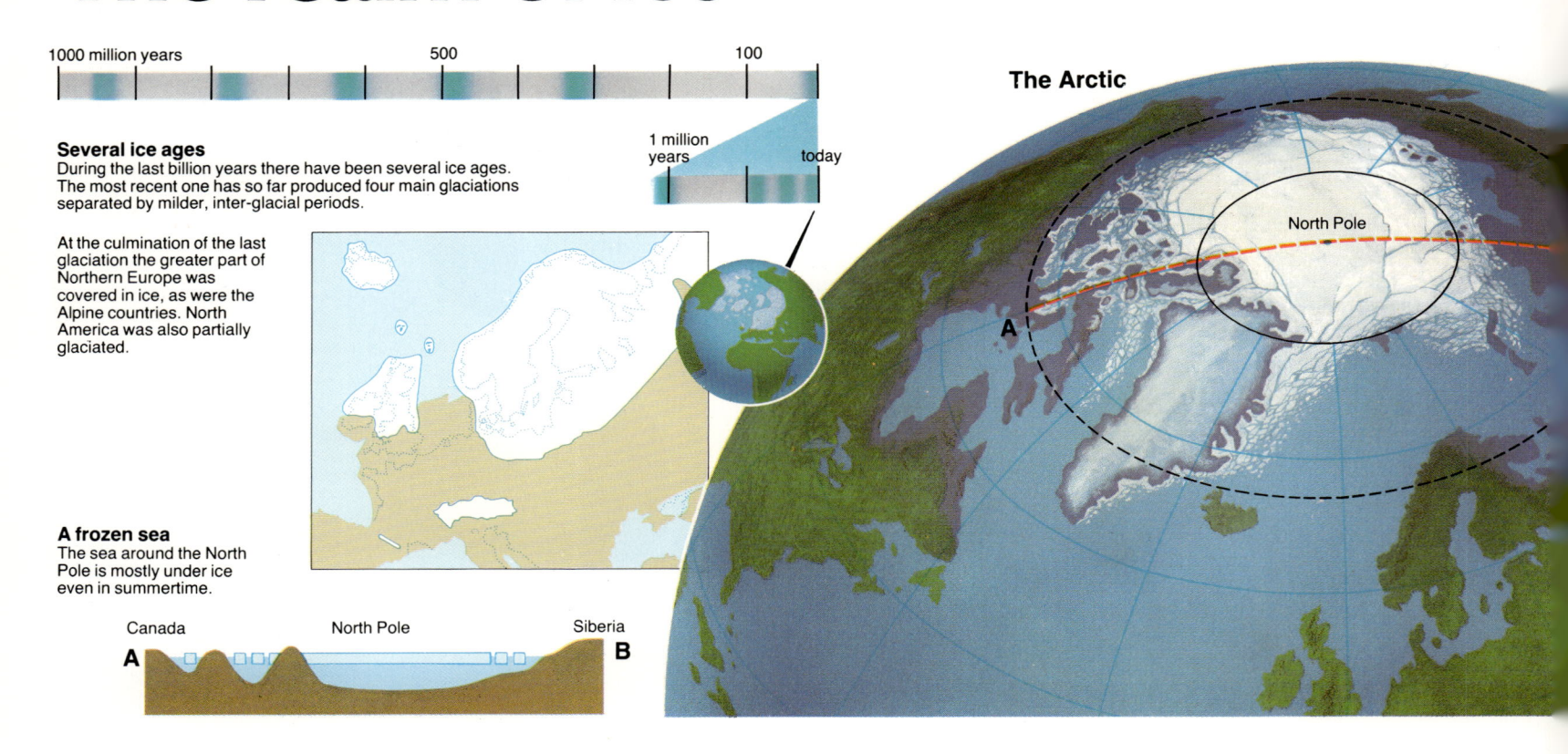

Several ice ages
During the last billion years there have been several ice ages. The most recent one has so far produced four main glaciations separated by milder, inter-glacial periods.

At the culmination of the last glaciation the greater part of Northern Europe was covered in ice, as were the Alpine countries. North America was also partially glaciated.

A frozen sea
The sea around the North Pole is mostly under ice even in summertime.

The Arctic

The Earth has two extensive ice covers: the arctic region around the North Pole and the antarctic region of the South Pole. At these extreme latitudes the sun never climbs very high in the heavens and it thus provides little heat. The ice regions also have their outposts all the way down to the equator; wherever there is enough precipitation and sufficient elevation above sea-level to keep temperatures below freezing glaciers can form.

The Earth has not always had these ice covers however. When snow falls on to open sea the flakes immediately melt. On a planet where over 70% of the surface is covered in water, the poles are within sea areas most of the time and thus no ice forms around them. Polar ice can form in two conditions only: either the pole must be on a continent or else in a closed sea basin, so that the exchange of water with warm seas is counteracted and pack ice can form. Our present geological epoch is unusual in that both these requirements are fulfilled, at the South Pole and the North Pole respectively. The result is an ice age in both hemispheres, though we have the good fortune to exist in one of its milder inter-glacial periods. Most of the Earth's earlier ice ages have apparently affected only one hemisphere. The current ice age will continue until the continental drift opens up the Arctic Ocean to warm currents from the south and pushes the antarctic continent away from the South Pole.

Between them the very warm tropics and the cold polar tracts create a gigantic heat engine where the equatorial belts are the boiler and the polar regions serve as the cooling system. This engine drives the global air circulation which transports enormous quantities of air around the world. In other words the climate and weather is determined to a large extent by the polar regions. Oceanic currents also transport ice from the polar regions and thereby influence local climate.

Man reached the Arctic as long ago as the close of the last ice age, but not until this century has he succeeded in penetrating the Antarctic. In both places in our time the pursuit of natural resources has become a grave threat to the delicately balanced polar environments.

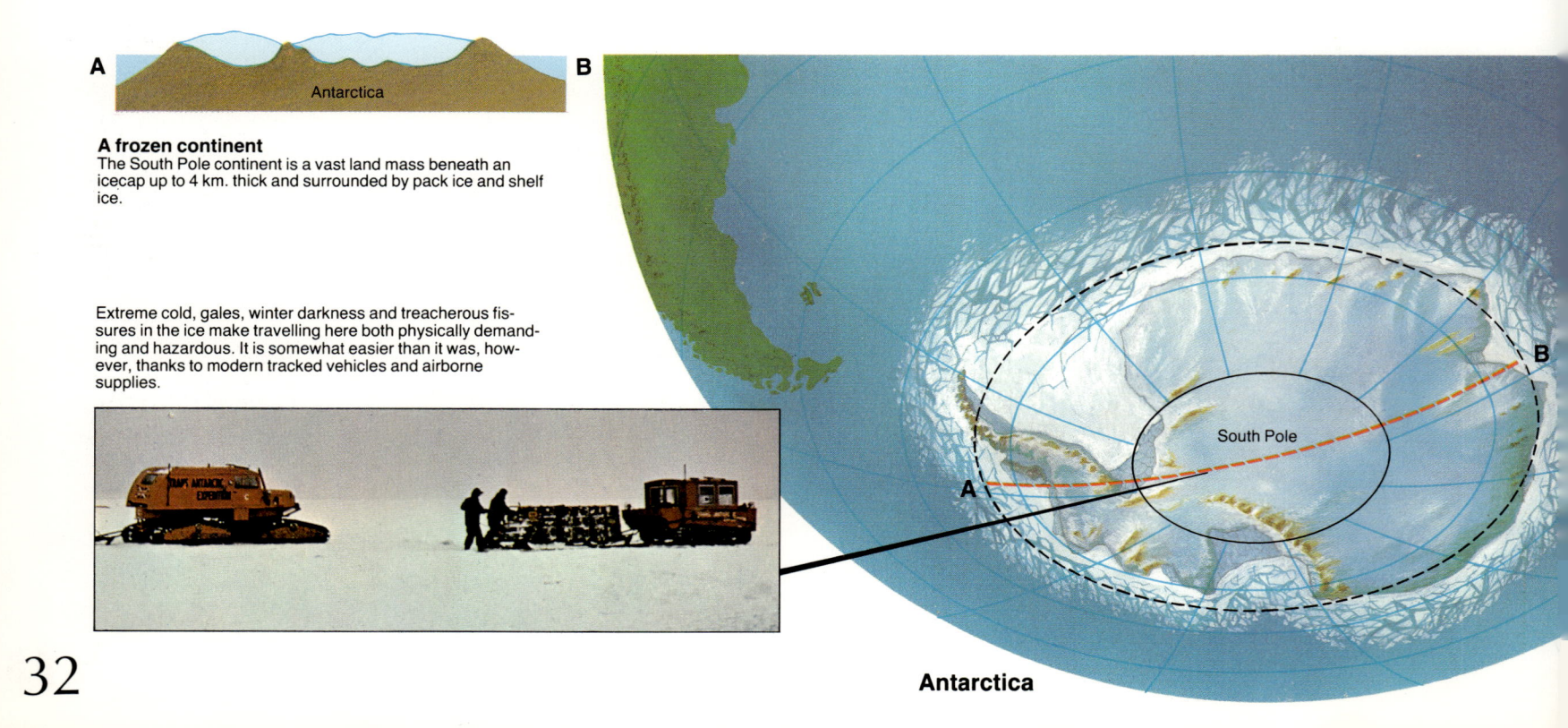

A frozen continent
The South Pole continent is a vast land mass beneath an icecap up to 4 km. thick and surrounded by pack ice and shelf ice.

Extreme cold, gales, winter darkness and treacherous fissures in the ice make travelling here both physically demanding and hazardous. It is somewhat easier than it was, however, thanks to modern tracked vehicles and airborne supplies.

Antarctica

Glaciers and currently glaciated areas

The glacier—a river of ice
The ice mass of the glacier increases at the upper end (the accumulation zone) where the winter's snow is converted by compaction into ice. This moves downward like a plastic mass. Meanwhile at the lower end (the waste zone) the ice diminishes through melting and evaporation.

Labels on diagram: snowfall; snow limit; crevasse; snow is packed together and becomes ice; accumulation zone; solid rock; loose material from rocks forms ground moraine; waste zone; the glacial till, sharp-edged stones and gravel, can form terminal moraine ridges at the glacier snout; glacial water; till

The glacial landscape
Glacial erosion cuts niches (cirques) in the mountain sides and produces characteristic U-shaped valleys. Terminal moraines are often found at the foot of the glaciers. Similar but larger glacial landscapes were formed during the glaciations and when the land ice melted.

The antarctic icecap contains enormous quantities of water and if it were to melt, the world's sea level would rise several tens of metres.

The antarctic waters from 40°S ("the roaring forties") southwards are among the roughest in the world. The waves rage unimpeded all round the continent.

Annual cold cycles
The ice area in the northern polar region multiplies every winter. In the summer season shipping is hindered by ice along the Siberian coast and has to be assisted by ice breakers. During winter this is the case as far south as the Baltic Sea. Cold fronts and blizzards cause chaos practically every winter both in Europe and in the USA, leaving motorists stranded among the snowdrifts.

33

The oceans

Viewed from space the Earth is an oceanic planet which might have more aptly been named Water, since 71% of its area is covered by seas. The deep seas comprise about 55% of the Earth's surface.

The beds of the deep seas and their unique geology were far beyond our reach until well into the present century. After World War II when studies were finally begun, the findings created a scientific revolution. The oceanic crust is not, as was formerly believed, one of Earth's oldest geological formations, instead it is among the most recent. Nowhere is it more than 200 million years old, while the earliest known continental rocks are almost four *billion* years old. The reason why the oceanic crust is not particularly ancient is because it is constantly being melted down and renewed.

The scientific study of the Earth's oceans is known as oceanography. As early as the 17th century mariners and geographers attempted to chart the oceanic currents, a task made more difficult due to their lack of instruments for precise navigation. Oceanic research in the modern sense of the term did not emerge until the 19th century. Since the seabed was still inaccessible this research was then directed mainly at marine biology, although important geophysical and geological discoveries were also made. One of the first of these was Darwin's theory on the origin of atolls: islands sink beneath the sea but the coral polyps, which can only live near the surface, tend constantly to build their reefs upwards towards the surface. It was Darwin's observations on the origins of new species on isolated oceanic islands which provided him with the material for his theory on evolution through natural selection. Thus our studies of the sea have given rise to not one but two scientific revolutions: biological and geophysical.

We now have a good knowledge of the basic features of ocean bed topography and are learning more about the sedimentation and rock types. Oceanic research is still by no means a complete science. New technology, especially in space, constantly provides us with fresh knowledge. From satellites it is now possible not only to chart the seabeds by gravimetry (the measurement of gravitational forces exerted by the bedrock and sediments on the ocean floor) but we can also measure the phytoplankton content of the water. There is little doubt that many more surprises await us in the depths of the oceans.

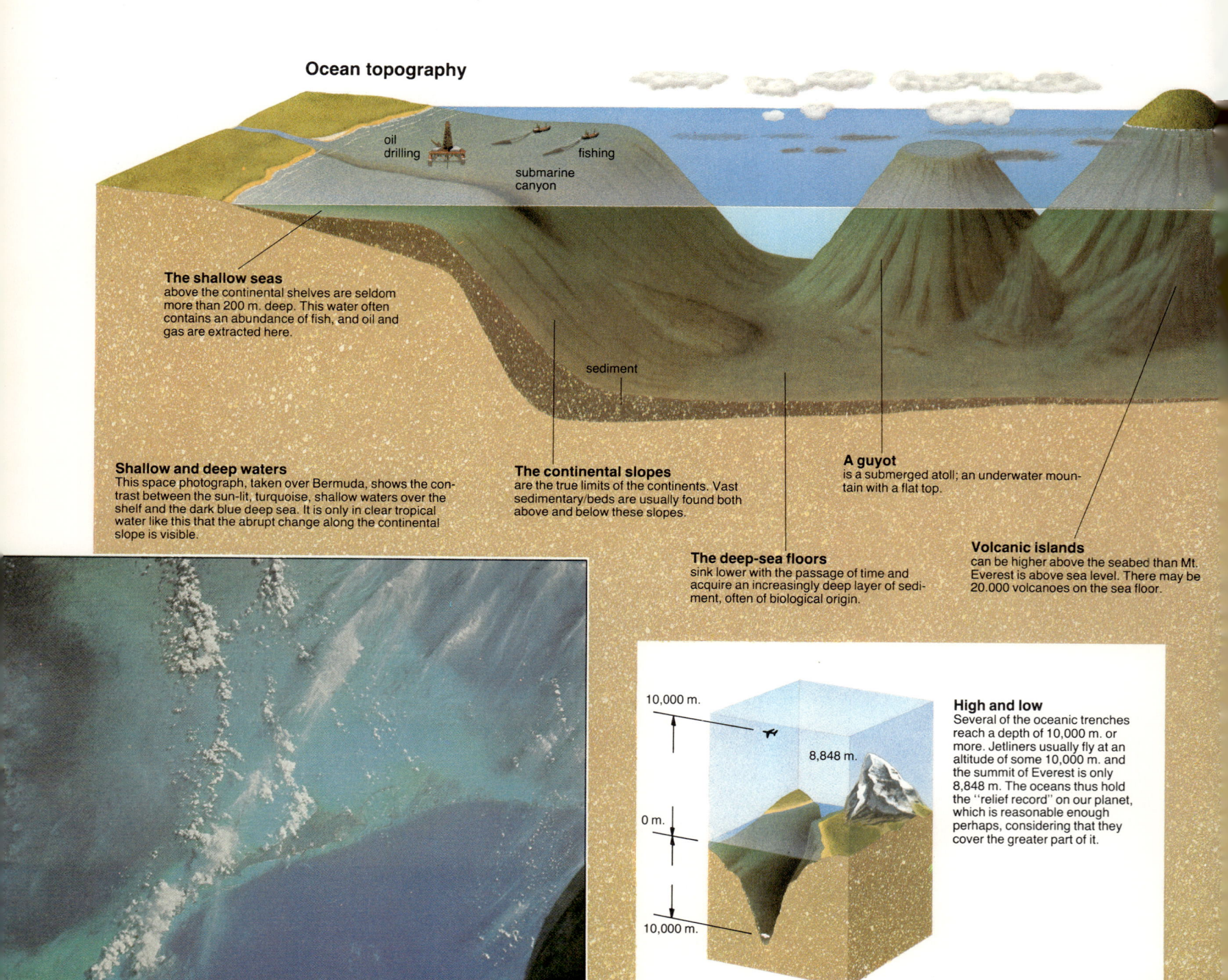

Ocean topography

The shallow seas above the continental shelves are seldom more than 200 m. deep. This water often contains an abundance of fish, and oil and gas are extracted here.

Shallow and deep waters This space photograph, taken over Bermuda, shows the contrast between the sun-lit, turquoise, shallow waters over the shelf and the dark blue deep sea. It is only in clear tropical water like this that the abrupt change along the continental slope is visible.

The continental slopes are the true limits of the continents. Vast sedimentary beds are usually found both above and below these slopes.

The deep-sea floors sink lower with the passage of time and acquire an increasingly deep layer of sediment, often of biological origin.

A guyot is a submerged atoll; an underwater mountain with a flat top.

Volcanic islands can be higher above the seabed than Mt. Everest is above sea level. There may be 20,000 volcanoes on the sea floor.

High and low Several of the oceanic trenches reach a depth of 10,000 m. or more. Jetliners usually fly at an altitude of some 10,000 m. and the summit of Everest is only 8,848 m. The oceans thus hold the "relief record" on our planet, which is reasonable enough perhaps, considering that they cover the greater part of it.

34

The four oceans
The oceans and their percentage shares of the planet's total sea area.

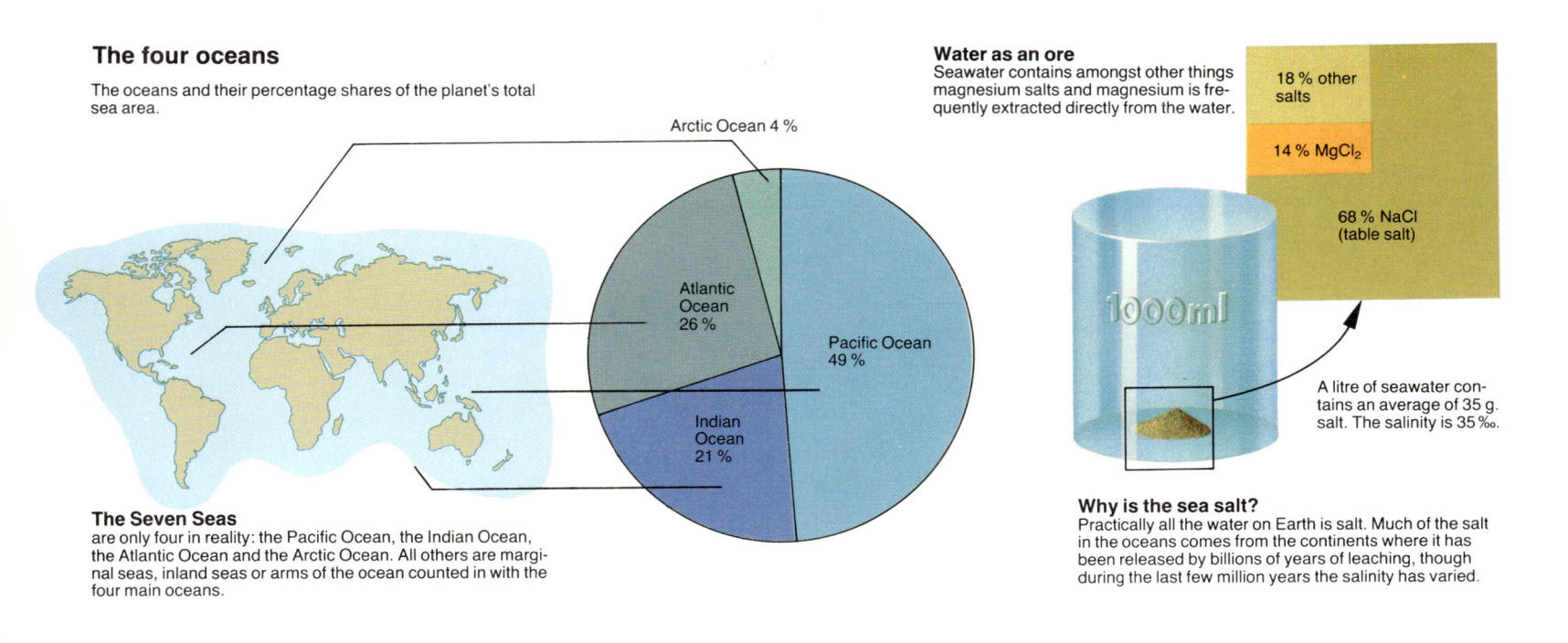

Arctic Ocean 4 %
Atlantic Ocean 26 %
Pacific Ocean 49 %
Indian Ocean 21 %

The Seven Seas
are only four in reality: the Pacific Ocean, the Indian Ocean, the Atlantic Ocean and the Arctic Ocean. All others are marginal seas, inland seas or arms of the ocean counted in with the four main oceans.

Water as an ore
Seawater contains amongst other things magnesium salts and magnesium is frequently extracted directly from the water.

18 % other salts
14 % MgCl$_2$
68 % NaCl (table salt)

A litre of seawater contains an average of 35 g. salt. The salinity is 35‰.

Why is the sea salt?
Practically all the water on Earth is salt. Much of the salt in the oceans comes from the continents where it has been released by billions of years of leaching, though during the last few million years the salinity has varied.

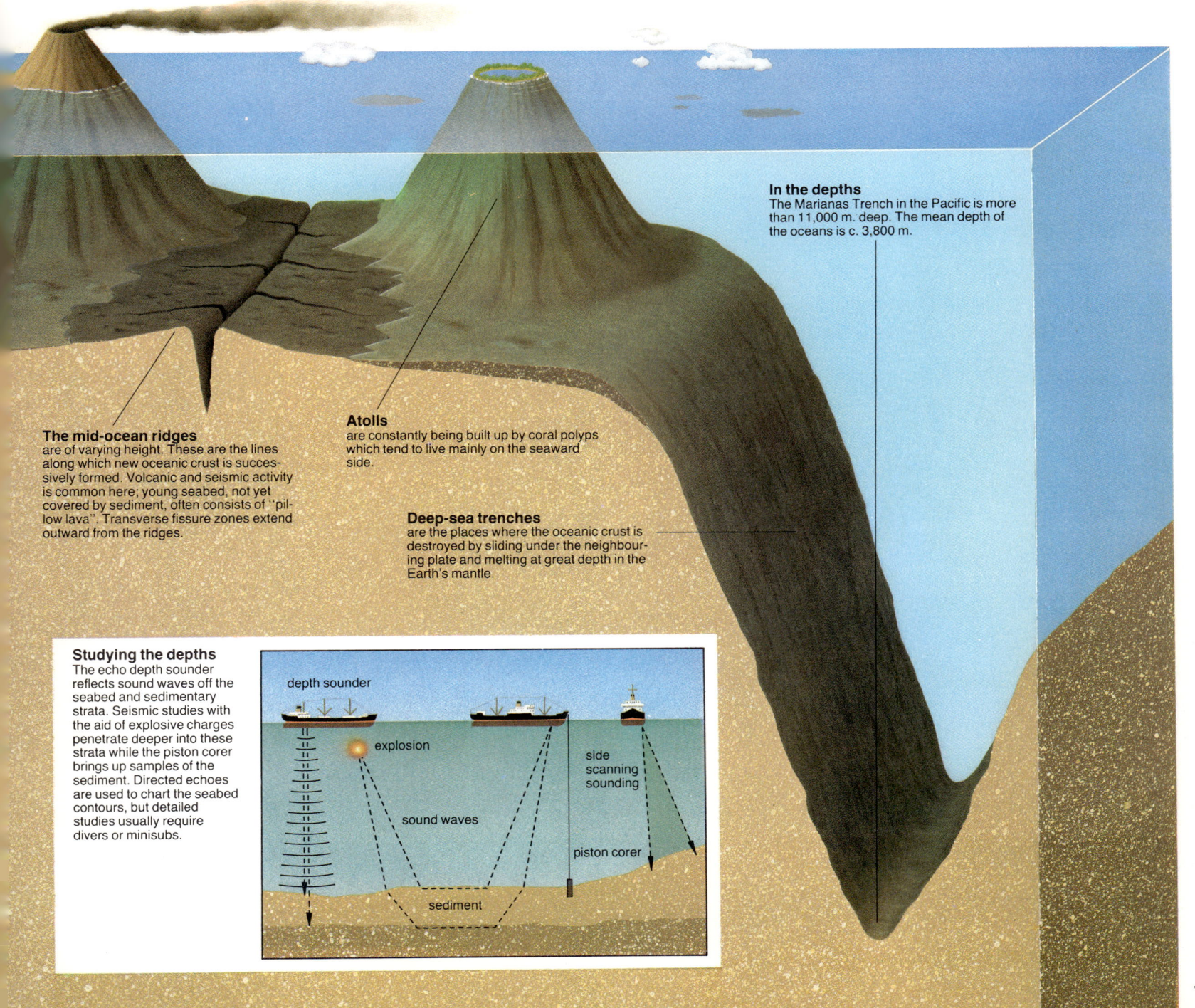

In the depths
The Marianas Trench in the Pacific is more than 11,000 m. deep. The mean depth of the oceans is c. 3,800 m.

The mid-ocean ridges
are of varying height. These are the lines along which new oceanic crust is successively formed. Volcanic and seismic activity is common here; young seabed, not yet covered by sediment, often consists of "pillow lava". Transverse fissure zones extend outward from the ridges.

Atolls
are constantly being built up by coral polyps which tend to live mainly on the seaward side.

Deep-sea trenches
are the places where the oceanic crust is destroyed by sliding under the neighbouring plate and melting at great depth in the Earth's mantle.

Studying the depths
The echo depth sounder reflects sound waves off the seabed and sedimentary strata. Seismic studies with the aid of explosive charges penetrate deeper into these strata while the piston corer brings up samples of the sediment. Directed echoes are used to chart the seabed contours, but detailed studies usually require divers or minisubs.

depth sounder
explosion
sound waves
side scanning sounding
piston corer
sediment

35

The powerful sea

Standing on a rocky coast during a gale makes one dramatically aware of the enormous energy contained in the sea. The movements of the sea, the waves and currents, represent solar energy converted mainly by winds in the atmosphere.

Atmosphere and sea
The interplay between air and water is complex. One example is the apparently simple oceanic current, driven by the wind. On the surface there is a flow of water along the direction of the wind, as would be expected. With increasing depth, however, this flow is deflected by the rotation of the Earth—so much so that at a depth of about 100 m. it is running in the opposite direction to the wind. The net or mean current runs at right-angles to the wind direction—to the right in the northern hemisphere and to the left in the southern hemisphere. Normal surface currents move at an average of a few km. every 24 hours.

There is also a chemical exchange, between the atmosphere and the sea, principally of carbon dioxide and oxygen, thereby stabilizing the content of these gases in both air and sea alike. This gas exchange takes place mainly through diffusion, i.e. the direct exchange of atoms. The wind also whips up aerosols consisting of almost invisible droplets of water which contain dissolved salts. When the water has evaporated the salt crystals are carried by the wind and then serve as condensation nuclei around which form larger water drops, producing mist, cloud and rain.

The wind creates small ripples on the water surface and these quickly grow into waves. The waves catch much of the wind, thereby absorbing even more of the wind's energy. This energy does not penetrate very far, however, diminishing to a mere 4–5% at a depth corresponding to one third the distance between the wave crests. As the wave rolls forward a small part of this energy is lost through friction, though the ocean swell can carry energy across great distances. Finally the energy is lost altogether when the waves break on the shore—the shore being eroded and re-formed by this process.

Oceanic currents
Currents can be activated by density and temperature variations in different masses of water, but the big surface current systems of the oceans are driven by the winds. The trade winds determine the patterns of the equatorial currents and counter-currents. The Gulf Stream is created by water which is carried by the Northern Equatorial Current towards the Antilles and on

Wind and waves
Seventy-one percent of the surface of our planet is covered by water and over this area a complex physical interplay takes place between atmosphere and hydrosphere. The waves are an easily observed and dramatic example of this.

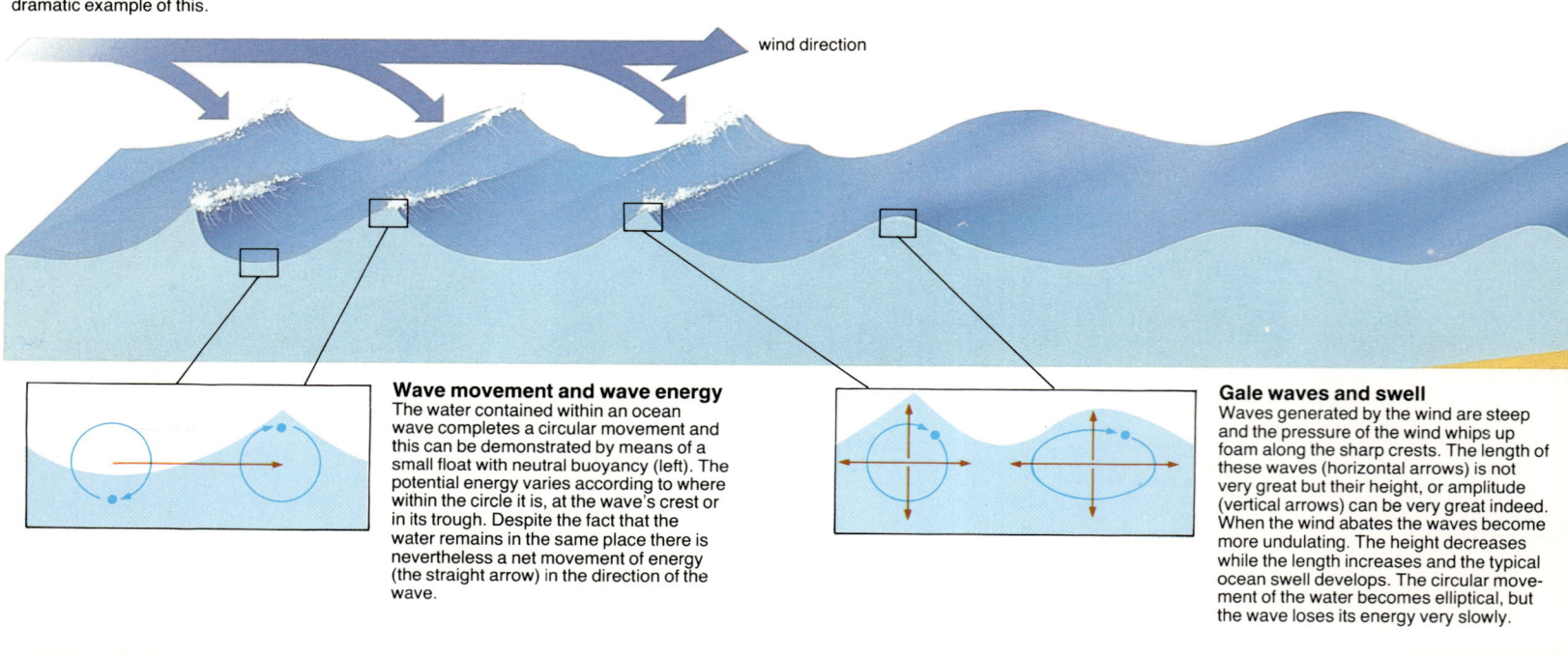

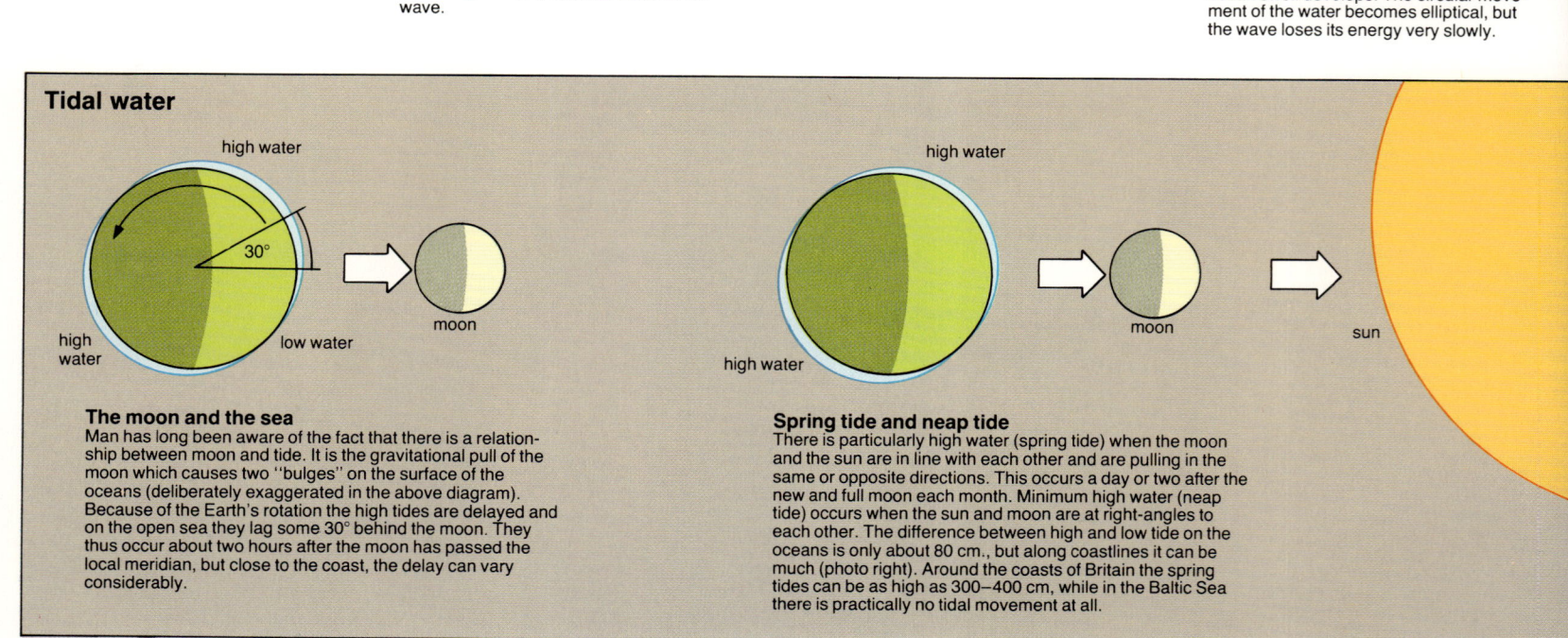

Wave movement and wave energy
The water contained within an ocean wave completes a circular movement and this can be demonstrated by means of a small float with neutral buoyancy (left). The potential energy varies according to where within the circle it is, at the wave's crest or in its trough. Despite the fact that the water remains in the same place there is nevertheless a net movement of energy (the straight arrow) in the direction of the wave.

Gale waves and swell
Waves generated by the wind are steep and the pressure of the wind whips up foam along the sharp crests. The length of these waves (horizontal arrows) is not very great but their height, or amplitude (vertical arrows) can be very great indeed. When the wind abates the waves become more undulating. The height decreases while the length increases and the typical ocean swell develops. The circular movement of the water becomes elliptical, but the wave loses its energy very slowly.

Tidal water

The moon and the sea
Man has long been aware of the fact that there is a relationship between moon and tide. It is the gravitational pull of the moon which causes two "bulges" on the surface of the oceans (deliberately exaggerated in the above diagram). Because of the Earth's rotation the high tides are delayed and on the open sea they lag some 30° behind the moon. They thus occur about two hours after the moon has passed the local meridian, but close to the coast, the delay can vary considerably.

Spring tide and neap tide
There is particularly high water (spring tide) when the moon and the sun are in line with each other and are pulling in the same or opposite directions. This occurs a day or two after the new and full moon each month. Minimum high water (neap tide) occurs when the sun and moon are at right-angles to each other. The difference between high and low tide on the oceans is only about 80 cm., but along coastlines it can be much (photo right). Around the coasts of Britain the spring tides can be as high as 300–400 cm., while in the Baltic Sea there is practically no tidal movement at all.

36

into the Caribbean Sea and which then "spills over" in a north-easterly direction. A steady westerly drift flows around the Antarctic where there are no continents to hinder it.

Where winds and currents drive the surface water out from the coast this is replaced by other water rising from deeper levels. The latter is often rich in nutrients, yielding an abundance of fish. Currents of nutritious water from the polar seas create other productive fisheries, to the east of Japan for example.

Dangerous aspects
The energy of sea can sometimes become a hazard even on land. A combination of spring tides and strong on-shore winds can cause devastating floods, as have occurred along the coast of Holland. Seabed earthquakes or volcanic explosions can produce sea waves, called tsunamis. Out at sea these may be no more than half a metre or so high and perhaps 20 km. from one crest to the next. But they can travel at several hundred km/h, striking land with tremendous force. The wave which was created when the island of Krakatau between Java and Sumatra exploded in 1883 rose to a height of 35 m. when it hit the coast of Java. Small ships were thrown far up onto the land and 35,000 people are believed to have perished.

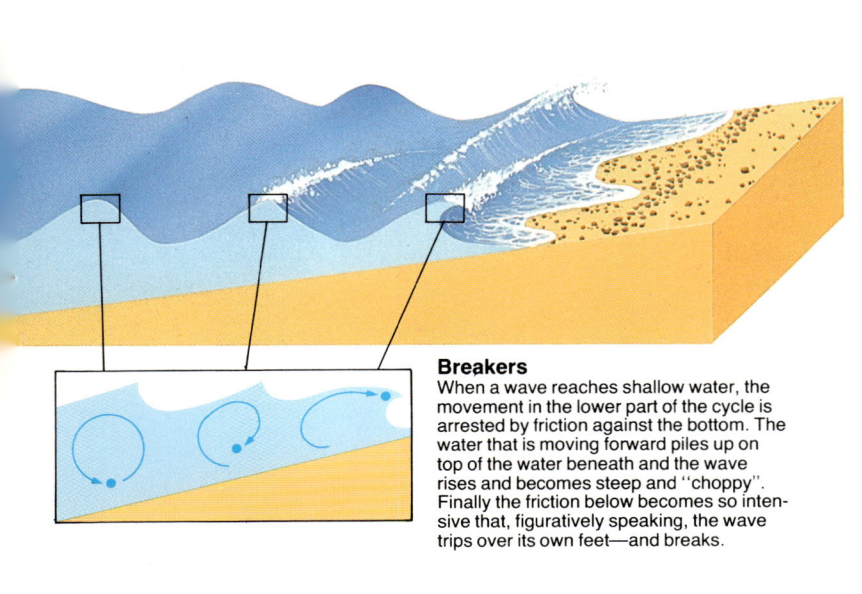

Energy from the sea

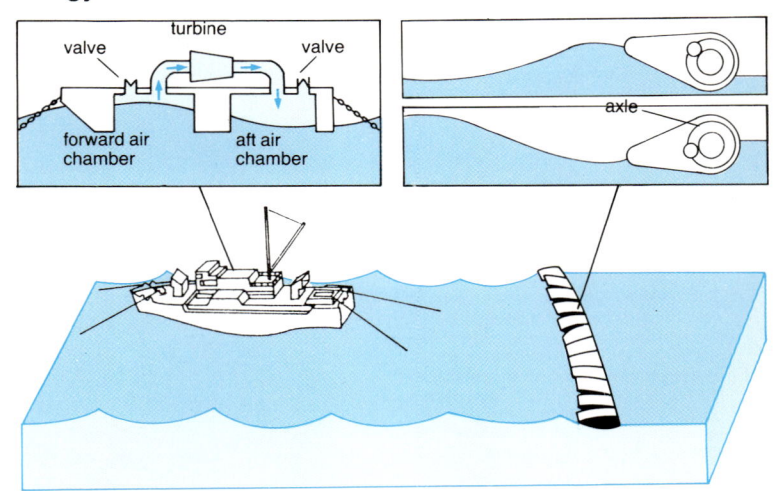

Wave energy
One way of deriving energy from waves is to anchor barges in the sea, each barge having two air chambers, separated by half a wavelength. When waves pass under the barges air is pumped in through the intake wave in the force chamber, from there through the turbine to the aft chamber and then out again.

In a sea inlet duckbill-shaped floats mounted on flexible axles can be used. The movements of the floats are transmitted via gears to the axles which in their turn drive electric generators set up ashore.

Breakers
When a wave reaches shallow water, the movement in the lower part of the cycle is arrested by friction against the bottom. The water that is moving forward piles up on top of the water beneath and the wave rises and becomes steep and "choppy". Finally the friction below becomes so intensive that, figuratively speaking, the wave trips over its own feet—and breaks.

Solar energy from the sea
Ocean Thermal Energy Conversion (OTEC) is a technique regarded as being particularly applicable in tropical waters. Here the sun-warmed surface water is used to gasify a suitable agent, for example freon or ammonia, whereupon the gas is harnessed to drive a turbine generator. The agent is subsequently condensed by means of deeper, cold water brought up by a syphon system. The agent, now in liquid form, is passed on again to the heat exchanger and the circuit is complete. Plans exist to build floating power stations and bring the electricity ashore through flexible cables.

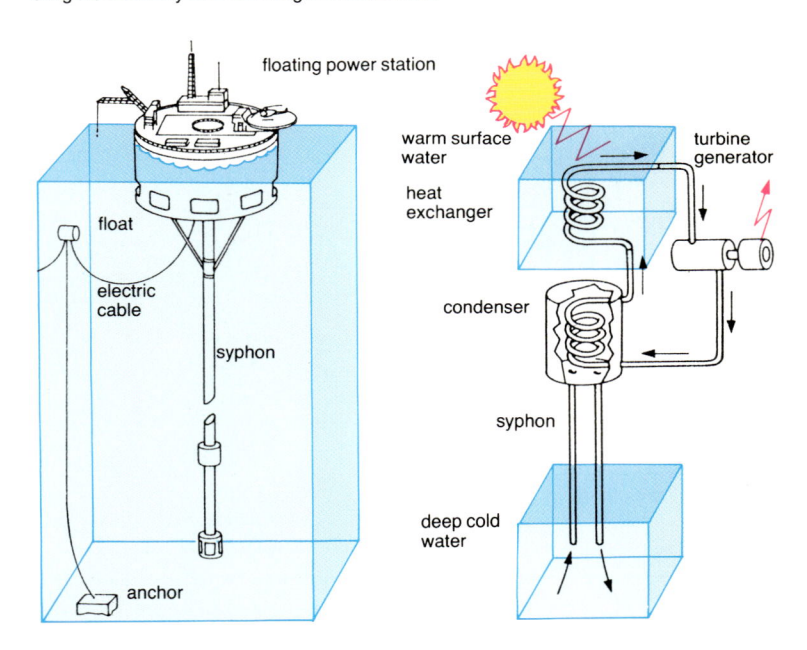

Tidal energy
In places where tides run high a narrow bay can be transformed into a power station reservoir by building a dam across the entrance, so that both inflowing and outflowing water can be used to drive reversible propeller turbines. There are not many places, however, with the right combination of a deep, narrow bay and sufficient ebb and flow.

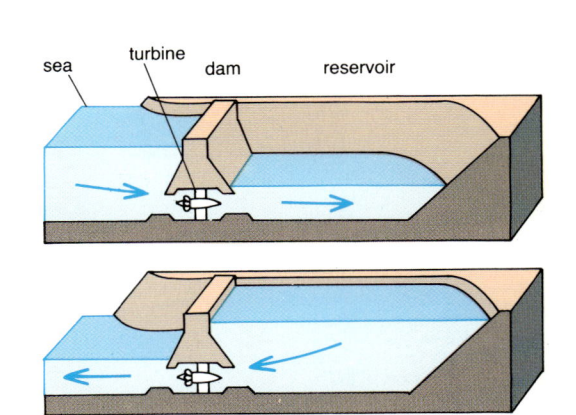

37

Aquatic life

The ocean's four depth zones

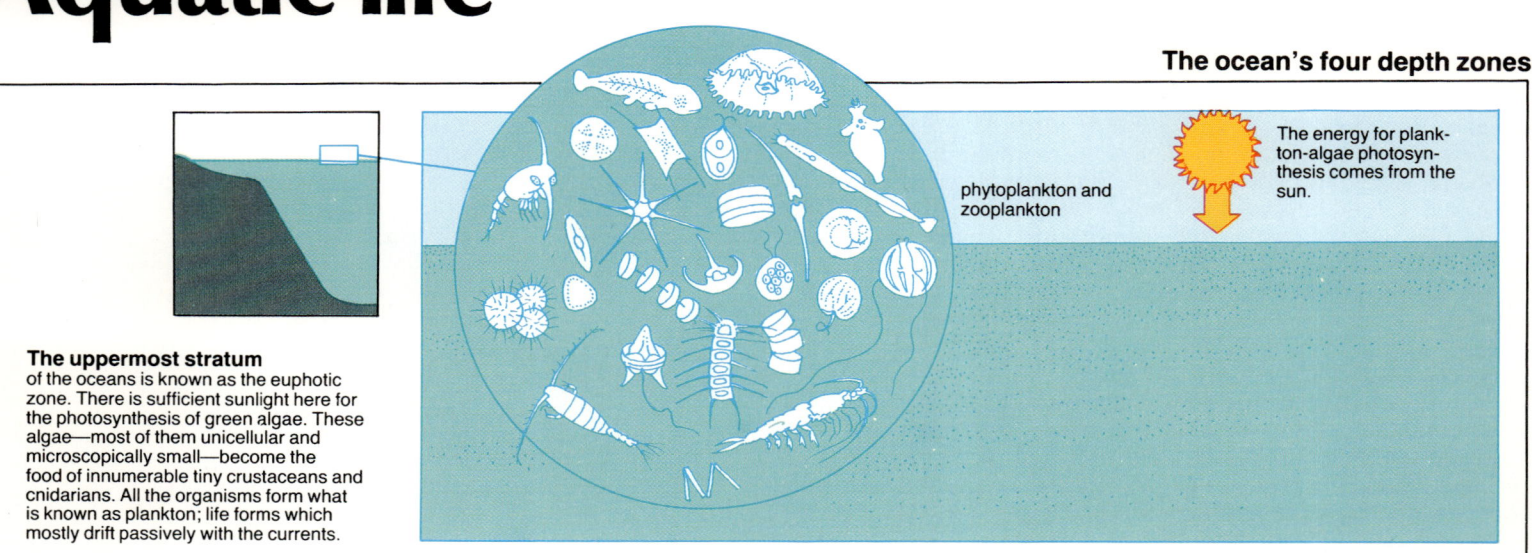

phytoplankton and zooplankton

The energy for plankton-algae photosynthesis comes from the sun.

The uppermost stratum of the oceans is known as the euphotic zone. There is sufficient sunlight here for the photosynthesis of green algae. These algae—most of them unicellular and microscopically small—become the food of innumerable tiny crustaceans and cnidarians. All the organisms form what is known as plankton; life forms which mostly drift passively with the currents.

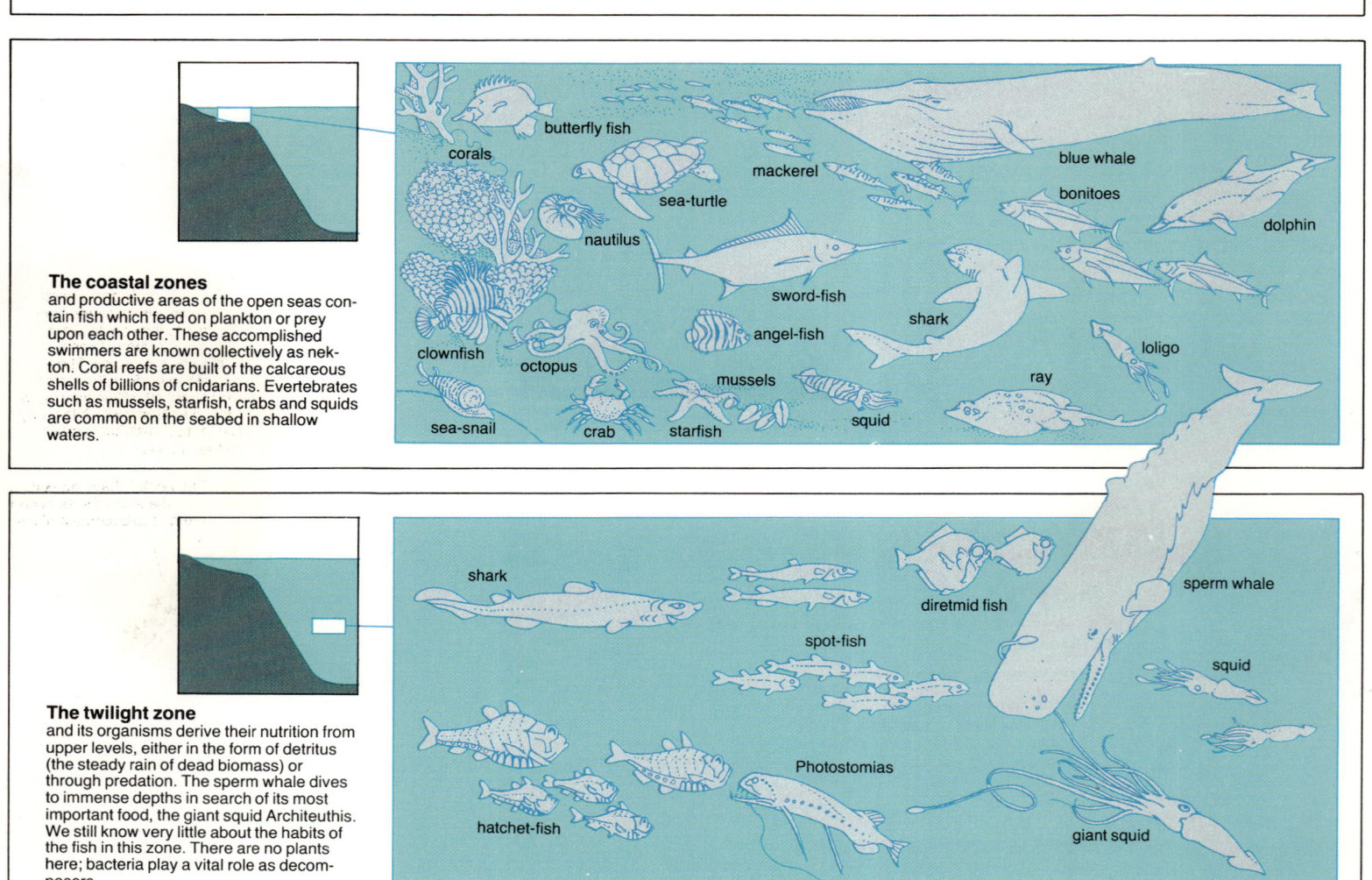

corals, butterfly fish, sea-turtle, nautilus, mackerel, blue whale, bonitoes, dolphin, sword-fish, angel-fish, shark, clownfish, octopus, loligo, mussels, ray, sea-snail, crab, starfish, squid

The coastal zones and productive areas of the open seas contain fish which feed on plankton or prey upon each other. These accomplished swimmers are known collectively as nekton. Coral reefs are built of the calcareous shells of billions of cnidarians. Evertebrates such as mussels, starfish, crabs and squids are common on the seabed in shallow waters.

shark, diretmid fish, sperm whale, spot-fish, squid, Photostomias, hatchet-fish, giant squid

The twilight zone and its organisms derive their nutrition from upper levels, either in the form of detritus (the steady rain of dead biomass) or through predation. The sperm whale dives to immense depths in search of its most important food, the giant squid Architeuthis. We still know very little about the habits of the fish in this zone. There are no plants here; bacteria play a vital role as decomposers.

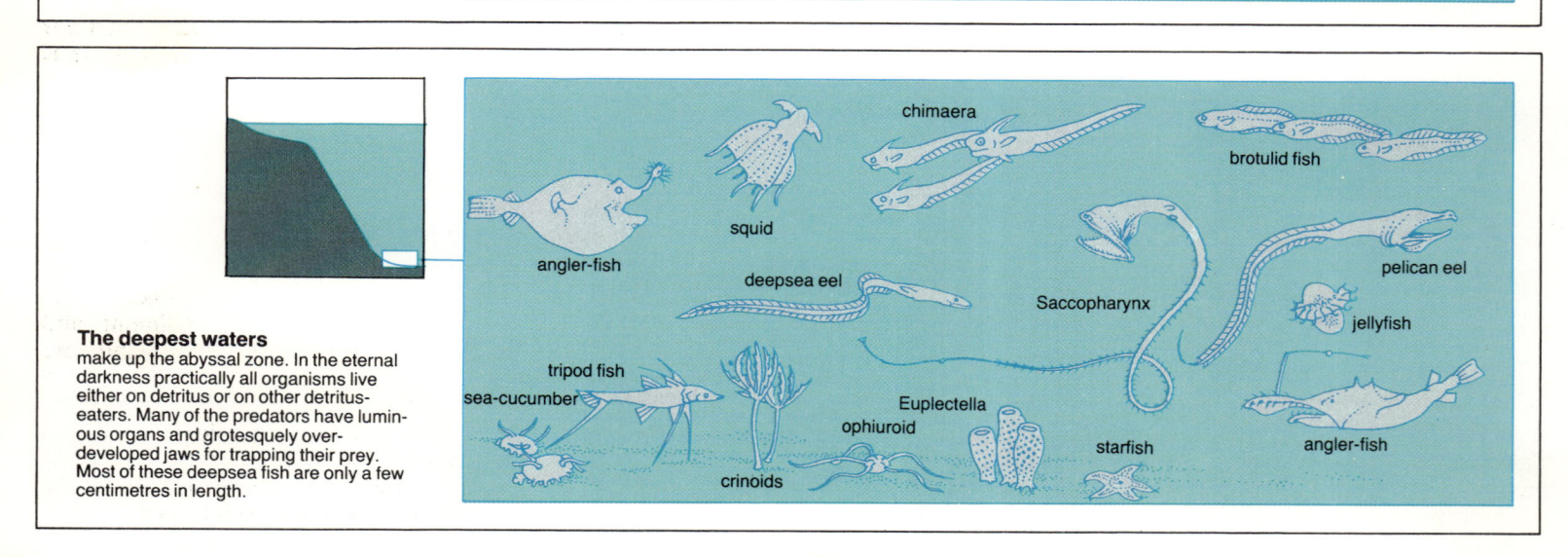

chimaera, brotulid fish, squid, angler-fish, deepsea eel, Saccopharynx, pelican eel, jellyfish, tripod fish, sea-cucumber, Euplectella, ophiuroid, starfish, angler-fish, crinoids

The deepest waters make up the abyssal zone. In the eternal darkness practically all organisms live either on detritus or on other detritus-eaters. Many of the predators have luminous organs and grotesquely over-developed jaws for trapping their prey. Most of these deepsea fish are only a few centimetres in length.

38

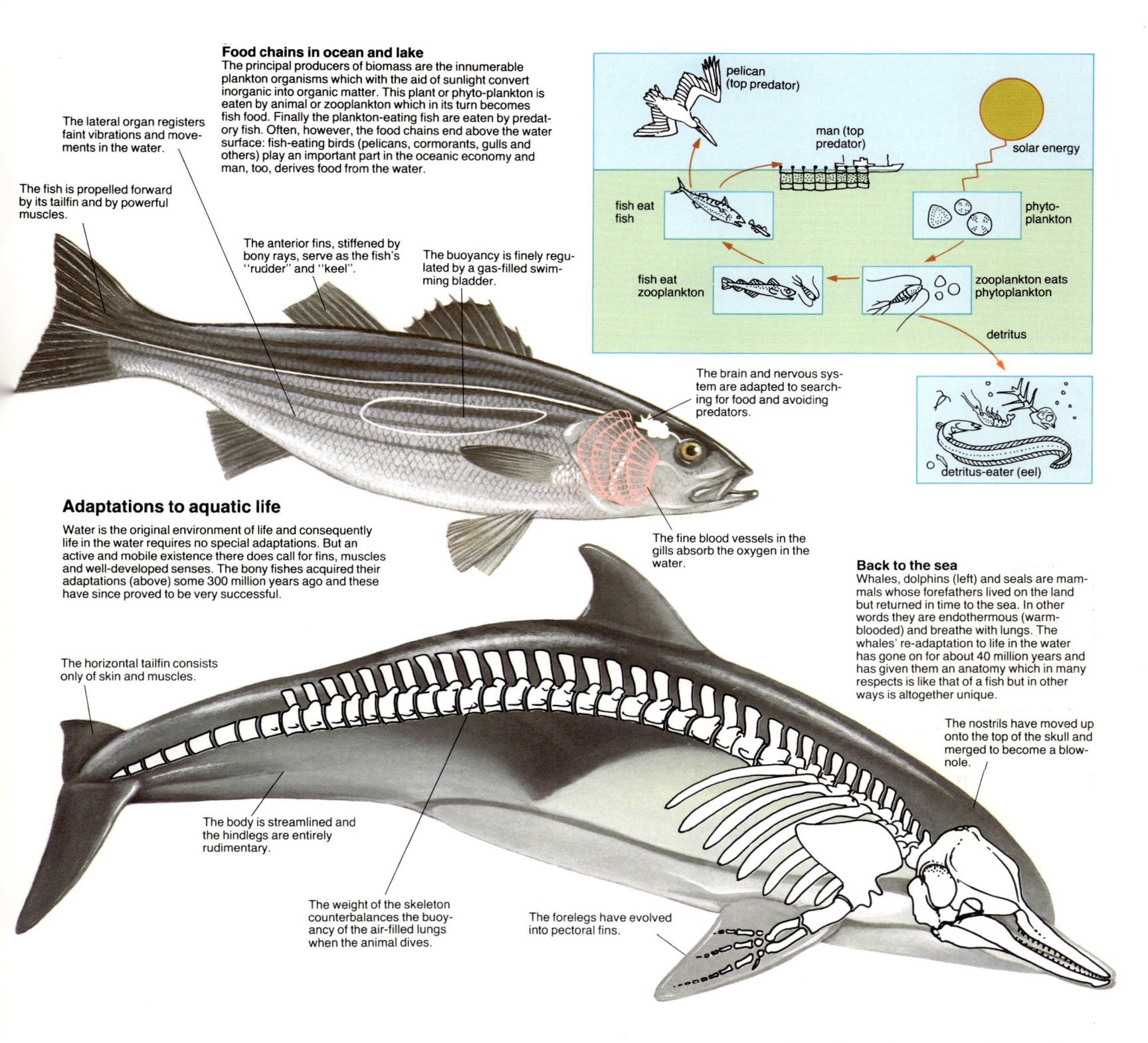

Food chains in ocean and lake
The principal producers of biomass are the innumerable plankton organisms which with the aid of sunlight convert inorganic into organic matter. This plant or phyto-plankton is eaten by animal or zooplankton which in its turn becomes fish food. Finally the plankton-eating fish are eaten by predatory fish. Often, however, the food chains end above the water surface: fish-eating birds (pelicans, cormorants, gulls and others) play an important part in the oceanic economy and man, too, derives food from the water.

The lateral organ registers faint vibrations and movements in the water.

The fish is propelled forward by its tailfin and by powerful muscles.

The anterior fins, stiffened by bony rays, serve as the fish's "rudder" and "keel".

The buoyancy is finely regulated by a gas-filled swimming bladder.

The brain and nervous system are adapted to searching for food and avoiding predators.

The fine blood vessels in the gills absorb the oxygen in the water.

Adaptations to aquatic life
Water is the original environment of life and consequently life in the water requires no special adaptations. But an active and mobile existence there does call for fins, muscles and well-developed senses. The bony fishes acquired their adaptations (above) some 300 million years ago and these have since proved to be very successful.

pelican (top predator)
man (top predator)
solar energy
fish eat fish
phyto-plankton
fish eat zooplankton
zooplankton eats phytoplankton
detritus
detritus-eater (eel)

Back to the sea
Whales, dolphins (left) and seals are mammals whose forefathers lived on the land but returned in time to the sea. In other words they are endothermous (warm-blooded) and breathe with lungs. The whales' re-adaptation to life in the water has gone on for about 40 million years and has given them an anatomy which in many respects is like that of a fish but in other ways is altogether unique.

The horizontal tailfin consists only of skin and muscles.

The body is streamlined and the hindlegs are entirely rudimentary.

The weight of the skeleton counterbalances the buoyancy of the air-filled lungs when the animal dives.

The forelegs have evolved into pectoral fins.

The nostrils have moved up onto the top of the skull and merged to become a blow-nole.

Fluid is the natural environment of the living cell. Ingenious molecular mechanisms pump vital substances from the surrounding fluid in through the cell membrane and pump the waste out in the opposite direction. Thus unicellular organisms do not need any particular adaptation to life in the water. An organism which moves requires a means of locomotion—in the case of fish, muscles and fins. Muscles in their turn have to be supplied with large quantities of oxygen, hence the gills. Finally, senses and a nervous system are essential to ensure that movement is both purposeful and effective.

The demands made by water of its inhabitants are the same in principle for practically all of them. Animals which re-adapt to life in the water have therefore many anatomical features in common with fishes. This applies to whales and seals, and, to the same extent, to the Mesozoic ichthyosaurs of 200 million years ago. All these share or shared the same handicap in that their forefathers' fundamental adaptation to life on land, the breathing of air, has been impossible to reverse.

The principal agents of organic production of ocean and lake are the green plankton plants. In order to grow, they need not only sunlight but also oxygen, carbon dioxide and salts. It is often the availability of phosphates which determines how much biomass, i.e. living matter, can exist in a cubic metre of water. Too little phospate means sterile water, while too much can lead to an algal bloom which consumes the oxygen in the water. The phosphates then move on through the food chain from phytoplankton via zooplankton and predators to top predators such as pelicans and man. At the same time phosphates, in the form of organic waste, descend constantly into the depths.

In the open seas this detritus sinks beyond the reach of the organic producers and is incorporated with sediment and sedimentary rocks. The shallow seas, on the other hand, are supplied with nutrients (nitrates and phosphates) from two sources: from water draining off the land and from the decomposition of organic matter in the sea. The organic production is high because almost all available nutrients are incorporated in biomass. The shallow seas are therefore very important fishing areas and one shoal can run into hundreds of thousands.

39

Food from the deep

Man has not always been a fisherman. It was not until the close of the Ice Age that ecological changes and the demands of an increasing population compelled the former big game hunters to turn to small game and ultimately to seafood in the form of mussels and oysters. This development can be studied archaeologically at certain sites through statistical analysis of household refuse. Fishing in the general sense of the term emerged during the Mesolithic period (c. 8,000 years ago) when the basic implements were devised: hook, spear, net and creel.

Fishing remained a largely local trade until first the steam engine and then the diesel engine brought about its industrialization during the last hundred years. Canning and refrigeration have further increased the scope of fishing. Fishing fleets are now accompanied by factory ships and mechanical equipment makes the hard work somewhat easier.

During the 1950's and '60's it was generally thought that food from the seas would be sufficient to provide for a limitless world population. But overfishing resulted in greatly diminished catches at the beginning of the 1970's. Today the total annual haul, including fish farming and algae, is around 68 million tons. Nearly 40% consists of different herring and cod species. Aquaculture (mussel and oyster beds, fish breeding in coastal and inland waters, etc.) contributes about nine per cent, a proportion which is increasing rapidly. In south-east Asia in particular the breeding of carp in pools is an important source of protein.

The most important fishing grounds are the shallow waters above the continental shelves, and those areas where water rising from the deep, or currents from the polar regions provide nutritive salts, primarily phosphates. Here biological productivity is at its greatest and the food chains are usually shorter than in the more complex ecological systems of the open oceanic waters. However these highly productive areas are more vulnerable to interference. At the beginning of the 1970's the Peruvian anchovy catches – then the world's largest fishing industry – suddenly failed when a cold, very nutritious oceanic current changed course. When this nutrition disappeared the anchovies did likewise, and the entire industry collapsed.

Traditional fishing is biologically ineffective. One ton of plankton can never become more than 10–20 kg of mackerel since mackerel are high up in the food chain, top predators like ourselves. It is a tempting idea to resort to the lowest possible trophic level and utilize the sea's primary producers, algae, and the secondary, pelagic crustaceans such as krill. This might become possible in the near future. Meanwhile one thing remains quite clear: if we are to use the Earth's waters for the production of food then we must cease polluting them. The oceans are no longer inexhaustible.

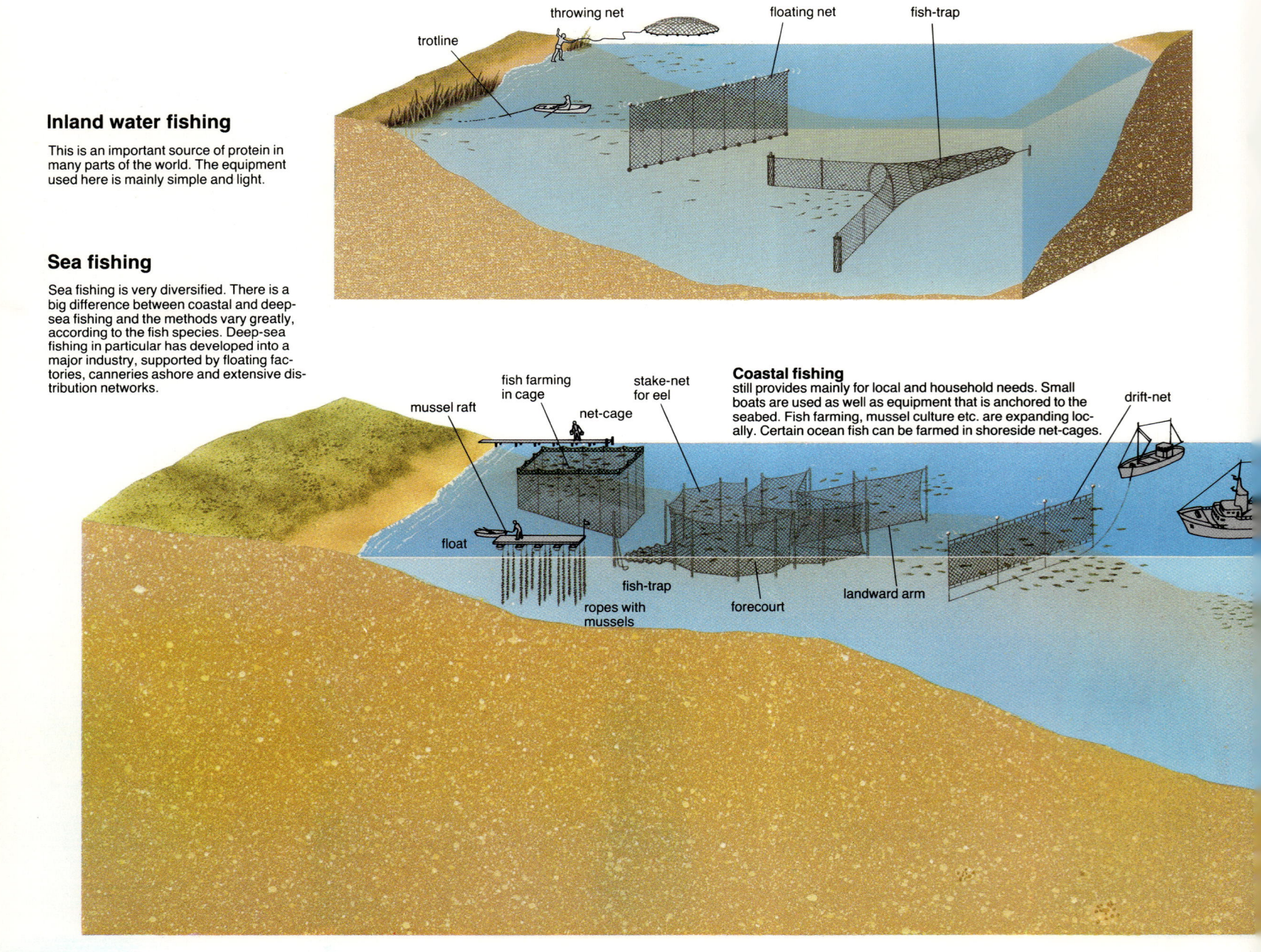

Inland water fishing

This is an important source of protein in many parts of the world. The equipment used here is mainly simple and light.

Sea fishing

Sea fishing is very diversified. There is a big difference between coastal and deep-sea fishing and the methods vary greatly, according to the fish species. Deep-sea fishing in particular has developed into a major industry, supported by floating factories, canneries ashore and extensive distribution networks.

Coastal fishing

still provides mainly for local and household needs. Small boats are used as well as equipment that is anchored to the seabed. Fish farming, mussel culture etc. are expanding locally. Certain ocean fish can be farmed in shoreside net-cages.

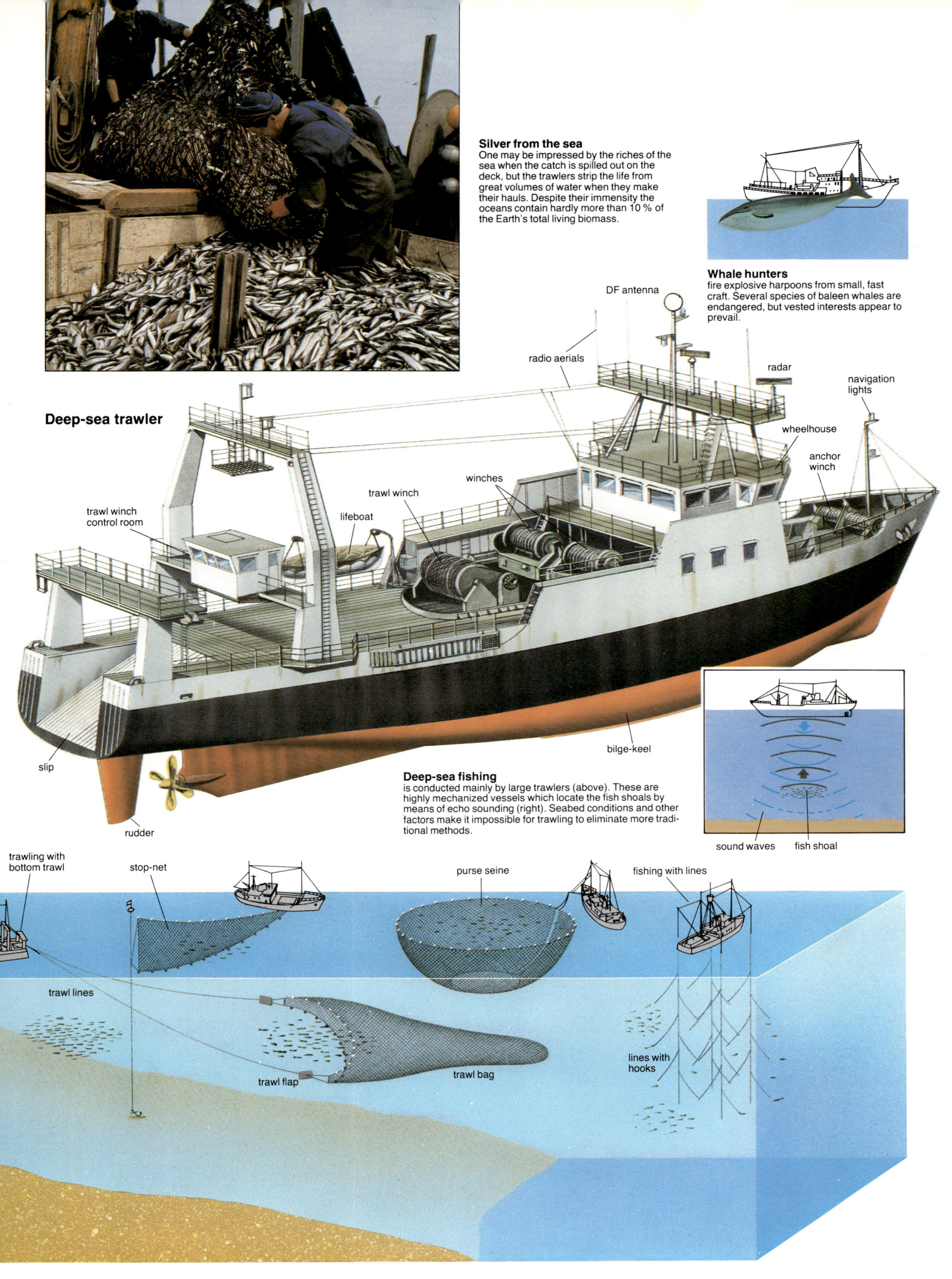

Silver from the sea
One may be impressed by the riches of the sea when the catch is spilled out on the deck, but the trawlers strip the life from great volumes of water when they make their hauls. Despite their immensity the oceans contain hardly more than 10 % of the Earth's total living biomass.

Whale hunters
fire explosive harpoons from small, fast craft. Several species of baleen whales are endangered, but vested interests appear to prevail.

Deep-sea trawler

- DF antenna
- radio aerials
- radar
- navigation lights
- wheelhouse
- anchor winch
- winches
- trawl winch
- lifeboat
- trawl winch control room
- bilge-keel
- slip
- rudder

Deep-sea fishing
is conducted mainly by large trawlers (above). These are highly mechanized vessels which locate the fish shoals by means of echo sounding (right). Seabed conditions and other factors make it impossible for trawling to eliminate more traditional methods.

- sound waves
- fish shoal

- trawling with bottom trawl
- stop-net
- purse seine
- fishing with lines
- trawl lines
- trawl flap
- trawl bag
- lines with hooks

41

The conquest of the seas

The Vikings
reached the Caspian Sea in the east and "Vinland" (presumably Newfoundland) in the west. In the 10th century they settled in Iceland and Greenland, although their voyages along the rivers of Russia were economically and historically more significant.

Early explorers
There were bold mariners on the seas long before the era of the great voyages of discovery. Chinese, Arabs, Polynesians and Vikings voyaged far beyond their own coastlines, but their fields of activity (map) were limited nevertheless. It was not until the 16th century that Europeans began voyaging all over the world.

The Chinese
were probably the best shipbuilders of the Middle Ages. Their junks carried several masts, they were fitted with a sternpost rudder and had watertight bulkheads. In the early 15th century Chinese explorers found their way as far west as India and East Africa.

The Polynesians
sailed vast distances during their voyages of colonization in the Pacific about 2,000 years ago. Their craft were outrigger canoes with a triangular sail. They used simple charts made of sticks and shells.

The Arabs
were accomplished seamen. In their lateen-rigged ships and aided by the steady monsoon winds they traded by sea during the Middle Ages from East Africa ("Azania") in the west to the Indonesian spice islands in the east.

Great seafarers
In 1492 Columbus sailed westward in search of a new sea route from Europe to India. Instead he discovered a new continent: America. The voyages of Columbus were followed by intensive colonization by the Spanish and Portuguese.

In 1496 Vasco da Gama sailed the eastward route to India, around Africa, using an Arab pilot on the last leg of the voyage. This was the culmination of eighty years of Portuguese maritime explorations.

In 1519 Ferdinand Magellan set forth on the first circumnavigation of the globe. Three years later one ship of the three returned to Portugal, with only 18 remaining of the original 265 men. Magellan himself was killed in the Philippines.

The geographic science
Critically minded geographers and careful cartographers compiled the accounts of the seafarers into a cohesive scientific survey of the world. The voyages of discovery in the 16th and 17th centuries had more far-reaching consequences than, for example, the expeditions of the Vikings.

In 1768–79 Captain James Cook explored great parts of the Pacific Ocean and Antarctic waters. His fine seamanship, scientific interests and humanitarian behaviour reflect an enlightened spirit in this crude and ruthless era of geographical discovery.

With increasing competence in shipbuilding came the development of the high seas as important travel routes. Busy shipping traffic developed early in the Mediterranean and the Baltic, for example, where the waters were fairly protected and landfall distances relatively short. In the Mediterranean, Cretans, Phoenicians, Greeks, Romans, Arabs and Italians succeeded each other as the leading seafarers—until world trade moved out to the great oceans and the Mediterranean declined into an economic backwater.

The new trade routes were the result of the great discoveries of the 15th and 16th centuries. Hundreds of years of voyaging along stormy coastlines had compelled western Europeans to develop good ships but the real impetus behind their maritime expansion was the idea of by-passing the Arab-Italian monopoly to trade with the Far East. Though it was not scientific fervour which sent Columbus and da Gama to sea, nevertheless, their voyages had important scientific consequences.

It is often asserted that it was the Indians and not Columbus who first discovered America. It is true that the original inhabitants of the New World knew their own hunting grounds well, but they had no idea that this land was an isolated continent separated by sea from other continents, such as Europe, Asia and Africa. They possessed no geographical science. The Europeans, however, developed one and this gave them a practical grasp of world geography unparalleled in earlier history. The epoch of the great voyages of discovery can be said to have terminated with Cook's travels in the 1770's. These represented the transition to the golden age of scientific expeditions in the 19th century: the Challenger expedition, Darwin, Nordenskiöld and many more.

Fishermen and mariners have always had some knowledge of sea depths, but the skindivers' capacity is limited to a few dozen metres and a duration of a couple of minutes. In the 17th century the diving bell was invented for salvaging operations and in the 1830's Siebe designed the modern diving suit for the same purpose. Breathing sets for "frogmen" were introduced in World War II. Today divers work as a matter of routine at depths of down to several hundred metres.

It was the invention of the torpedo around the close of the 19th century which turned the submarine into a practical military weapon. It remained a military craft until the 1960's when marine researchers developed specially built diving craft for scientific use. Since then the quest for oil under the sea has brought rapid advances in diving techniques.

Man is now beginning to probe the mysteries of the ocean depths. The "inner space" of the sea, is, like outer space, a new and promising frontier.

Exploring the depths

Divers breathing oxygen are limited to depths of 10–15 metres. Under pressure oxygen has a poisonous effect.

Using the simplest possible equipment pearl and sponge divers ("skindivers") reach depths of 30–50 m. for brief periods.

Frogmen using scuba equipment can go down to about 60 m. Beyond that depth special gas mixtures are needed.

Helmet divers can work at depths of 150–250 m. breathing heliox, a mixture of helium and oxygen.

Commercial submarines can be used for repairs and maintenance work at a depth of 400–500 m., in the offshore oilfields for example.

In 1934, using a bathysphere, a steel ball suspended on a cable from a ship, the American zoologist William Beebe descended to a depth of more than 900 m. This hazardous device made it possible for man to observe for the first time the eternally dark world of the ocean depths.

Research submarines built of new materials such as titanium, aluminium and plexiglass are being used to carry out scientific observations at depths of several thousand metres. With the aid of this type of craft important biological and geological discoveries have been made along the mid-ocean ridges.

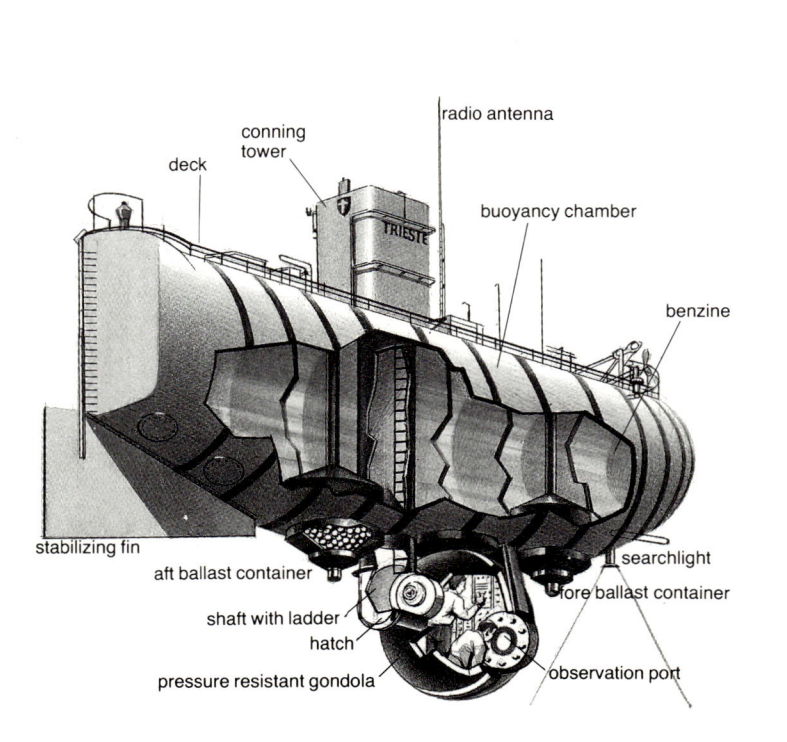

The greatest depths

The greatest known depth in the world's oceans is the MARINA TRENCH in the Pacific: 11,034 m. Here, in 1960, a bathyscaphe (right and in greater detail, left) descended to 10,916 m. In principle a bathyscaphe is a sort of underwater zeppelin. The hull is filled with benzine which is lighter than water, just as the gas in an airship is lighter than air. Beneath this hull or buoyancy chamber there is a steel, pressure resistant gondola with observation ports. The buoyancy is trimmed by means of steel balls released from two containers. The crew numbers two or three. The vehicle can remain on the seabed for a few hours at depths of 10,000 m. or more.

Sea routes

The Egyptians are believed to have built the first sailing ships. They collected luxury goods such as hard woods, gold, ivory and slaves from Lebanon and Punt (probably Somalia). For a long time shipping remained something which hardly affected or concerned ordinary people. The Greeks and after them the Romans, were the first to be dependant upon transport of staple goods across the seas: grain, olive oil, wine and metals. With the collapse of the Roman Empire around 500 AD this traffic ceased and it was not until the late Middle Ages that everyday commodities once again began to become an important factor in shipping. During all this time most ships sailed more or less inshore, passing from point to point along the coasts. The Arabs and Chinese conducted some oceanic traffic, aided by the monsoon winds, in the Middle Ages. But the Europeans did not embark on such ventures until around 1500.

Nowadays the major part of shipping freight consists of bulk goods like oil, ore, minerals, industrial chemicals and grain. Manufactured goods for shipment comprise mainly of heavy industrial products such as machinery, vehicles and various semi-finished goods. Passenger traffic is largely restricted to cruises and ferry lines, aircraft having taken over the transoceanic passenger trade. During the course of the last hundred years there have been immense advances in shipbuilding. The modern cargo liner has the same size crew as a clipper ship, 20 to 30 men, while the freight capacity can be as much as one hundred times greater; 30,000 tons or more. Noise, vibration and stress are the principal complaints of the modern seaman, just as accidents, cramped conditions, cold, heat and damp plagued his predecessors.

Ports, like ships, have changed as well. Increasingly large ships and the growing demands for freight-handling space have resulted in the ports being moved out of the towns to new deep water sites. Another significant change is the container. The idea is not new; the Middle Ages had their own unit load system in the barrel or cask. The French word for cask, "tonne", gave its name to the unit of measurement. The modern standard containers (24 and 48 ft. in length) have already greatly altered designs and routines of ports and ships alike. Ships now have a very short turn-round time and shipping tends to be concentrated on fewer and larger centres. The world's busiest port today is considered to be Rotterdam with a turnover of some 270 million tons of freight in 1978.

Ships from two centuries

Greyhounds of the seas
Centuries of development in square-rigged sailing vessels culminated in the British and American clippers of the mid-19th century. These swift ships were created to fulfill a particular requirement: costly and perishable cargoes from the Far East, especially tea, had to be carried to Europe and North America. The season's first deliveries could fetch very high prices and this led to the famous races across the high seas. The golden era of the clippers was brief for within a few decades they were replaced by steamships.

A modern cargo vessel
Because of industrial demands for fast, regular, sea transport services the tramp steamers of yesterday, the "casual workers" of the sea, have been almost eclipsed by regular-service cargo liners. These ships are swift and specially built for different cargoes. They usually have two crews who alternate, since it costs too much to have a ship lying idle while the entire crew is on leave.

The container revolution
Non-bulk cargo is no longer loaded and unloaded bit by bit, it is handled instead in unit loads, i.e. large standard-sized containers. This has reduced the alongside time of ships in port from days to hours. Special roll on-roll off ships carry cars and lorries on short routes between ports. The illustration below portrays both types of cargo in one vessel.

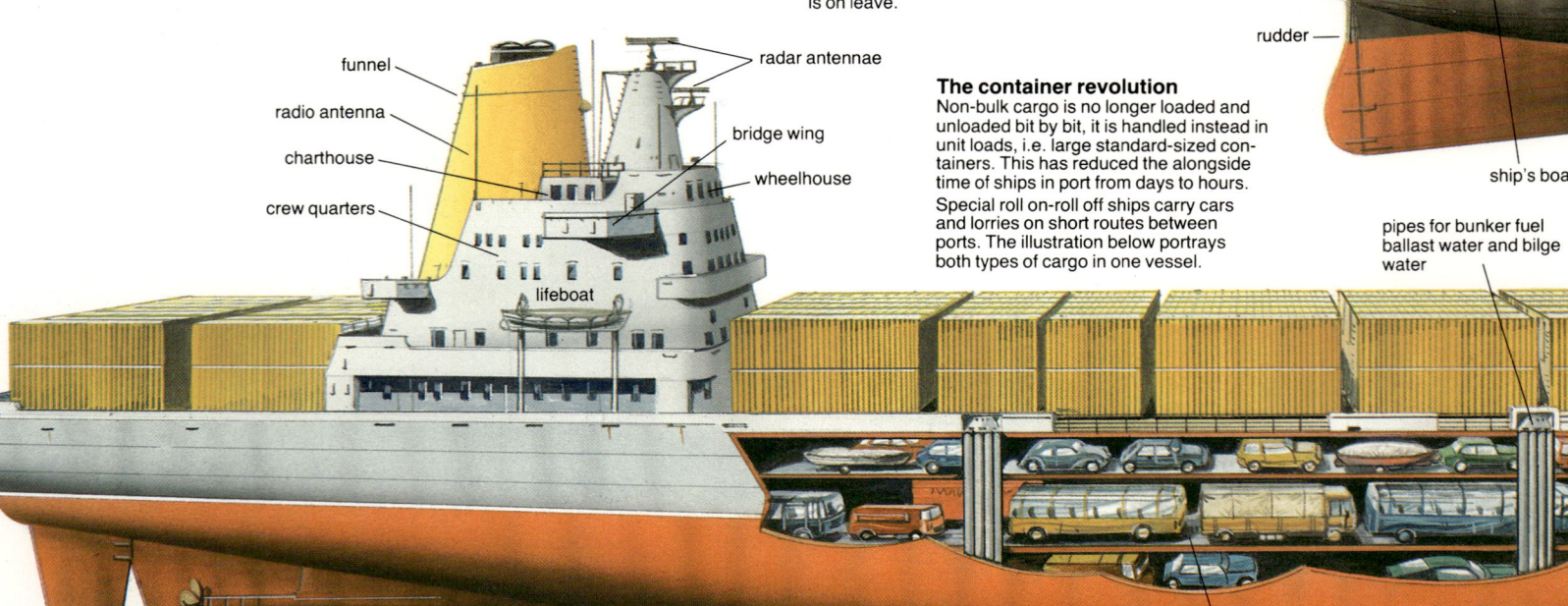

Finding the way at sea
On the high seas and in dangerous coastal waters alike, it is of vital importance to know a vessel's exact location. Modern navigators make use of many different methods:

Astronavigation
The height over the horizon of the sun or a suitable star when in a position due south, gives the latitude. Longitude can be established by recording the exact moment when the reading takes place. The altitude of the sun is measured with a sextant.

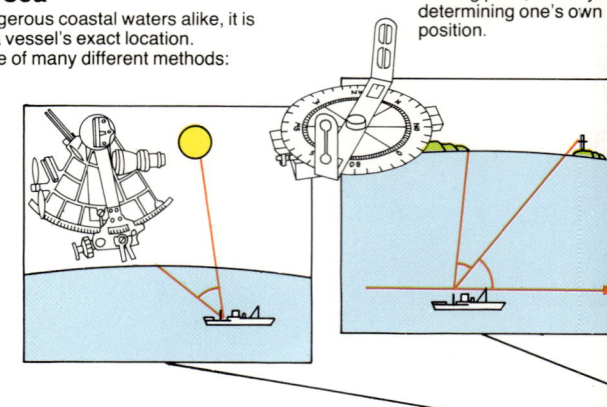

Bearings
The bearings (horizontal angles) of two landmarks of known positions can be read off on a bearing plate, thereby determining one's own position.

44

Sea routes past and present

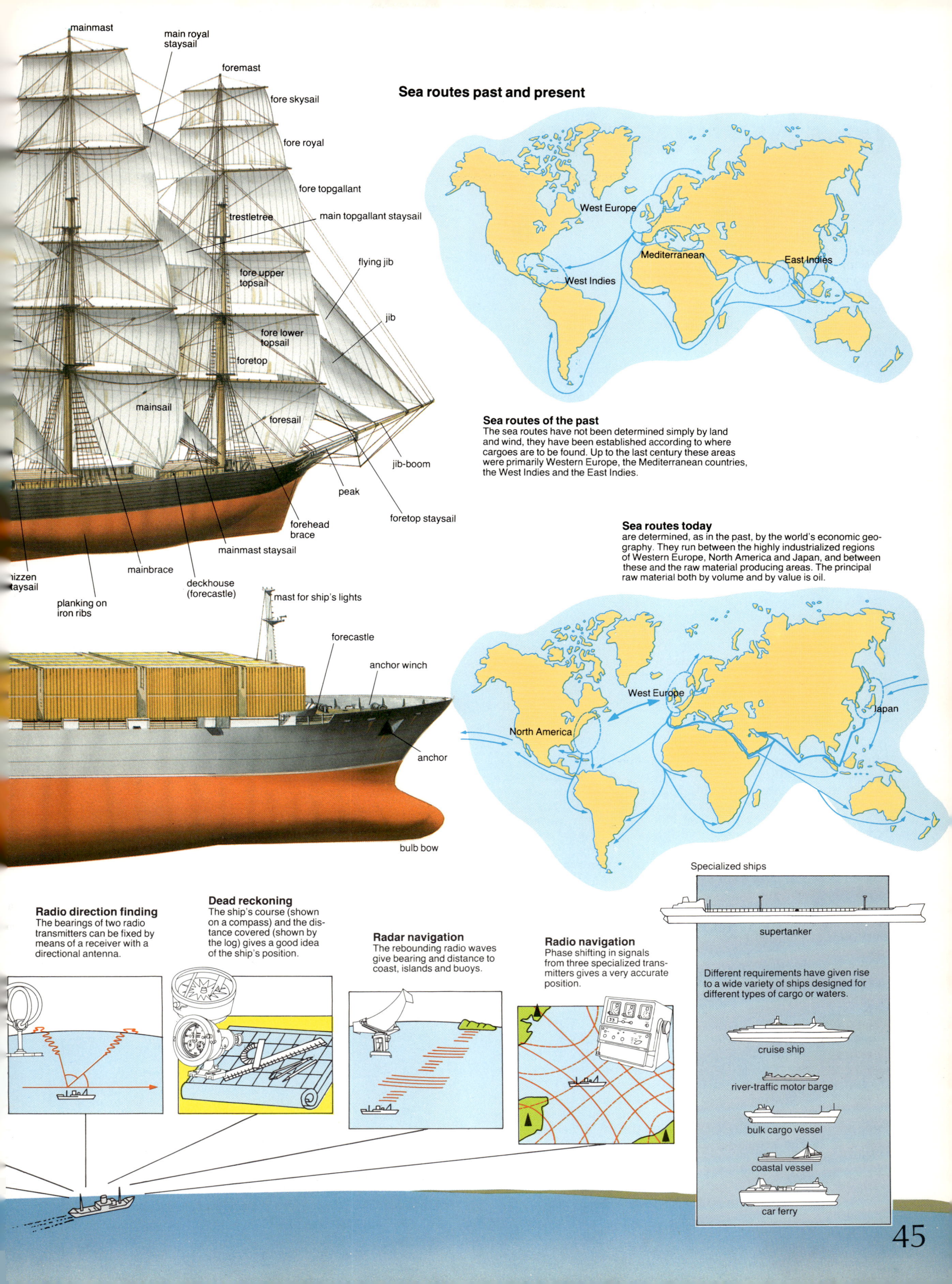

Sea routes of the past
The sea routes have not been determined simply by land and wind, they have been established according to where cargoes are to be found. Up to the last century these areas were primarily Western Europe, the Mediterranean countries, the West Indies and the East Indies.

Sea routes today
are determined, as in the past, by the world's economic geography. They run between the highly industrialized regions of Western Europe, North America and Japan, and between these and the raw material producing areas. The principal raw material both by volume and by value is oil.

Radio direction finding
The bearings of two radio transmitters can be fixed by means of a receiver with a directional antenna.

Dead reckoning
The ship's course (shown on a compass) and the distance covered (shown by the log) gives a good idea of the ship's position.

Radar navigation
The rebounding radio waves give bearing and distance to coast, islands and buoys.

Radio navigation
Phase shifting in signals from three specialized transmitters gives a very accurate position.

Specialized ships

Different requirements have given rise to a wide variety of ships designed for different types of cargo or waters.

- supertanker
- cruise ship
- river-traffic motor barge
- bulk cargo vessel
- coastal vessel
- car ferry

45

Man's impact on the hydrosphere

In dry regions and industrialized areas alike clean water is a scarce and valuable substance.

Surface and sub-surface water
The ancient Persians living in steppe and desert tracts regarded all running water as sacred. In rain-abundant Europe this healthy reverence for water has been lacking. The water in rivers flowing through the big cities was recognized as being dangerous to drink more than five hundred years ago and industrialization, growing population and new, toxic chemicals have steadily worsened the problem.

The laying of drainage systems and the increased use of cleaning agents have added growing quantities of phosphates to our waterways and lakes. This excessive nourishment, or eutrophication, results in an explosive growth of algae which in turn consumes the oxygen in the water and leads to the death of fish and the impoverishment of the ecological system. Serious water contamination has also resulted from the careless disposal of mercury compounds and other heavy metals from industry. During its progress through the food chains, mercury becomes increasingly concentrated until it causes acute nerve damage to fish-eating birds or human beings.

Waste water can be cleansed. Formerly this was a mechanical process involving sedimentation and filtering. Nowadays chemical methods are being used to precipitate the nutritive salts and biological methods to add oxygen to the waste water, thus accelerating the decomposition of organic matter. Thanks to a successful sewage treatment programme the River Thames now boasts 105 species of fish and in August 1983 a salmon was caught with rod and line for the first time in 150 years.

Sub-surface water is threatened as well, partly because too much of it is being drawn off and used. Oil and phenols from refuse dumps and nitrogen fertilizers can poison ground water. Once in the ground the nitrates in nitrogen fertilizers are converted into nitrite which in the human body can be transformed into substances that breed cancer.

Inland seas and oceans
Inland seas with their limited water turnover have much in common with lakes. Eutrophication leads to a shortage of oxygen in deep water. Hydrogen sulphide is generated in the water when the normal decomposition of organic matter no longer functions. Poisons like mercury and chlorinated hydrocarbons can reach high concentrations and in the Baltic these have affected fish and, indirectly, seals and eagles.

In the oceans with their much greater water masses these problems are not as manifest, but in the long term they are equally serious. There is a danger that the production of vegetable plankton will be reduced by chlorinated hydrocarbons such as DDT insecticide, which has even been traced in penguins in the Antarctic. The dumping of chemical and radio-active waste in deepsea areas has aroused equal anxiety in recent years. We do not know enough about the circulation of seawater between deep and surface strata and these poisons may well invade the food chains and become concentrated within them.

Land and sea water rights
The right to use the waters of rivers which cross national frontiers has frequently caused local conflict. Sea rights, by comparison, create dissent on a global scale. The "freedom of the seas" doctrine of the 18th and 19th centuries is now a thing of the past. In the 1970's nations began to claim vast areas of sea, and land-enclosed waters like the North Sea are now entirely divided up into economic zones. Disputes over the right to utilize the resources of the remaining free oceans have created international disagreement. The industrial nations with the necessary technology assert their right to exploit the high seas. Poorer countries and those without coastline demand that these resources should be administered supranationally as the common inheritance of all mankind. The tension has diminished to some extent now that the exaggerated expectations of high-profit seabed mining have abated.

The prospects are not entirely negative. International agreements on the release of oil in especially vulnerable waters have been introduced and implemented, even though these are all to often violated. This shows that agreements can be reached on individual issues, and it is in this spirit that we should continue.

Surface and sub-surface water

Human mismanagement
Destruction of ground vegetation and the draining of wetlands diminishes the infiltration of surface water and thereby lowers the water table. The latter can be lowered further by excessive demand for municipal and industrial purposes: fresh water is pumped up, used in households and industries and then released again as polluted surface water. Intensive irrigation, on the other hand, can increase infiltration until the water table reaches the surface. Then in dry regions, exceptional evaporation from the water-logged ground causes the precipitation of salts from this sub-surface water and in time the salty soil becomes useless for farming.

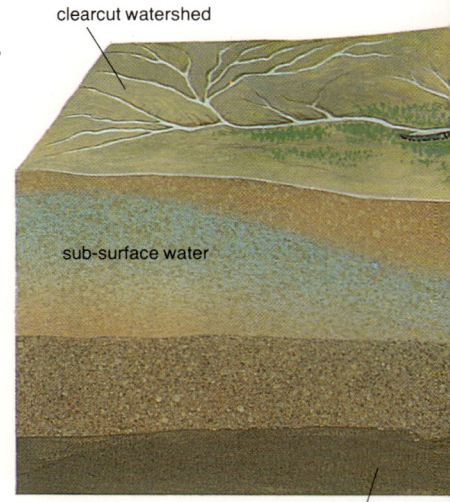

Death by oil
The dumping of ballast water mixed with oil is illegal in many waters, but it still occurs. The real oil disasters take place, however, when big tankers founder (below). The subsequent cleaning up is a costly and time-consuming undertaking. The death of many seafowl (right) arouses widespread public indignation, but the oil pollution is even more dangerous to organisms beneath the surface: fish and fish fry, crustaceans and algae. This is why we now try to remove the oil from the water instead of sinking it by the application of chemicals.

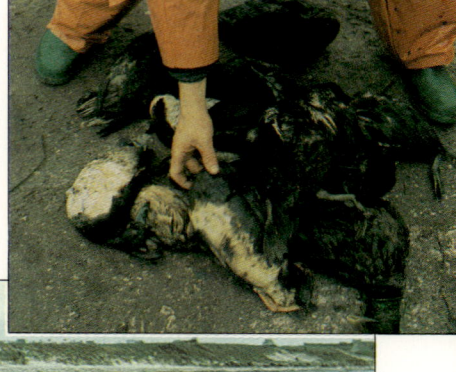

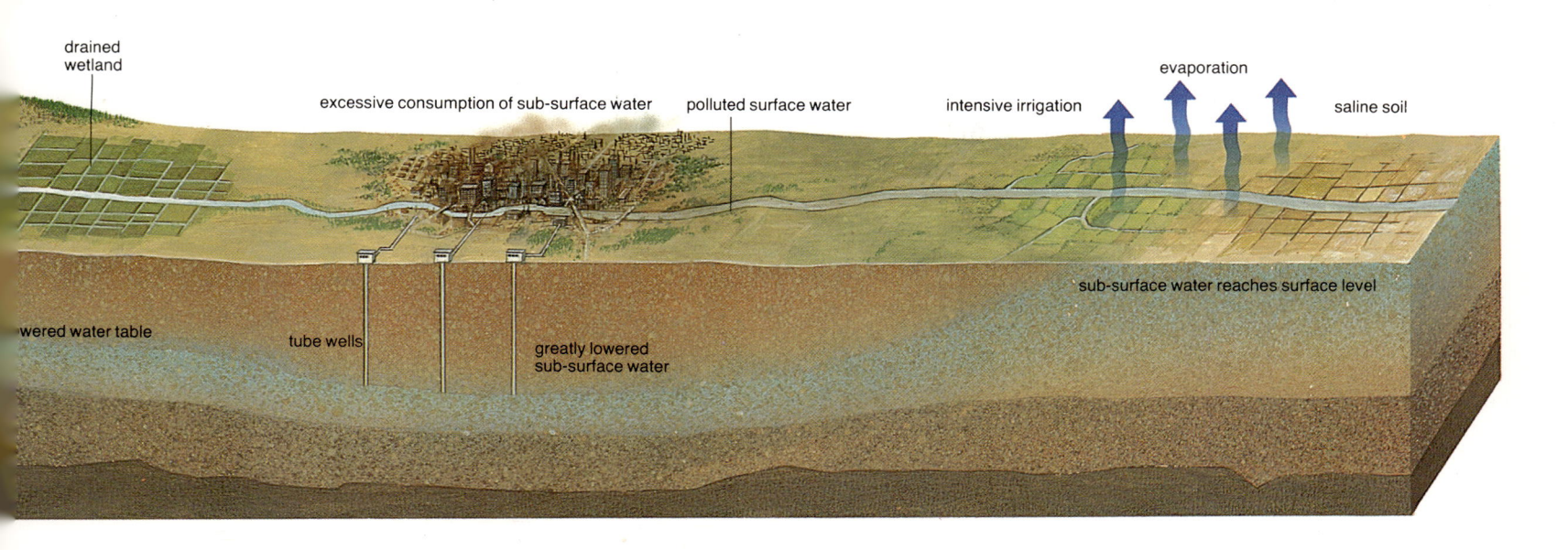

drained wetland · excessive consumption of sub-surface water · polluted surface water · intensive irrigation · evaporation · saline soil

sub-surface water reaches surface level

wered water table · tube wells · greatly lowered sub-surface water

Poisoning the world's water

Dumping at sea
The practice of dumping chemical and radio-active waste in the sea's depths has been going on for years. In time, however, containers can erode away and the poisonous contents can be released into the sea water. We do not know a great deal about the circulation of deep and surface water (arrows) and this process may take place faster than we formerly realized, so that the poisons spread to the biologically active water strata. Oceanographers have discovered currents even in the very deepest parts of the oceans.

Eutrophication
the over-nourishing of water results in algal blooms and lack of oxygen in the water. This can be caused by phosphorus of nitrogen in sewage or, as here, by nitrogen fertilizer draining off agricultural land.

Environmental poisons
are spread mainly by industry and agriculture. Poisonous substances such as DDT and PCB cause serious damage to inland seas like the Baltic where the water exchange rate is not very great.

Excessive fishing
does not necessarily lead to extermination but it does upset the balance between the different fish species. When catches diminish drastically serious problems arise for both fishermen and industries based on fish.

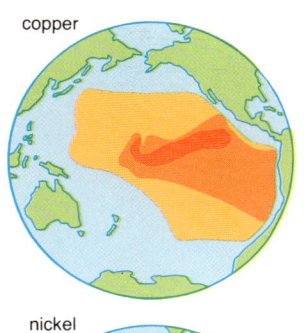

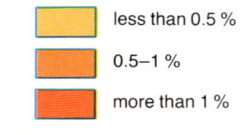

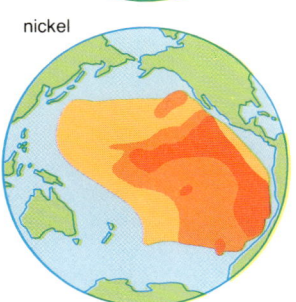

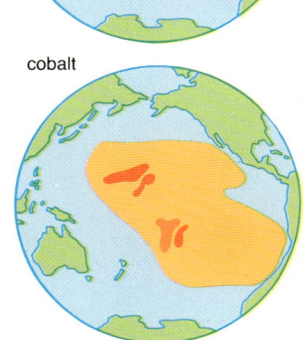

copper · nickel · cobalt

- less than 0.5 %
- 0.5–1 %
- more than 1 %

Mining on the seabed
Large areas of the ocean floors are scattered with fist-sized mineral nodules. These contain principally manganese plus a certain amount of copper, nickel and cobalt, varying in proportion according to where they are found (map, left). There are advanced plans to exploit these mineral resources. One such project is to dredge them up from the bed of the Pacific by means of a vast bucket dredger system (below).

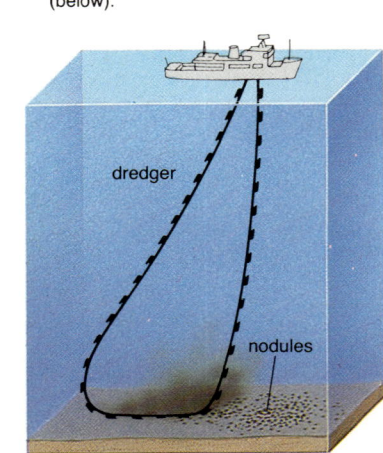

dredger · nodules

Fences in the sea
have become a reality in recent years, not physically but legally. The continental shelves have been divided among the nations bordering the seas, giving each of these the right to exploit the natural resources (below, the North Sea). Countries with a short coastline or no coast at all have been the losers.

Faroe Islands · **Danish zone** · **Norwegian zone** · Shetland Islands · Orkney Islands · **British zone** · Oslo · Stavanger · Aberdeen · **Danish zone** · **West German zone** · Copenhagen · **Dutch zone** · Hamburg · London · Amsterdam

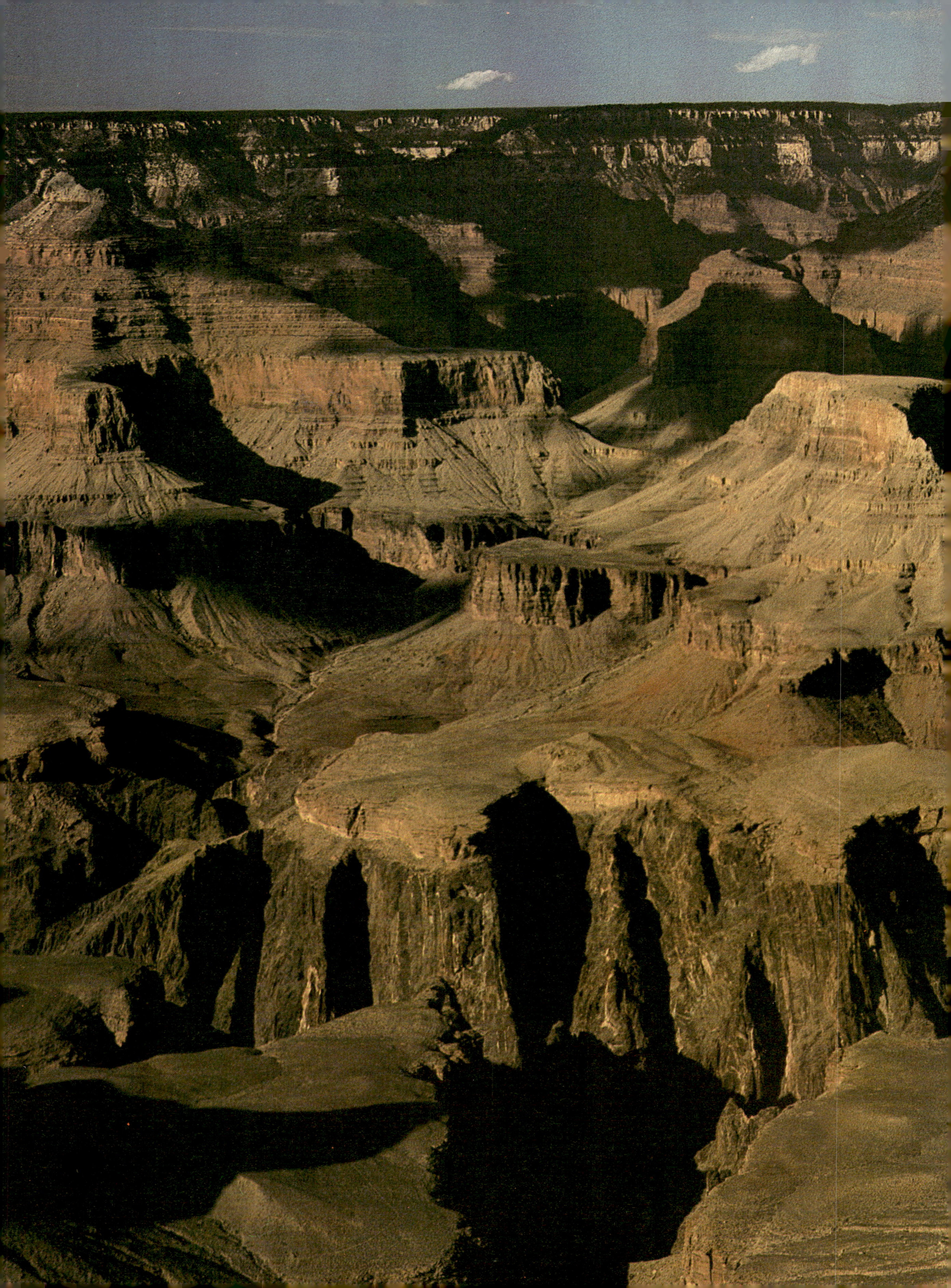

Earth

Earth is a tangible substance. There is nothing immediately remarkable about it so perhaps its elevation to one of the four primary elements occurred reluctantly and only because matter in the solid state also demanded a place among the primary substances, alongside gaseous air and fluid water. It is not surprising that none of the early philosophers recognised earth's fundamental importance.

This is not to say, however, that the Earth's crust and the matter contained in it were not subjected to philosophical speculation. Metals were extracted from the ground, and their transformation from grey ore through incandescent fire to gleaming metal fired man's imagination: if stone could become metal then could not lead and other base metals be transmuted into gold?

Thus alchemy was born in ancient Alexandria and was passed via the Arabs to mediaeval Europe. Alchemists' theories consisted almost entirely of occult speculation. But their practical experiments produced new techniques: for example, distillation led to the discovery of new elements such as phosphorus and, in time, sowed the seeds of scientific chemistry.

Geology, the science of the Earth's crust, originated as late as 1830, when the English scientist Lyell had the courage to assert in print that our Earth was not created in the year 4004 BC as claimed by the learned theologians, but was in fact millions of years old. Geophysics, geology and mineralogy form the basis for a group of special sciences which are collectively known as earth science. In our generation a revolution has occurred in the way we view the Earth. The crust is now seen as a mosaic of plates with the continents moving across the face of the globe. This new theory of "plate-tectonics" has enabled insight into the formation of minerals and ores, but it has also forced scientists to re-evaluate seemingly unrelated disciplines such as palaeontology, the science of extinct animals and plants.

Man has himself become a geological force, excavating and blasting, draining and filling in, to such an extent that in many places his ruthless activities have exposed the ground to the ravages of erosion. The shallow stratum of life that covers the Earth's crust – the biosphere – is essentially dependent upon the fragile layer of soil that exists beneath the green surface. We are ourselves part of that vulnerable stratum even though we usually overlook this in our pursuit of short-term gains.

The crust

The structure of the Earth

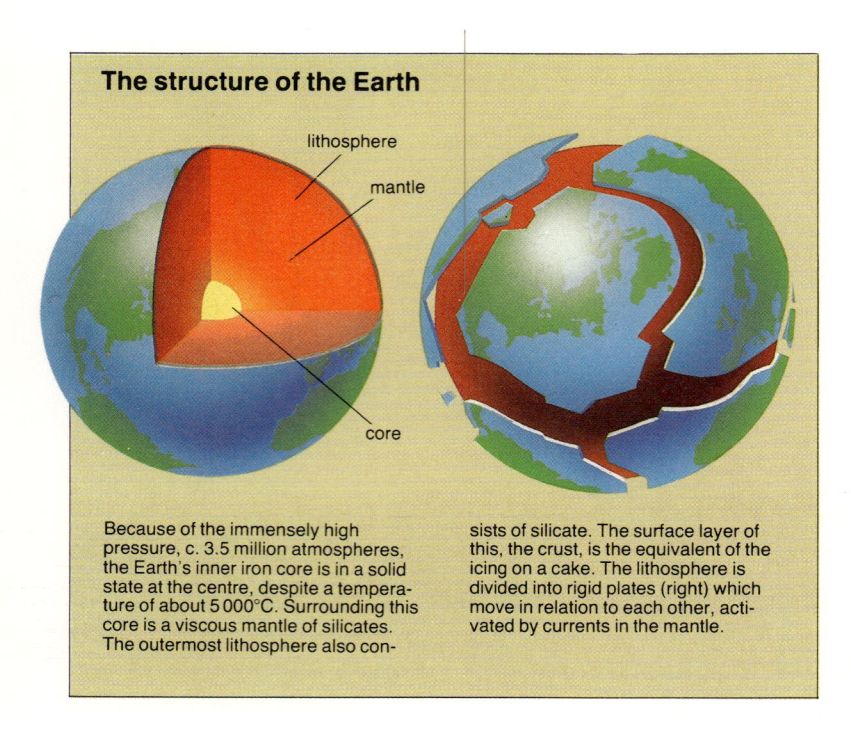

Because of the immensely high pressure, c. 3.5 million atmospheres, the Earth's inner iron core is in a solid state at the centre, despite a temperature of about 5 000°C. Surrounding this core is a viscous mantle of silicates. The outermost lithosphere also consists of silicate. The surface layer of this, the crust, is the equivalent of the icing on a cake. The lithosphere is divided into rigid plates (right) which move in relation to each other, activated by currents in the mantle.

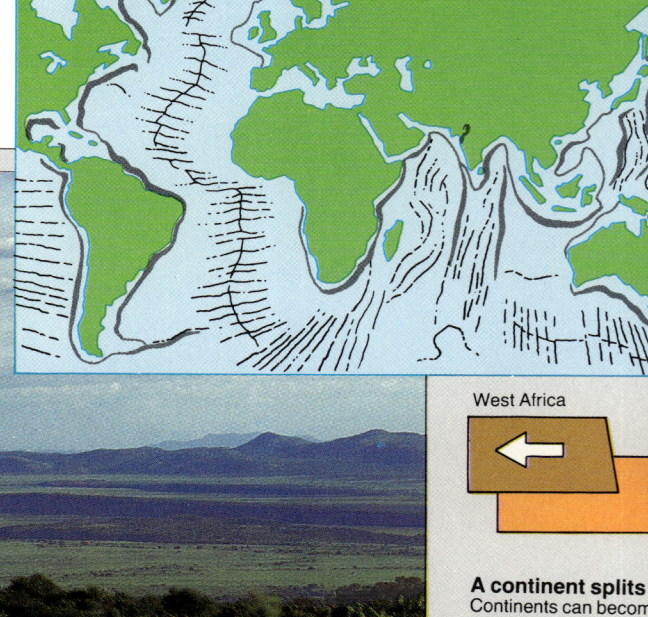

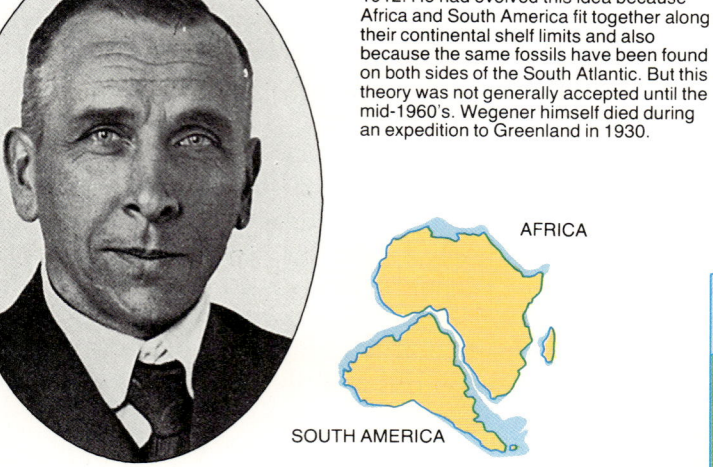

Alfred Wegener

published his theory on "continental drift" in 1912. He had evolved this idea because Africa and South America fit together along their continental shelf limits and also because the same fossils have been found on both sides of the South Atlantic. But this theory was not generally accepted until the mid-1960's. Wegener himself died during an expedition to Greenland in 1930.

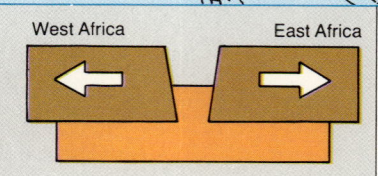

Drifting continents

With the aid of palaeomagnetic data scientists are seeking to reconstruct the appearance of the Earth during earlier geological periods. Palaeomagnetic data relates to how magnetic particles in minerals were aligned by the Earth's magnetic field at the time when the mineral was formed. This is a complicated task, however, and the various reconstructions can often differ in detail.

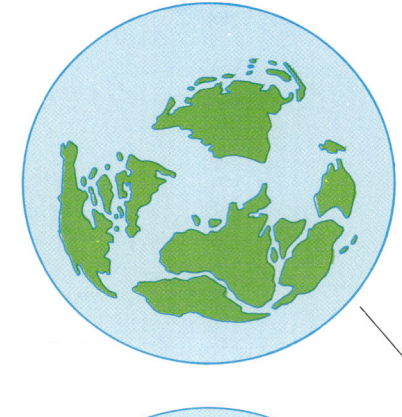

The Earth 300 million years ago

During the Carboniferous period the continents moved towards each other. Then in the Mesozoic era they formed a super-continent, Wegener's "Pangaea".

180 million years ago

By the time of the Jurassic period the super-continent had begun to split up. This was the heyday of the dinosaurs.

60 million years ago

At the beginning of the Cainozoic era, after the dinosaurs had become extinct, the South Atlantic had already opened up. India was moving towards Asia, but Australia was still attached to the Antarctic.

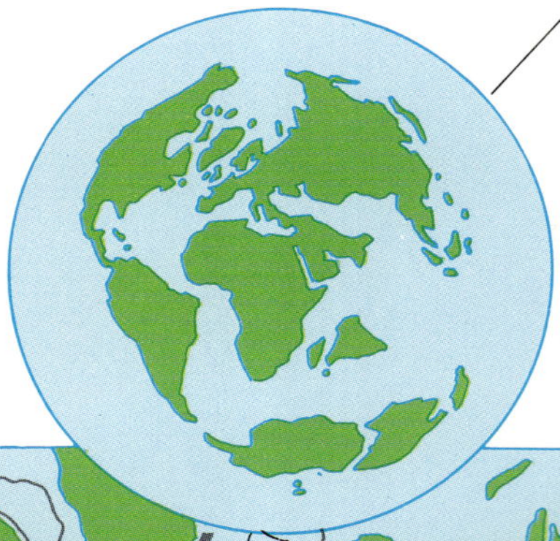

The Earth today

The contours of the continents have not altered much in 300 million years. But their present positions represent merely the latest phase in a constantly shifting pattern. Studies of mid-ocean ridges (below) and fracture zones have enabled scientists to decipher the movements of the crustal plates.

A continent splits

Continents can become welded together and they can split up. The latter process is taking place today along East Africa's Rift Valley (photo). West and East Africa are being pulled apart along this 4,000 km. fault line (above). Vulcanism is common in the Rift Valley. When, in the future, East Africa from southern Ethiopia to northern Mozambique becomes a "mini-continent", the Rift Valley will be an arm of the sea.

By studying the way in which earthquake shock waves progress through the Earth, scientists have found that it is vertically stratified. The molten iron core is surrounded by a mantle of viscous silicates. The Earth's crust is 20–70 km. thick beneath the continents but only about 6–7 kms. under the oceans, i.e. roughly one thousandth part of the Earth's radius. Combined with the upper stratum of the mantle, the crust forms a zone known as the lithosphere.

As recently as a couple of decades ago we believed that this thin crust was rigid and motionless. At the beginning of the century, the German climatologist Alfred Wegener observed that the climate had varied in an apparently erratic fashion during the past geological epochs. He attempted to explain this by postulating that the continents had "drifted". During the early Mesozoic era about 200 million years ago all the land on Earth formed a single huge continent, "Pangaea", which subsequently split up. Wegener declared that the continents had actively ploughed their way through the immobile oceanic crust. With good reason, geologists refused to accept this theory.

But in the early 1960's, using new instruments, oceanographers began measuring gravitation, magnetism and heat flow along the mid-ocean ridges. They discovered that these ridges are fractures where new oceanic crust is constantly formed until, possibly 150–200 million years later, it disintegrates in the oceanic trenches, far from its origin.

We know now that the lithosphere is divided up into plates which are comparatively rigid. They move in relation to each other like ice-floes in a current of water. These plates incorporate blocks of continental crust or "cratons". While, geologically speaking, the seabeds are recent and consist of homogenous volcanic rocks, the continents are extremely ancient and are made up of many different types of rock. They have repeatedly split and collided and fragments of oceanic sediment and rock have fastened on to their flanks. These movements have resulted in folding, faulting and vulcanism around the periphery of the continents. This new plate-tectonic theory has created a veritable revolution in geology.

Scientific studies into the structure of the continents have been going on for two hundred years and have produced important knowledge as to the origins of rocks and soils. Even as early as the 18th century we understood how magmatic rocks rise from the Earth's interior, how they are then weathered and how the mineral fragments form sediment far away from the original rocks. In time, chemical processes cement these fragments into sedimentary rock. High pressures and temperatures in the crustal collision zones can then convert the sedimentary rock into metamorphic rock. If this is raised to the surface and is exposed to weathering the entire rock cycle begins again: transportation, sedimentation, consolidation, metamorphosis. On land, this cycle is fragmentary and erratic when compared with the immense geological machinery of the oceans.

Vertical crustal movements
The large-scale movements in the Earth's crust are almost entirely horizontal, but the local shifts are often vertical. These derive their motive power mainly from the horizontal movements of the plates, but they can occur a long way from the plate limits. The mechanics of geological faulting (right) were being studied in detail long before the geologists themselves understood or even suspected any movement of the plates.

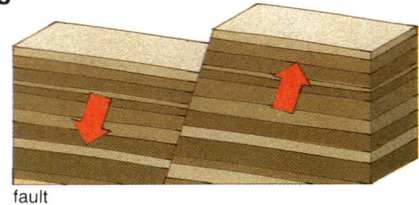

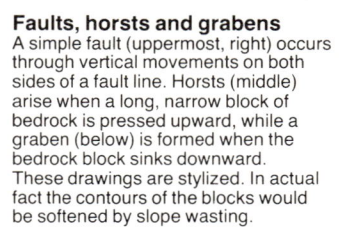

Faults, horsts and grabens
A simple fault (uppermost, right) occurs through vertical movements on both sides of a fault line. Horsts (middle) arise when a long, narrow block of bedrock is pressed upward, while a graben (below) is formed when the bedrock block sinks downward. These drawings are stylized. In actual fact the contours of the blocks would be softened by slope wasting.

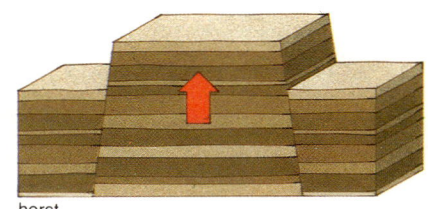

fault

horst

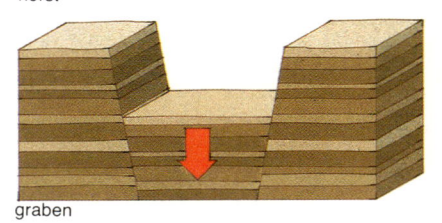

graben

Rocks of the Earth's crust

Magmatic rocks are formed when molten magma wells up from the Earth's upper mantle. Shown here is a coarse-grained granite. Magma on the surface is called lava.

Sedimentary rocks are usually deposited in water. This Jurassic period limestone has a clearly stratified structure.

Metamorphic rocks (shown here: gneiss) are formed when magmatic or sedimentary rocks are transformed through high pressure and/or high temperatures.

How rock types are formed
Unlike the homogenous oceanic crust, the continental crust is a patchwork of rock types from different periods and different origins. The magmatic rocks are the most primitive, though not always the oldest. The other rock types—with the exception of organic formations such as coal—are secondary products from the weathering, erosion, transportation, deposition and transformation of older rocks. Because of movements in the crust these rocks can now be found far from the places where they were originally formed. But their structure and composition give scientists important clues in determining their origin.

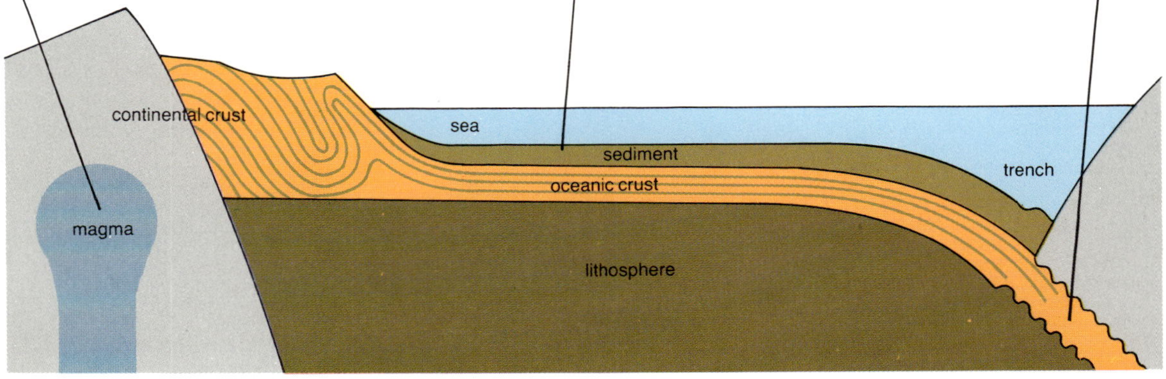

continental crust · sea · sediment · oceanic crust · trench · magma · lithosphere

The restless Earth

The interiors of the continents
are built around large granitic shields which have long been unaffected by the more dramatic geological processes. Consequently the continental rocks are the oldest in the world—as much as 3.8 billion years.

The shallow seas over the shelves
are strictly speaking flooded continents. Some of these sea areas were dry land in earlier epochs, while elsewhere the sea covered areas that form the continents of today. Small fluctuations of the sea level cause major changes in the coastline.

The mid-ocean ridges
are zones where new crust is constantly being formed. Active vulcanism sometimes raises parts of such a ridge above the surface of the sea. Typical examples of this include Iceland, Ascension Island and Tristan da Cunha.

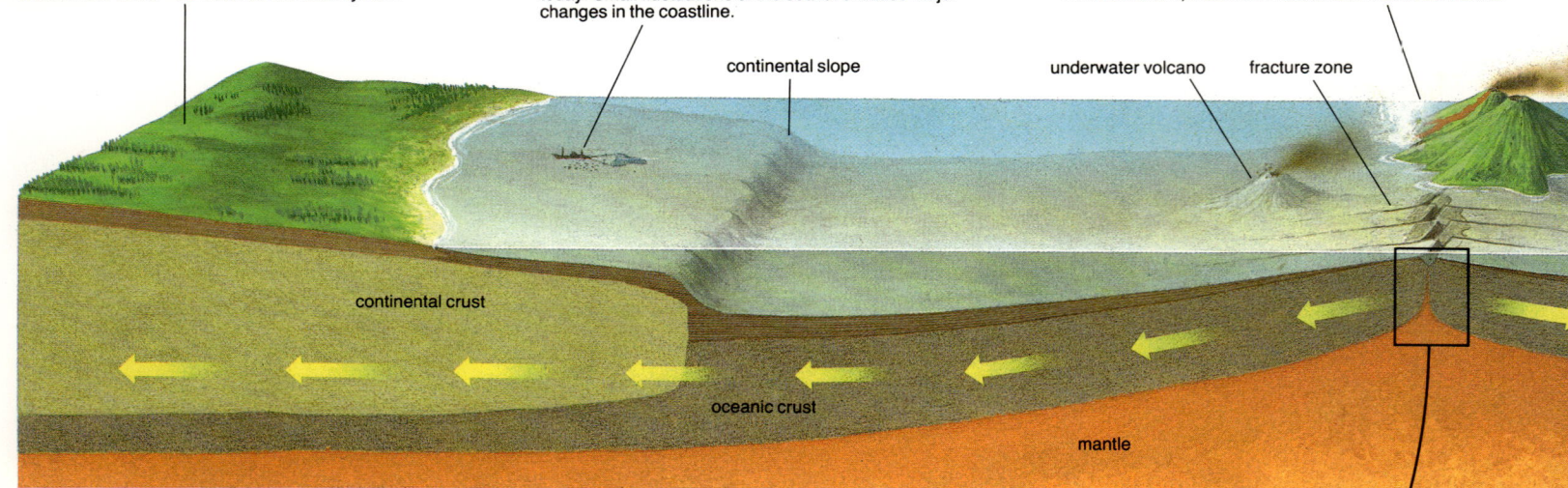

Continental and oceanic crust

Two types of crust
The continental crust is c.16 % lighter than the basalts of the oceanic crust. The continents can thus be said to be floating like ice floes on the oceanic beds. This isostatic effect explains why the surfaces of the continents are mainly above sea level. It also explains why the continents are not drawn down into the Earth's mantle like the seabed and, therefore, why the continents are older than the oceanic crust. Beneath the highest mountain ranges the Earth's crust is thickest.

How new crust is formed:

New crust is formed where two plates are drawn apart by movements in the underlying mantle, which consists of liquid magma. New formation takes place mainly along the mid-ocean ridges, but can also occur where continents are splitting up.

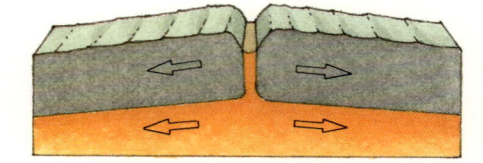

The newly formed fracture between the plates is immediately sealed by magma welling up from the mantle beneath. The oceanic crust is formed by these lava rocks, which develop a cushion-like shape when they harden rapidly beneath the water.

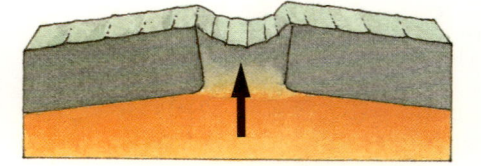

Meanwhile the movements in the mantle continue so that the process is quickly repeated: fractures form, fractures are sealed, fractures re-form...

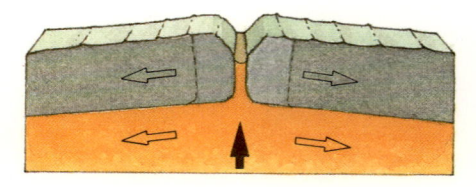

Because of this repeated process the oceanic crust is made up of long strips of simultaneously formed rock running parallel with the mid-ocean ridge. This ridge often has a central valley which is where the fissure is found. Transversal fracture zones extend outward from the ridge. Along these zones the crust is somewhat displaced, since the mantle movements are not equally great at all points along the mid-ocean ridge.

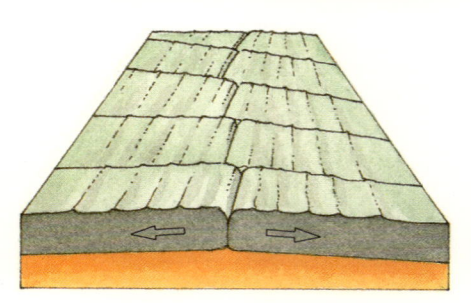

The movement of the continents across the face of the Earth is only one consequence of the phenomenon known as "seafloor spreading". This begins at the mid-ocean ridges where oceanic Earth crust is constantly being formed. The crust then moves away from the spreading zone at a rate of one to ten cm. a year. At first the newly formed seabed lava is fully exposed but gradually it becomes covered by sediment. Thus a recently formed seabed near the spreading zone has only a thin layer of sediment, while older parts farther away can be covered by sediment several km. deep. By its own weight this sediment becomes compressed to form sedimentary rock such as sandstone.

At the same time that the oceanic plate is being renewed in the spreading zones, it is disintegrating in the subduction or consumption zones. These are found in oceanic trenches, which form the greatest depths in the oceans. Here the plate is pressed downward beneath the adjoining plate and finally melted in the Earth's viscous mantle. This "consumption" of oceanic crust explains why we have never encountered a seabed with sediment more than 135 million years old.

By comparison the continental granite shields are almost incomprehensibly ancient—as much as one quarter to one third of the estimated age of the universe itself. These shields are believed to be eroded root zones from earlier mountain ranges. During the course of millions of years the continents have built up around them as the movements of the plates have heaped up sediment and fragments of oceanic crust in the surrounding areas. These formations have subsequently been folded, metamorphosed and jumbled together with rocks that have risen from the mantle. At the same time sediment has been deposited on top of them in inland basins and on the shelves. Geologically, therefore, continents and oceanic beds are totally different from each other.

All major earthquakes result from the movements of the plates against each other. Surface tremors occur when two adjacent plates move in opposite directions, as along the San Andreas fault in California. Deep earthquakes take place when a plate penetrates the mantle at an angle of about 45°. Consequently the very deepest tremors occur at quite a distance beneath the upper plate, sometimes at a depth of more than 700 km. Both surface and deep-level earthquakes have their true centres far beneath the surface. No matter how great the devastation may be at the epicentre on the surface, this is nevertheless a mere echo of what has taken place deep down in the bowels of the Earth.

Vulcanism is a common enough phenomenon throughout the solar system, but plate-tectonic processes appear to be restricted to Earth. It will be for the scientists of the future to determine just what special features of the Earth's interior structure give our planet this unique status.

Subduction zones are areas where the oceanic crust is disintegrating. If the subduction zone is in the open sea then the result is a volcanic island arch, but if it adjoins a continent a mountain range like the Andes is formed.

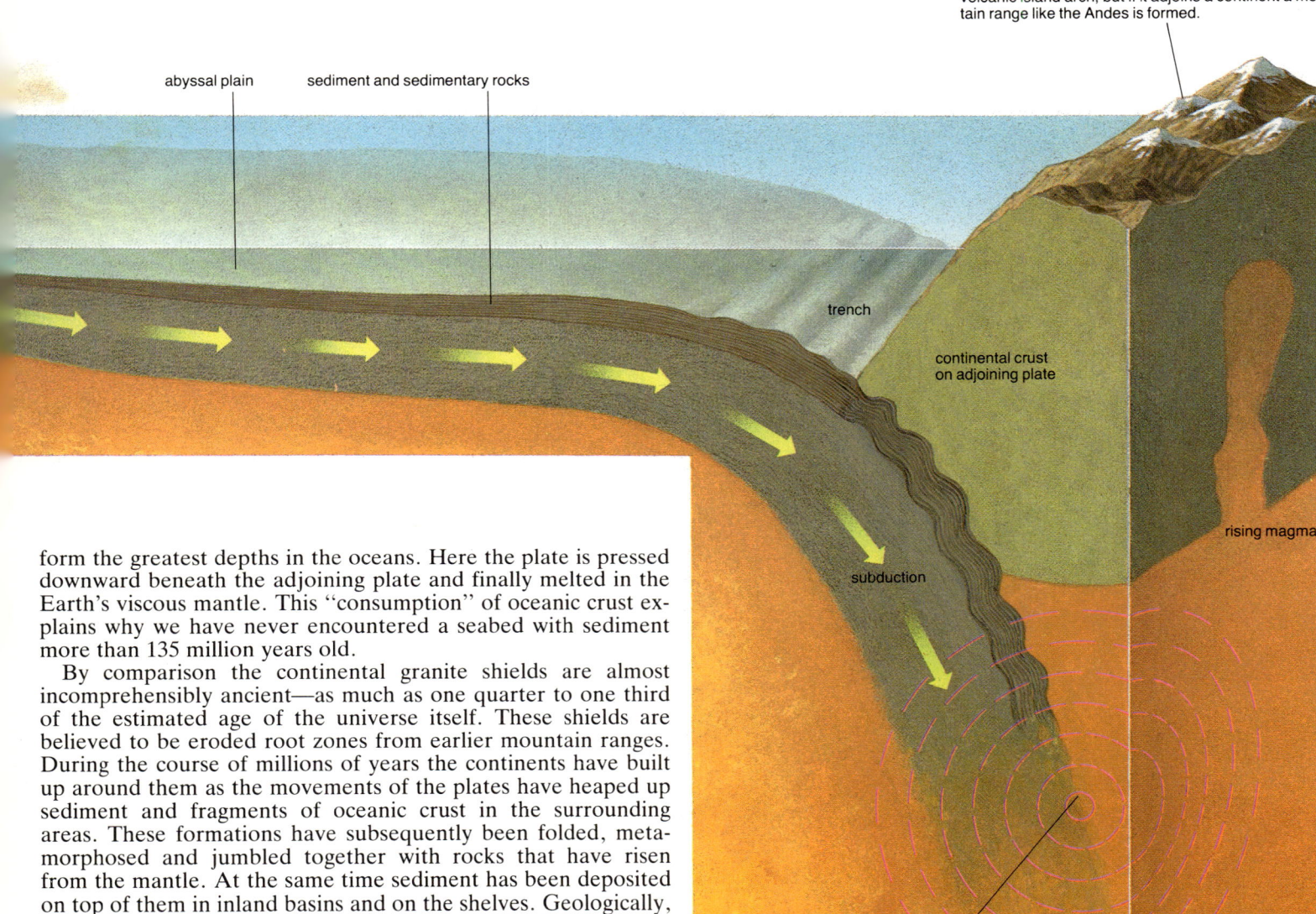

Subduction The movements of the plate when it is drawn down (subducted) into the mantle cause deep earthquakes.

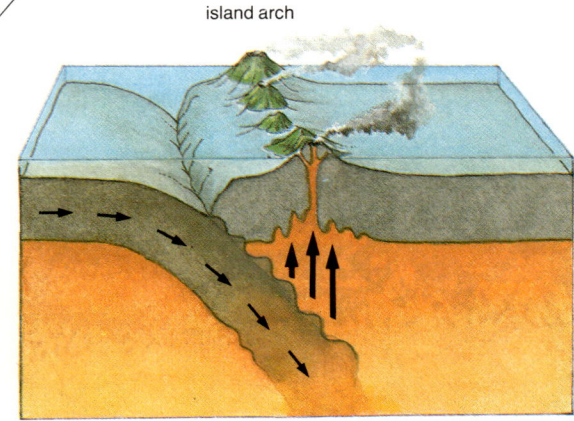

When the plate melts, lighter parts of the molten mass rise upward. These thicken the continental plate from beneath which results in isostatic lifting. They also cause vulcanism.

Weathering

Weathering is the common term for a series of mechanical and chemical processes which decompose both rock and soil. Nearly all of these processes are governed to some extent by climate. Precipitation and temperature are key factors which, along with the hardness and chemical composition of the rocks and soils, determine how the weathering process develops.

Mechanical weathering
In cold climates frost action is the most common form of weathering. Changes in temperature cause small inclusions of moisture in rock and earth to freeze and thaw alternately. Frost action will only occur where local temperatures vary above and below zero and where liquid water is present.

The pressure of growing ice crystals can shatter boulders and bedrock. There are other types of crystal, however, which can have the same shattering effect. All surface and sub-surface water contains dissolved salts which have been leached out of minerals and soils. When the moisture evaporates, salt crystals can split porous rocks.

This salt shattering action occurs particularly in sandstone and in desert regions where there is exceptional evaporation. Even in very arid conditions there is sufficient moisture present in rocks to cause this form of shattering. The process attacks not only rock formations, however, but also buildings. In modern times dam building and large scale irrigation have raised the water table in the Nile valley to such an extent that ancient monuments there are becoming damaged by the saline water that is soaking upward through the porous stone. In European cities, too, the foundations of historic buildings are being damaged by salt. This penetrates the masonry via dampness from the surrounding ground and then crystallizes.

Extreme changes of temperature between day and night can shatter stone through the constant expansion and contraction that takes place. This is a common phenomenon in the desert where, because of the dry air, there is a great difference between daytime and night-time temperatures. This type of shattering is consequently related to the absence, rather than to the presence, of moisture. One form of mechanical weathering which is of secondary significance is the shattering effect of growing roots.

Chemical weathering
This takes place primarily when weak acids in surface and sub-surface water dissolve different minerals. When carbon dioxide dissolves in water, part of it combines with the water and produces carbonic acid, H_2CO_3. This acid in turn dissolves the calcium carbonate in limestone. Water circulation in this pervious type of bedrock can thus form caves and tunnels. When the calcareous water evaporates, the calcium carbonate is precipitated again as limestone formations. In regions with a limestone bedrock and abundant precipitation this type of weathering is associated with karst landscapes (named after the ancient province of Karst on the Yugoslavian-Italian border) with ravines, dolines, poljes and caverns.

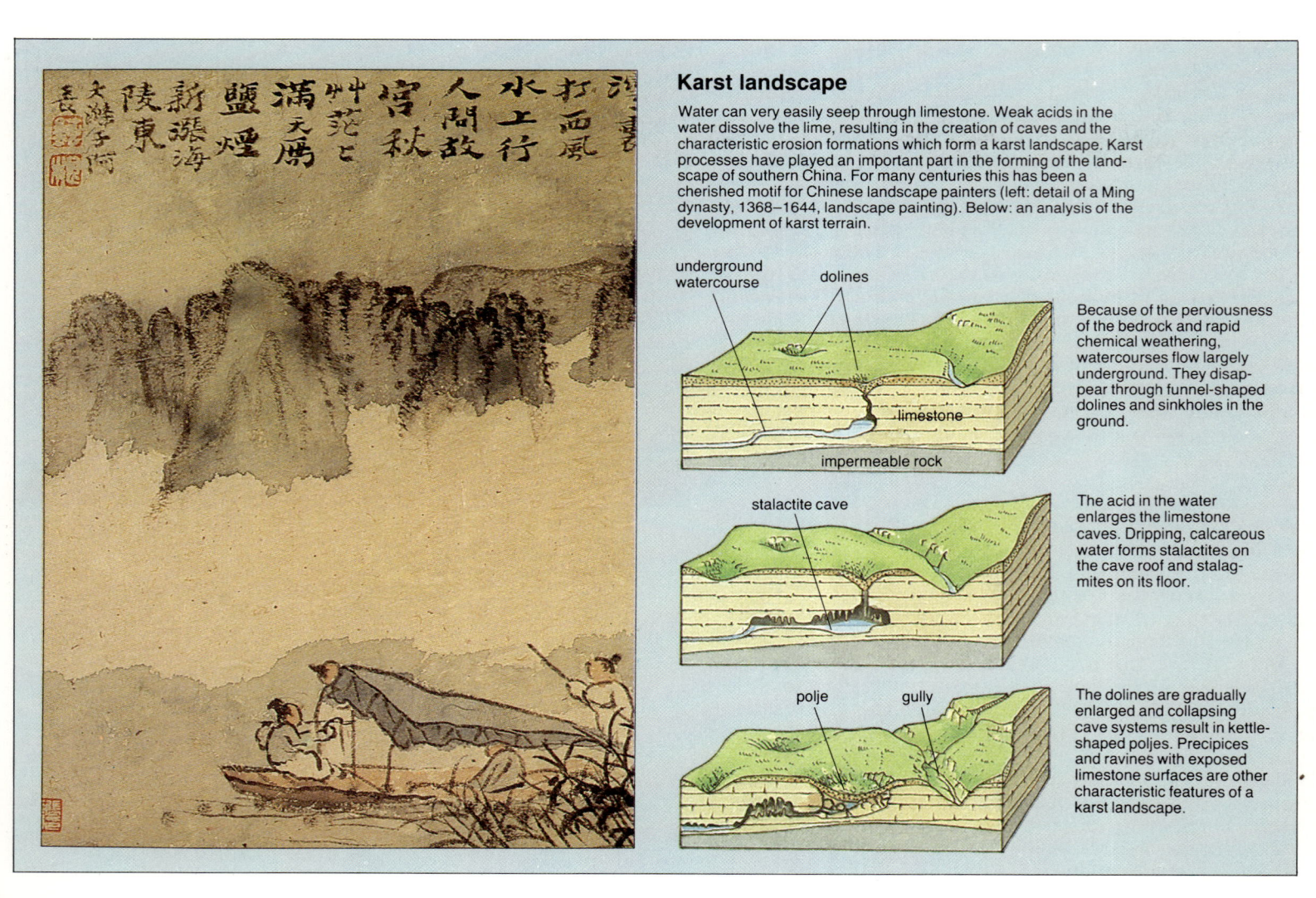

Karst landscape
Water can very easily seep through limestone. Weak acids in the water dissolve the lime, resulting in the creation of caves and the characteristic erosion formations which form a karst landscape. Karst processes have played an important part in the forming of the landscape of southern China. For many centuries this has been a cherished motif for Chinese landscape painters (left: detail of a Ming dynasty, 1368–1644, landscape painting). Below: an analysis of the development of karst terrain.

Because of the perviousness of the bedrock and rapid chemical weathering, watercourses flow largely underground. They disappear through funnel-shaped dolines and sinkholes in the ground.

The acid in the water enlarges the limestone caves. Dripping, calcareous water forms stalactites on the cave roof and stalagmites on its floor.

The dolines are gradually enlarged and collapsing cave systems result in kettle-shaped poljes. Precipices and ravines with exposed limestone surfaces are other characteristic features of a karst landscape.

In places where the air is polluted, limestone masonry suffers damage as airborne sulphuric acid decomposes the stone. The Acropolis, the hill citadel of Athens, is threatened with disintegration and the authorities are now considering removing these edifices altogether to a museum with purified air and erecting plastic models instead on the site—a solution which it is thought would be less expensive than attempting to clean up the notoriously polluted atmosphere of the Greek capital.

Organic acids, formed in a surface layer of humus, are an important factor in wet climates. Not only acids destroy stone, however; oxidation (attack by the oxygen in the air) and hydrolysis (minerals in the rocks dissolving in water), also result in weathering. Feldspar and mica in even the hardest of granites can break down and cause the stone to disintegrate. The feldspar and mica are transformed into hydrous oxides of iron and aluminium and hydrous alumino-silicates, clay minerals which form kaolin and bauxite. All that remains of the granite is loose grains of quartz. These can then sedimentate and become converted into rocks. When these rocks in their turn are weathered the geological rock cycle is completed.

In nature the process of weathering is so slow that it is often difficult to discern. But it is nevertheless highly significant for it is the first stage in denudation, the levelling out of the landscape. The products of weathering also form soils which in their turn are essential to the existence of vegetation and animal life on land. Weathering has therefore been a factor of fundamental importance in the creation of life environments on our planet.

Folding and denudation

The history of the Earth's surface constitutes a constant struggle between constructive and destructive forces. The most significant building-up processes are uplifting and folding while the principle disintegrating processes are weathering and erosion. The disintegration is part of a process known as denudation—a process which through geological time reduces even the highest mountains to mere hillocks (below). Weathering makes this process possible by breaking down even the hardest of rocks.

Horizontal forces in the Earth's crust fold the formerly level strata of sedimentary rocks. This diagram is schematic only—in reality no landforms such as these occur...

...since denudation is taking place simultaneously with folding and uplifting. Rapid uplifting and erosion together produce an "Alpine" relief with dramatic precipices, ridges and peaks.

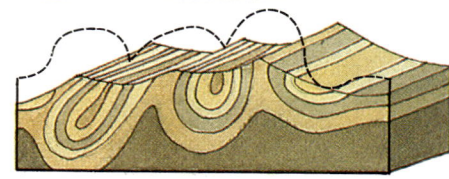

The ultimate result of denudation is a low, undulating relief, the highest points of which are much lower in many cases than the original mountain ridge (dotted line).

Frost action

The volume of water increases by 9 % when it freezes—a unique quality among naturally occurring fluids. In this way the water that always exists in cracks and pores in stone can shatter and split bedrock and boulders alike (left). In rocky regions with pronounced variations between warm and cold temperatures, frost action produces "boulder fields" or "felsenmeers", whole areas consisting of sharp-edged, split boulders and smaller stones.

Weathering in the tropics

In warm, humid climates weathering processes penetrate to 80 m. or more beneath the surface. Deep weathering of the bedrock often creates red, ferruginous laterite soil (right). A recently exposed "inselberg" reveals the results of weathering in earlier, wetter epochs in the form of rounded blocks and rock surfaces (below).

55

Erosion

Abraded coast

The kinetic energy in waves makes wave erosion, or abrasion, very effective, especially along exposed, rocky coasts. The waves undermine the rock until part of it falls away. It is this process which creates the steep faces of rock known as cliffs, for example the famous white cliffs of Dover in England. Harder parts remain standing as isolated pillars or "stacks". In front of the cliff an abrasion platform is formed and this is usually exposed at low water on tidal coasts. Loose material brought down by erosion gathers here. The stones are kept in constant movement by the waves and become rounded into smooth pebbles. On softer faces the abrasion process is more rapid and of a somewhat different nature.

Resistant rock forms promontories.

niche

sea arch

isolated pillar or stack

Abraded cliff formed in horizontally stratified limestone.

Erosion takes place mainly at the surface level of the water and an abrasion platform thus forms below this

Eroded material is moved by the waves to form an abrasion platform.

In a rockslide rocks or a whole cliff face will fall away. This usually happens on very steep slopes.

Rock, soil and gravity

When weathering or excessive moisture reduces the cohesion in a slope the force of gravity can set it in motion downward. This slope wasting may vary in manner according to the nature of the material (solid rock, boulders, moist or dry soils) and also according to the angle of the slope. When the material is dry and the slope only moderate then the process is normally slow. Creep and solifluction can take place almost indiscernibly and this occurs to some extent on all slopes. Rockslides or landslides on the other hand happen suddenly and violently and if this occurs in a built-up area the loss of life and property can be enormous. Landslides can take place on quite moderate slopes. When the moisture content in very fine-grained material, especially clays, rises beyond a specific limit the cohesion of that material diminishes dramatically.

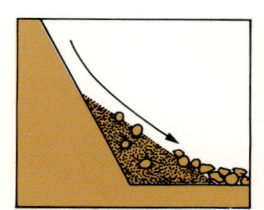

A talus is formed when repeated small slides pile up debris at the foot of a steep face. The "angle of repose" of the talus is about 35°, depending on the material in it.

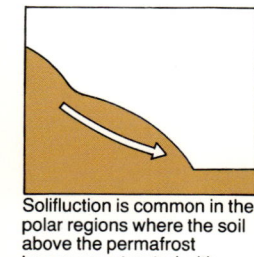

Solifluction is common in the polar regions where the soil above the permafrost becomes saturated with water in the summer.

Creep in loose ground can create steep ravines (right). Trees and posts are displaced from the vertical.

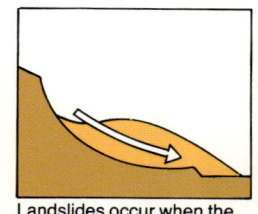

Landslides occur when the moisture content in fine-grained soils exceeds a certain limit, abruptly transforming the ground into mush.

Erosion is part of an extensive process which earth scientists call denudation—the stripping of the ground by the forces of wind, ice and running water. Denudation causes the gradual lowering of the ground level. It has been calculated that this takes place at a mean rate of 50–90 m. per million years, at least during the present geological epoch.

Denudation embraces a whole series of processes. Climatic conditions cause disintegration by weathering when particles and larger fragments break away from the bedrock. Gravity, water, ice and strong winds set this loose material in motion and erosion as such takes place when the particles, and the medium which carries them along, wears away the surface of the ground. Denudation could be described as the sum total of weathering, slope wasting and erosion.

The ground is most effectively eroded by running water and consequently heavy rainfall often results in severe erosion. Steep slopes increase the kinetic energy of the water and thereby further intensify the erosion process, as in the Alps or the Himalayas for example. The loose material which rivers and streams carry along with them is sooner or later deposited in deltas or sedimentation basins. This occurs at the point where the flow of water has diminished to the extent that the loose material is no longer kept moving.

The process of erosion has not continued at the same rate throughout geological time. For long periods the continents were considerably flatter than at present because the formation of mountain ranges proceeded slowly or did not take place at all. During other epochs when the plates in the Earth's crust collided with each other, new mountain ranges were folded and large areas of the continents were raised relative to sea level. Erosion then increased again. In dry regions wind erosion has been predominant while in the polar regions it is the slowly advancing ice of the glaciers which is the erosive element, but the principal factor on a global scale has always been running water.

The flow of water, in miniature gullies and great rivers alike, wears away the surface in characteristic V-shaped grooves. Glaciers carve out a broader valley, with a U-shaped profile. The valley sides are then smoothed out by slope wasting, especially in moist climates. The contours of the landscape become increasingly gentle, finally levelling out into a plain. By then denudation can have lowered the ground level so much that the slow flow of rivers is no longer sufficient to sustain erosion. This "peneplain" is the final product of denudation.

The surface of the Earth has never been reduced to one great peneplain since at many times in the past a new rising movement in the Earth's crust has increased the flow of water, transformed quiet rivers into raging torrents and thereby speeded up erosion once again. This struggle between the disintegrating forces of atmosphere and hydrosphere and the building forces of the crust will continue as long as the heat in the Earth's interior is sufficient to sustain the plate-tectonic processes.

Erosion's agents

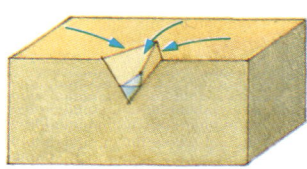

Running water dislodges and carries away bedrock fragments and soil particles, thereby forming ravines.

Waves abrade exposed coasts forming steep cliffs—anything from less than a metre to a hundred metres or more high.

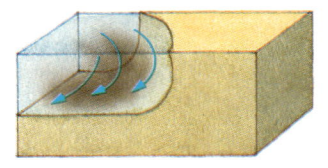

The river current erodes the shoreline, especially on the outer side of a bend. Rivers thus tend to develop an increasingly winding or meandering course.

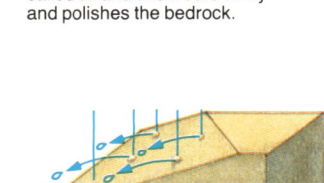

Glaciers contain stone debris, called till and this wears away and polishes the bedrock.

In dry areas the wind carries innumerable grains of sand which "blast" and sculpture exposed rocks.

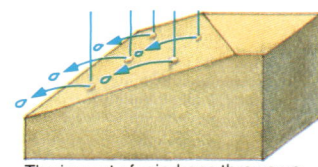

The impact of raindrops throws up loose particles which gradually move downward over a slope.

From plain to peneplain

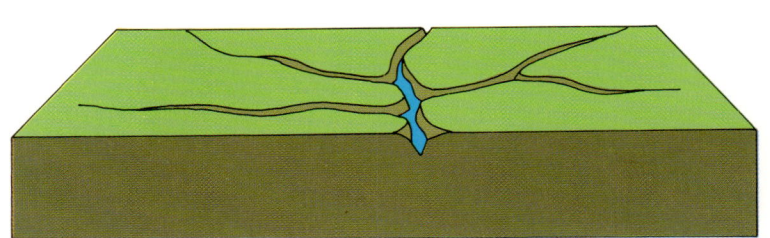

On a plain, rivers and streams run slowly and the valleys and gullies which these cut have the typical V-shaped profile of fluvial erosion. However, they are shallow—the slower the current, the less the erosion.

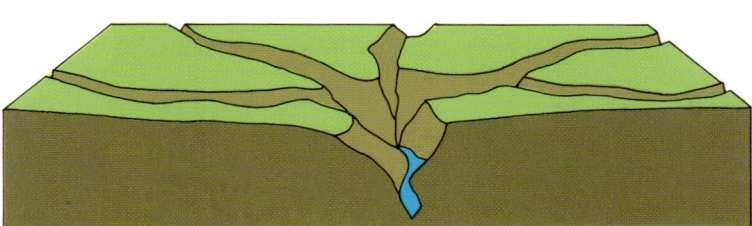

If a plain is raised by forces in the Earth's interior then the swiftness of the waterflow increases, and the rivers cut deep gorges with steep sides. In dry regions the areas between these gorges can remain intact for a long time...

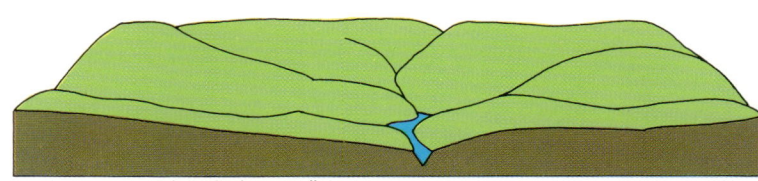

...but in wetter regions the intermediate areas are worn away by slope wasting. The entire plain becomes "denuded" and as its level sinks the flow of the rivers becomes slower and slower.

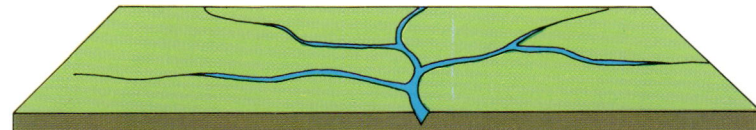

Finally denudation flattens out the entire area into a "peneplain". Erosion is now very slow because of the leisurely flow of the water. Peneplains are found in the granite regions of Canada and Scandinavia. Details of the terrain here have often been modified by glacial processes during the final stages of the last Ice Age.

Life on land

Living in water
A fish is a relatively uncomplicated creature. Its means of locomotion—muscles, fins—are simpler than those of terrestrial animals. The fish has no urgent need to regulate its body temperature.

Adaptations to life on dry land
The elephant, the largest and heaviest of all living terrestrial animals, can be used here as a fairly drastic example of the biological adaptations necessary for survival ashore. Mammals, with their complex temperature control mechanism, are the animals which have most efficiently adapted themselves to living on land.

Rigid supporting skeleton with complicated joints and muscle attachments.

Internal fertilization through copulation; fewer offspring.

The skin protects the animal against desiccation.

Adaptations for breathing air: respiratory tracts and lungs.

Legs and feet for walking on solid ground.

Life began in the sea and the life environment of those organisms which still live there is not particularly harsh. It protects them against desiccation and sudden changes in temperature. Filter feeders from the sea-cucumber to the baleen whale can treat the water quite simply as a nutrient solution. On the other hand the move on to land – a step which the multicellular plants took about 400 million years ago – required drastic biological adaptations.

Two of these adaptations are especially manifest. The first of them relates to locomotion. In order to be able to move on land the terrestrial animal had to evolve a complex motive apparatus with legs and feet, an apparatus which had, and continues to have, a low degree of energy efficiency. A small, running quadruped, a dog for example, has to use five times more energy than a swimming salmon to move one kilometre.

The second of these adaptations concerns reproduction. In the water fertilization is an external process: the female cod ejects her spawn whereupon the male secretes his milt over it. Fertilization occurs freely in the water and tens of thousands of offspring are left to their own resources.

Reproduction on land demands internal fertilization by means of copulation, incubation and usually care of the offspring. The mammal has gone a stage further; an "internal incubation" of the fertilized ovum is followed by delivery, i.e. birth. The tendency, in other words, has been towards greater attention to each individual offspring.

Yet despite these severe demands the colonization of the continents has been extraordinarily successful. The first amphibian to make a brief but arduous land crossing – probably from one pool of water to another – has through an incredible process of adaptation given rise to some 13,000 vertebrate species now dwelling on, in and above the ground, and also in the seas (seals and whales). The adaptation programme of the insects has been even more successful; there are now about one million insect species. The number of terrestrial plant species is probably in the region of 300,000. One reason for this vast variation may be that land, in contrast to water, is divided into numerous environments with different attributes.

In response to varying environmental characteristics organisms have been compelled to develop more differentiated forms and more complex behaviour patterns than would ever have been necessary in water. This is a course of development which has led to our own species.

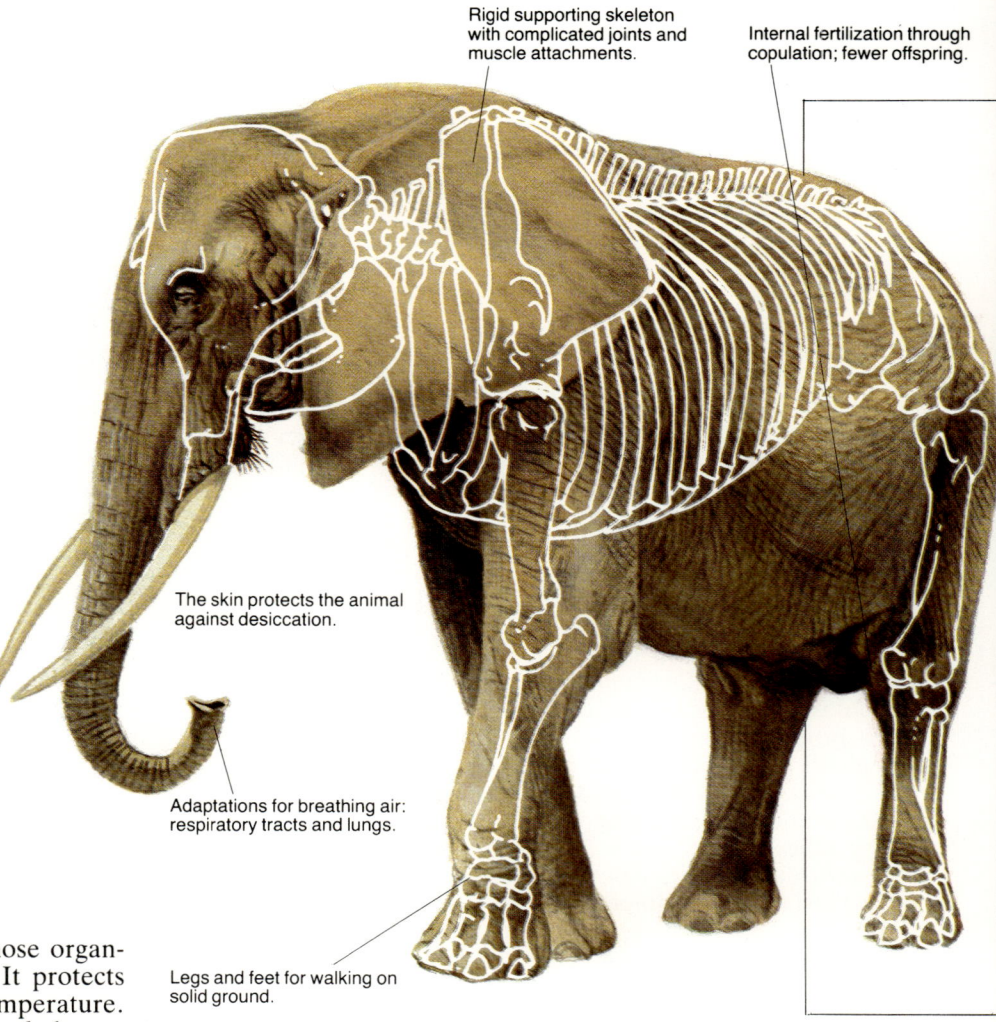

Life has colonized the land
The invasion of life on dry land has totally transformed the environment. This photograph shows lifeforms of different levels of sophistication, from grassplants to elephants.

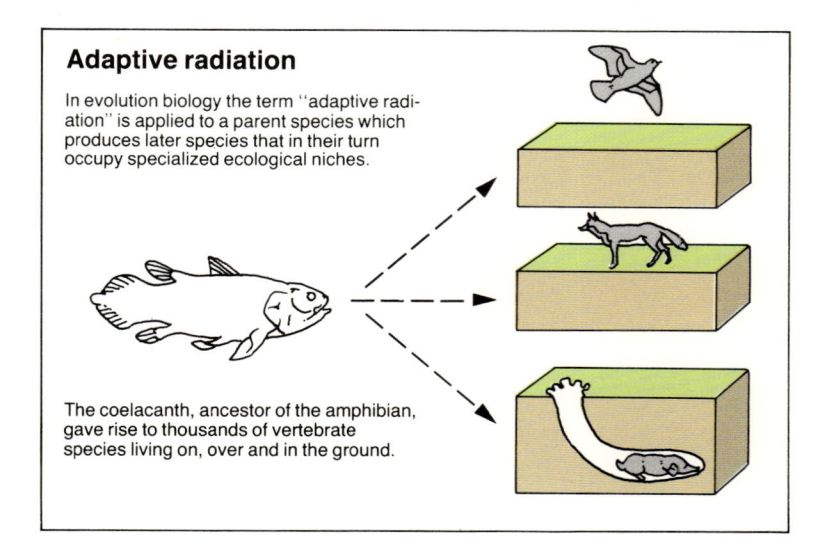

Adaptive radiation
In evolution biology the term "adaptive radiation" is applied to a parent species which produces later species that in their turn occupy specialized ecological niches.

The coelacanth, ancestor of the amphibian, gave rise to thousands of vertebrate species living on, over and in the ground.

Plants on dry land

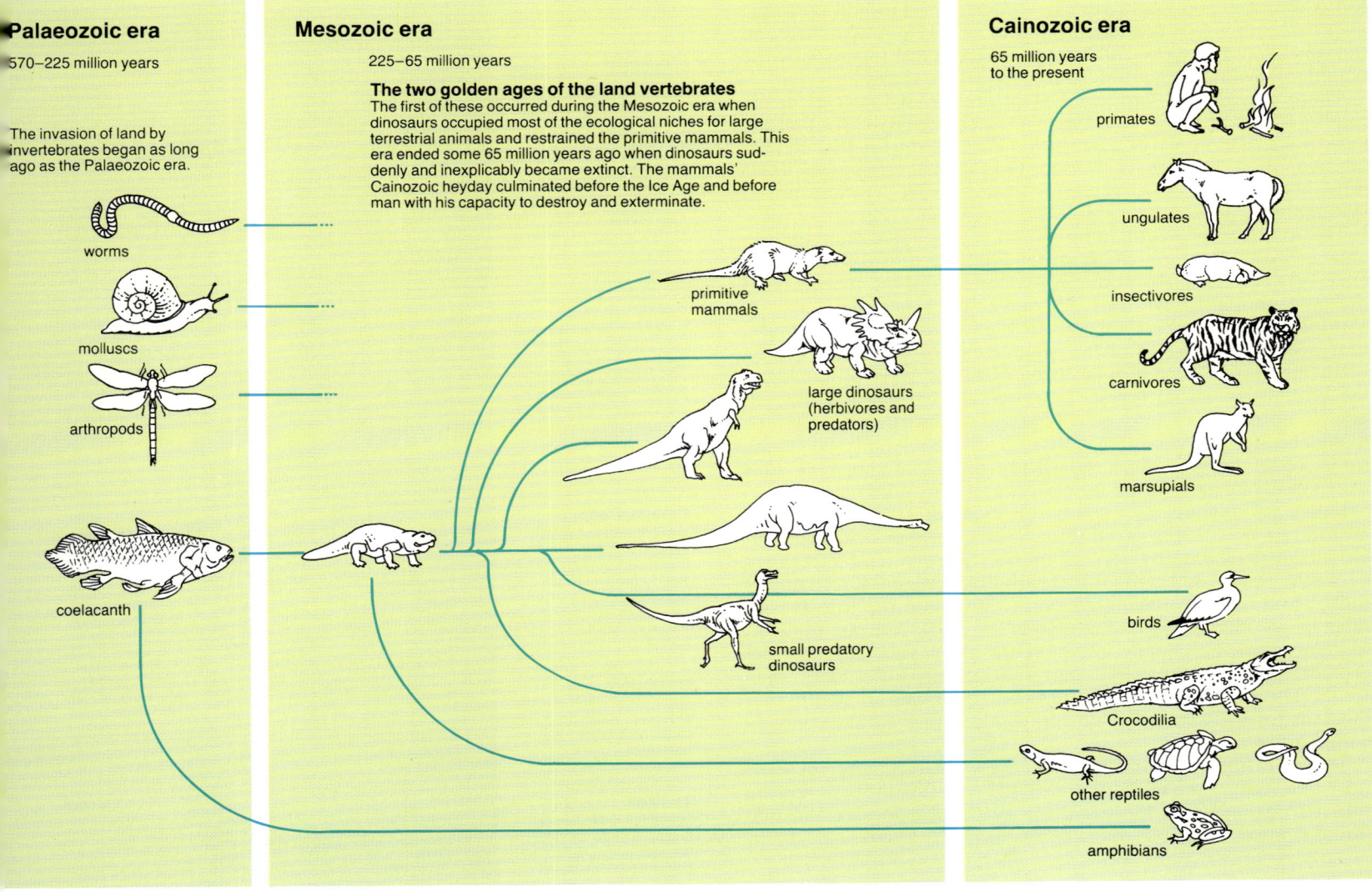

Aquatic plants are not lignified. They do not need structural rigidity since they are of almost the same density as water. Sub-arctic seaweed species can attain a length of several dozen metres and form veritable forests. At the other end of the scale microscopic plants can float as plankton, aided by tiny drops of oil in the cell plasm.

Bark protects the tree from desiccation.

Xylem tissue conveys moisture from the roots up through the tree.

The dead, hard heartwood is the tree's internal "skeleton".

The architecture of the tree is conditioned almost entirely by gravitation. The inner heartwood makes the trunk rigid and raises the crown of the tree towards the light. Moisture is conveyed from the roots up to the foliage by means of capillarity.
Why are trees so tall? Partly because they compete with each other for light, but also in order to protect their foliage against browsing animals. The trees evolved at a time when herbivorous dinosaurs roamed the continents.

Palaeozoic era
570–225 million years

The invasion of land by invertebrates began as long ago as the Palaeozoic era.

worms

molluscs

arthropods

coelacanth

Mesozoic era
225–65 million years

The two golden ages of the land vertebrates
The first of these occurred during the Mesozoic era when dinosaurs occupied most of the ecological niches for large terrestrial animals and restrained the primitive mammals. This era ended some 65 million years ago when dinosaurs suddenly and inexplicably became extinct. The mammals' Cainozoic heyday culminated before the Ice Age and before man with his capacity to destroy and exterminate.

primitive mammals

large dinosaurs (herbivores and predators)

small predatory dinosaurs

Cainozoic era
65 million years to the present

primates

ungulates

insectivores

carnivores

marsupials

birds

Crocodilia

other reptiles

amphibians

59

Tropical forests

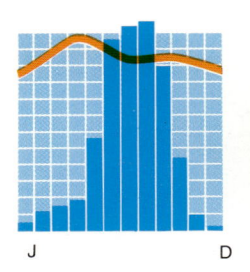

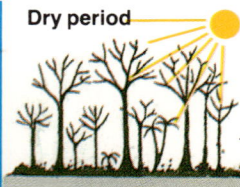

Monsoon and rain forests
form distinct ecological systems, because of climatic differences. Monsoon forest (above) has an annual dry period; the columns in the climate diagram show the rainfall distribution over the year. During the dry period most of the trees shed their leaves. The rain forest (below) remains green all the year round, because the rainfall is more evenly distributed. The temperature (graph curves) remains high and steady in all tropical lowland areas.

Monsoon forests (above) are found in south and southwest Asia. Lowland rain forests grow in an equatorial belt and are most extensive in the Amazon and Congo river basins (below).

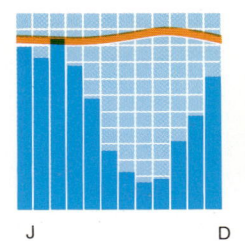

Forest requires moisture. In tropical regions where there is abundant rain, monsoon or rain forests flourish according to how the rainfall is distributed over the year. Lowland rain forests and the more unusual mountain rain forests are also distinctly different to each other. In regions where there is less rain, savanna and other types of vegetation emerge.

It is the competition for the sun's energy which gives the rain forest its particular character. The plants cling to and scramble over each other to reach upward to the light. The forest floor, on the other hand, is dark and humid. The tropical forests lack the abundant ground vegetation of the temperate zones.

There is a greater variety of plant and animal species in the rain forests than in any other ecosystem; probably half of all the known species on Earth exist here. The reason for this enormous wealth of species is that the equatorial ecosystems have remained stable for several million years. No Ice Age has moved through these regions.

The rain forests give the impression of superabundant vitality, and yet this is to some extent misleading. There is a great difference between the high-productive conditions of the treetops and the inhospitable forest floor. Moreover the rain forest environment is exceptionally delicate. In the temperate zone forest, only a small proportion of the organic carbon present occurs in the living plants; most of it is stored in a thick layer of humus on the ground. In a rain forest, however, the carbon is converted almost immediately into new vegetation. In other words, the humus stratum is very thin and is destroyed rapidly when the forest cover disappears. Beneath the humus are infertile soils which easily become fused into laterite, a brick-like mass.

Man's endeavours to exploit the rain forests can therefore have disastrous results. Traditional land clearance is not particularly hazardous but poverty and desperation can lead to reckless stripping that can be totally destructive. When international timber and food producing concerns move into the forests with their heavy machinery and demands for quick returns, the consequences can be equally grave. After a few good harvests the ground becomes exhausted and can sustain little more than scrub. The process of devastation is now moving so swiftly that the rain forests and their life-forms could face total extinction within a few decades.

The rain forests of the Old and New Worlds differ in their flora and fauna. Shown here is a South American forest, but the threat to existence is the same for all tropical forests and that threat is man.

The canopy
Because of the abundance of sunlight, the biomass production is highest among the treetops. Consequently large numbers of birds, insects and monkeys have their habitat on this level.

The lower trees
Lower down there are other treetop strata. These intermediate levels consist of tree species which are better adapted to shade than the trees that form the canopy. These lower levels, too, harbour their particular fauna.

Epiphytes
Many plants, for example lianas and some orchids, grow up among the trees. Certain of these epiphytes are parasites which feed on their host plants, while others merely make use of the trees to climb upwards towards the light. Other epiphytes are saprophytes, living on decaying organic matter.

Palms
do not normally grow as tall as deciduous trees. They are thus not common in the shadowy interior of the rain forests though they do occur where the sun can reach them, along the watercourses, for example.

Constant shade
prevails over the forest floor so that this environment is not very productive. Fallen leaves are decomposed by various organisms which have their habitat here.

Stranglers
Many of the epiphytes are stranglers which gradually choke and destroy the host plant.

The soil
beneath the thin layer of humus is often infertile, latosolic earth, reddish in colour from iron oxides.

The highest trees

protruding above the canopy and known as "emergents" harbour a number of bird species, including swifts that are closely related to the species of the Old World. The harpy eagle preys chiefly on the monkeys of the canopy.

The treetops

are the habitat of a great variety of fauna. There are many bird species here, from grotesque toucans to graceful humming birds that are often no bigger than a large butterfly. The green tree-boa slithers through the foliage in pursuit of monkeys and birds. Nocturnal vampire bats sleep away the hours of daylight while orchids bloom in branch-forks and bark fissures. Brilliant butterflies swarm among and over the tree crowns.

In the lower trees

great troops of howler monkeys greet the sunrise in clamorous chorus. Their screams can be heard several kilometres away. The two-toed sloth ambles leisurely through the branches; this creature has no natural enemies and thus no need for speed or agility. Unlike the heavier jaguar, the agile ocelot hunts up among the branches with ease.

On the ground

the giant armadillo roots among fallen leaves while the agouti, a rodent, scuttles about in search of fallen fruit. The jaguar frequents the tracts around the watercourses in which swim anacondas, the largest snakes in the world, up to ten metres in length.

Underground

a multitude of invertebrates, fungi and bacteria decompose dead organic matter to recycle the nutrients for further biological production.

61

The grasslands

Tropical or temperate zone forest thins out and becomes grassland because the rainfall there is inadequate in relation to evaporation, or because it is not sufficiently evenly distributed over the year to sustain an overall woodland coverage. The great grasslands of the world are located in places where the global air circulation system produces a predominance of dry, descending air masses.

The grasslands of the world
The grass plains constitute not one but several environments. The tropical savannas, the temperate zone prairies and the continental steppes differ in many ways. First and foremost the savannas have no winter; located as they are between the tropics of Cancer and Capricorn the savannas merely have two dry periods each year. Where the savanna gives way to steppe the vegetation becomes lower and sparser, more thorny and with smaller leaves, as the climate becomes drier. Lowland steppe forms the transitional zone between savanna and desert. Another type of steppe is the continental plateau as in Anatolia and central Asia.

The East African savannas are the best studied of all the world's grasslands. Compared with the monotonous and impoverished steppes the savannas are varied and highly productive. The prairie is a sort of intermediate environment between savanna and steppe, though it scarcely exists any longer in its natural state; most of it has been modifed by cultivation. The savanna can have the appearance of sparse woodland, have a park landscape, or be almost treeless, depending upon the humidity. The watercourses are lined by a narrow strip of forest often little more than a few dozen metres in breadth.

The food chain
Grasses represent the basic element in the food chain although they emerged only during the last 50–60 million years, i.e. in the Cainozoic era. The same also applies to the grazing animals. The teeth and the digestive systems of the ungulates have become adapted to the cellulose-abundant grass diet, especially in the case of the ruminants, while the grass in its turn has also adapted to the grazers. Unlike most other vascular plants, grass does not grow at the top but out from the bottom so that the stems can survive being constantly nibbled off.

Herbivores have specialized eating habits. Giraffes eat leaves and twigs from high up on the trees, elephants leaves and branches farther down, and zebras, antelopes and gazelles graze on grasses of different height and coarseness. In this way the herbivores make maximum use of the flora. The huge herds of animals represent an adaptation to the threat from predators. Large animals are unable to conceal themselves on the plains, but they can hide among their own kind. Thus the strong animals of high status are found in the herd's centre while the weaker individuals have to stay on the periphery.

The predators of the plains are interesting subjects of study, though their total living weight is at most one tenth that of the herbivores. There is not always a clear difference between the so-called predators and carrion-eaters. Nocturnal studies using image intensifiers have revealed that the hyena is an accomplished hunter and when one sees lions and hyenas around the same carcass it is by no means certain that it was the lions which brought down the prey.

Man on the grasslands
The human race evolved on the grass plains of Africa and man has continued to live on the savannas and steppes as hunter/gatherer, livestock nomad, and farmer. Hunters and nomads alike follow the animals which in their turn follow the rain seasons and vegetation cycles. The farmer departs from this pattern. In many places increasing population results in imprudent methods of cultivation, over-grazing and the laying waste of delicately balanced environments. In this way the productive savanna can become impoverished and reduced to steppe which in its turn can deteriorate into desert. Finally the soil itself can be blown away leaving only a sterile layer of small stones—a desert pavement.

Grassland regions
All the continents, except the Antarctic, have their grasslands: North America's prairies, South America's llanos and pampas, Africa's savanna and steppe belts north and south of the equatorial forests, Eastern Europe and central Asia's steppes. The "grass continent" of them all, however, is Australia, the vast "outback" consisting of grassland enclosing an inner core of desert.

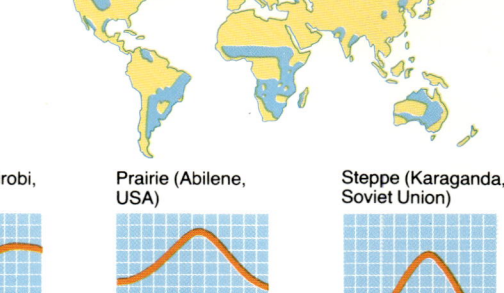

Savanna, prairie, steppe
These diagrams show the climates of savanna, prairie and steppe. Precipitation (columns) often has two annual peak periods but is greater on the savanna than on the steppe. The temperatures (graph curves) are constantly high on the savanna while on the steppe the winter is cold. For both precipitation and temperature the prairie is intermediate. It is found between humid and arid climates.

Savanna flora
is not as well adapted to drought as that of the desert; the dry periods on the savanna are shorter than in the desert. Grasses are the principal producers of biomass and thereby also the main sustenance for the animals, but trees like umbrella thorn and baobab are also characteristic plants.

umbrella thorn · Kigelia · Lobelia · baobab · Cenecio · aloe · elephant grass

Savanna animals
Hunters and scavengers
The puff-adder hunts stealthily on its own, the lions hunt in prides. Hunting dogs chase their prey until it collapses. Hyenas are not only carrion-eaters but also skilled nocturnal hunters. Vultures are specialized carrion-eaters – and outstanding gliders.

hooded vulture · hunting dog · puff-adder · spotted hyena · lion

The great herds
do not wander at random over the East African savannas. They undertake regular seasonal migrations governed ultimately by the periodic variations in rainfall and vegetation. Herd behaviour is an adaptation to the threat of predators, reducing the danger for the individual animal. Shown here is a mixed herd of wildebeest and zebra in East Africa.

A grazing succession

After the rain the new grass grows very rapidly and this is grazed by an ordered succession of animals: zebras move in first, eating the tallest and coarsest grass followed by the wildebeest that eat the medium-length stalks. Finally the Thomson gazelles nibble off the tenderest leaves. This grazing succession makes maximum use of the grass.

Savanna year

January | February | March | April | May | June | July | August | September | October | November | December

The two annual rain periods are most pronounced on the African savannas. The "long rains" continue for a couple of months, the "short rains" for about one month. The rain causes the ground to change its hue abruptly from yellow-brown to green. Between these rain periods the ground gradually resumes the colour of the dry period.

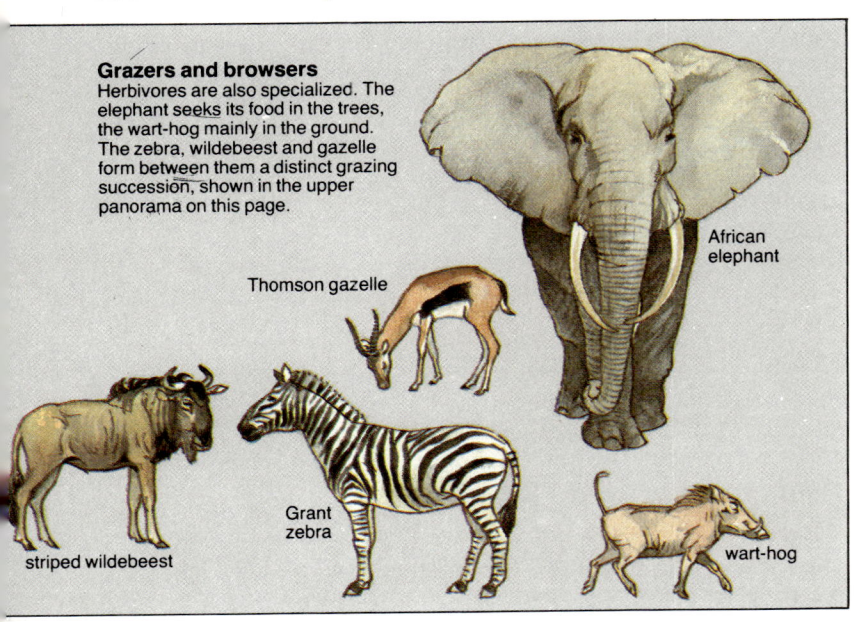

Grazers and browsers
Herbivores are also specialized. The elephant seeks its food in the trees, the wart-hog mainly in the ground. The zebra, wildebeest and gazelle form between them a distinct grazing succession, shown in the upper panorama on this page.

African elephant
Thomson gazelle
striped wildebeest
Grant zebra
wart-hog

Man and the grasslands
On the dry savanna, agricultural productivity is low. But commercial monoculture is more dangerous to the environment than varied subsistence farming. Intensive livestock rearing often causes the total destruction of the ground vegetation. One introduced species—cattle—makes less efficient use of the pasture than animals in a natural grazing succession. Rational game protection and game ranching would give the highest yield but this is difficult to organize and tends also to conflict with customs and traditions. A nomad's wealth is reckoned in terms of how many head of livestock he owns and without such affluence dowry payments and many other social transactions become impossible.

Deserts

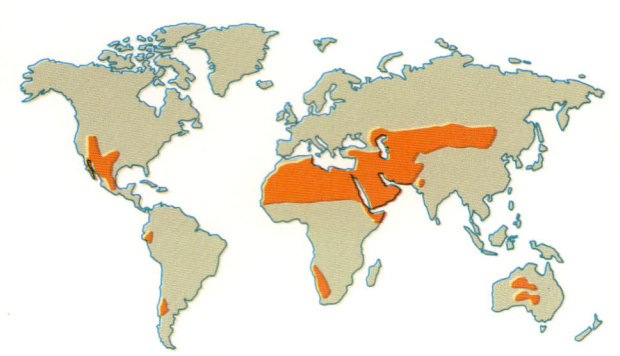

From bushland to desert
The dry bushland (above, far left) has a continuous cover of drought-resistant grasses and thorn bushes. The semi-desert has patches of vegetation, surrounded by bare ground, while the desert itself (far right) is barren with only isolated plantlife here and there.

Deserts of the world
These cover some 15 % of the Earth's land area and are located mainly between the tropics and the subtropical regions where dry air masses descend towards the ground. A vast belt of desert extends from the Atlantic to central Asia.

Sand, stone and rock

Desert types:
Local geology, elevation and winds create different types of desert. The principal ones are sand desert ("erg" in Arabic), stony desert ("sarir") and rock desert ("hammamet"). All of these types are represented in many desert regions.

Wind and sand
Barchan dunes are formed when the wind moves the sand up on the windward side. Eddies behind the crest cause the sand to be deposited and the dune to move forward. These dunes arise in areas where the wind blows in one direction only and they form at right angles to the wind direction.

A sea of sand
is what we generally envisage when we think of a desert. In fact, however, the sand desert is not very common – it is only nine percent of the Sahara, for example. The wind moves the sand into the area from adjacent rock and stone deserts and deposits it as dunes (above, right).

Sand desert
is characterized by dunes which do not always cover the entire area. Shifting dunes can bury cultivated land and sometimes entire communities.

Stony desert
is littered with stones of varying size, from boulders to coarse gravel. These stones are often so densely packed that they create a "desert pavement".

sand dunes — oasis — butte — playa

The deserts are the outcome of the large-scale air circulation system which distributes precipitation unevenly over the surface of the Earth. The large deserts are located along the border regions between the tropic and sub-tropic zones. Here, tropical air, which has risen in the equatorial convergence zone and thereby disposed of its moisture, descends again on the other side of the convection cell. Local conditions can also contribute. Mountain ranges can function as gigantic dehumidifiers whereupon areas sheltered by them can easily become desert or semi-desert. The main cause of coastal deserts is cold oceanic currents which compel the sea winds to deposit their rain out over the water.

It rains only seldom in the desert – but when it does rain the effect is dramatic. Roaring flash floods surge down the dry river beds, salt-pans become short-lived lakes and millions of seeds which have lain dormant in the ground are transformed into dazzling vegetation. Soon afterwards the desert becomes its customary, arid self again, but the rain has replenished the aquifers which often lie beneath the surface.

Deserts vary greatly in appearance. Most common are different types of stone and rock desert. Sand desert is created when over a long period steady winds bring in mineral particles from adjacent desert areas. A common feature of all dry deserts, however, is the extreme range in temperature; a result of the dry, clear air which produces very strong insolation in the daytime and equally strong loss of heat through outward radiation at night.

Survival in this extreme environment demands far-reaching biological adaptation. Desert plants often have a leathery or wax-like skin which protects them against desiccation. Certain animals, for example the desert rats, can manage without access to water. Through their behaviour, too, animals have contrived to adjust to desert conditions. Burying themselves by day and moving about by night, aided by very keen hearing, is a tactic used by both predators and their prey.

The deserts have varied in magnitude during different geological epochs. In our day, however, a new influence has entered the scene – man. Attempts to farm land and raise livestock in places where the precipitation is inadequate have resulted in large areas becoming desert which should otherwise have been bushland, savanna or even forest. As a rule the inhabitants are well aware of what is happening, yet poverty is forcing them to ruin their environment by overgrazing, overfarming and fuel collecting simply for the sake of day-to-day survival.

Wind and dust
Light dust particles are often carried away from desert areas by winds and deposited elsewhere as aeolian soils, e.g. the northern Chinese loess. Such soils are usually extremely fertile, if there is sufficient water present. Dust carried out over the sea produces red deep-sea clays.

How a salt-pan is formed
The infrequent but very heavy rains and intensive evaporation – the potential evaporation can be tens of times greater than the actual annual precipitation – produce salt pans ("chott" in Arabic), shallow saline lakes which often dry out altogether.

Wadis lead the rainwater out into the desert where it can form an extensive, though shallow and temporary lake. The water contains salts which have been leached out of the soil strata higher up in the drainage area.

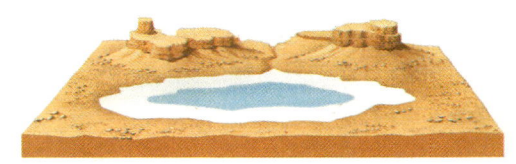

Evaporation is rapid and the lake shrinks. Pure water disappears into the atmosphere while the salts remain. The salinity of the water increases and salts – chlorides and sulphates – are precipitated.

The open water is transformed into a corrosive salt slush, or disappears altogether. A smooth, firm "playa" is left if the water has had a high clay and sand content. Salt from salt-pans has been an important commodity in the north-south caravan trade through the Sahara for thousands of years.

Sandstorm over the Atlantic
Strong winds can carry desert dust very great distances. This satellite photograph shows how an easterly gale has blown a vast cloud of dust out over the Atlantic and all the way to the Cape Verde Islands, a distance of some 1,000 km. The smallest particles can remain airborne long enough to cross the Atlantic.

Rock desert
is bedrock where the wind has stripped off all loose soil. Like the stony desert, it is criss-crossed by wadis, riverbeds that are usually dry.

Wind and rock
The desert winds carry sand with which they carve out many characteristically rounded shapes in the hard desert rocks. This process is known as abrasion.

Desert adaptations
Desert flora and fauna are very characteristic. This cross-section is from western North America, but parallel adaptations are found in many deserts. Both the fox and the mouse below, for example, have almost exact counterparts in the Sahara.

The desert mammals are often nocturnal and bury themselves in the daytime, both as a protection against the heat and to avoid predators. The fox has enormous ears, an adaptation to enable it to locate its prey almost solely by hearing. The kangaroo mouse is built so as to have minimum possible contact with the hot sand. Insects, arachnids and reptiles which have difficulty in regulating their body temperatures, survive by shifting between sun and shade. Snakes are common in sand desert where they can move more easily than quadrupeds. Most of the desert plants have a tough, leather-like skin as protection against dehydration, and thorns or prickles to save them from the animals that seek their stored water. Flowering occurs at infrequent intervals and is greatly dependent upon moisture and temperature. But certain plants can survive many years of drought, by lying dormant as seeds. When the rain does come, leaves, flowers and seeds are produced with a suddenness which seems little short of miraculous. The cacti in this panorama are typical of the New World's deserts and semi-deserts.

Temperate forests

Northern forests
The most extensive temperate forest regions are in the northern hemisphere. Between the tundra limit and roughly 50°N a belt of coniferous forest extends through northern North America, Europe and Asia. South of this there is another belt, of varying width, comprising mixed and deciduous woodland. Areas with a Mediterranean climate have permanently green deciduous trees.
The diagrams show two temperate climate types: right, a dry continental climate with greatly varying temperatures (graph lines) and maximum precipitation in summertime (columns); far right, a Mediterranean-type climate where the annual temperature is more even and precipitation greatest in wintertime.

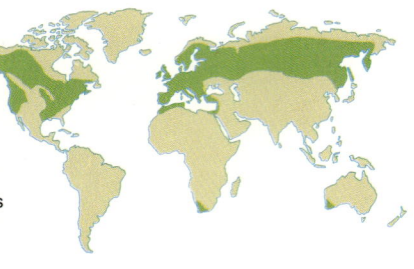

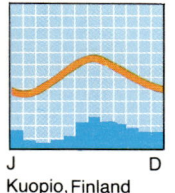

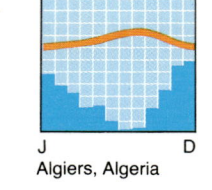

Kuopio, Finland   Algiers, Algeria

Coniferous forest
The coniferous forest regions are an important raw material source for sawn timber, wood pulp and fuel. As a rule the same tree species grow over very big areas which facilitates large-scale, highly mechanized forestry. Towards the tree limit, both on mountain slopes and adjoining the tundra in the north, the conifers give way to birch and brush vegetation which becomes increasingly stunted as conditions grow more severe.

Throughout the greater part of the Earth's temperate zones forest is the natural vegetation. The climatic requirements for temperate forest are relatively abundant precipitation, moderate temperatures and a distinct difference between summer and winter. A belt of coniferous forest runs from east to west through Asia, Europe and North America, the southernmost limit of which generally coincides with the southern limit of the snow climate according to the Austrian climatologist Köppen's definition, i.e. where the mean temperature of the coldest month is below −3°C. In the southern hemisphere these latitudes are mostly sea areas so there is practically no temperate forest at all. That which does exist, in South Africa and south-west Australia, is of the evergreen Mediterranean type.

In areas with a cold temperate or snow climate podsolic soils are the most common. Precipitation leaches out the humus substances of the uppermost layer and deposits these as a brown stratum deeper down. Farther south deciduous forest grows on soils which have not been leached but are brown with humus, from the surface layer's rotting vegetation down to the subsoil.

During the last Ice Age, temperate forest gave way to ice and tundra in Europe, forest survived only in a few sheltered places. When the ice retreated northward the tundra withdrew in its wake and the forest advanced again. The spruce, or fir, which now flourishes in large areas throughout the northern forests, was a latecomer. Pollen analysis (the use of pollen grains collected from peat bogs and sediment to determine plant species in ancient times) has revealed that during the post-glacial warm period deciduous forest extended very far northward in Europe. Thickets of hazel were common.

For the hunters and gatherers of the early Stone Age the forest was both a source of food and a habitat. During the late Stone Age the inhabitants cleared ground in the deciduous forest regions, establishing in time the first agricultural settlements. Greeks and Romans deforested large areas around the Mediterranean, but it was not until the Middle Ages that serious inroads were made on the European forests (in North America not before the colonists began to settle in the 19th century). The fact that hunting was a jealously guarded feudal privilege was the salvation of many forests in Western Europe. "Forest" and "hunting ground" were synonymous words in many languages. When the Swedish peasants were granted the right to hunt in the late 18th century on the other hand, the large animals were driven to the brink of extinction in a few years.

In deciduous forest areas income from game rights is still a significant consideration and ecologically productive mixed forest environments are permitted to survive to some extent. In the sparsely populated coniferous regions, on the other hand, the forests are used more specifically as a source of raw materials for the timber and pulp industries.

Mixed forest
In the mixed forestland hardy deciduous trees, such as birch and various Salix species (sallow, willow etc.), are commonest. Conifers grow mainly in meagre soils. The varied environments of the mixed woodlands offer a wide selection of specialized ecological niches and thereby a very diversified fauna. Such mixed forest is rare nowadays however. Large areas of it have been cleared for cultivation and what remains is in danger of being replaced by the fast-growing and commercially more attractive coniferous monoculture.

Deciduous forest
The deciduous forest consists mainly of hardwood trees such as oak, beech, elm, lime and maple. In areas with a distinctly maritime climate the evergreen holly is a characteristic feature. Because of the dense, shadowing canopy the ground vegetation is not as profuse here as in mixed forest, though the environment is still very productive. Hardwood forest of this type is even more scarce than mixed forest because, ever since the Middle Ages, it has been subject to clearance to facilitate cultivation.

The annual cycle
The deciduous forest undergoes seasonal changes with a growing season lasting from spring to autumn, followed by a period of dormancy throughout winter.

spring   summer   autumn   winter

Woodland flora and fauna

The species, left, are native to Europe and Asia. North America has similar plants and animals, however, in corresponding ecological niches. In the coniferous forestlands the species are to a large extent identical on both sides of the Atlantic.

Coniferous forest regions

Pines grow mostly in meagre soils while spruce, or fir, prefer richer, moister soils. The twinflower is used here to represent the relatively abundant ground vegetation of the coniferous forest. The marten is a carnivore which catches a lot of its prey in the trees. The capercaillie is encountered mainly in old, tall-trunked forest. The brown bear is Europe's only bear species. It is both herbivore and carnivore. The lynx is found from northern to southern Europe, mainly in mountainous areas. The elk is the largest of the deer family, feeding on broad-leaf foliage and the young twigs and shoots of the conifers. Bear, lynx (bobcat) and elk (moose) are also native to North America.

Mixed forest

The birch is the most typical tree of northern deciduous forestlands, while the larch is a "deciduous conifer" which sheds its needles in winter. The dog-rose is common in open places where there is plenty of light, for example forest edge and pastureland. The wide variety of vegetation supports an abundance of bird species. The great tit is found throughout temperate Eurasia. The tawny owl is specifically nocturnal and thus more often heard than seen. The red deer is primarily a leaf-eater. The fox is an opportunist frequenting both the depths of the forests and farmland or suburb, while the beaver confines itself exclusively to aquatic surroundings.

Deciduous forest

Oak and beech are typical of the European deciduous woodlands and their fruit, acorn and beechnut, are a vital source of food for wild boar and many other woodland animals. The oak lets in more light than the beech, thereby permitting a more diversified ground vegetation. Wood anemones bloom in profusion during early spring, before and while the trees are budding. The roe-deer move about mostly at twilight and dawn and can thus adapt themselves to environments which are modified by man. The wild boar likewise is mainly nocturnal. The European, red squirrel is not limited to deciduous woodland but can survive just as well on pine seeds as acorns. The sparrow hawk preys on small birds and the wood pigeon modestly conceals itself in the very depths of the woods.

The forest floor

In temperate climates the decomposition of dead biomass is a slow process and consequently the ground is covered in a deep layer of last year's leaves, pine needles, twigs, and so on, the layer beneath this being more thoroughly broken down. Consequently there is plenty of nutrition available at ground level and instead light is the limiting factor for the growth of ground vegetation. The beech forest (left) with its extremely dense canopy has very little ground flora and it is only those plants which bloom early in spring that can survive here.

67

The tundras

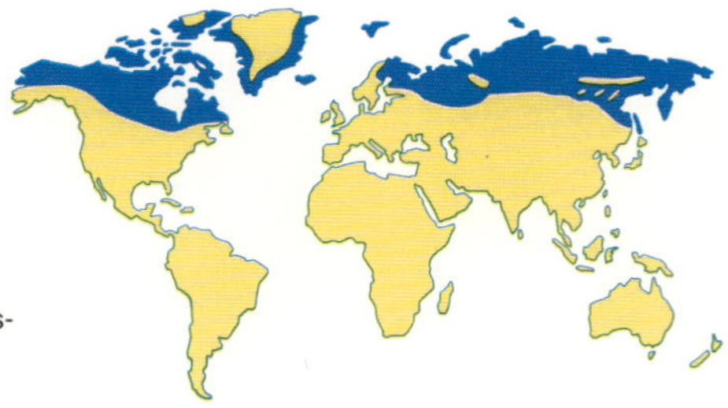

Tundra climate
can vary greatly from place to place. Both the precipitation and its yearly distribution (columns in the climate diagrams) and the temperature (graph curves) depend upon whether the location is maritime or continental. The sea evens out changes in temperature and produces precipitation. The common factor, that which prevents the forest from invading the tundra, is the long, severe winter and the brief summer. The warmest month does not exceed +10°C on average.

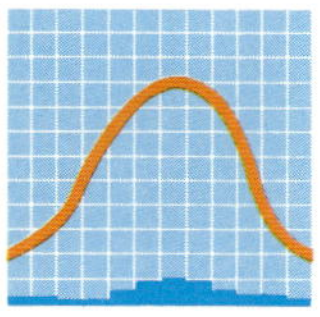

Verkhoyansk, USSR

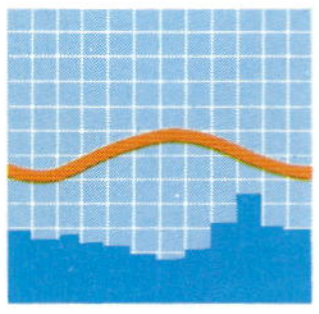

Godthåb, Greenland

The world's tundra
Tundra is the vegetation zone between the coniferous forest and the arctic wasteland. The line of demarcation between forest and tundra is determined by the climate; it runs farther south in the New than in the Old World. Height above sea-level is another determining factor: tundra-like vegetation is encountered far south of the normal tundra limit in mountainous areas like the Rockies and the Urals.

No tundra in the south
In the southern hemisphere the regions which could be covered with tundra (shown on map below) are nearly all sea. Consequently environments similar to maritime tundra are found only at Tierra del Fuego and in certain oceanic islands. For the same reasons there is no equivalent in the southern hemisphere to the northern coniferous forest region.

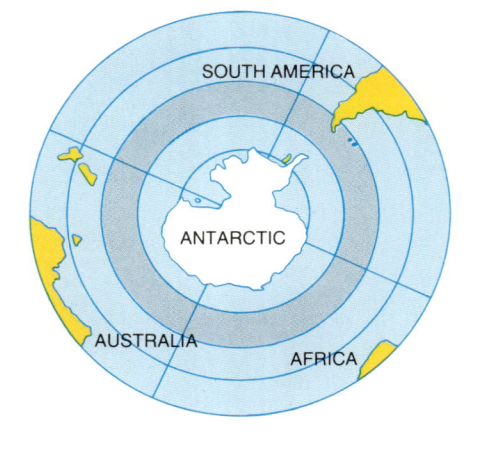

Earth, frost and water
When very wet ground freezes, cracks form and fine earth particles fall down into these cracks. Thus every winter fine material moves downwards and coarse material upwards. This process produces different types of stony terrain which on slopes often becomes terraced.

The climatologists have a simple definition for tundra: an area in which the highest monthly mean temperature is between 0 and +10°C. For ecologists and Eskimos the tundra is the zone between the termination of the forest belt and the ice and barren ground of the arctic wasteland. The climate and natural environment of the tundra is a question not only of latitude but also of elevation. Tundra-like environments are common in mountain ranges far from the normal tundra limits. The tundra climate may be of the maritime type with relatively moderate temperature variations and abundant precipitation, or the continental type: very dry and with extremely cold winters.

The tundra is a world of dramatic seasonal changes. In summertime the landscape throngs with animals and birds which depart in the autumn. Only a few cold-adapted species remain behind and survive the winter. The nature of the ground also changes with the seasons. All year round the permafrost keeps the ground deep-frozen. In northern Siberia it is as deep as 1,500 metres. In the summer a few decimetres on the surface thaw out, forming an "active zone" in which biological production is possible.

During the most recent glaciation, which came to an end about 10,000 years ago, the greater part of Europe, Asia and North America became tundra. The Ice Age environment and today's tundra have much in common. They are both characterized by few species but many individuals. One single plant species can cover a very large area and birds and mammals are often present in vast flocks or herds. In this unstable environment evolution has not yet had time to create any refined ecological niches.

The hunters and nomads of the tundra employed a simple but sophisticated technology. They did not upset the balance of nature, contenting themselves instead with a "tithe" of the summer's abundant biological production. The food standard could be very high, even though meagre years and hunger were by no means unusual. From the mid-18th century onwards Europeans began to move into the arctic regions. The pursuit of furred animals for profit decimated the fauna while at the same time the natives became stricken by disease and alcohol. Military operations in World War II, post-war industrial fishing and drilling for oil have all imposed further strains on the tundra environment.

Newcomers to the tundra have been made to realize, however, that this is an alien world. Those who devote a winter to removing the upper, insulating layer of the ground for the purpose of building an airfield, for example, may find that in the summer when the permafrost thaws out it sinks down into a mire of mud. Destroying the tundra environment is easy enough. To live with it, on the other hand, is difficult; this demands a properly adapted technology and adequate consideration—things with which industrial man is not always over-endowed.

Permafrost

Frozen ground
During winter the tundra ground is frozen to a great depth (above) and during the brief summer season only a shallow stratum of surface ground thaws out (right). Below that the ground remains permanently frozen, hence the term permafrost. Because this permafrost prevents the absorption of the surface water, the surface layer is water-logged and marshy in summertime.

Why the tundra is treeless
Permafrost prevents tree roots from penetrating deep into the ground. Shallow roots are only poorly anchored in the marshy ground and such trees as might grow are blown down by high winds.

Tundra environment

Marshland
The permafrost hinders ground drainage since the surface water is unable to seep down into the subsoil. As a result, during the summer season, large areas turn into marshland where billions of blood-sucking midges are hatched which can drive grazing reindeer into frenzy and death.

Sea and shore
The arctic waters contain abundant nutrition and produce large quantities of crustaceans. As soon as the ice disappears in the spring, large flocks of seafowl and waders appear. Because of the plentiful food they nest in the region, though once their young have learned to fly they return southwards again.

Man and the tundra
The early hunters did little harm to the environment. Industrial man does not live on the tundra but he exploits its natural resources, such as oil. Because the season of biological acitivity is brief, nature has only a limited capacity for decomposing wastes and repairing damage to the vegetation.

Mountain plateaus
Mountain plateaus, worn away and rounded off during past geological epochs, are a common feature of the tundra landscape. The word tundra itself, of Finnish derivation, means a low, barren mountain ridge.

Summer fauna
The few very long summer days produce a wealth of food and this attracts reindeer, for example, and many different species of birds which have spent the winter in the forest belts or even farther south. But the ecological balance is unstable and the animal populations can vary greatly from year to year.

The tundra's vegetation
consists of scrub, mosses, lichens and algae. It seldom grows above knee-height because perennials need the protection of insulating snow in order to survive the winter. Persistent winds also contribute to keeping the brush vegetation low and flattened.

Tundra flora and fauna
On the tundra the winter is the main taskmaster; the "bottleneck" through which all forms of life have to pass. Adaptations are many and varied: fur, small ears, feathered legs reduce loss of heat. The reindeer move southwards, the lemmings burrow into the ground. The lemmings are well known for their fluctuating population though in fact they share this characteristic with voles and other small rodents. The "rodent explosions" and subsequent population collapses lead to corresponding variations among predators such as the snowy owl and the arctic fox. The non-migratory bird species like the ptarmigan normally turn white during wintertime. The perennial plants adapt themselves to winter conditions by growing low to the ground.

Turf and ice

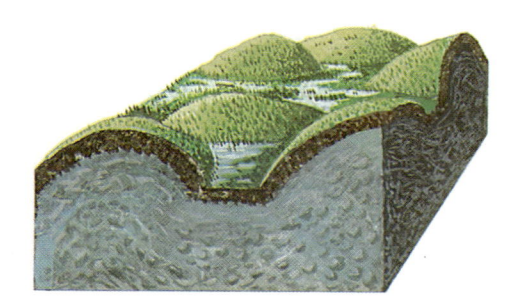

The marshlands of the tundra are made up of small rises, palsas, with swampy depressions between them. When the wet turf freezes it rises to form miniature hills. In the summer only the few top cm. thaw out. The following winter more water is absorbed and this freezes, causing the palsas to grow.

Winter camouflage
The appearance of the tundra landscape changes drastically from summer to winter. The lack of protective vegetation makes it doubly necessary for predators and prey alike to assume a white winter camouflage. Because of its white coat the hare is in less danger of being spotted, while the arctic fox's winter colour makes it easier for it to stalk its prey. This change in hue is not triggered directly by the snow but by the waning and increasing daylight. Therefore, during winters with little snow, white-coloured animals are clearly discernible against the dark ground, while the opposite applies in springs with a lot of snow. Animals that migrate (reindeer) and those that burrow (lemmings) do not need to change colour.

Mountain environments

In relation to the size of the Earth even the highest mountains are mere wrinkles on its face. Mt. Everest's height is only one seven hundredth part of the globe's radius and the Himalayas would scarcely be discernible from space, except for the varying colours in the vegetation at different levels. The really high mountain areas are equally small in relation to the lowland plains.

Seemingly minor differences in height above sea-level result in major differences in climate, flora and fauna. With an increase of a few hundred metres the environment can change as much as with a shift of several hundred km. towards one of the poles. The ecology of the mountains is therefore very distinct compared with that of the adjoining lowlands. The mountains also influence the lowland climate by affecting air circulation, precipitation and river flow.

Mountains' ecological zones
The mountainside's clearly visible arrangement of "storeys", each with its own vegetation, demonstrates the relationship between ecology and elevation. In many instances the highest peaks are entirely devoid of vegetation, with bare rock, permanent snow and glaciers. Glaciers are most usual on the leeward side of the peaks where air turbulence builds up deep snowdrifts.

Below the snow line is found alpine pasture and scrub-covered moorland. The species here are not usually the same as on the arctic tundra but the conditions are similar. In mountainous regions where there are steep slopes the treeline is very sharply demarcated, while on lower subarctic mountains is found a transitional zone frequently like that between coniferous forest and tundra with increasingly stunted birch forest. It is mainly temperature which determines the level of the treeline, just as it determines the boundary between woodland and tundra, although the wind and the duration of spring snows also play important parts. In tropical mountain regions one encounters specific, very distinctive transitional areas with cloud and mist forest.

In temperate areas the coniferous forest sometimes begins directly at the treeline without the transitional zone of stunted birch forest. In the Alps the silver fir is the most characteristic tree. In this zone pasture is also common. The term "Alp" in German does, in fact, mean a mountain pasture. As the woodland descends the mountainside the proportion of deciduous trees increases steadily, though further down the natural vegetation has been considerably changed through the influence of agriculture.

On account of their mobility, animals are less confined than plants to specific zones. Even above the treeline there are numerous large animal species including reindeer, golden eagles and, in Asia, snow leopards.

Mountains and man
Precipitation is abundant in mountainous regions. Streams tumble down the slopes from mountains and glaciers, forming rapids and waterfalls. Lower down these streams merge into rivers. The Alps are the source of Europe's largest rivers (Rhine,

Vertical zones
Mountain vegetation varies with elevation, from the agricultural land and deciduous and mixed forest of the lowest slopes, through the higher coniferous forest, upland pasture and moorland to the rocks and glaciers of the peaks. Each type of vegetation has its own fauna, even though many species can live at various altitudes, especially the birds. Right, an example from the Alps.

Mountains of four continents
Right, profiles across North America, South America, Africa, all in a west/east direction along one line of latitude, and north/south through Asia, i.e. along a meridian. They are all on the same longitudinal scale though the vertical scale is greatly exaggerated. The impression that the plain and mountain regions are distinctly delimited is nevertheless correct.

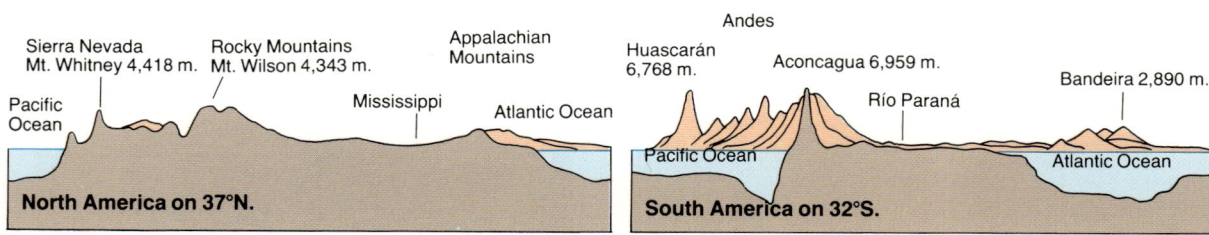

North America on 37°N. — Pacific Ocean, Sierra Nevada Mt. Whitney 4,418 m., Rocky Mountains Mt. Wilson 4,343 m., Mississippi, Appalachian Mountains, Atlantic Ocean

South America on 32°S. — Pacific Ocean, Andes Huascarán 6,768 m., Aconcagua 6,959 m., Río Paraná, Bandeira 2,890 m., Atlantic Ocean

Rhone, Danube, Po) while the Indus, the Ganges, the Mekong and the Chang Jiang all rise in the Himalayas. The water flows more slowly through the valleys, depositing sediment. Consequently the valley floors are usually fertile and thickly populated.

In contrast the mountain environment is harsh. Many of man's customary crops will not grow at high altitudes. The tribes and peoples who were able to settle in the lowlands preferred to remain there, thereby engendering the traditional antagonism between the "civilized" lowlanders and the "barbaric" mountain folk found all over the world. In the West even in quite recent times "educated" people regarded the mountain world as a horrifying wilderness. From the Renaissance onward there were exceptions – Petrarch and Rousseau among others— though the great change in attitude did not occur before the development of Romanticism in the early 19th century. By this time, roads, railways, bridges and tunnels had made it easier for people to cross and to visit the mountains. Today the mountains of Europe and North America are recreational areas where holidaymakers seek relaxation and peace, increasingly elusive objectives in the frenzy of modern resorts.

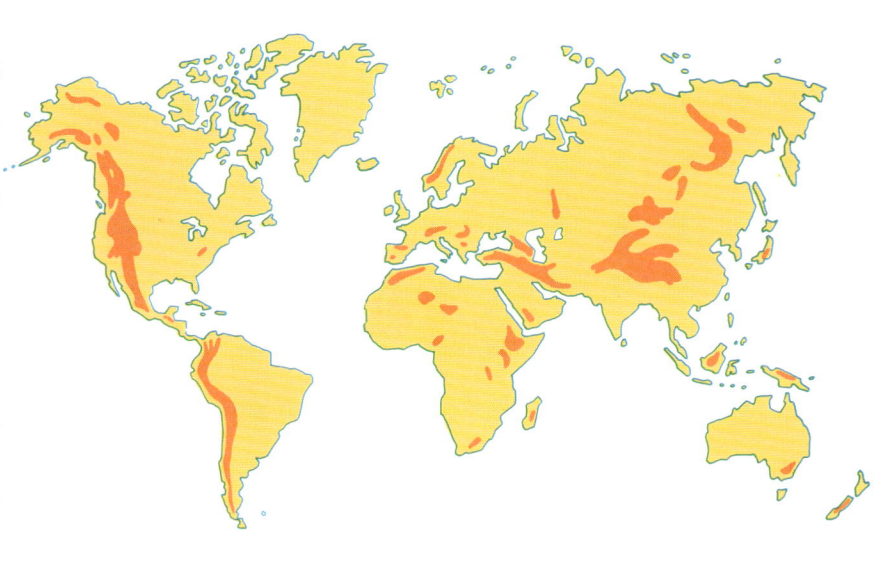

The world's mountain regions are located where the plates of the Earth's crust have collided, resulting in folding. The Andes, Alps and Himalayas are still being formed through continuing plate movement. The mountains of Scandinavia and Scotland, on the other hand, were first formed some 500 million years ago.

Mountain building

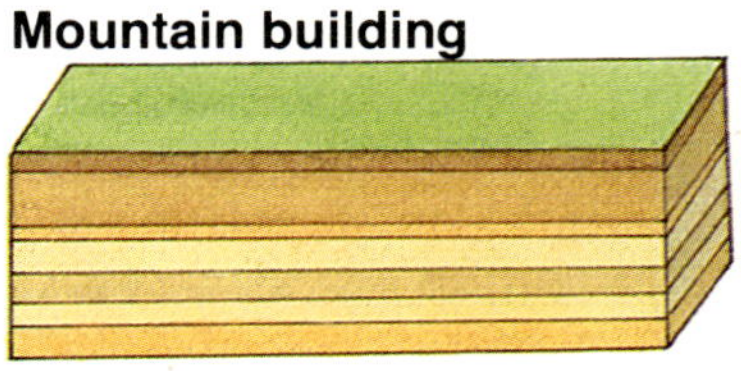

As a rule the rocks that make up the Earth's crust lie in horizontal layers over each other, because the sediments were deposited in water. Uppermost is a layer of loose soils with vegetation.

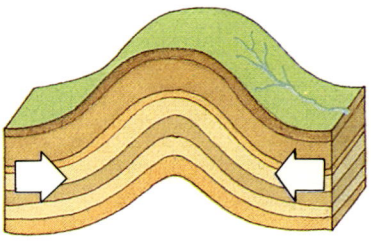

Compression forces of plate-tectonic origin cause the crust to fold, thereby forming a mountain range. The water runs very swiftly down the steep slopes, causing exceptionally rapid erosion.

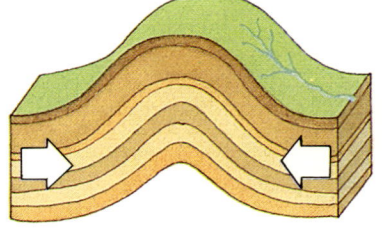

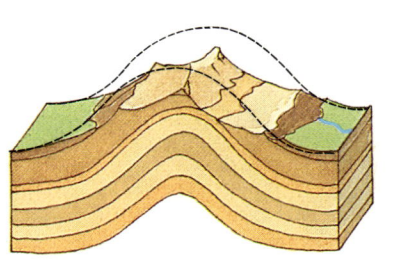

Erosion by running water and glaciers carves out the typical mountain terrain with its pinnacles and precipices, though at the same time this erosion also lowers the ground surface beneath its original level (marked with broken line).

Mountain climbing is a dramatic and dangerous hobby cherished by few. Other, less well trained people also seek recreation in the mountains, instead of avoiding such surroundings as they did in the past.

Elevation zones and climate
The vegetation zones of mountains are largely the same everywhere. The snows of Kilimanjaro and Mt. Kenya are fragments of the Arctic on the equator and below these are moorland tracts and tundra-like vegetation. The snow line is much higher in Africa than it is in Canada, just as are the other zones. The equatorial mountains of Africa also have a belt of mountain rain forest which exists only in the tropics. In Canada, the chilly climate and abundant precipitation causes the west coast glaciers to extend down the mountainsides all the way to the shores of the Pacific.

Subarctic and tropical mountains

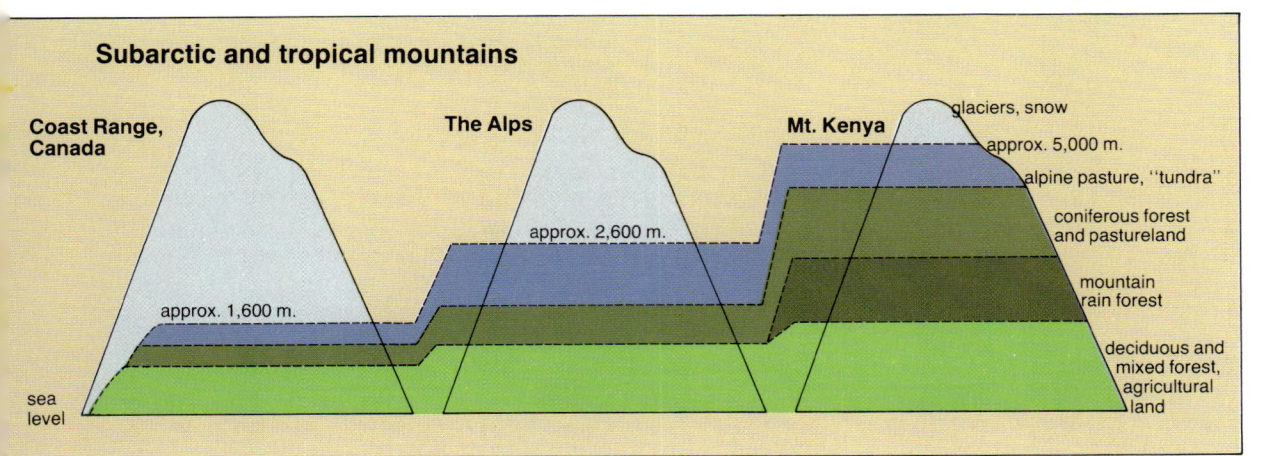

Coast Range, Canada — approx. 1,600 m.
The Alps — approx. 2,600 m.
Mt. Kenya — glaciers, snow, approx. 5,000 m.

alpine pasture, "tundra"
coniferous forest and pastureland
mountain rain forest
deciduous and mixed forest, agricultural land
sea level

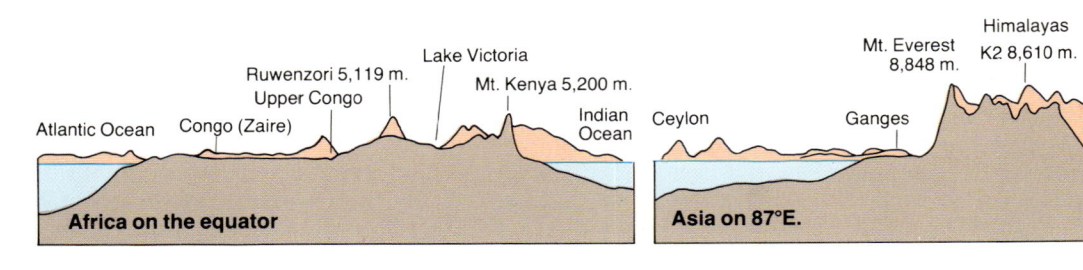

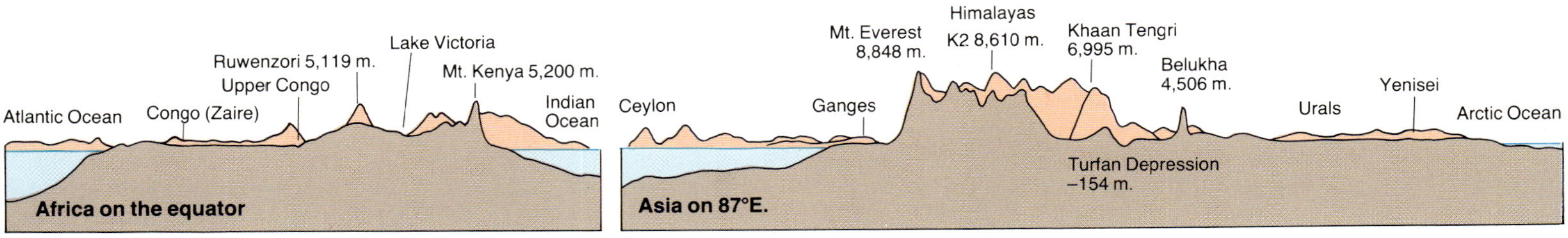

Africa on the equator: Atlantic Ocean, Congo (Zaire), Upper Congo, Ruwenzori 5,119 m., Lake Victoria, Mt. Kenya 5,200 m., Indian Ocean

Asia on 87°E.: Ceylon, Ganges, Mt. Everest 8,848 m., Himalayas K2 8,610 m., Khaan Tengri 6,995 m., Belukha 4,506 m., Turfan Depression −154 m., Urals, Yenisei, Arctic Ocean

Living off the land

The crop cycle

Tropical land clearance
Clearance by burning in forest and savanna regions is one of the earliest of all forms of farming. This is how it is employed (right) in the mountains of New Guinea. After 14–24 months the fields are abandoned and the forest reclaims the land, which is then left undisturbed for several decades. If the revegetation is allowed to continue uninterrupted then the effects on the environment are minimal. But where an expanding population and indigence lead to more ruthless clearing methods the outcome can be a breakdown in the entire ecological system.

clearing the ground

The ground is cleared and trees and branches burned. Minerals in the ash add to the soil's nutrition. Tree stumps and large trunks are left where they are, which prevents erosion in steep mountainous terrain.

fencing in and planting

The fields are fenced in to keep animals out. Taro, yams, beans, bananas, etc. are planted in mixed lots so that several layers of foliage protect the ground against violent rains, while the maximum benefit is derived from the sun.

Rice growing
Of all the world's cereals rice is the most widely used as a staple food, and most of this is paddy rice which requires an efficient irrigation system. The communities of S.E. Asia and S. China are greatly influenced by the needs and routines of rice growing. Depending upon the local climate a rice field can give as much as three crops a year though most farmers use a crop rotation system, growing rice during only part of the growing season. An alternative "crop" is fish, which can be bred in the flooded paddy fields.

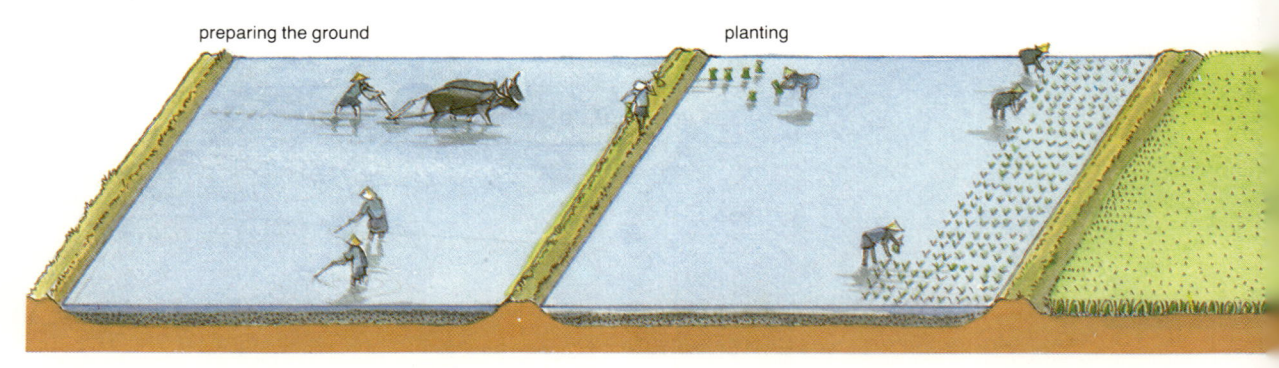

preparing the ground

The field is inundated. The ground is prepared with hoes, water buffalo-hauled ploughs and motor-cultivators. This produces a layer of mud on the bottom. Banks between the fields retain the water and serve as pathways.

planting

The rice plants, germinated in seed beds, are set out by hand in the mud. Rice growing requires a large workforce, but labour is abundant and so cheap that full mechanization of the system would not be worthwhile.

Autumn wheat
is an important crop in the temperate zones. All cereals are cultivated grass species and the autumn sowing of wheat imitates the normal reproductive cycle of the grasses: the mature plants spread their seed in the autumn, these lie dormant during the winter and germinate in the spring. Another variety is spring wheat: the seed is sown in the spring and harvested the same autumn. In this latter case, however, harvesting has to be later in the season. Autumn wheat is therefore more suitable in regions where the growing season is short.

ploughing and harrowing   *sowing*   *winter*

The land is first ploughed and harrowed. This keeps the weeds down and gives the wheat shoots a vital head-start. Sowing, formerly done by hand, is now entirely mechanized.

It is an advantage if during the winter season the ground is protected against frost by an insulating layer of snow. A cold winter with a shortage of snow often leads to a poor crop. As soon as the snow melts and the sun warms the ground the seeds begin to germinate.

In many cases a transition to farming has occurred in response to a local food crisis. People who hunt and gather have an excellent knowledge of practical biology and it is not usually ignorance that deters them from farming. But as long as they can continue the free life of the hunter they are disinclined to become involved in the arduous and monotonous toil of agriculture. Farming emerges in areas where a growing population has already initiated permanent settlement and where the traditional sources of food have begun to fail. In the Near East this took place some eight to ten thousand years ago. There the Triticum genus of cereal grasses came to play an important role as food. When the seeds were no longer collected from wild stands but were harvested from cultivated fields, then grass became domesticated wheat.

Earlier prehistorians regarded the rearing of livestock as more "primitive" and therefore of older date than arable farming. This is not the case. It was the farmers who first began rearing sheep and goats, cattle and pigs in order to add meat and milk to their cereal diet. Livestock nomadism is an ecological adaptation to arid areas where agriculture is an uncertain occupation.

The transition to permanent inhabitation and farming was a revolution: the population could increase and taxes could be extracted from the peasants to feed kings, priests, scribes and soldiers. Farming paved the way for social differentiation and specialization, though for all that it was not altogether a blessing. Unbalanced diet and contagious disease are believed to have shortened the average lifespan and many early settlements literally became buried in their own refuse.

The greater part of the world's population is still engaged in farming. Between 75–90% of Third World inhabitants work the land, though what they produce is scarcely sufficient to meet their needs. The saleable surplus is small: the farming is aimed at self-subsistence. In the industrial countries, on the other hand, seldom more than five to ten per cent of the people are engaged in commercial farming, yet their "cash crops" feed the nation. Just how has this difference come about?

Agriculture "fixes" solar energy in energy-abundant foodstuffs. This output of comestible energy requires an input of work energy. In "primitive" farming the input consists mainly of muscle work—the energy of men and animals which in turn derives from food that has recently been produced. This agricultural energy balance yields a surplus which can be utilized for

harvest   revegetation

New trees start growing even during the short cultivation period and the farmers encourage these; the fences protect them against animals. Thus when these fields are ultimately abandoned the revegetation process is very swift.

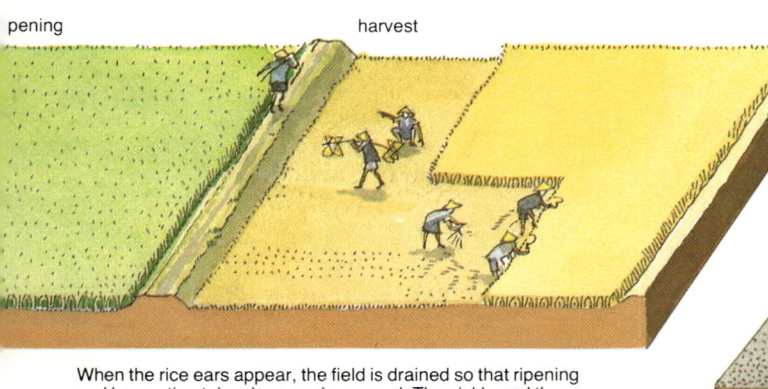

pening   harvest

When the rice ears appear, the field is drained so that ripening and harvesting take place on dry ground. The sickle and the carrying pole are still the most important implements in the Asian rice-growing areas.

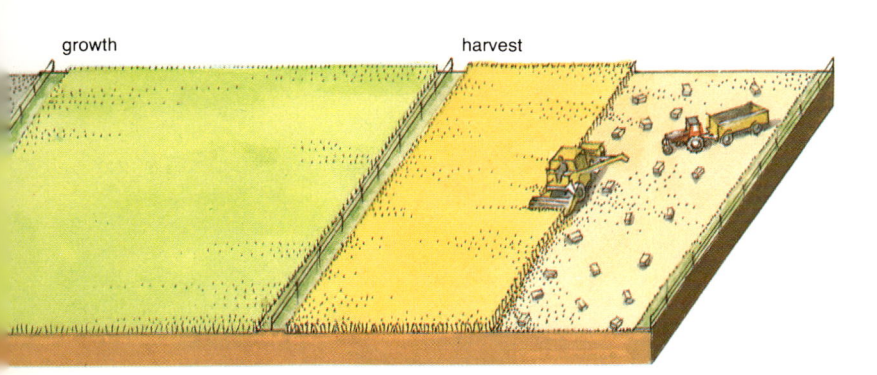

growth   harvest

Weeds usually have to be combatted during the growing season. The harvest is a critical operation, dependent on fine weather since wet grain quickly deteriorates. Harvesting thus has to be a rapid process and is therefore highly mechanized.

Agricultural revolutions
The earliest advance from hunting and gathering to farming occurred independently in at least four regions: the Iran highlands, S.E. Asia, W. Africa and Central America. Many important cultivated plants have also been domesticated outside these areas.

bare ground | grasses and annuals | perennials and bushes | young wood | climax forest

The natural succession
If a piece of land is cleared, and then left untended, grasses and annuals are the first plants to grow there. After 1–2 years perennials emerge and these are followed by young trees. In climatically favourable areas the final vegetation consists of full-grown forest. In the first stage of this succession (dotted rectangle) the growth rate of the biomass is greatest. The farmer keeps his land at this peak-production stage by combatting weeds, periodic harvests and ploughing-in of surplus biomass.

Using productive land
Subsistence agriculture using simple implements is still practised in most parts of the Third World. Terraced rice fields have created a unique "rice landscape" in E. Asia. Wheat and milk production are predominant in the temperate zones while extensive livestock rearing is important where there is little rainfall and irrigation is not possible. Forestry is a mechanized industry. Trees grow slowly, maturing from 20 years in the tropics to as much as 150 years in cold climates.

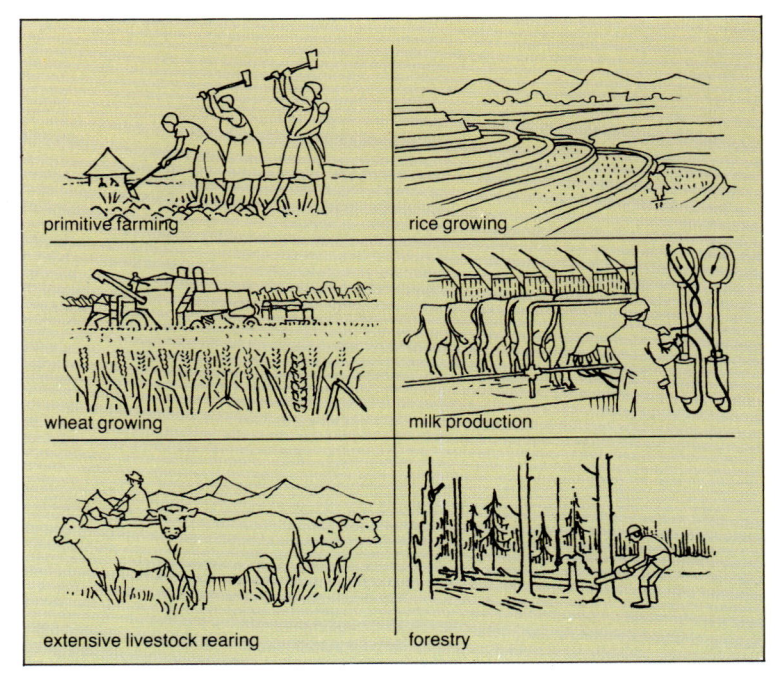

primitive farming | rice growing
wheat growing | milk production
extensive livestock rearing | forestry

other activities. Modern farming methods are far more productive, but this high productivity is attained through a massive contribution of energy from elsewhere—industrially generated energy invested in fuels, fertilizers, biocides, mechanized irrigation and transport. This overall contribution is so great that it cannot be derived from fixed solar energy; most of it originates in coal and oil. Thus, strictly in terms of energy, modern agriculture produces a deficit. But the overall yield is impressive, even though the labour intensive farming of south-east Asia probably gives the greatest return per unit area.

Modern agriculture is thus impossible without an industrial foundation. But the food we consume in the industrial society comes almost exclusively from farming and in that respect we all live in an agricultural society. If our agricultural system were to break down then no amount of advanced industrial technology could save us from starvation.

Urbanization

Urbanization of the landscape
The sites upon which our great cities stand were once virgin land onto which man gradually encroached. Populations have grown steadily through the centuries. This gradual, continuous process does not in itself lead to urbanisation, but at one stage in the progression the town forms. It usually becomes clearly demarcated from the surrounding countryside and an exchange and interaction develops between these two environments.

Mediaeval town
Villages at an intersection of two trade routes or where a temporal or church authority is established begin to turn to trade. The inhabitants protect their property and privileges by building a city wall. But for a long time to come there remain both orchards and cowsheds within the walls. It is not until an increase in prosperity and population has taken place that the towns begin to assume a really urban character.

Natural landscape
The greater part of northern Europe was once primeval forest with an occasional simple shelter for hunters or smallholders engaged in primitive farming. The only forms of transport were foot and packhorse. People still lived in tribes and clans.

The pioneers
Because of the shortage of land in the farming districts, people clear new ground in the forests. Increasing populations make shifting agriculture difficult and necessitate a more settled life. This in its turn demands improved farming methods and a more established social organization.

Farming landscape
The clearings merge and form farming districts and the farms grow into villages. Woods are now permitted to remain only on land that is difficult to work. Marginal land is used for grazing and this and the woodland are common land belonging to the village.

A collection of buildings or a gathering of people in one place does not necessarily create a town. There are farming areas on Java, for example, where the population density is greater than in many European cities, yet these areas are not urban. The definition of the city or town is primarily functional: the inhabitants specialize in things other than the production of foodstuffs and raw materials. They are engaged in industry, trade, service, administration, research and development.

The town-country relationship has not always been a benign one. In most early civilizations, the rural population would have managed just as well or even better without towns. It was not until the emergence of the industrial town that the urban community was able to offer its rural counterpart something worthwhile in exchange for the latter's foodstuffs and raw materials: industrial products (machines, chemicals) which could increase agricultural production.

The earliest towns
The villages where those in power resided and where they gathered in the surplus products of their subjects, grew into the first towns. Here dwelled not only the rulers but also the priests who vindicated the rulers' powers, the soldiers who slaughtered the rulers' enemies, the clerks, the craftsmen and the servants, and the merchants who managed the exchange of goods between the different towns. This pattern existed not only in the city-states of the Near East some 5,000 years ago (Sumerian, Egyptian) but throughout all Asia.

The oldest cities grew organically and with little planning. Successive layers of refuse gradually accumulated in Ur and Troy and beneath the foundations of modern London lie the remains of Roman Londinium. Defence and traffic sometimes gave rise to a certain degree of planning but first and foremost it was the ruling faction which determined developments according to its own particular requirements. Broad avenues and palaces contrasted harshly with the hovels of the poor.

The cities of western Asia often have a continuous history extending back to the most ancient civilizations. Jericho is probably the world's oldest inhabited city (from c. 8000 BC) and Damascus is believed to be the next oldest.

Town planning
In the West the Romans were the first to engage in large-scale town planning. Most of the European mediaeval towns expanded spontaneously, but newly established towns were planned with a regular network of streets. Renaissance and Baroque planning was aesthetic and symbolic in intention; to the honour of God or a worldly prince. The achievements of this planning can still be studied in papal Rome and the Paris of the absolute monarchs. Practical, social and hygienic needs were ignored. In the 18th century the traveller could recognize the stench of Hamburg long before the city came into sight. The urban population growth arising from industrialization was accompanied by appalling sanitation and social misery. A series of cholera epidemics in the mid-19th century compelled the authorities to install sewer and water pipes and to introduce elementary building by-laws at least in the western European cities. This legislation represented the advent of the highly regulated urban communities of our day.

Megalopolis—and afterwards?
The cities of the industrial world have grown very large, but more characteristic still of our century is the tendency for these large cities to merge into urban agglomerations. Typical examples of this are the Boston-Washington area ("Boswash") in the USA, Randstad in the Netherlands and the Rhine-Ruhr district in Germany. In the Third World it is the core cities which are growing or which, rather, are being stifled by their explosively expanding peripheral slums.

The latest censuses in the USA indicate that the agglomeration growth there has come to a standstill. Is the centuries-old urbanisation trend about to turn? It has occurred before in history that big cities have reverted to mere villages, or disappeared altogether as the fates of Babylon, Carthage and Troy amply testify.

Industrial town
Towns now develop a more regular layout with paved streets and piped water and drainage systems. Factories grow up on the outskirts, their chimneys competing with church towers and steeples to form the skyline. A structural pattern is established with administrative and commercial acitivities in the centre and industry and workers' accommodation around the outskirts.

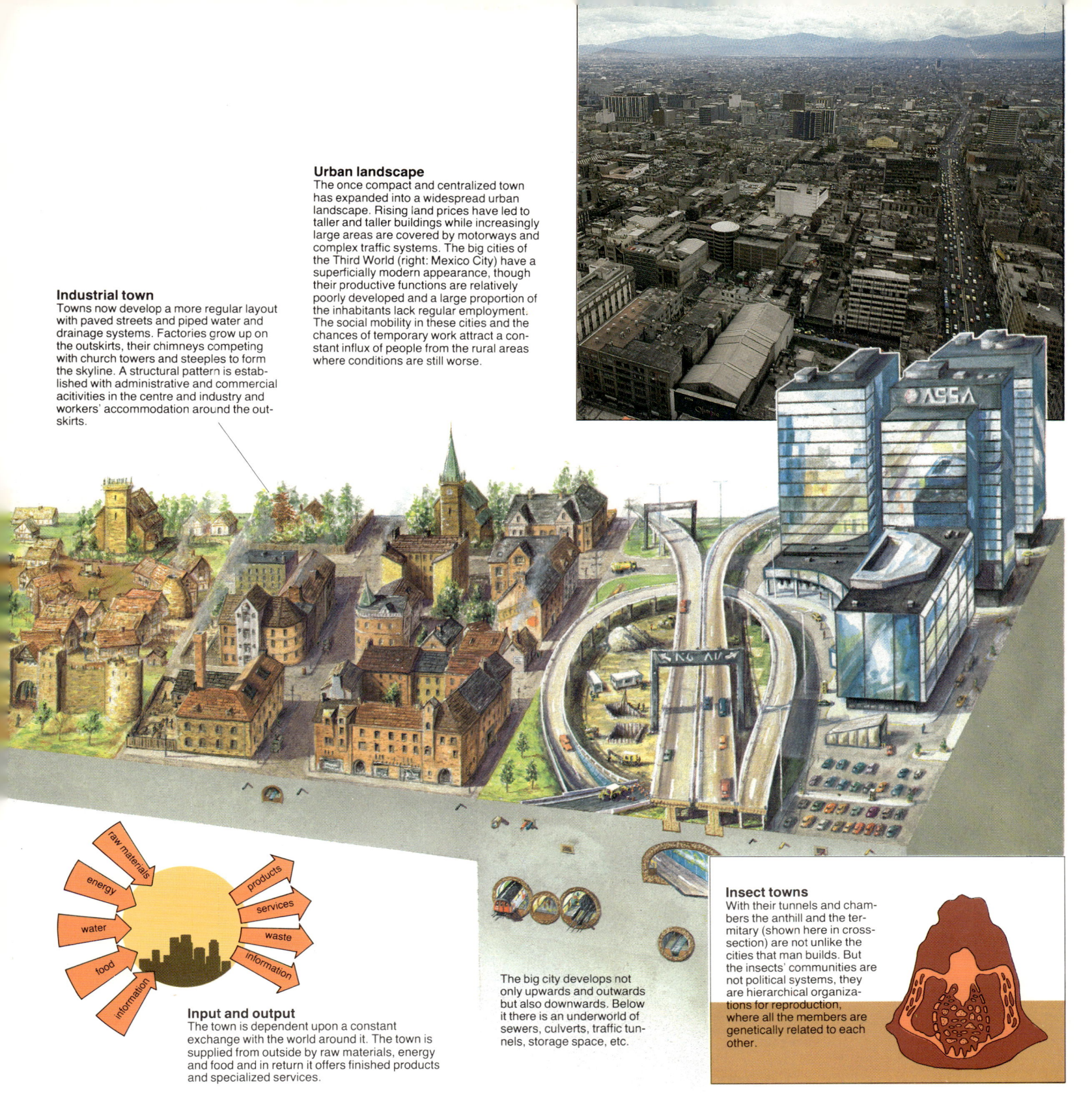

Urban landscape
The once compact and centralized town has expanded into a widespread urban landscape. Rising land prices have led to taller and taller buildings while increasingly large areas are covered by motorways and complex traffic systems. The big cities of the Third World (right: Mexico City) have a superficially modern appearance, though their productive functions are relatively poorly developed and a large proportion of the inhabitants lack regular employment. The social mobility in these cities and the chances of temporary work attract a constant influx of people from the rural areas where conditions are still worse.

Input and output
The town is dependent upon a constant exchange with the world around it. The town is supplied from outside by raw materials, energy and food and in return it offers finished products and specialized services.

The big city develops not only upwards and outwards but also downwards. Below it there is an underworld of sewers, culverts, traffic tunnels, storage space, etc.

Insect towns
With their tunnels and chambers the anthill and the termitary (shown here in cross-section) are not unlike the cities that man builds. But the insects' communities are not political systems, they are hierarchical organizations for reproduction, where all the members are genetically related to each other.

The expanding towns

The largest cities
The trading and industrial centres of Europe and North America were once the biggest cities in the world. Presently, however, the growing cities of the Third World often contain larger populations. Lack of consistency between administrative and demographic limits and uncertain statistics make comparisons difficult. Consequently the following table of the ten largest cities of the world must be regarded as approximate only:

Mexico City	14.0 million inhabitants
Tokyo	11.6 million inhabitants
Shanghai	10.8 million inhabitants
Buenos Aires	10.3 million inhabitants
New York	9.2 million inhabitants
Beijing (Peking)	8.5 million inhabitants
Paris	8.4 million inhabitants
Moscow	8.0 million inhabitants
Seoul	7.8 million inhabitants
São Paulo	7.2 million inhabitants

How the city expands
The growth of a city creates a system of differentiated zones. The historical nucleus, comprising administrative and commercial functions, is surrounded by densely built older housing. Beyond this there is a belt of industry and beyond that again more recent housing areas. Pressure on the city centre is relieved by satellite towns, which are smaller editions of the city itself with their own centres and industrial areas. The system of radial transport routes reveals that their independence is illusory. This city plan is based on Paris; for historical reasons other cities, especially those outside Europe, may have quite another structure.

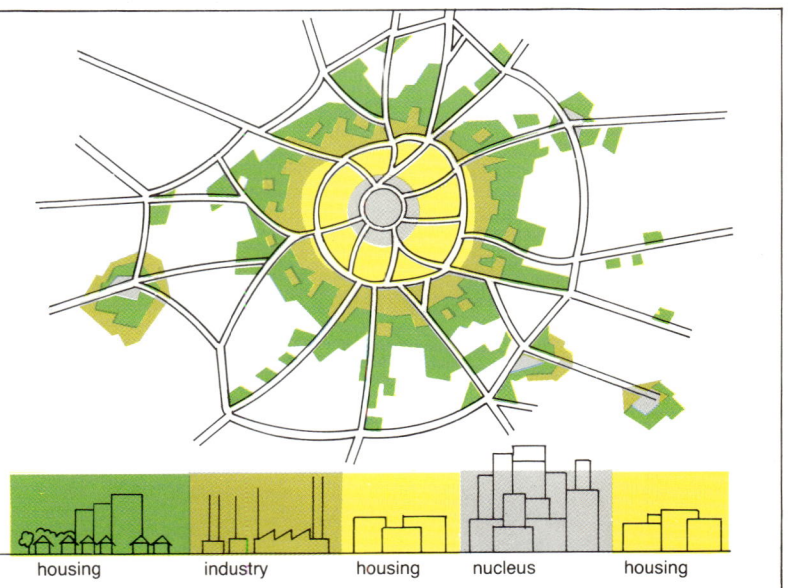

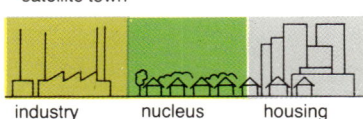

75

Treasures underground

Ore is a mineral which contains a concentration of metal that is worth extracting. Consequently, the definition of "ore" is essentially an economic matter. Because of great variations in raw material prices a mineral that is not worth mining today may easily be worth mining tomorrow, and vice versa. But it is not only ores that are of economic significance; numerous industrial minerals are also mined, from quartzite and dolomite for steel mill furnaces to sand and clay for the cement and building industries.

Metal ores
Metals are rare components of the Earth's crust. Workable ores appear either when metal-abundant magma rises from deeper strata within the Earth's interior, or when metal compounds in the ground or beneath the sea become concentrated through natural processes.

We have long known how ores form in the continental crust, but we remained ignorant for a long time of how they formed under the sea. Remarkable discoveries were made at the close of the 1970's when research submarines descended to the mid-ocean ridges along the bed of the Pacific. Scientists observed how hot springs spewed up black, metalliferous water and built up cones of metal minerals. The plate-tectonic theory also explains how other ores are formed; showing how, why and where magma rises upwards through the crust. This takes place mainly in areas adjoining those where an oceanic crustal plate is pressed down under a neighbouring plate to become re-melted within the mantle.

Mining through the ages
Mining is of earlier origin than man's use of metals. A number of flint mines from the late Stone Age have been found in northwest and central Europe. Extracting metals from ores required metallurgic skills and the ability to generate and regulate heat. The mine and mining operations did not change very much, however, before the end of the Middle Ages. By then the mines of central Europe had become so deep that they required pumps and haulage equipment driven by water power. During the 19th century mining operations became mechanized through such innovations as steam-powered lift-cages and fans. The deepest mine in the world today is a South African gold mine which reaches 3,859 m. in depth.

Many ores come mainly from open-cast mines, others from underground. Nowadays the ore is concentrated at the site of the mine and further refined as pulverized ore concentrate or as small pellets. Non-ferrous ores, principally sulphide ores, contain various metals which have to be separated by chemical and physical processes.

Metallurgy
Until the 18th century practically all metallurgic processes used charcoal, which served both as a source of heat and as an agent for reducing the oxides in the ore. Later, however, the steel industry moved on to coke processes. The modern steel industry

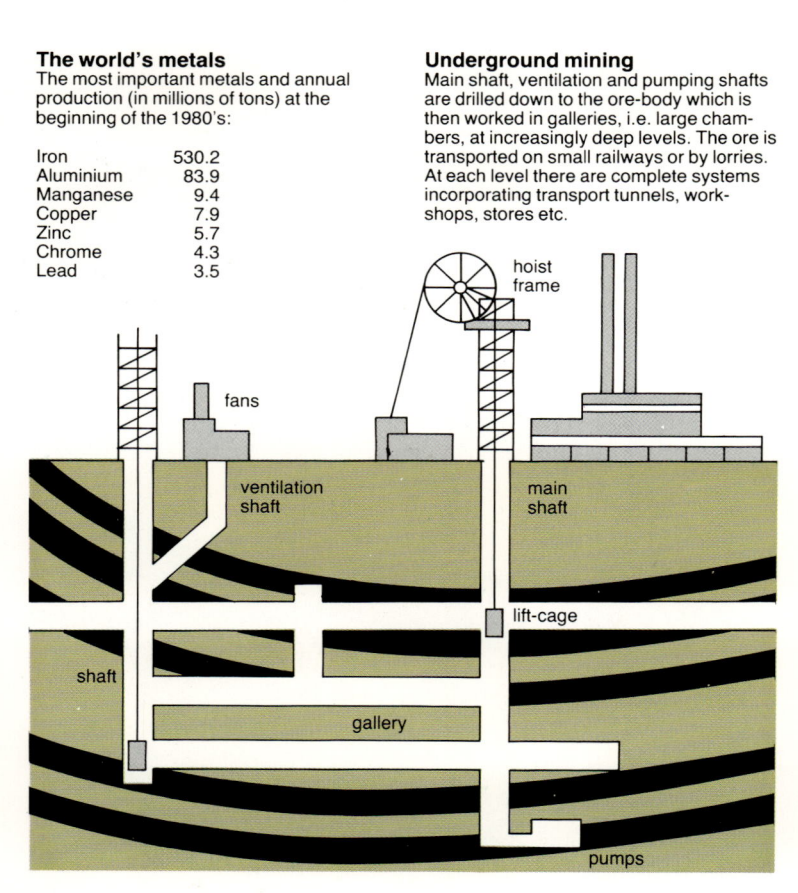

How ores are formed:
Most of the metals used by man are heavy elements, but these are not often encountered in the Earth's crust, the principal components of which are silica and aluminium. The heavier metals, mainly iron, sank downwards into the Earth's interior when the young planet began to heat up from the inside and developed its present structure with a core, a mantle and a lithosphere, each with different chemical compositions. Ores are formed when metalliferous magmas or solutions move upwards from the Earth's mantle. We still know very little about the processes in the mantle, but we do know what happens when the molten minerals reach the crust. The more significant of these processes are analyzed on the right.
Ores of magmatic origin can subsequently be weathered, swept away as grains or nuggets and then be deposited by sedimentation far from their place of origin. Finally, certain ores may have formed by precipitation from metalliferous solutions in marshland with a high content of hydrogen sulphide.

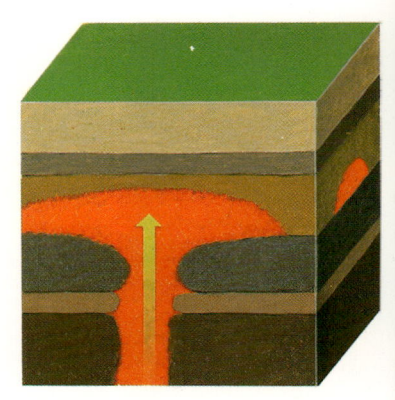

Intrusion
Metalliferous magma rises from below in the Earth's mantle and forms a distinctly defined ore-body higher up in the Earth's crust, or on the surface as lava.

The world's metals
The most important metals and annual production (in millions of tons) at the beginning of the 1980's:

Iron	530.2
Aluminium	83.9
Manganese	9.4
Copper	7.9
Zinc	5.7
Chrome	4.3
Lead	3.5

Underground mining
Main shaft, ventilation and pumping shafts are drilled down to the ore-body which is then worked in galleries, i.e. large chambers, at increasingly deep levels. The ore is transported on small railways or by lorries. At each level there are complete systems incorporating transport tunnels, workshops, stores etc.

Mining—then and now
The Stone Age flint mines, the Bronze Age copper mines and the mediaeval iron mines all looked much the same (left). The modern mine on the other hand is a highly mechanized, large-scale industry. Below: open-cast iron mining in Liberia. Many important mining areas are now located far away from traditional industrial centres.

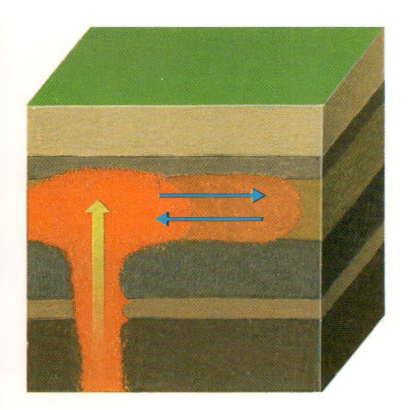

Contact metamorphosis
The magma heats up and transmutes the rock with which it comes into contact. An exchange of atoms occurs so that metal atoms from the magma move into the transmuted (metamorphic) rock.

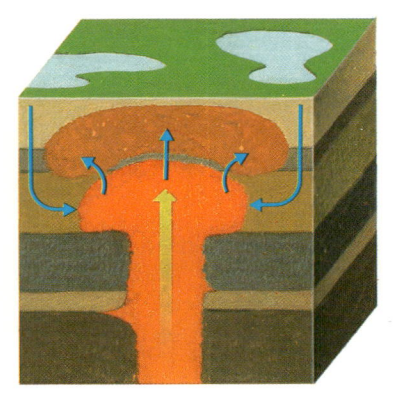

Water-carried minerals
Water from above, seeping down to a magma intrusion, can dissolve certain ion complexes which are subsequently precipitated and left behind in adjacent rock.

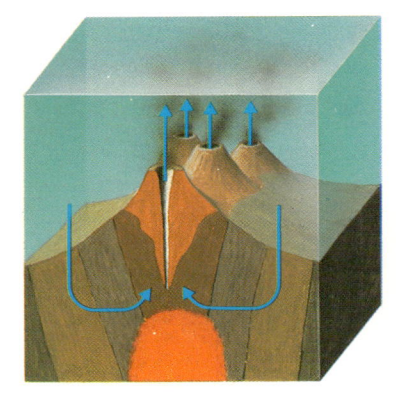

Mineral springs under the sea
Along the mid-ocean ridges, sea water can penetrate downwards to meet the rising magma. When the now hot and metalliferous water is suddenly cooled off through contact with sea water, copper, nickel and manganese minerals are precipitated on the seabed.

Sedimentation
Decomposition products from an ore-body that has reached the surface can result in metal in the sediment. An example of this process is gold sand and nuggets on the beds of river valleys and deltas.

primarily uses electricity for heat, and oxygen as a reducing agent. Electro-chemical separation processes are becoming more and more common since these conserve more energy: the metal does not have to be heated repeatedly as it did formerly.

Metallurgy has developed new products such as alloy steel and various light metals. Also, metals now have competition in the form of new, synthetic materials. Yet despite this and despite the immense recycling capacity of the scrap-metal industry, our civilization remains dependent upon ore production. A medium-sized car contains 800 kg. steel and 130 kg. of non-ferrous metals. However the treasures under the ground are not inexhaustible and if the level of car ownership in the world as a whole were as high per capita as that in western Europe and the USA, then the car industry alone would exhaust all known reserves of iron ore.

From blast furnace to scrap yard
In the modern steel mill many of the manufacturing phases are integrated in a semi-continuous process. The blast furnace is charged with ore, limestone and coke which reduce the oxides in the ore. The coal content in the molten iron is lowered by injection of oxygen or air. Alloying materials are added in an electrically heated oven. The molten steel is then cast in blocks which are afterwards reheated and rolled into sheeting or sections in a hydraulically powered rolling mill.

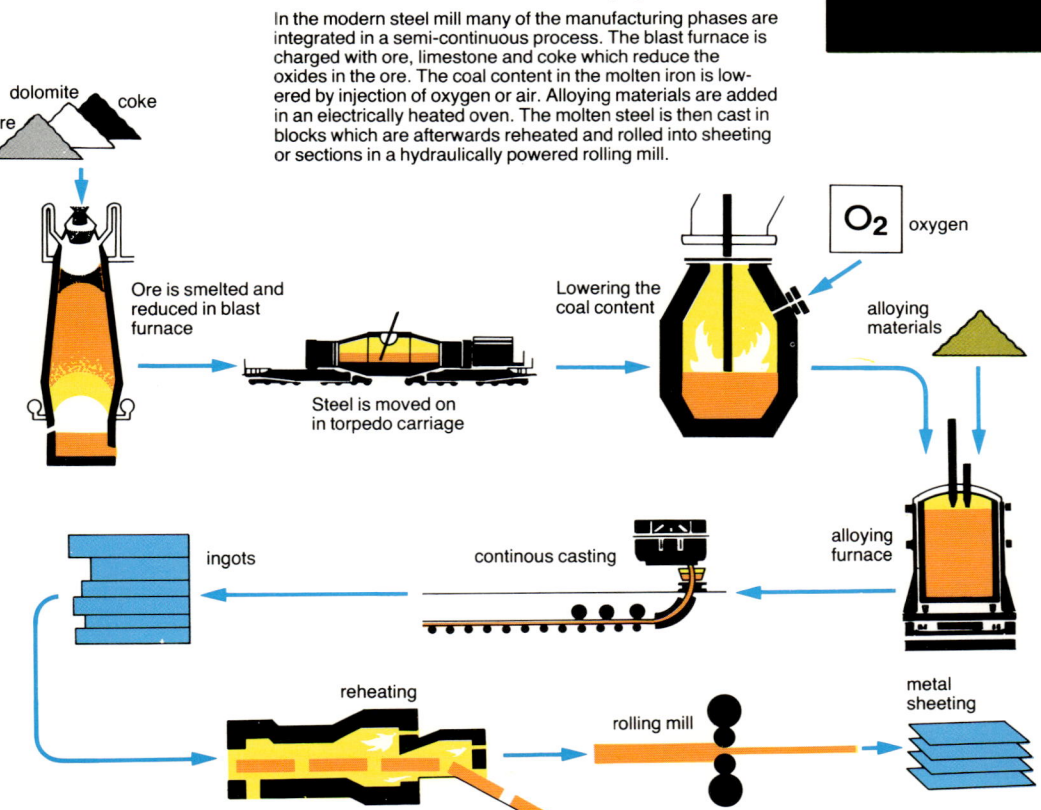

The tapping, when the molten steel is run off into transport vessels or moulds, is a critical phase in the manufacturing process.

The scrap yard is the final resting place of the car, but not of the steel in that car. Scrap metal is one of the most important raw materials of the industrial world and forms the basis of a busy international trade.

The ravaged Earth

Gone for ever
No species survives for ever. But a large number of plant and animal species has been exterminated prematurely with the help of man.

The migration of mankind to America via the Bering Strait (arrow on map, left) probably had disastrous consequences for the continent's fauna.

Man is suspected
At the close of the Ice Age there were large numbers of animal species on the North American prairies, including the giant ground sloth Mylodon (left). This "megafauna" suddenly died out at about the time of man's arrival on the scene. Many scientists suspect it was man that exterminated them. Slow moving and slow thinking creatures like the mylodon had no chance of survival against the super-predator, man.

Man is guilty
The dodo was a turkey-sized, flightless bird which lived on Mauritius in the Indian Ocean. When European seafarers arrived they began killing and eating the dodos and any that managed to escape became the victims of feral dogs and swine. The last specimen died around 1680 and all that remains of the dodo today is a preserved head in Copenhagen and a foot in London.

Threatened environments

Deforestation
The greatest threat to the world's flora and fauna is the destruction of living environments. No species can survive outside the environment to which it has been adapted. One of the most species-abundant habitats in the world is the rain forest, which is now being destroyed at an increasing rate. In fact all natural forests throughout the world are threatened. At best they are replaced by commercial forest monoculture, at worst by a meagre scrub terrain broken up by erosion.

Cultivating the grass plains
The prairies of North America have more or less disappeared. The growing population of Africa is burning off the savannas with their wealth of animal life to make way for an agriculture of doubtful viability. Traditional farming methods are both uncertain and dangerous in dry areas. Attempts to cultivate the steppes of Central Asia have led to many disastrous setbacks.

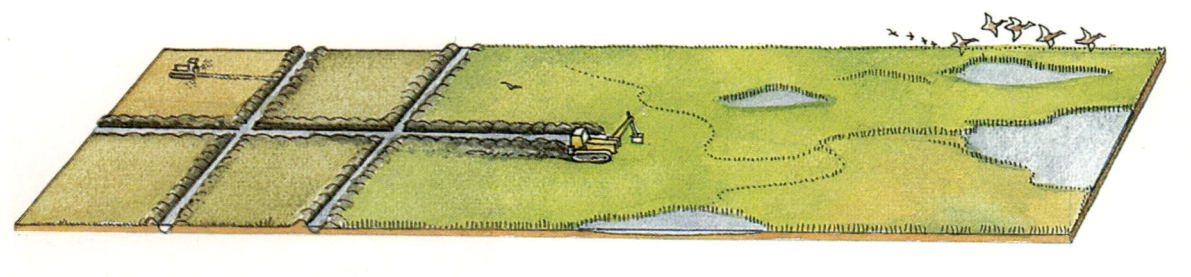

Draining the wetlands
The wetlands are not only living environments in themselves, they also play an important part in the hydrological cycle. They even out the flow rate of the rivers and improve the sub-surface water supply. But many wetlands are either drained off or filled in to make industrial or housing developments. Attempts to turn wetlands into arable land usually result in a low yield from poor soil.

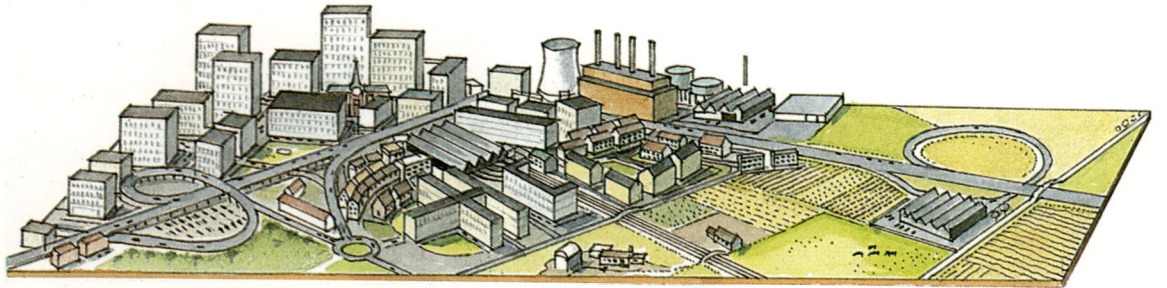

Asphalting the fields
Towns usually develop in good agricultural areas and urbanisation has often meant the sacrifice of productive land for housing developments, streets and car parks. In this way arable land is transformed into a biologically unproductive wasteland. It will be economically and probably physically impossible to restore such land to farmland again.

Endangered animal species

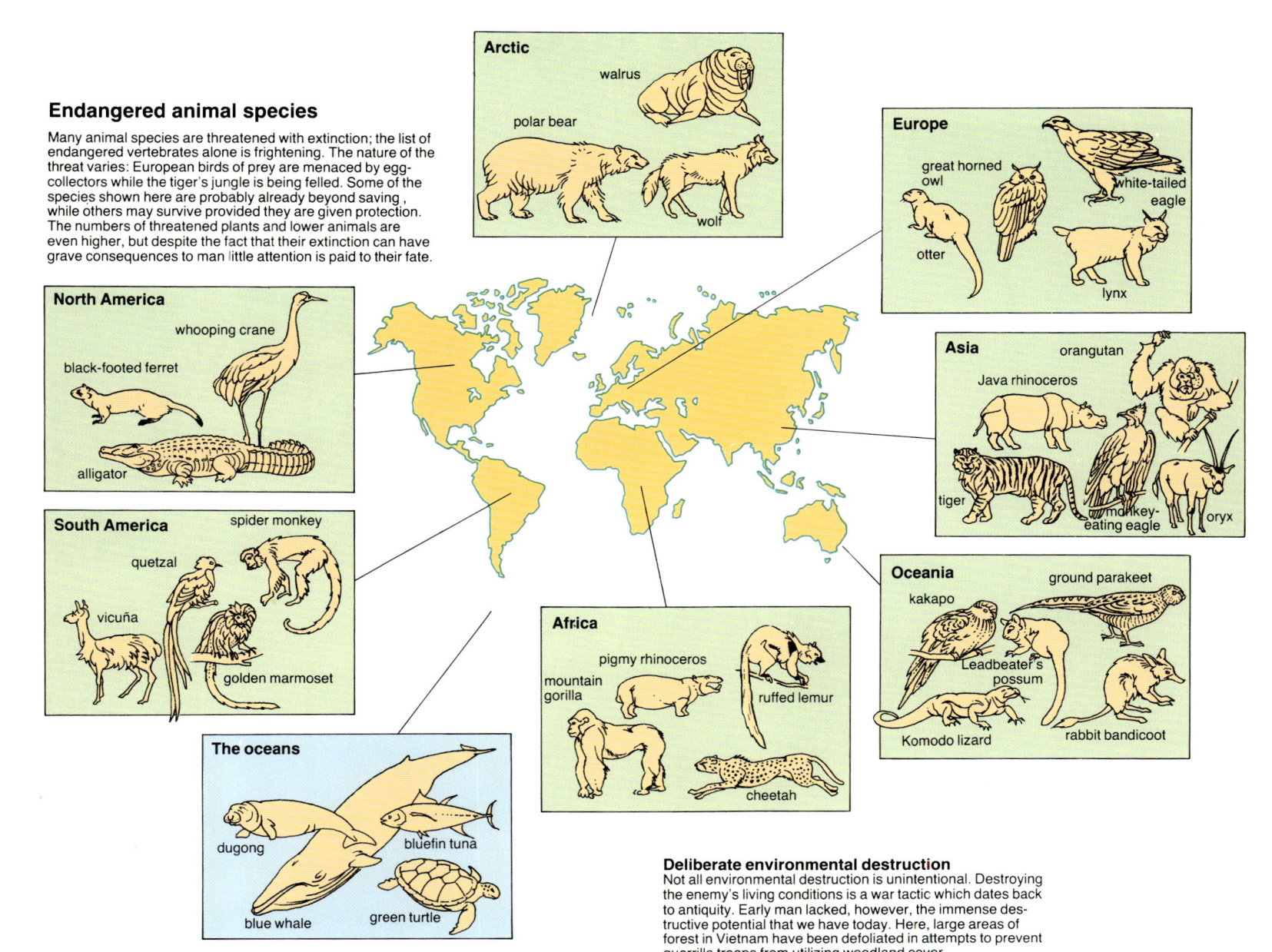

Many animal species are threatened with extinction; the list of endangered vertebrates alone is frightening. The nature of the threat varies: European birds of prey are menaced by egg-collectors while the tiger's jungle is being felled. Some of the species shown here are probably already beyond saving, while others may survive provided they are given protection. The numbers of threatened plants and lower animals are even higher, but despite the fact that their extinction can have grave consequences to man little attention is paid to their fate.

Deliberate environmental destruction
Not all environmental destruction is unintentional. Destroying the enemy's living conditions is a war tactic which dates back to antiquity. Early man lacked, however, the immense destructive potential that we have today. Here, large areas of forest in Vietnam have been defoliated in attempts to prevent guerrilla troops from utilizing woodland cover.

Through evolution every animal and plant species has adapted to its particular habitat; its living environment. This environment is shaped by climate and soil, but above all by the other species within it. About 300 years ago one of the species of tree on Mauritius suddenly ceased reproducing and today only a few specimens remain. Research has revealed that the seeds in the tree's fruit would only grow after having first passed through the digestive system of the dodo—and this bird became extinct towards the end of the 17th century. Indirect extermination through the destruction of a habitat is even more disastrous than direct assault with gun and axe.

Man considers that he has "conquered" nature and made himself independent of it, but that is not so. Man is a biological creature with biological needs. Without nature civilization is impossible. We are therefore dependent upon other animals and plants in our habitat, from whales and tigers to microscopic bacteria. No species can destroy its own living environment without perishing.

Because of this man must safeguard his own environment by protecting threatened species and vulnerable habitats—partly through the establishment of nature reserves but above all by learning how to use the world prudently and considerately. Ultimately, however, all this is both insufficient and impossible; the laws of change and evolution prescribe that no species can live for ever and that no environment can be made eternally stable. Man has to accept the responsibility to not only preserve but also create living environments for himself and for the other species he is going to share them with. Man the destroyer must become man the creator. Only then can the Earth be made permanently inhabitable for mankind, and for the species into which he will ultimately evolve.

Man's impact on the Earth's crust

Man, the digger
Ever since the late Stone Age, man has been engaged in re-arranging the surface of the Earth using the simplest of tools such as spades, mattocks, baskets, carts and wheelbarrows. These laborious but cheap methods are still useful in developing countries where large numbers of people can be mobilized for large undertakings. Such methods were an important factor in China's huge water regulating projects in the 1950's and 1960's (right). Industrialized countries use fewer people and larger machines (left).

Man, the geological force
In the long term man's interference with the Earth can have unfortunate consequences (right). The destruction is usually of an indirect nature, when the protective covering of vegetation is removed and erosion commences. Drainage, irrigation projects and open-cast mining are other examples of man's modification of the land. The destruction of the land is sometimes the result of a deliberate undertaking for immediate financial gain, though more often it is caused by poor people's day-to-day struggle for survival; need rather than profit being the motivation.

Forest is felled excessively for timber or fuel, to make way for commercial agriculture or, in many countries, for primitive, subsistence farming.

When the protective trees are felled the humus layer is easily destroyed and running water erodes the land.

The draining of wetlands eliminates important eco-systems and also reduces the percolation of sub-surface water.

Open-cast mining leaves lasting scars. The water-table often sinks and waste heaps can leak heavy metals.

Man creates his own landscape, for better or for worse. This fact is immediately evident in the agricultural regions of Western Europe, China and south-east Asia, but even in the more sparsely populated countries the landscape is scarcely "natural". Maps showing "natural vegetation" tend to show how things would have looked without man's intervention.

Man does not only interfere with the vegetation however, he also alters the Earth's crust. Even the simplest of tools such as shovels and carts are sufficient to bring about large scale changes on the face of the Earth. The methods used to build the great Pyramids and the Chinese Wall are still employed today. The scope for re-forming the landscape is, of course, much greater in industrial countries where use is made of earth-moving machinery, heavy trucks and explosives. When man operates as a geological force it is usually in an indirect fashion, by modifying or removing the vegetation. The results can be destructive (soil erosion, desert spreading or waterlogging), though he also creates stable, highly productive environments. In south-east Asia, for example, there are terraced fields which, according to archaeologists, have been used continuously for five or six thousand years. On the other hand, in the American prairie States a few decades of ruthless cultivation in a dry climate led in the 1930's to the dustbowl disasters when the wind carried all the soil away. Vast, fertile areas around the Euphrates, the Tigris and the Indus which once sustained the earliest civilizations, have since become sterile or waterlogged and excessively saline because of imprudent farming methods.

Interference with vegetation also leads to changes in the hydrological cycle which in their turn can cause changes in the landscape. A high proportion of silt in river water can clog up reservoirs and irrigation ditches and even cause the river itself to change course. A high silt content often derives from deforestation around the upper reaches of the river. Silting up of this kind can be combatted by reafforestation and other anti-erosion measures. A high silt content can sometimes have advantages. Silt from the Nile fertilized the Egyptian fields every year until the Aswan High Dam terminated the annual flooding. Damming has increased the need for expensive, imported artificial fertilizers, has ruined fishing in the delta and has put the delta itself, the most fertile region in Egypt, in danger of being washed away altogether by the sea. Man's capacity to change the face of the Earth is great, but his willingness to recognize the consequences of his actions is often considerably less.

Changing the course of rivers

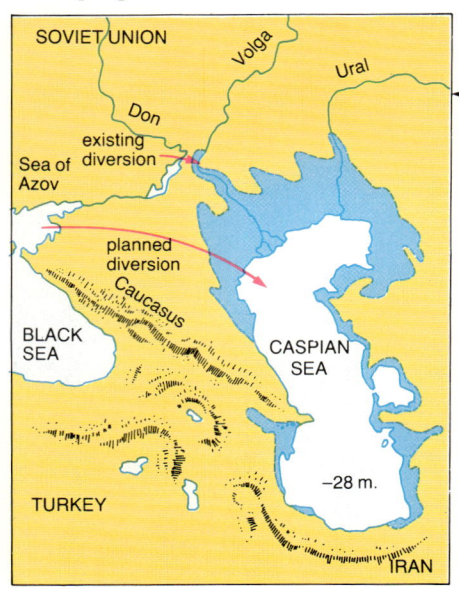

Six million years ago the Caspian Sea was a deep basin in an inland sea which stretched from the Carpathians to the Aral Sea. Today it is in danger of drying up because of the high rate of evaporation and inadequate inflow from the rivers. Large areas (dark blue on map, left) are below sea level. Already some of the Don's water is being redirected into the Volga (shorter red arrow) and there are plans to lead water from the Sea of Azov to the Caspian (long arrow). This would make it possible to stabilize the water in the latter at its existing level.

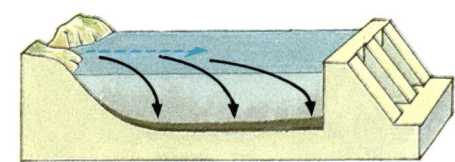

Dams and silting

The rivers' silt transport capacity depends upon the flow of water. If a river is dammed up the speed of the current is reduced. The silt particles can no longer remain suspended in the water...

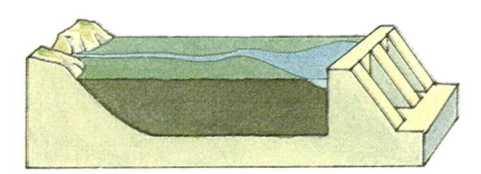

...but sink to the bottom. This process covers the bottom with an increasingly thick layer of sediment and the reservoir above the dam becomes progressively shallower.

In the end the reservoir is completely silted up except for a channel down the centre. This process is a long-term threat to regulated, silt-abundant rivers like the Nile and the Huang He.

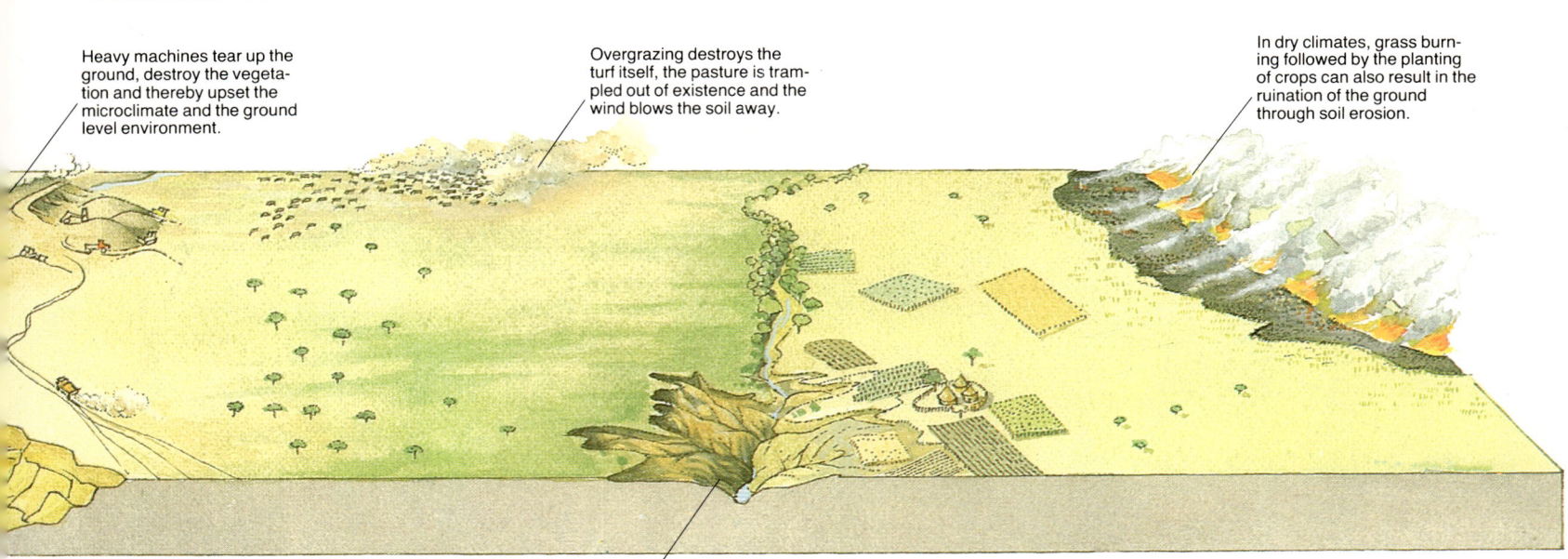

Heavy machines tear up the ground, destroy the vegetation and thereby upset the microclimate and the ground level environment.

Overgrazing destroys the turf itself, the pasture is trampled out of existence and the wind blows the soil away.

In dry climates, grass burning followed by the planting of crops can also result in the ruination of the ground through soil erosion.

In dry climates with periodic heavy rains excessive cultivation can lead to gully erosion.

Man's landscape
A landscape like the one below (north-east USA) is the product of our civilization. There is no natural vegetation at all. Prudent farming methods properly adapted to terrain and climate can make such an environment stable and productive for centuries.

Dust storms
arise when strong winds stir up fine particles on the ground and carry them away. This can only happen where there is no ground vegetation to impede the wind and consequently dust storms are common in desert regions. As a result of extensive farming, the farmlands of the US prairie States were turned into barren dustbowls by storms in the 1930's. Measures to restore ground vegetation are now overcoming the wind-erosion problem, but local dust storms do still occur (below).

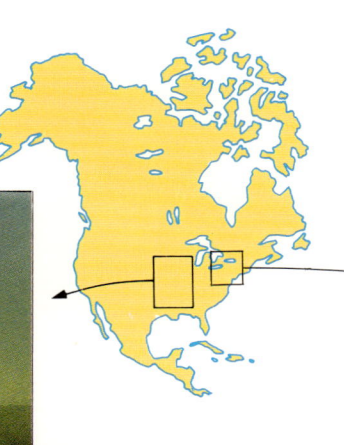

The land can be protected
Careful cultivation methods, the retaining of woodland and new shelter plantations can give protection against wind erosion. Contour ploughing, with the furrows parallel to the elevation contours of the terrain, prevents water from washing the soil away. These methods have been applied on the farmland, right.

81

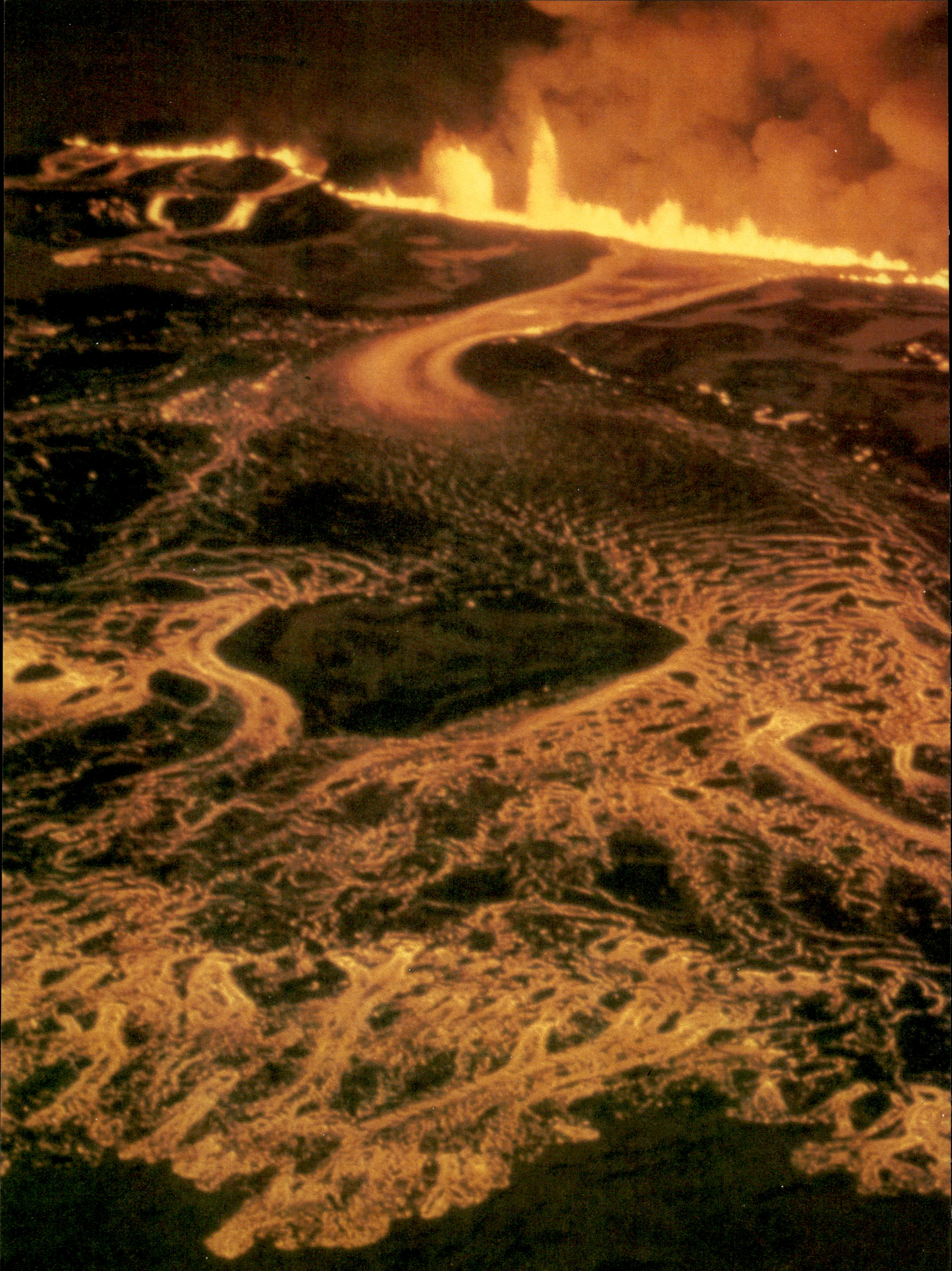

Fire

Crouched around their night fires our early forefathers gazed out into the darkness. Occasionally they saw the gleam of a pair of eyes. That blackness beyond the circle of their fire was a realm of terror, the haunt of real beasts of prey and imagined spirits and monsters.

According to Greek mythology the cultural awakening came when Prometheus stole fire from the gods and gave it to man. As myth gave way to philosophy, fire found a new advocate in Heracleitus—a thinker who lived around 500 BC in the Greek city of Ephesus in Asia Minor.

Heracleitus was a dialectic philosopher. He regarded the world not as an object or as a state but as a continuous process, a flux. He claimed that everything flows, that one cannot step twice into the same river because the water in it is never the same. In the all-consuming and constantly changing fire he saw the primary element. Today we know that fire is not an element at all, but a transformation, a process.

As recently as the 18th century chemists regarded heat as a physical substance called phlogiston. Warm bodies contained more phlogiston than cold bodies. In combustion, it was believed, the phlogiston was released from the fuel.

With the discovery of oxygen by the English chemist Priestley and the Swede Scheele, it became evident that combustion was an oxidization process and the phlogiston theory was rendered untenable. It was finally dispelled through the study of thermodynamics, a science which was inspired by the steam engine and which describes energy conversions, such as the conversion of heat into motion. Today the term heat describes a form of electro-magnetic radiation and also molecular movements.

Heracleitus has to some extent been vindicated by modern cosmology. Scientists are now inclined to believe that the universe was actually born in the fireball of the "big bang". All the energy around us, from the heat in the bowels of the Earth and the light of the sun's nuclear fires, to the cosmic background radiation only a few degrees above absolute zero, is ultimately a remnant of the "big bang": the primary fire. Sometime in the incomprehensibly far-off future fire may fail and darkness fall over the cosmos.

The primordial fire

No matter how often we gaze up at the stars we are unlikely to observe any changes from one night to the next. The idea of the universe being in a steady state with neither beginning nor end seems natural enough. Nevertheless every civilization has had its own legend about creation. The biblical account is found in the Book of Genesis: "And God said: Let there be Light; and there was Light".

The idea of the steady state was reinforced by natural science and this, despite biblical beliefs, was the predominant cosmological theory well into our century. In the 1920's the American astronomer Hubble discovered that light from distant galaxies is shifted further towards the red, longwave end of the spectrum, the farther away these galaxies are. Not until after prolonged debate did scientists accept the most simple explanation for this: the shifting results from the Doppler effect and the galaxies are moving out and away from us at tremendous speed. Finally by the 1960's it became clear that the universe is indeed expanding. It was then a simple matter for the cosmologists to determine the age of the universe on the basis of its present rate of expansion. It was concluded that the universe probably originated in a single dimensionless point, a "singularity" without extent in either space or time, containing the entire mass of the cosmos. The universe and space itself exploded out of this point at least 12–15 billion years ago. This "creation" was dubbed the "big bang".

As the universe expanded so it cooled. A few minutes after the bang the temperature had fallen to around one billion degrees and the first elementary particles were then formed. Two to three billion years later the first stars appeared among the hydrogen gas clouds. In this initial generation of stars, nuclear reactions fused hydrogen nuclei into the heavier elements, from helium to carbon and uranium, which subsequently became incorporated in the present stars and planets—and in our own bodies.

What, then of the future? There are two possibilities. One is that the expansion will continue for ever, the universe becoming increasingly sparse and cold, with the stars burning out and expiring, until finally matter itself decays and nothing remains but cosmic background radiation—cold radio noise a fraction of a degree above absolute zero. The other alternative is more dramatic; the expansion ceases and is replaced by contraction. Finally the universe reverts to a singularity—an implosion which the irreverent cosmologists refer to as the "big crunch".

Which of the alternatives is most likely depends upon the total mass of the universe, a value physicists are unable to calculate. If it is less than a certain critical value then the expansion will continue. If it is greater than that value then we are heading for the "big crunch". Does the neutrino, the most common of the elementary particles, have any mass? Are there large quantities of non-radiant, invisible matter in the cosmos? If the answer to either of these questions is yes then the total gravitational force is sufficient to halt the expansion and the history of the universe will become a leap from the primordial frying-pan into the ultimate fire.

The creation

In the Bible's account of the creation (above, detail from Michelangelo's painting) God made the difference between light and darkness, thereby establishing the visible universe.

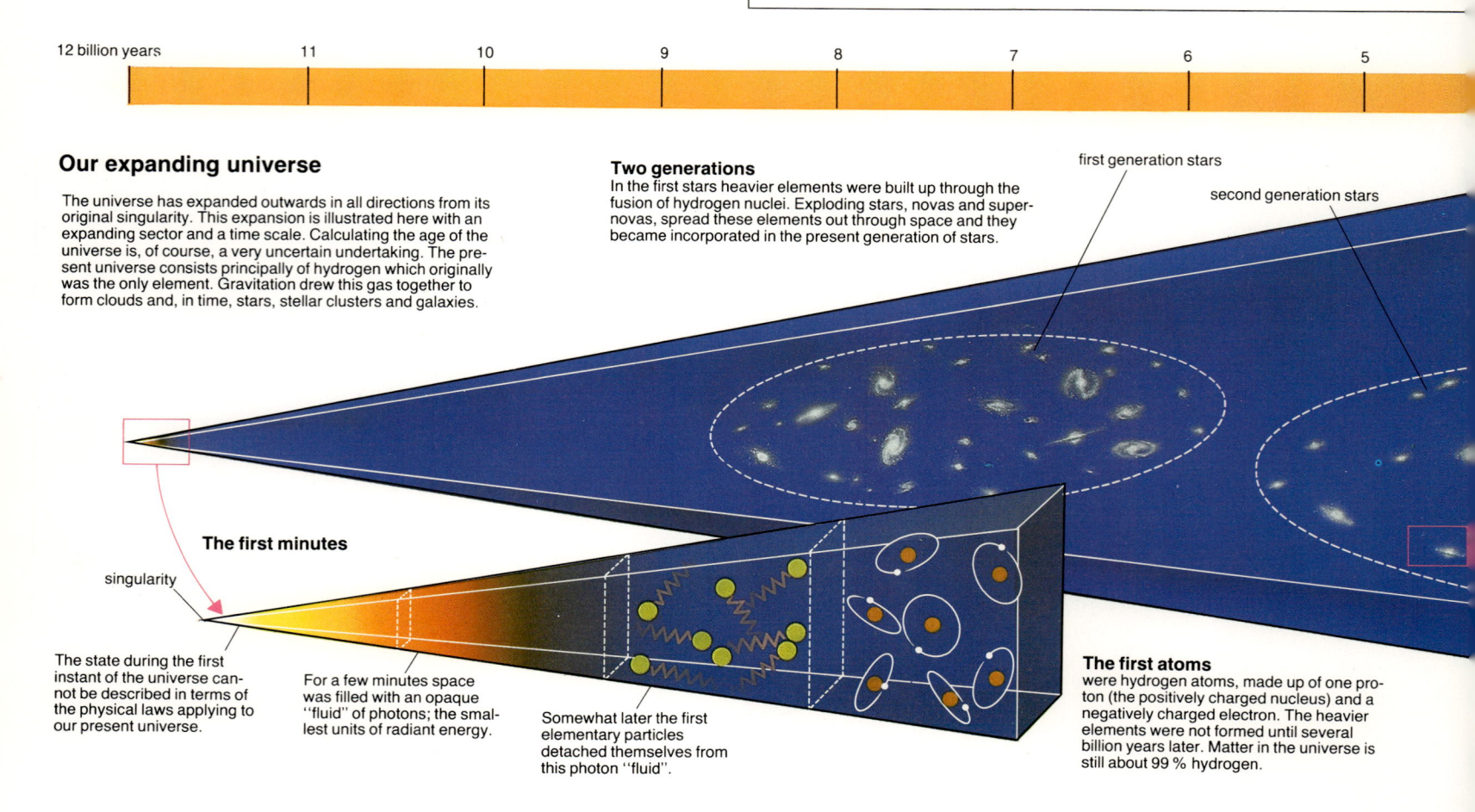

Our expanding universe

The universe has expanded outwards in all directions from its original singularity. This expansion is illustrated here with an expanding sector and a time scale. Calculating the age of the universe is, of course, a very uncertain undertaking. The present universe consists principally of hydrogen which originally was the only element. Gravitation drew this gas together to form clouds and, in time, stars, stellar clusters and galaxies.

Two generations

In the first stars heavier elements were built up through the fusion of hydrogen nuclei. Exploding stars, novas and supernovas, spread these elements out through space and they became incorporated in the present generation of stars.

The first minutes

singularity

The state during the first instant of the universe cannot be described in terms of the physical laws applying to our present universe.

For a few minutes space was filled with an opaque "fluid" of photons; the smallest units of radiant energy.

Somewhat later the first elementary particles detached themselves from this photon "fluid".

The first atoms

were hydrogen atoms, made up of one proton (the positively charged nucleus) and a negatively charged electron. The heavier elements were not formed until several billion years later. Matter in the universe is still about 99 % hydrogen.

Steady state...
For centuries scientists believed that the universe had not changed essentially, but only in minor detail. This theory could no longer be maintained, however, when it was discovered that space itself was expanding.

... or a big bang?
Cosmologists—scientists who study the structure and development of the universe—now believe that in the comparatively short space of some 12–15 billion years the universe has expanded out of a single point. The first explosive expansion is referred to as the "big bang".

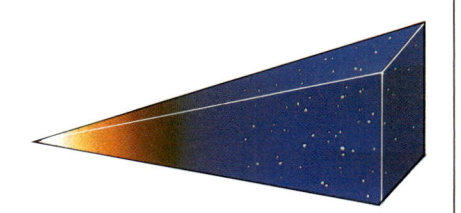

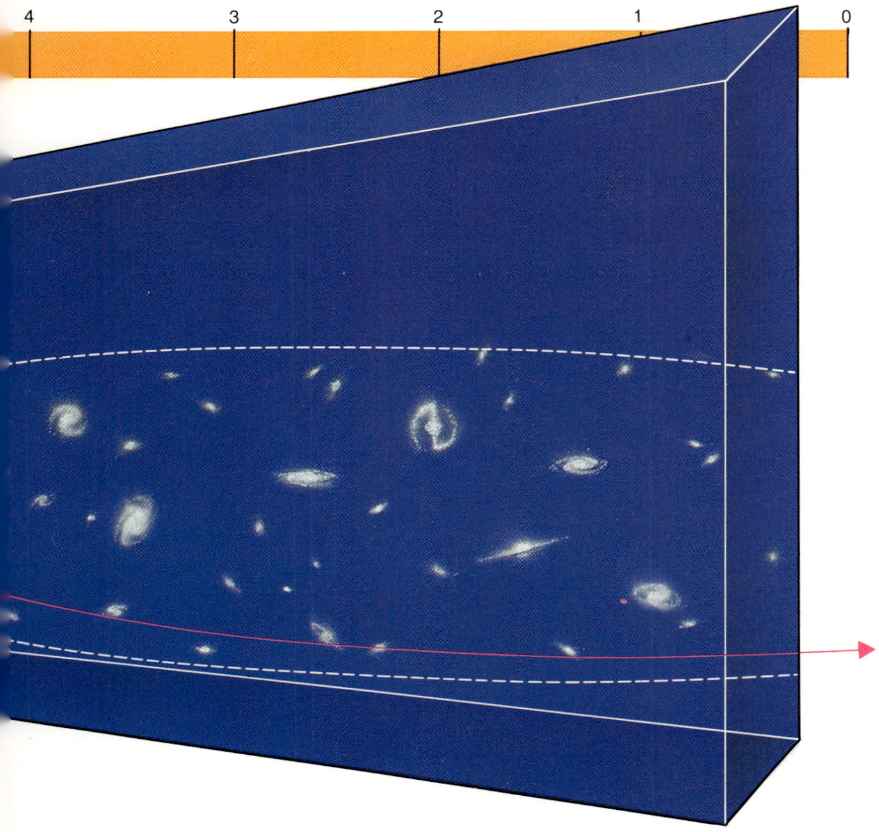

The curvature of space

From Euclid to Newton
geometric space was conceived of as being rectilinear, rightangled and basically uniform everywhere. In the universe described by Einstein, (right) however, space is deformed or bent by the masses present within it (below).

Space and mass
The curvature of three-dimensional space is almost impossible to visualize. We show it below as a two-dimensional plane deformed by the mass of a star. The curvature of space is conformed to not only by masses and particles but also by light rays. It was, in fact, the bending of light rays adjacent to a star which confirmed the correctness of Einstein's theory, when this phenomenon was first observed in the 1920's.

On a non-deformed plane a mass particle or a photon describes a straight line.

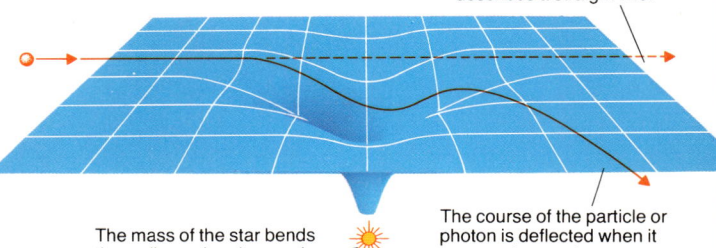

The mass of the star bends three-dimensional space in the same way that it bends this two-dimensional plane.

The course of the particle or photon is deflected when it passes close to the mass which is bending the space.

Our own sun
and its planetary system was formed between 4½ and 5 billion years ago. The sun thus belongs to the second generation of stars in the universe.

The red-shift

The red-shift (caused by the Doppler effect, right) shows that the distant galaxies are moving away from us. This does not imply, however, that the Earth or our galaxy is the centrepoint of the universe. A simple experiment can demonstrate this. Stick a number of pieces of tape to a deflated balloon and then blow up the balloon (below, right). It can be seen that all the pieces move away from each other, i.e. in all instances the distance from one piece to all the others increases.

The Doppler effect
Light or radio waves have a specific wavelength (top). If the radiation source moves towards us we perceive the wavelength as shorter (middle). If the source moves away from us the wavelength increases—the frequency diminishes—and the light is red-shifted (bottom). Police traffic speed control radar is based on the Doppler effect.

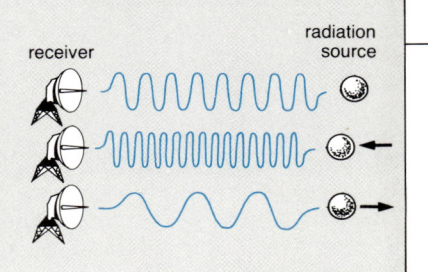

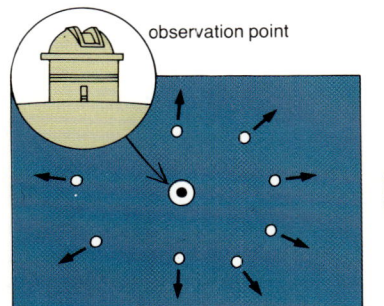

observation point

two observation points

The same everywhere
Since the universe expands uniformly it makes no difference where in the cosmos the astronomer sets up his instruments. From either of the two observation points in the diagram (left) he can see how all the other points are retreating (arrows).

85

The sun and its offspring

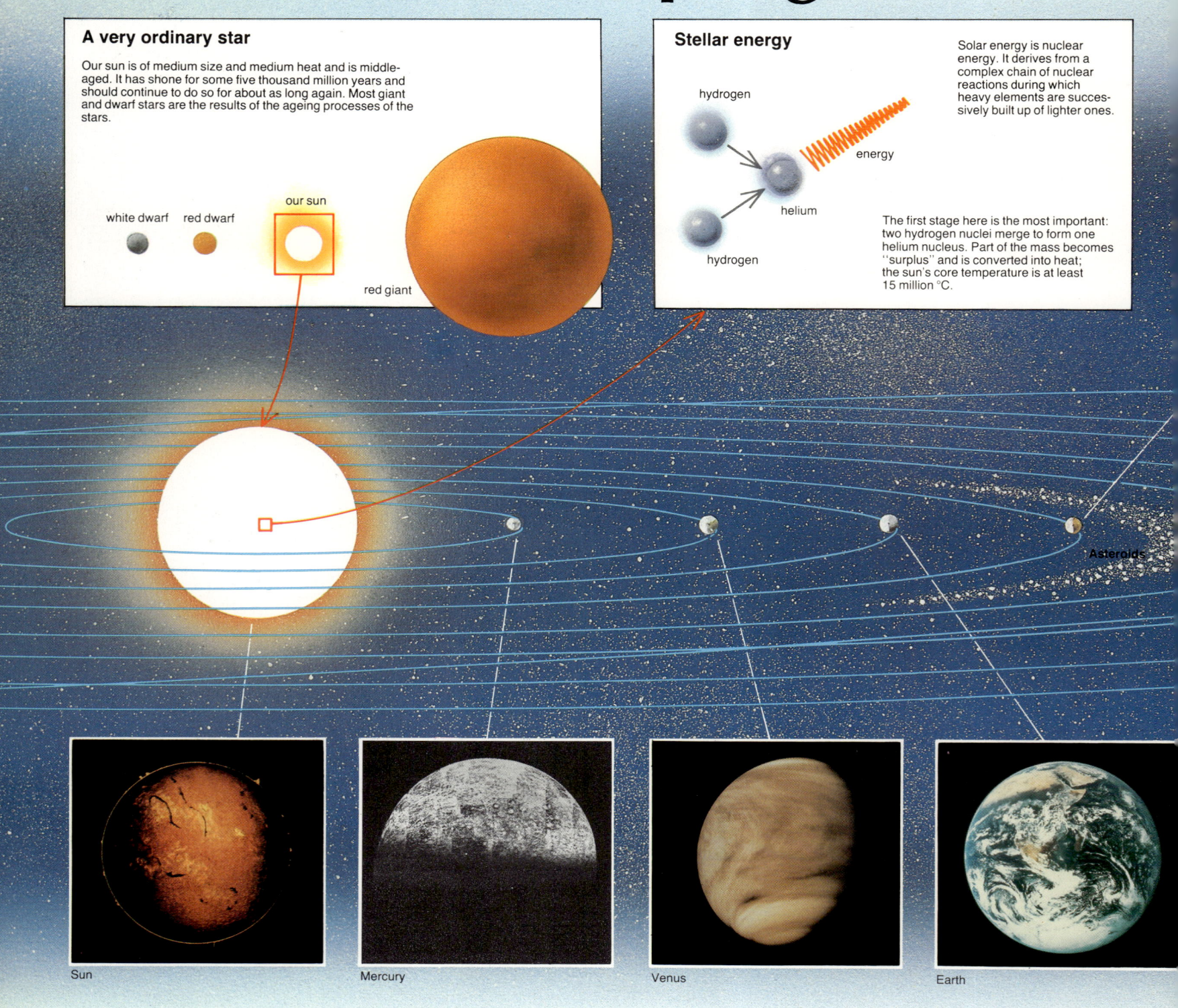

A very ordinary star

Our sun is of medium size and medium heat and is middle-aged. It has shone for some five thousand million years and should continue to do so for about as long again. Most giant and dwarf stars are the results of the ageing processes of the stars.

white dwarf   red dwarf   our sun   red giant

Stellar energy

hydrogen
helium
hydrogen
energy

Solar energy is nuclear energy. It derives from a complex chain of nuclear reactions during which heavy elements are successively built up of lighter ones.

The first stage here is the most important: two hydrogen nuclei merge to form one helium nucleus. Part of the mass becomes "surplus" and is converted into heat; the sun's core temperature is at least 15 million °C.

Asteroids

Sun   Mercury   Venus   Earth

Our sun is an average star, neither very large nor very small; neither hot nor cold; neither old nor recent. It is located on the edge of a very common type of spiral galaxy. If it is usual for such stars to have a planetary system – and most astronomers believe it is – then there must be many Earth-like planets in the universe, and on some of these there ought also to be life.

The planets in our solar system are of two entirely different categories. The inner planets, *Mercury*, *Venus*, *Earth* and *Mars*, are what are sometimes known as "cannonball worlds": compact mineral orbs encompassed by a shallow belt of atmosphere. The outer planets are mainly gaseous.

Mercury, in fact, lacks atmosphere altogether and is not unlike our moon, though its ground-level temperature would melt lead. Venus is a hot desert shrouded in a yellowish fog of carbon dioxide. It is only our Earth that has an oxygenous atmosphere and liquid water. So far as we know it is also the only one of the planets with life on its surface. Mars has a rarefied atmosphere consisting principally of carbon dioxide, like that of Venus. But the surface of Mars is a frigid wasteland where only dust storms move. Contrary to earlier theories *asteroids* are not fragments of an exploded planet, instead they are the material for a planet which never actually formed, because the gravitational force of the giant planet Jupiter constantly dissipated the pieces.

The outer planets, *Jupiter*, *Saturn*, *Uranus* and *Neptune*, are gigantic balls of very cold gases, primarily hydrogen, helium, methane and ammonia. The density is low—in Neptune's case lower than water—but because of their enormous size the gravitational fields of these planets are of immense power. The rings around Saturn consist of ice particles. Uranus and Neptune, too, have faint ring systems. Each of these planets also has its imposing array of moons, many of these being as big as the planet Mercury. *Pluto*, finally, is an erratic among the planets. Its orbit is oblique and eccentric, and it is a "cannonball world" like the inner planets. Pluto could possibly be an adopted planet; a celestial body recruited from elsewhere.

Mars   Saturn   Pluto

Panorama of planets
In this diagram, for the sake of clarity, both distances and differences in magnitude have had to be diminished. The system's radius out to Pluto's orbit is 8,500 times that of the sun's radius and almost 10,000 times that of Earth. In correct scale the planets would not be visible. The small pictures are photographs, except for Uranus, Neptune and Pluto which are drawings.

Jupiter   Uranus   Neptune

The first steps in space

When in 1969 Neil Armstrong set foot on the moon (right) it was, as he put it, "a giant leap for mankind". But because of the enormous costs of manned space travel, the further study of the planets is being conducted with remote-controlled devices. These have photographed Mercury, Jupiter and Saturn, penetrated the atmosphere of Venus and landed on Mars. In 1983 a US space-probe in the Pioneer series became the first man-made device to leave our solar system and continue on out into interstellar space.

87

Mountains of fire

Most geological processes are so slow that we do not have the time during our brief lifespan to observe them directly. Their cumulative effects do not emerge for thousands or millions of years. But vulcanism is an exception. A volcanic cone can be built up in only a few days, a mountain can explode and be thrown up into the stratosphere as fine dust in a matter of seconds.

Vulcanism occurs when magma rises up through the Earth's crust. Why it takes place, when and where it does, remained a mystery until the emergence of the modern plate-tectonic theory. We now know that the Earth's "fire belts" generally follow the limits of the geological plates. Ninety percent of all the active volcanoes are located either along the spreading lines (e.g. in Iceland) or in the subduction zones (Andes, Japan). In the spreading areas new earth-crust is formed when magma wells upward from the mantle, while in the subduction zones it is destroyed by being forced down into the mantle and re-melted. The magma which formed the Andean volcanoes, for example, consists mainly of "re-cycled" crust. The hot spots which give rise to whole chains of volcanoes as the earth-crust slides over the top of them are still a scientific riddle however; they appear to have remained in the same place in the mantle for millions of years.

The nature of vulcanism varies according to the composition of the magma. Certain volcanoes, in addition to nitrogen, water vapour and gasified sulphur, produce mainly stones—volcanic "bombs" and smaller "lapilli"—and ash. One example is Vesuvius which buried Pompeii in 79 AD. It is this type of volcano which builds up the characteristically steep cone profile. Other volcanoes erupt incandescent gas clouds, like Mont Pelée on Martinique which killed 30,000 people in 1902. Very liquid lava produces the more shallow contoured shield volcanoes. Volcanic domes caused by magma intrusions, hot springs and gas vents are other characteristic phenomena.

We tend to regard volcanoes as basically destructive. They have caused the death of vast numbers of people and lava flows and ash have had disastrous economic consequences. So much dust was spouted into the atmosphere during the eruption of Tambora in Indonesia in 1815 that there was practically no summer at all the following year. But there is another aspect to this. All the organic carbon and all the water on our planet is believed to be of volcanic origin—it was not part of the primeval atmosphere but came out of the Earth's mantle. Thus, vulcanism may be regarded as a prerequisite for life on our planet.

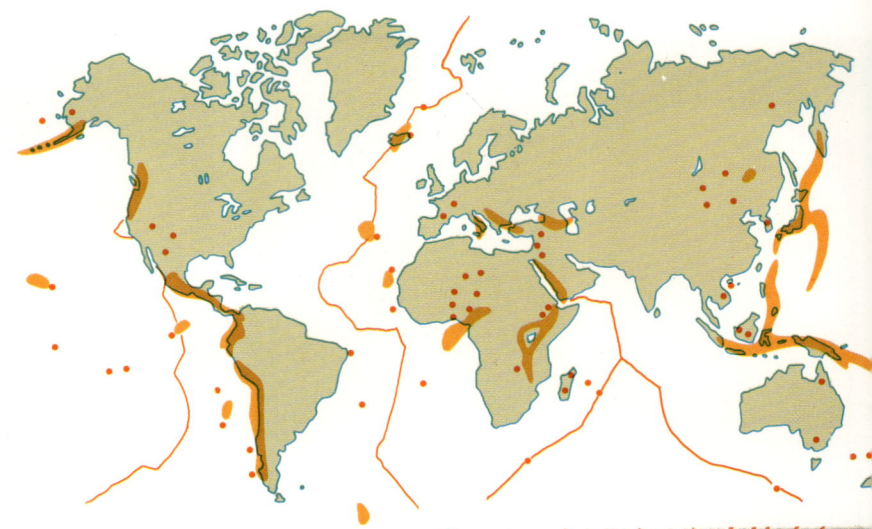

The earthquake zones (orange colour) are also where most volcanoes are found (red dots). These fire belts are areas where the crustal plates move relative to each other. Other important volcanic areas include the mid-ocean ridges (lines) and the "hot spots".

Stratovolcanoes are steep cones built up of layers of ash, lava and pumice.

crater

volcanic cone

funnel

Magma rises upward from deep down in the Earth's mantle. The consistency of the magma, and thereby the nature of the eruption, depends to a large extent upon its composition, especially the gas and silicic acid content.

Extraterrestrial vulcanism

Our solar system's biggest volcano is Olympus Mons on Mars. This is a gigantic shield volcano with a diameter of nearly 600 km. and the summit, a caldera, some 23,000 m. above the surrounding desertland. The gradually sloping sides terminate abruptly in a 4000 m. sheer fall down to the ground level. This is all clearly discernible in the mosaic, composed of a series of vertical photographs taken by a space probe in orbit. There appears also to be volcanic activity on a couple of Jupiter's satellites, though the familiar craters on our moon and Mercury have nothing to do with vulcanism. These are merely impact craters caused by falling meteorites back in the time when the celestial bodies were being formed.

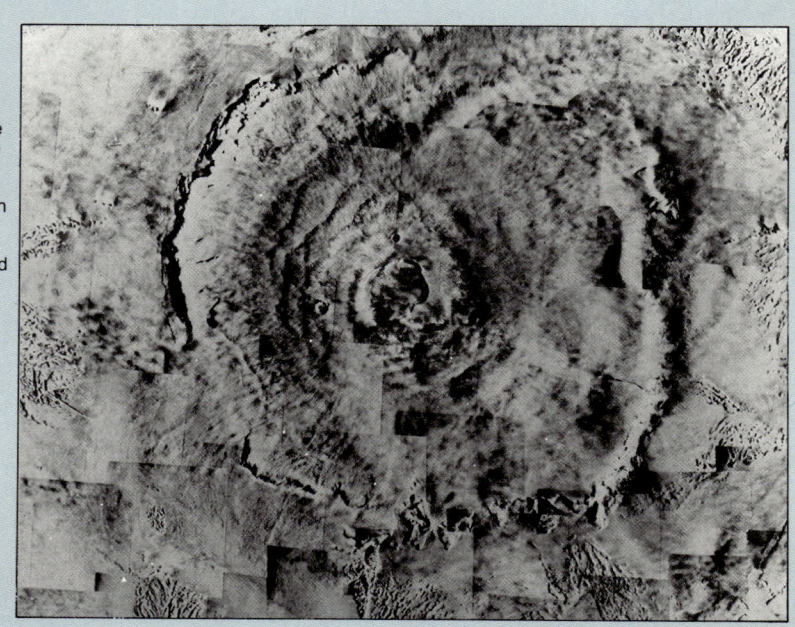

Mount Saint Helens—a volcanic case study

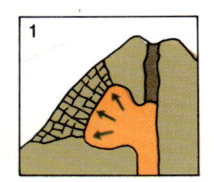

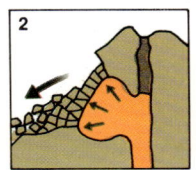

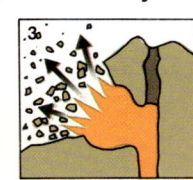

Mount Saint Helens in the northwestern USA produced a violent eruption in 1980. The funnel to the top crater had become blocked and the pressure of the magma caused the entire side of the mountain to bulge and fracture (1). A landslide then released the pressure that enclosed the magma (2) and the whole mountainside burst (3). The result was probably the most photographed volcanic eruption in history.

Boulders and small stones fall down around the crater, but the ash is spread over vast areas.

Lateral fissures can release lava or gas but also widen into lateral craters.

Shield volcanoes are formed from fluid and gaseous lavas. They are lower and flatter but also larger than typical stratovolcanoes.

Geysers and other hot springs arise when ground water reaches hot geological strata. These eruptions occur at intervals when the water comes to a violent boil.

How a caldera is formed:

A caldera is formed after a large magma chamber has developed underground. No normal funnel has formed here.

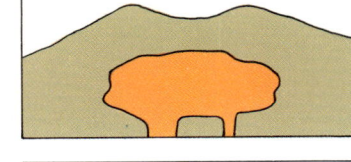

Instead the pressure is relieved through an explosion which shatters the rock above the chamber. The lighter material is then ejected into the air...

...but most of the heavy rock falls down into the empty chamber. The waning volcanic activity can build up a small volcanic cone out in the caldera.

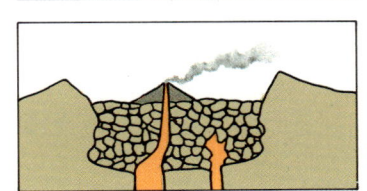

The final result is a circular depression enclosed by a ridge and often containing a lake. The diameter can be 20 km. or more.

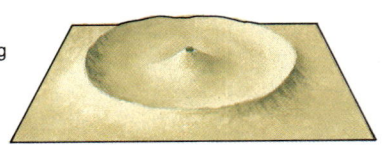

Hawaii's hot spot

The islands northwest of Hawaii itself are extinct volcanic cones.

Kauai, Oahu, Molokai, Maui, Hawaii, Mauna Loa

The hot spot remains in the same place in the mantle while the Pacific plate slides over it in a northwesterly direction (arrow). In this way a series of islands has been created, of which only the main one, Hawaii, exhibits active vulcanism today.

Energy from the Earth's interior

Industrial society is sustained by energy resources in the ground beneath our feet—coal and oil. Both of these are, in fact, fossilized solar energy from remote geological epochs.

Pit coal was formed during the Carboniferous Period about 300 million years ago. In conditions of immense pressure and heat, dead vegetation was gradually transformed into the mineral we now mine. Brown coal or lignite is of somewhat more recent origin. It is not as completely transformed as black or pit coal and its energy content is less. Petroleum and natural gas are also of organic origin, although in their case it was unicellular organisms which absorbed the sun's rays during the era of the dinosaurs a couple of hundred million years ago. According to another theory, however, at least some natural gas is "deep gas", hydrocarbons which have existed in the Earth's interior even since the planet was formed, seeping out during the course of billions of years. Some of this gas has been trapped beneath impenetrable rock strata in the same way as the organic gas.

Early interest in coal and oil developed through the availability of surface deposits. Fossil fuel was first used on a large scale in 16th century England where deforestation had resulted in a shortage of firewood for the expanding towns. Coal was later used to fuel the steam engines of the industrial revolution. The large-scale exploitation of petroleum began in the USA in the 1850's, the principal products at that time being axle grease and lamp paraffin. Petrol was a useless by-product. A little of it was sold for spot-removing while the rest was simply burned as a last means of disposal.

A further sort of energy in the Earth's interior is geothermal; heat in the bowels of our planet. This is a legacy from the creation of the solar system five thousand million years ago. The heat has been generated through the decay of radio-active elements which gathered in the core of Earth when the planet was formed.

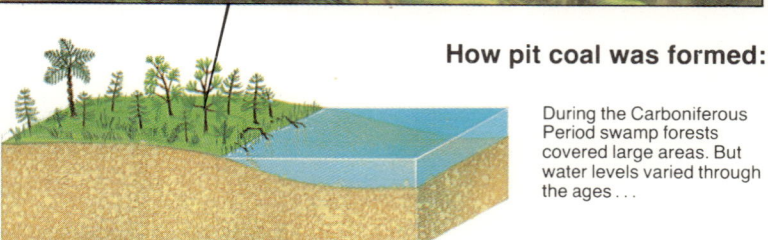

The world's coal
The USA, Western Europe, the Soviet Union, China and Australia are the principal producers.

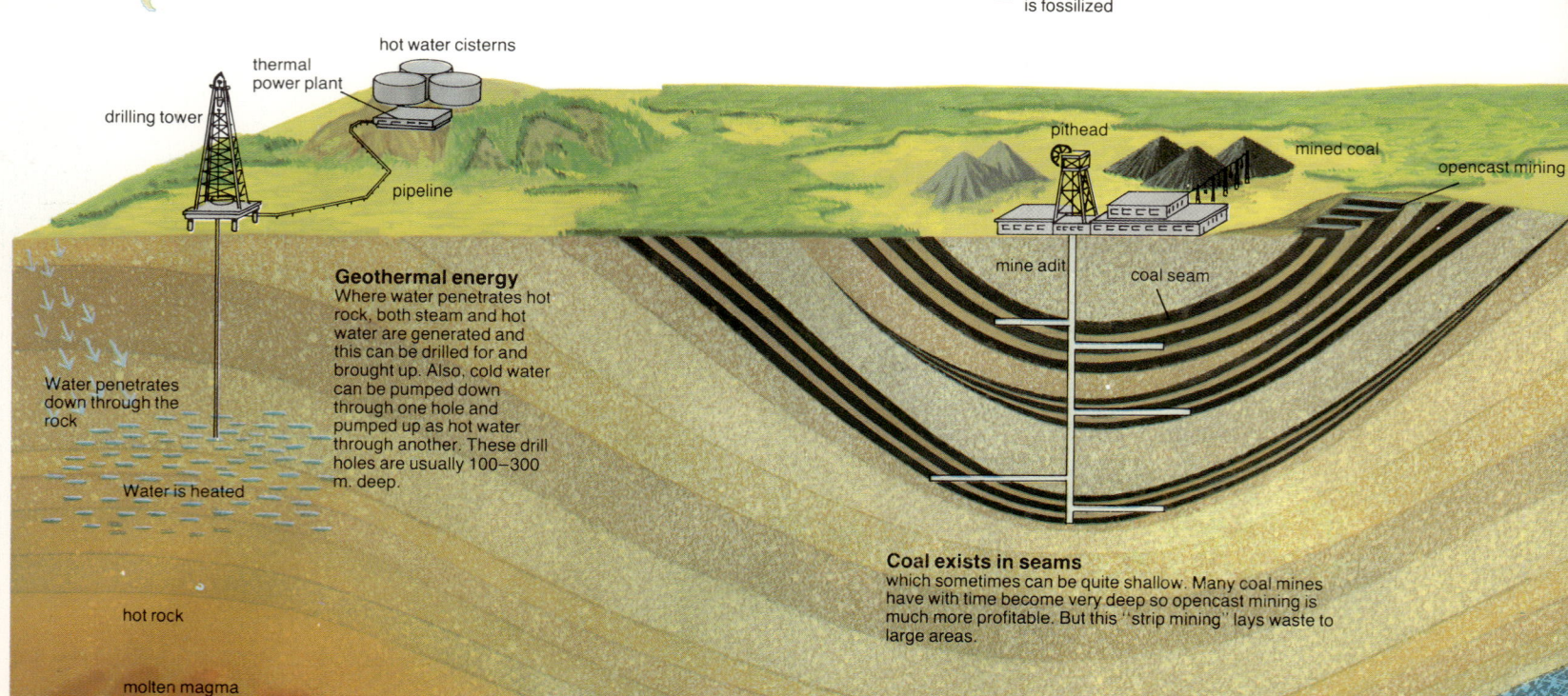

How pit coal was formed:

During the Carboniferous Period swamp forests covered large areas. But water levels varied through the ages...

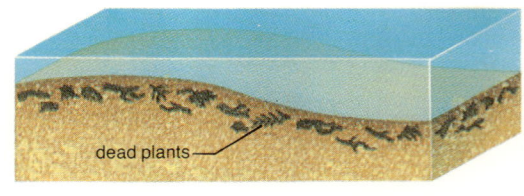

...and when the water rose the vegetation died. If the dead vegetation was covered so that oxygen could not reach it, it did not disintegrate but formed an organic stratum in the ground instead.

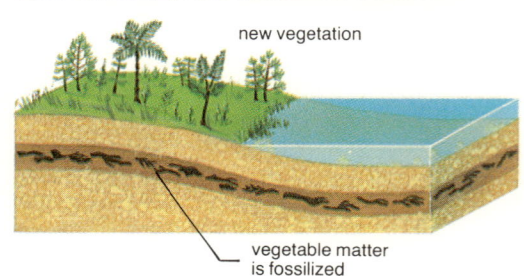

In time this stratum would be transformed into a coal seam. In the soil on top of the seam a new swamp forest grew—this would become the next coal seam.

Geothermal energy
Where water penetrates hot rock, both steam and hot water are generated and this can be drilled for and brought up. Also, cold water can be pumped down through one hole and pumped up as hot water through another. These drill holes are usually 100–300 m. deep.

Coal exists in seams
which sometimes can be quite shallow. Many coal mines have with time become very deep so opencast mining is much more profitable. But this "strip mining" lays waste to large areas.

How oil was formed:

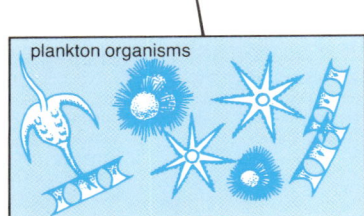

From seabed mud...
In shallow lakes and lagoons multitudes of tiny water organisms thrived. When they expired they sank to the bottom and formed a layer of mud rich in organic matter. A dinosaur or two probably went the same way, but these, of course, were not the main contributors to the process.

Dead organisms sink downward

plankton organisms

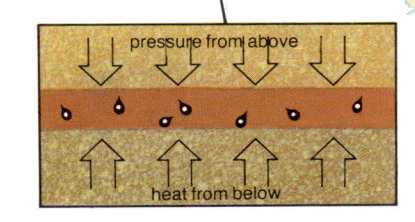

...to petroleum
The water at the bottom, containing little oxygen, protected the hydrocarbons in the dead organisms against disintegration. Pressure and heat converted simple hydrocarbons into the large molecules of petroleum. In this way oil-yielding sandstone, oil shale and tar sand were formed.

pressure from above
heat from below

Immense energy sources are concealed beneath the desolate surface of the desert.

The world's oil
is usually found far from where it is most in demand. The search for new reserves goes on constantly and rising prices have made it worthwhile to bring up oil from the continental shelves and in the Arctic.

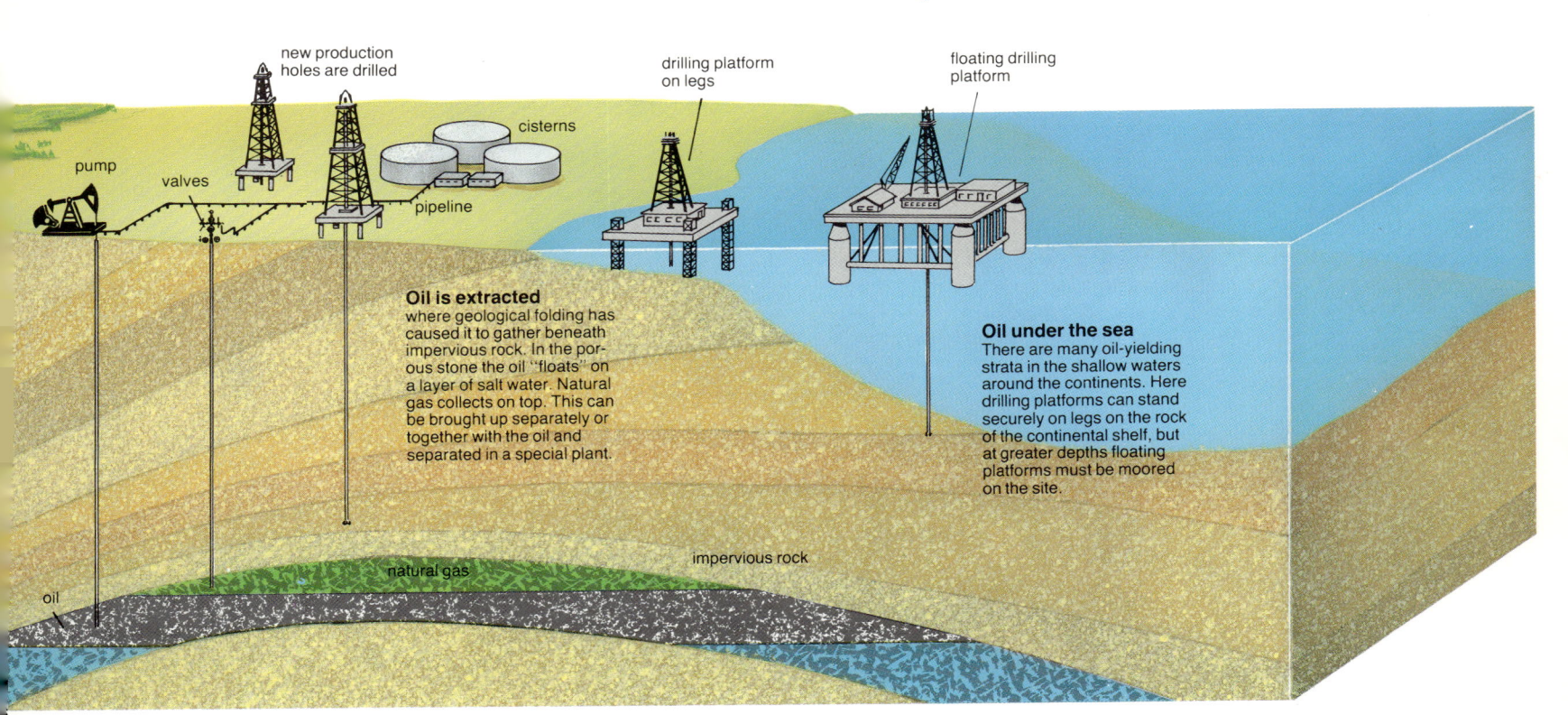

new production holes are drilled
drilling platform on legs
floating drilling platform
pump
valves
cisterns
pipeline

Oil is extracted
where geological folding has caused it to gather beneath impervious rock. In the porous stone the oil "floats" on a layer of salt water. Natural gas collects on top. This can be brought up separately or together with the oil and separated in a special plant.

Oil under the sea
There are many oil-yielding strata in the shallow waters around the continents. Here drilling platforms can stand securely on legs on the rock of the continental shelf, but at greater depths floating platforms must be moored on the site.

natural gas
impervious rock
oil

Fire, the servant of man

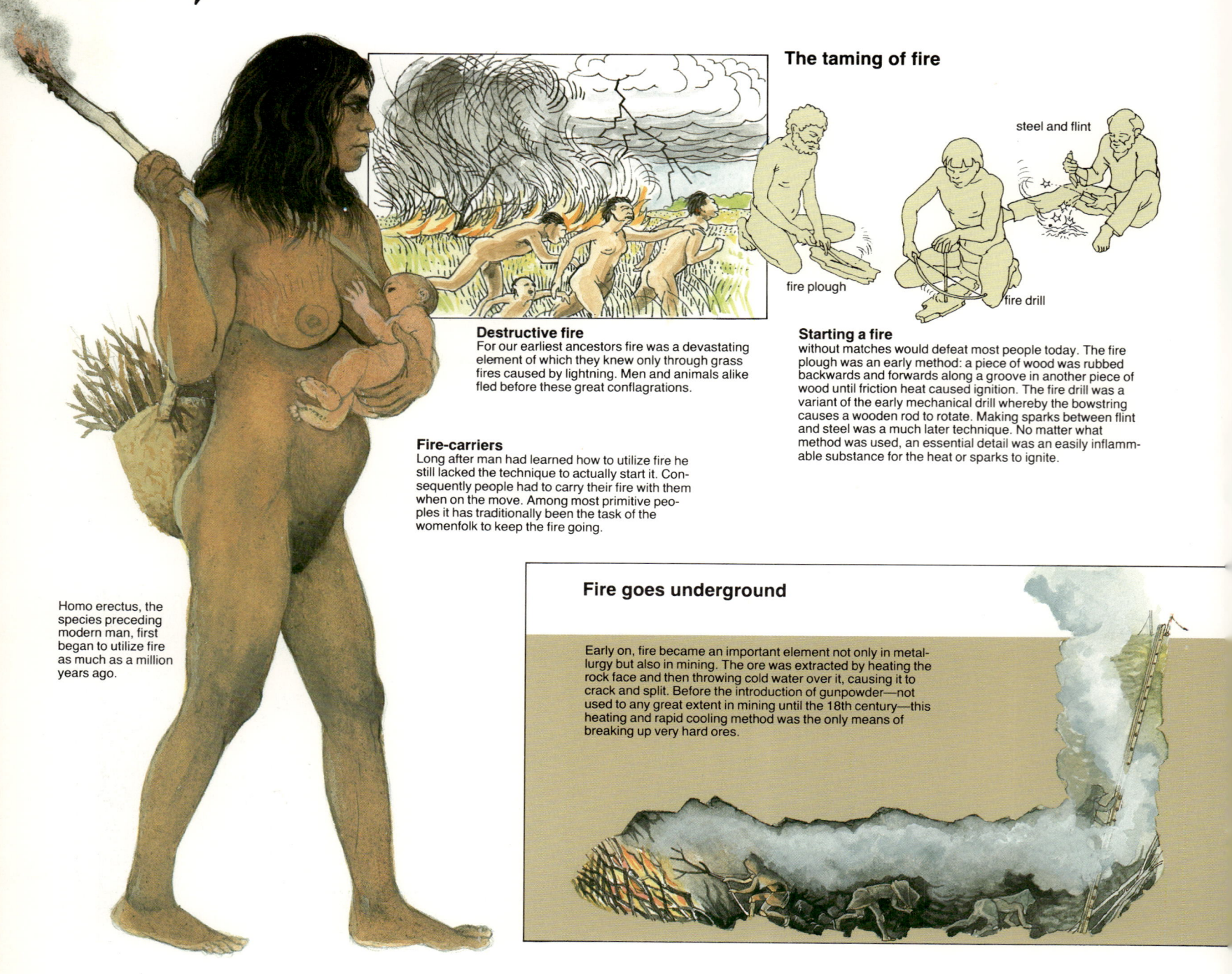

Homo erectus, the species preceding modern man, first began to utilize fire as much as a million years ago.

The taming of fire

Destructive fire
For our earliest ancestors fire was a devastating element of which they knew only through grass fires caused by lightning. Men and animals alike fled before these great conflagrations.

Fire-carriers
Long after man had learned how to utilize fire he still lacked the technique to actually start it. Consequently people had to carry their fire with them when on the move. Among most primitive peoples it has traditionally been the task of the womenfolk to keep the fire going.

Starting a fire
without matches would defeat most people today. The fire plough was an early method: a piece of wood was rubbed backwards and forwards along a groove in another piece of wood until friction heat caused ignition. The fire drill was a variant of the early mechanical drill whereby the bowstring causes a wooden rod to rotate. Making sparks between flint and steel was a much later technique. No matter what method was used, an essential detail was an easily inflammable substance for the heat or sparks to ignite.

fire plough

steel and flint

fire drill

Fire goes underground

Early on, fire became an important element not only in metallurgy but also in mining. The ore was extracted by heating the rock face and then throwing cold water over it, causing it to crack and split. Before the introduction of gunpowder—not used to any great extent in mining until the 18th century—this heating and rapid cooling method was the only means of breaking up very hard ores.

Ask a chemist to define fire and he or she will probably reply that it is an exothermic oxidation reaction. If certain carbon or hydrogen compounds are heated sufficiently then the carbon or hydrogen will combine with the oxygen in the air (oxidation). This process gives off large quantities of heat (it is exothermic)—so much so that it heats up the rest of the fuel sufficiently for the oxidation to continue and spread. Fire, in other words, is a chemical chain reaction.

On the grass plains where early man developed, fire played an important role as a periodic regenerator of the vegetation. When our ancestors first began to make use of fire for their own purposes—between 1,500,000 and 500,000 years ago—they probably employed it to raise game in their organized hunts. It was not until later, around 7000 BC, that Neolithic man began to utilize it regularly as a source of warmth and light and as a means of keeping nocturnal predators at bay. And it was much later still that man learned how to use the heat from fire to roast food. Fire probably became a necessity in the movement from the warm plains of Africa to colder, more inhospitable regions.

The initial, simple hearth, a ring of stones, was gradually built higher. The next step, to the oven, was soon achieved and in time the potter's kiln developed into the early metalworker's primitive smelting furnace. The enclosed oven made it possible to control simple oxidation and reduction processes. Subsequently, development remained largely at a standstill until about the 15th century when the low smelting furnace was replaced by a tall blast furnace with improved fuel economy and better process regulation.

In early Alexandria, Greek inventors had examined the idea of converting heat energy into kinetic energy. The concept was revived in the latter part of the 17th century when European mines had become so deep that it was impossible to pump them out manually. The first steam engines were therefore built to power the mine pumps. These were of the atmospheric type. Steam was injected into the cylinder when the piston was in its outermost position. Water was then added and the cooling-down process created a vacuum, causing the piston to be drawn inwards. The piston rate was about one stroke a minute and the machines had to be of enormous size to attain the required power.

The man who changed all this was James Watt. In 1769 he added a condenser to the steam engine. This greatly improved the fuel economy and the stroke rate. He introduced the piston rod, which converted the piston's backwards and forwards

Early iron manufacturing
For thousands of years iron was smelted in low beehive-shaped furnaces. These were filled with alternate layers of iron ore and charcoal. When the latter had burned out it left behind a sponge-like cake of iron at the bottom. There were many local variations of the process. Furnaces of this type were being used in Africa up until this century.

Large quantities of wood were used to produce charcoal for the smelting furnaces.

A blower, manual or wind-driven, increased the temperature in the furnace to iron's melting point, 1,528°C.

Slag inclusions were removed from the still red-hot iron by hammering.

Process heat

Early heat technology
The metallurgy of ancient peoples was part of a development which had been going on for thousands of years. The potter's kiln was adopted by the bronze-founder and when the blower was added this furnace could be used for iron smelting. The simple furnace could likewise be used for making glass (above: an oriental glassblower).

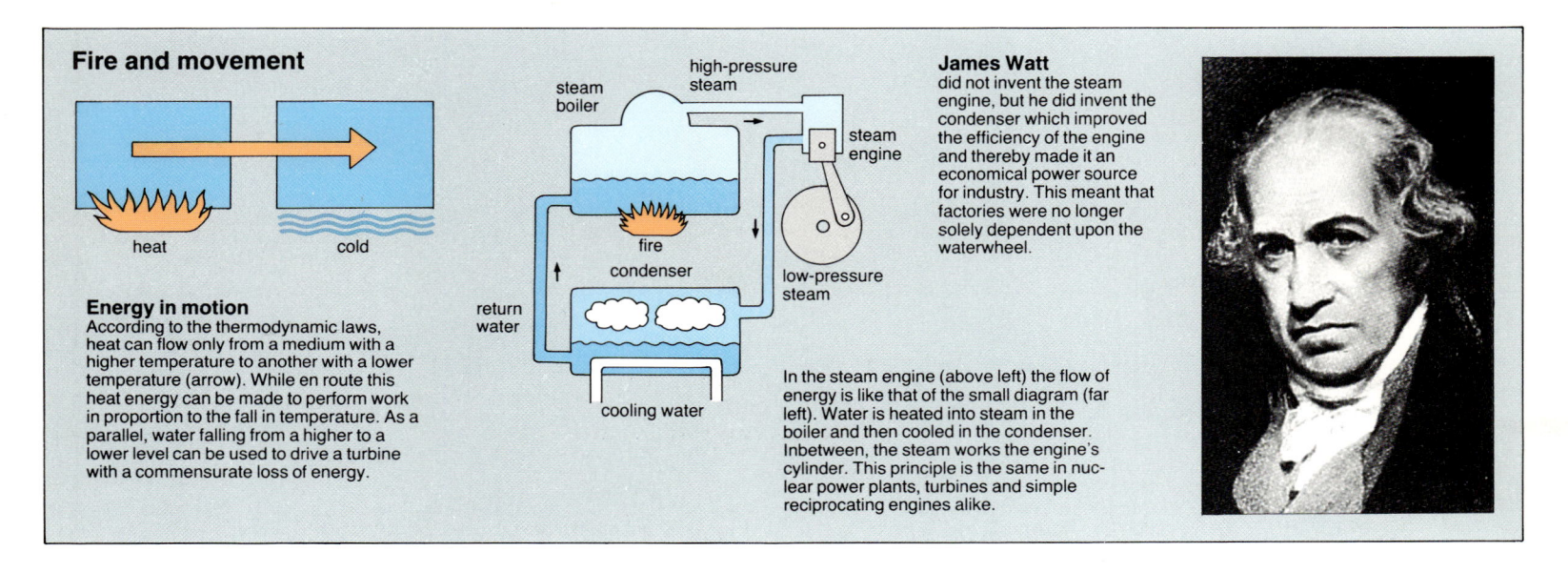

Fire and movement

Energy in motion
According to the thermodynamic laws, heat can flow only from a medium with a higher temperature to another with a lower temperature (arrow). While en route this heat energy can be made to perform work in proportion to the fall in temperature. As a parallel, water falling from a higher to a lower level can be used to drive a turbine with a commensurate loss of energy.

heat — cold

high-pressure steam — steam boiler — steam engine — fire — condenser — low-pressure steam — return water — cooling water

James Watt
did not invent the steam engine, but he did invent the condenser which improved the efficiency of the engine and thereby made it an economical power source for industry. This meant that factories were no longer solely dependent upon the waterwheel.

In the steam engine (above left) the flow of energy is like that of the small diagram (far left). Water is heated into steam in the boiler and then cooled in the condenser. Inbetween, the steam works the engine's cylinder. This principle is the same in nuclear power plants, turbines and simple reciprocating engines alike.

movement to a rotational movement, and also the governor which controlled the stroke rate. Watt was a self-taught mill-builder and instrument-maker and it was pure intuition which inspired him to invent the condenser. The scientific analysis of this invention was made by the Frenchman Sadi Carnot in 1824, who thereby founded thermodynamics, the science of energy conversion.

The role of steam in Europe's industrialization has often been misconstrued. Steam did not create industrialization—industry and machines had existed prior to Watt. As much as half a century after Watt's first patent, the waterwheel was just as important as steam as a power source in British industry—the most advanced in the world at that time. The steam engine did however liberate industry from the limitations of water power with regard to factory location and size.

It was in the realm of transport that the real revolution arose. Steamboats opened up the Mississippi valley, steam locomotives opened the way to the American West and Siberia for international trade and development. Steam helped carry the products of the industrialized nations out across the world, and brought back the raw materials to these same nations. The rise of steam signalled the advent of the modern world.

The factories of the 19th century
were run by steam engines, the power being distributed to the different machines through a maze of shafts and belts. Production increased, though it also became more centralized since the individual craftsmen could not afford their own steam engines. The many exposed belt drives in the early factory made working conditions there exceedingly dangerous.

93

Using energy

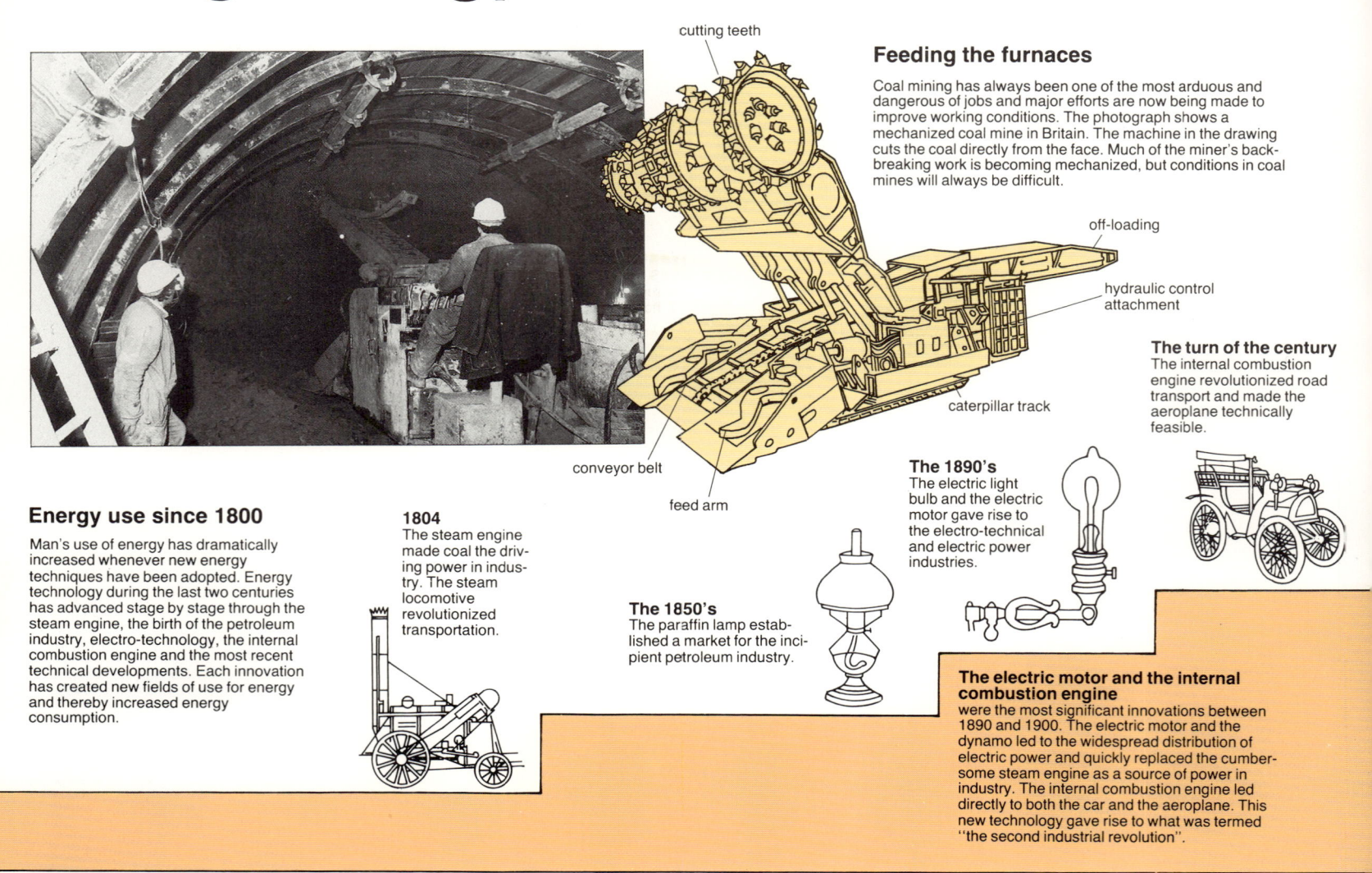

Feeding the furnaces
Coal mining has always been one of the most arduous and dangerous of jobs and major efforts are now being made to improve working conditions. The photograph shows a mechanized coal mine in Britain. The machine in the drawing cuts the coal directly from the face. Much of the miner's back-breaking work is becoming mechanized, but conditions in coal mines will always be difficult.

Labels: cutting teeth, off-loading, hydraulic control attachment, caterpillar track, feed arm, conveyor belt

Energy use since 1800
Man's use of energy has dramatically increased whenever new energy techniques have been adopted. Energy technology during the last two centuries has advanced stage by stage through the steam engine, the birth of the petroleum industry, electro-technology, the internal combustion engine and the most recent technical developments. Each innovation has created new fields of use for energy and thereby increased energy consumption.

1804
The steam engine made coal the driving power in industry. The steam locomotive revolutionized transportation.

The 1850's
The paraffin lamp established a market for the incipient petroleum industry.

The 1890's
The electric light bulb and the electric motor gave rise to the electro-technical and electric power industries.

The turn of the century
The internal combustion engine revolutionized road transport and made the aeroplane technically feasible.

The electric motor and the internal combustion engine
were the most significant innovations between 1890 and 1900. The electric motor and the dynamo led to the widespread distribution of electric power and quickly replaced the cumbersome steam engine as a source of power in industry. The internal combustion engine led directly to both the car and the aeroplane. This new technology gave rise to what was termed "the second industrial revolution".

The sun is the main source of energy in our planetary system. Electromagnetic radiation of almost incomprehensible magnitude floods out into space from its surface. This flow can be calculated at 4×10^{23} kilowatts, i.e. a 4 followed by twenty-three zeros. Of this vast output the Earth picks up about 127,500 billion kW on its daylight side, or 1 kW/m². This energy then streams through the atmosphere and hydrosphere until it again flows out into space. All life processes are sustained by the energy which organisms divert from this flow in order to utilize it in their own metabolism and life environment.

This applies to man. Our earliest forefathers had no more energy at their disposal than their own muscular strength. Two major steps were taken when man tamed fire about a million years ago and when he learned to harness draught animals during the agricultural revolution some 8,000 years ago. But the principle remained unchanged. The wood with which man fuelled his fires and the fodder that sustained his animals were reconstituted solar energy, as was the food that he himself consumed.

The situation changed drastically when man began using fossil fuels; coal and oil. It then became possible to utilize large amounts of energy in transport, industry and agriculture and this prepared the way for increasingly high productivity. It seemed as though all the natural limitations had been overcome. This energy optimism culminated with the advent of nuclear power when mankind was promised almost costless energy in unlimited quantities for ever.

Now, however, we are becoming aware that our energy resources are not inexhaustible, that their exploitation is costly and that such exploitation is ultimately harmful to the environment.

The laws of thermodynamics indicate that energy is indestructible. We can neither produce nor consume energy, merely harness it by converting it from one form to another. The electric current from a wall socket may amount to only 40% of the energy in oil, uranium or running water which has been used to keep the power station generators going. The light from an electric bulb represents about one tenth of the bulb's rated power, i.e. ten watts out of a hundred. What happens to the rest and where does the light go when the lamp is switched off? All this energy, including light energy, is converted into low-grade heat which flows out into space as long-wave infra-red radiation.

Radiation from a body is proportional to that body's temperature. The Earth's temperature has become stabilized at a point where incoming and outgoing radiation balance each other exactly. Heat emanating from fossil fuels and nuclear reaction does not derive from the sun, however. It is additional heat, thermal pollution, which increases the temperature of the atmosphere. As a result, the mean temperature of the Earth must increase in order that a radiation balance may once more be achieved. Until now this thermic environmental upset has been apparent only at the local level when cooling towers and cooling water releases have affected the microclimate in the immediate vicinity. What has been described above shows that there are limits to energy production. The way to greater prosperity is no longer an increased output of energy, but rather production processes and life styles that are more energy-saving and less environmentally destructive.

The 1950's:
The development of commercial nuclear power began: unlimited access to cheap energy was still regarded as the key to every form of technical and economic progress. The technology behind this "peaceful" nuclear power derived from the military nuclear weapons programmes, however.

Clean energy?
The processing of fuel and distribution of energy takes place under far more tolerable conditions than are found below ground. The photograph shows the control room at a nuclear power plant. The control room of a coal-fired power plant looks much the same, although the instrument panels may be somewhat less imposing. Despite the cleanliness of the power plant control room, threats to the environment do exist. All technical energy conversion, even the domestic fire, results in environmental damage of some sort. Large energy systems are very efficient, but they can break down. A major power failure can bring an entire region practically to a standstill.

The energy-saturated community
During the 1950's and 1960's energy consumption increased rapidly in industrial countries; doubling every five years in some cases. This increase was caused less by nuclear power than by the expansion of electric power networks and gas pipeline systems on a continental scale. During the 1970's energy consumption stagnated, partly because of the need to save expensive oil and partly because of a general slowdown in economic expansion. Industrial countries now foresee their energy consumption levelling off while the needs of Third World will continue to increase.

Man and the energy staircase
Homo sapiens and his predecessors have always been somewhere on the "energy staircase", but there were thousands or even millions of years from one step to another. Fire and the utilizing of beasts of burden such as oxen, donkeys and horses, were the most important advances until the advent of industrialism. Between these big changes the energy consumption per capita remained at a fairly steady level.

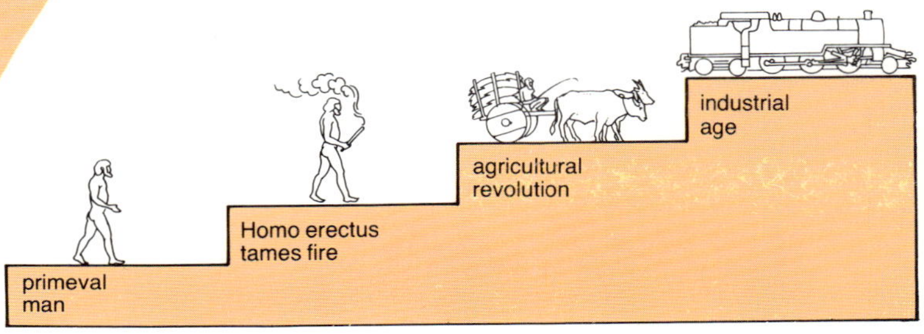

primeval man — Homo erectus tames fire — agricultural revolution — industrial age

Flowing versus capital energy
Utilizing flowing energy sources means that we divert solar energy on its way through the atmosphere, hydrosphere and biosphere, just as our forefathers did. With properly developed techniques this energy might even be sufficient for the needs of modern times. Capital energy on the other hand is energy from non-replenishable sources, such as fossil fuels and uranium. No matter where the energy comes from, it all ends up as waste heat in the atmosphere.

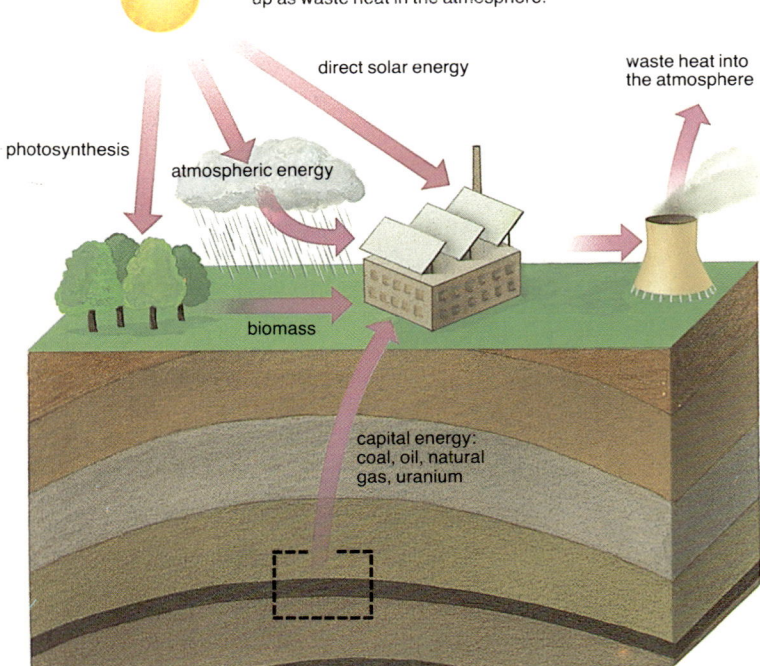

constantly flowing solar energy
photosynthesis
direct solar energy
atmospheric energy
biomass
waste heat into the atmosphere
capital energy: coal, oil, natural gas, uranium

Energy-impoverished societies
Energy resources are unevenly distributed. Industrialized countries use 90 % of the available energy while for the most part people in the developing countries have to manage with whatever "subsistence energy" they can find. Their pursuit of fuel (below) takes up an immense amount of time and labour, and often causes great damage to the vegetation.

95

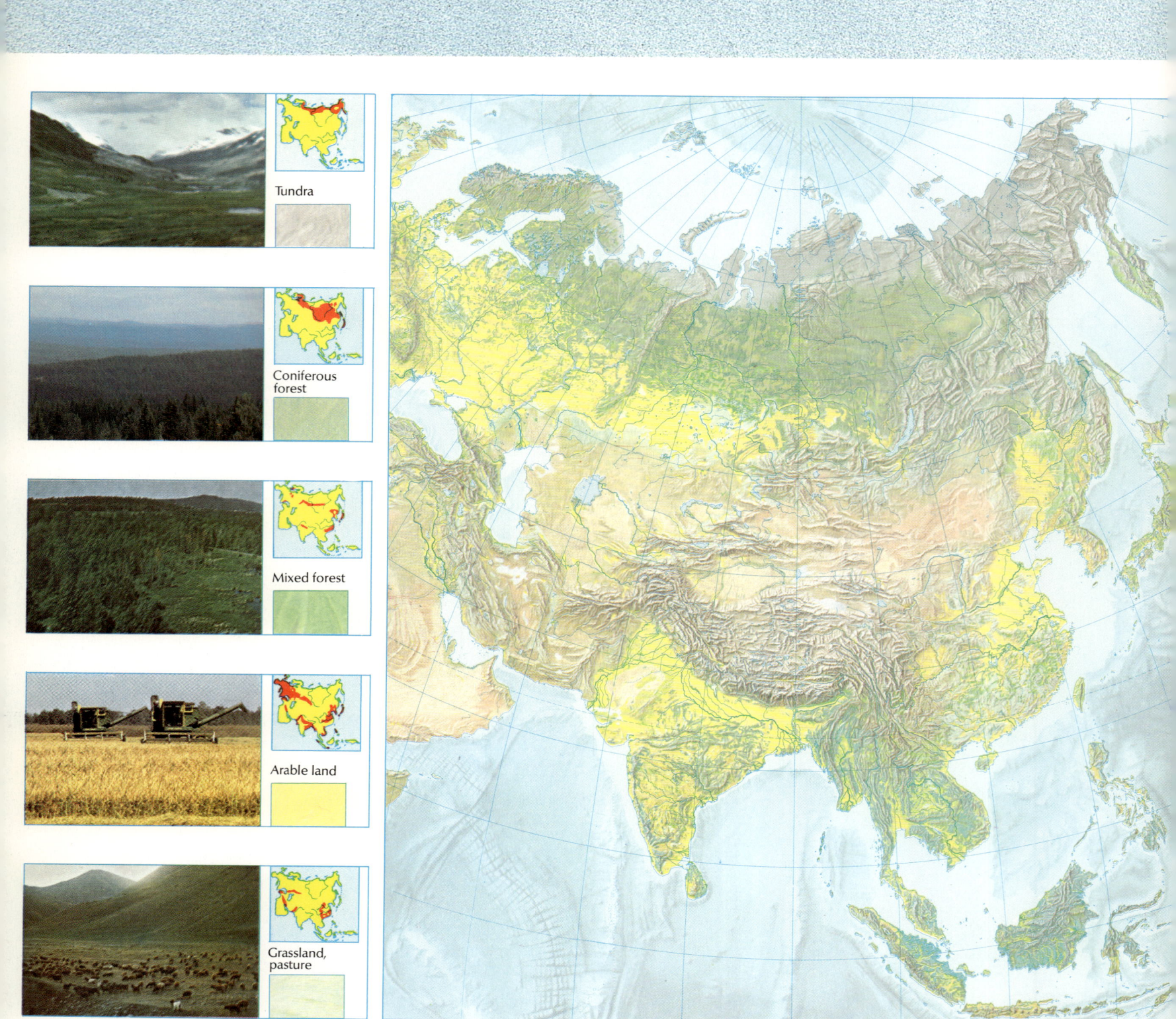

Tundra

Coniferous forest

Mixed forest

Arable land

Grassland, pasture

Semi-desert, Steppe

Other desert

Sand desert

Mountain

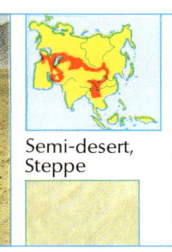

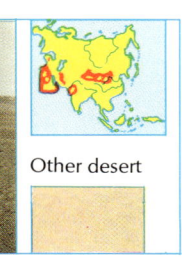

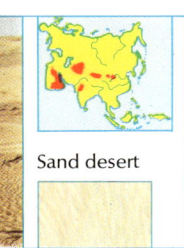

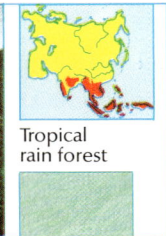

Tropical rain forest

THE WORLD in maps

A map is a representation of the face of the Earth. It lacks, however, the realism of an aerial photograph since it is abstract; mountains, rivers, seas and cities are indicated by signs and colours. The Earth's surface in all its endless variety has to be sorted out and arranged so that it may be presented in a form that is easily understood. In the past cartography has perhaps been a little too abstract; most people will recall the traditional school atlas where the lowland Sahara was shown in lush green, while upland Africa's rich vegetation was represented in parched brown; the map gave no intimation of the specific characteristics of the landscape with its forests and grasslands, its deserts and cultivated plains.

Satellite imagery and photographs of the Earth taken from space have inspired a new era in cartography. The environmental maps in this atlas bring the representation of the Earth's surface much closer to reality. The former, schematic levels of elevation have been succeeded by plastic relief effects and colours which are closer to those of the natural world. This new form of cartography represents the surface of the Earth at a level of detail never achieved before in an atlas of this kind.

The key on the left indicates the main classes into which different environments have been grouped. Certain specific environments not shown here have their own unique colour classification. A complete display of all the classes can be found inside the front cover. It should be noted that the British Isles has a separate series of colour classifications which is also displayed inside the front cover.

SCOTLAND

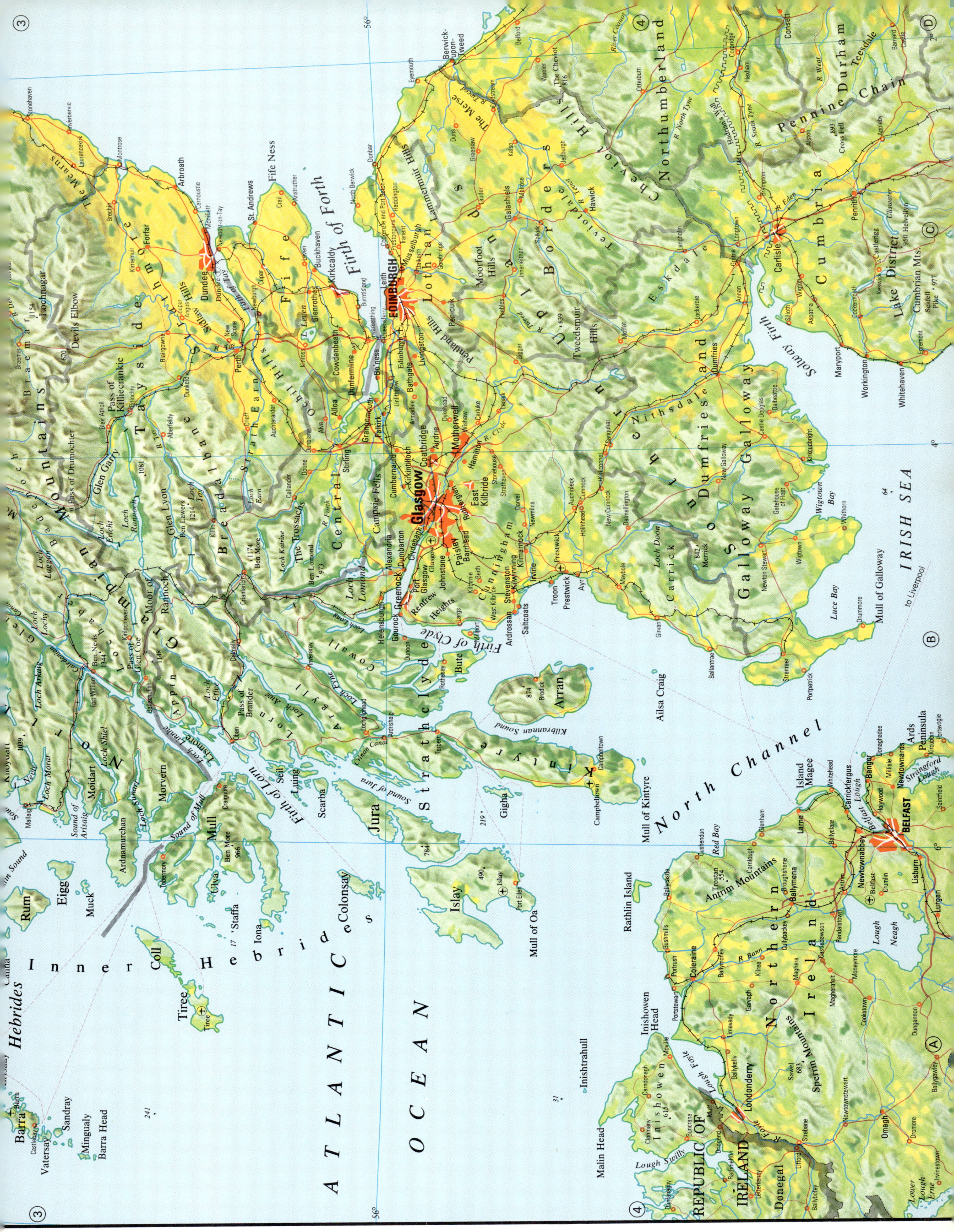

NORTHERN ENGLAND AND NORTHERN IRELAND

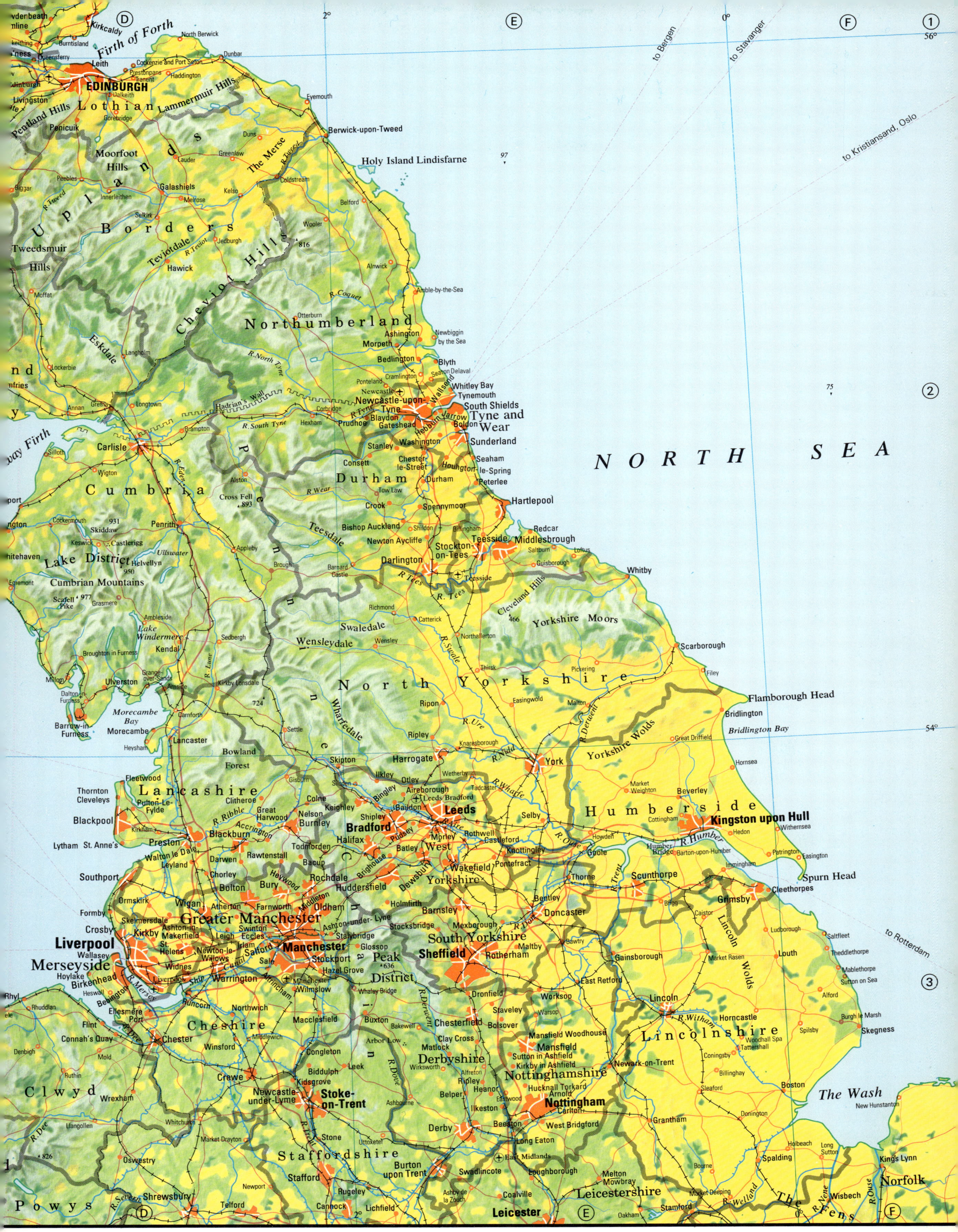

Scale 1:1250000

0 10 20 30 50 km

0 10 20 30 miles

102

WALES, CENTRAL AND SOUTHERN ENGLAND   103

UNITED KINGDOM, population

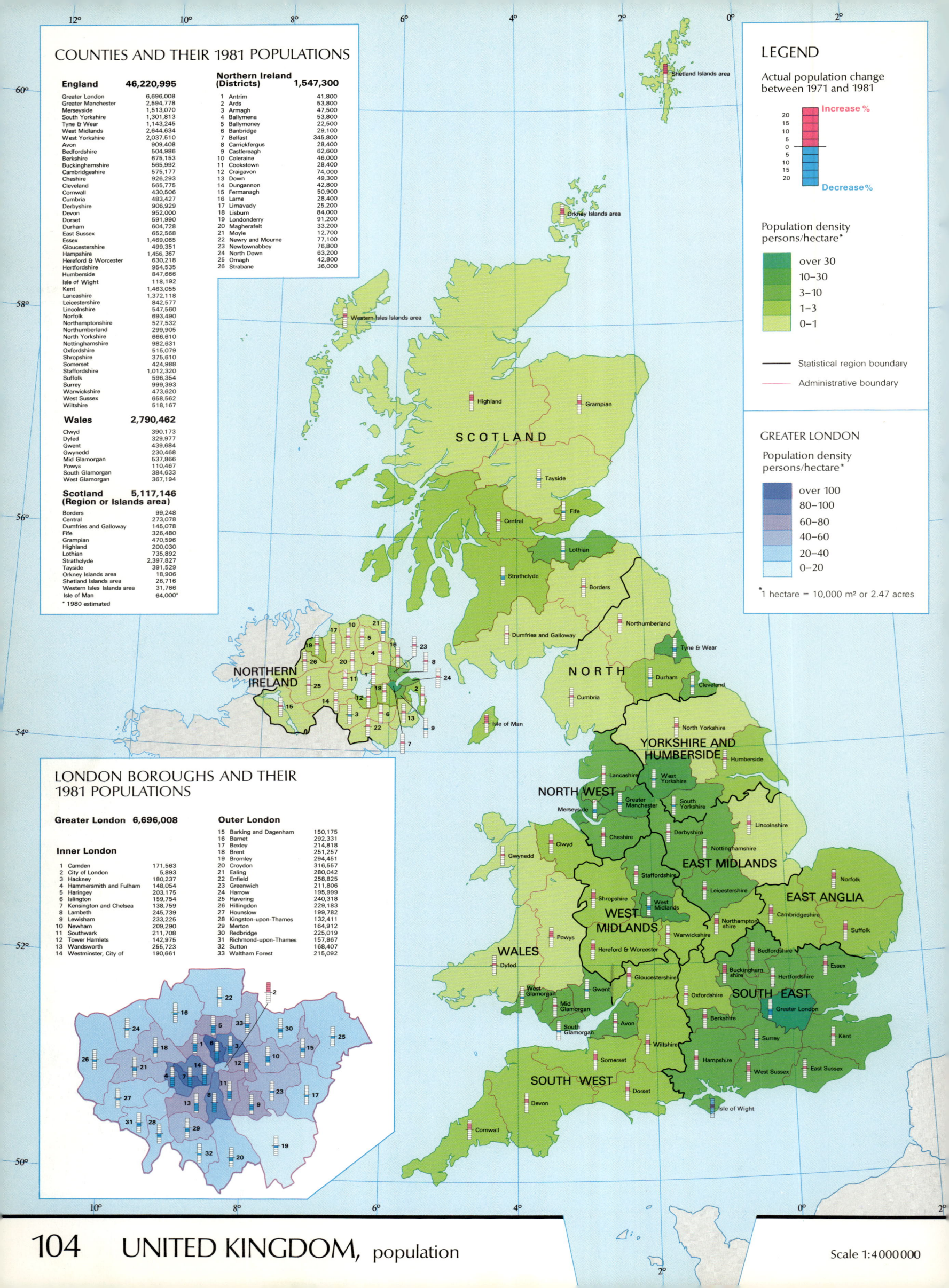

COUNTIES AND THEIR 1981 POPULATIONS

England 46,220,995

County	Population
Greater London	6,696,008
Greater Manchester	2,594,778
Merseyside	1,513,070
South Yorkshire	1,301,813
Tyne & Wear	1,143,245
West Midlands	2,644,634
West Yorkshire	2,037,510
Avon	909,408
Bedfordshire	504,986
Berkshire	675,153
Buckinghamshire	565,992
Cambridgeshire	575,177
Cheshire	926,293
Cleveland	565,775
Cornwall	430,506
Cumbria	483,427
Derbyshire	906,929
Devon	952,000
Dorset	591,990
Durham	604,728
East Sussex	652,568
Essex	1,469,065
Gloucestershire	499,351
Hampshire	1,456,367
Hereford & Worcester	630,218
Hertfordshire	954,535
Humberside	847,666
Isle of Wight	118,192
Kent	1,463,055
Lancashire	1,372,118
Leicestershire	842,577
Lincolnshire	547,560
Norfolk	693,490
Northamptonshire	527,532
Northumberland	299,905
North Yorkshire	666,610
Nottinghamshire	982,631
Oxfordshire	515,079
Shropshire	375,610
Somerset	424,988
Staffordshire	1,012,320
Suffolk	596,354
Surrey	999,393
Warwickshire	473,620
West Sussex	658,562
Wiltshire	518,167

Wales 2,790,462

County	Population
Clwyd	390,173
Dyfed	329,977
Gwent	439,684
Gwynedd	230,468
Mid Glamorgan	537,866
Powys	110,467
South Glamorgan	384,633
West Glamorgan	367,194

Scotland 5,117,146 (Region or Islands area)

Region	Population
Borders	99,248
Central	273,078
Dumfries and Galloway	145,078
Fife	326,480
Grampian	470,596
Highland	200,030
Lothian	735,892
Strathclyde	2,397,827
Tayside	391,529
Orkney Islands area	18,906
Shetland Islands area	26,716
Western Isles Islands area	31,766
Isle of Man	64,000*

*1980 estimated

Northern Ireland (Districts) 1,547,300

#	District	Population
1	Antrim	41,800
2	Ards	53,800
3	Armagh	47,500
4	Ballymena	53,800
5	Ballymoney	22,500
6	Banbridge	29,100
7	Belfast	345,800
8	Carrickfergus	28,400
9	Castlereagh	62,600
10	Coleraine	46,000
11	Cookstown	28,400
12	Craigavon	74,000
13	Down	49,300
14	Dungannon	42,800
15	Fermanagh	50,900
16	Larne	28,400
17	Limavady	25,200
18	Lisburn	84,000
19	Londonderry	91,200
20	Magherafelt	33,200
21	Moyle	12,700
22	Newry and Mourne	77,100
23	Newtownabbey	76,800
24	North Down	63,200
25	Omagh	42,800
26	Strabane	36,000

LEGEND

Actual population change between 1971 and 1981
- Increase % (20, 15, 10, 5)
- 0
- Decrease % (5, 10, 15, 20)

Population density persons/hectare*
- over 30
- 10–30
- 3–10
- 1–3
- 0–1

— Statistical region boundary
— Administrative boundary

GREATER LONDON
Population density persons/hectare*
- over 100
- 80–100
- 60–80
- 40–60
- 20–40
- 0–20

*1 hectare = 10,000 m² or 2.47 acres

LONDON BOROUGHS AND THEIR 1981 POPULATIONS

Greater London 6,696,008

Inner London

#	Borough	Population
1	Camden	171,563
2	City of London	5,893
3	Hackney	180,237
4	Hammersmith and Fulham	148,054
5	Haringey	203,175
6	Islington	159,754
7	Kensington and Chelsea	138,759
8	Lambeth	245,739
9	Lewisham	233,225
10	Newham	209,290
11	Southwark	211,708
12	Tower Hamlets	142,975
13	Wandsworth	255,723
14	Westminster, City of	190,661

Outer London

#	Borough	Population
15	Barking and Dagenham	150,175
16	Barnet	292,331
17	Bexley	214,818
18	Brent	251,257
19	Bromley	294,451
20	Croydon	316,557
21	Ealing	280,042
22	Enfield	258,825
23	Greenwich	211,806
24	Harrow	195,999
25	Havering	240,318
26	Hillingdon	229,183
27	Hounslow	199,782
28	Kingston-upon-Thames	132,411
29	Merton	164,912
30	Redbridge	225,019
31	Richmond-upon-Thames	157,867
32	Sutton	168,407
33	Waltham Forest	215,092

Scale 1:4 000 000

ENERGY

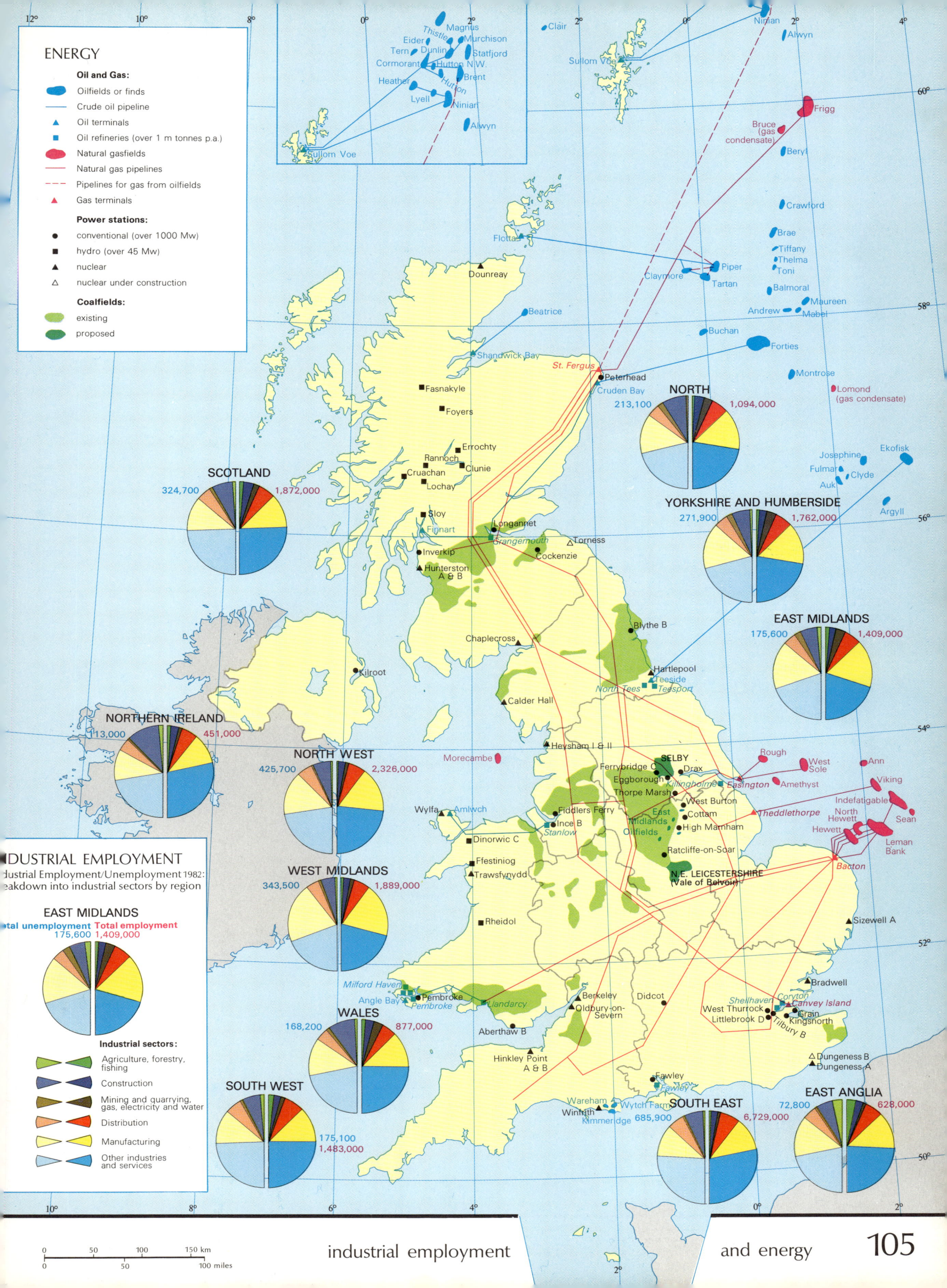

Oil and Gas:
- Oilfields or finds
- Crude oil pipeline
- Oil terminals
- Oil refineries (over 1 m tonnes p.a.)
- Natural gasfields
- Natural gas pipelines
- Pipelines for gas from oilfields
- Gas terminals

Power stations:
- conventional (over 1000 Mw)
- hydro (over 45 Mw)
- nuclear
- nuclear under construction

Coalfields:
- existing
- proposed

INDUSTRIAL EMPLOYMENT
Industrial Employment/Unemployment 1982: breakdown into industrial sectors by region

EAST MIDLANDS
Total unemployment: 175,600
Total employment: 1,409,000

Industrial sectors:
- Agriculture, forestry, fishing
- Construction
- Mining and quarrying, gas, electricity and water
- Distribution
- Manufacturing
- Other industries and services

Regional figures (unemployment / employment)

- **NORTH** 213,100 / 1,094,000
- **SCOTLAND** 324,700 / 1,872,000
- **YORKSHIRE AND HUMBERSIDE** 271,900 / 1,762,000
- **EAST MIDLANDS** 175,600 / 1,409,000
- **NORTHERN IRELAND** 113,000 / 451,000
- **NORTH WEST** 425,700 / 2,326,000
- **WEST MIDLANDS** 343,500 / 1,889,000
- **WALES** 168,200 / 877,000
- **SOUTH WEST** 175,100 / 1,483,000
- **SOUTH EAST** 685,900 / 6,729,000
- **EAST ANGLIA** 72,800 / 628,000

Oil and Gas Fields
Magnus, Thistle, Murchison, Eider, Tern, Dunlin, Statfjord, Cormorant, Hutton N.W., Heather, Brent, Hutton, Clair, Ninian, Alwyn, Lyell, Niniari, Sullom Voe, Frigg, Bruce (gas condensate), Beryl, Crawford, Brae, Tiffany, Thelma, Toni, Piper, Claymore, Tartan, Balmoral, Andrew, Maureen, Mabel, Buchan, Forties, Josephine, Fulmar, Ekofisk, Auk, Clyde, Argyll, Montrose, Lomond (gas condensate), Rough, West Sole, Ann, Amethyst, Viking, Indefatigable, North Hewett, Sean, Hewett, Leman Bank, Bacton

Power stations and places
Dounreay, Beatrice, Flotta, Shandwick Bay, St. Fergus, Peterhead, Cruden Bay, Fasnakyle, Foyers, Errochty, Rannoch, Clunie, Cruachan, Lochay, Sloy, Finnart, Longannet, Grangemouth, Inverkip, Hunterston A & B, Torness, Cockenzie, Chapelcross, Kilroot, Blyth B, Hartlepool, Teeside, Teesport, North Tees, Calder Hall, Heysham I & II, Morecambe, Selby, Ferrybridge C, Drax, Eggborough, Killingholme, Easington, Thorpe Marsh, West Burton, Cottam, High Marnham, Fiddlers Fiddlers Ferry, Ince B, Stanlow, Wylfa, Amlwch, Dinorwic C, Ffestiniog, Trawsfynydd, Rheidol, Ratcliffe-on-Soar, East Midlands Oilfields, N.E. Leicestershire (Vale of Belvoir), Theddlethorpe, Sizewell A, Bradwell, Milford Haven, Angle Bay, Pembroke, Llandarcy, Berkeley, Oldbury-on-Severn, Didcot, Shellhaven, Coryton, West Thurrock, Canvey Island, Littlebrook D, Grain, Tilbury B, Kingsnorth, Dungeness A, Dungeness B, Aberthaw B, Hinkley Point A & B, Fawley, Wareham, Wytch Farm, Winfrith, Kimmeridge

industrial employment and energy

105

POLITICAL DIVISIONS

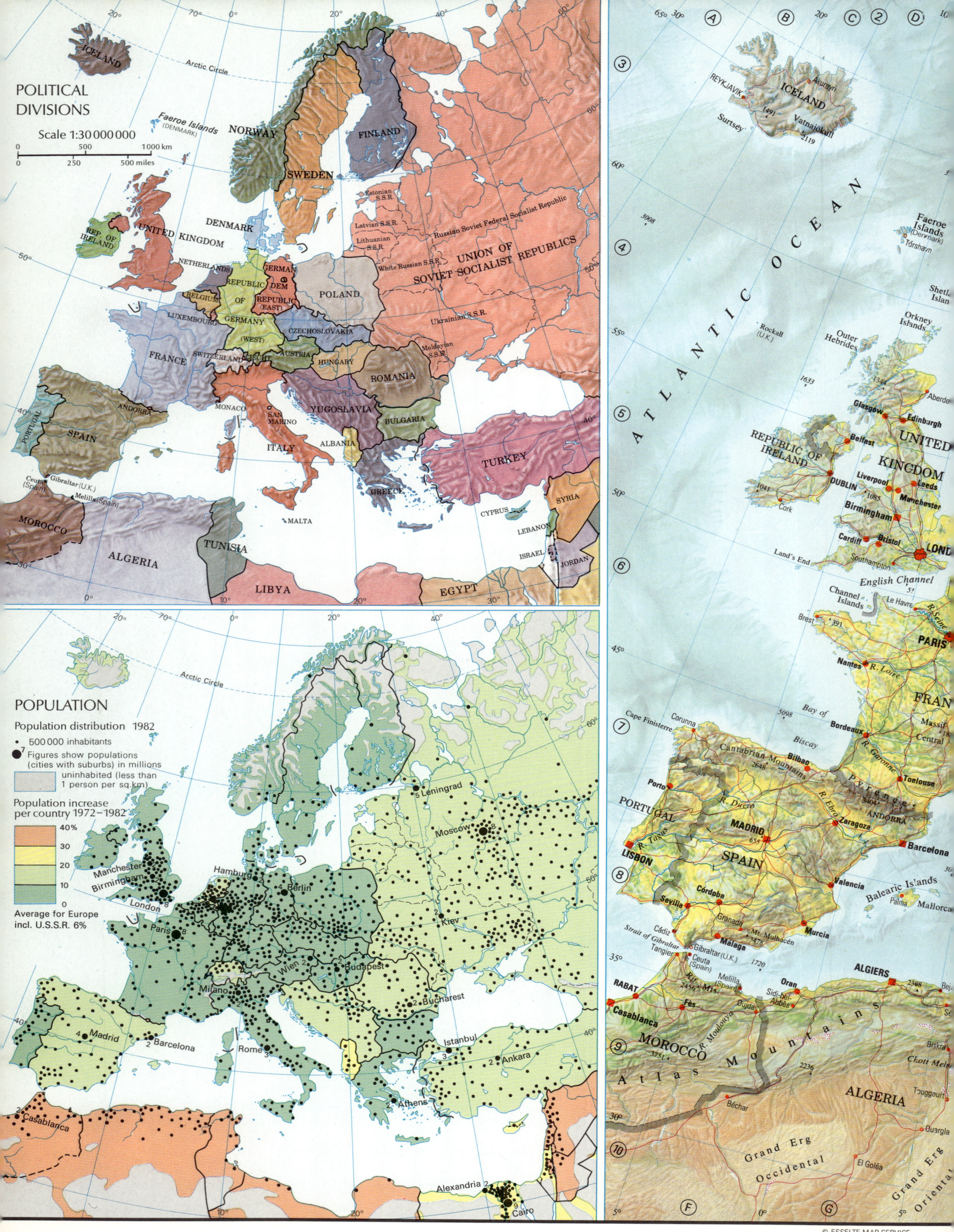

Scale 1:30 000 000

POPULATION

Population distribution 1982
- 500 000 inhabitants
- 7 Figures show populations (cities with suburbs) in millions
- uninhabited (less than 1 person per sq. km)

Population increase per country 1972–1982
- 40%
- 30
- 20
- 10
- 0

Average for Europe incl. U.S.S.R. 6%

106 EUROPE, environment, political divisions, population

© ESSELTE MAP SERVICE

LAMBERT'S CONFORMAL CONIC PROJECTION

Scale 1:15 000 000 — 0, 200, 400, 600 km; 0, 200, 300, 400 miles

ORGANIC PRODUCTION

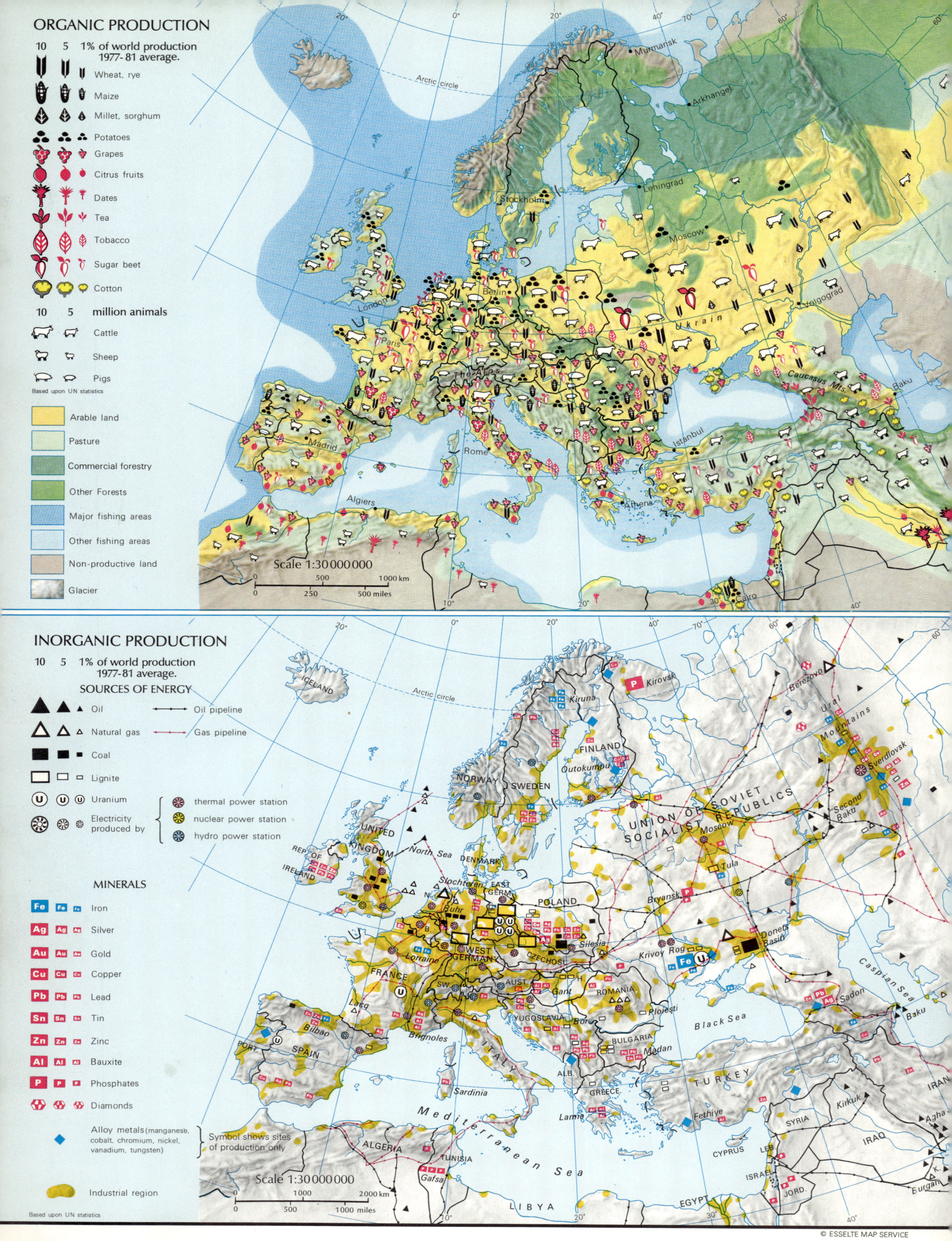

10 5 1% of world production
1977-81 average.

- Wheat, rye
- Maize
- Millet, sorghum
- Potatoes
- Grapes
- Citrus fruits
- Dates
- Tea
- Tobacco
- Sugar beet
- Cotton

10 5 million animals
- Cattle
- Sheep
- Pigs

Based upon UN statistics

- Arable land
- Pasture
- Commercial forestry
- Other Forests
- Major fishing areas
- Other fishing areas
- Non-productive land
- Glacier

Scale 1:30 000 000

INORGANIC PRODUCTION

10 5 1% of world production
1977-81 average.

SOURCES OF ENERGY
- Oil — Oil pipeline
- Natural gas — Gas pipeline
- Coal
- Lignite
- Uranium
- Electricity produced by:
  - thermal power station
  - nuclear power station
  - hydro power station

MINERALS
- Fe — Iron
- Ag — Silver
- Au — Gold
- Cu — Copper
- Pb — Lead
- Sn — Tin
- Zn — Zinc
- Al — Bauxite
- P — Phosphates
- Diamonds
- Alloy metals (manganese, cobalt, chromium, nickel, vanadium, tungsten)

Symbol shows sites of production only

- Industrial region

Based upon UN statistics

Scale 1:30 000 000

© ESSELTE MAP SERVICE

108 EUROPE, physical, economic

RELIEF

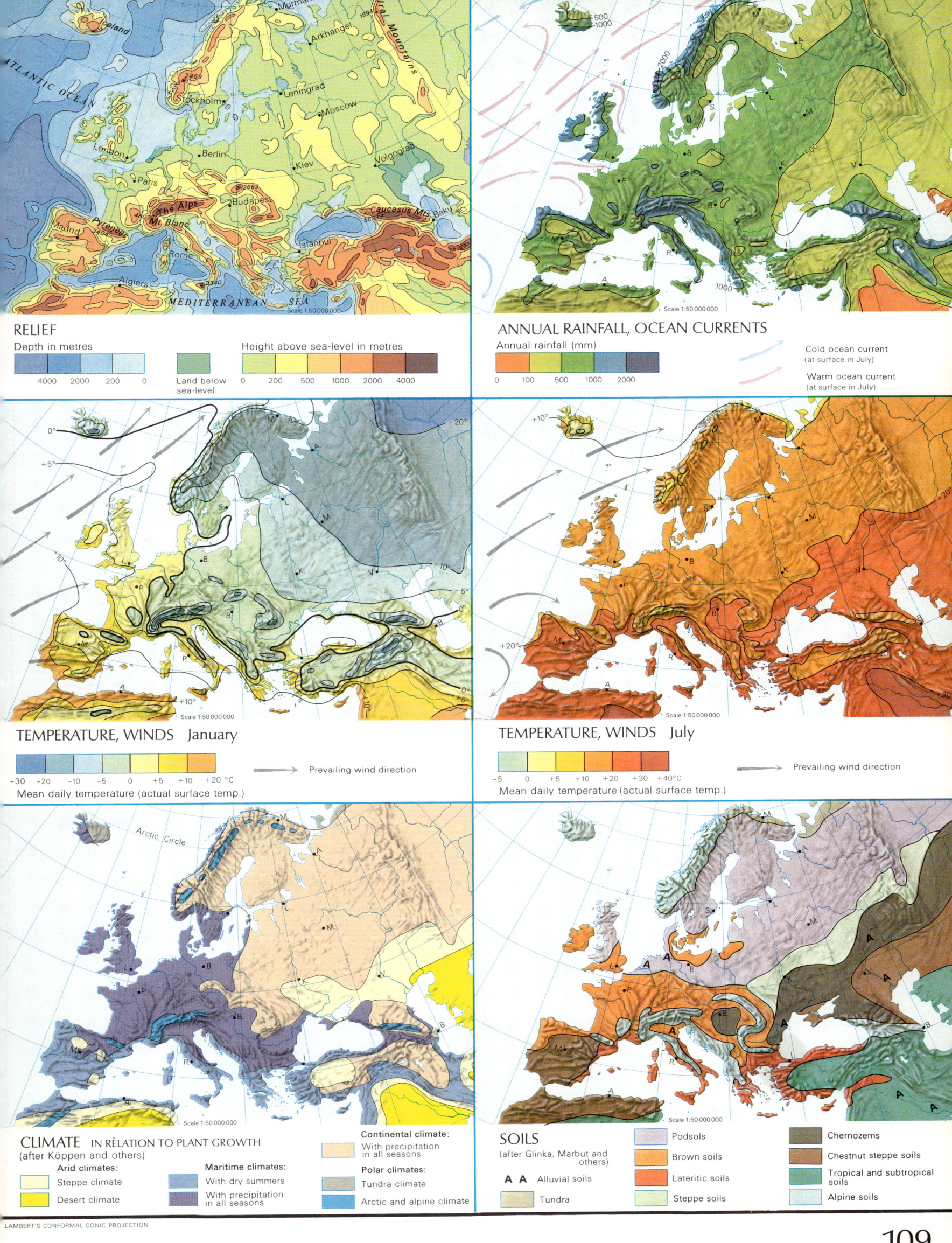

Depth in metres
4000 | 2000 | 200 | 0

Height above sea-level in metres
Land below sea-level | 0 | 200 | 500 | 1000 | 2000 | 4000

ANNUAL RAINFALL, OCEAN CURRENTS

Annual rainfall (mm)
0 | 100 | 500 | 1000 | 2000

Cold ocean current (at surface in July)
Warm ocean current (at surface in July)

TEMPERATURE, WINDS January

−30 | −20 | −10 | −5 | 0 | +5 | +10 | +20 °C

→ Prevailing wind direction

Mean daily temperature (actual surface temp.)

TEMPERATURE, WINDS July

−5 | 0 | +5 | +10 | +20 | +30 | +40 °C

→ Prevailing wind direction

Mean daily temperature (actual surface temp.)

CLIMATE IN RELATION TO PLANT GROWTH
(after Köppen and others)

Arid climates:
- Steppe climate
- Desert climate

Maritime climates:
- With dry summers
- With precipitation in all seasons

Continental climate:
- With precipitation in all seasons

Polar climates:
- Tundra climate
- Arctic and alpine climate

SOILS
(after Glinka, Marbut and others)

- Podsols
- Brown soils
- Lateritic soils
- Chernozems
- Chestnut steppe soils
- Tropical and subtropical soils
- A A Alluvial soils
- Tundra
- Steppe soils
- Alpine soils

LAMBERT'S CONFORMAL CONIC PROJECTION

109

THE BRITISH ISLES AND CENTRAL EUROPE

111

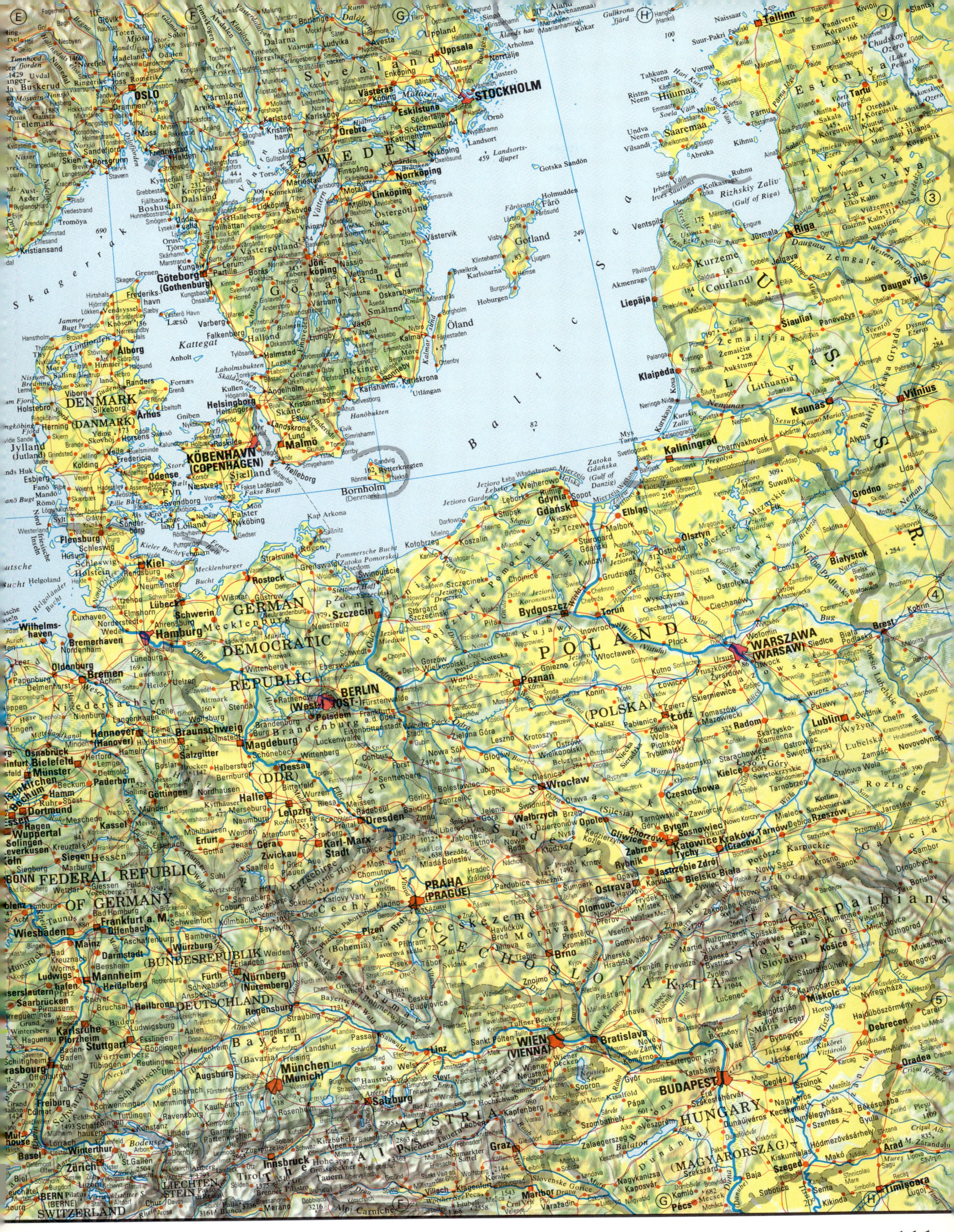

NORTHERN EUROPE

Scale 1:5 000 000

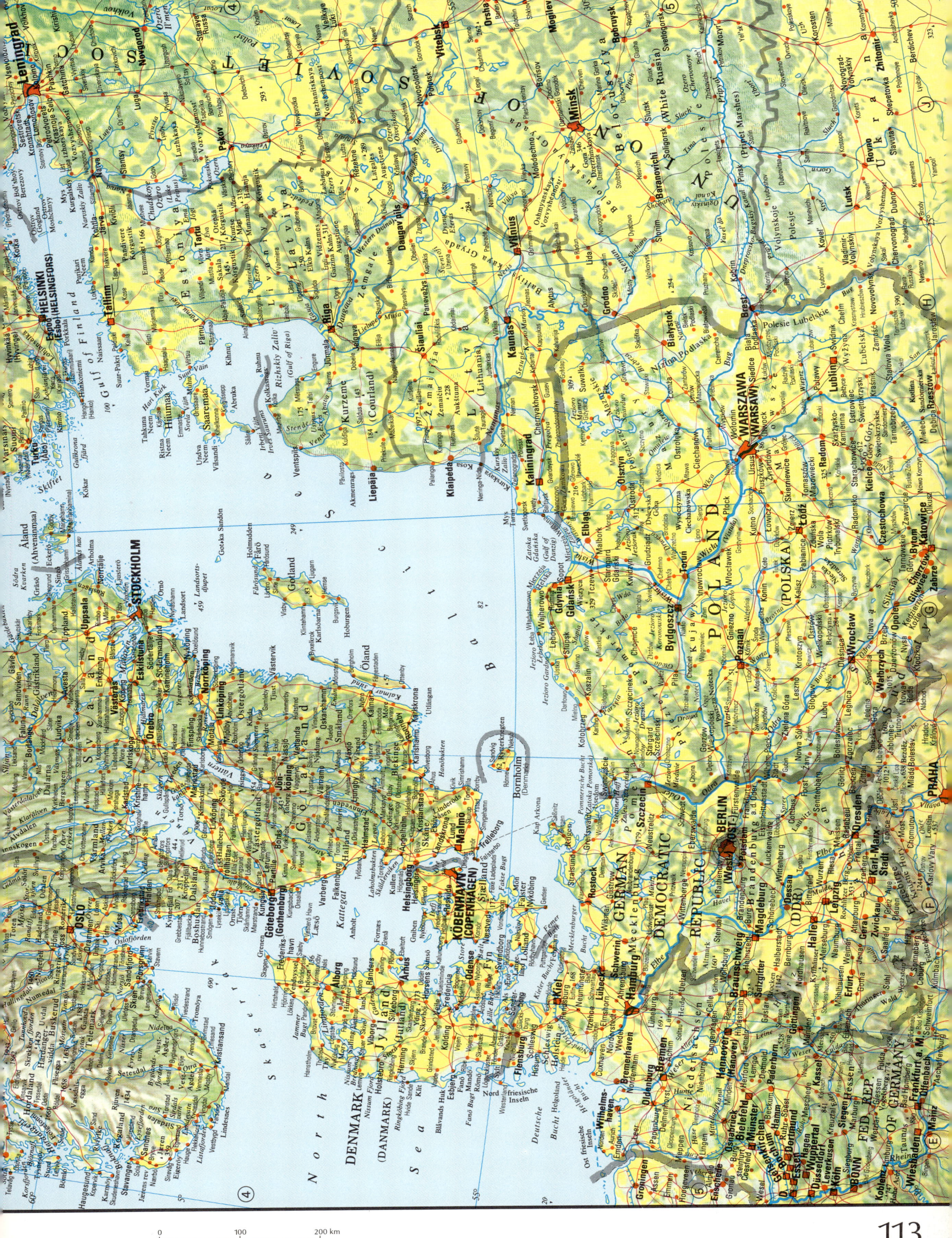

113

ATLANTIC OCEAN
Bay of Biscay
La Manche (English Channel)
UNITED KINGDOM
Channel Islands (U.K.)
FRANCE
PARIS
SPAIN
ESPAÑA
PORTUGAL
MADRID
LISBOA (LISBON)
ANDORRA
Islas Baleares (Balearic Islands) (Spain)
AL JAZĀ'IR (ALGIERS)
MOROCCO
MEDITER
Plymouth
Guernsey
Jersey
Brest
Nantes
Bordeaux
Toulouse
Montpellier
Perpignan
Barcelona
Valencia
Zaragoza
Bilbao
Santander
Oviedo
Gijón
La Coruña
Vigo
Porto (Oporto)
Coimbra
Salamanca
Valladolid
Burgos
Pamplona
Sevilla
Córdoba
Granada
Málaga
Cádiz
Murcia
Cartagena
Alicante
Palma
Mallorca
Ibiza
Formentera
Gibraltar (U.K.)
Ceuta (Sp.)
Tanger
Alborán (Sp.)
Cordillera Cantábrica
Pyrénées
Sierra Morena
Sierra Nevada
Massif Central
Golfe de Gascogne
Golfo de Cadiz
Estrecho de Gibraltar (Str. of Gibraltar)

FEDERAL REPUBLIC OF GERMANY
BUNDESREPUBLIK DEUTSCHLAND
LUXEMBOURG
CZECHOSLOVAKIA
AUSTRIA
HUNGARY (MAGYARORSZÁG)
SWITZERLAND
LIECHTENSTEIN
YUGOSLAVIA
ITALY (ITALIA)
SAN MARINO
MONACO
VATICAN STATE (CITTA DEL VATICANO)
TUNISIA
MALTA
Corse (Corsica) (Fr.)
Sardegna (Sardinia) (Italy)
Sicilia (Sicily)
Ligurian Sea
Tyrrhenian Sea
Adriatic Sea
MEDITERRANEAN SEA
Gulf of Venice
Golfo di Genova
Golfo di Taranto
Golfo di Manfredonia
Strait of Bonifacio
Canale di Sicilia
Canale di Malta
Alpi Carniche
Appennino
PRAHA (PRAGUE)
WIEN (VIENNA)
BUDAPEST
Bratislava
München (Munich)
Frankfurt a. M.
Stuttgart
Nürnberg (Nuremberg)
Salzburg
Innsbruck
Graz
Zagreb
Ljubljana
Sarajevo
Split
Bern (Berne)
Zürich
Genève
Lyon
Marseille
Nice
Torino (Turin)
Milano (Milan)
Genova (Genoa)
Venezia (Venice)
Trieste
Verona
Bologna
Firenze (Florence)
Pisa
Livorno
Ancona
Perugia
Pescara
ROMA (ROME)
Napoli (Naples)
Bari
Brindisi
Taranto
Salerno
Reggio di Calabria
Messina
Palermo
Catania
Siracusa
Cagliari
Sassari
Ajaccio
Bastia
Tunis
Bizerta
Annaba
Constantine
VALLETTA
Gozo
Pantelleria
Elba
Isole Eolie o Lipari
Stromboli
3500
3000

116 THE BALKANS

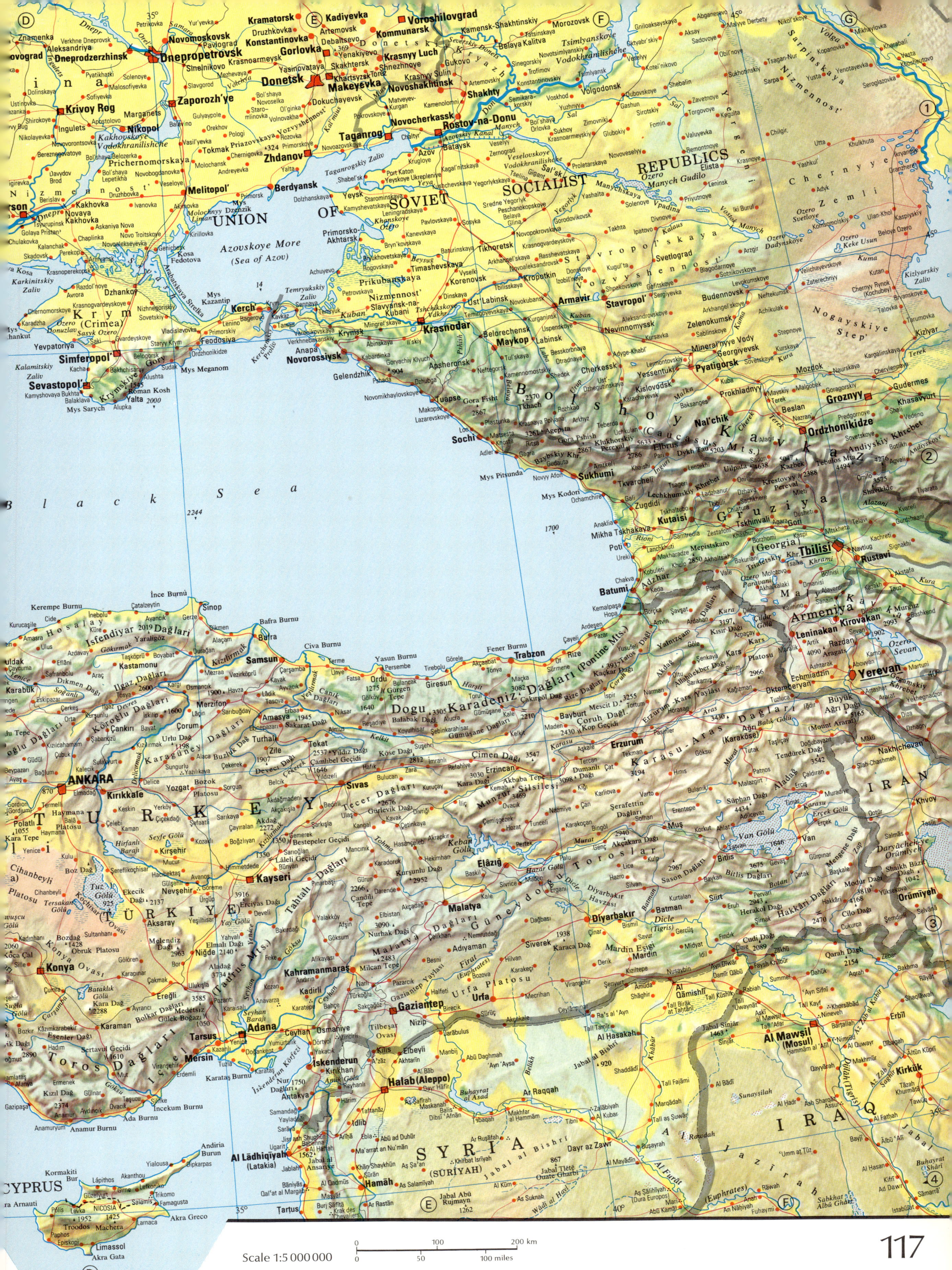

Scale 1:5 000 000 — 0 100 200 km; 0 50 100 miles

WESTERN SOVIET UNION

119

NORTHERN ASIA

121

122 SOUTHERN ASIA

LAMBERT'S AZIMUTHAL EQUAL-AREA PROJECTION

Scale 1:25 000 000

0 500 1000 km
0 200 400 600 miles

ASIA, economic

CLIMATE IN RELATION TO PLANT GROWTH
(after Köppen and others)

Tropical rain climates:
- Tropical rain forest climate
- Savanna climate

Arid climates:
- Steppe climate
- Desert climate

Maritime climates:
- With dry summers
- With dry winters
- With precipitation in all seasons

Continental climates:
- With precipitation in all seasons
- With dry winters

Polar climates:
- Tundra climate
- Arctic and alpine climate

Scale 1:90 000 000

ORGANIC PRODUCTION
10 5 1% of world production 1977-81 average.

- Wheat, rye
- Maize
- Rice
- Millet
- Potatoes
- Natural rubber
- Copra
- Ground nuts
- Palm oil
- Soya beans
- Cashew nuts
- Grapes
- Citrus fruits
- Bananas
- Dates
- Coffee
- Tea
- Cocoa
- Sugar cane
- Sugar beet
- Tobacco
- Cotton

10 5 million animals
- Cattle
- Sheep
- Pigs

- Arable land
- Pasture
- Commercial forestry
- Other forests
- Major fishing areas
- Other fishing areas
- Non-productive land
- Glacier

Scale 1:50 000 000
0   500   1000   2000 km
0   500   1000 miles

124

SOILS
(after Glinka, Marbut and others)

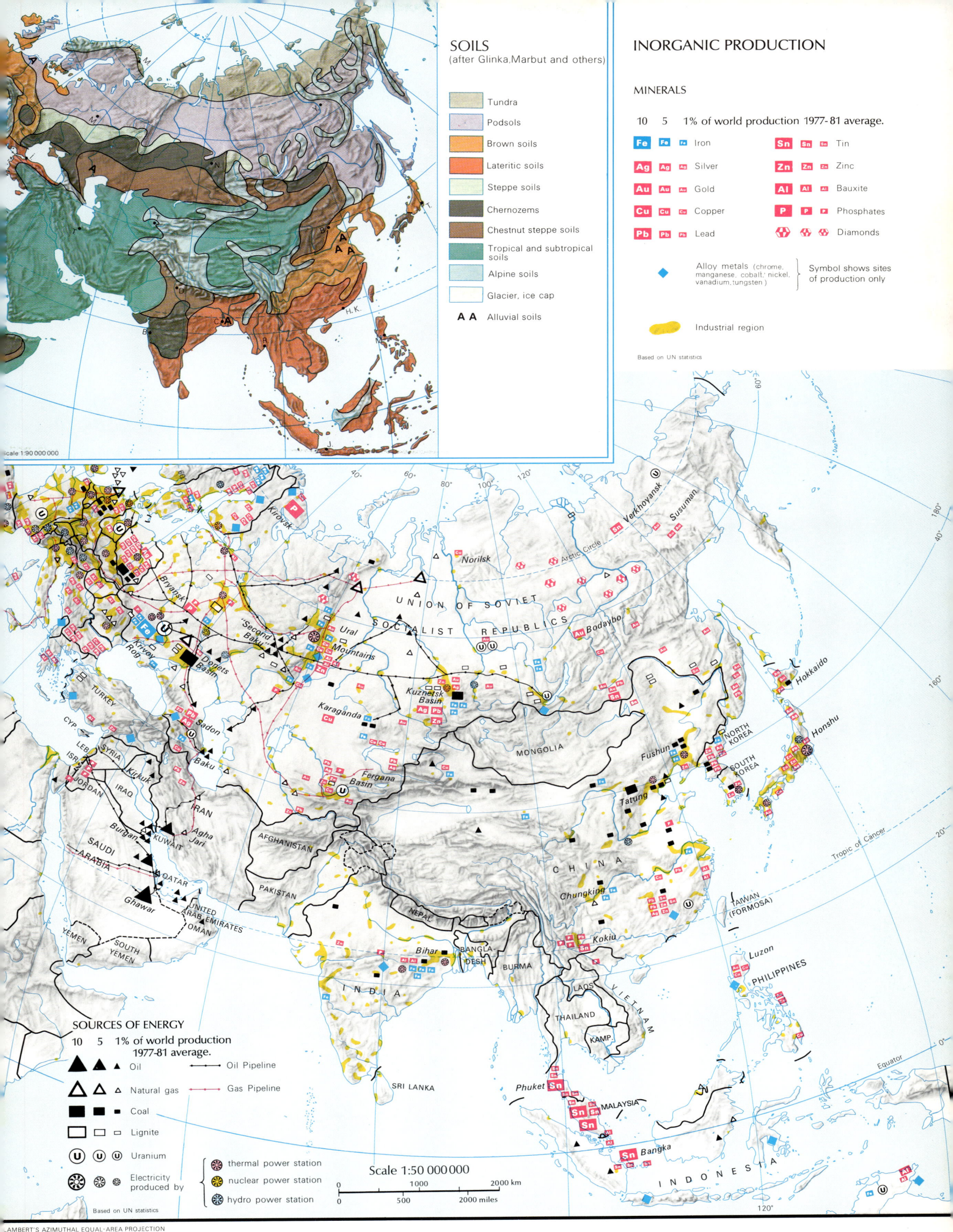

- Tundra
- Podsols
- Brown soils
- Lateritic soils
- Steppe soils
- Chernozems
- Chestnut steppe soils
- Tropical and subtropical soils
- Alpine soils
- Glacier, ice cap
- A A Alluvial soils

Scale 1:90 000 000

INORGANIC PRODUCTION

MINERALS

10 5 1% of world production 1977-81 average.

Fe	Iron	Sn	Tin
Ag	Silver	Zn	Zinc
Au	Gold	Al	Bauxite
Cu	Copper	P	Phosphates
Pb	Lead	◆	Diamonds

◆ Alloy metals (chrome, manganese, cobalt, nickel, vanadium, tungsten) — Symbol shows sites of production only

Industrial region

Based on UN statistics

SOURCES OF ENERGY

10 5 1% of world production 1977-81 average.

- ▲ Oil — Oil Pipeline
- △ Natural gas — Gas Pipeline
- ■ Coal
- ▭ Lignite
- Ⓤ Uranium
- ✶ Electricity produced by:
  - thermal power station
  - nuclear power station
  - hydro power station

Scale 1:50 000 000

Based on UN statistics

LAMBERT'S AZIMUTHAL EQUAL-AREA PROJECTION

125

ASIA, physical, population, political divisions

TEMPERATURE, WINDS

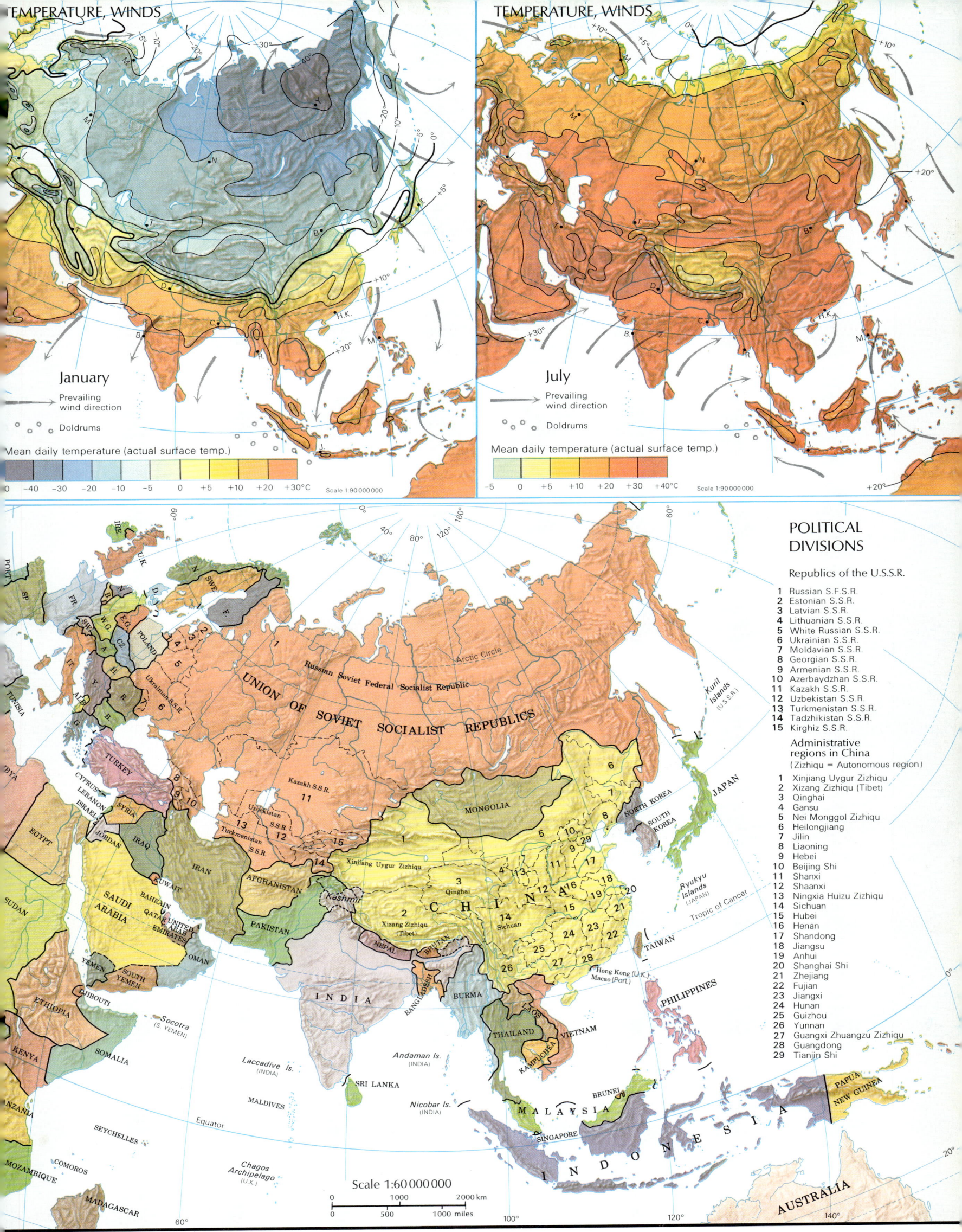

January
- → Prevailing wind direction
- ○ Doldrums

Mean daily temperature (actual surface temp.)

−40 −30 −20 −10 −5 0 +5 +10 +20 +30°C

Scale 1:90 000 000

TEMPERATURE, WINDS

July
- → Prevailing wind direction
- ○ Doldrums

Mean daily temperature (actual surface temp.)

−5 0 +5 +10 +20 +30 +40°C

Scale 1:90 000 000

POLITICAL DIVISIONS

Republics of the U.S.S.R.
1. Russian S.F.S.R.
2. Estonian S.S.R.
3. Latvian S.S.R.
4. Lithuanian S.S.R.
5. White Russian S.S.R.
6. Ukrainian S.S.R.
7. Moldavian S.S.R.
8. Georgian S.S.R.
9. Armenian S.S.R.
10. Azerbaydzhan S.S.R.
11. Kazakh S.S.R.
12. Uzbekistan S.S.R.
13. Turkmenistan S.S.R.
14. Tadzhikistan S.S.R.
15. Kirghiz S.S.R.

Administrative regions in China
(Zizhiqu = Autonomous region)

1. Xinjiang Uygur Zizhiqu
2. Xizang Zizhiqu (Tibet)
3. Qinghai
4. Gansu
5. Nei Monggol Zizhiqu
6. Heilongjiang
7. Jilin
8. Liaoning
9. Hebei
10. Beijing Shi
11. Shanxi
12. Shaanxi
13. Ningxia Huizu Zizhiqu
14. Sichuan
15. Hubei
16. Henan
17. Shandong
18. Jiangsu
19. Anhui
20. Shanghai Shi
21. Zhejiang
22. Fujian
23. Jiangxi
24. Hunan
25. Guizhou
26. Yunnan
27. Guangxi Zhuangzu Zizhiqu
28. Guangdong
29. Tianjin Shi

Scale 1:60 000 000

LAMBERT'S AZIMUTHAL EQUAL-AREA PROJECTION

128 THE MIDDLE EAST

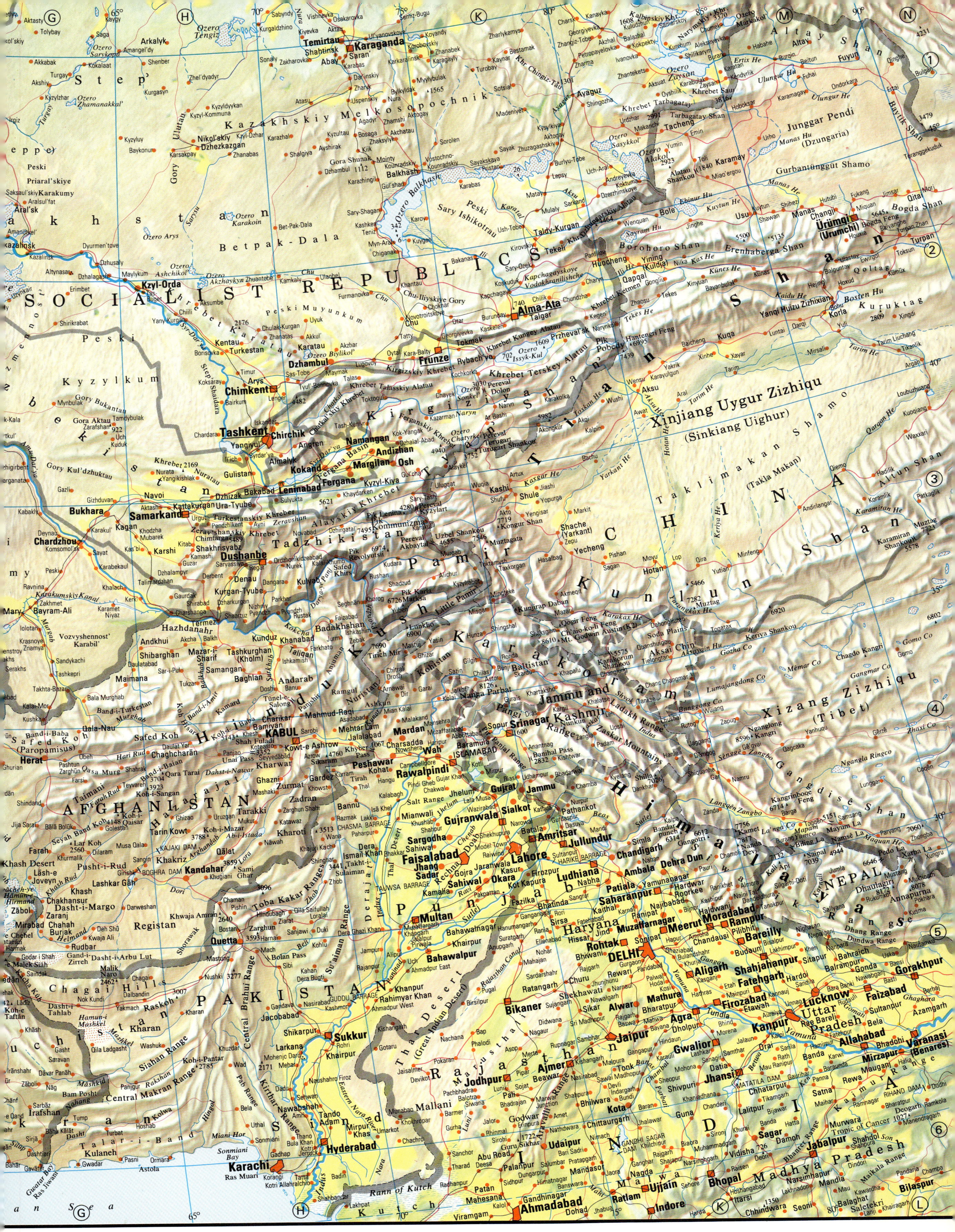

Scale 1:10 000 000

0 100 200 300 400 km

0 100 200 miles

UNION OF SOVIET SOCIALIST
MONGOLIA
(MONGOL ARD ULS)
Sredne Sibirskoye Ploskogor'ye
(Central Siberian Plateau)
Zapadno Sibirskoye Nizmennost'
(West Siberian Plain)
Severo Sibirskaya Nizmennost'
Poluostrov Taymyr
(Taymyr Peninsula)
Gory Putorana
Gory Byrranga
More Laptevykh
Poluostrov Yamal
(Yamal Peninsula)
Gydanskiy Poluostrov
Obskaya Guba
(Gulf of Ob')
Arctic Circle
Plato Syverma
Plato Putorana
Vilyuyskoye Plato
Anabarskoye Ploskogor'ye
Tunguska Plato
Prianagarskoye Plato
Yenisey
Lena
Angara
Vilyuy
Ozero Baykal
(Lake Baikal)
Bratskoye Vodokhranilishche
Vilyuyskoye Vodokhranilishche
Stanovoye Nagor'ye
Patomskoye Nagor'ye
Vitimskoye Ploskogor'ye
Yablonovyy Khrebet
Yablonovyy Range
Khrebet Khamar Daban
Zapadnyy Sayan
Vostochnyy Sayan
Tannu Ola
Altay
Hangayn Nuruu
Gichgeniyn Nuruu
Khrebet Ulan-Burgasy
Noril'sk
Nizhnevartovskoye
Tomsk
Novosibirsk
Kemerovo
Anzhero-Sudzhensk
Achinsk
Krasnoyarsk
Kansk
Leninsk-Kuznetskiy
Belovo
Kiselevsk
Prokop'yevsk
Novokuznetsk
Biysk
Abakan
Bratsk
Angarsk
Irkutsk
Ulan-Ude
Chita
Borzya
Manzhouli
ULAANBAATAR
(ULAN BATOR)
Hövsgöl Nuur
Hulun Nur
Buir Nur
Ural

131

CHINA AND JAPAN

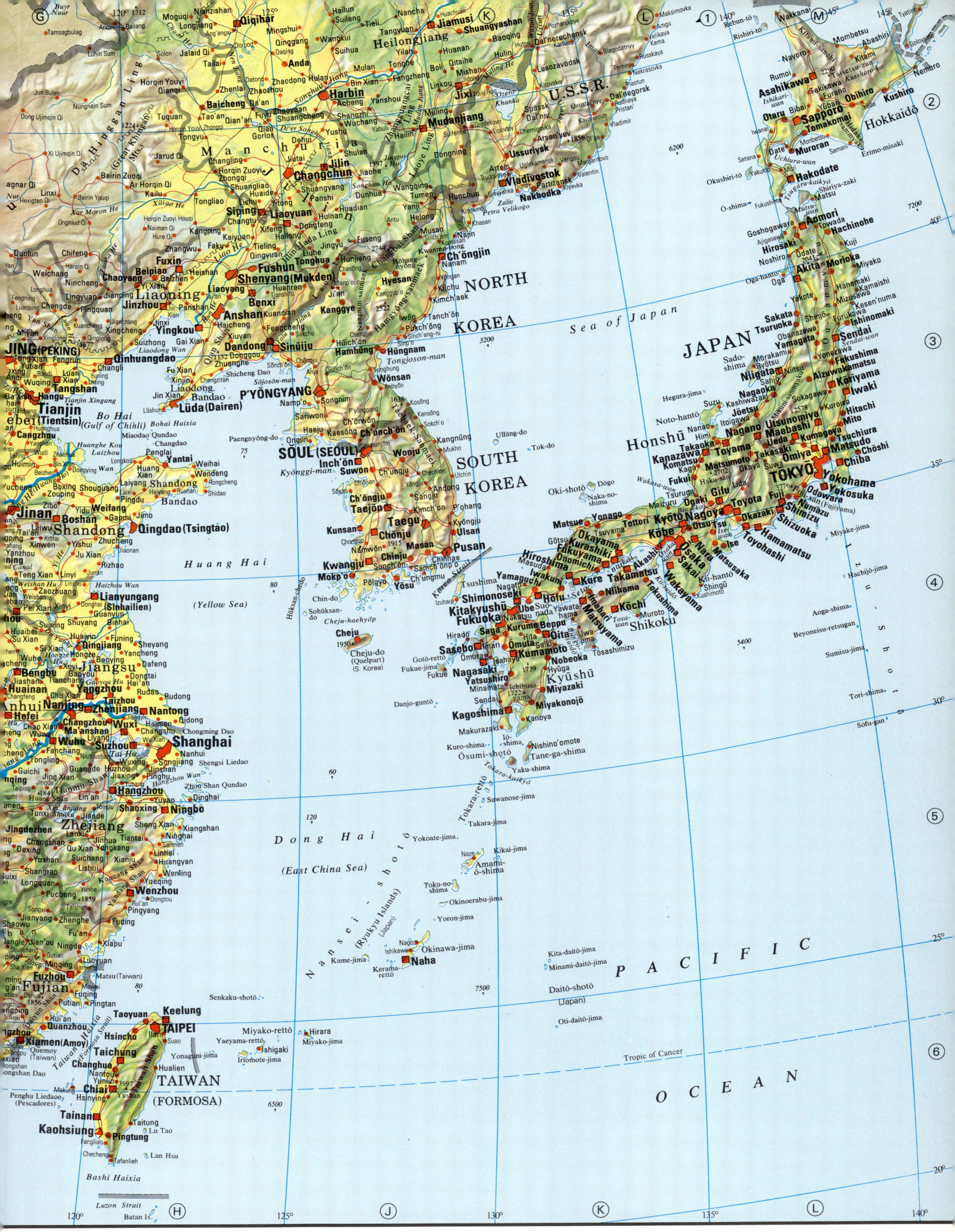

Scale 1:10 000 000 — 0 100 200 300 400 km; 0 100 200 miles

134 INDIA AND S-E ASIA

135

136 THE EAST INDIES

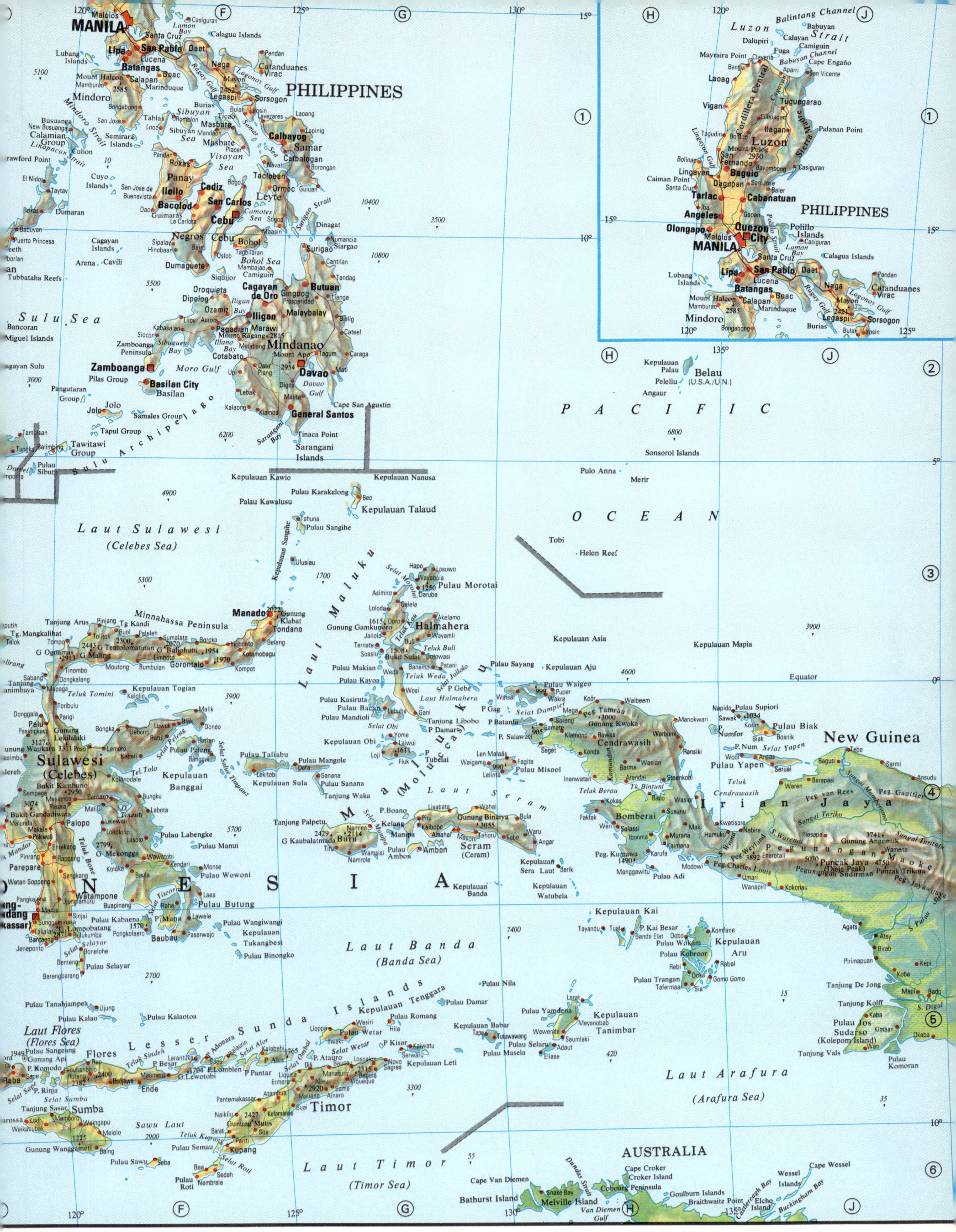

Scale 1:10 000 000

0 100 200 300 400 km

0 100 200 miles

138 AUSTRALASIA, environment, political divisions, population

POLITICAL DIVISIONS
Scale 1:60 000 000

POPULATION
Population distribution 1982
- 500 000 inhabitants
- ³ Figures show populations (cities with suburbs) in millions
- uninhabited (less than 1 person per sq. km)

Population increase per country 1972–1982: 0, 10, 20, 30, 40, 50 %
Average for Oceania 17%

© ESSELTE MAP SERVICE

139

RELIEF

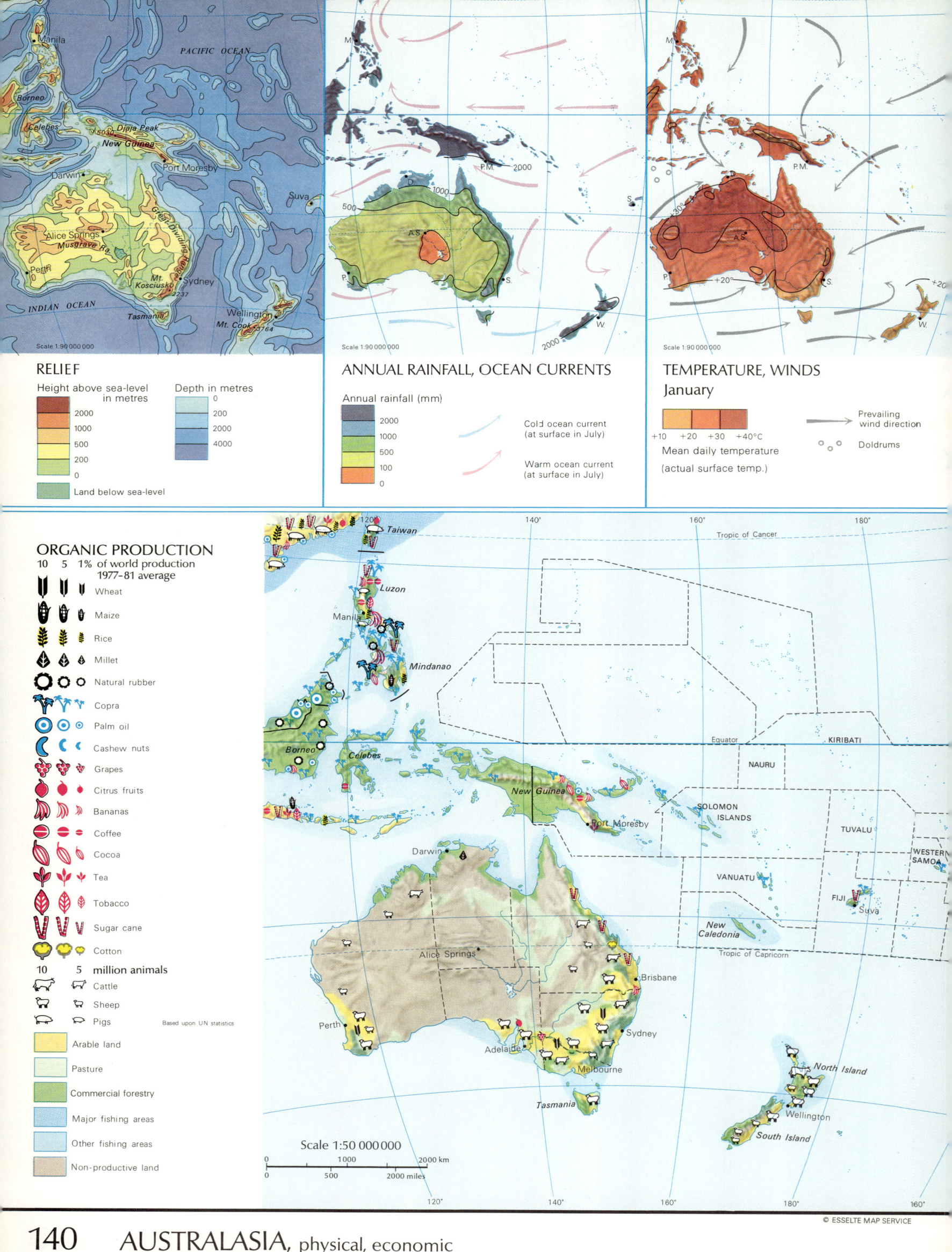

Height above sea-level in metres
- 2000
- 1000
- 500
- 200
- 0
- Land below sea-level

Depth in metres
- 0
- 200
- 2000
- 4000

Scale 1:90 000 000

ANNUAL RAINFALL, OCEAN CURRENTS

Annual rainfall (mm)
- 2000
- 1000
- 500
- 100
- 0

→ Cold ocean current (at surface in July)
→ Warm ocean current (at surface in July)

Scale 1:90 000 000

TEMPERATURE, WINDS
January

Mean daily temperature (actual surface temp.)
+10 +20 +30 +40°C

→ Prevailing wind direction
○○○ Doldrums

Scale 1:90 000 000

ORGANIC PRODUCTION

10 5 1% of world production
1977–81 average

- Wheat
- Maize
- Rice
- Millet
- Natural rubber
- Copra
- Palm oil
- Cashew nuts
- Grapes
- Citrus fruits
- Bananas
- Coffee
- Cocoa
- Tea
- Tobacco
- Sugar cane
- Cotton

10 5 million animals
- Cattle
- Sheep
- Pigs

Based upon UN statistics

- Arable land
- Pasture
- Commercial forestry
- Major fishing areas
- Other fishing areas
- Non-productive land

Scale 1:50 000 000

140 AUSTRALASIA, physical, economic

© ESSELTE MAP SERVICE

TEMPERATURE, WINDS
July

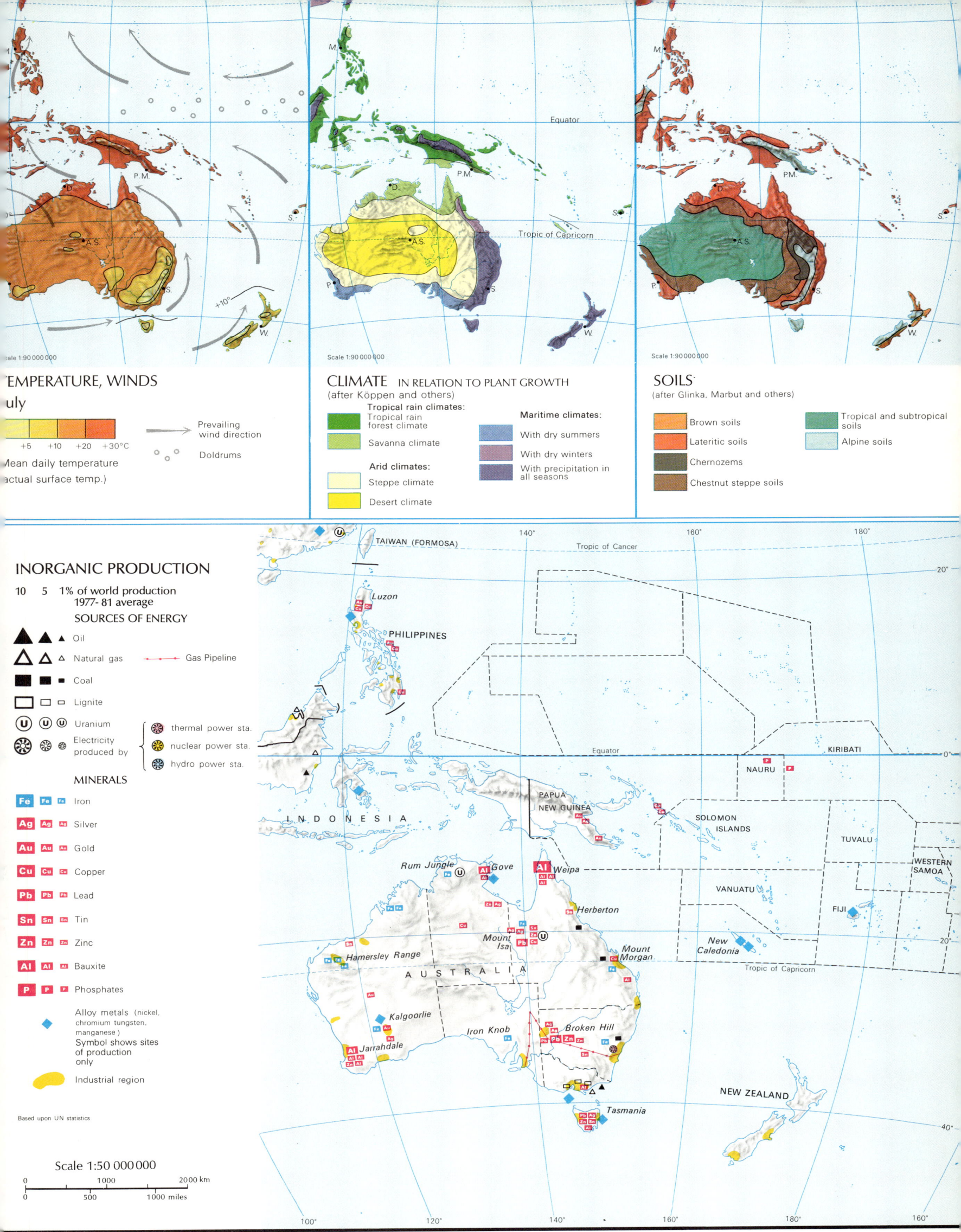

| +5 | +10 | +20 | +30°C |

→ Prevailing wind direction
○ Doldrums

Mean daily temperature (actual surface temp.)

CLIMATE IN RELATION TO PLANT GROWTH
(after Köppen and others)

Tropical rain climates:
- Tropical rain forest climate
- Savanna climate

Arid climates:
- Steppe climate
- Desert climate

Maritime climates:
- With dry summers
- With dry winters
- With precipitation in all seasons

SOILS
(after Glinka, Marbut and others)

- Brown soils
- Lateritic soils
- Chernozems
- Chestnut steppe soils
- Tropical and subtropical soils
- Alpine soils

Scale 1:90 000 000

INORGANIC PRODUCTION

10 5 1% of world production
1977-81 average

SOURCES OF ENERGY
- ▲ ▲ ▲ Oil
- △ △ △ Natural gas — Gas Pipeline
- ■ ■ ■ Coal
- ▭ ▭ ▭ Lignite
- Ⓤ Ⓤ Ⓤ Uranium
- ✺ ✺ ✺ Electricity produced by:
  - thermal power sta.
  - nuclear power sta.
  - hydro power sta.

MINERALS
- Fe Iron
- Ag Silver
- Au Gold
- Cu Copper
- Pb Lead
- Sn Tin
- Zn Zinc
- Al Bauxite
- P   Phosphates

◆ Alloy metals (nickel, chromium tungsten, manganese)
Symbol shows sites of production only

▨ Industrial region

Based upon UN statistics

Scale 1:50 000 000
0 — 1000 — 2000 km
0 — 500 — 1000 miles

LAMBERT'S AZIMUTHAL EQUAL-AREA PROJECTION

141

142 AUSTRALIA

143

144 NEW GUINEA AND NEW ZEALAND

Map 145 — Southwest Pacific

Main map labels

PACIFIC OCEAN

SOLOMON ISLANDS

VANUATU (New Hebrides)

Nouvelle-Calédonie (New Caledonia) (France)

NEW ZEALAND

North Island

Coral Sea

Solomon Sea

Tropic of Capricorn

Equator

Place names (north section)

Kapingamaringi · Nauru · Banaba (Ocean I.)

Emira · New Hanover · Kavieng · Meteran · Tabar Islands · Lakuramau · Djaul · Silom · Lihir Group · New Ireland · Namatanai · Danu · Tanga Islands · 1871 · Feni Islands · Cape Lambert · Rabaul · Taron · Green Islands · Nuguria Islands · Karavia · Gazette Peninsula · Lembon · Cape Saint George · Kilinailau Islands · Tauu Islands · Nukumanu Islands · Kimbe Bay · Marunga · Sampun · Buka · Gagan · Sohano · Hoskins · Pal Malmal · Mount Balbi 2743 · Bougainville · Ontong Java · Whiteman Range · Ovul · Torokina · Kieta · Bougainville Strait · New Britain · Taki · Mamagota · Choiseul · Panggoe · Alu · Fauro · Sasamungga · 1067 · Vaghena · Roncador · Planet Deep · Mono · Vella Lavella · Kolombangara · Kia · New Georgia Sound · Santa Isabel · Bradley Reefs · Ranongga · 1128 · Dadali · Trobriand or Kiriwina Islands · Simbo · Gizo · New Georgia · Sughe · Stewart Islands · Nelson · Rendova · Vangunu · San Jorge · Malaita · Fergusson · Madau · Woodlark · Tetepare · Nggatokae · Russell Islands · Aoki · Wapompiwa · Guasopa · Florida Islands · 1433 · D'Entrecasteaux Islands · Maravovo · HONIARA · Tetere · Apio · Marimasike · West Hunt Strait · Normanby Island · Ulawa · Duff Islands · Goschen Strait · Louisiade · Misima Island · Guadalcanal · 2331 · Pio · Reef Islands · Santa Cruz · Samarai · Archipelago · Deboyne Island · Pocklington Reef · Kirakira · 1250 · Nea · 549 · Nendo · Islands · San Cristobal · Santa Ana · Bellona · Rennell · Utupua · Tagula · Rossel Island · Tagula Island · Vanikolo Islands · Anuta · Fataka · Tikopia

Vanuatu / New Caledonia

Torres Islands · Vetaounde · Vanoua Lava · Banks Islands · Lakon · Espiritu Santo 1879 · Maewo · Luganville · Pentecôte · Bougainville Strait · Norsoup · Ranon · Ambrym · Malakula 1879 · Epi · VILA · Efate · Huon · Récifs d'Entrecasteaux · Grand Passage · Erromango · Potnarhvin · Récifs de l'Astrolabe · Iles Belep · Tanna · Aniwa · Futuna · Loméméri · Mont Panié 1628 · Koumac · Ouvéa · Iles Loyauté (Loyalty Islands) · Lifou · We · Pouébo · Poya · Tiga · La Roche · Bourail · Aoumou · Thio · Maré · Bouloupari · 1618 · Nouméa · Yaté-Village · Ile des Pins · Durand · Ile Walpole · Ile Matthew · Ile Hunter

New Zealand inset

Three Kings Islands · Te Hapua · North Cape · Cape Maria van Diemen · Great Exhibition Bay · Awanui · Kaitaia · Kaikohe · Russell · Cape Brett · Whangarei · Dargaville · Ruawai · Great Barrier Island · Wellsford · Coromandel Channel · Kaipara Harbour · Helensville · Devonport · **Auckland** · Coromandel Peninsula · Maukatu · Thames · Waihi · Cape Runaway · **Hamilton** · Bay of Plenty · Hikurangi 1754 · East Cape · Albatross Point · Tauranga · Whakatane · Opotiki · Tokomaru Bay · Te Kuiti · Kawerau · Rotorua · NATIONAL PARK · Gisborne · North Taranaki Bight · Taupo · Makorako · Wairoa · New Plymouth · Waitara · Mahia Peninsula · Cape Egmont · Mount Egmont 2518 · Hawke Bay · South Taranaki Bight · 1722 · Napier · Cape Kidnappers · Wanganui · Hastings · Waipukurau · Marton · Dannevirke · Cape Farewell · Levin · Collingwood · D'Urville I. · Palmerston North · ABEL TASMAN NATIONAL PARK · Masterton · Whakatake · The Twins · Motueka · Porirua · Karamea · Mount 1875 · Nelson · Blenheim · **Wellington** · Red Hill · Cape Palliser · Karamea Bight · Mount Owen 1790 · Cook Strait · Cape Foulwind · LAKES NATIONAL PARK · Westport · Cape Campbell · 1826 · Manakau 2610 · Greymouth · Springs Junction · Kaikoura · Hokitika · Southern Alps · Waipara · Cheviot · Mount Arrowsmith · Pegasus Bay · 2795 · **Christchurch** · Banks Peninsula · Canterbury Plains · Timaru · Canterbury Bight · Chatham 284 · Chatham Islands (New Zealand) · Pitt · Waimate · Hampden · Palmerston · Oamaru · Port Chalmers · Dunedin

Scale 1:10 000 000

0 100 200 300 400 km
0 100 200 miles

145

146 OCEANIA

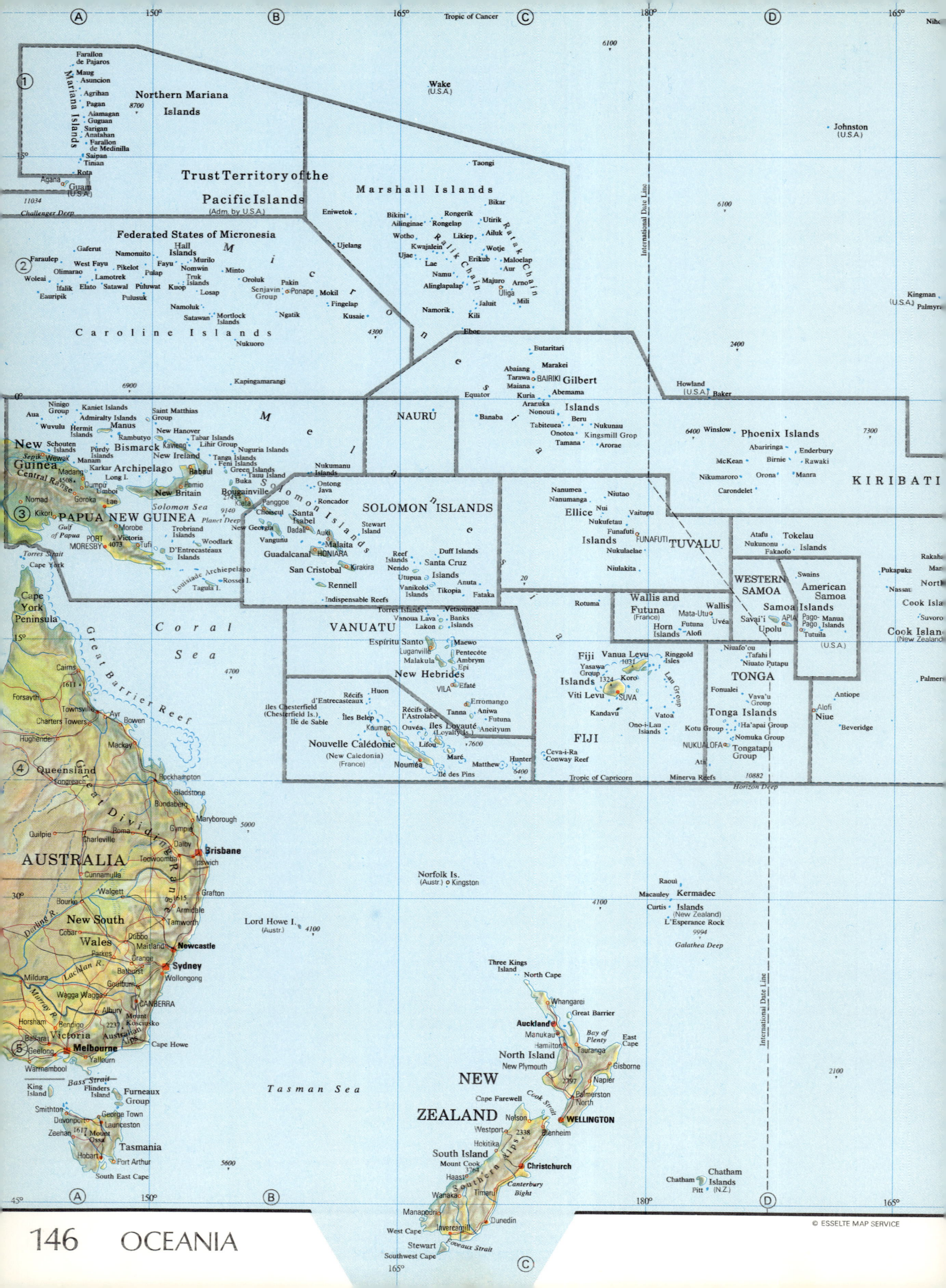

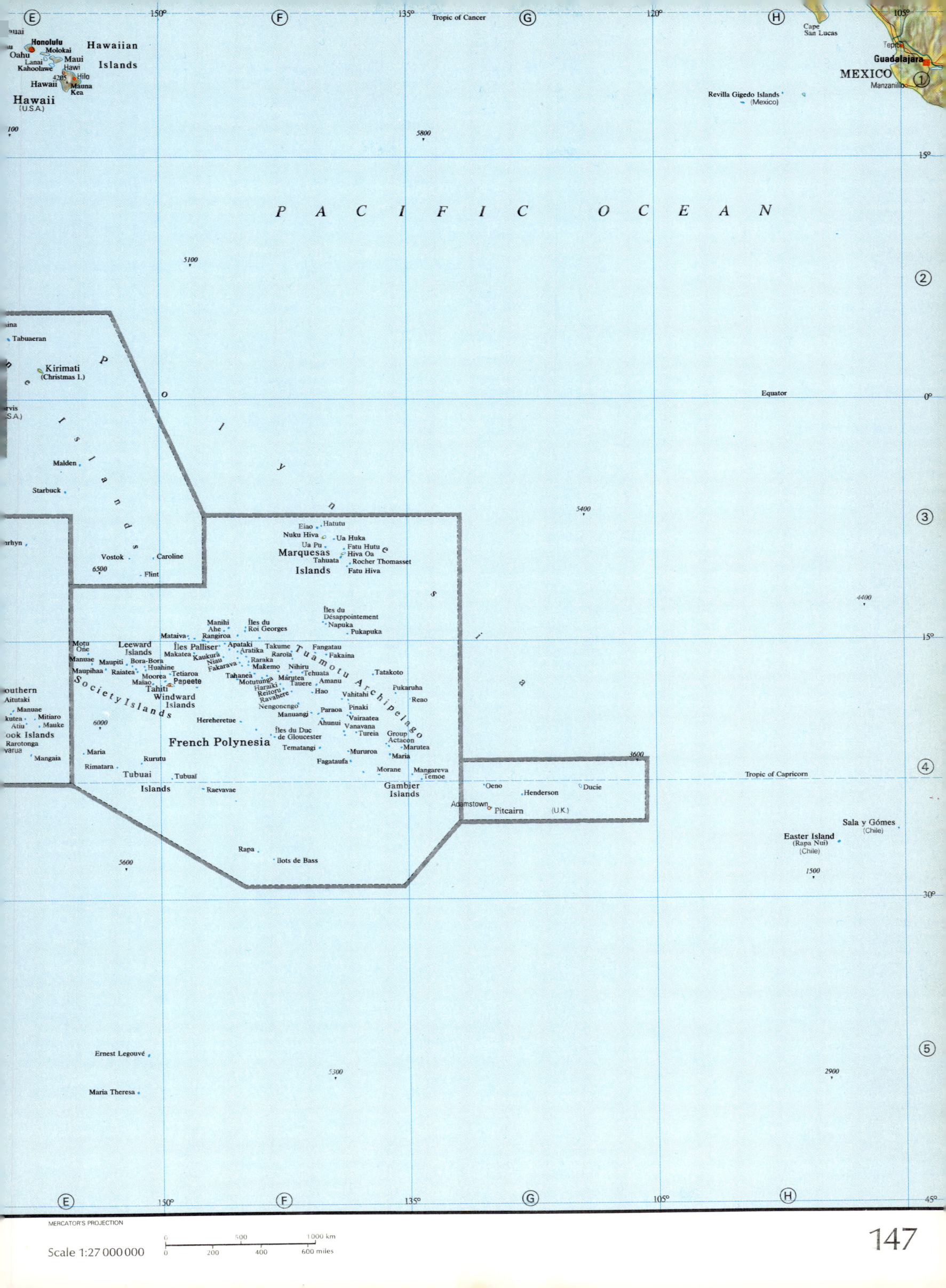

Pacific Ocean — French Polynesia and Hawaiian Islands

Hawaiian Islands (U.S.A.)
- Honolulu
- Oahu
- Molokai
- Lanai
- Maui
- Kahoolawe
- Hawi
- Hilo
- Hawaii
- Mauna Kea (4205)

HAWAII (U.S.A.)

Mexico
- Cape San Lucas
- Tepic
- Guadalajara
- Manzanillo
- Revilla Gigedo Islands (Mexico)

PACIFIC OCEAN

Line Islands
- Tabuaeran
- Kirimati (Christmas I.)
- Jarvis (U.S.A.)
- Malden
- Starbuck

French Polynesia

Marquesas Islands
- Eiao, Hatutu
- Nuku Hiva, Ua Huka
- Ua Pu, Fatu Hutu
- Hiva Oa
- Tahuata, Rocher Thomasset
- Fatu Hiva

Tuamotu Archipelago
- Vostok, Caroline
- Flint
- Manihi, Îles du Roi Georges
- Ahe, Rangiroa
- Mataiva
- Îles du Désappointement
- Napuka, Pukapuka
- Îles Palliser, Apataki, Takume, Fangatau
- Makatea, Kaukura, Aratika, Raroia, Fakaina
- Niau, Raraka
- Huahine, Makemo, Nihiru, Tatakoto
- Tahanea, Tehuata
- Tetiaroa, Motutunga, Marutea, Amanu
- Maiao, Haraiki, Tauere, Hao
- Papeete, Reitoru, Vahitahi, Pukaruha
- Ravahere, Reao
- Nengonengo, Pinaki
- Manuangi, Paraoa, Vairaatea
- Ahunui, Vanavana
- Tureia
- Hereheretue, Group Actaeon, Marutea
- Tematangi, Mururoa
- Morane, Mangareva, Temoe
- Fagataufa

Society Islands
- Motu One, Leeward Islands
- Manuae, Maupiti, Bora-Bora
- Maupihaa, Raiatea, Moorea
- Tahiti, Windward Islands

Tubuai Islands (Austral)
- Maria
- Rimatara, Kurutu
- Tubuai
- Raevavae
- Rapa
- Îlots de Bass

Gambier Islands
- Mangareva

Cook Islands (Southern)
- Aitutaki
- Manuae, Mitiaro
- Atiu, Mauke
- Rarotonga
- Mangaia

Pitcairn (U.K.)
- Oeno, Henderson, Ducie
- Adamstown
- Pitcairn

Chile
- Easter Island (Rapa Nui) (Chile)
- Sala y Gómes (Chile)

- Ernest Legouvé
- Maria Theresa

Tropic of Cancer
Equator
Tropic of Capricorn

MERCATOR'S PROJECTION
Scale 1:27 000 000
0 500 1000 km
0 200 400 600 miles

147

148 AFRICA, environment, political divisions, population

POLITICAL DIVISIONS
Scale 1:60 000 000

POPULATION

Population distribution 1982
- • 500 000 inhabitants
- ● 5 Figures show populations (cities with suburbs) in millions
- uninhabited (less than 1 person per sq. km)

Population increase per country 1972–1982
%
- 50
- 40
- 30
- 20 — Average for Africa 28%
- 10
- 0

© Esselte Map Service

ALGIERS
TUNISIA
TUNIS
ITALY
Palermo
Mt. Etna
Catania
VALLETTA
MALTA
GREECE
ATHENS
Crete
TURKEY
ANKARA
Izmir
Adana
CYPRUS
NICOSIA
SYRIA
Aleppo
DAMASCUS
LEBANON
BEIRUT
ISRAEL
Tel Aviv-Yafo
JERUSALEM
AMMAN
JORDAN
IRAQ
BAGHDAD
Mosul
R. Tigris
R. Euphrates
Basra
KUWAIT
IRAN
TEHRAN
Esfahan
Shiraz
Zagros Mountains
Mediterranean Sea
TRIPOLI
Benghazi
Tripolitania
Cyrenaica
LIBYA
Fezzan
Libyan Desert
Kufra Oases
Alexandria
Port Said
Suez Canal
CAIRO
Giza
Suez
Sinai Pen.
Qattara Depr.
EGYPT
Aswan
L. Nasser
Wadi Halfa
Nubian Desert
Port Sudan
Nubia
Red Sea
Hejaz
Nafud
SAUDI ARABIA
RIYADH
Nejd
Jiddah
Mecca
Medina
Rub al Khali
Persian Gulf
BAHRAIN
QATAR
DOHA
UNITED ARAB EMIRATES
Gulf of Oman
MUSCAT
OMAN
Tropic of Cancer
YEMEN
SAN'A
SOUTH YEMEN
ADEN
Hadramawt
Gulf of Aden
Socotra (S.Yemen)
Ahaggar
Tamanrasset
Sahara
Aïr
Tibesti
Emi Koussi
Faya-Largeau
Agadez
NIGER
CHAD
L. Chad
N'DJAMENA
R. Chari
SUDAN
Omdurman
KHARTOUM
R. Atbara
Blue Nile
White Nile
El Obeid
El Fasher
Marra Mts.
Eritrea
Asmara
Massawa
Ras Dashan
L. Tana
Gondar
DJIBOUTI
Berbera
Hargeisa
ADDIS ABABA
ETHIOPIA
Ogaden
SOMALIA
MOGADISHU
R. Juba
NIGERIA
Kano
Zaria
Kaduna
Jos
Sokoto
Maiduguri
R. Niger
R. Benue
Ibadan
Ogbomosho
LAGOS
Enugu
Onitsha
Port Harcourt
Adamaoua Mts.
CAMEROON
Mt. Cameroon
YAOUNDÉ
Douala
Bioko
MALABO
EQUATORIAL GUINEA
SÃO TOMÉ AND PRINCIPE
GABON
LIBREVILLE
Oubangui-Chari
CENTRAL AFRICAN REPUBLIC
BANGUI
R. Oubangui
R. Uele
R. Zaire
CONGO
R. Congo
BRAZZAVILLE
KINSHASA
Pointe Noire
Cabinda (Angola)
ZAIRE
L. Mai-Ndombe
Kisangani
Boyoma Falls
Kananga
Mbuji-Mayi
R. Kasai
R. Lualaba
Shaba
Lubumbashi
Kolwezi
UGANDA
KAMPALA
L. Albert
Kabarega Falls
Mount Elgon
Mt. Ruwenzori
L. Rutanzige (L. Edward)
Lake Kivu
RWANDA
KIGALI
BURUNDI
BUJUMBURA
Lake Victoria
KENYA
L. Turkana
NAIROBI
Mount Kenya
Mt. Kilimanjaro
Mombasa
SERENGETI NAT. PARK
TANZANIA
Masai Steppe
Dodoma
Tabora
L. Tanganyika
Rift Valley
Zanzibar
DAR ES SALAAM
Pemba I.
Equator
LUANDA
ANGOLA
R. Cuanza
Lobito
Benguela
Huambo
R. Cunene
R. Cubango
R. Kwango
ZAMBIA
LUSAKA
R. Kafue
R. Zambezi
Kitwe
Ndola
L. Bangweulu
L. Mweru
L. Malawi
MALAWI
LILONGWE
Blantyre
R. Ruvuma
MOZAMBIQUE
Mozambique Channel
L. Kariba
Victoria Falls
HARARE
ZIMBABWE
Bulawayo
Mutare
Beira
Ovambo
NAMIBIA
Namib Desert
WINDHOEK
Swakopmund
Walvis Bay (S. Africa)
Caprivi Strip
Okavango Swamp
Makgadikgadi Pans
BOTSWANA
Kalahari Desert
GABORONE
R. Limpopo
KRUGER NAT. PARK
PRETORIA
Johannesburg
MAPUTO
MBABANE
SWAZILAND
R. Vaal
R. Orange
Kimberley
Bloemfontein
MASERU
LESOTHO
Drakensberg
Durban
Pietermaritzburg
Richards Bay
REP. SOUTH AFRICA
CAPE TOWN
Cape of Good Hope
C. Agulhas
Port Elizabeth
East London
Lüderitz
MORONI
COMORO ISLANDS
Mayotte (France)
MADAGASCAR
ANTANANARIVO
Mahajanga
Toamasina
Fianarantsoa
Toliara
Tropic of Capricorn
C. d'Ambre
Antseranana
Mt. Tsaratanana
C. Sainte Marie
INDIAN OCEAN
SEYCHELLES
VICTORIA
Amirante Is. (Sey.)
Aldrabra Is. (Sey.)
Tromelin (Reun.)
MAURITIUS
PORT LOUIS
Réunion (France)
St. Denis
ATLANTIC OCEAN
Gulf of Guinea
C. Guardafui
MILLER'S STEREOGRAPHIC PROJECTION
Scale 1:25 000 000
0 500 1000 km
0 200 400 600 miles

Legend (Relief)

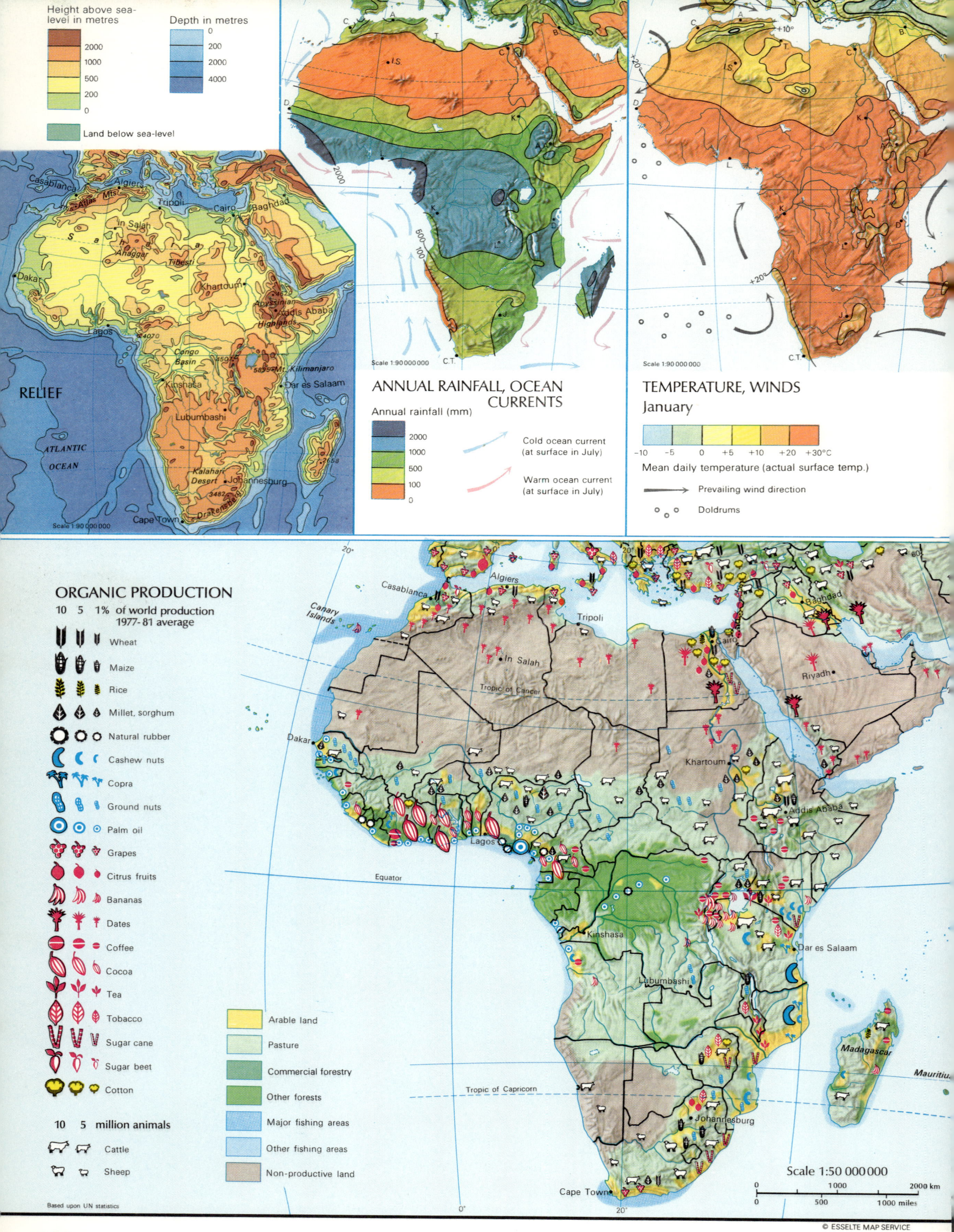

Height above sea-level in metres
- 2000
- 1000
- 500
- 200
- 0

Depth in metres
- 0
- 200
- 2000
- 4000

Land below sea-level

RELIEF

Scale 1:90 000 000

Places labelled: Casablanca, Algiers, Tripoli, Cairo, Baghdad, Atlas Mts., In Salah, Ahaggar, Tibesti, Dakar, Khartoum, Abyssinian Highlands, Addis Ababa, Lagos, Congo Basin, Kinshasa, Mt. Kilimanjaro, Dar es Salaam, Lubumbashi, Kalahari Desert, Johannesburg, Drakensberg, Cape Town, Atlantic Ocean

ANNUAL RAINFALL, OCEAN CURRENTS

Scale 1:90 000 000

Annual rainfall (mm)
- 2000
- 1000
- 500
- 100
- 0

→ Cold ocean current (at surface in July)
→ Warm ocean current (at surface in July)

TEMPERATURE, WINDS

January

Scale 1:90 000 000

Mean daily temperature (actual surface temp.): −10, −5, 0, +5, +10, +20, +30°C

→ Prevailing wind direction
○ ○ Doldrums

ORGANIC PRODUCTION

10 5 1% of world production 1977–81 average

- Wheat
- Maize
- Rice
- Millet, sorghum
- Natural rubber
- Cashew nuts
- Copra
- Ground nuts
- Palm oil
- Grapes
- Citrus fruits
- Bananas
- Dates
- Coffee
- Cocoa
- Tea
- Tobacco
- Sugar cane
- Sugar beet
- Cotton

10 5 million animals
- Cattle
- Sheep

Based upon UN statistics

- Arable land
- Pasture
- Commercial forestry
- Other forests
- Major fishing areas
- Other fishing areas
- Non-productive land

Scale 1:50 000 000
0   1000   2000 km
0   500   1000 miles

© ESSELTE MAP SERVICE

150 AFRICA, physical, economic

TEMPERATURE, WINDS July

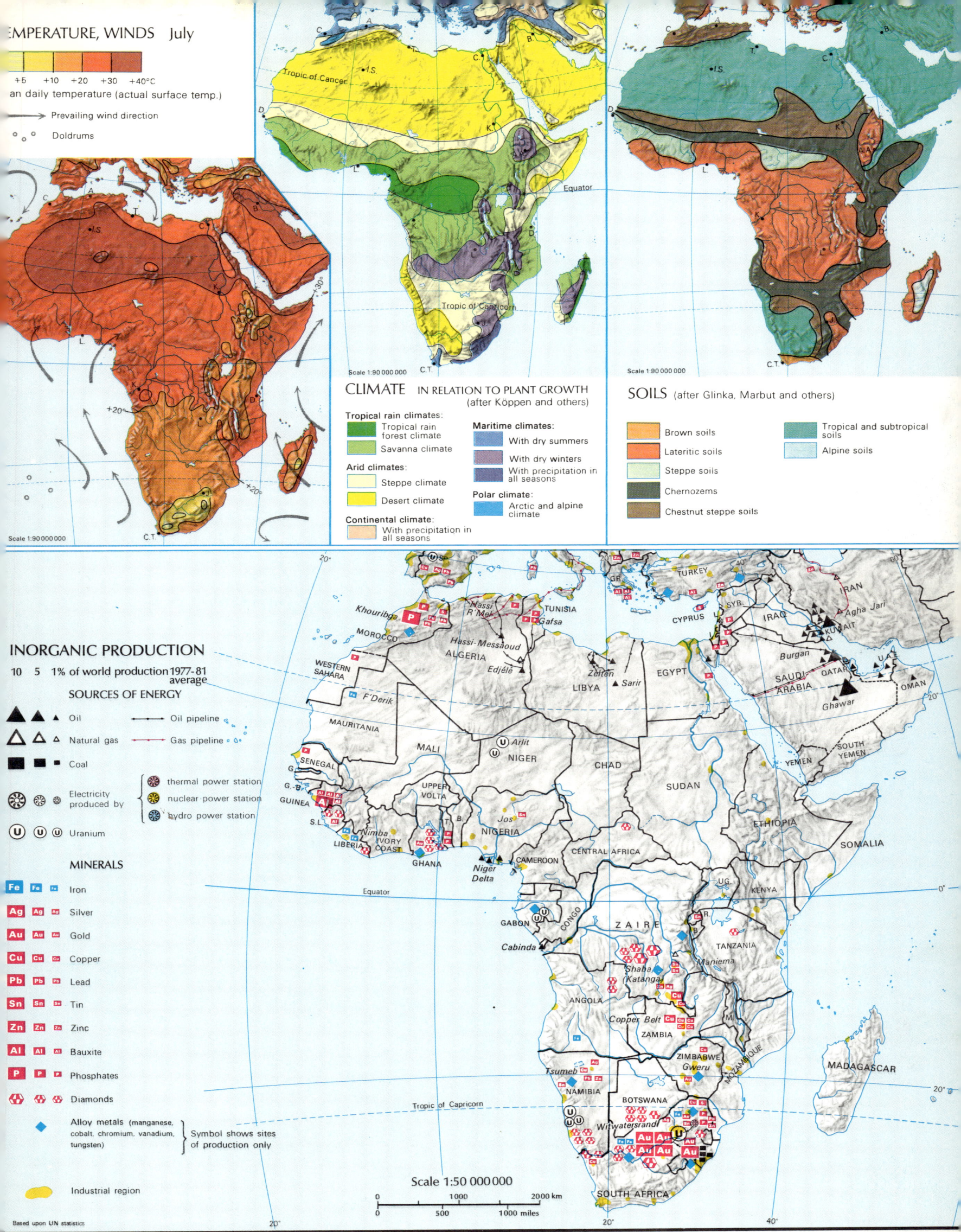

- +5 +10 +20 +30 +40°C
- Mean daily temperature (actual surface temp.)
- → Prevailing wind direction
- ° Doldrums

Scale 1:90 000 000

CLIMATE IN RELATION TO PLANT GROWTH
(after Köppen and others)

Tropical rain climates:
- Tropical rain forest climate
- Savanna climate

Arid climates:
- Steppe climate
- Desert climate

Continental climate:
- With precipitation in all seasons

Maritime climates:
- With dry summers
- With dry winters
- With precipitation in all seasons

Polar climate:
- Arctic and alpine climate

SOILS (after Glinka, Marbut and others)

- Brown soils
- Lateritic soils
- Steppe soils
- Chernozems
- Chestnut steppe soils
- Tropical and subtropical soils
- Alpine soils

Scale 1:90 000 000

INORGANIC PRODUCTION

10 5 1% of world production 1977–81 average

SOURCES OF ENERGY

- ▲ ▲ ▲ Oil   ●—● Oil pipeline
- △ △ △ Natural gas ●—● Gas pipeline
- ■ ■ ■ Coal

Electricity produced by:
- thermal power station
- nuclear power station
- hydro power station

Ⓤ Ⓤ Ⓤ Uranium

MINERALS

- Fe Iron
- Ag Silver
- Au Gold
- Cu Copper
- Pb Lead
- Sn Tin
- Zn Zinc
- Al Bauxite
- P   Phosphates
- ⬢   Diamonds
- ◆   Alloy metals (manganese, cobalt, chromium, vanadium, tungsten) — Symbol shows sites of production only
- ▨   Industrial region

Scale 1:50 000 000
0   500   1000   2000 km
0   500   1000 miles

Based upon UN statistics
MILLER'S STEREOGRAPHIC PROJECTION

151

152 NORTH-WEST AFRICA

Scale 1:10 000 000

153

154 THE NILE VALLEY AND ARABIA

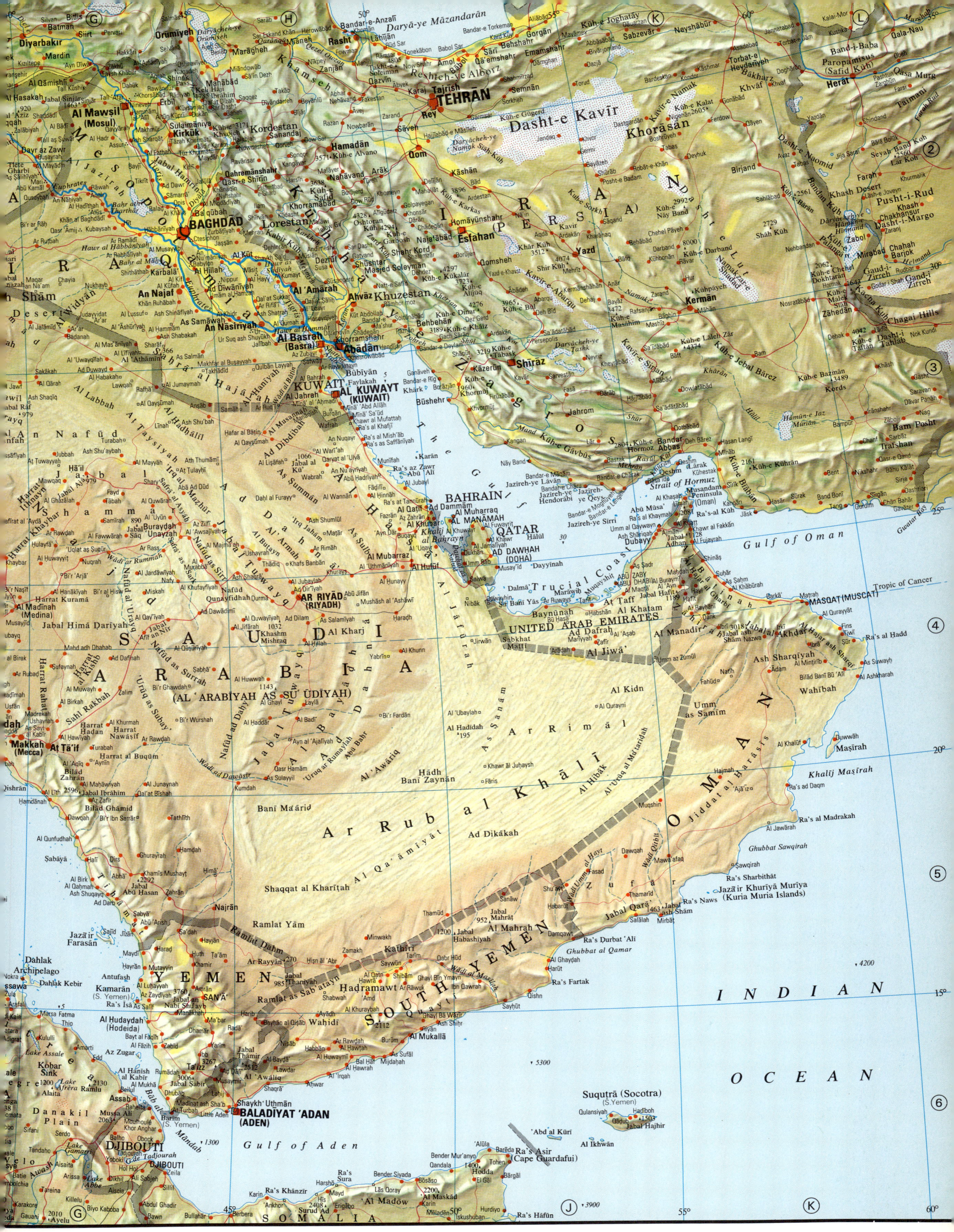

Scale 1:10 000 000

0 100 200 300 400 km

0 100 200 miles

WEST AFRICA

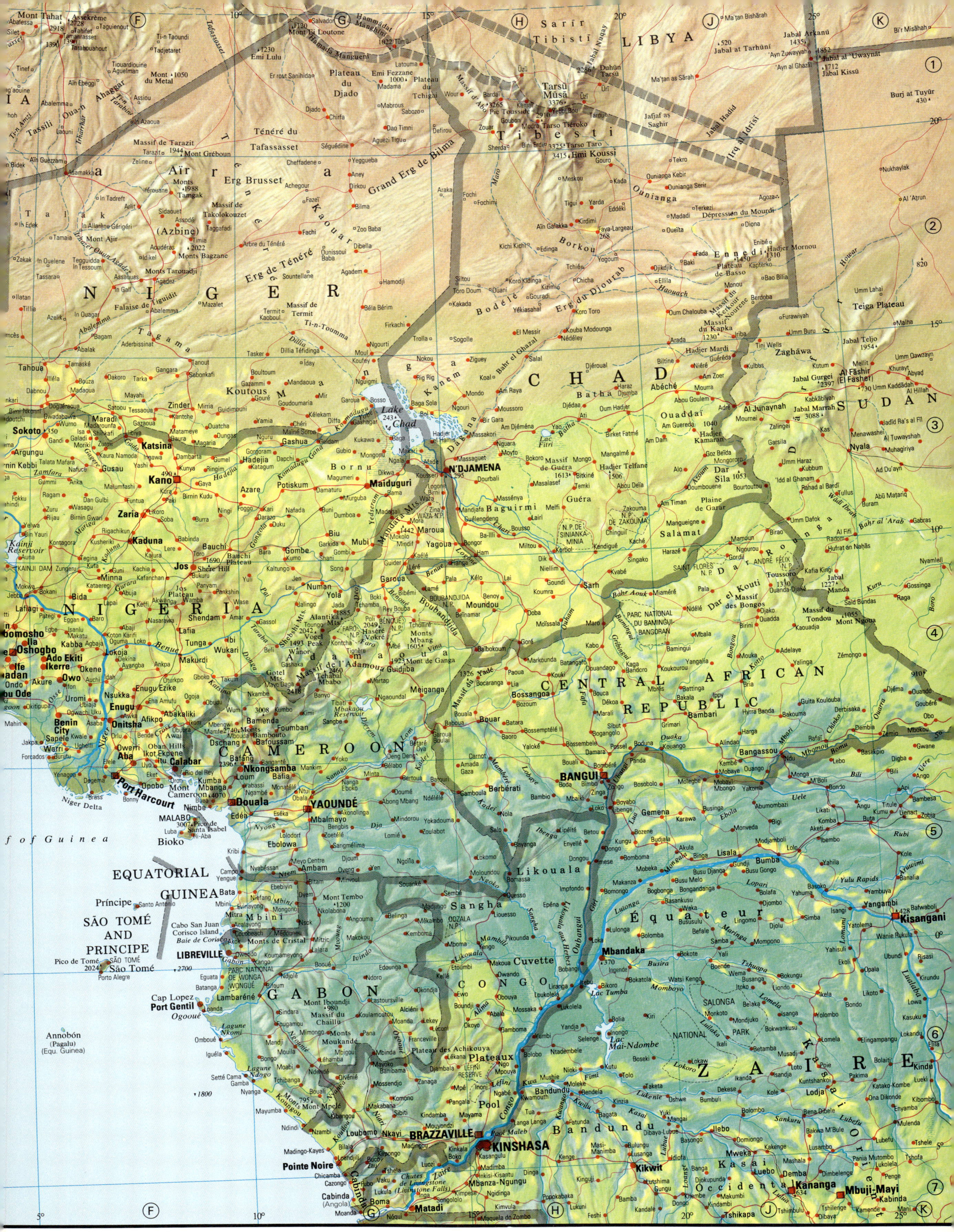

Scale 1:10 000 000

0 100 200 300 400 km
0 100 200 miles

EAST AFRICA

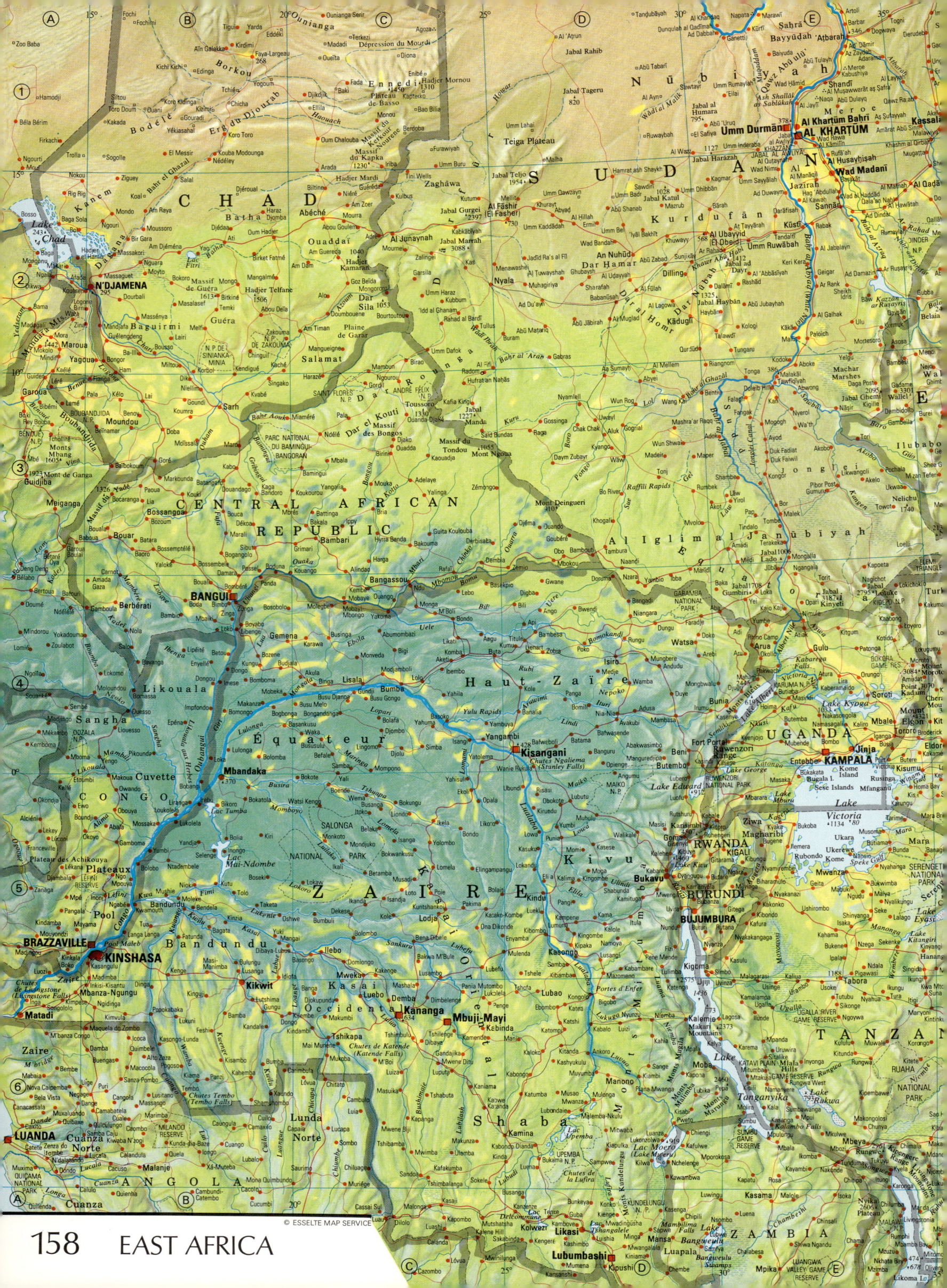

159

160 SOUTHERN AFRICA

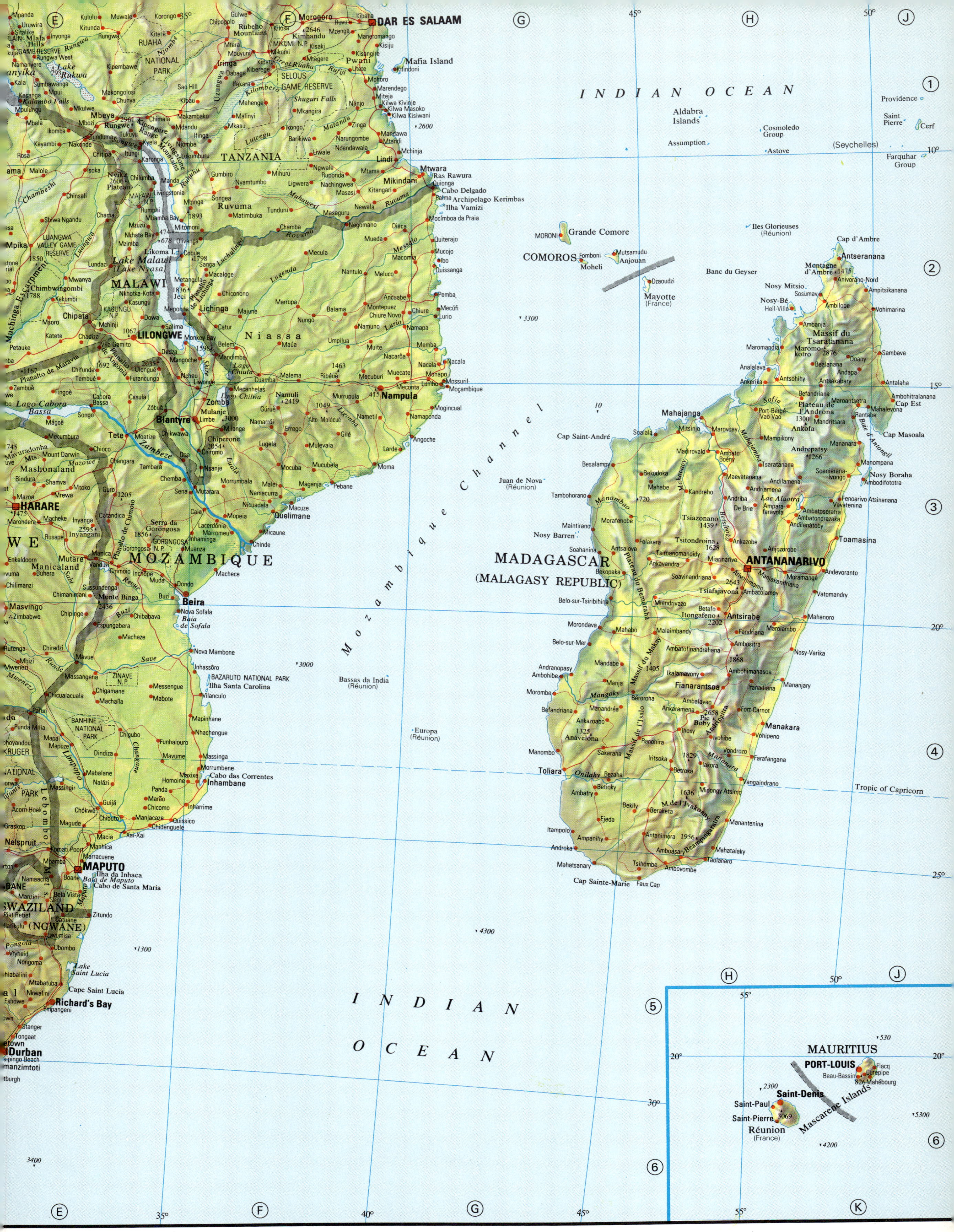

Scale 1:10 000 000 0 100 200 300 400 km 0 100 200 miles

POLITICAL DIVISIONS

Names of the American states, with their standard abbreviations

AL.	Alabama
AK.	Alaska
AZ.	Arizona
AR.	Arkansas
CA.	California
CO.	Colorado
CT.	Connecticut
DE.	Delaware
FL.	Florida
GA.	Georgia
HI.	Hawaii
ID.	Idaho
IL.	Illinois
IN.	Indiana
IA.	Iowa
KS.	Kansas
KY.	Kentucky
LA.	Louisiana
ME.	Maine
MD.	Maryland
MA.	Massachusetts
MI.	Michigan
MN.	Minnesota
MS.	Mississippi
MO.	Missouri
MT.	Montana
NE.	Nebraska
NV.	Nevada
N.H.	New Hampshire
N.J.	New Jersey
N.M.	New Mexico
N.Y.	New York
N.C.	North Carolina
N.D.	North Dakota
OH.	Ohio
OK.	Oklahoma
OR.	Oregon
PA.	Pennsylvania
R.I.	Rhode Island
S.C.	South Carolina
S.D.	South Dakota
TN.	Tennessee
TX.	Texas
UT.	Utah
VT.	Vermont
VA.	Virginia
WA.	Washington
W.V.	West Virginia
WI.	Wisconsin
WY.	Wyoming
D.C.	District of Colombia (Federal)

POPULATION

Population distribution 1982
- · 500 000 inhabitants
- ● 3 Figures show populations (cities with suburbs) in millions
- uninhabited (less than 1 person per sq.km)

Population increase per country 1972–1982

- 50%
- 40
- 30
- 20 Average for North and Central America 15%
- 10
- 0

Scale 1:60 000 000

0   1000   2000 km
0   500   1000 miles

162 NORTH AMERICA, environment, political divisions, population

© ESSELTE MAP SERVICE

MILLER'S BIPOLAR PROJECTION

Scale 1:25 000 000

0 500 1000 km

0 200 400 600 miles

RELIEF

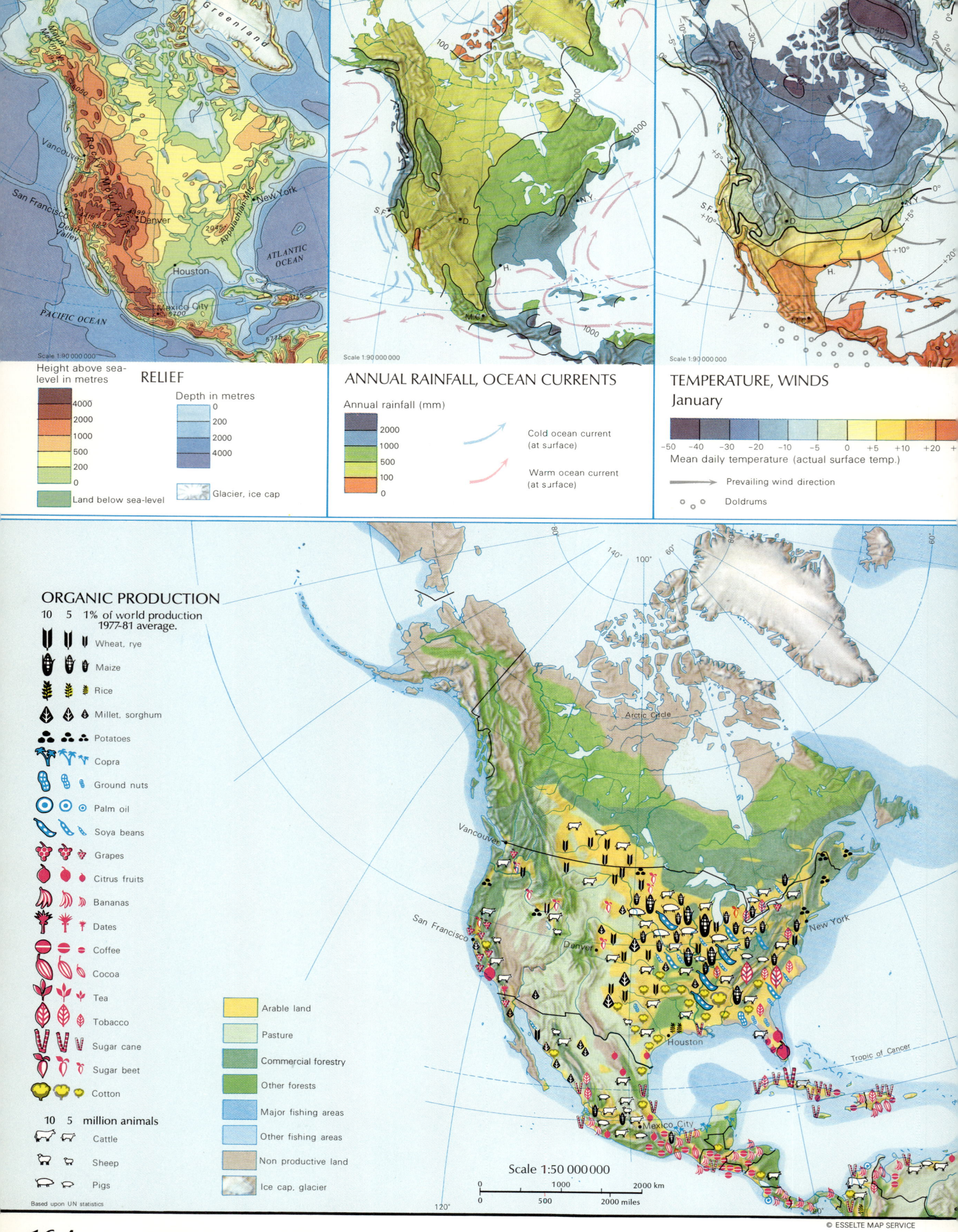

Height above sea-level in metres
- 4000
- 2000
- 1000
- 500
- 200
- 0
- Land below sea-level

Depth in metres
- 0
- 200
- 2000
- 4000

Glacier, ice cap

Scale 1:90 000 000

ANNUAL RAINFALL, OCEAN CURRENTS

Annual rainfall (mm)
- 2000
- 1000
- 500
- 100
- 0

Cold ocean current (at surface)
Warm ocean current (at surface)

Scale 1:90 000 000

TEMPERATURE, WINDS
January

Mean daily temperature (actual surface temp.)
−50 −40 −30 −20 −10 −5 0 +5 +10 +20 +

Prevailing wind direction
Doldrums

Scale 1:90 000 000

ORGANIC PRODUCTION

10 5 1% of world production 1977-81 average.

- Wheat, rye
- Maize
- Rice
- Millet, sorghum
- Potatoes
- Copra
- Ground nuts
- Palm oil
- Soya beans
- Grapes
- Citrus fruits
- Bananas
- Dates
- Coffee
- Cocoa
- Tea
- Tobacco
- Sugar cane
- Sugar beet
- Cotton

10 5 million animals
- Cattle
- Sheep
- Pigs

Based upon UN statistics

- Arable land
- Pasture
- Commercial forestry
- Other forests
- Major fishing areas
- Other fishing areas
- Non productive land
- Ice cap, glacier

Scale 1:50 000 000

© ESSELTE MAP SERVICE

164 NORTH AMERICA, physical, economic

TEMPERATURE, WINDS
July

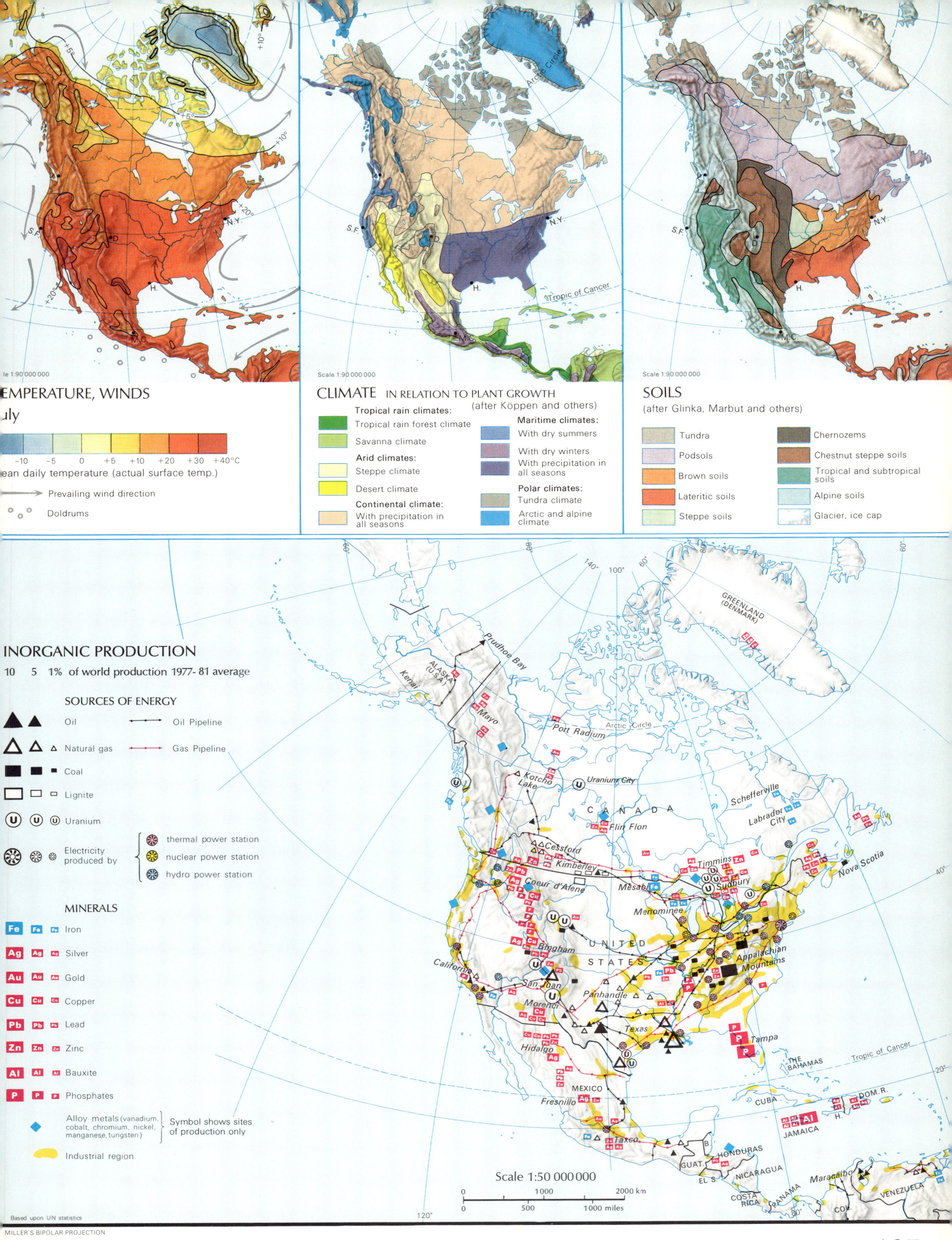

-10 -5 0 +5 +10 +20 +30 +40°C

Mean daily temperature (actual surface temp.)
→ Prevailing wind direction
○ ○ Doldrums

Scale 1:90 000 000

CLIMATE IN RELATION TO PLANT GROWTH
(after Köppen and others)

Tropical rain climates:
- Tropical rain forest climate
- Savanna climate

Arid climates:
- Steppe climate
- Desert climate

Continental climate:
- With precipitation in all seasons

Maritime climates:
- With dry summers
- With dry winters
- With precipitation in all seasons

Polar climates:
- Tundra climate
- Arctic and alpine climate

Scale 1:90 000 000

SOILS
(after Glinka, Marbut and others)

- Tundra
- Podsols
- Brown soils
- Lateritic soils
- Steppe soils
- Chernozems
- Chestnut steppe soils
- Tropical and subtropical soils
- Alpine soils
- Glacier, ice cap

Scale 1:90 000 000

INORGANIC PRODUCTION

10 5 1% of world production 1977-81 average

SOURCES OF ENERGY
- ▲ ▲ ▲ Oil — Oil Pipeline
- △ △ △ Natural gas — Gas Pipeline
- ■ ■ ■ Coal
- □ □ □ Lignite
- Ⓤ Ⓤ Ⓤ Uranium
- Electricity produced by:
  - thermal power station
  - nuclear power station
  - hydro power station

MINERALS
- Fe — Iron
- Ag — Silver
- Au — Gold
- Cu — Copper
- Pb — Lead
- Zn — Zinc
- Al — Bauxite
- P — Phosphates

◆ Alloy metals (vanadium, cobalt, chromium, nickel, manganese, tungsten) — Symbol shows sites of production only

Industrial region

Scale 1:50 000 000
0   1000   2000 km
0   500   1000 miles

Based upon UN statistics
MILLER'S BIPOLAR PROJECTION

165

ALASKA AND WESTERN CANADA

Scale 1:10 000 000

167

168 EASTERN CANADA

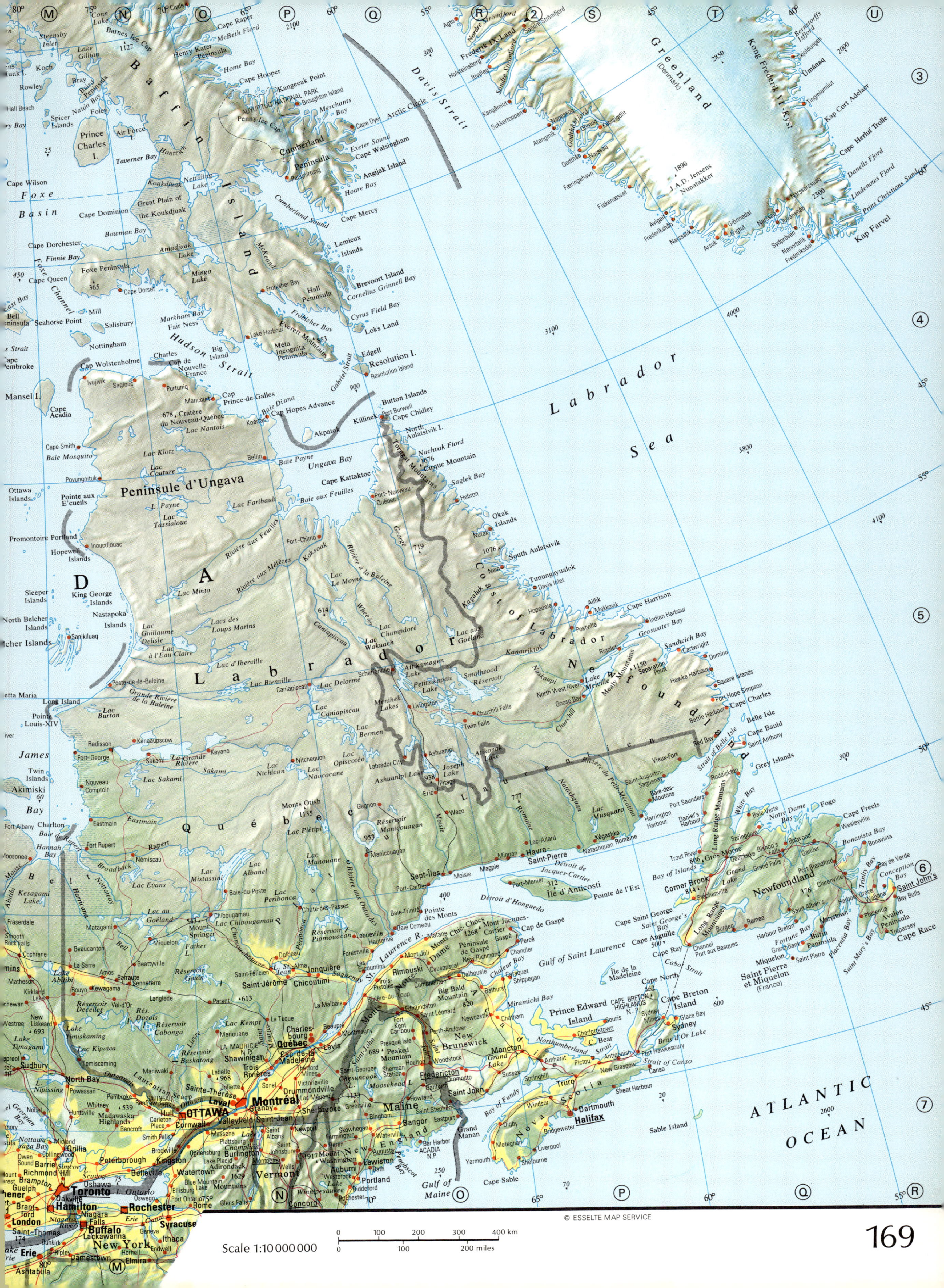

170 THE UNITED STATES

CANADA
Ontario
Québec
Maine
New Brunswick
Minnesota
Wisconsin
Michigan
Iowa
Illinois
Indiana
Ohio
Pennsylvania
New York
Vermont
New Hampshire
Massachusetts
Connecticut
Rhode Island
New Jersey
Delaware
Maryland
West Virginia
Virginia
Kentucky
Tennessee
North Carolina
South Carolina
Georgia
Alabama
Mississippi
Louisiana
Arkansas
Missouri
Florida
UNITED STATES
Lake Superior
Lake Michigan
Lake Huron
Lake Erie
L. Ontario
Thunder Bay
Duluth
Minneapolis
Saint Paul
Milwaukee
Chicago
Detroit
Toronto
Hamilton
Buffalo
Rochester
Syracuse
Ottawa
Montreal
Quebec
Albany
Boston
Providence
Hartford
New Haven
New York
Newark
Philadelphia
Baltimore
WASHINGTON
Pittsburgh
Cleveland
Columbus
Cincinnati
Indianapolis
Louisville
Lexington
Nashville
Memphis
Saint Louis
Kansas City
Des Moines
Tulsa
Little Rock
Dallas
Shreveport
Jackson
Birmingham
Atlanta
Chattanooga
Knoxville
Charlotte
Greensboro
Raleigh
Richmond
Norfolk
Virginia Beach
Charleston
Savannah
Jacksonville
Tallahassee
Montgomery
Mobile
New Orleans
Baton Rouge
Houston
Beaumont
Galveston
Orlando
Tampa
Saint Petersburg
West Palm Beach
Fort Lauderdale
Hollywood
Miami
Key West
Gulf of Maine
Cape Cod
Cape Hatteras
Cape Fear
ATLANTIC OCEAN
Gulf of Mexico
THE BAHAMAS
Grand Bahama
Great Abaco Island
NASSAU
Andros Island
CUBA
LA HABANA (HAVANA)
Santiago de Cuba
Camagüey
Holguín
Guantánamo
Isla de la Juventud
MEXICO
Tropic of Cancer
© ESSELTE MAP SERVICE
Scale 1:10 000 000
0 100 200 300 400 km
0 100 200 miles

172 CENTRAL AMERICA AND THE WEST INDIES

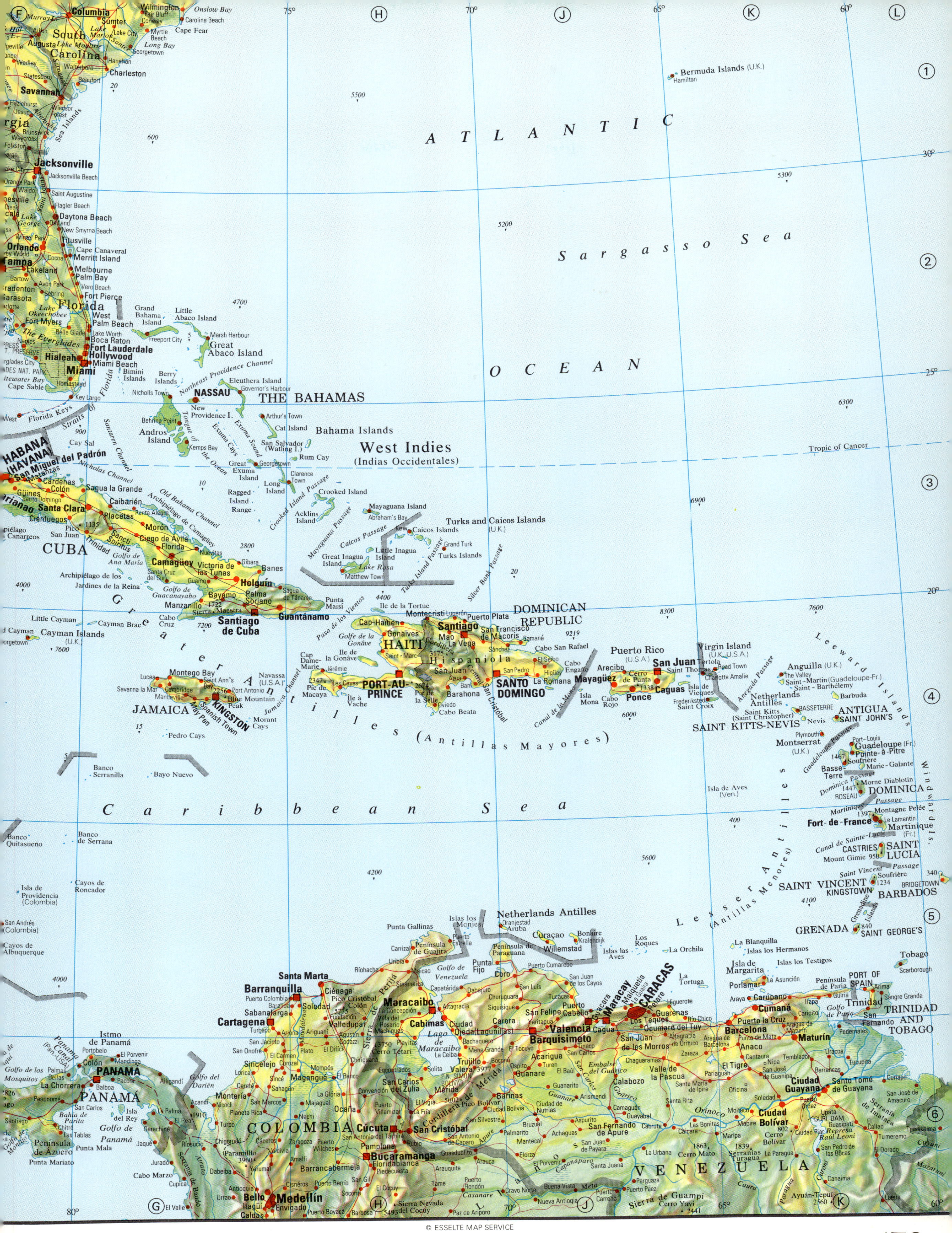

Scale 1:10 000 000

0 100 200 300 400 km

0 100 200 miles

POLITICAL DIVISIONS

Scale 1:60 000 000

POPULATION

Population distribution 1982
- · 500 000 inhabitants
- ● Figures show populations (cities with suburbs) in millions

□ uninhabited (less than 1 person per sq.km)

Population increase per country 1972–1982
- 50 %
- 40
- 30 — Average for South America 24%
- 20
- 10
- 0

174 SOUTH AMERICA, environment, political divisions, population

Scale 1:25 000 000

© ESSELTE MAP SERVICE

Caribbean Sea
JAMAICA
Puerto Rico (U.S.A.)
ST. KITTS-NEVIS
ANTIGUA
Guadeloupe (France)
Pointe-à-Pitre
DOMINICA
Martinique (France)
Fort-de-France
ST. LUCIA
BARBADOS
BRIDGETOWN
ST. VINCENT
GRENADA
Lesser Antilles
Aruba I.
Curaçao I. (Neth.)
TRINIDAD AND TOBAGO
PORT OF SPAIN
P. Gallinas
Barranquilla
Santa Marta
Cartagena
Maracaibo
Barquisimeto
Maracay
CARACAS
Valencia
Barcelona
Cumaná
Ciudad Bolívar
Ciudad Guayana
VENEZUELA
Orinoco R.
Angel Falls
Mt. Roraima
Kaieteur Falls
GUYANA
GEORGETOWN
PARAMARIBO
SURINAM
French Guiana
Cayenne
Cúcuta
San Cristóbal
Medellín
Bucaramanga
Manizales
BOGOTÁ
Ibagué
Cali
Buenaventura
Llanos
Meta R.
Guaviare R.
COLOMBIA
Pasto
QUITO
Mt. Cotopaxi
Chimborazo
Ambato
ECUADOR
Guayaquil
Cuenca
Tumbes
Piura
Putumayo R.
Amazon R.
Marañón R.
Iquitos
Leticia
Fonte Boa
Amazonas
Selvas
Negro R.
Branco R.
Boa Vista
Roraima
Manaus
Santarém
Amapá
Macapá
Marajó I.
Belém
São Luís
Pará
Xingu R.
Tapajós R.
Madeira R.
Purus R.
Juruá R.
Ucayali R.
Acre
Pôrto Velho
Rio Branco
Cobija
Rondônia
Guaporé R.
Guajará Mirim
Beni R.
BRAZIL
Caatingas
Maranhão
Tocantins R.
Araguaia R.
Parnaíba
Fortaleza
Sobral
Ceará
Teresina
Piauí
Juàzeiro do Norte
Mossoró
Natal
C. São Roque
João Pessoa
Paraíba
Recife
Pernambuco
Campina Grande
Caruaru
Alagoas
Maceió
Sergipe
Aracaju
Juàzeiro
Bahia
Barreiras
Feira
Salvador
Alagoinhas
Campos
S. Francisco R.
Goiás
Mato Grosso
Cuiabá
Distrito Federal
BRASÍLIA
Anápolis
Goiânia
Vitória
Jequié
Itabuna
Ilhéus
Montes Claros
Brazilian Highlands
Minas Gerais
Belo Horizonte
Teófilo Otoni
Governador Valadares
Espírito Santo
Paranaíba R.
Uberlândia
Uberaba
Mato Grosso do Sul
Campo Grande
São José
São Paulo
Ribeirão Prêto
Juiz de Fora
Rio de Janeiro
Niterói
Volta Redonda
C. Frio
Presidente Prudente
Bauru
Campinas
Sorocaba
Santos
Ponta Porã
Londrina
Paraná
Ponta Grossa
Curitiba
Joinville
Iguaçu Falls
Santa Catarina
Blumenau
Florianópolis
Passo Fundo
Rio Grande do Sul
Caxias do Sul
Pôrto Alegre
Santa Maria
L. dos Patos
Pelotas
Rio Grande
Lake Mirim
Uruguaiana
Salto
Paysandú
URUGUAY
MONTEVIDEO
River Plate
PARAGUAY
ASUNCIÓN
Gran Chaco
Paraguay R.
Paraná R.
Pilcomayo R.
Bermejo R.
Formosa
Posadas
Resistencia
Corrientes
Uruguay R.
PERU
Cajamarca
Trujillo
Chimbote
Mt. Huascarán
Huánuco
Cerro de Pasco
LIMA
Callao
La Oroya
Huancayo
Huancavelica
Ayacucho
Cuzco
Pisco
Ica
Mt. Coropuna
Arequipa
Puno
Lake Titicaca
LA PAZ
Mt. Ancohuma
Mt. Illimani
BOLIVIA
Trinidad
Cochabamba
Santa Cruz
Oruro
SUCRE
Potosí
Lake Poopó
Tarija
Mollendo
Tacna
Arica
Iquique
Tocopilla
Antofagasta
Atacama Desert
Mt. Llullaillaco
Salta
Mt. Galán
Tucumán
Mt. Ojos del Salado
Copiapó
Santiago del Estero
Catamarca
La Rioja
Salinas Grandes
Salado R.
Santa Fe
Paraná
Córdoba
Rosario
San Juan
La Serena
CHILE
Mt. Aconcagua
Viña del Mar
Valparaíso
SANTIAGO
Mendoza
San Luis
Río Cuarto
Junín
Zárate
BUENOS AIRES
La Plata
ARGENTINA
Rancagua
Talca
Santa Rosa
Azul
Tandil
Mar del Plata
Pampas
Colorado R.
Bahía Blanca
Talcahuano
Concepción
Chillán
Temuco
Neuquén
Plaza Huincul
Valdivia
Osorno
San Carlos de Bariloche
Viedma
Gulf of San Matías
Puerto Montt
Chiloé I.
Rawson
Patagonia
Puerto Aisén
Cerro San Valentín
Comodoro Rivadavia
Gulf of San Jorge
Puerto Deseado
Río Gallegos
Strait of Magellan
Tierra del Fuego
Ushuaia
Cape Horn
Punta Arenas
Falkland Islands (U.K.)
Stanley
South Georgia (U.K.)
Juan Fernández Islands (Chile)
S. Félix I. (Chile)
S. Ambrosio I.
ATLANTIC OCEAN
Equator
St. Peter and St. Paul Rocks (Braz.)
Fernando de Noronha I. (Braz.)
Trindade I. (Braz.)
Martin Vaz Is. (Braz.)
Tropic of Capricorn
Peru-Chile Trench
Andes Mountains
MILLER'S BIPOLAR PROJECTION
500 1000 km
200 400 600 miles

RELIEF

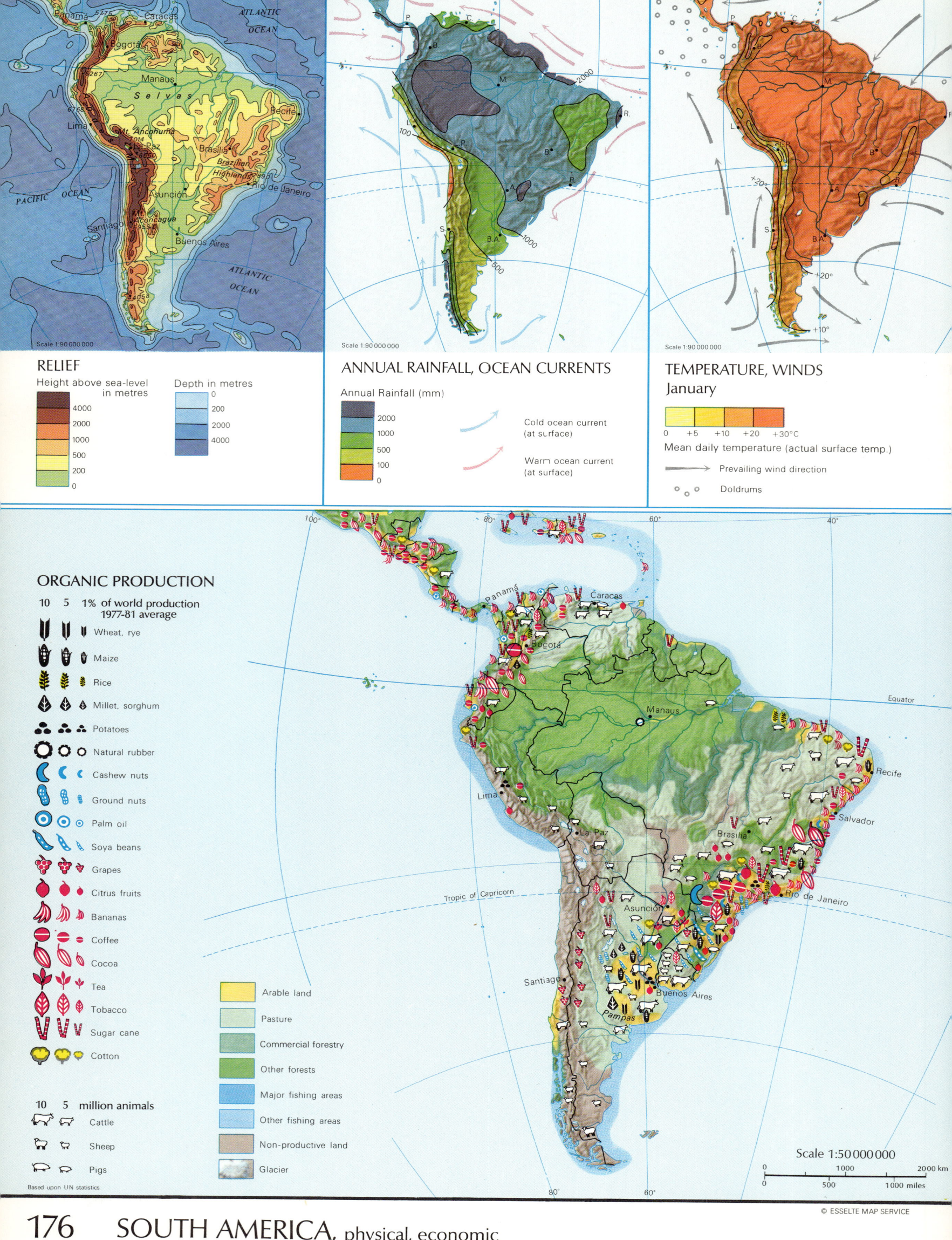

Height above sea-level in metres: 4000, 2000, 1000, 500, 200, 0
Depth in metres: 0, 200, 2000, 4000

Scale 1:90 000 000

ANNUAL RAINFALL, OCEAN CURRENTS

Annual Rainfall (mm): 2000, 1000, 500, 100

- Cold ocean current (at surface)
- Warm ocean current (at surface)

Scale 1:90 000 000

TEMPERATURE, WINDS
January

Mean daily temperature (actual surface temp.): 0, +5, +10, +20, +30°C

- Prevailing wind direction
- Doldrums

Scale 1:90 000 000

ORGANIC PRODUCTION

10 5 1% of world production 1977-81 average

- Wheat, rye
- Maize
- Rice
- Millet, sorghum
- Potatoes
- Natural rubber
- Cashew nuts
- Ground nuts
- Palm oil
- Soya beans
- Grapes
- Citrus fruits
- Bananas
- Coffee
- Cocoa
- Tea
- Tobacco
- Sugar cane
- Cotton

10 5 million animals
- Cattle
- Sheep
- Pigs

Based upon UN statistics

- Arable land
- Pasture
- Commercial forestry
- Other forests
- Major fishing areas
- Other fishing areas
- Non-productive land
- Glacier

Scale 1:50 000 000

© ESSELTE MAP SERVICE

176 SOUTH AMERICA, physical, economic

TEMPERATURE, WINDS
July

| | 0 | +5 | +10 | +20 | +30°C |

Mean daily temperature (actual surface temp.)

→ Prevailing wind direction

∘ ∘ Doldrums

CLIMATE IN RELATION TO PLANT GROWTH
(after Köppen and others)

Tropical rain climates:
- Tropical rain forest climate
- Savanna climate

Arid climates:
- Steppe climate
- Desert climate

Maritime climates:
- With dry summers
- With dry winters
- With precipitation in all seasons

Polar climate:
- Arctic and alpine climate

SOILS
(after Glinka, Marbut and others)

- Tundra
- Lateritic soils
- Steppe soils
- Chernozems
- Chestnut steppe soils
- Tropical and subtropical soils
- Alpine soils
- A A Alluvial soils

INORGANIC PRODUCTION

10 5 1% of world production
1977-81 average

SOURCES OF ENERGY
- ▲ ▲ ▲ Oil
- △ △ △ Natural gas
- ⊛ ⊛ ⊛ Electricity produced by:
  - thermal power station
  - nuclear power station
  - hydro power station
- ── Oil pipeline
- ── Gas pipeline

MINERALS
- Fe Iron
- Ag Silver
- Au Gold
- Cu Copper
- Pb Lead
- Sn Tin
- Zn Zinc
- Al Bauxite
- ⬡ Diamonds

◆ Alloy metals (chromium, manganese, nickel, tungsten) — Symbol shows sites of production only

▬ Industrial region

Based upon UN statistics

Scale 1:50 000 000

MILLER'S BIPOLAR PROJECTION

177

SOUTH AMERICA, NORTH

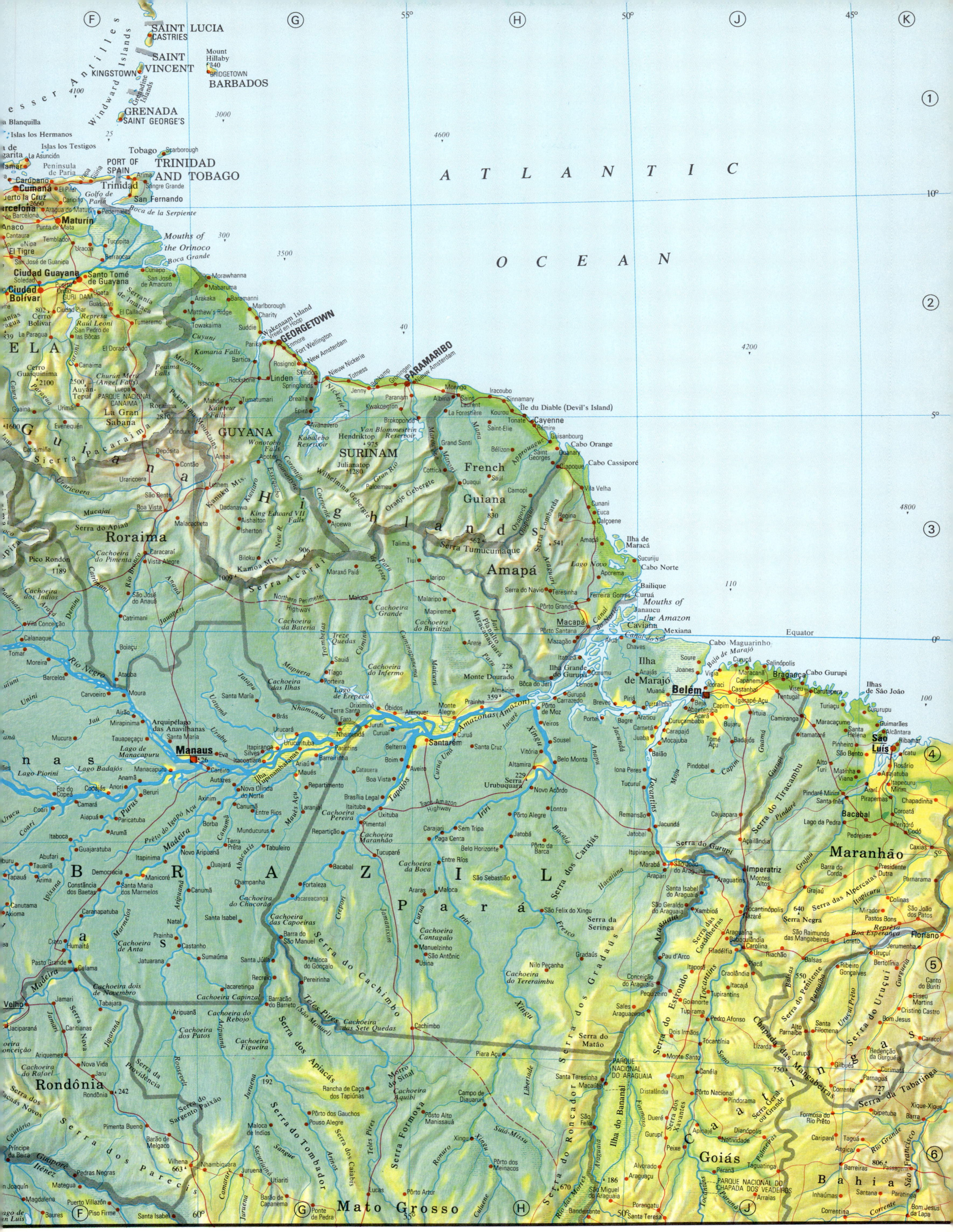

Scale 1:10 000 000

0 100 200 300 400 km

0 100 200 miles

180 SOUTH AMERICA, CENTRAL

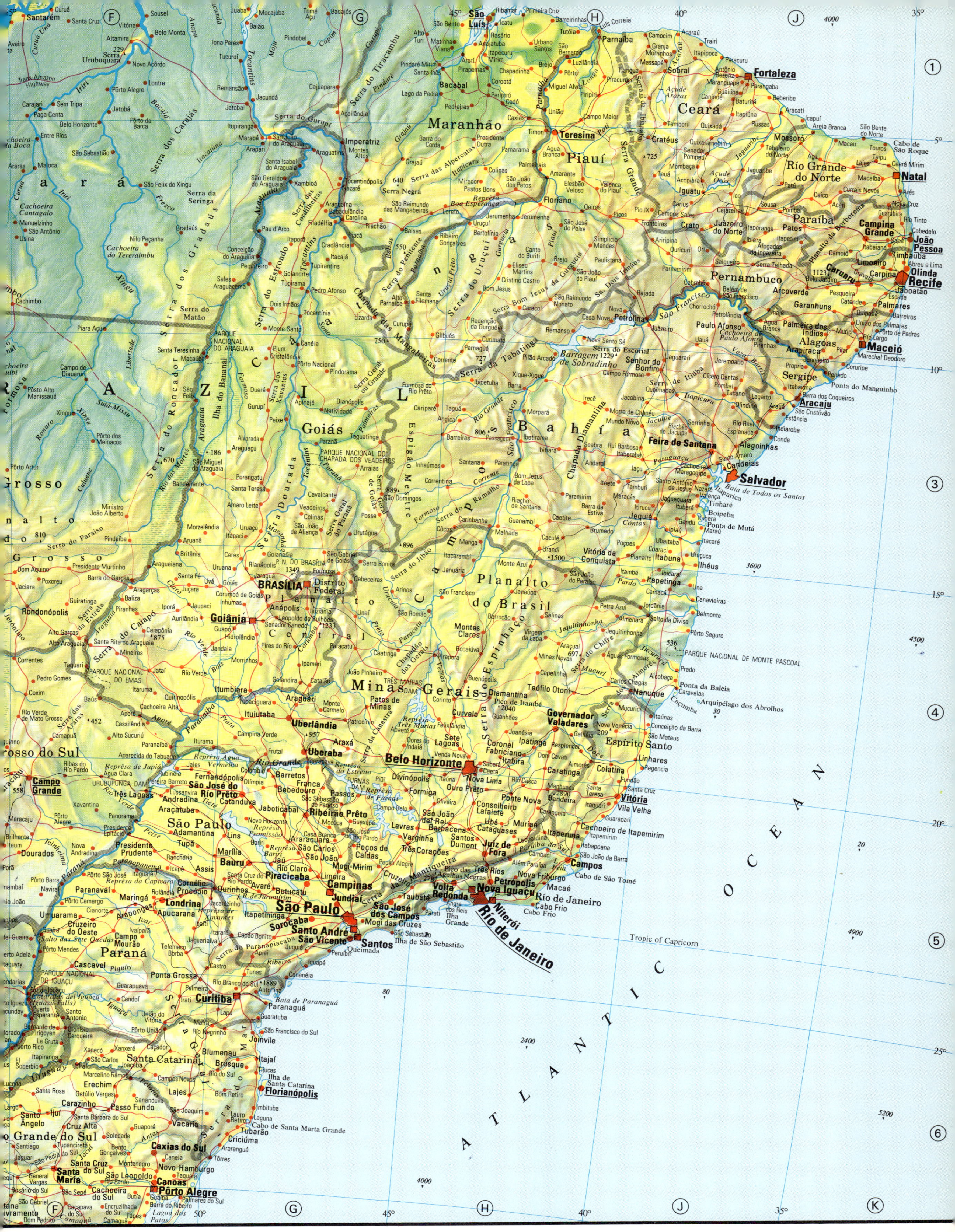

Scale 1:10 000 000

0 100 200 300 400 km

0 100 200 miles

SOUTH AMERICA, SOUTH

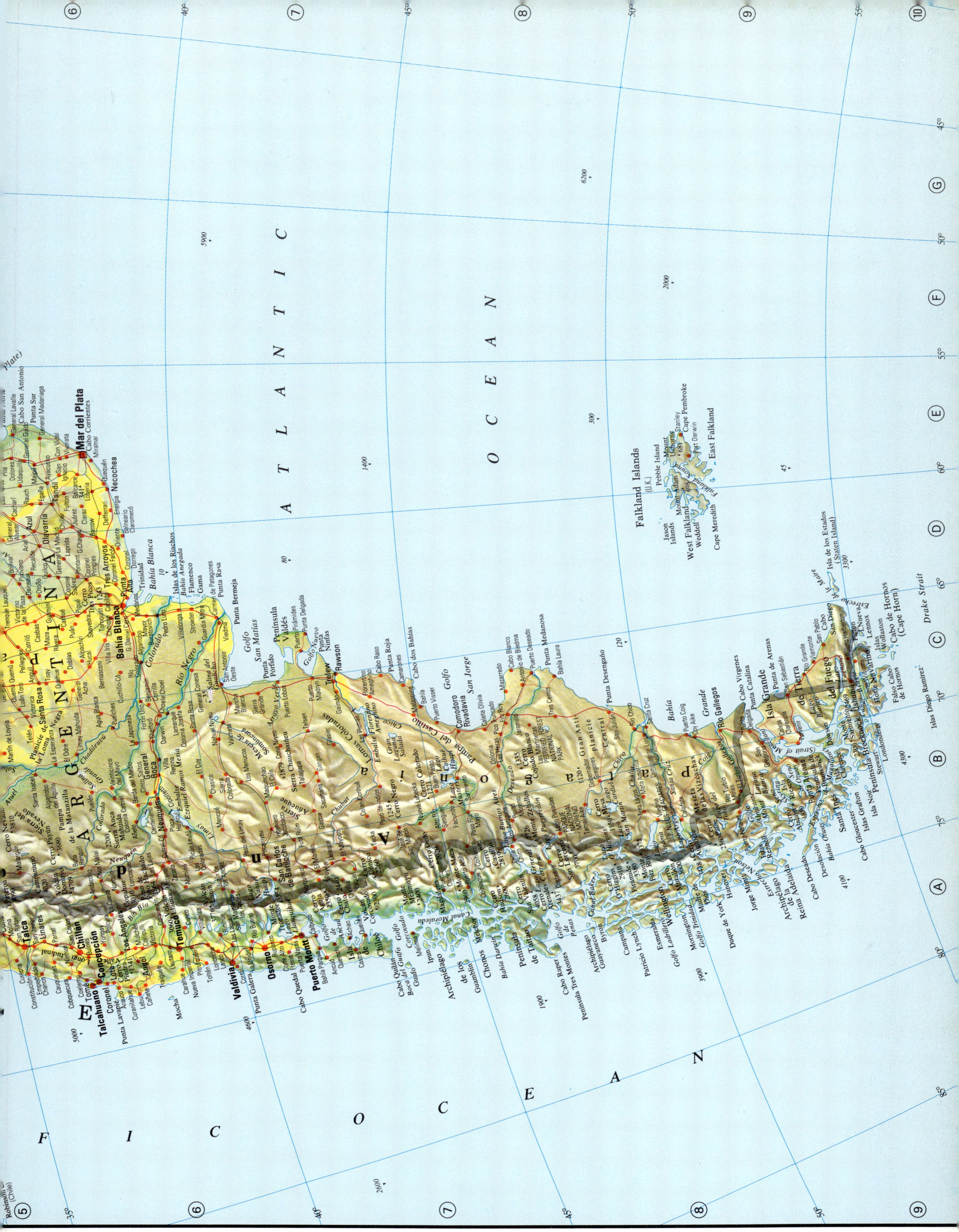

Scale 1:10 000 000

0 100 200 300 400 km

0 100 200 miles

184 THE ARCTIC

Scale 1:30 000 000

ANTARCTICA

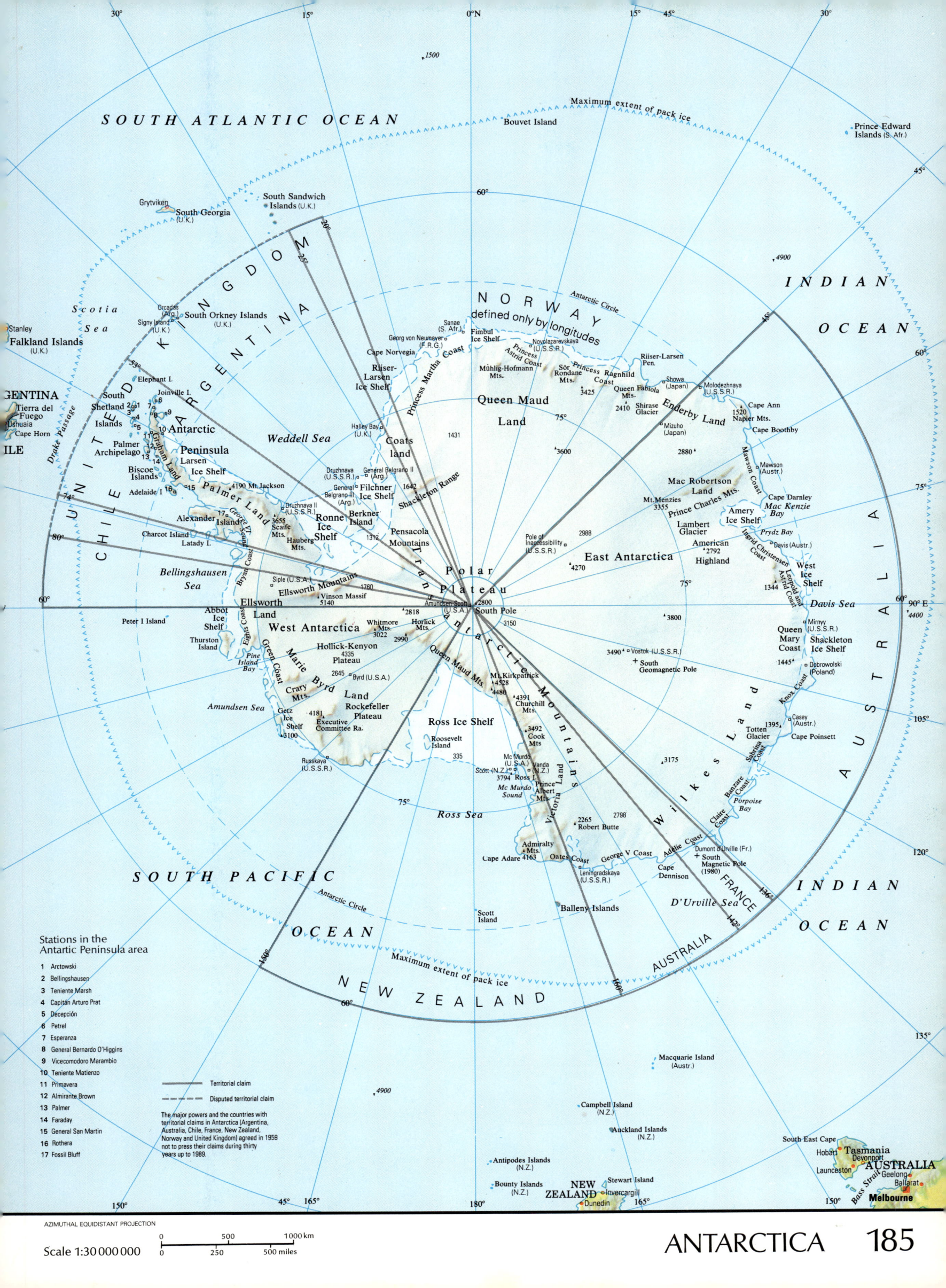

186 THE WORLD, environment

Map labels

North America region:
- Kamchatka
- Bering Sea
- Bering Strait
- Alaska
- Mount McKinley 6194
- Aleutian Islands
- Mackenzie River
- Victoria Island
- Baffin Bay
- Baffin Island
- Greenland
- Arctic Circle
- Rocky Mountains
- Hudson Bay
- Labrador
- Iceland
- NORTH AMERICA
- Labrador Current
- North Atlantic Drift
- California Current
- Missouri R.
- Chicago
- New York
- Newfoundland
- Los Angeles
- Mississippi R.
- Gulf Stream
- Sargasso Sea
- Canary Current
- Mexico City
- West Indies
- Tropic of Cancer
- Caribbean Sea
- Central America
- Hawaiian Islands

Oceans:
- PACIFIC OCEAN
- ATLANTIC OCEAN

South America region:
- Polynesia
- R. Amazon
- Equator
- Andes Mountains
- Peru Current
- Mount Ancohuma 6388
- SOUTH AMERICA
- São Paulo
- Rio de Janeiro
- Brazil Current
- Tropic of Capricorn
- Mount Aconcagua
- R. Paraná
- Buenos Aires
- New Zealand
- Mount Cook 3764
- Cape Horn
- Drake Passage

Legend

- ■ Million city
- → Warm current } at surface in January
- → Cold current
- Pack and drift ice
- — International boundary

Environment types

- Glacier, ice cap
- Tundra
- Coniferous forest
- Rain forest

© ESSELTE MAP SERVICE

| Cultivated land | Savanna | Steppe | Desert |

187

PRECIPITATION PRESSURE WINDS

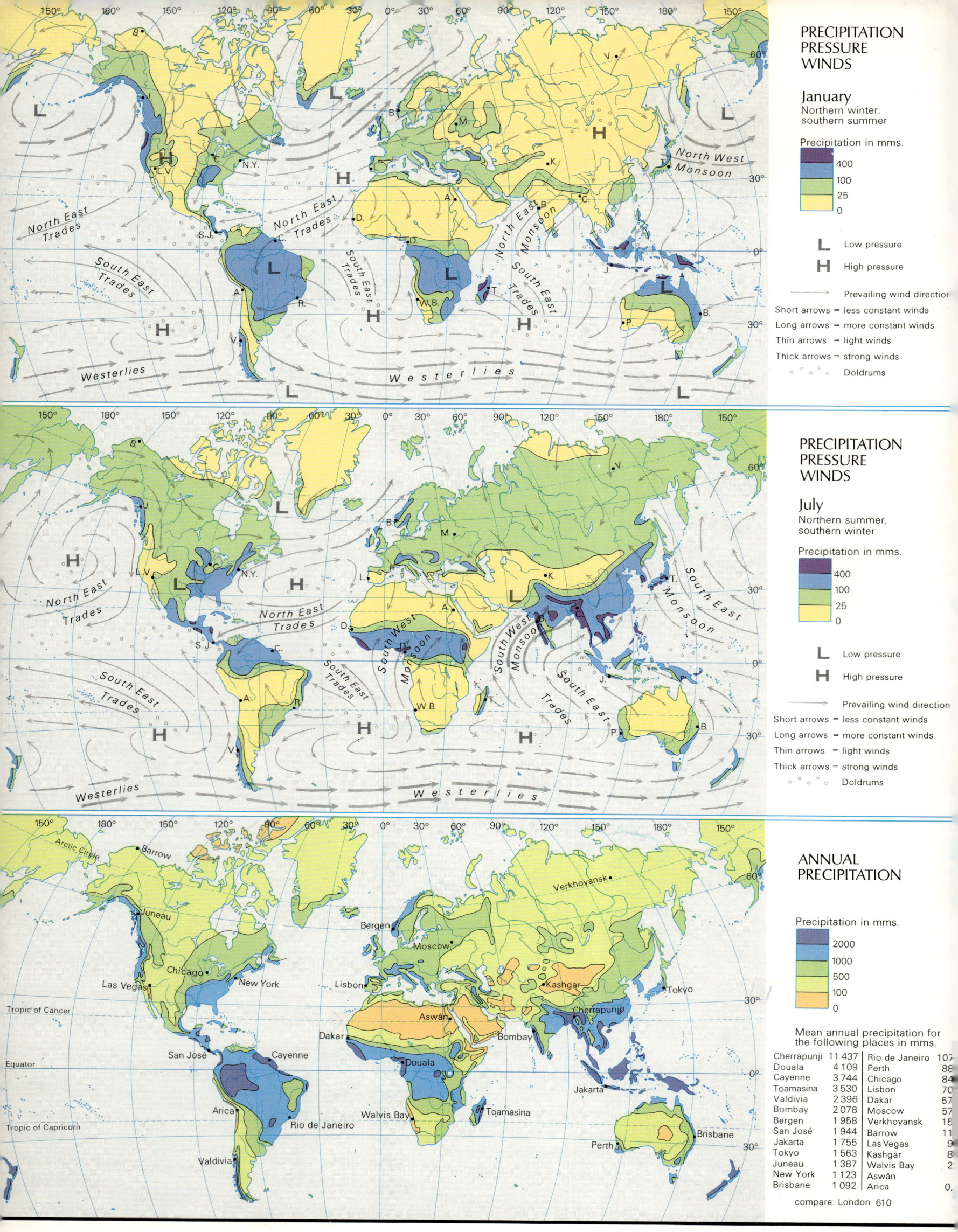

January
Northern winter, southern summer

Precipitation in mms.
- 400
- 100
- 25
- 0

L Low pressure
H High pressure

→ Prevailing wind direction
Short arrows = less constant winds
Long arrows = more constant winds
Thin arrows = light winds
Thick arrows = strong winds
∘ ∘ ∘ Doldrums

PRECIPITATION PRESSURE WINDS

July
Northern summer, southern winter

Precipitation in mms.
- 400
- 100
- 25
- 0

L Low pressure
H High pressure

→ Prevailing wind direction
Short arrows = less constant winds
Long arrows = more constant winds
Thin arrows = light winds
Thick arrows = strong winds
∘ ∘ ∘ Doldrums

ANNUAL PRECIPITATION

Precipitation in mms.
- 2000
- 1000
- 500
- 100
- 0

Mean annual precipitation for the following places in mms.

Place	mm	Place	mm
Cherrapunji	11 437	Rio de Janeiro	107...
Douala	4 109	Perth	88...
Cayenne	3 744	Chicago	84...
Toamasina	3 530	Lisbon	70...
Valdivia	2 396	Dakar	57...
Bombay	2 078	Moscow	57...
Bergen	1 958	Verkhoyansk	15...
San José	1 944	Barrow	11...
Jakarta	1 755	Las Vegas	9...
Tokyo	1 563	Kashgar	8...
Juneau	1 387	Walvis Bay	2...
New York	1 123	Aswân	0...
Brisbane	1 092	Arica	0...

compare: London 610

188 THE WORLD, climate

TEMPERATURE OCEAN CURRENTS

January
Northern winter, southern summer
Daily mean temperature (actual surface temp.)

- +30°C
- +20°C
- +10°C
- 0°C
- –10°C
- –20°C
- –30°C
- –40°C

Cold ocean current
Warm ocean current

Short arrows = less constant currents
Long arrows = more constant currents
Thin arrows = slow currents
Thick arrows = fast currents

TEMPERATURE OCEAN CURRENTS

July
Northern summer, southern winter
Daily mean temperature (actual surface temp.)

- +30°C
- +20°C
- +10°C
- 0°C
- –10°C

Cold ocean current
Warm ocean current

Short arrows = less constant currents
Long arrows = more constant currents
Thin arrows = slow currents
Thick arrows = fast currents

CLIMATE IN RELATION TO PLANT GROWTH
(after Köppen and others)

Tropical rain climates:
- Tropical rain forest climate
- Savanna climate

Arid climates:
- Steppe climate
- Desert climate

Maritime climates:
- With dry summers
- With dry winters
- With precipitation in all seasons

Continental climates:
- With precipitation in all seasons
- With dry winters

Polar climates:
- Tundra climate
- Arctic and alpine climate

VAN DER GRINTEN'S PROJECTION
Scale 1:220 000 000 at the equator

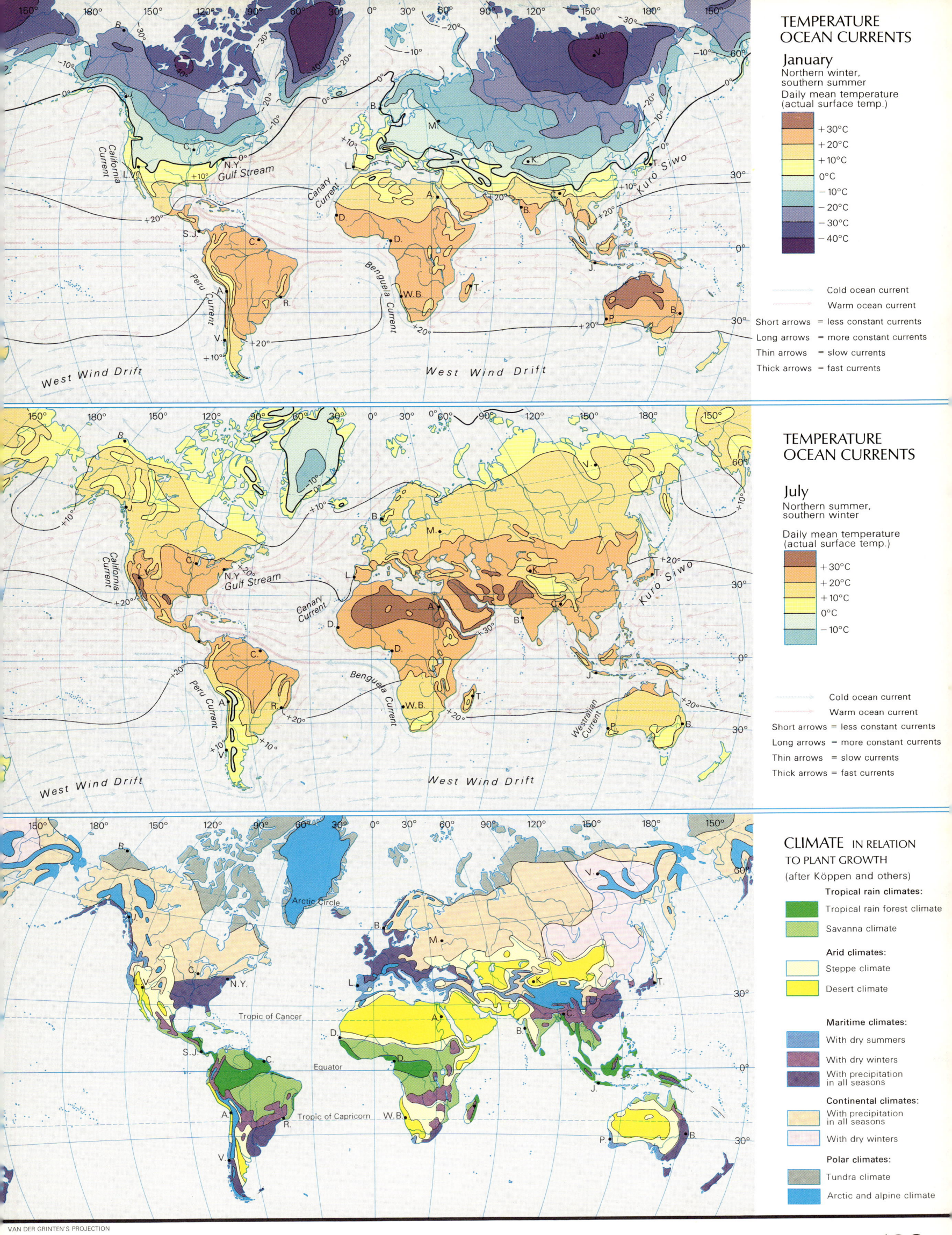

190 THE WORLD, geology

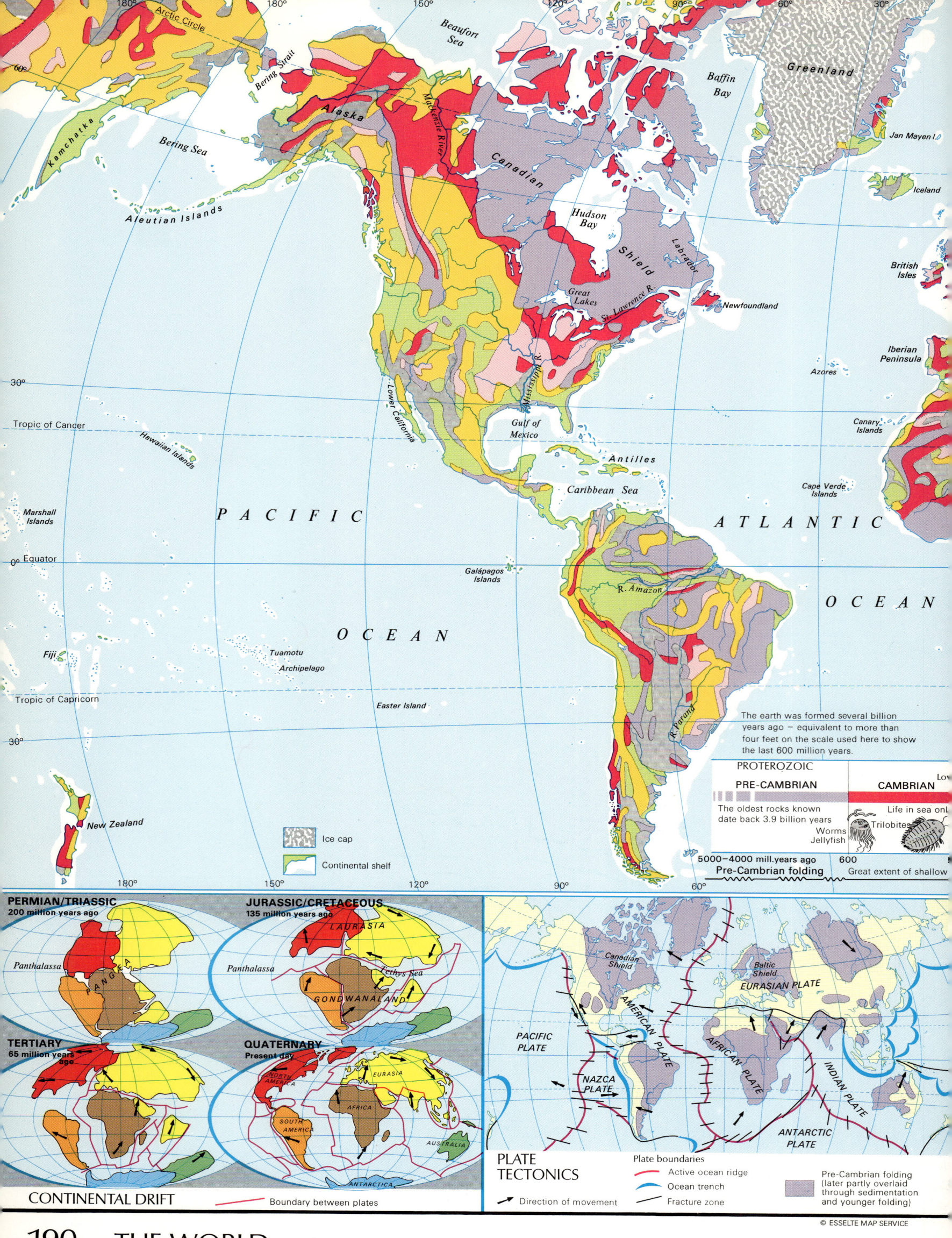

Geological Map of Eurasia, Africa and Australia

Time Scale — Geological Periods

Era	PRIMARY (Palaeozoic)			Upper Palaeozoic		SECONDARY (Mesozoic)			QUATERNARY TERTIARY (Caenozoic)
Period	OVICIAN	SILURIAN	DEVONIAN	CARBONIFEROUS	PERMIAN	TRIASSIC	JURASSIC	CRETACEOUS	

Fauna/Flora indicators: raptolites, Nautiloids, Shellfish, Sea lilies, Bony fishes, Primitive amphibians, Giant insects, Ichthyosaurs, First Mammals, Primitive birds, Giant reptiles, Mammals, Birds, Man

440 — 400 — 350 — 300 — 270 — 225 — 200 — 180 — 136 — 100 — 65 — Present day

Caledonian folding · Great swamps · Hercynian folding · Great lava flows · Extensive swamps and shallow seas · Alpine folding

Scale 1:90 000 000

MOUNTAIN BUILDING

- Main trend lines
- Main fault zones
- Sediment overlaid plateau
- Pre-Cambrian folding (stable shields)
- Caledonian folding
- Hercynian folding
- Alpine folding

EARTHQUAKES AND VOLCANOES

- Zone of strong seismic activity (frequent earthquakes)
- Zones of less frequent seismic activity (earthquakes can occasionally occur even in other areas)
- Active volcano or zone of volcanic activity (several minor volcanoes)

VAN DER GRINTEN'S PROJECTION

192 THE WORLD, oceans

MAJOR STORM AREAS

- Area subject to tropical storms
- Storm track
- Pack ice during northern winter
- Drift ice limit
- Coast subject to seismic surges (tsunamis)
- Sea areas where fog often occurs

193

194 THE WORLD, population

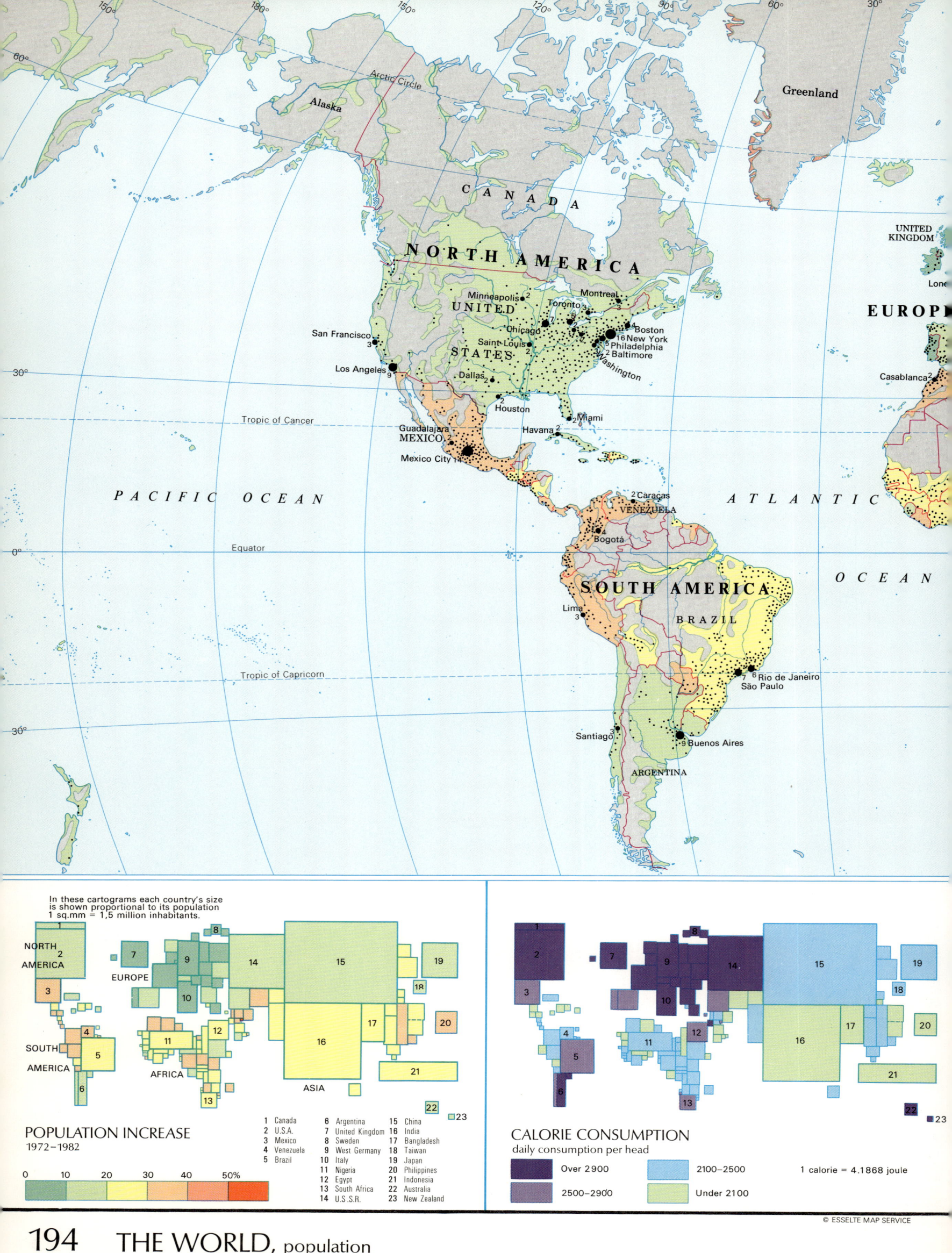

POPULATION INCREASE
1972–1982

0 — 10 — 20 — 30 — 40 — 50%

CALORIE CONSUMPTION
daily consumption per head

- Over 2900
- 2500–2900
- 2100–2500
- Under 2100

1 calorie = 4.1868 joule

In these cartograms each country's size is shown proportional to its population
1 sq.mm = 1,5 million inhabitants.

1. Canada
2. U.S.A.
3. Mexico
4. Venezuela
5. Brazil
6. Argentina
7. United Kingdom
8. Sweden
9. West Germany
10. Italy
11. Nigeria
12. Egypt
13. South Africa
14. U.S.S.R.
15. China
16. India
17. Bangladesh
18. Taiwan
19. Japan
20. Philippines
21. Indonesia
22. Australia
23. New Zealand

© ESSELTE MAP SERVICE

POPULATION DISTRIBUTION 1982
- • 500 000 inhabitants
- •5 Figures show populations (cities with suburbs) in millions
- uninhabited (less than 1 person per sq. km)

POPULATION INCREASE
per country 1972–1982

0 — 10 — 20 — 30 — 40 — 50 %

18% world average

Scale 1:90 000 000 at the equator

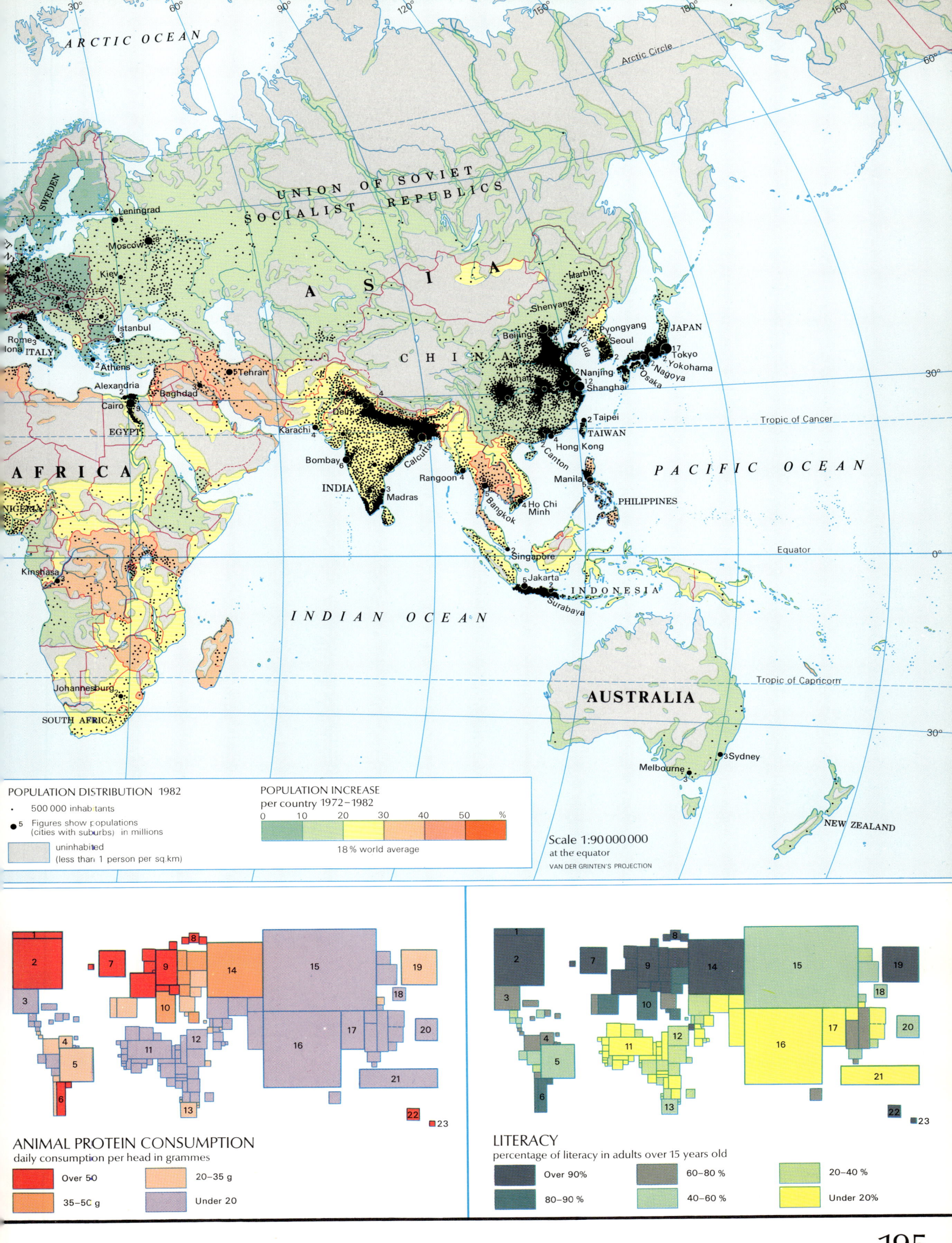

VAN DER GRINTEN'S PROJECTION

ANIMAL PROTEIN CONSUMPTION
daily consumption per head in grammes

- Over 50
- 35–50 g
- 20–35 g
- Under 20

LITERACY
percentage of literacy in adults over 15 years old

- Over 90%
- 80–90%
- 60–80%
- 40–60%
- 20–40%
- Under 20%

195

THE WORLD, political

MILITARY POLITICS

- N.A.T.O., A.N.Z.U.S.
- Warsaw Pact
- Other communist states
- Arab League
- Other states

AMERICAN ASPECT (centre Chicago)

EUROPEAN ASPECT (centre London)

EAST ASIATIC ASPECT (centre Peking)

W. William-Ols projection

© ESSELTE MAP SERVICE

196

TRADE POLITICS

Scale 1:90 000 000

- ● National capital
- ─── International boundary
- ─ ─ ─ Disputed boundary

VAN DER GRINTEN'S PROJECTION

AMERICAN ASPECT — centre Chicago
EUROPEAN ASPECT — centre London
EAST ASIATIC ASPECT — centre Peking

Legend:
- E.E.C.
- E.E.C. associated, Commonwealth
- E.F.T.A.
- L.A.I.A.
- Comecon
- Other countries
- ○ O.P.E.C.

197

198 THE WORLD, energy

PRODUCTION OF ENERGY
Total annual production of primary energy (crude oil, natural gas, coal, lignite, peat, hydro-electric and nuclear power)

primary energy expressed in million tons coal

537 — 1981
99 — 1962
AFRICA

- NORTH AMERICA: 2359 / 1533
- CENTRAL AMERICA (INCL. VENEZUELA AND COLOMBIA): 285 / 428
- SOUTH AMERICA: 133 / 46
- WESTERN EUROPE: 832 / 572
- AFRICA: 500 / 99
- MIDDLE EAST: 1193 / 408
- COMMUNIST COUNTRIES INCL. CHINA: 3089 / 1349
- REST OF ASIA: 365 / 186
- OCEANIA: 128 / 34

THE WORLD'S SOURCES OF ENERGY
- Hydro-electric & nuclear power: 3,6%
- Natural gas: 21,4%
- Coal, lignite: 29,4%
- Crude oil: 45,6%

CONSUMPTION OF ENERGY
Total annual consumption of primary energy per person by country (expressed in kilograms of coal)

100 | 1000 | 3000 | 6000 kilograms per person

LAND
- sedimentary basin (partly oil-bearing)
- bedrock without thick sediment cover
- hydro electric power > 500 Mw

deposits of:
- uranium
- crude oil
- tar sands or oil shales
- natural gas
- coal
- lignite

SEA
- sedimentary basin (partly oil-bearing)
- shallow seabed without thick sediment cover
- shallow sea (continental shelf) 200 m
- deep sea 2000 m

Scale 1:90 000 000 at the equator

VAN DER GRINTEN'S PROJECTION

199

THE WORLD, languages, religions, time zones

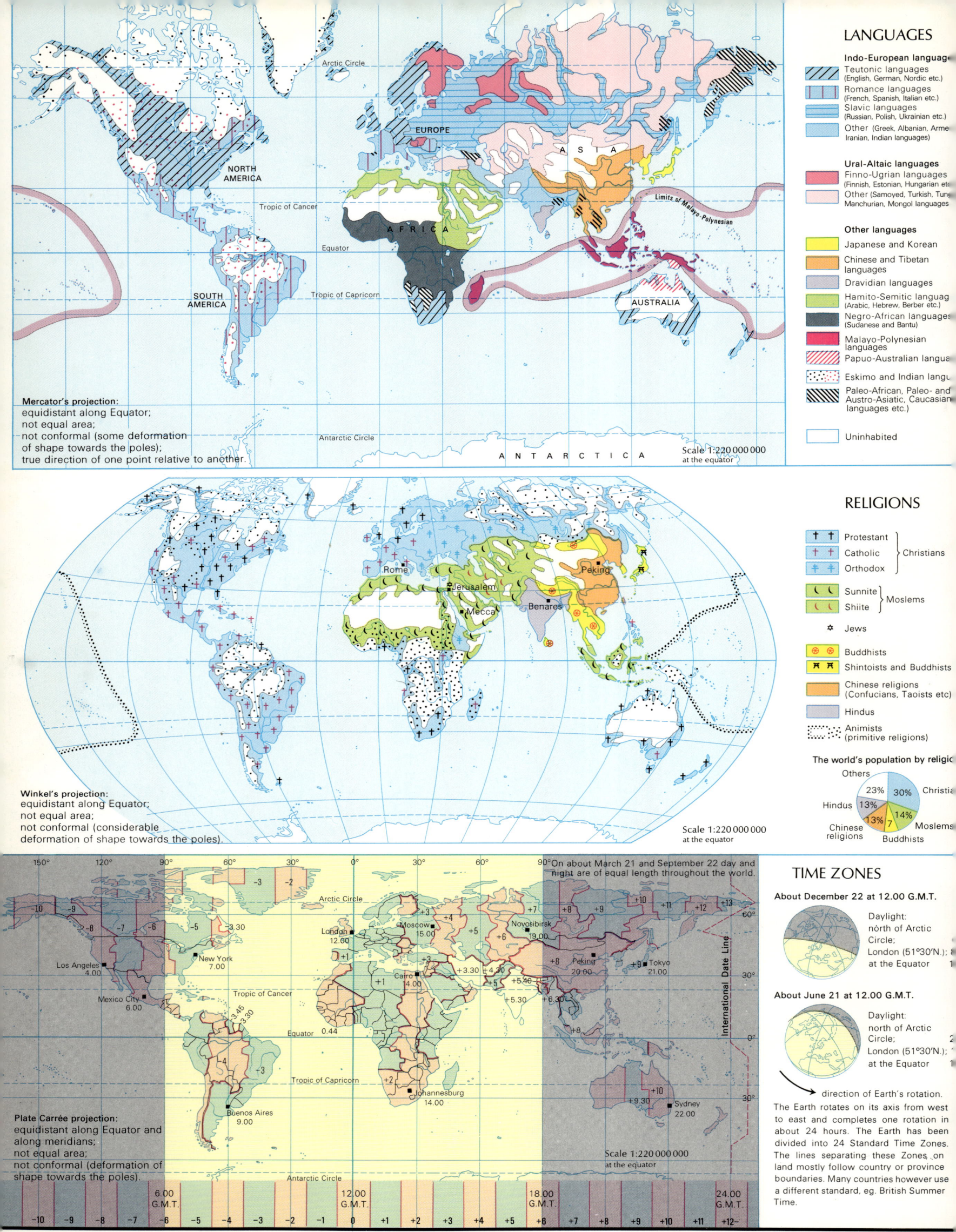

LANGUAGES

Indo-European languages
- Teutonic languages (English, German, Nordic etc.)
- Romance languages (French, Spanish, Italian etc.)
- Slavic languages (Russian, Polish, Ukrainian etc.)
- Other (Greek, Albanian, Armenian, Iranian, Indian languages)

Ural-Altaic languages
- Finno-Ugrian languages (Finnish, Estonian, Hungarian etc.)
- Other (Samoyed, Turkish, Tungusian, Manchurian, Mongol languages)

Other languages
- Japanese and Korean
- Chinese and Tibetan languages
- Dravidian languages
- Hamito-Semitic languages (Arabic, Hebrew, Berber etc.)
- Negro-African languages (Sudanese and Bantu)
- Malayo-Polynesian languages
- Papuo-Australian languages
- Eskimo and Indian languages
- Paleo-African, Paleo- and Austro-Asiatic, Caucasian languages etc.
- Uninhabited

Mercator's projection:
equidistant along Equator;
not equal area;
not conformal (some deformation of shape towards the poles);
true direction of one point relative to another.

Scale 1:220 000 000 at the equator

RELIGIONS

- Protestant ⎫
- Catholic   ⎬ Christians
- Orthodox   ⎭
- Sunnite ⎫ Moslems
- Shiite ⎭
- Jews
- Buddhists
- Shintoists and Buddhists
- Chinese religions (Confucians, Taoists etc)
- Hindus
- Animists (primitive religions)

The world's population by religion
- Christians 30%
- Moslems 14%
- Buddhists 7%
- Chinese religions 13%
- Hindus 13%
- Others 23%

Winkel's projection:
equidistant along Equator;
not equal area;
not conformal (considerable deformation of shape towards the poles).

Scale 1:220 000 000 at the equator

TIME ZONES

About December 22 at 12.00 G.M.T.
Daylight:
north of Arctic Circle;
London (51°30'N.);
at the Equator

About June 21 at 12.00 G.M.T.
Daylight:
north of Arctic Circle;
London (51°30'N.);
at the Equator

→ direction of Earth's rotation

The Earth rotates on its axis from west to east and completes one rotation in about 24 hours. The Earth has been divided into 24 Standard Time Zones. The lines separating these Zones on land mostly follow country or province boundaries. Many countries however use a different standard, eg. British Summer Time.

Plate Carrée projection:
equidistant along Equator and along meridians;
not equal area;
not conformal (some deformation of shape towards the poles).

Scale 1:220 000 000 at the equator

On about March 21 and September 22 day and night are of equal length throughout the world.

City times:
- Los Angeles 4.00
- Mexico City 6.00
- New York 7.00
- Buenos Aires 9.00
- London 12.00
- Cairo 14.00
- Johannesburg 14.00
- Moscow 15.00
- Novosibirsk 19.00
- Peking 20.00
- Tokyo 21.00
- Sydney 22.00

© ESSELTE MAP SERVICE

200

GLOSSARY and INDEX

The **GLOSSARY**, p. 201–203, provides an English translation of those geographical names and words which are presented on the maps in the langue of the area concerned. For languages using non-Latin alphabets, official transcriptions have been used throughout the entire atlas—in maps, glossary and index.

The words in the glossary are mostly single words, but some prefixes and suffixes are also translated into English. In some cases the name on the map is abbreviated, for instance **Khr.** for the Russian **Khrebet** (mountain chain or range). In the glossary both the full name and its abbreviation is given.

The **INDEX**, p. 205–296, contains about 45.000 names found in the map section. As a general rule each entry is referred to the map page where the place or feature is shown at the largest scale and where it is best seen in its national and environmental context. The oceans and some oceanic islands are referred to small-scale maps to show the extent of the oceans and, for the islands, their correct location.

Each name in the index is located by a map page number and an index square on that particular page. The locational reference is to the name and not, for instance, the extent of country or the position of the town. The squares are defined by letters and figures. For example the town Nyeri in Kenya is found in the index with the reference 159 F 5 which means that Nyeri is found on page 159 in index square F (marked at the top and at the bottom of the map spread) and 5 (marked at the sides of the spread).

Some names are given only a page number as reference. Some of these names appear on the maps of the Polar regions, where an index with letters and figures would be confusing. Other entries refer to names on the thematical maps of the continents which do not have index squares.

The order of names in the index is strictly alphabetical and unaffected by diacritical signs such as dots or accents.

GLOSSARY

A

å *Dan., Nor., Swe.*	river
açude *Portugese*	reservoir
adrar *Berber*	mountains
ákra, akrotition *Greek*	cape
Alb, Alp *German*	mountains, peak
alpes *French*	mountains
alpi *Italian*	mountains
-älv, -älven *Swedish*	river
ao *Thai*	bay
archipiélago *Spanish*	archipelago
arquipélago *Portugese*	archipelago
arrecife *Spanish*	reef
arroyo *Spanish*	brook
-ås, -åsen *Swedish*	hills
atol *Portugese*	atoll
aïn *Arabic*	spring

B

bab *Arabic*	strait
bælt *Danish*	strait
bahia *Spanish*	bay
bahr, baḥr *Arabic*	river, sea
baia *Portugese*	bay
baie *French*	bay
ballon *French*	mountain
balta *Romanian*	marsh
bañados *Spanish*	marsh
-bandao *Chinese*	peninsula
barrage *French*	dam
baraji *Turkish*	reservoir
batang *Indonesian*	river
batu *Malay*	mountain
Becken *German*	basin
ben *Gaelic*	mountain
Berg *German*	mountain, hill
berg *Afrikaan, Dutch*	mountains
-berg *Swedish*	mountain, hill
Berge *German*	mountains
-bergen *Swedish*	mountains
-berget *Swedish*	mountain, hill
bi'r *Arabic*	well
birkat *Arabic*	lake
boca *Spanish*	river mouth
boğazi *Turkish*	strait
bogd *Mongolian*	range
bol'shoy *Russian*	river, brook
bong *Korean*	mountain
-breen *Norwegian*	glacier
Bucht *German*	bay
bugt *Danish*	bay
buḥayrah *Arabic*	lake
buḥayrat *Arabic*	lake, lagoon

bukit *Indon., Malay*	mountain
-bukten *Swedish*	bay
burnu, burun *Turkish*	cape

C

c., cabo *Spanish*	cape
c., cabo *Port.*	cape
cachoeira *Portugese*	waterfall
canal *Fr., Port., Sp.*	canal, channel
canale *Italian*	canal, channel, strait
cao nguyen *Vietnamese*	plateau
c., cap *French*	cape
capo *Italian*	cape
causse *French*	upland
c., co., cerro *Spanish*	mountain
c., co., cerros *Spanish*	mountains
chapada *Portugese*	hills
chott *Arabic*	intermittent lake, salt marsh
chuŏr phnum *Cambod.*	mountains
ciudad *Spanish*	city
co *Chinese*	lake
col *French*	pass
colina *Spanish*	hill
colinas *Spanish*	hills
colli *Italian*	hills
collines *French*	hills
con *Vietnamese*	islands
cord., cordillera *Sp.*	mountains
corno *Italian*	mountain
costa *Spanish*	coast
côte *French*	coast, hills
crêt *French*	peak
cuevas *Spanish*	caves

D

dağ, dağı *Turkish*	mountain
dāgh *Persian*	mountains
dağlar, dağlan *Turkish*	mountains
dahr *Arabic*	hill
-dal, -dalen *Nor., Swe.*	valley
danau *Indonesian*	lake
-dao *Chinese, Vietnam.*	island
daryācheh *Persian*	lake
dasht *Persian*	desert
deniz, denizi *Turkish*	sea
desierto *Spanish*	desert
détroit *French*	strait
dhar *Arabic*	escarpment
-dian *Chinese*	lake
dijk *Dutch*	dike
djebel *Arabic*	mountain, mountains
-djupet *Swedish*	deep

-do *Korean*	island
doi *Thai*	mountain
dolina *Russian*	valley
dolok *Indonesian*	mountain

E

-egga *Norwegian*	mountain
-elv, -elva *Nor.*	river
embalse *Spanish*	reservoir
erg *Arabic*	desert
espigão *Portugese*	highland
estero *Spanish*	estuary
estrecho *Spanish*	strait
étang *French*	pond
-ey *Icelandic*	island

F

falaise *French*	cliff
farsh *Arabic*	upland
-fell *Icelandic*	mountain
-feng *Chinese*	mountain
firth *Gaelic*	estuary, strait
-fjäll *Swedish*	hill, mountain
-fjällen *Swedish*	mountain, mountains
-fjället *Swedish*	mountain
-fjell, -fjellet *Norwegian*	mountain
-fjöll *Icelandic*	mountain
-fjord *Norwegian*	fjord
-fjorden *Nor., Swe.*	fjord, lake
-fjördur *Icelandic*	fjord, bay
-flói *Icelandic*	bay
foci *Italian*	river mouths
-fonni *Norwegian*	glacier
fontaine *French*	spring
-foss *Icelandic*	waterfall

G

g., gora *Russian*	mountain, hill
G., gunung *Malay*	mountain
G., gunung *Indonesian*	mountain
gebergte *Dutch*	mountains
Gebirge *German*	mountains
greçidi *Turkish*	pass
ghubbat *Arabic*	bay
Gipfel *German*	peak
gji *Albanian*	bay
gol *Mongol*	river
göl, gölü *Turkish*	lake
golfe *French*	gulf
golfo *It., Sp.*	gulf
gora *Serbo-Croatian*	mountains

201

Term	Language	Meaning
góra	Polish	mountain
gorje	Serbo-Croatian	mountains, hills
gory	Russian	mountains, hills
góry	Polish	mountains
grotte	French	grotto
gryada	Russian	mountain
guba	Russian	bay
guelb	Arabic	mountain
-guntō	Japanese	islands

H

Term	Language	Meaning
Haff	German	lagoon
-hai	Chinese	sea, lake
-haixia	Chinese	strait
-halvøya	Norwegian	peninsula
-hama	Japanese	beach
hamada	Arabic	desert
hammādat	Arabic	plateau
hāmūn	Persian	lake, marsch
harrat	Arabic	lava flow
-hav	Swedish	sea, bay
havre	French	harbor
hawr	Arabic	lake
-he	Chinese	river
Heide	German	heath
hka	Burmese	river
-holm	Danish	island
horn	German	cape, mountain
hory	Czech., Slovenian	mountains
-hu	Chinese	lake

I

Term	Language	Meaning
i., isla	Spanish	island
idhan	Arabic	dunes
île	French	island
îles	French	islands
ilha	Portuguese	islands
Insel	German	island
Inseln	German	islands
Insulá	Romanian	island
'irq	Arabic	dunes
islas	Spanish	islands
isola	Italian	island
isole	Italian	islands
istmo	Spanish	isthmus

J

Term	Language	Meaning
jabal	Arabic	mountain, mountains
järv	Estonian	lake
-järvi	Finnish	lake
-jaur	Lappish	lake
-javre	Lappish	lake
jazā'ir	Arabic	islands
jazīrat	Arabic	island
jazīreh	Persian	island
jebel	Arabic	mountain
jezero	Serbo-Croatian, Albanian	lake
jezioro	Polish	lake, lagoon
-jiang	Chinese	river
jibāl	Arabic	mountains
-jima	Japanese	island
-joki	Finnish	river
-jøkulen	Norwegian	glacier
-jökull	Icelandic	glacier

K

Term	Language	Meaning
kabīr	Persian	mountains
-kaikuō	Japanese	strait
-kaise	Lappish	mountain
kalns	Latvian	mountain
Kamm	German	ridge
kanaal	Dutch	canal
kanal	Rus., S.C., Swe., Ger.	canal, channel
kanava	Finnish	canal, channel
Kap	German	cape
-kapp	Norwegian	cape
kas	Cambodian	island
kavīr	Persian	desert
kep	Albanian	cape
k., kep., kepulauan	Indon.	islands
khalīj	Arabic	gulf
khashm	Arabic	mountain
Khr., Khrebet	Russian	mountain range
ko	Thai	island
-ko	Japanese	lake, lagoon
koh	Afgan.	mountains
kólpos	Greek	bay
körfezi	Turkish	gulf, bay
Kórgustik	Estonian	mountain
kosa	Russian	spit
kotlina	Polish	basin
-kou	Chinese	bay, pass
krueng	Indonesian	river
kryazh	Russian	mountains
kuala	Malay	bay
kūh	Persian	mountain

Term	Language	Meaning
kūhha	Persian	mountains
-kulle	Swedish	hill
kyun	Burmese	island

L

Term	Language	Meaning
l., lac	French	lake
la	Tibethan	pass
lacs	French	lakes
lacul	Bulgarian	lake
lago	It., Sp. Port.	lake
lagoa	Portuguese	lake, lagoon
lagos	Port., Sp.	lakes
lag., laguna	Spanish	lagoon, lake
l., laut	Indonesian	sea
les	Czechoslovakian	mountains, forest
liman	Russian	estuary, bay
limni	Greek	lake
-ling	Chinese	peak
llano	Spanish, Port.	plain
llanos	Spanish, Port.	plains
loch	Gaelic	lake, inlet
lough	Gaelic	lake

M

Term	Language	Meaning
m., munţii	Romanian	mountains
mae	Thai	river
-mak	Turkish	river
-man	Korean	bay
mar	Spanish	sea
marais	French	marsch
mare	Italian	sea
massif	French	mountain, mountains
Meer	German	sea, lake
meer	Afrikaans, Dutch	sea, lake
mer	French	sea
mesa	Spanish	mesa
meseta	Spanish	plateau
mierzeja	Polish	spit
-misaki	Japanese	cape
mont	French	mount
montagna	Italian	mountain
montagne	French	mountain
montagnes	French	mountains
montaña	Spanish	mountain
montañas	Spanish	mountains
monte	It., Port., Sp.	mount
montes	Port., Sp.	mountains
monti	Italian	mountains
monts	French	mountains
more	Russian	sea
morro	Port., Sp.	hill, mountain
motu	Polynesian	island, rock
mui	Vietnamese	point
munkhafad	Arabic	depression
munţii	Romanian	mountains
mys	Russian	cape

N

Term	Language	Meaning
nafūd	Arabic	desert
najor'ye	Russian	plateau, mountains
namakzār	Persian	salt flat
-nås	Swedish	peninsula
nasjonal park	Nor.	national park
neem	Estonian	cape
-nes	Ice., Nor.	peninsula, point
ness	Gaelic	promontory
nev., nevado	Spanish	mountain
ngoc	Vietnamese	mountain
niso	Greek	islands
nizmennost'	Russian	plain
nunatakk	Eskimo	peak
nuruu	Mongol	mountains
nuur	Mongol	lake

O

Term	Language	Meaning
-ö	Swe., Dan., Nor.	island
o., ostrov	Russian	island
-öarna	Swedish	islands
-ön	Swedish	island
óri	Greek	mountains
óros	Greek	mountain, mountains
ostrov	Russian	island
ostrova	Russian	islands
ostrovul	Romanian	island
otok	Serbo-croatian	island
-øy, -øya	Norwegian	island
oz., ozero	Russian	lake
ozera	Russian	lakes

P

Term	Language	Meaning
pahorkatina	Czech.	hills
palla	Italian	peak
pampa	Spanish	plain
pantanal	Port., Sp.	swamp
parc national	French	national park
parq. nac., parque nacional	Port., Sp.	national park
pas	French	strait

Term	Language	Meaning
paso	Spanish	pass
Pass	German	pass
passe	French	passage
passo	Italian	pass
pasul	Romanian	pass
peg., pegunungan	Indonesian	mountains
pélagos	Greek	sea
peña	Spanish	peak, rock
-pendi	Chinese	basin
peninsula	Spanish	peninsula
pereval	Russian	pass
pertuis	French	strait
peski	Russian	desert
phnum	Cambodian	mountain
pic	French	peak
pico	Port., Sp.	peak
picos	Port., Sp.	peaks
-piggen	Norwegian	mountains
pik	Russian	peak
plaine	French	plain
planalto	Portuguese	plateau
planina	Serbo-Croatian	mountain
plato	Bulgarian, Russian	plateau
playa	Spanish	beach
ploskogorje	Russian	plateau
pointe	French	point
poluostrov	Russian	peninsula
ponta	Portuguese	point
porog	Russian	waterfall
presa	Spanish	reservoir, dam
prohod	Bulgarian	pass
proliv	Russian	strait
promontorio	It., Sp.	promonotyr
puerto	Spanish	pass
puig	Catalonian	peak
pulau	Indon., Malay	island
puna	Spanish	upland
punta	It., Sp.	point, peak
puncak	Indonesian	peak
puo	Laotian, Thai	mountain
puy	French	peak

Q

Term	Language	Meaning
qanāt	Arabic	canal
-quando	Chinese	islands
qurnat	Arabic	mountains

R

Term	Language	Meaning
r.	Port., Sp.	river
rags	Latvian	cape
ramlat	Arabic	dunes
ras, ra's	Arabic	cape
räs	Persian	cape
ravnina	Russian	plain
récif	French	reef
récifs	French	reefs
représa	Portuguese	dam, reservoir
-retto	Japanese	islands
ria	Spanish	estuary
rio	Portugese	river
rio	Spanish	river
riviera	Italian	coast
rivière	French	river
rt	Serbo-Croatian	cape
Ruck	German	mountain

S

Term	Language	Meaning
sa.	Portuguese	mountains
saar	Estonian	island
sabkhat	Arabic	lagoon, salt marsh
sadd	Arabic	dam
saguia	Arabic	wadi
şahrā'	Arabic	desert
salar	Spanish	salt flat
salina, salinas	Spanish	salt marsh, salt flat
-sälkä	Finnish	ridge
-sanmyaku	Japanese	range
-san	Jap., Korean	mountain
-sanchi	Japanese	mountains
-sanmaek	Korean	mountains
sarīr	Arabic	desert
Sattel	German	pass
saurums	Latvian	strait
sebkha	Arabic	salt flat
sebkra	Arabic	intermittent lake
See	German	lake
Seen	German	lakes
selat	Indonesian	strait
serra	Portuguese	mountains, mountain
serania, serranias	Sp.	mountains
shamo	Chinese	desert
-shan	Chinese	mountains, mountain, island
-shankou	Chinese	pass
sharm	Arabic	bay
-shima	Japanese	island
-shotō	Japanese	islands
-shuiku	Chinese	reservoir
sierra	Spanish	mountains

202

silsilesi *Turkish*	mountains	
-sjö *Norwegian*	lake	
-sjön *Swedish*	lake, bay	
serrania *Spanish*	mountains	
sopka *Russian*	mountain	
Spitze *German*	peak	
sierra *Spanish*	mountains	
step' *Russian*	plain	
štit *Slovenian*	peak	
stretto *Italian*	strait	
-suidō *Japanese*	channel	
-sund *Swedish*	sound	
s., sungai *Indonesian*	river	

T

tg., tanjung *Indones.*	cape
-tangar-, tangi *Icelandic*	point
tassili *Berber*	plateau
taung *Burmese*	mountain
teluk *Indonesian*	bay
ténéré *Berber*	desert
tepe, tepesi *Turkish*	peak, hill
thiu khao *Thai.*	mountains
-tind, -tindane *Nor.*	mountain
-tō *Japanese*	island
tónlé *Cambodian*	lake
-top *Dutch*	peak
-träsk *Swedish*	lake
-tunturi *Finnish*	mountain

U–V

uul *Mongol*	mountain, mountains
-vaara *Finnish*	hill
val *French, Italian*	valley
valle *Italian, Spanish*	valley
vallée *French*	valley
-vatn *Ice., Nor.*	lake
-vesi *Finnish*	lake
-vidda *Norwegian*	plateau
-viken *Swedish*	gulf
Virful *Romanian*	mountain
vodokhranilishche *Russian*	reservoir
vol., volcán *Spanish*	volcano
vozvyshennost *Russian*	upland
vrh., vrchovina *Czech., Slo.*	mountains
-väin *Estonian*	strait
-vötn *Icelandic*	lake

W–Z

wādi *Arabic*	wadi
wāhat *Arabic*	oasis
Wald *German*	forest, mountains
-wan *Ch., Jap.*	bay
-xan *Chinese*	strait
-yama *Japanese*	mountain
y., yarimadasi *Turkish*	peninsula
yoma *Burmese*	mountains
-zaki *Japanese*	point
zalew *Polish*	lagoon
zaliv *Russian*	gulf, bay
zatoka *Polish*	gulf
zee *Dutch*	sea, lake

INDEX

A

Å 112 F 2
Aachen 110 E 4
Aalen 111 F 5
Äänekoski 112 J 3
Aansluit 160 C 5
Aare 115 E 2
Aargub 152 B 4
Aạ Sumayḥ 158 D 3
Aba 132 D 4
Aba (Nigeria) 157 F 4
Aba (Zaire) 158 E 4
Abā Ad Dūd 155 G 3
Abacaxis 179 G 5
Abadab, Jabal 154 F 5
Ābādān 128 D 4
Ābādeh 128 E 4
Abadla 152 E 2
Abaeté 181 G 4
Abaetetuba 179 J 4
Abagnar Qi 133 G 2
Abai 182 E 4
Abaiang 146 C 2
Abaji 157 F 4
Abakaliki 157 F 4
Abakan 130 E 5
Abakan 130 F 5
Abakanskiy Khrebet 119 R 5
Abakwasimbo 158 D 4
Abala (Congo) 157 H 6
Abala (Niger) 156 E 3
Abalak 157 F 2
Abalemma (Algeria) 153 G 4
Abalemma (Niger) 157 F 2
Abalessa 153 F 4
Aban 130 G 4
Abancay 180 B 3
Abanga 157 G 5
Abant Silsilesi 116 D 2
Abār al Kanā'is 154 D 2
Abariringa 146 D 3
Abarqu 128 E 4
Abashiri 133 M 2
Abatskoye 119 O 4
Abau 144 E 4
Abau 143 H 5
Abava 113 H 4
Abay 119 O 6
Abaya, Lake 159 F 3
Abaza 130 F 5
Abbai 158 F 2
Abbāsābād 128 F 3
Abbe, Lake 159 G 2
Abbeville (France) 114 D 1
Abbeville (LA, U.S.A.) 171 H 6
Abbeyleix 100 B 3
Abborrträsk 112 G 2
Abbot Ice Shelf 185
Abbottabad 129 J 4
'Abd al Azīz, Jabal 155 G 1
'Abd al Kūrī 159 J 2
Abdul Ghadir 159 G 2
Abdulino 118 K 5
Abéché 157 J 3
Abel Tasman National Park 145 Q 9
Abelvær 112 F 3
Abemama 146 C 2
Abenab 160 B 3
Abengourou 156 D 4
Åbenrå 113 E 4
Åbenrå Fjord 113 E 4
Abeokuta 156 E 4
Aberaeron 102 B 1
Aberchirder 98 C 3
Aberdare 102 C 2
Aberdare National park 159 F 5
Aberdares → Nyanda Rua 159 F 5
Aberdeen 98 C 3
Aberdeen (Airport) 98 C 3
Aberdeen (Andaman Isl.) 135 F 5
Aberdeen (S. Afr.) 160 C 6
Aberdeen (S.D., U.S.A.) 170 G 3
Aberdeen (WA, U.S.A.) 170 B 2
Aberdeen Lake 167 R 3
Aberfeldy 99 C 3
Aberffraw 102 B 1
Aberfoyle 143 H 3
Abergavenny 102 C 2
Abergele 102 C 1

Abersoch 102 B 1
Abersychan 102 C 2
Abertillery 102 C 2
Aberystwyth 102 B 1
Abez' 119 M 2
Abganerevo 117 F 1
Abhā 155 G 5
Abhar 128 D 3
Abi Addi 159 F 2
Abidjan 156 D 4
Ab-i-Istada 129 H 4
Abilene 170 G 5
Abingdon 103 D 2
Abinsk 117 E 2
Abisko 112 G 2
Abitibi 169 L 5
Abja-Paluoja 112 J 4
Abkit 131 T 3
Abnūb 154 E 3
Åbo 113 H 3
Aboisso 156 D 4
Aboke 158 E 3
Abo, Massif d' 157 H 1
Abomey 156 E 4
Abong Abong, Gunung 136 A 3
Abong Mbang 157 G 5
Aborigen, Pik 131 R 3
Aborlan 137 EF 2
Abou Deïa 157 H 3
Abou Goulem 157 J 3
Abovyan 117 F 2
Aboyne 99 C 3
Abqayq → Buqayq 155 H 3
Abraham's Bay 173 H 3
Abrantes 114 B 4
Abreu e Lima 181 K 2
'Abrī 154 E 4
Abrolhos, Arquipélago dos 181 J 4
Abruka 113 H 4
Abruzzo 115 F 3
Absaroka Range 170 D 2
Abtenau 115 F 2
Abū ad Duhūr 154 F 1
Abū 'Alī 155 H 3
Abū 'Arīsh 155 G 5
Abū Baḥr 155 H 4
Abū Ballaṣ 154 D 4
Abu Dhabi 155 J 4
Abū Ḍulayq 154 E 5
Abufari 179 F 5
Abū Ḥadrīyah 155 H 3
Abū Ḥamad 154 E 5
Abū Ḥasan, Jabal 155 G 5
Abuja 157 F 4
Abū Jābirah 154 D 6
Abū Jifān 155 H 4
Abū Jubayhah 154 E 6
Abū Kamāl 155 G 2
Abū Madd, Ra's 154 F 4
Abū Maṭariq 154 D 6
Abu Mendi 158 F 2
Abumombazi 158 C 4
Abū Mūsa' 128 F 5
Abunā (Bolivia) 180 C 3
Abunā (Brazil) 178 E 5
Abū Njaym 153 J 2
Abūqrīn 153 J 2
Abu Road 134 B 3
Abū Rubayq 155 F 4
Abū Rujmayn, Jabal 154 F 2
Abū Shajarah, Ra's 154 F 4
Abū Shanab 154 D 6
Abu Simbel → Abū Sunbul 154 E 4
Abū Sunbul 154 E 4
Abū Ṭabarī 154 D 5
Abū Tīj 154 E 3
Abū Tulayh 154 E 5
Abū 'Uruq 154 E 5
Abuya Myeda 159 F 2
Abū Zabad 154 D 6
Abū Ẓaby 155 J 4
Abū Zanīmah 154 E 3
Abwong 158 E 3
Abyad 154 D 6
Abyaḍ, Jabal 154 D 5
Abyaḍ, Ra's al 154 F 4
Abyār 'Alī 155 F 4
Abydos 154 E 3
Abyei 158 D 3

Ābyek 128 E 3
Aby, Lagune 156 D 4
Åbyn 112 H 2
Abyy 131 QR 2
Acadia, Cape 169 M 3
Acadia National Park 171 N 3
Acadie 169 O 6
Açailândia 179 J 4
Acajutla 172 E 5
Acalayong 157 F 5
Acámbaro 172 B 3
Acandí 178 C 2
Acaponeta 172 A 3
Acapulco 172 C 4
Acará 179 J 4
Acarai, Serra 179 G 3
Acaraú 181 J 1
Acaraú 181 HJ 1
Acari (Brazil) 181 J 2
Acarí (Peru) 180 B 4
Acarigua 178 E 2
Acatlán de Osorio 172 C 4
Acayucan 172 D 4
Accomac 171 L 4
Accra 156 D 4
Accrington 101 D 3
Acebuches 172 B 2
Acerra 115 F 3
Achaguas 178 E 2
Achalpur 134 C 3
Achao 183 B 7
Achar 182 E 5
Achayvayam 131 W 3
Achegour 157 G 2
Acheloós 116 B 3
Acheng 133 N 2
Achikouya, Plateau des 157 G 6
Achikulak 117 F 2
Achill 110 A 4
Achim 111 E 4
Achinsk 130 EF 4
Achit Nuur 130 F 6
Achuyevo 117 E 1
Acı Gölü 116 C 3
Acil Barké 156 C 3
Acipayam 116 C 3
Acireale 115 G 4
Acklins Island 173 H 3
Aconcagua, Cerro 182 C 5
Acopiara 181 J 2
Acorizal 180 E 4
Acquasanta Terme 115 F 3
Acqui Terme 115 E 3
Acre 178 D 5
Acre 180 C 3
Acre → 'Akko 154 F 2
Acri 115 G 4
Actéon, Group 147 F 4
Actopan 172 C 3
Açu 181 J 2
Açude Araras 181 H 1
Açude Orós 181 J 2
Acuracay 178 D 5
Ada 171 G 5
Ada 156 E 4
Adaba 159 F 3
Ada Burnu 117 D 3
'Adad 159 H 3
Adädle 159 G 3
Adafer 152 CD 5
Adair, Bahia 170 D 5
Adak (AK, U.S.A.) 166 B 5
Adak (Sweden) 112 G 2
'Adale 159 H 4
Ådalen 112 G 3
'Adam 155 K 4
Adama Nazareth → Adama 159 F 3
Adamantina 181 F 5
Adamaoua 157 G 4
Adamello 115 F 2
Adam, Mount 183 E 9
Adamoua, Massif de l' 157 G 4
Adams 167 O 5
Adams Bridge 134 C 6
Adams Peak 134 D 6
Adamstown 147 G 4
Adana 117 E 3
Adang, Teluk 136 E 4

Adapazarı 116 D 2
Adarama 154 E 5
Adare, Cape 185
Adaut 137 H 5
Adavale 143 G 4
Adda 115 E 2
Aḍ Ḍab'ah 154 D 2
Ad Dabbah 154 E 5
Ad Dafīnah 155 G 4
Aḍ Ḍafrah 155 J 4
Aḍ Dahnā' 155 H 3
Aḍ Ḍālī' 155 G 6
Ad Damazin 154 E 6
Ad' Dāmir 154 E 5
Ad Dammām 155 HJ 3
Ad Dār al Ḥamrā' 154 F 3
Ad Darb 155 G 5
Ad Dawādimī 155 G 4
Ad Dawḥah 155 J 3
Ad Dawr 155 G 2
Ad Dibdibah 155 H 3
Aḍ Ḍiffah 153 K 2
Ad Dikākah 155 J 5
Ad Dilam 155 H 4
Ad Dindar 154 E 6
Ad Dir'īyah 155 H 4
Ad Dīwānīyah 155 GH 2
Ad Du'ayn 154 D 6
Ad Duwayd 155 G 2
Ad Duwaym 154 E 6
Addis Ababa 159 F 3
Addis Alam 159 F 3
Addis Derra 159 F 2
Addis Zemen 159 F 2
Adelaide (Australia) 143 F 5
Adelaide (S. Afr.) 160 D 6
Adelaide Island 185
Adelaide Peninsula 167 S 2
Adelaide River 142 E 1
Adele Island 142 C 2
Adélie Coast 185
Aden 155 H 6
Aden, Gulf of 155 H 6
Aderbissinat 157 F 2
Adhan, Jabal 155 K 3
Adh Dhahībāt 153 H 2
Adh Dhayd 155 K 3
Adi 158 E 4
Adiaké 156 D 4
Adi Arkai 159 F 2
Adige 115 F 2
Adigrat 159 F 2
Adıgüzel Barajı 116 C 3
Adi Kaie 159 F 2
Adilabad 134 C 4
Adilcevaz 117 F 3
Adi, Pulau 137 H 4
Adi Quala 159 F 2
Adirondack Mountains 171 M 3
Adi Ugri 159 F 2
Adıyaman 117 E 3
Adjud 116 C 1
Adler 117 E 2
Admer, Erg d' 153 G 4
Admiralty 166 L 4
Admiralty Gulf 142 D 1
Admiralty Island National Monument 166 L 4
Admiralty Islands 144 E 2
Admiralty Mountains 185
Ado 156 E 4
Ado Ekiti 157 F 4
Adok 158 E 3
Adolphus Island 142 D 2
Adonara, Pulau 137 F 5
Adoni 134 C 4
Adour 114 C 3
Ad Ouzzeïne 156 E 2
Adra 114 C 4
Adrano 115 F 4
Adrar (Algeria) 152 E 3
Adrar (Algeria) 153 G 3–4
Adrar des Iforas 156 E 2
Adrar Sotuf 152 B 4
Adré 157 J 3
Adria 115 F 2
Adrian 171 K 3
Adriatic Sea 115 FG 3
Adulis 159 F 1
Adusa 158 D 4

Adwa 159 F 2
Adyakit, Gora 130 G 2
Adycha 131 P 2
Adygalakh 131 R 3
Adyge-Khabl' 117 F 2
Adyk 117 G 1
Adzhar 117 F 2
Adzhima 131 P 6
Adzopáe 156 D 4
Adzva 119 M 2
Adz'va 119 L 2
Aegean Sea 116 BC 3
Ærö 113 F 5
Æroskøbing 113 F 5
Aesculapium 116 C 3
Afade 157 G 3
Afao, Mont 153 G 3
Affollé 152 C 5
Afghanistan 129 GH 4
Afgöye 159 H 4
'Afīf 155 G 4
Afikpo 157 F 4
Aflou 153 F 2
Afmadōw 159 G 4
Afognak 166 G 4
Afore 114 E 3
Afragola 115 F 3
Afrēra, Lake 159 G 2
African Islands 159 J 5
Afşin 117 E 3
Afsluitdijk 110 E 4
Aftout 152 C 5
Afuá 179 H 4
Afuá 179 H 4
Afyonkarahisar 116 D 3
Agadem 157 G 2
Agadez 157 F 2
Agadir 152 D 2
Agadyr' 119 O 6
Agaiáls 152 C 4
Agalta, Sierra de 172 E 4
Agan 119 O 3
Agana 146 A 2
Agapa 130 D 1
Agapitovo 119 R 2
Agapovka 119 L 5
Agara 117 F 2
Agaro 159 F 3
Agartala 135 F 3
Agata 130 F 2
Agata, Ozero 130 F 3
Agats 131 F 2
Agattu 166 A 5
Agawa Bay 171 K 2
Agbaja 157 F 4
Agboville 156 D 4
Agdam 128 D 2
Agdary 131 M 3
Agde 114 D 3
Agdz 152 D 2
Agen 114 D 3
Agenta 115 F 3
Agepsta 117 F 2
Agger 114 E 2
Agha Jari 125
Aghireşu 116 B 1
Aghrejit 152 C 4
Agía Pelagía 116 B 3
Aginskoye 130 K 5
Aginskoye 131 R 5
Agmar 152 C 3
Agmumuit 152 B 4
Agnew 142 C 4
Agnibilékrou 156 D 4
Agnita 116 B 1
Agön 112 G 3
Agordat 159 F 1
Agout 114 D 3
Agoza 157 F 2
Agra 134 C 2
Agreda 114 C 3
Agrihan 146 A 1
Agrinion 116 B 3
Agrour Sfaya 152 C 4
Agto 169 R 2
Agua Blanca 183 C 6
Água Branca (Alagoas, Brazil) 181 J 2
Água Branca (Piauí, Brazil) 181 H 2

205

Agu – Ale

Aguachica 178 D 2
Água Clara 181 F 5
Aguaclara 178 D 3
Aguadas 178 C 2
Aguadulce 178 B 2
Aguapeí, Serra do 180 E 4
Agua Prieta 170 E 5
Aguaray 180 D 5
Aguarico 178 C 4
Aguascalientes 172 B 3
Águas Formosas 181 H 4
Agua Vermelha, Reprêsa 181 FG 4–5
Águeda 114 B 3
Aguelhok 156 E 2
Aguelt el Melha 152 D 4
Aguelt Némadi 152 C 5
Aguemour 153 F 3
Aguenit 152 C 4
Agueraktem 152 D 4
Aguerguer 152 B 4
Aguezi Tigu 157 G 1
Aguilar de Campóo 114 C 3
Aguilas 114 C 4
Aguililla 172 B 4
Aguja, Cerro 183 B 7
Agulhas, Cape 160 C 6
Agulhas Negras, Pico das 181 H 5
Agung, Gunung 136 E 5
Aguscalientes 172 B 3
Ağva 116 C 2
Agvali 117 G 2
Ahaggar 153 G 4
Aha Hills 160 C 3
Ahar 128 D 3
Ahe 147 F 3
Ahiri 134 D 4
Ahlat 117 F 3
Ahmadabad 134 B 3
Ahmadnagar 134 B 4
Ahmadpur West 129 J 5
Ahmar Mountains 159 G 3
Ahmeyim 152 C 4
Ahnet 153 F 4
Ahome 170 E 6
Ahraura 134 D 2
Ahrensburg 111 F 4
Ähtäri 112 G 3
Ähtärinjärvi 112 H 3
Ahtaung 135 G 4
Ähtävänjoki 112 H 3
Ahunui 147 F 4
Åhus 170 D 5
Ahvāz 128 D 4
Ahvenanmaa (Åland) 113 G 3
Aḩwar 155 H 6
Ai-Ais 160 B 5
Aiapuá 179 F 4
Aigoual, Mont 114 D 3
Aigua 182 F 5
Aigues-Mortes 114 D 3
Aiguilete, Cerro 183 B 9
Aiguillon 114 D 3
Aihui 131 N 5
Aiken 171 K 5
Ailao Shan 132 D 6
Aileu 137 G 5
Ailigandí 178 C 2
Ailinginae 146 C 2
Aillik 169 Q 4
Ailsa Craig 99 B 4
Ailuk 146 C 2
Aim 131 O 4
Aimorés 181 H 4
Aimorés, Serra dos 181 H 4
Ain 115 E 2
Aïn Afalelah 153 G 4
'Ain al Khaleifa 154 D 3
'Ain al Wādī 154 D 3
Ain Amenas 153 G 3
Aïn Amguel 153 G 4
Ainaro 137 G 5
Aïn Athil 152 C 4
Aïn Azaoua 153 G 3
Ainaži 112 H 4
Aïn Beïda 153 G 1
Aïn Beni Mathar 152 E 2
Aïn ben Tili 152 D 3
Aïn Ebeggi 153 G 4
Aïn Ekker 153 G 4
Aïn el Barka 152 D 3
Aïn el Hadjadj 153 G 3
Aïn Ezzane 153 H 4
Aïn Galakka 157 H 2
Aïn Guezzam 153 G 5
Aïn Ouzzal 153 F 4
Aïnos Óros 116 B 3
Aïn Safra 152 C 5
Aïn Salah 153 F 3
Aïn Sefra 152 E 2
Aïn Souf 153 F 3
Aïn Taya 114 D 4
Aïn Témouchent 152 E 1

Aïn Tidjoubar 153 F 3
Aïn Tiguelguemine 153 F 3
Aïn Ziza 153 F 4
Aïoun Abd el Malek 152 D 4
Aioun el Atrouss 152 D 5
Aipley 103 D 1
Aiquile 180 C 4
Aïr 157 F 2
Airao 179 F 4
Airdrie 99 C 4
Aireborough 101 E 3
Aire, Canal d' 114 D 1
Aire, River 101 E 3
Aire-sur-l'Adour 114 C 3
Air Force Island 169 N 2
Air Komering 136 B 4
Air Musi 136 B 4
Air Ogan 136 B 4
Airolo 115 E 2
Aisaita 159 G 2
Aiscia 159 G 2
Aisega 144 E 3
Aishalton 179 G 3
Aishihik 166 K 3
Aisne 114 D 2
Aïssa, Djebel 152 E 2
Aitana, Pico 114 C 4
Aitape 144 D 2
Aitolikón 116 B 3
Aitutaki 147 E 4
Aiud 116 B 1
Aix-en-Provence 115 E 3
Aix-les-Bains 115 E 2
Aiyaíon Pélagos 116 BC 3
Aíyina 116 B 3
Aiyion 116 B 3
Aizawl 135 F 3
Aizuwakamatsu 133 L 3
Ajab Shīr 128 D 3
Ajaccio 115 E 3
'Ajā 'ız 155 K 5
Ajā', Jabal 155 G 3
Ajajú 178 D 3
Ajanta Range 134 C 3
Aj Bogd Uul 132 C 2
Ajdīr, Ra's 153 H 2
Ajdovščina 115 F 2
Ajigasawa 133 M 2
Ajir, Mont 157 F 2
Ajka 116 A 1
'Ajmān 155 K 3
Ajmer 134 B 2
Ajo 170 D 5
Ajo, Cabo de 114 C 3
Ajoewa 179 G 3
Ajtos 116 C 2
Aju, Kepulauan 137 H 3
Akabli 153 F 3
Akademii, Zaliv 131 P 5
Akal 154 F 5
Akalkot 134 C 4
Akanthou 117 D 3
Akarnaniká Ori 116 B 3
Akaroa 145 Q 9
'Akasha 154 E 4
Akashi 133 K 4
Akbaba Tepe 117 E 3
Akbaytal, Pereval 129 J 3
Akbulak 118 L 5
Akçaabat 117 E 2
Akçadağ 117 E 3
Akçakale 117 E 3
Akçakara Dağı 117 F 3
Akçakışla 117 E 3
Akçakoca 116 D 2
Akchatau 119 O 6
Akchar, Dunes de l' 152 C 4
Akdağ 117 F 2
Ak Dağ 116 C 3
Akdağ 117 E 3
Ak Dağ 116 C 3
Akdağmadeni 117 E 3
Ak Dovurak 130 F 5
Akelamo 137 G 3
Akelo 158 E 3
Akeonic 166 E 1
Akespe 128 G 1
Aketi 158 C 4
Ak 'Abbāsīyah 154 E 6
Akharnai 116 B 3
Akhḍar, Jabal al 155 K 4
Akhiny 130 J 5
Akhisar 116 C 3
Akhmīm 154 E 3
Akhsu 128 D 2
Akhtarīn 154 F 1
Akhtubinsk 118 J 6
Akhtyrka 118 F 5
Akimiski 169 L 5
Akimovka 117 E 1
Akita 133 M 3
Akjoujt 152 C 5

Akka 152 D 3
Akkabak 129 G 1
Akkajaure 112 G 2
'Akko 154 F 2
Akköy 116 C 3
Akkul' 129 J 2
Aklavik 166 L 2
Akmeqit 129 K 3
Akniste 113 J 4
Akobo 158 E 3
Akok 157 F 5
Akola 134 C 3
Al Akhḍar, Al Jabal 153 K 2
Alakol', Ozero 119 Q 6
Alakurtti 113 K 2
Al 'Alamayn 154 D 2
Al 'Amādīyah 155 G 1
Alamagan 146 A 1
'Alam al Rūm, Ra's 154 D 2
Al 'Amārah 155 H 2
Alamitos, Sierra de los 172 B 2
Alamogordo 170 E 5
Alamos 170 E 6
Alamosa 170 E 4
Alamos, Sierra 170 E 6
Åland 113 G 3
Ålands hav 113 G 4
Alaniemi 112 J 3
Alantika Mountains 157 G 4
Alanya 117 D 3
Alaotra, Lac 161 H 3
Alapaha River 171 K 5
Alapayevsk 119 M 4
Alaplı 116 D 2
Al 'Aqabah 154 F 3
Al 'Aqaylah 153 J 2
Al 'Aqīq 155 G 4
Al 'Araj 154 D 3
Alarçon, Embalse de 114 C 4
Al 'Arīsh 154 E 2
Al 'Armah 155 H 3
Al 'Aşāb 155 J 4
Alaşehir 116 C 3
Al Ashkharah 155 K 4
Al 'Āshūrīyah 155 G 2
Alaska 166 F–H 2
Alaska, Gulf of 166 J 4
Alaska Peninsula 166 E 4
Alaska Range 166 G 3
Aksay Kazakzu Zizhixian 132 B 3
Al 'Assāfīyah 155 F 3
Alas, Selat 136 E 5
Alassio 115 E 3
Alatau Shankou 129 L 1
Al 'Athāmīn 155 G 2
Alatna 166 G 2
Alatri 115 F 3
Al 'Aṭrun 154 D 5
Alatyr' 118 J 5
Alavus 112 G 3
Al 'Awāliq 155 H 6
Al 'Awāriq 155 H 4
Al 'Awaynāt 153 H 3
Al 'Awsajīyah 155 G 3
Al Awshazīyah 155 G 3
Alaykël' 129 J 2
Al Ayn 154 D 5
Al 'Ayn 155 K 4
Alayskiy Khrebet 129 J 3
Alayunt 116 D 3
Alazani 117 G 2
Alazeya 131 S 1
Alazeyskoye Ploskogor'ye 131 R 2
Al Azīzīyah 153 H 2
Alba 115 E 3
Al Bāb 154 F 1
Albacete 114 C 4
Al Badārī 154 E 3
Al Badī (Iraq) 155 G 1
Al Badī' (Saudi Arabia) 155 H 4
Ålbæk Bugt 113 F 4
Al Bahrah 155 H 3
Al Baḥrayn 154 D 3
Alba Iulia 116 B 1
Ålbæk Bugt 113 F 4
Al Balyanā 154 E 3
Albanel, Lac 169 N 5
Albania 116 AB 2
Albano Laziale 115 F 3
Albany 142 B 5
Albany (GA, U.S.A.) 171 K 5
Albany (N.Y., U.S.A.) 171 M 3
Albany (Ont., Can.) 168 K 5
Albany (OR, U.S.A.) 170 B 3
Albany Downs 143 H 4
Albardón 182 C 5
Al Barkāt 153 H 5
Al Barrah 155 H 4
Al Baṣrah 155 H 2
Al Bāṭinah 155 K 4
Albatross Bank 166 G 4
Albatross Bay 143 G 1

Alagoas 181 J 2
Alagoinhas 181 J 3
Alagón 114 B 3
Alagon 114 C 3
Alahanpanjang 136 B 4
Alahärmä 112 H 3
Alaid 131 T 5
Alaita 159 G 2
Alajärvi 112 G 3
Alajuela 172 F 5
Alakanuk 166 E 3

Albatross Plateau 193 D 3
Albatross Point 145 Q 8
Al Bawīṭi 154 D 3
Al Bayāḍ 155 H 4
Al Bayḍā' (Libya) 153 K 2
Al Bayḍā' (S. Yemen) 155 H 6
Albemarle Sound 171 L 4
Albenga 115 E 3
Albères, Chaine de 114 D 3
Alberga River 142 E 4
Alberta 167 O 5
Albert Edward Bay 167 R 2
Alberti 182 D 6
Albertkanaal 110 D 4
Albert Lake (OR, U.S.A.) 170 B 3
Albert, Lake (Uganda/Zaire) 158 A 4
Albert Lea 171 H 3
Albert Nile 158 E 4
Albert River 143 F 2
Albertville 115 E 2
Albi 114 D 3
Albina 179 H 2
Al Bi'r 154 F 3
Al Birk 155 G 5
Al Birkah 155 G 4
Alborán 114 C 4
Ålborg 113 E 4
Ålborg Bugt 113 F 4
Albox 114 C 4
Al Brayqah 153 J 2
Albro 143 H 3
Albuquerque 170 E 4
Albuquerque, Cayos de 173 F 5
Al Buraymī 155 K 4
Al Burdī 153 K 2
Al Burmah 153 G 2
Al Buṭayn 155 H 3
Alcañices 114 B 3
Alcañiz 114 C 3
Alcácer do Sal 114 B 4
Alcáçovas 114 B 4
Alcala de Chivert 114 D 3
Alcalá de Henares 114 C 3
Alcalá de Marchena 114 B 4
Alcalá la Real 114 C 4
Alcamo 115 F 4
Alcántara 179 K 4
Alcántara, Embalse de 114 B 4
Alcantarilla 114 C 4
Alcaraz 114 C 4
Alcaraz, Sierra de 114 C 4
Alcaudete 114 C 4
Alcázar de San Juan 114 C 4
Alcira 115 F 3
Alcobaça 181 J 4
Alcobendas 114 C 3
Alcolea del Pinar 114 C 3
Alcoutim 114 B 4
Alcoy 114 C 4
Alcudi 115 F 4
Alcudia 114 D 4
Aldabra Islands 159 H 6
Aldama 170 E 6
Aldan 131 O 3
Aldan 131 N 4
Aldano-Uchurskiy Khrebet 131 N 4
Aldanskoye Nagor'ye 131 MN 4
Aldarhaan 130 G 6
Aldeburgh 110 D 4
Aldeburgh 103 E 1
Alderney 103 E 2
Aldershot 103 D 2
Aldoma 131 P 4
Aldridge 103 D 1
Aleg 152 C 5
Alegrete 182 E 4
Aleknagik 166 F 4
Aleksandriya (Ukraina, U.S.S.R.) 117 D 1
Aleksandrov 118 G 4
Aleksandrov Gay 118 J 5
Aleksandrovsk 119 M 4
Aleksandrovskiy 130 L 5
Aleksandrovskiy Shiyuzo 119 R 4
Aleksandrovskoye 119 P 3
Aleksandrovskoye 119 R 4
Aleksandrovskoye 117 F 2
Aleksandrovsk-Sakhalinskiy 131 Q 5
Alekseyevka 119 O 5
Alekseyevka 119 R 6
Alekseyevka 119 M 3
Alekseyevka 118 G 5
Alekseyevo 131 R 1
Alekseyevsk 130 K 4
Aleksikovo 118 H 5
Aleksinac 116 B 2
Alemania (Arg.) 182 C 4
Alemania (Chile) 182 B 4
Além Paraíba 181 H 5

Alençon 114 D 2
Alenquer 179 H 4
Alépé 156 D 4
Aleppo 154 F 1
Aléria 115 E 3
Alerta 180 B 3
Alès 114 D 3
Aleshkino 130 H 4
Alessandria 115 E 3
Ålestrup 113 E 4
Ålesund 112 E 3
Aleutian Basin 193 C 2
Aleutian Islands 166 F 4
Aleutian Range 166 F 4
Aleutian Trench 193 D 2
Alexander Archipelago 166 K 4
Alexander Bay 160 B 5
Alexander Island 185
Alexandra 144 P 10
Alexandra Channel 135 F 5
Alexandra Falls 167 O 3
Alexandria (U.K.) 99 B 4
Alexandria (Australia) 143 F 2
Alexandria (Egypt) 154 D 2
Alexandria (LA, U.S.A.) 171 H 5
Alexandria (MD, U.S.A.) 171 L 4
Alexandria (Romania)116 C 2
Alexandria (S. Afr.) 160 D 6
Alexandrina, Lake 143 F 6
Alexandroúpolis 116 C 2
Aley 119 Q 5
Aleysk 119 Q 5
Alfabia, Sierra de 114 D 4
Alfambra 114 C 3
Alfaro (Ecuador) 178 C 4
Alfaro (Spain) 114 C 3
Al Fāshir 154 D 6
Al Fashn 154 E 3
Al Fatḥah 155 G 1
Al Fawwārah 155 G 3
Al Fayyūm 154 E 3
Al Fāzih 155 G 6
Alferovka 119 P 5
Al Fifi 154 C 6
Al Fijāj, Shaṭṭ 153 G 2
Alfios 116 E 3
Alföld 116 AB 1
Alford (Grampian) 98 C 3
Alford (Lincolnshire) 103 E 1
Alfreton 103 D 1
Al Fujayrah 155 K 3
Al Fūlah 154 D 6
Al Fuqahā 155 H 3
Al Fuwayrit 155 J 3
Alga 128 F 1
Al Gāga 154 E 4
Al Galhak 154 E 6
Algama 131 N 4
Alganskaya 131 W 3
Algarrobo 183 D 6
Algarrobo del Águila 183 C 6
Algarve 114 B 4
Algasovo 118 H 5
Algeciras 114 B 4
Alger 153 F 1
Algeria 152–153 EF 3
Al Gharbi 153 H 2
Al Ghāṭ 155 GH 3
Al Ghaydah 153 J 5
Al Ghayl 155 H 4
Al Ghazālah 155 G 3
Alghero 115 E 3
Al Ghrayfah 153 H 3
Al Ghurdaqah 154 E 3
Algibe 114 B 4
Algiers 153 F 1
Algoa Bay 160 D 6
Algona 171 H 3
Al Ḥabakah 155 G 3
Al Ḥadabat al Ma'āzah 154 E 3
Al Ḥadd 155 K 4
Al Ḥaddār 155 H 4
Al Ḥadḥāli 155 H 4
Al Ḥadīdah 155 J 4
Al Ḥadīthah 155 G 2
Al Ḥadr 155 G 1
Al Ḥā'ir 155 H 4
Al Hajar al Gharbī 155 K 4
Al Hajar ash Sharqī 155 K 4
Alhama de Murcia 114 C 4
Al Ḥammām 155 G 2
Al Ḥamrā' 154 F 4
Al Ḥamrā', al Ḥamādah 153 H 3
Al Ḥanākīyah 155 H 3
Al Ḥanīyah 155 H 3
Al Ḥarīq 155 H 4
Al Ḥarrah 154 F 2
Al Ḥarūj al Aswad 153 J 3
Al Ḥasā' 155 H 3
Al Ḥasakah 155 G 1
Al Ḥasānī 154 F 3

Al Ḥawā'ish, Jabal 153 K 4
Al Ḥawātah 154 E 6
Al Ḥawīyah 155 G 4
Al Ḥawjā' 154 F 3
Al Ḥawrah 155 H 6
Al Ḥawṭah 155 H 6
Al Ḥawwārī 153 K 4
Al Ḥayy 155 H 2
Al Ḥayz 154 D 3
Al Hibāk 155 J 4–5
AlḤijāz 154 F 3
Al Ḥillah (Iraq) 155 G 2
Al Ḥillah (S. Arabia) 155 H 4
Al Ḥillah (Sudan) 154 D 6
Al Ḥinnāh 155 H 3
Al Hoceima 152 E 1
Al Ḥudaydah 155 G 6
Al Ḥufrah 153 J 3
Al Ḥufrah 154 F 3
Al Ḥufūf 155 H 3
Al Hūj 154 F 3
Al Ḥunayy 155 H 4
Al Ḥusayḥiṣah 154 E 6
Al Ḥuwaymī 155 H 6
Al Ḥuwayyiṭ 155 G 3
Al Ḥuwwah 155 H 4
Alīābād 128 F 5
Alīābād 128 E 3
Aliákmon 116 B 2
Alibag 134 B 4
Ali Bayramly 128 D 3
Alibey, Ozero 116 D 1
Alibo 159 F 3
Alibori 156 E 3
Alicante 114 C 4
Alice 170 G 6
Alice, Punta 115 G 4
Alice River 143 H 3
Alice Springs 142 E 3
Alichur 129 J 3
Aligarh 134 C 2
Al Iglim al Janūbīyah 158 DE 3
Aligūdarz 128 D 4
Alikayası 117 E 3
Alima 157 H 6
Alindao 158 E 4
Alinglapalap 146 C 2
Alingsås 113 F 4
Alinskoye 119 R 3
Alipur 129 J 5
Alipur Duar 134 E 2
Al 'Irq 153 K 3
Al 'Irqah 155 H 6
Ali Sabjeh 159 G 2
Al Iskandarīyah 154 D 2
Al Ismā'īlīyah 154 E 2
Alitak, Cape 166 G 4
Aliwal North 160 D 5
Al Jabal al Akhḍar 153 K 2
Al Jabalayn 154 E 6
Al Jadīdah 154 D 3
Al Jafr 154 F 2
Al Jāfūrah 155 J 4
Al Jaghbūb 153 K 3
Al Jahrah 155 H 3
Al Jalāmīd 155 G 2
Al Jamalīyah 155 J 3
Al Jamm 153 H 1
Al Jardāwīyah 155 G 3
Al Jarid, Shaṭṭ 153 G 2
Al Jawārah 155 K 5
Al Jawf 155 F 3
Al Jawf → Al Kufrah 153 K 4
Al Jaylī 154 E 5
Al Jazā'ir 153 F 1
Al Jazīrah 154 E 6
Al Jazīrah 155 G 2
Al Jifārah 155 H 4
Al Jiwā' 155 J 4
Al Jīzah 154 E 2
Al Jubayl 155 H 3
Al Jubaylah 155 H 4
Al Jufrah Oasis → Wāḥāt al Jufrah 153 J 3
Al Jufrah, Wāḥāt 153 J 3
Al Jumaymah 155 G 3
Al Junaynah 155 H 4
Al Junaynah 154 C 6
Aljustrel 114 B 4
Al Kāf 153 G 1
Al Kahfah 155 G 3
Al Kāmilīn 155 E 6
Al Karak 154 F 2
Al Karnak 154 E 3
Al Kawah 154 E 6
Al Khābūrah 155 K 4
Al Khāliṣ 155 G 2
Al Khalūf 155 K 4
Al Khandaq 154 E 5
Al Khārijah 154 E 3
Al Kharj 155 H 4

Al Kharṭūm 154 E 5
Al Kharṭūm Baḥrī 154 E 5
Al Khaṣab 155 K 3
Al Khatam 155 J 4
Al Khaṭṭ 155 K 3
Al Khawr 155 J 3
Al Khiḍr 155 H 2
Al Khubar 155 J 3
Al Khufayfīyah 155 G 4
Al Khums 153 H 2
Al Khunfah 155 F 3
Al Khunn 155 H 4
Al Khuraybah 155 H 5–6
Al Khurmah 155 G 4
Al Khuwayr 155 J 3
Al Kidn 155 J 4
Al Kifl 155 G 2
Al Kirbekan 154 E 5
Al Kūfah 155 G 2
Al Kufrah 153 K 4
Al Kufrah, Wāḥāt 153 K 4
Al Kumayt 155 H 2
Al Kuntillah 154 E 2
Al Kūt 155 H 2
Al Kuwayt (Kuwait) 155 H 3
Al Labbah 155 G 3
Allada 156 E 4
Al Lādhiqīyah 154 F 1
Al Lagowa 154 D 6
Allahabad 134 D 2
Allahüekber Daği 117 F 2
Allakaket 166 G 2
Allakh-Yun' 131 P 3
Allanmyo 135 G 4
Allanridge 160 D 5
'Allāqī, Wādī al 154 E 4
Al Layyah 154 F 5
Alldays 160 D 4
Allegheny Mountains 171 KL 4
Allegheny Plateau 171 K 4
Allegheny River 171 L 3
Allende 172 B 2
Allen, Lough 100 A 2
Allentown 171 L 3
Alleppey 134 C 6
Aller 111 E 4
Allevard 115 E 2
Allgäuer Alpen 115 F 2
Alliance 170 F 3
Allier 114 D 2
Al Liffyah 155 G 2
Alligator River, East 142 E 1
Alligator River, South 142 E 1
Al Liṣāfah 155 H 3
Al Līth 155 G 4
Alloa 99 C 3
Allones 114 D 2
Allora 143 J 4
Allsensk 101 E 2
Alma 171 M 2
Alma-Ata 129 K 2
Almada 114 B 4
Almadén 114 C 4
Al Madīnah 155 F 4
'Al Madōw 159 H 2
Al Mafraq 143 H 3
Al Maghrah 154 D 2
Al Maḥallah al Kubrā 154 E 2
Al Maḥārīg 154 E 3
Al Maḥāwiyah 155 G 4
Al Maḥdīyah 153 H 1
Al Maḥrah 155 J 5
Al Majma'ah 155 H 3
Al Makhaylī 153 F 1
Al Maks al Qiblī 154 E 4
Al Mallāḥah al Baḥrīyah 153 H 2
Al Mallāḥah al Gharbīyah 153 H 2
Almalyk 129 H 2
Al Manādir 155 K 4
Al Manāmah 155 J 3
Al Manāqil 154 E 6
Almanor, Lake 170 B 3
Almansa 114 C 4
Al Manshāh 154 E 3
Al Manṣūrah 154 E 2
Al Māqnāh 154 E 3
Al Maqrūn 153 K 2
Al Maqṭā' 155 J 4
Al Marj 153 K 2
Al Ma'rūf 153 J 3
Al Mas'ānīyah 155 HJ 3
'Al Maskād 159 H 2
Al Matnah 154 F 6
Al Mayādīn 155 G 2
Al Mayyāh 155 G 3
Almazán 114 C 3

Almaznyy 130 K 3
Almeirim 179 H 4
Al Mellem 158 D 3
Almelo 110 E 4
Almenara 181 H 4
Almenara, Sierra de 114 C 4
Almendra, Embalse de 114 B 3
Almendralejo 114 B 4
Almeria 114 C 4
Almeria, Golfo de 114 C 4
Al'met'yevsk 118 K 5
Älmhult 113 F 4
Al Midhnab 155 G 3
Al Milḥ, Ra's 153 L 2
Al Mintirīb 155 K 4
Al Minyā 154 E 3
Al Mīqdādīyah 155 GH 2
Almirante 178 B 2
Almirante Brown 185
Almirante Montt, Golfo 183 B 9
Almirós 183 B 9
Almodôvar 114 B 4
Almogasta 182 C 4
Almonte 114 B 4
Almora 134 C 2
Almoustaret 156 E 2
Almuñécar 114 C 4
Al Mubarraz 155 H 3
Al Mudarraj 154 F 3
Al Mudawwarah 154 F 3
Al Mughayrā' 154 F 3
Al Muglad 154 D 6
Al Muharraq 155 J 3
Al Mukallā 155 H 6
Al Mukhā 155 G 6
Al Muknīn 153 H 1
Al Munastir 153 H 1
Al Murabbā' 155 G 3
Al Musannah 155 H 3
Al Musawwarat aṣ Ṣafra 170 E 5
Al Muṣawwart aṣ Ṣafra 154 E 5
Al Musayyid 155 J 3
Al Musayyib 155 G 2
Al Muwayh 155 G 4
Al Muwayliḥ 155 F 3
Al Nasser 154 E 4
Alness 98 B 3
Alney, Gora 131 T 4
Alnön 112 G 3
Alnwick 101 E 2
Alo 157 J 3
Alofi (Cook Islands) 146 D 4
Alofi (Wallis and Futuna) 146 D 3
Alomata 159 F 2
Along 135 F 2
Alongshan 131 M 5
Álora 114 C 4
Alor, Pulau 137 F 5
Alor, Selat 137 F 5
Alor Setar 136 B 2
Alotau 145 F 4
Alotaw 143 J 1
Alpachiri 183 D 6
Alpena 171 K 2
Alpercatas, Serra das 179 JK 5
Alpes Mancelles 114 C 2
Alpha 143 H 3
Alpha River 143 H 3
Alphonse 159 J 6
Alpi Carniche 115 F 2
Alpi Dolomitiche 115 F 2
Alpi Dolomitiche 115 F 2
Alpi le Pontine 115 E 2
Alpi Marittime 115 E 3
Alpine (TX, U.S.A.) 170 F 5
Alpine (WY, U.S.A.) 170 D 3
Alpi Orobie 115 EF 2
Alpi Pennine 115 E 2
Al Qa'āmīyāt 155 H 5
Al Qaḍārif 154 F 6
Al Qaddāḥīyah 153 J 2
Al Qadīmah 155 F 4
Al Qāhirah 154 E 2–3
Al Qaḥmah 155 G 4
Al Qalībah 154 F 3
Al Qāmishlī 155 G 1
Al Qanṭarah 154 E 2
Al Qarābullī 153 H 2
Al Qārah 155 G 3
Al Qarḍah 153 H 3
Al Qaryāt 153 H 2
Al Qaryatayn 154 F 2
Al Qaṭīf 155 HJ 3
Al Qaṭn 155 H 5
Al Qaṭrānī 153 H 5
Al Qay'īyah 155 G 4
Al Qayrawān 153 GH 1
Al Qayṣūmah 155 G 3

Al Qayṣūmah 155 H 3
Alqueva, Barragem de 114 B 4
Al Qunayṭirah 154 F 2
Al Qunfudhah 155 G 5
Al Qurayni 155 J 4
Al Qurayyah 154 F 3
Al Qurayyāt 155 K 4
Al Qurnah 155 H 2
Al Qusaymah 154 E 2
Al Quṣayr 154 E 3
Al Qūṣīyah 154 E 3
Al Qūṣūrīyah 155 G 4
Al Quṭayfah 154 F 2
Al Quṭaynah 154 E 6
Al Quwārah 155 G 3
Al Quwayīyah 155 H 4
Al Qwārshah 153 JK 2
Al Rabyānah 153 K 4
Al Rabyānah, Wāḥāt 153 K 4
Als 113 E 5
Alsask 167 Q 5
Alsasua 114 C 3
Alsek 166 J 4
Alsfeld 111 E 4
Alsh, Lake 98 B 3
Al'skiy Khrebet 131 P 5
Alsten 112 F 2
Alston 101 D 2
Alta 112 H 2
Altaelva 112 H 2
Altafjorden 112 H 1
Alta Gracia 182 D 5
Altagracia de Orituco 178 E 2
Altamachi 180 C 4
Altamaha River 171 K 5
Altamira 179 H 4
Altamira, Cuevas de 114 C 3
Altamont 170 B 3
Altamura 115 G 3
Altan 130 J 6
Altanbulag 130 J 5
Altar 170 D 5
Altas, Rías 114 B 3
Altat 130 F 4
Altata 170 E 7
Altatump 119 MN 3
Altay (Sinkiang, China) 129 M 1
Altay (U.S.S.R.) 119 R 5
Altay (U.S.S.R.) 119 N 3
Altay Shan 129 M 1
Altayskoye 119 R 5
Al Tāzirbū, Wāḥāt 153 K 3
Altdorf 115 E 2
Altenburg 111 F 4
Altevatnet 112 G 2
Altıntaş 116 D 3
Altiplanicie Mexicana 172 B 2
Altiplano 180 C 4
Altkirch 115 E 2
Altmark 111 F 4
Altmühl 111 F 5
Altnaharra 98 B 2
Alto - Alentejo 114 B 4
Alto Araguaia 181 F 4
Alto Chicapa 160 B 2
Alto Garças 181 F 4
Alto Molócuè 161 F 3
Alton (IL, U.S.A.) 171 H 4
Alton (U.K.) 103 D 2
Altona 111 E 4
Alton Downs 143 F 4
Altoona 171 L 3
Alto Paraguai 180 E 3
Alto Parnaíba 181 G 2
Alto Purus 178 D 6
Alto Río Senguerr 183 B 8
Alto Sucuriú 181 F 4
Alto Turi 181 G 1
Alto Zaza 160 B 1
Altrincham 101 D 3
Altun Ha 172 E 4
Altun Köprī 155 G 1
Altun Shan 132 A 3
Alturas 170 B 3
Altus 170 G 5
Altynasar 129 G 1
Alu 145 G 2
Al 'Ubaylah 155 J 4
Al Ubayyid 154 E 6
Alucra 117 E 2
Al Uḍayd 154 D 6
Al Ugsur 154 E 3
Aluk 158 D 3
Al 'Ulā 154 F 3
'Alūla 159 J 2
Aluminé 183 B 6
Alupka 117 D 2
Al 'Uqayr 155 J 3
Alur 134 C 4
Al Urayq 155 F 3
Al Urdun 154 F 2
Al 'Urūq al Mu'tariḍah 155 J 4

Alu – Ant

'Ālūs 155 G 2
Aluşta 117 D 2
Al 'Uthmānīyah 155 H 3
Al 'Uwaynidhīyah 154 F 3
Al 'Uwayqīlah 155 G 2
Al 'Uyūn 155 G 3
Al 'Uyūn 155 F 4
Al 'Uzayr 155 H 2
Alva (OK, U.S.A.) 170 G 4
Alva (U.K.) 99 C 3
Alvarães 179 F 4
Älvdal 112 F 3
Älvdalen 113 F 3
Älvdalen 112 F 3
Alvear 182 E 4
Alvelos, Serra de 114 B 4
Alvesta 113 F 4
Ålvik 113 E 3
Älvkarleby 113 G 3
Alvorada 181 G 3
Alvord Valley 170 C 3
Älvsbyn 112 H 2
Al Wāḥah 153 K 3
Al Wajh 154 F 3
Al Wannān 155 H 3
Alwar 134 C 2
Al Warī'ah 155 H 3
Al Wāsiṭah 154 E 3
Al Waṭyah 153 H 2
Al Wazz 154 E 5
Al Widyān 155 G 2
Al Wīgh 153 J 4
Al Wīgh, Ramlat 153 J 4
Alxa Youqi 132 D 3
Alxa Zuoqi 132 E 3
Alyangula 143 F 1
Alyaskitovyy 131 Q 3
Alygdzher 130 G 5
Alys-Khaya 131 P 2
Alysy-Garakh 131 Q 2
Alytus 113 H 5
Alzamay 130 G 4
Amada 154 E 4
Amada Gaza 158 B 4
Amadeus, Lake 142 E 3
Amadi 158 E 3
Amadjuak Lake 169 N 2
Amadora 114 B 4
Amahai 137 G 4
Amain, Monts d' 114 D 2
Amakinskiy 130 K 1
Åmål 113 F 4
Åmål 153 K 3
Amalfi (Italy) 115 F 3
Amalfi (Colombia) 178 D 2
Amalias 116 B 3
Amambaí 181 E 5
Amami-ō-shima 133 J 5
Amanã, Lago 179 F 4
Amangel'dy 119 N 5
Amanino 131 T 4
Amanotkel' 129 G 1
Amanu 147 F 4
Amanzimtoti 161 E 6
Amapá 179 H 3
Amar 157 FG 4
'Amara 154 E 4
Amarante 181 H 2
Amârat Abū Sinn 154 F 5
Amarillo 170 F 4
Amaro Leite 181 G 3
Amarti 159 G 2
Amasra 117 D 2
Amasya 117 E 2
Amataurá 178 E 4
Amazar 130 M 5
Amazonas 178–179 EF 4
Amazonas 179 H 4
Amba Farit 159 F 2
Ambala 134 C 1
Ambalavao 161 H 4
Ambam 157 G 5
Ambanja 161 H 2
Ambar 130 F 2
Ambarchik 130 G 4
Ambarchik 131 U 2
Ambardakh 131 P 1
Ambarnyy 113 K 2
Ambato 178 C 4
Ambato Boény 161 H 3
Ambatofinandrahana 161 H 4
Ambatolampy 161 H 3
Ambatondrazaka 161 H 3
Ambatosoratra 161 H 3
Ambatry 161 G 4
Ambelos, Ákra 116 B 3
Amberg 111 F 5
Ambérieu-en-Bugey 115 E 2
Ambgaon 134 C 3
Ambidédi 156 B 3
Ambikapur 134 D 3
Ambilobe 161 H 2
Amble-by-the-Sea 101 E 2

Ambleside 101 D 2
Ambo 180 A 3
Amboasary 161 H 5
Ambodifototra 161 H 3
Ambohibe 161 G 4
Ambohimahasoa 161 H 4
Ambohitralanana 161 J 3
Ambon 137 G 4
Ambon, Pulau 137 G 4
Amboseli, Lake 159 F 5
Ambositra 161 H 4
Ambovombe 161 H 5
Ambre, Dap d' 161 H 2
Ambre, Montagne d' 161 H 2
Ambriz 160 A 1
Ambrym 145 J 5
Ambur 134 C 5
Amchitka 166 A 5
Amchitka Pass 166 A 5
'Amd 155 H 5
Am Dam 157 J 3
Amderma 119 M 2
Am Djéména 157 H 3
Amdo 132 B 4
Ameca 172 B 3
Amendolara 115 G 4
American Falls Reservoir 170 D 3
American Highland 185
American Samoa 146 D 4
Americus 171 K 5
Amersham 103 D 2
Amery Ice Shelf 185
Ames 171 H 3
Amesbury 103 D 2
Amet 134 B 2
Ametlla de Mar 114 D 3
Amfilokia 116 B 3
Amfissa 116 B 3
Amga 131 O 3
Amgu 133 L 1
Amguema 166 B 2
Amguid Bordj 153 G 3
Amgun' 131 P 5
Amhara 159 F 2
Amherst 169 P 6
Amherst Island 171 L 3
Amiata, Monte 115 F 3
Amiens 114 D 2
Amik Gölü 117 E 3
Amili 135 G 2
Amindivi Islands 134 B 5
Aminuis 160 B 4
Amirante Islands 159 J 6
Amisk Lake 167 R 5
Amka 131 Q 4
Amlia 166 C 5
Amlwch 102 B 1
'Amm Adām 154 F 5
Ammān 154 F 2
Ammanford 102 B 2
Ammarfjället 112 G 2
Ammarnäs 112 G 2
Ammokhostos → Famagusta
  117 D 3
Amo 130 H 3
Åmol 128 E 3
Amolar 180 E 4
Amorgos 116 C 3
Amos 171 L 2
Amot 113 E 4
Amour, Djebel 153 F 2
Amourj 152 D 5
Amoy 133 G 6
Ampanihy 161 G 4
Amparafaravola 161 H 3
Ampitsikanana 161 H 2
Amposta 114 D 3
Ampthill 103 D 1
'Amrān 155 G 5
Amravati 134 C 3
Am Raya 157 H 3
Amri 129 H 5
Amritsar 134 B 1
Amroha 134 C 2
Amsa'ad 153 K 2
Amsterdam (Netherl.) 110 D E 4
Amsterdam (N.Y., U.S.A.)
  171 M 3
Amstetten 115 F 2
Am Timan 157 J 3
Amu-Dar'ya 129 G 2
Amudat 158 E 4
Amukta Pass 166 C 5
Amundsen Gulf 167 N 1
Amundsen-Scott 185
Amundsen Sea 185
Amungen 112 G 3
Amuntai 136 E 4
Amur 131 P 5
Amursk 131 P 5
Amvrakikos Kólpos 116 B 3
Amysakh 130 L 2

Am Zoer 157 J 3
An 155 H 2
Anabar 130 K 1
Anabarskiy Zaliv 130 KL 1
Anabarskoye Ploskogor'ye
  130 J 1–2
Anaco 179 F 2
Anaconda 170 D 2
Anadoli 116 CD 3
Anadyr' 131 X 3
Anadyrskaja Nizmennost 131 X 2
Anadyrskiy Liman 131 X 3
Anadyrskiy Zaliv 131 X 3
Anadyrskoye Ploskogor'ye
  131 VW 2
Anáfi 116 C 3
Anåfjället 112 F 3
Anaghit 159 F 1
Anagni 115 F 3
'Ānah 155 G 2
Anáhuac 172 B 2
Anaï 153 H 4
Anaimalai Hills 134 C 5
Anajás 179 J 4
Anajatuba 181 H 1
Anakapallei 134 D 4
Anaklia 117 F 2
Anaktuvuk Pass 166 G 2
Analalava 161 H 2
Anamá 171 F 4
Ana Maria, Golfo de 173 G 3
Anambas, Kepulauan 136 C 3
Anamur 117 D 3
Anamur Burun 117 D 3
Anamuryum 117 D 3
Anangravnen, Sopka 131 U 4
Anantapur 134 C 5
Anantnag 129 K 4
Anan'yev 116 C 1
Anapa 117 E 2
Anapka 131 U 4
Anápolis 181 G 4
Anapu 179 H 4
Anār 128 F 4
Anarisfjällen 112 F 3
Anatahan 146 A 1
Anatolia 116 CD 3
Añatuya 182 D 4
Anauá 179 F 3
Anavarza 117 E 3
Anavelona 161 G 4
Anavilhanas, Arquipélago das
  179 F 4
'Anazah, Jabal 155 F 2
Anazarba 117 J 6
Anbyŏn 133 J 3
Ancares, Sierra de 114 B 3
Ancasti, Sierra de 182 C 4
Ancenis 114 C 2
Ancha 131 P 3
Anchorage 166 H 3
Anchor Bay 170 B 4
Anci 131 P 5
Ancohuma 180 C 4
Ancon (Ecuador) 178 B 4
Ancón (Peru) 180 A 3
Ancona 115 F 3
Ancuabe 161 F 2
Ancud 183 B 7
Ancud, Golfo de 183 B 7
Anda 133 J 1
Andacollo (Argentina) 183 B 6
Andacollo (Chile) 182 B 5
Andahuaylas 180 B 3
Andalgala 182 C 4
Åndalsnes 112 E 3
Andalucía 114 BC 4
Andaman Islands 135 F 5
Andaman Sea 135 G 5–6
Andamooka 143 F 5
Andapa 161 H 2
Andara 160 C 3
Andarab 129 H 3
Andaraí 181 H 3
Andeg 118 K 2
Andenes 112 G 2
Andéranboukane 156 E 2
Anderson (IN, U.S.A.) 171 J 3
Anderson (N.W.T., Can.) 166 M 2
Anderson (S.C., U.S.A.) 171 K 5
Anderstorp 113 F 4
Andes (Col.) 178 C 2
Andevoranto 161 H 3
Andfjorden 112 G 2
Andhra Pradesh 134 C 4
Andikira 116 B 3
Andikíthira 173 K 4
Andilamena 161 H 3
Andilanatoby 161 H 3
Andīmeshk 128 D 3
Andípaxoi 116 B 3
Andiria Burun 117 D 3
Andırın 117 E 3

Andirlangar 129 L 3
Andiyskiy Khrebet 117 G 2
Andiyskoye 117 G 2
Andizhan 129 J 2
Andkhui 129 H 3
Andoas 178 C 4
Andomskiy Pogost 118 G 3
Andong 133 J 3
Andorra 114 D 3
Andorra la Vella 114 D 3
Andover 103 D 2
Andöya 112 G 2
Andradina 181 F 5
Andraitx 114 D 4
Andranopasy 161 G 4
Andreanof Islands 166 B 5
André Félix National Park 158 C 3
Andrews 170 F 5
Andreyevka 117 E 1
Andreyevka 119 Q 6
Andreyevka 118 K 5
Andreyevo-Ivanovka 116 D 1
Andreyevsk 130 K 4
Andreyevskiy 130 K 4
Andria 115 G 3
Andriamena 161 H 3
Andriba 161 H 3
Andringitra 161 H 4
Androka 161 G 5
Androna, Plateau de l'Andrepatsy
  161 H 3
Andropov 118 G 4
Ándros 116 B 3
Andros Island 173 G 3
Androsovka 118 J 5
Androth 134 B 5
Andryushka 131 S 2
Andselv 112 G 2
Andudu 158 D 4
Andújar 114 C 4
Andulo 160 B 2
Andu Tan 136 D 2
Andyngda 130 L 2
Aneby 113 F 4
Anécho 156 E 4
Anéfis 156 E 2
Anegada, Bahía 183 D 7
Anegada Passage 173 K 4
Aneityum 146 C 4
Aneityum 145 J 6
Añelo 183 C 6
Aneto, Pico de 114 D 3
Aney 157 G 2
Angamos, Punta 180 B 5
Ang'angxi 131 M 6
Angar 137 H 4
Angara 130 F 4
Angarsk 130 H 5
Angas Downs 142 E 4
Angaul 130 H 5
Angaur 137 H 2
Ånge 112 G 3
Ángel de la Guarda, Isla 170 D 6
Angel Falls → Salto Angel
  179 F 2
Ängelholm 113 F 4
Angemuk, Gunung 137 J 4
Ångermanälven 112 G 3
Ångermanland 112 G 3
Angers 114 C 2
Angerville (France) 114 D 2
Angical 181 H 3
Angijak Island 169 P 2
Angikuni Lake 167 S 3
Angkor 135 H 5
Anglem, Mount 144 P 10
Anglesey 102 B 1
Angmagssalik 184
Ango 158 D 4
Angoche 161 G 3
Angol 183 B 6
Angola 160 B 2
Angola Basin 192 B 4
Angónia, Planalto de 161 E 2
Angoram 144 D 2
Angostura 170 E 6
Angostura, Salto 178 D 3
Angoulême 114 D 2
Angouma 157 G 5
Angra do Heroismo 152 A 1
Angra dos Reis 181 H 5
Angren 129 J 2
Ang Thong 135 H 5
Angu 158 C 4
Anguil 183 D 6
Anguilla 173 K 4
Anguille, Cape 169 Q 6
Angul 134 E 3
Angumu 158 D 5
Anguo 132 G 3
Angutikha 119 R 2
Anholt 113 F 4

Anh Son 135 J 4
Anhua 132 F 5
Anhui 133 G 4
Aniak 166 F 3
Aniakchak National Monument
  and Preserve 166 F 4
Anié 156 E 4
Animas Peak 170 E 5
Anina 116 B 1
Aniva 113 J 3
Aniva, Mys 131 Q 6
Aniva, Zaliv 131 Q 6
Anivorano-Nord 161 H 2
Aniwa 146 C 4
Aniwa 145 J 5
Anjala 113 J 3
Anjou 114 C 2
Anjouan 161 G 2
Anjozorobe 161 H 3
Anju 133 J 3
Anjuman 129 J 3
Anka 157 F 3
Ankacho 130 J 3
Ankang 132 E 4
Ankara 117 D 3
Ankaramena 161 H 4
Ankavandra 161 H 3
Ankazoabo 161 G 4
Ankazobe 161 H 3
Ankerika 161 H 2
'Ankhor (Somalia) 159 H 2
Anklam 111 F 4
Anklesvar 134 B 3
Ankober 159 F 3
Ankofa 161 H 3
Ankoro 158 D 6
Ankpa 157 F 4
Anlong 132 E 5
Anlu 132 F 4
Ånn 112 F 3
Anna (U.S.S.R.) 118 H 5
Anna (IL, U.S.A.) 171 J 4
Annaba 153 G 1
An Nabk 154 F 2
An Nabk Abū Qaşr 154 F 2
An Nafīdah 115 F 4
An Nafūd 155 G 3
An Nāfūrah 153 K 3
An Nāhiyah 155 G 2
Annai 179 G 3
An Najaf 155 G 2
An Nakhl 154 E 3
Annam 135 J 4
An Nāmūs, Jabal 153 J 4
Annan 101 D 2
Annandale 143 H 3
Anna Plains 142 C 2
Annapolis 171 L 4
Ann Arbor 171 K 3
An Nāsirīyah 155 H 2
Ann, Cape 185
Annean, Lake 142 B 4
Annecy 115 E 2
Annemasse 115 E 2
Annenskiy-Most 118 G 3
An Nhon 135 J 5
Anniston 171 J 5
Annobón 157 F 6
Annonay 115 D 2
An Nu'ayrīyah 155 H 3
An Nuhūd 154 D 6
An Nu'mān 154 F 3
An Nuqayr 155 H 3
An Nūwfalīyah 153 J 2
Anoka 171 H 2
Anori 179 F 4
Anoshkinsk 131 N 1
Anou 156 E 2
Anoumaba 156 D 4
Anou-n Bidek 153 F 5
Anqing 133 G 4
Anṣāb (S. Arabia) 155 G 3
Ansas 137 J 4
Ansbach 111 F 5
Anserma 178 C 2
Anshan 133 H 2
Anshun 132 E 5
Ansina 182 E 5
Ansley 170 G 3
Anson Bay 142 D 1
Ansongo 156 E 2
Anstruther 99 C 3
Ansudu 137 J 4
Anta 180 B 3
Anta, Cachoeira de 179 F 5
Antakya 117 E 3
Antalaha 161 J 2
Antalya 116 D 3
Antalya Körfezi 116 D 3
Antananarivo 161 H 3
Antanimora 161 H 4
Antarctic Peninsula 185

Ant – Art

Antas 182 F 4
Antela, Laguna de 114 B 3
Antequera 114 C 4
Antequera 180 E 5
Anthony 170 E 5
Anthony Lagoon 142 F 2
Anti-Atlas 152 D 2–3
Antibes 115 E 3
Antico 180 B 4
Anticosti, Île de 169 P 6
Antifer, Cap d' 114 D 2
Antigonish 169 P 6
Antigua 173 K 4
Antigua Guatemala 172 D 5
Antillas Mayores 173 GHJ 4
Antillas Menores 173 K 5
Antioche, Pertuis d' 114 C 2
Antiope 146 D 4
Antioquia 178 C 2
Antipayuta 119 P 2
Antipinskiy 131 N 1
Antipodes Islands 185
Antlāt 153 K 2
Antnäs 112 H 2
Antofagasta 180 B 5
Antofagasta de la Sierra 182 C 4
Antofalla, Salar de 182 C 4
Antofalla, Volcán 182 C 4
Antongil, Baie d' 161 HJ 3
Antonina 181 G 6
Antônio Bezerra 181 J 1
Antonio de Biedma 183 C 8
Antônio João 180 CD 6
Antonovo 128 E 1
Antonto 182 C 4
Antrim 100 B 2
Antrim Mountains 100 B 2
Antrodoco 115 F 3
Antsakabary 161 H 2
Antsalova 161 G 3
Antseranana 161 H 2
Antsirabe 161 H 3
Antsohihy 161 H 2
Antu 133 J 2
An Tuc 135 J 5
Antufash 155 G 5
Antwerpen 110 D 4
Antykan 131 P 5
An Uaimh 100 B 3
Añueque, Sierra 183 C 7
Anupgarh 134 B 2
Anuradhapura 134 D 6
Anuta 145 J 2
Anvik 166 E 3
Anxi 133 G 5
Anxi 132 C 2
An Xian 132 D 4
Anxiang 132 F 5
Anxious Bay 142 E 5
Anyama 156 D 4
Anyang 132 F 3
A'nyemaqen Shan 132 C 3
Anyuan 132 G 5
An'yudin 119 L 3
Anyue 132 E 4
Anyuysk 131 U 2
Anyuyskiy Khrebet, Severnyy 131 U 2–W 2
Anyuyskiy Khrebet, Yuzhnyy 131 U 2–V 2
Anzhero-Sudzhensk 119 R 4
Ao Ban Don 135 G 6
Aoga-shima 133 LM 4
Aomori 133 M 2
Aosta 115 E 2
Aoudaghost 152 C 5
Aoudéras 157 F 2
Aouinat Legraa 152 D 3
Aouker 152 CD 5
Aoulef el Arab 153 F 3
Aoumou 145 J 6
Apacha 131 T 5
Apahida 116 B 1
Apalachee Bay 171 K 6
Apan 172 C 4
Apaporis 178 D 3
Aparecida do Tabuado 181 F 5
Aparri 137 J 1
Apataki 147 F 3
Apatin 116 A 1
Apatity 113 K 2
Apatzingán 172 B 4
Ape 113 J 4
Apeldoorn 110 E 4
Apennino Calabro 115 G 4
Apennino Ligure 115 E 3
Apere 180 C 3
Aphrodisias 116 C 3
Api (Nepal) 134 D 2
Api (Zaire) 158 D 4
Apia 146 D 3
Apiacás, Serra dos 180 E 2–3
Apiai 181 G 5

Apiaú, Serra do 179 F 3
Api, Gunung 137 E 5
Apinajé 181 G 3
Api, Tanjung 136 C 3
Apizaco 172 C 4
Apolinario Saravia 180 D 5
Apollo Bay 143 G 6
Apolo 180 C 3
Apo, Mount 137 G 2
Aporé 181 F 4
Aporema 179 H 3
Apóstoles 182 E 4
Apostolovo 117 D 1
Apoteri 179 G 3
Appalachian Mountains 171 K 4
Appenno Lucano 115 G 3–4
Appenno Tosco-Emiliano 115 F 3
Appenzell 115 E 2
Appin 99 B 3
Appleby 101 D 2
Appleton 171 J 3
Appollonia → Sūsah 153 K 2
Approuague 179 H 3
Aprilia 115 F 3
Apsheronsk 117 E 2
Apt 115 E 3
Apucarana 181 F 5
Apuka 131 W 3
Apuka Chukotskaya 131 W 3
Apure 178 D 2
Apurimac 180 B 3
Aqār 'Atabah 153 H 3
Aqdā 128 E 4
'Aqīq 154 F 5
'Aqrah 155 G 1
Aquibi, Cachoeira 181 E 3
Aquidauana 180 E 5
Ara 114 D 3
Arabatskaya Strelka 117 E 1
Arabian Basin 192 B 3
Arabian Desert → Aş Şaḩrā' ash-Sharqīyah 154 E 2
Arabian Sea 187
Araç 117 D 2
Araçá 179 F 3
Aracaju 181 J 3
Aracati 181 J 1
Araçatuba 181 F 5
Aracena, Sierra de 114 B 4
Árachthos 116 B 3
Araçuai 181 H 4
Arad 116 B 1
Arada 157 J 2
'Arādah 155 J 4
Aradanskiy Khrebet 130 F 5
Arafali 159 F 1
Arafura, Laut 137 H 5
Arafura Sea 137 HJ 5
Arafura Shelf 193 C 4
Aragarças 181 F 4
Aragats 117 F 2
Aragón 114 C 3
Araguacema 181 J 5
Aragua de Barcelona 179 F 2
Aragua de Maturín 179 F 1–2
Araguaia 181 J 5
Araguaiana 181 F 4
Araguaia, Parco Nacional do 179 HJ 6
Araguaia, Parque Nacional do 181 FG 3
Araguaína 179 J 5
Araguari (Amapá, Brazil) 179 H 3
Araguari (Minas Gerais, Brazil) 181 G 4
Araguatins 179 J 5
Arāk (Iran) 128 D 4
Arak (Algeria) 153 F 3
Araka 157 H 2
Arakaka 179 G 2
Arakan Yoma 135 FG 4
Arak Bordj 153 F 3
Araks 128 D 3
Aral 129 L 2
Aral Sea 128 F 1,2
Aral'sk 129 G 1
Aral'skoye More 128 F 1,2
Aralsul'fat 129 G 1
Aramac 143 H 3
Arambaza 178 D 4
Aranda de Duero 114 C 3
Arandai 137 H 4
Arandelovac 116 B 2
Aran Island 110 B 3
Aran Islands 110 B 4
Aranjuez 114 C 3
Aranos 160 B 4
Aranuka 146 C 2
Aranyaprathet 135 H 5
Araouane 156 D 2
Arapa, Lago 180 BC 4

Arapari 179 J 5
Arapey 182 E 5
Arapiraca 181 J 2
Arapongas 181 F 5
Araquara 181 G 5
Ar'ar 155 G 2
Araracuara, Cerros de 178 D 3–4
Araranguá 181 G 6
Ararat (Armeniya, U.S.S.R.) 117 F 3
Ararat (Australia) 143 G 6
Ararat, Mount (Turkey) 117 F 3
Ararí 181 H 1
Araro 159 F 4
Aras 128 D 3
Aras Dağları 117 F 3
Araticu 179 J 4
Aratika 147 F 4
Arauá 181 J 3
Arauca 178 D 2
Arauco 183 B 6
Arauquita 178 D 2
Aura 178 C 2
Aravalli Range 134 B 2
Arawale Game Reserve 159 G 5
Araxá 181 G 4
Áraxos, Ákra 116 B 3
Araya 179 F 1
Arba Minch 159 F 3
Arbatax 115 E 4
Arboga 113 G 4
Arbon 115 E 2
Arbor Low 101 E 3
Arbrá 112 G 3
Arbre du Ténéré 157 G 2
Arbroath 99 C 3
Arbyn 131 N 3
Arcachon 114 C 3
Arcata 170 B 3
Arcelia 172 B 4
Archer River 143 G 1
Archer River National Park 143 G 1
Archer's Post 159 F 4
Archidona 114 C 4
Archipelago Kerimbas 161 G 2
Archipelago of the Recherche 142 C 5
Archipiélago de Camagüey 173 G 3
Archipiélago de Colón 178 B 6
Archipiélago de la Reina Adelaida 183 A 9
Archipiélago de los Canarreos 173 F 3
Archipiélago de los Chonos 183 B 7–5
Archipiélago de los Jardines-de la Reina 173 G 3
Archipiélago Guayaneco 183 A 8
Arckaringa River 142 E 4
Arco 170 D 3
Arco 115 F 2
Arcos de Jalón 114 C 3
Arcos de la Frontera 114 B 4
Arcos de Valdevez 114 B 3
Arcoverde 181 J 2
Arctic Ocean 184
Arctic Red River 166 L 2
Arctic Village 166 H 2
Arctowski 185
Arda 116 C 2
Ardabīl 128 D 3
Ardahan 117 F 2
Ardakān 128 E 4
Årdalsfjorden 112 E 3
Ardalstangen 112 E 3
Arḍ aş Şawwān 154 F 2
Ardatov 118 H 4
Ardee 110 B 4
Ardee 100 B 3
Ardennes 110 E 5
Ardennes, Canal des 115 D 2
Ardeşen 117 F 2
Ardestan 128 E 4
Ardglass 100 C 2
Ardhas 116 C 2
Ardila 114 B 4
Ardmore 171 G 5
Ardnamurchan 99 A 3
Ardrishaig 99 B 4
Ardrossan 99 B 4
Ards Peninsula 110 B 4
Ards Peninsula 100 C 2
Åre 112 F 3
Arebi 158 D 4
Arecibo 173 J 4
Areia Branca 181 J 1
Arena, Point 170 B 4

Arenápolis 180 E 3
Arenas, Punta de 183 C 9
Arendal 113 E 4
Aréopolis 116 B 3
Arequipa 180 B 4
Arere 179 H 4
Arés 181 J 2
Áreskutan 112 F 3
Arevaldé 114 C 3
Arezzaf 156 D 2
Arezzo 115 F 3
Arga 131 R 2
Argadargada 143 F 3
Arga-Emneke, Gora 131 Q 2
Argan 132 A 2
Arganda 114 C 3
Argens 115 E 3
Argentan 114 C 2
Argent, Côte d' 114 C 3
Argentina 183 CD 3
Argentine Basin 192 A 5
Argentino, Lago 183 B 9
Argenton-sur-Creuse 114 D 2
Arges 115 D 2
Arghandab 129 H 4
Argio 115 F 3
Argo 154 E 5
Argolikós Kólpos 116 B 3
Argonne 115 D 2
Árgos 116 B 3
Argostólion 116 B 3
Arguin, Cap d' 152 B 4
Argun' 130 L 5
Argungu 157 E 3
Argyle, Lake 142 D 2
Argyll 99 B 3
Arholma 113 G 4
Ar Horqin Qi 133 H 2
Århus 113 F 4
Århus Bugt 113 F 4
Ariari 178 D 3
Arias 182 D 5
Ariaú 179 F 4
Aribinda 156 D 3
Arica (Chile) 180 B 4
Arica (Colombia) 178 D 4
Aridal 152 C 3
Arid, Cape 142 C 5
Ariège 114 D 3
Ariel 183 D 6
Ariguaní 178 D 1
Ariḥā 154 F 1
Arima (Brazil) 179 F 5
Arima (Trinidad) 179 F 1
Arinos (Mato Grosso, Brazil) 180 E 3
Arinos (Minas Gerais, Brazil) 181 G 4
Aripero 178 D 2
Aripuanã 179 F 5
Ariquemes 179 F 5
Ariripina 181 H 2
Arisa 159 G 2
Arismendi 178 E 2
Aritzo 115 E 3
Arivonimamo 161 H 3
Ariza 114 C 3
Arizaro, Salar de 180 C 5
Arizona (U.S.A.) 170 D 5
Arizona (Arg.) 183 C 6
Årjäng 113 F 4
Arjasa 136 E 5
Arjeplog 112 G 2
Arjona 178 C 1
Arka 131 Q 3
Arkadak 118 H 5
Arkadelphia 171 H 5
Arkaig, Loch 99 B 3
Arkalyk 119 N 5
Arkansas 171 H 4
Arkansas City 171 G 4
Arkansas River 171 H 5
Arkanü, Jabal 153 K 4
Arkatag Shan 132 A 3
Arkhangel'sk 118 H 3
Arkhangel'skaya 117 F 1
Arkhangel'skoye 117 F 2
Arkhangel'skoye 118 G 5
Arkhara 131 O 6
Arkhyz 117 F 2
Arklow 100 B 3
Arkonam 134 C 5
Arlberg 115 EF 2
Arles 115 D 3
Arlington (OR, U.S.A.) 170 B 2
Arlington (TX, U.S.A.) 171 G 5
Arlington (VA, U.S.A.) 171 L 4
Arlington Heights 171 J 3
Arlit 157 F 2
Arlon 110 E 5

Armagh 100 B 2
Armagnac, Collines de l' 114 D 3
Arman 131 S 4
Armant 154 E 3
Armavir 117 F 1
Armenia 178 C 3
Armeniya 117 F 2
Armentieres 114 D 1
Armeria 172 B 4
Armero 178 D 3
Armidale 143 J 5
Armori 134 C 3
Armstrong 168 K 5
Armur 134 C 4
Armyansk 117 D 1
Arnawai 129 J 3
Arnhem 110 E 4
Arnhem Bay 143 F 1
Arnhem, Cape 143 F 1
Arnhem Land 142 EF 1
Arnhem Land Reserve 142 EF 1
Arni 134 C 5
Arno (Marshall Isl.) 146 C 2
Arno (Italy) 115 F 3
Arno Bay 143 F 5
Arnold 103 D 1
Arnøy 112 H 1
Arnside 101 D 2
Aroab 160 B 5
Aroche, Pico de 114 B 4
Aroma 154 F 5
Arona 144 E 3
Arorae 146 C 3
Arosa 115 E 2
Arosa, Ría de 114 B 3
Årosund 113 E 4
Arpaçay 117 F 2
Arpajon 114 D 2
Arpavla 119 MN 3
Arquipélago das Anavilhanas 179 F 4
Arquipélago dos Abrolhos 181 J 4
Arquipélago dos Bijagós 156 A 3
Ar Rachidiya 152 E 2
Ar Radīsīyah Baḥrī 154 E 4
Arrah 134 D 2
Ar Rahad 154 E 6
Ar Rahad 154 F 6
Ar Raḩḩālīyah 155 G 2
Arraias 181 G 3
Ar Ramādī 155 G 2
Ar Ramlah 154 F 3
Arran 99 B 4
Ar Raqqah 155 F 1
Ar Rāqūbah 153 J 3
Arras 114 D 1
Ar Rass 155 G 3
Ar Rastān 154 F 2
Ar Rawdah 154 E 6
Ar Rawdah 155 G 4
Ar Rawdah 155 G 3
Ar Rawdatayn 155 H 3
Ar Rāwuk 155 H 5
Ar Rayḥānī 155 K 4
Ar Rayyān 155 H 5
Arrecifal 178 E 3
Arrecife 152 C 3
Arrecife Cabeza 172 C 4
Arrecifes 182 D 5
Arrecifes Triángulos 172 D 3
Arrée, Montagnes d' 114 C 2
Arriaga 172 D 4
Ar Rifā'ī 155 H 2
Ar Rimāh 155 H 3
Ar Rimāl 155 J 4
Ar Riyāḍ 155 H 4
Arroio Grande 182 F 5
Arrowsmith, Mount 145 Q 9
Arroyito 182 D 5
Arroyo de las Flores 183 D 6
Arroyos y Esteros 180 E 5
Arroyo Verde 183 C 7
Ar Rubaḑ 155 H 4
Ar Rub' al Khālī 155 H 5–J 4
Ar Ruq'ī 155 H 3
Ar Ruşāfah 154 F 1
Ar Ruşayriş 154 E 6
Ar Rutbah 155 G 2
Ar Ruwayḑah 155 G 3
Ar Ruways 155 J 4
Års 113 E 4
Arsen'yev 133 K 2
Årskogen 112 G 3
Arsuk 169 S 3
Árta 116 B 3
Artá, Cuevas de 114 D 4
Artashat 117 F 3
Arteaga 172 B 4
Artem 133 K 2
Artemisa 172 F 3
Artémou 152 C 5
Artemovsk 130 F 5

Art – Ayd

Artemovsk 117 E 1
Artemovskiy 117 F 1
Artesia 170 F 5
Artherstone 103 D 1
Arthur's Town 173 G 3
Artigas 182 E 5
Artik 117 F 2
Artillery Lake 167 Q 3
Artois, Collines de l' 114 D 1
Artoli 154 E 5
Artsyz 116 C 1
Artux 129 K 3
Artvin 117 F 2
Artybash 119 R 5
Artyk 131 R 3
Aru 158 E 4
Arua 158 E 4
Aruaja 178 E 5
Aruanã 181 F 3
Aruba 178 E 1
Aru Islands 144 C 3
Aru, Kepulauan 137 H 5
Aruma 179 F 4
Arunachal 135 F 2
Arundel 103 D 2
Arun Qi 131 M 6
Aruppukkottai 134 C 6
Arusha 159 F 5
Arusha Chini 159 F 5
Arus, Tanjung 137 F 3
Aru, Tanjung 136 E 4
Aruwimi 158 C 4
Arvada 170 E 4
Arvayheer 132 D 1
Arvidsjaur 112 G 2
Arvika 113 F 4
Årviksand 112 H 1
Arxan 130 L 6
Ary 130 M 1
Arys' 129 H 2
Arys, Ozero 129 H 1
Aryta 131 N 3
Arzamas 118 H 4
Aržano 115 G 3
Arzgir 117 F 1
Arzhan 130 G 5
Asab 160 B 5
Asaba 157 F 4
Asadabad (Afghanistan) 129 J 4
Asadābād (Iran) 128 F 3
Asahikawa 133 M 2
Asamakka 157 F 2
Asansol 134 E 3
Åsarna 112 F 3
Asba Tafari 159 G 3
Asbest 119 M 4
Ascensión (Bolivia) 180 D 4
Aschaffenburg 111 E 5
Ascoli Piceno 115 F 3
Ascot 103 D 2
Ascotán 180 C 5
Åseda 113 G 4
Asedjrad 153 F 4
Aseksemé 153 F 3
Åsele 112 G 3
Aselle 159 F 3
Åsen 112 F 3
Asendabo 159 F 3
Åseral 113 E 4
Asha 119 L 4
Ashanti 156 D 4
As Ḥasāwinah, Jabal 153 H 3
Ashbourne 101 E 3
Ashburton 145 Q 9
Ashburton River 142 B 3
Ashby de la Zouch 103 D 1
Ashchikol', Ozero 129 H 1
Ashdod 154 E 2
Asheville 171 K 4
Ashford 103 E 2
Ashington 101 E 2
Ashkhabad 128 F 3
Ashkidah 153 H 3
Ashkun 129 J 3
Ashland (KS, U.S.A.) 170 G 4
Ashland (KY, U.S.A.) 171 K 4
Ashland (OR, U.S.A.) 170 B 3
Ashland (WI, U.S.A.) 171 H 2
Ashmore Reef 142 C 1
Ash Shabakah 155 G 2
Ash Shabb 154 D 4
Ash Shallāl al Khamis 154 E 5
Ash Shallāl ar Rābi' 154 E 5
Ash Shallāl as Sablūkah 154 E 5
Ash Shallāl ath Thālith 154 E 5
Ash Shaqīq 155 G 3
Ash Shaqrā' 155 H 3
Ash Sha'rā 155 G 4
Ash Shārīqah 155 K 3
Ash Sharmah 154 F 3
Ash Sharqāt 155 G 1–2
Ash Sharqī 153 H 2
Ash Sharqīyah 155 K 4

Ash Shāṭi', Wādī 153 H 3
Ash Shaṭrah 155 H 2
Ash Shiḥr 155 H 6
Ash Shināfīyah 155 G 2
Ash Shu'aybah 155 G 3
Ash Shu'bah 155 G 3
Ash Shumlūl 155 H 3
Ash Shuqayq 155 G 5
Ash Shurayf → Khaybar 155 F 3
Ash Shuraykh 154 E 5
Ash Shwayrif 153 H 3
Ashtabula 171 K 3
Ashtarak 117 F 2
Ashton 170 D 3
Ashton-in-Makerfield 101 D 3
Ashton-under-Lyne 101 D 3
Ashuanipi 169 O 5
Ashuanipi Lake 169 O 5
Ashur → Assur 155 G 1–2
Asia, Kepulauan 137 H 3
Asilah 152 D 1
Asimiro 137 G 3
Asinara 115 E 3
Asinara, Golfo dell' 115 E 3
Asino 119 R 4
Asir, Ra's 159 J 2
Aska 134 D 4
Aşkale 117 F 3
Askaniya Nova 117 D 1
Asker 113 F 4
Askersund 113 F 4
Askim 113 F 4
Askiz 130 F 5
Askja 112 B 2
Askvoll 112 E 3
Asmara 159 F 1
Asni 112 D 2
Asop 134 B 2
Asosa 158 E 2
Asoteriba, Jabal 154 F 4
Asouf Mellene 153 F 3
Aspatria 99 C 4
Aspen 170 E 4
Aspendos 116 D 3
Aspermont 170 F 5
Aspiring, Mount 144 P 9
Aspurito 178 E 2
Asqueimat 152 B 4
Assa 152 D 3
Assab 159 G 2
Assâba 152 C 5
As Sab'ān 155 G 3
Aṣ Ṣadr 155 J 4
Aş Şafra' 154 F 5
Aş Şahm 155 K 4
Aş Şaḥrā' al Gharbīyah 154 D 3
Aş Şaḥrā' al Janūbīyah 154 D 4
Aş Şaḥrā' an Nūbīyah 154 E 4
Aş Şaḥrā' ash Sharqīyah 154 E 3
Aş Şaḥrā' at Tīh 154 E 3
As Salamīyah 154 F 1
As Salamīyah 155 H 4
Assale, Lake 159 G 2
As Salīf 155 G 5
Aş Şāliḥīyah 155 G 2
As Sallūm 154 D 2
As Salmān 155 G 2
As Salt 154 F 2
Assam 135 F 2
As Samāwah 155 H 2
As Şanām 155 J 4
Assaouas 157 F 2
As Sarīr 153 K 3
As Sawdā, Jabal 153 HJ 3
As Sawrah 154 F 3
Assaye 147 E 4
As Sayl al Kabīr 155 G 4
Assekaifaf 153 G 3
Assekrème 153 G 4
Assen 110 E 4
Assens 113 E 4
As Sidrah 153 J 2
Assiniboia 167 Q 6
Assiniboine 167 S 6
Assiniboine, Mount 167 O 5
Assiou 153 G 4
Assis 181 F 5
Assisi 115 F 3
Assodé 157 F 2
As Subū' 154 E 4
As Sūdān 154 DE 6
As Sufal 155 H 6
Aş Şufayyah 154 E 5
As Suknah 154 F 2
As Sulaymī 155 G 3
As Sulayyil 155 H 4
Aş Şulb 155 H 3
Aş Şummān 155 H 3
Assumption 159 H 6
Assur 155 G 1–2
As Suwaydā' 154 F 2

As Suwayḥ 155 K 4
As Suways 154 E 3
Astakh 131 P 2
Astārā (Iran) 128 D 3
Astara (U.S.S.R.) 128 D 3
Asti 115 E 3
Astillero 180 C 3
Astipálaia 116 C 3
Astola 129 G 5–6
Astor 129 J 3
Astorga 114 B 3
Astoria 170 B 2
Astove 159 H 6
Astrakhan 128 D 1
Astrolabe, Récifs de l' 146 C 4
Asunción (Mariana Isl.) 146 A 1
Asunción (Paraguay) 182 E 4
Aswa 158 E 4
Aswad, Ra's al 154 F 4
Aswān 154 E 4
Aswān High Dam 154 E 4
Asyūţ 154 E 3
Ata 146 D 4
Ataki 116 C 1
Atakora, Chaîne de l' 156 E 3
Atakpamé 156 E 4
Atalándi 116 B 3
Atalaya 180 B 3
Atalaya, Cerro (Chile) 183 B 9
Atalaya, Cerro (Peru) 180 B 3
Atalayasa 114 D 4
Atamanon Óri 116 B 3
Atambua 137 F 5
Atamgmik 169 R 3
Atar 152 C 4
Atas Bogd Uul 132 C 2
Atascadero 170 B 4
Atasu 119 O 6
Atauba 179 F 4
Atauro, Pulau 137 G 5
Ataviros 116 C 3
Atbalmin 144 D 2
Aţbarah 154 F 5
'Atbarah 145 E 4
Atbasar 119 N 5
At-Bash 119 K 3
Atchafalaya Bay 171 H 6
Atchison 171 G 4
Atebubu 156 D 4
Ateca 114 C 3
Atemble 144 D 3
Athabasca (Alb., Can.) 167 P 5
Athabasca (Alb., Can.) 167 P 4
Athabasca River 167 O 5
Athens (GA, U.S.A.) 171 K 5
Athens (TN, U.S.A.) 171 K 4
Athens → Athínai 116 B 3
Atherton (Australia) 143 H 2
Atherton (U.K.) 101 D 3
Athi 159 F 5
Athi River 159 F 5
Athlone 100 B 3
Athni 134 C 4
Áthos 116 B 2
Ath Thumāmī 155 G 3
Athy 100 B 3
Ati 157 H 3
Atiak 158 E 4
Atikokan 168 J 6
Atikonak Lake 169 P 5
Atitlán, Volcán 172 D 5
Atiu 147 E 4
Atka (AK, U.S.A.) 166 C 5
Atka (U.S.S.R.) 131 S 3
Atkarsk 118 H 5
Atkinson (N.C., U.S.A.) 171 L 5
Atkinson (NE, U.S.A.) 170 G 3
Atlanta 171 K 5
Atlanta (IA, U.S.A.) 171 H 3
Atlantic City 171 M 4
Atlantic-Indian Rise 192 B 5
Atlantic Ocean 186
Atlas Mountains 152 D–F 2
Atlasova, Ostrov 131 T 5
Atlin 166 L 4
Atlin Lake 166 L 4
Atmore 171 J 5
Atna Peak 167 M 5
Atocha 180 C 5
Atoka 171 G 5
Atouat 135 J 4
Atoyac de Alvarez 172 B 4
Åtran 113 F 4
Atrato 178 C 2
Atrek 128 E 3
Atsy 137 J 5
Aţ Ţaff 155 J 4

Aţ Ţafīlah 154 F 2
Aţ Ţā'if 155 G 4
At Tamīmī 153 K 2
At Tarhūnī, Jabal 153 K 4
Attawapiskat 168 L 5
Attawapiskat Lake 168 K 5
Aţ Ṭawīl 155 F 3
Aţ Ṭaysīyah 155 G 3
Aţ Ṭayyārah 154 E 6
Attersee 115 F 2
Aţ Ṭīb, Ra's 153 H 1
At Tin, Ra's 153 K 2
Attikamagen Lake 169 O 5
Attleborough 103 E 1
Attopeu 135 J 5
Attu 166 A 5
Attur 134 C 5
Aţ Ţulayhī 155 G 3
Aţ Ţullāb 153 K 4
Aţ Tuwayshah 154 D 6
Aţ Tuwayyah 155 G 3
Atuel 183 C 6
Atura 158 E 4
Åtvidaberg 113 G 4
Atyr-Meyite 131 O 2
Aua 144 D 2
Auadi 152 C 4
Auas Mountains 160 B 4
Auati Paraná 178 E 4
Auatu 159 G 3
Aubagne 115 E 3
Aubrac, Monts d' 114 D 3
Aubry, Lake 167 M 2
Aubusson 114 D 2
Auca Mahuida, Sierra 183 C 6
Auch 114 D 3
Auchi 157 F 4
Auchinleck 99 B 4
Auchterarder 99 C 3
Auckland 145 Q 8
Auckland Islands 185
Aude 114 D 3
Audierne, Baie de 114 C 2
Audo Range 159 G 3
Aue 111 F 4
Augathella 143 H 4
Aughrabies Falls 160 C 5
Augsburg 111 F 5
Augusta (Italy) 115 G 4
Augusta (Australia) 142 A 5
Augusta (AR, U.S.A.) 171 H 4
Augusta (GA, U.S.A.) 171 K 5
Augusta (ME, U.S.A.) 171 N 3
Augustín Codazzi 178 D 1
Augustów 111 H 4
Augustus, Mount 142 B 3
Auki 145 H 3
Auld, Lake 142 C 3
Auna 156 E 3
Auning 113 F 4
Auraiya 134 C 2
Aurangabad 134 D 3
Aurangaband 134 C 4
Auray 114 C 2
Aure 112 E 3
Aurès, Massif de l' 153 G 1
Aurich 111 E 4
Aurilândia 181 F 4
Aurillac 114 D 3
Aurlandsfjorden 112 E 3
Aurlandsvangen 112 E 3
Aurora (Philippines) 137 F 2
Aurora (CO, U.S.A.) 170 F 4
Aursunden 112 F 3
Aurukun 143 G 1
Aurunci, Monti 115 F 3
Aus 160 B 5
Ausangate, Nevado 180 B 3
Ausert 152 C 4
Aust-Agder 113 E 4
Austin (Australia) 142 B 4
Austin (MN, U.S.A.) 171 H 3
Austin (NV, U.S.A.) 170 C 4
Austin (TX, U.S.A.) 170 G 5
Austin, Lake 142 B 4
Austral Downs 143 F 3
Australia 142–143 CG 3
Australian Alps 143 H 6
Australian-Antarctic Basin 192 B 5
Australian-Antarctic Discordance 193 C 5
Australian-Antarctic Rise 193 C 5
Australian Capital Territory 143 H 6
Austria 115 F 2

Austurhorn 112 C 3
Austvågöy 112 F 2
Autazes 179 G 4
Autlán 172 B 4
Autun 114 D 2
Auvézère 114 D 2
Auxerre 114 D 2
Auxonne 115 E 2
Auyuittuq National Park 169 O 2
Avakubi 158 D 4
Avallon 114 D 2
Avalon Peninsula 169 R 6
Avan 128 G 1
Avanavero 179 G 3
Avanos 117 D 3
Avaré 181 G 5
Avarua 147 E 4
Avaz 128 G 4
Avdhira 116 B 2
Aveiro (Portugal) 114 B 3
Aveiro (Brazil) 179 G 4
Åvej 128 D 3
Āvej, Gardaneh-ye 128 D 3
Avekova 131 U 3
Avellaneda 182 E 5
Avellino 115 F 3
Averøya 112 E 3
Aversa 115 F 3
Avesnes 114 D 1
Avesta 113 G 3
Aveyron 114 D 3
Avezzano 115 F 3
Aviá Terai 182 D 4
Aviemore 98 C 3
Avigait 169 R 3
Avignon 115 D 3
Ávila 114 C 3
Avilés 114 B 3
Avington 143 G 3
Aviz 114 B 3
Avola 115 G 4
Avon Downs 143 F 2
Avonmouth 102 C 2
Avon Park 171 K 6
Avon River (Australia) 142 B 5
Avon, River (Avon) 102 C 2
Avon, River (Grampian) 98 C 3
Avon, River (Warwickshire) 103 D 1
Avranches 114 C 2
Avrora 117 D 1
Awai 157 F 4
Awanui 145 Q 8
Awara Plain 159 G 4
Awareh 159 G 3
Awasa 159 F 3
Awash 159 G 2
Awash 159 G 3
Awasib Mountains 160 B 5
Awaso 156 D 4
Awat 129 L 2
'Awaynat Wanīn 153 H 3
Awbārī 153 H 3
Awbārī, Idhān 153 H 3
Awdêgle 159 G 4
Awe, Loch 99 B 3
Awjilah 153 K 3
Awka 157 F 4
Axel Heiberg Island 184
Axim 156 D 5
Aximim 179 G 4
Axioma 179 F 5
Axios 116 B 2
Ax-les-Thermes 114 D 3
Axminster 102 C 2
Ayabaca 178 C 4
Ayachi, Jbel 152 DE 2
Ayacucho (Arg.) 183 E 6
Ayacucho (Peru) 180 B 3
'Ayādh 155 G 3
Ayaguz 119 Q 6
Ayagurz 119 P 6
Ayakkum Hu 132 A 3
Ayakli 130 G 2
Ayamé 156 D 4
Ayamé Dam 156 D 4
Ayamonte 114 B 4
Ayan 130 J 3
Ayan 131 P 4
Ayan 130 J 4
Ayan 130 F 2
Ayanaka 131 V 3
Ayancık 117 D 2
Ayangba 157 F 4
Ayanka 131 U 3
Ayaş 117 D 2
Ayaturku, Ozero 130 F 1
Ayava 130 H 4
Ayaviri 180 B 3
Ayaya 131 O 3
Aydın 116 C 3
Aydıncık 117 D 3

Aydingkol Hu 132 A 2
Aydyrlinskiy 119 L 5
Ayelu 159 G 2
Ayerbe 114 C 3
Ayers Rock – Mount Olga National Park 142 E 4
Áyion Óros 116 B 2
Áyios Evstrátios 116 BC 3
Áyios Kirikos 116 C 3
Áyios Nikólaos 116 C 3
Aykhal 130 K 4
Aylesbury 103 D 2
Aylmer Lake 167 Q 3
Aylsham 103 E 1
Ayna 114 C 4
'Aynabo 159 H 3
'Ayn al 'Ajalīyah 155 H 4
'Ayn al Ghazāl 153 K 4
'Ayn 'Aysa 154 F 1
'Ayn Dāllah 154 D 3
'Ayn Dār 155 H 3
'Ayn Dīwār 155 G 1
Ayni 129 H 3
'Aynīn 155 G 4
'Ayn Sukhnah 154 E 3
'Ayn Zuwayyah 153 K 4
Ayod 158 E 3
Ayon 131 V 2
Ayon, Ostrov 131 V 2
Ayorou 156 E 3
Ayr (U.K.) 100 C 2
Ayr (Australia) 143 H 2
Ayrag Nuur 130 F 6
Ayrancı 117 D 3
Ayrolle, Étang de l' 114 D 3
Ayrshire Downs 143 G 3
Aysary 119 O 5
Ayshirak 119 O 6
Aytré 114 C 2
Ayuán-Tepuí 179 F 2
Ayutla 172 C 4
Ayutthaya 135 H 5
Ayvacık 117 E 2
Ayvacık 116 C 3
Ayvalık 116 C 3
Azaila 114 C 3
Azambuja 114 B 4
Azamgarh 134 D 3
Azanka 119 M 4
Azaouad 156 D 2
Azaouak, Vallée de l' 156 E 2
Azarān 128 D 3
Azare 157 G 3
Azbine → Aïr 157 F 2
Az Daro 159 F 2
Azdavay 117 D 2
Azéffal, Dunes de l' 152 BC 4
Azelik 157 F 2
Azemmour 152 D 2
Azennezal 152 F 4
Azerbaydzhan 128 D 2
Azilal 152 D 2
Azogues 178 C 4
Azopol'ye 118 J 2
Azores 152 A 1
Azoum 157 J 3
Azov 117 E 1
Azovskiy Kanal 117 EF 1
Azovskoye More 117 E 1
Azovy 119 N 2
Azozo 159 F 2
Azrou 152 D 2
Azrow 129 H 4
Aztec ruins 170 E 4
Az Tibaghbagh 154 D 3
Azua 173 H 4
Azuaga 114 B 4
Azuero, Península de 178 B 2
Azul 183 E 6
Azul, Cordillera 178 C 5
Azur, Côte d' 115 E 3
Azzaba 153 G 1
Az Zafir 155 G 5
Az Zahrah 153 J 3
Az Zahrān 155 HJ 3
Az Zaqāzīq 154 E 2
Az Zarqā' 154 D 3
Az Zawiyah 153 H 2
Az Zaydab 154 E 5
Az Zaydīyah 155 G 5
Az Zaytūn 154 D 3
Azzel Matti, Sebkha 152 E 3
Az Zilfī 155 G 3
Az Zubayr 155 H 2
Az Zugar 155 G 6
Azzuwaytīnah 153 JK 2

B

Bañados de Izozog 180 D 4

Baa 136 F 6
Baä 142 C 1
Ba'ādwēyn 159 H 3
Baan Baa 143 H 5
Baba Burnu 116 D 2
Baba Burun 116 C 3
Babaculândia 179 J 5
Babadag 116 C 2
Babaeski 116 C 2
Babahoyo 178 C 4
Babai Gaxun 132 D 2
Bāb al Māndab 155 G 6
Babanūsah 154 D 6
Babar, Kepulauan 137 G 5
Babati 159 F 5
Babayevo 118 G 4
Babinda 157 F 3
Babine 167 M 5
Babine Lake 167 M 5
Babino Polje 115 G 3
Babi, Pulau 136 A 3
Babo 137 H 4
Bābol 128 E 3
Babol Sar 128 E 3
Baborigame 170 E 6
Baboua 158 A 3
Babushkin 130 J 5
Babuyan 137 J 1
Babuyan Channel 137 J 1
Babylon 155 G 2
Bacabal (Maranhão, Brazil) 181 G 1
Bacabal (Pará, Brazil) 179 G 5
Bacajá 179 H 4
Bacău 116 C 1
Bac Can 135 J 3
Bachaquero 178 D 2
Bacho 135 H 6
Bachu 129 K 3
Back 167 R 2
Bačka Palanka 116 A 1
Bačka Topola 116 A 1
Bačkovski Manastir 116 B 2
Bac Ninh 135 J 3
Bacolod 137 F 1
Bac Quang 135 H 3
Bacton 103 E 1
Bacup 101 D 3
Bād 128 E 4
Badagara 134 C 5
Badain Jaran Shamo 132 D 2
Badajós 179 J 4
Badajós, Lago 179 F 4
Badajoz 114 B 4
Badakhshan 129 J 3
Badalona 114 D 3
Badami 134 C 4
Badanah 155 G 2
Badarma 130 H 4
Bad Aussee 115 F 2
Badda 159 F 3
Baden (Austria) 115 G 2
Baden (Ethiopia) 159 F 1
Baden (Switzerland) 115 E 2
Baden-Baden 111 E 5
Badenoch 99 B 3
Baden-Württemberg 111 E 5
Badgastein 115 F 2
Bad Godesberg 111 E 4
Bad Hersfeld 111 E 4
Bad Homburg 111 E 4
Badin 129 H 6
Badiraguato 170 E 6
Bad Ischl 115 F 2
Bādiyat ash Shām 154–155 FG 2
Badjawa 137 F 5
Bad Kissingen 111 F 4
Bad Kreuznach 111 E 5
Badlands 170 F 2
Bado 137 J 5
Ba Dong 135 J 4
Badoumbé 156 B 3
Bad Reichenhall 111 F 5
Badr Hunayn 154 E 4
Bad Schwartau 111 F 4
Bad Tölz 111 F 5
Badulla 134 D 6
Badyarikha 131 R 2
Badzal'skiy Khrebet 131 O 5
Badzhal 131 O 5
Baena 114 C 4
Baeza (Spain) 114 C 4
Baeza (Ecuador) 178 C 4
Bafa Gölü 116 C 3
Bafang 157 FG 5
Bafatá 156 B 3
Baffin Bay 184
Baffin Island 169 NO 2
Bafia 157 G 5
Bafing 156 B 3
Bafing Makana 156 B 3
Bafoulabé 156 B 3
Bafoussam 157 G 4
Baf → Paphos 117 D 4
Bāfq 128 F 4
Bafra 117 E 2
Bafra Burnu 117 E 2
Bāft 128 F 5
Bafwaboli 158 D 4
Bafwasende 158 D 4
Baga 157 G 3
Bagadzha 130 L 3
Bagalkot 134 C 4
Bagam 157 F 3
Bagamoyo 159 F 6
Baganalakh 130 L 3
Bagansiapapi 136 B 3
Baga Sola 157 G 3
Bagata 158 B 5
Bagdarin 130 K 5
Bagé 182 F 5
Bagerovo 117 E 1
Baghdād 155 G 2
Bagheria 115 F 4
Bāghīn 128 F 4
Baghlan 129 H 3
Bagley 171 G 2
Baglung 134 D 2
Bagn 113 E 3
Bagnères-de-Bigorre 114 D 3
Bagoé 156 C 3
Bagrawia → Meroe 154 E 5
Bagrax → Bohu 132 A 2
Bagre 179 H 4
Bagua 178 C 5
Baguia 137 G 5
Baguio 137 J 1
Baguirmi 157 H 3
Bagusi 137 J 4
Bagzane, Monts 157 F 2
Bahadale 159 F 5
Bahá de Punta Gorda 172 F 5
Bahama Islands 173 H 3
Bahamas 173 H 3
Bahar Dar 159 F 2
Bahariya Oasis → Wāḥat al Baḥarīyah 154 D 3
Bahau 136 B 3
Bahaur 136 D 4
Bahawalnagar 129 J 5
Bahawalpur 129 J 5
Bahçe 117 E 3
Bahi 158 E 6
Bahía (Arg.) 183 C 8
Bahía (Brazil) 181 H 3
Bahia Adair 170 D 5
Bahía Ballenas 170 D 6
Bahía Blanca 183 D 6
Bahía Blanca 183 D 6
Bahia Chamela 172 A 4
Bahía Coatzacoalcos 172 D 4
Bahía Concepción 170 D 6
Bahía de Amatique 172 E 4
Bahia de Banderas 172 A 3
Bahia de Campeche 172 D 4
Bahia de Caráquez 178 B 4
Bahía de Chetumal 172 E 4
Bahía de Coronado 172 E 6
Bahia de La Paz 170 D 7
Bahia de Manzanillo 172 B 4
Bahia de Petacalco 172 B 4
Bahia de San Jorge 170 D 5
Bahía de San Quintin 170 C 5
Bahia de Santa Elena 172 E 5
Bahia de Santa Maria 170 E 6
Bahía de Sechura 178 B 5
Bahia de Tepoca 170 D 5
Bahía de Topolobampo 170 E 6
Bahia Dulce 172 C 4
Bahía Grande 183 C 9
Bahia, Islas de la 172 E 4
Bahía Kino 170 D 6
Bahia Laura 183 C 8
Bahia Magdalena 170 D 7
Bahia Negra 180 E 5
Bahia Otway 183 B 9
Bahía Pargua 183 B 7
Bahia Rosario 170 C 6
Bahia → Salvador (Brazil) 181 J 3
Bahía Samborombón 183 E 6
Bahía San Luis Gonzaga 170 D 5
Bahia Santa Ines 170 D 6
Bahías, Cabo dos 183 C 8
Bahía Sebastián Vizcaíno 170 D 6
Bahindi 157 E 3
Bahrah 155 F 4
Bahraich 134 D 2
Bahrain 155 J 3

Baḥr al Abyaḍ 154 E 6
Baḥr al 'Arab 154 D 6
Baḥr al Azraq 154 E 6
Baḥr al Ghazāl 158 D 3
Baḥr al Jabal 158 E 3
Baḥr al Milh 155 G 2
Bahr Aouk 158 B 3
Baḥr ar Rimāl al 'Azīm 154 D 3
Bahr ath Tharthār 155 G 2
Bahr el Ghazal 157 H 3
Bāhu Kālāt 129 G 5
Baião 179 J 4
Baía de Maputo 161 E 5
Baia de Paranaguá 181 G 2
Baía de Setúbal 114 B 4
Baía de Sofala 161 F 4
Baia de Todos os Santos 181 J 3
Baía do Bengo 160 A 1
Baía dos Tigres 160 A 3
Baía Farta 160 A 2
Baia Mare 116 B 1
Baíbokoum 157 H 4
Baicang 135 F 1
Baicheng 133 H 1
Baicheng 129 L 2
Baie aux Feuilles 169 O 4
Baie Comeau 169 O 6
Baie d'Antongil 161 HJ 3
Baie d'Audierne 114 C 2
Baie de Corisco 157 F 5
Baie de Lannion 114 C 2
Baie de la Seine 114 C 2
Baie de Rupert 169 M 5
Baie-des-Moutons 169 Q 5
Baie Diana 169 O 3
Baie du Poste 169 N 5
Baie Mosquito 169 N 4
Baie Payne 169 O 4
Baie Trinité 169 O 6
Baie Verte 169 Q 6
Baihe 132 F 4
Baikal, Lake 130 J 4 5
Baikha 119 R 3
Bailang 130 M 6
Baildon 101 D 3
Baile Atha Cliath 100 B 3
Bailén 114 C 4
Băileşti 116 B 2
Bailique 179 J 3
Ba-Illi 157 H 3
Bailundo 160 B 2
Baima 132 D 4
Baimuru 144 D 3
Bainang 134 E 2
Bainbridge 171 K 5
Bain-de-Bretagne 114 C 2
Baing 136 F 6
Baingoin 134 E 1
Baiquan 131 N 6
Baird Inlet 166 E 3
Baird Mountains 166 E 2
Baird Peninsula 169 M 1
Bairiki 146 C 2
Bairin Youqi 133 G 2
Bairin Zuoqi 133 G 2
Bairkum 129 H 2
Bairnsdale 143 H 6
Bais 137 F 2
Baisha 132 E 7
Bai Thuong 135 J 4
Baix-Alentejo 114 B 4
Baixo-Longa 160 B 3
Baiyanghe 129 M 2
Baiyer River 144 D 3
Baiyü 132 C 4
Baiyuda 154 E 5
Baiyuda Desert → Ṣaḥrā' Bayyūdah 154 E 5
Baja 116 A 1
Baja California Norte 170 C 5
Baja California Sur 170 D 6
Baja de Marajó 179 J 4
Bājah 153 G 1
Bajas, Rías 114 B 3
Bājgīrān 128 F 3
Bajitpur 135 F 3
Bajun Islands 159 G 5
Baka 158 E 4
Bakadžicite 116 C 2
Bakal 119 L 5
Bakala 158 C 3
Bakanas 129 K 2
Bakan Mts 116 B 2
Bakar 115 F 2
Bakayan, Gunung 136 E 3
Bakchar 119 Q 4
Bake 136 B 4
Bakel 156 B 3
Baker (CA, U.S.A.) 170 C 4
Baker (MT, U.S.A.) 170 F 2
Baker (Oceania) 146 C 2
Baker (OR, U.S.A.) 170 C 3
Baker, Canal 183 B 8

Ayd – Bal

Baker Lake (NWT., Canada) 167 S 3
Baker Lake (Australia) 142 D 4
Bakersfield 170 C 4
Bakewell 103 D 1
Bakharden 128 F 3
Bakhardok 128 F 3
Bākharz 128 G 4
Bakhchisaray 117 D 2
Bakhmach 118 F 5
Bakhta 119 R 3
Baki 157 J 2
Bakinskikh Komissarov, Imeni 26 128 D 3
Bakir 116 C 3
Bakırdağı 117 E 3
Bakkaflói 112 C 2
Bako (Ethiopia) 159 F 3
Bako (Ivory Coast) 156 C 4
Bakony 116 A 1
Bakouma 158 C 3
Bakoye 156 C 3
Baksanges 117 F 2
Baku 128 D 2
Bakungan 136 A 3
Bakuriani 117 F 2
Bakwa M'Bule 158 C 5
Balâ (Turkey) 117 D 3
Bala (U.S.S.R.) 131 O 2
Bala (U.K.) 102 C 1
Bala (Guinea) 156 C 3
Bala (Senegal) 156 B 3
Balabac 136 E 2
Balabac Strait 136 E 2
Balabak Dağları 117 E 2
Balabalangan, Kepulauan 136 E 4
Balad 155 G 2
Bal'ad 159 H 4
Baladek 131 O 5
Baladīyat 'Adan 155 GH 6
Balagannakh 131 O 2
Balagannoye 131 R 4
Balaghat 134 D 3
Balaghat Range 134 C 4
Balaguer 114 D 3
Balakhna 118 H 4
Balakhnya 130 H 1
Balakhta 130 F 4
Balaklava 117 D 2
Balakleya 118 G 6
Balakovo 118 J 5
Balama 161 F 2
Balambangam 136 E 2
Bala Murghab 129 G 3
Balas 158 F 2
Balashov 118 H 5
Balasore 134 E 3
Balassagyarmat 116 A 1
Balāt 154 D 3
Balaton 116 A 1
Balaurin 137 F 5
Balavino 117 E 1
Balazhal 119 Q 6
Balazote 114 C 4
Balbi, Mount 145 F 3
Balboa 178 C 2
Balbriggan 100 B 3
Balcarce 183 E 6
Balclutha 144 P 10
Balde 182 C 5
Bald Head 142 B 6
Baldock 103 D 2
Baldy Peak 170 E 5
Bale 159 G 3
Baleares, Islas 114 D 3–4
Balearic Islands 114 D 3
Baleia, Ponta da 181 J 4
Baleine, Grande Rivière de la 169 MN 5
Baleine, Rivière à la 169 O 4
Baler 137 J 1
Baley 130 L 5
Balezino 118 K 4
Balgazin 130 G 5
Balguntay 129 M 2
Bal Hāf 155 H 6
Balho 159 G 2
Bali 159 F 4
Balia 156 B 4
Balıkesir 116 C 3
Balık Gölü 117 F 3
Balikpapan 136 E 4
Balikpapan, Gunung 136 E 4
Balikpapan, Teluk 136 E 4
Bali, Laut 136 D 5
Balimbing 137 EF 2
Balimo 144 D 3
Balintang Channel 137 J 1
Baliza 181 F 4
Balkan Mountains 116 C 2
Balkashino 119 N 5
Balkh 129 H 3

211

Bal – Bas

Balkhab 129 H 3
Balkhash 119 O 6
Balkhash, Ozero 119 OP 6
Ballachulish 99 B 3
Balladonia 142 C 5
Ballangen 112 G 2
Ballantrae 100 C 2
Ballarat 143 G 6
Ballard, Lake 142 C 4
Ballater 99 C 3
Ballé 156 C 2
Ballenas, Bahía 170 D 6
Ballenita, Punta 182 B 4
Balleny Islands 185
Ballia 134 D 2
Ballina (Australia) 143 J 4
Ballina (Rep. of Ireland) 110 B 4
Ballinamore 100 B 2
Ballinger 170 G 5
Ballinrobe 110 B 4
Ballitore 100 B 3
Balls Pyramid 143 K 5
Ballybofey 100 B 2
Ballycastle 100 B 2
Ballyclare 100 B 2
Ballygawley 100 B 2
Ballyhaunis 110 B 4
Ballykelly 100 B 2
Ballymena 100 B 2
Ballymoney 100 B 2
Ballynahinch 100 C 2
Ballyshannon 100 A 2
Balmoral Castle 99 C 3
Balneario Claromecó 183 D 6
Balombo 160 B 2
Balonne River 143 H 4
Balotra 134 B 2
Balovale 160 C 2
Bal Qaf 153 J 3
Balrampur 134 D 2
Balranald 143 G 5
Balş 116 B 2
Balsas (Brazil) 181 G 2
Balsas (Mexico) 172 C 4
Balsas, Rio 172 B 4
Bålsta 113 G 4
Balta 116 C 1
Balta Brăilei 116 C 2
Balta Ialomiţei 116 C 2
Baltasar Brum 182 E 5
Baltaţi 116 C 1
Baltic Sea 113 GH 4
Baltīm 154 E 2
Baltim 154 DE 3
Baltimore (MD, U.S.A.) 171 L 4
Baltimore (S. Afr.) 160 D 4
Baltistan 129 K 3
Baltiysk 113 GH 5
Baltiyskaja Grjada 113 H J 4–5
Baluchistan 129 G 5
Balurghat 134 E 2
Balva 116 C 3
Balvi 113 J 4
Balygychan 131 S 3
Balyksa 119 R 5
Bam 128 F 5
Bama 157 G 3
Bamaga 143 G 1
Bamako 156 C 3
Bāmbā (Libya) 153 K 2
Bamba (Mali) 156 D 2
Bamba (Zaire) 158 B 6
Bambafouga 156 B 3
Bambama 157 G 6
Bambamarca 178 C 5
Bambangando 160 C 3
Bambari 158 C 3
Bambaroo 143 H 2
Bamberg 111 F 5
Bambesa 158 D 4
Bambesi 158 E 3
Bambey 156 A 3
Bambio 158 B 4
Bamboi 156 D 4
Bambouti 158 D 3
Bambouto, Monts 157 F 4
Bamenda 157 G 4
Bami 128 F 3
Bamingui 158 C 3
Bamingui 158 B 3
Bamingui-Bangoran, Parc National du 158 BC 3
Bamiyan 129 H 4
Bam Posht 129 G 5
Bampūr 129 G 5
Ban 135 J 5
Banaadir 159 GH 4
Banaba 145 J 2
Banagher 100 B 3
Banagi 158 E 5
Banalia 158 D 4
Banamba 156 C 3
Banana 143 J 3

Banana Islands 156 B 4
Bananal, Ilha do 181 F 3
Bananga 135 F 6
Banas 134 C 2
Banās, Ra's 154 F 4
Banat 116 B 1
Banaz 116 C 3
Ban Ban 135 H 4
Banbar 132 B 4
Banbridge 100 B 2
Banbury 103 D 1
Banc du Geyser 161 H 2
Banchory 99 C 3
Banco Chinchorro 172 E 4
Banco de Serrana 173 FG 5
Banco Quitasueño 173 F 5
Bancoran 137 E 2
Banco Serranilla 173 G 4
Bancroft 171 L 2
Banda 134 D 2
Banda 134 C 3
Banda Aceh 136 A 2
Banda del Río Sali 182 D 4
Banda Elat 137 H 5
Bandahara, Gunung 136 A 3
Banda, Kepulauan 137 G 5
Banda, Laut 137 G 5
Bandama 156 D 4
Bandama Blanc 156 C 4
Bandan Kūh 128 G 4
Bandar Abbas 128 F 5
Bandarban 135 F 3
Bandar-e-Anzalī 128 D 3
Bandar-e Chārak 128 E 5
Bandar-e Chāru 128 E 5
Bandar-e Deylam 128 E 3
Bandar-e Khomeyni 128 D 4
Bandar-e Lengeh 128 E 5
Bandar-e Māqām 128 E 5
Bandar-e Moghūyeh 128 E 5
Bandar-e Rig 128 E 5
Bandar-e Shah → Bandar-e Torkeman 128 E 3
Bandar-e Shahpur → Bandar-e Khomeyni 128 D 4
Bandar-e Torkeman 128 E 3
Bandarlampung 136 C 4
Bandar → Machilipatnami 134 D 4
Bandar Ma'shur 128 D 4
Bandarpunch 134 C 1
Bandar Seri Begawan 136 D 3
Banda Sea 137 G 5
Bandau 136 E 2
Band Bonī 128 F 5
Bandeira 181 H 5
Bandeirante 181 F 3
Bandera 182 D 4
Banderas, Bahia de 172 A 3
Bandiagara 156 D 3
Band-i-Amir 129 H 3–4
Band-i-Baba 129 G 3
Band-i-Baian 129 H 4
Bandırma 116 C 2
Band-i-Turkestan 129 G 3
Ban Don 135 J 5
Bandundu 158 B 5
Bandung 136 C 5
Baneh 128 D 3
Banemo 137 G 3
Banes 173 G 3
Banff (U.S.A.) 167 O 5
Banff (U.K.) 98 C 3
Banff National Park 167 O 5
Banfora 156 CD 3
Banga 158 C 6
Bangadi 158 D 4
Bangalore 134 C 5
Banganté 157 G 4
Bangar 136 E 3
Bangassou 158 C 4
Bangeta, Mount 144 E 3
Banggai 137 F 4
Banggai, Kepulauan 137 F 4
Banggi 136 E 2
Banggong Co 134 C 1
Bang Hieng 135 J 4
Bangil 136 D 5
Bangkalan 136 D 5
Bangka, Pulau 136 C 4
Bangkaru, Pulau 136 A 3
Bangka, Selat 136 C 4
Bangko 159 F 1
Bangkok 135 H 5
Bangkok, Bight of 135 H 5
Bangladesh 134 EF 3
Bang Mun Nak 135 H 4
Bangor (U.S.A.) 171 N 3
Bangor (U.K.) 100 C 2
Bang Saphan Yai 135 G 5
Bangsund 112 F 3
Bangui (Phil.) 137 J 1
BanguiMbaiki 158 B 4
Banguru 158 D 4

Bangweulu Swamps 160 D 2
Banhã 154 E 2
Banhine National Park 161 E 4
Bani 156 C 3
Banī 173 H 4
Baniara 145 E 3
Bani Bangou 156 E 3
Banihal Pass 129 K 4
Bani, Jbel 152 D 3
Banī Ma'ārid 155 H 5
Banī Mazār 154 E 3
Banī Suwayf 154 E 3
Banī Walīd 153 H 2
Bāniyās (Jordan) 154 F 2
Bāniyās (Syria) 154 F 1
Banja Koviljača 115 G 3
Banjarmasin 136 D 4
Banja Luka 115 G 3
Banjul 156 A 3
Banka 134 E 3
Bankas 156 D 3
Bankeryd 113 F 4
Banket 161 E 3
Ban Khemmarat 135 J 4
Banks, Îles 146 C 3
Banks Island (Australia) 143 G 1
Banks Island (U.S.A.) 167 N 1
Banks Islands (Vanuatu) 146 C 3
Banks Lake 170 C 2
Banks Peninsula 145 Q 9
Banks Strait 144 L 9
Bankura 134 E 3
Banmauk 135 G 3
Ban Me Thuot 135 J 5
Bann 110 B 4
Ban Nabo 135 J 4
Ban Na Shan 135 G 6
Ban Ngon 135 H 4
Bann, River 100 B 2
Bannu 129 J 4
Bāno 112 G 2
Ban Sao 135 H 4
Bansi 134 D 2
Banská Bystrica 111 J 5
Ban Sop Huai Hai 135 G 4
Banstead 103 D 2
Banswara 134 B 3
Ban Taup 135 J 4
Bantry 110 B 4
Bantry Bay 110 B 4
Banu 129 H 3
Banyo 157 G 4
Banyuls-sur-Mer 114 D 3
Banyuwangi 136 D 5
Banzare Coast 185
Bao Bilia 157 J 2
Baode 132 F 3
Baodi 133 G 3
Baoding 132 G 3
Baofeng 132 F 4
Bao Ha 135 H 3
Baoji 132 E 4
Baokang 132 F 4
Bao Loc 135 J 5
Baoqing 133 K 1
Baoro 158 B 3
Baoshan 132 C 5
Baotou 132 E 3
Baoulé 156 C 3
Baoxing 132 D 4
Baoying 133 G 4
Bap 134 B 2
Bapatla 134 D 4
Bapuyu 136 D 4
Baqen 132 B 4
Baquedano 180 C 5
Ba'qūbah 155 G 2
Bar 116 A 2
Barāo de Capanema 180 E 3
Barão de Melgaço 180 D 3
Barão de Melgaço 180 E 4
Bara 157 G 3
Barabal 136 E 4
Bara Banki 134 D 2
Barabinsk 119 P 4
Barabinskaya Step' 119 P 5
Baracaldo 114 C 3
Baragoi 159 F 4
Bärah 154 E 6
Barakāt 154 E 6
Barakkul' 119 N 5
Baram 136 D 3
Baramanni 179 G 2
Baramula 129 J 4
Baran (India) 134 C 2
Baran (U.S.S.R.) 113 K 5
Barangbarang 137 F 5
Barani 156 D 3
Baranikha, Malaya 131 V 2
Baranoa 178 D 1

Baranof 166 K 4
Baranovichi 113 J 5
Baranovka 118 J 5
Barapasi 137 J 4
Baratang 135 F 5
Barati 137 F 5
Barāwe 159 G 4
Barbacena 181 H 5
Barbacoas 178 C 3
Barbados 173 L 5
Barbar 154 E 5
Bárbara 178 D 4
Barbas, Cabo 152 B 4
Barbastro 114 D 3
Barbate de Franco 114 B 4
Barberton (S. Africa) 161 E 5
Barberton (U.S.A.) 171 K 3
Barbezieux 114 C 2
Barbosa 178 D 2
Barbuda 173 K 4
Barcaldine 143 H 3
Barce → Al Marj 153 K 2
Barcellona Pozzo di Gotto 115 G 4
Barcelona (Spain) 114 D 3
Barcelona (Ven.) 179 F 2
Barcelonette 115 E 3
Barcelos 179 F 4
Barcoo or Cooper Creek 143 F 4
Barcoo River 143 G 3
Barda del Medio 183 C 6
Bardaï 157 H 1
Bardejov 111 H 5
Bărđĕre 159 G 4
Bardeskan 128 F 3
Bardhhaman 134 E 3
Bardonecchia 115 E 2
Bardsey 110 BC 4
Bardsey Island 102 B 1
Barēda 159 J 2
Bareilly 134 C 2
Barentsovo More 118 GJ 1
Barents Sea 184
Barentu 159 F 1
Bårgă 112 G 2
Barga 130 D 1
Bārgāl 159 J 2
Bargarh 134 D 3
Bargoed 102 C 2
Barguzin 130 J 4 5
Barguzinskiy Khrebet 130 J 4 5
Barhaj 134 D 2
Barhau 136 B 5
Bari 115 G 3
Baria 178 E 3
Barīdī, Ra's 154 F 4
Barikiwa 159 F 6
Barim 155 G 6
Bari, Mola di 115 G 3
Barinas 178 D 2
Baring, Cape 167 O 2
Baringo, Lake 159 F 4
Baripada 134 E 3
Bariri 181 G 5
Bariri, Represa 181 G 5
Bărīs 154 E 4
Bari Sadri 134 B 3
Barisal 135 F 3
Barisan, Pegunungan 136 B 4
Bari, Terra di 115 G 3
Barito, Sungai 136 D 4
Barkā' 155 K 4
Barkam 132 D 4
Barker, Mount 142 B 5
Barkley, Lake 171 J 4
Barkly East 160 D 6
Barkly Tableland 143 F 2
Barkly West 160 C 5
Barkol Hu 129 N 2
Barkol Kazak Zizhixian 132 B 2
Barladağı 116 D 3
Bar-le-Duc 115 E 2
Barlee, Lake 142 B 4
Barlee Range 142 B 3
Barletta 115 G 3
Barlovento, Islas de 173 K 4
Barma 137 H 4
Barmer 134 B 2
Barmera 143 G 5
Barmouth 102 B 1
Barnard Castle 101 E 2
Barnaul 119 Q 5
Barnes Ice Cap 169 N 1
Barnsley 101 E 3
Barnstaple 102 B 2
Barnstaple or Bideford Bay 102 B 2

Barotseland 160 C 3
Barouéli 156 C 3
Barq al Bishārīyīn 154 E 5
Barquisimeto 178 E 1
Barra (Brazil) 181 H 3
Barra (U.K.) 99 A 3
Barra (Airport) 99 A 3
Barraba 143 J 5
Barracão do Barreto 179 G 5
Barra da Estiva 181 H 3
Barra do Corda 181 G 2
Barra do Dande 160 A 1
Barra do Garças 181 F 4
Barra do Ribeiro 182 F 5
Barra do São Manuel 179 G 5
Barra dos Coqueiros 181 J 3
Barragem da Rocha de Galé 114 B 4
Barragem de Alqueva 114 B 4
Barragem de Sobradinho 181 H 3
Barra Head 110 B 3
Barra Head 99 A 3
Barranca (Peru) 178 C 4
Barranca (Peru) 178 C 6
Barrancabermeja 178 D 2
Barrancas 179 F 2
Barranqueras 182 E 4
Barranquilla 178 D 1
Barra Patuca 172 F 4
Barraute 169 M 6
Barreiranha 179 G 4
Barreirinhas 181 H 1
Barreiras 181 H 3
Barreiro 114 B 4
Barreiros 181 J 2
Barren Island 135 F 5
Barren Islands 166 G 4
Barrenitos 170 F 6
Barren Lands 166 FH 2
Barretos 181 G 5
Barrhead (Canada) 167 P 5
Barrhead (U.K.) 99 B 4
Barri 102 C 2
Barrie 171 L 3
Barrocão 181 H 4
Barrow (Argentina) 183 D 6
Barrow (AK, U.S.A.) 166 F 1
Barrow Creek 142 E 3
Barrow-in-Furness 101 D 2
Barrow Island 142 A 3
Barrow, Point 166 F 1
Barrow Range 142 D 4
Barrow, River 100 B 3
Barry 110 C 4
Barsa-Kel'mes, Ostrov 128 F 1
Barsi 134 C 4
Barstow 170 C 5
Bar-sur-Aube 115 D 2
Bartazuga, Jabal 154 E 4
Bartibougou 156 E 3
Bartica 179 G 2
Bartın 117 D 2
Bartlesville 171 G 4
Barton-upon-Humber 101 E 3
Bartow 171 K 6
Bāruni 134 E 2
Baruun Urt 132 F 1
Barú, Volcán 178 B 2
Barvas 98 A 2
Barwa 134 D 3
Barwani 134 B 3
Barwon River 143 H 4
Barycz 111 G 3
Barylas 131 O 2
Barzas 119 R 4
Bãsa'idū 128 F 5
Basankusu 158 B 4
Basauri 114 C 3
Basekpio 158 C 4
Basel 115 E 2
Bashi Haixia 133 H 6
Bashkend 117 G 2
Basian 137 F 2
Basilan 137 F 2
Basilan City 137 F 2
Basildon 103 E 2
Basilio 182 E 5
Basingstoke 103 D 2
Başkale 117 F 3
Baskatong, Réservoir 171 L 2
Baskil 117 E 3
Baskol' 119 P 5
Basmat 134 C 4
Basoko 158 C 4
Basongo 158 C 5
Baso, Pulau 136 B 4
Basque Provinces 114 C 3
Basra 155 H 2
Bassano del Grappa 115 F 2
Bassari 156 E 4
Bassas da India 161 F 4
Bassein 135 F 4
Bassein → Vasai 134 B 4

212

Basse Santa Su 156 B 3
Basse Terre 173 K 4
Bassikounou 152 D 5
Bassila 156 E 4
Bassinde Rennes 114 C 2
Bassin de Thau 114 D 3
Basso, Plateau de 157 J 2
Bass Strait 144 L 8
Båstad 113 F 4
Bastak 128 E 5
Bastevarri 112 H 2
Basti 134 D 2
Bastia 115 E 3
Basto, Terra de 114 B 3
Bastrop 171 H 5
Bastuträsk 112 H 3
Basuto 160 D 3
Bata 157 F 5
Batabanó, Golfo de 172 F 3
Batagay 131 O 2
Batagay-Alyta 131 O 2
Batai, Gunung 136 B 5
Bata Islands 133 H 6
Bataklık Gölü 117 D 3
Batala 134 C 1
Batama (U.S.S.R.) 130 H 5
Batama (Zaire) 158 D 4
Batamay 131 N 3
Batam, Pulau 136 B 3
Batamshinskiy 119 L 5
Batang (China) 132 C 4
Batang (Indonesia) 136 C 5
Batanga 157 F 6
Batangafo 158 B 3
Batangas 137 F 1
Batang Hari 136 B 4
Batanta, Pulau 137 H 4
Batara 158 B 3
Batavia 182 C 5
Bataysk 117 E 1
Batchawana Mountain 168 L 6
Batchelor 142 E 1
Batemans Bay 143 J 6
Bateria, Cachoeira 179 G 3
Bath (U.S.A.) 171 N 3
Bath (U.K.) 102 C 2
Batha 157 H 3
Bathalha 114 B 4
Bathgate 99 C 4
Bathurst (Canada) 169 O 6
Bathurst (Australia) 143 H 5
Bathurst → Banjul 156 A 3
Bathurst, Cape 166 M 1
Bathurst Inlet 167 Q 2
Bathurst Island (Australia) 142 D 1
Bathurst Island (The Arctic) 184
Batié 156 D 4
Batie 159 G 2
Bāṭin, Wādī al 155 H 3
Batkanu 156 B 4
Bātlāq-e Gavkhūnī 128 E 4
Batley 101 E 3
Batman 117 F 3
Batna 153 G 1
Batn al Hajar 154 E 4
Batoka 160 D 3
Batomga 131 P 4
Baton Rouge 171 H 5
Batopilas 170 E 6
Batouri 157 G 5
Batrā, Jabal 154 F 3
Båtsfjord 112 J 1
Battambang 135 H 5
Batticaloa 134 D 6
Batti Malv 135 F 6
Battinga 158 C 3
Battle (Canada) 167 P 5
Battle (U.K.) 103 E 2
Battle Creek 171 J 3
Battleford 167 Q 5
Battle Harbour 169 Q 5
Battle Mountain 170 C 3
Batu 159 F 3
Batui 137 F 4
Batulantee, Gunung 136 E 5
Batumi 117 F 2
Batu Pahat 136 B 3
Batu Puteh, Gunung 136 B 3
Batuputih 137 E 3
Baturaja 136 B 4
Baturino 119 R 4
Baturinskaya 117 E 1
Baturité 181 J 1
Bau 136 D 3
Baubau 137 F 5
Baucau 137 G 5
Bauchi 157 F 3
Bauchi Plateau 157 G 3–4
Baud 114 C 2
Baudo 178 C 2
Baudó, Serranía de 178 C 2
Bauhinia Downs 143 H 3
Baula 137 F 4

Bauld, Cape 169 Q 5
Baumann, Pic 156 E 4
Baunei 115 E 3
Baunt 130 K 4
Bauple 143 J 4
Baures 180 D 3
Bauru 181 G 5
Baús 181 F 4
Bauska 113 H 4
Bautzen 111 F 4
Bavaria 111 F 5
Bavispe 170 E 5
Bāw 115 E 6
Bawdwin 135 G 3
Bawean, Pulau 136 D 5
Bawku 156 D 3
Bawmi 135 F 4
Bawn 159 G 2
Bawtry 101 E 3
Ba Xian 133 G 3
Ba Xian 132 E 5
Baxoi 132 C 4
Bayamo 173 G 3
Bayan 130 J 6
Bayana 134 C 2
Bayan-Adraga 130 K 6
Bayan-Agt 130 H 6
Bayan-Aul 119 P 5
Bayanbaraat 132 E 1
Bayanbulag 130 G 6
Bayanbulak 129 L 2
Bayanchandman 130 J 6
Bayandalay 132 D 2
Bayanday 130 J 5
Bayandzurh 130 J 6
Bayanga 158 B 2
Bayangol 130 H J 5
Bayan Har Shan 132 C 4
Bayan Har Shankou 132 C 4
Bayanhongor 130 H 6
Bayan Mod 132 D 2
Bayanmönh 132 E 1
Bayan Obo 132 E 2
Bayan-Öndör 132 E 2
Bayan-Öndör 132 D 1
Bayantsagaan 132 E 1
Bayantsogt 130 J 6
Bayan-Uul 130 K 6
Bayan-Uul 130 G 6
Bayat 117 D 2
Bayāz 128 F 4
Bayāzeh 128 F 4
Baychunas 128 E 1
Bay City (MI, U.S.A.) 171 K 3
Bay City (TX, U.S.A.) 171 G 6
Baydaratskaya Guba 119 N 2
Bay de Verde 169 R 6
Baydrag Gol 132 C 1
Bayerischer Wald 111 F 5
Bayern 111 F 5
Bayeux 114 C 2
Bayḥān al Qiṣāb 155 H 6
Bayındır 116 C 3
Bayjī 155 G 2
Baykal 130 H 5
Baykalovo 119 N 4
Baykal, Ozero 130 J 4 5
Baykal'skiy Khrebet 130 JK 4–5
Baykal'skoye 130 J 4
Baykal'skoye Nagor'ye, Severo 130 K 4
Baykan 117 F 3
Bay-Khak 130 F 5
Baykit 130 G 3
Baykitskiy 130 G 3
Baykonur 129 H 1
Baymak 119 L 5
Baynūnah 155 J 4
Bay of Bengal 134 EF 4
Bay of Biscay 114 C 2–3
Bay of Fundy 169 O 7
Bay of Gods Mercy 167 U 3
Bay of Islands 169 Q 6
Bay of Plenty 145 R 8
Bay of Plenty 146 C 5
Bayombong 137 J 1
Bayonne 114 C 3
Bayo Nuevo 173 G 4
Bayovar 178 B 5
Bayram-Ali 129 G 3
Bayramiç 116 C 3
Bayreuth 111 F 5
Bayrūt 154 EF 2
Baysa 130 K 5
Bay Springs 171 J 5
Bay-Syut 130 G 5
Bayt al Faqīh 155 G 6
Baytik Shan 129 N 1
Bayt Laḥm 154 F 2
Baytown 171 H 6
Bayunglincir 136 B 4

Bayy al Kabīr, Wādī 153 H 2
Bayyūdah, Ṣaḥrā' 154 E 5
Baza 114 C 4
Bazar Dyuzi, Gora 128 D 2
Bazarnyy Syzgan 118 J 5
Bazaruto National Park 161 F 4
Bazhong 132 E 4
Bei'an 131 N 6
B Bua Chum 135 H 4
Beach 170 F 2
Beachy Head 103 E 2
Beacon 142 B 5
Beaconsfield 103 D 2
Beagle Bay 142 C 2
Beagle, Canal 183 C 9
Beagle Gulf 142 DE 1
Bealanana 161 H 2
Beal Range 143 G 4
Beaminster 102 C 2
Beampingaratra 161 H 4
Bear Cape 169 P 6
Bear Island 184
Bear Lake 170 D 3
Bear Lodge Mountains 170 F 3
Bearpaw Mountains 170 D 2
Bearskin Lake 168 J 5
Beas 134 C 1
Beas de Segura 114 C 4
Beata, Cabo 173 H 4
Beatini, Monti 115 F 3
Beatrice 171 G 3
Beatrice, Cape 143 F 1
Beatton 167 N 4
Beatton River 167 N 4
Beatty 170 C 4
Beattyville 169 M 6
Beau-Bassin 161 K 6
Beaucaire 115 D 3
Beaucanton 169 M 6
Beaufort 171 K 5
Beaufort 136 E 2
Beaufort Sea 166 J–L 1
Beaufort West 160 C 6
Beaujolais, Monts du 115 D 2
Beauly 98 B 3
Beauly Firth 98 B 3
Beaumaris 102 B 1
Beaumont (France) 114 C 2
Beaumont (U.S.A.) 171 H 5
Beaune 115 D 2
Beaupré 171 M 2
Beausejour 167 S 5
Beauvais 114 D 2
Beaver (AK, U.S.A.) 166 H 2
Beaver (Sask., Can.) 167 Q 5
Beaver (UT, U.S.A.) 170 D 4
Beaver Dam 171 J 3
Beaver Island 171 J 2
Beaverton 170 B 2
Beawar 134 B 2
Beazley 182 C 5
Bebedouro 181 G 5
Beberibe 181 J 1
Bebington 101 D 3
Becan 172 E 4
Beccles 103 E 1
Becerreá 114 B 3
Béchar 152 E 2
Becharof Lake 166 F 4
Becharof National Monument 166 F 4
Bechevin Bay 166 E 4
Beckley 171 K 4
Beckum 111 E 4
Bełczyna 111 G 4
Bedeli 159 F 3
Bedford (U.K.) 103 D 1
Bedford (IN, U.S.A.) 171 J 4
Bedford (PA, U.S.A.) 171 L 3
Bedfordshire 103 D 1
Bedirka 143 E 4
Bedirli 117 E 3
Bedlington 101 E 2
Bednodem'yanovsk 118 H 5
Bedoba 130 G 4
Bedourie 143 F 3
Bedworth 134 D 1
Beech Grove 171 J 4
Beecroft Head 143 J 5
Beenleigh 143 J 4
Be'er Sheva 154 E 2
Beeston 103 D 1
Beetaloo 142 E 2
Beeville 170 G 6
Befale 158 C 4
Befandriana 161 G 4
Bega 143 H 6
Begejski Kanal 116 B 1
Begna 113 E 3

Begoml' (Belorussiya, U.S.S.R.) 112 J 5
Behābād 128 F 4
Behbehān 128 E 4
Behleg 132 B 3
Behring Point 173 G 3
Behshahr 128 E 3
Bei'an 131 N 6
Beibu Wan 132 E 6
Beichuan 132 D 4
Beida 153 K 2
Beihai 132 E 6
Bei Hulsan Hu 132 C 3
Beijing 133 G 3
Beiliu 132 F 6
Beilul Heyan 132 B 4
Beilul 159 G 2
Beilun He 132 E 6
Beinamar 157 H 4
Beinn Dearg 98 B 3
Beinn Dhorain 98 C 2
Beipiao 133 H 2
Beira 161 EF 3
Beirut 154 EF 2
Bei Shan 132 B 2
Beishan 132 C 2
Beitbridge 160 D 4
Beitstad 112 F 3
Beith 99 B 4
Beizhen 133 G 3
Beizhen 133 H 2
Beja 179 J 4
Béjar 114 B 3
Beji 129 H 5
Bejaïa 153 F 1
Bekabad 129 H 2
Bekasi 136 C 5
Bekdash 128 E 2
Bekily 161 H 4
Bekodoka 161 H 3
Bekopaka 161 G 3
Bekwai 156 D 4
Bela 161 E 5
Bela 134 D 2
Béla Bérim 157 G 2
Bélabo 157 G 5
Bela Crkva 116 B 2
Bela Dila 134 D 4
Belaga 136 D 3
Bel'Agach 119 Q 5
Belaia 158 F 2
Belaka 158 C 5
Bela Kanrach 129 G 5
Belang 137 F 3
Belau 137 H 2
Bela Polanka 116 B 2
Bela Vista (Angola) 160 A 1
Bela Vista (Brazil) 180 E 5
Belawan 136 A 3
Belaya (U.S.S.R.) 118 K 4
Belaya (U.S.S.R.) 117 F 2
Belaya Glina 117 F 1
Belaya Kalitva 117 F 1
Belaya Tserkov 118 F 6
Belbel 153 F 3
Belcher Islands 169 M 4
Belcik 117 E 3
Beled Weyne 159 H 4
Belem (Mexico) 170 D 6
Belém (Amazonas, Brazil) 178 E 4
Belem (Mozambique) 161 F 2
Belém (Pará, Brazil) 179 J 4
Belen (U.S.A.) 170 E 5
Belén (Argentina) 182 C 4
Belén (Colombia) 178 C 3
Belén (Paraguay) 180 E 5
Belep, Îles 146 B 4
Beleuli 128 F 2
Belfast 100 C 2
Belfast (Airport) 100 B 2
Belfield 167 R 6
Belford 101 E 2
Belfort 115 E 2
Belgaum 134 B 4
België 110 D 4
Belgique 110 D 4
Belgium 110 D 4
Belgorod 118 G 5
Belgorod-Dnestrovskiy 116 D 1
Belgrade 116 B 2
Bel Guerdane 152 C 3
Bel Haïrane 153 G 2
Beli 157 G 4
Belice 115 F 4
Beli Drim 116 B 2
Beli Lom 116 C 2
Beli Manastir 115 G 2
Belimbing 136 B 5

Belin 114 C 3
Belinga 157 G 5
Belingwe → Mberengwa 160 D 4
Belinskiy 118 H 5
Belinyu 136 C 4
Belitung, Pulau 136 C 4
Belize 172 E 4
Belize City 172 E 4
Belize River 172 E 4
Bélizon 179 H 3
Beljanica 116 B 2
Bel'kachi 131 O 4
Bell 169 M 6
Bella Bella 167 M 5
Bellac 114 D 2
Bellaco 182 E 5
Bella Coola 167 M 5
Bellary 134 C 4
Bella Vista (Argentina) 182 E 4
Bellavista (Peru) 178 C 5
Bellavista (Peru) 178 C 4
Bell Bay 168 K 1
Bellbrook 143 J 5
Belle Fourche River 170 F 3
Bellegarde-sur-Valserine 115 E 2
Belle Glade 171 K 6
Belle Ile 114 C 2
Belle Isle 169 Q 5
Belle Isle, Strait of 169 Q 5
Belleville 115 D 2
Belleville (IL, U.S.A.) 171 J 4
Belleville (KA, U.S.A.) 170 G 4
Belleville (Ont., Can.) 171 L 3
Bellevue (NE, U.S.A.)171 G 3
Bellevue (WA, U.S.A.) 170 B 2
Belley 115 E 2
Belle Yella 156 B 4
Bellin 169 N 3
Bellingen 143 J 5
Bellingham 170 B 2
Bellingshausen 185
Bellingshausen Sea 185
Bellinzona 115 E 2
Bello 178 C 2
Bellona 145 G 4
Bellona, Récifs 143 K 3
Bellot Strait 167 T 1
Bell Peninsula 167 V 3
Belluno 115 F 2
Bell Ville 182 D 5
Bellyk 130 F 5
Belmonte (Brazil) 181 J 4
Belmonte (Portugal) 114 B 3
Belmonte (Spain) 114 C 4
Belmopan 172 E 4
Belogolovoye 131 T 4
Belogorsk (U.S.S.R.) 131 N 5
Belogorsk (U.S.S.R.) 117 D 1
Belogor'ye 119 N 3
Belogradčik 116 B 2
Belo Horizonte (Minas Gerais, Brazil) 181 H 4
Belo Horizonte (Pará, Brazil) 179 H 4
Beloit 171 J 3
Belo Jardim 181 J 2
Belokholunitskiy 118 K 4
Belo Monta 179 H 4
Belomorsk 112 K 3
Belopol'ye 118 F 5
Belorechensk 117 E 2
Beloretsk 119 L 5
Belorussiya 113 J 4
Belorusskaya Gryada 113 H 5
Belo-sur-Mer 161 G 4
Belo-sur-Tsiribihina 161 G 3
Belot, Lac 167 M 2
Belousovka 116 D 2
Belovo 119 R 5
Beloyarovo 119 N 5
Beloye More 118 G 2
Beloye Ozero 118 G 3
Beloye Ozero 117 G 1
Belozerka 117 D 1
Belozersk 118 G 4
Belper 101 E 3
Beloretsk 119 L 5
Belterra 179 GH 4
Belt'sy 116 C 1
Belturbet 100 B 2
Belukha, Gora 119 R 6
Belush'ya Guba 184
Belyando River 143 H 3
Belyayevka 116 D 1
Belyy 118 F 4
Belyy Yar 119 R 4
Bemaraha, Plateau du 161 G 3–H 4
Bembe 160 A 1
Bemidji 171 H 2
Benāb 128 D 3
Ben Ahmadu 152 C 3
Benalla 143 H 6

Ben – Bir

Benares 134 D 2
Benasque 114 D 3
Benavente 114 B 3
Benbecula 98 A 3
Benbecula (Airport) 98 A 3
Bencubbin 142 B 5
Bend 170 B 3
Bendaja 156 B 4
Bende 157 F 4
Bendela 158 B 5
Bendemeer 143 J 5
Bender Bāyla 159 J 3
Bender Cassim → Bōsāso 159 H 2
Bender Mur'anyo 159 J 2
Bender Siyada 159 H 2
Bendery 116 C 1
Bendigo 143 G 6
Benešov 111 F 5
Benevento 115 F 3
Bengal, Bay of 134 EF 4
Bengal, West 134 E 3
Bengara 136 E 3
Bengbis 157 G 5
Bengbu 133 G 4
Benghazi 153 J 2
Benghisa Point 115 F 4
Bengkalis 136 B 3
Bengkalis, Pulau 136 B 3
Bengkulu 136 B 4
Bengo, Baía do 160 A 1
Bengtsfors 113 F 4
Benguela 160 A 2
Benguerir 152 D 2
Ben Hee 98 B 2
Ben Hope 98 B 2
Beni (Zaire) 158 D 4
Beni (Bolivia) 180 C 3
Beni Abbès 152 E 2
Benicarló 114 D 3
Benicasim 114 D 3
Benidorm 114 C 4
Beni Mellal 152 D 2
Benin 156 E 3–4
Benin, Bight of 156 E 4
Benin City 157 F 4
Beni Ounif 152 E 2
Beni Saf 152 E 1
Beni Suef → Banī Suwayf 154 E 3
Benito Juárez 172 D 4
Benjamin Constant 178 D 4
Benjamin Corrilla 183 C 6
Benkelman 170 F 3
Ben Kilbreck 98 B 2
Benkovac 115 G 3
Ben Lawers 99 B 3
Benllech 102 B 1
Ben Lomond 99 B 3
Ben Macdhui 99 C 3
Ben Macdhui 110 C 3
Ben Mehidi 115 E 4
Ben More 99 A 3
Ben More Assynt 98 B 2
Ben Nevis 99 B 3
Bennichab 152 B 5
Benoud 152 F 2
Bénoué 157 G 4
Bénoué National Park 157 G 4
Benoy 157 H 4
Bensané 156 B 3
Bensheim 111 E 5
Benson 170 D 5
Bent 128 F 5
Benteng 137 F 5
Bentiaba 160 A 2
Bentinck 135 G 5
Bentinck Island 143 F 2
Bentiu 158 D 3
Bentley 101 E 3
Bento Gonçalves 182 F 4
Benton 171 H 5
Bentong 136 B 3
Benue 157 F 4
Ben Wyvis 98 B 3
Benxi 133 H 2
Benzerta 153 GH 1
Beo 137 G 3
Beograd 116 B 2
Beoumi 156 C 4
Beppu 133 K 4
Bera 134 E 3
Beraketa 161 H 4
Berati 116 A 2
Berau, Teluk 137 H 4
Berbera 159 H 2
Berbérati 158 B 4
Berberia, Cabo 114 D 4
Berca 116 C 1
Berchogur 128 F 1
Berchtesgaden 111 F 5
Berck 114 D 1
Berdāle 159 H 3
Berdale 159 G 4
Berdichev 113 J 6

Berdigestyakh 131 N 3
Berdoba 157 J 2
Berdsk 119 Q 5
Berdyansk 117 E 1
Berdyuzh'ye 119 N 4
Beregovo 116 B 1
Bereina 144 E 3
Bereko 159 F 5
Berekum 156 D 4
Berenice → Mīnā' Baranīs 154 F 4
Berens 167 S 5
Berens River 167 S 5
Berettyóújfalu 116 B 1
Bereza 113 J 5
Berezhany 118 D 6
Bereznegovatoye 117 D 1
Berezniki 118 L 4
Berezovka (R.S.F.S.R., U.S.S.R.) 119 Q 4
Berezovka (R.S.F.S.R., U.S.S.R.) 130 L 4
Berezovka (R.S.F.S.R., U.S.S.R.) 131 T 2
Berezovka (Ukraina, U.S.S.R.) 116 D 1
Berezovo 119 MN 3
Berezovo 131 W 3
Berezovskaya 118 H 5
Berezovskiy 119 R 4
Berezovskiy 119 L 5
Berezovy 112 J 3
Berg 112 F 3
Berga 114 D 3
Bergama 116 C 3
Bergamo 115 E 2
Bergby 113 G 3
Bergen (B.R.D.) 111 F 4
Bergen (Norway) 113 E 3
Bergerac 114 D 3
Bergkvara 113 G 4
Bergland 160 B 4
Bergö 112 H 3
Bergslagen 113 F 3
Berguent 152 E 2
Bergviken 112 G 3
Berhala, Selat 136 B 4
Berhampore 134 E 3
Berhampur 134 D 4
Berikul'skiy 119 R 4
Beringarra 142 B 4
Bering Glacier 166 J 3
Bering Land Bridge National Preserve 166 E 2
Beringovskiy 131 X 3
Bering Strait 166 D 2
Berislav 117 D 1
Berkakit 131 M 4
Berkane 152 E 2
Berkeley 170 B 4
Berkner Island 185
Berkovica 116 B 2
Berkshire 103 D 2
Berlevåg 112 J 1
Berlin 111 F 4
Berlin (N.H., U.S.A.) 171 M 3
Bermeja, Punta 183 D 7
Bermeja, Sierra 114 B 4
Bermejo (Argentina) 182 C 5
Bermejo (Argentina) 182 D 4
Bermen, Lac 169 O 5
Bermeo 114 C 3
Bermuda Islands 173 K 1
Bern 115 E 2
Bernalillo 170 E 4
Bernardo de Irigoyen 182 F 4
Bernasconi 183 D 6
Bernay 114 D 2
Bernburg 111 F 4
Berne 115 E 2
Berner Alpen 115 E 2
Berneray 98 A 3
Bernier Bay 168 K 1
Bernier Island 142 A 3
Bernina 115 E 2
Bernkastel-Kues 111 E 5
Bernstorffs Isfjord 169 T 3
Béroroha 161 H 4
Beroubouaye 156 E 3
Beroum 111 F 5
Berovo 116 B 2
Berrechid 152 D 2
Berriane 153 F 2
Berry 114 D 2
Berry Islands 173 G 2
Berseba 160 B 5
Bershad 116 C 1
Bertolínia 181 H 2
Bertoua 157 G 5
Beru 146 C 3
Beruri 179 F 4
Beruwala 134 CD 6

Berwick-upon-Tweed 101 E 2
Besalampy 161 G 3
Besançon 115 E 2
Besar, Gunung 136 E 4
Besar, Pulau 137 F 5
Beskidy Zachodny 115 GH 2
Beslan 117 F 2
Besna Kobila 116 B 2
Besni 117 E 3
Bessarabiya 116 C 1
Bessemer 171 J 5
Bessines-sur-Gartempe 114 D 2
Besskorbnaya 117 F 2
Bestamak 119 P 6
Bestepeler Geçidi 117 E 3
Bestobe 119 O 5
Bestuzhevo 118 H 3
Bestyakh 131 O 3
Bestyakh 131 M 2
Beswick 142 E 1
Bësyuke 131 N 2
Betafo 161 H 3
Betamba 158 C 5
Betanzos 114 B 3
Bétaré Oya 157 G 4
Bethal 160 D 5
Bethanie 160 B 5
Bethany (IA, U.S.A.) 171 H 3
Bethany (OK, U.S.A.) 170 G 4
Bethel 166 E 3
Bethesda 102 B 1
Bethlehem (S. Afr.) 160 D 5
Bethlehem → Bayt Laḥm 154 F 2
Bethor 159 F 2
Bethulie 160 D 5
Betioky 161 G 4
Betling Sib 135 F 3
Betong (Indonesia) 136 D 3
Betong (Thailand) 135 H 6
Betoota 143 G 4
Betou 157 H 5
Betpak-Dala 129 HJ 1
Bet-Pak-Dala 119 O 6
Betroka 161 H 4
Betsiboka 161 H 3
Bettiah 134 D 2
Bettles Field 166 G 2
Bettola 115 E 3
Betul 134 C 3
Betwa 134 C 3
Betws-y-Coed 102 C 1
Beveridge 146 D 4
Beverley (Australia) 142 B 5
Beverley (U.K.) 101 E 3
Bexhill 103 E 2
Beyānlū 128 D 3
Bey Dağları 116 CD 3
Beykoz 116 C 2
Beyla 156 C 4
Beyneu 128 F 1
Beyoneisu-retsugan 133 LM 4
Beypazarı 117 D 2
Beypore 134 C 5
Beyra 159 H 3
Beyşehir 117 D 3
Beyşehir Gölü 116 D 3
Beysug 117 E 1
Bezaha 161 G 4
Bezdez 111 F 4
Bezhanitsy 113 J 4
Bezhetsk 118 G 4
Béziers 114 D 3
Bezmein 128 F 3
Beznosova 130 H 5
Bezwada → Vijayawadai 134 D 4
Bhadarwah 129 K 4
Bhadgaon 134 E 2
Bhadohi 134 D 2
Bhadrachalam 134 D 4
Bhadrajan 134 B 2
Bhadrakh 134 E 3
Bhadravati 134 C 5
Bhagalpur 134 E 2
Bhakkar 129 J 4
Bhalki 134 C 4
Bhamo 135 G 3
Bhandara 134 C 3
Bhanrer Range 134 C 3
Bharatpur 134 C 2
Bharatpur 134 D 3
Bharuch 134 B 3
Bhatinda 134 B 1
Bhatpara 134 E 3
Bhavnagar 134 B 3
Bhawanipatna 134 D 3
Bhilwara 134 B 2
Bhima 134 C 4
Bhind 134 C 2
Bhiwani 134 C 2

Bhongir 134 C 4
Bhopal 134 C 3
Bhopalpatnam 134 D 4
Bhor 134 B 4
Bhuban 134 E 3
Bhuban Hills 135 F 3
Bhubaneswar 134 E 3
Bhumiphol Dam 135 G 4
Bhusawal 134 C 3
Bhutan 134–135 EF 2
Bhuj 134 A 3
Biafra 157 F 5
Biafra, Bight of 157 F 5
Biak (Sulawesi) 137 J 4
Biak (New Guinea) 137 F 4
Biak, Pulau 137 J 4
Biala Podlaska 111 H 4
Biala Slatina 116 B 2
Bianco 115 G 4
Biankouma 156 C 4
Białogard 111 G 4
Białowieża 111 H 4
Biały stok 111 H 4
Bibā 154 E 3
Bibai 133 M 2
Bibala 160 A 2
Bibémi 157 G 4
Biberach 111 E 5
Bibiani 156 D 4
Bicester 103 D 2
Bichura 130 J 5
Bickerton Island 143 F 1
Bicuari National Park 160 B 3
Bida 157 F 4
Bidar 134 C 4
Biddeford 171 M 3
Biddulph 103 C 1
Bideford 102 B 2
Bidon 5 153 F 4
Bidzhan 131 O 6
Bié 160 B 2
Biebrza 111 H 4
Biel 115 E 2
Bielefeld 111 E 4
Bielsko-Biała 111 G 5
Bielsk Podlaski 111 H 4
Bien Hoa 135 J 5
Bienville, Lac 169 N 4
Biferno 115 F 3
Bifoum 157 G 6
Biga 116 C 2
Big Bald Mountain 169 O 6
Big Bell 142 B 4
Big Belt Mountains 170 D 2
Big Bend National Park 170 F 6
Bigbury Bay 102 C 2
Big Cypress National Preserve 171 K 6
Big Delta 166 H 3
Biger 132 C 1
Big Falls 171 H 2
Biggar 167 Q 5
Biggar 99 C 4
Biggleswade 103 D 1
Bighorn Basin 170 E 3
Bighorn Lake 170 E 2
Bighorn Mountains 170 E 3
Bighorn River 170 E 2
Bight of Bangkok 135 H 5
Bight of Benin 156 E 4
Bight of Biafra 157 F 5
Bigi 158 C 4
Big Island 169 N 3
Bignona 156 A 3
Bigobo 158 D 6
Bigorre, Pic du Midi de 114 D 3
Big Quill Lake 167 R 5
Big Rapids 171 J 3
Big River 167 Q 5
Big Sand Lake 167 S 4
Big Sheep Mountains 170 E 2
Big Sioux 171 G 3
Big Smoky Valley 170 C 4
Big Snowy Mountains 170 E 2
Big Spring 170 F 5
Big Trout Lake 168 K 5
Bihać 115 G 3
Bihar 134 E 3
Biharamulo 158 E 5
Bijapur 134 C 4
Bījār 128 D 3
Bijawar 134 C 2
Bijeljina 115 G 3
Bijelo Polje 116 A 2
Bijiang 132 C 5
Bijie 132 E 5
Bijnor 134 C 2
Bijoutier 159 J 6
Bikaner 134 B 2

Bikar 146 C 2
Bikin 131 P 6
Bikin 131 O 6
Bikoro 158 B 5
Bilād Banī Bū 'Alī 155 K 4
Bilād Ghāmid 155 G 5
Bilād Zahrān 155 G 4
Bilala 157 G 3
Bilanga 156 E 3
Bilaspur 134 D 3
Bilauktaung Range 135 G 5
Bilbao 114 C 3
Bil'chir 130 K 5
Bileća 115 G 3
Bilecik 116 D 2
Bilesha Plain 159 G 4
Bili 115 F 2
Bili 158 D 4
Bilibino 131 V 2
Biling La 134 D 1
Bilir 131 O 2
Billabalong 142 B 4
Billericay 103 E 2
Billiluna 142 D 2
Billingham 101 E 2
Billinghay 101 E 3
Billings 170 E 2
Billingsfors 113 F 4
Billingshurst 103 D 2
Bilma 157 G 2
Bilma, Grand Erg de 157 G 2
Biloela 143 J 3
Bilogord 115 G 2
Biloku 179 G 3
Biloxi 171 J 5
Biltine 157 J 3
Bilugyun 135 G 4
Bilyarsk 118 K 5
Bima 137 E 5
Bima 158 D 4
Bima, Teluk 137 E 5
Bimbéréke 156 E 3
Bimberi, Mount 143 H 6
Bimbila 156 DE 4
Bimbo 158 B 4
Bimini Islands 173 G 2
Bimlipatam 134 D 4
Bin 153 H 2
Binaiya, Gunung 137 G 4
Binatang 135 D 3
Binchuan 132 D 5
Binder 130 K 6
Bindura 161 E 3
Binga (Zaire) 160 D 3
Binga (Zimbabwe) 158 C 4
Binga, Monte 161 E 3
Bingara 143 J 4
Bingen 111 E 5
Bingham 171 N 2
Binghamton 171 L 3
Bin Ghanīmah, Jabal 153 J 3–4
Bingley 101 E 3
Bingöl 117 F 3
Binhai 153 J 3
Binh Son 135 J 4
Bini Erdi 157 H 1
Binjai 156 C 3
Binjai 136 A 3
Binnaway 143 H 5
Binongko, Pulau 137 F 5
Bint Bayyah 153 H 3
Bintan, Pulau 136 B 3
Bintuan 136 B 4
Bintulu 136 D 3
Bintuni, Teluk 137 H 4
Bin Xian 133 J 1
Bin Xian 133 G 3
Bin Xian 132 E 3
Bin Yauri 157 E 3
Binongko, Pulau 137 F 5
Bío Bío 183 B 6
Biograd na Moru 115 G 3
Bioko 157 F 5
Bir 134 C 4
Bira 131 P 6
Bira 131 O 6
Birab 137 J 5
Bi'r Abraq 154 E 4
Bi'r Abū Algharab 153 H 2
Bi'r Abū al Ḥusayn 154 E 4
Bi'r Abū Gharādiq 154 D 2
Bi'r Abū Hashim 154 E 4
Bi'r Abū Mingat 154 D 3
Bi'r Adh Dhikār 153 K 3
Birakan 131 O 6
Bi'r al Ḥakīm 153 K 2
Bi'r al Ḥamrā' 153 H 2
Bi'r al Ḥisw 155 G 4
Bi'r al Jadīd 154 F 3
Bi'r al Khamsah 154 D 2
Bi'r 'Allāq 153 H 2
Bi'r al Mushayqīq 153 H 2

Bir al War 157 G 1
Birao 158 C 2
Bi'r 'Arjā' 155 G 3
Bi'r ar Rāh 155 G 2
Bi'r ar Rūmān 153 G 2
Biratnagar 134 E 2
Bi'r Baydā 154 F 3
Bi'r Baylī 154 D 2
Bi'r Bin Ghunaymah 153 K 2
Bi'r Bū Ḩawsh 153 K 3
Bi'r Bū Zurayyq 153 K 3
Bir Chali 156 C 1
Birch Creek 166 H 2
Birch Lake 168 J 5
Birch Mountains 167 P 4
Bird 167 T 4
Bi'r Dibis 154 D 4
Bir Djedid 153 G 2
Birdsville 143 F 4
Bi'r Dūfān 153 H 2
Birdum River 142 E 2
Birecik 117 E 3
Bir ed Deheb 152 E 3
Birekte 130 L 2
Bir el Ater 153 G 2
Bir el Hadjaj 152 E 3
Bir el Khzaim 152 D 4
Bir el Ksaib 156 C 1
Bir Enzaran 152 C 4
Bireuen 136 A 2
Bi'r Fajr 154 E 3
Bi'r Fardān 155 H 4
Bi'r Fu'ād 154 D 2
Bir Gandus 152 B 4
Bir Gara 157 H 3
Bi'r Ghawdah 155 G 4
Bi'r Ḩabs adh Dhur'ānī 153 K 2
Bi'r Ḩaymir 154 F 4
Bi'r Ibn Sarrār 155 G 5
Bir Igueni 152 BC 4
Birikao → Būr Gābo 159 G 5
Biriluyssy 158 F 4
Birini 158 C 3
Birjand 128 F 4
Birkat Nasser 154 E 4
Birkat Qārūn 154 E 3
Birkenhead 101 D 3
Birket Fatmé 157 H 3
Birksgate Range 142 D 4
Bi'r Kusaybah 154 E 4
Bîrlad 116 C 1
Bir Lehlú 152 D 3
Bir Lehmar 152 C 3
Birmingham (U.K.) 103 D 1
Birmingham (Airport) 103 D 1
Birmingham (AL, U.S.A.) 171 J 5
Bi'r Misāhah 154 D 4
Bir Moghreim 152 C 3
Bi'r Murr 154 E 4
Bi'r Murrah 154 E 4
Bi'r Nāhid 154 D 2
Bi'r Naṣīf 155 F 4
Birni 156 E 3
Birnie 146 D 3
Birni Ngaoure 156 E 3
Birnin Gwari 157 F 3
Birnin Kebbi 157 E 3
Birnin-Konni 157 F 3
Birnin Kudu 157 F 3
Birobidzhan 131 O 6
Bir Ould Brini 152 E 3
Bir Ounane 156 D 1
Birr 100 B 3
Bir Rhoraffa 153 G 2
Birrindudu 142 D 2
Bi'r Safājah 154 E 3
Bi'r Saḩrā' 154 D 4
Bi'r Salālah 154 F 5
Bi'r Shalatayn 154 F 4
Bi'r Sīdī Madhkūr 153 H 2
Birsilpur 134 B 2
Birsk 118 L 4
Bi'r Ţarfāwī (Egypt) 154 D 4
Bi'r Ţarfāwī (Sudan) 154 E 4
Bi'r Tlākshīn 153 H 2
Biru 132 B 4
Bi'r Ungāt 154 E 4
Biruni 128 G 2
Biryusa 130 G 4
Biryusinsk 130 G 4
Biržai 113 H 4
Birzebbuga 115 F 4
Bir Zreigat 152 D 4
Bisaccia 115 G 3
Bisalpur 134 C 2
Bisbee 170 E 5
Biscarrosse, Étang de 114 C 3
Biscay, Bay of 114 C 2-3
Bisceglie 115 G 3
Bischofshofen 115 F 2
Biscoe Islands 185
Bisekera 131 X 3

Bisert' 119 L 4
Bishan 132 E 5
Bishārīyīn, Barq al 154 E 5
Bishnath 135 F 2
Bishop 170 C 4
Bishop Auckland 101 E 2
Bishop Rock 110 B 5
Bishop's Falls 169 Q 6
Bishops Stortford 103 E 2
Bishr 153 J 2
Bishrī, Jabal al 154 171 F 1
Bishui 131 M 5
Biskia 159 F 1
Biskra 153 G 2
Bislig 137 G 2
Bismarck 170 F 2
Bismarck Archipelago 144 E 2
Bismarck Range 144 D 3
Bismarck Sea 144 E 2
Bismil 117 F 3
Bison 167 R 6
Bispfors 112 G 3
Bissau 156 A 3
Bissett 167 S 5
Bissikrima 156 B 3
Bistcho Lake 167 O 4
Bistrica 116 B 2
Bistriţa 116 C 1
Bitam 157 G 5
Bitchana 159 F 2
Bitkin 157 H 3
Bitlis 117 F 3
Bitlis Dağları 117 F 3
Bitola 116 B 2
Bitonto 115 G 3
Bitterfeld 111 F 4
Bitterfontein 160 B 6
Bitterroot Range 170 D 2-3
Bittou 156 D 3
Biu 157 G 3
Bivolari 116 C 1
Biwa-ko 133 L 3
Bixad 116 C 1
Biya 119 R 5
Biyang 132 F 4
Biyārjomand 128 F 3
Biylikol' 129 J 2
Biyo Kaboba 159 G 2
Biysk 119 R 5
Bizerta → Banzart 153 GH 1
Bjargtangar 112 A 2
Bjelovar 115 G 2
Bjerkvik 112 G 2
Bjerringbro 113 E 4
Björköby 112 H 3
Björna 112 G 3
Björnafjorden 113 E 3
Björneborg 112 H 3
Björnevatn 112 J 2
Björnöya 184
Bjurholm 112 G 3
Bjuröklubb 112 H 3
Bjuv 113 F 4
Bla 156 C 3
Blackall 143 H 3
Blackbull 143 G 2
Blackburn 101 D 3
Blackburn, Mount 166 J 3
Black Escarpment 160 B 5
Blackfoot 170 D 3
Black Hills 170 F 3
Black Isle 98 B 3
Black Lake 167 R 4
Black Mountain 171 K 4
Black Mountains 102 C 2
Black Pagoda → Konarak 134 E 4
Blackpool 101 D 3
Black Range 170 E 5
Black River Falls 171 H 3
Black Rock Desert 170 C 3
Black Sea 116–117 CF 2
Black Volta 156 D 4
Blackwater (Rep. of Ireland) 110 B 4
Blackwater (Australia) 143 H 3
Blackwater, River 103 E 2
Blackwell 170 G 4
Blackwood River 142 B 5
Blaenau Ffestiniog 102 C 1
Blaenavon 102 C 2
Blåfjellhatten 112 F 3
Blagodarnyy 117 F 1
Blagodatnoye 116 D 1
Blagodatnyy 133 J 2
Blagojevgrad 116 B 2
Blagoveshchenka 119 P 5
Blagoveshchensk 131 N 5
Blagoveshchensk 118 K 4
Blain 114 C 2
Blaine 171 H 2
Blair 171 G 3
Blair Atholl 99 C 3

Blairgowrie 99 C 3
Blaj 116 B 1
Blanca, Cordillera 178 C 5
Blanca, Laguna 183 B 9
Blanc, Cap (Mauritania) 152 B 4
Blanche, Lake (South Australia, Australia) 143 F 4
Blanche, Lake (Western Australia, Australia) 142 C 3
Blanco, Cape 170 B 3
Blanco, Lago 183 C 9
Blanda 112 B 2
Blandford Forum 103 C 2
Blanes 114 D 3
Blangy-sur-Bresle 114 D 2
Blansko 111 G 5
Blantyre 161 E 3
Blåsjön, Stora 112 F 3
Blåskavlen 112 E 3
Blato 115 G 3
Blåvands Huk 113 E 4
Blaver 115 F 2
Blaydon 101 E 2
Blaye 114 C 2
Bled 115 G 2
Blei, Monti i 115 F 4
Blenheim 145 Q 9
Bletchley 103 D 2
Bleus, Monts 158 E 4
Blida 153 F 1
Blind River 171 K 2
Blitar 136 D 5
Blitta 156 E 4
Bloemfontein 160 D 5
Bloemhof 160 D 5
Bloemhof Dam 160 D 5
Blois 114 D 2
Blönduós 112 A 2
Bloomington (IL, U.S.A.) 171 J 3
Bloomington (IN, U.S.A.) 171 J 4
Bloomington (MN, U.S.A) 171 H 3
Blora 136 D 5
Blosseville Coast 184
Blouberg 160 D 4
Bluefield 171 K 4
Bluefields 172 F 5
Blue Mountain Lake 171 L 2
Blue Mountain Peak 173 G 4
Blue Mountains 143 J 5
Blue Mountanis National Park 143 J 5
Blue Mud Bay 143 F 1
Blue Nile 154 E 6
Bluenose Lake 167 O 2
Blue Ridge 171 K 4
Blue Stack 110 B 4
Blue Stack Mountains 100 A 2
Bluff 144 P 10
Bluff Knoll 142 B 5
Bluff Point 142 A 4
Blumenau 181 G 6
Blyth 101 E 2
Blythe 170 D 5
Blytheville 171 J 4
Bo 156 B 4
Boac 137 F 1
Boaco 172 E 5
Boa Esperança, Reprêsa 181 H 2
Boane 161 E 5
Boano, Pulau 137 G 4
Boatasyn 131 Q 5
Boatman 143 H 4
Boa Vista (Cape Verde) 156 B 6
Boa Vista (Pará, Brazil) 179 G 4
Boa Vista (Roraima, Brazil) 179 F 3
Bobai 132 E 6
Bobangi 158 B 5
Bobbili 134 D 4
Bobo Dioulasso 156 D 3
Bobonazo 178 C 4
Bobonong 160 D 4
Bobrinets 117 D 1
Bobrov 118 H 5
Bobruysk 113 J 5
Boby, Pic 161 H 4
Boca, Cachoeira da 179 H 5
Boca de la Serpiente 179 F 1-2
Boca del Guafo 183 B 7
Boca del Rio 170 E 6
Bôca do Acre 178 E 5
Bôca do Curuquetê 178 E 5
Bôca do Jari 179 H 4
Bôca do Moaço 178 E 5
Bocage Normand 114 C 2
Bocage Vendéen 114 C 2
Boca Grande 179 F 2
Bocaiúva 181 H 4
Boca Mavaca 178 E 3
Bocaranga 158 B 3
Boca Raton 171 K 6
Bocas del Toro 178 B 2

Boche di Bonifacio 115 E 3
Bochnia 111 H 5
Bochum 111 E 4
Bocoio 160 A 2
Boconó 178 D 2
Boçşa 116 B 1
Boda 158 B 4
Bodaybo 130 K 4
Boddington 142 B 5
Bodélé 157 H 2
Boden 112 H 2
Bodensee 115 E 2
Bodmin 102 B 2
Bodmin Moor 102 B 2
Bodø 112 F 2
Bodoquena, Serra da 180 E 5
Bodrum 116 C 3
Boduna 158 B 3
Boën 114 D 2
Boende 158 C 5
Boffa 156 B 3
Bogachevka 131 U 5
Bogale 135 G 4
Bogalusa 171 J 5
Bogandé 156 DE 3
Bogangolo 158 B 3
Bogan River 143 H 5
Bogbonga 158 B 4
Bogcang Zangbo 134 E 1
Bogda Feng 129 M 2
Bogdan 116 B 2
Bogda Shan 129 M 2
Bogen 112 G 2
Bogense 113 F 4
Bogetkol'skiy 119 M 5
Boggabilla 143 J 4
Boggeragh Mountains 110 B 4
Boghari → Ksar el Buokhari 153 F 1
Boghra Dam 129 G 4
Bogia 144 D 2
Bognor Regis 103 D 2
Bogo 137 F 1
Bogodukhov 118 G 5
Bog of Allen 100 B 3
Bogol Manya 159 G 4
Bogor 136 C 5
Bogoroditsk 118 G 5
Bogorodskoye 131 Q 5
Bogorodskoye 118 K 4
Bogotá 178 D 3
Bogotol 119 R 4
Bogöy 112 G 2
Bogra 134 E 3
Böhmerwald 111 F 5
Bohemia 111 F 5
Bohemia Downs 142 D 2
Bohicon 156 E 4
Bohodoyou 156 C 4
Bohol 137 F 2
Bohol Sea 137 F 2
Bohu 132 A 2
Bo Hai 133 G 3
Bohai Haixia 133 H 3
Boiaçu 179 F 4
Boim 179 G 4
Boipeba 181 J 3
Bois 181 F 4
Boise 170 C 3
Boise City 170 F 4
Boise River 170 C 3
Bois, Lac des 167 N 2
Boissevain 167 R 6
Boizenburg 111 F 4
Bojador, Cabo 152 C 3
Bojnegoro 136 D 5
Bojnūrd 128 F 3
Bojuru 182 F 5
Bok 144 E 3
Boka Kotorska 116 A 2
Bokani 157 F 4
Bokatola 158 B 5
Boké 156 B 3
Bokhapcha 131 S 3
Boki 144 E 3
Boknafjorden 113 E 4
Boko 157 G 6
Bokora Game Reserve 158 E 4
Bokoro 157 H 3
Bokote 158 C 5
Bokpyin 135 G 5
Boksitogorsk 118 F 4
Bokspits 160 C 5
Bokwankusu 158 C 5
Bol (Chad) 157 G 3
Bol (Yugoslavia) 115 G 3
Bolafa 158 C 4
Bolaiti 158 C 5

Bir – Bom

Bolama 156 A 3
Bolangir 134 D 3
Bolan Pass 129 G 5
Boldon 101 E 2
Bole (China) 129 L 2
Bole (Ethiopia) 159 F 3
Bole (Ghana) 156 D 4
Boles1awiec 111 G 4
Bolgatanga 156 D 3
Bolgrad 116 C 1
Boli 133 K 1
Bolia 158 B 5
Boliden 112 H 3
Bolinao 137 F 1
Bolintin Vale 116 C 2
Boliohutu, Gunung 137 F 3
Bolívar (Arg.) 183 D 6
Bolívar (Colombia) 178 C 3
Bolívar, Cerro 179 F 2
Bolívar, Pico 178 D 2
Bolivia 180 D 4
Bolkar Dağları 117 D 3
Bolkhov 118 G 5
Bolléne 115 D 3
Bollnäs 112 G 3
Bollon 143 H 4
Bollstabruk 112 G 3
Bolmen 113 F 4
Bolnisi 117 F 2
Bolobo 158 B 5
Bologna 115 F 3
Bolognesi 180 B 3
Bologoye 118 F 4
Bologur 131 O 3
Bolomba 158 B 4
Bolombo 158 C 5
Bolon 116 B 2
Bol'shaya Belozerka 117 D 1
Bol'shaya Chernigovka 118 K 5
Bol'shaya Glushitsa 118 K 5
Bol'shaya Lepetikha 117 D 1
Bol'shaya Murta 119 R 4
Bol'shaya Novoselka 117 E 1
Bol'shaya Orlovka 117 F 1
Bol'shaya Pyssa 118 J 3
Bol'shaya Vladimirovka 119 P 5
Bol'shaya Yerema 130 J 3
Bol'shekinskoye 130 H 4
Bol'sherech'ye 119 O 4
Bol'sheretsk 131 T 5
Bol'shezemel'skaya Tundra 118 KLM 2
Bol'shiye Khatymy 131 N 4
Bol'shiye Klyuchsishchi 118 J 5
Bol'shiye Lar'yak 119 Q 3
Bol'shiye Uki 119 O 4
Bol. Shogany 119 M 3
Bol'shoy Anyuy 131 U 2
Bol'shoy Balkhan, Khrebet 128 E 3
Bol'shoy Begichev, Ostrov 130 K 1
Bol'shoy Berezovy, Ostrov 112 J 3
Bol'shoye Vlas'evo 131 Q 5
Bolshoy Kavkaz 117 F 2
Bol'shoy Lyakhovskiy, Ostrov 131 Q 1
Bol'shoy Nimnyr 131 N 4
Bol'shoy Oloy 131 U 2
Bol'shoy Onguren 130 J 4 5
Bol'shoy Patom 130 L 3
Bol'shoy Porog 130 F 2
Bol'shoy Salym 119 O 3
Bol'shoy Shantar, Ostrov 131 P 4–5
Bol'shoy Uluy 130 F 4
Bol'shoy Yenisey 130 G 5
Bol'shoy Yeravnoye, Ozero 130 K 5
Bol'shoy Yugan 119 O 4
Bolsjoj Morskeye, Ozero 131 T 1
Bolsón de Mapimi 170 E 6
Bolsover 103 D 1
Bolton 101 D 3
Bolu 116 D 2
Bolungarvík 112 A 2
Boluntay 132 B 3
Bolvadin 116 D 3
Bolvanskiy Nos, Mys 119 L 1
Bolzano 115 F 2
Bom 144 E 3
Boma 157 G 7
Bomassa 157 H 5
Bombala 143 H 6
Bombarai 137 H 4

Bom – Bri

Bombarral 114 B 4
Bombay 134 B 4
Bombéré 158 B 4
Bombo 158 E 4
Bomboma 158 B 4
Bom Comercio 178 E 5
Bomdila 135 F 2
Bomi 132 C 5
Bomi Hills 156 B 4
Bomili 158 D 4
Bom Jardin 178 E 5
Bom Jesus 181 H 2
Bom Jesus da Gurguéia, Serra 181 H 2
Bom Jesus da Lapa 181 H 3
Bömlo 113 E 4
Bomokandi 158 D 4
Bomongo 158 B 4
Bom Retiro 181 G 6
Bomu 158 C 4
Bonaire 178 E 1
Bona, Mount 166 J 3
Bonampak 172 D 4
Bonanza 172 F 5
Bonaparte Archipelago 142 C 1
Bonar Bridge 98 B 3
Bonavista 169 R 6
Bonavista Bay 169 R 6
Bondo 158 C 5
Bondo 158 C 4
Bondowoso 136 D 5
Bône → Annaba 153 G 1
Bonelohe 137 F 5
Boneng 135 H 4
Bo'ness 99 C 3
Bonete, Cerro 182 C 4
Bone, Teluk 137 F 4
Bonga 159 F 3
Bongabong 137 F 1
Bongandanga 158 C 4
Bongka 137 F 4
Bong Mountains 156 C 4
Bongo 157 G 6
Bongor 157 H 3
Bongos, Massif des 158 C 3
Bongou 158 C 3
Bongouanou 156 D 4
Bonifacio 115 E 3
Bonifacio, Boche di 115 E 3
Bonifacio, Strait of 115 E 3
Bonifati, Capo 115 G 4
Boni Game Reserve 159 G 5
Bonin Islands 121 R 7
Bonito 180 E 5
Bonkoukou 156 E 3
Bonn 111 E 4
Bonners Ferry 170 C 2
Bonnet Plume 166 L 2–3
Bonneville Saltflats 170 D 3
Bonnie Rock 142 B 5
Bonny 157 F 5
Bonobono 136 E 2
Bontang 136 E 3
Bonthe 156 B 4
Bontoc 137 J 1
Bonwapitse 160 D 4
Bonyhád 116 AB 1
Boogardie 142 B 4
Boola 156 C 4
Boolaloo 142 B 3
Booligal 143 G 5
Boologoero 142 A 3
Boon 168 L 6
Boonah 143 J 4
Boone 171 H 3
Boongoondoo 143 H 3
Böön Tsagaan Nuur 132 C 1
Boonville 171 H 4
Booroorban 143 G 5
Boothby, Cape 185
Boothia, Gulf of 167 T 1
Boothia Peninsula 167 T 1
Boué 157 G 5–6
Bophuthatswana 160 C 5
Bopolu 156 B 4
Boqueirão 182 F 5
Boquete 178 B 2
Boquillagas del Carmen 172 B 2
Bor (Sudan) 158 E 3
Bor (U.S.S.R.) 118 H 4
Bor (Turkey) 117 D 3
Bor (Yugoslavia) 116 B 2
Bora-Bora 147 E 4
Borah Peak 170 D 3
Böramo 159 G 3
Borås 113 F 4
Borasambar 134 D 3
Borāzjān 128 E 5
Borba 179 G 4
Borborema, Planalto da 181 J 2
Borçka 117 D 2
Bordeaux 114 C 3
Borders 99 C 4

Bordertown 143 G 6
Bordj Bou Arreridj 153 F 1
Bordj Fly Sainte Marie 152 E 3
Bordj Messouda 153 G 2
Bordj Moktar 153 F 4
Bordj Omar Driss 153 G 3
Bordj Sif Fatima 153 G 2
Borgå (Porvoo) 113 J 3
Borgarnes 112 A 3
Börgefjellet 112 F 2
Borgholm 113 G 4
Borislav 111 H 5
Borisoglebsk 118 H 5
Borisov 113 J 5
Borisovka 129 H 2
Borispol 118 F 5
Bo River 158 D 3
Borja 178 C 4
Borjas Blancas 114 D 3
Borkou 157 H 2
Borlänge 113 G 3
Borlu 116 C 3
Borneo 136 D 3
Bornholm 113 F 5
Bornu 157 G 3
Boro 158 D 3
Borodino 130 G 4
Borodyanka 118 E 5
Borogontsy 131 O 3
Borohoro Shan 129 L 2
Boroko 137 F 3
Borolgustakh 130 M 2
Boromo 156 D 3
Borongan 137 G 1
Borong, Khrebet 131 P 2
Bororen 143 J 3
Borotou 156 C 4
Borovichi 118 F 4
Borovichi 113 J 4
Borovlyanka 119 Q 5
Borovo 115 G 2
Borovoye 119 O 5
Borovskiy 119 N 4
Borovskoye 119 M 5
Borrãn 159 H 2
Borrby 113 F 4
Borris 100 B 3
Borroloola 143 F 2
Borşa 116 B 1
Börselv 112 J 1
Borshchev 118 E 6
Borshchovochnyy Khrebet 130 K 6–L 5
Boru 131 Q 1
Borūjen 128 E 4
Borūjerd 128 D 4
Borzhomi 117 F 2
Borzya 130 L 5
Bosa 115 E 3
Bosaga 119 O 6
Bosanska Gradiška 115 G 2
Bosanska Krupa 115 G 3
Bosanski Novi 115 G 2
Bosanski Petrovac 115 G 3
Bosanski Samac 115 G 2
Bösäso 159 H 2
Bose 132 E 6
Boseki 158 B 5
Boshan 133 G 3
Boshnyakovo 131 Q 6
Boshrūyeh 128 F 4
Boshuslän 113 F 4
Bosilegrad 116 B 2
Boskamp 179 G 2
Bosna 115 G 3
Bosnik 137 J 4
Bosobolo 158 B 4
Bosporus 116 C 2
Bosque Bonito 170 E 5
Bossangoa 158 B 3
Bossé Bangou 156 E 3
Bossembele 158 B 3
Bossemptélé II 158 B 3
Bossier City 171 H 5
Bosso 157 G 3
Bossut, Cape 142 C 2
Bostan 129 H 4
Bostandyk 118 J 6
Bosten Hu 132 B 2
Bostona (MA, U.S.A.) 171 M 3
Boston (U.K.) 103 D 1
Boston Mountains 171 H 4
Botan 117 F 3
Botevgrad 116 B 2
Bothaville 160 D 5
Botletle 160 C 4
Botlikh 117 G 2
Boto 159 F 2
Botomoyu 130 L 3
Botoşani 116 C 1
Bo Trach 135 J 4
Botrange 110 E 4
Botswana 160 CD 4

Botte Donato 115 G 4
Bottrop 111 E 4
Botucatu 181 G 5
Botuobuya, Ulakhan 130 K 3
Botwood 169 Q 6
Bouaflé 156 C 4
Bouaké 156 CD 4
Bouala 158 B 3
Bouali (Centr.Afr. Rep.) 158 B 4
Bouali (Gabon) 157 G 6
Bouânane 152 E 2
Bouar 158 B 3
Bouârfa 152 E 2
Bou Arfa 152 E 2
Boubandjida 157 GH 4
Boubandjida National Park 157 GH 4
Boubin 111 F 5
Boubout 152 E 3
Bouca 158 B 3
Boucle de Baoulé 156 C 3
Boucle de Baoulé, Parc 156 C 3
Boudenib 152 E 2
Bou Djébiha 156 D 2
Boufarik 114 D 4
Bougainville 145 G 2
Bougainville Reef 143 H 2
Bougainville Strait (N. Hebr.) 145 J 5
Bougainville Strait (Sol. Is.) 145 G 2
Bou Garfa 152 D 3
Bougar'oûn, Cap 153 G 1
Bougaroun, Cap 153 G 1
Bougie → Bejaïa 153 F 1
Bougouni 156 C 3
Bougtob 152 EF 2
Bouïra 153 F 1
Bou Ismaïl 114 D 4
Bou Izakarn 152 D 3
Bou Kadir 114 D 4
Boulanouar 152 B 4
Boulder 142 C 5
Boulder 170 E 3
Boulder City 170 D 4
Boulia 143 F 3
Boulogne-sur-Mer 114 D 1
Boulouli 156 C 2
Bouloupari 145 J 6
Boulsa 156 D 3
Boultoum 157 G 3
Bouly 152 C 5
Boumdeïd 152 C 5
Bouna 156 D 4
Bou Naga 152 C 5
Boundiali 156 C 4
Boundji 157 H 6
Boundou 156 B 3
Boundoukou 156 D 4
Boun Neua 135 H 3
Bounoum 156 B 3
Bountiful 170 D 3
Bounty Islands 185
Bourail 145 J 6
Bourem 156 D 2
Bouressa 156 E 2
Bourganeuf 114 D 2
Bourg-en-Bresse 115 E 2
Bourges 114 D 2
Bourget, Lac du 115 E 2
Bourgogne 115 DE 2
Bourgogne, Canal de 114 D 2
Bourgoin-Jallieu 115 E 2
Bou Rjeima 152 B 5
Bourke 143 H 5
Bourkina Fasso → Upper Volta 156 DE 3
Bourne 103 D 1
Bournemouth 103 D 2
Bournemouth (Airport) 103 D 2
Bouroum 156 D 3
Bourtoutou 157 J 3
Bou Saâda 153 F 1
Boussens 114 D 3
Bousso 157 H 3
Bouvet Island 185
Bouza 157 F 3
Bova Marina 115 G 4
Bovril 182 E 5
Bow 167 P 5
Bowen (Argentina) 182 C 5
Bowen (Australia) 143 H 2
Bowland Forest 101 D 2
Bowling Green 171 J 4
Bowling Green, Cape 143 H 2
Bowman 170 F 2
Bowman Bay 169 N 2
Bowral 143 J 5
Boxholm 113 G 4
Bo Xian 132 G 4
Boxing 133 G 3
Boyabat 117 D 2
Boyabo 158 B 4

Boyang 133 G 5
Boyang Hu 132 G 5
Boyarka 130 G 1
Boyarsk 130 J 4
Boyle 110 B 4
Boyne 110 B 4
Boyne, River 100 B 3
Boyuibe 180 D 5
Bozcaada 116 C 3
Bozdağ 117 D 3
Boz Dağı 116 C 3
Bozdoğan 116 C 3
Bozeman 170 D 2
Bozene 158 B 4
Bozkır 117 D 3
Bozok Platosu 117 DE 3
Bozouls 114 D 3
Bozoum 158 B 3
Bozova 117 E 3
Bozshakul' 119 O 5
Bozüyük 116 D 3
Bra 115 E 3
Brač 115 G 3
Bracciano, Lago di 115 F 3
Bräcke 112 G 3
Brački Kanal 115 G 3
Brackley 103 D 1
Bracknell 103 D 2
Brad 116 B 1
Bradano 115 G 3
Bradda Head 100 C 2
Bradenton 171 K 6
Bradford (U.S.A.) 171 L 3
Bradford (U.K.) 101 E 3
Bradford-on-Avon 103 C 2
Bradley Reefs 145 H 3
Bradshaw 142 E 2
Brady 170 G 5
Brady Mountains 170 G 5
Braemar 99 C 3
Braga 114 B 3
Bragado 182 D 6
Bragança 179 J 4
Bragança 114 B 3
Bragina 131 X 3
Brahman Baria 135 F 3
Brahmaputra 135 F 2
Brăila 116 C 1
Brainerd 171 H 2
Braintree 103 E 2
Braithwaite Point 142 E 1
Bråk 153 H 3
Brakna 152 C 5
Brålanda 113 F 4
Bramhapuri 134 C 3
Brampton (U.K.) 101 D 2
Brampton (U.S.A.) 171 L 3
Bramsche 111 E 4
Brandberg 160 A 4
Brandberg West Mine 160 A 4
Brande 113 E 4
Brandenburg 111 F 4
Brandon 167 R 6
Brandon 103 E 1
Brandvlei 160 C 6
Braniewo 111 G 4
Brantford 171 K 3
Brás 179 G 4
Bras d'Or Lake 169 P 6
Brasiléia 180 C 3
Brasília 181 G 4
Brasília Legal 179 G 4
Brasília, Parque Nacional do 181 G 4
Brasil, Planalto do 181 H 4
Braslav 113 J 4
Braşov 116 C 1
Brass 157 F 5
Brassey, Mount 142 E 3
Bratca 116 B 1
Bratislava 111 G 5
Bratsk 130 H 4
Bratskoye Vodokhranilishche 130 H 4
Bratslav 116 C 1
Brattleboro 171 M 3
Brattvåg 112 E 3
Bratul Borcea 116 C 2
Bratul Chilia 116 C 1
Bratul Cremenea 116 C 2
Bratul Sfintu Gheorghe 116 C 1
Bratul Sulina 116 C 1
Braunau am Inn 115 F 2
Braunschweig 111 F 4
Braunton 102 B 2
Brava 156 A 7
Bråviken 113 G 4
Bravo, Cerro 178 C 5
Brawley 170 C 5
Bray (S. Africa) 160 C 5
Bray (U.K.) 100 B 3
Brazil 180–181 E–G 3
Brazil Basin 192 A 4

Brazo 178 E 3
Brazos River 171 G 5
Brčko 115 G 3
Brda 111 G 4
Brea, Cerros de la 178 B 4
Breadalbane 99 B 3
Breaden, Lake 142 D 4
Breaza 116 C 1
Brebes 136 C 5
Brechin 99 C 3
Breckenridge 170 G 5
Brecknock, Península 183 B 9
Breclav 111 G 5
Brecon 102 C 2
Breda 110 D 4
Bredasdorp 160 C 6
Bredbyn 112 G 3
Breiðafjörður 112 A 2
Bredy 119 M 5
Bregalnica 116 B 2
Bregenz 115 E 2
Breiðdalur 112 C 3
Breivikbotn 112 H 1
Brejo (Maranhão, Brazil) 181 H 1
Brejo (Piauí, Brazil) 181 H 2
Brekhovskije Ostrova 130 D 1
Brekken 112 F 3
Brekstad 112 E 3
Bremangerlandet 112 D 3
Bremen 111 E 4
Bremer Bay 142 B 5
Bremerhaven 111 E 4
Bremerton 170 B 2
Brenner 115 F 2
Brenta 115 F 2
Brenta, Gruppo di 115 F 2
Brentwood 103 E 2
Brescia 115 F 2
Bressanone 115 F 2
Bressay 98 D 1
Brest (Belorussiya, U.S.S.R) 112 H 5
Brest (France) 114 C 2
Brestova 115 F 2
Bretagne 114 C 2
Breteuil 114 D 2
Breton, Pertuis 114 C 2
Brett, Cape 145 Q 8
Breves 179 H 4
Brevik 113 E 4
Brevoort Island 169 P 3
Brewarrina 143 H 4
Brewerville 156 B 4
Brewning 170 D 2
Brewster, Kap 184
Brewton 171 J 5
Brezhnev 118 K 4
Brežice 115 G 2
Brézina 153 F 2
Bria 158 C 3
Briançon 115 E 3
Brichany 116 C 1
Bridgend (Mid-Glamorgan) 102 C 2
Bridgeport (CA, U.S.A.) 170 C 4
Bridgeport (CT, U.S.A.) 171 M 3
Bridger Peak 170 E 3
Bridgetown (Barbados) 173 L 5
Bridgetown (Australia) 142 B 5
Bridgewater 169 P 7
Bridgnorth 102 C 2
Bridgwater 102 C 2
Bridgwater Bay 102 C 2
Bridlington 101 E 2
Bridlington Bay 101 E 2
Bridport 102 C 2
Brig 115 E 2
Brigg 101 E 3
Brigham City 170 D 3
Brighouse 101 E 3
Bright 143 H 6
Brightlingsea 103 E 2
Brighton 103 D 2
Brignoles 108
Brijunio 115 F 3
Brikama 156 A 3
Brindisi 115 G 3
Brinkene 152 E 3
Brisbane 143 J 4
Bristol 102 C 2
Bristol (Airport) 102 C 2
Bristol (TN, U.S.A.) 171 K 4
Bristol Bay 166 F 4
Bristol Channel 102 C 2
Britânia 181 F 4
British Columbia 167 N 5
British Mountains 166 J 2
Brits 160 D 5
Britstown 160 C 6
Brive-la-Gaillarde 114 D 2
Briviesca 114 C 3

Bri – Bzy

Brixham 102 C 2
Brno 111 G 5
Broadback 169 M 5
Broad Bay 98 A 2
Broadford 98 B 3
Broad Sound 143 H 3
Broadstairs 103 E 2
Broadus 170 E 2
Broadview 167 R 5
Broadwey 102 C 2
Brochet 167 R 4
Brocken 111 F 4
Brockman, Mount 142 B 3
Brock's Creek 142 E 1
Brockville 171 L 3
Brod 116 B 2
Broderick 158 E 4
Brodick 99 B 4
Brodnica 111 G 4
Brody 113 J 5
Broken Hill 143 G 5
Brokhovo 131 S 4
Brokopondo 179 GH 3
Brokopondomeer 179 G 3
Bromölla 113 F 4
Brønderslev 113 E 4
Bronnikovo 119 N 4
Brønnøysund 112 F 2
Bronte 115 F 4
Brooke's Point 136 E 2
Brookfield 171 H 4
Brookhaven 171 H 5
Brookings (CA, U.S.A.) 170 B 3
Brookings (S.D., U.S.A.) 171 G 3
Brooks 167 P 5
Brooks Range 166 F 2
Brookston 171 H 2
Brookton 142 B 5
Brookville 143 H 3
Broome 142 C 2
Broome, Mount 142 D 2
Broom, Loch 98 B 3
Brora 98 C 2
Brora, River 98 B 2
Brough 101 D 2
Brough Head 98 C 2
Broughshane 100 B 2
Broughton in Furness 101 D 2
Broughton Island 169 P 2
Broutona, Ostrov 131 S 6
Brovst 113 E 4
Browne Range Nature Reserve 142 D 3
Brownfield 170 F 5
Brownhills 103 D 1
Brown Lake 167 T 2
Brown River 143 G 2
Brownsville 171 G 6
Brownwood 170 G 5
Browse Island 142 C 1
Bruay-en-Artois 114 D 1
Bruce Crossing 171 J 6
Bruce, Mount 142 B 3
Bruce Peninsula 171 K 3
Bruchsal 111 E 5
Bruck 115 G 2
Brugge 110 D 4
Brumado 181 H 3
Bruncio 115 F 2
Bruneau 170 C 3
Brunei 136 D 2
Brunflo 112 F 3
Brunsbüttel 111 E 4
Brunswick 171 K 5
Brunswick Bay 142 C 2
Brunswick, Peninsula de 183 B 9
Bruny 144 L 9
Brusilovka 118 KL 5
Brus, Laguna de 172 F 4
Brusovo 119 R 3
Brusque 181 G 6
Brussel 110 D 4
Brusset, Erg 157 FG 2
Bruxelles 110 D 4
Bruzual 178 E 2
Bryan 171 G 5
Bryan Coast 185
Bryanka 130 F 4
Bryansk 118 F 5
Bryanskoye 117 G 2
Bryne 113 E 4
Bryn'kovskaya 117 E 1
Bryukhovetskaya 117 E 1
Bryungyadinskiye Gory 131 P 3
Brza Palanka 116 B 2
Brzeg 111 G 4
Buandougou 156 C 4
Buapinang 137 F 4
Búðardalur 112 A 2
Bua Yai 135 H 4
Buba 156 AB 3
Bubanza 158 D 5
Bubaque 156 A 3

Būbīyān 155 H 3
Bucak 116 D 3
Bucaramanga 178 D 2
Buccaneer Archipelago 142 C 2
Buchan 98 C 3
Buchanan 156 B 4
Buchanan, Lake 170 G 5
Buchanan, Lake (Queensland, Austr.) 143 H 3
Buchanan, Lake (Western Australia) 142 C 4
Buchan Ness 98 D 3
Buchardo 182 D 5
Bucharest 116 C 2
Bucharest → București 116 C 2
Buchs 115 E 2
Buckeye 170 D 5
Buckfastleigh 102 C 2
Buckhaven 99 C 3
Buckie 98 C 3
Buckingham 103 D 2
Buckingham Bay 143 F 1
Buckinghamshire 103 D 2
Buck, Lake 142 E 2
Buckland 166 E 2
Buckland Tableland 143 H 3
Buckley 102 C 1
Buco Zau 157 G 6
Bu Craa 152 C 3
București 116 C 2
Bucyrus 171 K 3
Budapest 116 A 1
Budaun 134 C 2
Bud Bud 159 H 4
Budleigh Salterton 102 C 2
Bude 102 B 2
Bude Bay 102 B 2
Budennovka 118 K 5
Budennovsk 117 F 2
Budjala 158 B 4
Budleigh Salterton 102 C 2
Buea 157 F 5
Buenaventura (Mexico) 170 E 6
Buenaventura (Colombia) 178 C 3
Buena Vista 178 E 2
Buenavista 170 E 7
Buendia, Embalse de 114 C 3
Buengas 160 B 1
Buenópolis 181 H 4
Buenos Aires 182 E 5
Buenos Aires, Lago 183 B 8
Buen Pasto 183 C 8
Buffalo (N.W.T., Can.) 167 P 4
Buffalo (N.Y., U.S.A.) 171 L 3
Buffalo (OK, U.S.A.) 170 G 4
Buffalo (S. D, U.S.A.) 170 F 2
Buffalo (WY, U.S.A.) 170 E 3
Buffalo Lake 167 O 3
Buffalo Narrows 167 Q 4
Buftea 116 C 2
Bug 111 H 4
Buga 178 C 3
Bugala Island 158 E 5
Bugarach, Pech de 114 D 3
Bugarikhta 130 K 5
Bugat 130 H 6
Bugel, Tanjung 136 D 5
Bugene 158 E 5
Bugku 137 F 4
Bugojno 115 G 3
Bugorkan 130 J 3
Bugöynes 112 J 2
Bugrino 118 J 2
Bugsuk 136 E 2
Bugt 131 M 6
Bugul'deyka 130 J 5
Bugul'ma 118 K 5
Buguruslan 118 K 5
Bū Ḥasā' 155 J 4
Buhera 161 E 3
Buh He 132 C 3
Bühödle 159 H 3
Bui Dam 156 D 4
Builth Wells 102 C 1
Buinsk 118 J 5
Búðir 112 C 2
Buir Nur 130 L 6
Buitepos 160 B 4
Buítrago del Lozoya 114 C 3
Bujaraloz 114 C 3
Bujaru 179 J 4
Buje 115 F 2
Bujumbura 158 D 5
Buka 145 E 2
Bukachacha 130 L 5
Bukadaban Feng 132 B 3
Bukakata 158 E 5
Bukama 158 D 6
Bukantau, Gory 129 G 2
Bukavu 158 D 5
Bukene 158 E 5
Bu Khanum 135 H 5
Bukhara 129 G 3
Bukit 136 C 3

Bukit Gandadiwata 137 E 4
Bukit Harun 136 E 3
Bukit Kambuno 137 E 4
Bukit Masurai 136 B 4
Bukit Mawa 136 D 3
Bukit Raya 136 D 4
Bukit Sulat 137 G 3
Bukittinggi 136 B 4
Bukoba 158 E 5
Bukukun 130 K 6–L 5
Bukuru 157 F 2
Bukwimba 158 E 5
Bula 137 H 4
Bulambuk 130 G 5
Bulan 137 F 1
Bulancak 117 E 2
Bulandshahr 134 C 2
Bulanık 117 F 3
Būlāq 154 E 3
Bulawayo 160 D 4
Bulayevo 119 O 5
Buldan 116 C 3
Buldana 134 C 3
Buldir 166 A 5
Bulgan 130 G 5
Bulgan 130 H 6
Bulgan 130 F 6
Bulgaria 116 C 2
Buli 137 G 3
Buli, Teluk 137 G 3
Bulki 159 F 3
Bullahär 159 G 2
Bulla Regia 115 E 4
Bullfinch 142 B 5
Bullion Mountains 170 C 5
Bullita 142 E 2
Bulloo River 143 G 4
Bull Shoals Lake 171 H 4
Bulnes 183 B 6
Bulo Berde 159 H 4
Bulolo 144 E 3
Bulucan 117 E 2
Bulukumba 137 F 5
Bulun 131 T 2
Bulun 131 Q 4
Bulun 131 N 1
Bulungu 158 B 5
Bumba 158 C 4
Bumba 158 B 6
Bumbulan 137 F 3
Bumbuli 158 C 5
Bumbuna 156 B 4
Buna 159 F 4
Bunbeg 100 A 2
Bunbury 142 B 5
Buncrana 100 B 2
Bunda 158 E 5
Bundaberg 143 J 3
Bunda Bunda 143 G 3
Bundi 134 C 2
Bundooma 142 E 3
Bundoran 110 B 4
Bungay 103 E 1
Bungku 137 F 4
Bungo-suidō 133 K 4
Bung Sai 135 J 4
Buni 157 G 3
Bunia 158 E 4
Bunji 129 J 3
Bunkeya 160 D 2
Bunkie 171 H 5
Buntok 136 D 4
Bünyan 117 E 3
Bun Yun 135 H 4
Buol 137 F 3
Buolkalakh 130 L 1
Buorkhaya, Guba 131 O 1
Buorkhaya, Mys 131 O 1
Buotama 131 N 3
Bupul 144 D 3
Buqayq 155 H 3
Buqūm, Ḥarrat al 155 G 4
Bur 130 J 4
Bura 159 F 5
Buram 154 D 6
Buran 119 R 6
Burang 134 D 2
Bura'o 159 H 3
Buraydah 155 G 3
Burdēre 159 H 4
Burdekin River 143 H 2
Burdur 116 D 3
Burdur Gölü 116 C 3
Burdwan 134 E 3
Bureå 112 H 3
Burei 158 F 3
Bureinskiy, Khrebet 131 O 5
Büren 130 H 6

Bure, River 103 E 1
Bureya 131 N 6
Bureya 131 O 5
Burfjord 112 H 2
Burg 111 F 4
Būr Gābo 159 G 5
Burgakhcha 131 Q 3
Burgan 125
Burgas 116 C 2
Burgaski zaliv 116 C 2
Burgdorf 115 E 2
Burgeo 169 Q 6
Burgersdorp 160 D 5
Burgess Hill 103 D 2
Burgfjället 112 G 3
Burghausen 115 F 2
Burgh le Marsh 101 F 3
Burgos (Spain) 114 C 3
Burgos (Mexico) 172 C 3
Burgsteinfurt 111 E 4
Burgsvik 113 G 4
Bür Hakkaba 159 G 4
Burhan Budai Shan 132 C 3
Burhaniye 116 C 3
Burhanpur 134 C 3
Burias 137 F 1
Buribay 119 L 5
Burica, Punta 172 F 6
Burin Peninsula 169 Q 6
Buriram 135 H 5
Buriti 180 E 4
Buritizal 180 E 4
Buritizal, Cachoeira do 179 H 3
Burjasot 114 C 3
Burj at Tuyūr 154 D 4
Burji 159 F 3
Burke River 143 F 3
Burketown 143 F 2
Burkhala 131 R 3
Burkhaybyt 131 P 2
Burla 119 P 5
Burley 170 D 3
Burlington (CO, U.S.A.) 170 F 4
Burlington (IA, U.S.A.) 171 H 3
Burlington (VT, U.S.A.) 171 M 3
Burlyu-Tobe 119 P 6
Burma 135 G 3
Burmantovo 119 MN 3
Burnett River 143 J 4
Burney 170 B 3
Burnham 102 C 2
Burnham-on-Crouch 103 E 2
Burnie 144 L 9
Burnley 101 D 3
Burns 170 C 3
Burnside 167 Q 2
Burns Lake 167 M 5
Burntisland 99 C 3
Burntwood 167 S 4
Burqān 155 H 3
Burqin 129 M 1
Burra (Nigeria) 157 F 3
Burra (Australia) 143 F 5
Burray 98 C 2
Burriana 114 C 4
Burry Port 102 B 2
Bursa 116 C 2
Būr Sa'īd 154 E 2
Bur Sūdān 154 F 5
Burtnieku ezers 113 J 4
Burton, Lac 169 M 5
Burton Latimer 103 D 1
Burton upon Trent 103 D 1
Burträsk 112 H 3
Buru 137 G 4
Burūm 155 H 6
Burunday 129 K 2
Burundi 158 DE 5
Bururi 158 D 5
Burutu 157 F 4
Burwell 103 E 1
Bury 101 D 3
Burye 159 F 2
Bury St. Edmunds 103 E 1
Bury St. Edmunds 110 D 4
Busalla 115 E 3
Busanga (Zaire) 160 D 2
Busanga (Zaire) 158 C 5
Busanga Swamp (Zambia) 160 D 2
Buşayrah 155 G 1
Büshehr 128 E 5
Bushimaie 158 C 6
Bushman Land 160 B 5
Bushmills 100 B 2
Busia 158 E 4
Businga 158 C 4
Busira 158 B 5
Busko-Zdrój 111 H 4
Buskul' 119 M 5
Busse 131 N 5
Busselton 142 A 5
Bussol', Proliv 131 S 6

Bustakh, Ozero 131 Q 1
Busuanga 137 F 1
Busu Djanoa 158 C 4
Busu Gongo 158 C 4
Busu Melo 158 C 4
Bususulu 158 C 4
Buta 158 C 4
Butajira 159 F 3
Butang Group 135 G 6
Buta Ranquil 183 C 6
Butare 158 D 5
Butaritari 146 C 2
Bute 100 C 2
Butemba 158 E 4
Butembo 158 D 4
Butere 158 E 4
Butha Qi 131 M 6
Buthidaung 135 F 3
Butía 182 F 5
Butiaba 158 E 4
Butiama 158 E 5
Butkan 118 J 3
Butler 100 B 2
Butte 170 D 2
Butte de Vaudémont 115 E 2
Butterworth (Malaysia) 136 B 2
Butterworth (S. Africa) 160 D 6
Butt of Lewis 98 A 2
Button Bay 167 T 4
Button Islands 169 P 3
Butuan 137 G 2
Buturlinovka 118 H 5
Butung, Pulau 137 F 4
Butuy 130 K 5
Bu Tu Suay 135 J 5
Buwayrāt al Ḥasūn 153 J 2
Buxton 171 L 4
Buxton 101 E 3
Buy 118 H 4
Buyant-Ovoo 132 E 2
Buynaksk 128 D 2
Buyo 156 C 4
Buyr Nuur 130 L 6
Büyük Ağrı Daği 117 F 3
Büyük Menderes 116 C 3
Buyunda 131 S 3
Buzachi, Poluostrov 128 E 1
Buzău 116 C 1
Buzet 115 F 2
Buzi 161 E 3
Buzi 161 E 4
Buzluk Dağ 117 E 2
Buzuluk 118 K 5
Bwendi 158 D 4
Byblos 154 F 2
Byczyna 111 G 4
Bydgoszcz 111 G 4
Bygdeå 112 H 3
Bygdeträsket 112 H 3
Byglandsfjord 113 E 4
Byglandsfjorden 113 E 4
Bykhov 118 F 5
Bykle 112 E 4
Bykov 131 Q 6
Bykovo 118 J 3
Bykovskiy 131 N 1
Bylkyldak 119 P 6
Bylot Island 184
Bynoe River 143 G 2
Byrka 130 L 5
Byro 142 B 4
Byrock 143 H 5
Byron Bay 143 J 4
Byron, Cape 143 J 4
Byron, Isla 183 A 8
Byrranga, Gory 130 E 1–H 1
Byserovo 118 K 4
Byske 113 H 3
Byskeälven 112 H 2
Bystraya 131 T 5
Bystrinskiy Golets, Gora 130 JK 6
Bytča 111 G 5
Bytom 111 G 4
Bytów 111 G 4
Byuchennyakh 131 Q 3
Byxelkrok 113 G 4
Byzantium 143 H 4
Bzimah 153 K 4
Bzybskiy Khrebet 117 F 2

C–Can

C

Cañada de Gómez 182 D 5
Cañada Verde → Villa Huidobro 182 D 5
Cañaveral 114 B 4
Cañete (Chile) 183 B 6
Cañete (Peru) 180 A 3
Cañuelas 182 E 6
Caaguazu 182 E 4
Caála 160 B 2
Caatinga (Minas Gerais, Brazil) 181 G 4
Cáatingas 181 GH 2
Caazapa 182 E 4
Caballeria, Cabo de 114 D 3
Caballococha 178 D 4
Caballo Res. 170 E 5
Cabanatuan 137 J 1
Čabar 115 F 2
Cabeceiras 181 G 4
Cabedelo 181 K 2
Cabeza del Buey 114 B 4
Cabezas 180 D 4
Cabildo (Argentina) 183 D 6
Cabildo (Chile) 182 B 5
Cabimas 178 D 1
Cabinda 157 G 7
Cabinet Mountains 170 C 2
Cabo 161 G 2
Cabo Barbas 152 B 4
Cabo Bascuñan 182 B 4
Cabo Beata 173 H 4
Cabo Blanco 183 C 8
Cabo Bojador 152 C 3
Cabo Camarón 172 E, F 4
Cabo Carvoeiro 114 B 4
Cabo Cassiporé 179 H 3
Cabo Catoche 172 E 3
Cabo Choros 182 B 4
Cabo Corrientes (Argentina) 183 E 6
Cabo Corrientes (Colombia) 178 C 2
Cabo Cruz 173 G 4
Cabo das Correntes 161 F 4
Cabo de Ajo 114 C 3
Cabo de Caballeria 114 D 3
Cabo de Cala Figuera 114 D 4
Cabo de Creus 114 D 3
Cabo de Finisterre 114 B 3
Cabo de Formentor 114 D 4
Cabo de Gata 114 C 4
Cabo de Hornos 183 C 10
Cabo de la Nao 114 C 4
Cabo Delgado 161 G 2
Cabo de Palos 114 C 4
Cabo de Peñas 114 B 3
Cabo de São Brás 160 A 2
Cabo de São Roque 181 J 2
Cabo de São Tomé 181 H 5
Cabo de São Vicente 114 B 4
Cabo de Salinas 114 D 4
Cabo de San Francisco 178 B 3
Cabo de Santa Maria (Portugal) 114 B 4
Cabo de Santa Maria (Mozambique) 161 E 5
Cabo de Santa Marta 160 A 2
Cabo de Santa Marta Grande 181 G 6
Cabo Deseado 183 AB 6
Cabo de Sines 114 B 4
Cabo de Tortosa 114 D 3
Cabo dos Bahías 183 C 8
Cabo Engaño 173 J 4
Cabo Espichel 114 B 4
Cabo Francés 171 K 7
Cabo Freu 114 D 4
Cabo Frio 181 H 5
Cabo Gloucester 183 B 9
Cabo Gracias a Dios 172 F 5
Cabo Gurupi 179 J 4
Cabo Ledo 160 A 1
Cabo Maguarinho 179 J 4
Cabo Manglares 178 C 3
Cabo Marzo 178 C 2
Cabo Mondego 114 B 3
Cabonga, Réservoir 171 L 2
Cabo Norte 179 J 3
Cabo Orange 179 H 3
Cabo Ortegal 114 B 3
Cabo Pasado 178 B 4
Cabo Polonio 182 F 5
Cabo Quedal 183 B 7
Cabo Quilán 183 B 7
Cabora Bassa 161 E 3
Cabora Bassa, Lago 161 E 3
Cabo Raper 183 A 8
Cabo Raso 183 C 7
Caborca 170 D 5

Cabo Rojo (Mex.) 172 C 3
Cabo Rojo (Puerto R.) 173 J 4
Cabo San Antonio (Cuba) 172 F 3
Cabo San Antonio (Argentina) 183 E 6
Cabo San Diego 183 C 9
Cabo San Juan 157 F 5
Cabo San Lorenzo 178 B 4
Cabo San Lucas 170 E 7
Cabo San Rafael 173 J 4
Cabo Santa Elena 172 E 5
Cabo Touriñán 114 B 3
Cabo Trafalgar 114 B 4
Cabot Strait 169 Q 6
Cabourg 114 C 2
Cabo Verde 156 A 6
Cabo Virgenes 183 C 9
Cabras, Stagno di 115 E 4
Cabrera 114 D 4
Cabrera, Sierra de la 114 B 3
Cabriel 114 C 4
Cabrobó 181 J 2
Cabruta 178 E 2
Cabuyaro 178 D 3
Caçador 182 F 4
Cacequí 182 F 4
Cáceraes 180 E 4
Cáceres (Colombia) 178 C 2
Cáceres (Spain) 114 B 4
Cacharí 183 E 6
Cacheu 156 A 3
Cachimbo 179 H 5
Cachimbo, Serra do 179 G 5
Cachinal 180 C 5
Cachi, Nevado de 180 D 5
Cachingues 160 B 2
Cachoeira 181 J 3
Cachoeira Alta 181 F 4
Cachoeira Aquibi 181 E 3
Cachoeira Cantagalo 179 H 5
Cachoeira Capinzal 179 G 4–5
Cachoeira da Bateria 179 G 3
Cachoeira da Boca 179 H 5
Cachoeira da Conceição 179 F 5
Cachoeira das Capoeiras 179 G 4–5
Cachoeira das Ilhas 179 G 4
Cachoeira das Sete Quedas 179 G 4–5
Cachoeira de Anta 179 F 5
Cachoeira de Paulo Afonso 181 J 2
Cachoeira do Buritizal 179 H 3
Cachoeira do Chacorão 179 G 4–5
Cachoeira do Inferno 179 G 4
Cachoeira do Rafael 180 D 3
Cachoeira do Rebojo 179 G 4–5
Cachoeira dos Índios 179 F 3
Cachoeira dos Patos 179 F 5
Cachoeira do Sul 182 F 5
Cachoeira do Tereraimbu 179 H 5
Cachoeira Figueira 179 G 4–5
Cachoeira Grande 179 G 3
Cachoeira Maranhão 179 G 4
Cachoeira Pereira 179 G 4
Cachoeira de Itapemirim 181 H 5
Cachos, Punta 182 B 4
Cacine 156 AB 3
Cacolo 160 B 2
Caconda 160 B 2
Cacuaco 160 A 1
Cacula 160 A 2
Caculé 181 H 3
Caçumba 181 J 4
Cacuso 160 B 1
Cadaqués 114 D 3
Cadarga 143 J 4
Cadena del Pantiacolla 180 B 3
Cader Idris 102 C 1
Cadillac 171 J 3
Cadi, Sierra del 114 D 3
Cádiz (Spain) 114 B 3
Cadiz (Phil.) 137 F 1
Caliente 170 D 4
California 170 B 4
California, Golfo de 170 D 6
Calilegua 180 D 5
Calimere, Point 134 C 5
Calingasta 182 C 5
Callabonna, Lake 143 F 4
Callac 114 C 2
Callao 180 A 3
Callander 99 B 3
Callao 180 A 3
Callernish 98 A 2
Callytharra Springs 142 B 4
Calne 103 C 2
Calpe 114 D 4
Caen 114 C 2
Caerleon 102 C 2
Caernarfon 102 B 1
Caernarfon Bay 102 B 1
Caerphilly 102 C 2
Caete 181 H 4
Caetite 181 H 3
Cagayan 137 J 1
Cagayan de Oro 137 F 2
Cagayan Islands 137 F 2
Cagayan Sulu 137 E 2
Cagliari 115 E 4
Cagnes-sur-Mer 115 E 3
Cagua 178 E 1

Caguas 173 J 4
Cagüén 178 D 3
Cahama 160 A 3
Caha Mountains 110 B 4
Cahersiveen 110 A 4
Cahore Point 102 A 1
Cahors 114 D 3
Caia 161 F 3
Caiabis, Serra dos 180 E 3
Caianda 160 C 2
Caiapônia 181 F 4
Caiapó, Serra do 181 F 4
Caibarién 173 G 3
Caicara 178 E 2
Caico 181 J 2
Caicos Islands 173 H 3
Cailloma 180 B 4
Caiman Point 137 H 1
Cainde 160 A 3
Cai Nuoc 135 HJ 6
Cairngorm Mountains 98 C 3
Cairns 143 H 2
Cairo 154 E 2–3
Caister-on-Sea 103 E 1
Caistor 101 E 3
Caiundo 160 B 3
Cajamarca 178 C 5
Cajazeiras 181 J 2
Cajuapara 179 J 4
Caka 132 C 3
Čakirgöl Dağ 117 E 2
Çakmak 117 D 3
Čakovec 115 G 2
Cakrani 116 A 2
Çal 116 C 3
Calabar 157 F 5
Calabozo 178 E 2
Calabria 115 G 4
Calabro, Appennino 115 G 4
Calafate 183 B 9
Cala Figuera, Cabo de 114 D 4
Calagua Islands 137 F 1
Calahorra 114 C 3
Calai 160 B 3
Calais 114 D 1
Calais, Pas de 110 D 4
Calakmul 172 E 4
Calama (Brazil) 179 F 5
Calama (Chile) 180 C 5
Calamar 178 D 3
Calamarca 180 C 4
Calamian Group 137 E 1
Calamocha 114 C 3
Calanaque 179 F 4
Calanda 114 C 3
Calandula 160 B 1
Calang 136 A 3
Calapan 171 H 2
Călăraşi 116 C 2
Cala Ratjada 114 D 4
Calatayud 114 C 3
Calatrava, Campo de 114 C 4
Calayan 137 J 1
Calbayog 137 F 1
Calbuco 183 B 7
Calchaquí 182 D 4
Calçoene 179 H 3
Calcutta 134 E 3
Caldas 178 C 2
Caldas da Rainha 114 B 4
Caldeirão, Serra de 114 B 4
Caldera 182 B 4
Calderina 114 C 4
Calderina, Sierra de la 114 C 4
Caldicot 102 C 2
Caldron 117 F 3
Caldwell 170 C 3
Caldy Island 102 B 2
Caledonia 171 H 3
Caledonian Canal 99 B 3
Caleta Buena 180 B 4
Caleta Clarencia 183 B 9
Caleta Olivia 183 C 8
Calf of Man 100 C 2
Calgary 167 P 5
Cali 178 C 3
Calicut 134 C 5

Caltagirone 115 F 4
Caltanissetta 115 F 4
Calulo 160 A 2
Caluquembe 160 A 2
Calvi 115 E 3
Calvinia 160 B 6
Calvitero 114 B 3
Cama 172 F 5
Camabatela 160 B 1
Camacá 181 J 4
Camacupa 160 B 2
Camaguán 178 E 2
Camagüey 173 G 3
Camagüey, Archipiélago de 173 G 3
Camaná 180 B 4
Camapuã 181 F 4
Camaquã 182 F 5
Camara 179 F 4
Camararo 180 E 3
Camarat, Cap 115 E 3
Camargo 180 C 5
Camariñas 114 B 3
Camarón, Cabo 172 E, F 4
Camarones (Argentina) 183 C 7
Camarones (Chile) 180 B 4
Camas 113 B 3
Camatindi 180 D 5
Camaxilo 160 B 1
Cambados 114 B 3
Cambay → Khambhat 134 B 3
Camberley 103 D 2
Cambodia 135 HJ 5
Camboon 143 J 4
Camborne 102 B 2
Cambrai 114 D 1
Cambrian Mountains 102 C 1
Cambridge (U.K.) 103 E 1
Cambridge (Airport) 103 E 1
Cambridge (ID, U.S.A.) 170 C 3
Cambridge (Jamaica) 173 G 4
Cambridge (MA, U.S.A.) 171 M 3
Cambridge (MD., U.S.A.) 171 L 4
Cambridge Bay 167 Q 2
Cambridge Downs 143 G 3
Cambridge Gulf 142 D 1
Cambridgeshire 103 D 1
Cambuci 181 H 5
Cambulo 160 C 1
Cambundi-Catembo 160 B 2
Camden 171 H 5
Camden Bay 166 J 1
Camelford 102 B 2
Camerá 179 J 4
Camerino 115 F 3
Cameron 171 H 2
Cameron Hills 167 O 4
Cameroon 157 G 4
Cameroun, Mont 157 F 5
Camiña 180 C 4
Camiguin 137 J 1
Camiranga 179 J 4
Camiri 180 D 5
Camisea 180 B 3
Çamlıbel Geçidi 117 E 2–3
Camocim 181 H 1
Camoió 181 J 2
Camoola 143 G 3
Camooweal 143 F 2
Camopi 179 H 3
Camorta 135 F 6
Camotes Sea 137 F 1
Campana 182 E 5
Campana, Isla 183 A 8
Campanario 183 B 6
Campbell, Cape 145 Q 9
Campbell Island 185
Campbell Plateau 193 C 5
Campbellpore 129 J 4
Campbell River 167 M 6
Campbellton 169 O 6
Campbeltown (Australia) 143 J 5
Campbeltown (U.K.) 100 C 2
Campbeltown (Airport) 100 C 2
Camp Century 184
Campeche 172 D 4
Campeche, Bahia de 172 D 4
Camperdown 143 G 6
Campidano 115 E 4
Campiglia 115 F 3
Campina Grande 181 J 2
Campinas 181 G 5
Campina Verde 181 G 4
Campo 157 F 5
Campo Belo 181 G 5
Campobasso 115 F 3
Campo de Calatrava 114 C 4
Campo de Criptana 114 C 4
Campo de Diauaruri 181 F 3

Campo de Montiel 114 C 4
Campo Formoso 181 H 3
Campo Gallo 182 D 4
Campo Grande 181 F 5
Campo Maior 181 H 1
Campo Mourão 181 F 5
Campo Quijano 180 C 5
Campos 181 H 5
Campos Novos 182 F 4
Campos Sales 181 HJ 2
Campos, Tierra de 114 BC 3
Campo Troso 178 E 3
Campsie Fells 100 C 1
Camp Verde 170 D 5
Cam Ranh 135 J 5
Camrose 167 P 5
Camsell 167 O 2
Camsell Portage 167 Q 4
Camucuio 160 A 2
Çan (Turkey) 116 C 3
Çan (Turkey) 117 F 3
Ca Na 135 J 5
Canacassala 160 A 1
Canada 166–169
Canada Basin 193 D 1
Canadian River 170 F 4
Canadian River North 170 G 4
Canaima 179 F 2
Canaima, Parque Nacional 179 F 2
Çanakkale 116 C 2
Çanakkale Boğazı 116 C 2
Canal Baker 183 B 8
Canal Beagle 183 C 9
Canal de Ballenas 170 D 6
Canal de Bourgogne 114 D 2
Canal de Briare 114 D 2
Canal de la Dominique 173 K 4
Canal de la Marne à la Saône 115 E 2
Canal de la Marne au Rhin 115 E 2
Canal de la Mona 173 J 4
Canal de la Sambre à l'Oise 114 D 2
Canal de Sainte-Lucie 173 K 5
Canal de Yucatán 172 E 3
Canal do Norte 179 H 3
Canal do Sul 179 J 4
Canal du Midi 114 D 3
Canal du Rhone au Rhin 115 E 2
Canale Cavour 115 E 2
Canale de Sicilia 115 F 4
Canale di Corsica 115 E 3
Canale di Malta 115 F 4
Canalejas 183 C 6
Canal lateral de la Garonne 114 D 3
Canal Moraleda 183 B 7
Canama 178 D 5
Canamari 180 C 3
Cananea 170 D 5
Cananéia 181 G 5
Cananguchal 178 C 3
Canapiari, Cerro 178 E 3
Canary Islands 152 B 3
Canastra, Serra da 181 G 4
Canaveral, Cape 171 K 6
Canavieiras 181 J 4
Canberra 143 H 6
Canby 171 G 3
Canchas 182 B 4
Canchyuaya, Cerros de 178 D 5
Cancún 172 E 3
Candamom Hills 134 C 6
Çandarlı 116 C 3
Candeias 181 J 3
Candelaria 172 D 4
Çandili Tepe 117 E 3
Cando 167 S 6
Candoí 182 F 4
Canéia 181 G 5
Canela 182 F 4
Canelones 182 E 5
Cangamba 160 B 2
Cangandala 160 B 1
Cangas 114 B 3
Cangas de Narcea 114 B 3
Cangola 160 B 1
Cangombé 160 B 2
Cangumbe 160 B 2
Cangwu 132 F 6
Cangyuan 132 C 6
Cangzhou 133 G 3
Caniapiscau 169 O 5
Caniapiscau, Lac 169 O 5
Canicatti 115 F 4
Canık Dağları 117 E 2
Canindé (Amazonas, Brazil) 178 D 5

Can–Cas

Canindé (Ceará, Brazil) 181 J 1
Canipiscau 169 O 4
Çankırı 117 D 2
Canna 99 A 3
Cannanore 134 C 5
Cannes 115 E 3
Canning Basin 142 C 2
Cannock 103 C 1
Cann River 143 H 6
Canoas 182 F 4
Canobie 143 G 2
Canon City 170 E 4
Canora 167 R 5
Canosa di Puglia 115 G 3
Canso 169 P 6
Canso, Strait of 169 P 6
Canta 180 A 3
Cantabrian Mountains 114 BC 3
Cantagalo, Cachoeira 179 H 5
Cantaura 179 F 2
Canterbury 103 E 2
Canterbury Bight 145 Q 9
Canterbury Plains 145 Q 9
Can Tho 135 J 5
Cantilan 137 G 2
Canto do Buriti 181 H 2
Canton (China) 132 F 6
Canton (MS, U.S.A.) 171 H 5
Canton (OH, U.S.A.) 171 K 3
Cantù 115 E 2
Cantwell 166 H 3
Canumã (Amazonas, Brazil) 179 G 4
Canumã (Amazonas, Brazil) 179 F 5
Canutama 179 F 5
Canvey 103 E 2
Canyon 170 F 4
Cao Bang 135 J 3
Caombo 160 B 1
Caonguyen Dac Lac 135 J 5
Càorle 115 E 2
Cao Xian 132 G 4
Capão Bonito 181 G 5
Capaccio 115 G 3
Capaia 160 C 1
Capanaparo 178 E 2
Capanema 179 J 4
Capatárida 178 D 1
Cap Blanc (Mauritania) 152 B 4
Cap Blanc → Ra's al Abyaḍ 153 G 1
Cap Bon → Ra's aṭ Ṭīb 153 H 1
Cap Bougar'oûn 153 G 1
Cap Camarat 115 E 3
Cap Corse 115 E 3
Cap Croisette 115 E 3
Cap d'Ambre 161 H 2
Cap Dame-Marie 173 H 4
Cap d'Antifer 114 D 2
Cap d'Arguin 152 B 4
Cap de Fer 153 G 1
Cap de Gaspé 169 P 6
Cap de la Hague 114 C 2
Cap-de-la-Madeleine 171 M 2
Cap-de-Nouvelle France 169 N 3
Cap Drâa 152 C 3
Cape Abyssal Plain 192 B 5
Cape Acadia 169 M 3
Cape Adare 185
Cape Agulhas 160 C 6
Cape Alava 170 A 2
Cape Alitak 166 G 4
Cape Anguille 169 Q 6
Cape Ann 185
Cape Arid 142 C 5
Cape Arid National Park 142 C 5
Cape Arnhem 143 F 1
Cape Baring 167 O 2
Cape Barren Island 144 L 9
Cape Basin 192 B 5
Cape Bathurst 166 M 1
Cape Bauld 169 Q 5
Cape Bear 169 P 6
Cape Beatrice 143 F 1
Cape Blanco 170 B 3
Cape Boothby 185
Cape Bossut 142 C 2
Cape Bowling Green 143 H 2
Cape Breton Highlands National Park 169 P 6
Cape Breton Island 169 P 6
Cape Brett 145 Q 8
Cape Byron 143 J 4
Cape Campbell 145 Q 9
Cape Canaveral 171 K 6
Cape Capricorn 143 J 3
Cape Catastrophe 143 F 6
Cape Chapman 167 U 2
Cape Charles (Newfoundl., Can.) 169 Q 5
Cape Charles (VA, U.S.A.) 171 L 4

Cape Chelyuskin 184
Cape Chidley 169 P 3
Cape Churchill 167 T 4
Cape Clear 110 B 4
Cape Coast 156 D 4
Cape Cod 171 N 3
Cape Cod Bay 171 M 3
Cape Columbine 160 B 6
Cape Colville 167 T 2
Cape Comorin 134 C 6
Cape Constantine 166 F 4
Cape Coral 171 K 6
Cape Cornwall 102 B 2
Cape Cretin 144 E 3
Cape Croker 142 E 1
Cape Cross 160 A 4
Cape Cuvier 142 A 3
Cape Dalhousie 166 M 1
Cape Darnley 185
Cape de la Hague 103 D 3
Cape Dennison 185
Cape Dominion 169 N 2
Cape Dorchester 169 M 1
Cape Dorset 169 M 3
Cape du Couedic 143 F 6
Cape Dyer 169 P 2
Cape Egmont 145 Q 8
Cape Engaño 137 J 1
Cape Farewell 145 Q 9
Cape Farquhar 142 A 3
Cape Fear 171 L 5
Cape Felix 167 S 2
Cape Finniss 142 E 5
Cape Flattery (Australia) 143 H 1
Cape Flattery (U.S.A.) 170 B 2
Cape Foulwind 145 Q 9
Cape Freels 169 R 6
Cape Fria 160 A 3
Cape Girardeau 171 J 4
Cape Grenville 143 G 1
Cape Grim 144 K 9
Cape Guardafui 159 J 2
Cape Halkett 166 G 1
Cape Harrison 169 Q 5
Cape Hatteras 171 L 4
Cape Henrietta Maria 169 L 4
Cape Herluf Trolle 169 T 3
Cape Hooper 169 O 2
Cape Hope 167 O 2
Cape Horn 183 C 10
Cape Howe 143 J 6
Cape Inscription 142 A 4
Cape Jaffa 143 F 6
Cape Jones 167 T 3
Cape Kattaktoc 169 O 4
Cape Keer-Weer 143 G 1
Cape Kellett 167 M 1
Cape Kendall 167 U 3
Cape Kidnappers 145 R 8
Cape Knox 166 L 5
Cape Krusenstern National Monument 166 E 2
Cape Lambert 145 F 2
Cape Lambton 167 N 1
Cape Latouche Treville 142 C 2
Cape Leeuwin 142 A 5
Cape Lévêque 142 C 2
Cape Lisburne 166 D 2
Cape Londonderry 142 D 1
Cape Lookout 171 L 5
Cape Low 167 U 3
Cape Maria van Diemen 145 Q 7
Cape May 171 M 4
Cape Melville 143 G 1
Cape Mendocino 170 B 3
Cape Mercy 169 P 3
Cape Meredith 183 D 9
Cape Michelsen 167 R 1
Cape Mohican 166 D 3
Cape Monze → Ras Muari 129 H 6
Cape Morris Jesup 184
Cape Naturaliste 142 A 5
Cape Negrais 135 F 4
Cape Nelson 143 G 6
Cape Newenham 166 E 4
Cape North 169 P 6
Cape Norvegia 185
Cape of Good Hope 160 B 6
Cape Otway 143 G 6
Cape Palliser 145 R 9
Cape Palmas 156 C 5
Cape Parry 167 N 1
Cape Pembroke (Canada) 169 L 3
Cape Pembroke (Falkland Islands) 183 E 9
Cape Poinsett 185
Cape Portland 144 L 9
Cape Prince Alfred 167 N 1
Cape Prince of Wales 166 D 2
Cape Providence 144 P 10

Cape Province 160 CD 6
Cape Queen 169 M 3
Cape Race 169 R 6
Cape Raper 169 O 2
Cape Ray 169 Q 6
Cape River 143 H 3
Cape Rodney (Papua New Guinea) 144 E 4
Cape Rodney (Alaska) 166 D 3
Cape Romanzof 166 D 3
Cape Runaway 145 R 8
Cape Sable (FL, U.S.A.) 171 K 6
Cape Sable (N.Br., Can.) 169 O 7
Cape Saint Francis 160 C 6
Cape Saint George (Canada) 169 Q 6
Cape Saint George (Papua New Guinea) 145 F 2
Cape Saint James 166 L 5
Cape Saint Lucia 161 E 5
Cape San Agustin 137 G 2
Cape San Blas 171 J 6
Cape Scott 167 M 5
Cape Scott 142 D 1
Cape Smith 169 M 3
Cape Southampton 167 V 3
Cape Spencer 143 F 6
Cap Est 161 J 3
Cape Swinburne 167 S 1
Cape Tatnam 167 T 4
Cape Three Points 156 D 5
Cape Town 160 B 6
Cape Townshend 143 J 3
Cape Van Diemen 142 D 1
Cape Verde 156 A 6
Cape Verde (Senegal) 152 B 6
Cape Walsingham 169 P 2
Cape Wessel 143 F 1
Cape Wickham 144 K 8
Cape Wilson 167 V 2
Cape Wrath 98 B 2
Cape Wrottesley 167 N 1
Capcross 166 L 3
Cape Yakataga 166 J 3
Cape York Peninsula 143 G 1
Cape Zhelaniya 184
Cap Ferret 114 C 3
Cap Fréhel 114 C 2
Cap Gris-Nez 114 D 1
Cap-Haïtien 173 H 4
Cap Hopes Advance 169 O 3
Capibara 178 E 3
Capilla 182 E 5
Capim 179 J 4
Capinota 180 C 4
Capinzal, Cachoeira 179 G 4–5
Capitán Arturo Prat 185
Capitan Bado 180 E 5
Capitán Meza 182 E 4
Capivara, Reprêsa da 181 F 5
Cap Juby 152 C 3
Cap Lopez 157 F 2
Cap Masoala 161 J 3
Capo Bonifati 115 G 4
Capo Carbonara 115 E 4
Capo Circeo 115 F 3
Capo delle Colonne 115 G 4
Capo di Pula 115 E 4
Capoeiras, Cachoeira das 179 G 4–5
Capo Gallo 115 F 4
Capo Linaro 115 F 3
Capo Mannu 115 E 3
Capo Marargiu 115 E 3
Capo Murro di Porco 115 G 4
Capoompeta 143 J 4
Capo Palinuro 115 G 3
Capo Passero 115 G 4
Capo San Marco 115 E 4
Capo Santa Maria di Leuca 115 G 4
Capo Scaramia 115 F 4
Capo Sferracavallo 115 E 4
Capo Spartivento 115 E 4
Capo Testa 115 E 3
Capo Vaticano 115 G 4
Capraia 115 E 3
Capreol 169 L 6
Cap Rhir 152 CD 2
Capri 115 F 3
Capricorn, Cape 143 J 3
Capricorn Channel 143 J 3
Capricorn Group 143 J 3
Caprivi Game Park 160 C 3
Caprivi Strip 160 C 3
Cap Roxo 156 A 3
Cap Saint-André 161 G 3
Cap Sainte-Marie 161 H 5
Cap Spartel 152 D 1
Captains Flat 143 H 6
Captieux 114 C 3
Cap Timiris 152 B 5
Cap Tres Forcas 152 E 1

Capunda 160 B 2
Cap Verga 156 B 3
Cap Vert 156 A 3
Cap Wolstenholme 169 M 3
Caquetá 178 D 4
Carabaya, Cordillera de 180 B 3
Caracal Roșiori de Vede 116 B 2
Caracarai 179 F 3
Caracas 178 E 1
Caracol 181 H 2
Caraga 137 G 2
Carahue 183 B 6
Carajari 179 H 4
Carajás, Serra dos 179 H 5
Caramulo, Serra do 114 B 3
Caranapatuba 179 F 5
Carandotta 143 F 3
Carangola 181 H 5
Caransebes 116 B 1
Carantuohill 110 B 4
Carapajó 179 J 4
Carapé 179 P 6
Caratasca, Laguna de 172 F 4
Caratinga 181 H 4
Carauari 178 E 4
Caravaca 114 C 4
Caraveli 180 B 4
Caravelas 181 J 4
Caraz 178 C 5
Carazinho 182 F 4
Carballo 114 B 3
Carbonara, Capo 115 E 4
Carboneras 114 C 4
Carbonia 115 E 4
Carcajou 167 O 4
Carcans 114 C 3
Carcans-Plage 114 C 2
Carcarañá 182 D 5
Carcar Mountains → Karkär 159 H 3
Carcassonne 114 D 3
Carcross 166 L 3
Cardamomes, Chaine des 135 J 5
Cárdenas (Cuba) 173 F 3
Cárdenas (Mex.) 172 C 3
Cardiel, Lago 183 B 8
Cardiff 102 C 2
Cardiff (Airport) 102 C 2
Cardigan 102 B 1
Cardigan Bay 102 B 1
Cardona 114 D 3
Cardozo 182 E 5
Cardston 167 P 6
Carei 116 B 1
Careiro 179 G 4
Carentan 114 C 2
Carey 170 D 3
Carey, Lake 142 C 4
Cargèse 115 E 3
Carhaix-Plouguer 114 C 2
Carhué 183 D 6
Cariñena 114 C 3
Cariati 115 G 4
Caribbean Sea 173 G–J 4
Cariboo Mountains (Br.Col., Can.) 167 N 5
Caribou 171 N 2
Caribou Lake, North 168 J 5
Caribou Mountains (Alb., Can.) 167 O 4
Carimbula 160 B 1
Carinhanha 181 H 3
Caripare 181 G 3
Caripito 179 F 1
Caritianas 179 F 5
Carius 181 J 2
Carleton Place 171 L 2
Carletonville 160 D 5
Carlingford Lough 100 B 2
Carlisle 101 D 2
Carloforte 115 E 4
Carlos Casares 183 D 6
Carlos Chagas 181 H 4
Carlow 100 B 3
Carloway 98 A 2
Carlsbad (CA, U.S.A.) 170 C 5
Carlsbad (N.M., U.S.A.) 170 F 5
Carlsberg Ridge 192 B 3
Carlton 103 D 1
Carlton Hill 142 D 2
Carluke 100 D 2
Carlyle 167 R 6
Carmacks 166 K 3
Carmagnola 115 E 3
Carmarthen 102 B 2
Carmarthen Bay 102 B 2
Carmaux 114 D 3
Carmel 170 B 4
Çarmelı 116 C 3
Carmelo 182 E 5
Carmen 182 E 4
Carmen Alto 180 C 5
Carmen de Patagones 183 D 7
Carmen, Isla 170 D 6

Carmensa 183 C 6
Carmi 171 J 4
Carmila 143 H 3
Carmona 114 B 4
Carnac 114 C 2
Carnamah 142 B 4
Carnarvon 142 A 3
Carnarvon Range 142 C 4
Carndonagh 100 B 2
Carnegie 142 C 4
Carnegie, Lake 142 C 4
Carn Eige 110 B 3
Carnforth 101 D 2
Carniche, Alpi 115 F 2
Car Nicobar 135 F 6
Carnlough 100 C 2
Carnot 158 B 3
Carnoustie 99 C 3
Carnsore Point 102 A 1
Carolina (Brazil) 179 J 5
Carolina (Ecuador) 178 C 3
Carolina Beach 171 L 5
Caroline (Kiribati) 147 E 3
Caroline Basin 193 C 3
Caroline Islands 146 AB 2
Carondelet 146 D 3
Caroní 179 F 2
Carpathian Mountains 116 C 1
Carpaţii Meridionali 116 B 1
Carpentaria Gulf of 143 F 1
Carpentras 115 E 3
Carpi 115 F 3
Carpina 181 J 2
Carpra 178 D 1
Carrara 115 F 3
Carrazedo 179 H 4
Carrera 180 E 5
Carreta, Punta 180 A 3
Carribou Lake, North 168 J 5
Carrick 100 C 2
Carrickfergus 100 C 2
Carrickmacross 100 B 3
Carrick-on-Shannon 100 A 3
Carrillo 170 F 6
Carrión de los Condes 114 C 3
Carrizal (Mexico) 170 E 5
Carrizal (Colombia) 178 D 1
Carrizal Bajo 182 B 4
Carrizos 170 E 5
Carrizo Springs 170 G 6
Carrizozo 170 E 5
Carroll 171 H 3
Carrollton 171 J 5
Carron, Loch 98 B 3
Çarşamba 117 E 2
Çarşamban 117 D 3
Carson 170 B 2
Carson City 170 C 3
Cartagena 114 C 4
Cartagena (Col.) 178 C 1
Cartago (Col.) 178 C 3
Cartago (Costa Rica) 172 F 6
Carter, Mount 143 G 1
Carthage (IL, U.S.A.) 171 H 3
Carthage (MO, U.S.A.) 171 H 4
Carthage (Tunisia) 115 F 4
Carthage (Tunisia) → Karthago 153 H 1
Cartier Island 142 C 1
Cartwright 169 Q 5
Caruaru 181 J 2
Carúpano 179 F 1
Carutapera 179 J 4
Carvoeiro 179 F 4
Carvoeiro, Cabo 114 B 4
Casablanca 152 D 2
Casablanca (Chile) 182 B 5
Casa Branca 181 G 5
Casa Grande 170 D 5
Casalbordino 115 F 3
Casale Monferrato 115 E 2
Casalmaggiore 115 F 3
Casalvasco 180 E 4
Casal Velino 115 G 3
Casamance 156 A 3
Casanare 178 C 2
Casa Nova 181 H 2
Casaux, Étang de 114 C 3
Casbas 183 D 6
Cascade 170 C 3
Cascade Range 170 B 2–3
Cascadia Basin 193 D 2
Cascais 114 B 4
Cascata della Marmore 115 F 3
Cascavel 181 F 5
Cascina 115 F 3
Caserta 115 F 3
Casey 185
Casiguran 137 F 1
Casilda 182 D 5
Casino 143 J 4
Casiquiare 178 E 3

219

Cas–Cha

Cáslav 111 G 5
Casma 178 C 5
Casper 170 E 3
Caspian Depression 128 DE 1
Caspian Sea 128 DE 2–3
Cassai 160 C 2
Cassai Sul 160 C 2
Cassamba 160 C 2
Cassiar Mountains 166 M 4
Cassilândia 181 F 4
Cassinga 160 B 3
Cassino (Brazil) 182 F 5
Cassino (Italy) 115 F 3
Cassiporé, Cabo 179 H 3
Cassongue 160 A 2
Castañar, Sierra del 114 C 4
Castaño 182 C 5
Castanhal 179 J 4
Castanho 179 F 5
Castelarrasin 114 D 3
Castel di Sangro 115 F 3
Castelfranco Veneto 115 F 2
Castellabate 115 E 3
Castellammare, Golfo di 115 F 4
Castellane 115 E 3
Castellaneta 115 G 3
Castelli 183 E 6
Castellón de la Plana 114 C 4
Castelnaudary 114 D 3
Castelnau-de-Médoc 114 C 2
Castelo Branco 114 B 4
Castelvetrano 115 F 4
Castets 114 C 3
Castiglione della Pescaia 115 F 3
Castilla (Chile) 182 B 4
Castilla (Peru) 178 B 5
Castilla la Nueva 114 C 3–4
Castilla la Vieja 114 C 3
Castillejo 114 B 3
Castillo, Cerro 183 B 8
Castillo Incasico de Ingapirca 178 C 3
Castillonnes 114 D 3
Castillos 182 F 5
Castlebar 110 B 4
Castlebay 99 A 3
Castleblayney 100 B 2
Castle Cary 102 C 2
Castledawson 100 B 2
Castle Douglas 100 D 2
Castleford 101 E 3
Castlegar 167 O 6
Castlemaine 143 G 6
Castlereagh Bay 142 F 1
Castlereagh River 143 H 5
Castlerigg 101 D 2
Castletown 100 C 2
Castlewellan 100 C 2
Castor 167 P 5
Castres 114 D 3
Castries (Saint Lucia) 173 K 5
Castrignano del Capo 115 G 4
Castro (Chile) 183 B 7
Castro (Paraná, Brazil) 181 G 5
Castro Daire 114 B 3
Castro del Río 114 C 3
Castro-Urdiales 114 C 3
Castro Verde 114 B 4
Castrovillari 115 G 4
Castuera 114 B 4
Casuarina, Mount 142 D 1
Casula 161 E 3
Çat 117 F 2
Catabola 160 B 2
Catacaos 178 B 5
Cataguases 181 H 5
Çatak 117 F 3
Catalão 181 G 4
Çatal Balkan 116 C 2
Catalina, Punta 183 C 9
Catalonia → Catalūna 114 D 3
Çatalzeytin 117 D 2
Catamarca 182 C 4
Catamayo 178 BC 4
Catandica 161 E 3
Catanduanes 137 F 1
Catanduva 181 G 5
Catania 115 G 4
Catanzaro 115 G 4
Cataratas del Iguazú 182 F 4
Catastrophe, Cape 143 F 6
Catauera 179 G 4
Catbalogan 137 F 1
Cateel 137 G 2
Catende 181 J 2
Caterham 103 D 2
Catete 160 A 1
Catherine, Mount 170 D 4
Catinzaco 182 C 4
Catió 156 A 3
Catisimiña 179 F 3
Cat Island 173 G 3
Cat Lake 168 J 5

Catoche, Cabo 172 E 3
Cato Island and Bank 143 K 3
Catora 180 D 4
Catrilo 183 D 6
Catrimani 179 F 3
Catuane 161 E 5
Catuile 160 C 3
Catuna 182 C 5
Catur 161 F 2
Catwick Islands 135 J 6
Cauca 178 C 2
Caucasia 178 C 2
Caucasus Mountains 117 F 2
Caudry 114 D 1
Caulonia 115 G 4
Caungula 160 B 1
Cauquenas 183 B 6
Caura 179 F 2
Causapscal 169 O 6
Caussade 114 D 3
Causse de Gramat 114 D 3
Causse de Limogne 114 D 3
Causse du Larzac 114 D 3
Causse Mejean 114 D 3
Cautário 180 D 3
Cauvery 134 C 5
Cavaillon 115 E 3
Cavalcante 181 G 3
Cavally 156 C 4
Cavan 100 B 3
Cavarzere 115 F 2
Çavdarhisar 116 C 3
Cavell 168 K 5
Caviana, Ilha 179 H 3
Cavignac 114 C 2
Cavour, Canale 115 E 2
Cavtat 115 G 3
Çavuşcu Gölü 117 D 3
Caxias (Amazonas, Brazil) 178 D 4
Caxias (Maranhão, Brazil) 181 H 1
Caxias do Sul 182 F 4
Caxito 160 A 1
Çay 116 D 3
Cayambe 178 C 3
Çaycuma 117 D 2
Çayeli 117 F 2
Cayenne 179 H 3
Çayıralan 117 E 3
Çayırhan 116 D 2
Cayman Brac 173 G 4
Cayman Islands 173 F 4
Cayo Arenas 172 D 3
Cayo Nuevo 172 D 3
Cayos Arcas 172 D 3
Cayos de Albuquerque 173 F 5
Cayos de Roncador 173 FG 5
Cayos Miskitos 172 F 5
Cay Sal 173 F 3
Cazombo 160 C 2
Cazongo 157 G 7
Ceanannus Mor 100 B 3
Ceará 181 J 1
Ceara Abyssal Plain 192 A 3
Ceará Mirim 181 J 2
Ceballos 172 B 2
Cebollar 182 C 4
Cebolleti 182 F 5
Cebu 137 F 1
Cebu 137 F 2
Čechy 111 F 5
Cecina 115 F 3
Cedar City 170 D 4
Cedar Creek Reservoir 171 G 5
Cedar Falls 171 H 3
Cedar Key 171 K 6
Cedar Lake 167 R 5
Cedar Rapids 171 H 3
Cedar River 171 H 3
Cedros, Isla 170 C 6
Ceduna 142 E 5
Cefalù 115 F 4
Cefn-Mawr 102 C 1
Cegléd 116 A 1
Cejal 178 E 3
Çekerek 117 E 2
Celaya 172 B 3
Celebes 137 E 4
Celebes Sea 137 F 3
Çelebi 117 D 3
Celestún 172 D 3
Çelikhan 117 E 3
Celje 115 G 2
Celle 111 F 4
Celorico da Beira 114 B 3
Celtic Sea 110 B 4
Celtic Shelf 192 A 2
Çeltikçi Geçidi 116 D 3
Çemişgezek 117 E 3
Cenajo, Embalse de 114 C 4
Cencia 159 F 3
Cendrawasih 137 H 4
Cendrawasih, Teluk 137 H 4

Centenario 183 C 6
Center 171 H 5
Centerville 171 H 3
Cento 115 F 3
Central 99 B 3
Central African Republic 158 BC 3
Central Arctic District 167 QR 1
Central Brahui 129 G 5
Centralia 170 B 2
Central Kalahari Game Reserve 160 C 4
Central Makran Range 129 G 5
Centralno Tungusskoye Plato 130 H 3–4
Central Pacific Basin 193 D 3
Central Range (Papua New Guinea) 144 D 3
Central Siberian Plateau 130 GK 3
Centreville 171 H 5
Čepin 115 G 2
Cepu 136 D 5
Ceram 137 G 4
Cercal 114 B 4
Cereal 167 P 5
Ceremai, Gunung 136 C 5
Ceres (S. Africa) 160 B 6
Ceres (Brazil) 181 G 4
Cereté 178 C 2
Cerf 159 J 6
Cerignola 115 G 3
Çerkeş 117 D 2
Čermenika 116 B 2
Cernavoda 116 C 1
Černi vrah 116 B 2
Černo More 116 C 2
Cerralvo, Isla 170 D 7
Cerra Viejo 170 D 5
Cerritos 172 B 3
Cerro Aconcagua 182 C 5
Cerro Agua Caliente 172 A 2
Cerro Aguja 183 B 7
Cerro Aiguilete 183 B 9
Cerro Ángel 172 B 3
Cerro Arenales 183 B 8
Cerro Ataláya (Chile) 183 B 9
Cerro Atalaya (Peru) 180 B 3
Cerro Azul 172 C 3
Cerro Blanco 170 E 6
Cerro Bolívar 179 F 2
Cerro Bonete 182 C 4
Cerro Bravo 178 C 5
Cerro Canapiari 178 E 3
Cerro Candelaria 172 B 3
Cerro Castillo 183 B 8
Cerro Champaquí 182 D 5
Cerro Chato 183 B 7
Cerro Chirripó 172 F 6
Cerro Chochis 180 E 4
Cerro Cibuta 170 D 5
Cerro Coan 178 C 5
Cerro Coatepetl 172 C 4
Cerro Cofre de Perote 172 C 4
Cerro Cojudo Blanco 183 C 8
Cerro Colorado 170 C 5
Cerro Cónico 183 B 7
Cerro Dedo 183 B 7
Cerro de la Asunción 172 C 3
Cerro de la Encantada 170 C 5
Cerro de las Mesas 172 C 4
Cerro del Tigre 172 C 3
Cerro del Toro 182 C 4
Cerro de Pasco 180 A 3
Cerro de Punta 173 J 4
Cerro de San Felipe 114 C 3
Cerro Desmoronado 172 B 3
Cerro de Tocorpuri 180 C 5
Cerro el Cóndor 182 C 4
Cerro el Nevada 178 D 3
Cerro el Potro 182 C 4
Cerro Galán 182 C 4
Cerro Grande 172 B 3
Cerro Guaiquinima 179 F 2
Cerro Hudson 183 B 8
Cerro La Ardilla 172 B 3
Cerro Largo 182 F 4
Cerro Las Casilas 170 E 7
Cerro Las Minas 172 E 5
Cerro Lechiguiri 172 C 4
Cerro Lejia 180 D 5
Cerro León 180 D 5
Cerro Marahuaca 178 E 3
Cerro Mariquita 172 C 3
Cerro Mato 178 E 2
Cerro Mercedario 182 B 5
Cerro Mesa 183 B 8
Cerro Mohinora 170 E 6
Cerro Morado 180 CD 5
Cerro Moreno 180 B 5
Cerro Munchique 178 C 3
Cerro Murallón 183 B 8
Cerro Negro 183 C 7
Cerro Nevado 183 C 6
Cerro Nuevo Mundo 180 C 5

Cerro O'Higgins 183 B 8
Cerro Ojos del Salado 182 C 4
Cerro Paine Medio 183 B 9
Cerro Payún 183 C 6
Cerro Peña Gorda 172 B 3
Cerro Peña Nevada 172 C 3
Cerro Piedra 183 B 6
Cerro Potosí 172 B 3
Cerro San Lorenzo 183 B 8
Cerro Santiago 178 B 2
Cerro Santiago 173 F 6
Cerro San Valentín 183 B 8
Cerros de Araracuara 178 D 3–4
Cerros de Canchyuaya 178 D 5
Cerros de la Brea 178 B 4
Cerro Tetari 178 D 2
Cerro Toroni 180 C 4
Cerro Tres Cruces 172 D 4
Cerro Tres Picos 183 D 6
Cerro Tunari 180 C 4
Cerro Veijo 178 C 4
Cerro Ventana 172 A 3
Cerro Yavi 178 E 2
Cerro Yucuyácua 172 C 4
Cerro Yumari 178 E 3
Cervera 114 D 3
Cervia 115 F 3
Cesano 115 F 3
Cesena 115 F 3
Cēsis 113 J 4
Česká Lípa 111 F 4
Česká Třebová 111 G 5
České Budějovice 111 F 5
Českézemě 111 G 5
Československo 111 F 5
Český les 111 F 5
Çeşme 116 C 3
Cess 156 C 4
Cessford 165
Cessnock 143 J 5
Cetina 115 G 3
Cetinje 116 A 2
Çetinkaya 117 E 3
Cetraro 115 G 4
Ceuta 152 D 1
Ceva-i-Ra 146 C 4
Cévennes 114 D 3
Ceyhan 117 E 3
Ceylanpınar 117 F 3
Ceylon → Sri Lanka 134 D 6
Cézallier 114 D 2
Chañaral 182 B 4
Chabas 182 D 5
Chacabuco 182 D 5
Chacance 180 C 5
Chachani, Nevado 180 B 4
Chachapoyas 180 B 2
Chachoengsao 135 H 5
Chachro 129 J 5
Chaco 180 B 4
Chaco Austral 182 D 4
Chaco Boreal 180 D 5
Chaco Central 180 DE 6
Chaco, Parque Nacional de 182 E 4
Chacorão, Cachoeira do 179 G 4–5
Chad 157 H 3
Chadan 130 F 5
Chādegān 128 E 4
Chadileuvú 183 C 6
Chadiza 161 E 2
Chad, Lake 157 G 3
Chadobets 130 G 4
Chadron 170 F 3
Chagai 129 G 5
Chagai Hills 129 G 5
Chagda 131 O 4
Chagdo Kangri 134 D 1
Chaghcharān 129 H 4
Chagny 115 D 2
Chagodoshcha 118 G 4
Chagos Archipelago 122 F 7
Chaguaramos 178 E 2
Chagyl 128 F 2
Chahah Burjak 129 G 4
Chah Bahār 129 G 5
Chai Badan 135 H 5
Chaibassa 134 E 3
Chai Buri 135 H 4
Chaillu, Massif du 157 G 6
Chainat 135 GH 4
Chaiyaphum 135 H 4
Chajari 182 E 5
Chakari 160 D 3
Chak Chak 158 D 3
Chake Chake 159 F 6
Chakhansur 129 G 4
Chakwal 129 J 4
Chala 180 B 4

Chalabesa 161 E 2
Chalafat 116 B 2
Chalbi Desert 159 F 4
Chaleur Bay 169 O 6
Chalhuanca 180 B 3
Chalía 183 B 8
Chaling 132 F 5
Chalisgaon 134 C 3
Challapata 180 C 4
Challenger Deep 193 C 3
Challis 170 D 3
Chalmette 171 J 6
Chalna 135 F 3
Châlons-sur-Marne 115 D 2
Chalon-sur-Saône 115 D 2
Chaltry' 117 E 1
Cham 111 F 4
Chama 161 E 2
Chamais 160 B 5
Chaman 129 H 4
Chamaya 178 C 5
Chamba (India) 134 C 1
Chamba (Tanzania) 161 F 2
Chambal 134 C 2
Chamberlain River 142 D 2
Chambery 115 E 2
Chambeshi 161 E 2
Chambishi 160 D 2
Chamela 172 B 4
Chamela, Bahia 172 A 4
Chamiapatna 134 C 5
Chamical 182 C 5
Chamo, Lake 159 F 3
Chamoli 134 C 2
Chamonix-Mont-Blanc 115 E 2
Chamouchouane 169 N 6
Champa 134 D 3
Champagne 114–115 D 2
Champaign 171 J 3
Champanha 179 G 4–5
Champaquí, Cerro 182 D 5
Champdoré, Lac 169 O 4
Champlain, Lake 171 M 3
Champotón 172 D 4
Chamrajnagar 134 C 5
Chamutete 160 B 3
Chanc Changmar 134 C 1
Chan Chan 178 C 5
Chanchur 130 J 5
Chanco 183 B 6
Chandalar 166 H 2
Chandarnagar 134 E 3
Chandausi 134 C 2
Chandeleur Islands 171 J 6
Chanderi 134 C 3
Chandigarh 134 C 1
Chandler 169 P 6
Chandmanī 132 C 1
Chandon 131 P 1
Chandpur 135 F 3
Chandrakona 134 E 3
Chandrapur 134 C 4
Chanf 129 G 5
Changane 161 E 4
Changara 161 E 3
Changbai Shan 133 J 2
Changcheng (Chinese Wall) 132 E 3
Changchun 133 J 2
Changdao 133 H 3
Changde 132 F 5
Changfeng 133 G 4
Changhua 133 H 6
Changji 129 M 2
Changjiang 132 E 7
Chang Jiang 133 G 4
Changjin 133 J 2
Changli 133 G 3
Changling 133 H 2
Changlung 129 K 4
Changning 132 C 6
Changsha 132 F 5
Changshan 133 G 5
Changshu 133 H 4
Changshun 132 E 5
Changting 133 G 5
Changtu 133 H 2
Changwu 132 E 3
Changzhi 132 F 3
Changzhou 133 G 4
Channel Islands (U.S.A.) 170 C 5
Channel Islands (U.K.) 103 C 3
Channel Islands National Park 170 BC 5
Channel Port aux Basques 169 Q 6
Channing 170 F 4
Chantada 114 B 3
Chanthaburi 135 H 5
Chantilly 114 D 2
Chantrey Inlet 167 S 2
Chany 119 P 4
Chany, Ozero 119 P 5
Chao 178 C 5

220

Cha–Cho

Chao'an 132 G 6
Chao Hu 133 G 4
Chaor He 133 H 1
Chao Xian 133 G 4
Chaoyang 132 G 6
Chaoyang 133 GH 2
Chaoyangcun 131 M 5
Chaozhong 131 M 5
Chapa 131 N 4
Chapadão dos Gerais 181 G 4
Chapada das Mangabeiras 181 G 2–3
Chapada Diamantina 181 H 3
Chapada dos Veadeiros, Parque Nacional do 181 G 3
Chapadinha 181 H 1
Chapala 143 H 4
Chapala, Lago de 172 B 3
Chapanda 131 O 4
Chaparral 178 C 3
Chapa Tong 135 F 3
Chapayevo 118 K 5
Chapayevsk 118 J 5
Chapayev-Zheday 130 L 3
Chapchachi 118 J 6
Chapiquy 182 E 5
Chapleau 168 L 6
Chaplinka 117 E 1
Chaplygin 118 G 5
Chapman, Cape 167 U 2
Chapoma 118 G 2
Chapra 134 D 2
Chaqui 180 C 4
Char 152 C 4
Chara 130 L 4
Charaña 180 C 4
Charagua 180 D 4
Charcas 172 B 3
Charcot Island 185
Chard (Alberta, Can.) 167 P 4
Chard (U.K.) 102 C 2
Chardara 129 H 2
Chardzhou 129 G 3
Charente 114 C 2
Chari 157 H 3
Charikar 129 H 3
Charity 179 G 2
Charkabozh 129 J 4
Charkayuvom 118 K 2
Charleroi 110 D 4
Charles 169 N 3
Charlesbourg 171 M 2
Charles, Cape (Newfoundl., Can.) 169 Q 5
Charles City 171 H 3
Charles Louis, Pegunungan 137 J 4
Charles Peak 142 C 5
Charleston (S.C., U.S.A.) 171 L 5
Charleston (W.V., U.S.A.) 171 K 4
Charleville 143 H 4
Charleville-Mézières 115 D 2
Charlotte 171 K 4
Charlotte Amalie 173 K 4
Charlotte Harbor 171 K 6
Charlottenberg 113 F 4
Charlottesville 171 L 4
Charlottetown 169 P 6
Charlton 169 M 5
Charlton 143 G 6
Charmes 115 E 2
Charouïne 152 E 3
Charsadda 129 J 4
Charshanga 129 H 3
Charsk 119 Q 6
Charters Towers 143 H 3
Chartres 114 D 2
Chartreuse, Grande 115 E 2
Charyn 129 K 2
Charysh 119 Q 5
Charyshskoye 119 Q 5
Chascomus 182 E 6
Chasel'ka 119 Q 2
Chashniki 113 J 5
Chasico 183 C 7
Chasma Barrage 129 J 4
Chasnachorr, Gora 113 K 2
Chasŏng 133 J 2
Chasovnya Uchurskaya 131 O 4
Chât 128 F 3
Chatanga 130 K 5
Châteaubriant 114 C 2
Château-Chinon 114 D 2
Château-du-Loir 114 D 2
Châteaudun 114 D 2
Châteaulin 114 C 2
Châteauneuf-sur-Loire 114 D 2
Châteauroux 114 D 2
Château-Salins 115 E 2
Chateau-Thierry 114 D 2
Chateaux-Arnoux 115 E 3
Châtellerault 114 D 2

Chatham (New Zealand) 145 S 9
Chatham (U.K.) 103 E 2
Chatham (N.Br., Can.) 169 O 6
Chatham (Ont., Can.) 171 K 3
Chatham Islands 147 D 5
Chatham Strait 166 L 4
Chatkal 129 J 2
Chato, Cerro 183 B 7
Chatra 134 D 3
Chatrapur 134 E 4
Chattahoochee 171 K 5
Chattahoochee River 171 J 5
Chattanooga 171 J 4
Chatteris 103 E 1
Chatyrkel', Ozero 129 K 2
Chauchaiñeu, Sierra 183 C 7
Chauk 135 F 3
Chaullay 180 B 3
Chaumont 115 E 2
Chaunskaya Guba 131 V 2
Chauny 114 D 2
Chau Phu 135 J 5
Chaura 135 F 6
Chaves (Portugal) 114 B 3
Chaves (Brazil) 179 H 4
Cháviva 178 D 3
Chavuma 160 C 2
Chayatyn, Khrebet 131 P 5
Chaydakh 131 O 2
Chayek 129 J 2
Chayia 155 G 2
Chaykovskiy 118 K 4
Chayvo, Zaliv 131 Q 5
Chazhegovo 118 K 3
Chazón 182 D 5
Cheaha Mountain 171 J 5
Cheb 111 F 4
Chebarkul' 119 M 5
Cheboksary 118 J 4
Chechaouen 152 D 1
Checheng 133 H 6
Chech, Erg 152 E 3–4
Chech'on 133 J 3
Chechuysk 130 J 4
Cheduba 135 F 4
Cheffadene 157 G 2
Cheg 152 C 3
Chegdomyn 131 O 5
Chegga (Algeria) 153 G 2
Chegga (Mauritania) 152 D 2
Chegutu 160 DE 3
Chegytun 166 C 2
Chehel Päyeh 128 F 4
Cheikria 152 D 3
Cheil, Ra's el 159 H 3
Cheju 133 J 4
Cheju-do 133 J 4
Cheju-haehyŏp 133 J 4
Chekhov 131 Q 6
Chekunda 131 O 5
Chekurovka 131 N 1
Chekuyevo 118 G 3
Chelan, Lake 170 B 2
Chela, Serra da 160 A 3
Cheleken 128 E 3
Chelforó 183 C 6
Chélia, Djebel 153 G 1
Cheliff 153 F 1
Chelkar 128 F 1
Chellala 153 F 1
Chelmsford 103 E 2
Chelmuzhi 118 G 3
Chelosh 119 R 5
Cheltenham 103 C 2
Chelyabinsk 119 M 4
Chełm 111 H 4
Chemal 119 R 5
Chemba 161 E 3
Chembe 160 D 2
Chemdal'sk 130 H 4
Chemer 118 F 5
ChemilléCholet 114 C 2
Chełmno 111 G 4
Chemult 170 B 3
Chełmża 111 G 4
Chenab 129 J 4
Chenachane 152 E 3
Chen Barag Qi 130 L 6
Chencoyi 172 D 4
Cheng'an 132 F 3
Chengcheng 132 E 3
Chengde 133 G 2
Chengdu 132 D 4
Chenggong 132 D 5
Chengjiang 132 D 5
Chengkou 132 E 4
Chengmai 132 F 7
Cheng Xian 132 E 4
Chengzitan 133 H 3
Chenxi 132 F 5
Chenzhou 132 F 5
Cheom Ksan 135 H 5

Chepen 178 C 5
Chepes 182 C 5
Chepstow 102 C 2
Cher 114 D 2
Cherangani Mountains 158 F 4
Cherbaniani Reef 134 B 5
Cherbourg 114 C 2
Cherchell 153 F 1
Cherdyn' 118 L 3
Cherek 117 F 2
Cheremkhovo 130 H 5
Cherendey 130 L 3
Cherepanovo 119 Q 5
Chereponi 156 DE 3
Cherepovets 118 G 4
Chergui, Chott ech 152 EF 2
Chergui, Chott Ech 152 E 2
Chéri 157 G 3
Cherkashina 130 J 4
Cherkassy 118 F 6
Cherkessk 117 F 2
Cherlak 119 O 5
Cherlakskiy 119 O 5
Chernaya 118 L 2
Chernaya 130 E 1
Chernigov 118 F 5
Chernigovka 133 K 2
Chernigovka 117 E 1
Chernikovsk 118 L 5
Chernobyl 118 F 5
Chernogorsk 130 F 5
Chernolesskaya 131 P 3
Chernomorskoye 117 D 1
Chernoostrovskoye 119 R 3
Chernovtsy 116 C 1
Chernushka 118 L 4
Chernyakhovsk 112 H 5
Chernyanka 118 G 5
Chernyshevsk 130 L 5
Chernyshevskiy 130 K 3
Chernyye Brat'ya, Ostrova 131 S 6
Chernyye Zemli 117 G 1
Chernyy Ostrov 130 F 3
Chernyy Rynok 117 G 2
Cherokee 171 G 3
Cherokees, Lake O' The 171 H 4
Cherskiy Range 131 Q 2
Cherskogo, Khrebet 130 K 5
Cherskogo, Khrebet 131 P 2
Chertkovo 118 H 6
Chertsey 103 D 2
Cherven 113 J 5
Chervlennaya 117 G 2
Chervonograd 113 H 5
Chervonoye, Ozero 113 J 5
Chervonoznamenka 116 D 1
Chervyanka 130 G 4
Cherwell 110 C 4
Cherwell, River 103 D 2
Chesham 103 D 2
Cheshire 101 D 3
Chëshskaya Guba 118 J 2
Cheshunt 103 D 2
Chester 101 D 3
Chesterfield 103 D 1
Chesterfield Inlet 167 T 3
Chesterfield, Récifs et Iles 143 K 2
Chester-le-Spring 101 E 2
Chesuncook Lake 171 N 2
Chetlat 134 B 5
Chetumal 172 E 4
Chetumal, Bahia de 172 E 4
Chetvertyy Kuril'skiy Proliv 131 S 6,7
Cheugda 131 O 5
Cheulik 131 P 2
Cheviot (New Zealand) 145 Q 9
Cheviot Hills 101 D 2
Cheyenne 170 F 3
Cheyenne River 170 F 3
Cheyenne Wells 170 F 4
Cheyne Bay 142 B 5
Chhatarpur 134 C 3
Chhindwara 134 C 3
Chiai 133 H 6
Chiamboni, Ra's 159 G 5
Chiang Dao 135 G 4
Chiange 160 A 3
Chiang Kham 135 H 4
Chiang Khan 135 H 4
Chiang Mai 135 G 4
Chiang Rai 135 G 4
Chiang Saen 135 H 3
Chiapas 172 D 4
Chiatura 117 F 2

Chiavari 115 E 3
Chiba 133 M 3
Chibabava 161 E 4
Chibagalakh 131 P 2
Chibemba 160 A 3
Chibia 160 A 3
Chibit 119 R 5
Chibougamau 169 N 6
Chibougamau, Lac 169 N 6
Chibuto 161 E 4
Chibwe 160 D 2
Chicacole → Srikakulami 134 D 4
Chicago 171 J 3
Chicago Heights 171 J 3
Chicamba 157 G 7
Chicapa 160 C 1
Chic-Chocs, Mounts 169 O 6
Chicha 157 H 2
Chichagof 166 K 4
Chichaoua 152 D 2
Chicheng 133 G 2
Chichén-Itzá 172 E 3
Chichester 103 D 2
Chichester Range National Park 142 B 3
Chickasha 170 G 4
Chicken 166 J 3
Chiclana de la Frontera 114 B 4
Chiclayo 178 C 5
Chico 170 B 4
Chico (Chile) 183 C 7
Chico (Chile) 183 C 8
Chicoana 182 C 4
Chicomba 160 A 2
Chicomo 161 E 4
Chiconono 161 F 2
Chicoutimi 171 M 2
Chicualacuala 161 E 4
Chicuma 160 A 2
Chidambaram 134 C 5
Chidenguele 161 E 4
Chidley, Cape 169 P 3
Chiemsee 111 F 5
Chiengi 160 D 1
Chieri 115 E 2
Chieti 115 F 3
Chifeng 133 G 2
Chifre, Serra do 181 H 4
Chifunde 161 E 2
Chigamane 161 E 4
Chiganak 119 O 6
Chignik 166 F 4
Chigorodó 178 C 2
Chigubo 161 E 4
Chihli, Gulf of 133 G 3
Chihuahua 170 E 3
Chikan 130 J 5
Chikayevo 131 W 3
Chik Ballapur 134 C 5
Chikhacheva 131 R 1
Chikmagalur 134 C 5
Chikoy 130 J 5
Chikwawa 161 E 3
Chilabombwe 160 D 2
Chilas 129 J 3
Chilaw 134 C 6
Chilca, Cordillera de 180 B 4
Chilca, Punta de 178 C 6
Childers 143 J 4
Childress 170 F 5
Chile 182 B 5
Chile Basin 193 E 5
Chile Chico 183 B 8
Chilecito 182 C 4
Chilete 178 C 5
Chilgir 117 G 1
Chilik 129 K 2
Chilimanzi 161 E 3
Chilipa de Alvarez 172 C 4
Chilka Lake 134 E 4
Chillagoe 143 G 2
Chillán 183 B 6
Chillar 183 E 6
Chillicothe (MO, U.S.A.) 171 H 4
Chillicothe (OH, U.S.A.) 171 K 4
Chiloé, Isla de 183 B 7
Chiloquin 170 B 3
Chilpancingo 172 C 4
Chiltern Hills 103 D 2
Chiluage 143 G 2
Chiluba 160 D 1
Chilumba 161 E 2
Chilumbo 161 E 2
Chilwa, Lake 161 F 3
Chimala 158 E 6
Chimalavera 160 A 2
Chimaltenango 172 D 5
Chimán 178 C 2
Chimanimani 161 E 3
Chimbay 128 F 2
Chimborazo 178 C 4
Chimbote 178 C 5

Chimbwingombi 161 E 2
Chimeyevo 119 N 4
Chimishliya 116 C 1
Chimkent 129 H 2
Chimoio 161 E 3
Chimoio, Planalto de 161 E 3
Chimtarga 129 H 3
Chin 135 F 3
China 132–133
Chinandega 172 E 5
Chincha Alta 180 A 3
Chinchilla 143 J 4
Chinchilla de Monte-Aragon 114 C 4
Chinchorro, Banco 172 E 4
Chindagatuy 119 R 6
Chinde 161 F 3
Chin-do 133 J 4
Chindu 132 C 4
Chindwin 135 F 3
Chinese Wall 132 E 3
Chingirlau 118 K 5
Chingiz-Tau, Khrebet 119 P 6
Chingola 160 D 2
Chinguetti 152 C 4
Chinguil 157 H 3
Chinhae 133 J 3
Chínipas 170 E 6
Chinju 133 J 3
Chinko 158 C 3
Chinnur 134 C 4
Chinon 114 D 3
Chinsali 161 E 2
Chintalnar 134 D 4
Chioco 161 E 3
Chipata 161 E 2
Chipepo 160 D 3
Chiperone 161 F 3
Chipili 160 D 2
Chipindo 160 B 2
Chipinge 160 E 4
Chipogolo 159 F 6
Chipoia 160 B 2
Chippenham 103 C 2
Chippewa Falls 171 H 3
Chippewa, Lake 171 H 2
Chipping Norton 103 D 2
Chipping Ongar 103 E 2
Chipping Sodbury 102 C 2
Chipurupalle 134 D 4
Chiquián 179 C 5
Chiquibamba 180 B 4
Chiquinquirá 178 D 2
Chiquitos, Llanos de 180 D 4
Chirala 134 D 4
Chirchik 129 H 2
Chiredzi 160 E 4
Chirfa 157 G 1
Chiriguaná 178 D 2
Chiriguanos 180 D 5
Chirikof 166 F 4
Chirinda 131 H 3
Chirinkotan, Ostrov 131 S 6
Chiriquí 178 B 2
Chiriquí, Golfo de 178 B 2
Chiriquí → Volcán Barú 178 B 2
Chiromo 161 F 3
Chirue, Lago 161 F 3
Chirundu 160 D 3
Chisamba 160 D 2
Chishmy 118 L 5
Chishui 132 E 5
Chishui He 132 E 5
Chisimaio → Kismāyu 159 G 5
Chiskovo 130 G 3
Chistoozernoye 119 P 5
Chistopol 118 K 4
Chita 130 K 5
Chitado 160 A 3
Chitato 160 C 1
Chitembo 160 B 2
Chitina 166 J 3
Chitipa 161 E 1
Chitokoloki 160 C 2
Chitradurga 134 C 5
Chitral 129 J 3
Chitré 178 B 2
Chittagong 135 F 3
Chittaurgarh 134 B 3
Chittoor 134 C 5
Chiumbe 160 C 1
Chiume 160 C 3
Chiure 161 F 2
Chiure Novo 161 F 2
Chiuta, Lago 161 F 2
Chivasso 115 E 2
Chivay 180 B 4
Chivilcoy 182 D 5
Chizha 118 H 2
Chkalovo 119 O 5
Choba 159 F 4
Chobe National Park 160 C 3

Cho–Col

Chochis, Cerro 180 E 4
Chocontá 178 D 2
Chocope 178 C 5
Chodzież 111 G 4
Choele Choel 183 C 6
Choggia 115 F 2
Choique 183 D 6
Choiseul 145 G 2
Choix 170 E 6
Chojna 111 F 4
Chojnice 111 G 4
Choke Mountains 159 F 2
Choknar 129 J 2
Chokurdakh 131 R 1
Chókwè 161 E 4
Chola Shan 132 C 4
Cholila 183 B 7
Choluteca 172 E 5
Choma 160 D 3
Chomo Yummo 134 E 2
Chomutov 111 F 4
Chona 130 J 3
Ch'ŏnan 133 J 3
Chon Buri 135 H 5
Chone 178 B 4
Ch'ŏngjin 133 J 2
Chŏngju 133 J 3
Ch'ŏngju 133 J 3
Chong Kal 135 H 5
Chongkü 132 C 4
Chongming Dao 133 H 4
Chongoroi 160 A 2
Chongqing 132 E 5
Chongup 133 J 3
Chongxin 132 E 3
Chongzuo 132 E 6
Chŏnju 133 J 3
Chonos, Archipiélago de los 183 B 7–5
Chon Thanh 135 J 5
Chop 116 B 1
Cho Ra 135 J 3
Chorito, Sierra del 114 C 4
Chorley 101 D 3
Chorolque 180 C 5
Choros, Cabo 182 B 4
Chorregon 143 G 3
Chorrillos 180 A 3
Chorrochó 181 J 2
Ch'örwön 133 J 3
Chorzów 111 G 4
Chōshi 133 M 3
Chosica 180 A 3
Chos Malal 183 B 6
Choszczno 111 G 4
Chota 178 C 5
Chotanagpur 134 D 3
Chota Udaipur 134 B 3
Chott Ech Chergui 152 EF 2
Chott el Hodna 153 F 1
Chott el Rharsa 153 G 2
Chott Melrhir 153 G 2
Chott Merouane 153 G 2
Choum 152 C 4
Choybalsan 130 K 6
Christchurch (New Zealand) 146 C 5
Christchurch (U.K.) 103 D 2
Christiana 160 D 5
Christian Sound 166 L 4
Christie Bay 167 P 3
Christie, Mount 142 B 4
Christmas (Kiribati) 147 E 2
Christmas Island 136 C 6
Christmas Island → Kiritimati 162 E 2
Chrzanow 111 G 4
Chtakal'skiy Khrebet 129 J 2
Chu 129 J 2
Chuña 182 D 5
Chubut 183 C 7
Chuchukan 130 L 3
Chucuito 180 BC 4
Chucul 182 D 5
Chudinovo 119 M 5
Chudleigh Park 143 G 2
Chudovo 113 K 4
Chudskoye Ozero 113 J 4
Chugach Mountains 166 H 3
Chuginadak 166 C 5
Chuhuichupa 170 E 6
Chu-Iliyskiye Gory 129 J 2
Chukai 136 B 3
Chukar 130 L 3
Chukchagirskoye, Ozero 131 P 5
Chukchi Sea 166 CD 2
Chuken 131 P 6
Chukhloma 118 H 4
Chukoch'ye 131 T 2
Chukotskiy, Mys 166 C 3
Chukotskiy Poluostrov 166 BC 2
Chukotskiy Range 184
Chukuchany 131 R 2

Chulak-Kurgan 129 H 2
Chulakovka 117 D 1
Chulasa 118 J 3
Chula Vista 170 C 5
Chulitna 166 H 3
Chulkovo 119 R 3
Chul'man 131 M 4
Chulucanas 178 BC 5
Chulym 119 Q 4
Chulym 130 F 4
Chum 119 M 2
Chumakovo 119 P 4
Chumbicha 182 C 4
Chumek 119 R 6
Chumikan 131 P 5
Chum Phae 135 H 4
Chumphon 135 G 5
Chumysh 119 Q 5
Chuna 130 G 4
Ch'unch'ŏn 133 J 3
Chundzha 129 K 2
Chunga 160 D 2
Ch'ungju 133 J 3
Chungking → Chongqing 132 E 5
Ch'ungmu 133 J 4
Chunhua 133 K 2
Chunskiy 130 G 4
Chunya 130 G 3
Chunya (Tanzania) 158 E 6
Chuor Phnum Kravanh 135 H 5
Chupa 112 K 2
Chuquicamata 180 C 5
Chuquillanqui 178 C 5
Chur 115 E 2
Churapcha 131 O 3
Churchill (Lab., Can.) 169 P 5
Churchill (Man., Can.) 167 T 4
Churchill (Sask., Can.) 167 R 4
Churchill, Cape 167 T 4
Churchill Falls 169 P 5
Churchill Lake 167 Q 4
Churchill Mountains 185
Churchill Peak 167 N 4
Chureg-Tag, Gora 130 F 5
Churia Range 134 E 2
Churkino 118 H 3
Churu 134 C 2
Churuguara 178 E 1
Churún Merú 179 F 2
Chushal 129 K 4
Chushkakyl' 128 F 1
Chusovaya 119 L 4
Chusovoy 119 L 4
Chusovskoy 118 L 3
Chute-des-Passes 169 N 6
Chutes de Katende (Katende Falls) 158 C 6
Chutes de la Lufira 158 D 6
Chutes de Livingstone (Livingstone Falls) 158 A 6
Chutes Ngaliema (Stanley Falls) 158 D 4
Chutes Tembo (Tembo Falls) 158 B 6
Chuval 119 L 3
Chuvanskiye Gory 131 V 3
Chu Xian 133 G 4
Chuxiong 132 D 5
Chuy 182 F 5
Chuya 130 K 4
Chuyengo 130 H 3
Chybydat 130 M 3
Chyul'be 131 O 4
Chyulu Range 159 F 5
Ciamis 136 C 5
Cianjur 136 C 5
Cianorte 181 F 5
Cibuta, Cerro 170 D 5
Çiçekdağı 117 D 3
Cícero Dantas 181 J 3
Ćićevac 116 B 2
Cide 117 D 2
Ciechanów 111 H 4
Ciego de Ávila 173 G 3
Ciénaga 178 D 1
Cienfuegos 173 F 3
Çifteler 117 D 3
Cifuentes 114 C 3
Cihanbeyli 117 D 3
Cihanbeyli Platosu 117 D 3
Cihara 136 C 5
Cihuatlán 172 B 4
Cijara, Embalse de 114 C 4
Cijulang 136 C 5
Cilacap 136 C 5
Çıldır 117 F 2
Çıldır Gölü 117 F 2
Cilo Dağı 117 F 3
Cimahi 136 C 5
Cimarron River 170 G 4
Çimen Dağı 117 E 3

Cimone 115 F 3
Cîmpia Bărăganului 116 C 2
Cîmpia Burnazului 116 C 2
Cîmpia Turzii 116 B 1
Cîmpina 116 C 1
Cîmpulung Moldovenesc 116 C 1
Çinar 117 F 3
Cina, Tanjung 136 B 5
Cinca 114 D 3
Cincinatti 171 K 4
Cinco Saltos 183 C 6
Çine 116 C 3
Cintalapa de Figueroa 172 D 4
Cinto, Monte 115 E 3
Cintra, Golfo de 152 B 4
Cipolletti 183 C 6
Circeo, Capo 115 F 3
Circle (AK, U.S.A.) 166 J 2
Circle (MT, U.S.A.) 167 Q 6
Cirebon 136 C 5
Cirencester 110 C 4
Cirencester 103 D 2
Ciriè 115 E 2
Ciro Marina 115 G 4
Cirpan 116 C 2
Cirque Mountain 169 P 4
Cisco 170 G 5
Ciskei 160 D 6
Cisne, Islas del 172 F 4
Cisnéros (Colombia) 178 D 2
Citac, Nevado 180 A 3
Citlaltépetl, Volcán 172 C 4
Citrusdal 160 B 6
Città del Vaticano 115 F 3
Città di Castello 115 F 3
Ciudad Acuña 172 B 2
Ciudad Altamirano 172 B 4
Ciudad Bolívar 179 F 2
Ciudad Bolivia 178 D 2
Ciudad Camargo 170 E 6
Ciudad Cuauhtémoc 172 D 4
Ciudad de Dolores Hidalgo 172 B 3
Ciudad del Carmen 172 D 4
Ciudad Delicias 170 E 6
Ciudad del Maíz 172 C 3
Ciudad de México 172 C 4
Ciudad de Rio Grande 172 B 3
Ciudad Guayana → Santo Tomé 179 F 2
Ciudad Guzmán 172 B 4
Ciudad Hidalgo 172 D 5
Ciudad Hidalgo 172 B 4
Ciudad Juárez 170 E 5
Ciudad Lerdo 172 B 2
Ciudad Madero 172 C 3
Ciudad Mante 172 C 3
Ciudad Mendoza 172 C 4
Ciudad Obregón 170 E 6
Ciudad Ojeda 178 D 1
Ciudad Piar 179 F 2
Ciudad Real 114 C 4
Ciudad Río Bravo 172 C 2
Ciudad-Rodrigo 114 B 3
Ciudad Valles 172 C 3
Ciudad Victoria 172 C 3
Civa Burnu 117 E 2
Civita Castellana 115 F 3
Civitanova Marche 115 F 3
Civitavecchia 115 F 3
Çivril 116 C 3
Cizre 117 F 3
Clacton-on-Sea 103 E 2
Claire Coast 185
Claire Engle Lake 170 B 3
Claire, Lake 167 P 4
Clamey 114 D 2
Clanwilliam 160 B 6
Clara 100 B 3
Claraz 183 E 6
Clare 143 F 5
Claremont 171 M 3
Clarence Strait (Alaska) 166 L 4
Clarence Strait (Australia) 142 E
Clarence Town 173 H 3
Clarendon 170 F 5
Clarenville 169 R 6
Claresholm 167 P 5
Clarinda 171 H 3
Clarion 169 R 6
Clarion Fracture Zone 193 D 3
Clarke 144 L 9
Clarke Range 143 H 3
Clark Fork 170 C 2
Clark Hill Lake 171 K 5
Clark, Lake 166 H 2
Clark River 143 H 2
Clarksburg 171 K 4
Clarksdale 171 H 5
Clarkston 170 C 2
Clarksville 171 J 4

Claveria 137 J 1
Clay Belt 168 L 5
Clay Cross 101 E 3
Claydon 103 E 1
Clay Head 100 C 2
Clearfield 170 D 3
Clear Lake 170 B 4
Clear Lake Reservoir 170 B 3
Clearwater 171 K 6
Clearwater Mountains 170 C 2
Cleethorpes 101 E 3
Clere, Mount 142 B 4
Clermont 143 H 3
Clermont-Ferrand 114 D 2
Clevedon 102 C 2
Cleveland (MS, U.S.A.) 171 H 5
Cleveland (OH, U.S.A.) 171 K 3
Cleveland (U.K.) 101 E 2
Cleveland Hills 101 E 2
Cleveland, Mount 170 D 2
Clew Bay 110 B 4
Clifton 171 J 3
Clifton Hills 143 F 4
Clinton (Br.Col., Can.) 167 N 5
Clinton (IO, U.S.A.) 171 H 3
Clinton (OK, U.S.A.) 170 G 4
Clinton-Colden Lake 167 Q 3
Clipperton Fracture Zone 193 D 3
Clipperton Island 147 H 2
Clitheroe 101 E 2
Cloates, Point 142 A 3
Clodomira 182 D 4
Cloncurry 143 F 3
Cloncurry River 143 G 3
Clones 100 B 2
Clonmany 100 B 2
Clonmel 110 B 4
Cloppenburg 111 E 4
Cloquet 171 H 2
Clorinda 182 E 4
Cloud Peak 170 E 3
Clough 100 C 2
Clovis 170 F 5
Cluj-Napoca 116 B 1
Cluny 115 D 2
Cluses 115 E 2
Clutha River 144 P 10
Clwyd 101 D 3
Clyde (Can.) 169 O 1
Clydebank 100 C 2
Clyde, Firth of 110 C 3
Clyde, River 100 D 2
Cnossus 116 C 3
Côa 114 B 3
Coahuila 172 B 2
Coalcoman, Sierra de 172 B 4
Coalinga 170 B 4
Coal River 167 M 4
Coalville 103 D 1
Coan, Cerro 178 C 5
Coaraci 181 J 3
Coari 179 F 4
Coast Mountains 167 M 5
Coast of Labrador 169 P 4
Coast Range (U.S.A.) 170 B 3–4
Coast Range (Austr.) 143 J 4
Coatbridge 100 C 2
Coatepec 172 C 4
Coats Island 167 V 3
Coats land 185
Coatzacoalcos 172 D 4
Coatzacoalcos, Bahia 172 D 4
Coba 172 E 3
Cobán 172 D 4
Cobar 143 H 5
Cobh 110 B 4
Cobija 180 C 3
Cobourg Peninsula 142 E 1
Cobquecura 183 B 6
Cobue 161 EF 2
Coburg 111 F 4
Cocachacra 180 B 4
Cocamá 180 B 3
Cocanada → Kakinadai 134 D 4
Cochabamba 180 C 4
Cochin 134 C 6
Cochinoca 180 C 5
Cochrane (Chile) 183 B 8
Cochrane (Man., Can.) 167 R 4
Cochrane (Ont., Can.) 169 L 6
Cockburn 143 G 5
Cockenzie and Port Seton 99 C 4
Cockermouth 101 D 2
Cocklebiddy 142 D 5
Cocoa 171 K 6
Cocobeach 157 F 5
Coco Channel 135 F 5
Coco Island (Costa Rica) 174 B 2
Coco Islands (India) 135 F 5
Coco o Segovia, Rio 172 F 5
Cocuy, Sierra Nevada de 178 D 2
Cocula 172 B 3

Codajás 179 F 4
Cod, Cape 171 N 3
Codigoro 115 F 3
Codlea 116 C 1
Codó 181 H 1
Cody 170 D 3
Coelemu 183 B 6
Coen 143 G 1
Coeroenie 179 G 3
Coesfeld 111 E 4
Coetivy 159 K 6
Coeur d'Alene 170 C 2
Coffeyville 171 G 4
Coffin Bay 143 F 5
Coff's Harbour 143 J 5
Cofrentes 114 C 4
Cognac 114 C 2
Cogne 115 E 2
Coiba, Ilha de 178 B 2
Coig 183 B 9
Coihaique 183 B 8
Coihaique Alto 183 B 8
Coimbatore 134 C 5
Coimbra 114 B 3
Coin 114 C 4
Coipasa, Salar de 180 C 4
Cojimies 178 B 3
Cojudo Blanco, Cerro 183 C 8
Cojutepeque 172 E 5
Colac 143 G 6
Colalao del Valle 182 C 4
Colan-Conhué 183 C 7
Colatina 181 H 4
Colchester 103 E 2
Cold Bay 166 E 4
Col de Larche 115 E 3
Col de Perthus 114 D 3
Col de Tenda 115 E 3
Cold Lake 167 P 5
Coldstream 99 C 4
Coleman 170 G 5
Coleman River 143 G 2
Coleraine 100 B 2
Coles Bay 144 L 9
Colesberg 160 D 5
Coleshill 103 D 1
Colfax 170 C 2
Colhué Huapí, Lago 183 C 8
Colima 172 B 4
Colinas (Goiás, Brazil) 181 G 3
Colinas (Maranhão, Brazil) 181 H 2
Coll 99 A 3
Collahuasi 180 C 5
College 166 H 3
College Station 171 G 5
Collie 142 B 5
Collier Bay 142 C 2
Collier Ranges National Park 142 B 3
Colli Euganei 115 F 2
Collines de la Puisaye 114 D 2
Collines de l'Armagnac 114 D 3
Collines de l'Artois 114 D 1
Collines du Perche 114 D 2
Collines du Sancerrois 114 D 2
Collingwood (New Zealand) 145 Q 9
Collingwood (Canada) 171 K 3
Collins 167 R 1
Collinsville 143 H 3
Collipulli 183 B 6
Collo 115 E 4
Collon 100 B 3
Colmar 115 E 2
Colmena 182 D 4
Colmenar Viejo 114 C 3
Colne 101 D 3
Cologne → Köln 111 E 4
Cololo, Nevado 180 C 4
Colombia 178 D 3
Colombia (Brazil) 181 G 5
Colombo 134 C 6
Colon (Argentina) 182 D 5
Colón (Cuba) 173 F 3
Colón (Arg.) 182 E 5
Colón (Pan.) 178 C 2
Colona 142 E 5
Colón, Archipiélago de 178 B 6
Colón Cristóbal, Pico 178 D 1
Colonet 170 C 5
Colonia Catriel 183 C 6
Colonia Dalmacia 182 E 4
Colonia del Sac 182 E 5
Colonia Josefa 183 C 6
Colonia Las Heras 183 C 8
Colonia Morelos 170 E 5
Colonne, Capo 115 G 4
Colonsay 99 A 3
Colorado (U.S.A.) 170 EF 4
Colorado (Arg.) 183 CD 3
Colorado, Cerro 170 C 5
Colorado, Pico 182 C 4

222

Col–Cua

Colorado Plateau 170 D 4
Colorado, Rio 170 C 5
Colorado River (AZ, U.S.A.) 170 D 5
Colorado River (TX, U.S.A.) 171 G 6
Colorado Springs 170 F 4
Colotlán 172 B 3
Colquechaca 180 C 4
Columbia (Br.Col., Can.) 167 O 5
Columbia (MS, U.S.A.) 171 H 4
Columbia (S.C., U.S.A.) 171 K 5
Columbia (TN, U.S.A.) 171 J 4
Columbia (WA, U.S.A.) 171 BC 2
Columbia Basin 170 C 2
Columbia Falls 170 D 2
Columbia, Mount 167 O 5
Columbia Mountains 167 N 5
Columbia Plateau 170 C 3
Columbine, Cape 160 B 6
Columbria 143 H 3
Columbus (GA, U.S.A.) 171 K 5
Columbus (IN, U.S.A.) 171 J 4
Columbus (MS, U.S.A.) 171 J 5
Columbus (NE, U.S.A.) 170 G 3
Columbus (OH, U.S.A.) 171 K 4
Columbus (TX, U.S.A.) 171 G 6
Colville 166 G 2
Colville, Cape 167 T 2
Colville Channel 145 R 8
Colville Lake 167 M 2
Colwyn Bay 102 C 1
Comacchio 115 F 3
Comai 135 F 2
Comalcalco 172 D 4
Comandante Luis 183 C 8
Comandante Salas 182 C 5
Comănești 116 C 1
Comayagua 172 E 5
Combarbalá 182 B 5
Combermere Bay 135 F 4
Comeragh Mountains 110 B 4
Comet 143 H 3
Comet River 143 H 3
Comiguin 137 HJ 1
Comilla 135 F 3
Comitán 172 D 4
Commentry 114 D 2
Commercy 115 E 2
Committee Bay 167 U 2
Como 115 E 2
Como, Lago di 115 E 2
Comondú 170 D 6
Comorin, Cape 134 C 6
Comoro Islands 161 G 2
Compiègne 114 D 2
Cona 135 F 2
Conakry 156 B 4
Cona Niyeo 183 C 7
Concarneau 114 C 2
Conceição, Cachoeira da 179 F 5
Conceição da Barra 181 J 4
Conceição do Araguaia 179 J 5
Concepción (Arg.) 182 C 4
Concepción (Bolivia) 180 D 4
Concepción (Bolivia) 180 C 4
Concepción (Chile) 183 B 6
Concepción (Paraguay) 180 E 5
Concepción, Bahía 170 D 6
Concepción del Oro 172 B 3
Concepción del Uruguay 182 E 5
Conception Bay (Canada) 169 R 6
Conception Bay (Namibia) 160 A 4
Conception, Point 170 B 5
Conchi 180 C 5
Conchos, Rio 170 E 6
Concord 171 M 3
Concórdia (Amazonas, Brazil) 178 E 4
Concordia (Argentina) 182 E 5
Concordia (KS, U.S.A.) 170 G 4
Concordia (Mex.) 172 A 3
Concordia (Peru) 178 C 4
Conda 160 A 2
Condamine 143 J 4
Conde 181 J 3
Condobolin 143 H 5
Condom 114 D 3
Condon 170 B 2
Condor, Cordillera del 178 C 4
Condoto 178 C 4
Conecuh River 171 J 5
Conegliano 115 F 2
Conejera 114 C 4
Conejo 170 D 7
Conero 115 F 3
Conghua 132 F 6
Congleton 103 C 1
Congo 156 CD 2
Cónico, Cerro 183 B 7
Coningsby 101 E 3

Connah's Quay 102 C 1
Connaught 110 B 4
Connecticut 171 M 3
Connellsville 171 L 3
Connemara, Mountains of 110 B 4
Conn Lake 169 N 1
Conn, Lough 110 B 4
Connor, Mount 142 D 1
Conrad 170 D 2
Conrad Rise 192 B 5
Conroe 171 G 5
Conselheiro Lafaiete 181 H 5
Consett 101 E 2
Con Son 135 J 6
Constância dos Baetas 179 F 5
Constanţa 116 C 2
Constantina 114 B 4
Constantine 153 G 1
Constantine, Cape 166 F 4
Constitución 183 B 6
Contão 179 F 3
Contai 134 E 3
Contamana 178 D 5
Cóntas 181 H 3
Contreras, Embalse de 114 C 4
Contreras, Puerto de 114 C 4
Contwoyto Lake 167 Q 2
Convención 178 D 2
Con Vidal 183 E 6
Conway (AR, U.S.A.) 171 H 4
Conway (S.C., U.S.A.) 171 L 5
Conway Reef → Ceva-i-Ra 146 C 4
Conwy 102 C 1
Coober Pedy 142 E 4
Cooch Bihar 134 E 2
Cookes Peak 170 E 5
Cookeville 171 J 4
Cook Inlet 166 G 3
Cook Islands 147 E 4
Cook, Mount 145 Q 9
Cook Mountains 185
Cookstown 100 B 2
Cook Strait 145 Q 9
Cooktown 143 H 2
Coolgardie 142 C 5
Coolibah 142 E 2
Coolidge 170 D 5
Coolon, Mount 143 H 3
Cooma 143 H 6
Coombe Martin 102 B 2
Coonabarabran 143 H 5
Coonamble 143 H 5
Coondapoor 134 B 5
Coongoola 143 H 4
Coonoor 134 C 5
Coon Rapids 171 H 2
Cooper Creek 143 G 4
Coorow 142 B 4
Cooroy 143 J 4
Coosa River 171 J 5
Coos Bay 170 B 3
Cootamundra 143 H 5
Cootehill 100 B 2
Copahue 183 B 6
Copan 172 E 5
Copana 178 E 4
Copenhagen 113 F 4
Copiapó 182 B 4
Čopköy 116 C 2
Copper 166 J 3
Copperbelt 160 D 2
Copper Center 166 H 3
Copper Cliff 171 K 2
Copper Harbor 171 J 2
Coppermine 167 O 2
Copper Queen 160 D 3
Coqên 134 E 1
Coquet, River 101 E 2
Coquimbo 182 B 4
Corabia 116 B 2
Coral Harbour 167 V 3
Coral Sea 145 H 4
Coral Sea Islands Territory 143 H 1
Corantijn 179 G 3
Corato 115 G 3
Corbridge 101 D 2
Corby 103 D 1
Corcaigh 110 B 4
Corcovado, Golfo 183 B 7
Corcovado, Volcán 183 B 7
Cordele 171 K 5
Cordilheiras, Serra das 179 J 5
Cordillera Azul 178 C 5
Cordillera Blanca 178 C 5
Cordillera Cantábrica 114 BC 3
Cordillera Central (Colombia) 178 C 3
Cordillera Central (Dom. Rep.) 173 H 4

Cordillera Central (Phil.) 137 J 1
Cordillera de Carabaya 180 B 3
Cordillera de Chichas 180 C 4–5
Cordillera de Chilca 180 B 4
Cordillera de Huanzo 180 B 3
Cordillera de la Costa 178 E 2
Cordillera del Condor 178 C 4
Cordillera de Lípez 180 C 5
Cordillera de Mérida 178 D 2
Cordillera Domeyko 180 C 5
Cordillera Isabella 172 E 5
Cordillera Negra 178 C 5
Cordillera Occidental 178 C 2–3
Cordillera Oriental 178 C 3
Cordillera Real (Bolivia) 180 C 4
Cordillera Real (Ecuador) 178 C 4
Cordillera Uilcabamba 180 B 3
Cordillera Volcanica 172 B 4
Córdoba (Mexico) 172 C 4
Córdoba (Spain) 114 C 4
Córdoba (Arg.) 182 D 5
Córdoba, Sierra de 182 D 5
Córdova (Peru) 180 A 3
Cordova (AK, U.S.A.) 166 H 3
Corfu 116 A 3
Corguinno 181 E 4
Coria 114 B 4
Corigliano Calabro 115 G 4
Corinda 143 F 2
Coringa Islands 143 J 2
Corinth (Greece) 116 B 3
Corinth (U.S.A.) 171 J 5
Corinto 181 H 4
Corisco, Baie de 157 F 5
Corisco Island 157 F 5
Cork (Rep. of Ireland) 110 B 4
Cork (Australia) 143 G 3
Corleone 115 F 4
Cornélio Procópio 181 F 5
Cornelius Grinnel Bay 169 P 3
Corner Brook 169 Q 6
Corno Grande 115 F 3
Cornwall (U.K.) 102 B 2
Cornwall (Ont., Can.) 171 M 2
Coro 178 E 1
Coroatá 181 H 1
Corocoro 180 C 4
Coroico 180 C 4
Coromandel Coast 134 D 5
Coromandel Peninsula 145 R 8
Coronado, Bahía de 172 F 6
Coronation 167 P 5
Coronation Gulf 167 P 2
Corondo 182 D 5
Coronel 183 B 6
Coronel Dorrego 183 D 6
Coronel Fabriciano 181 H 4
Coronel Falcón 183 D 6
Coronel Pringles 183 D 6
Coronel Suárez 183 D 6
Corongo 178 C 5
Coropuna, Nevado 180 B 4
Corozal 178 C 2
Corozal 172 E 4
Corpus 180 E 5
Corpus Christi 171 G 6
Corque 180 C 4
Corquin 172 E 5
Corral 183 B 6
Corrales 182 E 5
Corrente (Bahía, Brazil) 181 H 3
Corrente (Piauí, Brazil) 181 G 3
Correntes 181 F 4
Correntes, Cabo das 161 F 4
Correntina 181 GH 3
Corrib, Lough 110 B 4
Corrientes (Argentina) 182 E 4
Corrientes (Peru) 178 C 4
Corrientes, Cabo 172 A 3
Corrientes, Cabo (Argentina) 183 E 6
Corrientes, Cabo (Colombia) 178 C 2
Corrigin 142 B 5
Corryong 143 H 6
Corse 115 E 3
Corse, Cap 115 E 3
Corsica 115 E 3
Corsica, Canale di 115 E 3
Corsicana 171 G 5
Corte 115 E 3
Corte Alto Fresia 183 B 7
Cortegana 114 B 4
Cortez 114 C 3
Cortez 170 E 4
Cortona 115 F 3
Corubal 156 B 3
Coruche 114 B 4
Çoruh 117 F 2
Çoruh Dağları 117 F 2
Çorum 117 D 2

Corumbá (Mato Grosso du Sul, Brazil) 180 E 4
Corumbá de Goiás 181 G 4
Corumba de Goiás (Goiàs, Brazil) 181 G 4
Corunna 114 B 3
Coruripe 181 J 3
Corvallis 170 B 3
Corvo 152 A 1
Corwen 102 C 1
Cosamaloapan 172 C 4
Cosenza 115 G 4
Coshocton 171 K 3
Cosmoledo Group 159 H 6
Cosne-sur-Loire 114 D 2
Costa Blanca 114 CD 4
Costa Brava 114 D 3
Costa de la Luz 114 B 4
Costa del Azahar 114 D 3–4
Costa del Sol 114 C 4
Costa de Mosquitos 172 F 5
Costa Dorada 114 D 3
Costa Rica 172 F 6
Costa Verde 114 B 3
Cotabato 137 F 2
Cotagaita 180 C 5
Cotahuasi 180 B 4
Coteau du Missouri 170 F 2
Côte d'Argent 114 C 3
Côte d'Azur 115 E 3
Côte de l'Ile de France 114 D 2
Côte d'Ivoire 156 CD 4
Côte d'Or 115 D 2
Cotentin 114 C 2
Cotherstone 143 H 3
Cotonou 156 E 4
Cotopaxi 178 C 4
Cotswold Hills 103 C 2
Cottbus 111 F 1
Cottica 179 H 3
Cottingham 101 E 3
Cotulla 170 G 6
Coubre, Pointe de la 114 C 2
Couhé 114 D 2
Čoukkarašša 112 H 2
Coulommiers 114 D 2
Council 166 E 3
Council Bluffs 171 G 3
Coupar Angus 99 C 3
Courantyne 179 G 3
Courland 113 H 4
Courmayeur 115 E 2
Courtennai 167 M 6
Coutances 114 C 2
Coutras 114 C 2
Couvin 110 D 4
Coventry 103 D 1
Covilhã 114 B 3
Covington (GA, U.S.A.) 171 K 5
Covington (KY, U.S.A.) 171 K 4
Covington (VA, U.S.A.) 171 L 4
Cowal 99 B 3
Cowal, Lake 143 H 5
Cowan, Lake 142 C 5
Cowargarze 132 C 4
Cowbridge 102 C 2
Cowdenbeath 99 C 3
Cowell 143 F 5
Cowes 103 D 2
Cowra 143 H 5
Cox's Bazar 135 F 3
Coy Aike 183 C 9
Coyame 170 E 6
Coyle → Coig 183 B 9
Coyotitan 172 A 3
Cracow 143 J 4
Cradock 160 D 6
Craig (AK, U.S.A.) 166 L 4
Craig (CO, U.S.A.) 170 E 3
Craigavon 100 B 2
Craignure 99 B 3
Craigs Range 143 J 4
Crail 99 C 3
Craiova 116 B 2
Cramlington 101 E 2
Crampel 152 E 2
Crampel → Kaga Bandoro 158 B 3
Cranbrook (Australia) 142 B 5
Cranbrook (Canada) 167 O 6
Cranleigh 103 D 2
Craolândia 179 J 5
Crary Mountains 185
Cratère du Nouveau-Québec 169 N 3
Cratéus 181 H 2
Crato (Amazonas, Brazil) 179 F 5
Crato (Ceará, Brazil) 181 J 2
Cravo Norte 178 D 2
Crawford 170 F 3
Crawford Point 137 E 1

Crawfordsville 171 J 3
Crawley 103 D 2
Crawley (U.K) 110 C 4
Crazy Peak 170 D 2
Crediton 102 C 2
Cree 167 Q 5
Creel 170 E 6
Cree Lake 167 Q 4
Creil 114 D 2
Crema 115 E 2
Cremona 115 F 2
Crepori 179 G 5
Cres 115 F 3
Crescent City 170 B 3
Crest 115 E 3
Creston 171 H 3
Crestview 171 J 5
Crêt de la Neige 115 E 2
Crete 116 BC 3
Cretin, Cape 144 E 3
Creus, Cabo de 114 D 3
Creuse 114 D 2
Crevillente 114 C 4
Crewe 101 D 3
Crewkerne 102 C 2
Crianlarich 99 B 3
Criccieth 102 B 1
Cricklade 103 D 2
Crieff 99 C 3
Crinan Canal 99 B 3
Cristalândia 181 G 3
Cristallo 115 F 2
Cristal, Monts de 157 G 5
Cristino Castro 181 H 2
Crişu Negru 116 B 1
Crişur Repede 116 B 1
Crkvena Planina 116 B 2
Crna Gora 116 B 2
Crna Reka 116 B 2
Crni Drim 116 B 2
Crni Vrh (Yugoslavia) 115 G 2
Crni Vrh (Yugoslavia) 115 G 3
Croatia 115 G 2
Crockett 171 G 5
Croissette, Cap 115 E 3
Croker, Cape 142 E 1
Croker Island 142 E 1
Cromarty 98 B 3
Cromarty Firth 98 B 3
Cromer 103 E 1
Crook 101 E 2
Crooked Creek 166 F 3
Crooked Island 173 H 3
Crooked Island Passage 173 H 3
Crookston 171 G 2
Crosby (N.D., U.S.A.) 170 F 2
Crosby (U.K.) 101 D 3
Cross (Nigeria) 157 F 4
Cross, Cape 160 A 4
Cross City 171 K 6
Crossett 171 H 5
Cross Fell 101 D 2
Crossgar 100 C 2
Cross Lake 167 S 5
Cross Sound 166 K 4
Crotone 115 G 4
Crottmaglen 100 B 2
Crow Agency 170 E 2
Crowborough 103 C 2
Crowell 170 G 5
Crow Lake 168 J 6
Crowley 171 H 5
Crowley Ridge 171 H 4
Crown Prince Frederik Island 167 U 2
Crows Nest 143 J 4
Crowsnest Pass 167 P 6
Croydon 143 G 2
Crozon 114 C 2
Cruden Bay 98 D 3
Crumlin 100 B 2
Cruz Alta (Argentina) 182 D 5
Cruz Alta (Brazil) 182 F 4
Cruz, Cabo 173 G 4
Cruz del Eje 182 D 5
Cruz Grande (Chile) 182 B 4
Cruz Grande (Mexico) 172 C 4
Crvanj 115 G 3
Crystal Brook 143 F 5
Ctesiphon 155 G 2
Cuale 160 B 1
Cuamba 161 F 2
Cuando Cubango 160 BC 3
Cuangar 160 B 3
Cuango 160 B 1
Cuanza 160 B 1
Cuanza Norte 160 AB 1
Cuanza Sul 160 B 2
Cua Rao 135 H 4

Cua–Das

Cuareim 182 E 5
Cuarteron Reef 136 D 2
Cuarto 182 D 5
Cuauhtémoc 170 E 6
Cuba 173 F 3
Cubal 160 A 2
Cubango 160 B 3
Cubati 160 B 3
Cubuk 117 D 2
Cúcata 178 D 2
Cuchi 160 B 2
Cuchilla de Santa Ana 183 EF 2
Cuchilla Grande 183 EF 2
Cuchillo-Có 183 D 6
Cuchumatanes, Sierra de los 172 D 4
Cuckfield 103 D 2
Cucuí 178 E 3
Cucumbi 160 B 2
Cucurpe 170 D 5
Cuddalore 134 C 5
Cuddapah 134 C 5
Cudi Dağı 117 F 3
Cue 142 B 4
Cuéllar 114 C 3
Cuemba 160 B 2
Cuenca (Spain) 114 C 3
Cuenca (Ecuador) 178 C 4
Cuencamé de Ceniceros 172 B 3
Cuerda del Pozo, Embalse de la 114 C 3
Cuernavaca 172 C 4
Cuero 171 G 6
Cuevas de Artá 114 D 4
Cuevo 180 D 5
Cufra Oasis → Wāḥāt al Kufrah 153 K 4
Cuiabá 180 E 4
Cuiari 178 E 3
Cuilapa 172 D 5
Cuillin Hills 98 A 3
Cuillin Sound 99 A 3
Cuilo 160 B 1
Cuito Cuanavale 160 B 3
Cuiuni 179 F 4
Cujmir 116 B 2
Cukurca 117 F 3
Culan 114 D 2
Cu Lao Cham 135 J 4
Cu Lao Hon 135 J 5
Cu Lao Re 135 J 4
Culcairn 143 H 6
Culgoa River 143 H 4
Culiacán, Rosales 170 E 7
Culion 137 E 2
Cullen 98 C 3
Culleoka 171 J 3
Cullera 114 C 4
Cullman 171 J 5
Cullompton 102 C 2
Cullybackey 100 B 2
Culrain 98 B 3
Cultowa 143 G 5
Culuene 181 F 3
Culver, Point 142 C 5
Cumaná 179 F 1
Cumaria 178 D 5
Cumbal 178 C 3
Cumberland 171 L 4
Cumberland Islands 143 H 3
Cumberland, Lake (KY, U.S.A.) 171 J 4
Cumberland Lake (Sask., Can.) 167 R 5
Cumberland Peninsula 169 O 2
Cumberland Plateau 171 J 4
Cumberland River 171 J 4
Cumberland Sound 169 O 2
Cumbernauld 99 B 4
Cumbrian Mountains 101 D 2
Cumerna 116 C 2
Cumia 160 B 2
Cûmina 179 G 4
Cuminapanema 179 GH 4
Cummins 143 F 5
Cumnock 99 B 4
Çumra 117 D 3
Cunani 179 H 3
Cunco 183 B 6
Cunene 160 B 3
Cunene 160 A 3
Cuneo 115 E 3
Cungena 142 E 5
Cunnamulla 143 H 4
Cunningham 99 B 4
Cupar 99 C 3
Cupica 178 C 2
Cuprija 116 B 2
Curaçao 178 E 1
Curacautin 183 B 6
Curanilahue 183 B 6
Curaray 178 CD 4
Curare 178 E 3

Curdimurka 143 F 4
Curepipe 161 K 6
Curepto 183 B 6
Curiapo 179 F 2
Curicó 182 B 5
Curicuriari 178 E 4
Curimatá 181 H 2–3
Curious, Mount 142 A 4
Curiplaya 178 CD 3
Curitiba 181 G 6
Curnamona 143 F 5
Curoca 160 A 3
Currais Novos 181 J 2
Curralinho 179 J 4
Currie 143 G 6
Curtea de Argeş 116 B 1
Curtici 116 B 1
Curtina 182 E 5
Curtis 146 D 5
Curtis Channel 143 J 3
Curtis Island 143 J 3
Curuá 179 H 5
Curuá (Amapá, Brazil) 179 J 3
Curuá (Pará, Brazil) 179 H 4
Curuaí 179 G 4
Curuá Una 179 H 4
Curuça 179 J 4
Curuçambaba 179 J 4
Curuguaty 180 E 5
Curumu 179 H 4
Curupá 179 J 5
Curupuru 181 H 1
Curuzú Cuatiá 182 E 4
Curvelo 181 H 4
Cushendun 100 B 2
Cushing 171 G 4
Cushing, Mount 167 M 4
Cusset 114 D 2
Cutervo 178 C 5
Cutral-Có 183 C 6
Cuttack 134 E 3
Cuvelai 160 B 3
Cuvette 157 H 6
Cuvier, Cape 142 A 3
Cuxhaven 111 E 4
Cuya 180 B 4
Cuyo Islands 137 F 1
Cuyuni 179 G 2
Cuzco 180 B 3
Cuzna 114 C 4
Cwmbran 102 C 2
Cyangugu 158 D 5
Cyclades 116 BC 3
Cypress Hills 167 P 6
Cyprus 117 D 3
Cyrenaica 153 K 3
Cyrene → Shaḥḥāt 153 K 2
Cyrus Field Bay 169 P 3
Częstochowa 111 G 4
Czechoslovakia 111 G 5
Czechowice-Dziedzice 111 G 5
Czeremcha 111 H 4
Czersk 111 G 4

D

Da'an 133 H 1
Dabaga 159 F 6
Dabajuro 178 D 1
Dabakala 156 D 4
Daba Shan 132 E 4
Dabat 159 F 2
Dabbāgh, Jabal 154 F 3
Dabeiba 178 C 2
Dabhoi 134 B 3
Dabie Shan 132 G 4
Dabnou 157 F 3
Dabo 136 B 3
Dabola 156 B 3
Daborów 159 H 3
Dabou 156 D 4
Daboya 156 D 4
Dabraš 115 B 2
Dabu 132 G 6
Dăbuleni 116 B 2
Dacca 135 F 5
Dachau 111 F 5
Dadali 145 G 3
Dadanawa 179 G 3
Dadu 129 G 5
Dadu He 132 D 5
Dadynskoye, Ozero 117 G 1
Daet 137 F 1
Dafang 132 E 5
Dafeng 133 H 4
Daflar 135 F 2
Dagabur 159 G 3
Dagadzhik 128 E 3
Daga Medo 159 G 3
Dagana (Chad) 157 H 3

Dagana (Senegal) 156 A 2
Daga Post 158 E 3
Dagary 130 J 4
Dagash 154 E 5
Dağbası 117 E 3
Dagi 131 Q 5
Daguan 132 D 5
Dagupan 137 J 1
Dagur 132 C 3
Dagworth 143 G 2
Dagzê 135 F 2
Dagzê Co 134 E 1
Dagzhuka 134 E 2
Dahabān 155 F 4
Dahanu 134 B 4
Daheiding Shan 131 N 6
Dahei He 132 F 2
Da Hinggan Ling 133 G 2
Dahlak Archipelago 159 FG 1
Dahlak Kebir 159 G 1
Dahl al Furayy 155 H 3
Dahongliutan 129 K 3
Dahra (Senegal) 156 A 2
Dahra (Algeria) 114 D 4
Dahūk 155 G 1
Daḥy, Nafūd ad 155 H 4
Daïa 153 F 2
Daicheng 133 G 3
Daik-u 135 G 4
Daingean 100 B 3
Dainkog 132 C 4
Daintree River National Park 143 G 2
Daireaux 183 D 6
Dairen → Lüda 133 H 3
Daitō-shotō 133 K 5
Dai Xian 132 F 3
Daiyun Shan 133 G 5
Dajarra 143 F 3
Daka 156 D 4
Dakala 156 C 3
Dakar 156 A 3
Dakha 135 F 3
Dakham 101 E 3
Dakhla 152 B 4
Dakhla Oasis → Wāḥāt ad Dākhilah 154 D 3
Dakhlet Nouadhibou 152 B 4
Dak Kon 135 J 5
Dako 156 D 2
Dakoro 157 F 3
Daktuy 131 N 5
Dákura 172 F 5
Dala 160 C 2
Dalaba 156 B 3
Dalad Qi 132 F 2
Dalai Nur 133 G 2
Dalälven 113 G 3
Dalaman 116 C 3
Dalāmī 154 E 6
Dalandzadgad 132 D 2
Dalanjargalan 132 E 1
Dalarna 113 F 3
Da Lat 135 J 5
Dalbandin 129 G 5
Dalbeattie 99 C 4
Dalbosjön 113 F 4
Dalby 143 J 4
Dalbyrdakh 131 P 2
Dale 113 E 3
Dale Hollow Lake 171 J 4
Dalen 113 E 4
Daletme 135 F 3
Dalgonally 143 G 3
Dalhart 170 F 4
Dalhouse, Cape 166 M 1
Dalhousie 169 O 6
Dali 132 D 5
Dali 132 E 4
Daliang Shan 132 D 5
Dalian → Lüda 133 H 3
Dalias 114 C 4
Dalimiel 114 C 4
Dalj 115 G 2
Daljā' 154 E 3
Dalkeith 99 C 4
Dall 166 L 5
Dalli 134 D 3
Dall Lake 166 E 3
Dallol Bosso 156 E 3
Dalmā' 155 J 4
Dalmally 99 B 3
Dalmellington 99 B 4
Dal'negorsk 133 L 2
Dal'nerechensk 133 K 1
Dal'nyaya 131 Q 6
Daloa 156 C 4
Dalou Shan 132 E 5
Dalqān 155 H 4
Dalqū 154 E 4

Dalrymple, Mount 143 H 3
Dalsfjorden 112 D 3
Dalsland 113 F 4
Dals Långed 113 F 4
Dalstroy 131 P 3
Dalton 171 K 5
Daltonganj 134 D 3
Dalton-in-Furness 101 D 2
Daluo 132 D 6
Dalupiri 137 J 1
Dalvik 112 B 2
Dalwallinu 142 B 5
Daly Bay 167 U 3
Daly River 142 E 1
Daly Waters 142 E 2
Daman 134 B 3
Damanhûr 154 E 2
Damara 158 B 3
Damaraland 160 B 4
Damar, Pulau 137 G 5
Damar, Pulau 137 G 4
Damascus → Dimashq 154 F 2
Damaturu 157 G 3
Damavand 128 E 3
Damāvand, Qolleh-ye 128 E 3
Damba 160 B 1
Dambarta 157 F 3
Dame Marie, Cap 173 H 4
Dāmghan 128 E 3
Damietta → Dumyāt 154 E 2
Damlataş 117 D 3
Damoh 134 C 3
Damongo 156 D 4
Damot 159 H 3
Dampier 142 B 3
Dampier Archipelago 142 B 3
Dampier Land 142 C 2
Dampier, Selat 137 H 4
Dampier Strait 144 E 3
Damqawt 155 J 5
Damxung 135 F 1
Dana 131 U 3
Danakil Depression → Kobar 159 G 2
Danakil Plain 159 G 2
Danan 159 G 3
Danané 156 C 4
Da Nang 135 J 4
Danau Jempang 136 E 4
Danau Melintang 136 E 4
Danau Toba 136 A 3
Danau Towuti 137 F 4
Danba 132 D 4
Dandarah 154 E 3
Dande 160 A 1
Dandeldhura 134 D 2
Dandeli 134 B 4
Dandong 133 H 2
Danells Fjord 169 T 3
Danfa 156 C 3
Danfeng 132 F 4
Danforth 171 N 2
Dangara 129 H 3
Dangchang 132 D 4
Dange 160 B 1
Danghe Nanshan 132 C 3
Dangila 159 F 2
Dangjin Shankou 132 B 3
Dang Khe 135 J 3
Dang Krien 135 J 5
Dangriga 172 E 4
Dangshan 133 G 4
Dan Gulbi 157 F 3
Dangyang 132 F 4
Daniel 170 F 4
Daniel 170 D 3
Daniel's Harbour 169 Q 5
Danielskuil 160 C 5
Danilov 118 H 4
Danilovka 118 H 5
Daning 132 F 3
Danjiangkou Shuiku 132 F 4
Danjo-guntō 133 J 4
Dank 155 K 4
Dankhar 134 C 1
Danlí 172 E 5
Danmark 113 E 4
Danmarks Havn 184
Dannevirke 145 R 9
Danompari 136 E 3
Dan Sai 135 H 4
Dante → Hāfūn 159 J 2
Dantewara 134 D 4
Danu 145 F 2
Danube 116 C 1
Danville (IL, U.S.A.) 171 J 3
Danville (KY, U.S.A.) 171 K 4
Danville (VA, U.S.A.) 171 L 4
Dan Xian 132 E 7
Danyang 133 G 4
Danzhai 132 E 5
Danzig 111 G 4
Dao 137 F 1

Daocheng 132 D 5
Daora 152 C 3
Dao Timni 157 G 1
Daoukro 156 D 4
Daoura 152 E 2
Dao Xian 132 F 5
Dapango 156 E 3
Dapchi 157 G 3
Daphabum 135 G 2
Dapoli 134 B 4
Da Qaidam 132 C 3
Daqing 133 J 1
Dar'ā 154 F 2
Dārāb 128 E 5
Darabani 116 C 1
Daraçya Yarımadası 116 C 3
Darāfisah 154 E 6
Dar al Ḥomr 154 D 6
Dārān 128 E 4
Darapap 144 D 2
Darasun 130 K 5
Daravica 116 B 2
Darāw 154 E 4
Darazo 157 G 3
Darband 128 F 4
Darbat 'Alī, Ra's 155 J 5
Darbhanga 134 E 2
Dārboruk 159 G 3
Darda 115 G 2
Dardanelle Lake 171 H 4
Dardanelles → Canakkale Boğazı 116 C 2
Dar el Beida 152 CD 2
Dar el Kouti 158 C 3
Darende 117 E 3
Dar es Salaam 159 F 6
Darfo Boario Terme 115 F 2
Dārfūr 154 C 6
Darganata 129 G 2
Dargaville 145 Q 8
Dargo 143 H 6
Dargol 156 E 3
Dar Ḥamar 154 D 6
Dar Ḥamid 154 DE 6
Darhan 130 J 6
Darhan Muminggan Lianheqi 132 F 2
Darién 178 C 2
Darién, Golfo del 178 C 2
Darién, Serranía del 178 C 2
Dar'inskiy 119 O 6
Darj 153 H 2
Darjeeling 134 E 2
Darkan 142 B 5
Darkhovīn 128 D 4
Darlag 132 C 4
Darling Downs 143 H 4
Darling Range 142 B 5
Darling River 143 G 5
Darlington 101 E 2
Darlot, Lake 142 C 4
Darmstadt 111 E 5
Darnah 153 K 2
Darnley Bay 167 N 2
Darnley, Cape 185
Dar Nūbah 154 DE 6
Daroca 114 C 3
Darłowo 111 G 4
Darreh Gaz 128 F 3
Dar Rounga 158 C 2–2
Darsi 134 C 4
Dar Sila 157 J 3
Dartford 103 E 2
Dartmoor 102 B–C 2
Dartmouth (U.K.) 102 C 2
Dartmouth (New Brunsw., Can.) 169 P 7
Dartuch, Cabo 114 D 4
Daru 144 D 3
Daruba 137 G 3
Daruvar 115 G 2
Darvaza 128 F 2
Darvel 99 B 4
Darvel, Teluk 137 E 3
Darvi 130 F 6
Darwen 101 D 3
Darweshan 129 G 4
Darwin (Australia) 142 E 1
Darwin (Arg.) 183 C 6
Darwin (Galapagos Islands) 178 A 4
Darwin, Bahía 183 AB 5
Darwin, Port 142 E 1
Daryācheh-ye Bakhtegān 128 E 5
Daryācheh-ye Hāmūn-e Hirmand 128 G 4
Daryācheh-ye Namak 128 E 4
Daryācheh-ye Orūmīyeh 128 D 3
Daryācheh-ye Tashk 128 E 5
Daryā-ye Māzandarān 128 E 3
Darya-ye Panj 129 J 3
Dās 155 J 3
Dashbalbar 130 K 6

Dasht (Iran) 128 F 3
Dasht (Pakistan) 129 G 5
Dasht-e Kavīr 128 E 4
Dasht e Lut 128 F 4
Dasht-e Naomid 128 G 4
Dasht-i Arbu Lut 129 G 5
Dashtiari 129 G 5
Dasht-i-Margo 129 G 4
Dasht-i-Nawar 129 H 4
Dasht-i Tahlab 129 G 5
Daspalla 134 D 3
Dastgardān 128 F 4
Dasuya 134 C 1
Datça 116 C 3
Date 133 M 2
Datha 134 B 3
Datia 134 C 2
Datian 133 G 5
Datong 132 F 2
Datong 133 H 1
Datong 132 D 3
Datong Shan 132 D 3
Datta 131 Q 6
Datumakuta 136 E 3
Datu Piang 137 F 2
Dāuarzan 128 F 3
Daugava 113 H 4
Daugav'pils 113 J 4
Daulatabad 129 G 3
Daulat Yar 129 H 4
Daule 178 C 4
Daung Kyun 135 G 5
Dauphin 167 R 5
Dauphiné 115 E 3
Dauphin Lake 167 S 5
Daura 157 F 3
Daurskoye 130 F 4
Davangere 134 C 5
Davao 137 G 2
Davao Gulf 137 G 2
Dāvar Panāh 129 G 5
Davenport 171 H 3
Davenport Downs 143 G 3
Daventry 103 D 1
David 178 B 2
Davidson Mountains 166 J 2
Davies, Mount 142 E 4
Davis (CA, U.S.A.) 170 B 4
Davis (Antarctica) 185
Davis Inlet 169 P 4
Davis, Mount 171 L 4
Davis River 142 C 3
Davis Sea 185
Davis Strait 169 Q 2
Davlekanovo 118 K 5
Davos 115 E 2
Davydov Brod 117 D 1
Dawa 159 G 4
Dawāsir, Wādī ad 155 G 4
Dawes Range 143 J 3
Dawḥat as Salwā 155 J 3
Dawlish 102 C 2
Dawna Range 135 G 4
Dawqah (Oman) 155 J 5
Dawqah (Saudi Arabia) 155 G 5
Dawson 166 K 3
Dawson Creek 167 N 4
Dawson Inlet 167 T 3
Dawson, Isla 183 B 9
Dawson Range 166 K 3
Dawson River 143 H 3
Dawu 132 D 4
Dawu 132 F 4
Dax 114 C 3
Daxian 132 E 4
Daxin 132 E 6
Daxing 133 G 3
Daxue Shan 132 D 4
Daya Abeidi 156 C 1
Daya Hamami 152 C 4
Dayangshu 131 M 6
Dayao 132 D 5
Dayet en Naharat 156 D 2
Daym Zubayr 158 D 3
Dayong 132 F 5
Dayr az Zawr 155 G 1
Dayr, Jabal ad 154 E 3
Dayrūṭ 154 E 3
Dayton 171 K 4
Daytona Beach 171 K 6
Dayu 132 F 5
Da Yunhe 133 G 4
Dayyīnah 155 J 4
Dazhu 132 E 4
Dazjā 128 F 3
Dazkırı 116 C 3
Dazu 132 E 5
Dębica 111 H 4
Deblin 111 H 4
Debno 111 H 4
De Aar 160 C 6
Deadhorse 166 H 1
Dead Sea 154 F 2

Deal 103 E 2
Deal Island (Australia) 143 H 6
Dealu Mare 116 C 1
Dean 167 M 5
De'an 132 G 5
Deán Funes 182 D 5
Dease 166 M 4
Dease Arm 167 O 2
Dease Lake 166 L 4
Dease Strait 167 Q 2
Death Valley 170 C 4
Death Valley National Monument 170 C 4
Debak 136 D 3
Debaltsevo 117 E 1
Debao 132 E 6
Debar 116 B 2
Debark 159 F 2
Debdou 152 E 2
De Behagle → Lai 157 H 4
Débo, Lac 156 D 2
Deborah, Lake 142 B 5
Deboyne Island 143 J 1
Debra Birhan 159 F 3
Debra Libanos 159 F 3
Debra Markos 159 F 2
Debra Sina 159 FG 3
Debra Tabor 159 F 2
Debra Zeit 159 F 3
Debrecen 116 B 1
De Brie 161 H 3
Decamere 159 F 1
Decatur (AL, U.S.A.) 171 J 5
Decatur (IL, U.S.A.) 171 J 4
Decazeville 114 D 3
Deccan 134 C 5–D 5
Decelles, Réservoir 171 L 2
Decepción 185
Dechang 132 D 5
Děčín 111 F 4
Deda 116 B 1
Dedegöl Dağı 116 D 3
Dedo, Cerro 183 B 7
Dédougou 156 D 3
Dedovichi 112 K 4
Dedu 131 N 6
Dedza 161 E 2
Deep Well 142 E 3
Deering 166 E 2
Deering, Mount 142 D 3
Dee, River (Clwyd) 102 C 1
Dee, River (Grampian) 98 C 3
Deer Lake (Newf., Can.) 169 Q 6
Deer Lake (Ont., Can.) 168 J 5
Deer Lodge 170 D 2
Deesa 134 B 3
Defah 153 JK 3
Defferrari 183 E 6
Defirou 157 H 1
Degema 157 F 5
Dêgê 132 C 4
Dêgên 135 F 1
Degerfors 113 F 4
Deggendorf 111 F 5
de Gras, Lac 167 P 3
De Grey River 142 C 3
Dehaj 128 E 4
Dehak 129 G 5
Deh Bārez 128 F 5
Deh Bīd 128 E 4
Dehdez 128 E 4
Dehlorān 128 D 3
Dehra Dun 134 C 1
Deh Shū 129 G 4
Dehua 133 G 5
Dehui 133 J 2
Deingueri, Mont 158 D 3
Dej 116 B 1
Dejiang 132 E 5
De Jong, Tanjung 137 J 5
De Kalb 171 J 3
De Kalk 160 B 4
Dekar 160 C 4
Dekese 158 C 5
Dekina 157 F 4
Dékoa 158 B 3
De Land 171 K 6
Delarof Islands 166 B 5
Delaware 171 K 4
Delaware Bay 171 L 4
Delaware River 171 L 3
Del Campillo 182 D 5
Del City 170 G 4
Delcommune, Lac 160 D 2
De Peré 171 J 3
Delegate 143 J 6
Delémont 115 E 2
Delft (Netherl.) 110 D 4
Delft (Sri Lanka) 134 C 6
Delfzijl 110 E 4
Delgado, 161 G 2
Delger 130 G 6
Delgereh 132 F 1
Delgerhaan 132 D 1
Delgerhaan 130 J 4

Delgerhangay 132 D 1
Delgerhet 132 F 1
Delgertsogt 132 E 1
Delhi 134 C 2
Deliblatska Peščara 116 B 2 3
Deličal Dağı 116 C 2–3
Delice 117 D 3
Delicermak 117 D 3
Delījān 128 E 4
Delingha 132 C 3
Dellen 112 G 3
Dellys 153 F 1
Delmarva Peninsula 171 L 4
Delmenhorst 111 E 4
Delnice 115 F 2
Del Norte 170 E 4
Delorme, Lac 169 O 5
Delos → Dhílos 116 C 3
Delphi 116 B 3
Delphi → Dhelfoí 116 B 3
Del Rio 170 F 6
Delsbo 112 G 3
Delta (CO, U.S.A.) 170 E 4
Delta (UT, U.S.A.) 170 D 4
Delta del Ebro 114 D 3
Delta Downs 143 G 2
Delta Dunării 116 C 1
Delta Junction 166 H 3
Delvina 116 B 3
Delyankyr 131 R 3
Delyatin 116 B 1
Demanda, Sierra de la 114 C 3
Demavend, Mount 128 E 3
Demba 158 C 6
Dembi 159 F 3
Dembia 158 C 3
Dembidollo 158 E 3
Deming 170 E 5
Demini 179 F 3
Demirci 116 C 3
Demir Kapija 116 B 2
Demirköprü Barajı 116 C 3
Demmin 111 F 4
Demnate 152 D 2
Democracia 179 F 5
Demópolis 171 J 5
Dempo, Gunung 136 B 4
Dêmqog 134 C 1
Demre 116 C 3
Dem'yanka 119 O 4
Dem'yanovka 119 N 5
Dem'yanskoye 119 N 4
Dena Dibile 158 C 5
Denain 114 D 1
Denali 166 H 3
Denali National Park and Preserve 166 G 3
Denau 129 H 3
Denbigh 102 C 1
Dendang 136 C 4
Dendi 159 F 3
Denezhkin Kamen', Gora 119 L 3
Denezhkino 119 R 2
Deng Deng 157 G 4
Dêngqên 132 C 4
Deng Xian 132 F 4
Den Haag 110 D 4
Denham 142 A 4
Denham Sound 142 A 4
Den Helder 110 D 4
Denia 114 D 4
Deniliquin 143 G 6
Denio 170 C 3
Denizli 116 C 3
Denkou 132 E 2
Denmark 113 E 4
Denmark (Australia) 142 B 5
Denmark Strait 184
Dennison, Cape 185
Denpasar 136 E 5
Denton 171 G 5
D'Entrecasteaux Islands 145 F 3
D'Entrecasteaux, Point 142 B 5
Denver 170 F 4
Deo 157 G 4
Deogarh 134 D 3
Deoghar 134 E 3
Deolali 134 B 4
Deori 134 C 3
Deosai, Plains of 129 K 3
De Peré 171 J 3
Depoe Bay 170 B 3
Depósita 179 F 3
Dépression del Balsas 172 B 4
Dépression du Mourdi 157 J 2
Deputatskiy 131 P 2
Deqên 132 C 5
Deqing 132 F 6
De Queen 171 H 5

Dera Bugti 129 G 5
Dera Ghazi Khan 129 J 4
Deraheib 154 F 4
Dera Ismail Khan 129 J 4
Derajat 129 J 4
Derbeke 131 P 2
Derbent 128 D 2
Derbent 131 H 3
Derbino 130 F 4
Derbisaka 158 C 3
Derbur 130 M 5
Derby (U.K.) 103 D 1
Derby (Australia) 142 C 2
Derbyshire 103 D 1
Derdap 116 B 2
Dereköy 116 C 2
Dergachi 118 J 5
De Ridder 171 H 5
Derik 117 F 2
Der, Lac du 115 D 2
Derm 160 B 4
Dermott 171 H 5
Derna → Darnah 153 K 2
Dêrong 132 C 5
Derryveagh Mountains 100 A 2
Derudeb 154 F 5
Derventa 115 G 3
Derwent, River (U.K.) 101 E 2
Derwent River (Tasmania, Austr.) 144 L 9
Deryabino 119 Q 1
Derzhavinsk 119 N 5
Desaguadero, Sierra de la 114 C 3
Desaguadero (Argentina) 182 C 5
Desaguadero (Bolivia) 180 C 4
Désappointement, Îles du 147 F 3
Desborough 103 D 1
Descalvado 180 E 4
Deschambault Lake 167 R 5
Deschutes River 170 B 2
Deseado 183 C 8
Deseado, Cabo 183 AB 6
Desengaño, Punta 183 C 8
Desert Center 170 C 5
Desierto de Altar 170 D 5
Desierto de Sechura 178 B 5
Desierto de Vizcaíno 170 D 6
Desierto do Atacama 180 C 5
Des Moines 171 H 3
Des Moines River 171 H 3
Desna 118 F 5
Desrouches, Île 159 J 6
Dessau 111 F 4
Dessye 159 F 2
Destruction Bay 166 K 3
Deta 116 B 1
Detmold 111 E 4
Detroit 171 K 3
Détroit de Jaques-Cartier 169 P 6
Détroit d'Honguedo 169 P 6
Detroit Lakes 171 G 2
Dett 160 D 3
Dettifoss 112 B 2
Deutsche Bucht 111 E 4
Deutsche Demokratische Republik 111 F 4
Deutschlandsberg 115 G 2
Deva 116 B 1
Devakottai 134 C 6
Devarkonda 134 C 4
Deveci Dağı 117 E 2
Develi 117 E 3
Deveron, River 98 C 3
Devikot 134 B 2
Devils Elbow 99 C 3
Devil's Island → Île du Diable 179 H 2
Devils Lake 170 G 2
Devils Paw 166 L 4
Devizes 103 D 2
Devli 134 C 2
Devolli 116 B 2
Devon 102 C 2
Devon Island 184
Devonport (Tasmania, Austr.) 144 L 9
Devonport (N. Zealand) 145 Q 8
Devrek 117 D 2
Devrez 117 D 2
Dewangiri 135 F 2
Dewsbury 101 E 3
Dexing 133 G 5
Dexter 171 K 5
Deyang 132 D 4
Dey Dey, Lake 142 E 4
Deyhuk 128 F 4
Deynau 129 G 3
Dez 128 D 3
Dez Gerd 128 E 4
Dezfūl 128 D 3
Dezhneva, Mys 166 D 2
Dezhou 133 G 3
Dháfni 116 B 3
Dhahab 154 E 3

Dhahran → Aẓ Ẓahrān 155 HJ 3
Dhamār 155 G 6
Dhamra 134 E 3
Dhamtari 134 D 3
Dhanbad 134 E 3
Dhangain 134 D 2
Dhankuta 134 E 2
Dhar 134 C 3
Dhar Adrar 152 C 4
Dharinavaram 134 C 5
Dharmapuri 134 C 5
Dharmjaygarh 134 D 3
Dhar Oualata 152 D 5
Dhar Tagant 152 C 5
Dhar Tichit 152 D 5
Dharwar 134 C 4
Dhaulagiri 134 D 2
Dhelfoí 116 B 3
Dhenkanal 134 E 3
Dhiavlos Thásou 116 B 2
Dhíavlos Zakínthou 116 B 3
Dhiekplous Kafiréos 116 B 3
Dhílos 116 C 3
Dhirfis Óros 116 B 3
Dhisoron Óros 116 B 2
Dhofar → Ẓufār 155 J 5
Dholpur 134 C 2
Dhomokós 116 B 3
Dhone 134 C 5
Dhoraji 134 B 3
Dhubāb 155 G 6
Dhule 134 B 3
Dhulian 134 E 3
Día 116 C 3
Diabakagna 156 B 3
Diable, Île du 179 H 2
Diablo Range 170 B 4
Diaca 161 F 2
Diafarabe 156 C 3
Dialafara 156 B 3
Dialakoto 156 B 3
Diamante (Argentina) 182 D 5
Diamante (Italy) 115 G 4
Diamante, Punta del 172 C 4
Diamantina (Australia) 143 G 3
Diamantina (Brazil) 181 H 4
Diamantina Lakes 143 G 3
Diamantino 180 E 3
Diamantina Fracture Zone 192 C 5
Diamond Harbour 134 E 3
Diamond Jenness Peninsula 167 O 1
Diamond Peak 170 C 4
Diamou 156 B 3
Diamouguel 156 B 2
Diana, Baie 169 O 3
Dianbai 132 F 6
Dian Chi 132 D 6
Diane Bank 143 H 2
Dianjiang 132 E 4
Dianópolis 181 G 3
Diapaga 156 E 3
Dibaya 158 C 6
Dibaya-Lubue 158 B 5
Dibella 157 G 2
Dibete 160 D 4
Dibo 159 G 3
Dibrugarh 135 F 2
Dickinson 170 F 2
Dicle 117 F 3
Didcot 103 D 2
Didiéni 156 C 3
Didwana 134 B 2
Didyma 116 C 3
Die 115 E 3
Diébougou 156 D 3
Diéké 156 C 4
Diéma 156 C 3
Dien Bien Phu 135 H 3
Diepholz 111 E 4
Dieppe 114 D 2
Di'er Songhua Jiang 133 J 2
Dif 159 G 4
Diffa 157 G 3
Digba 158 D 4
Digby 169 O 7
Dighir 134 C 4
Digne 115 E 3
Digoin 114 D 2
Digos 137 G 2
Digranes 112 C 2
Digul, Sungai 137 J 5
Dihang 135 G 2
Dijon 114 D 2
Dik 157 H 4
Dikanäs 112 G 2
Dikchu 134 E 2
Dikebeye 160 D 4
Dikhil 159 G 2
Dikili 116 C 3

Dik – Dub

Dikmen 117 E 2
Dıkmen Dağı 117 D 2
Dikodougou 156 C 4
Dikson 184
Dikwa 157 G 3
Dilaram 129 G 4
Di Linh 135 J 5
Dilizhan 117 F 2
Dilj 115 G 2
Dilla 159 F 3
Dilli 137 G 5
Dillia 157 G 2
Dillia Téfidinga 157 G 2
Dilling 154 D 6
Dillingham 166 F 4
Dillon 170 D 2
Dilly 156 C 2
Dilolo 160 C 2
Dimashq (Damascus) 154 F 2
Dimbelenge 158 C 6
Dimbokro 156 D 4
Dimboola 143 G 6
Dimitrovgrad 118 J 5
Dimitrovgrad 116 B 2
Dimitrovgrad 116 C 2
Dimitrya Laptevа, Proliv 131 Q 1
Dimovo 116 B 2
Dinagat 137 G 1
Dinajpur 134 E 2
Dinangourou 156 D 3
Dinant 110 D 4
Dınar 116 D 3
Dinara Planina 115 G 3
Dinard 114 C 2
Dinder National Park 154 EF 6
Dindigul 134 C 5
Dindiza 161 E 4
Dindori 134 D 3
Dinga 158 B 6
Dingbian 132 E 3
Dinggyê 134 E 2
Dinghai 133 H 4
Dingle 110 A 4
Dingle Bay 110 A B 4
Dingtao 132 G 3
Dinguiraye 156 B 3
Dingwall 98 B 3
Dingxi 132 D 3
Ding Xian 132 G 3
Dingxian 132 F 3
Dingxing 132 G 3
Dinh Lap 135 J 3
Diniapur 135 F 2
Dinokwe 160 D 4
Dinskaya 117 E 1
Dïnsör 159 G 4
Diois, Massif du 115 E 3
Dioka 156 B 3
Diomida, Ostrova 166 D 2
Dion 156 C 4
Diona 157 J 2
Dionísio Cerqueira 182 F 4
Diouloulou 156 A 3
Dioundiou 156 E 3
Dioura 156 C 3
Diourbel 156 A 3
Dipkarpas 117 D 3
Dipolog 137 F 2
Dir 129 J 3
Diré 156 D 2
Diredawa 159 G 3
Dirico 160 C 3
Dirk Hartog Island 142 A 4
Dirkou 157 G 2
Dirranbandi 143 H 4
Ḍirs 155 G 5
Disappointment, Lake 142 C 3
Discovery Great Reef 136 D 1
Dishnā 154 E 3
Disko 184
Disko Bugt 184
Disna 113 J 4
Dispur 135 F 2
Diss 103 E 1
District of Columbia (U.S.A.) 171 L 4
District of Fort Smith 167 O 3
District of Franklin 167 P 1
District of Inuvik 166 LM 3
District of Keewatin 167 S 2
District of Mackenzie 167 N 3
Distrito Federal 181 G 4
Ditdak 135 F 6
Diu 134 B 3
Diudad de l'maiz 172 C 5
Dīvāndarreh 128 D 3
Divénié 157 G 6
Divenskaya 113 JK 4
Divinopolis 181 G 5
Divisor, Serra do 178 D 5
Divnogorsk 130 F 4
Divnoye 117 F 1
Divo 156 C 4

Divriği 117 E 3
Dixon 171 J 3
Dixon Entrance 166 L 5
Diyālā 155 G 2
Diyarbakır 117 F 3
Diyarbakır Havzası 117 F 3
Diza 117 G 2
Dja 157 G 5
Djado 157 G 1
Djado, Plateau du 157 G 1
Djafou 153 F 3
Djaja Peak 144 C 2
Djako 158 C 3
Djamaa 153 G 2
Djambala 157 G 6
Djanet 153 G 4
Djaret 153 F 3
Djaul 145 F 2
Djebel 153 G 2
Djebel Aïssa 152 E 2
Djebel Amour 153 F 2
Djebel Chélia 153 G 1
Djebel Edough 115 E 4
Djebel Onk 153 G 2
Djebel Ounane 153 G 3
Djebel Telerhteba 153 G 4
Djebobo 156 E 4
Djédaa 157 H 3
Djedi 153 F 2
Djelfa 153 F 2
Djéma 158 D 3
Djemila 153 G 1
Djenienbou Rezg 152 E 2
Djénné 156 D 3
Djerba → Jarbah 153 H 2
Djerem 157 G 4
Djéroual 157 H 3
Djibo 156 D 3
Djibouti 159 G 2
Djiguéni 152 D 5
Djikdjik 157 J 2
Djilbabo Plain 159 F 4
Djokupunda 158 C 6
Djolu 158 C 4
Djombo 158 C 4
Djougou 156 E 4
Djoum 157 G 5
Djourab, Erg du 157 H 2
Djugu 158 E 4
Djúpivogur 112 C 2
Dmanisi 117 F 2
Dnepr 118 J 5
Dneprodzerzhinsk 117 D 1
Dnepropetrovsk 117 E 1
Dneprovskiy Liman 116 D 1
Dneprovsko-Bugskiy Kanal 112 H 5
Dnestr 116 C 1
Dnestrovskiy Liman 116 D 1
Dno 113 K 4
Doa 161 E 3
Doany 161 H 2
Doba (Chad) 157 H 4
Doba (China) 134 E 1
Dobbiaco 115 F 2
Dobel 159 F 4
Dobele 113 H 4
Döbeln 111 F 4
Doblas 183 D 6
Dobo 137 H 5
Doboj 115 G 3
Dobreta Turnu Severin 116 B 2
Dobrogea 116 C 2
Dobrowolski 185
Dobroye 131 R 7
Dobrudžansko Plato 116 C 2
Dobruja 116 C 2
Dobryanka 118 L 4
Doce 181 H 4
Docksta 112 G 3
Doctor Arroyo 172 B 3
Doda Betta 134 C 5
Dod Ballapur 134 C 5
Dodecanese 116 C 3
Dodge City 170 E 7
Dodman Point 102 B 2
Dodoma 159 F 6
Dofa 137 G 4
Dogai Coring 134 E 1
Doğankent 117 E 3
Dog Creek 167 N 5
Dogger Bank 110 D 4
Doghārūn 128 G 4
Dōgo 133 K 3
Dogondoutchi 157 F 3
Doğubayazıt 117 F 3
Doguéraoua 157 F 3
Doğu Karadeniz Dağlari 117 EF 2
Dogwaya 154 E 5
Do'gyaling 134 E 1
Doha 155 J 3
Dohad 134 B 3
Dohazan 135 F 3

Dōhō Nugāled 159 H 3
Doi Inthanon 135 G 4
Doilungdêqen 135 F 2
Dois de Novembro, Cachoeira 179 F 5
Dois Irmãos 179 J 5
Dois Irmãos, Serra 181 H 2
Doka (Indonesia) 137 H 5
Doka (Sudan) 154 F 6
Dokka 113 F 3
Doko 158 D 4
Dokshitsy 113 J 5
Dokuchayevsk 117 E 1
Dô, Lac 156 D 2
Dolak Island 144 C 3
Dolbeau 169 N 6
Dôle 115 E 2
Doleib Hill 158 E 3
Dolgellau 102 C 1
Dolgiy-Most 130 G 4
Dolgiy, Ostrov 119 L 2
Dolinovka 131 T 4
Dolinsk 131 Q 6
Dolinskaya 117 D 1
Dolo 159 G 4
Dolok Island 144 C 3
Dolomadare 159 G 4
Domaniç 116 C 3
Doma Peaks 144 C 3
Dom Aquino 181 F 4
Domažlice 111 F 5
Domba 132 C 1
Dombarovskiy 119 L 5
Dombás 112 E 3
Dombóvár 116 A 1
Dom Cavati 181 H 4
Dome, Monts 114 D 2
Domeyko 180 C 5
Domeyko, Cordillera 180 C 5
Dominica 173 K 4
Dominican Republic 173 J 4
Dominica Passage 173 K 4
Dominion, Cape 169 N 2
Domino 169 Q 5
Domiongo 158 C 5
Domo → Damot 159 H 3
Domodossola 115 E 2
Dom Pedrito 182 F 5
Dompierre-sur-Besbre 114 D 2
Dompu 137 E 5
Domuyo, Volcán 183 B 6
Don (U.S.S.R.) 118 H 6
Don (Mex.) 170 E 6
Donadeu 182 D 4
Donaghadee 100 C 2
Donald 143 G 6
Donau 115 F 2
Donauwörth 111 F 5
Don Benito 114 B 4
Doncaster 101 E 3
Dondo (Indonesia) 137 F 4
Dondo (Angola) 160 A 1
Dondo (Mozambique) 161 E 3
Dondra Head 134 D 6
Donegal 100 A 2
Donegal Bay 110 B 4
Donegal Mountains 110 B 4
Donets Basin 108
Donetsk 117 E 1
Donetskiy Kryazh 117 E 1
Donets, Severskiy 117 F 1
Donfeng 133 J 2
Donga 157 G 4
Dong'an 132 F 5
Dongara 142 A 4
Dongargarh 134 D 3
Dongchuan 132 D 5
Donges 114 C 2
Dongfang 132 E 7
Donggala 137 E 4
Donggi Cona 132 C 3
Donggou 133 H 3
Dongguan 132 F 6
Dong Ha 135 J 4
Donghai 133 G 4
Dong Hai 133 HJ 5
Donghai Dao 132 F 6
Dong He 132 D 2
Dong Hoi 135 J 4
Dong Jiang 132 F 6
Dongkalang 137 F 5
Donglan 132 E 6
Donglük 132 A 3
Dong Nai 135 J 5
Dongning 133 K 2
Dongo (Angola) 160 B 2
Dongo (Zaire) 158 B 6

Dongo (Zaire) 158 B 4
Dongou 157 H 5
Dongoura 156 C 3
Dongping 133 G 3
Dongshan 133 G 6
Dongshan Dao 133 G 6
Dongsha Qundao 132 G 6
Dongsheng 132 F 3
Dongtai 133 H 4
Dong Taijnar Hu 132 B 3
Dongting Hu 132 F 5
Dongtou 133 H 5
Dong Ujimqin Qi 133 G 1
Dongwe 160 C 2
Dongxiang 132 G 5
Dongying 133 G 3
Dongzhen 132 D 3
Dongzhi 133 G 4
Donington 101 E 3
Donja Brela 115 G 3
Donjek 166 K 3
Donji Miholjac 115 G 2
Donji Vakuf 115 G 3
Don Khi 135 H 4
Dönna 112 F 2
Donner Pass 170 B 4
Donnybrook 142 B 5
Don, River (Grampian) 98 C 3
Don, River (S. Yorkshire) 101 E 3
Donskoye 117 F 1
Donuzlav, Ozero 117 D 1
Doonerak, Mount 166 G 2
Doon, Loch 100 C 2
Door Peninsula 171 J 3
Dora Baltea 115 E 2
Dora, Lake 142 C 3
Doramarkog 132 C 4
Dorbod 133 H 1
Dorchester 102 C 2
Dorchester, Cape 169 M 1
Dordogne 114 C 2
Dordrecht 110 D 4
Dore Lake 167 Q 5
Dore, Monts 114 D 2
Dores do Indaiá 181 G 4
Dori 129 H 4
Doring 160 B 6
Dorking 103 D 2
Dormidontovka 131 O 6
Dornbin 115 E 2
Dornoch 98 B 3
Dornoch Firth 98 B 3
Dornod 130 K 6
Dornogovĭ 132 E 2
Dorohoi 116 C 1
Dorogobuzh 118 F 5
Dorogorskoye 118 H 2
Dörööö Nuur 130 F 6
Dorotea 112 G 3
Dorre Island 142 A 4
Dorrigo 143 J 5
Dorset 103 C 2
Dortmund 111 E 4
Dörtyol 117 E 3
Doruma 158 D 4
Doruokha 130 K 1
Dosatuy 130 L 5
Dos de Mayo 178 D 5
Dos Hermanas 114 B 4
Doshi 129 H 3
Dosso 156 E 3
Dossor 128 E 1
Dothan 171 J 5
Douai 114 D 1
Douala 157 F 5
Douandago 158 B 3
Doubs 115 E 2
Doubtful Sound 144 P 10
Douentza 156 D 3
Dougga 153 G 1
Douglas (South Africa) 160 C 5
Douglas (U.K.) 100 C 2
Douglas (AK, U.S.A.) 166 L 4
Douglas (AZ, U.S.A.) 170 E 5
Douglas (WY, U.S.A.) 170 E 3
Douglas (GA, U.S.A.) 171 K 5
Douglas, Mount 143 H 3
Doumbouene 157 J 3
Doumé 157 G 5
Doune 99 B 3
Douobé 156 C 4
Dourada, Serra 181 G 3
Dourado, Monte 179 H 4
Dourados 181 F 5
Dourbali 157 H 3
Douro 114 B 2
Dover (DE, U.S.A.) 171 L 4
Dove, River 103 D 1
Dover, Strait of 110 D 4

Dovre 112 E 3
Dovrefjell 112 E 3
Dowa 161 E 2
Dowlatābād 128 F 5
Downham Market 103 E 1
Downpatrick 100 C 2
Dow Rūd 128 D 4
Dow Sar 128 D 3
Dozois, Réservoir 169 M 6
Drâa, Cap 152 C 3
Drâa, Hamada du 152 D 3
Drâa, Wadi 152 D 3
Drac 115 E 3
Dragan 112 G 3
Drăgășani 116 B 2
Dragonera 114 D 4
Dragör 113 F 4
Draguignan 115 E 3
Drain 170 B 3
Drake 143 J 4
Drakensberg 160 D 5–6
Drake Strait 183 C 10
Dráma 116 B 2
Drammen 113 F 4
Drangajökull 112 A 2
Drangedal 113 E 4
Drangsnes 112 A 2
Dranka 131 U 4
Drava 115 G 2
Dravograd 115 G 2
Drawa 111 G 4
Drawsko, Jezioro 111 G 4
Drayton 143 J 4
Drayton Valley 167 O 5
Drean 115 E 4
Dresden 111 F 4
Dreux 114 D 2
Drevsjö 112 F 3
Drina 115 G 3
Drini 116 B 2
Driva 112 E 3
Drjanovo 116 C 2
Drniš 115 G 3
Drøbak 113 F 4
Drogheda 100 B 3
Drogobych 111 H 5
Droichead Átha 110 B 4
Droichead Nua 100 B 3
Droitwich 103 C 1
Drokiya 116 C 1
Drôme 115 E 3
Dromore 100 B 2
Dronfield 101 E 3
Dromore 100 B 3
Drosh 129 J 3
Drumheller 167 P 5
Drummond 170 D 2
Drummond Range 143 H 3
Drummondville 169 N 6
Drummore 100 C 2
Drumod 100 B 3
Druskininkai 113 H 5
Druzhina 131 R 2
Druzhkovka 117 E 1
Druzhnaya 185
Druzhnaya II 185
Drvar 115 G 3
Drvenik 115 G 3
Drweca 111 G 4
Dryden 168 J 6
Dry River 142 E 2
Drysdale River 142 D 1
Drysdale River National Park 142 D 2
Dry Tortugas 171 K 7
Dschang 157 FG 4
Dua 158 C 4
Duale 178 C 4
Duaringa 143 H 3
Dubai → Dubayy 155 K 3
Dubawnt 167 R 3
Dubawnt Lake 167 R 3
Dubayy 155 K 3
Dubbo 143 H 5
Dubenskiy 118 L 5
Dubica 115 G 2
Dublin (Rep. of Ireland) 100 B 3
Dublin (Airport) 100 B 3
Dublin (GA, U.S.A.) 171 K 5
Dubna 118 G 4
Dubna 118 G 5
Dubno 112 H 2
Du Bois 171 L 3
Dubossary 116 C 1
Dubovka 118 J 6
Dubovskoye 117 F 1
Dubreka 156 B 4
Dubrovitsa 113 J 5
Dubrovnik 115 G 3
Dubrovnoye 119 N 4
Dubuque 171 H 3

226

Duc de Gloucester, Îles du 147 F 4
Duchesne 170 D 3
Duchess 143 F 3
Ducie 147 G 4
du Couedic, Cape 143 F 6
Dudhi 134 D 3
Dudinka 119 R 2
Dudley 103 C 1
Ḏūdo 159 J 3
Dudub 159 H 3
Dudypta 130 F 1
Duékoué 156 C 4
Dueré 181 G 3
Duff Islands 145 J 3
Dufftown 98 C 3
Dugi Otok 115 FG 3
Dugo Selo 115 G 2
Duhūn Tarsū 153 J 4
Duifken Point 143 G 1
Duirinish 98 A 3
Duisburg 110 D E 4
Duitama 178 D 2
Dujūma 159 G 4
Dukagjini 116 A 2
Dukān 155 G 1–2
Dukana 159 F 4
Duke of York Bay 167 V 2
Duk Fadiat 158 E 3
Duk Faiwil 158 E 3
Dukhān 155 J 3
Duki (Pakistan) 129 H 4
Duki (U.S.S.R.) 131 P 5
Dukku 157 G 3
Dukou 132 D 5
Dukwe 160 D 4
Dulan 132 C 3
Dulce 182 D 4
Dulce, Bahia 172 C 4
Dulce, Golfo 172 F 6
Dul'durga 130 K 5
Dulga-Kyuyel' 130 K 3
Dulgalakh 131 O 2
Dulla 159 F 3
Duluth 171 H 2
Dūmā 154 F 2
Dumaguete 137 F 2
Dumai 136 B 3
Dumanlı Dağı 117 F 3
Dumaran 137 EF 1
Dumaring 136 E 3
Dumbarton 99 B 4
Dumboa 157 G 3
Dumfries 99 C 4
Dumfries and Galloway 99 C 4
Dumont d'Urville 185
Dumpu 144 E 3
Dumraon 134 D 2
Dumyāṭ 154 E 2
Duna 116 A 1
Dunafőldvár 116 A 1
Dunajec 111 G 5
Dunántúl 116 A 1
Dunărea 116 C 1
Dunaújváros 116 A 1
Dunav 116 C 2
Dunay 130 M 1
Dunay 133 K 2
Dunayevtsy 118 E 6
Dunbar (Australia) 143 G 2
Dunbar (U.K.) 99 C 3
Dunblane 99 C 3
Duncan 170 G 5
Duncan Passage 135 F 5
Duncansby Head 98 C 2
Dundalk 100 B 3
Dundalk Bay 100 B 3
Dundas, Lake 142 C 5
Dundas Peninsula 167 P 1
Dundas Strait 142 E 1
Dún Dealgan 110 B 4
Dundee (U.K.) 99 C 3
Dundee (Airport) 99 C 3
Dundee (S. Afr.) 160 DE 5
Dundgovĭ 132 E 1
Dundwa Range 134 D 2
Dunedin 145 Q 10
Dunes de l'Akchar 152 C 4
Dunes de l'Azéffal 152 BC 4
Dunfanaghy 100 B 2
Dunfermline 99 C 3
Dungannon 100 B 2
Dungarpur 134 B 3
Dungas 157 F 3
Dungeness 103 E 2
Dungog 143 J 5
Dungu 158 D 4
Dungul 154 E 3
Dunhua 133 J 2
Dunhuang 132 B 2
Dunkeld 99 C 3
Dunkerque 114 D 1
Dunkirk 171 L 3

Dunkur 158 F 2
Dunkwa 156 D 4
Dun Laoghaire 100 B 3
Dunlavin 100 B 3
Dunleer 100 B 3
Dunmanway 110 B 4
Dunmarra 142 E 2
Dunmore 171 L 3
Dunnet Head 98 C 2
Dunoon 99 B 4
Dunqulah al 'Ordi 154 E 5
Dunqulah al Qadīmah 154 E 5
Dunqunāb 154 F 4
Dunrankin 171 K 2
Duns 99 C 4
Dunsmuir 170 B 3
Dunstable 103 D 2
Dunstan 144 P 9–10
Dunvegan 98 A 3
Dunvegan Head 98 D 3
Duolun 133 G 2
Duong Dong 135 H 5
Duque de York 183 A 9
Durack Range 142 D 2
Durağan 117 D 2
Durance 115 E 3
Durand 145 J 6
Durango (Spain) 114 C 3
Durango (CO, U.S.A.) 170 E 4
Durango (Mex.) 172 B 3
Durant 171 G 5
Duratón 114 C 3
Durazno 182 E 5
Durban 161 E 4
Düren 110 E 4
Durg 134 D 3
Durgapur (Bangla Desh) 135 F 2
Durgapur (India) 134 E 3
Durham (N.C., U.S.A.) 171 L 4
Durham (U.K.) 101 E 2
Durham Downs 143 G 4
Durmā 155 H 4
Durmitor 116 A 2
Durness 98 B 2
Duro Europos → Aş Şāliḥīyah 155 G 2
Duroy 130 L 5
Durresi 116 A 2
Durrow 100 B 3
Dursunbey 116 C 3
Duruksi 159 H 3
Durusu Gölü 116 C 2
Durūz, Jabal ad 154 F 2
D'Urville Island 145 Q 9
D'Urville Sea 185
Dusa Mareb 159 H 3
Dushak 128 G 3
Dushan 132 E 5
Dushanbe 129 H 3
Dushekan 130 J 3
Dusheti 117 F 2
Düsseldorf 110 D E 4
Dutch Harbor 166 D 5
Dutlwe 160 C 4
Duved 112 F 3
Duvno 115 G 3
Duvogero 118 H 3
Duwayhin 155 J 4
Duwwāh 155 K 4
Duye 158 D 4
Duyun 132 E 5
Düz 153 G 2
Düzce 116 D 2
Dvina, Severnyy 118 H 3
Dvinskaya Guba 118 G 2
Dvurechnaya 118 G 6
Dwarka 134 A 3
Dworshak Reservoir 170 C 2
Dyadmo 130 J 4
Dyatkovo 118 F 5
Dyatlovo 113 J 5
Dyersburg 171 J 4
Dyfed 102 B 2
Dyga-Zapadnaya, Mys 131 R 4
Dygdy-Sise, Khrebet 131 O 4
Dyje 111 G 5
Dykehead 99 C 4
Dykh Tau 117 F 2
Dylewska Góra 111 G 4
Dysný Ežeras 113 J 5
Dytike Rodhopi 116 B 2
Dyurmen'tove 129 G 1
Dyurtyuli 118 K 4
Dzag 130 G 6
Dzamīn Üüd 132 F 2
Dzaoudzi 161 H 3
Dzavhan Gol 130 F 6
Dzenzik, Mys 117 E 1
Dzerzhinsk 113 J 5
Dzerzhinsk 118 H 4
Dzerzhinskaya, Gora 113 J 5

Dzerzhinskoye 119 Q 6
Dzerzhinskoye 130 G 4
Dzhagdy, Khrebet 131 O 5
Dzhagry 117 G 2
Dzhaki-Unakhta Yakbyyana, Khrebet 131 OP 6
Dzhaksy 119 N 5
Dzhalagash 129 G 1
Dzhalal-Abad 129 J 2
Dzhalampyr 129 H 3
Dzhalilabad 128 D 3
Dzhalinda 131 M 5
Dzhaltyr 119 N 5
Dzhambul 119 M 5
Dzhambul 119 O 6
Dzhamm 131 O 1
Dzhanga 128 E 2
Dzhankoy 117 D 1
Dzhanybek 118 J 6
Dzhardzhan 131 MN 2
Dzharkurgan 129 H 3
Dzhava 117 F 2
Dzhebariki 131 P 3
Dzhebel 128 E 3
Dzhelinde 130 K 1
Dzhetygara 119 M 5
Dzhezkazgan 129 H 1
Dzhigirbent 129 G 2
Dzhigudzhak 131 T 3
Dzhirgatal' 129 J 3
Dzhizak 129 H 2
Dzhubga 117 E 2
Dzhugdzhur, Khrebet 131 OP 4
Dzhugdzhur Range 131 Q 4
Dzhungarskiy Alatau, Khrebet 119 Q 6
Dzhunkun 130 K 3
Dzhurin 116 C 1
Dzhusaly 129 G 1
Dzibalchén 172 E 4
Dzierżoniów 111 G 4
Dzioua 153 G 2
Dziuche 172 E 4
Dzungaria 129 M 1
Dzüünbayan 132 E 2
Dzuunbulag 132 F G 1

E

Eagle (Seychelles) 166 J 3
Eagle (AK, U.S.A.) 159 J 6
Eagle Lake (CA, U.S.A.) 170 B 3
Eagle Lake (Ont., Can.) 168 J 6
Eagle Pass 170 F 6
Eagle Peak 170 B 3
Eagle River 166 H 3
Eagle Summit 166 H 2
Ear Falls 168 J 5
Earn, Loch 99 B 3
Easington 101 F 3
Easingwold 101 E 2
Easley 171 K 5
East Alligator River 142 E 1
East Antarctica 185
East Bay 167 V 3
Eastbourne 103 E 2
East Cape 145 R 8
East China Sea 133 HJ 5
East Dereham 103 E 1
Easter Island 147 H 5
Eastern Ghats 134 D 4
Eastern Nard River 129 G 5
Easter Ross 98 B 3
East Falkland 183 E 9
East Grinstead 103 E 2
East Kilbride 99 B 4
Eastleigh 103 D 2
East London 160 D 6
Eastmain 169 M 5
Eastman 171 K 5
East Midlands (Airport) 103 D 1
Easton 171 L 3
East Pacific Basin 193 D 4
East Pacific Ridge 193 D 5
East Point 171 K 5
East Retford 101 E 1
East Siberian Sea 184
East Sussex 103 E 2
Eastwood 103 D 1
Eaton, Lake 142 B 4
Eatonville 170 B 2
Eau Claire 171 H 3
Eau-Claire, Lac à l' 169 N 4
Eauripik 146 A 2
Eba, Mount 143 F 5
Ebano 172 C 3
Ebbw Vale 102 C 2

Ebe 131 Q 3
Ebe-Basa 131 N 3
Ebebiyin 157 G 5
Ebeltoft 113 F 4
Eber Gölü 116 D 3
Eberswalde 111 F 4
Ebinur Hu 129 L 1
Ebo 160 A 2
Eboli 115 G 3
Ebolowa 157 G 5
Ebombo 158 D 6
EbonKili 146 C 2
Ebony 160 B 4
Ebro 114 C 3
Ebro, Delta del 114 D 3
Ebro, Embalse del 114 C 3
Ebyakh 131 S 2
Ecbatana 128 D 4
Eccles 101 D 3
Ech Cheliff 153 F 1
Echdeiria 152 C 3
Echeng 132 F 4
Echmiadzin 117 F 2
Echo Bay 167 O 2
Echuca 143 G 6
Écija 114 B 4
Eckernförde 111 E 4
Eckerö 113 G 3
Ecuador 178 B 4
Ed 113 F 4
Eday 98 C 2
Edchera 152 C 3
Ed Damer → Ad' Dāmir 154 E 5
Eddaré 152 D 4
Eddéki 157 H 2
Ede 157 E 4
Edéa 157 G 5
Edefors 112 H 2
Edel Land 142 A 4
Eden (Australia) 143 H 6
Edenburg 160 D 5
Edenderry 100 B 3
Eden, River 101 D 2
Edenton 171 L 4
Eder 111 E 4
Edgar Range 142 C 2
Edgell 169 P 3
Edgemont 170 F 3
Edgeøya 184
Edgeworthstown 100 B 3
Edhampur 129 K 4
Edhessa 116 B 2
Edina 171 H 3
Edinburgh 99 C 4
Edinburgh (Airport) 99 C 4
Edinga 157 H 2
Edirne 116 C 2
Edjeleh 153 G 3
Edmonds 170 B 2
Edmonton 167 P 5
Edmundston 169 O 6
Edough, Djebel 115 E 4
Edounga 157 G 6
Edremit 116 C 3
Edremit Körfezi 116 C 3
Edrengiyn Nuruu 132 C 2
Edsbyn 112 G 3
Edson 167 O 5
Eduni, Mount 166 M 3
Edward 171 M 3
Edward, Lake 158 D 5
Edward River 143 G 1
Edwards Creek 143 F 4
Edwards Plateau 170 F 5
Edzhen 131 P 3
Edzo 167 O 3
Eek 166 E 3
Eenhana 160 B 3
Efate 145 J 5
Efāni 117 D 2
Efes 116 C 3
Effingham 171 J 4
Eforie 116 C 2
Egaña 183 E 6
Egan Range 170 D 4
Egbe 157 F 4
Egegik 166 F 4
Eger 116 B 1
Egersund 113 E 4
Egerton, Mount 142 B 3
Eggan 157 F 4
Eg Glab Tiguesmat 152 D 3–4
Égletons 114 D 2
Egmont, Cape 145 Q 8
Egmont, Mount 145 Q 8

Egremont 101 D 2
Eğridir 116 D 3
Eğridir Gölü 116 D 3
Eguata 157 F 6
Egvekinot 166 B 2
Egypt 154 DE 3
Eha Amufu 157 F 4
Ehcel 156 E 2
Eiao 147 F 3
Eibar 114 C 3
Eidet 112 F 3
Eidfjord 113 E 3
Eidslandet 112 E 3
Eidsvåg 112 E 3
Eidsvoll 113 F 3
Eifel 110 E 4
Eigat, Jabal 154 F 5
Eigerøy 113 E 4
Eigg 99 A 3
Eight Degree Channel 134 B 6
Eights Coast 185
Eighty Mile Beach 142 C 2
Eigrim, Jabal 154 F 5
'Eilai 154 E 5
Eildon 143 H 6
Ei Loutone, Mont 157 G 1
Einasleigh 143 G 2
Einasleigh River 143 G 2
Eindhoven 110 DE 4
Eindpaal 160 B 5
Eire 110 B 4
Eiríksjökull 112 A 3
Eirunepé 178 DE 5
Eisenach 111 F 4
Eisenerz 115 F 2
Eisenhüttenstadt 111 F 4
Eisenstadt 115 G 2
Ejeda 161 G 4
Ejin Horo Qi 132 E 3
Ejin Qi 132 D 2
Ejura 156 D 4
Ekarma, Ostrov 131 S 6
Ekecik Dağı 117 D 3
Ekenäs (Tammisaari) 113 H 3
Eket 157 F 5
Ekibastuz 119 P 5
Ekimchan 131 O 5
Ekoli 158 C 5
Ekonda 130 H 2
Eksjö 113 F 4
Ekwan 168 L 5
El Aaiún 152 C 2
El Aatf 152 B 2
El Abiodh Sidi Cheikh 152 F 2
El Adeb Larache 153 G 3
El Affroum 114 D 4
El Agreb 153 G 2
El Alamein → Al 'Alamayn 154 D 2
El Alamo 170 C 5
El Alia 153 G 2
El Arahal 114 B 4
El Arâich → Larache 152 D 1
El Aricha 152 E 2
El Arrouch 115 E 4
Elassón 116 B 3
Eláti 116 B 3
Elato 146 A 2
El Attar 153 F 2
Elâzığ 117 E 3
Elba 115 F 3
El'ban 131 P 5
El Banco 178 D 2
El Barco 114 B 3
El Barco de Ávila 114 B 3
Elbasani 116 B 2
El Baul 178 E 2
El Bayadh 153 F 2
El Bema 153 F 4
Elbert, Mount 170 E 4
Elbeyli 117 E 3
El Bir → Teouit 153 G 3
Elbistan 117 E 3
Elblag 111 G 4
Elbow 167 Q 5
Elbrus 117 F 2
'El Būr 159 H 4
El Burgo de Osma 114 C 3
El Buro 172 B 3
Elburz Mountains 128 E 3
El Caín 183 C 7
El Cajon 170 C 5
El Callao 179 F 2
El Canelo 172 B 3
El Carre 159 G 3
El Casco 172 B 3
El Carmen (Bolivia) 180 D 3
El Carmen (Colombia) 178 C 2
El Centro 170 C 5
El Cerito 178 C 3

El C – Esp

El Cerro 180 D 4
Elche 114 C 4
Elcho Island 142 F 1
El Chorro 180 D 5
El Cocuy 178 D 2
El Cóndor, Cerro 182 C 4
El Cuy 183 C 6
Elda 114 C 4
El Dab 159 H 3
El Daoud 152 D 4
El Der 159 G 3
'El Dēre 159 H 4
El Descanso 170 C 5
El Difícil 178 D 2
El'dikan 131 P 3
El Diviso 178 C 3
El Djezair (Alger) 153 F 1
El Djouf 152 D 4
Eldorado (Argentina) 182 F 4
El Dorado (AR, U.S.A.) 171 H 5
El Dorado (KS, U.S.A.) 171 G 4
El Dorado (Mex.) 170 E 4
El Dorado (Ven.) 179 F 2
Eldoret 158 F 4
Eldsberga 113 F 4
El Eglab 152 DE 3
Eleja 112 H 4
Elektrostal' 118 G 4
Elele 157 F 4
Elemi Triangle 158 EF 4
El Encanto 178 D 4
Elephant Butte Reservoir 170 E 5
Elephant Island 185
Elesbão Veloso 181 H 2
El Espina 178 D 3
El Eulma 153 G 1
Eleuthera Island 173 G 2
Elevtheroúpolis 116 B 2
El Farsia 152 D 3
El Fasher 154 D 6
El Ferrol 114 B 3
El Fud 159 G 3
El Fuerte 172 B 3
Elgåhogna 112 F 3
El'gakan 131 M 4
'El Gâl 159 J 2
El Gassi 153 G 2
Elghena 159 F 1
El'gi 131 Q 3
Elgin (OR, U.S.A.) 170 C 2
Elgin (U.K.) 98 C 3
El'ginskoye Ploskogor'ye 131 PQ 2
El Goléa 153 F 2
Elgon, Mount 158 E 4
El Goran 159 G 3
El Guamo 178 C 3
El Guettara 156 D 1
El'gyay 130 L 3
El'gygytgyn, Ozero 131 W 2
El Hachchana 153 F 3
El Hajeb 152 D 2
'El Hamurre 159 H 3
El Hank 152 D 4
El Homr 153 F 3
Elhovo 116 C 2
Eliase 137 H 5
Eliki 157 F 3
Elila 158 D 5
Elim 166 E 3
Elingampangu 158 C 5
Elisabethtown 171 J 4
Elisejna 116 B 2
Elisenvaara 112 J 3
Eliseu Martins 181 H 2
Elista 117 F 1
Elizabeth 143 F 5
Elizabeth City 171 L 4
Elizabeth Falls 167 Q 4
Elizabeth, Mount 142 D 2
Elizabeth Reef 145 K 4
Elizabethton 171 K 4
El Jadida 152 D 2
El Jicaral 172 E 5
El Kala 153 G 1
El Kantara 153 G 1
Elk City 170 G 4
El Kelaa 152 D 2
El Kharga → Al Khārijah 154 E 3
Elkhart 171 J 3
El Khnâchîch 152 E 4
Elkhorn River 170 G 3
Elkhotovo 117 F 2
Elkins 171 L 4
Elko 170 C 3
El Kseïbat 152 E 3
Elku Kalns 113 J 4
El Lagodei → Qardo 159 H 3
Ellef Ringnes Island 184
Ellenabad 134 B 2
Ellendale 170 G 2
Ellensburg 170 B 2
Ellesmere Island 184

Ellesmere Port 101 D 3
Ellice Islands 146 C 3
Ellila 157 J 2
Elliot (Australia) 142 E 2
Elliot (South Africa) 160 D 6
Elliot, Mount 143 H 2
Ellisburg 171 L 3
Elliston 143 E 5
Ell, Lake 142 D 4
Ellon 98 C 3
Ellsworth Land 185
Ellsworth Mountains 185
Elm 111 F 4
Elmadağ 117 D 3
El Maestrazgo 114 C 3
El Mahia 156 D 1
El Maitén 183 B 7
Elmalı 116 C 3
Elmalı Dağı 117 E 3
El Mamoun 156 D 2
El Mansour 152 E 3
El Mayoco 183 B 7
El Medo 159 G 3
El Meghaïer 153 G 2
El Meghair 153 G 2
El Mereié 152 D 5
El Messir 157 H 2
Elmhurst 171 J 3
El Milhéas 152 D 3
El Milia 115 E 4
Elmira 171 L 3
El Mirador 172 E 4
El Moïnane 152 C 5
El Mreiti 152 D 4
El Mreyer 152 D 4
El Mzerif 156 D 1
Elne 114 D 3
El Niabo 159 F 4
El Nido 137 E 1
El Nihuil 182 C 5
El Novillo 170 E 6
El Obeid 154 E 6
El Odre 183 C 6
Elorza 178 E 2
El Oso 178 E 3
El Oued 153 G 2
El Ousseukh 153 F 2
Eloy 170 D 5
El Palmito 172 A 2
El Palquí 182 B 5
El Paso 170 E 5
Elphinstone 143 H 3
El Pico 180 D 4
El Pilar 179 F 1
El Pintado 180 D 5
El Portugues 178 C 5
El Porvenir (Panama) 178 C 2
El Porvenir (Venezuela) 178 E 2
El Potro, Cerro 182 C 4
El Progreso 172 E 4
El Puerto 170 D 6
El Puerto de Santa Maria 114 B 4
El Real 178 C 2
El Reno 170 G 4
El Salto 172 A 3
El Salvador 172 E 5
El Sauca 170 D 7
El Sáuz 170 E 6
El Seibo 173 J 4
Elsen Nur 132 B 3
Elsey 142 E 1
El Sharana 142 E 1
El Soberbio 182 F 4
El Sueco 170 E 6
Eltajin 172 C 3
Eltanin Fracture Zone System 193 D 5
El Tigre (Colombia) 178 E 3
El Tigre (Venezuela) 179 F 2
El Tocuyo 178 E 2
El Tofo 182 B 4
Elton 118 J 6
El Tránsito 182 B 4
El Trapiche 178 C 3
El Triumfo 170 D 7
El Tuito 172 A 3
El Tunal 182 D 4
El Tuparro, Parque Nacional 178 E 2
El Turbio 183 B 9
Eluru 134 D 4
Elva 113 J 4
El Valle 178 C 2
Elvas 114 B 4
Elverum 113 F 3
El Vigía 178 D 3
Elvira 178 D 5
Elvire River 142 D 2
El Wak 159 G 4
Ely (U.K.) 103 E 1
Ely (MN, U.S.A.) 171 H 2
Ely (NV, U.S.A.) 170 D 4

Ema Jõgi 113 J 4
Emali 159 F 5
Emāmrūd 128 E 3
Emån 113 G 4
Emas, Parque Nacional do 181 F 4
Embalse de Alarcón 114 C 4
Embalse de Alcántara 114 B 4
Embalse de Almendra 114 B 3
Embalse de Buendia 114 C 3
Embalse de Cenajo 114 C 4
Embalse de Cijara 114 B 4
Embalse de Contreras 114 C 4
Embalse de Entrepeñas 114 C 3
Embalse de Gabriel y Galan 114 B 3
Embalse de la Cuerda del Pozo 114 C 3
Embalse de la Sotonera 114 C 3
Embalse del Ebro 114 C 3
Embalse del Guárico 178 E 2
Embalse del Río Negro 182 E 5
Embalse de Mequinenza 114 CD 3
Embalse de Ricobayo 114 B 3
Embalse de Valdecañas 114 B 4
Embalse de Yesa 114 C 3
Embalse Ezequiel Ramos Mexia 183 C 6
Embalse Florentino Ameghino 183 C 7
Embarcación 180 D 5
Embarras Portage 167 P 4
Embira 178 D 5
Embu 159 F 5
Emden 111 E 4
Emei Shan 132 D 5
Emel'dzak 131 N 4
Emerald 143 H 3
Emerson 167 S 5
Emet 116 C 3
Emgayet 153 H 3
Emi 130 G 5
Emi Fezzane 157 G 1
Emiliano Zapata 172 D 4
Emi Lulu 157 G 1
Emin 129 L 1
Emira 145 E 2
Emirdağ 116 D 3
Emmaboda 113 G 4
Emmaste 113 H 4
Emmen 110 E 4
Emmet 143 G 3
Emmett 170 C 3
Emmonak 166 E 3
Emory Peak 170 F 6
Empalme 170 D 6
Empangeni 161 E 5
Empedrado (Argentina) 182 E 4
Empedrado (Chile) 183 B 6
Emperor Seamount Chain 193 C 2
Empoli 115 F 3
Emporia (KS, U.S.A.) 171 G 4
Emporia (VA, U.S.A.) 171 L 4
Ems 111 E 4
Emumägi 112 J 4
Enånger 112 G 3
Enard Bay 98 B 2
Enarotali 137 J 4
Encantada, Sierra de la 170 C 5
Encarnación 182 E 4
Enchi 156 D 4
Encinal 170 G 6
Encón 182 C 5
Encontrados 178 D 2
Encounter Bay 143 F 6
Encruzilhada do Sul 182 F 5
Enda Salassie 159 F 2
Ende 137 F 5
Endeavour 143 H 2
Endeavour Strait 143 G 1
Enderbury 147 D 3
Enderby Abyssal Plain 192 B 5
Enderby Land 185
Endicott Mountains 166 G 2
Endwell 171 L 3
Endybal 131 O 2
Energia 183 E 6
Enez 116 C 2
Enfer, Portes d' 158 D 6
Enfield 100 B 3
Engaño, Cabo 173 J 4
Engaño, Cape 137 J 1
Engel's 118 J 5
Engerdyakh 130 L 3
Engershatu 159 F 1
Enggano, Pulau 136 B 5
Engiabaia 159 F 2
English Bazar 134 E 2–3
English Channel 103 D 2
Engozero 112 K 2

Engozero, Ozero 112 K 2
Engure 113 H 4
Enibé 157 J 2
Enid 170 G 4
Eniwetok 146 B 2
Enji 152 D 5
Enkan 131 Q 4
Enkan, Mys 131 Q 4
Enkeldoorn 161 E 3
Enköping 113 G 4
Enmore 179 G 2
Enna 115 F 4
Ennadai 167 R 3
Ennadai Lake 167 R 3
Ennedi 157 J 2
Ennis 110 B 4
Enniscorthy 102 A 1
Enniskillen 100 B 2
Ennistymon 110 B 4
Ennore 134 D 5
Enns 115 F 2
Eno 112 K 3
Enontekiö 112 H 2
Enrekang 137 E 4
Enschede 110 E 4
Ensenada 170 C 5
Enshi 132 E 4
Entebbe 158 E 4
Enterprise (NWT., Can.) 167 O 3
Enterprise (OR, U.S.A.) 170 C 2
Entrecasteaux, Récifs d' 146 B 4
Entrepreñas, Embalse de 114 C 3
Entre Rios (Amazonas, Brazil) 179 G 4
Entre Ríos (Bolivia) 180 D 5
Entre Rios (Pará, Brazil) 179 H 5
Entrevaux 115 E 3
Entroncamento 114 B 4
Enugu 157 F 4
Enugu Ezike 157 F 4
Enurmino 166 C 2
Envigado 178 C 2
Envira 178 D 5
Enyamba 158 C 5
Enyellé 157 H 5
Eolie o Lipari, Isole 115 F 4
Epanomi 116 B 2
Epembe 160 A 3
Épéna 157 H 5
Épernay 114 D 2
Ephesus 116 C 3
Epi 145 J 5
Epidhavros 116 B 3
Épinal 115 E 2
Epira 179 G 2
Episkopi 117 D 4
Epping 103 E 2
Epsom 103 D 2
Epukiro 160 B 4
Epukiro 160 C 4
Epupa Falls 160 A 3
Epuyén 183 B 7
Équateur 158 BC 4
Equatoria 158 DE 3
Equatorial Guinea 157 FG 5
Eraclea 115 G 3
Erap 144 E 3
Erbaa 117 E 2
Erba, Jabal 154 F 4
Erbeskopf 111 E 5
Erbîl 155 G 1
Erçek 117 F 3
Erçek Gölü 117 F 3
Erciş 117 F 3
Erciyas Daği 117 E 3
Érd 116 A 1
Erdaogou 132 B 4
Erdek 116 C 2
Erdemli 117 D 3
Erdene 132 F 2
Erdenedalay 132 D 1
Erechim 182 F 4
Ereentsav 130 L 6
Ereğli (Turkey) 117 D 3
Ereğli (Turkey) 116 D 2
Erenhaberga Shan 129 M 2
Erenhot 132 F 2
Erentepe 117 F 3
Erepecu, Lago de 179 G 4
Eresma 114 C 3
Erfoud 152 E 2
Erfurt 111 F 4
Erg Afarag 153 F 4
Ergani 117 E 3
Erg Atouila 156 D 1
Erg Brusset 157 FG 2
Erg Chech 152 E 3
Erg d'Admer 153 G 4
Erg de Ténéré 157 G 2
Erg du Djourab 157 H 2
Ergedzhey 130 L 3
Ergene 116 C 2
Erg er Raoui 152 E 3

Erg Iabès 152 E 3
Erg Iguidi 152 DE 3
Erg in Sakkane 156 D 1
Ergli 113 J 4
Erg N-Ataram 153 F 4
Ergun He 130 M 5
Ergun Youqi 130 M 5
Ergun Zuoqi 131 M 5
Er Hai 132 D 5
Eriba 154 F 5
Eriboll, Loch 98 B 2
Eric 169 O 5
Erice 115 F 4
Ericeira 114 B 4
Erichsen Lake 169 L 2
Ericht, Loch 99 B 3
Erie 171 K 3
Erie Canal 171 L 3
Erie, Lake 171 K 3
'Erigābo 159 H 2
Erikub 146 C 2
Erimanthos Óros 116 B 3
Erimbet 129 G 2
Erimo-misaki 133 M 2
Erinpura 134 B 2
Eriskay 99 A 3
Eritrea 159 F 1–G 2
Erkowit 154 F 5
Erlangen 111 F 5
Erldunda 142 E 4
Ermelo 160 DE 5
Ermenek 117 D 3
Ermera 137 G 5
Ermesinde 114 B 3
Ermil 154 D 6
Ermióni 116 B 3
Ermoupolis 116 B 3
Ernakulam 134 C 6
Erne, Lower Lough 110 B 4
Erne, River 100 A 2
Ernest Legouvé 147 E 5
Erode 134 C 5
Erongo 160 B 4
Erongo Mountains 160 B 4
Erota 159 F 1
Erozionnyy 131 R 2
Errego 161 F 3
Er Rif 152 E 2
Erris Head 110 A 1
Erromango 145 J 5
Er Roseires → Ar Ruṣayriṣ 154 E 6
Er rout Sanihida 157 G 1
Ertai 129 N 1
Ertil 118 H 5
Ertix He 129 M 1
Eruh 117 F 3
Erundu 160 B 4
Eryuan 132 C 5
Erzgebirge 111 F 4
Erzin 129 Q 3
Erzincan Kalan 117 E 3
Erzurum 117 F 3
Erzurum-Kars Yaylâsı 117 F 2
Esa-ala 145 F 3
Esbjerg 113 E 4
Esbo 113 H 3
Escada 181 J 2
Escalante 170 D 4
Escalón 170 E 6
Escalona 114 C 3
Escanaba 171 J 2
Escatrón 114 C 3
Escaut 114 D 1
Esch (sur-Alzette) 115 E 2
Eschan 131 R 3
Eschwege 111 F 4
Escondido 170 C 5
Escorial, Serra do 181 H 3
Escudo, Puerto de 114 C 3
Escuintla 172 D 5
Eşenler Daği 117 D 3
Esfahān 128 E 3
Eshowe 161 E 5
Eskdale 99 C 4
Eskifjörður 112 C 2
Eskilstuna 113 G 4
Eskimo Lakes 166 L 2
Eskimo Point 167 T 3
Eskipazar 117 D 2
Eskişehir 116 D 3
Esk River 144 L 9
Esla 113 F 3
Eslāmābād 128 D 4
Eslöv 113 F 4
Eşme 116 C 3
Esmeralda 178 E 3
Esmeralda, Isla 183 A 8
Esmeraldas 178 C 3
España 114 C 4
Española, Isla 178 B 6
Espanola 170 E 4

Esperance 142 C 5
Esperance Bay 142 C 5
Esperanza (Mexico) 170 E 6
Esperanza (Antarctica) 185
Esperanza (Argentina) 182 D 5
Esperanza (Peru) 178 D 5
Espichel, Cabo 114 B 4
Espigão Mestre 181 G 3
Espinal 180 E 4
Espinar 180 B 3
Espinazo del Diablo, Sierra 172 A 3
Espinhaço, Serra do 181 H 4
Espinho 114 B 3
Espírito Santo 181 J 4
Espiritu Santo 145 J 5
Esplanada 181 J 3
Espoo (Esbo) 113 H 3
Espungabera 161 E 4
Esquel 183 B 7
Esquina 182 E 5
Esquinapa de Hidalgo 172 A 3
Essaouira 152 CD 2
Essen 111 E 4
Essendon, Mount 142 C 3
Essequibo 179 G 3
Essex 103 E 2
Essex Mountain 170 E 3
Essexvale 160 D 4
Esslingen 111 E 5
Esso 131 T 4
Essouk 156 E 2
Estados, Isla de los 183 D 9
Estância 181 J 3
Estancias, Sierra de la 114 C 4
Estarreja 114 B 3
Estats, Pic d' 114 D 3
Est, Cap 161 J 3
Estcourt 160 D 5
Este 115 F 2
Estelí 172 E 5
Estella 114 C 3
Estepona 114 B 4
Estero de Agiabampo 170 E 6
Esteros 180 D 5
Esteros del Iberá 182 E 4
Estevan 167 R 6
Estherville 171 H 3
Estoniya 113 J 4
Estrecho de Gibraltar 114 B 4
Estrecho de le Maire 183 CD 9–10
Estrecho de Magallanes 183 B 9
Estrecho Nelson 183 B 9
Estreito, Reprêsa do 181 G 4–5
Estrela, Serra da (Brazil) 181 F 4
Estrêla, Serra de (Portugal) 114 B 3
Estrella 114 C 4
Estremadura 114 B 4
Estremoz 114 B 4
Estrondo, Serra do 179 J 5
Esztergom 116 A 1
Etadunna 143 F 4
Etah 134 C 2
Étain 115 E 2
Étampes 114 D 2
Étang de Berre Arc 115 E 3
Étang de Biscarrosse 114 C 3
Étang de Carcans 114 C 2
Étang de Cazaux 114 C 2
Étang de Lacanau 114 C 3
Étang de Leucate 114 D 3
Étang de Sigean 114 D 3
Étang d'Hourtin 114 C 2
Etawah 134 C 2
Etengua 160 A 3
Ethel Creek 142 C 3
Ethiopia 159 FG 3
Ethiopian Plateau 159 FG 3
Etna 115 FG 4
Etolin 166 L 4
Etolin Strait 166 E 3
Etosha National Park 160 B 3
Etosha Pan 160 B 3
Etoumbi 157 G 5
Etykan 131 R 2
Etzná Tixmucuy 172 D 4
Euca 179 H 3
Eucla 142 D 5
Eudora 171 H 5
Eufaula 171 J 5
Eufaula Lake 171 G 4
Eugene 170 B 3
Eugenia, Punta 170 C 6
Eugenio Garay 180 D 5
Eugmo 112 H 3
Eungella National Park 143 H 3
Euphrates 155 G 2
Eura 112 H 3
Eure 114 D 2
Eureka (CA, U.S.A.) 170 B 3
Eureka (NV, U.S.A.) 170 C 4
Europa 161 F 4

Europa, Picos de 114 B 3
Europa, Punta de 114 B 4
Euston 143 G 5
Eutin 111 F 4
Eva 179 G 4
Evans, Lac 169 M 5
Evans Strait 167 V 3
Evanston (IL, U.S.A.) 171 J 3
Evanston (WY, U.S.A.) 170 D 3
Evansville 171 J 4
Evenequén 179 F 3
Evensk 131 T 3
Everard, Lake 143 F 5
Everard Range 142 E 4
Everest, Mount 134 E 2
Everett 170 B 2
Everett Mountains 169 O 3
Everglades City 171 K 6
Everglades National Park 171 K 6
Evergreen 171 J 5
Evesham 103 D 1
Evijärvi 112 H 3
Evinayong 157 G 5
Évora 114 B 4
Évreux 114 D 2
Evros 116 C 2
Evrótas 116 B 3
Evvoia 116 B 3
Evzono 116 B 2
Ewaso Ngiri 159 F 4
Ewasse 145 F 3
Ewe, Loch 98 B 3
Ewenkizu Zizhqi 130 L 6
Ewirgol 129 M 2
Ewo 157 G 6
Exaltacion 180 C 3
Excelsior Springs 171 H 4
Executive Committee Range 185
Exe, River 102 C 2
Exeter 102 C 2
Exeter Sound 169 P 2
Exmoor 102 C 2
Exmouth (U.K.) 102 C 2
Exmouth (Australia) 142 A 3
Exmouth Gulf 142 A 3
Expedition Range 143 H 3
Extremadura 114 B 4
Extremo 180 B 3
Exuma Cays 173 G 3
Exuma Sound 173 G 3
Eyakit-Tërdë 130 K 2
Eyasi, Lake 158 E 5
Eye 103 E 1
Eyemouth 99 C 4
Eye Peninsula 98 A 2
Eygurande 114 D 2
Eyik 130 L 2
Eyjafjallajökull 112 A 3
Eyjafjörður 112 B 2
Eyl 159 H 3
Eyrarbakki 112 A 3
Eyre 142 D 5
Eyre, Lake 143 F 4
Eyre Peninsula 143 F 5
Eyre River 143 F 3
Eysturoy 110 A 1
Ezequiel Ramos Mexia, Embalse 183 C 6
Ezine 116 C 3
Ezinepazari 117 E 2
Ezop, Gora 131 S 3

F

Fabala 156 C 4
Fabens 170 E 5
Faber Lake 167 O 3
Fabriano 115 F 3
Facatativa 178 D 3
Fada 157 J 2
Fada Ngourma 156 E 3
Fādilī 155 H 3
Faenza 115 F 3
Færingehavn 169 R 3
Faeroe Islands 110 A 1
Fafa (Centr.Afr. Rep.) 158 B 3
Fafa (Mali) 156 E 2
Fafan 159 G 3
Fafen 159 G 3
Făgăraş 116 B 1
Fagatoufa 147 F 4
Fagernes 112 E 3
Fagersta 113 G 3
Fagita 137 H 4
Fagnano 183 C 9
Faguibine, Lac 156 D 2
Fahūd 155 K 4
Faial 152 A 1
Fairbanks 166 H 3

Fair Bluff 171 L 5
Fairborn 171 K 4
Fairfield 170 B 4
Fair Isle 98 D 2
Fairmont (MN, U.S.A.) 171 H 3
Fairmont (W.V., U.S.A.) 171 K 4
Fair Ness 169 N 3
Fairview 143 G 2
Fairweather, Mount 166 K 4
Faisalabad 129 J 4
Faith 170 F 2
Faizabad (Afghanistan) 129 J 3
Faizabad (India) 134 D 2
Fajardo 173 J 4
Fajr, Wādī 154 F 3
Fakahina 147 F 4
Fakaofo 146 D 3
Fakarava 147 F 4
Fakenham 103 E 1
Fakfak 137 H 4
Fakse Bugt 113 F 4
Fakse Ladeplats 113 F 4
Faku 133 H 2
Falaba 156 B 4
Falagh 158 E 3
Falaise 114 C 2
Falaise de Tiguidit 157 F 2
Falam 135 F 3
Fălciu 116 C 1
Falconara Marittima 115 F 3
Falcone, Punta 115 E 3
Faléa 156 B 3
Falémé 156 B 3
Faleshty 116 C 1
Falfurrias 170 G 6
Falkenberg 113 C 4
Falkirk 99 C 3
Falkland Islands 183 DE 9
Falkland Sound 183 DE 9
Falköping 113 F 4
Fallon 170 C 4
Fall River 171 M 3
Falls 158 E 4
Falls City 171 G 3
Falmouth 102 B 2
Falmouth Bay 102 B 2
False Bay 160 B 6
False Pass 166 E 3
Falso Cabo de Hornos 183 C 10
Falster 113 F 5
Falsterbo 113 F 4
Falterona 115 F 3
Falticeni 116 C 1
Falun 113 G 3
Famagusta 117 D 3
Famatina 182 C 4
Famatina, Sierra de 182 C 4
Fana 156 C 3
Fanchang 133 G 4
Fandriana 161 H 4
Fangak 158 E 3
Fangatau 147 F 4
Fangcheng 132 E 6
Fangcheng 132 F 4
Fangliao 133 H 6
Fangshan 133 G 3
Fang Xian 132 F 4
Fangzheng 133 J 1
Fanning → Tabuaeran 147 E 2
Fanø 113 E 4
Fano 115 F 3
Fanø Bugt 113 E 4
Fan si Pan 135 H 3
Faraba 156 B 3
Faraday 185
Faradje 178 D 4
Farāfirah, Wāḥāt al 154 D 3
Farafra Oasis → Wāḥāt al Farāfirah 154 D 3
Farah 129 G 4
Farah Rud 129 G 4
Farallon de Medinilla 146 A 1
Farallon de Pajaros 146 A 1
Faranah 156 B 3
Farasān, Jazā'ir 155 G 5
Faraulep 146 A 2
Farāyid, Jabal al 154 E 4
Fardes 114 C 4
Fareham 103 D 2
Farewell 166 G 3
Farewell, Cape 145 Q 9
Farewell, Cape 166 C 5
Färgelanda 113 F 4

Färjestaden 113 G 4
Farkhato 129 H 3
Farkovo 119 R 2
Farkwa 159 F 6
Farmington (MN, U.S.A.) 171 M 3
Farmington (N.M., U.S.A.) 170 E 4
Farnborough 103 D 2
Farnham 103 D 2
Farnworth 101 D 3
Faro (NWT, Canada) 166 L 3
Faro (Cameroon) 157 G 4
Faro (Portugal) 114 B 4
Fårö 113 G 4
Faro (Brazil) 179 G 4
Faro National Park 157 G 4
Faro, Sierra del 114 B 3
Fårösund 113 G 4
Farquhar, Cape 142 A 3
Farquhar Group 159 J 6
Farrar 110 C 3
Farrars Creek 143 G 3
Farsi 129 G 4
Farsö 113 E 4
Farsund 113 E 4
Fartak, Ra's 155 J 5
Fasā 128 E 5
Fasad 155 J 5
Fasano 115 G 3
Fastov 118 E 5
Fataka 145 J 4
Fatala 156 B 3
Fatehabad 134 C 2
Fatehgarh 134 C 2
Fatehpur 134 D 2
Father Lake 169 M 6
Fatick 156 A 3
Fatsa 117 E 2
Fatu Hiva 147 F 3
Fatu Hutu 147 F 3
Fatunda 158 B 5
Făurei 116 C 1
Fauro 145 G 2
Fauske 112 G 2
Faux Cap 161 H 5
Favang 112 F 3
Favara 115 F 4
Faversham 103 C 2
Favignana 115 F 4
Fayd 155 G 3
Fayette 158 B 6
Fayetteville (AR, U.S.A.) 171 H 4
Fayetteville (N.C., U.S.A.) 171 L 4
Faylakah 155 H 3
Faysh Khābūr 155 G 1
Fayu 146 B 2
Fazeī 157 G 2
Fazrān 155 H 3
Fazilka 134 B 1
F. D. Roosevelt Lake 170 C 2
Fear, Cape 171 L 5
Feathertop, Mount 143 H 6
Fécamp 114 D 2
Federación 182 E 5
Federal Republic of Germany 111 E 5
Federated States of Micronesia 146 AB 2
Fedorovka 119 M 5
Fehmarn 111 F 4
Feicheng 133 G 3
Feijó 178 D 5
Feixiang 132 F 3
Fejø 113 F 5
Feke 117 E 3
Feklistova, Ostrov 131 P 5
Felanitx 114 D 4
Feldberg 111 E 5
Feldkirch 115 E 2
Felipe Carrillo Puerto 172 E 4
Felix, Cape 167 S 2
Felixlândia 181 H 4
Felixstowe 103 E 2
Feltre 115 F 2
Feltwell 103 E 1
Femer Bælt 113 F 5
Femö 113 F 5
Femund 112 F 3
Fenaroa 159 F 2
Fener Burnu 117 E 2
Fengcheng 133 H 2
Fengcheng 133 H 3
Fengdu 132 E 5
Fenghuang 132 E 5
Fengjie 132 F 4
Fengning 133 G 2
Fengqing 132 C 6

Fengqiu 132 F 3
Fengrun 133 G 3
Fengshuba Shuiku 132 G 6
Fengshui Shan 131 M 5
Fengtai 133 G 4
Feng Xian 133 G 4
Feng Xian 132 E 4
Fengxiang 132 E 4
Fengxin 132 G 5
Fengzhen 132 F 2
Fen He 132 F 3
Feni Islands 145 F 2
Fenoarivo Atsinanana 161 H 3
Fensfjorden 112 D 3
Fentani, Monti dei 115 F 3
Fenxi 132 F 3
Fenyang 132 F 3
Fenyi 132 F 5
Feodosiya 117 E 1
Fer, Cap de 153 G 1
Ferdow 128 F 3
Feren 112 F 3
Ferfer 159 H 3
Fergana 129 J 2
Fergana Basin 129 J 2
Ferganskiy Khrebet 129 J 2
Fergus 98 D 3
Fergus Falls 171 G 2
Ferguson Lake 167 Q 2
Fergusson 145 F 3
Fergusson River 142 E 1
Ferjukot 112 A 3
Ferkéssédougou 156 C 4
Ferlo 156 B 3
Fermo 115 F 3
Fermoselle 114 B 3
Fernandina, Isla 178 B 6
Fernando de la Mora 182 E 4
Fernando de Noronha Island 175 G 3
Fernandópolis 181 F 5
Fernando Póo → Bioko 157 F 5
Ferrara 115 F 3
Ferreira Gomes 179 H 3
Ferrenafe 178 C 5
Ferret, Cap 114 C 3
Ferriday 171 H 5
Fertilia 115 E 3
Fès 152 E 2
Feshi 158 B 6
Festus 171 H 4
Feteşti 116 C 2
Fethiye 116 C 3
Fethiye Körfezi 116 C 3
Fetisovo 128 E 2
Fetlar 98 D 1
Feuilles, Baie aux 169 O 4
Feuilles, Rivière aux 169 N 4
Fezzan 153 HJ 3
Ffestiniog 102 C 1
Fiambalá 182 C 4
Fianarantsoa 161 H 4
Fianga 157 H 4
Fich 159 G 3
Fiche 159 F 3
Fichtelgebirge 111 F 4
Ficksburg 160 D 5
Fidenza 115 F 3
Fieri 116 A 2
Fierras 112 G 2
Fiery Cross Reef 136 D 2
Fife 99 C 3
Fife Ness 99 C 3
Fifth Cataract → Ash Shallāl al Khamis 154 E 5
Figeac 114 D 3
Figtree 160 D 4
Figueira, Cachoeira 179 G 4–5
Figueira da Foz 114 B 3
Figueras 114 D 3
Figuig 152 E 2
Fiji 146 C 4
Fiji Islands 146 C 4
Filadélfia (Brazil) 179 J 5
Filadélfia (Paraguay) 180 D 5
Filchner Ice Shelf 185
Filey 101 E 2
Filiaşi 116 B 2
Filiatra 116 B 3
Filicudi 115 F 4
Filingué 156 E 3
Filipstad 113 F 4
Filtu 159 G 3
Fimbul Ice Shelf 185
Fimi 158 B 5
Findhorn, River 98 C 3
Findık 117 F 3
Findlay 171 K 3
Fingoè 161 E 3
Finike 116 C 3
Finisterre, Cabo de 114 B 3
Finke 142 E 4
Finke Flood Flats River 143 F 4

Esp–Fin

229

Fin – Fue

Finke Gorge National Park 142 E 3
Finke, Mount 142 E 5
Finke River 142 E 4
Finland 112 J 3
Finland, Gulf of 113 J 4
Finlay 167 M 4
Finlay Forks 167 N 4
Finley 143 H 6
Finnie Bay 169 M 2
Finniss, Cape 142 E 5
Finnmark 112 H 2
Finnmarksvidda 112 H 2
Finnskogen 113 F 3
Finnsnes 112 G 2
Finnveden 113 F 4
Fins 155 K 4
Finspång 113 G 4
Finsterwalde 111 F 4
Fiordland National Park 144 P 9–10
Fırat 117 E 3
Firenze 115 F 3
Firghia 156 B 3
Firkachi 157 G 2
Firmat 182 D 5
Firminy 114 D 2
Firovo 118 F 4
Firozabad 134 C 2
Firozpur 134 B 1
First Cataract → Sadd al Aswān 154 E 4
Firth of Clyde 99 B 4
Firth of Forth 99 C 3
Firth of Inverness 98 B 3
Firth of Lorn 99 B 3
Firth of Tay 99 C 3
Firūzābād 128 E 5
Fischersbrunn 160 A 4
Fisher Strait 167 V 3
Fishguard 102 B 2
Fish River (South Africa) 160 C 6
Fish River (Namibia) 160 B 5
Fish River 143 F 2
Fisht, Gora 117 E 2
Fiskåfjället 112 F 3
Fiskárdhon 116 B 3
Fiskenæsset 169 R 3
Fitful Head 98 D 2
Fitri, Lac 157 H 3
Fitzcarrald 180 B 3
Fitzgerald 167 P 4
Fitzgerald River National Park 142 B 5
Fitz Roy 183 C 8
Fitzroy Crossing 142 D 2
Fitz Roy, Monte 183 B 8
Fitzroy River (Queensland, Austr.) 143 J 3
Fitzroy River (Western Australia) 142 C 2
Fiumicino 115 F 3
Fivizzano 115 F 3
Fizi 158 D 5
Fizuli 128 D 3
Fjällbacka 113 F 4
Fjällfjällen 112 F 2
Fkih Ben Salah 152 D 2
Flacq 161 K 6
Flagler Beach 171 K 6
Flagstaff 170 D 4
Flamborough Head 101 E 2
Flamenco (Argentina) 183 D 7
Flamenco (Chile) 182 B 4
Flaming Gorge Reservoir 170 E 3
Flanders 110 D 4
Flannan Isles 98 A 2
Flasher 170 F 2
Flåsjön 112 G 3
Flat 166 F 3
Flatey 113 A 2
Flateyri 112 A 2
Flathead Lake 170 D 2
Flat Island 136 E 1
Flattery, Cape (WA, U.S.A.) 170 A 2
Flattery, Cape (Australia) 143 H 1
Flåvatnet 113 E 4
Fleet 103 D 2
Fleetwood (U.K.) 101 D 3
Fleetwood (Australia) 143 H 3
Flekkefjord 113 E 4
Flen 113 G 4
Flensburg 111 E 4
Flers 114 C 2
Flesberg 113 E 4
Fleurance 114 D 3
Flevoland 110 E 4
Flinders 144 L 8
Flinders Bay 142 B 5
Flinders Chase National Park 143 F 6
Flinders Island 143 H 6
Flinders Passage 143 H 2

Flinders Range 143 F 5
Flinders Ranges National Park 143 F 5
Flinders Reefs 143 H 2
Flinders River 143 G 2
Flin Flon 167 R 5
Flint (Kiribati) 147 E 3
Flint (MI, U.S.A.) 171 K 3
Flint (U.K.) 101 D 3
Flint Hills 171 G 4
Flinton 143 H 4
Flint River 171 K 5
Flisa 113 F 3
Flisegga 113 E 4
Flora 112 E 3
Florac 114 D 3
Floraville 143 F 2
Florence (Italy) 115 F 3
Florence (AL, U.S.A.) 171 J 5
Florence (OR, U.S.A.) 170 B 3
Florence (S.C., U.S.A.) 171 L 5
Florencia 178 C 3
Florentino Ameghino 183 C 7
Florentino Ameghino, Embalse 183 C 7
Flores (Guatemala) 172 E 4
Flores (Azores) 152 A 1
Flores (Indonesia) 137 F 5
Floreshty 116 C 1
Flores, Laut 137 E 5
Floriano 181 H 2
Floriano Pleixoto 178 E 5
Florianópolis 181 G 6
Florida 171 K 6
Florida (Cuba) 173 G 3
Florida (Uruguay) 182 E 5
Florida Bay 171 K 7
Floridablanca 178 D 2
Florida Islands 145 H 3
Florida Keys 171 K 7
Flórina 116 B 2
Flotta 98 C 2
Fluk 137 G 4
Flumendosa 115 E 4
Flying Fish Cove 136 C 6
Fly River 144 D 3
Foča 115 G 3
Fochi 157 H 2
Fochville 157 H 2
Foci del Po 115 F 2–3
Focsani 116 C 1
Foggaret ez Zoua 153 F 3
Foggia 115 G 3
Foggo 157 G 3
Fogo (Cape Verde) 156 B 7
Fogo (Newfoundl., Can.) 169 R 6
Fohnsdorf 115 F 2
Foix 114 D 3
Fokku 157 E 3
Folakara 161 H 3
Folda 112 F 2
Folégandros 116 B 3
Foley (Botswana) 160 D 4
Foley (NWT., Can.) 169 M 1
Foleyet 168 L 6
Foligno 115 F 3
Folkestone 103 E 2
Folkston 171 K 5
Folldal 112 E 3
Föllinge 112 F 3
Fomboni 161 G 2
Fomich 130 J 1
Fomin 117 F 1
Fond du-Lac (Sask., Can.) 167 Q 4
Fond du Lac (WI, U.S.A.) 171 J 3
Fongen 112 F 3
Fonseca, Golfo de 172 E 5
Fontainebleau 114 D 2
Fontas 167 N 4
Fonte Boa 178 E 4
Fonte do Pau-d'Agua 180 E 3
Fontenay-le-Comte 114 C 2
Fontur 112 C 1
Fonualei 146 D 4
Foraker, Mount 166 G 3
Forbes 143 H 5
Forcados 157 F 4
Ford City 170 C 4
Förde 112 E 3
Fördefjorden 112 E 3
Forecariah 156 B 4
Forest 171 J 5
Forest Fawr 102 C 2
Forest of Dean 102 C 2
Forestville 169 O 6
Forêt d'Ecouves 114 C 2
Forez, Plaine du 114 D 2
Forfar 99 C 3
Forín Linares 180 D 5
Forkas 156 E 3
Forli 115 F 3
Formby 101 D 3
Formentera 114 D 4

Formentor, Cabo de 114 D 4
Formia 115 F 3
Formiga 181 G 5
Formigas 152 A 1
Formosa (Taiwan) 133 H 6
Formosa (Argentina) 182 E 4
Formosa (Goias, Brazil) 181 G 4
Formosa do Rio Prêto 181 G 3
Formosa, Serra 181 E 3
Formosa Strait → Taiwan Haixia 133 GH 6
Formoso 181 G 3
Fornæs 113 F 4
Foroyar 110 A 1
Forres 98 C 3
Forrest 142 D 5
Forrest City 171 H 5
Forsayth 143 G 2
Forshaga 113 F 4
Forsmark 113 G 3
Forsnäs 112 G 2
Forssa 113 H 3
Forst 111 F 4
Fort Albany 169 L 5
Fortaleza (Ceará, Brazil) 181 J 1
Fortaleza (Pará, Brazil) 179 G 5
Fortaleza de Ituxi 178 E 5
Fortaleza de Santa Teresa 182 F 5
Fort Archambault → Sarh 157 H 4
Fort Assiniboine 167 OP 5
Fort Augustus 98 B 3
Fort Beaufort 160 D 6
Fort Benton 170 D 2
Fort Black 167 Q 4
Fort Bragg 170 B 4
Fort Bridger 170 D 3
Fort Brussaux → Markounda 158 B 3
Fort-Carnot 161 H 4
Fort Charlet → Djanet 153 G 4
Fort Chimo 169 O 4
Fort Chipewyan 167 P 4
Fort Collins 170 E 3
Fort Collinson 167 O 1
Fort-de-France 173 K 5
Fort de Polignac → Illizi 153 G 3
Fort Dodge 171 H 3
Fortescue River 142 B 3
Fort Flatters → Bordj Omar Driss 153 G 3
Fort Foureau → Kousseri 157 G 3
Fort Frances 168 J 6
Fort Franklin 167 N 2
Fort Gardel → Zaouatallaz 153 G 4
Fort George 169 M 5
Fort Good Hope 166 M 2
Fort Gouraud → Fdérik 152 C 4
Fort Hope 168 K 5
Forth, River 99 B 3
Fortín Carlos Antonio López 180 E 5
Fortín Coronel 180 D 5
Fortín Falcon 180 E 5
Fortín Galpón 180 E 5
Fortín General Aquino 180 E 5
Fortín General Pando 180 E 4
Fortín Ingavi 180 D 4
Fortín Lavalle 182 D 4
Fortín Madrejón 180 E 5
Fortín Madrejoncito 180 E 5
Fortín Ravelo 180 D 4
Fortín Rojas Silva 180 E 5
Fortín Suárez Arana 180 D 4
Fortín Uno 183 C 6
Fort Kent 169 O 6
Fort Knox 171 J 4
Fort Lallemand → Belhirane 153 G 2
Fort Lamy → N'Djamena 157 H 3
Fort Laperrine → Tamanrasset 153 G 4
Fort Lauderdale 171 K 6
Fort Liard 167 N 3
Fort Mackay 167 P 4
Fort Macleod 167 P 6
Fort Madison 171 H 3
Fort McMahon → El Homr 153 F 3
Fort McMurray 167 P 4
Fort McPherson 166 L 2
Fort Miribel 153 F 3
Fort Morgan 170 F 3
Fort Motylinski → Tarahouahout 153 G 4
Fort Myers 171 K 6
Fort Nelson 167 N 4
Fort Norman 167 M 3
Fort Peck 167 Q 6
Fort Peck Dam 170 E 2
Fort Peck Lake 170 E 2
Fort Pierce 171 K 6

Fort Portal 158 E 4
Fort Providence 167 O 3
Fort Qu'Appelle 167 R 5
Fort Randell Dam 170 G 3
Fortrose 98 B 3
Fort Rupert 169 M 5
Fort Saint James 167 N 5
Fort Saint John 167 N 4
Fort Saskatchewan 167 P 5
Fort Scott 171 H 4
Fort Severn 168 K 4
Fort Shevchenko 128 E 2
Fort Simpson 167 N 3
Fort Smith (Can.) 167 P 4
Fort Smith (OK, U.S.A.) 171 H 4
Fort Stockton 170 F 5
Fort Sumner 170 F 5
Fort Trinquet → Bir Moghreim 152 C 3
Fortune Bay 169 Q 6
Fortuneswell 102 C 2
Fort Vermilion 167 O 4
Fort Victoria → Masvingo 160 E 4
Fort Walton Beach 171 J 5
Fort Wayne 171 J 3
Fort Wellington 179 G 2
Fort William 99 B 3
Fort Worth 171 G 5
Fort Yukon 166 H 2
Foshan 132 F 6
Fosna 112 F 3
Foso 156 D 4
Fossano 115 E 3
Fossil Bluff 185
Foster 143 H 6
Foster, Mount 166 K 4
Fougamou 157 G 6
Fougères 114 C 2
Foula 98 D 1
Fouladou 156 AB 3
Foulaba 156 C 3
Foula Morie 156 B 3
Foul Bay → Khalīj Foul 154 F 4
Foulness Island 103 E 2
Foulwind, Cape 145 Q 9
Foumban 157 G 4
Foum Zguid 152 D 2
Foundiougne 156 A 3
Fourmies 114 D 1
Four Mountains, Islands of 166 C 5
Fourth Cataract → Ash Shallāl ar Rābi' 154 E 3
Fouta Djallon 156 B 3
Fouta Ferlo 156 B 2
Foveaux Strait 144 P 10
Fowey 102 B 2
Fowlers Bay 142 E 5
Fowman 128 D 3
Foxe Basin 167 W 2
Foxe Channel 169 M 3
Foxe Peninsula 169 M 3
Fox Islands 166 D 5
Fox River 171 J 3
Foyle, Lough 100 B 2
Foyle, River 100 B 2
Foz do Breu 178 D 5
Foz do Copeá 179 F 4
Foz do Cunene 160 A 3
Foz do Gregório 178 D 5
Foz do Iguaçu 182 F 4
Foz do Jordão 178 D 5
Foz do Jutaí 178 E 4
Foz Tarauacá 178 E 5
Fraga 114 D 3
Franca 181 G 5
France 114–115 CE 2
Frances 166 M 3
Francés, Cabo 171 K 7
Franceville 157 G 6
Francis Case, Lake 170 G 3
Francisco de Orellana (Ecuador) 178 C 4
Francisco Escárcega 172 D 4
Francistown 160 D 4
Francofonte 115 F 4
Francs Peak 170 D 3
Frankenberg 111 E 4
Frankfort (KY, U.S.A.) 171 K 4
Frankfort (MI, U.S.A.) 171 J 3
Frankfurt am Main 111 E 4
Frankfurt an der Oder 111 F 4
Franklin Bay 167 M 1
Franklin, District of 167 P 1
Franklin Lake 167 S 2
Franklin Mountains 167 M 2
Franklin Strait 167 S 1
Fransfontein 160 A 4
Fransfontein Mountains 160 B 4
Fransisco de Orellana (Peru) 178 D 4

Franz 168 L 6
Franz Josef Land 184
Fraser 167 N 5
Fraser (South Africa) 160 C 6
Fraserburg (South Africa) 160 C 6
Fraserburgh (U.K.) 98 D 3
Fraserdale 169 L 6
Fraser, Mount 142 B 4
Fraser or Great Sandy Island 143 J 4
Fraser Plateau 167 N 5
Fraser Range 142 C 5
Frauenfeld 115 E 2
Fray Bentos 182 E 5
Fredericia 113 E 4
Frederick 170 G 5
Frederick Hills 142 F 1
Frederick Reef 143 J 3
Fredericksburg 171 L 4
Fredericton 169 O 6
Frederik IX-Land 169 R 2
Frederiksdal 169 S 3
Frederikshåb 169 S 3
Frederikshavn 113 F 4
Frederikssund 113 F 4
Fredriksted 173 J 4
Frederiksværk 113 F 4
Fredônia 178 C 2
Fredrika 112 G 3
Fredrikshamn 113 J 3
Fredrikstad 113 F 4
Fredvang 112 F 2
Freeling Heights 143 F 5
Freels, Cape 169 R 6
Freeport (IL, U.S.A.) 171 J 3
Freeport (TX, U.S.A.) 171 G 6
Freeport City 173 G 2
Freetown 156 B 4
Fréhel, Cap 114 C 2
Freiberg 111 F 4
Freilassing 111 F 5
Freirina 182 B 4
Freising 111 F 5
Freistadt 115 F 2
Freital 111 F 4
Fréjus 115 E 3
Fremantle 142 B 5
French Frigate Shoals 147 D 1
French Guiana 179 H 3
Frenchman 167 Q 6
French Polynesia 147 F 4
Frenda 153 F 1
Fresco (Ivory Coast) 156 C 5
Fresco (Brazil) 179 H 5
Fresnillo 172 B 3
Fresno 170 C 4
Freu, Cabo 114 D 4
Freycinet Peninsula 144 L 9
Fria 156 B 3
Fria, Cape 160 A 3
Frías 182 C 4
Fribourg 115 E 2
Friedberg 115 G 2
Friedrichshafen 111 E 5
Friesach 115 F 2
Friesland 110 E 4
Frinton 103 E 2
Frio, Cabo 181 H 5
Frisian Islands 110 E 4
Frobisher Bay 169 O 3
Frobisher Lake 167 Q 4
Frolovo 118 H 6
Frome 103 C 2
Frome, Lake 143 F 5
Fronteiras 181 H 2
Frontera 172 D 4
Fronteras 170 E 5
Front Range 170 E 3–4
Frosinone 115 F 3
Frösö 112 F 3
Frotín Cañada Oruro 180 D 5
Frøya 112 E 3
Fröysjöen 112 D 3
Frozen Strait 167 V 2
Frumos 116 C 1
Frunze 129 J 2
Frunzovka 116 C 1
Fruška Gora 116 A 1
Frutal 181 G 4
Frýdek Mistek 111 G 5
Fryken, Mellan 113 F 4
Fryken, Övre 113 F 3
Ftéri 116 B 3
Fu'an 133 G 5
Fubo 157 G 7
Fuchuan 132 F 6
Fuding 133 H 5
Fuengirola 114 C 4
Fuente de Cantos 114 B 4
Fuentesaúco 114 B 3
Fuentes de Andalucia 114 B 4
Fuerte Olimpo 180 E 5
Fuerteventura 152 C 3

230

Fuga 137 J 1
Fuglafjorður 110 A 1
Fugong 132 C 5
Fugou 132 F 4
Fugu 132 F 3
Fuhai 129 M 1
Fuji 133 L 3
Fujian 133 G 5
Fujin 131 O 6
Fuji-san 133 L 3
Fujiyama 133 L 3
Fūka 154 D 2
Fukang 129 M 2
Fukue 133 J 4
Fukue-jima 133 J 4
Fukui 133 L 3
Fukuoka 133 K 4
Fukushima 133 M 3
Fukushima 133 M 2
Fukuyama 133 K 4
Fulda 111 E 4
Fuling 132 E 5
Fulton 183 E 6
Fulufjället 112 F 3
Funafuti 146 C 3
Funäsdalen 112 F 3
Funchal 152 B 2
Fundão 114 B 3
Fundão 181 H 4
Fundación 178 D 1
Fundy, Bay of 169 O 7
Funhalouro 161 E 2
Funing 133 G 3
Funing 133 G 4
Funing 132 E 6
Funiu Shan 132 F 4
Funnel River 143 H 3
Funsi 156 D 3
Funtua 157 F 3
Fuping 132 E 4
Fuping 132 F 3
Fuqing 133 G 5
Furana 153 F 4
Furancungo 161 E 2
Furano 133 M 2
Furawiyah 154 C 5
Furmanov 118 H 4
Furmanovka 129 J 2
Furmanovo 118 J 6
Furnas Dam 181 G 5
Furneaux Group 146 A 5
Fürstenfeld 115 G 2
Fürstenfeldbrück 111 F 5
Fürstenwalde 111 F 4
Fürth 111 F 5
Furth im Wald 111 F 5
Furudal 112 G 3
Furukawa 133 M 3
Fury and Hecla Strait 168 K 1
Fusagasugá 178 D 3
Fushë-Lura 116 B 2
Fushun 133 H 2
Fusong 133 J 2
Fusui 132 E 6
Futa, Passo della 115 F 3
Futa Ruím 183 B 7
Futuna (Vanuatu) 145 K 5
Futuna (Wallis and Futuna) 146 D 3
Fu Xian 132 E 3
Fu Xian 133 H 3
Fuxian Hu 132 D 6
Fuxin 133 H 2
Fuyang 132 G 4
Fuyu 131 M 6
Fuyu 133 H 1
Fuyuan (China) 132 D 5
Fuyuan (U.S.S.R.) 131 O 6
Fuyun 129 M 1
Fuzhou 132 G 5
Fyn 113 F 4
Fyne, Loch 99 B 3
Fyresvatn 113 E 4
Fyrsjön 112 G 3

G

Gabba' 159 J 3
Gabbs 170 C 4
Gabela 160 A 2
Gabès 153 H 2
Gabon 157 G 6
Gaborone 160 D 4
Gaboto 182 D 5
Gabras 154 D 6
Gabredarre 159 G 3
Gabrey, Vozvyshennost' 130 F 1
Gabriel Strait 169 O 3
Gabriel y Galan, Embalse de 114 B 3

Gabrovo 116 C 2
Gacé 114 D 2
Gach Sārān 128 E 4
Gacko 115 G 3
Gada 157 F 3
Gadag 134 C 4
Gadamai 154 F 5
Gadame 158 E 3
Gäddede 112 F 3
Gadê 132 C 4
Gadhap 129 G 5
Gadsden 171 J 5
Gadwal 134 C 4
Gaeta 115 E 3
Gaeta, Golfo di 115 F 3
Gaferut 146 A 2
Gaffney 171 K 4
Gafsa 151
Gafsa → Qafşah 153 G 2
Gagan 145 F 3
Gagarin 118 F 4
Gagere 157 F 3
Gagnoa 156 C 4
Gagnon 169 O 5
Gag, Pulau 137 G 4
Gagra 117 F 2
Gagshor 118 K 3
Gaibanda 134 E 2
Gaillac 114 D 3
Gaillimh 110 B 4
Gaimán 183 C 7
Gainesville (FL, U.S.A.) 171 K 6
Gainesville (GA, U.S.A.) 171 K 5
Gainesville (TX, U.S.A.) 171 G 5
Gainsborough 103 D 1
Gairdner, Lake 143 F 5
Gairloch 98 B 3
Gai Xian 133 H 2
Gaizina Kalns 113 J 4
Gakankoy 131 T 4
Gakarosa 160 C 5
Gakona 166 H 3
Gala (Tibet, China) 134 E 2
Gala (Greece) 116 C 2
Gălăbovo 116 C 2
Galadi (Ethiopia) 159 H 3
Galadi (Nigeria) 157 F 3
Galana 159 F 5
Galán, Cerro 182 C 4
Galanino 130 F 4
Galápagos Islands 178 B 6
Galashiels 99 C 4
Galaţi 116 C 1
Galatina 115 G 3
Galbraith 143 G 2
Galdhöpiggen 112 E 3
Galeana (Mex.) 172 B 3
Galeana (Mex.) 170 E 5
Galela 137 G 3
Galena 166 F 3
Galera, Punta 183 B 6-4
Galesburg 171 H 3
Gali 117 F 2
Galich 118 H 4
Galicia (Poland) 111 H 5
Galicia (Spain) 114 B 3
Galilee, Lake 143 H 3
Galilea 181 H 4
Galimyy 131 T 3
Gälka'yo 159 H 3
Gallan Head 98 A 2
Gallarate 115 E 2
Galle 134 D 6
Gallego 114 C 3
Gallegos 183 B 9
Gallinas, Punta 178 D 1
Gallipoli 115 G 3
Gällivare 112 H 2
Gallo 114 C 3
Gallo, Capo 115 F 4
Gallo Mountains 170 E 5
Galloway 99 B 4
Gallup 170 E 4
Galole 159 F 5
Gal Tardo 159 H 4
Galty Mountains 110 B 4
Galveston 171 H 6
Galveston Bay 171 H 6
Galvez 182 D 5
Galway 110 B 4
Galway Bay 110 B 4
Gam 160 C 4
Gama 183 D 7
Gamarri, Lake 159 G 2
Gamba (Gabon) 157 F 6
Gamba (Tibet, China) 134 E 2
Gambaga 156 D 3
Gambeila 158 E 3
Gambell 166 C 3
Gambia 156 A 3
Gambie 156 B 3
Gambier Islands 147 FG 4
Gambier, Mount 143 F 6

Gamboma 157 H 6
Gamboola 143 G 2
Gamboula 158 B 4
Gamleby 113 G 4
Gammelstad 112 H 2
Gamo Gofa 159 F 3
Gamud 159 F 4
Gamvik 112 J 1
Ganale 159 G 3
Ganāveh 128 E 3
Ganaly 131 T 5
Ganda 160 A 2
Gandadiwata, Bukit 137 E 4
Gandajika 158 C 6
Gandak 134 D 2
Gandaua 129 G 5
Gander 169 R 6
Gandesa 114 D 3
Gandhinagar 134 B 3
Gandhi Sagar Dam 134 C 3
Gandi 157 F 3
Gandía 114 C 4
Gand-i-Zirreh 129 G 4
Gand-i-Zirreh 129 G 5
Gandu 181 J 3
Ganeb 152 C 5
Gangakher 134 C 4
Ganga, Mont de 157 G 4
Ganga 134 E 2
Gangan 183 C 7
Ganganagar 134 B 2
Gangapur 134 C 2
Gangara 132 F 3
Gangaw 135 F 3
Gangawati 134 C 4
Gangca 132 D 3
Gangdisê Shan 134 D 1
Ganges 134 E 3
Ganges Cone 192 B 3
Ganges, Mouths of the 134-135 EF 3
Ganghar 134 C 3
Gangmar Co 134 D 1
Gangotri 134 C 1
Gangtok 134 E 2
Gangu 132 E 4
Gani 137 G 4
Ganina Gar' 130 F 4
Gan Jiang 132 G 5
Gannan 131 M 6
Gannat 114 D 2
Gannett Peak 170 E 3
Ganquan 132 E 3
Gant 108
Ganta 156 C 4
Gantang 132 D 3
Ganyesa 160 C 5
Ganzhou 132 G 5
Ganzurino 130 J 5
Gao 156 D 2
Gao'an 132 G 5
Gaohe 132 F 6
Gaolan 132 D 3
Gaoligong Shan 132 C 5
Gaomi 133 G 3
Gaona 182 D 4
Gaoping 132 F 3
Gaotai 132 C 3
Gaotang 133 G 3
Gaoua 156 D 3
Gaoual 156 B 3
Gao Xian 132 D 5
Gaoyi 132 F 3
Gaoyou 133 G 4
Gaoyou Hu 133 G 4
Gaozhou 132 F 6
Gap 115 E 3
Gapan 137 J 1
Gar 134 C 1
Gara'ad 159 H 3
Garachiné 178 C 2
Garai 129 J 3
Garaina 144 E 3
Garamba National Park 158 D 4
Garanhuns 181 J 2
Garantah 136 E 5
Garara 144 E 3
Garar, Plaine de 157 J 3
Garba Harrey 159 G 4
Garbakaray 130 G 5
García Salinas 172 B 3
Garco 134 E 1
Garda, Lago di 115 F 2
Gardaneh-ye Āvej 128 D 3
Gardemoen 171 K 2
Garden City 170 F 4
Gardez 129 H 2
Gardiner 170 D 2
Gardo → Qardo 159 H 3

Gardula 159 F 3
Gareloi 166 B 5
Garet el Djenoun 153 G 3
Gargano 115 G 3
Gargano, Promontorio del 115 G 3
Gargnäs 112 G 2
Gargouna 156 E 2
Gari 119 M 4
Garies 160 B 6
Garissa 159 F 5
Garkida 157 G 3
Garmal 159 J 3
Garmisch-Partenkirchen 111 F 5
Garmsar 128 E 3
Garnett 171 G 4
Garonne 114 C 3
Garonne, Canal lateral de la 114 D 3
Garoua (Cameroon) 157 G 4
Garoua (Niger) 157 G 3
Garoua Boulai 157 G 4
Garôwe 159 H 3
Garphyttan 113 F 4
Garrison Dam 170 F 2
Garry Bay 167 U 2
Garry Lake 167 R 2
Garsen 159 F 5
Garsila 154 C 6
Garut 136 C 5
Garvagh 100 B 2
Garwa 134 D 3
Garwolin 111 H 4
Gary 171 J 3
Garyn' 130 F 4
Garza 182 D 4
Garze 132 C 4
Garzón 178 C 3
Gasan-Kuli 128 E 3
Gascogne 114 CD 3
Gascoyne Junction 142 B 4
Gascoyne River 142 A 3
Gashagar 157 G 3
Gashaka 157 G 4
Gasht 129 G 5
Gas Hu 132 B 3
Gashua 157 G 3
Gashun 117 F 1
Gaspar, Selat 136 C 4
Gaspé 169 P 6
Gaspé, Cap de 169 P 6
Gaspé, Péninsule de 169 O 6
Gassi Touil 153 G 2
Gassol 157 G 4
Gastello, Iméni 131 R 3
Gastonia 171 K 4
Gaston, Lake 171 L 4
Gastre 183 C 7
Gästrikland 113 G 3
Gata, Cabo de 114 C 4
Gata, Sierra de 114 B 3
Gatchina 112 K 4
Gateshead (U.K.) 101 C 2
Gateshead (NWT, Canada) 167 S 1
Gates of the Arctic National Park and Preserve 166 G 2
Gatineau Park 171 L 2
Gatooma → Kadoma 160 D 3
Gattinara 115 E 2
Gatton 143 J 4
Gatvand 128 D 4
Gatwick (Airport) 103 D 2
Gauaburi 178 E 3
Gauani 159 G 2
Gauhati 135 F 2
Gauja 112 H 4
Gaula 112 F 3
Gauldalen 112 F 3
Gallup 170 E 4
Gausta 113 E 4
Gauttier, Pegunungan 137 J 4
Gavanka 131 T 4
Gåvdhos 116 B 4
Gave de Pau 114 C 3
Gåv Koshī 128 F 5
Gävle 113 G 3
Gävlebukten 113 G 3
Gawler 143 F 5
Gawler Ranges 143 F 5
Gawso 156 D 4
Gaxun Nur 132 D 2
Gaya (India) 134 E 1
Gaya (Niger) 156 E 3
Gaya (Nigeria) 157 F 3
Gaylord 171 K 2
Gayndah 143 J 4
Gayny 118 K 3
Gaysin 116 C 1
Gayvoron 116 C 1
Gaza → Ghazzah 154 E 2

Gazammi 157 G 3
Gazaoua 157 F 3
Gazelle Peninsula 145 F 2
Gaziantep 117 E 3
Gaziantep Yaylası 117 E 3
Gazimur 130 L 5
Gazimurskiy Zavod 130 L 5
Gazipaşa 117 D 3
Gazli 129 G 2
Gbarnga 156 C 4
Gboko 157 F 4
Gcoverega 160 C 3
Gdańsk 111 G 4
Gdansk, Gulf of 111 G 4
Gdov 113 J 4
Gdynia 111 G 4
Gearhart Mountain 170 B 3
Géba 156 A 3
Gebe, Pulau 137 G 4
Gebze 116 C 2
Gechia 158 F 3
Gedi 159 F 5
Gediz 116 C 3
Gedser 113 F 5
Gedser Odde 113 F 5
Geelong 143 G 6
Geelvink Channel 142 A 4
Gefara Plain → Jifārah Plain 153 H 2
Gegamskiy Khrebet 117 G 2-3
Ge'gyai 134 D 1
Geidam 157 G 3
Geigar 154 E 6
Geikie 167 R 4
Geilo 113 E 3
Geiranger 112 E 3
Geita 158 E 5
Gejiu 132 D 6
Gel 158 D 3
Gela 115 F 4
Gelai 159 F 5
Gelendzhik 117 E 2
Gelibolu 116 C 2
Gelibolu Yarimadasi 116 C 2
Gellinsör 159 H 3
Gelsenkirchen 111 E 4
Gemas 136 C 3
Gemena 158 B 4
Gemerek 117 E 3
Gemlik 116 C 2
Gemlik Körfezi 116 C 2
Gemona del Friuli 115 F 2
Gemsbok National Park 160 C 4-5
Gemuru 136 C 3
Genç 117 F 3
Gencek 116 D 3
Geneina → Al Junaynah 154 C 6
General Acha 183 D 6
General Alvear (Argentina) 183 E 6
General Alvear (Argentina) 182 C 5
General Belgrano 183 E 6
General Belgrano II 185
General Belgrano III 185
General Bernardo O'Higgins 185
General Bravo 172 C 2
General Carrera, Lago 183 B 8
General Chaves 183 E 6
General Conesa 183 D 7
General Daniel Cerri 183 D 6
General Guido 183 E 6
General La Madrid 183 D 6
General Lavalle 183 E 6
General Madariaga 183 E 6
General Martín Miguel de Güemes 180 D 5
General Paz 182 E 4
General Pico 183 D 6
General Pinedo 182 D 4
General Pinto 182 D 5
General Roca 183 C 6
General San Martin 185
General Santos 137 G 2
General Treviñe 172 C 2
General Trias 170 E 6
General Vargas 182 F 4
General Villegas 182 D 6
Geneva (N.Y., U.S.A.) 171 L 3
Geneva, Lake 115 E 2
Genève 115 E 2
Genghis Khan, Rampart of 130 K L 6
Gengma 132 C 6
Genichesk 117 D 1
Genil 114 B 4
Genoa 115 E 3
Genova 115 E 3
Genova, Golfo di 115 E 3
Genovesa 178 B 6
Gent 110 D 4
Genteng 136 C 5
Genyem 144 D 3
Geographe Bay 142 B 5
Geographe Channel 142 A 3

231

Geo – Gor

Geok-Tepe 128 F 3
George (Quebec, Can.) 169 O 4
George (South Africa) 160 C 6
George, Lake (Uganda) 158 E 5
George, Lake (Australia) 142 C 3
George, Lake (FL, U.S.A.) 171 K 6
George, Lake (N.Y., U.S.A.) 171 M 3
Georgetown (Queensland, Austr.) 143 G 2
George Town (Tasmania, Austr.) 144 L 9
George Town (Malaysia) 136 A 2
Georgetown (Guyana) 179 G 2
Georgetown (Cayman Isl.) 173 F 4
Georgetown (Gambia) 156 AB 3
Georgetown (S.C., U.S.A.) 171 L 5
Georgetown (The Bahamas) 173 G 3
Georgetown (TX, U.S.A.) 170 G 5
George V Coast 185
George VI Sound 185
George West 170 G 6
Georgia (U.S.A.) 171 K 5
Georgia (U.S.S.R.) 117 F 2
Georgian Bay 171 K 2
Georgina River 143 F 3
Georgiu-Dezh 118 G 5
Georgiyevka 119 Q 6
Georgiyevka 129 J 2
Georgiyevsk 117 F 2
Georg von Neumayer 185
Gerâs, Serra do 114 B 3
Gera 111 F 4
Gerais, Chapadão dos 181 G 4
Geral de Goiás, Serra 181 G 3
Geraldine (Western Australia) 142 A 4
Geraldine (New Zealand) 145 Q 9
Geral do Paranã, Serra 181 G 3
Geraldton (Western Australia) 142 A 4
Geraldton (Ont., Canada) 168 K 6
Geral ou Grande, Serra 181 G 3
Geral, Serra 182 F 4
Gerasimovka 119 O 4
Gerba 131 S 3
Gerbichi, Gora 130 J 2
Gercüş 117 F 3
Gerðar 112 A 3
Gerecse Pilis 116 A 1
Gerede 117 D 2
Geriban → 'El Ḩamurre 159 H 3
Gering 170 F 3
Gerlachovský Štit 111 H 5
Gerlogubi 159 H 3
Gerlovo 116 C 2
German Democratic Republic 111 F 4
Germânia 180 C 3
Germanic 182 D 5
Germi 128 E 4
Germi 128 D 3
Gerona 114 D 3
Gerze 117 E 2
Gêrzê 134 D 1
Gesoa 144 D 3
Gestro, Webbe 159 G 3
Gesunda 113 F 3
Gesunden 112 G 3
Getafe 114 C 3
Gettysburg 170 G 2
Getúlio Vargas 182 F 4
Getz Ice Shelf 185
Geumpang, Krueng 136 A 3
Gevaş 117 F 3
Gevgelija 116 B 2
Geyser, Banc du 161 H 2
Geysir 112 A 3
Ghadāmis 153 G 2
Ghadduwah 153 H 3
Ghadīr ar Razzah 153 J 3
Ghaghara 134 D 2
Ghana 156 D 4
Ghanzi 160 C 4
Ghardaïa 153 F 2
Ghārib, Jabal 154 E 3
Gharyān 153 H 2
Ghashīr 153 H 2
Ghāt 153 H 5
Ghats, Eastern 134 D 4
Ghats, Western 134 B 4
Ghawar 125
Ghayl Bā Wāzīr 155 H 6
Ghayl Bīn Ymayn 155 H 5
Ghazaouet 152 E 1
Ghaziabad 134 C 2
Ghazipur 134 D 2
Ghazni 129 H 4
Ghazzah 154 E 2
Ghedo 159 F 3
Ghelemso 159 G 3
Ghemi, Jabal 158 E 3
Gheorghe Gheorghiu-Dej 116 C 1
Gheorghieni 116 C 1
Gherla 116 B 1
Ghimbi 158 F 3
Ghizao 129 H 4
Ghizar 129 J 3
Ghubaysh 154 D 6
Ghubbat al Qamar 155 J 5
Ghubbat Şawqirah 155 K 5
Ghurāb, Jabal al 154 F 2
Ghurayrah 155 G 5
Ghurd Abū Muḩarrik 154 D 3
Ghurian 129 G 4
Giamame → Jamāme 159 G 4
Giannutri 115 E 3
Gibara 171 L 7
Gibb River 142 D 2
Gibeon 160 B 5
Gibostad 112 G 2
Gibraltar 114 B 4
Gibraltar, Estrecho de 114 B 4
Gibraltar, Strait of 114 B 4
Gibson 142 C 5
Gibson Desert 142 C 3
Gichgeniyn Nuruu 132 C 1
Giddings 171 G 5
Gideå 112 G 3
Gideån 112 G 3
Gidgi, Lake 142 D 4
Gidole → Gardula 159 F 3
Gien 114 D 2
Giessen 111 E 4
Gifthorn 111 F 4
Gift Lake 167 O 4
Gifu 133 L 3
Gigant 117 F 1
Giganta, Sierra de la 170 D 6
Gigha 99 B 4
Giglio 115 F 3
Gjiri i Vlorës 116 A 2
Gijon 114 B 3
Gila Bend 170 D 5
Gila River 170 D 5
Gilbert Islands 146 C 2–3
Gilberton 143 G 2
Gilbert River 143 G 2
Gilbués 181 G 2
Gilé 161 F 3
Giles 142 D 4
Gilford 100 B 2
Gilgandra 143 H 5
Gilgau 116 B 1
Gilgil 159 F 5
Gilgit 129 J 3
Gilgunnia 143 H 5
Gillam 167 T 4
Gillen, Lake 142 C 4
Gillette 170 E 3
Gillian, Lake 169 M 1
Gillingham 103 E 2
Gilo 158 E 3
Gilroy 170 B 4
Gilyuy 131 N 4
Gimli 167 S 5
Gimolskoye, Ozero 112 K 3
Gingin 142 B 5
Gingoog 137 G 2
Ginir 159 G 3
Ginzo de Limia 114 B 3
Gioher → Jōwhar 159 H 4
Gioia del Colle 115 G 3
Gioia Tauro 115 G 4
Giralia 142 A 3
Girardot 178 D 3
Girdle Ness 98 D 3
Giresun 117 E 2
Gir Forest 134 B 3
Giri 158 B 4
Giridih 134 E 3
Girishk 129 G 4
Girna 134 C 3
Girne 117 D 3
Girón 178 C 4
Gironde 114 C 2
Girvan 99 B 4
Girvas 112 K 3
Gisborne 145 R 8
Gisburn 101 D 3
Gisenye 158 D 5
Gislaved 113 F 4
Gistral 114 B 3
Gitarama 158 D 5
Gitega 158 D 5
Giuba → Juba 159 G 4
Giulianova 115 F 3
Giurgiu 116 C 2
Give 113 E 4
Givors 115 D 2
Giza 154 DE 3
Gizhduvan 129 G 2
Gizhiga 131 U 3
Gizhiginskaya Guba 131 T 3
Gizo 145 G 2
Giżycko 111 H 4
Gjiri i Drinit 116 A 2
Gjiri i Karavastase 116 A 2
Gjirokastra 116 B 2
Gjoa Haven 167 S 2
Gjögur 112 B 2
Gjövik 113 F 3
Glace Bay 169 Q 6
Glaciares, Parque Nacional los 183 B 8
Glacier Bay 166 K 4
Glacier Bay National Park and Preserve 166 K 4
Glacier National Park (Brit. Col., Canada) 167 P 5
Glacier National Park (MT, U.S.A.) 170 D 2
Glacier Peak 170 B 2
Gladstone 171 J 2
Gladstone 143 J 3
Glåma 112 F 3
Gláma 112 A 2
Glärmisch 115 E 2
Glarus 115 E 2
Glasgow (U.K.) 99 B 4
Glasgow (Airport) 99 B 4
Glasgow (KY, U.S.A.) 171 J 4
Glasgow (MT, U.S.A.) 170 E 2
Glasier 183 C 7
Glastonbury 102 C 2
Glazov 118 K 4
Gleib Chileh 152 C 4
Gleisdorf 115 G 2
Glenarm 100 C 2
Glen Canyon National Recreation Area 170 D 4
Glendale 170 D 5
Glendive 170 F 2
Glen Garry 99 B 3
Glenhope 145 Q 9
Glen Innes 143 J 4
Glen Lyon 99 B 3
Glen More Monadhliath Mountains 98 B 3
Glennallen 166 H 3
Glenormiston 143 F 3
Glenrock 170 E 3
Glenrothes 99 C 3
Glens Falls 171 M 3
Glenwood Springs 170 E 4
Glina 115 G 2
Glittertind 112 E 3
Gliwice 111 G 4
Globe 170 D 5
Glomfjord 112 F 2
Glommersträsk 112 G 2
Gloppet 112 H 3
Glorieuses 161 H 2
Glorieuses, Iles 161 H 2
Glossop 101 E 3
Glottof, Mount 166 G 4
Gloucester (MA, U.S.A.) 171 M 3
Gloucester (U.K.) 103 C 2
Gloucester (New South Wales, Austr.) 143 J 5
Gloucester, Cabo 183 B 9
Gloucestershire 103 C 2
Glubokiy 117 F 1
Glubokiy 118 H 6
Glubokoye 119 Q 5
Glubokoye 112 J 4
Glücksburg 111 E 4
Glukhov 118 F 5
Glusha 113 J 5
Glusk 113 J 5
Glyboka 116 C 1
Gmelinka 118 J 5
Gmünd 115 G 2
Gmunden 115 F 2
Gnarp 112 G 3
Gniben 113 F 4
Gniezno 111 G 4
Gniloaksayskaya 117 F 1
Gnjilane 116 B 2
Gnowangerup 142 B 5
Goñi 182 E 5
Goa 134 B 4
Goageb 160 B 5
Goalpara 135 F 2
Goari 179 F 4
Goba 159 G 3
Gobabeb 160 B 4
Gobabis 160 B 4
Gobernador Crespo 182 D 5
Gobernador Gregores 183 B 8
Gobi 132 F 2
Goce Delčev 116 B 2
Gochas 160 B 4
Goðafoss 112 B 2
Godalming 103 D 2
Godar i Shah 129 G 5
Godavari 134 D 4
Godavari, Mouths of the 134 D 4
Godhra 134 B 3
Godinlave 159 H 3
Godmanchester 103 D 1
Godoy Cruz 182 C 5
Gods Lake 167 T 5
Gods Mercy, Bay of 167 U 3
Gods River 167 T 4
Godthåb 169 R 3
Godthåbfjord 169 R 3
Godwar 134 B 2
Goe 144 D 3
Goéland, Lac au 169 M 6
Goélands, Lac aux 169 P 4
Goes 110 D 4
Gofitskoye 117 F 1
Gogebic Range 171 J 2
Gogland, Ostrov 113 J 3
Gogolevskiy 119 O 5
Głogów 111 G 4
Gogrial 158 D 3
Gogui 156 C 2
Goiandira 181 G 4
Goianesia 181 G 4
Goiânia 181 G 4
Goianorte 179 J 5
Goiás 181 G 3
Göinge 113 F 4
Góis 114 B 3
Gojam 159 F 2
Gojra 129 J 4
Gökırmak 117 D 2
Goksu 117 D 3
Göksu (Turkey) 117 F 3
Göksu (Turkey) 117 E 3
Göksum 117 E 3
Göktepe 116 C 3
Gokwe 160 D 3
Gol 113 E 3
Golaghat 135 F 2
Golaya Pristan 117 D 1
Golconda 170 C 3
Gölcük 116 C 2
Gold Coast 156 D 5–E 4
Gold Coast (Australia) 143 J 4
Gołdap 111 H 4
Golden 167 O 5
Golden Gate 170 B 4
Golden Hinde 167 M 6
Golden Vale 110 B 4
Goldfield 170 C 4
Gold Rock 168 J 6
Goldsboro 171 L 4
Goldsworthy 142 B 3
Göle 117 F 2
Goleniów 111 F 4
Golestan 129 G 4
Golets-Inyaptuk, Gora 130 K 4
Golets-Longdor, Gora 130 L 4
Golets-Purpula, Gora 130 K 4
Golets Skalistyy, Gora 131 O 4
Golets-Skalistyy, Gora 130 L 4
Golfe de la Gonâve 173 H 4
Golfe de Saint-Florent 115 E 3
Golfe de Saint-Malo 114 C 2
Golfe de Tadjourah 159 G 2
Golfe de Valinco 115 E 3
Golfe du Lion 114–115 D 2
Golfito 172 F 6
Golfo Almirante Montt 183 B 9
Golfo Aranci 115 E 3
Golfo Corcovado 183 B 7
Golfo de Almeria 114 C 4
Golfo de Ana María 173 G 3
Golfo de Ancud 183 B 7
Golfo de Batabanó 172 F 3
Golfo de Cadiz 114 B 4
Golfo de California 170 D 6
Golfo de Chiriquí 178 B 2
Golfo de Cintra 152 B 4
Golfo de Fonseca 172 E 5
Golfo de Guacanayabo 173 G 3
Golfo de Guayaquil 178 B 4
Golfo de Honduras 172 E 4
Golfo del Darién 178 C 2
Golfo dell'Asinara 115 E 3
Golfo de los Mosquitos 178 B 2
Golfo del Papagayo 172 E 5
Golfo de Nicoya 172 F 6
Golfo de Panamá 178 C 2
Golfo de Paria 179 F 1
Golfo de Penas 183 B 8
Golfo de Rosas 114 D 3
Golfo de San Jorge 114 D 3
Golfo de Tehuantepec 172 D 4
Golfo de Valencia 114 CD 4
Golfo de Venezuela 178 D 1
Golfo di Castellammare 115 F 4
Golfo di Gaeta 115 F 3
Golfo di Genova 115 E 3
Golfo di Manfredonia 115 G 3
Golfo di Palmas 115 E 4
Golfo di Policastro 115 G 3
Golfo di Salerno 115 E 3
Golfo di Squillace 115 G 4
Golfo di Taranto 115 G 3–4
Golfo di Trieste 115 F 2
Golfo Dulce 172 F 6
Gulf of Venice 115 F 2
Golfo Ladrillero 183 A 8
Golfo Nuevo 183 D 7
Golfo San Jorge 183 C 8
Golfo San Matías 183 D 7
Golfo Trinidad 183 A 8
Gölgelı Dağları 116 C 3
Gölhisar 116 C 3
Golija 116 B 2
Goljak 116 B 2
Goljama Sjutkja 116 B 2
Goljam Persenk 116 B 2
Gölköy 117 E 2
Golmud 132 B 3
Golmud He 132 B 3
Golo 115 E 3
Gololcha 159 G 3
Gölören 117 D 3
Golovanevsk 116 D 1
Golovin 166 E 3
Golovnino 131 R 7
Golovskoye 130 J 4
Golpayegan 128 E 4
Gölpazarı 116 D 2
Golspie 98 C 3
Golubac 116 B 2
Golubovka 119 O 5
Golyayevka 118 H 5
Golygino 131 T 5
Golyshmanovo 119 N 4
Gol, Zaliv 128 E 2
Goma 158 D 5
Gomati 134 D 2
Gombe 157 G 3
Gombi 157 G 3
Gomel 118 F 5
Gomera 152 B 3
Goméz Palacio 172 B 2
Gomo 134 E 1
Gomo Co 134 E 1
Gomo Gomo 137 H 5
Gonābād 128 F 4
Gonaïves 173 H 4
Gonam 131 O 4
Gonâve, Golfe de la 173 H 4
Gonâve, Ile de la 173 H 4
Gonbad-e Qābus 128 F 3
Gonda 134 D 2
Gondal 134 B 3
Gondar 159 F 2
Gondia 134 D 3
Gondomar 114 B 3
Gönen 116 C 2
Gongan 132 F 4
Gongbo' gyamda 132 B 5
Gonggar 135 F 2
Gongga Shan 132 D 5
Gonghe 132 D 3
Gonglee 156 C 4
Gongliu 129 L 2
Gongola 157 G 3
Gongpoquan 132 C 2
Gongshan 132 C 5
Gonjo 132 C 4
Gonzales 172 C 3
Good Hope, Cape of 160 B 6
Goodhouse 160 B 5
Gooding 170 D 3
Goodland 170 F 4
Goodnews Bay 166 E 4
Goodooga 143 H 4
Goole 101 E 3
Goolgowi 143 H 5
Goomalling 142 B 5
Goondiwindi 143 J 4
Goongarrie 142 C 5
Goonyella 143 H 3
Goose Bay 169 P 5
Goose Lake 170 B 3
Göppingen 111 E 5
Gora Adyakit 130 G 2
Gora Aktau 129 G 2
Gora Alney 131 T 4
Gora Arga-Emneke 131 Q 2
Gora Bazar Dyuzi 128 D 2
Gora Belukha 119 R 6
Gora Bystrinskiy Golets 130 JK 6
Gora Chasnachorr 112 K 2
Gora Chureg-Tag 130 F 5
Gora Denezhkin Kamen' 119 L 3
Gora Dzerzhinskaya 113 J 5
Gora Ezop 131 S 3
Gora Fisht 117 E 2
Gora Gerbichi 130 J 2
Gora Golets-Inyaptuk 130 K 4
Gora-Golets-Longdor 130 L 4
Gora Golets-Purpula 130 K 4

Gor – Gru

Gora Golets-Skalistyy **130** L 4
Gora Golets Skalistyy **131** O 4
Goragorskiy **117** G 2
Gora Isherim **119** L 3
Gora Ivao **131** RS 6
Gora Kamen **130** F 2
Gora Kekurnaya **131** V 3
Gora Kelil'vun **131** V 2
Gora Khil'mi **131** S 1
Gora Khoydype **119** N 2
Gorakhpur **134** D 2
Gora Konus **131** O 4
Gora Konzhakovskiy Kamen' **119** L 4
Gora Kovriga **118** J 2
Gora Kroviga **130** F 3
Gora Kurkure-Bazhi **119** R 5
Gora Kuytun **119** R 6
Gora Ledyanaya **131** W 3
Gora Lopatina **131** Q 5
Gora Medvezh'ya **131** P 6
Gora More-Iz **119** M 2
Gora Moskva **130** F 5
Gora Munku-Sardyk **130** H 5
Gora Nachikinskaya **131** U 4
Gora Narodnaya **119** M 2
Gora Nelkuchan **131** P 3
Goransko **116** A 2
Gora Ostryak **131** W 3
Gora Pal-Pal **131** V 3
Gora Pay-Yer **119** M 2
Gora Pobeda **131** R 2
Gora Pshish **117** F 2
Gora Pyat'kovende **131** T 2
Gora Shunak **129** J 1
Gora Skalistaya **130** D 1
Gora Sokhondo **130** K 6–L 5
Gora Sokhor **130** J 5
Gora Syuge-Khaya **131** P 2
Gora Taklaun **131** Q 3
Gora Tardoki Yani **131** P 6
Gora Tel'pos-Iz **119** L 3
Gora Terpukhoy **131** V 2
Gora Topko **131** P 4
Gora Volna **131** T 3
Gora Yamantau **119** L 5
Gora Yenashimski Pol'kan **130** F 4
Góra Zamkowa **111** H 4
Gora Zubets **131** X 3
Gorda **170** B 4
Gördes **116** C 3
Gordil **158** C 3
Gordion **117** D 3
Gordium **117** D 3
Gordon (NE, U.S.A.) **170** F 3
Gordon (WI, U.S.A.) **171** H 2
Gordon Downs **142** D 2
Gordon Lake **167** P 3
Gordon River **144** L 9
Gordonvale **143** H 2
Gore (New Zealand) **144** P 10
Goré (Chad) **157** H 4
Gore (Ethiopia) **158** F 3
Gorebridge **99** C 4
Görele **117** E 2
Gorelova **131** T 2
Göreme **117** D 3
Gorey **100** B 3
Gorg **128** F 5
Gorgân **128** E 3
Gorgona (Italy) **115** E 3
Gorgona (Colombia) **178** C 3
Gorgora **159** F 2
Gorgoram **157** G 3
Gori **117** F 2
Gorizia **115** F 2
Gorjanci **115** G 2
Gorkha **134** D 2
Gorki **119** N 2
Gor'kiy **118** H 4
Gor'kovskoye Vodokhranilishche **118** H 4
Görlitz **111** F 4
Gorlovka **117** E 1
Gormanstown **144** L 9
Gorna Orjahovica **116** C 2
Gornji Vakuf **115** G 3
Gorno-Altaysk **119** R 5
Gorno-Chuyskiy **130** K 4
Gorno-Filinskoye **119** N 3
Gorno Slinkina **119** N 4
Gornostakhskiy Khrebet **131** P 3,4
Gornozavodsk **131** Q 6
Gornyak **119** Q 5
Gornyy **131** P 5
Gornyy Kazymsk **119** N 2
Gorodenka **116** C 1
Gorodets **118** H 4
Gorodnitsa **113** J 5
Gorodnya **118** F 4
Gorodok (Belorussiya, U.S.S.R.) **113** J 4
Gorodok (Ukraina, U.S.S.R.)**111** H 5
Gorodovikovsk **117** F 1
Goroka **144** E 3
Goromay **131** Q 5
Gorom-Gorom **156** D 3
Gorongosa **161** E 3
Gorongosa National Park **161** E 3
Gorongosa, Serra da **161** E 3
Gorontalo **137** F 3
Goroshikha **119** R 2
Górowo Haweckié **111** H 4
Gorrahei **159** G 3
Gorseinon **102** B 2
Gorstan **98** B 3
Goryachegorsk **119** R 4
Goryachenskiy **118** K 5
Goryachiy Klyuch **131** S 3
Goryachiy Klyuch **117** E 2
Gory Bukantau **129** G 2
Gory Byrranga **130** E 1–H 1
Gory Kul'dzhuktau **129** G 2
Goryn' **113** J 4
Gory Putorana **130** F 2–H 2
Gory Świetokrzyskie **111** H 4
Gory Ulutau **129** H 1
Gory Ushkan'iy **131** X 2
Gory Ushurakchan **131** U 2
Gory Yerementau **119** O 5
Gorzów Wielkopolski **111** G 4
Goschen Strait **143** J 1
Gosford **143** J 5
Goshogawara **133** M 2
Goslar **111** F 4
Gospic **115** G 3
Gosport **103** D 2
Gossi **156** D 2
Gossinga **158** D 3
Gostivar **116** B 2
Gostynin **111** G 4
Gotaru **134** B 2
Gotel Mountains **157** G 4
Gotha **111** F 4
Gothenburg (Sweden) **113** F 4
Gothenburg (NE, U.S.A.) **170** F 3
Gotheye **156** E 3
Gotland **113** G 4
Gotō-rettō **133** J 4
Gotowasi **137** G 3
Gotska Sandön **113** G 4
Gōtsu **133** K 3
Gottwaldov **111** G 5
Goubéré **158** D 3
Goubon **157** H 1
Goudge **182** C 5
Goudiri **156** B 3
Goudoumaria **157** G 3
Goulburn **143** H 5
Goulburn Islands **142** E 1
Gould, Mount **142** B 4
Goulimime **152** C 3
Goumbou **156** C 2
Goundam **156** D 2
Goundi **157** H 4
Gouradi **157** H 2
Gourara **152** EF 3
Gourcy **156** D 3
Gourdon **114** D 3
Gouré **157** G 3
Gourin **114** C 2
Gourma **156** E 3
Gourma-Rarous **156** D 2
Gouro **157** H 2
Gourock **100** C 2
Gourounsi **156** D 3
Gourrama **152** E 2
Gouzon **114** D 2
Gove (Angola) **160** B 2
Gove (Australia) **141**
Govena, Poluostrov **131** V 4
Goverla **116** B 1
Governador Valadares **181** H 4
Governor's Harbour **173** G 2
Govĭaltay **132** C 1
Govorovo **131** N 1
Gower **102** B 2
Goya **182** E 4
Goyder River **142** E 1
Goz Beïda **157** J 3
Goz Dağ **117** D 3
Gozha Co **134** D 1
Gozo **115** F 4
Göppingen **111** E 5
Graaff Reinet **160** C 6
Grabo **156** C 5
Gračac **115** G 3
Grace, Lake **142** B 5
Gracias a Dios, Cabo **172** F 5
Graciosa **152** A 1
Gradaús **179** H 5
Gradaús, Serra dos **179** H 5
Grado (Italy) **115** F 2
Grado (Spain) **114** B 3
Grafing **111** F 5
Grafton (N.D., U.S.A.) **170** G 2
Grafton (New South Wales, Austr.) **143** J 4
Grafton, Islas **183** B 9
Graham (Br.Col., Can.) **166** L 5
Graham Land **185**
Graham (Ont., Can.) **168** J 6
Grahamstown **160** D 6
Grain Coast **156** B 4–C 5
Grajaú **181** G 2
Grajewo **111** H 4
Gramat **114** D 3
Gramat, Causse de **114** D 3
Grampian **98** C 3
Grampian Mountains **99** B 3
Granada (Nicaragua) **172** E 5
Granada (Spain) **114** C 4
Gran Antiplanicie Central **183** C 8
Granard **100** B 3
Granby **169** N 6
Gran Canaria **152** B 3
Gran Chaco **180** D 5
Grand Bahama Island **173** G 2
Grand Ballon **115** E 2
Grand Bank **169** Q 6
Grand Bassam **156** D 4
Grand Béréby **156** C 5
Grand Canal (Rep. of Ireland) **100** B 3
Grand Canal (China) **133** G 3
Grand Canyon **170** D 4
Grand Canyon National Park **170** D 4
Grand Cayman **173** F 4
Grand Cess **156** C 5
Grand Coulee **170** C 2
Grand Coulee Dam **170** C 2
Grande Cache **167** O 5
Grande Chartreuse **115** E 2
Grande Comore **161** G 2
Grande, Ilha (Brazil) **181** H 5
Grande Prairie **167** O 4
Grand Erg de Bilma **157** G 2
Grand Erg Occidental **152–153** E 3–F 2
Grand Erg Oriental **153** G 2–3
Grande Ridge **192** A 5
Grande Rivière de la Baleine **169** MN 5
Grande Ronde River **170** C 2
Grande, Sierra **170** F 6
Grand Falls **169** Q 6
Grand Forks **170** G 2
Grandin, Lake **167** O 3
Grandioznyy, Pik **130** G 5
Grand Island **170** G 3
Grand Junction **170** E 4
Grand Lahou **156** C 4
Grand Lake (N. Brunsw., Can.) **169** O 6
Grand Lake (Newfoundl., Can.) **169** Q 6
Grand Lake Victoria **171** L 2
Grand Lieu, Lac de **114** C 2
Grand Manan **169** O 7
Grand Marais (MN, U.S.A.) **171** H 2
Grândola **114** B 4
Grândola, Serra de **114** B 4
Grand Passage **145** H 5
Grand Popo **156** E 4
Grand Portage **171** J 2
Grand Rapids (Man., Can.) **167** S 5
Grand Rapids (MI, U.S.A.) **171** J 3
Grand Rapids (MN, U.S.A.) **171** H 2
Grand River **171** J 3
Grand Santi **179** H 3
Grand Teton **170** D 3
Grand Teton National Park **170** D 3
Grand Traverse Bay **171** J 2
Grand Turk **173** H 3
Grand Valley **170** E 4
Grand Wintersberg **115** E 2
Graneros **182** B 5
Grangemouth **99** C 3
Grange-over-Sands **101** D 2
Grangeville **170** C 2
Granite City **171** H 4
Granite Peak (MT, U.S.A.) **170** E 2
Granite Peak (NV, U.S.A.) **170** C 3
Granitola, Punta **115** F 4
Granja **181** H 1
Gran Laguna Salada **183** C 7
Gran Morelos **170** E 5
Granön **112** G 3
Granollérs **114** D 3
Gran Paradiso **115** E 2
Gran Pilastro **115** F 2
Gran Río **179** G 3
Gran Sasso d'Italia **115** F 3
Grant **170** F 3
Grantham **103** D 1
Grantown-on-Spey **98** C 3
Grants **170** E 4
Grants Pass **170** B 3
Granville **114** C 2
Granville Lake **167** R 4
Graskop **161** E 4
Grasmere **101** D 2
Grasse **115** E 3
Graulhet **114** D 3
Gravatá **181** J 2
Gravelbourg **167** Q 6
Grave, Pointe de **114** C 2
Gravesend **103** E 2
Gravina in Puglia **115** G 3
Gray **115** E 2
Grayling **171** K 3
Grays **103** E 2
Grays Harbor **170** B 2
Graz **115** G 2
Grdelica **116** B 2
Gördes **116** C 3
Great Abaco Island **173** G 2
Great Artesian Basin **143** G 3–4
Great Australian Bight **142** D 5
Great Barrier **146** C 5
Great Barrier Island **145** R 8
Great Barrier Reef **143** G 1
Great Basin **170** C 3–4
Great Bear **167** N 2
Great Bear Lake **167** N 2
Great Bend **170** G 4
Great Berg **160** B 6
Great Bernera **98** A 2
Great Dividing Range **143** H 3–4
Great Driffield **101** E 2
Great Dunmow **103** E 2
Greater Antilles **173** G–J 4
Greater London **103** D 2
Greater Manchester **101** D 3
Great Exhibition Bay **145** Q 7
Great Exuma Island **173** G 3
Great Falls **170** D 2
Great Fisher Bank **110** D 3
Great Harwood **101** D 3
Great Inagua Island **173** H 3
Great Indian Basin **192** B 4
Great Indian Desert **134** B 2
Great Karas Mountains **160** B 5
Great Karroo **160** C 6
Great Khingan Mountains **133** G 2–H 1
Great Lake **144** L 9
Great Malvern **103** C 1
Great Mountains **160** A 3
Great Nicobar **135** F 6
Great North East Channel **144** D 3
Great Pee Dee River **171** L 5
Great Plain of the Koukdjuak **169** N 2
Great Plains **170** F 2–4
Great Ruaha **159** F 6
Great Salt Lake **170** D 3
Great Salt Lake Desert **170** D 3
Great Sand Sea → Baḥr ar Rimāl al Azim **154** D 3
Great Sandy Desert **142** C 3
Great Scarcies **156** B 4
Great Sitkin **166** B 5
Great Slave Lake **167** P 3
Great Torrington **102** B 2
Great Valley **171** K 4–5
Great Victoria Desert **142** D 4
Great Victoria Desert Nature Reserve **142** D 4–5
Great Yarmouth **103** E 1
Grebbestad **113** F 4
Grebenka **118** F 5
Gréboun, Mont **157** F 1–2
Greece **116** BC 2–3
Greeley (CO, U.S.A.) **170** F 3
Greeley (NE, U.S.A.) **170** G 3
Green (OR, U.S.A.) **170** B 3
Green Bay (WI, U.S.A.)**171** J 3
Green Coast **185**
Greenhorn Mountain **170** F 4
Green Island (New Zealand) **145** Q 10
Green Islands (Papua New Guinea) **145** F 2
Greenland **184**
Greenland Sea **184**
Greenlaw **99** C 4
Greenock **99** B 4
Greenough River **142** B 4
Green River (Papua New Guinea) **144** D 2
Green River (KY, U.S.A.) **171** J 4
Green River (UT, U.S.A.) **170** D 4
Green River (UT, U.S.A.) **170** E 4
Green River (WY, U.S.A.) **170** E 3
Greensboro (GA, U.S.A.) **171** K 5
Greensboro (N.C., U.S.A.) **171** L 4
Greenvale **143** H 2
Greenville (Liberia) **156** C 5
Greenville (AL, U.S.A.) **171** J 5
Greenville (MS, U.S.A.) **171** H 5
Greenville (N.C., U.S.A.) **171** L 4
Greenville (NE, U.S.A.) **171** N 2
Greenville (S.C., U.S.A.) **171** K 5
Greenville (TX, U.S.A.) **171** G 5
Greenwood **171** K 5
Gregorio **178** D 5
Gregory Downs **143** F 2
Gregory, Lake (Western Australia) **142** D 3
Gregory, Lake (South Australia) **143** F 4
Gregory, Lake (Western Australia) **142** B 4
Gregory Range **143** G 2
Gregory River **143** F 2
Greifswald **111** F 4
Grein **115** F 2
Greitz **111** F 4
Gremikha **118** G 2
Grenå **113** F 4
Grenada **173** K 5
Grenada (MS, U.S.A.) **171** J 5
Grenadine Islands **173** K 5
Grenchen **115** E 2
Grenen **113** F 4
Grenoble **115** E 2
Grense-Jakobselv **113** K 2
Grenville, Cape **143** G 1
Gresik **136** D 5
Gretna **99** C 4
Grevená **116** B 2
Grey Islands **169** Q 5
Greymouth **145** Q 9
Grey Range **143** G 4
Greystones **100** B 3
Greytown **161** E 5
Gribingui **158** B 3
Grico **178** E 2
Griffin **171** K 5
Griffith **143** H 5
Grigoriopol' **116** C 1
Grimari **158** C 3
Grim, Cape **144** K 9
Grime's Graves **103** E 1
Grimsá **112** A 3
Grimsby **101** E 3
Grímsey **112** B 2
Grimshaw **167** O 4
Grímsstaðir **112** B 2
Grimstad **113** E 4
Grímsvötn **112** B 3
Grindavik **112** A 3
Grindsted **113** E 4
Grinnel **171** H 3
Grintavec **115** G 2
Griquatown **160** C 5
Gris-Nez, Cap **114** D 1
Grisslehamn **113** G 3
Grizim **152** E 3
Grmeč **115** G 3
Groblersdal **160** D 5
Grodekovo **133** K 2
Grodno **113** H 5
Groix, Ile de **114** C 2
Grójek **111** H 4
Gronau **110** E 4
Gröndalen **112** F 3
Grong **112** F 3
Groningen (Netherlands) **110** E 4
Groningen (Surinam) **179** G 2
Grønnedal **169** S 3
Groote Eylandt **143** F 1
Grootfontein **160** B 3
Groot River **160** C 6
Groot Vloer **160** C 5
Groot Winter Berg **160** D 6
Gros Morne **169** Q 6
Grosser Arber **111** F 5
Grosseto **115** F 3
Groswater Bay **169** Q 5
Grötavær **112** G 2
Grotli **112** E 3
Grottaglie **115** G 3
Grotte de Lascaux **114** D 2
Groumania **156** D 4
Group Actéon **147** F 4
Grovfjord **112** G 2
Groznyy **117** G 2
Gruñidera **172** B 3
Grubišno Polje **115** G 2
Grudziądz **111** G 4
Gruesa, Punta **180** B 5
Grums **113** F 4

Grü – Had

Grünau 160 B 5
Grundy 171 K 4
Gruppo di Brenta 115 F 2
Gruziya 117 F 2
Gryada Khara-Tas 130 J 1
Gryazi 118 H 5
Gryazovets 118 H 4
Grycksbo 113 G 3
Grythyttan 113 F 4
Grytviken 185
Guañape 178 C 5
Guacamayas 178 CD 3
Guacanayabo, Golfo de 173 G 3
Guacara 178 E 1
Guadalajara (Mexico) 172 B 3
Guadalajara (Spain) 114 C 3
Guadalcanal 145 G 2
Guadalén 114 C 4
Guadalete 114 B 4
Guadalmena 114 C 4
Guadalquivir 114 BC 4
Guadalupe (Mex.) 172 B 2
Guadalupe (Mex.) 172 B 3
Guadalupe Bravos 170 E 5
Guadalupe Mountains 170 F 5
Guadalupe River 171 G 6
Guadalupe, Sierra de 114 B 4
Guadalupe, Isla de 170 C 6
Guadarrama, Sierra de 114 C 3
Guadelope (Spain) 114 C 3
Guadeloupe (Lesser Antilles) 173 K 4
Guadeloupe Passage 173 K 4
Guadiana 114 B 4
Guadix 114 C 4
Guafo, Boca del 183 B 7
Guafo, Isla 183 B 7
Guaíba 182 F 5
Guaina 179 F 2
Guainia 178 E 3
Guaiquinima, Cerro 179 F 2
Guaíra 181 F 5
Guaiúba 181 J 1
Guajará Mirim 180 C 3
Guajaturaba 179 F 5
Guajira, Península de 178 D 1
Gualaquiza 178 C 4
Gualeguay 182 E 5
Gualeguaychú 182 E 5
Gualicho, Salina del 183 CD 4
Guallatiri 180 C 3
Guam 146 A 2
Guamá 179 J 4
Guamblin 183 AB 4
Guaminí 183 D 6
Guamo 171 L 7
Guampi, Sierra de 178 E 2
Guamúchil 170 E 6
Gua Musang 136 B 3
Gu'an 133 G 3
Guanajuato 172 B 3
Guanambi 181 H 3
Guanare 178 E 2
Guanarito 178 E 2
Guandacol 182 C 4
Guane 172 F 3
Guang'an 132 E 4
Guangchang 132 G 5
Guangde 133 G 4
Guangdong 132 F 6
Guanghan 132 D 4
Guanghe 132 D 3
Guanghua 132 F 4
Guangji 132 G 5
Guangling 132 F 3
Guangnan 132 E 6
Guangning 132 F 6
Guangshan 132 F 4
Guangxi Zhuangzu Zizhiqu 132 E 6
Guangyuan 132 E 4
Guangze 133 G 5
Guangzhou 132 F 6
Guanhães 181 H 4
Guanling 132 E 5
Guantánamo 173 G 3
Guantao 132 G 3
Guan Xian 132 D 4
Guanyun 133 G 4
Guapí 178 C 3
Guapó 181 G 4
Guaporé (Rio Grande do Sul, Brazil) 182 F 4
Guaporé (Rondônia, Brazil) 180 D 3
Guaqui 180 C 4
Guarabira 181 J 2
Guaranda 178 C 4
Guarapari 181 H 5
Guarapuava 182 F 4
Guaratuba 181 G 6
Guarda 114 B 3
Guardafui, Cape 159 J 2

Guardal 114 C 4
Guardia Mitre 183 D 7
Guardo 114 C 3
Guarenas 178 E 1
Guárico 178 E 2
Guárico, Embalse del 178 E 2
Guascama, Punta 178 C 3
Guasdualito 178 D 2
Guasipati 179 F 2
Guasopa 145 F 3
Guatemala 172 D 4
Guatemala City 172 D 5
Guatire 178 E 1
Guaviare 178 E 3
Guaxupé 181 G 5
Guayabal 178 E 2
Guayabero 178 D 3
Guayaneco, Archipiélago 183 A 8
Guayaquil 178 C 4
Guayaquil, Golfo de 178 B 4
Guayaramerin 180 C 3
Guaymallén 182 C 5
Guaymas 170 D 6
Guba (Zaire) 160 D 2
Guba (U.S.S.R.) 118 F 3
Guba Buorkhaya 131 O 1
Guba Gusinaya 131 R 1
Gubakha 119 L 4
Guban 159 GH 2
Gubba 158 F 2
Gubbio 115 F 3
Gubin 111 F 4
Gubio 157 G 3
Gubkin 118 G 5
Guchin-Us 132 D 1
Gudar, Sierra de 114 C 3
Gudauta 117 F 2
Gudbrandsdalen 112 E 3
Guddu Barrage 129 H 5
Gudenå 113 E 4
Gudermes 117 G 2
Gudivada 134 D 4
Gudiyattam 134 C 5
Güdül 117 D 2
Gudur 134 C 5
Gudvangen 112 E 3
Guebwiller 115 E 2
Guékédou 156 B 4
Guelb er Richât 152 C 4
Guelma 153 G 1
Guelph 171 K 3
Guelta Zemmur 152 C 3
Guem 156 D 2
Guémar 153 G 2
Guéné 156 E 3
Guénéné-Penfao 114 C 2
Guéra 154 B 6
Güera 152 B 4
Guéra, Massif de 157 H 3
Guérande 114 C 2
Guerara 153 F 2
Guercif 152 E 2
Guéréda 157 J 3
Gueredong, Gunung 136 A 3
Guéret 114 D 2
Guernsey 103 C 3
Guernsey (Airport) 103 C 3
Guérou 152 C 3
Guerrara 153 F 2
Guerrero 172 B 4
Guerzim 152 E 3
Guga 131 P 5
Gughe 159 F 3
Guguan 146 A 1
Gugu Mountains 159 FG 3
Guiana Highlands 179 F–H 3
Guibes 160 B 5
Guichi 133 G 4
Guide 132 D 3
Guider 157 G 4
Guidimouni 157 F 3
Guiding 132 E 5
Guidjiba (Ngaoundéré) 157 G 4
Guidong 132 F 5
Guiers, Lac de 156 A 2
Giglo 156 C 4
Guijá 161 E 4
Gui Jiang 132 F 6
Guijuelo 114 B 3
Guildford 103 D 2
Guilin 132 F 5
Guillaume Delisle, Lac 169 M 4
Guilvinec 114 C 2
Guimarães 181 H 1
Guimaras 137 F 2
Guinan 132 D 3
Guinea 156 B 3
Guinea Basin 192 A 3
Guinea-Bissau 156 AB 3
Guinea Ecuatorial 157 FG 5
Guinea, Gulf of 157 EF 5
Guiné-Bissau 156 AB 3
Guinée 156 B 3

Güines 173 F 3
Guingamp 114 C 2
Guinguinéo 156 A 3
Guir 156 D 2
Guiratinga 181 F 4
Guir, Hamada du 152 EF 1
Guiria 179 F 1
Guisanbourg 179 H 3
Guisborough 101 E 2
Guita Koulouba 158 C 3
Guitiriz 114 B 3
Guiuan 137 G 1
Guixi 133 G 5
Gui Xian 132 E 6
Guiyang 132 E 5
Guizhou 132 E 5
Gujarat 134 B 3
Gujar Khan 129 J 4
Gujranwala 129 J 4
Gujrat 129 J 4
Gukovo 117 E 1
Gulang 132 D 3
Gulbarga 134 C 4
Gulbene 112 J 4
Gul'cha 129 J 2
Gülek Boğazı 117 D 3
Gulf of Aden 155 H 6
Gulf of Alaska 166 J 4
Gulf of Aqaba → Khalīj al 'Aqabah 154 E 3
Gulf of Boothia 167 T 1
Gulf of Bothnia 112 G 3
Gulf of Carpentaria 143 F 1
Gulf of Chihli 133 G 3
Gulf of Danzig 111 H 4
Gulf of Finland 113 J 4
Gulf of Guinea 157 EF 5
Gulf of Khambhat 134 B 3
Gulf of Kutch 134 A 3
Gulf of Maine 171 N 3
Gulf of Mannar 134 C 6
Gulf of Martaban 135 G 4
Gulf of Mexico 172 DE 2
Gulf of Ob 119 O 2
Gulf of Oman 128 F 5–6
Gulf of Papua 146 A 3
Gulf of Riga 113 H 4
Gulf of Saint Lawrence 169 P 6
Gulf of Sirt 153 J 2
Gulf of Suez → Khalīj as Suways 154 E 3
Gulf of Thailand 135 H 5
Gulf of Tongking 135 J 3–4
Gulf of Venice 115 F 2
Gulfport 171 J 5
Gulf Saint Vincent 143 F 6
Gulgong 143 H 5
Gulian 131 M 5
Gulin 132 E 5
Gulistan 129 H 2
Guliya Shan 131 M 6
Gulkana 166 H 3
Gullfoss 112 L 2
Gullkrona fjärd 113 H 4
Gull Lake 167 Q 5
Gullspång 113 F 4
Güllük 116 C 3
Gülnar 117 D 3
Gülşehir 117 D 3
Gul'shad 119 O 6
Gulstav 113 F 5
Gulu 158 E 4
Guluguba 143 J 4
Gulwe 159 F 6
Gulya 130 M 5
Gulyaypole 117 E 1
Gumbiri, Jabal 158 E 4
Gumbiro 161 F 2
Gumel 157 F 3
Gummi 157 F 3
Gumuru 158 E 3
Gümüşane Dağları 117 E 2
Gümüshane 117 E 2
Guna (Ethiopia) 159 F 2
Guna (India) 134 C 3
Gunda 130 K 5
Gundagai 143 H 6
Gundji 158 C 4
Gundoğmus 117 D 3
Gungu 158 B 6
Guni 157 F 4
Gunib 128 D 2
Günnariyn 132 D 1
Gunnar 167 Q 4
Gunnarn 112 G 2
Gunnedah 143 J 6
Gunnison 170 E 4
Gunnison River 170 E 4
Guntakal 134 C 4
Guntersville Lake 171 J 5
Guntur 134 D 4

Gunung Abong Abong 136 A 3
Gunung Agung 136 E 5
Gunung Angemuk 137 J 4
Gunung Api 137 E 5
Gunung Bakayan 136 E 3
Gunung Balikpapan 136 E 4
Gunung Bandahara 136 A 3
Gunung Batai 136 B 5
Gunung Batulantee 136 E 5
Gunung Batu Puteh 136 B 3
Gunung Besar 136 E 4
Gunung Binaiya 137 G 4
Gunung Boliohutu 137 F 3
Gunung Ceremai 136 C 5
Gunung Dempo 136 B 4
Gunung Gamkunoro 137 G 3
Gunung Gueredong 136 A 3
Gunung Kaubalatmada 137 G 4
Gunung Kerinci 136 B 4
Gunung Kinabalu 136 E 2
Gunung Klabat 137 G 3
Gunung Kongkemul 136 E 3
Gunung Kwoka 137 H 4
Gunung Lawit 136 D 3
Gunung Leuser 136 A 3
Gunung Lewotobi 137 F 5
Gunung Liangpran 136 D 3
Gunung Lokilalaki 137 F 4
Gunung Lompobatang 137 F 5
Gunung Longnawan 136 E 3
Gunung Maling 137 F 3
Gunung Mandasawu 137 F 5
Gunung Marapi 136 B 4
Gunung Mekongga 137 F 4
Gunung Menyapa 136 E 3
Gunung Mulu 136 E 3
Gunung Mutis 137 F 5
Gunung Niut 136 D 3
Gunung Ogoamas 137 F 3
Gunung Parango 136 C 5
Gunung Peuetsagu 136 A 3
Gunung Rabakah 137 F 5
Gunung Rinjani 136 E 5
Gunung Saran 136 D 4
Gunung Sarempaka 136 E 4
Gunung Sinabung 136 A 3
Gunung Sitoli 136 A 3
Gunung Slamet 136 C 5
Gunung Sombang 136 E 3
Gunung Sorikmerapi 136 A 3
Gunungsugih 136 C 4
Gunung Tahan 136 B 3
Gunung Talakmau 136 B 3
Gunung Tambora 137 E 5
Gunung Tentolomatinan 137 F 3
Gunung Wanggameti 137 F 6
Gunung Waukara 137 E 4
Guoiret es Soud 153 F 3
Guoyang 132 G 4
Gurais 129 J 4
Guran 130 H 5
Gurara 157 F 4
Gurban Obo 132 F 2
Gurbantünggüt Shamo 129 M 1
Gurdaspur 134 C 1
Gurdim 128 G 5
Gurdzhaani 117 G 2
Gurgaon 134 C 2
Gurgei, Jabal 154 C 6
Gürgen Tepe 117 E 2
Gurgueia 181 H 2
Gurha 134 B 2
Guri Dam 179 F 2
Gurimatu 144 D 3
Gürlevik Dağı 117 E 3
Guro 161 E 3
Gürpınar 117 F 3
Gurskoye 131 P 5
Gúruè 161 F 3
Gürün 117 E 3
Gurupá 179 H 4
Gurupá, Ilha Grande do 179 HJ 4
Gurupi (Brazil) 179 J 4
Gurupi (Goiás, Brazil) 181 G 3
Gurupi, Cabo 179 J 4
Gurupira, Sierra de 178 F 3
Gurupi, Serra do 179 J 4
Guru Sikhar 134 B 3
Guruve 161 E 3
Guruzala 134 C 4
Gurvanbulag 130 H 6
Gurvan Sayhan Uul 132 D 2
Gur'yev 128 E 1
Gur'yevsk 119 R 5
Gusau 157 F 3
Gusave 170 E 6
Gusev 113 H 5
Gushi 132 G 4
Gushiago 156 D 4
Gusikha 130 J 1
Gusinaya Zemlya, Poluostrov 118 K 1
Gusinoozersk 130 J 5

Gusinoye Ozero 130 J 5
Gus'Khrustal'nyy 118 GH 4
Gusmp, Ostrov 131 U 1–2
Guspini 115 E 4
Güssing 115 G 2
Gustavus 166 K 4
Güstrow 111 F 4
Guthrie (OK, U.S.A.) 170 G 4
Guthrie (TX, U.S.A.) 170 F 5
Gutian 133 G 5
Guyana 179 G 3
Guyenne 114 CD 3
Guyra 143 J 5
Guyuan 132 E 3
Guyuan 133 G 2
Guzar 129 H 3
Güzelhisar 116 C 3
Güzelyurt 117 D 3
Güzelyurt Körfezi 117 D 3
Guzhang 132 F 5
Guzhen 133 G 4
Gvardejsk 113 H 5
Gvarv 113 E 4
Gvardeyskoye 117 D 1
Gwa 135 F 4
Gwadabawa 157 F 3
Gwadar 129 G 5
Gwai 160 D 3
Gwalior 134 C 2
Gwanda 160 D 4
Gwane 158 D 4
Gwatar Bay 129 G 5
Gwda 111 G 4
Gwebin 135 F 3
Gwelo 160 D 3
Gwent 102 C 2
Gweta 160 D 4
Gwynedd 102 B 1
Gyaca 132 B 5
Gya La 134 D 2
Gyamysh 128 D 2
Gyangzê 134 E 2
Gyaring 132 C 3
Gyaring Co 134 E 1
Gyaring Hu 132 C 4
Gyda 119 P 1
Gydanskaya Guba 119 P 1
Gydanskiy Poluostrov 119 P 1
Gyirong 134 E 2
Gyitang 132 C 4
Gyldenlöves Fjord 169 T 3
Gympie 143 J 4
Gypsum Point 167 O 3
Gypsumville 167 S 5
Gyula 116 B 1
Gyurgyan 128 E 2
Gyöngyös 116 A 1
Győr 116 A 1

H

Haanhöniy Uul 130 F 6
Haanja Kõrgustik 112 J 4
Ha'apai Group 146 D 4
Haapajärvi 112 J 3
Haapasaari 112 J 3
Haapavesi 112 J 3
Haapsalu 113 H 4
Haarlem 110 D 4
Haast 144 P 9
Ḥabarūt 155 J 5
Habas 152 C 3
Ḥabashīyah, Jabal 155 J 5
Habaswein 159 F 4
Habay (Somalia) 159 G 4
Habay (Alb., Canada) 167 O 4
Ḥabbān 155 H 6
Ḥabbānīyah 155 G 2
Ḥabbānīyah, Hawr al 155 G 2
Habiganj 135 F 3
Ḥabshān 155 F 3
Hachijō-jima 133 L 4
Hachinohe 133 M 2
Hacıbektaş 117 D 3
Ḥaḍabat al Jilf al Kabīr 154 D 4
Ḥadabat Tayga 154 D 5
Hadada, Jabal 154 D 4
Ḥadan, Ḥarrat 155 G 4
Ḥadāribah, Ra's al 154 F 4
Ḥaddā' 155 F 4
Hadded 159 H 2
Haddington 99 C 2
Hadd, Ra's al 155 K 4
Hadejia 157 G 3
Hadejia 157 F 3
Hadeland 113 F 3
Hadera 154 E 2
Haderslev 113 E 4

Ḥādh Banī Zaynān 155 H 4
Ḥadīboh 159 J 2
Hadid, Jabal 153 K 4
Hadilik 129 M 3
Hadım 117 D 3
Hadjer el Hamis 157 GH 3
Hadjer Kamaran 157 J 3
Hadjer Mardi 157 J 3
Hadjer Mornou 157 J 2
Hadjer Telfane 157 H 3
Hadjout 114 D 4
Hadleigh 103 E 1
Hadley Bay 167 Q 1
Ha Dong 135 J 3
Ḥaḍramawt 155 H 5
Hadrian's Wall 101 D 2
Hadsund 113 F 4
Haeju 133 J 3
Ḥafar al 'Atk 155 H 3
Ḥafar al Bāṭin 155 H 3
Hafik 117 E 3
Ḥafīrat al 'Aydā 155 F 3
Ḥafīt 155 K 4
Ḥafīt, Jabal 155 K 4
Hafnarfjörður 112 A 3
Häfūn 159 J 2
Häfūn, Ra's 159 J 2
Hag 'Abdullah 154 E 6
Hagadera 159 G 4
Hagari 134 C 5
Hagemeister 166 E 4
Hagen 111 E 4
Hagen, Mount 144 D 3
Hagerstown 171 L 4
Hagfors 113 F 3
Häggenås 112 F 3
Ha Giang 135 H 3
Hags Head 110 B 4
Hague, Cap de la 114 C 2
Haguenau 115 E 2
Hagunia 152 C 3
Hai'an 133 H 4
Haicheng 133 H 2
Hai Duong 135 J 3
Haifa 154 E 2
Haifeng 132 G 6
Hai He 133 G 3
Haikang 132 F 6
Haikou 132 F 6
Hā'il 155 G 3
Hailakandi 135 F 3
Hailar 130 L 6
Hailar He 130 M 6
Hailin 133 J 2
Hailing Dao 132 F 6
Hailong 133 J 2
Hailsham 103 E 2
Hailun 131 N 6
Hailuoto 112 H 2
Haimen 133 H 4
Hainan Dao 132 F 7
Hainburg an der Donau 115 G 2
Haines 166 K 4
Haines Junction 166 K 3
Hai Phong 135 J 3
Haiqing 131 O 6
Haïti 173 H 4
Haiware 144 D 3
Haiyan 132 G 4
Haiyang 133 H 3
Haiyuan 132 E 3
Haizhou Wan 133 G 4
Ḥajārah, Ṣaḥrā' al 155 G 2–H 3
Hajdúböszörmény 116 B 1
Hajduság 116 B 1
Hajhir, Jabal 159 J 2
Hajipur 134 E 2
Ḥājjīābād 128 F 5
Ḥājjīābād-e Māsīleh 128 E 4
Hajmah 155 K 5
Haka 135 F 3
Hakkâri 117 F 3
Hakkâri Dağları 117 F 3
Hakkas 112 H 2
Hakksund 113 E 4
Hakodate 133 M 2
Haku-san 133 L 3
Halab 154 F 1
Halabjah 155 H 1
Ḥalā'ib 154 F 4
Halali 160 B 3
Halberstadt 111 F 4
Halcon, Mount 137 F 1
Halden 113 F 4
Haldia 134 E 3
Haldwani 134 C 2
Hale, Mount 142 B 4
Halesowen 103 C 1
Halesworth 103 E 1
Halfeti 117 E 3
Ḥalī 155 G 5
Halia 134 D 3

Halicarnassus 116 C 3
Halifax (Queensland, Austr.) 143 H 2
Halifax (New Brunsw., Can.) 169 P 7
Halifax (U.K.) 101 E 3
Halifax Bay 143 H 2
Halifax, Mount 143 H 2
Hālīl 128 F 5
Halin 159 H 3
Halkett, Cape 166 G 1
Halkırk 98 C 2
Hall 166 C 3
Halland 113 F 4
Hallat 'Ammār 154 F 3
Hall Beach 167 V 2
Halle 111 F 4
Halleberg 113 F 4
Hällefors 113 F 4
Hallettsville 171 G 6
Halley Bay 185
Hallingdal 113 E 3
Hallingdalselva 113 E 3
Hallingskarvet 113 E 3
Hall Islands 146 B 2
Hall Lake 167 V 2
Hällnäs 112 G 3
Hall Peninsula 169 O 3
Hallsberg 113 G 4
Halls Creek 142 D 2
Hallstahammar 113 G 4
Hallstatt 115 F 2
Hallstavik 113 G 3
Halmahera 137 G 3
Halmahera, Laut 137 G 4
Halmstad 113 F 4
Hals 113 F 4
Hälsingeskogen 112 G 3
Hälsingland 112 G 3
Halsön 112 H 3
Halstead 103 E 2
Haltia 112 H 2
Ḥālūl 155 J 3
Ham 157 H 3
Hamab 160 B 5
Hamada de Tindouf 152 D 3
Hamada de Tinrhert 153 G 3
Hamada du Drâa 152 D 3
Hamada du Guir 152 E 2
Hamada el Haricha 156 D 1
Hamada Mangueni 157 G 1
Hamadān 128 D 4
Hamada Safia 156 D 1
Hamada Tounassine 152 DE 3
Ḥamādat Tingharat 153 H 3
Ḥamāh 154 F 1
Hamamatsu 133 L 4
Hamar 113 F 3
Hamarro Hadad 159 G 3
Ḥamāṭah, Jabal 154 F 4
Hambantota 134 D 6
Hamburg 111 E F 4
Ḥamḍah 155 G 5
Ḥamdānah 155 G 5
Ḥamḍ, Wādī al 154 F 3
Häme 112 H 3
Hämeenlinna (Tavastehus) 112 H 3
Hämeenselkä 112 H 3
Hamelin Pool 142 A 4
Hameln 111 E 4
Hamersley Range 142 B 3
Hamersley Range National Park 142 B 3
Hamgyŏng-sanmaek 133 J 2
Hamhŭng 133 J 3
Hami 132 B 2
Hamilton (Bermuda Isl.) 173 K 1
Hamilton (MT, U.S.A.) 170 D 2
Hamilton (New Zealand) 145 R 8
Hamilton (Ont., Can.) 171 L 3
Hamilton (Queensland, Austr.) 143 G 3
Hamilton (U.K.) 99 B 4
Hamilton (Victoria, Austr.) 143 G 6
Hamilton River 143 G 3
Ḥamīm, Wādī 153 K 2
Hamina (Fredrikshamn) 113 J 3
Hamirpur 134 D 2
Hamm 111 E 4
Ḥammādat Mānghīnī 153 H 5
Hammām al 'Alīl 155 G 1
Hammām al Anf 153 H 1
Ḥammāmāt 153 H 1
Hammami 152 C 4
Ḥammār, Hawr al 155 H 2
Hammarstrand 112 G 3
Hammerdal 112 G 3
Hammerfest 112 H 1
Hammond (IN, U.S.A.) 171 J 3
Hammond (LA, U.S.A.) 171 H 5
Hammur Koke 159 F 3

Hamodji 157 G 2
Hamoyet, Jabal 154 F 5
Hampden 145 Q 10
Hampshire 103 D 2
Hampton 171 L 4
Hamra 112 G 3
Ḥamrat ash Shaykh 154 D 6
Ḥamrīn, Jabal 155 G 2
Hamuku 137 J 4
Hamum i Mashkel 129 G 5
Hāmūn-e Jaz Mūriān 128 F 5
Han 156 D 3
Hanahan 171 K 5
Ḥanak 154 F 3
Hanamaki 133 M 3
Hanang 128 F 5
Hanbogd 132 E 2
Hanceville 167 N 5
Hancheng 132 F 3
Hanchuan 132 F 4
Handan 132 F 3
Handen 113 G 4
Handeni 159 F 6
Hangay 130 G 6
Hangayn Nuruu 130 G H 6
Hanggin Houqi 132 E 2
Hanggin Qi 132 E 3
Hangö (Hanko) 113 H 3
Hangsdorf 115 G 2
Hangu (China) 133 G 3
Hangu (Pakistan) 129 J 4
Hangya 132 C 3
Hangzhou 133 H 4
Hangzhou Wan 133 H 4
Hanh 130 H 5
Han Jiang 132 G 6
Hankasalmi 112 J 3
Hanko 113 H 3
Hankoniemi 113 H 4
Hanksville 170 D 4
Hanle 129 K 4
Hanna 167 P 5
Hannah Bay 169 L 5
Hannibal 171 H 4
Hannover (B.R.D.) 111 E 4
Hanöbukten 113 F 4
Ha Noi 135 J 3
Hanover (S. Afr.) 160 C 6
Hanover, Islas 183 B 9
Han Shui 132 F 4
Hanstholm 113 E 4
Hantengri Feng 129 L 2
Hantzsch 169 N 2
Hanumangarh 134 B 2
Han-Uul 130 K 6
Hanuy Gol 130 H 6
Hanyuan 132 D 5
Hanzhong 132 E 4
Hao 147 F 4
Haora → Howrah 134 E 3
Haouach 157 J 2
Haoud el Hamra 153 G 2
Haparanda 112 H 2
Hapo 137 G 3
Hapur 134 C 2
Ḥaql 154 F 3
Hara 130 J 6
Ḥarad 155 G 5
Ḥaraḍ 155 H 4
Hara Fanna 159 G 3
Haraiki 147 F 4
Harara 159 G 3
Hararḍēre 159 H 4
Harare 161 E 3
Ḥarāsīs, Jiddat al 155 K 4–5
Harāwah 153 J 2
Har-Ayrag 132 E 1
Haraz 157 H 3
Harāzah, Jabal 154 E 5
Harazé 157 J 4
Harbel 156 B 4
Harbin 133 J 1
Harbor Beach 171 K 3
Harbour Breton 169 Q 6
Harbour Grace 169 R 6
Harburg 111 E 4
Harda 134 C 3
Hardangerfjorden 113 E 3–4
Hardangerjøkulen 113 E 3
Hardangervidda 113 E 3
Hardap Dam 160 B 4
Hardin 170 E 2
Hardoi 134 D 2
Hardwar 134 C 2
Harēri Mālīn Warfā 159 H 4
Hargeysa 159 G 3
Har Hu 134 C 3
Harib 155 H 6
Hari, Batang 136 B 4
Harihari 145 Q 9

Harike Barrage 134 C 1
Hari Kurk 113 H 4
Ḥārim 154 F 1
Ḥarīm, Jabal al 155 K 3
Haringhat 134 E 3
Haripur 129 J 4
Hari Rud 129 G 4
Harjavalta 112 H 3
Härjedalen 112 F 3
Harlech 102 B 1
Harleston 103 E 1
Harlingen (Netherlands) 110 E 4
Harlingen (TX, U.S.A.) 171 G 6
Harlow 103 E 2
Harlu 112 K 3
Harmak 128 G 4
Harmancık 116 C 3
Harmånger 112 G 3
Harmanli 116 C 2
Harnai 129 H 4
Harney Basin 170 BC 3
Harney Lake 170 C 3
Harney Peak 170 F 3
Härnön 112 G 3
Härnösand 112 G 3
Har Nuur 130 F 6
Haröyfjorden 112 E 3
Harpenden 103 D 2
Harper 156 C 5
Harqin 132 G 2
Ḥarrat al Buqūm 155 G 4
Ḥarrat al Kishb 155 G 4
Ḥarrat al 'Uwayrid 154 F 3
Ḥarrat ar Raḥāh 154 F 3
Ḥarrat Ḥaḍan 155 G 4
Ḥarrat Ithnayn 155 G 3
Ḥarrat Khaybar 155 FG 3
Ḥarrat Kurāmā 155 G 4
Ḥarrat Lunayyir 154 F 3
Ḥarrat Nawāṣif 155 G 4
Ḥarrat Raḥaṭ 155 G 4
Harricana 169 M 5
Harrington Harbour 169 Q 5
Harris 98 A 3
Harrisburg 171 L 3
Harrismith 160 D 5
Harrison 171 H 4
Harrison Bay 166 G 1
Harrisonburg 171 L 4
Harrison, Cape 169 Q 5
Harrisville 171 K 3
Harrogate 101 E 3
Harrs Range 142 E 3
Hartwell Lake 171 K 5
Hartz Mountains National Park 144 L 9
Haruchas 160 B 4
Harun, Bukit 136 E 3
Har Us Nuur 130 F 6
Ḥarūṭ 155 J 5
Harvey (Western Australia) 142 B 5
Harvey (N.D., U.S.A.) 170 G 2
Harwich 103 E 2
Haryana 134 C 2
Hasalbag 129 K 3
Hasan 133 K 2
Hasançelebi 117 E 3
Hasan Langī 128 F 5
Ḥasār 128 E 4
Hase 113 E 5
Hasekijata 116 C 2
Haskovo 116 C 2
Haslemere 103 D 2
Haslev 113 F 4
Hassan 134 C 5
Hassela 112 G 3
Hassi Barouda 153 F 3
Hassi Bel Guebbour 153 G 3
Hassi Bou Akba 152 D 3
Hassi Bou Krechba 153 G 3
Hassi Bou Zid 153 F 2
Hassi Chaamba 152 E 2
Hassi Djafou 153 F 2
Hassi el Hadadra 153 F 2
Hassi el Krenig 153 F 2

Hassi Erg Sedra 153 F 2
Hassi Fokra 152 E 2
Hassi Habadra 153 F 3
Hassi Imoulaye 153 G 3
Hassi Inifel 153 F 3
Hassi Insokki 153 F 3
Hassi Krezrez 153 F 3
Hassi Marroket 153 F 2
Hassi Messaoud 153 G 2
Hassi Ouchen 152 EF 2
Hassi R'Mel 153 F 2
Hassi Serouenout 153 G 4
Hassi Tartrat 153 G 2
Hassi Timellouline 153 G 2
Hassi Tin Fouchaye 153 G 3
Hassi Zemmoul 152 D 3
Hassi Zirara 153 F 2
Hässleholm 113 F 4
Hastings (U.K.) 103 E 2
Hastings (MN, U.S.A.) 171 H 3
Hastings (NE, U.S.A.) 170 G 3
Hastings (New Zealand) 145 R 8
Hasvik 112 H 1
Ḥasy Hague 153 H 3
Hatanbulag 132 E 2
Haṭeg 116 B 1
Hatfield 103 D 2
Hatgal 130 G H 5
Hat Hin 135 H 3
Hathras 134 C 2
Ḥāṭibah, Ra's 154 F 4
Ha Tien 135 H 5
Ha Tinh 135 J 4
Hatisar 135 F 2
Hatta 134 C 3
Hattah 143 G 5
Hatteras, Cape 171 L 4
Hatteras Island 171 L 4
Hattfjelldal 112 F 2
Hattiesburg 171 J 5
Hatton Bank 192 A 2
Hatutaa 147 F 3
Hat Yai 135 H 6
Hauberg Mountains 185
Haud 159 GH 3
Hauge 113 E 4
Haugesund 113 E 4
Haugsdorf 115 G 2
Haukeligrend 113 E 4
Haukipudas 112 J 2
Haukivesi 112 J 3
Haukivuori 112 J 3
Hauraki Gulf 145 R 8
Hausa 152 C 3
Hausruck 115 F 2
Haut Atlas 152 DE 2
Hauterive 169 O 6
Haute-Saône, Plateau de 115 E 2
Haute-Volta 156 DE 3
Hauts Plateaux 152 EF 2
Haut-Zaïre 158 CD 4
Havana 173 F 3
Havant 103 D 2
Havel 111 F 4
Havelock Island 135 F 5
Haverfordwest 102 B 2
Haverhill (U.K.) 103 E 1
Haverhill (MA, U.S.A.) 171 M 3
Havern 112 G 3
Havířov 111 G 5
Havøysund 112 H 1
Havran 116 C 3
Havre 170 D 2
Havre-Saint-Pierre 169 P 5
Havsa 116 C 2
Havza 117 E 2
Hawaii 147 E 1
Hawaiian Islands 147 E 1
Hawaiian Ridge 193 D 3
Hawera 145 Q 8
Hawi 147 E 1
Hawick 99 C 4
Hawick Wooler 101 D 2
Hawke Bay 145 R 8
Hawke Harbour 169 Q 5
Hawker 143 F 5
Hawkers Gate 143 G 4
Hawkwood 143 J 4
Hawmat as Sūq 153 H 2
Hawng Luk 135 G 3
Ḥawrā' 155 H 5
Hawr al Ḥabbānīyah 155 G 2
Hawr al Ḥammār 155 H 2
Hawr as Sa'dīyah 155 H 2
Hawthorne 170 C 4
Hay (Alberta, Can.) 167 O 4
Hay (New South Wales, Austr.) 143 G 5
Haybān 154 E 6
Haybān, Jabal 154 E 6
Hayes 167 T 4
Hayes, Mount 166 H 3

Hay – Hor

Hayjān 155 G 5
Hayl 155 K 4
Haymana 117 D 3
Haymana Platosu 117 D 3
Hay-on-Wye 102 C 1
Hayraboly 116 C 2
Hayrān 155 G 5
Hay River (NWT, Canada) 167 O 3
Hay River (Northern Terr., Austr.) 143 F 3
Hays 170 G 4
Hayward 170 B 4
Haywards Heath 103 D 2
Haywood, Mount 167 N 3
Hayyā 154 F 5
Hazarajat 129 H 4
Hazard 171 K 4
Hazar Gölü 117 E 3
Hazaribagh 134 E 3
Hazaribagh Range 134 D 3
Hazebrouck 114 D 1
Hazel Grove 101 D 3
Hazelton 167 M 4
Hazhdanahr 129 H 3
Hazlehurst 171 K 5
Hazleton 171 L 3
Hazlett, Lake 142 D 3
Hazro 117 F 2
Head of Bight 142 E 5
Heales-ville 143 H 6
Heanor 103 D 1
Hearne 171 G 5
Hearst 168 L 6
Heathfield 103 E 2
Heathrow (Airport) 103 D 2
Hebei 133 G 3
Hebel 143 H 4
Hebi 132 F 3
Hebian 132 F 3
Hebron (Can.) 169 P 4
Heby 113 G 4
Hecate Strait 166 L 5
Hechi 132 E 6
Hechuan 132 E 4
Hede 112 F 3
Hedemora 113 G 3
Hedmark 112 F 3
Hedon 101 E 3
Heerenveen 110 E 4
Hefa 154 E 2
Hefei 133 G 4
Hegang 131 O 6
Hegura-jima 133 L 3
Heide (Namibia) 160 B 4
Heide (B.R.D.) 111 E 4
Heidelberg 111 E 5
Heidenheim 111 F 5
Heilbron 160 D 5
Heilbronn 111 E 5
Heiligenblut 115 F 2
Heiligenstadt 111 F 4
Heilongjiang 133 J 1
Heilong Jiang 131 O 6
Heimaey 112 A 3
Heimahe 132 C 3
Heimdal 112 F 3
Heinola 112 J 3
Heirnkut 135 FG 2
Heishan 133 H 2
Heishui 132 D 4
Hejian 133 G 3
Hejiang 132 E 5
Hejing 132 A 2
Heka 132 C 3
Hekimhan 117 E 3
Hekla 112 B 3
Helagsfjället 112 F 3
Helan 132 E 3
Helan Shan 132 E 3
Helena (AR, U.S.A.) 171 H 5
Helena (MT, U.S.A.) 170 D 2
Helen Reef 137 H 3
Helensburgh 99 B 3
Helensville 145 Q 8
Helga å 113 F 4
Helgeland 112 F 2
Helgoland 111 E 4
Helgoländer Bucht 111 E 4
Helikarnassos 116 C 3
Helikon Öros 116 B 3
Heljulja 112 K 3
Hella 112 A 3
Hellas 116 BC 2–3
Hellin 114 C 4
Hells Canyon 170 C 2
Hell-Ville 161 H 2
Helmand 129 G 4
Helmeringhausen 160 B 5
Helmsdale 98 C 2
Helmstedt 111 F 4
Helong 133 J 2
Helsingborg 113 F 4

Helsingfors 113 J 3
Helsingör 113 F 4
Helsinki (Helsingfors) 113 J 3
Helston 102 B 2
Helvellyn 101 D 2
Helwan → Hulwān 154 E 3
Hemel Hempstead 103 D 2
Hemnesberget 112 F 2
Hemsby 103 E 1
Hemse 113 G 4
Hemsö 112 G 3
Henan 132 F 4
Henan 132 D 4
Henares 114 C 3
Henbury 142 E 3
Hendek 116 D 2
Henderson (Oceania) 147 G 4
Henderson (N.C., U.S.A.) 171 L 4
Henderson (N.C., U.S.A.) 171 H 5
Henderson (TX, U.S.A.) 170 D 4
Hendersonville (N.C., U.S.A.) 171 K 4
Hendersonville (TN, U.S.A.) 171 J 4
Hendījān 128 D 4
Hendriktop 179 G 3
Hendrik Verwoerd Dam 160 D 5
Henganon 144 E 3
Hengduan Shan 132 C 5
Heng Shan 132 F 5
Heng Shan 132 F 3
Hengshan 132 E 3
Hengshui 132 G 3
Hengue 160 B 2
Heng Xian 132 E 6
Hengyang 132 F 5
Henik Lakes 167 S 3
Henley-on-Thames 103 D 2
Hennan 112 G 3
Henrietta Maria, Cape 169 L 4
Henryetta 171 G 4
Henry Kater Peninsula 169 O 2
Henties Bay 160 A 4
Hentiy 130 J 6
Hentiyn Nuruu 130 J 6
Henzada 135 G 4
Hepu 132 E 6
Hequ 132 F 3
Heraklia 154 F 1
Herakol Daği 117 F 3
Herald Cays 143 H 2
Herat 129 G 4
Herault 114 D 3
Herbert 167 Q 5
Herberton 141
Herbert River 143 F 3
Hercegnovi 116 A 2
Hercegovina 115 G 3
Herðubreið 112 B 2
Heredia 172 F 5
Hereford (TX, U.S.A.) 170 F 5
Hereford (U.K.) 102 C 1
Hereford and Worcester 102 C 1
Hereheretue 147 F 4
Herford 111 E 4
Herlen Gol 130 K 6
Herlen He 130 L 6
Herluf Trolle, Cape 169 T 3
Herm 103 C 3
Hermagor 115 F 2
Hermanas 172 B 2
Herma Ness 98 D 1
Hermanus 160 B 6
Hermidale 143 H 5
Hermiston 170 C 2
Hermit Islands 144 E 2
Hermosillo 170 D 6
Hernandarias 182 F 4
Hernani 114 C 3
Herne Bay 103 E 2
Herning 113 E 4
Heroica 172 B 4
Heroica Alvarado 172 C 4
Heroica Tlapacoyan 172 C 4
Herrera 182 D 4
Herrera de Pisuerga 114 C 3
Herrljunga 113 F 4
Herschel 166 K 2
Hertford 103 D 2
Hertfordshire 103 D 2
's-Hertogenbosch 110 D E 4
Hervey Bay 143 J 4
Heshun 132 F 3
Hess 166 L 3
Hessen 111 E 4
Heswall 101 D 3
Hexham 101 D 2
He Xian 132 F 6
Hexigten Qi 133 G 2
Heysham 101 D 2
Heyuan 132 F 6

Heywood (U.K.) 101 D 3
Heywood (Victoria, Austr.) 143 G 6
Heze 132 G 3
Hezheng 132 D 3
Hialeah 171 K 6
Hibbing 171 H 2
Hibernia Reef 142 C 1
Hickley 103 D 1
Hidaka-sammyaku 133 M 2
Hidalgo 172 C 3
Hidalgo del Parral 170 E 6
Hidcolândia 181 G 4
Hierro 152 B 3
Higginsville 142 C 5
Higham Ferrers 103 D 1
High Desert 170 B 3
Highland 98 B 3
High Level 167 O 4
High Point 171 L 4
High Prairie 167 O 4
High River 167 P 5
Highrock Lake (Man., Can.) 167 R 4
Highrock Lake (Sask., Can.) 167 Q 4
Highworth 103 D 2
High Wycombe 103 D 2
Higüey 173 J 4
Hiitola 112 J 3
Hiiumaa 113 H 4
Hijar 114 C 3
Hikurangi 145 R 8
Hila 137 G 5
Hildesheim 111 F 4
Hill 171 M 3
Hill Bank 172 E 4
Hillcrest Center 170 C 4
Hilleröd 113 F 4
Hill Grove 143 H 2
Hill Island Lake 167 Q 3
Hill of Tara 100 B 3
Hills 171 G 4
Hillsboro (IL, U.S.A.) 171 J 4
Hillsboro (TX, U.S.A.) 171 G 5
Hillston 143 H 5
Hillswick 98 D 1
Hilo 147 E 1
Hilvan 117 E 3
Hilversum 110 E 4
Himā' 155 G 5
Himachal Pradesh 134 C 1
Himā Ḍarīyah, Jabal 155 G 4
Himalaya 134–135 D–F 2
Himanka 112 H 3
Himara 116 A 2
Himatnagar 134 B 3
Himi 133 L 3
Himmelbjerget 113 E 4
Himmerland 113 E 4
Himmetdede 117 E 3
Himo 159 F 5
Ḥimṣ 154 F 2
Hinchin Brook 166 H 3
Hinchinbrook Island 143 H 2
Hindarun 134 C 2
Hindmarsh, Lake 143 G 6
Hindubagh 129 H 4
Hindu Kush 129 J 3
Hindupur 134 C 5
Hinganghat 134 C 3
Hingol 129 G 5
Hingoli 134 C 4
Hin Heup 135 H 4
Hinnöya 112 G 2
Hinobaan 137 F 2
Hinton 167 O 5
Hiquerote 178 E 1
Hirado 133 J 4
Hirakud Reservoir 134 D 3
Hirara 133 J 6
Hirfanlı barajı 117 D 3
Hirhafok 153 G 4
Hiriyur 134 C 5
Hirosaki 133 M 2
Hiroshima 133 K 4
Hirson 114 D 2
Hirtshals 101 E 4
Hirvensalmi 112 J 3
Hirwaun 102 C 2
Hīs 159 H 2
Ḥismā 154 F 3
Ḥiṣn āl 'Abr 155 H 5
Hispaniola 173 H 4
Hīt 155 G 2
Hita 133 K 4
Hitachi 133 M 3
Hitchin 103 D 2
Hite 170 D 4
Hitra 112 E 3
Hiva Oa 147 F 3

Hjälmaren 113 G 4
Hjelmsöya 112 H 1
Hjerkinn 112 E 3
Hjo 113 F 4
Hjörring 113 E 4
Hlatikulu 161 E 5
Ho 156 E 4
Hoa Binh 135 J 3
Hoachanas 160 B 4
Hoai Nhon 135 J 5
Hoanib 160 A 3
Hoare Bay 169 P 2
Hoaseb Store 160 B 4
Hobart (Tasmania, Austr.) 144 L 9
Hobart (OK, U.S.A.) 170 G 4
Hobbs 170 F 5
Hobburn 101 E 2
Hobo 178 C 3
Hoboksar 129 M 1
Hobo Shamo 132 E 2
Hobro 113 E 4
Hoburgen 113 G 4
Hobyā 159 H 3
Hochalmspitze 115 F 2
Hochfeld 160 B 4
Ho Chi Minh 135 J 5
Hodal 134 C 2
Hodda 159 J 2
Hoddesdon 103 E 2
Hodeida 155 G 6
Hodgson Downs 142 E 2
Hódmezővásárhely 116 B 1
Hodna, Chott el 153 F 1
Hodna, Monts du 153 F 1
Hodonin 115 G 5
Hof 111 F 4
Höfðakaupstaður 112 A 2
Höfn 112 B 3
Hofors 113 G 3
Hofsá 112 B 2
Hofsjökull 112 B 3
Hōfu 133 K 4
Höganäs 113 F 4
Hogback Mountain 170 D 3
Hoggar 153 F 4
Hoggar → Ahaggar 153 G 4
Högstegia 112 F 3
Höhang-nyŏng 133 J 2
Hohe Acht 115 E 1
Hohes Venn 110 E 4
Hohe Tauern 115 F 2
Hohhot 132 F 2
Hohoe 156 E 4
Hoh Sai Hu 132 B 3
Hoh Xil Hu 132 B 3
Hoh Xil Shan 132 A 3
Hoi An 135 J 4
Hoima 158 E 4
Hoi Xuan 135 J 3
Hökensås 113 F 4
Hokitika 145 Q 9
Hokkaidō 133 M 2
Hokmābād 128 F 3
Hol 113 E 3
Holanda 180 C 3
Holbæk 113 F 4
Holbeach 103 D 1
Holbox, Isla 172 E 3
Holbrook 170 D 5
Holdenville 171 G 4
Holdrege 170 G 3
Hole 134 C 5
Holguín 173 G 3
Hol Hol 159 G 2
Holitna 166 F 3
Höljes 113 F 3
Hollabrunn 115 G 2
Holland 171 J 3
Hollandsbird 160 A 4
Hollick-Kenyon Plateau 185
Holly Springs 171 J 5
Hollywood (CA, U.S.A.) 170 C 5
Hollywood (FL, U.S.A.) 171 K 6
Holman Island 167 O 1
Hólmavík 112 A 2
Holmes Reefs 143 H 2
Holmestrand 113 F 4
Holmfirth 101 E 3
Holmhead 99 B 4
Holmön 112 H 3
Holmsjön 112 G 3
Holmsland Klit 113 E 4
Holmsund 112 H 3
Holmsveden 112 G 3
Holmudden 113 G 4
Holoog 160 B 5
Holstebro 113 E 4
Holsteinsborg 169 R 2
Holsworthy 102 B 2
Holy Cross 166 E 3
Holyhead 102 B 1
Holy Island 101 E 2

Holy Island Lindisfarne 102 B 1
Holyoke (CO, U.S.A.) 170 F 3
Holyoke (MA, U.S.A.) 171 M 3
Holywell 102 C 1
Holywood (U.K.) 100 C 2
Homa Bay 158 E 5
Homalin 135 G 3
Homāyūnshahr 128 E 4
Hombori 156 D 2
Hombori, Monts du 156 D 2
Hombori Tondo 156 D 2–3
Hombre Muerto, Salar de 182 C 4
Home Bay 169 O 2
Home Hill 143 H 2
Homer 166 G 4
Homestead (FL, U.S.A.) 171 K 6
Homestead (Queensland, Austr.) 143 H 3
Homewood 171 J 5
Hommelstö 112 F 2
Homnabad 134 C 4
Homoine 161 F 4
Homoljske Planina 116 B 2
Homosassa 171 K 6
Homs 154 F 2
Homs → Al Khums 153 H 2
Honavar 134 B 5
Honda 178 D 2
Hondeklip Baai 160 B 6
Honduras 172 E 5
Hönefoss 113 F 3
Honey Lake 170 B 3
Hon Gai 135 J 3
Hong Kong 132 F 6
Hongbe 132 D 6
Hongliuhe 132 B 2
Hongliuyuan 132 C 2
Hongor 132 F 1
Hongqizhen 132 E 7
Hongsa 135 H 4
Hongshui He 132 E 6
Honguedo, Détroit d' 169 P 6
Hongyuan 132 D 4
Hongze 132 G 3
Hongze Hu 133 G 4
Honiara 145 G 2
Honiton 102 C 2
Honkajoki 112 H 3
Hon Khoci 135 H 6
Honnali 134 C 5
Honningsvåg 112 J 1
Honolulu 147 E 1
Hon Panjang 135 H 6
Honrubia 114 C 4
Honshū 133 L 3
Hood, Mount 170 B 2
Hood Point 142 B 5
Hood River 170 B 2
Hoogeveen 110 E 4
Hooghly 134 E 3
Hooker Creek 142 E 2
Hook Island 143 H 3
Hoonah 166 K 4
Hooper, Cape 169 O 2
Hoorn 110 E 4
Hoover Dam 170 D 4
Hopa 117 F 2
Hope (AR, U.S.A.) 171 H 5
Hope (AZ, U.S.A.) 170 D 5
Hope, Cape 167 O 2
Hopedale 169 P 4
Hope, Mount 143 F 5
Hope, Point 166 D 2
Hopes Advance, Cap 169 O 3
Hopetoun (Victoria, Austr.) 143 G 6
Hopetoun (Western Australia) 142 C 5
Hopetown 160 C 5
Hopewell Islands 169 M 4
Hopin 135 G 3
Hopkins, Lake 142 D 3
Hopkinsville 171 J 4
Hopton 103 E 1
Hoquiam 170 B 2
Hora Kalifo 159 G 3
Horasan 117 F 2
Hordaland 113 E 3
Hordio → Hurdiyo 159 J 2
Horgen 115 E 2
Horgos 116 A 1
Hörh Uul 132 E 2
Horinger 132 F 2
Horley 103 D 2
Horlick Mountains 185
Hormoz 128 F 5
Hormuz, Strait of 155 K 3
Horn (Austria) 115 G 2
Horn (Iceland) 112 A 2
Hornad 111 H 5
Hornavan 112 G 2

Hornby Bay 167 O 2
Horn, Cape 183 E 10
Horncastle 101 E 3
Hörnefors 112 G 3
Hornell 171 L 3
Hornepayne 168 L 6
Horn Islands 147 D 3
Hornos, Cabo de 183 C 10
Hornos, Falso Cabo de 183 C 10
Horn Plateau 167 O 3
Hornsea 101 E 3
Hornslandet 112 G 3
Horqin Youyi Qianqi 133 H 1
Horqin Youyi Zhongqi 133 H 1
Horqin Zuoyi Houqi 133 H 2
Horqin Zuoyi Zhongqi 133 H 2
Horqueta 180 E 5
Horred 113 F 4
Horsens 113 E 4
Horsham 103 D 2
Horsham 143 G 6
Hørsholm 113 F 4
Hortobágy 116 B 1
Horton 167 N 2
Hosalay 117 D 2
Hose Mountains 136 D 3
Hosenofu 153 K 4
Hoseynīyeh 128 D 4
Hoshab 129 G 5
Hoshangabad 134 C 3
Hoskins 145 F 3
Hospet 134 C 4
Hospitalet de Llobregat 114 D 3
Hosseina 159 F 3
Hoste, Isla 183 C 10
Hot 135 G 4
Hotagen 112 F 3
Hotan 129 K 3
Hotan He 129 L 3
Hotazel 160 C 5
Hoting 112 G 3
Hot Springs 170 F 3
Hot Springs National Park 171 H 5
Hottah Lake 167 O 2
Houei Sai 135 H 3
Houghton 171 J 2
Houghton Lake 171 K 3
Houlton 171 N 2
Houma (LA, U.S.A.) 171 H 6
Houma (China) 132 F 3
Houndé 156 D 3
Hourn, Loch 99 B 3
Hourtin, Étang d' 114 C 2
House, Mount 142 D 2
Houston 171 G 6
Houtman Abrolhos 142 A 4
Houxia 129 M 2
Hovd 132 D 2
Hovd 130 F 6
Hovd Gol 130 F 6
Hove 103 D 2
Hövsgöl 132 E 2
Hövsgöl Nuur 130 H 5
Howar 154 D 5
Howard 143 J 4
Howden 101 E 3
Howe, Cape 143 J 6
Howland (Oceania) 146 D 2
Howland (ME, U.S.A.) 171 N 2
Howrah 134 E 3
Howth Head 100 B 3
Höxter 111 E 4
Hoxud 132 A 2
Hoy 98 C 2
Höyanger 112 E 3
Hoylake 101 D 3
Hoyos 114 B 3
Höytiäinen 112 J 3
Hozat 117 E 3
Hpunhpu 135 G 2
Hradec Králové 111 G 4
Hraun 112 BC 3
Hrebny 111 F 5
Hron 115 G 5
Hrubieszow 111 H 4
Hrvatska 115 G 2
Hsi-hseng 135 G 3
Hsinchu 133 H 6
Hsinying 133 H 6
Hsipaw 135 G 3
Hua'an 133 G 5
Huab 160 A 4
Huachinango 172 C 3
Huacho 179 C 6
Huachuan 131 O 6
Huacrachuco 178 C 5
Huade 132 F 2
Huadian 133 J 2
Hua Hin 135 GH 5
Huahine 147 L 6
Huahuapán 172 A 3
Huai'an 132 F 2

Huaibei 133 G 4
Huaibin 132 G 4
Huaide 133 H 2
Huaihua 132 E 5
Huaiji 132 F 6
Huailai 132 G 2
Huainan 133 G 4
Huairen 132 F 3
Huaiyin 133 G 4
Huajuapan de León 172 C 4
Hualien 133 H 6
Huallaga 178 C 5
Huallanca 178 C 5
Hualong 132 D 3
Huambo 160 B 2
Huanan 133 K 1
Huancabamba 178 C 5
Huancané 180 C 4
Huancavelica 180 A 3
Huanchaca 180 C 5
Huanchasa 180 C 5
Huangchuan 132 G 4
Huang Hai 133 H 4
Huang He 133 G 3
Huanghe Kou 133 G 3
Huanghetan 132 C 3
Huanghua 133 G 3
Huangling 132 E 3
Huanglong 132 E 3
Huangnihe 132 E 7
Huang Shan 133 G 4
Huangshi 132 G 4
Huang Shui 132 D 3
Huang Xian 133 H 3
Huangyan 133 H 5
Huangyangzhen 132 D 3
Huangyuan 132 D 3
Huangzhong 132 D 3
Huanren 133 J 2
Huanta 180 B 3
Huánuco 178 C 5
Huan Xian 132 E 3
Huanzo, Cordillera de 180 B 3
Huaping 132 D 5
Huara 180 C 4
Huaral 180 A 3
Huaraz 178 C 5
Huariaca 180 A 3
Huarmey 179 C 6
Huasago 178 C 4
Hua Sai 135 H 6
Huascarán, Nevado 178 C 5
Huasco 182 B 4
Huashixia 132 C 3
Huatabampo 170 E 6
Huating 132 E 3
Huautla 172 C 4
Hua Xian 132 F 3
Hua Xian 132 F 6
Huayllay 180 A 3
Huayuri, Pampa de 180 A 3
Huazhou 132 F 6
Hubbart Point 167 T 4
Hubei 132 F 4
Hubli 134 C 4
Hucal 183 D 6
Hucknall Torkard 103 D 1
Hudat 159 F 4
Huddersfield 101 E 3
Huddinge 113 G 4
Huddun 159 H 3
Huddur Hadama 159 G 4
Huder 131 N 6
Hudiksvall 112 G 3
Hudson Bay (Sask., Can.) 167 R 5
Hudson Bay 168 KL 3–4
Hudson, Cerro 183 B 8
Hudson River 171 M 3
Hudson's Hope 167 N 4
Hudson Strait 169 N 3
Hue 135 J 4
Huehuetenango 172 D 4
Huelma 114 C 4
Huelva 114 B 4
Huercal-Overa 114 C 4
Huesca 114 C 3
Huéscar 114 C 4
Huesco, Sierra del 170 E 5
Hufrat an Nahās 158 C 3
Hughenden 143 G 3
Hughes (South Australia) 142 D 5
Hughes (AK, U.S.A.) 166 G 2
Hugh Town 102 A 3
Hugo 171 G 5
Hui'an 133 G 5
Huiarau Range 145 R 8
Huichang 132 G 5
Huicholes, Sierra de los 172 B 3
Hŭich'ŏn 133 J 2
Huidong 132 F 6

Huihe 130 L 6
Huila 160 AB 2
Huila 178 C 3
Huilai 132 G 6
Huili 132 D 5
Huimin 133 G 3
Huinan 133 J 2
Huishui 132 E 5
Huiten Nur 132 B 3
Huittinen 112 H 3
Hui Xian 132 E 4
Huixtla 172 D 4
Huize 132 D 5
Ḫŭksan-chedo 133 HJ 4
Hukuntsi 160 C 4
Hulan 133 J 1
Hulayfā' 155 G 3
Huld 132 E 1
Hulin 133 K 1
Hull (Canada) 171 L 2
Hull (Kiribati) → Orona 146 D 3
Hultsfred 113 G 4
Hulun Buir Meng 130 L 6
Hulun Nur 130 L 6
Ḥulwān 154 E 3
Huma 131 N 5
Huma He 131 M 5
Humahuaca 180 C 5
Humaitá (Amazonas, Brazil) 179 F 5
Humaitá (Paraguay) 182 E 4
Humansdorp 160 C 6
Humara, Jabal al 154 E 5
Humay 180 A 3
Humber 110 C 4
Humber Bridge 101 E 3
Humber, River 101 E 3
Humberside 101 E 3
Humboldt (Sask., Can.) 167 R 5
Humboldt (TN, U.S.A.) 171 J 4
Humboldt River 170 C 3
Humeburn 143 H 4
Humenné 111 H 5
Hummelfjell 112 F 3
Humpata 160 A 2
Hūn 153 J 3
Húnaflói 112 A 2
Hunan 132 F 5
Hunchun 133 K 2
Hunedoara 116 B 1
Hungary 116 A 1
Hungerford (Queensland Austr.) 143 G 4
Hungerford (U.K.) 103 D 2
Hŭngnam 111 J 3
Hungry Horse Reservoir 170 D 2
Hun He 133 H 2
Huni Valley 156 D 4
Hunjiang 133 J 2
Hunnebostrand 113 F 4
Huns Mountains 160 B 5
Hunsrück 111 E 5
Hunsur 134 C 5
Hunte 111 E 4
Hunter 144 K 3
Hunter, Ile 145 K 6
Hunter's Bay 135 F 3–4
Huntingdon 103 D 1
Huntington 171 K 4
Huntly 98 C 3
Huntsville (AL, U.S.A.) 171 J 5
Huntsville (Ont., Can.) 171 L 2
Huntsville (TX, U.S.A.) 171 G 5
Hun Xieng Hung 135 H 3
Hunyani 161 E 3
Hunyuan 132 F 3
Hunza 129 J 3
Huocheng 129 L 2
Huolongmen 131 N 6
Huon 145 H 5
Huong Khe 135 J 4
Huong Thuy 135 J 4
Huon Gulf 144 E 3
Huon Peninsula 144 E 3
Huoshan 132 G 4
Huo Xian 132 F 3
Hur 128 F 4
Huraymilah 155 H 4
Hurdiyo 159 J 2
Hure Qi 133 H 2
Hurghada → Al Ghurdaqah 154 E 3
Huri Hills 159 F 4
Huron 170 F 3
Huron, Lake 171 K 3
Huron Mountains 171 J 2
Hurricane 170 D 4
Hurst 171 G 5
Húsavík 112 B 2
Huşi 116 C 1
Huskvarna 113 F 4
Huslia 166 F 2

Husum (B.R.D.) 111 E 4
Husum (Sweden) 112 G 3
Hutag 130 H 6
Hutchinson (KS, U.S.A.) 170 G 4
Hutchinson (MS, U.S.A.) 171 H 3
Huth 155 G 5
Huthi 135 G 4
Hutou 133 K 1
Hutton, Mount 143 H 4
Hutubi 129 M 2
Huzhou 133 H 4
Hvaler 113 F 4
Hvammstangi 112 A 2
Hvar 115 G 3
Hvarski Kanal 115 G 3
Hverageröi 112 A 3
Hveravellir 112 B 3
Hvide Sande 113 E 4
Hvita 112 AB 3
Hvitá 112 AB 3
Hvítárvatn 112 AB 3
Hwang Ho 133 G 3
Hyannis 171 M 3
Hyargas Nuur 130 F 6
Hyden 142 B 5
Hyderabad (India) 134 C 4
Hyderabad (Pakistan) 129 H 5
Hyères 115 E 3
Hyères, Iles d' 115 E 3
Hyesan 133 J 2
Hyllekrog 113 F 5
Hyltebruk 113 F 4
Hyrra Banda 158 C 3
Hyrynsalmi 112 J 3
Hysham 170 E 2
Hythe 103 E 2
Hyūga 133 K 4
Hyvinge 113 H 3
Hyvinkää (Hyvinge) 113 H 3

I

Iñapari 180 C 3
Iacó 180 C 3
Iaçu 181 H 3
īah-Chashmeh 128 C 3
Iakora 161 H 4
Ialomiţa 116 C 2
Iaripo 179 H 3
Iaşi 116 C 1
Iauareté 178 E 3
Iława 111 J 3
Iba 137 J 1
Ibadan 156 E 4
Ibagué 178 C 3
Ibaiti 181 F 5
Ibar 116 B 2
Ibarra 178 C 3
Ibb 155 G 6
Ibba 158 D 4
Ibembo 158 C 4
Ibenga 157 H 5
Iberá, Esteros del 182 E 4
Iberia 180 C 3
Iberville, Lac d' 169 N 4
Ibestad 112 G 2
Ibi 157 F 4
Ibiapaba, Serra da 181 H 1–2
Ibiara 181 J 2
Ibicaraí 181 J 4
Ibicui 182 E 4
Ibicuy 182 E 5
Ibipetuba 181 H 3
Ibitiara 181 H 3
Ibiza 114 D 4
Ibn Qawrah 155 J 5
Ibo 161 G 2
Ibonma 137 H 4
Ibotirama 181 H 3
Iboundji, Mont 157 G 6
Ibrā' 155 K 4
Ibrāhīm, Jabal 155 G 4
Ibrah, Wādī 154 C 6
'Ibrī 155 K 4
Ibrīm 154 E 4
Icá (Amazonas, Brazil) 178 E 4
Ica (Peru) 180 A 3
Icana (Amazonas, Brazil) 178 E 3
Icapuí 181 J 2
Icatu 181 H 1
İçel 117 D 3
Icepê 181 F 5
Icha 131 T 4
Ichaf 152 D 3
Ichalkaranji 134 B 4
Ichchapuram 134 D 4
Ichera 130 J 4
Ichibusa-yama 133 K 4
Ichig → Chegga 152 D 3

Ichigemskiy Khrebet 131 U 3
Ichinskaya Sopka 131 T 4
Ichnya 118 F 5
Ichourad 156 D 1
Ico 181 J 2
Icoca 160 B 1
Icoraci 179 J 4
Icy Cape 166 E 1
Idabel 171 H 5
Idah 157 F 4
Idaho 170 CD 3
Idaho Falls 170 D 3
Idän 159 H 3
Íday 157 G 3
'Idd al Ghanam 154 C 6
Idel 112 K 3
Idelès 153 G 4
Idélimen 156 E 2
Idfū 154 E 4
Idhān Awbārī 153 H 3
Idhān Murzuq 153 H 5
Ídhi Óros 116 B 3
Ídhra 116 B 3
Idikel 157 F 2
Ierisós 116 B 2
Idil 117 F 3
Idiofa 158 B 5
Idjil, Sebkhet 152 C 4
Idlib 154 F 1
Idre 112 F 3
Idrī 153 H 3
Idrigill Point 98 D 3
Idrija 115 F 2
Idutywa 160 D 6
Idyum 131 O 4
Ierápetra 116 C 4
Iesi 115 F 3
Iet 59 G 2
Ifag 159 F 2
Ifakara 159 F 6
Ifaki 157 F 4
Ifalik 146 A 2
Ifanadiana 161 H 4
Ife 157 E 4
Iferouane 157 F 2
Ifetesene 153 F 3
Ifinga 158 F 6
Ifjord 112 J 1
Ifon 157 F 4
Iganga 158 E 4
Igara Paraná 178 D 4
Igarapava 181 G 5
Igarka 119 R 3
Igatimí 181 E 5
Igatpuri 134 B 4
Igbetti 157 E 4
Igdet, Jbel 152 D 2
Iğdır (Iran) 128 D 3
Iğdır (Turkey) 117 F 3
Ige 152 B 3
Iggesund 112 G 3
Ighil Mgoun, Jbel 152 D 2
Iglesia 182 C 5
Iglesias 115 E 4
Igli 152 E 2
Ignace 171 J 6
Iğneada 111 C 2
Ignashino 131 M 5
Igoumenitsá 116 B 3
Igra 118 K 4
Igrim MN 3
Iguaçu 182 F 4
Iguaçu, Parque Nacional do 182 F 4
Iguaçu, Saltos do 182 F 4
Iguala 172 C 4
Igualada 114 D 3
Igualdade 178 E 4
Iguatu 181 J 2
Iguazú, Cataratas del 182 F 4
Iguazú Falls 182 F 4
Iguéla 157 F 6
Iguetti, Sebkha 152 D 3
Iguidi, Erg 152 DE 3
Iguigik 166 F 4
Igusi 160 D 3
Ih Bogd Uul 132 D 2
Ihelum 132 J 4
Iherene 153 F 4
Ihosy 161 H 4
Ihsaniye 116 D 3
Ihtamir 130 H 6
Ii 112 J 2
Iijärvi 112 J 2
Iijoki 112 J 2
Iisalmi 112 J 3
Iivaara 112 J 2
Ijebu Ode 157 E 4
Ijsselmeer 110 E 4
Ijuí 182 F 4
Ikaalinen 112 H 3
Ikalamavony 161 H 4

Ika–Isi

Ikali 158 C 5
Ikanda 158 C 5
Ikaría 116 C 3
Ikast 113 E 4
Ikatskiy Khrebet 130 K 5
Ikeda 133 M 2
Ikeja 156 E 4
Ikela 158 C 5
Ikelemba 158 B 4
Ikerre 157 F 4
Ikey 130 H 5
Iki Burul 117 F 1
Ikom 157 F 4
Ikomba 161 E 1
Ikongo 159 F 6
Ikopa 161 H 3
Ikot Ekpene 157 F 4
Ikryanoye 117 G 1
Ikungi 158 E 6
Ikungu 158 E 6
Ila 157 E 4
Ilabaya 180 B 4
Ilad 159 H 2
Ilaferh 153 F 4
Ilagan 137 J 1
Ilam 128 D 4
Ilan 133 H 6
Ilanskiy 130 G 4
Ilaro 156 E 4
Ilatan 157 E 2
Ilbenge 131 M 3
Ile-à-la-Crosse 167 Q 4
Île à Vache 173 H 4
Ilebo 158 C 5
Île d'Anticosti 169 P 6
Ile de France 114 D 2
Ile de France, Côte de l' 114 D 2
Ile de Groix 114 C 2
Ile de la Gonâve 173 H 4
Île de la Madeleine 169 P 6
Ile de la Tortue 173 H 3
Île de Ré 114 C 2
Île de Sable 146 B 4
Ile des Noefs 159 J 6
Ile des Pins 145 J 6
hes 159 J 6
Ile d'Oléron 114 C 2
Ile d'Ouessant 114 B 2
Île du Diable 179 H 2
Ile d'Yeu 114 C 2
Ile Hunter 145 K 6
Ilek 118 L 5
Ile Matthew 145 K 6
Ilemera 158 E 5
Iles Banks 145 J 4
Iles Belep 145 H 5
Îles de Los 156 B 4
Îles d'Hyères 115 E 3
Îles du Désappointement 147 F 3
Îles du Duc de Gloucester 147 F 4
Îles du Roi Georges 147 F 3
Îles Glorienses (Reunion) 161 H 2
Ilesha 156 E 4
Iles Loyauté 145 J 6
Îles Palliser 147 F 4
Iles Torres 145 J 4
Ile Tidra 152 B 5
Ile Walpole 145 J 6
Ilford 167 S 4
Ilfracombe 102 B 2
Ilgaz 117 D 2
Ilgaz Dağları 117 D 2
Ilgın 117 D 3
Ilha Caviana 179 H 3
Ilha da Inhaca 161 E 5
Ilha de Coiba 178 B 2
Ilha de Maracá 179 H 3
Ilha de Marajó 179 HJ 4
Ilha de Orango 156 A 3
Ilha de São Sebastião 181 G 5
Ilha de Santa Catarina 181 G 6
Ilha de Tinharé 181 J 3
Ilha do Bananal 181 F 3
Ilha Grande (Brazil) 181 H 5
Ilha Grande (Brazil) 178 E 4
Ilha Grande do Gurupá 179 H 4
Ilha Janauca 179 H 3
Ilha Mexiana 179 J 3
Ilha Santa Carolina 161 F 4
Ilhas, Cachoeira das 179 G 4
Ilhas de São João 179 K 4
Ilhas Selvagens (Port.) 152 B 2
Ilha Tupinambaranas 179 G 4
Ilha Vamizi 161 G 2
Ilhea Point 160 A 4
Ilhéus 181 J 3
Ili 129 K 2
Ilia 116 B 1
Iliamna 166 G 4
Iliamna Lake 166 F 4
İliç 117 E 3
Il'ich 129 H 2
Ilichevsk 116 D 1

Ilidza 115 G 3
Iligan 137 F 2
Iligan Bay 137 F 2
Ili He 129 L 2
Ilim 130 H 4
Ilimniir 131 S 2
Ilimsk 130 H 4
Ilimskiy, Ust'-, Vodokhrani-
 lishche 130 H 4
Ilinskiy 131 Q 6
Ilinsky 113 K 3
Ilir 130 H 4
Ilirgytkin, Ozero 131 T 1
Ilirney 131 V 2
Ilirska Bistrica 115 F 2
Il'ka 130 J 5
Ilkeston 103 D 1
Ilkley 101 E 3
Illana Bay 137 F 2
Illapel 182 B 5
Illescas 114 C 3
Illéta 157 F 3
Illimani, Nevado 180 C 4
Illinois 171 J 3–4
Illinois River 171 H 4
Illizi 153 G 3
Illo 156 E 3
Ilmajoki 112 G 3
Il'men, Ozero 113 K 4
Ilminster 102 C 2
Ilmuvye 131 W 3
Ilo 180 B 4
Iloilo 137 F 1
Ilok 115 G 2
Ilomantsi 112 K 3
Ilorin 157 E 4
Ilots de Bass 147 F 4
Ilovlinskaya 118 H 6
Il'pi 131 W 3
Il'pyrskiy 131 U 4
Ilskiy 117 E 2
Ilubabor 158 EF 3
Ilunde 158 E 6
Ilwaki 137 G 5
Ilych 118 L 3
Ima 130 L 4
Imabari 133 K 4
Imām al Ḥamzah 155 GH 2
Iman 133 L 1
Imandra, Ozero 112 K 2
Imari 133 J 4
Imasa 154 F 5
Imataca, Serranía de 179 F 2
Imatra 112 J 3
Imbituba 181 G 6
Imenas 156 E 2
Imeni 26 Bakinskikh Komissarov
 128 D 3
Iméni Gastello 131 R 3
Iméni Lazo 131 S 3
Iméni Mariny 131 R 3
Iméni Peliny Osipenko 131 P 5
Imese 158 B 4
Imgytskoye Boloto 119 O 4
Imi 159 G 3
Imilac 180 C 5
Imilili 152 B 4
Imi n'Tanoute 152 D 2
Imishli 128 D 3
Imola 115 F 3
Imonda 144 D 2
Imotski 115 G 3
Imperatriz (Amazonas, Brazil)
 178 E 5
Imperatriz (Maranhão, Brazil)
 179 J 5
Imperia 115 E 3
Impfondo 157 H 5
Imphal 135 F 3
Imphy 114 D 2
İmralı 116 C 2
İmranlı 117 E 3
İmroz 116 C 2
Imst 115 F 2
Imtonzha 131 N 2
In 153 F 3
In Abalene 156 E 2
Inagua Island, Great 173 H 3
Inagua Island, Little 173 H 3
Inajá 181 J 2
In Akhmed 156 D 2
In Alay 156 D 2
In Allarène Gérigéri 157 F 2
Inanwatan 137 H 4
Inanya 131 S 3
Inari 157 H 6
Inarigda 130 J 3
Inarijärvi 112 J 2
In Azaoua 157 F 1
In Beriem 156 D 2
Inca 114 D 4

Inca de Oro 182 B 4
Ince Burun 117 D 2
İncekum Burnu 117 D 3
Inchiri 152 C 5
Inchôpe 161 E 3
Inch'ŏn 133 J 3
In Dagouber 156 D 1
Indalsälven 112 G 3
Indargarh 134 C 2
Independence (KS, U.S.A.)
 171 G 4
Independence (MO, U.S.A.)
 171 H 4
Independencia, Isla 180 A 3
Independenta 116 C 1
Inderagiri, Sungai 136 B 4
Inderapura 136 B 4
Inderborskiy 128 EF 1
India 134 CD 3
Indiana 171 J 3
Indianapolis 171 J 4
Indian Harbour 169 Q 5
Indian Ocean 187
Indian Springs 170 C 4
Indiaroba 181 J 3
Indiga 118 J 2
Indigirka 131 R 2
Indigirskaya Nizmennost'
 131 QR 2
Indija 116 B 1
Índios, Cachoeira dos 179 F 3
Indispensable Reefs 146 B 3
Indispensable Strait 145 H 3
Indonesia 136–137 DG 4
Indore 134 C 3
Indramayu 136 C 5
Indravati 134 D 3
Indre 114 D 2
Indus 129 H 6
Indus Cone 192 B 3
Indus, Mouths of the 129 H 6
İnebolu 117 D 2
İnecik 116 C 2
İnegöl 116 C 2
Inezgane 152 D 2
In Zekouane 156 E 2
Inzia 158 B 6
Ioánnina 116 B 3
Iolotan 129 G 3
Ioma 144 E 3
Iona (Angola) 160 A 3
Iona (U.K.) 99 A 3
Iona National Park 160 A 3
Iona Peres 179 J 4
Iongo 160 B 1
Ionian Islands 116 AB 3
Ionian Sea 116 AB 3
Ionioi Nísoi 116 AB 3
Iónion Pélagos 116 AB 3
Iony, Ostrov 131 Q 4
Íos 116 C 3
Iõ-shima 133 K 4
Iosser 118 K 3
Iowa 171 H 3
Iowa City 171 H 3
Ipala 158 E 5
Ipameri 181 G 4
Ipatovo 117 F 1
Ipatunga 181 H 4
Ipiales 178 C 3
Ipiaú 181 J 3
Ipiranga 178 E 4
Ípiros 116 B 3
Ipixuna (Amazonas, Brazil)
 179 F 5
Ipixuna (Amazonas, Brazil)
 178 D 5
Ipoh 136 B 3
Iporá 181 F 4
Ippy 158 C 3
İpsala 116 C 2
Ipswich (U.K.) 103 E 1
Ipswich (Australia) 143 J 4
Ipu 181 H 1
Ipun 183 B 7
Iqarapé-Açu 179 J 4
Iqe He 132 B 3
Iquape 181 G 5
Iquique 180 B 5
Iquitos 178 D 4
Iracoubo 179 H 2
Iraí 182 F 4
Iráklion 116 C 3
Iran 128 E 4
Iran, Pegunungan 136 D 3
Îrânshahr 129 G 5
Irapa 179 F 1
Irapuato 172 B 3
Iraq 155 G 2
Irati 182 F 4
Irazú, Volcán 178 B 1
Irbeni Väin 113 H 4
Irbid 154 F 2
Irbit 119 M 4
Irebu 158 B 5
Irecê 181 H 3
Ireland 110 B 4

In Rhar 153 F 3
In Salah 153 F 3
Inscription, Cape 142 A 4
Insein 135 G 4
Insiza 160 D 3
Insiza → Nsiza 160 D 3
Insulă Sacalin 116 C 2
Inta 119 M 2
In Tadreft 157 F 2
In Talak 156 E 2
In Tebezas 156 E 2
Intepe 116 C 2–3
Interlaken 115 E 2
Interview Island 135 F 5
Intletovy 119 P 3
Intuto 178 D 4
Inuvik 166 L 2
Inuvik, District of 166 LM 2
Inveraray 99 B 3
Invergordon 98 B 3
Inverbervie 99 C 3
Invercargill (New Zealand)
 144 P 10
Invercargill (New Zealand) 146 C 6
Inverell 143 J 4
Inverkeithing 99 C 3
Invermoriston 98 B 3
Inverness 98 B 3
Inverness (Airport) 98 B 3
Inverurie 98 C 3
Inverway 142 D 2
Investigator Shoal 136 D 2
Investigator Strait 143 F 6
Inya 131 R 3
Inya 119 Q 4
Inya 119 R 5
Inyanga 161 E 3
Inyangani 161 E 3
Inyati 160 D 3
Inyonga 158 E 6

Iret' 131 S 3
Irgiz 118 J 5
Irgiz 129 G 1
Irharen 153 F 4
Irharhar 153 G 3
Irharharene 153 G 3
Irharrhar 153 G 4
Irhazer Ouan Agadez 157 F 2
Irherm 152 D 2
Irian Jaya 137 H 4
Iriba 119 J 2
Iriklinskiy 119 L 5
Iringa 159 F 6
Iriomote-jima 133 H 6
Iriona 172 E 4
Iriri 179 H 5
Irish Sea 100 C 3
Iritsoka 161 H 4
Irkeneyeva 130 G 4
Irkut 130 H 5
Irkutsk 130 H 5
İrmasan Geçidi 116 D 3
Irminger Basin 192 A 2
Irnijärvi 112 J 2
Iroise 114 C 2
Iron gate → Portile de Fier
 116 B 2
Iron Knob 143 F 5
Iron Mountain 171 J 2
Iron Mountains 100 B 2
Iron Range 143 G 1
Irosin 137 F 1
'Irq al Idrīsī 153 K 4–5
'Irq al Mazhūr 155 G 3
'Irq Jahām 155 H 3
Irrawaddy 135 G 4
Irrawaddy, Mouths of the 135 F 4
Irrigi 156 CD 2
Irthlingborough 103 D 1
Irtuia 179 J 4
Irtysh 119 N 4
Irtysh 119 O 5
Irtyshskoye 119 O 5
Irumu 158 D 4
Irún 114 C 3
Irves Šaurums 113 H 4
Irvine 99 B 4
Irvinestown 100 B 2
Irving 171 G 5
Îrwân, Wādī 153 H 3
Isa 157 F 3
Isabel 167 R 6
Isabela, Isla (Ecuador) 178 B 6
Ísafjörður 112 A 2
Isahaya 133 K 4
Isaka 158 E 5
Isá Khel 129 J 4
Isakogorka 118 H 3
Isalo, Massif de l' 161 H 4
Isa, Mount 143 F 3
Isaouane N-Irharharene 153 G 3
Isar 181 J 3
Íshã, Ra's 155 G 5
Isarco 115 F 2
Isăwah 153 H 3
Isayevskiy 130 G 1
Ischia 115 F 3
Iscia Baidoa → Isha Bayḏabo
 159 G 4
Ise 133 L 4
Isefjord 113 F 4
Iséo, Lago d' 115 F 2
Isère 115 E 2
Isernia 115 F 3
Iset' 119 M 4
Ise-wan 133 L 4
Iseyin 156 E 4
Isfahan → Esfahan 128 E 4
Isfendiyar Dağları 117 DE 2
Isha Bayḏabo 159 G 4
Isherim, Gora 119 L 3
Isherton 179 G 3
Ishigaki 133 H 6
Ishikari-wan 133 M 2
Ishikawa 133 J 5
Ishikhly 128 D 3
Ishim 119 N 4
Ishimbay 118 L 5
Ishimskaya Step' 119 O 5
Ishinomaki 133 M 3
Ishkamish 129 H 3
Ishkashim 129 J 3
Ishulli i Sazanit 116 A 2
Isiboro 180 C 4
Isigny-sur-Mer 114 C 2
Işıklar Dağı 116 C 2
Isikli Gölü 116 C 3
Isil'kul 119 O 5

Isi – Jal

Isinga 130 K 5
Isiolo 159 F 4
Isipingo Beach 161 E 6
Isiro 158 D 4
Isisford 143 G 3
Isit' 131 N 3
Is, Jabal 154 F 4
Iskamen', Khrebet 166 B 2
Iskander 129 H 2
Iskăr 116 B 2
İskenderun 117 E 3
İskenderun Körfezi 117 E 3
İskilip 117 D 2
Iskitim 119 Q 5
Iskup 119 R 3
Iskushuban 159 J 2
Iskut River 166 L 4
Isla Ángel de la Guarda 170 D 6
Isla Byron 183 A 8
Isla Campana 183 A 8
Isla Carmen 170 D 6
Isla Cedros 170 C 6
Isla Cerralvo 170 D 7
Isla Clarence 183 B 9
Isla-Cristina 114 B 4
Isla Dawson 183 B 9
Isla de Altamura 170 E 7
Isla de Aves 173 K 4
Isla de Chiloé 183 B 7
Isla de Coiba 173 F 6
Isla de Cozumel 172 E 3
Isla de Guadelupe 170 C 6
Isla de la Juventud 172 F 3
Isla del Maíz 172 F 5
Isla de los Estados 183 D 9
Isla del Rey 178 C 2
Isla del Toro 172 C 3
Isla de Margarita 179 F 1
Isla de Ometepe 172 E 5
Isla de Providencia (CA, U.S.A.) 173 F 5
Isla de San Ignacio 170 E 6
Isla de Santa Margarita 170 D 7
Isla de Vieques 173 J 4
Isla Esmeralda 183 A 8
Isla Española 178 B 6
Isla Fernandina 178 B 6
Isla Grande de Tierra del Fuego 183 C 9
Isla Guafo 183 B 7
Isla Holbox 172 E 3
Isla Hoste 183 C 10
Isla Independencia 180 A 3
Isla Isabela (Ecuador) 178 B 6
Isla Jorge Montt 183 B 9
Isla Lennox 183 C 10
Isla Londonderry 183 B 9–7
Islamabad 129 J 4
Isla Madre de Dios 183 AB 6
Isla Magdalena (Chile) 183 B 7
Isla Magdalena (Mexico) 170 D 7
Isla Marchena 178 B 6
Isla Maria Madre 172 A 3
Isla Maria Magdalena 172 A 3
Isla Melchor 183 B 8
Isla Mocha 183 B 6
Isla Mona 173 J 4
Isla Montague 170 D 5
Isla Mornington 183 A 8
Isla Navarino 183 C 9–7
Ísland 112 AB 2–3
Island Lake 167 T 5
Island Magee 100 C 2
Islands, Bay of 169 Q 6
Islands of Four Mountains 166 C 5
Isla Noir 183 B 9
Isla Nueva 183 C 10
Isla Pinta 178 B 6
Isla Riesco 183 B 9
Isla San Cristóbal 178 B 6
Isla San José 170 D 6
Isla San Marcos 170 D 6
Isla San Salvador 178 B 6
Isla Santa Catalina 170 D 6
Isla Santa Cruz 178 B 6
Isla Santa Inés 183 B 9
Isla Santa María 178 B 6
Islas Baleares 114 D 3–4
Islas Canarias 152 B 3
Islas de Barlovento 173 K 4
Islas de la Bahía 172 E 4
Islas del Cisne 172 F 4
Islas de los Riachos 183 D 6
Islas de Sotavento 178 E 1
Islas Diego Ramírez 183 BC 10
Islas Grafton 183 B 9
Islas Hanover 183 B 9
Islas las Aves 178 E 1
Islas Lobos de Afuera 178 B 5
Islas los Hermanos 179 F 1
Islas los Monjes 178 D 1
Islas los Testigos 179 F 1

Islas Malvinas → Falkland Islands 183 DE 9
Islas Marias 172 A 3
Islas Rennell 183 B 9
Islas Wollaston 183 C 10
Isla Tiburon 170 D 6
Isla Tortuga 170 D 6
Isla Trinidad (Arg.) 183 D 6
Isla Wellington 183 AB 5
Islay 110 B 3
Islay 99 A 4
Islay (Airport) 99 A 4
Isle of Man 100 C 2
Isle of Man (Airport) 100 C 2
Isle of Portland 102 C 2
Isle of Sheppey 103 E 2
Isle of Wight 103 D 2
Isle Royale 171 J 2
Isles of Scilly 102 A 3
Ísles Tristao 156 A 3
Islos del Cisne (Hond.) 172 F 4
Isluga 180 C 4
Ismailia → Al Ismā'īlīyah 154 E 2
Isnā 154 E 3
Isny 111 F 5
Isojärvi 112 H 3
Isoka 161 E 2
Isole Egadi 115 F 4
Isole Eolie o Lipari 115 F 4
Isole Ponziane 115 F 3
Isole Tremiti 115 G 3
Isosyöte 112 J 2
Ísparta 116 D 3
İspir 117 F 2
Israel 154 E 2
Issano 179 G 2
Issia 156 C 4
Issoire 114 D 2
Issoudun 114 D 2
Issyk-Kul, Ozero 129 K 2
İstanbul 116 C 2
İstanbul Boğazı 116 C 2
Isteren 112 F 3
Isthmus of Kra 135 G 5
Istiaía 116 B 3
Istmina 178 C 2
Istmo de Panamá 178 C 2
Istmo de Tehuantepec 172 D 4
Isto, Mount 166 J 2
Istra 115 F 2
Istria 116 C 2
Itabaiana (Paraíba, Brazil) 181 J 2
Itabaiana (Sergipe, Brazil) 181 J 3
Itabapoana 181 H 5
Itaberaba 181 H 3
Itabira 181 H 4
Itaboca 179 F 4
Itabuna 181 J 3
Itacaiúna 179 H 5
Itacajá 179 J 5
Itacarambi 181 H 3–4
Itacaré 181 J 3
Itacoatiara 179 G 4
Itaete 181 H 3
Itaguajé 181 F 5
Itagüí 178 C 2
Itaitaba 179 G 4
Itajaí 181 G 6
Itaka 130 L 5
Italia 115 E–G 2–4
Italy 115 E–G 2–4
Itamataré 179 J 4
Itambé 181 H 4
Itambé, Pico de 181 H 4
Itampolo 161 G 4
Itapaci 181 G 3
Itaparica 181 J 3
Itapemirim 181 H 5
Itaperucu Mirim 181 H 1
Itaperuna 181 H 5
Itapetim 181 J 2
Itapetinga 181 H 4
Itapetininga 181 G 5
Itapicura 181 H 2
Itapicuru 181 J 1
Itapinima 179 F 5
Itapipoca 181 J 1
Itapiranga (Amazonas, Brazil) 179 G 4
Itapiranga (Sta. Catarina, Brazil) 182 F 4
Itapiúna 181 J 1
Itaporã 179 J 5
Itaporanga 181 J 2
Itaquari 181 H 5
Itaqui 182 E 4
Itaquyry 181 E 5
Itararé 181 G 5
Itarsi 134 C 3
Itaruma 181 F 4
Itatupá 181 H 4
Itaum 181 EF 5
Itaúna 181 H 5

Itaúnas 181 J 4
Itbāy 154 E 3–4
Itchen Lake 167 P 2
Iténez 180 D 3
Iteshi-Teshi, Lake 160 D 3
Ithaca 171 L 3
Ithaca 171 L 3
Itháki 116 B 3
Ithnayn, Harrat 155 FG 3
Ithra 154 F 2
Itigi 158 E 6
Itiopya 159 FG 3
Itiquira 180 E 4
Itirucu 181 H 3
Itivdleg 169 R 2
Itoigawa 133 L 3
Itoko 158 C 5
Itongafeno 161 H 4
Itu 157 F 4
Itu Aba 136 D 1
Itubera (Bahia, Brazil) 181 J 3
Ituberá (Bahia, Brazil) 181 J 3
Ituí 178 D 5
Ituiutaba 181 G 4
Itumbiara 181 G 4
Itungi 158 E 6
Iturama 181 F 4
Iturbe 180 C 5
Ituri 158 D 4
Iturup, Ostrov 131 R 7
Ituxi 178 E 5
Itzehoe 111 E 4
Iul'tin 166 B 2
Ivaí 181 F 5
Ivaiporã 181 F 5
Ivakoany, Massif de l' 161 H 4
Ivalo 112 J 2
Ivalojoki 112 J 2
Ivangorod 113 J 4
Ivangrad 116 A 2
Ivanhoe 143 G 3
Ivaničgrad 115 G 2
Ivanjska 115 G 3
Ivankov 118 E 5
Ivano-Frankovsk 118 D 6
Ivanovka 131 N 5
Ivanovka 119 Q 6
Ivanovka 118 K 5
Ivanovka 117 D 1
Ivanovo 118 H 4
Ivao, Gora 131 RS 6
Ivashka 131 U 4
Ivdel' 119 MN 3
Ivindo 157 G 5
Ivinheima 181 F 5
Ivohibe 161 H 4
Ivory Coast 156 CD 4
Ivrea 115 E 2
Ivujivik 169 M 3
Iwaki 133 M 3
Iwakuni 133 K 4
Iwanai 133 M 2
Iwo 157 E 4
Iwo Jima 121 R 7
Iwŏn 133 J 2
Ixiamas 180 C 3
Ixopo 160 DE 6
Iya 130 G 5
'Iyāl Bakhīt 154 D 6
Izamal Balankanche 172 E 3
Izberbash 128 D 2
Izegem 111 D 5
Izhevsk 118 K 4
Izhma 118 K 3
Izhorskaya Vozvyshennost' 112 J 4
Izkī 155 K 4
Izmail 116 C 1
İzmir 116 C 3
İzmir Körfezi 116 C 3
İzmit 116 C 2
İznik Gölü 116 C 2
Izobil'nyy 117 F 1
Izozog, Bañados de 180 D 4
Iztočni Rodopi 116 C 2
Izuhara 133 J 4
Izu-shotō 133 L 4
Izynda 128 F 1
Izyum 118 G 6

J

Jõgeva 112 J 4
Jaala 112 J 3
Jaama 113 J 4
Jääsjärvi 112 J 3
Jabal Abadab 154 F 5
Jabal 'Abd al 'Azīz 155 G 1

Jabal Abū Ḥasan 155 G 5
Jabal Abū Rujmayn 154 F 2
Jabal ad Dayr 154 E 6
Jabal ad Durūz 154 F 2
Jabal Adhan 155 K 3
Jabal Ajā' 155 G 3
Jabal al Akhḍar 155 K 4
Jabal al Awlīyā' 154 E 5
Jabal al Bishrī 154 171 F 1
Jabal al Fārayid 154 E 4
Jabal al Ḥarīm 155 K 3
Jabal al Ḥawā'ish 153 K 4
Jabal al Humara 154 E 5
Jabal al Kū' 155 H 3
Jabal al Lawz 154 F 3
Jabal al Ung 115 E 4
Jabal al 'Uwaynāt 154 D 4
Jabal 'Anazah 155 F 2
Jabal an Nabī Shu'ayb 155 G 5
Jabal an Nāmūs 153 J 4
Jabal an Nīr 155 G 4
Jabal Arkanū 153 K 4
Jabal as Ḥasāwinah 153 H 3
Jabal ash Shām 155 J 5
Jabal ash Shīfā' 154 F 3
Jabal Asoteriba 154 F 4
Jabal as Sawdā 153 HJ 3
Jabal as Sibā'ī 153 E 3
Jabal at Ṭanf 154 F 2
Jabal at Tarhūnī 153 K 4
Jabal aṭ Ṭubayq 154 F 3
Jabal Bartazuga 154 E 4
Jabal Batrā 154 F 3
Jabal Bin Ghanīmah 153 J 3–4
Jabal Dabbāgh 154 F 3
Jabal Eigat 154 EF 4
Jabal Eigrim 154 F 5
Jabal Erba 154 F 4
Jabal Ghārib 154 E 3
Jabal Ghemi 158 E 3
Jabal Gumbiri 158 E 4
Jabal Gurgei 154 C 6
Jabal Ḥabashīyah 155 HJ 5
Jabal Ḥadada 154 D 4
Jabal Hadid 153 K 4
Jabal Ḥafīt 155 K 4
Jabal Hajhir 159 J 2
Jabal Ḥamāṭah 154 F 4
Jabal Hamoyet 154 F 5
Jabal Ḥamrīn 155 H 2
Jabal Ḥarāzah 154 E 6
Jabal Haybān 154 E 6
Jabal Ḥimā Dārīyah 155 G 4
Jabal Ibrāhīm 155 G 4
Jabal Is 154 F 4
Jabal Kātrīna 154 E 3
Jabal Katul 154 D 6
Jabal Kissū 154 D 4
Jabal Kurur 154 E 4
Jabal Lado 158 E 3
Jabal Lotuke 158 E 4
Jabal Mahrāt 155 J 5
Jabal Manda 158 C 3
Jabal Marrah 154 C 6
Jabal Nafūsah 153 H 2
Jabal Natityāy 154 E 4
Jabal Nuqay 153 J 4
Jabal Nuqrus 154 E 4
Jabal Oda 154 F 4
Jabalón 114 C 4
Jabalpur 134 C 3
Jabal Qarā 155 J 5
Jabal Raḍwā 154 F 4
Jabal Rāf 155 F 3
Jabal Rahib 154 D 5
Jabal Ramm 154 F 3
Jabal Sabidana 154 F 5
Jabal Ṣabīr 155 G 6
Jabal Sāq 155 G 3
Jabal Shā'ib al Banāt 154 E 3
Jabal Shammar 155 G 3
Jabal Sharshar 154 E 4
Jabal Sinjār 155 G 1
Jabal Tageru 154 D 5
Jabal Teljo 154 D 6
Jabal Thāmir 155 H 6
Jabal Thanīyah 155 H 5
Jabal Tlētē Ouate Gharbī 155 F 1
Jabal Ṭuwayq 155 H 3–4
Jabal Waddān 153 J 3
Jabjabah, Wādī 154 E 4
Jablah 154 F 1
Jablanica 115 G 3
Jablaničko Jezero 115 G 3
Jablonec 111 G 4
Jaboatão 181 J 2
Jaboticabal 181 G 5
Jabung, Tanjung 136 B 4
Jaburu 179 F 5
Jaca 114 C 3
Jacaré 179 H 4
Jacareacanga 179 G 5

Jacaretinga 179 G 5
Jacarézinho 181 G 5
Jáchal 182 C 5
Jaciafa 181 F 4
Jaciparaná 179 F 5
Jack Mountain 170 B 2
Jackpot 170 D 3
Jacksboro 170 G 5
Jackson (MI, U.S.A.) 171 K 3
Jackson (MS, U.S.A.) 171 H 5
Jackson (TS, U.S.A.) 171 J 4
Jackson Head 144 P 9
Jackson Lake 170 D 3
Jackson, Mount (Western Austr.) 142 B 5
Jackson, Mount (Antarctica) 185
Jacksonville (FL, U.S.A.) 171 K 5
Jacksonville (IL, U.S.A.) 171 H 4
Jacksonville (N.C., U.S.A.) 171 L 5
Jacksonville (TX, U.S.A.) 171 G 5
Jacksonville Beach 171 K 5
Jacobabad 129 J 4
Jacobina 181 H 3
Jacob Lake 170 D 4
Jacona 172 B 4
Jacques Cartier, Détroit de 169 P 6
Jacques Cartier, Mont 169 O 6
Jacuí 182 F 4
Jacuipe 181 HJ 3
Jacundá (Pará, Brazil) 179 H 4
Jacundá (Pará, Brazil) 179 J 4
Jada 157 G 4
Jadal 157 E 2
Jade-Kanal 111 E 4
Jadīd Ra's al Fīl 154 D 6
J.A.D. Jensens Nunatakker 169 S 3
Jādū 153 H 2
Jaén 114 C 4
Jæren 113 E 4
Jærens rev 113 E 4
Jaffa, Cape 143 F 6
Jaffa → Tel Aviv-Yafo 154 E 2
Jaffna 134 D 6
Jafjaf aṣ Ṣaghīr 153 K 4
Jagdalpur 134 D 4
Jagdaqi 131 M 5
Jagersfontein 160 D 5
Jaggang 134 C 2
Jagtial 134 C 4
Jaguaquara 181 J 3
Jaguarão 182 F 5
Jaguarari 181 HJ 3
Jaguari 182 F 4
Jaguariaíva 181 G 5
Jaguaribe 181 J 2
Jagüé 182 C 4
Jahām, 'Irq 155 H 3
Jahrom 128 E 5
Jaice 115 G 3
Jailolo 137 G 3
Jailolo, Selat 137 G 4
Jaina 172 D 3
Jainca 132 D 3
Jaipur 134 C 2
Jaisalmer 134 B 2
Jaitpur 134 C 2
Jajapura 144 D 2
Jakarta 136 C 5
Jakhan 134 A 3
Jakin 128 E 5
Jakobshavn 184
Jakobstad 112 H 3
Jakpa 157 EF 5
Jakupica 116 B 2
Jalaid Qi 133 H 1
Jalājil 155 H 3
Jalalabad 129 J 4
Jalalpur Pirwala 129 J 5
Jalapa 178 F 2
Jalapa Enríquez 172 C 4
Jalasjärvi 112 G 3
Jalaun 134 C 2
Jaldessa 159 G 3
Jales 181 F 5
Jalgaon 134 C 3
Jalībah 155 H 2
Jalingo 157 G 4
Jalisco 172 B 3
Jālitah 153 G 1
Jalkot 129 J 3
Jalna 134 C 4
Jalón 114 C 3
Jalo Oasis → Wāḥāt Jālū 153 K 3
Jalor 134 B 2
Jalostotitlán 172 B 3
Jalpa 172 B 3
Jalpaiguri 134 E 2
Jālū 153 K 3
Jaluit 146 C 2
Jalūlā' 155 H 2

Jal – Juq

Jālū Wāḥāt 153 K 3
Jama 178 B 4
Jamaica 173 G 4
Jamaica Channel 173 G 4
Jamalpur 134 F 3
Jamāme 159 G 4
Jamanixim 179 G 5
Jamari 179 F 5
Jamba 160 B 2
Jambi 136 B 4
Jamboaye 136 A 3
Jambol 116 C 2
Jambuair, Tanjung 136 A 2
Jambusar 134 B 3
James (N.D., U.S.A.) 170 G 3
James Bay 169 L 5
James River (VA, U.S.A.) 171 L 4
James Ross Strait 167 S 2
Jamestown (South Australia) 143 F 5
Jamestown (N.D., U.S.A.) 170 G 2
Jamestown (N.Y., U.S.A.) 171 L 3
Jamiltepec 172 C 4
Jamkhandi 134 C 4
Jamkhed 134 C 4
Jammer Bugt 113 E 4
Jammu 129 K 4
Jammu and Kashmir 129 K 4
Jamnagar 134 B 3
Jampur 129 J 5
Jämsä 112 J 3
Jamsah 154 E 3
Jämsänkoski 112 J 3
Jamshedpur 134 E 3
Jämtland 112 F 3
Jamuna 134 E 3
Jamundí 178 C 3
Janakpur 134 E 2
Janaúba 181 H 4
Janaucu, Ilha 179 H 3
Jandaia 181 F 4
Jandaq 128 E 4
Jándula 114 C 4
Janesville 171 J 3
Janjira 134 B 4
Jan Mayen Island 184
Jan Mayen Ridge 192 A 1
Jannatabad 128 G 3
Janos 170 E 5
Jansenville 160 C 6
Jäntra 116 C 2
Januária 181 H 4
Jaora 134 C 3
Japan 133 L 3
Japan, Sea of 133 KL 3
Japan Trench 193 C 2
Japiim 178 D 5
Japurá 178 E 4
Japvo Mountain 135 F 2
Jaqué 178 C 2
Jarābulus 154 F 1
Jaraguá 181 G 4
Jarandilla 114 B 3
Jaranwala 129 J 4
Jarbah 153 H 2
Jardim 180 E 5
Jardine River National Park 143 G 1
Jardines de la Reina, Archipiélago de los 173 G 3
Jargalant 132 F G 1
Jargalant→Hovd 130 F 6
Jari 179 H 3
Jarjīs 153 H 2
Jarlshof 98 D 2
Jarny 115 E 2
Jarocin 111 G 4
Jarosław 111 H 4
Järpen 112 F 3
Jarrahdale 141
Jarrow 101 E 2
Jartai 132 E 3
Jaru 180 D 3
Jarud Qi 133 H 2
Järvenpää 113 J 3
Jarvis 147 E 2–3
Järvsö 112 G 3
Jashpurnagar 134 D 3
Jasikan 156 E 4
Jasīra 159 H 4
Jāsk 128 F 5
Jasło 111 H 5
Jason Islands 183 D 9
Jasper (Alb., Can.) 167 O 5
Jasper (AL, U.S.A.) 171 J 5
Jasper (TX, U.S.A.) 171 H 5
Jasper National Park 167 O 5
Jaṣṣān 155 H 2
Jastrzebie Zdrój 111 G 5
Jászberény 116 A 1
Jászság 116 AB 1

Jataí 181 F 4
Jatapu 179 G 4
Jath 134 C 4
Jatisiri, Pulau 136 E 4
Játiva 114 C 4
Jatobá 179 H 4
Jatobal 179 H 4
Jatuarana 179 F 5
Jaú (Amazonas, Brazil) 179 F 4
Jaú (São Paulo, Brazil) 181 G 5
Jaua, Meseta del Cerro 179 F 2–3
Jauaperi 179 F 3
Jauja 180 A 3
Jaumave 172 C 3
Jaunjelgava 113 J 4
Jaunpur 134 D 2
Jaupaci 181 F 4
Java 136 C 5
Javari 178 D 5
Java Sea 136 C 5
Java Trench 193 C 4
Jávea 114 D 4
Javhlant → Uliastay 130 G 6
Javorie 111 G 5
Javor Osat 115 G 3
Javorová skála 111 F 4
Jävre 112 H 2
Jawa 136 C 5
Jawi 136 C 4
Jayanca 178 C 5
Jaya, Puncak 137 J 4
Jayapura 144 D 2
Jayawijaya, Pegunungan 137 J 4
Jazā'ir Farasān 155 G 5
Jazā'ir Khurīyā Murīya 155 K 5
Jazīreh-ye Hendorābī 128 E 5
Jazīreh-ye Lāvān 128 E 5
Jazīreh-ye Qeys 128 E 5
Jazīreh-ye Sīrrī 128 E 5
Jbel Ayachi 152 DE 2
Jbel Bani 152 D 3
Jbel Igdet 152 D 2
Jbel Ighil Mgoun 152 D 2
Jbel Lekst 152 D 3
Jbel Mousaaou Salah 152 E 2
Jbel Ouarkziz 152 D 3
Jbel Sarhro 152 D 2
Jbel Tidirhine 152 E 2
Jbel Toubkal 152 D 2
Jebba 157 E 4
Jebel 153 JK 3
Jeberos 178 C 5
Jedburgh 101 D 2
Jedda → Jiddah 154 F 4
Jedrzejów 111 H 4
Jefferson City 171 H 4
Jefferson, Mount (NV, U.S.A.) 170 C 4
Jefferson, Mount (OR, U.S.A.) 170 B 3
Jefferson River 170 D 2
Jega 157 E 3
Jēkabpils 112 J 4
Jelenia Góra 111 G 4
Jelgava 113 H 4
Jelica 116 B 2
Jelling 113 E 4
Jelöy 113 F 4
Jemaja, Pulau 136 C 3
Jember 136 D 5
Jembongan 136 E 2
Jempang, Danau 136 E 4
Jen 157 G 4
Jena 111 F 4
Jeneponto 137 E 5
Jenny 179 G 2
Jenny Lind Island 167 R 2
Jens Munk Island 169 L 2
Jeqoia 170 C 4
Jequié 181 H 3
Jequitinhonha 181 H 4
Jerada 152 E 2
Jérémie 173 H 4
Jeremoabo 181 J 3
Jerevan 117 F 2
Jerez de Garcia Salinas 172 B 3
Jerez de la Frontera 114 B 4
Jerez de los Caballeros 114 B 4
Jerik 137 H 4
Jerome 170 D 3
Jerruck 129 G 5
Jersey 103 C 3
Jersey (Airport) 103 C 3
Jerumenha 181 H 2
Jerusalem 154 F 2
Jervis Bay 143 J 6
Jesenice 115 G 3
Jessheim 113 F 3
Jessore 134 E 3
Ještěd 111 F 4

Jesup 171 K 5
Jesus Carranza 172 C 4
Jesús María 182 D 5
Jevnaker 113 F 3
Jeypore 134 D 4
Jezerces 116 A 2
Jezero 115 G 3
Jeziorak, Jegioro 111 G 4
Jezioro Drawsko 111 G 4
Jezioro Łebsko 111 G 4
Jezioro Gardno 111 G 4
Jezioro Gopło 111 G 4
Jezioro Jeziorak 111 G 4
Jezioro Koronowski 111 G 4
Jezioro Mamry 111 H 4
Jezioro Miedwie 111 F 4
Jezioro Sniardwy 111 H 4
Jhabua 134 B 3
Jhalawar 134 C 3
Jhang Maghiana 129 J 4
Jhansi 134 C 2
Jhelum 129 J 4
Jhunjhunu 134 C 2
Jiahe 132 F 5
Jialing Jiang 132 E 4
Jiamusi 133 K 1
Ji'an (China) 132 F 5
Ji'an (N. Korea) 133 J 2
Jianchang 133 G 2
Jianchuan 132 C 5
Jiande 133 G 5
Jiang'an 132 DE 5
Jiangao Shan 132 C 5
Jiangbiancun 132 G 5
Jiangcheng 132 D 5
Jiangchuan 132 D 6
Jiange 132 E 4
Jianghua 132 F 5
Jiangjin 132 E 5
Jiangle 133 G 5
Jiangling 132 F 4
Jiangmen 132 F 6
Jiangsu 133 G 4
Jiangxi 132 G 5
Jiangyin 133 H 4
Jiangyong 132 F 5
Jiangyou 132 D 4
Jianli 132 F 5
Jianning 132 G 5
Jian'ou 133 G 5
Jianping 133 G 2
Jianshi 132 E 4
Jianshui 132 D 6
Jianyang 132 D 4
Jianyang 133 G 5
Jiaocheng 132 F 3
Jiaohe 133 J 2
Jiaonan 133 G 3
Jiaozuo 132 F 3
Jiashan 133 G 4
Jiashi 129 K 3
Jia Xian 132 F 3
Jiaxing 133 H 4
Jiayin 131 O 6
Jiayu 132 F 5
Jiayuguan 132 C 3
Jibāl ash Sharāh 154 F 2
Jibiya 157 F 3
Jiddah 154 F 4
Jiddat al Ḥarāsīs 155 K 4–5
Jidong 133 K 1
Jiekkevarre 112 G 2
Jiešjavrre 112 H 2
Jiexi 132 G 6
Jiexiu 132 F 3
Jieyang 132 G 6
Jieznas 112 H 5
Jifārah Plain 153 H 2
Jigzhi 132 D 4
Jihlava 111 G 5
Jija Sarai 129 G 4
Jijel 153 G 1
Jijiga 159 G 3
Jijona 114 C 4
Jilib 159 G 4
Jilin 133 J 2
Jilin Hada Ling 133 J 2
Jiloca 114 C 3
Jimbolia 116 B 1
Jimena de la Frontera 114 B 4
Jiménez 170 E 6
Jimma 159 F 3
Jimo 133 H 3
Jimsar 129 M 2
Jinan 133 G 3
Jincheng 132 F 3
Jinchuan 132 D 4
Jind 134 C 2
Jingbian 132 E 3
Jingde 133 G 4
Jingdezhen 133 G 5
Jinggu 132 D 6
Jinghai 133 G 3

Jinghe 129 L 2
Jinghong 132 D 6
Jingle 132 F 3
Jingmen 132 F 4
Jingning 132 E 3
Jingpo Hu 133 J 2
Jingtai 132 D 3
Jing Xian 132 E 5
Jing Xian 133 G 4
Jingyu 133 J 2
Jinhua 133 G 5
Jining 132 F 2
Jining 133 G 3
Jinja 158 E 4
Jinkouhe 132 D 5
Jinotega 172 E 5
Jinotepe 172 E 5
Jinping 132 E 5
Jinping 132 D 6
Jinsha 132 E 5
Jinshan 133 H 4
Jinshi 132 F 5
Jinst 132 D 1
Jinta 132 C 3
Jinxi 133 H 2
Jin Xian 132 G 3
Jin Xian 133 H 2
Jin Xian 133 H 3
Jinxiang 133 G 3
Jinyang 132 D 5
Jinzhai 132 G 4
Jinzhou 133 H 2
Jiparaná 179 F 5
Jipijapa 178 B 4
Jirjā 154 E 3
Jirwān 155 J 4
Jishan 132 F 3
Jishou 132 E 5
Jishui 132 G 5
Jisr ash Shughūr 154 F 1
Jiu 116 B 2
Jiujiang 132 G 5
Jiulong 132 D 5
Jiuquan 132 C 3
Jiutai 133 J 2
Jiwani, Ras 129 G 6
Jiwen 131 M 5
Jixi 133 K 1
Jize 132 F 3
Jīzān 155 G 5
João Pessoa 181 K 2
João Pinheiro 181 G 4
Joaçaba 182 F 4
Joal-Fadiout 156 A 3
Joanes 179 J 4
Joanésia 181 H 4
Joaquín V. González 182 D 4
Jódar 114 C 4
Jodhpur 134 B 2
Joensuu 112 J 3
Jōetsu 133 L 3
Jóf di Montasio 115 F 2
Johannesburg 160 D 5
John Day 170 C 3
John Day River 170 B 3
John, Mount 142 D 2
John o' Groats 98 C 2
Johnson 170 F 4
Johnsonburg 171 L 3
Johnson City (TN, U.S.A.) 171 K 4
Johnson City (TX, U.S.A.) 170 G 5
Johnsons Crossing 166 L 3
Johnston (U.K.) 102 B 2
Johnston (Oceania) 146 D 1
Johnstone 99 B 4
Johnstown 171 L 3
Johor Baharu 136 B 3
Joigny 114 D 2
Joinville 181 G 6
Joinville 115 E 2
Joinville Island 185
Jokk 112 H 2
Jökulsá 112 B 3
Jökulsá á Dal 112 B 2
Jökulsá á Fjöllum 112 B 2
Jolfa 128 D 3
Joliette 171 M 2
Jolo 137 F 2
Jombang 136 D 5
Jomda 131 L 5
Jonava 113 H 4
Jonê 132 D 4
Jonesboro 171 H 4
Jones, Cape 167 T 3
Jonglei 158 E 3
Jonglei Canal 158 E 3
Jonk 134 D 3
Jönköping 113 F 4
Jonquière 171 M 2

Jontoy 159 G 5
Jonuta 172 D 4
Joplin 171 H 4
Jordan 154 F 2
Jordan (MT, U.S.A.) 170 E 2
Jordânia 181 H 4
Jordan Valley 170 C 3
Jorge Montt, Isla 183 B 9
Jorhat 135 F 2
Jörn 112 H 2
Joroinen 112 J 3
Jørpeland 113 E 4
Jos 157 F 4
José de San Martín 183 B 7
Joseph Bonaparte Gulf 142 D 1
Joseph Lake 169 O 5
Josephstaal 144 E 2
Joshua Tree National Monument 170 C 5
Jos Plateau 157 F 4
Josselin 114 C 2
Jos Sodarso, Pulau 137 J 5
Jostedalen 112 E 3
Jostedalsbreen 112 E 3
Jotunheimen 112 E 3
Joutsa 112 J 3
Joutseno 112 J 3
Jöwhar 159 H 4
Jreïda 152 B 5
Juaba 179 J 4
Juan Aldama 172 B 3
Juancheng 132 G 3
Juan de Nova 161 G 3
Juan Fernández Islands 175 B 6
Juan José 182 D 4
Juanjuí 178 C 5
Juankoski 112 J 3
Juan L. Lacaze 182 E 5
Juárez 183 E 6
Juarez, Ciudad 170 E 5
Juarez, Sierra de 170 C 5
Juàzeiro 181 H 2
Juàzeiro do Norte 181 J 2
Juba (Somalia) 159 G 4
Jūbā (Sudan) 158 E 4
Jubaland 159 G 4
Jubayt 154 F 5
Jubayt 154 F 4
Jubbah 155 G 3
Jubilee Lake 142 D 4
Jubileo 182 E 5
Juby, Cap 152 C 3
Júcar 114 C 4
Juçara 181 F 4
Jucurucú 181 J 4
Juchitán de Zaragoza 172 C 4
Judayyidat 'Ar'ar 155 G 2
Juelsminde 113 F 4
Jugoslavija → Yugoslavia 115–116 G 3–A 3
Juigalpa 172 E 5
Juiz de Fora 181 H 5
Juktån 112 G 2
Julaca 180 C 5
Juli 180 C 4
Juliaca 180 B 4
Julia Creek 143 G 3
Julianatop 179 G 3
Julianehåb 169 S 3
Julimes 170 E 6
Jullundur 134 C 1
Jumanggoin 132 C 4
Jumbo 159 G 5
Jumilla 114 C 4
Jumla 134 D 2
Junagadh 134 B 3
Junagarh 134 D 4
Junan 133 G 3
Jun Bulen 133 G 1
Junction 170 G 5
Junction City 171 G 4
Jundah 143 G 3
Jundiaí 181 G 5
Jundūbah 153 G 1
Juneau 166 L 4
Junee 143 H 5
Jungar Qi 132 F 3
Junggar Pendi 129 M 1
Junín (Argentina) 182 D 5
Junín (Chile) 180 B 4
Junín (Peru) 180 A 3
Junín de los Andes 183 B 6
Junín, Lago de 180 A 3
Jūniyah 154 F 2
Junlian 132 D 5
Junosuando 112 H 2
Junqueiro 181 J 2
Junsele 112 G 3
Jun Xian 132 F 4
Juoksengi 112 H 2
Jupiá, Représa de 181 F 5
Juquiá 181 G 5

Jur–Kan

Jura (Switzerland) 115 E 2
Jura (U.K.) 99 B 3
Jurado 178 C 2
Juratiški 113 J 5
Jurbarkas 113 H 4
Jurby Head 100 C 2
Jurhen Ul Shan 132 B 4
Jurien Bay 142 A 5
Jurm 129 J 3
Jūrmala 113 H 4
Juruá (Amazonas, Brazil) 178 E 4
Juruá (Amazonas, Brazil) 178 D 5
Juruena 180 E 3
Jurumirim, Reprêsa de 181 G 5
Juruti 179 G 4
Jushkozero 113 K 3
Justo Daract 182 C 5
Jutaí (Amazonas, Brazil) 178 E 5
Jutaí (Amazonas, Brazil) 178 E 4
Jutiapa 172 E 5
Juticalpa 172 E 5
Jutland 113 E 4
Juuka 112 J 3
Juva 112 J 3
Juventud, Isla de la 172 F 3
Ju Xian 133 G 3
Juzna Morava 116 B 2
Južni Rodopi 116 C 2
Juzur Qarqannah 153 H 2
Jylland 113 E 4
Jyväskylä 112 J 3

K

Ka 157 E 3
Kaabong 158 E 4
Kaakhka 128 F 3
Kaamanen 112 J 2
Kaap Plato 160 C 5
Kaarta 156 C 3
Kaba 137 J 5
Kabaena, Pulau 137 F 5
Kabakly 129 G 3
Kabala 156 B 4
Kabale 158 D 5
Kabalebo Reservoir 179 G 3
Kabali 137 F 4
Kabalo 158 D 6
Kabambare 158 D 5
Kabanjahe 136 A 3
Kabanovka 118 K 5
Kaban'ya 131 P 6
Kabardinka 117 E 2
Kabare 158 D 5
Kabasalan 137 F 2
Kābāw 153 H 2
Kabba 157 F 4
Kâbdalis 112 G 2
Kaberamaido 158 E 4
Kabinakagami Lake 168 L 6
Kabinda 158 C 6
Kabir Kūh 128 D 4
Kabkābīyah 154 C 6
Kabna 154 E 5
Kabo 158 B 3
Kabompo 160 C 2
Kabondo Dianda 158 D 6
Kabongo 158 D 6
Kabūdiyāh, Ra's 153 H 1
Kabul 129 H 3
Kabuli 144 E 2
Kabunda 160 D 2
Kabushiya 154 E 5
Kabwe 160 D 2
Kabwe Katanda 158 C 6
Kabylie 153 G 1
Kacha 117 D 2
Kacha Kuh 129 G 5
Kaché 157 H 3
Kachia 157 F 4
Kachikattsy 131 N 3
Kachikau 160 C 3
Kachin 135 G 2
Kachiry 119 P 5
Kachkanar 119 L 4
Kachreti 117 G 2
Kachug 130 J 5
Kaçkar Dağı 117 F 2
Kada 157 H 2
Kadali 130 K 4
Kadami, Point 158 E 4
Kadan Kyun 135 G 5
Kade 156 D 4
Kadeï 158 B 4
Kadiana 156 C 3
Kadina 143 F 6
Kadınhanı 117 D 3
Kadiolo 156 C 3
Kadiri 134 C 5

Kadirli 117 E 3
Kadiyevka 117 E 1
Kadmat 134 B 5
Kadoka 170 F 3
Kadoma 160 D 3
Kadonkani 135 G 4
Kāduglī 154 D 6
Kaduna 157 F 3
Kadur 134 C 5
Kadusam 135 G 2
Kadyr-Egi-Tayga, Khrebet 130 G 5
Kadzherom 118 L 3
Kaédi 152 C 5
Kaélé 157 G 3
Kaesŏng 133 J 3
Kāf 154 F 2
Kafakumba 158 C 6
Kafan 128 D 3
Kafanchan 157 F 4
Kaffrine 156 A 3
Kafia Kingi 158 C 3
Kafiréus, Ákra 116 B 3
Kafta 159 F 2
Kafu 158 E 4
Kafue 160 D 3
Kafue (River) 160 D 2
Kafue Dam 160 D 3
Kafue National Park 160 D 2–3
Kafulwe 160 D 1
Kafura 158 E 5
Kaga 133 L 3
Kaga Bandoro 158 B 3
Kagalaska 166 B 5
Kagal'nitskaya 117 F 1
Kagaluk 169 P 4
Kagan 129 G 3
Kagera 158 E 5
Kagera National Park 158 E 5
Kağızman 117 F 2
Kagmar 154 E 6
Kagoshima 133 K 4
Kagua 144 D 3
Kagul 116 C 1
Kahal Tabelbala 152 E 3
Kahama 158 E 5
Kahan 129 G 5
Kahe 159 F 5
Kahemba 158 B 6
Kahia 158 D 6
Kahoolawe 147 E 1
Kahramanmaras 117 E 3
Kahrāmān 157 E 4
Kai Besar, Pulau 137 H 5
Kaibobo 137 G 4
Kaiduhe 129 M 2
Kaieteur Falls 179 G 2
Kaifeng 132 F 4
Kai, Kepulauan 137 H 5
Kaikohe 145 Q 8
Kaikoura 145 Q 9
Kaikoura Range 145 Q 9
Kailahun 156 B 4
Kaili 132 E 5
Kailu 133 H 2
Kaimana 137 H 4
Kaimur Range 134 D 3
Kainantu 144 E 3
Kainji Dam 157 E 4
Kainji Reservoir 157 E 3
Kaintragarh 134 D 3
Kaipara Harbour 145 Q 8
Kaiping 132 F 6
Kairouan → Al Qayrawān 153 H 1
Kairuku 144 E 3
Kaiserslautern 111 E 5
Kaitaia 145 Q 8
Kaithal 134 C 2
Kaiti 159 F 5
Kaitumälven 112 GH 2
Kaiwatu 137 G 5
Kai Xian 132 E 4
Kaiyang 132 E 5
Kaiyuan 132 D 6
Kaiyuan 133 H 2
Kaiyuh Mountains 166 F 3
Kajaani 112 J 3
Kajabbi 143 E 3
Kajaki Dam 129 H 4
Kajiado 159 F 5
Kajo Kaji 158 E 4
Kajura 157 F 3
Kākā (Sudan) 154 E 6
Kaka (Ethiopia) 159 F 3
Kakada 157 H 2
Kakamas 160 C 4
Kakamega 158 E 4
Kakana 135 F 6
Kakata 156 B 4
Kakdwip 134 E 3
Kakenge 158 C 5
Kakhonak 166 G 4

Kakhovka 117 D 1
Kakhovskoye Vodokhranilishche 117 D 1
Kakhtana 131 T 4
Kākī 128 E 5
Kakinada 134 D 4
Kakisa 167 O 3
Kakisa Lake 167 O 3
Kakpin 156 D 4
Kaktovik 166 J 1
Kakuma 158 E 4
Kakumbi 161 E 2
Kakya 159 F 5
Kalabagh 129 J 4
Kalabáka 116 B 3
Kalabakan 136 E 3
Kalabana 156 C 3
Kalabo 160 C 3
Kalach 118 H 5
Kalach-na-Donu 118 H 6
Kaladan 135 F 3
Kaladan 130 L 4
Kalámai 116 B 3
Kalamazoo 171 J 3
Kalambo Falls 158 E 6
Kalamitskiy Zaliv 117 D 1,2
Kalampising 136 E 3
Kalanchak 117 D 1
Kalanshiyū 153 K 3
Kalaong 137 F 2
Kalao, Pulau 137 F 5
Kalaotoa, Pulau 137 F 5
Kalar 130 L 4
Kalarash 116 C 1
Kalasin (Indonesia) 136 D 3
Kalasin (Thailand) 135 H 4
Kalat 134 A 2
Kalaus 117 F 1
Kalavárdha 116 C 3
Kalávrita 116 B 3
Kalaw 135 G 3
Kalbarri 142 A 4
Kalbarri National Park 142 A 4
Kalbinskiy Khrebet 119 Q 6
Kaldbakur 112 A 2
Kaldfarnes 112 G 2
Kale (Turkey) 117 E 3
Kale (Turkey) 117 E 2
Kale (Turkey) 116 D 3
Kale (Turkey) 116 C 3
Kalecik 117 D 2
Kalegauk 135 G 4
Kalehe 158 D 5
Kalemie 158 D 6
Kalemyo 135 F 3
Kāl-e Shūr 128 F 3
Kalevala 112 K 2
Kalewa 135 F 3
Kálfshamarsvík 112 A 2
Kalga 130 L 5
Kalianda 136 C 5
Kaliganj 135 F 3
Kalima 158 D 5
Kalimantan 136 D 3
Kálimnos 116 C 3
Kalingapatam 134 D 4
Kalinin (U.S.S.R.) 128 F 2
Kalinin (U.S.S.R.) 118 G 4
Kaliningrad 143 H 5
Kalinino 117 F 2
Kalinkovichi 113 J 5
Kalinovik 115 G 3
Kaliro 158 E 4
Kalis 159 H 3
Kalispell 170 D 2
Kalisz 111 G 4
Kaliua 158 E 5–6
Kalix 112 H 2
Kalixälven 112 H 2
Kalkah 143 G 1
Kalkan 116 C 3
Kalkfeld 160 B 4
Kalkfontein 160 C 4
Kalkrand 160 B 4
Kall 112 F 3
Kallaktjåkkå 112 G 2
Kållandsö 113 F 4
Kallavesi 112 J 3
Kallinge 113 G 4

Kallonis, Kólpos 116 C 3
Kallsjön 112 F 3
Kalmar 113 G 4
Kalmarsund 113 G 4
Kal'mius 117 E 1
Kalmykovo 128 E 1
Kalni 135 F 3
Kalnik 115 G 2
Kaloko 158 D 6
Kalol 134 B 3
Kalole 158 D 5
Kalolio 137 F 4
Kalomo 160 D 3
Kalpa 134 C 1
Kalpákion 116 B 3
Kalpeni 134 B 5
Kalpi 134 C 2
Kalpin 129 K 2
Kalskag 166 E 3
Kalsubai 134 B 4
Kaltag 166 F 3
Kaltunga 157 G 4
Kaluga 118 G 5
Kalukalukuang, Pulau 136 E 5
Kalulushi 160 D 2
Kalumburu 142 D 1
Kalundborg 113 F 4
Kalush 118 D 6
Kalutara 134 C 6
Kalvarija 113 H 5
Kalya 158 DE 6
Kalyazin 118 G 4
Kama (U.S.S.R.) 118 K 4
Kama (Zaïre) 158 D 5
Kamaï 153 J 2
Kamaishi 133 M 3
Kamal 136 D 5
Kamalampa 158 E 6
Kamalia 129 J 4
Kaman 117 D 3
Kamanjab 160 A 3
Kamanyola 158 D 5
Kamarān 155 G 5
Kamaran, Hadjer 157 J 3
Kamard 129 H 3
Kamareddi 134 C 4
Kamaria Falls 179 G 2
Kamashi 129 H 3
Kambalda 142 C 5
Kambal'naya Sopka 131 T 5
Kambanós, Ákra 116 B 3
Kambia 156 B 4
Kambove 160 D 2
Kambuno, Bukit 137 E 4
Kambūt 153 K 2
Kamchatka, Poluostrov 131 T 4
Kamchatskiy Poluostrov 131 U 4
Kamchatskiy Zaliv 131 U 4
Kamčijska Plato 116 C 2
Kamende 158 C 6
Kamenets-Podolskiy 116 C 1
Kamen, Gora 130 F 2
Kamenjak, Rt 115 F 3
Kamenka 130 G 4
Kamenka 118 G 5
Kamenka 118 H 5
Kamenka 118 H 5
Kamen-na-Obi 119 Q 5
Kamennogorsk 112 J 3
Kamennomostskiy 117 F 2
Kamennoye, Ozero 112 K 3
Kamennyy, Khrebet 131 U 3
Kamenolomni 117 F 1
Kamenskoye 131 V 3
Kamensk 130 J 5
Kamensk-Shakhtinskiy 117 F 1
Kamensk-Ural'skiy 119 M 4
Kameshki 131 U 3
Kamet 134 C 1
Kamieskroon 160 B 6
Kamileroi 143 H 5
Kamilukuak, Lake 167 S 3
Kamina 158 D 6
Kaminak Lake 167 S 3
Kaminuriak Lake 167 S 3
Kamituga 158 D 5
Kamkaly 129 J 2
Kamla 130 H 2
Kamla 134 E 2
Kamloops 167 N 5
Kamnik 115 G 2
Kamnrokan 130 K 4
Kamo 117 G 2
Kamoa Mountains 179 G 3
Kampala 158 E 4
Kampanda 160 C 2
Kampar 136 B 3
Kampar, Sungai 136 B 3
Kampen 110 E 4
Kampene 158 D 5
Kamphaeng Phet 135 G 4
Kampot 135 H 5
Kamptee 134 C 3

Kampti 156 D 3
Kampuchea 135 HJ 5
Kampungtengah 136 D 4
Kamsack 167 R 5
Kamsar 156 B 3
Kamskoye Vodokhranilishche 118 L 4
Kam Summa 159 G 4
Kamundan 137 H 4
Kamyshevatskaya 117 E 1
Kamyshin 118 J 5
Kamyshlov 119 M 4
Kamyshnyy 119 N 4
Kamyshovaya Bukhta 117 D 2
Kamyzyak 128 D 1
Kan (Sudan) 158 E 3
Kan (Burma) 135 F 3
Kan (U.S.S.R.) 130 G 4
Kanaaupscow 169 M 5
Kanab 170 D 4
Kanaga 166 B 5
Kanairiktok 169 P 5
Kanā'is, Ra's al 154 D 2
Kananga 158 C 6
Kanangra Boyd National Park 143 H 5
Kanayka 119 Q 6
Kanazawa 133 L 3
Kanbalu 135 G 3
Kanchanaburi 135 G 5
Kanchipuram 134 C 5
Kandagach 128 F 1
Kandahar 129 H 4
Kandalaksha 113 K 2
Kandalakshskaya Guba 113 K 2
Kandale 158 B 6
Kandangan 136 E 4
Kandavu 146 C 4
Kande 156 E 4
Kandi 156 E 3
Kandıra 116 D 2
Kandi, Tanjung 137 F 3
Kandla 134 B 3
Kandreho 161 H 3
Kandrian 145 E 2
Kandukur 134 C 4
Kandy 134 D 6
Kandychan 131 S 3
Kane Fracture Zone 192 A 2–3
Kanem 157 GH 3
Kánestron, Ákra 116 B 3
Kanevskaya 117 E 1
Kang 160 C 4
Kanga 159 F 6
Kangaba 156 C 3
Kangal 117 E 3
Kangalassy 131 N 3
Kangāmiut 169 R 2
Kangān 128 F 5
Kangan 128 E 5
Kangar 136 B 2
Kangare 156 C 3
Kangaroo Island 143 F 6
Kangasala 112 H 3
Kangâtsiaq 169 R 2
Kangasniemi 112 J 3
Kangāvar 128 D 3
Kangbao 132 F 2
Kangchenjunga 134 E 2
Kangding 132 D 4
Kangean, Kepulauan 136 E 5
Kangeeak Point 169 P 2
Kangen 158 E 3
Kangetet 159 F 4
Kanggup'o 133 J 2
Kanggye 133 J 2
Kangle 132 D 3
Kangmar 134 E 1
Kangmar 134 E 1
Kangnŭng 133 J 3
Kango 157 G 5
Kangping 133 H 2
Kang Xian 132 E 4
Kanghan 134 C 3
Kangrinboqe Feng 134 D 1
Kangto 135 F 2
Kangynin 166 B 2
Kanhan 134 C 3
Kani 156 C 4
Kaniama 158 C 6
Kaniet Islands 144 E 2
Kanigiri 134 C 4
Kaningo 159 F 5
Kanin Nos 118 H 2
Kanin Nos, Mys 118 H 2
Kanin, Poluostrov 118 H 2
Kaninskiy Bereg 118 H 2
Kanioumé 156 D 2
Kanjiža 116 B 1
Kankaanpää 112 H 3
Kankakee 171 J 3
Kankakee River 171 J 3
Kankan 156 C 3

Kan – Kaz

Kanker 134 D 3
Kankesanturai 134 D 6
Kankossa 152 C 5
Kankunskiy 131 N 4
Kanmaw Kyun 135 G 5
Kannapolis 171 K 4
Kannauj 134 C 2
Kannonkoski 112 J 3
Kannus 112 H 3
Kano 157 F 3
Kanona 161 E 2
Kanovlei 160 B 3
Kanowit 136 D 3
Kanoya 133 K 4
Kanozero, Ozero 112 K 2
Kanpur 134 D 2
Kansanshi 160 D 2
Kansas 170 G 4
Kansas City 171 H 4
Kansk 130 G 4
Kansŏng 133 J 3
Kantang 135 G 6
Kantaralak 135 H 5
Kantchari 156 E 3
Kantche 157 F 3
Kantemirovka 118 G 6
Kantishna 166 G 3
Kanton (Kiribati) → Abariringa 146 D 3
Kanton (China) → Guangzhou 132 F 6
Kanturk 110 B 4
Kanuku Mountains 179 G 3
Kanye 160 D 4–5
Kanyu 160 C 4
Kanzenze 160 D 2
Kaohsiung 133 H 6
Kaolack 156 A 3
Kaoma 160 C 2
Kaouadja 158 C 3
Kaouar 157 G 2
Kapanga 158 C 6
Kap Arkona 111 F 4
Kapatu 161 E 1
Kap Brewster 184
Kapchagay 129 K 2
Kapchagayskoye Vodokhranilishche 129 K 2
Kap Cort Adelaer 169 T 3
Kap Farvel 169 T 4
Kapfenberg 115 G 2
Kapıdağı Yarımadası 116 C 2
Kapili 135 F 2
Kapingamaringi 145 F 1
Kapiri Moposhi 160 D 2
Kapisigdlit 169 RS 3
Kapiskau 168 L 5
Kapit 136 D 3
Kapitanskaya Zaseka 131 P 3
Kapitonovka 118 F 6
Kapka, Massif du 157 J 2
Kapoe 135 G 6
Kapoeta 158 E 4
Kapombo 160 C 2
Kapona 158 D 6
Kaposvár 116 A 1
Kapp 113 F 3
Kapsukas 113 H 5
Kapterko 157 J 2
Kapuas, Sungai 136 D 4
Kapuas, Sungai 136 C 4
Kapuskasing 168 L 6
Kapustoye 112 K 2
Kaputir 158 F 4
Kaquengue 160 C 2
Kara 119 M 2
Kara-Balty 129 J 2
Karabas 119 P 6
Karabas 119 O 6
Karabekaul 129 G 3
Karabiga 116 C 2
Karabil', Vozvyshennost' 129 G 3
Kara-Bogaz 128 E 2
Kara-Bogaz-Gol 128 E 2
Karabük 117 D 2
Karabula 130 G 4
Karabulak 119 Q 6
Karabutak 128 G 1
Karaca Dağ 117 E 3
Karacaköy 116 C 2
Karacapey 116 C 2
Karacasu 116 C 3
Karachayevsk 117 F 2
Karachev 117 F 5
Karachi 129 H 6
Karad 134 B 4
Kara Dağ 117 D 3
Kara Dağı 117 E 3
Karadoruk 117 E 3
Karadzha 117 D 1
Karaftit 130 K 5
Karaga 131 U 4
Karagan 130 M 5

Karaganda 119 O 6
Karagayly 119 P 6
Karaginskiy, Ostrov 131 U 4
Karaginskiy Zaliv 131 U 4
Karagüney Dağları 117 DE 2
Karaikkudi 134 C 5
Karaisalı 117 E 3
Karaitivu 134 C 6
Karaj 128 E 3
Kara-Kala 128 F 3
Karakax He 129 K 3
Karakeçi 117 E 3
Karakelong, Pulau 137 G 3
Karakoçan 117 F 3
Karakoin, Ozero 129 H 1
Karakolka 129 K 2
Karakoram 129 K 3
Karakore 159 G 2
Karakorum 130 H 6
Karakorum Shankou 129 K 3
Karaköse 117 F 3
Karakuduk 119 P 5
Karakul' 129 G 3
Karakul' 129 J 3
Karakum, Peski 128 E 1
Karakumskiy Kanal 129 G 3
Karakumy, Peski 128 F 3–G 3
Karakuwisa 160 B 3
Karalundi 142 B 4
Karam 130 J 4
Karamagay 129 M 1
Karaman 117 D 3
Karama, Sungai 137 E 4
Karamay 129 L 1
Karamea 145 Q 9
Karamea Bight 145 Q 9
Karamet Niyaz 129 G 3
Karamıkbataklığı 116 D 3
Karamiran He 129 M 3
Karamiran Shankou 129 M 3
Karamysheva 130 H 4
Karan 155 H 3
Karapınar 117 D 3
Karasburg 160 B 5
Kara Sea 184
Karashoky 119 P 5
Karasjåkka 112 H 2
Karasjok 112 J 2
Karasu (Turkey) 117 F 3
Karasu (Turkey) 116 D 2
Karasu-Aras Dağları 117 F 3
Karasuk 119 P 5
Karatal 119 P 6
Karatan 119 R 3
Karataş 117 E 3
Karataş Burun 117 E 3
Karatau 129 J 2
Karatau, Khrebet 129 H 2
Karatboe 128 E 1
Kara Tepe 117 D 3
Karatepe 117 E 3
Karathuri 135 G 5
Karatj 112 G 2
Karatogay 128 F 1
Karaton 128 E 1
Kartal 116 C 2
Karaul 119 Q 1
Karauli 134 C 2
Karaulkel'dy 128 F 1
Karavat 145 F 2
Karawa 158 C 4
Karawang 136 C 4
Karayulgun 129 L 2
Karazhal 119 O 6
Karazhingil 119 O 6
Karbalā' 155 G 2
Kårböle 112 G 3
Karcag 116 B 1
Karchyk, Poluostrov 131 V 2
Kardhámila 116 C 3
Kardhítsa 116 B 3
Kärdla 112 H 4
Kärdžali 116 C 2
Kareliya 112 K 3
Karema 158 E 6
Karen 135 F 5
Karenga 130 L 5
Karepino 118 L 3
Karesuando 112 H 2
Karet 152 D 4
Kargalinskaya 117 G 2
Karganay 131 X 2
Kargasok 119 Q 4
Kargat 119 Q 4
Kargı 117 E 2
Kargil 129 K 4
Kargopol' 118 G 3
Karhijärvi 112 H 3
Kari 157 G 3
Kariai 116 B 2
Kariba 160 D 3
Kariba Dam 160 D 3
Kariba, Lake 160 D 3
Karibib 160 B 4

Karigasniemi 112 J 2
Karikal 134 C 5
Karimata, Pulau 136 C 4
Karimata, Selat 136 C 4
Karimganj 135 F 3
Karimnagar 134 C 4
Karimunjawa, Pulau 136 D 5
Karin 159 H 2
Karis (Karjaa) 113 H 3
Karisimbi 158 D 5
Kárjaa 113 H 3
Karkabat 159 F 1
Karkār 159 H 3
Karkaralinsk 119 P 6
Karkar Island 144 E 2
Karkheh 128 D 4
Karkinitskiy Zaliv 117 D 1
Karkkila 113 H 3
Karkūma, Ra's 154 F 3
Karla Marksa, Pik 129 J 3
Karleby 112 H 3
Karlik Shan 132 B 2
Karlino 111 G 4
Karliova 117 F 3
Karl-Marx-Stadt 111 F 4
Karlobag 115 G 3
Karlovac 115 G 2
Karlovy Vary 111 F 4
Karlsborg 113 F 4
Karlshamn 113 F 4
Karlskoga 113 F 4
Karlskrona 113 G 4
Karlsöarna 113 G 4
Karlsruhe 111 E 4
Karlstad (Sweden) 113 F 4
Karlstad (MN, U.S.A.) 171 G 2
Karluk 166 G 4
Karma 156 E 3
Karmah 154 E 5
Karmala 134 C 4
Karmøy 113 E 4
Karnafuli Reservoir 135 F 3
Karnal 134 C 2
Karnali 134 D 2
Karnataka 134 C 4
Karnobat 116 C 2
Karokpi 135 G 4
Karong 135 F 2
Karonga 161 E 1
Karonie 142 C 5
Karora 154 F 5
Karossa, Tanjung 137 E 5
Karoy 119 O 6
Kárpathos 116 C 3
Karpenision 116 B 3
Kars 117 F 2
Karsakpay 129 H 1
Kärsämäki 112 J 3
Kärsava 113 J 4
Karshi 129 H 3
Karskiye Vorota, Proliv 118 L 1
Karskoye More 119 M 1
Kars Platosu 117 F 2
Karstula 112 G 3
Kartago 153 H 1
Kartalay 119 M 5
Karthago 153 H 1
Kartun 133 K 1
Karufa 137 H 4
Karuma National Park 158 E 4
Karumba 143 G 2
Kārūn 128 D 4
Karungi 112 H 2
Karungu 158 E 5
Karunjie 142 D 2
Karunki 112 H 2
Karur 134 C 5
Karvia 112 H 3
Karvina 111 G 5
Karwar 134 B 5
Karwi 134 D 3
Karym 119 N 3
Karymskoye 130 K 5
Karzala 118 K 4
Kas (U.S.S.R.) 119 R 4
Kaş (Turkey) 116 C 3
Kas (Sudan) 154 C 6
Kasai 158 B 5
Kasai Occidental 158 C 6
Kasai Oriental 158 C 5
Kasaji 160 C 2
Kasama 161 E 2
Kasane 160 CD 3
Kasanga 158 E 6
Kasangulu 158 B 5
Kasaragod 134 B 5
Kasba Lake 167 R 3
Kasba Tadla 152 D 2
Kas'bi 129 H 3
Kasempa 160 D 2
Kasenga 160 D 2
Kasenye 158 E 4

Kasese (Uganda) 158 E 4
Kasese (Zaire) 158 D 5
Kasganj 134 C 2
Kashaf 128 G 3
Kāshān 128 E 4
Kashi 129 K 3
Kashimbo 160 D 2
Kashin 118 G 4
Kashipur 134 C 2
Kashitu 160 D 2
Kashiwazaki 133 L 3
Kashken Teniz 119 O 6
Kāshmar 128 F 3
Kashmir 129 H 5
Kashyukulu 158 D 6
Kasigao, Mount 159 F 5
Kasimov 118 H 5
Kasindi 158 D 4
Kasiruta, Pulau 137 G 4
Kasisty 130 JK 1
Kas Kong 135 H 5
Kaskaskia River 171 J 4
Kaskelen 129 K 2
Kaskinen 112 G 3
Kaskö (Kaskinen) 112 G 3
Kasli 119 M 4
Kasongo 158 D 5
Kasongo-Lunda 158 B 6
Kásos 116 C 3
Kaspi 117 F 2
Kaspiysk 128 D 2
Kaspiyskiy 117 G 1
Kaspiyskoye More 128 D 2
Kas Rong 135 H 5
Kasr, Ra's 154 F 5
Kassalā 154 F 5
Kassándra 116 B 2–3
Kassándras, Kólpos 116 B 2
Kasserine → Al Qaşrayn 153 G 1
Kassel 111 E 4
Kastamonu 117 D 2
Kastaneaí 116 C 2
Kastéllion 116 B 3
Kastellós, Ákra 116 C 3
Kastoria 116 B 2
Kástron 116 BC 3
Kasuku 158 D 5
Kasulu 158 E 5
Kasumbalesa 160 D 2
Kasumkent 128 D 2
Kasungan 136 D 4
Kasungu 161 E 2
Kasungu National Park 161 E 2
Kasur 129 J 4
Kata 130 H 4
Kataeregi 157 F 4
Kataba 160 C 3
Katako-Kombe 158 C 5
Katagum 157 G 3
Katanga 151
Katangli 131 Q 5
Katanning 142 B 5
Katav-Ivanovsk 119 L 5
Katawaz 129 H 4
Katchiungo 160 B 2
Katea 158 D 6
Katende Falls 158 C 6
Katenga 158 D 6
Katerini 116 B 2
Katesh 158 F 5
Katete 161 E 2
Katha 135 G 3
Katherine 142 E 1
Katherine Gorge National Park 142 E 1
Katherine River 142 E 1
Kathiawar 134 B 3
Kathīrī 155 H 5
Kathleen Falls 142 E 1
Kathmandu 134 E 2
Kathua 129 K 4
Kati 156 C 3
Katihar 134 E 2
Katima Mulilo 160 C 3
Katima Rapids 160 C 3
Katiola 156 CD 4
Katla 112 B 3
Katlanovo 116 B 2
Katlavia 116 C 3
Katmai, Mount 166 G 4
Katmai National Park and Preserve 166 G 4
Katompi 158 D 6
Katonga 158 E 4
Katon-Karagay 119 R 6
Kato Olimbos 116 B 3
Katoomba 143 J 5
Katowice 111 G H 4
Kātrīna, Jabal 154 E 3

Katrineholm 113 G 4
Katrine, Loch 99 B 3
Katshi 158 D 6
Katsina 157 F 4
Katsina 157 F 3
Kattaktoc, Cape 169 O 4
Kattakurgan 129 H 3
Kattegat 113 F 4
Katul, Jabal 154 D 6
Katulu 159 G 4
Katumba 158 D 6
Katun' 119 R 5
Katunskiy Khrebet 119 R 6
Katyl'ga 119 P 4
Katyryk 130 G 1
Kauai 147 E 1
Kaubalatmada, Gunung 137 G 4
Kaufbeuren 111 F 5
Kau → Bender 159 H 2
Kauhajoki 112 G 3
Kauhava 112 G 3
Kaukkwe Hills 135 G 3
Kaukonen 112 H 2
Kaukura 147 F 4
Kaul 144 E 1
Kaula 147 E 1
Kaulishishi 160 D 3
Kaunas 113 H 5
Kaunispää 112 J 2
Kaunomarios 113 H 5
Kaura Namoda 157 F 3
Kaustinen 112 H 3
Kau, Teluk 137 G 3
Kautokeino 112 H 2
Kavacha 131 V 3
Kavadarci 116 B 2
Kavaja 116 A 2
Kavak (Turkey) 117 E 2
Kavak (Turkey) 117 E 3
Kavak (Turkey) 116 C 2
Kavak Dağı 116 C 3
Kavála 116 B 2
Kavalerovo 133 K 2
Kavali 134 D 5
Kaval'kan 131 P 4
Kavār 128 E 5
Kavendou, Mont 156 B 3
Kavieng 146 B 3
Kavieng 145 F 2
Kavir 128 E 4
Kavīr-e Abarqu 128 E 4
Kavīr-e Namak 128 F 4
Kavīr-e Namak 128 F 3
Kavīr-e Sirjan 128 F 5
Kavirondo Gulf 158 E 5
Kavkaz 117 E 1
Kawa 154 E 5
Kawalusu, Pulau 137 F 3
Kawambwa 160 D 1
Kawardha 134 D 3
Kawerau 145 R 8
Kawich Peak 170 C 4
Kawio, Kepulauan 137 F 3
Kawkareik 135 G 4
Kawm Umbū 154 E 4
Kawthaung 135 G 5
Kaxgar He 129 K 3
Kax He 129 L 2
Kaya 156 D 3
Kayah 135 G 4
Kayak (U.S.S.R.) 130 H 1
Kayak (AK, U.S.A.) 166 J 4
Kayambi 161 E 1
Kayan 135 G 4
Kayan, Sungai 136 E 3
Kayenta 170 D 4
Kayes 156 B 3
Kaygy 119 M 5
Kaymysovy 119 P 4
Kaynar 119 P 6
Kayoa, Pulau 137 G 3
Kayseri 117 E 3
Kayuagung 136 B 3
Kayyerkan 119 R 2
Kazachinskoye 130 J 4
Kazachinskoye 130 F 4
Kazach'ye 131 P 1
Kazakh 117 G 2
Kazakhskiy Melkosopochnik 119 NO 5,6
Kazakhstan 144–145 F–K 5
Kazalinsk 129 G 1
Kazan' (U.S.S.R.) 118 J 4
Kazan (N.W.T., Can.) 167 R 3
Kazan Islands (Japan) 127 QR 7
Kazandzhik 128 F 4
Kazanka 117 D 1
Kazanlŭk 116 C 2
Kazanlı 117 D 3
Kazanskoye 119 N 4
Kazantip, Mys 117 E 1
Kazantsevo 119 Q 2

242

Kazarman 129 J 2
Kazatin 118 E 6
Kazbek 117 F 2
Kaz Dağı 116 C 3
Kāzerūn 128 E 5
Kazgorodok 119 N 5
Kazhim 118 K 3
Kazi Magomed 128 D 2
Kâzımkarabekir 117 D 3
Kazincbarcika 116 B 1
Kaztalovka 118 J 6
Kazungula 160 D 3
Kazym 119 N 3
Kazymskaya 119 N 3
Kazymskiy Mys 119 N 3
Kazzān ar Ruşayriş 154 E 6
Kéa 116 B 3
Keams Canyon 170 D 4
Kearney 170 G 3
Kearns 170 D 3
Keban Gölü 117 E 3
Ke Bao 135 J 4
Kebbi 157 E 3
Kébémer 156 A 2
Kebnekaise 112 G 2
Kebumen 136 C 5
Kecskemét 116 A 1
Keda 117 F 2
Kėdainiai 113 H 4
Kediat Idjil 152 C 4
Kediri 136 D 5
Kedjaman 136 D 3
Kedong 131 N 6
Kédougou 156 B 3
Kedva 118 K 3
Kedzierzyn Koźle 111 G 4
Keele 167 M 3
Keele Peak 166 L 3
Keelung 133 H 6
Keer-Weer, Cape 143 G 1
Keestekraal 160 D 5
Keetmanshoop 160 B 5
Keewatin 168 J 6
Keewatin, District of 167 S 2
Kefa 159 F 3
Kefallania 116 B 3
Kéfalos 116 C 3
Kefamanau 137 F 5
Keffi 157 F 4
Kefken 117 D 2
Keflavík 112 A 3
Kegalla 134 D 6
Kégashka 169 P 5
Kegen' 129 K 2
Kegulta 117 F 1
Kehl 111 E 5
Kehsi Mansam 135 G 3
Keighley 101 E 3
Keila 113 H 4
Keimoes 160 C 5
Keitele 112 J 3
Keith (U.K.) 98 C 3
Keith (South Austr.) 143 G 6
Keith Arm 167 N 2
Keketa 144 D 3
Keke Usun, Ozero 117 G 1
Kekurnaya, Gora 131 V 3
Kel' 131 N 2
Kelam 159 F 4
Kelan 132 F 3
Kelang 136 B 3
Kelang, Pulau 137 G 4
Kelantan 136 B 2
Këlcyra 116 B 2
Kele 131 O 2
Kélekam 157 G 3
Keles 116 C 3
Keli Hâji Ibrāhīm 155 GH 1
Kelil'vun, Gora 131 V 2
Kelkit 117 E 2
Kellé 157 E 5
Kellerberrin 142 B 5
Kellett, Cape 167 M 1
Kellog (U.S.S.R.) 119 R 3
Kellogg (ID, U.S.A.) 170 C 2
Kelloselkä 112 J 2
Kells 100 B 3
Kélo 157 H 4
Kelokan 136 E 3
Kelowna 167 O 6
Kelsey 167 S 4
Kelsey Bay 167 M 5
Kelso (WA, U.S.A.) 170 B 2
Kelso (U.K.) 101 D 2
Kel'terskiy Khrebet 131 N 3
Keluang 136 B 3
Kelyeḫed 159 H 3
Kem' 112 K 3
Ké Macina 156 C 3
Kemah 117 E 3
Kemalpaşa (Turkey) 116 C 3
Kemalpaşa (Turkey) 117 F 2
Kembé 158 C 4

Kemboma 157 G 5
Kemer 116 C 3
Kemer Barajı 116 C 3
Kemerovo 119 R 4
Kemi 134 H 2
Kemijärvi 112 J 2
Kemijoki 112 J 2
Kemkra 131 P 4
Kempele 112 J 3
Kempendyayi 130 L 3
Kemp, Lake 170 G 5
Kemps Bay 173 G 3
Kempsey 143 J 5
Kempten 111 F 5
Kempt, Lac 171 M 2
Kenadsa 152 E 2
Kenai 166 G 3
Kenai Fjords National Park 166 G 4
Kenai Mountains 166 G 4
Kenai Peninsula 166 G 4
Kenaliasam 136 B 4
Kencha 131 P 3
Kendal 101 D 2
Kendall, Cape 167 U 3
Kendallville 171 J 3
Kendari 137 F 4
Kendawangan 136 C 4
Kendigué 157 H 3
Kendyrlik 119 R 6
Kenema 156 B 4
Kenga 119 Q 4
Kenge 158 B 5
Kengere 160 D 2
Kengtung 135 G 3
Kenhardt 160 C 5
Kéniéba 156 B 3
Kenilworth 103 D 1
Kenitra 152 D 2
Keniut 131 X 3
Kenkeme 131 N 3
Ken Koel 134 D 3
Kenmare (ND, U.S.A.) 167 R 6
Kenmare (Rep. of Ireland) 110 B 4
Kennedy Peak 135 F 3
Kennedy Range National Park 142 B 3
Kennet 110 C 4
Kennet, River 103 D 2
Kennett 171 H 4
Kennewick 170 C 2
Kenn Reef 143 K 3
Kennya 131 P 3
Kenogami 168 K 5
Keno Hill 166 K 3
Kenora 168 J 6
Kent (U.K.) 103 E 2
Kent (Sierra Leone) 156 B 4
Kentau 129 H 2
Ken Thao 135 H 4
Kent Peninsula 167 Q 2
Kents 171 M 3
Kentucky 171 J 4
Kentucky Lake 171 J 4
Kentucky River 171 K 4
Kenya 159 F 4
Kenya, Mount 159 F 5
Keokuk 171 H 3
Keonihargarh 134 E 3
Kepahiang 136 B 4
Kepe 112 K 2
Kepi 137 J 5
Kep i Gjuhës 116 A 2
Kep i Rodonit 116 A 2
Kepno 111 G 4
Keppyul'skaya 131 P 4
Keptin 131 M 3
Kepulauan Aju 137 H 3
Kepulauan Anambas 136 C 3
Kepulauan Aru 137 H 5
Kepulauan Asia 137 H 3
Kepulauan Babar 137 G 5
Kepulauan Balabalangan 136 E 4
Kepulauan Banda 137 G 4
Kepulauan Banggai 137 F 4
Kepulauan Kai 137 H 5
Kepulauan Kangean 136 E 5
Kepulauan Kawio 137 F 3
Kepulauan Leti 137 G 5
Kepulauan Lingga 136 B 4
Kepulauan Mapia 137 HJ 3
Kepulauan Mentawai 136 A 4
Kepulauan Nanusa 137 G 3
Kepulauan Natuna 136 C 3
Kepulauan Obi 137 G 4
Kepulauan Palau 137 H 2
Kepulauan Riau 136 B 3
Kepulauan Sangihe 137 G 3
Kepulauan Seram Laut 137 H 4
Kepulauan Sula 137 F 4
Kepulauan Talaud 137 G 3
Kepulauan Tambelan 136 C 3
Kepulauan Tanimbar 137 H 5

Kepulauan Tenggara 137 G 5
Kepulauan Togian 137 F 4
Kepulauan Tukangbesi 137 F 5
Kepulauan Watubela 137 H 4
Kerala 134 C 5
Kerama-rettō 133 J 5
Kerandin 136 B 4
Kerang 143 G 6
Kerava 112 J 3
Kerch 117 E 1
Kerchel' 119 M 4
Kerchenskiy Proliv 117 E 1
Kerchevskiy 118 L 4
Kerekityakh 131 N 3
Kerekyano 131 N 3
Kerema 144 E 3
Kerempe Burnu 117 D 2
Keren 159 F 1
Keret', Ozero 112 K 2
Kerets, Mys 118 G 2
Kerewan 156 A 3
Kerguelen-Gaussberg Ridge 192 B 5
Kericho 158 F 5
Kerimäki 112 J 3
Kerimbas, Archipelago 161 G 2
Kerimbas, Ilhas 161 G 2
Kerinci, Gunung 136 B 4
Kerio 159 F 4
Keriske 131 O 2
Keriya He 129 L 3
Keriya Shankou 129 J 3
Kerkennah Islands → Juzur 153 H 2
Kerkhardt 160 C 3
Kerki 118 K 3
Kerki 129 H 3
Kérkira 116 A 3
Kerkour Nourene, Massif du 157 J 3
Kermadec Islands 146 D 4–5
Kermadec Trench 193 D 5
Kermān 128 F 4
Kermānshāhān 128 E 4
Kerme Körfezi 116 C 3
Kermit 170 F 5
Kérouané 156 C 4
Kerrobert 167 Q 5
Kerrville 170 G 5
Kerry, Mountains of 110 AB 4
Kertamulia 136 C 4
Kerteh 136 B 3
Kerulen 130 K 6
Kerzaz 152 E 3
Kesagami Lake 169 L 5
Kesälahti 112 J 3
Keşan 116 C 2
Kesen'numa 133 M 3
Keshan 131 N 6
Keskin 117 D 3
Keskozero 118 F 3
Kestenga 112 K 2
Keswick 110 C 4
Keswick 101 D 2
Keszthely 116 A 1
Ket' 119 Q 4
Ket' 130 F 4
Keta 156 E 4
Ketanda 131 Q 3
Keta, Ozero 130 F 2
Ketapang 136 C 4
Ketchikan 166 L 4
Ketchum Mountain 170 F 5
Kete Krachi 156 D 4
Ketmen', Khrebet 129 KL 2
Ketou 156 E 4
Ketoy, Ostrov 131 S 6
Ketrzyn 111 H 4
Kettering 103 D 1
Kettle River Range 170 C 2
Keul' 130 H 4
Keurusselkä 112 H 3
Keuruu 112 G 3
Kew 173 H 3
K'ewagama 169 M 6
Kewanee 171 J 3
Keweenaw Peninsula 171 J 2
Keyano 169 N 5
Key Largo 171 K 6
Keynsham 102 E 2
Keystone Lake 171 G 4
Key West 171 K 7
Kezhma 130 H 4
Kezi 160 D 4
Kghoti 160 C 4
Khabalakh 130 K 3
Khabarikha 118 K 2
Khabarovsk 131 P 6
Khabary 119 P 5
Khachmas 128 D 2
Khadki 134 B 4

Khafs Banbān 155 H 3
Khairagarh 134 D 3
Khairpur 129 J 5
Khaishi 117 F 2
Khajuri Kach 129 H 4
Khakhar 131 P 4
Khakhea 160 C 4
Khakhsyn 131 M 2
Khakriz 129 H 4
Khalach 129 G 3
Khalatse 129 K 4
Khalesavoy 119 P 3
Khalīj al 'Aqabah 154 E 3
Khalīj al Baḥrain 155 J 3
Khalīj as Suways 154 E 3
Khalīj Foul 154 F 4
Khalīj Maṣīrah 155 K 5
Khalīj Qābis 153 H 2
Khalkhāl 128 D 3
Khálki 116 C 3
Khalkidhiki 116 B 2
Khalkis 116 B 3
Khal'mer-Yu 119 M 2
Khalturin 118 J 4
Khalygras 131 N 2
Khamaky 130 K 3
Khamar Daban, Khrebet 130 H J 5
Khambhat 134 B 3
Khambhat, Gulf of 134 B 3
Khambi Yakha 119 O 2
Khamgaon 134 C 3
Khamir 155 G 5
Khamīs Mushayṭ 155 G 5
Kham Keut 135 H 4
Khammam 134 D 4
Khampa 131 M 3
Khampa 130 L 3
Khamra 130 K 3
Khamsa a 130 G 5
Khamseh 128 D 3
Khanabad 129 H 3
Khān al Baghdādī 155 G 2
Khanapur 134 B 4
Khānaqin 155 H 2
Khand 129 H 4
Khandagayty 130 F 5
Khandwa 134 C 3
Khandyga 131 P 3
Khangarh 129 J 5
Khanglasy 119 MN 3
Khangokurt 119 MN 3
Khanh Hung 135 J 6
Khani 130 M 4
Khaniadhana 134 C 2
Khanion, Kólpos 116 B 3
Khanka, Ozero 133 K 1
Khannya 130 L 2
Khanovey-Sede 119 P 2
Khanpur 129 J 5
Khān Ruḥābah 155 G 2
Khān Shaykhūn 154 F 1
Khanskoye Ozero 117 E 1
Khantau 129 J 2
Khantayka 119 R 2
Khantayskoye, Ozero 130 F 2
Khantayskoye Vodokhranilishche 119 R 2
Khanty-Mansiysk 119 N 3
Khanu 135 G 4
Khanyangda 131 Q 4
Khanyardakh 131 N 3
Khānzīr, Ra's 159 H 2
Khao Lang 135 G 6
Khao Luang 135 G 6
Khao Sai Dao Tai 135 H 5
Khapa 134 C 3
Khapalu 129 K 3
Khapcheranga 130 K 6–L 5
Khappyrastakh 131 M 4
Khara 130 G 5
Khara-Aldan 131 O 3
Khara Astakh 130 K 3
Kharabali 117 G 1
Kharagpur 134 E 3
Kharagun 130 K 5
Kharakas 116 C 4
Kharampur 119 P 3
Khārān (Iran) 128 F 5
Kharan (Pakistan) 129 G 5
Khārānaq 128 E 4
Kharanor 130 L 5
Khara-Tala 131 S 2
Khara-Tas, Gryada 130 J 1
Kharaulakhskiy Khrebet 131 N 1
Kharauz 131 J 5
Kharga Oasis → Wāḥāt al Khārijah 154 E 3
Kharik 130 H 5
Kharimkotan, Ostrov 131 S 6
Khārk 128 E 5
Kharkov 118 G 6

Khār Kūh 128 E 4
Kharlovka 118 G 2
Kharoti 129 H 4
Kharovsk 118 H 4
Kharstan 131 Q 1
Khartaksho 129 K 4
Khartoum → Al Kharṭūm 154 E 5
Khartoum North → Al Kharṭūm-Baḥrī 154 E 5
Khartsyzsk 117 E 1
Kharutayuvam 119 L 2
Kharwar 129 H 4
Khasan 133 K 2
Khasavyurt 117 G 2
Khash (Afghanistan) 129 G 4
Khāsh (Iran) 129 G 5
Khash Desert 129 G 4
Khashgort 119 N 2
Khashm al Qirbah 154 F 6
Khashm Mishraq 155 H 4
Khash Rud 129 G 4
Khashuri 117 F 2
Khasi Jaintia 135 F 2
Khatanga 130 H 1
Khatangskiy Zaliv 130 J 1
Khataren 131 T 3
Khatyngnakh 131 O 3
Khatyrka 131 X 3
Khatystakh 130 M 4
Khawr Abū Habl 154 E 6
Khawr al Fakkān 155 K 3
Khawr āl Juḥaysh 155 J 4
Khawr al Muffattaḥ 155 H 3
Khaya 131 P 3
Khaybar 155 F 3
Khaybar, Ḥarrat 155 FG 3
Khaydarken 129 J 3
Khaylino 131 V 3
Khaylyulya 131 U 4
Khaypudyrskaya Guba 119 L 2
Khayryuzovka 135 H 5
Khayryuzovo 131 T 4
Khayyr 131 O 1
Khazzān Jabal al Awliyā' 154 E 5
Khe Bo 135 H 4
Kheda 134 B 3
Khemchik 130 F 5
Khemis Miliana 153 F 1
Khemisset 152 D 2
Khenchela 153 G 1
Khenifra 152 D 2
Kheri 134 D 2
Kherpuchi 131 P 5
Khersan 128 E 4
Kherson 117 D 1
Khe Sanh 135 J 4
Khesh 129 H 4
Kheta 130 H 1
Kheta 130 G 1
Kheta 119 Q 2
Khetta, Levaya 119 O 3
Kheyrābād 128 F 5
Khibiny 112 K 2
Khilchipur 134 C 3
Khil'mi, Gora 131 S 1
Khilok 130 K 5
Khilok 130 J 5
Khimki 118 G 4
Khíos 116 C 3
Khirbat Isrīyah 154 F 1
Khlong Makham 135 H 5
Khmelev 118 F 5
Khmel'nik 118 E 6
Khmel'nitskiy 118 E 6
Khobol'chan 131 Q 2
Khodzha Mubarek 129 H 3
Khodzheyli 128 F 2
Khoe 131 Q 5
Khogali 158 D 3
Khokhropar 129 J 5
Khokiley 119 Q 2
Khok Kloi 135 G 6
Kholm (Afghanistan) 129 H 3
Kholm (U.S.S.R.) 113 K 4
Kholmogory 118 H 3
Kholmsk 131 Q 6
Kholodnoye 119 MN 3
Kholzun, Khrebet 119 Q 5
Khomān 128 E 3
Khomas Highland 160 B 4
Khomeyn 128 E 4
Khomokashevo 130 J 3
Khong 135 J 5
Khongkhoyuku 131 O 3
Khongo 131 S 3
Khong Sedone 135 J 4
Khon Kaen 135 H 4
Khonsār 128 E 4
Khonu 131 O 2
Khoper 118 H 5
Khoppuruo 130 L 4
Khor 131 P 6
Khora 116 B 3

Kho–Kiz

Khor Anghar 159 G 2
Khorāsān 128 F 4
Khorat Plateau 135 H 4
Khorb el Ethel 152 D 3
Khordogoy 130 L 3
Khorgo 130 K 1
Khorinsk 130 J 5
Khorintsy 130 M 3
Khorixas 160 A 4
Khorog 129 J 3
Khoronkhu 131 O 3
Khoronnokh 130 M 2
Khorramābād 128 E 4
Khorramshahr 128 D 4
Khorsābād 155 G 1
Khosheutovo 117 G 1
Khosrowābād 128 D 4
Khosta 117 E 2
Khotin 116 C 1
Khouribga 152 D 2
Khovu-Aksy 130 F 5
Khowst 129 H 4
Khoydype, Gora 119 N 2
Khoyniki 118 F 5
Khrami 117 F 2
Khrebet Bol'shoy Balkhan 128 E 3
Khrebet Borong 131 P 2
Khrebet Bureinskiy 131 O 5
Khrebet Chayatyn 131 P 5
Khrebet Cherskogo 130 K 5
Khrebet Cherskogo 131 P 1–2
Khrebet Chingiz-Tau 119 P 6
Khrebet Dygdy-Sise 131 O 4
Khrebet Dzhagdy 131 O 5
Khrebet Dzhaki-Unakhta Yakbyyana 131 OP 6
Khrebet Dzhugdzhur 131 OP 4
Khrebet Dzhungarskiy Alatau 119 Q 6
Khrebet Iskamen' 166 B 2
Khrebet Kadyr-Egi-Tayga 130 G 5
Khrebet Kamennyy 131 U 3
Khrebet Karatau 129 H 2
Khrebet Ket-Kap 131 O 4
Khrebet Ketmen' 129 KL 2
Khrebet Khamar Daban 130 H J 5
Khrebet Kholzun 119 Q 5
Khrebet Khugdyungda 130 G 3
Khrebet Kivun 131 P 5
Khrebet Kodar 130 L 4
Khrebet Kolymskiy 131 S 3–U 3
Khrebet Kopet-Dag 128 F 3
Khrebet Kungey Alatau 129 K 2
Khrebet Mayskiy 131 O 5
Khrebet Nuratau 129 H 2
Khrebet Orulgan 131 N 2
Khrebet Pay-Khoy 119 M 2
Khrebet Pekul'ney 131 W 2
Khrebet Pribrezhnyy 131 P 4
Khrebet Rarytkin 131 WX 3
Khrebet Saur 119 R 6
Khrebet Semmedaban 131 P 3
Khrebet Sette Daban 131 P 3–4
Khrebet Suntar Khayata 131 PQ 3
Khrebet Taaga 131 N 4
Khrebet Talasskiy Alatau 129 J 2
Khrebet Tarbagatay 119 Q 6
Khrebet Taskyl 130 G 5
Khrebet Tas-Kystabys 131 Q 3
Khrebet Terskey Alatau 129 K 2
Khrebet Tukuringra 131 N 5
Khrebet Turana 131 O 5
Khrebet Udokan 130 L 4
Khrebet Ulakhan-Chistay 131 R 2–3
Khrebet Ulan-Burgasy 130 J 5
Khrebet Umnyn Syverma 130 GH 3
Khrebet Yam-Alin' 131 OP 5
Khrebet Yankan 130 L 4
Khrebet Yuzhno Chuyskiy 119 R 6
Khroma 131 Q 1
Khromskaya Guba 131 R 1
Khrom-Tau 119 L 5
Khudoseya 119 Q 2–3
Khudumelapye 160 C 4
Khudzhakh 131 R 3
Khuff 153 J 3
Khugdyungda, Khrebet 130 G 3
Khugiani 129 H 4
Khuis 160 C 5
Khulga 119 M 3
Khulkhuta 117 G 1
Khulna 134 E 3
Khulo 117 F 2
Khummi, Ozero 131 P 5
Khurai 134 C 3
Khūran 128 F 5
Khurayṣ 155 H 3
Khurayt 154 D 6

Khurchan 131 S 4
Khurda 134 E 3
Khuren 131 R 4
Khurīyā Murīya, Jazā'ir 155 K 5
Khurja 134 C 2
Khurmalik 129 G 4
Khushab 129 J 4
Khust 116 B 1
Khutse 160 C 4
Khuwayy 154 D 6
Khuzdar 129 G 5
Khūzestan 128 D 4
Khuzhir 130 J 5
Khvāf 128 G 4
Khvalynsk 118 J 5
Khvor 128 F 4
Khvormūj 128 E 5
Khvoy 128 D 3
Khwaja Amran 129 H 4
Khwaja Kuram 129 H 4
Khyber Pass 129 J 4
Kia 145 G 3
Kiama 158 B 6
Kiamba 137 F 2
Kiambi 158 D 6
Kiana 166 D 2
Kiantajärvi 112 J 2
Kiapulka 158 D 6
Kibaha 159 F 6
Kibali 158 D 4
Kibamba 158 D 5
Kibangou 157 G 6
Kibau 158 F 6
Kibaya 159 F 6
Kiberege 159 F 6
Kiberg 112 K 1
Kiboko 159 F 5
Kibombo 158 D 5
Kibondo 158 E 5
Kibre Mengist 159 F 3
Kibris → Cyprus 117 D 3
Kibungu 158 E 5
Kibuye 158 D 5
Kibwezi 159 F 5
Kicevo 116 B 2
Kichiga 131 U 4
Kichi Kichi 157 H 2
Kicking Horse Pass 167 O 5
Kidal 156 E 2
Kidatu 159 F 6
Kidderminster 103 C 1
Kidepo National Park 158 E 4
Kidira 156 B 3
Kidnappers, Cape 145 R 8
Kidsgrove 103 C 1
Kidwelly 102 B 2
Kiel 111 F 4
Kielce 111 H 4
Kieler Bucht 111 F 4
Kienge 160 D 2
Kieta 145 G 2
Kiffa 152 C 5
Kifissós 116 B 3
Kifri 155 G 2
Kigali 158 E 5
Kiği 117 F 3
Kigille 158 E 3
Kigilyakh 131 Q 1
Kignan 156 C 3
Kigoma 158 D 5
Kigosi 158 E 5
Kihelkonna 112 H 4
Kihnu 113 H 4
Kii-hantō 133 L 4
Kiik 119 O 6
Kiiminki 112 J 2
Kii-suidō 133 K 4
Kikai-jima 133 JK 5
Kikiakki 119 Q 3
Kikinda 116 B 1
Kikladhes 116 BC 3
Kikori 144 D 3
Kikwit 158 B 6
Kil 113 F 4
Kilafors 112 G 3
Kilakkarai 134 C 6
Kilambé 172 E 5
Kilbirnie 99 B 4
Kilbrannan Sound 99 B 4
Kilbuck Mountains 166 F 3
Kilchu 133 J 2
Kilcormac 100 B 3
Kilcoy 143 J 4
Kildare 100 B 3
Kil'din, Ostrov 112 K 2
Kilembe 158 B 6
Kilibo 156 E 4
Kılıç Dağları 116 C 3
Kilifi 159 F 5
Kilimanjaro 159 F 5
Kilimanjaro National Park 159 F 5
Kilinailau Islands 145 G 2
Kilindini 159 F 5

Kilindoni 159 F 6
Kilis 117 E 3
Kilitbahir 116 C 2
Kiliya 116 C 1
Kilkee 110 B 4
Kilkeel 100 C 2
Kilkenny 100 B 3
Kilkis 116 B 2
Killarney 110 B 4
Killeen 170 G 5
Killelu 159 G 2
Killin 99 B 3
Killinek 169 P 3
Killini Óros 116 B 3
Kilmarnock 99 B 4
Kil'mez' 118 K 4
Kilmore 143 H 6
Kilombero 159 F 6
Kilosa 159 F 6
Kilpisjärvi 112 H 2
Kilp-Javr 112 K 2
Kilrea 100 B 2
Kiltan 134 B 5
Kilwa 158 D 6
Kilwa Kisiwani 159 F 6
Kilwa Kivinje 159 F 6
Kilwa Masoko 159 F 6
Kilwinning 99 B 4
Kilyos 116 C 2
Kimaan 137 J 5
Kimba 143 F 5
Kimball 170 G 3
Kimball, Mount 166 J 3
Kimbe Bay 145 F 3
Kimberley (Western Austr.) 142 D 2
Kimberley (South Africa) 160 C 5
Kimberley (Alb., Can.) 167 O 6
Kimberley Downs 142 D 2
Kimberley Plateau 142 D 2
Kimch'aek 133 J 2
Kimch'on 133 J 3
Kimhandu 159 F 6
Kimi (Cameroon) 157 G 4
Kimi (Greece) 116 B 3
Kimito 113 H 3
Kimongo 157 G 6
Kimovsk 118 G 5
Kimparana 156 C 3
Kimpese 158 A 6
Kimry 118 G 4
Kimvula 158 B 6
Kinabalu, Gunung 136 E 2
Kinabatangan 136 E 2
Kinbrace 98 C 2
Kinchang 135 G 2
Kinchega National Park 143 G 5
Kinda (Zaire) 158 C 6
Kinda (Sweden) 113 G 4
Kindamba 157 G 6
Kindambi 158 C 6
Kindat 135 F 3
Kinder 111 H 4
Kindersley 167 Q 5
Kindia 156 B 3
Kindu 158 D 5
Kineshma 118 H 4
King 144 K 8
Kingaroy 143 J 4
King Christian IX Land 184
King Christian X Land 184
King City 170 B 4
King Edward VII Falls 179 G 3
King Frederik VIII Land 184
King George Islands 169 M 4
King George Sound 142 B 6
Kingisepp (U.S.S.R.) 113 J 4
Kingissepp (Estoniya, U.S.S.R.) 113 H 4
King Leopold Ranges 142 CD 2
Kingman (Oceania) 147 E 2
Kingman (AZ, U.S.A.) 170 D 4
Kingombe 158 D 5
Kingoonya 143 F 5
Kingsbridge 102 C 2
Kings Canyon National Park 170 C 4
Kingscote 143 F 6
Kings Island 143 G 6
King's Lynn 103 E 1
King Sound 142 C 2
Kings Peak (CA, U.S.A.) 170 B 3
Kings Peak (UT, U.S.A.) 170 D 3
Kingsport 171 K 4
Kingsteignton 102 C 2
Kingston (Jamaica) 173 G 4
Kingston (NY, U.S.A.) 171 M 3
Kingston (Norfolk Is., Austr.) 146 C 4
Kingston (N.Y., U.S.A.) 171 L 3
Kingston (South Australia) 143 F 6
Kingston Peak (Ont., Can.) 170 C 4

Kingston upon Hull 101 E 3
Kingstown 173 K 5
Kingsville 170 G 6
Kington 102 C 1
Kinguji 158 B 6
Kingussie 99 B 3
King William Island 167 S 2
King Williams Town 160 D 6
Kiniama 160 D 2
Kinkala 157 G 6
Kinlochewe 98 B 3
Kinlochleven 99 B 3
Kinmaw 135 F 4
Kinna 113 F 4
Kinnairds Head 110 C 3
Kinnaird's Head 98 D 3
Kinnegad 100 B 3
Kinnekulle 113 F 4
Kinoosao 167 R 4
Kinross 99 C 3
Kinsale 110 B 4
Kinsarvik 113 E 3
Kinshasa 158 B 5
Kinston 171 L 4
Kintampo 156 D 4
Kintap 136 E 4
Kintinku 158 F 6
Kintyre 99 B 4
Kinyangiri 158 E 5
Kinyeti 158 E 4
Kinzia 158 B 5
Kipaka 158 D 5
Kiparissiakós Kolpós 116 B 3
Kipawa, Lac 171 L 2
Kipembawe 158 E 6
Kipengere Range 158 E 6
Kipili 158 E 6
Kipini 159 G 5
Kipnuk 166 E 4
Kipushi 160 D 2
Kirakira 145 H 4
Kirané 156 B 2
Kiraz 116 C 3
Kirbey 130 H 2
Kirbey 130 K 2
Kircubbin 100 C 2
Kirdimi 157 H 2
Kirenga 130 J 4
Kirensk 130 J 4
Kirghiz Steppe 128 FG 1
Kirgiziya 129 JK 2
Kirgizskiy Khrebet 129 J 2
Kirgiz Step' 128 EF 1
Kiri 158 B 5
Kiribati 147 DE 3
Kırıkhan 117 E 3
Kırıkkale 117 D 3
Kirillovka 117 E 1
Kirimati 147 E 2
Kirishi 113 K 4
Kırkağaç 116 C 3
Kirkby 101 D 3
Kirkby in Ashfield 103 D 1
Kirkby Lonsdale 101 D 2
Kirkcaldy 99 C 3
Kirkconnel 99 B 4
Kirkcudbright 99 B 4
Kirkee → Khadki 134 B 4
Kirkenes 112 K 2
Kirkham 101 D 3
Kirkintilloch 99 B 4
Kirkjubæjarklaustur 112 B 3
Kirkland Lake 171 K 2
Kirklareli 116 C 2
Kirkpatrick, Mount 185
Kirksville 171 H 3
Kirkūk 155 G 1
Kirkwall 98 C 2
Kirkwall (Airport) 98 C 2
Kirkwood (South Africa) 160 D 6
Kirkwood (MO, U.S.A.) 171 H 4
Kırlangıç Burun 116 D 3
Kirov 118 J 4
Kirov 118 F 5
Kirovabad 128 D 2
Kirovakan 117 F 2
Kirovo Chepetsk 118 JK 4
Kirovograd 117 D 1
Kirovsk 128 G 3
Kirovsk 113 K 4
Kirovsk 112 C 1
Kirovsk 131 T 5
Kirovskiy 129 K 2
Kirovskiy 133 K 1
Kirriemuir 99 C 3
Kirs 118 K 4
Kirşehir 117 D 2
Kirtachi 156 E 3
Kirthar Range 129 G 5
Kiruna 112 H 2
Kirundu 158 D 5
Kir'yanovskaya Kontora 130 H 4
Kisa 113 G 4

Kisabi 158 D 6
Kisaki 159 F 6
Kisalföld 116 A 1
Kisambo 158 B 6
Kisangani 158 D 4
Kisangire 159 F 6
Kisar, Pulau 137 G 5
Kiselevsk 119 R 5
Kishangarh 134 B 2
Kishb, Ḥarrat al 155 G 4
Kishi 156 E 4
Kishinev 116 C 1
Kishorganj 135 F 3
Kishtwar 129 K 4
Kisii 158 E 5
Kisiju 159 F 6
Kızılırmak 117 D 2
Kısır Dağı 117 F 2
Kiska 158 A 5
Kiska Volcano 166 A 5
Kiskunfélegyháza 116 A 1
Kiskunhalas 116 A 1
Kiskőrei viztároló 116 B 1
Kiskőrös 116 A 1
Kislovodsk 117 F 2
Kismāyu 159 G 5
Kisoro 158 D 5
Kissidougou 156 B 4
Kissū, Jabal 154 D 4
Kisumu 158 E 5
Kisvárda 116 B 1
Kita 156 B 3
Kitab 129 H 3
Kita-daitō-jima 133 K 5
Kitai, Ozero 116 C 1
Kitakyushū 133 K 4
Kitale 158 F 4
Kitami 133 M 2
Kitami-sanchi 133 M 2
Kitanda 158 D 6
Kitangari 161 F 2
Kitangiri, Lake 158 E 5
Kitchener 171 K 3
Kitee 112 K 3
Kiteiyab 154 E 4
Kitepskaya 131 U 3
Kitete 158 E 6
Kitgum 158 E 4
Kíthira 116 B 3
Kithnos 116 B 3
Kitimat 166 M 5
Kitimat Ranges 166 M 5
Kitinen 112 J 2
Kitoboynyy 131 S 6
Kitoy 130 H 5
Kit's Coty House 103 E 2
Kitsman 116 C 1
Kittanning 171 L 3
Kittilä 112 H 2
Kitui 159 F 5
Kitunda 158 E 6
Kitwe 160 D 2
Kitzbühel 115 F 2
Kitzbüheler Alpen 115 F 2
Kiunga (Kenya) 159 G 5
Kiunga (Papua New Guinea) 144 D 3
Kiuruvesi 112 J 3
Kivak 166 C 3
Kivalina 166 E 2
Kiviöli 113 J 4
Kivijärvi 112 J 3
Kivik 113 F 4
Kivu 118 F 5
Kivun, Khrebet 131 P 5
Kiwaba N'zogi 160 B 1
Kiya 119 R 4
Kiyamaki Dāgh 128 D 3
Kiyeng-Kyuyel' 131 S 2
Kiyeng-Kyuyel', Ozero 130 J 1
Kiyev 118 F 5
Kiyevka 119 O 5
Kiyevka 133 K 2
Kiyevskoye Vodokhranilishche 118 F 5
Kıyıköy 116 C 2
Kıyma 119 N 5
Kizel 119 L 4
Kizema 118 H 3
Kizha 130 J 5
Kizhinga 130 J 5
Kızılcahamam 117 D 2
Kızıl Dağ 117 D 3
Kızılırmak 117 D 2
Kizil'skoye 119 L 5
Kızıltepe 117 F 3
Kızıl Tepe 116 F 2
Kizimen, Sopka 131 U 4
Kizimi 157 H 2
Kizlyar 117 G 2
Kizlyarskiy Zaliv 117 G 2
Kizyl-Arvat 128 F 4
Kizyl-Atrek 128 E 3

Kizyl-Su 128 E 3
Kjöllefjord 112 J 1
Kjölur 112 B 3
Kjöpsvik 112 G 2
Kjustendil 116 B 2
Klabat, Gunung 137 G 3
Kladanj 115 G 3
Kladno 111 F 4
Klagan 136 E 2
Klagenfurt 115 F 2
Klaipėda 113 H 4
Klamath Falls 170 B 3
Klamath Mountains 170 B 3
Klamath River 170 B 3
Klamono 137 H 4
Klarälven 113 F 3
Klaten 136 D 5
Klatovy 111 F 5
Klawer 160 B 6
Klea → Abū Tulayh 154 E 5
Klein Aub 160 B 4
Kleinsee 160 B 5
Klerksdorp 160 D 5
Klevan' 113 J 5
Klichka 130 L 5
Klin 118 G 4
Klina 116 B 2
Klintehamn 113 G 4
Klintsovka 118 J 5
Klintsy 118 F 5
Klipgat 160 C 4
Klippan 113 F 4
Klondike Plateau 166 K 3
Klosi 116 B 2
Klosterneuburg 115 G 2
Klotz, Lac 169 M 3
Klotz, Mount 166 JK 2
Kluane Lake 166 K 3
Kluane National Park 166 K 3
Kluczbork 111 G 4
Klukhorskiy Pereval 117 F 2
Klyavlino 118 K 5
Klyazma 118 H 4
Klyuchevaya 118 H 2
Klyuchevskaya Sopka 131 U 4
Klyuchi 130 K 5
Klyuchr 131 U 4
Knaresborough 101 E 2
Kneža 116 B 2
Kniet 135 J 5
Knighton 102 C 1
Knin 115 G 3
Knittelfeld 115 F 2
Knjaževac 116 B 2
Knokke-Heist 110 D 4
Knomi, Lagune 157 F 6
Knösen 113 F 4
Knosós 116 C 3
Knottingley 101 E 3
Knox, Cape 166 L 5
Knox Coast 185
Knoxville (IA, U.S.A.) 171 H 3
Knoxville (TN, U.S.A.) 171 K 4
Knoydart 99 B 3
Knud Rasmussen Land 184
Knutsford 102 C 1
Knyazhevo 118 H 4
Knysna 160 C 6
Koal 157 H 3
Koani 157 F 6
Koartac 169 O 3
Koba 137 J 5
Koba 136 C 4
Kobar Sink 159 G 2
Kobbo 157 F 6
Kobdo → Hovd 130 F 6
Kōbe 133 L 4
København 113 F 4
Kobenni 152 D 5
Koblenz 111 E 4
Koboldo 131 O 5
Kobrin 113 H 5
Kobuk 166 F 2
Kobuk Valley N.P. 166 F 2
Kobuleti 117 F 2
Kobyai 131 N 3
Koca Çal 117 D 3
Koca Çay 116 C 3
Kocaeli 116 C 2
Kočani 115 B 3
Kocasu 116 C 3
Koch 169 M 1
Ko Chan 135 G 6
Ko Chang 135 H 5
Kochechum 130 H 4
Kochegarovo 130 L 4
Kochenga 130 H 4
Kochevo 118 K 4
Kōchi 133 K 4
Kochikha 130 G 1
Koçhisar Ovası 117 D 3
Kochkorka 129 K 2
Kochmes 119 M 2

Kochubey 117 G 2
Kock 111 H 4
Kočmar 116 C 2
Kodar, Khrebet 130 L 4
Kodi 137 E 5
Kodiak 166 G 4
Kodiak Island 166 G 4
Kodima 118 H 3
Kodino 118 G 3
Kodok 158 E 3
Kodori, Mys 117 F 2
Kodyma 116 D 1
Kodža Balkan 116 C 2
Kłodzko 111 G 4
Köes 160 B 5
Kofçaz 116 C 2
Koffiefontein 160 C 5
Koforidua 156 D 4
Køge 113 F 4
Køge Bugt 113 F 4
Koggala 134 D 6
Kogil'nik 116 C 1
Kogon 156 B 3
Kohat 129 J 4
Koh-Hisar 129 H 4
Koh-i-Baba 129 H 4
Kohima 135 F 2
Koh-i-Mazar 129 H 4
Koh-i-Pantar 129 G 5
Koh i Qaisar 129 G 4
Koh-i-Sangan 129 H 4
Kohistan 129 J 3
Kohlu 129 G 5
Kohtla-Järve 113 J 4
Kohunlich 172 E 4
Koitere 113 K 3
Kojonup 142 B 5
Kokalaat 129 G 1
Kokand 129 J 2
Kōkar 113 H 4
Kokaral, Ostrov 128 G 1
Kokas 137 H 4
Kokcha 129 H 3
Kokchetav 119 N 5
Kokemäenjoki 112 H 3
Kokemäki 112 H 3
Kokiu 125
Kokkola 112 H 3
Koko 158 F 2
Kokoda 144 E 3
Kokomo 171 J 3
Kokonau 137 J 5
Kokong 160 C 4
Koko Nor 132 D 3
Kokora, Ozero 130 H 1
Koksaray 129 H 2
Kokshaga 118 J 4
Koksoak 169 O 4
Kokstad 160 D 6
Koktuma 119 Q 6
Kokuora 131 Q 1
Ko Kut 135 H 5
Kok-Yangak 129 J 2
Kola 112 K 2
Kolahun 156 BC 4
Kolai 129 J 3
Kolaka 137 F 4
Ko Lanta 135 G 6
Kola Peninsula 118 G 2
Kolar 134 C 5
Kolar Gold Fields 134 C 5
Kolari 112 H 2
Kolbachi 135 M 5
Kolbio 159 G 5
Kolda 156 AB 3
Kolding 113 E 4
Kole 158 C 5
Kole 158 D 4
Koléa 114 D 1
Kolepom Island 137 J 6
Kolesnoye 116 C 1
Kolesovo 131 S 1
Kolgompja, Mys 112 J 4
Kolguyev, Ostrov 118 J 2
Kolhapur 134 B 4
Koli 112 J 3
Koliganek 166 F 4
Kolka 113 H 4
Kolkasrags 113 H 4
Kollegal 134 C 5
Kollumúli 112 C 2
Kolmanskop 160 B 5
Kolmården 113 G 4
Kolmogorovo 130 F 4
Köln 111 E 4
Kolo 111 G 4
Kologi 154 E 6
Kolokani 156 C 3
Kololo 159 G 3
Kolombangara 145 G 2

Kolomna 118 G 4
Kolomyya 116 C 1
Kolondieba 156 C 3
Kolonodale 137 F 4
Kolosovka 119 O 4
Kolozero, Ozero 112 K 2
Kolpakovo 131 T 5
Kolpashevo 119 Q 4
Kolpino 113 K 4
Kólpos Ierisou 116 B 2
Kólpos Kallonis 116 C 3
Kólpos Kassándras 116 B 2
Kólpos Khanion 116 B 3
Kol'skiy, Poluostrov 118 G 2
Kon Plong 135 J 5
Koluton 119 N 5
Kolva 118 L 2
Kolvitskoye, Ozero 113 K 3
Kolwa 129 G 5
Kolwezi 160 D 2
Kolyma 131 T 2
Kolyma Range 131 U 3
Kolymskaya 131 T 2
Kolymskaya 131 V 2
Kolymskaya Nizmennost' 131 ST 2
Kolymskiy, Khrebet 131 SU 3
Kolymskoye Nagor'ye 131 RS 3
Kolyshley 118 H 5
Kolyuchinskaya Guba 166 C 2
Kolyvan' 119 Q 5
Koma 159 F 3
Komadugu Gana 157 G 3
Komadugu Yobe 157 G 3
Komandorski Islands 127 T 4
Komandorskije Ostrova 127 T 4
Komarichi 118 F 5
Komárno 111 G 5
Komarom 116 A 1
Komati Poort 161 E 5
Komatsu 133 L 3
Komba 158 C 4
Kombat 160 B 3
Kombissiguiri 156 D 3
Kombolcha 159 F 2
Komdi 135 G 2
Kome Island 158 E 5
Komelek 131 O 3
Komering, Air 136 B 4
Komfane 137 H 5
Komló 116 A 1
Kommunarka 119 R 2
Kommunarsk 117 E 1
Kommunizma, Pik 129 J 3
Kommunist 131 X 3
Komodo, Pulau 137 E 5
Komoé 156 D 3
Komoé, Parc National de la 156 D 4
Komono 157 G 6
Komoran, Pulau 137 J 5
Komotini 116 C 2
Kompas Berg 160 C 6
Kompong Cham 135 J 5
Kompong Chhnang 135 H 5
Kompong Som 135 H 5
Kompong Speu 135 H 5
Kompong Sralao 135 J 5
Kompong Thom 135 H 5
Kompot 137 F 3
Komrat 135 H 6
Komsa 119 R 3
Komsomolets 119 M 5
Komsomol'sk 129 G 3
Komsomol'skiy 119 M 2
Komsomol'skiy 128 E 1
Komsomolskiy 117 E 1
Komsomol'sk-na-Amure 131 P 5
Komusan 133 J 2
Kona 156 D 3
Konakovo 118 G 4
Konarak 134 E 4
Konda 119 M 3
Kondagaon 134 D 4
Kondakara 131 T 2
Kondakovo 131 S 2
Kondinin 142 B 5
Kondoa 159 F 5
Kondon 131 P 5
Kondopoga 118 F 3
Kondor 128 F 3
Kondut 142 B 5
Konetsbor 118 L 3
Konevits, Ostrov 112 K 3
Konevo 118 G 3
Kong 156 D 4
Kong Frederik VI-Kyst 169 T 3
Konginskiye Gory 131 T 3
Kongkemul, Gunung 136 E 3
Kongola 160 C 3
Kongolo 158 D 6
Kongor 158 E 3
Kongsberg 113 E 4
Kongsvinger 113 F 3

Kongur Shan 129 K 3
Kongwa 159 F 6
Koniakar 156 B 3
Konin 111 G 4
Koni, Poluostrov 131 S 4
Konitsa 116 B 2
Konkan 134 B 4
Konko 160 D 2
Konkouré 156 B 3
Konkudera 130 K 4
Konosha 118 H 3
Konoshchel'ye 119 R 2
Konotop 118 F 5
Konqi He 132 A 2
Konstantinovka 117 E 1
Konstantinovsk 117 F 1
Konstanz 111 E 5
Kontagora 157 F 3
Kontcha 157 G 4
Kontiomäki 112 J 3
Kontum 135 J 5
Kontum, Plateau du 135 J 5
Konus, Gora 131 O 4
Konya 117 D 3
Konya Ovası 117 D 3
Konza 159 F 5
Konzaboy 131 T 2
Konzhakovskiy Kamen', Gora 119 L 4
Kołobrzeg 111 G 4
Kookynie 142 C 4
Kooline 142 B 3
Koolivoo, Lake 143 F 3
Koonalda 142 D 5
Koör 137 H 4
Koorda 142 B 5
Koör 137 H 4
Kootenai River 170 C 2
Kootenay National Park 167 O 5
Kooussa 156 C 4
Kopanovka 117 G 1
Kópasker 112 B 2
Kópavogur 112 A 3
Koper 115 F 2
Kopervik 113 E 4
Kopet-Dag, Khrebet 128 F 3
Kopeysk 119 M 4
Kop Geçidi 117 F 3
Ko Phangan 135 H 6
Ko Phuket 135 G 6
Köping 113 G 4
Kopliku 116 A 2
Köpmanholmen 112 G 3
Koppang 112 F 3
Kopparberg 113 G 4
Koprivnica 115 G 2
Kopychintsy 118 E 6
Kop'yevo 119 R 5
Kopylovka 119 Q 4
Kor 128 E 4
Koralpe 115 G 2
Koramlik 129 M 3
Korangi 129 H 6
Koraput 134 D 4
Korarou, Lac 156 D 2
Korba 134 D 3
Korbach 111 E 4
Korbol 157 H 3
Korça 116 B 2
Korchino 119 Q 5
Korčula 115 G 3
Korčulanski Kanal 115 G 3
Kordestan 128 D 3
Kord Kūy 128 E 3
Kordofan → Kurdufān 154 DE 6
Korea Strait 133 J 4
Korelaksha 112 J 3
Korennoye 130 J 1
Korenovsk 117 E 1
Korenshty 117 C 1
Korets 113 J 5
Korf 131 V 3
Korfa, Zaliv 131 V 3
Korfovskiy 131 P 6
Korgen 112 F 2
Korhogo 156 C 4
Korienza 156 D 2
Korim 137 J 4
Korinthiakos Kólpos 116 B 3
Kórinthos 116 B 3
Korioliei 159 G 4
Kōriyama 133 M 3
Korkino 130 J 5
Korkodon 131 S 3
Korkodon 131 T 3
Korkut 117 F 3
Korkuteli 116 D 3
Korla 132 A 2
Korliki 119 Q 3
Kormakiti Burun 117 D 3
Kornat 115 G 3

Korneuburg 115 G 2
Kórnik 111 G 4
Kornilovo 119 Q 5
Koro (Fiji) 146 C 4
Koro (Ivory Coast) 156 C 4
Koro (Mali) 156 D 3
Korobovskiy 119 P 6
Köroğlu Dağları 117 D 2
Köroğlu Tepe 117 D 2
Korogwe 159 F 6
Koroit 143 G 6
Koro Kidinga 157 H 2
Korongo 158 E 6
Kőrös 113 F 3
Korosten 113 J 5
Korostyshev 113 J 5
Koro Toro 157 H 2
Korovin Volcano 166 C 5
Korpilahti 112 J 3
Korpilombolo 112 H 2
Korsakov 131 Q 6
Korsfjorden 113 D 3
Korshunovo 130 K 4
Korskrogen 112 G 3
Korsnäs 112 H 3
Korsör 113 F 4
Kort Creek 134 A 3
Koryak Range 131 W 3
Koryakskaya Sopka 131 T 5
Koryakskiy Khrebet 131 VX 3
Koryazhma 118 J 3
Kos 116 C 3
Kosa (U.S.S.R.) 130 J 5
Kosa (Mauritania) 152 D 5
Kosa Fedotova 117 E 1
Ko Samui 135 G 6
Ko Samui 135 H 6
Koschagyl 128 E 1
Kościan 111 G 4
Kosciusko 171 J 5
Kosciusko, Mount 143 H 6
Kose 113 J 4
Köse Dağı 117 E 2
Kosha 154 E 4
Kosh-Agach 119 R 6
Kosi 134 C 2
Košice 111 H 5
Koskuduk 129 K 2
Kosmaj 116 B 2
Kosŏng 133 J 3
Kosovo Polje 116 B 2
Kosovska Mitrovica 116 B 2
Kossou, Lac de 156 C 4
Kossovo 113 J 5
Kostajnica 115 G 2
Kostamus 112 K 3
Koster 160 D 5
Kosteröarna 113 F 4
Kostino 119 R 2
Kostomuksa 112 K 3
Kostopol' 113 J 5
Kostroma 118 H 4
Kostrzyn 111 F 4
Kos'yu 119 L 2
Koszalin 111 G 4
Kota 134 C 2
Kota Baharu (Malaysia) 136 B 2
Kotabaharu (Indonesia) 136 D 4
Kotabaru 136 E 4
Kota Belud 136 E 2
Kotabumi 136 B 4
Kota Kinabalu 136 E 2
Kotamobagu 137 F 3
Ko Tao 135 G 6
Kotapad 134 D 4
Ko Tarutao 135 G 6
Kota Tinggi 136 B 3
Kotchandpur 134 E 3
Kotcho, Lake 165
Koteasro 129 H 4
Kotel'nich 118 J 4
Kotel'nikovo 117 F 1
Kotel'nyy, Ostrov 131 P 1
Kotido 158 E 4
Kotikovo 131 Q 6
Kotka 113 J 3
Kotkino 119 P 4
Kotlas 118 J 3
Kotli 129 J 4
Kotlik 166 E 3
Kotlina Sandomierska 111 H 4
Koto 131 P 6
Koton Karifi 157 F 4
Kotor 116 A 2
Kotor Varoš 115 G 3
Kotovsk 116 C 1
Kotovsk 118 H 5
Kotri 129 J 5
Kotri Allahrakhio Shah 129 H 6
Kotr-Tas 128 F 1

Kiz–Kot

245

Kot – Kur

Kötschach 115 F 2
Kottagudem 134 D 4
Kottayam 134 C 6
Kotto 158 C 3
Kotton 159 J 3
Kotturu 134 C 5
Kotu Group 146 D 4
Kotuy 130 H 2
Kotuykan 130 H 1
Kotzebue 166 E 2
Kotzebue Sound 166 E 2
Kouango 158 BC 3
Kouba Modounga 157 H 2
Koudougou 156 D 3
Kouére 156 D 3
Koufey 157 G 3
Kougaberge 160 C 6
Kouilou 157 G 6
Koukdjuak 169 N 2
Kouki 158 B 3
Koukourou 158 C 3
Koula Moutou 157 G 6
Koulen 135 H 5
Koulikoro 156 C 3
Koumac 145 H 6
Koumala 143 H 3
Koumameyong 157 G 5
Koumbia 156 B 3
Koumbi-Saleh 152 D 5
Koumongou 156 E 3
Koumpentoum 156 B 3
Koumra 157 H 4
Koundara 156 B 3
Koundian 156 B 3
Koundougou 156 D 3
Koungheul 156 AB 3
Koungou, Monts 157 G 6
Kounradskiy 119 O 6
Koupéla 156 D 3
Kourou 179 H 2
Kouroussa 156 BC 3
Koussanar 156 B 3
Kousseri 157 G 3
Koutiala 156 C 3
Koutous 157 FG 3
Kouvola 112 J 3
Kouyou 157 H 6
Kova 130 H 4
Kovac 116 A 2
Kovdor 112 K 2
Kovdozero, Ozero 112 K 2
Kovel' 113 H 5
Kovinskaya Gora 130 H 4
Kovriga, Gora 118 J 2
Kovrizhka 131 U 3
Kovrov 118 H 4
Kovylkino 118 H 5
Kowares 160 A 3
Ko Way 135 H 6
Kowloon 132 F 6
Kowt-e Ashrow 129 H 4
Koyandy 119 P 6
Köyceğis 116 C 3
Koyda 118 H 2
Koyuk 166 E 3
Koyukuk 166 F 2
Koyulhisar 117 E 2
Kozakli 117 D 3
Kozan 117 E 3
Kozáni 116 B 2
Kozel'sk 118 G 5
Kozhevnikovo 130 K 1
Kozhevnikovo 119 Q 4
Kozhikode → Calicut 134 C 5
Kozhim 119 L 2
Kozhozero, Ozero 118 G 3
Kozhva 118 L 2
Kozlu 116 D 2
Kozul'ka 130 F 4
Kozyrevsk 131 T 4
Kpandu 156 E 4
Kpessi 156 E 4
Kra 156 E 4
Kra Buri 135 G 5
Krafla 112 B 2
Kragerö 113 E 4
Kragujevac 116 B 2
Kra, Isthmus of 135 G 5
Krajište 116 B 2
Krakatau → Pulau Rakata 136 C 5
Krakor 135 H 5
Kraków 111 G 4
Kralendijk 178 E 1
Kraljevica 115 F 2
Kraljevo 116 B 2
Kramatorsk 117 E 1
Kramfors 112 G 3
Kranj 115 G 2
Krapina 115 G 2
Krasilov 118 E 6
Krasino 118 K 1
Kraskino 133 K 2
Kräslava 113 J 4

Krasnaya Polyana 117 F 2
Krasnaya Yaranga 131 X 3
Krasnaya Yaranga 166 C 2
Krasneno 131 W 3
Kraśnik 111 H 4
Krasnoarmeyesk 119 N 5
Krasnoarmeysk 118 J 5
Krasnoarmeysk 117 E 1
Krasnoarmeyskiy 117 F 1
Krasnodar 117 E 1
Krasnogorsk 131 Q 6
Krasnograd 118 G 6
Krasnogvardeyskoye (Ukraina, U.S.S.R.) 117 D 1
Krasnogvardeyskoye (Ukraina, U.S.S.R.) 117 F 1
Krasnoje Selo 112 K 4
Krasnokamsk 118 L 4
Krasnokutskoye 119 P 5
Krasnoperekopsk 117 D 1
Krasnosel'kup 119 Q 2
Krasnoslobodsk 118 HJ 6
Krasnoturansk 130 F 5
Krasnotur'insk 119 M 4
Krasnoufimsk 119 L 4
Krasnoural'sk 119 M 4
Krasnousol'skiy 118 L 5
Krasnovishersk 118 L 3
Krasnovodsk 128 E 2
Krasnovodskoye Poluostrov 128 E 2
Krasnoyarovo 131 N 5
Krasnoyarsk 130 F 4
Krasnoyarskiy 119 L 5
Krasnoyarskoye Vodokhranilishehe 130 F 5
Krasnoye 117 F 1
Krasnoye, Ozero 131 W 3
Krasnoye Znamya 129 G 3
Krasnozatonskiy 118 K 3
Krasnozerskoye 119 P 5
Krasnoznamensk 119 N 5
Krasnystaw 111 H 4
Krasnyy Chikoy 130 J 5
Krasnyy Kut 118 J 5
Krasnyy Luch 117 E 1
Krasnyy Sulin 117 F 1
Krasnyy Yar 118 H 5
Krasnyy Yar 128 D 1
Krasnyy Yar 119 N 5
Krasnyy-Yar 119 O 4
Krasnyy Yar 119 Q 4
Kratie 135 J 5
Kratovo 116 B 2
Kray Lesov 131 U 2
Krefeld 110 D E 4
Kremastá, Limni 116 B 3
Kremenchug 118 F 6
Kremenchugskoye Vodokhranilishche 118 F 6
Kremenets 113 J 5
Kremmling 170 E 3
Krems an der Donau 115 G 2
Kreshchenka 119 Q 4
Kresta, Zaliv 166 B 2
Kresti 118 F 4
Krest-Khal'dzhayy 131 O 3
Krestovaya 130 K 4
Krestovka 118 K 2
Krestovskiy, Ostrov 131 U 1
Krestovyy Pereval 117 F 2
Kresty 130 E 1
Kretinga 113 H 4
Kreuzlingen 115 E 2
Kreuztal 111 E 4
Kribi 157 F 5
Krichev 118 F 5
Kričim 116 B 2
Kril'on, Mys 131 Q 6
Krimml 115 F 2
Krishna 134 C 4
Krishnagiri 134 C 5
Krishna, Mouths of the 134 D 4
Krishnanagar 134 E 3
Kristiansand 113 E 4
Kristianstad 113 F 4
Kristiansund 112 E 3
Kristiinankaupunki 112 G 3
Kristineberg 112 G 2
Kristinehamn 113 F 4
Kristinestad (Kristiinankaupunki) 112 G 3
Kristinovka 116 C 1
Kríti 116 BC 3
Kritikón Pélagos 116 BC 3
Kriva Palanka 116 B 2
Krivoy Rog 117 D 1
Krk 115 F 2
Krnov 111 G 4
Kroken 112 F 3
Krokodil River 160 D 4
Krokom 112 F 3
Kroměříž 111 G 5

Kronoki 131 U 5
Kronotskaya Sopka 131 U 5
Kronotskiy, Mys 131 U 5
Kronotskiy Poluostrov 131 U 5
Kronotskiy Zaliv 131 U 5
Kronotskoye Ozero 131 T 5
Kronshtadt 113 J 4
Kroonstad 160 D 5
Kropotkin 117 F 1
Kropotkin 130 L 4
Kroppefjäll 113 F 4
Krosno 111 H 5
Krotoszyn 111 G 4
Krotovka 118 K 5
Kroviga, Gora 130 F 3
Krško 115 G 2
Krstača 116 B 2
Krueng Geumpang 136 A 3
Kruger National Park 161 E 4
Krugersdorp 160 D 5
Krugloye 117 E 1
Krui 136 B 5
Krung Thep 135 H 5
Kruså 113 E 5
Kruševac 116 B 2
Krusne Hory 111 F 4
Krutinka 119 O 4
Kruzenshterna, Proliv 131 S 6
Kruzof 166 K 4
Kryazh Chernysheva 119 LM 2
Kryazh Kula 131 O 2
Kryazh Polousnyy 131 PQ 2
Kryazh Ulakhan-Sis 131 S 2
Krym (Ukraina, U.S.S.R.) 117 E 1
Krym (Ukraina, U.S.S.R.) 117 D 1
Krymsk 117 E 2
Krymskiye Gory 117 D 2
Krzyż 111 G 4
Ksabi 152 E 3
Ksar el Barka 152 C 5
Ksar el Boukhari 153 F 1
Ksar el Kebir 152 D 1
Ksar es Souk 152 E 2
Ksar Torchane 152 C 4
Ksen'yevka 130 L 5
Ksour, Monts des (Tunisia) 153 GH 2
Ksour, Monts des (Algeria) 152 EF 2
Kuala Belait 136 D 3
Kuala Dungun 136 B 3
Kuala Kangsar 135 F 2
Kuala Kapuas 136 D 4
Kuala Kerai 136 B 2
Kualakeriau 136 D 4
Kualakurun 136 D 4
Kuala Lipis 136 B 3
Kuala Lumpur 136 B 3
Kualamanjual 136 D 4
Kualapembuang 136 D 4
Kuala Pilah 136 B 3
Kuala Rompin 136 B 3
Kuala Selangor 136 B 3
Kualasimpang 136 A 2
Kuala Terengganu 136 B 2
Kualatungkal 136 B 4
Kuamut 136 E 2
Kuancheng 133 G 2
Kuandian 133 H 2
Kuantan 136 B 3
Kuba (Azerbaydzhan, U.S.S.R.) 128 D 2
Kuba (Russia, U.S.S.R.) 117 F 2
Kuban' 117 E 1
Kubaysah 155 G 2
Kubbe 112 G 3
Kubbum 154 C 6
Kubenskoye, Ozero 118 G 4
Kubkain 144 D 2
Kubumesaäi 136 E 3
Kubyshevskiy 119 N 5
Kuching 136 D 3
Kudara 129 J 3
Kūdasht 128 D 4
Kudaw 135 G 3
Kudat 136 E 2
Kudremukh 134 BC 5
Kudryashevo 119 Q 4
Kudu-Kyuyel't 130 M 4
Kudus 136 D 5
Kudymkar 118 K 4
Kufra Oases 153 K 3
Kufstein 115 F 2
Kugmallit Bay 166 L 2
Kugul'ta 117 F 1
Kūh 128 E 4
Kuḫaylī 154 E 5
Kūh-e Ālādāgh 128 F 3
Kūh-e Alījūq 128 E 4
Kūh-e Alvano 128 D 4
Kūh-e-Bārān 128 G 4
Kūh-e Bazmān 128 F 5

Kūh-e Biābān 128 F 5
Kūh-e Bozqūsh 128 D 3
Kūh-e Būl 128 E 4
Kūh-e Chehel Dokhtarān 128 G 4
Kūh-e Darband 128 F 4
Kūh-e Dinar 128 E 4
Kūh-e Garbosh 128 E 4
Kūh-e Garri 128 D 4
Kūh-e Gāvbūs 128 E 5
Kūh-e Gügerd 128 E 4
Kūh-e Hormoz 128 F 5
Kūh-e Jebal Bārez 128 F 5
Kūh-e Joghatāy 128 F 3
Kūh-e Kalat 128 F 4
Kūh-e Karkas 128 E 4
Kūh-e Khāīz 128 E 4
Kūh-e Khormūj 128 E 5
Kūh-e Khvojeh Lāk 128 D 3
Kūh-e Kūhrān 128 F 5
Kūh-e Kūkalār 128 E 4
Kūh-e Lāleh Zār 128 F 5
Kūh-e Malek Sīāh 129 G 5
Kūh-e Masāhīm 128 F 4
Kūh-e Nāy Band 128 F 4
Kūh-e Safid 128 D 4
Kūh-e Shah Jahān 128 F 3
Kūh-e Sorkh 128 EF 4
Kūh-e Sorkh 128 F 3
Kūhestak 128 F 5
Kūh-e Tābask 128 E 5
Kūh-e Taftān 129 G 5
Kūhhā-ye Bashākerd 128 F53
Kūhhā-ye Qorūd 128 E 4
Kūhhā-ye-Sabālān 128 D 3
Kūhhā-ye Zagros 128 E 5
Kūhhā Zagros 128 D 4
Kuhmo 112 J 3
Kuhmoinen 112 J 3
Kūhpāyeh 128 F 4
Kuikkavaara 112 J 3
Kui Nua 135 GH 5
Kuiseb 160 B 4
Kuito 160 B 2
Kuiu 166 L 4
Kuivaniemi 112 J 2
Kujani Game Reserve 156 D 4
Kujawy 111 G 4
Kuji 133 M 2
Kukan 131 O 6
Kukawa 157 G 3
Kukësi 116 B 2
Kukhtuy 131 Q 4
Kukushka 131 N 5
Kūl 128 F 5
Kula 116 C 3
Kulagino 128 E 1
Kula Kangri 135 F 2
Kulākh 155 G 4
Kulakovo 130 F 4
Kulakshi 128 F 1
Kulaneh 129 G 5
Kulanoy 128 F 1
Kulbus 154 C 6
Kul'chi 131 P 5
Kuldīga 113 H 4
Kuldja 129 L 2
Kul'dzhuktau, Gory 129 G 2
Kule 160 C 4
Kulen Vakuf 115 G 3
Kulgera 142 E 4
Kulinda 130 H 3
Kulinda 130 J 3
Kullen 117 F 2
Kulmasa 156 D 4
Kulmbach 111 F 4
Kulp 154 C 3
Kul'sary 128 E 1
Kul'skiy 130 J 5
Kultay 128 E 1
Kultsjön 112 G 3
Kultuk 130 H 5
Kulu (U.S.S.R.) 131 R 3
Kulu (Turkey) 117 D 3
Kuludzhun 119 Q 6
Kululli 159 G 2
Kululu 158 E 6
Kulunda 119 P 5
Kulundinskaya Step' 119 P 5
Kulundinskoye, Ozero 119 P 5
Kulyab 129 H 3
Kuma (Russia, U.S.S.R.) 112 K 2
Kuma (Russia, U.S.S.R.) 117 G 2
Kumagaya 133 L 3
Kumai 136 D 4
Kumai, Teluk 136 D 4
Kumak 119 M 5
Kumakhta 130 K 5
Kumamoto 133 K 4
Kumanovo 116 B 2
Kumara 131 N 5
Kumasi 156 D 4

Kumawa, Pegunungan 137 H 4
Kumba 157 F 5
Kumbakonam 134 C 5
Kumbe 144 D 3
Kumbo 157 G 4
Kum-Dag 128 E 3
Kumdah 155 H 4
Kume-jima 133 J 5
Kumertau 118 L 5
Kuminskiy 119 N 4
Kum Kuduk 132 B 2
Kumla 113 G 4
Kumluca 116 D 3
Kumo 157 G 3
Kumonda 130 K 4
Kumon Range 135 G 2
Kumora 130 K 4
Kumta 134 B 5
Kumu 158 D 4
Kümüx 132 A 2
Kunar 129 J 4
Künas 129 L 2
Kunashak 119 M 4
Kunda 113 J 4
Kunda-dia-Baze 160 B 1
Kunda Hills 134 C 5
Kundelungu, Monts 158 D 6
Kundelungu National Park 160 D 2
Kundur, Pulau 136 B 3
Kunduz 129 H 3
Kunene 160 A 3
Kunes 113 J 1
Künes He 129 L 2
Kungälv 113 F 4
Kungasalakh, Ozero 130 J 1
Kungsbacka 113 F 4
Kungu 158 B 4
Kungur 118 L 4
Kungurri 143 H 3
Kungur Tuk 130 G 5
Kungyangon 135 G 4
Kunhing 135 G 3
Kunjirap Daban 129 K 3
Kunlong 135 G 3
Kunlun Shan 129 KM 3
Kunlun Shankou 132 B 3
Kunming 132 D 5
Kunsan 133 J 3
Kuntshankoi 158 C 5
Kuntuk 131 R 4
Kununurra 142 D 2
Kunwak 167 S 3
Kunya 157 F 3
Kunya-Urgench 128 F 2
Kuocang 131 O 6
Kuocang Shan 133 H 5
Kuonamka 130 J 2
Kuonara 130 M 2
Kuop 146 B 2
Kuopio 112 J 3
Kuoqiang 132 A 3
Kuorboaivi 112 J 2
Kuoyka 130 M 1
Kupa 115 G 2
Kupang 136 F 6
Kupang, Teluk 137 F 6
Kupiano 144 E 4
Kupino 119 P 5
Kupiškis 113 J 4
Kupreanof 166 L 4
Kupyansk 118 G 6
Kuqa 129 L 2
Kur 131 P 5
Kura (U.S.S.R.) 128 D 2
Kura (Turkey) 117 F 2
Kura (Nigeria) 157 F 3
Kuragino 130 F 5
Kuramā, Ḥarrat 155 G 4
Kurashasayskiy 118 L 5
Kurashiki 133 K 4
Kuraymah 154 E 5
Kurbatovo 130 F 4
Kurbulik 130 J 5
Kurchum 119 Q 6
Kurdufān 154 DE 6
Kure 133 K 4
Küre 117 D 2
Kureyka 119 R 2
Kurgaldzhino 119 O 5
Kurgalski, Mys 113 J 4
Kurgan 119 N 4
Kurganinsk 117 F 2
Kurgan-Tyube 129 H 3
Kurgasyn 129 H 1
Kuria 146 C 2
Kuria Muria Islands 155 K 5
Kurikka 112 G 3
Kuril Islands 131 S 6
Kurilovka 118 J 5
Kuril'sk 131 R 6
Kuril'skiye Ostrova 131 RS 6

Kuril Trench 193 C 2
Kurkure-Bazhi, Gora 119 R 5
Kurleya 130 L 5
Kurmuk 154 E 6
Kurnool 134 C 4
Kuroiso 133 M 3
Kurort Družba 116 C 2
Kurort Slǎnčev brjag 116 C 2
Kurort Zlatni pjasčaci 116 C 2
Kuro-shima 133 J 4
Kurovskiy 131 N 5
Kurram 129 J 4
Kursavka 117 F 2
Kuršenai 113 H 4
Kursk 118 G 5
Kurskaja Kosa Neringa 113 H 4
Kurskaya 117 F 2
Kurski Zaliv 113 H 4
Kursu 112 J 2
Kuršumlija 116 B 2
Kurşunlu 117 D 2
Kurşunlu Daği 117 E 3
Kurtalan 117 F 3
Kurtamysh 119 M 5
Kürtī 154 E 5
Kuru 158 D 3
Kurucaşile 117 D 2
Kuruçay 117 E 3
Kuru Daği 116 C 2
Kuruktag 132 A 2
Kurum 144 E 2
Kuruman 160 C 5
Kurume 133 K 4
Kurumkan 130 K 5
Kurunegala 134 D 6
Kurung 130 L 2
Kurupka 166 C 5
Kurur, Jabal 154 E 4
Kur'ya 118 L 3
Kur'ya 119 Q 5
Kur'ya 130 E 1
Kurzeme 113 H 4
Kurzemes Augstiene 113 H 4
Kuşada Körfezi 116 C 3
Kuşadasi 116 C 3
Kusaie 146 B 2
Kuş Gölü 116 C 2
Kushchevskaya 117 E 1
Kusheriki 157 F 3
Kushimoto 133 L 4
Kushiro 133 M 2
Kushka 129 G 3
Kushkushara 118 H 3
Kushmurun 119 M 5
Kushmurun, Ozero 119 M 5
Kushva 119 L 4
Kuskokwim 166 E 3
Kuskokwim Bay 166 E 4
Kuskokwim Mountains 166 F 3
Kusma 134 D 2
Kussharo-ko 133 M 2
Kustanay 119 M 5
Kūstī 154 E 6
Kuta 157 F 4
Kūt Abdollah 128 D 4
Kütahya 116 C 3
Kutaisi 117 F 2
Kutai, Sungai 136 E 4
Kutan 117 G 2
Kutana 131 O 4
Kutch 134 AB 3
Kutch, Gulf of 134 A 3
Kutch, Rann of 134 AB 3
Kutima 130 J 4
Kutina 115 G 2
Kutno 111 G 4
Kutopy'egan 119 NO 2
Kutru 134 D 2
Kuttusvaara 112 J 2
Kutu 158 B 5
Kutulik 130 H 5
Kutum 154 C 6
Kuuli-Mayak 128 E 2
Kuusamo 112 J 2
Kuusankoski 112 J 3
Kuusivaara 112 H 2
Kuutse Mägi 112 J 4
Kuvango 160 B 2
Kuwait 155 H 3
Kuya 118 H 2
Kuybyshev 119 P 4
Kuybyshevo 131 R 6
Kuybyshevskoye Vodokhranilishche 118 J 5
Kuygan 119 O 6
Kūysanjaq 155 G 1
Kuytun (China) 129 LM 2
Kuytun (U.S.S.R.) 130 H 5
Kuytun, Gora 119 R 6
Kuytun He 119 L 2
Kuyucuk Daği 116 D 2
Kuyumba 130 G 3

Kuz'movka 130 F 3
Kuzmovka 118 J 5
Kuznetsk Basin 125
Kuznetskiy Alatau 119 R 4,5
Kuzomen 118 G 2
Kvænangen 112 H 1
Kvalöy 112 G 2
Kvalöya 112 H 1
Kvalsund 112 H 1
Kvareli 117 G 2
Kvarnbergsvattnet 112 F 3
Kvarner 115 F 2–3
Kvarnerič 115 F 3
Kverkfjöll 112 B 2
Kvichak Bay 166 F 4
Kvikkjokk 112 G 2
Kvinesdal 113 E 4
Kvissleby 112 G 3
Kviteseid 113 E 4
Kwa 158 B 5
Kwahu Plateau 156 D 4
Kwaja Ali 129 G 4
Kwajalein 146 C 2
Kwakoegron 179 G 2
Kwale (Kenya) 159 F 5
Kwale (Nigeria) 157 F 4
Kwamisa 156 D 4
Kwamouth 158 B 5
Kwa Mtoro 158 F 6
Kwangju 133 J 3
Kwangsi Chuang 132 E 6
Kwango 158 B 5
Kwanmo-bong 133 J 2
Kwatisore 137 H 4
Kwenge 158 B 6
Kwethluk 166 E 3
Kwidzyn 111 G 4
Kwigillingok 166 E 4
Kwikila 144 E 3
Kwilo 158 B 6
Kwilu 158 B 5
Kwitaro 179 G 3
Kwoka, Gunung 137 H 4
Kyabé 157 H 4
Kyabram 143 H 6
Kyaikkami 135 G 4
Kyaikto 135 G 4
Kyaka 158 E 5
Kyakhta 130 J 5
Kyancutta 143 F 5
Kyango 158 D 3
Kyaukkyi 135 G 4
Kyaukme 135 G 3
Kyaukpyu 135 F 4
Kyaukse 135 G 3
Kyauktaw 135 F 3
Kybartai 113 H 5
Kycham-Kyuyel' 131 R 2
Kychema 118 H 2
Kyeintali 135 F 4
Kyela 158 E 6
Kyelanq 134 C 1
Kyenjojo 158 E 4
Kyffhäuser 111 F 4
Kyjov 111 F 4
Kyle of Lochalsh 98 B 3
Kyll 115 E 1
Kymijoki 112 J 3
Kynnefjell 113 E 4
Kynuna 143 G 3
Kyoga, Lake 158 E 4
Kyong 135 G 3
Kyŏnggi-man 133 J 3
Kyŏngju 133 J 3
Kyōto 133 L 3
Kypros → Cyprus 117 D 3
Kyrbykan 131 N 3
Kyren 130 H J 5
Kyrenia → Girne 117 D 3
Kyrgyday 131 M 3
Kyrkheden 113 F 3
Kyrksæteröra 112 E 3
Kyrönjoki 112 H 3
Kyröjärvi 112 H 3
Kyrta 118 L 3
Kyrynniky 130 L 3
Kyshtovka 119 P 4
Kyshtym 119 M 4
Kystatam 130 M 2
Kysylkiya 119 P 6
Kysyl-Suluo 131 P 3
Kysyl-Syr 131 N 3
Kysyl-Yllyk 130 K 3
Kytalyktakh 131 O 2
Kyuekh-Bulung 130 K 2
Kyungyaung 135 G 4
Kyushe 128 E 1
Kyūshū 133 K 4
Kyzas 119 R 5
Kyusyur 131 N 1
Kyzyk 128 E 2

Kyzyl 130 F 5
Kyzyl 119 R 5
Kyzylart, Pereval 129 J 3
Kyzyldyykan 129 H 1
Kyzyl-Kiya 129 J 2
Kyzyl-Kommuna 129 H 1
Kyzylkum, Peski 129 G 2
Kyzylkoga 128 E 1
Kyzylrabot 129 J 3
Kyzyluy 129 H 1
Kyzylzhar 129 G 1
Kzyl-Dzhar 129 H 1
Kzyl-Orda 129 H 2
Kzyltu 119 O 5

L

Laa an der Thaya 115 G 2
La Asunción 179 F 1
Laba 117 F 2
La Babia 172 B 2
La Banda 182 D 4
Labang 136 D 3
La Barca 172 B 3
La Barge 170 D 3
Labazhskoye 118 K 2
Labaz, Ozero 130 G 1
Labbezenga 156 E 2
Labé (Guinea) 156 B 3
Labe (Czechoslovakia) 111 G 4
Labelle 171 M 2
Labengke, Pulau 137 F 4
Labenne 114 C 3
Laberge, Lake 166 K 3
Labinsk 117 F 2
Labis 136 B 3
La Blanquilla 179 F 1
Labota 137 F 4
Labouheyre 114 C 3
Laboulaye 182 D 5
Labrador 169 N 5
Labrador Basin 192 A 2
Labrador City 169 O 5
Labrador, Coast of 169 P 4
Labrador Sea 169 QR 4
Lábrea 179 F 5
Labrieville 169 O 6
Labuan (Indonesia) 136 C 5
Labuan (Malysia) 136 DE 2
Labuha 137 G 4
Labuhanbajo 137 E 5
Labuhanbilik 136 B 3
La Bureba 114 C 3
Labutta 135 F 4
Labuya 131 S 2
Labytnangi 119 N 2
Lac 116 A 2
La Cadena 172 B 2
Lac Alaotra 161 H 3
Lac Albanel 169 N 5
Lac à l'Eau-Claire 169 N 4
Lac Allard 169 P 5
La Campina 114 BC 4
Lacanau 171 H 3
Lacanau, Étang de 114 C 3
La Canourgue 114 D 3
Lacantún, Rio 172 D 4
La Carlota 137 F 1
La Carolina 114 C 4
Lac au Goéland 169 M 6
Lacaune, Monts de 114 D 3
Lac aux Goélands 169 P 4
Lac Belot 167 M 2
Lac Bermen 169 O 5
Lac Bienville 169 N 4
Lac Brochet 167 R 4
Lac Burton 169 M 5
Laccadive Islands 134 B 5
Lac Caniapiscau 169 O 5
Lac Champdoré 169 O 4
Lac Chibougamau 169 N 6
Lac Couture 169 M 3
Lac Débo 156 D 2
Lac de Grand Lieu 114 C 2
Lac de Gras 167 P 3
Lac de Guiers 156 A 2
Lac Delcommune 160 D 2
Lac Delorme 169 O 5
Lac de Neuchâtel 115 E 2
Lac des Bois 167 N 2
Lac d'Iberville 169 N 4
Lac Dô 156 D 2
Lac du Bourget 115 E 2
Lac du Der 115 D 2
La Cebollera 114 C 3
La Ceiba (Honduras) 172 E 4
La Ceiba (Venezuela) 178 D 2
Lacepede Bay 143 F 6
Lacepede Islands 142 C 2

Lacerdónia 161 F 3
Lac Evans 169 M 5
Lac Faguibine 156 D 2
Lac Faribault 169 N 4
Lac Fitri 157 H 3
Lac Guillaume Delisle 169 M 4
Lacha, Ozero 118 G 3
La Charité-sur-Loire 114 D 2
La Charlota 182 D 5
La Châtre 114 D 2
La Chaux-de-Fonds 115 E 2
Lachay, Punta 178 C 6
Lachlan River 143 H 5
La Chorrera 178 D 4
Lâçin 117 D 2
La Ciotat 115 E 3
Lackawanna 171 L 3
Lac Kempt 171 M 2
Lac Kipawa 171 L 2
Lac Klotz 169 N 3
Lac Korarou 156 D 2
Lac la Biche 167 P 5
Lac la Martre 167 O 3
Lac la Ronge 167 R 4
Lac Le Moyne 169 O 4
Lac Léman 115 E 2
Lac Mai-Ndombe 158 B 5
Lac Manouane 169 N 5
Lac Maunoir 167 N 2
Lac Mégantic 169 N 6
Lac Minto 169 N 4
Lac Mistassini 169 N 5
Lac Moero (Lake Mweru) 158 D 6
Lac Musquaro 169 P 5
Lac Nantais 169 N 3
Lac Naocoane 169 N 5
Lac Niangay 156 D 2
Lac Nichicum 169 N 5
La Cocha 182 C 4
La Colorada 170 D 6
Lacombe 167 P 5
La Concepción 178 D 1
La Coronilla 182 F 5
La Coruña 114 B 3
Lac Opiscotéo 169 O 5
Lac Payne 169 N 4
Lac Peribonca 169 N 5
Lac Plétipi 169 N 5
Lacq 108
La Crosse 171 H 3
La Cruz (Argentina) 182 E 4
La Cruz (Costa Rica) 172 E 5
La Cruz (Mexico) 170 E 7
La Cruz (Uruguay) 182 E 5
Lac Saint-Pierre 169 N 6
Lac Sakami 169 M 5
Lacs des Loups Marins 169 N 4
Lac Seul 168 J 5
Lac Tassialouc 169 N 4
Lac Tshangalele 160 D 2
Lac Tumba 158 B 5
La Cuesta 172 B 2
La Cueva 183 B 6
Lacul Razelm 116 C 2
Lacul Sinoe 116 C 2
Lac Upemba 158 D 6
Lac Wakuach 169 O 5
Ladakh Range 129 K 4
Ladário 180 E 4
Laddicea 116 C 3
La Digue 159 K 5
Lâdik 117 E 2
Ladismith 160 C 6
Lâdīz 129 G 5
Ladoga, Lake 112 K 3
Lado, Jabal 158 E 3
Ladong 132 E 6
La Dorada 178 D 2
Ladozhskoye Ozero 112 K 3
Ladrillcro, Golfo 183 A 8
Ladu 135 F 2
Ladybrand 160 D 5
Ladyga 119 R 2
Ladysmith 160 D 5
Ladyzhenka 119 N 5
Ladzhanur 117 F 2
Lae (Marshall Is.) 146 C 2
Lae (Papua New Guinea) 144 E 3
Lae (Papua New Guinea) 146 A 3
Laea 137 F 4
Laem Ngop 135 H 5
Lærdalsöyri 112 E 3
La Escala 114 D 3
La Esmeralda 180 D 5
Læsö 113 F 4
La Esperanza (Argentina) 183 C 6
La Esperanza (Bolivia) 180 D 3
La Estrada 114 B 3
La Estrella 180 D 5
Lafayette (IN, U.S.A.) 171 J 3
Lafayette (LA, U.S.A.) 171 H 5
Lafia 157 F 4
Lafiagi 157 F 4

Kur – Lag

La Flèche 114 C 2
La Flor 172 F 5
La Forestière 179 H 2–3
La Fría 178 D 2
La Fuente de San Esteban 114 B 3
Laful 135 F 6
Lagaao Feia 181 H 5
Laga Hida 159 G 3
Lagan 113 F 4
Lagarto 181 J 3
Lågen 112 E 3
Laggan, Loch 99 B 3
Laghouat 153 F 2
La Glória 178 D 2
Lagoa dos Patos 182 F 5
Lago Agrio 178 C 4
Lago Amanã 179 F 4
Lagoa Mangueira 182 F 5
Lagoa Mirim 182 F 5
Lago Arapa 180 BC 4
Lago Argentino 183 B 9
Lago Badajós 179 F 4
Lago Blanco 183 C 9
Lago Buenos Aires 183 B 8
Lago Cabora Bassa 161 E 3
Lago Cardiel 183 B 8
Lago Chilwa 161 F 3
Lago Colhué Huapí 183 C 8
Lago da Pedra 179 J 4
Lago de Chapala 172 B 3
Lago de Erepecu 179 G 4
Lago de Junín 180 A 3
Lago del Coghinas 115 E 3
Lago del Toro 183 B 9
Lago de Manacapuru 179 F 4
Lago de Managua 172 E 5
Lago de Maracaibo 178 D 1–2
Lago de Nicaragua 172 E 5
Lago de Poopó 180 C 4
Lago de San Luis 180 D 3
Lago de Yojoa 172 E 5
Lago di Bolsena 115 F 3
Lago di Bracciano 115 F 3
Lago di Como 115 E 2
Lago di Garda 115 F 2
Lago di Lesina 115 G 3
Lago di Lugano 115 E 2
Lago d'Iséo 115 F 2
Lago di Varano 115 G 3
Lago d'Ortà 115 E 2
Lago Fagnano 183 C 9
Lago General Carrera 183 B 8
Lago Llanquihue 183 B 7
Lago Maggiore 115 E 2
Lago Mandioré 180 E 4
Lago Musters 183 C 8
Lago Nahuel Huapi 183 B 7
Lagone Birni 157 G 3
Lago Novo 179 H 3
Lagonoy Gulf 137 F 1
Lago O'Higgins 183 B 8
Lago Omodeo 115 E 3
Lagoon, Island 143 F 5
Lago Piorini 179 F 4
Lago Posadas 183 B 8
Lago Pueyrredón 183 B 8
Lago Rogagua 180 C 3
Lago Rogoaguado 180 C 3
Lagos (Nigeria) 156 E 4
Lagos (Greece) 116 C 2
Lagos (Port.) 114 B 4
Lagosa 158 E 6
Lago San Martín 183 B 8
Lagos de Moreno 172 B 3
Lago Titicaca 180 C 4
Lago Trasimeno 115 F 3
Lago Uiñaimarca 180 C 4
Lago Viedma 183 B 8
La Grand-Combe 114 D 3
La Grande 170 C 2
La Grande-Motte 114 D 3
La Grande Rivière 169 M 5
La Grange 171 K 5
Lagrange 142 C 2
La Granja 114 C 3
La Gran Sabana 179 F 2–3
La Gruta 182 F 4
La Guaira 178 E 1
La Guardia (Argentina) 182 C 4
La Guardia (Bolivia) 180 D 4
La Guardia (Sp.) 114 B 3
Laguiole 114 D 3
Laguna 181 G 6
Laguna Agua Brava 172 A 3
Laguna Blanca 183 B 9
Laguna Canaranico 172 A 3
Laguna Concepción 180 D 4
Laguna de Antela 114 B 3
Laguna de Brus 172 F 4
Laguna de Caratasca 172 F 4
Laguna de Perlas 172 F 5
Laguna de Santa María 170 E 5

247

Lag–Lap

Laguna de Tamiahua 172 C 3
Laguna de Términos 172 D 4
Laguna Madre (Mexico) 172 C 3
Laguna Madre (TX, U.S.A.) 171 G 6
Laguna Mar Chiquita 182 D 5
Laguna Merín 182 F 5
Laguna Morales 172 C 3
Laguna Nahuala 172 C 4
Lagunas (Chile) 180 C 5
Lagunas (Peru) 178 C 5
Laguna Uberaba 180 E 4
Laguna Veneta 115 F 2
Lagune Aby 156 D 4
Lagune Ndogo 157 G 6
Lagune Nkomi 157 F 6
Lagunillas 180 D 4
Lagunitos 178 B 4
Laha 131 M 6
La Habana 173 F 3
Lahad Datu 137 E 2
Lahat 136 B 4
Lahdenpohja 112 K 3
Lahe 135 G 2
Lahewa 136 A 3
Lahij 155 G 6
Lāhījān 128 E 3
Laholm 113 F 4
Laholmsbukten 113 F 4
Lahore 129 J 4
Lahr 111 E 5
Lahti 112 J 3
La Huacan 172 B 4
Lai 157 H 4
Laiagam 144 D 3
Laibin 132 E 6
Lai Chau 135 H 3
Laide 98 B 3
Laihia 112 H 3
Lai-hka 135 H 3
Laingsburg 160 C 6
Lainioälven 112 H 2
Lairg 98 B 2
Lairi 157 H 3
Lais 136 B 4
Laisamis 159 F 4
Laisvall 112 G 2
Laitila 113 H 3
Laiwu 133 G 3
Laiwui 137 G 4
Laixi 133 H 3
Laiyang 133 H 3
Laiyuan 132 F 3
Laizhou Wan 133 G 3
La Japonesa 183 C 6
Lajes (Río Grande do Norte, Brazil) 181 J 2
Lajes (Sta. Catarina, Brazil) 182 F 4
La Junta (Bolivia) 180 D 4
La Junta (CO, U.S.A.) 170 F 4
La Junta (Mexico) 170 E 6
Lak Boggal 159 F 4
Lak Bor 159 F 4
Lak Dera 159 G 4
Lake Abaya 159 F 3
Lake Abbe 159 G 2
Lake Abitibi 171 K 2
Lake Afrēra 159 G 2
Lake Albert (Zaire/Uganda) 158 E 4
Lake Albert (OR, U.S.A.) 170 BC 3
Lake Alexandrina 143 F 6
Lake Almanor 170 B 3
Lake Alsh 98 B 3
Lake Amadeus 142 E 3
Lake Amboseli 159 F 5
Lake Annean 142 B 4
Lake Argyle 142 D 2
Lake Assale 159 G 2
Lake Athabasca 167 Q 4
Lake Aubry 167 M 2
Lake Auld 142 C 3
Lake Austin 142 B 4
Lake Baikal 130 J 4 5
Lake Ballard 142 C 4
Lake Bangweulu 160 D 2
Lake Baringo 159 F 4
Lake Barkley 171 J 4
Lake Barlee 142 B 4
Lake Berryessa 170 B 4
Lake Big Sand, 167 S 4
Lake Birch, 168 J 5
Lake Blanche (South Australia) 143 F 4
Lake Blanche (Western Australia) 142 C 3
Lake Breaden 142 D 4
Lake Brown, 167 T 2
Lake Buchanan (TX, U.S.A.) 170 G 5

Lake Buchanan (Queensland, Austr.) 143 H 3
Lake Buchanan (Western Australia) 142 C 4
Lake Buck 142 E 2
Lake Callabonna 143 F 4
Lake Carey 142 C 4
Lake Cargelligo 143 H 5
Lake Carnegie 142 C 4
Lake Chad 157 G 3
Lake Chamo 159 F 3
Lake Champlain 171 M 3
Lake Charles 171 H 5
Lake Chelan 170 B 2
Lake Chippewa 171 H 2
Lake City (FL, U.S.A.) 171 K 5
Lake City (N.C., U.S.A.) 171 L 5
Lake Claire 167 P 4
Lake Clark 166 G 3
Lake Clark National Park and Preserve 166 G 3
Lake Cowal 143 H 5
Lake Cowan 142 C 5
Lake Cumberland 171 J 4
Lake Dall, 166 E 3
Lake Darlot 142 C 4
Lake Deborah 142 B 5
Lake Dey Dey 142 E 4
Lake Disappointment 142 C 3
Lake District 101 D 2
Lake Dora 142 C 3
Lake Dundas 142 C 5
Lake Eaton 142 E 3
Lake Edward 158 D 5
Lake Ell 142 D 4
Lake Erie 171 K 3
Lake Everard 143 F 5
Lake Eyasi 158 E 5
Lake Eyre 143 F 4
Lake Eyre Basin 143 F 4
Lakefield 143 G 1
Lake Francis Case 170 G 3
Lake Frome 143 F 5
Lake Gairdner 143 F 5
Lake Galilee 143 H 3
Lake Gamarri 159 G 2
Lake Gaston 171 L 4
Lake Geneva 115 E 2
Lake George (Uganda) 158 E 5
Lake George (Western Austr.) 142 C 3
Lake George (FL, U.S.A.) 171 K 6
Lake George (N.Y., U.S.A.) 171 M 3
Lake Gidgi 142 D 4
Lake Gillen 142 C 4
Lake Gillian 169 M 1
Lake Gordon, 167 P 3
Lake Grace 142 B 5
Lake Grandin 167 O 3
Lake Gregory (South Australia) 143 F 4
Lake Gregory (Western Australia) 142 B 4
Lake Harbour 169 O 3
Lake Havasu City 170 D 5
Lake Hazlett 142 D 3
Lake Highrock, 167 Q 4
Lake Hill Island, 167 Q 3
Lake Hindmarsh 143 G 6
Lake Hopkins 142 D 3
Lake Huron 171 K 3
Lake Inle 135 G 3
Lake Itchen, 167 P 2
Lake Iteshi-Teshi 160 D 3
Lake Jackson 171 G 6
Lake Kariba 160 D 3
Lake Kemp 170 G 5
Lake King 142 B 5
Lake Kitangiri 158 E 5
Lake Koocanusa 170 C 2
Lake Koolivoo 143 F 3
Lake Kopiago 144 D 3
Lake Kotcho 165
Lake Kutubu 144 D 3
Lake Kyoga 158 E 4
Lake Laberge 166 K 3
Lake Ladoga 113 K 3
Lakeland 171 K 6
Lake Lapage 142 C 5
Lake Lefroy 142 C 5
Lake Lucas 142 D 3
Lake Macdonald 142 D 3
Lake Machattie 143 F 3
Lake Mackay 142 D 3
Lake Magenta 142 B 5
Lake Maitland 142 C 4
Lake Malawi (Lake Nyasa) 161 E 2
Lake Manitoba 167 S 5
Lake Manyara 159 F 5
Lake Marion 171 K 5

Lake Mason 142 B 4
Lake Maurepas 171 H 5
Lake Maurice 142 E 4
Lake Mburu 158 E 5
Lake Mc Leod 142 A 3
Lake Mead 170 D 4
Lake Mead National Recreation-Area 170 D 4
Lake Melville 169 Q 5
Lake Michigan 171 J 3
Lake Minchumina 166 G 3
Lake Minigwal 142 C 4
Lake Missisa, 168 K 5
Lake Monger 142 B 4
Lake Moore 142 B 4
Lake Moultrie 171 K 5
Lake Murray (SC, U.S.A.) 171 K 5
Lake Murray (Papua New Guinea) 144 D 3
Lake Mweru 158 D 6
Lake Nabberu 142 C 4
Lake Nash 143 F 3
Lake Nasser 154 E 4
Lake Natron 159 F 5
Lake Neale 142 E 3
Lake Ngami 160 C 4
Lakenheath 103 E 1
Lake Nipigon 168 K 6
Lake Nipissing 169 LM 6
Lake Norman 171 K 4
Lake Nyanga 142 D 4
Lake Nyasa 161 E 2
Lake Oahe 170 F 2
Lake of the Ozarks 171 H 4
Lake of the Woods 168 J 6
Lake Okeechobee 171 K 6
Lake Old Wives, 167 Q 5
Lake Ontario 171 L 3
Lake O' The Cherokees 171 H 4
Lake Owyhee 170 C 3
Lake Oxford, 167 S 5
Lake Peipus 113 J 4
Lake Pend Oreille 170 C 2
Lake Peter, 167 T 3
Lake Philippi 143 F 3
Lake Placid 171 M 3
Lake Pontchartrain 171 H 5
Lake Powell 170 D 4
Lake Raeside 142 C 4
Lake Rason 142 C 4
Lake Rebecca 142 C 5
Lake River 169 L 5
Lake Rosa 173 H 3
Lake Rudolf 159 F 4
Lake Rukwa 158 E 6
Lake Rutanzige (Lake Edward) 158 D 5
Lake Sagara 158 E 6
Lake Saint Clair 171 K 3
Lake Saint-Jean, 169 N 6
Lake Saint Joseph 168 J 5
Lake Saint Lucia 161 E 5
Lake Sakakawea 170 F 2
Lake Scugog 171 L 3
Lake Seabrook 142 B 5
Lakes Entrance 143 H 6
Lakes, Eskimo 166 L 2
Lake Shala 159 F 3
Lake Shepperd 142 C 4
Lake Shibogama, 168 K 5
Lake Simcoe 171 L 3
Lakes National Park 145 Q 9
Lake Stefanie 159 F 4
Lake Superior 171 J 2
Lake Tahirvuak, 167 P 1
Lake Tahoe 170 C 4
Lake Tana 159 F 2
Lake Tanganyika 158 DE 6
Lake Taupo 145 R 8
Lake Te Anau 144 P 10
Lake Throssel 142 C 4
Lake Timagami 171 K 2
Lake Timiskaming 171 L 2
Lake Tobin 142 D 3
Lake Torrens 143 F 5
Lake Turkana (Lake Rudolf) 159 F 4
Lake Victoria 158 E 5
Lakeview 170 B 3
Lake Volta 156 DE 4
Lake Wakatinu 144 P 10
Lake Wanaka 144 P 9
Lake Waukearly 142 C 3
Lake Way 142 C 4
Lake White 142 D 3
Lake Willkhuti 117 F 2
Lake Wills 142 D 3
Lake Windermere 101 D 2
Lake Winnebago 171 J 3
Lake Winnibigoshish 171 H 2
Lake Winnipeg 167 S 5
Lake Winnipegosis 167 R 5

Lake Winnipesaukee 171 M 3
Lakewood (CO, U.S.A.) 170 E 4
Lakewood (OH, U.S.A.) 171 K 3
Lake Woods 142 E 2
Lake Worth 171 K 6
Lake Wylie 171 K 4
Lake Xau 160 C 4
Lake Yamma Yamma 143 G 4
Lake Yeo 142 C 4
Lake Zwai 159 F 3
Lakhimpur 134 D 2
Lakhnadon 134 C 3
Lakhpat 134 A 3
Lakki 129 J 4
Lakmos Óros 116 B 3
Lakon 145 J 4
Lakonikos Kólpos 116 B 3
Lakota 156 C 4
Laksefjorden 112 J 1
Lakselv 112 J 1
Lakshadweep 134 B 5
Lakuramay 145 F 2
Lalago 158 E 5
Lala Musa 129 J 4
Lalibela 159 F 2
La Libertad 172 E 5
La Ligua 182 B 5
Lalin 114 B 3
La Linea 114 B 4
La Loche 167 Q 4
La Maddalena 115 E 3
La Maiella 115 F 3
Lama Kara 156 E 4
La Malbaie 171 M 2
La Mancha 114 C 4
La Manche 110 D 4
La Marina 114 C 4
La Mariscala 182 F 5
La Marmora 115 E 4
Lamarque 183 C 6
La Marque 171 H 6
Lamas 178 C 5
Lama Shillindi 159 G 4
La Mauricie National Park 171 M 2
Lamballe 114 C 2
Lambaréné 157 G 6
Lambay 110 B 4
Lambayeque 178 B 5
Lambay Island 100 B 3
Lambert, Cape 145 F 2
Lambert Glacier 185
Lamberts Bay 160 B 6
Lambon 145 F 2
Lambro 115 E 2
Lam Chi 135 H 4
Lamego 114 B 3
La Merced 182 C 4
Lamesa 170 F 5
La Meta 115 F 3
Lamezia Terme 115 G 4
Lamia 108
Lamía Stilis 116 B 3
Lamington National Park 143 J 4
Lammermoor 143 G 3
Lammermuir Hills 99 C 4
Lamon Bay 137 F 1
Lamont 171 K 5
La Montaña 180 B 2–3
Lamotrek 145 F 2
Lamotte-Beuvron 114 D 2
Lampang 135 G 4
Lam Pao Reservoir 135 H 4
Lampasas 170 G 5
Lampazos de Naranjo 172 B 2
Lampeter 102 B 1
Lamphun 135 G 4
Lamu 159 G 5
Lamud 178 C 5
Lanai 147 E 1
Lanark 99 C 4
Lanbi Kyun 135 G 5
Lancang 132 C 6
Lancang Jiang 132 D 6
Lancashire 101 D 3
Lancaster (U.K.) 101 D 2
Lancaster (CA, U.S.A.) 170 C 5
Lancaster (OH, U.S.A.) 171 K 4
Lanciano 115 F 3
Lanco 183 B 6
Łańcut 111 H 4
Landau 111 E 5
Landeck 115 F 2
Landegode 112 F 2

Lander 170 E 3
Landerneau 114 C 2
Landete 114 C 4
Landfall Island 135 F 5
Land's End 102 B 2
Landshut 111 F 5
Landskrona 113 F 4
Landsort 113 G 4
Landsortsdjupet 113 G 4
La Negra 180 B 5
La'nga Co 134 D 1
Langa Langa 158 B 5
Långan 112 F 3
Langanes 112 BC 2
Langarfoss 112 C 2
Langas 112 G 2
Langdon 170 G 2
Langeberg 160 BC 6
Lange Berg 160 B 6
Langeland 113 F 5
Längelmävesi 112 H 3
Langenhagen 111 E 4
Langesund 113 E 4
Langholm 101 D 2
Langjökull 112 AB 3
Langkawi 136 A 2
Langkon 136 E 2
Langlade 171 L 2
Langlo River 143 H 4
Langogne 114 D 3
Langon 114 C 3
Langöya 112 F 2
Langqên Zangbo 134 C 1
Langreo 114 B 3
Langres 115 E 2
Langres, Plateau de 115 DE 2
Langry 131 Q 5
Langsa 136 A 3
Långsele 112 G 3
Långseleån 112 G 3
Lang Shan 132 E 2
Lang Son 135 H 3
Lang Suan 135 G 6
Languedoc 114 D 3
Langzhong 132 E 4
Lan Hsu 133 H 6
Lanji 134 D 3
Lannemezan 114 D 3
Lannion 114 C 2
Lannion, Baie de 114 C 2
Lanping 132 C 5
Lansdowne House 168 K 5
Lanshan 132 F 5
Lansing (MI, U.S.A.) 171 K 3
Lansing (NWT, Can.) 166 L 3
Lansjärv 112 H 2
Lanxi 133 G 5
Lanzarote 152 C 3
Lanzhou 132 D 3
Laoag 137 J 1
Laoang 137 G 1
Lao Cai 135 H 3
Laodikeia 116 C 3
Laoha He 133 G 2
Laohekou 132 F 4
Laoie 100 B 3
Lao Ling 133 J 2
Laon 114 D 2
La Orchila 178 E 1
La Oroya 180 A 3
Laos 135 H 4
Laouni 153 G 4
Laoye Ling 133 J 2
Lapa 181 G 6
Lapage, Lake 142 C 5
Lapai 157 F 4
Lapalisse 114 D 2
La Palma (Canary Islands) 152 B 3
La Palma (Panama) 178 C 2
La Palma del Condado 114 B 4
La Paloma 182 F 5
La Paragua 179 F 2
La Paz (Arg.) 182 C 5
La Paz (Arg.) 182 E 5
La Paz (Bolivia) 180 C 4
La Paz (Honduras) 172 E 5
La Paz (México) 170 D 7
La Paz, Bahia de 170 D 7
La Pedrera 178 E 4
La Pelada 182 D 5
La Perouse Strait 133 M 1
La Pesca 172 C 3
La Piedad Cavadas 172 B 3
La Pine 170 B 3
Lapinig 137 G 1
Lapinlahti 112 J 3
Lápithos 117 D 3
Lapland 112 GH 2
La Plata 182 E 5
Lappajärvi 112 H 3
Lappeenranta (Villmanstrand) 112 J 3

Lappi 112 J 2
Lapri 131 N 4
Laprida (Argentina) 182 D 4
Laprida (Argentina) 183 D 6
Lapseki 116 C 2
Laptevo 118 G 5
Laptev Sea 130 NO 1
Laptev Sea 184
Laptevykh, More 130 L 1–O 1
Lapua 112 G 3
La Puebla de Cazalla 114 B 4
La Puerta 182 D 5
La Puntilla 178 B 4
Laqīyat al Arba'in 154 D 4
Laqīyat 'Umran 154 D 5
La Quemada 172 B 3
La Quiaca 180 C 5
L'Aquila 115 F 3
Lār 128 E 5
Lara 157 G 5
Larache 152 D 1
Laragne-Montéglin 115 E 3
Lārak 128 F 5
Laramate 180 B 3
Laramie 170 E 3
Laramie Mountains 170 E 3
Laramie River 170 E 3
Laranjal 179 G 4
Larantuka 137 F 5
Larat 137 H 5
La Raya Abra 180 B 3
Lärbro 113 G 4
Larche, Col de 115 E 3
Larde 161 F 3
Laredo (Spain) 114 C 3
Laredo (TX, U.S.A.) 170 G 6
La Réole 114 C 3
Lārestān 128 EF 5
Largs 99 B 4
La Ribera 114 C 3
La Rioja (Spain) 114 C 3
La Rioja (Argentina) 182 C 4
Lárisa 116 B 3
Larkana 129 G 5
Lar Koh 129 G 4
Larlomkriny 119 O 3
Larnaca 117 D 4
Lárnax → Larnaca 117 D 4
Larne 100 C 2
Larned 170 G 4
La Robla 114 B 3
La Roche 145 J 6
La Rochelle 114 C 2
La Roche-sur-Yon 114 C 2
La Roda 114 C 4
La Romana 173 J 4
La Ronge 167 Q 4
Larrey Point 142 B 2
Larrimah 142 E 2
Larsen Ice Shelf 185
Lartac, Causse du 114 D 3
La Rumorosa 170 C 5
Larvik 113 F 4
Lar'yak 119 Q 3
La Sabana (Argentina) 182 D 4
La Sabana (Colombia) 178 E 3
La Salina 170 D 5
La Salle 171 J 3
Läs 'Ānōd 159 H 3
La Sarre 169 M 6
Las Bonitas 178 E 2
Lascaux, Grotte de 114 D 2
Las Cejas 182 D 4
Las Colaradas 183 B 6
Las Cruces 170 E 5
Lās Dāred 159 H 2
Lās Dawa 159 H 2
La Serena (Chile) 182 B 4
La Serena (Spain) 114 B 4
La Seyne-sur-Mer 115 E 3
Las Flores 183 E 6
Lāsh-e Joveyn 129 G 4
Lashio 135 G 3
Lashkar 134 C 2
Lashkar Gāh 129 G 4
Lasia, Pulau 136 A 3
Las Lajas 183 B 6
Las Lanjitas 180 D 5
Las Lomitas 180 D 5
Las Marismas 114 B 4
Las Martinetas 183 C 8
Las Mestenas 170 E 6
La Solana 114 C 4
Lasolo 137 F 4
La Souterraine 114 D 2
Las Palmas 152 B 3
Las Palomas 170 E 5
Las Piedras 182 E 5
Las Pipinas 182 E 6
Las Plumas 183 C 7
Lās Qoray 159 H 2
Lassen Peak 170 B 3

Las Tablas 178 B 2
Las Tinajas 182 D 4
Last Mountain Lake 167 R 5
Lastoursville 157 G 6
Lastovo 115 G 3
Las Vegas (N.M., U.S.A.) 170 E 4
Las Vegas (NV, U.S.A.) 170 C 4
Latacunga 178 C 4
Latady Island 185
La Tagua 178 D 3–4
Latakia 154 F 1
Latheard 103 D 2
Lätäseno 112 H 2
La Teste 114 C 3
Latgale 113 J 4
Latgales Augstiene 113 J 4
Latheron 98 C 2
Latina 115 F 3
La Tortuga 178 E 1
Latouche Treville, Cape 142 C 2
Latouma 157 G 1
Latronico 115 G 3
La Tuque 171 M 2
Latur 134 C 4
Latviya 113 HJ 4
Lau 157 G 4
Lauder 99 C 4
Lauenburg 111 F 4
Laughlin Peak 170 F 4
Lau Group 146 D 4
Lauhanvuori 112 H 3
Laukaa 112 J 3
Launceston (Tasmania Austr.) 144 L 9
Launceston (U.K.) 102 B 2
Launggyaung 135 G 2
La Unión (Spain) 114 C 4
La Unión (Chile) 183 B 7
La Unión (Col.) 178 C 3
La Union (Mexico) 172 B 4
La Union (San Salv.) 172 E 5
Laura 143 G 2
La Urbana 178 E 2
Laurel 171 J 5
Laurencekirk 99 C 3
Laurentian Scarp 171 L 2
Lauria 115 G 3
Laurie River 167 R 4
Lauro Retiro 181 G 6
Lausanne 115 E 2
Laut Arafura 137 H 5
Lautaret, Col du 115 E 2
Lautaro 183 B 6
Laut Bali 136 E 5
Laut Banda 137 G 5
Laut Flores 137 E 5
Laut Halmahera 137 G 4
Laut Jawa 136 C 4
Laut Maluku 137 G 4
Laut, Pulau 136 E 4
Laut Seram 137 G 4
Laut Sulawesi 137 F 3
Laut Timor 137 G 5
Laval (France) 114 C 2
Laval (Quebec, Can.) 169 N 6
Lavalle 182 C 5
Lavapié, Punta 183 B 6
Lävar Meydān 128 E 4
La Vega 173 H 4
La Venta 172 D 4
La Ventana 172 B 3
Laverton 142 C 4
Lavezares 137 F 1
La Viña 178 C 5
Lavia 113 H 3
Lavka Integralsoyuza 131 V 2
Lavras 181 G 5
Lavrentiya 166 C 2
Lávrion 116 B 3
Lavumisa 161 E 5
Lāw 158 E 3
Lawas 136 E 3
Lawdar 155 H 6
Lawele 137 F 5
Lawit, Gunung 136 D 3
Lawksawk 135 G 3
Lawn Hill 143 F 2
Lawn Hill Creek 143 F 2
Lawqah 155 G 3
Lawra 156 D 3
Lawrence 171 G 4
Lawrenceburg 171 J 4
Lawton 170 G 5
Lawz, Jabal al 154 F 3
Laxå 113 F 4
Laxey Bay 100 C 2
Layar, Tanjung 136 E 4
Laydennyy, Mys 118 J 2
Laylā 155 H 4
Layton 170 D 3

La Zarca 172 B 2
Lazarev 131 Q 5
Lazarevac 116 B 2
Lazarevskoye 117 E 2
Lazo 131 T 4
Lazo, Iméni 131 S 3
Łębork 111 G 4
Leadville 170 E 4
League City 171 G 6
Leake, Mount 142 D 2
Le'an 132 G 5
Leatherhead 103 D 2
Leavenworth 171 H 4
Łeba 111 G 4
Lebak 137 F 2
Lebanon 154 F 2
Lebanon (MO, U.S.A.) 171 H 4
Lebanon (PA, U.S.A.) 171 L 3
Lebedin 118 F 5
Lebedyan' 118 G 5
Le Blanc 114 D 2
Lebo 158 C 4
Lebombo Mountains 161 E 4–5
Lebrija 114 B 4
Lebu 183 B 6
Lebyazh'ye 119 P 5
Lecce 115 G 3
Lecco 115 E 2
Lech 115 F 2
Le Champ du Feu 115 E 2
Lechang 132 F 5
Lechkhumskiy Khrebet 117 F 2
Le Creusot 115 E 2
Ledbury 102 C 1
Ledesma 114 B 3
Ledo, Cabo 160 A 1
Leduc 167 P 5
Ledyanaya, Gora 131 W 3
Leeds 101 E 3
Leeds Bradford (Airport) 101 E 3
Leek 101 D 3
Leer 111 E 4
Leeuwarden 110 E 4
Leeuwin, Cape 142 A 5
Leeward Islands (West Indies) 173 K 4
Leeward Islands (Fr. Polynesia) 147 E 4
Léfini 157 H 6
Léfini Reserve 157 H 6
Lefke → Levka 117 D 3
Lefkoniko 117 D 3
Lefkosa → Nicosia 117 D 3
Leganés 114 C 3
Legaspi 137 F 1
Legges Tor 144 L 9
Legionowo 111 H 4
Legnago 115 F 2
Legnano 115 E 2
Legnica 111 G 4
Legune 142 D 2
Leh 129 K 4
Lehamba 157 G 6
Le Havre 114 D 2
Lehi 170 D 3
Lehututu 160 C 4
Leibnitz 115 G 2
Leicester 103 D 1
Leicestershire 103 D 1
Leichardt River 143 F 2
Leiden 110 D 4
Leigh 101 D 3
Leigh Creek 143 F 5
Leighton Buzzard 103 D 2
Leikanger 112 E 3
Leine 111 E 4
Leinster 110 B 4
Leipzig 111 F 4
Leiria 114 B 4
Leirvik 113 E 4
Leisler, Mount 142 D 3
Leiston 103 E 1
Leitha 115 G 2
Leitrim 100 A 2
Leixlip 100 B 3
Leiyang 132 F 5
Leizhou Bandao 132 E 6
Leizhou Wan 132 F 6
Leje 110 D 4
Lejia, Cerro 180 C 5
Lek 110 D 4
Leka 112 F 2
Lékana 157 G 6
Lekemti → Nekemt 159 F 3
Lekey 157 G 6
Lekhainá 116 B 3
Lekitobi 137 F 4
Lekki Lagoon 157 E 4
Leknes 112 F 2
Lekrisovo 119 P 3
Leksand 113 F 3

Leksozero, Ozero 112 K 3
Lekst, Jbel 152 D 3
Leksvik 112 F 3
Le Lamentin 173 K 5
Lelâng 113 F 4
Lelekovka 117 D 1
Lelewau 137 F 4
Leling 133 G 3
Lelinta 137 H 4
Le Locle 115 E 2
Lema 157 E 3
Le Madonie 115 F 4
Le Maire, Estrecho de 183 CD 6
Léman, Lac 115 E 2
Le Mans 114 D 2
Le Mars 171 G 3
Lembolovskaya Vozvyshennost' 113 K 3
Lemesós → Limassol 117 D 4
Lemgo 111 E 4
Lemieux Islands 169 P 3
Lemluia 152 C 3
Lemmenjoki 112 J 2
Lemmon 170 F 2
Lemmon, Mount 170 D 5
Le Mont-Saint-Michel 114 C 2
Lemos 179 H 4
Le Moyne, Lac 169 O 4
Lempäälä 112 H 3
Lempa, Rio 172 E 5
Lemtybozh 118 L 3
Lemvig 113 E 4
Lena 131 N 1
Lendava 115 G 2
Lendery 112 K 3
Lenger 129 H 2
Lengshuijiang 132 F 5
Leninabad 129 H 2
Leninakan 117 F 2
Lenina, Pik 129 J 3
Leningrad 113 K 4
Leningradskaya 117 E 1
Leningradskaya 185
Leninka 131 X 3
Lenino 117 E 1
Leninogorsk 118 K 5
Leninogorsk 119 Q 5
Leninsk 117 F 1
Leninskiy 131 N 4
Leninsk-Kuznetskiy 119 R 5
Leninskoye 131 O 6
Len'ki 119 Q 5
Lenkoran' 128 D 3
Lennard River 142 C 2
Lennox 183 C 10
Lennox, Isla 183 C 10
Leno-Angarskoye Plato 130 HJ 4
Lensk 130 K 3
Lentekhi 117 F 2
Lentiira 112 J 3
Lentini 115 G 4
Lentua 112 J 3
Léo 156 D 3
Leoben 115 G 2
Leominster 102 C 1
León (Spain) 114 B 3
Leon (Mexico) 172 B 3
Leon (Nicaragua) 172 E 5
Léonard 169 O 6
Leonardville 160 B 4
León, Cerro 180 D 5
Leon, Montes de 114 B 3
León Nuevo (Mexico) 172 C 2
Leonora 142 C 4
Léon, Puerto de 114 C 4
Leopold and Astrid Coast 185
Leopoldina 181 H 5
Leopoldo de Bulhões 181 G 4
Leovo 116 C 1
Le Palais 114 C 2
Lepar, Pulau 136 C 4
Lepe 114 B 4
Lepel' 112 J 5
Le Petit Rhône 115 D 3
Lephepe 160 D 4
Leping 133 G 5
Lepini, Monti 115 F 3
Lepiske 131 N 2
Lepsy 119 P 6
Leptis Magna 153 H 2
Le Puy 114 D 2
Lercara Friddi 115 F 4
Lere (Nigeria) 157 F 3
Léré (Chad) 157 G 4
Lerma 114 C 3
Lermontov 117 F 2
Lermoos 115 F 2

Lermos 115 F 2
Léros 116 C 3
Leroy, Lake 142 C 5
Lerum 113 F 4
Lerwick 98 D 1
Lesbos 116 C 3
Les Cayes 173 H 4
Les Coëvrons 114 C 2
Les Escoumins 171 N 2
Lesina, Lago di 115 G 3
Lesjöfors 113 F 4
Leskino 130 C 1
Leskovac 116 B 2
Les Landes 114 C 3
Lesnaya 131 U 4
Lesnoy 119 N 4
Lesny 111 F 4
Lesogorsk 131 Q 6
Lesosibirsk 130 F 4
Lesotho 160 D 5
Lesozavodsk 133 K 1
Lesozavodskiy 112 K 2
Lesparre-Médoc 114 C 2
L'Esperance Rock 146 D 5
Les Sables-d'Olonne 114 C 2
Lessebo 113 G 4
Lesser Antilles 173 K 5
Lesser Khingan Mountains 131 N 5
Lesser Slave Lake 167 O 4
Lesser Sunda Islands 137 FG 5
Lestijärvi 112 H 3
Lestijoki 112 H 3
Lesueur, Mount 142 B 5
Lésvos 116 C 3
Le Tanargue 114 D 3
Letchworth 103 D 2
Letha Range 135 F 3
Lethbridge 167 P 6
Lethem 179 H 4
Le Thillot 115 E 2
Leticia 178 E 4
Leti, Kepulauan 137 G 5
Leting 133 G 3
Letlhakane 160 D 4
Letlhakeng 160 C 4
Letnerechenskiy 112 K 3
Letnyaya Zolotitsa 118 G 3
Letong 136 C 3
Le Touquet 114 D 2
Letovice 111 G 5
Le Tréport 114 D 1
Letsok-aw Kyun 135 G 5
Letterkenny 100 B 2
Léua 160 C 2
Leuca 115 G 4
Leucate, Étang de 114 D 3
Leuser, Gunung 136 A 3
Leuven 110 D 4
Levadhia 116 B 3
Levanger 112 F 3
Levante, Riviera di 115 E 3
Levanzo 115 F 4
Levashi 128 D 2
Levaya Khetta 119 O 3
Leven 99 C 3
Leven, Loch 99 C 3
Lévêque, Cape 142 C 2
Le Verdon-sur-Mer 114 C 2
Leverkusen 111 E 4
Lévézou 114 D 3
Levice 111 G 5
Levin 145 R 9
Levis 171 N 6
Levka 117 D 3
Levká Óri 116 B 3
Levkás 116 B 3
Levkosia → Nicosia 117 D 3
Levokumskoye 117 F 2
Levski 116 C 2
Lewe 135 G 4
Lewes 103 E 2
Lewis 98 A 2
Lewis Range 170 D 2
Lewiston (ID, U.S.A.) 170 C 2
Lewiston (ME, U.S.A.) 171 M 3
Lewistown (MI, U.S.A.) 171 K 3
Lewistown (MT, U.S.A.) 170 E 2
Lewistown (PA, U.S.A.) 171 L 3
Lewotobi, Gunung 137 F 5
Lexington 171 K 4
Leye 132 E 6
Leyland 101 D 3
Leyte 137 F 1
Lezha 116 A 2
Lezhi 132 E 4
Lezhi 132 B 4
Lézignan-Corbieres 114 D 3
L'gov 118 G 5
Lhari 132 B 4
Lhasa 135 F 2
Lhasa He 135 F 2

Lha–Lok

Lhazê 134 E 2
Lhazhong 134 E 1
Lhok Seumawe 136 A 2
Lhoksukon 136 A 2
Lhorong 132 C 4
Lhozhag 135 F 2
Lhünze 132 B 5
Lhünzhub 135 F 1
Lia 158 B 3
Liancheng 132 G 5
Lianga 137 G 2
Lianghe 132 C 6
Liangpran, Gunung 136 D 3
Lianhua Shan 132 G 6
Lianjiang 132 EF 6
Lianjiang 133 G 5
Lianping 132 F 6
Lian Xian 132 F 6
Lianyin 131 M 5
Lianyungang 133 G 4
Liaodong Bandao 133 H 3
Liaodong Wan 133 H 2
Liao He 133 H 2
Liaoning 133 H 2
Liaoyang 133 H 2
Liaoyuan 133 J 2
Liard 167 M 4
Liard River 167 M 4
Libby 170 C 2
Libenge 158 B 4
Liberal 170 F 4
Liberec 111 G 4
Liberia 156 BC 4
Liberia (Costa Rica) 172 E 5
Libertade 181 F 3
Libertador General San Martín 180 D 5
Libo 132 E 5
Libobo, Tanjung 137 G 4
Liboi 159 G 4
Libourne 114 C 3
Librazhdi 116 B 2
Libreville 157 F 5
Libya 153 H–K 3
Libyan Desert 154 CD 3–4
Licata 115 F 4
Lice 117 F 3
Lichfield 103 D 1
Lichinga 161 F 2
Lichinga, Planalto de 161 F 2
Lichtenburg 160 D 5
Lichuan 132 E 4
Licosa, Punta 115 E 3
Lida (U.S.S.R.) 113 J 5
Lida (Japan) 133 L 3
Liden 112 G 3
Lidhorikion 116 B 3
Lidingö 113 G 4
Lidköping 113 F 4
Lido di Ostia 115 F 3
Lidzbark Wárminski 111 H 4
Liebig, Mount 142 E 3
Liechtenstein 115 E 2
Liege 110 E 4
Lieksa 113 K 3
Lielupe 113 H 4
Lienart 158 D 4
Lienz 115 F 2
Liepāja 113 H 4
Lierne 112 F 3
Liestal 115 E 2
Lievestuoreenjärvi 112 J 3
Lievre 171 L 2
Liffey, River 100 B 3
Lifford 100 B 2
Lifou 145 J 6
Līgatne 113 H 4
Ligen Shkodrës 116 A 2
Ligonha 161 F 3
Ligure, Apennino 115 E 3
Liguria 115 E 3
Ligurian Sea 115 E 3
Ligwera 161 F 2
Lihir Group 145 F 2
Lihou Reef and Cays 143 J 2
Liinahamari 113 K 2
Lijiang 132 D 5
Likasi 160 D 2
Likati 158 C 4
Likenäs 113 F 3
Likhapani 135 G 2
Likiep 146 C 2
Likoma Islands 161 E 2
Likoro 157 F 3
Likoto 158 C 5
Likouala 157 H 5
Likouala aux Herbes 157 H 5
Likwangoli 158 E 3
Liling 132 F 5
Lilla Edet 113 F 4
Lille 114 D 1
Lille Bælt 113 E 4
Lillebonne 114 D 2

Lillehammer 112 F 3
Lillesand 113 E 4
Lilleström 113 F 4
Lillhärdal 112 F 3
Lilloet 167 N 5
Lilongwe 161 E 2
Liloy 137 F 2
Lim 116 A 2
Lima (Peru) 180 A 3
Lima (MT, U.S.A.) 170 D 3
Lima (OH, U.S.A.) 171 K 3
Lima (Port.) 114 B 3
Limache 182 B 5
Līmah 155 K 3
Limal 180 D 5
Limassol 117 D 4
Limavady 100 B 2
Limay 183 C 6
Limay Mahuida 183 C 6
Limbaži 113 H 4
Limbe 161 F 3
Limboto 137 F 3
Limburg 111 E 4
Limedsforsen 113 F 3
Limeira 181 G 5
Limerick 110 B 4
Limfjorden 113 E 4
Liminka 112 J 3
Limmen Bight 142 F 1
Limni Kremastá 116 B 3
Límni Mikre Prëspa 116 B 2
Limni Trikhonis 116 B 3
Limni Válvi 116 B 2
Limni Vegorritis 116 B 2
Limni Zistonis 116 C 2
Limnos 116 C 3
Limoeiro 181 J 2
Limoges 114 D 2
Limogne, Causse de 114 D 3
Limón (Costa Rica) 172 F 5
Limon (CO, U.S.A.) 170 F 4
Limone Piemonte 115 E 3
Limoquije 180 D 4
Limousin 114 D 2
Limoux 114 D 3
Limpopo 161 E 4
Limuru 159 F 5
Linaälven 112 H 2
Līnah 155 K 3
Lin'an 133 G 4
Linapacan Strait 137 E 1
Linares 114 C 4
Linares 183 B 6
Linares 172 C 3
Linaro, Capo 115 F 3
Lincang 132 D 6
Lincoln 103 D 1
Lincoln (Argentina) 182 D 5
Lincoln (IL, U.S.A.) 171 J 3
Lincoln (NE, U.S.A.) 171 G 3
Lincoln (U.K.) 110 C 4
Lincoln City 170 B 2
Lincoln Sea 184
Lincolnshire 103 D 1
Lincoln Wolds 101 E 3
Lindau 111 E 5
Linde 130 M 2
Linden 179 G 2
Lindenows Fjord 169 T 3
Linderödsåsen 113 F 4
Lindesberg 113 G 4
Lindesnes 113 E 4
Lindhos 116 C 3
Lindi (Tanzania) 159 F 6
Lindi (Zaire) 158 D 4
Lindian 131 M 6
Line Islands 147 E 2–3
Linfen 132 F 3
Lingao 132 E 7
Lingayan Gulf 137 H 1
Lingayen 137 H 1
Lingen 111 E 4
Lingga, Kepulauan 136 B 4
Lingga, Pulau 136 B 4
Lingling 132 F 5
Lingomo 158 C 4
Lingqiu 132 F 3
Lingshan 132 E 6
Lingshi 132 F 3
Lingshui 132 F 7
Lingsugur 134 C 4
Lingwu 132 E 3
Lingyuan 133 G 2
Linhai 133 H 5
Linhares 181 J 4
Linh Cam 135 J 4
Linhe 132 E 2
Linhpa 135 G 2
Linjanti 160 C 3
Linköping 113 G 4
Linkou 133 K 1

Linlithgow 99 C 4
Linnhe, Loch 99 B 3
Linosa 115 F 4
Linquan 132 G 4
Lins 181 G 5
Linshu 133 G 4
Lintan 132 D 4
Lintao 132 D 3
Linton 170 F 2
Lintong 132 E 4
Linxi 133 G 2
Linxia 132 D 3
Lin Xian 132 F 3
Linyi 133 G 3
Linyi 132 F 3
Linz 115 F 2
Linze 132 D 3
Liondo 158 C 5
Lion, Golfe de 114–115 D 2
Lioppa 137 G 5
Liouesso 157 H 5
Lipa 137 F 1
Lipari 115 F 4
Lipatkain 136 B 3
Lipéité 157 H 5
Lipetsk 118 GH 5
Lipin Bor 118 G 3
Liping 132 E 5
Lipkany 116 C 1
Lipno 111 G 4
Lipova 116 B 1
Lipovtsy 133 K 2
Lipu 132 F 6
Liquica 137 G 5
Lira 158 E 4
Liranga 157 H 6
Lircay 180 B 3
Lisa 116 A 2
Lisabata 137 G 4
Lisala 158 C 4
Lisboa 114 B 4
Lisbon (Portugal) 114 B 4
Lisbon (N.D., U.S.A.) 170 G 2
Lisburn 110 B 4
Lisburn 100 B 2
Lisburne, Cape 166 D 2
Lishi 132 F 3
Lishu 133 H 2
Lishui 133 G 5
Lisichansk 118 G 6
Lisieux 114 D 2
Liskeard 102 B 2
L'Isle-Jourdain 114 D 3
L'Isle-sur-la-Sorgue 115 E 3
Lismanovy 119 P 3
Lismore (U.K.) 99 B 3
Lismore (New South Wales, Austr.) 143 J 4
Lisnaskea 100 B 2
Listafjorden 113 E 4
Lištica 115 G 3
Litang 132 E 6
Litang 132 D 4
Litang Qu 132 D 5
Lithgow 143 J 5
Lithinon, Ákra 116 B 4
Lithuania 113 H 4
Litke 118 L 1
Litke 131 Q 5
Litoměřice 111 F 4
Litovko 131 P 6
Little Abaco Island 173 G 2
Little Aden 155 G 6
Little Andaman 135 F 5
Little Cayman 173 F 4
Little Colorado River 170 E 4
Little Desert National Park 143 G 6
Little Falls 171 H 2
Littlefield 170 F 5
Little Grand Rapids 167 S 5
Littlehampton 103 D 2
Little Inagua Island 173 H 3
Little Karroo 160 C 6
Little Minch 98 A 3
Little Minch 110 B 3
Little Missouri River 170 F 2
Little Nicobar 135 F 6
Little Ouse, River 103 E 1
Little Pamir 129 J 3
Little Rock 171 H 5
Little Sitkin 166 A 5
Little Smoky River 167 O 5
Little Tanaga 166 B 5
Littleton 170 E 4
Litva 113 H 4
Liuhe 133 J 2
Liujia Xia 132 D 3
Liuku 132 C 5
Liupanshui 132 D 5
Liushuquan 132 B 2
Liuwa Plain 160 C 2
Liuyuan 132 C 2

Liuzhou 132 E 6
Līvāni 113 J 4
Livengood 166 H 2
Liveringa 142 C 2
Livermore, Mount 170 F 4
Liverpool (U.K.) 101 D 3
Liverpool (Airport) 101 D 3
Liverpool (Canada) 169 P 7
Liverpool Bay 166 M 1–2
Liverpool Range 143 J 5
Livingston (U.K.) 99 C 4
Livingston (MT, U.S.A.) 170 D 2
Livingston (Newfoundl., Can.) 169 O 5
Livingstone 160 D 3
Livingstone Falls 157 G 7
Livingstone Memorial 161 E 2
Livingstone Mountains 158 E 6
Livingstonia 161 E 2
Livny 118 G 5
Livonia 113 J 4
Livorno 115 F 3
Livradois, Monts du 114 D 2
Livramento 182 E 5
Liwale 157 F 6
Liwonde 161 F 3
Li Xian 132 E 4
Li Xian 132 D 4
Li Xian 132 F 5
Liyang 133 G 4
Lizard 102 B 3
Lizard Point 102 B 3
Lizarda 179 J 5
Ljig 116 B 2
Ljubeli 115 F 2
Ljubinje 115 G 3
Ljubljana 115 G 2
Ljubovija 115 G 3
Ljugarn 113 G 4
Ljungan 112 F 3
Ljungaverk 112 G 3
Ljungby 113 F 4
Ljungdalen 112 F 3
Ljungskile 113 F 4
Ljusdal 112 G 3
Ljusnan 112 F 3
Ljusne 112 G 3
Ljusterö 113 G 4
Llallagua 177
Llandeilo 102 B 2
Llandovery 102 C 2
Llandovery 110 C 4
Llandrindod Wells 102 C 1
Llandudno 100 D 3
Llanelli 102 B 2
Llanes 114 C 3
Llanfairfechan 100 D 3
Llanfyllin 102 C 1
Llangefni 102 B 1
Llangollen 102 C 1
Llanidloes 102 C 1
Llano de la Magdalena 170 D 7
Llano Estacado 170 F 5
Llano River 170 G 5
Llanos 178 DE 2
Llanos de Chiquitos 180 D 4
Llanos de Moxos 180 CD 4
Llanos de Sinaloa 170 D 6
Llanos de Sonora 170 D 6
Llanos de Tabasco y Campeche 172 D 4
Llanos de Tamaulipas 172 C 2
Llanos de Urgel 114 D 3
Llanquihue, Lago 183 B 7
Llanrwst 102 C 1
Llantrisant 102 C 2
Llanwrtyd-Wells 102 C 1
Lleyn 102 B 1
Lliama, Volcán 183 B 6
Llica 180 C 4
Llico 182 B 5
L'Ile Rousse 115 E 3
Lluchmayor 114 D 3
Llullaillaco, Volcán 180 C 5
Loa 180 C 5
Loanda 157 F 6
Loandjili 157 G 6
Loange 158 C 5
Loano 115 E 3
Lobatse 160 D 5
Lobaye 158 B 4
Loberia 183 E 6
Lobito 160 A 2
Lobitos 178 B 4
Lobo 156 C 4
Lobos 182 E 5
Lobos de Afuera, Islas 178 B 5
Lobos de Tierra 178 B 5
Lobos, Islas de 172 C 3
Lobva 119 M 4
Locarno 115 E 2

Loch Arkaig 99 B 3
Loch Awe 99 B 3
Lochboisdale 98 A 3
Loch Broom 98 B 3
Loch Carron 98 B 3
Loch Doon 99 B 4
Loch Earn 99 B 3
Loch Eriboll 98 B 2
Loch Ericht 99 B 3
Loch Ettive 99 B 3
Loch Ewe 98 B 3
Loch Fyne 99 B 3
Lochgilphead 99 B 3
Loch Hourn 99 B 3
Lochinver 98 B 2
Lochinver 110 B 3
Loch Katrine 99 B 3
Loch Laggan 99 B 3
Loch Leven 99 C 3
Loch Linnhe 99 B 3
Loch Lochy 99 B 3
Loch Lomond 99 B 3
Loch Long 99 B 3
Lochmaddu 98 A 3
Lochmaddy 110 B 3
Loch Maree 98 B 3
Loch Morar 99 B 3
Lochnagar 99 C 3
Lochnagar 110 C 3
Loch Ness 98 B 3
Loch Nevis 99 B 3
Loch Rannoch 99 B 3
Loch Shiel 99 B 3
Loch Shin 98 B 2
Loch Sleat 98 B 3
Loch Snizort 98 A 3
Loch Sunart 99 B 3
Loch Tay 99 B 3
Loch Torridon 98 B 3
Lochy, Loch 99 B 3
Lock 143 F 5
Lockerbie 99 C 4
Lockhart River Mission 143 G 1
Locminé 114 C 2
Locri 115 G 4
Lod 154 E 2
Łódz 111 G 4
Loddon River 143 G 6
Lodève 114 D 3
Lodeynoye Pole 118 F 3
Lodi 115 E 2
Lödingen 112 G 2
Lodja 158 C 5
Lödöse 113 F 4
Lodwar 158 F 4
Loelli 158 E 3
Loeriesfontein 160 B 6
Lofa 156 B 4
Lofoten 112 F 2
Lofsdalen 112 F 3
Loftus 101 E 2
Lofty Ranges, Mount 143 F 6
Loga 156 E 3
Logan 170 D 3
Logan, Mount 166 J 3
Logan Mountains 166 M 3
Logansport 171 J 3
Logone 157 H 3
Logone Birni 157 G 3
Logoualé 156 C 4
Logroño 114 C 3
Logrosán 114 B 4
Lögstör 113 E 4
Lögumkloster 113 E 4
Lögurinn 112 C 2
Lohardaga 134 D 3
Lohit 135 G 2
Lohja (Lojo) 113 H 3
Lohjanjärvi 113 H 3
Lohjanselkä 113 H 3
Loholoho 137 F 4
Loikaw 135 G 4
Loile 158 C 5
Loimaa 113 H 3
Loimijoki 112 H 3
Loir 114 C 2
Loire 114 C 2
Loire, Val de 114 D 2
Loir, Vaux du 114 D 2
Loja 114 C 4
Loja 178 C 4
Loji 137 G 4
Lojo 113 H 3
Loka (Sudan) 158 E 4
Loka (Zaire) 158 B 4
Lokandu 158 D 5
Lokan tekojärvi 112 J 2
Lokwe 158 C 5
Löken 113 F 4
Lokgwabe 160 C 4
Lokhpodgort 119 N 2
Lokichar 158 F 4
Lokichoggio 158 E 4

Lok–Lup

Lokilalaki, Gunung 137 F 4
Lokka 112 J 2
Løkken (Denmark) 113 E 4
Løkken (Norway) 112 E 3
Loknya 113 K 4
Loko (Centr. Afr. Rep.) 158 B 4
Loko (Nigeria) 157 F 4
Lokoja 157 F 4
Lokolo 158 B 5
Lokomo 157 H 5
Lokoro 158 C 5
Lokosovo 119 O 3
Loksa 112 J 4
Lokshak 131 O 5
Loks Land 169 P 3
Lol 158 D 3
Lola 156 C 4
Loliondo 158 F 5
Lolland 113 F 5
Lolo 158 C 4
Loloda 137 G 3
Lolodorf 157 G 5
Lolowau 136 A 3
Lom (Cameroon) 157 G 4
Lom (Bulgaria) 116 B 2
Loma Bonita 172 C 4
Lomami 158 C 4
Loma Mountains 156 B 4
Loma Negra, Planicie de la 183 C 6
Lomas Colorados 183 C 7
Lomas de Zamora 182 E 6
Lombarda, Serra 179 H 3
Lombardia 115 EF 2
Lombarton 100 C 2
Lomblen, Pulau 137 F 5
Lombok 136 E 5
Lombok, Selat 136 E 5
Lomé 156 E 4
Loméméti, Jabal 135 J 5
Lomié 157 G 5
Lomond, Loch 99 B 3
Lomonosov 112 J 4
Lomonosovkiy 119 N 5
Lomovoye 118 H 3
Lomphat 135 J 5
Lompobatang, Gunung 137 E 5
Lompoc 170 B 5
Lom Sak 135 H 4
Łomża 111 H 4
Lo Nakpo 135 F 2
Loncoche 183 B 6
Loncopue 183 B 6
Londiani 158 F 5
London (U.K.) 103 D 2
London (Canada) 171 K 3
Londonderry 100 B 2
Londonderry, Cape 142 D 1
Londonderry, Isla (Chile) 183 B 9
Londrina 181 F 2
Lone Pine 170 C 4
Longa (Brazil) 181 H 1
Longa (Angola) 160 A 2
Longa (Angola) 160 B 2
Long Akah 136 D 3
Long Bay 171 L 5
Long Beach (CA, U.S.A.) 170 C 5
Long Beach (N.Y., U.S.A.) 171 M 3
Long Beach (WA, U.S.A.) 170 B 2
Longbleh 136 E 3
Longchuan Wandingzhen 132 C 6
Longde 132 E 3
Long Eaton 103 D 1
Longford (U.K.) 100 B 3
Longford (Tasmania, Austr.) 144 L 9
Longhai 133 G 6
Longhua 133 G 2
Longhui 132 F 5
Long Island (Canada) 169 M 5
Long Island (Papua New Guinea) 146 A 3
Long Island (Papua New Guinea) 144 E 3
Long Island (The Bahamas) 173 G 3
Longitudinal, Valle 183 B 6
Longjiang 131 M 6
Longkou 133 H 3
Longlac 168 K 6
Long Lake 168 K 6
Longleju 135 F 5
Longlin 132 E 6
Longling 132 C 6
Long, Loch 99 B 3
Longmen 132 F 6
Longmont 170 E 3
Longnan 132 F 6
Longnawan, Gunung 136 E 3
Longquan 133 G 5

Long Range Mountaines 169 Q 5–6
Longreach 143 G 3
Longsegah 136 E 3
Longshan 132 E 5
Longsheng 132 F 5
Longshou Shan 132 D 3
Longs Peak 170 E 3
Long Sutton 101 F 3
Longtown 99 C 3
Long Valley 170 D 5
Longview (TX, U.S.A.) 171 G 5
Longview (WA, U.S.A.) 170 B 2
Longwy 115 E 2
Longxi 132 D 3
Long Xian 132 E 4
Long Xuyen 135 J 5
Longyan 132 G 5
Longyao 132 F 3
Longzhou 132 E 6
Lonkin 135 G 2
Lons-le-Saunier 115 E 2
Lonton 135 G 2
Lontra 179 H 4
Loo 117 E 2
Looc 137 F 1
Looe 102 B 2
Lookout, Cape 171 L 5
Lookout Pass 170 C 2
Lookout Ridge 166 F 2
Loolmalasin 159 F 5
Loongana 142 D 5
Loop Head 110 B 4
Lopari 158 C 4
Lopatin 128 D 2
Lopatina, Gora 131 Q 5
Lopatka 131 T 5
Lopatka, Mys 131 T 5
Lopatki 119 N 5
Lop Buri 135 H 5
Lopcha 131 M 4
Lopez, Cap 157 F 6
Lop Nur 132 J 4
Lopphavet 112 H 1
Loppi 113 H 3
Lopud 115 G 3
Lopydino 118 K 3
Lora 129 H 4
Lora del Río 114 B 4
Loralai 129 H 4
Lorca 114 C 4
Lord Howe Island 143 K 5
Lord Mayor Bay 167 T 2
Lordsburg 170 E 5
Lorengau 144 E 2
Lorent 114 C 2
Lorenzo, Rio 170 E 7
Lorestan 128 D 4
Loreto (Amazonas, Brazil) 178 D 4
Loreto (Baja Calif., Mex.) 170 D 6
Loreto (Maranhão, Brazil) 179 J 5
Loreto (Mex.) 172 B 3
Lorica 178 C 2
Lorn 99 B 3
Lorne 143 G 6
Lörrach 111 E 5
Lorraine 115 E 2
Lorraine 143 F 2
Lorugumu 158 F 4
Los 112 G 3
Los Alamos 170 E 4
Los Andes 182 B 5
Los Ángeles 170 C 5
Los Ángeles (Chile) 183 B 6
Los Antiguos 183 B 8
Losap 146 B 2
Los Blancos 180 D 5
Los Frentones 182 D 4
Los Gatos 170 B 4
Los, Îles de 156 B 4
Lošinj 115 F 3
Losinoborskaya 119 R 4
Los Juríes 182 D 4
Los Lagos 183 B 6
Los Lavaderos 172 C 3
Los Menucos 183 C 7
Los Mochis 170 E 6
Los Monegros 114 CD 3
Los Palacios 171 K 7
Los Pozos 182 B 4
Los Reyes de Salgado 172 B 4
Los Roques 178 E 1
Lossen 112 F 3
Lossiemouth 98 C 3
Los Teques 178 E 1
Lost Trail Pass 170 D 2
Lostwithiel 102 B 2
Losuia 145 F 3
Losuwo 137 G 3
Los Vilos 182 B 5
Lot 114 D 3

Lota 183 B 6
Lothian 99 C 4
Loto 158 C 5
Lotoi 158 B 5
Lotta 112 J 2
Lotuke, Jabal 158 E 4
Lou 144 E 2
Loubomo 157 G 6
Loubuzhuang 132 A 3
Loudéac 114 C 2
Loudun 114 D 2
Loué 114 C 2
Louga 156 A 2
Lough Allen 100 A 2
Loughborough 103 D 1
Lough Conn 110 B 4
Lough Foyle 100 B 2
Lough Neagh 100 B 2
Lough Ree 100 B 3
Lough Ree 110 B 4
Lough Sheelin 100 B 3
Lough Swilly 100 B 2
Loughton 103 E 2
Louhans 115 E 2
Louisa 171 K 4
Louisa Reef 136 D 2
Louisiade Archipelago 145 F 4
Louisiana 171 H 5
Louis Trichardt 160 D 4
Louisville 171 J 4
Loukhi 112 K 2
Loukolela 157 H 6
Loukoléla 157 H 6
Loulan Yiji 132 A 2
Loum 157 F 5
Loup River 170 G 3
Loups Marins, Lacs des 169 N 4
Loups Peak 170 E 3
Lourdes 114 C 3
Loústin 111 F 4
Louth (Australia) 143 H 5
Louth (Lincolnshire U.K.) 101 E 3
Louth (Rep. of Ireland) 100 B 3
Loutrá Killinis 116 B 3
Louviers 114 D 2
Louwater 160 B 4
Lövånger 112 H 3
Lovat 113 J 4
Loveč 116 B 2
Loveland 170 E 3
Lovell 170 E 3
Lovelock 170 C 3
Loviisa 113 J 3
Lovington 170 F 5
Lovisa (Loviisa) 113 J 3
Lovoi 158 D 6
Lovozero 112 L 2
Lovozero, Ozero 112 L 2
Lóvua 160 C 1
Lówa 158 D 5
Low, Cape 167 U 3
Low Desert 170 B 3
Lowell 171 M 3
Lower California 170 D 6
Lower Hutt 145 R 9
Lower Lough Erne 100 B 2
Lower Post 166 M 4
Lower Red Lake 171 H 2
Lower Tunguska River 130 F 3
Lowestoft 103 E 1
Łowicz 111 G 4
Loxton (Australia) 143 G 5
Loxton (South Africa) 160 C 6
Loyalty Islands 145 J 6
Loyauté, Îles 145 J 6
Loyoro 158 E 4
Loyskiye Gory 131 U 2
Lozère, Mont 114 D 3
Loznica 116 A 2
Lozovaya 119 P 5
Loz'va 119 M 4
Lua 158 B 4
Luacano 160 C 2
Luahasibuka 136 A 4
Luala 161 F 3
Lualaba 158 D 5
Luama 158 D 5
Lu'an 133 G 4
Luan He 133 G 2
Luanping 133 G 2
Luanshya 161 E 2
Luán Toro 183 D 6
Luanza 158 D 6

Luapala 160 D 2
Luarca 114 B 3
Luashi 160 C 2
Luau 160 C 2
Lubānas Ezers 112 J 4
Luba 157 F 5
Lubalo 160 B 1
Luban 111 G 4
Lubang Islands 137 EF 1
Lubango 160 A 2
Lubao 158 D 6
Lubartów 111 H 4
Lübbenau 111 F 4
Lubbock 170 F 5
Lübeck 111 F 4
Lubefu 158 C 5
Lubero 158 D 5
Lubika 158 D 6
Lubilash 158 C 6
Lubin 111 G 4
Lublin 111 H 4
Lubnān, Jabal 154 F 2
Lubny 118 F 5
Luboń 115 G 4
Lubondaie 158 D 6
Lubuagan 137 J 1
Lubudi 158 D 6
Lubue 158 B 5
Lubuklinggau 136 B 4
Lubumbashi 160 D 2
Lubutu 158 D 5
Lubwe 160 D 2
Lucala 160 B 1
Lucan 100 B 3
Lucania, Mount 166 J 3
Lucano, Appenino 115 G 3–4
Lucapa 160 C 1
Lucas 180 E 3
Lucas, Lake 142 D 3
Lucca 115 F 3
Luce Bay 100 C 2
Lucena (Spain) 114 C 4
Lucena (Philippines) 137 F 1
Lučenec 111 G 5
Lucera 115 G 3
Lucero 170 E 5
Luchulingo 161 F 2
Lüchun 132 D 6
Lucira 160 A 2
Luckenwalde 111 F 4
Lucknow 134 D 2
Lucksta 112 G 3
Lucon 114 C 2
Lucusse 160 C 2
Lucy Greek 143 F 3
Lüda 133 H 3
Ludborough 101 E 3
Ludbreg 115 G 2
Ludendorf 160 C 1
Ludhiana 134 C 1
Ludian 132 D 5
Ludington 171 J 3
Ludlow 102 C 1
Ludogorije 116 C 2
Ludvika 113 G 3
Ludwigsburg 111 E 5
Ludwigshafen 111 E 5
Ludwigslust 111 F 4
Ludza 112 J 4
Ludus 116 B 1
Luebo 158 C 6
Lueki 158 D 5
Luembe 158 C 6
Luena (Angola) 160 B 2
Luena (River; Angola) 160 C 2
Luena (Zaire) 158 D 6
Luena (Zambia) 161 E 2
Luena Flats 160 C 2
Luepa 179 F 2
Lüeyang 132 E 4
Lufeng 132 G 6
Lufeng 132 D 5
Lufico 160 A 1
Lufira 158 D 6
Lufira, Chutes de la 158 D 6
Luga 112 J 4
Lugano 115 E 2
Lugano, Lago di 115 E 2
Lugansk → Voroshilovgrad 117 E 1
Luganville 145 J 5
Lugards Falls 159 F 5
Lugela 161 F 3
Lugenda 161 F 2
Lugnaquillia 100 B 3
Lugnquillia 110 B 4
Lugnvik 112 G 3
Lugo 114 B 3
Lugoj 116 B 1

Lugovskiy 130 K 4
Lugulu 158 D 5
Luhin Sum 133 G 1
Luhuo 132 D 4
Lui 160 B 1
Luia 160 C 1
Luiana 160 C 3
Luilaka 158 C 5
Luilu 158 C 6
Luimneach 110 B 4
Luing 99 B 3
Luino 115 E 2
Luiro 112 J 2
Luís Correia 181 H 1
Luis d'Abreu → Calchaguí 182 D 4
Luishia 160 D 2
Luiza 158 C 6
Luizi 158 D 6
Lujiang 133 G 4
Lukanga 160 D 2
Lukashkin Yar 119 P 3
Lukenie 158 B 5
Lukeville 170 D 5
Lukolela (Congo) 158 B 5
Lukolela (Zaire) 158 C 6
Lukonzolwa 158 D 6
Lukovit 116 B 2
Lukoyanov 118 H 4
Lukuga 158 D 6
Lukumburu 158 F 6
Lukuni 158 B 6
Lukusashi 161 E 2
Luleå 112 H 2
Luleälven 112 H 2
Lüleburgaz 116 C 2
Luliang 132 D 5
Lüliang Shan 132 F 3
Lulimba 158 D 5
Lulo 160 B 1
Lulonga 158 B 4
Lulua 158 C 6
Lulworth Cove 103 C 2
Luma Cassai 160 B 2
Lumajang 136 D 5
Lumajangdong Co 134 D 1
Lumbala 158 C 6
Lumberton 171 L 4
Lumbo 161 G 2
Lumbovka 118 H 2
Lumbrales 114 B 3
Lumding 135 F 2
Lumsden 144 P 10
Lumut, Tanjung 136 C 4
Lunayyir, Harrat 154 F 3
Lund 113 F 4
Lunda Norte 160 C 1
Lunda Sul 160 C 2
Lundazi 161 E 2
Lundevatn 113 E 4
Lundu 136 C 3
Lundy 110 CD 4
Lundy Island 102 B 2
Lüneburg 111 F 4
Lüneburger Heide 111 F 4
Lunel 114 D 3
Lune, River 101 D 2
Lunéville 115 E 2
Lunga 160 D 2
Lungarr 134 D 1
Lungleh 135 F 3
Lungue-Bungo 160 B 2
Luni 134 B 2
Luninets 113 J 5
Lunkho 129 J 3
Lunovayam 131 U 3
Lunsar 156 B 4
Lunsemfwa 160 D 2
Luntai 129 L 2
Luobei 131 O 6
Luocheng 132 E 6
Luochuan 132 E 3
Luodian 132 E 5
Luoding 132 F 6
Luofu 158 D 5
Luohe 132 F 4
Luonan 132 F 4
Luong Nam Tha 135 H 3
Luonteri 112 J 3
Luoshan 132 F 4
Luoxiao Shan 132 F 5
Luoyang 132 F 4
Luoyuan 133 G 5
Luozi 157 G 6
Lupa 158 E 6
Lupane 160 D 3
Lupan Shan 132 E 3
Lupeni 116 B 1
Luperón 173 H 4
Lupire 160 B 2

Lup–Mak

Luputa 158 C 6
Lūq 159 G 4
Luqu 132 D 4
Luquan 132 D 5
Luquembo 160 B 2
Lure, Montagne de 115 E 3
Lurgan 110 B 4
Lurgan 100 B 2
Luribay 180 C 4
Lurín 180 A 3
Lurio 161 G 2
Lurio 161 F 2
Lusaka 160 D 3
Lusambo 158 C 5
Lusanga 158 B 5
Lusangi 158 D 5
Lushan 132 D 4
Lushi 132 F 4
Lush, Mount 142 D 2
Lushnja 116 A 2
Lushoto 159 F 5
Lushui 132 C 5
Lüshun 133 H 3
Lusitano 160 B 1
Lusk (Rep. of Ireland) 100 B 3
Lusk (U.S.A.) 170 F 3
Lussanvira 181 F 5
Lustrafjorden 112 E 3
Lu Tao 133 H 6
Lutembo 160 C 2
Luton 103 D 2
Luton (Airport) 103 D 2
Lutong 136 D 3
Lutshima 158 B 6
Lutsk 113 J 5
Lutterworth 103 D 1
Lutuai 160 C 2
Luusua 112 J 2
Luvidjo 158 D 6
Luvua 158 D 6
Luvuei 160 C 2
Luwegu 159 F 6
Luwingu 160 D 2
Luwuk 137 F 4
Luxembourg 110 E 5
Luxi 132 C 6
Luxi 132 D 6
Luxor 154 E 3
Luza 118 J 3
Luzern 115 E 2
Luzhai 132 E 6
Luzhou 132 E 5
Luzhskaya Vozvyshennost' 113 J 4
Luziânia 181 G 4
Luzilândia 181 H 1
Luzino 119 R 2
Luzon 137 J 1
Luzon Strait 137 J 1
L'vovka 119 P 4
Lyady 112 J 4
Lyakhovskiy, Bol'shoy, Ostrov 131 Q 1
Lyakhovskiye Ostrova 131 P 1
Lyakhovskiy, Malyy, Ostrov 131 Q 1
Lyamin 119 O 3
Lycksele 112 G 3
Lydd 103 C 2
Lydd (Airport) 103 E 2
Lydenburg 160 DE 5
Lydney 102 C 2
Lygyy, Mys 130 L 1
Lyme Bay 102 C 2
Lyme Regis 102 C 2
Lymington 103 D 2
Lympne (Airport) 103 E 2
Lynchburg 171 L 4
Lynd 143 G 2
Lyndhurst (Australia) 143 G 2
Lyndhurst (U.K.) 103 D 2
Lyndon River 142 A 3
Lynd River 143 G 2
Lyngdal 113 E 4
Lyngen 112 H 2
Lyngseidet 112 H 2
Lynn Canal 166 K 4
Lynn Lake 167 R 4
Lynton 102 C 2
Lynx Lake 167 Q 3
Lyon 115 D 2
Lyon Inlet 167 V 2
Lyonnais, Monts du 115 D 2
Lyons River 142 B 3
Lysefjorden 113 E 4
Lysekil 113 F 4
Lyskovo 118 H 4
Łysa Gory 111 H 4
Lys'va 119 L 4
Lysye Gory 118 H 5
Lytham St. Anne's 101 D 3
Lytton 167 N 5
Lyuban' 113 K 4

Lyubertsy 118 G 4
Lyubeshov 113 J 5
Lyuboml 112 H 5
Lyucha 130 G 3
Lyudinovo 118 F 5
Lyuri 131 W 3

M

Maaia 161 G 2
Ma'ān 154 F 2
Maanselkä 112 J 3
Ma'anshan 133 G 4
Maarianhamina (Mariehamn) 113 G 3
Ma'arrat an Nu'mān 154 F 1
Maas 110 D E 4
Maasin 137 F 1
Maastricht 110 E 4
Maaza Plateau → Al Haḍabat al Ma'āzah 154 E 3
Mabaia 160 A 1
Mabalane 161 E 4
Ma'bar 155 G 6
Mabaruma 179 G 2
Mablethorpe 103 E 1
Mabote 161 E 4
Mabrous 157 G 1
Mabrūk 153 J 3
Mabuasehube 160 C 4–5
Mabuki 158 E 5
Ma'būs Yūsuf 153 K 3
Macadam Plains 142 B 4
Macaé 181 H 5
Macaíba 181 J 2
Macalister River 143 H 6
Macaloge 161 F 2
MacAlpine Lake 167 R 2
Maca, Monte 183 B 8
Macao 132 F 6
Macapá (Brazil) 179 H 3
Macará (Peru) 178 B 4
Macarena, Parque Nacional de la 178 D 3
Macas 178 C 4
Macau 181 J 2
Macaúba 181 F 3
Macauley 147 D 4–5
Macaya, Pic de 173 H 4
Macclesfield 101 D 3
Macclesfield 110 C 4
Macdonald, Lake 142 D 3
Macdonnell Ranges 142 E 3
Macduff 98 C 3
Macedo de Cavaleiros 114 B 3
Maceió 181 J 2
Macenta 156 C 4
Macerata 115 F 3
Mach 129 G 5
Macha 130 L 4
Machacamarca 180 C 4
Machachi 178 C 4
Machaïla 161 E 4
Machakos 159 F 5
Machala 178 C 4
Machar Marshes 158 E 3
Machattie, Lake 143 F 3
Machaze 161 E 4
Machece 161 F 3
Macheke 161 E 3
Macheng 132 G 4
Machera 117 D 4
Machevna 131 W 3
Machilipatnam 134 D 4
Machiques 178 D 1
Machupicchu 180 B 3
Machynlleth 102 C 1
Macia 161 E 5
Măcin 116 C 1
Macina 156 D 3
Maçka 117 E 2
Mackay 143 H 3
Mackay, Lake 142 D 3
Mackenzie 167 N 3
Mackenzie Bay 166 K 2
Mac Kenzie Bay 185
Mackenzie, District of 167 N 3
Mackenzie King Island 184
Mackenzie Mountains 166 M 3
Mackenzie River 143 H 3
Mackinaw City 171 K 2
Mac Kinlay River 143 G 3
Mackinnon Road 159 F 5
Maclean 143 J 4
Macmillan 166 L 3
Macmillan Pass 166 M 3
Macocola 160 B 1
Macomer 115 E 3
Macomia 161 FG 2
Mâcon (France) 115 D 2

Macon (GA, U.S.A.) 171 K 5
Macon (MS, U.S.A.) 171 J 5
Macondo 160 C 2
Mac Pherson Range 143 J 4
Macquarie Harbour 144 L 9
Macquarie Island 185
Macquarie River 143 H 5
Mac Robertson Land 185
Macugnaga 115 E 2
Macujer 178 D 3
Macumba 143 F 4
Macusani 180 B 3
Macuze 161 F 3
Mačva Podluzje 116 A B 2
Madadi 157 J 2
Madagali 157 G 3
Madagascar 161 G 4
Madā'in Şāliḥ 154 F 3
Madama 157 G 1
Madan 108
Madang 144 E 3
Madanīyīn 153 H 2
Madaoua 157 F 3
Madarounfa 157 F 3
Madau 145 F 3
Madawaska Highlands 171 L 2
Madaya 135 G 3
Maddaloni 115 F 3
Madeir 158 D 3
Madeira (Portugal) 152 B 2
Madeira (Brazil) 179 F 5
Madeleine, Île de la 169 P 6
Maden 117 E 3
Maden 117 E 3
Madeniyet 119 P 6
Madeniyet 128 F 2
Madera 170 B 4
Madero, Puerto del 114 C 3
Madesimo 115 E 2
Madetkoski 112 J 2
Madhipura 134 E 2
Madhubani 134 E 2
Madhupur Jungle 135 F 3
Madhya Pradesh 134 CD 3
Madidi 180 C 3
Madimba 158 B 5
Madina 156 B 3
Madīnat ash Sha'b 155 G 6
Madingo-Kayes 157 G 6
Madingou 157 G 6
Madirovalo 161 H 3
Madison (IN, U.S.A.) 171 J 4
Madison (MN, U.S.A.) 171 G 2
Madison (WI, U.S.A.) 171 J 3
Madison River 170 D 2
Madisonville (KY, U.S.A.) 171 J 4
Madisonville (TX, U.S.A.) 171 G 5
Madiun 136 D 5
Madjingo 157 G 5
Mado Gashi 159 F 4
Madoi 132 C 4
Madona 112 J 4
Madrakah 155 FG 4
Madrakah, Ra's al 155 K 5
Madras (India) 134 D 5
Madras (OR, U.S.A.) 170 B 3
Madre de Dios 180 B 3
Madre de Dios, Isla 183 AB 7
Madre del Sur, Sierra 172 B 4
Madre de Oaxaca, Sierra 172 C 4
Madre Oriental, Sierra 172 C 3
Madre, Sierra 172 D 4
Madrid 114 C 3
Madridejos 114 C 4
Madrona, Sierra 114 C 4
Madrūsah 153 H 5
Madurai 134 C 5
Madurantakam 134 C 5
Madura, Pulau 136 D 5
Madura, Selat 136 D 5
Madyan 154 F 3
Madzha 118 K 3
Maebashi 133 L 3
Mae Hong Son 135 G 4
Mae Nam Mun 135 H 4
Mae Nam Nan 135 H 4
Mae Nam Yom 135 G 4
Mae Rim 135 G 4
Mae Sariang 135 G 4
Maes Howe 98 C 2
Mae Sot 135 G 4
Maestég 102 C 2
Maevatanana 161 H 3
Maéwo 145 J 5
Mafeteng 160 D 5
Mafia Island 159 F 6
Mafikeng (Mmbatho) 160 D 5
Mafra 181 G 6
Magadan 131 S 4
Magadi 159 F 5
Magallanes, Estrecho de 183 B 9
Magalo 159 G 3
Magangue 178 D 2

Maganja 161 F 3
Magaria 157 F 3
Magarida 144 E 4
Magburaka 156 B 4
Magdagachi 131 N 5
Magdala 159 F 2
Magdalena (Bolivia) 180 D 3
Magdalena (Colombia) 178 D 1–2
Magdalena (Mexico) 170 D 5
Magdalena, Bahia 170 D 7
Magdalena, Isla (Mexico) 170 D 7
Magdalena, Isla (Chile) 183 B 7
Magdalena, Punta 178 C 3
Magdeburg 111 F 4
Magelang 136 C 5
Magellan, Strait of 183 B 9
Magenta 115 E 2
Magenta, Lake 142 B 5
Mageröya 112 J 1
Maggiorasca 115 E 3
Maggiore, Lago 115 E 2
Maghāgha 154 E 3
Maghama 152 C 5
Maghera 100 B 2
Magherafelt 100 B 2
Maghnia 152 E 2
Maglaj 115 G 3
Magnitogorsk 119 L 5
Magnolia 171 H 5
Magnor 113 F 4
Mago 131 Q 5
Mágoè 161 E 3
Magoša → Famagusta 117 D 3
Magpie 169 P 5
Magta Lahjar 152 C 5
Maguari, Cabo 179 J 4
Magude 161 E 4
Magumeri 157 G 3
Măgura Priei 116 B 1
Magwe 135 F 3
Magyarország 116 A 1
Magyichaung 135 F 3
Mahābād 128 D 3
Mahabalipuram 134 D 5
Mahabe 161 H 3
Mahabharat Range 134 E 2
Mahabo 161 G 4
Mahaddalay Weyne 159 H 4
Mahadeo Hills 134 C 3
Mahadeo Range 134 B 4
Mahagi 158 E 4
Mahajamba 161 H 3
Mahajan 134 B 2
Mahajanga 161 H 3
Mahakam, Sungai 136 E 3
Mahakos Kólpos 116 B 3
Mahalapye 160 D 4
Mahalevona 161 HJ 3
Mahallāt 128 E 4
Mahān 128 F 4
Mahanadi 134 D 3
Mahanoro 161 H 3
Maharashtra 134 C 4
Mahās 159 H 4
Mahasamund 134 D 3
Maha Sarakham 135 H 4
Mahatalaky 161 H 4
Mahatsanary 161 G 5
Mahavavy 161 H 3
Mahbés 152 D 3
Mahbubnagar 134 C 4
Mahd adh Dhahab 155 G 4
Maḥḍah 155 K 4
Mahdia (Algeria) 153 F 1
Mahdia (Guyana) 179 G 2
Mahé 134 C 5
Mahébourg 161 HJ 5
Mahendragiri 134 D 4
Mahenge 159 F 6
Mahesana 134 B 3
Maheshwar 134 C 3
Mahi 134 B 3
Mahia Peninsula 145 R 8
Mahin 157 E 4
Mahkene 112 F 3
Mahlabalini 161 E 5
Mahmudiye 116 D 3
Mahmud-Raqi 129 H 3
Mahnomen 171 G 2
Mahón 114 D 4
Mahonda 159 F 6
Mahrāt 155 J 5
Mahrāt, Jabal 155 J 5
Mahuva 134 B 3
Mahwa 134 C 2
Maiana 146 C 2
Maïao 147 F 4
Maicao 178 D 1
Maicurú 179 H 4
Maidenhead 103 D 2
Maidstone 103 E 2
Maiduguri 157 G 3
Maigudo 159 F 3

Maihar 134 D 3
Maijdi 135 F 3
Maikala Range 134 D 3
Maiko 158 D 5
Maiko National Park 158 D 5
Mai Munene 158 C 6
Main 111 E 5
Maínalon Óros 116 B 3
Main Barrier Range 143 G 5
Main Channel 171 K 2
Mai-Ndombe, Lac 158 B 5
Maine 171 N 2
Maïné Soroa 157 G 3
Mainland (Shetland Is., U.K.) 98 D 1
Mainland (Orkney Is., U.K.) 98 C 2
Mainling 132 B 5
Mainoru 142 E 1
Mainpuri 134 C 2
Maintirano 161 G 3
Mainz 111 E 5
Maio 156 B 6
Maipo, Volcán 182 C 5
Maipú (Arg.) 183 E 6
Maipú (Chile) 182 B 5
Maipuco 178 D 4
Maiquetía 178 E 1
Maisi, Punta 173 H 3
Maiskhal Island 135 F 3
Maitengwe 160 D 4
Maitland (New South Wales, Austr.) 143 J 5
Maitland (South Australia) 143 F 5
Maitland, Lake 142 C 4
Maiyu, Mount 142 D 2
Maizhokunggar 132 B 5
Maíz, Isla del 172 F 5
Maizuru 133 L 3
Majagual 178 D 2
Majardah 115 EF 4
Majdanpek 116 B 2
Majene 137 E 4
Mājerţen 159 HJ 3
Majevica 115 G 3
Maji 158 F 3
Majune 161 F 2
Majuriã 178 E 5
Majuro 146 C 2
Maka 156 B 3
Makabana 157 G 6
Makalamabedi 160 C 4
Makale (Ethiopia) 159 F 2
Makale (Indonesia) 137 E 4
Makalu, Mount 134 E 2
Makambako 158 E 6
Makanchi 119 Q 6
Makanrushi, Ostrov 131 S 6
Makanza 158 B 4
Makar 157 G 3
Makarikari 160 D 4
Makarikha 119 L 2
Makari Mountains 158 DE 6
Makarov 131 Q 6
Makarova 130 D 1
Makarovo 130 J 4
Makarovo 118 H 5
Makaryev 118 H 4
Makassar 137 E 5
Makassar, Selat 136 E 4
Makassar Strait 136 E 4
Makat 128 E 1
Makatea 147 F 4
Makaw 135 G 2
Makay, Massif du 161 H 4
Makedhonía 116 B 2
Makedonia 116 B 2
Makemo 147 F 4
Makeni 156 B 4
Makeyevka 117 E 1
Makgadikgadi Pan (Makarikari) 160 D 4
Makgadikgadi Pans Game Reserve 160 D 4
Makhachkala 128 D 2
Makharadze 117 F 2
Makhfar al Buşayyah 155 H 2
Makhmûr 155 G 1–2
Maki 137 H 4
Makinsk 119 O 5
Makkah 155 F 4
Makkovik 169 Q 4
Maknassy 153 G 2
Makó 116 B 1
Makokou 157 G 5
Makoli 160 D 3
Makongolosi 158 E 6
Makopse 117 E 2
Makorako 145 R 8
Makoua 157 H 6
Makovskoye 119 R 2
Makrai 134 C 3

Makran 129 G 5
Makri 134 D 4
Maksimkiy Yar 119 R 4
Maksimovka 133 L 1
Makteir 152 C 4
Mākū 128 C 3
Makumbi 158 C 6
Makunduchi 159 F 6
Makung 133 H 6
Makunza 158 C 6
Makurazaki 133 K 4
Makurdi 157 F 4
Makushino 119 N 4
Makushin Volcano 166 D 5
Makuyuni 159 F 5
Mal 152 C 5
Malå 112 G 2
Mala 180 A 3
Malabang 137 F 2
Malabar Coast 134 B 5–C 6
Malabo 157 F 5
Malacacheta 179 H 5
Malacca, Strait of 136 A 2
MalackyTrnava 111 G 5
Malad City 170 F 4
Malá Fatra 111 G 5
Málaga 114 C 4
Malagarasi 158 E 5–6
Malagarsi 158 E 5
Malagasy Republic 161 G 4
Malagón 114 C 4
Malaimbandy 161 H 4
Malaita 145 H 3
Malakāl 158 E 3
Malakanagiri 134 D 4
Malakand 129 J 4
Mala → Kapela 115 G 3
Malakula 145 J 5
Malam 144 D 3
Malang 136 D 5
Malanga 161 F 2
Malangen 112 G 2
Malanje 160 B 1
Malanville 156 E 3
Malao 145 J 5
Mälaren 113 G 4
Malargue 183 C 6
Malaripo 179 F 3
Malaspina (Argentina) 183 C 7
Malaspina Glacier 166 J 4
Malatayur, Tanjung 136 D 4
Malatya 117 E 3
Malatya Dağları 117 E 3
Malāwī (Iran) 128 D 4
Malawi 161 E 2
Malawi, Lake 161 E 2
Malawi National Park 161 E 2
Malawiya 154 F 5
Malax 112 H 3
Malaya 136 B 3
Malaya Baranikha 131 V 2
Malaya Sos'va 119 MN 3
Malaya Vishera 118 F 4
Malaya Viska 116 D 1
Malaybalay 137 G 2
Malāyer 128 D 4
Malaysia 136 B 3
Malazgirt 117 F 3
Malbon 143 G 3
Malbork 111 G 4
Malbrán 182 D 4
Malcolm 142 C 4
Malda 134 E 2
Maldon 103 E 2
Maldonado 182 F 5
Malé 115 F 2
Maleás, Ákra 116 B 3
Malegaon 134 B 3
Maléha 156 C 3
Malei 161 F 3
Malek 158 E 3
Malé Karpaty 111 G 5
Malema 161 F 2
Malemba-Nkulu 158 D 6
Maleta 130 J 5
Maleyevo 130 G 4
Maleza 178 E 3
Malgobek 117 F 2
Malgomaj 112 G 3
Malha 154 D 5
Malhada 181 H 3
Malheur Lake 170 C 3
Mali 156 D 3–E 2
Mali (Guinea) 156 B 3
Maliana 137 G 5
Malianjing 132 C 2
Mali Hka 135 G 2
Mali i Gribës 116 A 2
Mali i Ostrovicës 116 B 2
Mali i Tomorit 116 B 2
Malik 137 F 4
Mali Kanal 116 A 1

Malik Naro 129 G 5
Malik, Wādī al 154 D 5
Mali Kyun 135 G 5
Malili 137 F 4
Mali Lošinj 115 F 3
Malimba, Monts 158 D 6
Malinaloo 172 C 4
Malindi 159 G 5
Maling, Gunung 137 F 3
Malin Head 100 B 3
Malinovka 119 R 4
Malinovye Ozero 119 P 5
Malinyi 159 F 6
Malipo 132 D 6
Malita 137 G 2
Maljovica 116 B 2
Malka 117 F 2
Malkachan 131 S 4
Malkara 116 C 2
Malkhanskiy Khrebet 130 J K 5
Mallacoota 143 H 6
Mallaig 110 B 3
Mallaig 99 B 3
Mallani 134 B 2
Mallawī 154 E 3
Mallery Lake 167 S 3
Mallorca 114 D 4
Malm 112 F 3
Malmberget 112 H 2
Malmesbury (South Africa) 160 B 6
Malmesbury (U.K.) 103 C 2
Malmö 113 F 4
Maloca 179 G 3
Maloca 179 H 5
Maloca de Indios 180 E 3
Maloca do Gonçalo 179 G 4–5
Maloelap 146 C 2
Malole 161 E 2
Malolos 137 F 1
Malonga 160 C 2
Malorita 112 H 5
Maloshuyka 118 G 3
Malosofiyevka 117 D 1
Måløy 112 E 3
Malozemel'skaya Tundra 118 JK 2
Malpelo 178 B 3
Malpura 134 C 2
Malta 115 F 4
Malta (MT, U.S.A.) 170 E 2
Maltahöhe 160 B 4
Maltby 101 E 3
Malton 101 E 2
Maluku 137 G 4
Maluku, Laut 137 G 3
Malumfashi 157 F 3
Malunda 137 E 4
Malung 113 F 3
Malūṭ 154 E 6
Malvan 134 B 4
Malvern 110 C 4
Malvinas, Islas → Falkland Islands 183 DE 9
Malwa 134 C 3
Malya 158 E 5
Maly Kavkaz 117 FG 2
Malykay 130 L 3
Malyshevka 119 Q 2
Malyy Anyuy 131 U 2
Malyye Derbety 128 CD 1
Malyye Derbety 117 F 1
Malyy Lyakhovskiy, Ostrov 131 Q 1
Malyy Yenisey 130 F 5
Mama 130 K 4
Mamagota 145 G 3
Mamaia 116 C 2
Mamakan 130 K 4
Mamara 180 B 3
Mambajao 137 G 2
Mambasa 158 D 4
Mamberamo, Sungai 137 J 4
Mambéré 158 B 4
Mambili 157 H 5
Mambilima Falls 160 D 2
Mambrui 159 G 5
Mamburao 137 F 1
Mamfe 157 F 4
Mamiña 180 C 4
Mamlyutka 119 N 5
Mammamattawe 168 L 5
Mamonovo 113 H 5
Mamonta, Poluostrov 130 C 1
Mamoré 180 C 3
Mamou 156 B 3
Mamoun 158 C 2
Mampikony 161 H 3
Mampodre, Picos de 114 B 3
Mampong 156 D 4
Mamry, Jezioro 111 H 4
Mamuju 137 E 4

Mamuno 160 C 4
Man 156 C 4
Mana (U.S.S.R.) 130 F 4
Mana (French Guiana) 179 H 3
Manacacías 178 D 3
Manacapuru 179 F 4
Manacapuru, Lago de 179 F 4
Manacor 114 D 4
Manado 137 F 3
Managua 172 E 5
Managua, Lago de 172 E 5
Manakara 161 H 4
Manakau 145 Q 9
Manākhah 155 G 6
Manambao 161 G 3
Manam Island 144 E 2
Mananara 161 H 3
Mananara (River) 161 H 4
Manandréa 161 G 4
Manangoora 143 F 2
Mananjary 161 H 4
Manankoro 156 C 3
Manantenina 161 H 4
Manapouri 144 P 10
Manāqīsh 155 H 3
Manas (Bhutan) 135 F 2
Manas (China) 129 M 2
Manas He 129 M 2
Manas Hu 129 M 1
Manaslu 134 D 2
Manatuto 137 G 5
Manaus 179 F 4
Manavgat 116 D 3
Mancha Blanca 183 C 7
Mancheng 132 G 3
Manchester 101 D 3
Manchester (Airport) 101 D 3
Manchuria 133 HJ 2
Manciano 115 F 3
Mancınık 117 E 3
Mancınık Dağı 110 C 3
Máncora 178 B 4
Man, Isle of 110 C 4
Mand 128 E 5
Manda 161 E 2
Mandabe 161 G 4
Manda Hills 134 B 3
Manda Island 159 G 5
Manda, Jabal 158 C 3
Mandal (Mongolia) 130 H 6
Mandal (Norway) 113 E 4
Mandalay 135 G 3
Mandalgovĭ 132 E 1
Mandal-Ovoo 132 D 2
Mandan 170 F 2
Mandaon 137 F 1
Mandaoua 157 G 3
Mandara Mountains 157 G 3
Mandar, Teluk 137 E 4
Mandas 115 E 4
Mandasawu, Gunung 137 F 5
Mandasor 134 C 3
Mandawa 159 F 6
Mandera 159 G 4
Mandeville 173 G 4
Mandi 134 C 1
Mandiana 156 C 3
Mandimba 161 F 2
Mandinga 178 C 2
Mandingues, Monts 156 B 3
Mandioli, Pulau 137 G 4
Mandioré, Lago 180 E 4
Mandjafa 157 H 3
Mandji 157 G 6
Mandla 134 D 3
Mandö 113 E 4
Mandor 136 C 3
Mandora 142 C 2
Mandoúdhion 116 B 3
Mandritsara 161 H 3
Mandulya Körfezi 116 C 3
Mandurah 142 B 5
Manduria 115 G 3
Mandvi 134 A 3
Mandya 134 C 5
Manendragarh 134 D 3
Maneromango 159 F 6
Manevichi 113 J 5
Manfalūt 154 E 3
Manfredonia 115 G 3
Manfredonia, Golfo di 115 G 3
Manga (Niger/Chad) 157 GH 3
Manga (Brazil) 181 H 3
Mangabeiras, Chapada das 181 G 2–3
Mangai 158 B 5
Mangaia 147 E 4
Mangalia 116 C 2
Mangalmé 157 H 3
Mangalore 134 B 5
Mangareva 147 G 4
Manggawitu 137 H 4
Mangit 128 G 2

Mangkalihat, Tanjung 137 E 3
Manglar Alto 178 B 4
Manglares, Cabo 178 C 3
Mangnai 132 B 3
Mangoche 161 F 2
Mangoky 161 G 4
Mangole, Pulau 137 G 4
Mangueigne 157 J 3
Mangueira, Lagoa 182 F 5
Mangui 131 M 5
Manguinho, Ponta do 181 J 3
Manguredjipa 158 D 4
Mangut 130 K 6–L 5
Mangyshlak, Poluostrov 128 E 2
Manhan 130 F 6
Manhattan 171 G 4
Manhica 161 E 5
Manhuacu 181 H 5
Maní (Colombia) 178 D 3
Mani (Zaire) 158 D 6
Mania 161 H 4
Manianko 156 C 4
Manica 161 E 3
Manicaland 161 E 3
Manicore 179 F 5
Manicouagan 169 O 5
Manicouagan, Réservoir 169 O 5
Maniema 151
Maniganggo 132 C 4
Manihi 147 F 3
Manihiki 146 E 3
Manika, Plateau de la 158 D 6
Manila 137 F 1
Manimbaya, Tanjung 137 E 4
Maningrida 142 E 1
Maninian (Guinea) 156 C 3
Maninian (Ivory Coast) 156 C 4
Manipa, Pulau 137 G 4
Manipa, Selat 137 G 4
Manipur 137 F 3
Manisa 116 C 3
Manises 114 C 4
Manistique 171 J 2
Manitoba 167 S 5
Manitoba, Lake 167 S 5
Manitoulin Island 171 K 2
Manitou Springs 170 F 4
Manitowoc 171 J 3
Maniwaki 171 L 2
Manizales 178 C 2
Manja 161 G 4
Manjacaze 161 E 4
Manjakandriana 161 H 3
Manjil 128 D 3
Manjimup 142 B 5
Manjra 134 C 4
Mankato 171 H 3
Mankhere 134 D 3
Mankim 157 G 4
Mankono 156 C 4
Manlay 132 E 2
Manlleu 114 D 3
Manmad 134 B 3
Man Na 135 G 3
Manna 136 B 4
Mannahill 143 F 5
Mannar 134 C 6
Mannheim 111 E 5
Manning 167 O 4
Mannu, Capo 115 E 3
Mano 156 B 4
Manoa 158 E 5
Manoel Urbano 178 E 5
Manokwari 137 H 4
Manombo 161 G 4
Manompana 161 HJ 3
Manonga 158 E 5
Manono 158 D 6
Manoron 135 G 5
Manosque 115 E 3
Manouane, Lac 169 N 5
Manp'ojin 133 J 2
Manra 146 D 3
Manresa 114 D 3
Mansa 160 D 2
Mansa Konko 156 A 3
Mansehra 129 J 4
Mansel Island 169 LM 3
Mansfield (U.S.A.) 171 K 3
Mansfield (U.K.) 101 E 3
Mansfield Woodhouse 103 D 1
Mansi 135 G 3
Mansle 114 D 2
Mansôa 156 A 3
Manta 178 B 4
Mantalingajan, Mount 136 E 2
Mantaro 180 B 3
Mantecal 178 E 2
Manteo 171 L 4
Mantes-la-Jolie 114 D 2
Mantiqueira, Serra da 181 H 5
Mantova 115 F 2

Mäntsälä 113 J 3
Mänttä 112 G 3
Mäntyharju 112 J 3
Manú 180 B 3
Manuae 147 E 4
Manua Islands 146 D 3
Manuangi 147 F 4
Manuel Benavides 170 F 6
Manuelzinho 179 H 5
Manui, Pulau 137 F 4
Mănūk 154 F 2
Manukau 145 Q 8
Manukau Harbour 145 Q 8
Manu Ranipur 134 C 2
Manus 144 E 2
Manwat 134 C 4
Man'ya 119 MN 3
Manyara, Lake 159 F 5
Manych 117 F 1
Manych Gudilo, Ozero 117 F 1
Manychskaya Vpadina 117 F 1
Manyoni 158 E 6
Manzanares 114 C 3
Manzanillo (Cuba) 173 G 3
Manzanillo (Mexico) 172 B 4
Manzanillo, Bahia de 172 B 4
Manzhouli 130 L 6
Manzil Bū Ruqaybah 153 GH 1
Manzini 161 E 5
Manzurka 130 J 5
Mao 173 H 4
Maoke Mountains 144 D 2
Maoming 132 F 6
Maowen 132 D 4
Mapaga 137 E 4
Mapai 161 E 4
Mapam Yumco 134 D 1
Mapanza 160 D 3
Maper 158 D 3
Mapi 137 J 5
Mapia, Kepulauan 137 HJ 3
Mapinhane 161 F 4
Mapire 179 F 2
Mapireme 179 H 3
Mapiripana 178 D 3
Maple Creek 167 Q 6
Mapmakers Seamounts 193 C 3
Maprik 144 D 2
Mapuera 179 G 4
Mapuera 161 E 5
Maputo, Baía de 161 E 5
Maqar an Na'am 155 G 2
Maqên 132 D 4
Maqên Gangri 132 C 4
Maqu 132 D 4
Maquan He 134 D 2
Maquela do Zombo 160 B 1
Maquinchao 183 C 7
Marão 161 E 4
Marão, Serra do 114 B 3
Mara 158 E 5
Marañón 178 C 4
Maraá 178 E 4
Marabá 179 J 5
Marabahan 136 D 4
Mara Bridge 158 F 5
Maracaçume 179 J 4
Maracaibo 178 D 1
Maracaibo, Lago de 178 D 1–2
Maracá, Ilha de 179 H 3
Maracaju 181 F 5
Maracaju, Serra de 180–181 EF 5
Maracanã 179 J 4
Maracanaquará, Planalto 179 H 3–4
Maracás 181 H 3
Maracay 178 E 1
Marādah 153 J 3
Maradi 157 F 3
Marāgheh 128 D 3
Maragogipe 181 J 3
Marahuaca, Cerro 178 E 3
Marais Breton 114 C 2
Marajó, Baja de 179 J 4
Marajó, Ilha de 179 HJ 4
Marakei 146 C 2
Maralal 159 F 4
Maralaleng 160 C 5
Marali 158 B 3
Maralik 117 F 2
Maralinga 142 E 5
Maramasike 145 H 3
Maramba 160 D 3
Maran 136 B 2
Maränd 128 D 3
Marandellas → Maronderá 161 E 3
Marang 136 B 2
Maranguape 181 J 1
Maranhão (Brazil) 181 GH 2
Maranhão (Goiás, Brazil) 181 G 3
Maranoa River 143 H 4

Mar–Maw

Maraoue 156 C 4
Marapi, Gunung 136 B 4
Marargiu, Capo 115 E 3
Marari 178 E 5
Mărășești 116 C 1
Maratea 115 G 4
Marathon 116 B 3
Marathon (Can.) 168 K 6
Marathon (TX, U.S.A.) 170 F 5
Maraú 181 J 3
Marauá 178 E 4
Marávia, Planalto de 161 E 2
Maravovo 145 G 3
Marăwah 153 K 2
Marawī (Sudan) 154 E 5
Marawi (Philippines) 137 F 2
Marăwih 155 J 4
Maraxó Paiá 179 G 3
Maraza 128 D 2
Marbella 114 C 4
Marble Bar 142 B 3
Marble Canyon 170 D 4
Marble Hall 160 D 4
Marburg 111 E 4
Marcala 172 E 5
Marcelino Ramos 182 F 4
March (Austria) 115 G 2
March (U.K.) 103 E 1
Marche 115 F 3
Marche-en-Famenne 110 E 4
Marchena, Isla 178 B 6
Marche, Plateaux de la 114 D 2
Mar Chiquita, Laguna 182 D 5
Marcigny 114 D 2
Marcos Juárez 182 D 5
Marcus Baker, Mount 166 H 3
Mardan 129 J 4
Mar del Plata 183 E 6
Mardi, Hadjer 157 J 3
Mardin 117 F 3
Mardin Eşigi 117 F 3
Maré 145 J 6
Marea Neagră 116 C 2
Marechal Deodoro 181 J 2
Mareeba 143 H 2
Maree, Loch 98 B 3
Marēg 159 H 4
Maréna 156 C 3
Marendego 159 F 6
Marennes 114 C 2
Marettimo 115 F 4
Marfa 170 F 5
Margai Caka 129 M 3
Marganets 117 D 1
Margaret River (Western Australia) 142 A 5
Margaret River (Western Australia) 142 D 2
Margarida 180 E 5
Margarita, Isla de 179 F 1
Margaritovo 133 K 2
Margate (South Africa) 160 DE 6
Margate (U.K.) 103 E 2
Margherita di Savoia 115 G 3
Margherita → Jamāme 159 G 4
Margie 167 P 4
Margilan 129 J 2
Margyang 135 F 2
Marhoum 152 E 2
Mari (Syria) 155 G 2
Mari (Burma) 135 G 2
Mari (Papua New Guinea) 144 D 3
Maria (Tuamotu Is.) 147 F 4
Maria (Tubuai Is.) 147 E 4
Mariager Fjord 113 F 4
Maria Grande 182 E 5
Maria Island 143 F 1
Mariakani 159 F 5
Maria Madre, Isla 172 A 3
Maria Magdalena, Isla 172 A 3
Mariana Islands 146 A 1
Marianao 173 F 3
Mariana Trench 193 C 3
Marias, Islas 172 A 3
Marias River 170 D 2
María Teresa (Argentina) 182 D 5
Maria Theresa (Oceania) 147 E 5
Mariato, Punta 178 B 2
Maria van Diemen, Cape 145 Q 7
Mariazell 115 G 2
Maribo 113 F 5
Maribor 115 G 2
Marica 116 C 2
Marico 160 D 4
Maricourt 169 N 3
Marīdī 158 D 4
Marie Byrd Land 185
Marie-Galante 173 K 4
Mariehamn 113 G 3
Marie Louise 159 J 6
Mariental 160 B 4
Mariestad 113 F 4
Marietta 171 K 5

Mariga 157 F 3
Marignane 115 E 3
Mariinsk 119 R 4
Mariinskoye 131 Q 5
Marília 181 G 5
Marillana 142 B 3
Marimba 160 B 1
Marina Gorka 113 J 5
Marinduque 137 F 1
Marinette 171 J 2
Maringa (Zaire) 158 C 4
Maringá (Brazil) 181 F 5
Marino 115 F 3
Marinuma 178 E 3
Mariny, Iméni 131 R 3
Marion (IA, U.S.A.) 171 H 3
Marion (IL, U.S.A.) 171 J 4
Marion (IN, U.S.A.) 171 J 3
Marion (OH, U.S.A.) 171 K 3
Marion Downs 143 F 3
Marion, Lake 171 K 5
Marion Reef 143 J 2
Maripa 178 E 2
Mariscal Estigarribia 180 D 5
Marittime, Alpi 115 E 3
Mariu 144 D 3
Marīyyah 155 J 4
Märjamaa 112 H 4
Marka 159 GH 4
Markakol', Ozero 119 R 6
Markam 132 C 5
Markapur 134 C 4
Markaryd 113 F 4
Market Deeping 103 D 1
Market Drayton 101 D 3
Market Harborough 103 D 1
Market Rasen 101 E 2
Market Weighton 101 E 3
Markha 131 M 3
Markha 130 L 3
Markha 130 K 2
Markham Bay 169 N 3
Markit 129 K 3
Marko 112 G 2
Markounda 158 B 3
Markovo 131 W 3
Markovo 119 R 3
Marlborough (U.K.) 103 D 2
Marlborough (Australia) 143 H 3
Marlborough (Guyana) 179 G 2
Marlin 171 G 5
Marlow 103 D 2
Marmagao 134 B 4
Marmande 114 D 3
Marmara 116 C 2
Marmara Denizi 116 C 2
Marmara Gölü 116 C 3
Marmara, Sea of 116 C 2
Marmaris 116 C 3
Marmelos 179 F 5
Mar Menor 114 C 4
Marmolada 115 F 2
Marne 114 D 2
Marne à la Sane, Canal de la 115 E 2
Marne au Rhin, Canal de la 115 E 2
Mårnes 112 F 2
Marnpat 134 D 3
Maro 157 H 4
Maro (Wadi) 157 H 2
Maroa 178 E 3
Maroantsetra 161 H 3
Marolambo 161 H 4
Maromandia 161 H 2
Maromokotro 161 H 2
Marondera 161 E 3
Maroni 179 H 3
Maros 137 E 4
Marovoay 161 H 3
Maroua 157 G 3
Marowijne 179 H 3
Marquesas Islands 147 F 3
Marquette 171 J 2
Marracuene 161 E 5
Marradi 115 F 3
Marrah, Jabal 154 C 6
Marrakech 152 D 2
Marra Mountains 154 CD 6
Marrawah 144 K 9
Marree 143 F 4
Marrero 171 H 6
Marresale 119 N 2
Marromeu 161 F 3
Marrupa 161 F 2
Marryat River 142 E 4
Marsa al 'Alam 154 E 3
Marsa al Uwayjah 153 J 2
Marsabit 159 F 4
Marsabit National Reserve 159 F 4
Marsa Fatma 155 G 6
Marsala 115 F 4
Marsa Sha'b 154 E 4

Marsa Taklai 159 F 1
Marsden 143 H 5
Marseille 115 E 3
Mar, Serra do 181 G 6
Marsfjällen 112 G 2
Marshall 156 B 4
Marshall (AK, U.S.A.) 166 E 3
Marshall (MN, U.S.A.) 171 G 3
Marshall (TX, U.S.A.) 171 H 5
Marshall Islands 146 BC 2
Marshall River 143 F 3
Marshalltown 171 H 3
Marshfield 171 H 3
Marsh Harbour 173 G 2
Marsh Island 171 H 6
Märsta 113 G 4
Marstrand 113 F 4
Marta 115 F 3
Martaban 135 G 4
Martaban, Gulf of 135 G 4
Martap 157 G 4
Martapura 136 D 4
Martapura 136 B 4
Martés, Sierra de 114 C 4
Martigny 115 E 2
Martigues 115 E 3
Martin (Czechoslovakia) 111 G 5
Martin (U.S.A.) 170 F 3
Martina Franca 115 G 3
Martín de Loyola 183 C 6
Martínez de la Torre 172 C 3
Martinique 173 K 5
Martinique Passage 173 K 5
Martinsburg 171 L 4
Martinsville 171 L 4
Martin Vaz Islands 175 H 5
Marton 145 R 9
Martos 114 C 4
Martre, Lac la 167 O 3
Martti 112 J 2
Martūbah 153 K 2
Martuk 118 L 5
Martuni 117 G 2
Martyn 119 L 2
Marudi 136 D 3
Marungu, Monts 158 D 6
Marusthali 134 B 2
Marutea 147 F 4
Marvejols 114 D 3
Marwar Junction 134 B 2
Mary 129 G 3
Maryborough (Queensland, Austr.)143 J 4
Maryborough (Victoria, Austr.) 143 G 6
Marydale 160 C 5
Mar'yevka 119 N 5
Maryland 171 L 4
Maryport 101 D 2
Marystown 169 R 6
Marysville (CA, U.S.A.) 170 B 4
Marysville (KS, U.S.A.) 171 G 4
Maryville 171 H 3
Marzafal 156 D 2
Marzo, Cabo 178 C 2
Masaguru 161 F 2
Masai Steppe 159 F 5
Masaka 158 E 5
Masākin 153 H 1
Masalasef 157 H 3
Masalembo, Pulau 136 D 5
Masally 128 D 3
Masamba 137 F 4
Masan 133 K 4
Masasi 161 F 2
Masaya 172 E 5
Masbate 137 F 1
Mascara 152 EF 1
Mascarene Islands 161 HJ 5
Mascota 172 E 5
Masela, Pulau 137 G 5
Maseru 160 D 5
Masfinto 159 F 2
Mashaba 160 E 4
Mashaki 159 F 4
Mashala 158 C 6
Mashan 132 E 6
Mashewa 159 F 5
Mashhad 128 F 3
Mashīz 128 F 5
Mashkel 171 H 6
Mäshkīd 129 G 5
Mashonaland 161 E 3
Mashoro 160 E 4
Mashra'ar Raqq 158 D 3
Masīlah, Wādī al 155 J 5
Masi-Manimba 158 B 5
Masimbu 137 F 4
Masindi 158 E 4
Maṣīrah 155 K 4
Maṣīrah, Khalīj 155 K 5
Masisea 178 D 5

Masisi 158 D 5
Masjed Soleymān 128 D 4
Maskanah 154 F 1
Maslovare 115 G 3
Maslovo 119 MN 3
Maslyanskoye 119 O 4
Maso 156 D 4
Masoala, Cap 161 J 3
Masohi 137 G 4
Mason City 171 H 3
Mason, Lake 142 B 4
Masqat (Muscat) 155 K 4
Massa 115 F 3
Massachusetts 171 M 3
Massafra 115 G 3
Massaguet 157 H 3
Massakori 157 H 3
Massa Marittima 115 F 3
Massangena 161 E 4
Massango 160 B 1
Massapé 181 H 1
Massau 145 E 2
Massava 119 MN 3
Massawa 159 F 1
Massawarat es Sufra → Al Muṣawwarāt aṣ Ṣafra' 154 E 5
Massena 171 M 3
Massénya 157 H 3
Masset 166 L 5
Massif Central 114 D2–3
Massif d'Abo 157 H 1
Massif de Guéra 157 H 3
Massif de l'Adamaoua 157 G 4
Massif de l'Aurès 153 G 1
Massif de l'Isalo 161 H 4
Massif de l'Ivakoany 161 H 4
Massif de l'Ouarsenis 153 F 1
Massif des Bongos 158 C 3
Massif de Takolokouzet 157 F 2
Massif de Tarazit 157 F 1
Massif de Termit 157 G 2
Massif du Chaillu 157 G 6
Massif du Diois 115 E 3
Massif du Kapka 157 J 2
Massif du Kerkour Nourene 157 J 2
Massif du Makay 161 H 4
Massif du Pelvoux 115 E 3
Massif du Tamgué 156 B 3
Massif du Tondou 158 C 3
Massif du Tsaratanana 161 H 2
Massif du Yadé 158 B 3
Massigui 156 C 3
Massinga 161 F 4
Massingir 161 E 4
Masslo 159 F 3
Mastābah 155 F 4
Masteksay 128 E 1
Masterton 145 R 9
Mastuj 129 J 3
Mastung 129 G 5
Mastūrah 154 F 4
Masuda 133 K 4
Masuika 158 C 6
Masulipatnam → Machilipatnami 134 D 4
Masurai, Bukit 136 B 4
Masvingo 160 E 4
Mata Amarilla 183 B 8
Matabeleland 160 D 3–4
Matachewan 171 K 2
Matachic 170 E 6
Matadi 158 A 6
Matador 170 F 5
Matagalpa 172 E 5
Matagalpa, Río Grande de 172 F 5
Matagami 169 M 6
Mata Gassile 159 G 4
Matagorda Island 171 G 6
Matairie 171 H 5
Mataiva 147 F 3
Matakana 143 H 5
Matala 160 A 2
Matale 134 D 6
Matam 156 B 2
Matameye 157 F 3
Matamoros 172 B 2
Matancita 170 D 6
Matandu 159 F 6
Matane 169 O 6
Matankari 159 F 3
Matanzas 173 F 3
Matanzilla, Pampa de la 183 C 6
Matar 155 F 4
Matara (Etiopia) 159 F 2
Matara (Peru) 178 C 5
Matara (Sri Lanka) 134 D 6
Mataram 136 E 5
Matarani 180 B 4

Mataranka 142 E 1
Matarca 178 D 4
Matarka 152 E 2
Mataró 114 D 3
Matatiele 160 D 6
Matatila Dam 134 C 2
Mata-Utu 147 D 3
Matay 119 P 6
Mategua 180 D 3
Matehuala 172 B 3
Matera 115 G 3
Mátészalka 116 B 1
Matetsi 160 D 3
Matfors 112 G 3
Matheson 171 K 2
Mathura 134 C 2
Mati 137 G 2
Matiakouali 156 E 3
Matimbuka 161 F 2
Matinha 179 JK 4
Matīr 153 G 1
Matla 134 E 3
Matlock 101 E 3
Mato, Cerro 178 E 2
Mato Grosso 180–181 EF 3
Mato Grosso (Mato Grosso, Brazil) 180 E 3
Mato Grosso do Sul 180–181 EF 4
Matopo Hills 160 D 4
Matoque 182 D 4
Matozinhos 114 B 3
Mátra 116 AB 1
Maṭraḥ 155 K 4
Matru 156 B 4
Matrūh 154 D 2
Matsesta 117 E 2
Matsu (Japan) 133 M 2
Matsu (Taiwan) 133 H 5
Matsudo 133 L 3
Matsue 133 K 3
Matsumoto 133 L 3
Matsusaka 133 L 4
Matsuyama 133 K 4
Mattancheri 134 C 6
Matterhorn (NV, U.S.A.) 170 C 3
Matterhorn (Switzerland) 115 E 2
Matthew 146 C 4
Matthew, Ile 145 K 6
Matthews Range 159 F 4
Matthew's Ridge 179 FG 2
Matthew Town 173 H 3
Maṭṭī, Sabkhat 155 J 4
Mattoon 171 J 4
Matturai → Matara 134 D 6
Matu 136 D 3
Matua, Ostrov 131 S 6
Matucana 180 A 3
Maturín 179 F 2
Matveyev-Kurgan 117 E 1
Matyl'ka 119 R 3
Matyshevo 118 H 5
Matyushkinskaya 119 P 4
Mau 134 D 3
Maúa 161 F 2
Maubeuge 114 D 1
Maubin 135 G 4
Maude 143 G 5
Maués 179 G 4
Maués Açu 179 G 4
Maug 146 A 1
Mauganj 134 D 3
Maughold Head 100 C 2
Maui 147 E 1
Mauke 147 E 4
Mauléon 114 C 2
Maulvi Bazar 135 F 3
Maumere 137 F 5
Maun 160 C 4
Mauna Kea 147 E 1
Maungmagan Island 135 G 5
Maunoir, Lac 167 N 2
Maupihaa 147 E 4
Maupin 170 B 2
Maupiti 147 E 4
Mauralasan 136 E 3
Mau Range 159 F 5
Maurepas, Lake 171 H 5
Maurice, Lake 142 E 4
Mauritania 152 CD 5
Mauritius 161 HJ 5
Mauron 114 C 2
Mavasjaure 112 G 2
Mavinga 160 C 3
Mavue 161 E 4
Mavume 161 F 4
Mavuradonha Mountains 161 E 3
Mawa 136 C 3
Mawa'afaq 155 J 5
Mawa, Bukit 136 D 3
Mawk 133 G 5
Mawkmai 135 G 3
Mawlaik 135 F 3
Mawqaq 155 G 3

254

Mawson 185
Mawson Coast 185
Maxcanu 172 E 3
Maxixe 161 F 4
Maya 131 O 5
Mayaguana Island 173 H 3
Mayaguana Passage 173 H 3
Mayagüez 173 J 4
Mayahi 157 F 3
Mayakan 131 S 3
Mayama 157 G 6
Mayāmey 128 F 3
Maya Mountains 172 E 4
Mayang 132 E 5
Mayapán 172 E 3
Maya, Pulau 136 C 4
Maybole 100 C 2
Mayd 159 H 2
Maydān 155 H 2
Maydī 155 G 5
Mayenne 114 C 2
Maykain 119 P 5
Maykop 117 F 2
Maylykum 129 H 1
Maymak 129 J 2
Maymakan 131 P 4
Maymecha 130 H 1
Maymyo 135 G 3
Mayn 131 W 3
Mayna 130 F 5
Maynas 178 CD 4
Mayno-Amamkut 131 X 3
Maynopil'gyn 131 X 3
Mayn, Staryy 131 W 3
Mayo 166 K 3
Mayo Daga 157 G 4
Mayoko 157 G 6
Mayo Mayo 180 C 3
Mayo, Mountains of 110 B 4
Mayon 137 F 1
Mayor Buratovich 183 D 6
Mayor-Krest 131 Q 2
Mayotte 161 H 2
May Pen 173 G 4
Mayraira Point 137 HJ 1
May River 144 D 2
Maysk 119 P 4
Mayskiy 131 N 5
Mayskiy 117 F 2
Mayskiy, Khrebet 131 O 5
Mayskoye 119 P 5
Maysville 171 L 5
Mayumba 157 G 6
Mayum La 134 D 1
Mayvale 143 H 4
Mayya 131 O 3
Maza 183 D 6
Mazabuka 160 D 3
Mazagão 179 H 4
Mazalet 157 F 2
Mazamet 114 D 3
Mazar 129 K 3
Mazara dell Vallo 115 F 4
Mazar-i-Sharif 129 H 3
Mazarredo 183 C 8
Mazaruni 179 FG 2
Mazatenango 172 D 5
Mazatlán 172 A 3
Mažeikiai 113 H 4
Mazirbe 113 H 4
Mazomeno 158 D 5
Mazong Shan 132 C 2
Mazowe 161 E 3
Mazowsze 111 H 4
Mazrub 154 D 6
Mazunga 160 D 4
Mazury 111 H 4
Mbabane 161 E 5
Mbahiakro 156 D 4
Mbakaou Reservoir 157 G 4
Mbaké 156 A 3
Mbala (Centr. Afr. Rep.) 158 C 3
Mbala (Zambia) 161 E 1
Mbale 158 E 4
Mbalmayo 157 G 5
Mbam 157 G 4
Mbamba Bay 161 E 2
Mbandaka 158 B 4
Mbanga 157 F 5
Mbang, Monts 157 G 4
M'banza Congo 160 A 1
Mbanza-Ngungu 158 A 6
Mbarara 158 E 4
Mbari 158 C 3
Mbé 157 F 5
Mbengwi 157 F 4
Mbéré 157 H 4
Mberengwa 160 D 4
Mbeya 158 E 6
Mbigou 157 G 6
Mbinda 157 G 6
Mbini 157 F 5
Mbini River 157 G 5

Mbizi 160 E 4
M'Boi 158 C 6
Mbokou 158 D 3
M'Boli 158 C 4
Mboma 157 G 5
Mbomou 158 C 4
Mbouda 157 G 4
Mbour 156 A 3
Mbout 152 C 5
Mbozi 158 E 6
Mbrés 158 B 3
M'bridge 160 A 1
Mbuji-Mayi 158 C 6
Mbulu 158 F 5
Mburucuyá 182 E 4
Mburu, Lake 158 E 5
Mbuyuni 159 F 6
McAlester 171 G 5
McAllen 170 G 6
Mc Arthur River 143 F 2
McBeth Fjord 169 O 2
McCamey 170 F 5
McCammon 170 D 3
McCarthy 166 J 3
McComb 171 H 5
McCook 170 F 3
McDame 166 M 4
McDermitt 170 C 3
McGill 170 D 4
Mc Grath 166 F 3
McGregor 171 H 2
Mchenrrah 152 E 3
Mchinja 159 F 6
Mchinji 161 E 2
McKean 147 D 3
McKeand 169 O 3
McKeesport 171 L 3
McKenzie Island 168 J 5
McKinley, Mount 166 G 3
McKinley Park 166 H 3
McKinney 171 G 5
McLeod Bay 167 P 3
Mc Leod Lake 167 N 5
Mc Leod, Lake 142 A 3
M'Clintock 167 T 4
M'Clintock Channel 167 R 1
McLoughlin, Mount 170 B 3
M'Clure Strait 167 O 1
Mc Murdo 185
Mc Murdo Sound 185
McPherson 170 G 4
McVicar Arm 167 O 2
Mdandu 158 E 6
Mdennah 152 D 4
Meade 166 F 1–2
Meade Peak 170 D 3
Mead, Lake 170 D 4
Meadow 142 A 4
Meadow Lake 167 Q 5
Mealhada 114 B 3
Mealy Mountains 169 Q 5
Meander River 167 O 4
Meath 100 B 3
Meaux 114 D 2
Mecanhelas 161 F 3
Mecca 155 F 4
Mechelen 110 D 4
Mecheria 152 E 2
Mechigmenskiy Zaliv 166 C 2
Mecklenburg 111 F 4
Mecklenburger Bucht 111 F 4
Meconta 161 F 3
Mecrihan 117 E 3
Mecsek 116 A 1
Mecuburi 161 F 3
Mecúfi 161 G 2
Mecula 161 F 2
Mecumbura 161 E 3
Medaguine 153 F 2
Medak 134 C 4
Médala 152 D 5
Medan 136 A 3
Medano 183 D 6
Médanos 182 E 5
Medanosa, Punta 183 C 8
Médéa 153 F 1
Medellín 178 C 2
Medelpad 112 G 3
Mederdra 152 B 5
Medford 170 B 3
Medgidia 116 C 2
Medi 158 E 3
Media 116 B 1
Medical Lake 170 C 2
Medicine Bow 170 E 3
Medicine Hat 167 P 5
Medicine Lodge 170 G 4
Medigan 119 R 5
Medina 155 F 4
Medina del Campo 114 C 3
Medinipur 134 E 3
Medje 158 D 4

Medjerda, Monts de la 153 G 1
Mednogorsk 119 L 5
Mēdog 132 C 5
Médouneu 157 G 5
Medveditsa 118 H 5
Medvezh'i, Ostrova 131 U 1
Medvezhiy Var 130 F 1
Medvezh'ya, Gora 131 P 6
Medvezh'yegorsk 118 F 3
Medway, River 103 D 2
Meeberrie 142 B 4
Meekatharra 142 B 4
Meeker 170 E 3
Meerut 134 C 2
Mega (Indonesia) 137 H 4
Mega (Ethiopia) 159 F 4
Megalopolis 116 B 3
Meganom, Mys 117 E 2
Mega, Pulau 136 B 4
Mégara 116 B 3
Megasani Hill 134 E 3
Megève 115 E 2
Meghalaya 135 F 2
Megid 153 K 3
Megion 119 P 3
Megra 118 H 2
Meguidene 153 F 3
Meguinenza, Embalse de 114 CD 3
Mehadia 116 B 2
Mehar 129 G 5
Mehrān 128 EF 5
Mehran 128 D 4
Mehrīz 128 E 4
Mehtar Lam 129 J 4
Meia Meia 159 F 6
Meiganga 157 G 4
Meiktila 135 G 3
Meishan 132 D 5
Meissen 111 F 4
Meissner 111 E 4
Meitan 132 E 5
Mei Xian 132 G 6
Mejillones 180 B 5
Mékambo 157 G 5
Mekerrhane, Sebkha 153 F 3
Mekhé 156 A 2
Meknès 152 D 2
Meko 156 E 4
Mekong 135 J 5
Mekong, Mouths of the 135 J 6
Mekoryuk 166 D 3
Mekrou 156 E 3
Mēladēn 159 H 2
Melaka 136 B 3
Melanesia 146 A–C 3
Melanesia 145 GH 2–3
Melawi, Sungai 136 D 4
Melbourne 143 G 6
Melbourne (FL, U.S.A.) 171 K 6
Melchor, Isla 183 B 8
Melchor Múzquiz 172 B 2
Melchor Ocampo 172 B 4
Melendiz Daği 117 D 3
Melenki 118 H 4
Meletsk 130 F 4
Meleuz 118 L 5
Mélèzes, Rivière aux 169 N 4
Melfi (Italy) 115 F 4
Melfi (Chad) 157 H 3
Melfort 167 R 5
Melilla 152 E 1
Melimoyo, Monte 183 B 7
Melinca 183 B 7
Melincue 182 D 5
Melintang, Danau 136 E 4
Melipilla 182 B 5
Melitopol' 117 E 1
Melk 115 G 2
Melksham 103 C 2
Mellen 171 H 2
Mellerud 113 F 4
Mellish Reef 143 K 2
Mellit 154 D 6
Mellouline 153 F 4
Mel'nichnaya 119 R 2
Melo 182 F 5
Melolo 137 F 5
Melrhir, Chott 153 G 2
Melrose (U.S.A.) 170 D 2
Melrose (U.K.) 101 D 2
Melsetter → Chimanimani 161 E 3
Melsungen 111 E 4
Meltaus 112 J 2
Melton Mowbray 103 D 1
Melun 114 D 2
Melvich 98 C 2
Melville 167 R 5
Melville Bay 184
Melville, Cape 143 G 1
Melville Fracture Zone 192 B 5
Melville Hills 167 N 2

Melville Island 184
Melville Island 142 E 1
Melville, Lake 169 Q 5
Melville Peninsula 167 V 2
Melville Sound 167 Q 2
Melyuveyem 131 W 3
Meman 135 J 5
Mēmar Co 134 D 1
Memba 161 G 2
Memboro 137 E 5
Memmingen 111 F 5
Memphis 154 E 3
Memphis (TN, U.S.A.) 171 J 4
Mena (U.S.A.) 171 H 5
Mena (U.S.S.R.) 118 F 5
Menai Bridge 102 B 1
Menai Strait 102 B 1
Ménaka 153 F 5
Menawashei 154 D 6
Mencué 183 C 7
Mendawai, Sungai 136 D 4
Mende 114 D 3
Mendebo Mountains 159 FG 3
Mendi (Ethiopia) 158 F 3
Mendi (Papua New Guinea) 144 D 3
Mendip Hills 102 C 2
Mendocino, Cape 170 B 3
Mendoza (Argentina) 182 C 5
Mendoza (Peru) 178 C 3
Mene Grande 178 D 2
Menemen 116 C 3
Menez Hom 114 C 2
Mengcheng 133 G 4
Méngen 117 D 2
Mengene Daği 117 F 3
Menghai 132 C 7
Mengla 132 D 6
Menglian 132 C 6
Menglianggu 133 G 3
Mengzi 132 D 6
Menihek Lakes 169 O 5
Menindee 143 G 5
Meningie 143 F 6
Menkere 130 M 2
Menkere 131 NO 2
Menoikion Óros 116 B 2
Menominee 171 J 2
Menongue 160 B 2
Menorca 114 E 3
Menouarar 152 E 2
Men'shikova, Ostrov 131 P 5
Men'shikova, Mys 119 L 1
Mentarang, Sungai 136 E 3
Mentasta Lake 166 J 3
Mentawai, Kepulauan 136 A 4
Mentawai, Selat 136 A 4
Mentese 116 C 3
Mentok 136 C 4
Menton 115 E 3
Menyamya 144 E 3
Menyapa, Gunung 136 E 3
Menyuan 132 D 3
Menza 131 J 6
Menzel Bourgiba → Manzil Bū Ruquaybah 153 GH 1
Menzelinsk 118 K 4
Menzies 142 C 5
Menzies, Mount 185
Meoqui 170 E 6
Mepistskaro 117 F 2
Meponda 161 EF 2
Meppel 110 E 4
Meppen 111 E 4
Mepuze 161 E 4
Mer 115 E 3
Merak 136 C 5
Meråker 112 F 3
Meranggau 136 D 4
Merano 115 F 2
Meratus, Pegunungan 136 E 4
Merauke 144 D 3
Mercadal 114 D 4
Mercara 134 C 5
Merced 170 B 4
Mercedario, Cerro 182 B 5
Mercedes (Argentina) 182 E 4
Mercedes (Uruguay) 182 E 5
Merceditas 183 B 4
Mercês 178 E 5
Merchants Bay 169 P 2
Mercury 145 R 8
Mercy Bay 167 O 1
Mercy, Cape 169 P 3
Meredith, Cape 183 D 9
Merefa 118 G 6
Merenga 131 T 3
Merga → Nukhaylak 154 D 5
Mergenevo 128 E 1
Mergui 135 G 5

Mergui Archipelago 135 G 5
Meriç 116 C 2
Mérida (Spain) 114 B 4
Mérida (Venezuela) 178 D 2
Mérida (Mexico) 172 E 3
Mérida, Cordillera de 178 D 2
Meridian 171 J 5
Meridja 152 E 2
Merikarvia 112 H 3
Meringur 143 G 5
Merín, Laguna 182 F 5
Merinos 182 E 5
Merir 137 H 3
Merivale River 143 H 4
Merkushino 119 N 4
Merkushura Strelka 131 R 1
Meroe 154 E 5
Merouance, Chott 153 G 2
Merowe → Marawī 154 E 5
Merredin 142 B 5
Merrick 110 C 3
Merrick 99 B 4
Merrill 171 J 2
Merriman 170 F 3
Merritt 167 N 5
Merritt Island 171 K 6
Merseburg 111 F 4
Mersey, River 101 D 3
Merseyside 101 D 3
Mersin 117 D 3
Mersing 136 B 3
Mērsrags 112 H 4
Merta 134 B 2
Merthyr Tydfil 102 C 2
Merti 159 F 4
Mértola 114 B 4
Mertole Maryam 159 F 2
Meru (Kenya) 159 F 4
Meru (Tanzania) 159 F 5
Meru Game Reserve 159 F 4
Merutai 136 E 3
Merzifon 117 E 2
Mesabi 165
Mesabi Range 171 H 2
Mesa, Cerro 183 B 8
Mesa 170 D 5
Mesa de San Carlos 170 C 6
Mesa de Yambi 178 D 3
Mesapo 136 E 2
Mescalero 170 E 5
Meschede 111 E 4
Mescit Daği 117 F 2
Meseied 152 C 3
Meseta Central 172 B 3
Meseta de Chiapas 172 D 4
Meseta del Cerro Jaua 179 F 2–3
Meseta de Somuncurá 183 C 7
Mesetas de las Vizcachas 183 B 9
Meskou 157 H 2
Mesmiyah 154 F 2
Mesolóngion 116 B 3
Mesopotamia 155 GH 2
Mesquite 171 G 5
Messaad 153 F 2
Messalo 161 F 2
Messengue 161 E 4
Messerian 128 E 3
Messina (Italy) 115 F 4
Messina (S. Afr.) 160 D 4
Messiniakós Kólpos 116 B 3
Messo 119 P 2
Messoyakha 119 P 2
Mesta 116 B 2
Mesters Vig 184
Meta 178 E 2
Meta Incognita Peninsula 169 O 3
Metal, Mont du 153 G 4
Metamoros 172 G 2
Metán 182 D 4
Metangula 161 EF 2
Metapan 172 E 5
Metaponto 115 G 3
Meteghan 169 O 7
Metemma 158 F 2
Meteor Depth 192 A 5
Meteran 145 F 2
Méthana 116 B 3
Metković 115 G 3
Metlakatli 166 L 4
Metlika 115 G 2
Metlili Chaamba 153 F 2
Metro 136 C 5
Métsevon, Zigos 116 B 3
Metu 158 F 3
Metz 115 E 2
Meulaboh 136 A 3
Meureudu 136 A 2
Meuse 115 E 2
Mexborough 101 D 3
Mexiana, Ilha 179 J 3
Mexicala 170 C 5
Mexican Hat 170 E 4
Mexico 172 C 3

Mex–Mok

Mexico (MO, U.S.A.) 171 H 4
México City 172 C 4
Mexico, Gulf of 172 DE 2
Meyanobab 137 H 5
Meydān-e Gel 128 EF 5
Meyeihido 152 B 4
Meyísti 116 C 3
Meymeh 128 D 4
Meyo Centre 157 G 5
Mezcalapa, Rio 172 D 4
Mezdra 116 B 2
Mezen' 118 H 2
Mézenc, Mont 114 D 3
Mezenskaya Guba 118 H 2
Mezenskiy 130 G 1
Mezhdurechensk 119 R 5
Mezhdurechenskiy 119 N 4
Mezhdusharskiy, Ostrov 118 K 1
Mezhevaya 117 E 1
Mežica 115 G 2
Mezőtúr 116 B 1
Mezraa 117 E 2
Mfanganu Island 158 E 5
Mgachi 131 Q 5
Mgera 159 F 6
Mgori 158 F 5
Mhow 134 C 3
Miño 114 B 3
Miajadas 114 B 4
Miaméré 158 BC 3
Miami (AZ, U.S.A.) 170 D 5
Miami (FL, U.S.A.) 171 K 6
Miami (OK, U.S.A.) 171 H 4
Miami Beach 171 K 6
Miancaowan 132 C 3
Mianchi 132 F 4
Miǎndowǎb 128 D 3
Miandrivazo 161 H 3
Mianduhe 131 M 6
Miāneh 128 D 3
Miani Hor 129 G 5
Mian Kalai 129 J 4
Mianning 132 D 5
Mianwali 129 J 4
Mianyang 132 D 4
Mianzhu 132 D 4
Miaodao Qundao 133 H 3
Miao'ergou 129 L 1
Miarinarivo 161 H 3
Miaru 144 E 3
Miass 119 M 4
Miastko 111 G 4
Miazz 119 M 5
Micaune 161 F 3
Micay 178 C 3
Międzyrzec Podlaski 111 H 4
Międzyrzecz 111 G 4
Michalovce 111 H 5
Michelson, Mount 166 H 2
Micheweni 159 FG 5
Michigan 171 J 2
Michigan City 171 J 3
Michigan, Lake 171 J 3
Michipicoten Bay 171 J 2
Michipicoten Island 171 J 2
Michoacán 172 B 4
Michurinsk 118 H 5
Micronesia 146 A–C 2
Mičurin 116 C 2
Midai, Pulau 136 C 3
Mid-Atlantic Ridge 192 A 2–5
Middelburg 110 D 4
Middelburg (S. Afr.) 160 D 5
Middelburg (S. Afr.) 160 D 6
Middelfart 113 E 4
Middelwit 160 D 4
Middle Alkali Lake 170 C 3
Middle America Trench 193 D 3
Middle Andaman 135 F 5
Middlesboro 171 K 4
Middlesbrough 101 E 2
Middleton 101 D 3
Middleton 166 H 4
Middleton Reef 145 K 4
Middletown 171 K 4
Middlewich 101 D 3
Midelt 152 E 2
Mid Glamorgan 102 C 2
Midhordland 113 E 3
Midhurst 103 D 2
Midi, Canal du 114 D 3
Mid-Indian Ridge 192 B 4
Midland (MI, U.S.A.) 171 K 3
Midland (Ont., Can.) 171 L 3
Midland (TN, U.S.A.) 170 F 5
Midongy Atsimo 161 H 3
Midsummer Norton 102 C 2
Midwest 170 E 3
Midyat 117 F 3
Midžor 116 B 2
Miedwie, Jezioro 111 F 4
Miekojärvi 112 H 2
Mielan 114 D 3

Mielec 111 H 4
Mielno 111 G 4
Miercurea Ciuc 116 C 1
Mieres 114 B 3
Mierzeja Helska 111 G 4
Mierzeja Wiślana 111 G 4
Miesso 159 G 3
Migiurtinia 159 HJ 2
Miguel Alves 181 H 1
Mihăilesti 116 C 2
Mihajlovgrad 116 B 2
Mihalıççık 116 D 3
Mihuru 161 F 2
Mijares 114 C 3
Mijdahah 155 H 6
Mikha Tskhakaya 117 F 2
Mikhaylov 118 G 5
Mikhaylovka 128 D 1
Mikhaylovka 118 H 5
Mikhaylovka 117 G 1
Mikhaylovskiy 119 PQ 5
Mikinai 116 B 3
Mikindani 161 G 2
Mikkeli (Sankt Michel) 112 J 3
Míkonos 116 C 3
Mikré Préspa, Límni 116 B 2
Mikumi 159 F 6
Mikumi National Park 159 F 6
Mikun' 118 K 3
Mikuni-sanmyaku 133 L 3
Mila 115 E 4
Miladunmadulu Atoll 134 B 6
Milagro 178 C 4
Milan 115 E 2
Milando Reserve 160 B 1
Milange 161 F 3
Milano 115 E 2
Milas 116 C 3
Milazzo 115 G 4
Milcan Tepe 117 E 3
Mildenhall 103 E 1
Mildura 143 G 5
Mile 132 D 6
Miléai 116 B 3
100 Mile House 167 N 5
Miles 143 J 4
Miles City 170 E 2
Milet 116 C 3
Milford 170 D 4
Milford Haven 102 B 2
Milford Sound 144 P 9
Milgun 170 E 2
Milḥ, Baḥr al 155 G 2
Mili 146 C 2
Milkovo 131 T 5
Milk River 170 E 2
Mill 169 M 3
Millau 114 D 3
Milledgeville 171 K 5
Mille Lacs Lake 171 H 2
Millerovo 118 H 6
Millevaches, Plateau de 114 D 2
Millicent 143 F 6
Millington 171 J 4
Millisle 100 C 2
Millom 101 D 2
Millport 99 B 4
Mills Lake 167 O 3
Millstatt 115 F 2
Millstream 142 B 3
Millwood Lake 171 H 5
Milly Milly 142 B 4
Milo 156 C 3
Miflos 116 B 3
Milparinka 143 G 4
Milton (Australia) 143 J 6
Milton (U.S.A.) 171 L 4
Milton Keynes 103 D 1
Miltou 157 H 3
Miluo 132 F 5
Milwaukee 171 J 3
Milwaukie 170 B 2
Milyatino 118 F 5
Mimizan 114 C 3
Mimongo 157 G 6
Mina 130 F 5
Mīnā' 'Abd Allāh 155 H 3
Mīnā' al Aḥmadī 155 H 3
Mīnāb 128 F 5
Mīnā' Baranīs 154 F 4
Minamata 133 K 4
Minami-daitō-jima 133 K 5
Mina, Mont 156 C 3
Minas (Indonesia) 136 B 3
Minas (Uruguay) 182 E 5
Mīnā' Sa'ūd 155 H 3
Minas Gerais 181 GH 4
Minas Novas 181 H 4
Minas, Sierra de las 172 E 4
Minatitlán 172 D 4
Minbu 135 F 3

Minbya 135 F 3
Mincha 182 B 5
Mincio 115 F 2
Mindanao 137 F 2
Mindelo 156 A 6
Minden (FRG) 111 E 4
Minden (U.S.A.) 171 H 5
Minderoo 142 B 3
Mindif 157 G 3
Mindoro 137 F 1
Mindoro Strait 137 F 1
Mindorou 157 G 5
Mindyak 119 L 5
Mine Head 110 B 4
Minehead 102 C 2
Mineiros 181 F 4
Mineral'nyye Vody 117 F 2
Mineral Wells 170 G 5
Minerva Reefs 146 D 4
Minfeng 129 L 3
Minga 160 D 2
Mingan 169 P 5
Mingary 143 G 5
Mingechaur 128 D 2
Mingechaurskoye Vodokhrani-
lishche 128 D 2
Mingenew 142 B 4
Mingin Range 135 G 3
Mingo Lake 169 N 2
Mingon 135 G 3
Mingrel'skaya 117 E 2
Mingshui 132 C 2
Mingteke 129 K 3
Mingxi 133 G 5
Minhe 132 D 3
Minho 114 B 3
Minicoy 134 B 6
Minigwal, Lake 142 C 4
Minilya 142 A 3
Minilya River 142 A 3
Ministro João Alberto 181 F 3
Min Jiang 132 D 5
Min Jiang 133 G 5
Minle 132 D 3
Minna 157 F 4
Minnahassa Peninsula 137 F 1
Minneapolis (KS, U.S.A.) 170 G 4
Minneapolis (MN, U.S.A.) 171 H 3
Minnedosa 167 S 5
Minnesota 171 GH 2
Minnesota River 171 G 2
Minot 170 F 2
Minqin 132 D 3
Minqing 133 G 5
Min Shan 132 D 4
Minsin 135 G 2
Minsk 111 J 5
Minskaya Vozvyshennost' 113 J 5
Mińsk Mazowiecki 111 H 4
Minster 103 C 2
Minta 157 G 5
Minto (U.S.A.) 166 K 3
Minto (Oceania) 146 M 4
Minto Inlet 167 O 1
Minto, Lac 169 N 4
Minūdasht 128 F 3
Minusinsk 130 F 5
Minvoul 157 G 5
Minwakh 155 H 5
Min Xian 132 D 4
Miquan 129 M 2
Miquelon 169 Q 6
Miquelon 169 M 6
Miquelon et Saint Pierre 169 Q 6
Mir 157 G 3
Mira 115 F 2
Mirabad 129 G 4
Mirador 181 H 2
Miraflores 178 D 3
Miraj 134 B 4
Miramar 183 E 6
Mirambeau 114 C 2
Miramichi Bay 169 P 6
Miramont-de-Guyenne 114 D 3
Miran 129 M 3
Miranda 180 E 5
Miranda de Ebro 114 C 3
Mirandela 114 B 3
Mirandola 115 F 3
Mirapinima 179 F 4
Miravalles, Volcán 172 E 5
Miravete, Puerto de 114 B 4
Mirbāṭ 155 J 5
Mirdita 116 B 2
Mirgorod 118 F 6
Miri 136 D 3
Miriam Vale 143 J 3
Mirim, Lagoa 182 F 5
Mirina 116 C 3
Mirnoye 119 R 3
Mirnyy 130 K 3

Mirnyy 185
Mirpur 129 J 4
Mirpur Khas 129 G 5
Mirria 157 F 3
Mīrsāle 159 H 3
Mirsali 129 M 2
Mirtna 143 H 3
Mirtóon Pélagos 116 B 3
Mirzapur 134 D 2
Miósandur 112 A 3
Misgar 129 J 3
Mishan 133 K 1
Mishkino 118 L 4
Misima 145 F 4
Misima Island 143 J 1
Misión Cavinas 180 C 3
Miskah 155 G 4
Miskitos, Cayos 172 F 5
Miskolc 116 B 1
Mismār 129 M 2
Misoöl, Pulau 137 H 4
Misquah Hills 171 H 2
Misr → Al Mukhā 155 G 6
Miṣrātah 153 HJ 2
Miṣrātah, Ra's 153 J 2
Missinaibi 168 L 5
Missinipe 167 R 4
Missisa Lake 168 K 5
Mississippi 171 J 5
Mississippi Delta 171 J 6
Mississippi River 171 H 5
Missoula 170 D 2
Missour 152 E 2
Missouri 171 H 4
Missouri River 171 H 4
Mistassini, Lac 169 N 5
Misti, Volcán 180 B 4
Misty Fjords National Monument 166 L 4
Mitchell (U.S.A.) 170 G 3
Mitchell (Australia) 143 H 4
Mitchell, Mount 171 K 4
Mitchell River (Queensland, Austr.) 143 G 2
Mitchell River (Victoria, Austr.) 143 H 6
Miteja 159 F 6
Mithimna 116 C 3
Mitiaro 147 E 4
Mitilini 116 C 3
Mitina 118 J 2
Mitla 172 C 4
Mito 133 M 3
Mitomoni 161 F 2
Mitra 157 F 5
Mitsinjo 161 H 3
Mittersill 115 F 2
Mitú 178 D 3
Mitumba 158 D 6
Mitumba, Monts 158 D 5–6
Mitwaba 158 D 6
Mityayevo 119 MN 3
Mitzic 157 G 5
Mius 117 E 1
Mivec 152 C 4
Miyake-jima 133 L 4
Miyako 133 M 3
Miyako-jima 133 J 6
Miyakonojō 133 K 4
Miyako-rettō 133 J 6
Miyaly 128 E 1
Miyazaki 133 K 4
Miyi 132 D 5
Miyun 133 G 2
Mizan Teferi 158 F 3
Mizdah 153 H 2
Mizen Head 110 B 4
Mizhi 132 F 3
Mizil 116 C 2
Mizque 180 C 4
Mizoram 135 F 3
Mizusawa 133 M 3
Mizuho 185
Mjölby 113 G 4
Mjöndalen 113 F 4
Mjösa 113 F 3
Mkangira 159 F 6
Mkasu 159 F 6
Mkata 159 F 6
Mkoani 159 F 6
Mkokotoni 159 F 6
Mkomazi 159 F 5
Mkomazi Game Reserve 159 F 5
Mkuku 160 D 4
Mkulwe 158 E 6
Mkushi 160 D 2
Mladá Boleslav 111 F 4
Mladenovac 116 B 2
Mlala Hills 158 E 6
Mława 111 H 4
Mleihas 152 D 4
Mleti 117 F 2
Mljet 115 G 3

Mljetski kanal 115 G 3
Mmadinare 160 D 4
Mmbatho (Mafeking) 160 D 5
Moa 156 B 4
Moab 170 E 4
Moabi 157 G 6
Moamba 161 E 5
Moanda (Gabon) 157 G 6
Moanda (Zaire) 157 G 7
Moate 100 B 3
Moatize 161 E 3
Moba 158 D 6
Mobaye 158 C 4
Mobayi-Mbongo 158 C 4
Mobeka 158 B 4
Moberly 171 H 4
Mobile 171 J 5
Mobile Bay 171 J 5
Mobridge 170 F 2
Mocajuba 179 J 4
Moçambique 161 G 3
Moçambique Basin 192 B 5
Mocha → Al Mukhā 155 G 6
Mocha, Isla 183 B 6
Mochudi 160 D 4
Mocímboa da Praia 161 G 2
Mockfjärd 113 F 3
Mocoa 178 C 3
Mococa 181 G 5
Môco, Morro de 160 B 2
Moctezuma 172 B 3
Moctezuma 170 E 6
Mocuba 161 F 3
Modane 115 E 2
Model Town 129 J 4
Modena (Italy) 115 F 3
Modena (U.S.A.) 170 D 4
Modesto 170 B 4
Modica 115 F 4
Modjamboli 158 C 4
Mödling 115 G 2
Modowi 137 H 4
Modra 157 H 1
Modriča 115 G 3
Modur Dāği 117 F 3
Moe 143 H 6
Moelv 112 F 3
Moengo 179 H 2
Moero, Lac 158 D 6
Moffat 99 C 4
Moga 128 D 5
Mogadiscio → Muqdisho 159 H 4
Mogadishu 159 H 4
Mogadouro, Serra do 114 B 3
Mogaung 135 G 2
Mogdy 131 O 5
Mogi das Cruzes 181 G 5
Mogilev 113 K 5
Mogilev Podol'skiy 116 C 1
Mogil-Mogil 143 H 4
Mogi-Mirim 181 G 5
Mogincual 161 G 3
Mogocha 130 LM 5
Mogochin 119 Q 4
Mogogh 158 E 3
Mogok 135 G 3
Mogotoyevo, Ozero 131 R 1
Mogoyn 130 G 6
Mogocha 130 K 5
Mogu 159 G 4
Moguqi 131 M 6
Mogzon 130 K 5
Mohács 116 A 1
Mohall 170 F 2
Mohammedia 152 D 2
Mohe 131 M 5
Moheda 113 F 4
Moheli 161 G 2
Mohenjo Daro 129 H 5
Mohnyin 135 G 3
Mohon Peak 170 D 5
Mohoro 159 F 6
Moidart 99 B 3
Mointy 119 O 6
Mo i Rana 112 F 2
Moisie 169 O 5
Moissac 114 D 3
Moïssala 157 H 4
Moitaco 179 F 2
Mojácar 114 C 4
Mojave 170 C 4
Mojave Desert 170 C 4
Mojiang 132 D 6
Mojo 159 G 4
Moju 179 J 4
Mokambo 160 D 2
Mokhotlong 160 D 5
Mokhovaya 131 T 5
Mokil 146 B 2
Moklakan 130 L 5
Mokokchung 135 F 2

256

Mokolo 157 G 3
Mokp'o 133 J 4
Mokra Gora 116 B 2
Mokwa 157 E 4
Mol 110 E 4
Mola di Bari 115 G 3
Molagno 172 C 3
Molat 115 F 3
Molchanovo 119 Q 4
Mold 102 C 1
Moldau 111 F 4
Moldava 116 C 1
Moldaviya 116 C 1
Molde 112 E 3
Moldefjorden 112 E 3
Moldes 182 D 5
Moldova Nouă 116 B 2
Mole Game Reserve 156 D 4
Molegbe 158 C 4
Moleke 158 B 5
Molepolole 160 D 4
Molfetta 115 G 3
Molina (Argentina) 182 C 5
Molina (Chile) 183 B 6
Molina de Aragón 114 C 3
Molina de Segura 114 C 4
Moline 171 H 3
Moling 135 F 2
Moliro 158 E 6
Molkom 113 F 4
Mollendo 180 B 4
Molloy, Mount 143 H 2
Mölndal 113 F 4
Molochansk 117 E 1
Molochnyy Liman 117 E 1
Molodechno 113 J 5
Molodezhnaya 185
Molodo 130 M 2
Molodogvardeyskaya 119 O 5
Molokai 147 E 1
Molokai Fracture Zone 193 D 2
Molong 143 H 5
Molopo 160 C 5
Molotovo 117 F 2
Moloundou 157 H 5
Molteno 160 D 6
Moluccas 137 G 4
Molus Ridge 192 A 1
Moma (U.S.S.R.) 131 Q 2
Moma (Mozambique) 161 F 3
Mombaça 181 J 2
Mombasa 159 F 5
Mombetsu 133 M 2
Mombi New 135 F 3
Mombo 159 F 5
Mombotuta Falls 160 D 2
Momboyo 158 B 5
Momi 158 D 5
Mompono 158 C 4
Mompós 178 C 2
Momskiy Khrebet 131 QR 2
Mon 135 G 4–5
Mön 113 F 5
Mona, Canal de la 173 J 4
Monach Isles 98 A 3
Monaco 115 E 3
Monadhliath Mountains 110 C 3
Monaghan 100 C 3
Monahans 170 F 5
Mona, Isla 173 J 4
Monapo 161 G 2
Mona Quimbundo 160 B 1
Monarch Mountain 167 M 5
Monashee Mountains 167 O 5
Monasterevin 100 B 3
Monastery of Saint Catherine 154 E 3
Monatélé 157 G 5
Moncalieri 115 E 2
Moncayo, Sierra del 114 C 3
Monchegorsk 112 K 2
Mönchen-Gladbach 110 D E 4
Monclova 172 B 2
Moncton 169 P 6
Mondego 114 B 3
Mondego, Cabo 114 B 3
Mondjuko 158 C 5
Mondo 135 H 3
Mondoñedo 114 B 3
Mondovi 115 E 3
Mondragone 115 F 3
Mondy 130 H J 5
Money 135 K 4
Moneymore 100 B 2
Monfalcone 115 F 2
Monforte 114 B 4
Monga 158 C 4
Mongala 158 C 4
Mongalla 158 E 3
Mongbwalu 158 D 4
Mong Cai 135 J 3
Monger, Lake 142 B 4
Mong Hang 135 G 3

Mong Hpayak 135 G 3
Monghyr 134 E 2
Mong Lin 135 H 3
Mong Loi 135 H 3
Mong Nai 135 G 3
Mongo (Sierra Leone) 156 B 4
Mongo (Chad) 157 H 3
Mongol Ard Uls 130 G 3–6
Mongolia 130 G 3–6
Mongolo 130 J 2
Mongono 157 G 5
Mongonu 157 G 3
Mongororo 157 J 3
Mongu 160 C 3
Môngua 160 B 3
Monguel 152 C 5
Mong Yai 135 G 3
Mönhhaan 132 F 1
Monichkirchen 115 G 2
Monifieth Newport-on-Tay 99 C 3
Monigotes 182 D 5
Monjes, Islas los 178 D 1
Monkey Bay 161 E 2
Monkey River 172 E 4
Monkira 143 G 3
Monkoto 158 C 5
Monmouth 102 C 2
Mono (Togo) 156 E 4
Mono (Solomon Islands) 145 G 2
Mono Lake 170 C 4
Monolithos 116 C 3
Monong 160 C 4
Monopoli 115 G 3
Monor 116 A 1
Monou 157 J 2
Monreal del Campo 114 C 3
Monreale 115 F 4
Monroe (LA, U.S.A.) 171 H 5
Monroe (MI, U.S.A.) 171 K 3
Monroe (N.C., U.S.A.) 171 K 5
Monrovia 156 B 4
Mons 110 D 4
Monsanto 114 B 3
Monse 137 F 4
Monsefú 178 C 5
Möns Klint 113 F 5
Mönsterås 113 G 4
Mont Afao 153 G 3
Montagne d'Ambre 161 H 2
Montagne de Lure 115 E 3
Montagne Noire 114 D 3
Montagne Pelée 173 K 5
Montagnes d'Arrée 114 C 2
Montague 166 H 4
Montague, Isla 170 D 5
Mont Aigoual 114 D 3
Mont Ajir 157 F 2
Montalbán 114 C 3
Montalegre 114 B 3
Montana 170 D 2
Montargis 114 D 2
Montauban 114 D 3
Montauban 114 C 2
Mont aux Sources 160 D 5
Montbard 115 D 2
Montbéliard 115 E 2
Mont Blanc 115 E 2
Montbrison 114 D 2
Mont Cameroun 157 F 5
Montceau-les-Mines 114 D 2
Mont de Ganga 157 G 4
Mont Deingueri 158 D 3
Mont-de-Marsan 114 C 3
Mont du Guéra 157 H 3
Mont du Metal 153 G 4
Monte Alban 172 C 4
Monte Alegre 179 H 4
Monte Amiata 115 F 3
Monte Azul 181 H 4
Monte Bello Islands 142 AB 3
Monte Binga 161 E 3
Monte Carlo 115 E 3
Monte Carmelo 181 G 4
Monte Caseros 182 E 5
Montech 114 D 3
Monte Cinto 115 E 3
Monte Claros 181 H 4
Monte Comán 182 C 5
Montecristi 173 H 4
Monte Cristo 180 D 3
Montecristo 115 E 3
Monte d'Oro 115 E 3
Monte Dourado 179 H 4
Monte Fitz Roy 183 B 8
Montego Bay 173 G 4
Monte Ei Loutone 157 G 1
Montejinnie 142 E 2
Montelimar 115 D 3
Monte Lindo 180 E 4
Monte Maca 183 B 8
Monte Melimoyo 183 B 7
Montemoreios 172 C 2
Montemor-o-Novo 114 B 4

Montenegro 182 F 4
Monte Negro Falls 160 A 3
Monte Pascoal, Parque Nacional de 181 J 4
Montepuez 161 F 2
Montepulciano 115 F 3
Monte Quemado 182 D 4
Monterado 136 C 3
Monterey 170 B 4
Monterey Bay 170 B 4
Monteria 178 C 2
Montero 180 D 4
Monte Rosa 115 E 2
Monterotondo 115 F 3
Monterrey 172 B 2
Montes Altos 179 J 5
Monte Santo 179 J 5
Monte Sarmiento 183 B 9
Montesilvano 115 F 3
Montes de Leon 114 B 3
Montes de Toledo 114 C 4
Montes Universales 114 C 3
Montes Vascos 114 C 3
Monte Tronador 183 B 7
Montevarchi 115 F 3
Montevideo 182 E 5
Monte Zeballos 183 B 8
Montgomery 171 J 5
Montgomery 102 C 1
Mont Gréboun 157 F 1–2
Monthey 115 E 2
Monti Aurunci 115 F 3
Monti Beatini 115 F 3
Mont Iboundji 157 G 6
Monticello 170 E 4
Monti dei Frentani 115 F 3
Monti di Ala 115 E 3
Montiel, Campo de 114 C 4
Montigny-le-Roi 115 E 2
Montigny-les-Metz 115 E 2
Monti Iblei 115 F 3
Montijo, Golfo de 173 F 6
Monti Lepini 115 F 3
Montilla 114 C 4
Monti Peloritani 114 B 3
Monti Sabini 115 F 3
Monti Sicani 115 F 4
Monti Volsini 115 F 3
Mont Jacques-Cartier 169 O 6
Mont Joli 169 O 6
Mont Kavendou 156 B 3
Mont-Louis 114 C 2
Mont Lozére 114 D 3
Montluçon 114 D 2
Montmagny 169 N 6
Mont Mézenc 114 D 3
Mont Mina 156 C 3
Mont Mpelé 157 G 6
Mont Ngoua 158 C 3
Mont Niéndkoué 156 C 4
Monto 143 J 3
Montorïeda 114 B 3
Montoro 114 C 3
Mont Panié 145 H 6
Mont Pelat 115 E 3
Montpelier (ID, U.S.A.) 170 D 3
Montpelier (VT, U.S.A.) 171 M 3
Montpéllier 114 D 3
Mont Pinçon 114 C 2
Montréal 171 M 2
Montreal Lake 167 Q 5
Montréjeau 114 D 3
Montreux 115 E 2
Montrose (U.S.A.) 170 E 4
Montrose (U.K.) 99 C 3
Montsalvy 114 D 3
Montsant, Sierra de 114 D 3
Monts Bagzane 153 G 5
Monts Bambouto 157 G 4
Monts Bleus 158 E 4
Monts Chic-Chocs 169 O 6
Monts d'Amain 114 D 2
Monts d'Arrée 114 C 2
Monts d'Aubrac 114 D 3
Monts de Cristal 157 G 5
Monts de la Medjerda 153 G 1
Monts de Lacaune 114 D 3
Monts des Ksour (Algeria) 152 EF 2
Monts des Ksour (Tunisia) 153 GH 2
Monts des Oulad Naïl 153 F 2
Monts de Toura 156 C 4
Monts Dome 114 D 2
Monts Dore 114 D 2
Monts du Beaujolais 115 D 2
Monts du Hodna 153 F 1
Monts du Hombori 156 D 2
Monts du Livradois 115 D 2
Monts du Lyonnais 115 D 2
Montseck, Sierra del 114 D 3
Montseny, Sierra de 114 D 3
Montserrat 173 K 4

Monts Koungou 157 G 6
Monts Kundelungu 158 D 6
Monts Malimba 158 D 6
Monts Mandingues 156 B 3
Monts Marungu 158 D 6
Monts Mbang 157 G 4
Monts Mitumba 158 D 5–6
Monts Moukandé 157 G 6
Monts Mugila 158 D 6
Monts Nimba 156 C 4
Monts Notre-Dame 169 N 6
Monts Otish 169 N 5
Monts Tamgak 157 F 2
Monts Tarouadji 157 F 2
Monts Timétrine 156 DE 2
Mont Tahat 153 G 4
Mont Tembo 157 G 5
Mont Tonkou 156 C 4
Mont Ventoux 115 E 3
Mont Zedness 152 C 4
Monveda 158 C 4
Monviso 115 E 3
Mon Yul 135 F 2
Monywa 135 G 3
Monza 115 E 2
Monze 160 D 3
Monzón 114 D 3
Moonie 143 J 4
Moonie River 143 H 4
Moonta 143 F 5
Moora 142 B 5
Mooraberree 143 G 4
Moorea 147 EF 4
Moore, Lake 142 B 4
Moorfoot Hills 99 C 4
Moorhead 171 G 2
Moorlands 143 F 6
Moor of Rannoch 99 B 3
Moor of Rannoch 110 BC 3
Moorreesburg 160 B 6
Moose 169 L 5
Moose Jaw 167 Q 5
Moose Pass 166 H 3
Moosehead Lake 171 N 2
Moosomin 167 R 5
Moosonee 169 L 5
Mopeia 161 F 3
Mopipi 160 CD 4
Mopti 156 D 3
Moqokorei 159 H 4
Moquegua 180 B 4
Mora (Cameroon) 157 G 3
Mora (Spain) 114 C 4
Mora (Sweden) 113 F 3
Moraca 116 A 2
Moradabad 134 C 2
Mora de Ebro 114 D 3
Morado, Cerro 180 D 5
Morafenobe 161 G 3
Moraleda, Canal 183 B 7
Moraleya 114 B 3
Moramanga 161 H 3
Moran 170 D 3
Morane 147 F 4
Morant Cays 173 G 4
Morar, Loch 99 B 3
Morata, Puerto de 114 C 3
Moratuwa 134 C 6
Morava 142 B 4
Morava (Czechoslov.) 111 G 5
Morava (Yugoslavia) 116 B 2
Moravia 111 G 5
Moraviţa 116 B 1
Morawhanna 179 G 2
Moray 143 H 4
Moray Firth 110 C 3
Moray Firth 98 C 3
Morbi 134 B 3
Morcenx 114 C 3
Mordaga 130 M 5
Morden 167 S 6
Mordovo 118 H 5
Möre 113 G 4
Morecambe 101 D 2
Morecambe Bay 101 D 2
Moree 143 H 4
Morehead 144 D 3
Morehead City 171 L 5
Moreira 179 F 4
More-Iz, Gora 119 M 2
More Laptevykh 130 L 1–O 1
Morelia 172 B 4
Morelos 172 B 4
Morena 134 C 2
Morena, Sierra 114 BC 4
Morenci 170 E 5
Moreni 116 C 2
Moreno (Argentina) 183 B 6
Moreno (Peru) 178 C 5
Moreno National Park 183 B 8
Moreno, Parque Nacional 183 B 8
Möre og Romsdal 112 F 3
Moresby 166 L 5
Moreton 143 G 1

Moreton Island 143 J 4
Morgan 143 F 5
Morgan City 171 H 6
Morgan Mount 143 J 3
Morganton 171 K 4
Morges 115 E 2
Mori (China) 129 N 2
Mori (Japan) 133 M 2
Moriarty 170 E 4
Morichal 178 D 3
Moriki 157 F 3
Morin Dawa 131 M 6
Morioka 133 M 3
Morjärv 112 H 2
Morkoka 130 K 2
Morlaix 114 C 2
Morley 101 E 3
Mormanno 115 G 4
Morne Diablotin 173 K 4
Mornington Abyssal Plain 193 D 5
Mornington, Isla 183 A 8
Mornington Island 143 F 2
Morno 156 D 4
Mornou, Hadjer 157 J 2
Moro 156 D 4
Morobe 144 E 3
Morocco 152 D 2
Moroga 118 E 3
Morogoro 159 F 6
Moro Gulf 137 F 2
Moroleón 172 B 3
Morombe 161 G 4
Morón 173 G 3
Mörön 130 H 6
Morón 178 E 1
Morona 178 C 4
Morondava 161 G 4
Morón de la Frontera 114 B 4
Morondo 156 C 4
Moroni 161 G 2
Moroshechnoye 131 T 4
Morotai, Pulau 137 G 3
Morotai, Selat 137 G 3
Moroto 158 E 4
Moroto, Mount 158 E 4
Morozov 116 C 2
Morozovsk 117 F 1
Morpará 181 H 3
Morpeth 101 E 2
Morphou → Güzelyurt 117 D 3
Morrinhas 181 H 1
Morrinhos 181 G 4
Morris 167 S 6
Morristown 171 K 4
Morro de Chapéu 181 H 3
Morro de Môco 160 B 2
Morro do Sinal 181 E 3
Morro, Punta 182 B 4
Mörrum 113 F 4
Morrumbala 161 F 3
Morrumbene 161 F 4
Mörrumsån 113 F 4
Mors 113 E 4
Morshansk 118 H 5
Mörsil 112 F 3
Morskaya 131 X 3
Mortagne-sur-Sèvre 114 C 2
Mortain 114 C 2
Morteros 182 D 5
Mortesoro 154 E 6
Mortlake 143 G 6
Mortlock Islands 146 B 2
Moruya 143 J 6
Morven 143 H 4
Morvern 99 B 3
Morwell 143 H 6
Moryakovskiy Zaton 119 Q 4
Morzelândia 181 F 3
Mosby 113 E 4
Moscow (U.S.S.R.) 118 G 4
Moscow (ID, U.S.A.) 170 C 2
Mosel 110 E 5
Moselle 115 E 2
Moses Lake 170 C 2
Moses Point 166 E 3
Moseyevo 118 H 2
Mosgiel 144 Q 10
Moshchnyy, Ostrov 113 J 4
Moshi 159 F 5
Mosina 111 G 4
Mosjøen 112 F 2
Moskal'vo 131 Q 5
Moskenesöya 112 F 2
Moskosel 112 G 2
Moskva 118 G 4
Moskva, Gora 130 F 5
Moslavačka Gora 115 G 2
Mosomane 160 D 4
Mosonmagyaróvár 116 A 1
Mosquera 178 C 3
Mosquito, Baie 169 M 3
Mosquitos, Costa de 172 F 5
Mosquitos, Golfo de los 178 B 2

257

Mos–Mun

Moss 113 F 4
Mossaka 157 H 6
Mosselbaai 160 C 6
Mossendjo 157 G 6
Mossoró 181 J 2
Mossuril 161 G 2
Most 111 F 4
Mostaganem 152 EF 1
Mostar 115 G 3
Mostardas 182 F 5
Mostrim 100 B 3
Mosty 113 H 5
Mostyn 137 E 3
Mosul 155 G 1
Mösvatn 113 E 4
Mota 159 F 2
Motaba 157 H 5
Motajica 115 G 2
Motala 115 G 4
Motherwell 99 C 4
Motihari 134 D 2
Motilla del Palancar 114 C 4
Motovskiy Zaliv 112 K 2
Motril 114 C 4
Motru 116 B 2
Motueka 145 Q 9
Motul 172 E 3
Motu One 147 E 4
Mututunga 147 F 4
Motykleyka 131 R 4
Mouchard 115 E 2
Moudjéria 152 C 5
Mouila (Gabon) 157 G 6
Mouila (Algeria) 152 E 3
Mouka 158 C 3
Moukandé, Monts 157 G 6
Moul 157 G 2
Moulhoulé 159 G 2
Moulins 114 D 2
Moulmein 135 G 4
Moulouya 152 E 2
Moultrie 171 K 5
Moultrie, Lake 171 K 5
Moundou 157 H 4
Mount Adam 183 E 9
Mountain Ash 102 C 2
Mountain Grove 171 H 4
Mountain Home 170 C 3
Mountains of Connemara 110 B 4
Mountains of Mayo 110 B 4
Mountain Village 166 E 3
Mount Airy 171 K 4
Mount Anglem 144 P 10
Mount Apo 137 G 2
Mount Ararat 117 F 3
Mount Arrowsmith 145 Q 9
Mount Aspiring 144 P 9
Mount Assiniboine 167 O 5
Mount Augustus 142 B 3
Mount Balbi 145 F 3
Mount Bangeta 144 E 3
Mount Barker 142 B 5
Mount Bimberi 143 H 6
Mount Blackburn 166 J 3
Mount Bona 166 J 3
Mount Brassey 142 E 3
Mount Brockman 142 B 3
Mount Broome 142 D 2
Mount Bruce 142 B 3
Mount Brukkaros 160 B 5
Mount Carter 143 G 1
Mount Casuarina 142 D 1
Mount Catherine 170 D 4
Mount Christie 142 E 5
Mount Clark 167 N 3
Mount Clere 142 B 4
Mount Cleveland 170 D 2
Mount Columbia 167 O 5
Mount Connor 142 D 1
Mount Cook 145 Q 9
Mount Coolon 143 H 3
Mount Curious 142 A 4
Mount Cushing 167 M 4
Mount Dalrymple 143 H 3
Mount Darwin 161 E 3
Mount Davies 142 D 4
Mount Davis 171 L 4
Mount Deering 142 D 3
Mount Demavend 128 E 3
Mount Denison 166 G 4
Mount Doonerak 166 G 2
Mount Douglas 143 H 3
Mount Eba 143 F 5
Mount Eduni 166 M 3
Mount Egerton 142 B 3
Mount Egmont 145 Q 8
Mount Elbert 170 E 4
Mount Elgon 158 E 4
Mount Elizabeth 142 D 2
Mount Elliot 143 H 2
Mount Essendon 142 C 3
Mount Everest 134 E 2
Mount Fairweather 166 K 4

Mount Feathertop 143 H 6
Mount Finke 142 E 5
Mount Foraker 166 G 3
Mount Forel 184
Mount Forest 171 K 3
Mount Foster 166 K 4
Mount Fraser 142 B 4
Mount Frere 160 D 6
Mount Gambier 143 F 6
Mount Gimie 173 K 5
Mount Glottof 166 G 4
Mount Godwin Austin 129 K 3
Mount Gould 142 B 4
Mount Hagen 144 D 3
Mount Halcon 137 F 1
Mount Hale 142 B 4
Mount Halifax 143 H 2
Mount Harper 166 J 3
Mount Hayes 166 H 3
Mount Haywood 167 N 3
Mount Hillaby 179 G 1
Mount Hood 170 B 2
Mount Hope 143 F 5
Mount House 142 D 2
Mount Hutton 143 H 4
Mount Isa 143 F 3
Mount Isto 166 J 2
Mount Jackson 142 B 5
Mount Jackson 185
Mount Jefferson (NV, U.S.A.) 170 C 4
Mount Jefferson (OR, U.S.A.) 170 B 3
Mount John 142 D 2
Mount Kasigao 159 F 5
Mount Katmai 166 G 4
Mount Kenya 159 F 5
Mount Kenya National Park 159 F 5
Mount Kimball 166 J 3
Mount Kirkpatrick 185
Mount Klotz 166 JK 3
Mount Kosciusko 143 H 6
Mount Leake 142 D 2
Mount Leisler 142 D 3
Mount Lemmon 170 D 5
Mount Lesueur 142 B 5
Mount Liebig 142 E 3
Mount Livermore 170 F 5
Mount Lofty Ranges 143 F 6
Mount Logan 166 J 3
Mount Lucania 166 J 3
Mount Lush 142 D 2
Mount Magnet 142 B 4
Mount Maiyu 142 D 2
Mount Makalu 134 E 2
Mount Mantalingajan 136 E 2
Mount Marcus Baker 166 H 3
Mount McKinley 166 G 3
Mount McLoughlin 170 B 3
Mountmellick 100 B 3
Mount Menzies 185
Mount Michelson 166 H 2
Mount Mitchell 171 K 4
Mount Molloy 143 H 2
Mount Morgan 143 J 3
Mount Moroto 158 E 4
Mount Mowbullan 143 J 4
Mount Murchison 142 B 4
Mount Nurri 143 H 5
Mount Nyiru 159 F 4
Mount Oglethorpe 171 K 5
Mount Olga 142 E 4
Mount Olympos → Kato Olimbos 116 B 3
Mount Olympus 170 B 2
Mount Omatako 160 B 4
Mount Ord 142 D 2
Mount Ossa 144 L 9
Mount Owen 145 Q 9
Mount Palomar 170 C 5
Mount Pattullo 166 M 4
Mount Pinos 170 C 5
Mount Pleasant (MI, U.S.A.) 171 K 3
Mount Pleasant (UT, U.S.A.) 170 D 4
Mount Pulog 137 J 1
Mount Queen Bess 167 N 5
Mount Ragang 137 F 2
Mount Rainier 170 B 2
Mount Rainier National Park 170 B 2
Mountrath 100 B 3
Mount Ratz 166 L 4
Mount Redcliffe 142 C 4
Mount Richthofen 170 E 3
Mount Ritter 170 C 4
Mount Robe 143 G 5
Mount Roberts 143 J 4
Mount Robson 167 O 5
Mount Roosevelt 167 M 4
Mount Saint Elias 166 J 3

Mount Saint Helens 170 B 2
Mount Samuel 142 E 2
Mount Sandiman 142 B 3
Mount Sanford 166 J 3
Mount Shasta 170 B 3
Mount Shenton 142 C 4
Mount Singleton 142 B 4
Mount Sir Alexander 167 N 5
Mount Sir James MacBrian 166 M 3
Mount Sir Thomas 142 D 4
Mount Smythe 167 N 4
Mount Springer 169 N 6
Mount Squires 142 D 4
Mount Sulen 144 D 2
Mount Sunflower 170 F 4
Mount Tama 160 A 2
Mount Taylor 170 E 4
Mount Tenabo 170 C 3
Mount Thuillier 135 F 6
Mount Tipton 170 D 4
Mount Tom White 166 J 3
Mount Torbert 166 G 3
Mount Travers 145 Q 9
Mount Trumbull 170 D 4
Mount Usborne 183 E 9
Mount Veniaminof 166 F 4
Mount Vernon (Australia) 142 B 3
Mount Vernon (IL, U.S.A.) 171 J 4
Mount Vernon (KY, U.S.A.) 171 K 4
Mount Vernon (OH, U.S.A.) 171 K 3
Mount Victoria (Papua New Guinea) 144 E 3
Mount Victoria (Burma) 135 F 3
Mount Vsevidof 166 D 5
Mount Waddington 167 M 5
Mount Washington 171 M 3
Mount Whitney 170 C 4
Mount Wilhelm 144 D 3
Mount Willoughby 142 E 4
Mount Wilson 170 E 4
Mount Woodroffe 142 E 4
Mount Wrightson 170 D 5
Mount Ziel 142 E 3
Mourão 114 B 4
Moura 179 F 4
Mourdiah 156 C 3
Mourdi, Dépression du 157 J 2
Mourenx 114 C 3
Mournei 154 C 6
Mourne Mountains 100 B 2
Mourra 157 J 3
Mousaaou Salah, Jbel 152 E 2
Mouscron 114 D 3
Moussoro 157 H 3
Mouths of the Amazon 179 J 3
Mouths of the Danube 116 C 1
Mouths of the Ganges 134–135 EF 3
Mouths of the Godavari 134 D 4
Mouths of the Indus 129 H 6
Mouths of the Irrawaddy 135 F 4
Mouths of the Krishna 134 D 4
Mouths of the Mekong 135 J 6
Mouths of the Orinoco 179 FG 2
Moûtiers 115 E 2
Moutong 137 F 3
Mouydir 153 F 4
Mouyondzi 157 G 6
Movas 170 E 6
Moville 100 B 2
Mowbullan, Mount 143 J 4
Möwe Bay 160 A 3
Moxico 160 BC 2
Moxos, Llanos de 180 CD 4
Moyahua 172 B 3
Moyale 159 F 4
Moyamba 156 B 4
Moyen Atlas 152 DE 2
Moyeni 160 D 5
Moyero 130 N 2
Moyobamba 178 C 5
Moyowosi 158 E 5
Moyto 157 H 3
Moyu 129 K 3
Mozambique 161 E 4–F 2
Mozambique Channel 161 FG 3–4
Mozdok 117 F 2
Mozharka 130 F 5
Mozhga 118 K 4
Mozyr' 113 J 5
Mpala 158 D 6
Mpanda 158 E 6
Mpé 157 G 6
Mpelé, Mont 157 G 6
Mpika 161 E 2
Mpoko 158 B 3
Mporokosa 160 DE 1
Mpouya 157 H 6

Mpui 158 E 6
Mpulungu 161 E 1
Mpwapwa 159 F 6
Mrakovo 118 L 5
Mragowa 111 H 4
Mrewa 161 E 3
Msâk Mallat 153 H 3–5
Msâk Mastâfat 153 H 3
Msata 159 F 6
M'Sila 153 F 1
Msoro 161 E 2
Mstislavl' 118 F 5
Mtabatuba 161 E 5
Mtakuja 158 E 6
Mtama 161 F 2
Mtandi 159 F 6
Mtegere 159 F 6
Mtera 159 F 5
Mtito Andei 159 F 5
Mtoko 161 E 3
Mtsensk 118 G 5
Mtskheta 117 F 2
Mtwara 161 G 2
Mualang 130 D 3
Muanã 179 J 4
Muang 135 H 5
Muang Loei 135 H 4
Muang Long 135 G 4
Muang Moc 135 H 4
Muang Nan 135 H 4
Muang Ngao 135 G 4
Muang Oi 135 H 4
Muang Phayao 135 G 4
Muang Phichit 135 H 4
Muang Phrae 135 H 4
Muang Thoen 135 G 4
Muanza 161 EF 3
Muar 136 B 3
Muara 136 E 2
Muaraaman 136 B 4
Muarabenangin 136 E 4
Muarabungo 136 B 4
Muaraenim 136 B 4
Muaramawai 136 E 3
Muarapangean 136 E 3
Muarapayang 136 E 3
Muara Sekatak 136 E 3
Muarasiberut 136 A 4
Muaratebo 136 B 4
Muarateweh 136 D 4
Muarawahau 136 E 3
Muari, Ras 129 H 6
Muaro 136 B 4
Mubende 158 E 4
Mubi 159 G 3
Mucajaí 179 F 3
Muchinga Escarpment 161 E 2
Muck 99 A 3
Muckle Roe 98 D 1
Mucojo 161 G 2
Muconda 160 C 2
Mucubela 161 F 3
Mucur 117 D 3
Mucura 179 F 4
Mucuri 181 H 4
Mucurici 181 H 4
Mucusso 160 C 3
Muda 161 E 3
Mudanjiang 133 J 2
Mudan Jiang 133 J 1
Mudanya 116 C 2
Muddy Gap 170 E 3
Mudhol 134 C 4
Mudon 135 G 4
Mudug 159 H 3
Mudurnu 116 D 2
Muecate 161 F 2
Mueda 161 F 2
Mufulira 160 D 2
Mufu Shan 132 F 5
Muganskaya Step' 128 D 3
Mugatta 154 F 6
Mugila, Monts 158 D 6
Muğla 116 C 3
Mugodzhary 128 F 1
Muhagiriya 154 D 6
Muhammadgarh 134 C 3
Muhammad Qawl 154 F 4
Muhammad, Ra's 154 E 3
Muhesi 158 E 6
Mühlhausen 111 F 4
Mühlig-Hofmann Mountains 185
Muhos 112 J 3
Muhu 112 H 4
Muhulu 158 D 5
Muhuwesi 161 F 2
Mui Bai Bung 135 H 6
Muié 160 C 2
Muine Bheag 100 B 3
Muir of Ord 98 B 3
Muiron Islands 142 A 3

Muite 161 F 2
Mujimbeji 160 C 2
Mukachevo 116 B 1
Mukah 136 D 3
Mukdahan 135 H 4
Mukden → Shenyang 133 H 2
Mukhino 131 N 5
Mukho 133 J 3
Mukhomornoye 131 W 2
Mukhor-Shibir' 130 J 5
Mukinbudin 142 B 5
Mukoba 158 C 6
Mukomuko 136 B 4
Muktinath 134 D 2
Mukur (Afghanistan) 129 H 4
Mukur (U.S.S.R.) 128 E 1
Mukwe 160 C 3
Mula 114 C 4
Mulainagiri 134 C 5
Mulaly 119 P 6
Mulan 133 J 1
Mulanje 161 F 3
Mulata 159 G 3
Mulchatna 166 F 3
Mulchén 183 B 6
Mulde 111 F 4
Mulegé 170 D 6
Mulegé, Sierra de 170 D 6
Mulenda 158 C 5
Mulevala 161 F 3
Mulga Park 142 E 4
Mulgrave Island 144 D 4
Mulhacén 114 C 4
Mülheim 111 E 5
Mulhouse 115 E 2
Muli 132 D 5
Muling 133 K 2
Muling He 133 K 1
Mull 99 A 3
Mullaittivu 134 D 6
Mullaley 143 H 5
Muller, Pegunungan 136 D 3
Mullet Peninsula 110 A 4
Mullewa 142 B 4
Mulligan River 143 F 4
Mullingar 100 B 3
Mullion 102 B 2
Mull of Galloway 100 C 2
Mull of Kintyre 99 B 4
Mull of Oa 100 B 2
Mulobezi 160 D 3
Mulonga 158 D 6
Multan 129 J 4
Multanovy 119 O 3
Multia 112 J 3
Mulu, Gunung 136 E 3
Mulym'ya 119 MN 3
Mumbué 160 B 2
Mumbwa 160 D 2
Mumena 160 D 2
Mumra 128 D 1
Muna 130 M 2
Munabao 184 B 2
Munamägi 112 J 4
Muna, Pulau 137 F 5
Munayly 128 E 2
München 111 F 5
Munchique, Cerro 178 C 3
Muncho Lake 167 M 4
Muncie 171 J 3
Mundar 131 R 2
Munday 170 G 5
Münden 111 E 4
Mundo Nôvo 181 H 3
Mundra 134 A 3
Mundrabilla 142 D 5
Munducurus 179 G 4
Mundurachu 131 N 3
Mundybash 119 R 5
Mungar 143 J 4
Mungbere 158 D 4
Mungo 160 B 2
Munhango 160 B 2
Munich 111 F 5
Munifah 155 H 3
Munkedal 113 F 4
Munkfors 113 F 4
Munkhafad al Qattārah 154 D 3
Munku-Sardyk, Gora 130 H 5
Münster 111 E 4
Munster 110 B 4
Muntenia 116 C 2
Munţii Almăjului 116 B 2
Munţii Apuseni 116 B 1
Munţii Bihorului 116 B 1
Munţii Căliman 116 C 1
Munţii Harghita 116 C 1
Munţii Metaliferi 116 B 1
Munţii Poiana Ruscă 116 B 1
Munţii Rodnei 116 B 1
Munţii Sebeşului 116 B 1
Munţii Zărandului 116 B 1
Munugudzhak 131 U 3

Munzur Silsilesi 117 E 3
Muodoslompolo 112 H 2
Muojärvi 112 J 2
Muong Hiem 135 H 3
Muong Khoua 135 H 3
Muong Khuong 135 H 3
Muong Lam 135 H 4
Muong Nong 135 J 4
Muong Sai 135 H 3
Muong Sen 135 H 4
Muong Sing 135 H 3
Muong Son 135 H 3
Muong Te 135 H 3
Muonio 112 H 2
Muonioälven 112 H 2
Muonionjoki 112 H 2
Mupa National Park 160 B 3
Muqaddam 154 E 5
Muqayshiṭ 155 J 4
Muqdisho (Mogadishu) 159 H 4
Muqshin 155 J 5
Mur 115 G 2
Mura 115 G 2
Muradiye 117 F 3
Murakami 133 L 3
Murallón, Cerro 183 B 8
Murana 137 H 4
Murango 159 F 5
Murashi 118 J 4
Murat (France) 114 D 2
Murat (Turkey) 117 F 3
Murat Daği 116 C 3
Muratlı 116 C 2
Murau 115 F 2
Muravera 115 E 4
Murchison, Mount 142 B 4
Murchison River 142 A 4
Murcia 114 C 4
Murdo 170 F 3
Mureş 116 B 1
Muret 114 D 3
Murfreesboro 171 J 4
Murgab 129 G 3
Murgaš 116 B 2
Murghab 129 G 3
Murgon 143 J 4
Murgoo 142 B 4
Murguba 157 F 3
Murguz 117 G 2
Muriaé 181 H 5
Murici 181 J 2
Muriége 160 C 1
Murilo 146 B 2
Murin'ya 130 J 5
Muritz 111 F 4
Murjek 112 H 2
Murkong Selek 135 G 2
Murmansk 112 K 2
Murmashi 112 K 2
Murmino 118 H 5
Murnau 111 F 5
Murom 118 H 4
Muromtsevo 119 P 4
Muroran 133 M 2
Muros 114 B 3
Muroto 133 K 4
Murphysboro 171 J 4
Murray (KY, U.S.A.) 171 J 4
Murray (UT, U.S.A.) 170 D 3
Murray Bridge 143 F 6
Murray Downs 142 E 3
Murray Fracture Zone 193 D 2
Murray Islands 144 D 3
Murray, Lake 144 D 3
Murray, Lake 171 K 5
Murray River 143 G 5
Murraysburg 160 C 6
Murro di Porco, Capo 115 G 4
Murrumbidgee River 143 H 5
Murrupula 161 F 3
Mursala, Pulau 136 A 3
Murshidabad 134 E 3
Murska Sobota 115 G 2
Murten 115 E 2
Murukta 130 H 2
Mururoa 147 F 4
Murwara 134 D 3
Murwillumbah 143 J 4
Murzuq 153 H 3
Murzuq, Idhān 153 H 5
Mürzzuschlag 115 G 2
Muş 117 F 3
Muša 113 H 4
Musadi 158 C 5
Musala 116 B 2
Musan 133 J 2
Musandam Peninsula 155 K 3
Musao 158 D 6
Musa Qala 129 G 4
Musay'īd 155 J 4
Musayamir 155 G 6
Muscat 155 K 4
Musgrave 143 G 1

Musgrave Ranges 142 E 4
Mushāsh al 'Ashāwī 155 H 4
Mushie 158 B 5
Musi, Air 136 B 4
Mūsiān 128 D 4
Muskegon 171 J 3
Muskegon River 171 J 3
Muskogee 171 G 4
Musoma 158 E 5
Musqat 155 K 4
Musquaro, Lac 169 P 5
Mussa Ali 159 G 2
Musselburgh 99 C 4
Musselshell River 170 E 2
Mussende 160 B 2
Mussidan 114 D 2
Mustafa 131 P 3
Mustafakemalpaşa 116 C 3
Mustahil 159 G 3
Mustang 134 D 2
Musters, Lago 183 C 8
Mustla 113 J 4
Mustvee 113 J 4
Muswellbrook 143 J 5
Mut (Turkey) 117 D 3
Mūṭ (Egypt) 154 D 3
Mutanda 160 D 2
Mutá, Ponta de 181 J 3
Mutarara 161 F 3
Mutare 161 E 3
Mutayyin 155 G 5
Mutha 159 F 5
Mutis, Gunung 137 F 5
Mutnovskaya Sopka 131 T 5
Mutoray 130 H 3
Mutsamudu 161 G 2
Mutshatsha 160 C 2
Mutsu-wan 133 M 2
Muttaburra 143 G 3
Mutusjärvi 112 J 2
Muurasjärvi 112 J 3
Muurola 112 J 2
Mu Us Shamo 132 E 3
Muwale 158 E 6
Muxaluando 160 A 1
Muxima 160 A 1
Muya 130 K 4
Muya 130 L 4
Muyezerskiy 112 K 3
Muyinga 158 E 5
Muynak 128 F 2
Muyumba 158 D 6
Muzaffarabad 129 J 4
Muzaffargarh 129 J 4
Muzaffarnagar 134 C 2
Muzaffarpur 134 E 2
Muzhi 119 M 2
Muzillac 114 C 2
Muztag 129 L 3
Muztag 129 M 3
Muztagata 129 K 3
Mvolo 158 D 3
Mvomero 159 F 6
Mvoung 157 G 5
Mwadingusha 160 D 2
Mwangalala 160 D 2
Mwanya 161 E 2
Mwanza (Tanzania) 158 E 5
Mwanza (Zaire) 158 D 6
Mwatate 159 F 5
Mweelrea 110 B 4
Mweka 158 C 6
Mwene Biji 158 C 6
Mwene Ditu 158 C 6
Mwenezi 161 E 4
Mwenga 158 D 5
Mweru, Lake 160 D 1
Mwimba 158 C 6
Mwinilunga 160 C 2
Mya 153 F 2
Myakit 131 S 3
Myaksa 118 G 4
Myanaung 135 G 4
Myaundzha 131 R 3
Myaungmya 135 F 4
Mycenae → Mikinai 116 B 3
Myingyan 135 G 3
Myinmoletkat 135 G 5
Myinmu 135 G 3
Myitkyina 135 G 2
Myitta 135 G 5
Myittha 135 G 3
Mymensingh 135 F 3
Myn-Aral 119 O 6
Mynbulak 119 N 3
Myndagayy 131 O 3
Mynydd Prescelly 102 B 2
Mýrar 112 A 3
Mýrdalsjökull 112 B 3
Myre 112 F 2
Myrtle Beach 171 L 5
Mys Aniva 131 Q 6
Mys Bolvanskiy Nos 119 L 1

Mys Buorkhaya 131 O 1
Mys Chukotskiy 166 C 3
Mys Dezhneva 166 D 2
Mys Duga-Zapadnaya 131 R 4
Mys Dzenzik 117 E 1
Mysen 113 F 4
Mys Enkan 131 Q 4
Mys Kanin Nos 118 H 2
Mys Kazantip 117 E 1
Mys Kerets 118 G 2
Mys Kodori 117 F 2
Mys Kolgompja 113 J 4
Mys Kril'on 131 Q 6
Mys Kronotskiy 131 U 5
Mys Kurgalski 113 J 4
Mys Laydennyy 118 J 2
Mys Lopatka 131 T 5
Mys Lygyy 130 L 1
Mys Meganom 117 E 2
Mys Men'shikova 119 L 1
Mys Navarin 131 X 3
Mys Olyutorskiy 131 VW 4
Mys Ostrovnoy 131 T 3
Mysovaya 131 T 2
Mys Peschanyy 128 E 2
Mys Pitsunda 117 F 2
Mys Ratmanova 118 L 1
Mys Saryeh 117 D 2
Mys Sengiri 128 E 2
Mys Shipunskiy 131 U 5
Mys Svatoy Nos 118 J 2
Mys Svyatoy Nos 131 P 1
Mys Svyatoy Nos 118 G 2
Mys Taran 113 GH 5
Mys Tarkhankut 117 D 1
Mys Taygonos 131 U 3
Mys Terpeniya 131 Q 6
Mys Tolstoy 131 T 4
Mys Uengan 119 N 1
Mys Yelizavety 131 Q 5
Mys Yuzhnyy 131 T 4
My Tho 135 J 5
My Trach 135 J 5
Mývatn 112 B 2
Myylybulak 119 P 6
Mze 111 F 5
Mzenga 159 F 6
Mziha 159 F 6
Mzimba-Mzuzu 161 E 2
Mzuzu 161 E 2

N

Naab 111 F 5
Naama 152 EF 2
Naandi 158 D 3
Naantali (Nådendal) 113 H 3
Naas 100 B 3
Näätämöjoki 112 J 2
Naba 135 G 3
Nabadid 159 G 3
Na Baek 135 H 4
Nabberu, Lake 142 C 4
Nabha 134 C 1
Nabire 137 F 4
Nabī Shu'ayb, Jabal an 155 G 5
Nabou 156 D 3
Nābul 153 H 1
Nābulus 154 F 2
Nacala 161 G 2
Nacaroa 161 F 2
Nachana 134 B 2
Nachikinskaya, Gora 131 U 4
Nachingwea 161 F 2
Nachod 111 G 4
Nachuge 135 F 5
Nachvak Fiord 169 P 4
Nacozari 170 E 5
Nacunday 182 J 6
Nådendal 113 H 3
Nadiad 134 B 3
Nådlac 116 B 1
Nador 152 E 1
Nadvoicy 112 K 3
Nadvornaya 116 B 1
Nadym 119 O 2
Nærbö 113 E 4
Næstved 113 F 4
Nafada 157 G 3
Naft-e Safīd 128 D 4
Naftshahr 128 D 4
Nafuce 157 F 3
Nafūd ad Daḥy 155 H 4
Nafūd al 'Urayq 155 G 3–4
Nafūd as Sirr 155 G 3
Nafūd as Surrah 155 G 4

Nafūd Qunayfidhah 155 H 4
Nafūsah, Jabal 153 H 2
Nafy 155 G 3
Nag 129 G 5
Naga 137 F 1
Naga Hills 135 FG 2
Nagaland 135 F 2
Nagano 133 L 3
Nagaoka 133 L 3
Nagappattinam 134 C 5
Nagarzê 135 F 2
Nagasaki 133 J 4
Nagato 133 K 4
Nagaur 134 B 2
Nagavati 134 D 4
Nagda 134 C 3
Nagercoil 134 C 6
Nagichot 158 E 4
Nago 133 J 5
Nagornyy 131 N 4
Nagor'ye Sangilen 130 G 5
Nagoya 133 L 3
Nagpur 134 C 3
Nagqu 132 B 4
Nagyatád 116 A 1
Nagykanizsa 116 A 1
Nagykőrös 116 A 1
Naha 133 J 5
Nahan 134 C 1
Nahang 129 G 5
Nahanni Butte 167 N 3
Nahanni National Park 167 M, N 3
Nahāvand 128 D 4
Nahr ad Dindar 154 EF 6
Nahr an Nīl 154 E 3
Nahuel Huapi, Lago 183 B 7
Nahuel Niyeu 183 C 7
Nai 145 E 2
Nai Ga 135 G 2
Naikliu 137 F 5
Nailsworth 103 C 2
Naiman Qi 133 H 2
Nain (U.S.A.) 169 P 4
Naini Tal 134 C 2
Nā'īn (Iran) 128 E 4
Nairn 98 C 3
Nairobi 159 F 5
Naissaar 113 H 4
Naita 158 F 3
Naivasha 159 F 5
Najafābād 128 E 4
Najd 155 G 3–4
Najera 114 C 3
Naj' Ḥammādi 154 E 3
Najibabad 134 C 2
Najin 133 K 2
Najrān 155 G 5
Nakamti → Nekemt 159 F 3
Nakanno 130 J 3
Naka-no-shima 133 K 3
Nakasongola 158 E 4
Nakatsu 133 K 4
Nakfa 159 F 1
Nakhichevan' 128 D 3
Nakhichevan' 117 G 3
Nakhodka 133 K 2
Nakhodka 119 O 2
Nakhon Nayok 135 H 5
Nakhon Pathom 135 H 5
Nakhon Phanom 135 H 4
Nakhon Ratchasima 135 H 5
Nakhon Sawan 135 H 4
Nakhon Si Thammarat 135 G 6
Nakina 168 K 5
Nakło 111 G 4
Naknek 166 F 4
Nako 156 D 3
Nakonde 161 E 1
Nakop 160 B 5
Nakskov 113 F 5
Näkten 112 F 3
Nakuru 159 F 5
Nalayh 130 F 6
Nalázi 161 E 4
Nal'chik 117 F 2
Nálgimskaya 131 V 3
Nalgonda 134 C 4
Nallamala Range 134 C 4
Nallıhan 116 D 2
Nālūṭ 153 H 2
Namaacha 161 E 5
Namaki 157 G 3
Namakzar-e Shadād 128 F 4
Namaland 160 B 5
Namanga 159 F 5
Namangan 129 J 2
Namanyere 158 E 6
Namapa 161 F 2

Namaponda 161 F 3
Namaqualand 160 B 5
Namarrói 161 F 3
Namasagali 158 E 4
Namatanai 145 F 2
Nambour 143 J 4
Nam Ca Dinh 135 H 4
Nam Can 135 J 6
Namche Bazar 134 E 2
Nam Co 135 F 1
Namdalen 112 F 3
Nam Dinh 135 J 3
Nametil 161 F 3
Namib Desert 160 A 4–5
Namib Desert Park 160 B 4
Namibe 160 A 3
Namibe Reserve 160 A 3
Namibia 160 B 4
Namiquipa 170 E 6
Namjagbarwa Feng 132 C 5
Namkham 135 G 3
Namlan Pan 135 G 3
Namlea 137 G 4
Namling 134 E 2
Namoi River 143 H 5
Namoluk 146 B 2
Namonuito 146 A 2
Namorik 146 C 2
Nam Ou 135 H 3
Namoya 158 D 5
Nampa 170 C 3
Nampala 156 C 2
Nam Phang 135 H 4
Nam Phong 135 H 4
Namp'o 133 J 3
Nampula 161 F 3
Namrole 137 G 4
Namru 134 D 1
Namsang 135 G 3
Namsê La 134 D 2
Namsen 112 F 2–3
Namsos 112 F 3
Namsvattnet 112 F 2
Nam Teng 135 G 3
Namton 135 G 3
Namtsy 131 N 3
Namtu 135 G 3
Namu 146 C 2
Namuli 161 F 3
Namuno 161 F 2
Namur 110 D 4
Namutoni 160 B 3
Namwala 160 D 3
Namwǒn 133 J 3
Namy 131 O 2
Namya Ra 135 G 2
Namyit Island 136 D 1
Nanaimo 167 N 6
Nana Kru 156 C 5
Nanam 133 J 2
Nanambinia 142 C 5
Nanao 133 L 3
Nancha 131 N 6
Nanchang 132 G 5
Nancheng 132 G 5
Nanchong 132 E 4
Nanchuan 132 E 5
Nancowry 135 F 6
Nancy 115 E 2
Nanda Devi 134 C 1
Nandan 132 E 6
Nander 134 C 4
Nandod 134 B 3
Nandu Jiang 132 E 7
Nandurbar 134 B 3
Nandyal 134 C 4
Nanfeng 132 G 5
Nanga Emboko 157 G 5
Nangakelawit 136 D 3
Nanga Parbat 129 J 3
Nangapinoh 136 D 4
Nangatayap 136 D 4
Nangin 135 G 5
Nangnim-sanmaek 133 J 2
Nangong 132 G 3
Nangqên 132 C 4
Nanguneri 134 C 6
Nang Xian 132 B 5
Nan Hai 132 F 7
Nanhua 132 D 5
Nanhui 133 H 4
Nan Hulsan Hu 132 C 3
Nanjian 132 D 5
Nanjiang 132 E 4
Nanjing 133 G 4
Nanking → Nanjing 133 G 4
Nankova 160 B 3
Nanle 132 G 3
Nan Ling 132 F 5
Nannine 142 B 4
Nanning 132 E 6
Nannup 142 B 5

Nan–New

Nanortalik 169 S 3
Nanpan Jiang 132 D 6
Nanpara 134 D 2
Nanpi 133 G 3
Nanping 133 G 5
Nanping 132 D 4
Nansei-shotō 133 J 5
Nanshan Islands 136 D 2
Nansha Qundao 136 D 2
Nansikan, Ostrov 131 PQ 4
Nansio 158 E 5
Nantais, Lac 169 N 3
Nantes 114 C 2
Nanton 167 P 5
Nantong 133 H 4
Nantou 133 H 6
Nantucket Island 171 M 3
Nantucket Sound 171 M 3
Nantulo 161 F 2
Nantwich 102 C 1
Nantyglow 102 C 2
Nanumanga 146 C 3
Nanumea 146 C 3
Nanuque 181 H 4
Nanusa, Kepulauan 137 G 3
Nanwei Dao 136 D 2
Nanxiong 132 F 5
Nanyang 132 F 4
Nanyuki 159 F 4
Nanzhang 132 F 4
Nanzhao 132 F 4
Nanzhila 160 D 3
Nao, Cabo de la 114 C 4
Naococane, Lac 169 N 5
Naoli He 131 O 6
Náousa 116 B 2
Napaku 136 E 3
Napalkovo 119 O 1
Napana 131 T 4
Napas 119 Q 4
Napassoq 169 R 2
Napata 154 E 5
Nape 135 J 4
Napido 137 J 4
Napier 146 C 5
Napier Mountains 185
Naples (U.S.A.) 171 K 6
Naples (Italy) 115 F 3
Napo (China) 132 E 6
Napo (Peru) 178 D 4
Napoli 115 F 3
Napperby 142 E 3
Napuka 147 F 3
Naqa 154 E 5
Naqadeh 128 D 3
Nara (Mali) 156 C 2
Nara (Japan) 133 L 4
Nara (Pakistan) 129 H 6
Naracoorte 143 G 6
Naran 130 G 6
Naran 132 F 1
Naranjos 172 C 3
Narasapur 134 D 4
Narasun 130 K 5
Narathiwat 135 H 6
Narayanganj 135 F 3
Narberth 102 B 2
Narbonne 114 D 3
Nares Strait 184
Naretha 142 C 5
Narew 111 H 4
Narlı 117 E 3
Narmada 134 B 3
Narman 117 F 2
Narnaul 134 C 2
Naroch 113 J 5
Narodnaya, Gora 119 M 2
Naro-Fominsk 118 G 4
Narok 159 F 5
Narooma 143 J 6
Narowal 129 J 4
Närpes (Närpiö) 112 G 3
Närpiö 112 G 3
Narrabri 143 H 6
Narrandera 143 H 5
Narrogin 142 B 5
Narromine 143 H 5
Narsimhapur 134 C 3
Narsinghgarh 134 C 3
Narsinghpur 134 E 3
Narssaq 169 R 3
Narssalik 169 S 3
Narssaq 169 S 3
Narssarssuaq 169 S 3
Năruja 116 C 1
Narungombe 159 F 6
Narva 113 J 4
Narvik 112 G 2
Narvski Zaliv 113 J 4
Narwietooma 142 E 3
Nar'yan Mar 118 K 2
Narym 119 Q 4
Narymskiy Khrebet 119 QR 6

Naryn 130 G 5
Naryn 129 K 2
Naryn 129 JK 2
Narynkol' 129 KL 2
Nås 113 F 3
Näsåker 112 G 3
Nasarawa 157 F 4
Năsăud 116 B 1
Nashville 171 J 4
Našice 115 G 2
Näsijärvi 112 H 3
Nasik 134 B 3
Nāṣir 158 E 3
Nasirabad (India) 134 B 2
Nasirabad (Pakistan) 129 H 5
Naskaupi 169 P 5
Nasmah 153 H 2
Nasmgani 134 D 3
Nass 166 M 4
Nassau (The Bahamas) 173 G 2
Nassau (Cook Is.) 146 D 3
Nasser, Birkat 154 E 4
Nassian 156 D 4
Nässjö 113 F 4
Nastapoka Islands 169 M 4
Nasva 113 K 4
Nata 160 D 4
Natal (South Africa) 160–161 DE 5
Natal (Brazil) 181 J 2
Natal (Brazil) 179 F 5
Natal (Indonesia) 136 A 3
Natara 131 MN 2
Natashquan 169 P 5
Natchez 171 H 5
Natchitoches 171 H 5
Nathdwara 134 B 3
Natîh 155 K 4
Natitingou 156 E 3
Natityāy, Jabal 154 E 4
Natividade 181 G 3
Natkyizin 135 G 5
Natron, Lake 159 F 5
Natrūn, Wādī an 154 DE 2
Nattaung 135 G 4
Nattavaara 112 H 2
Natuna, Kepulauan 136 C 3
Natuna Utara 136 C 3
Naturaliste, Cape 142 A 5
Naturaliste Channel 142 A 4
Naturno 115 F 2
Nauchas 160 B 4
Nauja Bay 169 M 1
Naujoji-Akmene 113 H 4
Naukluft 160 B 4
Naumburg 111 F 4
Naungpale 135 G 4
Naupe 178 C 5
Naurskay 117 G 2
Nauru 145 J 2
Naurzum 119 M 5
Naushahro Firoz 129 G 5
Naushki 130 J 5
Nauta 178 D 4
Nautanwa 134 D 2
Nava 172 B 2
Navahermosa 114 C 4
Navajo Reservoir 170 E 4
Naval 137 F 1
Navalmoral de la Mata 114 B 4
Navan 100 B 3
Navarin, Mys 131 X 3
Navarino, Isla 183 C 9–7
Navarra 114 C 3
Navassa 173 GH 4
Navia (Spain) 114 B 3
Navia (Argentina) 182 C 5
Navidad 182 B 5
Naviraí 181 F 5
Navlya 118 F 5
Năvodari 116 C 2
Navoi 129 H 2
Navojoa 170 E 6
Navolato 170 E 7
Navolok 118 G 3
Navplion 116 B 3
Navrongo 156 D 3
Navsari 134 B 3
Navtlug 117 FG 2
Nawabganj 134 D 2
Nawabshah 129 G 5
Nāwah 129 H 4
Nawalgarh 134 C 2
Nawāṣif, Ḥarrat 155 G 4
Naws, Ra's 155 K 5
Náxos 116 C 3
Nayakhan 131 T 2
Nayarit 172 B 3
Nayarit, Sierra 172 B 3
Nāy Band 128 E 5
Nayoro 133 M 2
Naystenyarvi 112 K 3
Nazaré 114 B 4
Nazaré (Bahía, Brazil) 181 J 3

Nazaré (Goiás, Brazil) 179 J 5
Nazareth (Peru) 178 C 5
Nazarovka 118 H 5
Nazarovo 130 F 4
Nazas 172 B 2
Nazca 180 B 3
Nazca Ridge 193 E 4
Naze 133 J 5
Nazerat 154 F 2
Nazilli 116 C 3
Nazimovo 130 F 4
Nazina 119 P 3
Nazira 135 F 2
Nazmiye 117 E 3
Nazran' 117 F 2
Nazwa 155 K 4
Nchelenge 160 D 1
Ncheu 161 E 2
Ndaghamcha, Sebkra de 152 B 5
Ndala 158 E 5
N'dalatando 160 A 1
Ndali 156 E 4
Ndandawala 159 F 6
Ndélé 158 C 3
Ndélélé 157 G 5
Ndendé 157 G 6
Ndindi 157 G 6
Ndjamena 157 H 3
Ndjolé 157 G 6
Ndogo, Lagune 157 G 6
Ndola 160 D 2
Ndoro 157 G 6
Ndrhamcha, Sebkha de 152 BC 5
Ndu 158 C 4
Nea (Norway) 112 F 3
Nea (Solomon Islands) 145 J 4
Nea Filippías 116 B 3
Neagh, Lough 100 B 2
Néa Ionia 116 B 3
Néon Karlovásion 116 C 3
Neale, Lake 142 E 3
Neápolis 134 B 2
Neápolis 116 B 3
Near Islands 166 A 5
Neath 170 D 2
Néa Zikhni 116 B 2
Nebbou 156 D 3
Nebine River 143 H 4
Nebit-Dag 128 E 3
Neblina, Pico da 178 E 3
Nebo 143 H 3
Nebolchi 118 F 4
Nebraska 170 F 3
Nebraska City 171 G 3
Nechako 167 N 5
Nechako Plateau 167 N 5
Nechako Reservoir 167 M 5
Nechi 178 D 2
Neckar 111 E 5
Necker 147 E 1
Necochea 183 E 6
Nédéley 157 H 2
Nederland 110 D E 4
Nedong 132 B 5
Needles 170 D 5
Nefedovo 119 O 4
Neftah 153 G 2
Neftegorsk 118 K 5
Neftegorsk 117 E 2
Neftekamsk 118 K 4
Neftekumsk 117 F 2
Neftelensk 130 J 4
Nefteyugansk 119 O 3
Negage 160 B 1
Negala 156 C 3
Neganili Lake 167 S 4
Negelli 159 F 3
Negomano 161 F 2
Negombo 134 C 6
Negonego 147 F 4
Negotin 116 B 2
Negotka 119 Q 4
Negra, Cordillera 178 C 5
Negrais, Cape 135 F 4
Negra, Punta 178 B 5
Negra, Serra 179 J 5
Négrine 153 G 2
Negritos 178 B 4
Negro, Cerro 183 C 7
Negro, Río (Brazil) 179 F 4
Negro, Rio (Uruguay) 182 EF 2
Negros 137 F 2
Negru Vodă 116 C 2
Nehavand 128 D 3
Nehbandan 128 G 4
Nehe 131 M 6
Nehoiu 116 C 1
Nehone 160 B 3
Neige, Crêt de la 115 E 2
Neijiang 132 E 5
Neilton 170 B 2
Nei Monggol Zizhiqu 132 EF 2
Neiqiu 132 F 3
Neiva 178 C 3

Nejo 158 F 3
Nekemt 159 F 3
Nekrasovka 133 L 2
Neksikan 131 R 3
Neksö 113 G 4
Nelemnoye 131 S 2
Nel'gese 131 O 2
Nelichu 158 E 3
Nelidovo 118 F 4
Nel'kan 131 P 4
Nel'keskan 130 M 2
Nelkuchan, Gora 131 P 3
Nellore 135 F 2
Nel'ma 131 P 6
Nelson (New Zealand) 145 Q 9
Nelson (U.K.) 101 D 3
Nelson (Br.Col., Canada) 167 O 6
Nelson (Man., Can.) 167 S 5
Nelson, Cape 143 G 6
Nelson, Estrecho 183 B 9
Nelson Head 167 N 1
Nelson Island 166 D 3
Nelspruit 161 E 5
Nelyaty 130 L 4
Néma 152 D 5
Neman 113 H 5
Nembrala 137 F 6
Némiscau 169 M 5
Nemours → Ghazaouet 152 E 1
Nemrutdağı 117 E 3
Nemunas 113 H 4
Nemuro 133 N 2
Nemuy 131 P 4
Nenana 166 H 3
Nendo 145 J 4
Nene, River 103 E 1
Nen Jiang 133 H 1
Nenjiang 131 N 6
Néon Karlovásion 116 C 3
Nepa 130 J 4
Nepal 134 D 2
Nepalganj 134 D 2
Nepeña 178 C 5
Nephi 170 D 4
Nepoko 158 D 4
Nera 131 Q 3
Nérac 114 D 3
Neraw 111 H 4
Nercha 130 L 5
Nerchinsk 130 L 5
Nerchinskiy Khrebet 130 L 5
Nerekhta 118 H 4
Neretva 115 G 3
Neringa-Nida 113 H 4
Neriquinha 160 C 3
Neris 113 HJ 5
Neroy 130 G 5
Nerpich'ye, Ozero 131 T 2
Nerpio 114 C 4
Nerva 114 B 4
Nes' 118 H 2
Nesbyen 113 E 3
Nesebăr 116 C 2
Nesjöen 112 F 3
Neskaupstaður 112 C 2
Nesna 112 G 2
Ness, Loch 98 B 3
Nesterov 113 H 5
Nesterovo 131 J 5
Neston 102 C 1
Néstos 116 B 2
Nesvizh 113 J 5
Netanya 154 E 2
Netherlands Antilles 178 E 1
Netherlands 110 D–E 4
Netherlands Antilles 173 K 4
Nettilling Lake 169 N 2
Nettuno 115 F 3
Neubrandenburg 111 F 4
Neuchâtel 115 E 2
Neuchâtel, Lac de 115 E 2
Neufchâteau 115 E 2
Neufchâtel-en-Bray 114 D 2
Neum 115 G 3
Neumarkter Sattel 115 F 2
Neumünster 111 E 4
Neunkirchen (Austria) 115 G 2
Neunkirchen (B.R.D.) 111 E 5
Neuquén 183 C 6
Neuruppin 111 F 4
Neusiedler See 115 G 2
Neustadt 111 E 5
Neustrelitz 111 F 4
Nevada (U.S.A.) 170 C 4
Nevada (MO, U.S.A.) 171 H 4
Nevada, Cerro el 178 D 3
Nevada, Sierra 170 BC 4
Nevada, Sierra (Spain) 114 C 4
Nevado Ausangate 180 B 3
Nevado, Cerro 183 C 6
Nevado Chachani 180 B 4
Nevado Citac 180 A 3
Nevado Cololo 180 C 4

Nevado Coropuna 180 B 4
Nevado de Cachi 180 D 5
Nevado de Colima 172 B 4
Nevado Huascarán 178 C 5
Nevado Illimani 180 C 4
Nevado Sajama 180 C 4
Nevado Salcantay 180 B 3
Nevado Salluyo 180 C 3
Nevado, Sierra del 183 C 6
Nevado Yerupajá 179 C 6
Nevagissey 102 B 2
Nevel' 113 J 4
Nevel'sk 131 Q 6
Nevel'skogo, Proliv 131 Q 5
Never 131 M 5
Nevers 114 D 2
Neve, Serra da 160 A 2
Nevesinje 115 G 3
Nevinnomyssk 117 F 2
Nevis 173 K 4
Nevis, Loch 99 B 3
Nevon 130 H 4
Nevşehir 117 D 3
Nev'yansk 119 M 4
Newala 161 F 2
New Albany 171 J 4
New Amsterdam 179 G 2
Newark (N.J., U.S.A.) 171 M 3
Newark (OH, U.S.A) 171 K 3
Newark-on-Trent (U.K.) 103 D 1
New Bedford 171 M 3
New Bern 171 L 4
Newberry 171 J 2
Newbiggin by the Sea 101 E 2
New Braunfels 170 G 6
New Britain 145 F 3
New Brunswick (Can.) 169 O 6
New Brunswick (PA, U.S.A.) 171 M 3
New Buffalo 171 J 3
Newburgh (NY, U.S.A.) 171 M 3
Newburgh (U.K.) 99 C 3
Newbury 103 D 2
New Busuanga 137 E 1
New Caledonia 145 H 6
Newcastle 100 C 2
New Castle 171 K 3
Newcastle (Airport) 101 E 2
Newcastle (Austr.) 143 J 5
Newcastle (Canada) 169 O 6
Newcastle (S. Afr.) 160 D 5
Newcastle (WY, U.S.A.) 170 F 3
Newcastle Emlyn 102 B 1
Newcastle River 142 E 2
Newcastle-under-Lyme 101 D 3
Newcastle-upon-Tyne 101 E 2
Newcastle-upon-Tyne 110 C 3
Newcastle Waters 142 E 2
New Cumnock 100 C 2
New Delhi → Dehli 134 C 2
New England 171 MN 3
New England Range 143 J 5
Newenham, Cape 166 E 4
New Forest 103 D 2
Newfoundland 169 Q 6
Newfoundland 169 Q 4
New Galloway 99 B 4
New Georgia 145 G 2
New Georgia Sound 145 G 2
New Glasgow 169 P 6
Newgrange 100 B 3
New Guinea 137 H 4
New Hampshire 171 M 3
New Hampton 171 H 3
New Hanover 145 F 2
New Haven 171 M 3
Newhaven 103 D 2
New Hebrides 145 J 5
New Hunstanton 103 E 1
New Iberia 171 H 5
New Ireland 145 F 2
New Jersey 171 M 4
New Liskeard 171 L 2
New London 171 M 3
Newman 142 B 3
Newmarket 103 E 1
New Meadows 170 C 2
New Mexico 170 E 5
Newmilns 99 B 4
New Norcia 142 B 5
New Norfolk 144 L 9
New Orleans 171 HJ 5–6
New Plymouth 145 Q 8
Newport (AR, U.S.A.) 171 H 4
Newport (Gwent) 102 C 2
Newport (Isle of Wight) 103 D 2
Newport (OR, U.S.A.) 170 B 3
Newport, R.J. 2
Newport (Salop) 102 C 1
Newport (WA, U.S.A.) 170 C 2
Newport Beach 170 C 5
Newport Pagnell 103 D 1
New Providence Island 173 G 3
New Quay 102 B 1

Newquay 102 B 2
New Richmond 169 O 6
New River (WV, U.S.A.) 171 K 4
New River (Guyana) 179 G 3
New Rockford 170 G 2
New Romney 103 E 2
Newry (U.K.) 100 B 2
Newry (Australia) 142 D 2
New Scone 99 C 3
New Siberian Islands 184
New Smyrna Beach 171 K 6
New South Wales 143 G 5
New Stuyahok 166 F 4
Newton 171 H 3
Newtonabbey 110 B 4
Newton Abbot 102 C 2
Newton Aycliffe 101 E 2
Newton-le-Willows 101 D 3
Newtonmore 99 B 3
Newton Stewart 100 C 2
Newtown 102 C 1
Newtownabbey 100 B 2
Newtownards 100 C 2
Newtownstewart 100 B 2
New Ulm 171 H 3
New Westminster 167 N 6
New York 171 H 3
New York (N.Y., U.S.A.) 171 M 3
New York State Barge Canal 171 L 3
New Zealand 145 R 9
Neya 118 H 4
Neyland 102 B 2
Neyriz 128 E 5
Neyshābūr 128 F 3
Nezhin 118 F 5
Ngabé 157 H 6
Ngala 157 G 3
Ngambé 157 G 5
Ngami, Lake 160 C 4
Ngamiland 160 C 4
Ngamring 134 E 2
Ngangala 158 E 4
Ngangerabeli Plain 159 G 5
Ngangla Ringco 134 D 1
Nganglong Kangri 129 J 4
N'gangula 160 A 2
Ngangzê Co 134 E 1
Ngaoundal 157 G 4
Ngaoundéré → Guidjiba 157 G 4
Ngara 158 E 5
Ngathaingyaung 135 G 4
Ngatik 146 B 2
Nggatokae 145 G 2
Ngidinga 158 B 6
Ngo 157 H 6
Ngoc Linh 135 J 4
Ngoïla 157 G 5
Ngoko 157 H 5
Ngomeni, Ras 159 G 5
Ngom Qu 132 C 4
Ngong 159 F 5
Ngoring 132 C 3
Ngoring Hu 132 C 4
Ngorongoro Crater 158 F 5
Ngoua, Mont 158 C 3
Ngoui 156 B 2
Ngounié 157 G 6
Ngouri 157 H 3
Ngourou 158 C 3
Ngourti 157 G 2
Ngoussi 153 G 2
Ngoywa 158 E 6
Nguara 157 H 3
Ngudu 158 E 5
Nguigmi 157 G 3
N'guimbo 160 C 2
Ngum 135 H 4
Nguni 159 F 5
Nguru 157 G 3
Nguyen Binh 135 J 3
Ngwale 161 F 2
Ngwane 161 F 3
Nhachengue 161 F 4
Nhambiquara 180 E 3
Nhamundá 179 G 4
N'harea 160 B 2
Nhill 143 G 6
Nhoma 160 C 3
Nhommarath 135 J 4
Nhulunbuy 143 F 1
Niafounke 156 D 3
Niagara Falls 171 L 3
Niagara River 171 L 3
Niagassola 156 C 3
Niah 136 D 3
Niakaramandougou 156 C 4
Niamey 156 E 3
Niaming 156 E 4
Niamtougou 156 E 4
Niandan Koro 156 C 3
Niangay, Lac 156 D 2

Niangoloko 156 D 3
Nia-Nia 158 D 4
Nianzishan 131 M 6
Niari 157 G 6
Nias, Pulau 136 A 3
Niassa 161 F 2
Niau 147 F 4
Nibāk 155 J 4
Nibe 113 E 4
Nicaragua 172 E 5
Nicaragua, Lago de 172 E 5
Nice 115 E 3
Nichalakh 131 R 1
Nichicum, Lac 169 N 5
Nichnyaya Pesha 118 J 2
Nicholas Channel 173 F 3
Nicholls Town 173 G 2
Nicholson River 143 F 2
Nickerie 179 G 2
Nickol Bay 142 B 3
Nicobar Islands 135 F 6
Nicocli 178 C 2
Nicosia 117 D 3
Nicotera 115 G 4
Nicoya 172 E 5
Nicoya, Golfo de 172 F 6
Nicoya, Península de 172 E 6
Nicuadala 161 F 3
Nida 111 H 4
Nidd, River 101 E 3
Nidelva 113 E 4
Nido, Sierra del 170 E 6
Nidym 130 G 2
Nidzica 111 H 4
Niebüll 111 E 4
Niecka Sieradzka 111 G 4
Nieddu 115 E 3
Niedersachsen 111 E 4
Niedre Tauern 115 F 2
Niefang 157 G 5
Niellé 156 C 3
Niellim 157 H 4
Niemba 158 D 6
Niemisel 112 H 2
Nienburg 111 E 4
Niéndkoué, Mont 156 C 4
Niéré 157 J 3
Niete Mountains 156 C 4
Nieuw Amsterdam 179 H 2
Nieuw Nickerie 179 G 2
Nieuwoudtville 160 B 6
Nieves 180 C 3
Niğde 117 D 3
Nigenän 128 F 4
Niger (River) 157 F 4
Niger Delta 157 F 5
Nigeria 157 F 4
Nighasan 134 D 2
Nihau 147 E 1
Nihiru 147 F 4
Nihoa 146 E 1
Niigata 133 L 3
Niihama 133 K 4
Niitsu 133 L 3
Nijar 114 C 4
Nijmegen 110 D E 4
Nikel 112 K 2
Nikkaluokta 112 G 2
Nikki 156 E 4
Nikolajev 111 H 5
Nikolayev 116 D 1
Nikolayevka 117 D 1
Nikolayevka 119 N 5
Nikolayevo 113 F 4
Nikolayevskiy 131 N 5
Nikolayevskiy 119 M 5
Nikolayevsk-na-Amure 131 Q 5
Nikol'sk 118 J 4
Nikol'sk 130 F 4
Nikol'sk 118 J 5
Nikolski 166 C 4
Nikol'skiy 129 H 1
Nikol'skoye 117 G 1
Nikonga 158 E 5
Nikopol (Bulgaria) 116 B 2
Nikopol (Russia, U.S.S.R.) 117 D 1
Nīkpey 128 D 3
Niksar 117 E 2
Nikshahr 129 G 5
Nikšic 116 A 2
Nikumaroro 147 D 3
Nilakka 112 J 3
Nila, Pulau 137 G 5
Nile 154 E 3
Niles 171 J 3
Nili 153 F 2
Nilka 129 L 2
Nilo Peçanha 179 H 5
Nilsiä 112 J 3
Nimach 134 B 3

Nimba, Monts 156 C 4
Nimbe 157 F 5
Nimes 114 D 3
Nimmitable 143 H 6
Nimule 158 E 4
Nin 115 G 3
Nincheng 133 G 2
Ninda 160 C 2
Nine Degree Channel 134 B 6
Ninety East Ridge 192 B 5
Ninety Mile Beach 143 H 6
Nineveh 155 G 1
Ninfas, Punta 183 D 7
Ningaloo 142 A 3
Njombe 158 E 6
Ningbo 133 H 5
Ningde 133 G 5
Ningdu 132 G 5
Ninghai 133 H 5
Ningi 157 F 3
Ningjing Shan 132 C 4
Ninglang 132 D 5
Ningming 132 E 6
Ningnan 132 D 5
Ningshan 132 E 4
Ningwu 132 F 3
Ningxia Huizu Zizhiqu 132 E 3
Ning Xian 132 E 3
Ningxiang 132 F 5
Ninh Binh 135 J 3
Ninhue 183 B 6
Ninigo Group 146 A 3
Ninigo Islands 144 D 2
Ninyako-Vogumma 119 P 1
Nioki 158 B 5
Niokolo Koba, Parc National du 156 B 3
Niono 156 C 3
Nioro 156 A 3
Nioro du Sahel 156 C 2
Niort 114 C 2
Niou 156 D 3
Niout 152 D 5
Nipa 179 F 2
Nipani 134 B 4
Nipawin 167 R 5
Nipigon 168 K 6
Nipigon, Lake 168 K 6
Nipissing, Lake 169 LM 6
Nippur 155 H 2
Nīr, Jabal an 155 G 4
Nirmal 134 C 4
Nirmal Range 134 C 4
Nis 116 B 2
Nișāb → Anşāb 155 G 3
Nişāb (S. Yemen) 155 H 6
Nišava 116 B 2
Niscemi 115 F 4
Nishino'omote 133 K 4
Nisko 111 H 4
Nísoi 116 B 3
Nísoi Strofádhes 116 B 3
Nissan 113 F 4
Nisser 113 E 4
Nissum Bredning 113 E 4
Nissum Fjord 113 E 4
Niterói 181 H 5
Nithsdale 99 C 4
Nitiya 131 P 4
Nitra 111 G 5
Nitsa 119 M 4
Niuafo'ou 146 D 4
Niuato Putapu 146 D 4
Niue 146 D 4
Niulakita 146 C 3
Niutao 146 C 3
Niut, Gunung 136 D 3
Niutoushan 133 G 4
Nivala 112 H 3
Nivernais 114 D 2
Nivskiy 112 K 2
Nizamabad 134 C 4
Nizhneangarsk 130 J 4
Nizhnegoriskiy 117 D 1
Nizhne-Kamchatsk 131 U 4
Nizhne-Ozernaya 131 U 4
Nizhneshadrino 130 F 4
Nizhneudinsk 130 G 5
Nizhnevartovskoye 119 P 3
Nizhneyansk 131 P 1
Nizhneye Bugayevo 118 K 2
Nizhneye Karelina 130 J 4
Nizhniy Baskunchak 118 J 6
Nizhniy Chir 118 H 6
Nizhniye Kresty 131 U 2
Nizhniy Kholtoson 130 H J 5
Nizhniy Kuranakh 131 N 4
Nizhniy Lomov 118 H 5
Nizhniy Pyandzh 129 H 3
Nizhniy Tagil 119 M 4

Nizhniy Tsasuchey 130 L 5
Nizhniy Yenangsk 118 J 4
Nizhnyaya Mgla 118 H 2
Nizhnyaya Omka 119 O 4
Nizhnyaya Poyma 130 G 4
Nizhnyaya Tavda 119 N 4
Nizhnyaya Tunguska 130 F 2
Nizhnyaya Voch' 118 K 3
Nizhnyaya Zolotitsa 118 H 2
Nizina Podlaska 111 H 4
Nizip 117 E 3
Nízke Tatry 111 G 5
Njinjo 159 F 6
Njombe 158 E 6
Njudung 113 F 4
Njunes 112 G 2
Njurunda 112 G 3
Njutånger 112 G 3
Nkai 160 D 3
Nkambe 157 G 4
Nkawkaw 156 D 4
Nkayi 157 G 6
Nkhata Bay 161 E 2
Nkhotka-Kota 161 E 2
Nkolabona 157 G 5
Nkongsamba 157 FG 5
Nkululu 158 E 5
Nkusi 158 E 4
Nkwalini 161 E 5
Nmai Hka 135 G 2
Nömrög 130 G 6
Noakhali 135 F 3
Noanamá 178 C 3
Noatak 166 E 2
Noatak National Preserve 166 F 2
Noatak (River) 166 F 2
Nobel 171 K 2
Nobeoka 133 K 4
Noberé 156 D 3
Nobres 180 E 3
Noccundra 143 G 4
Noefs, Ile des 159 J 6
Nogales 170 D 5
Nogal Valley → Dōhō Nugālēd 159 H 3
Nogayskiye Step' 117 G 2
Nogent-le-Rotrou 114 D 2
Noginsk 118 F 3
Noginskiy 130 F 3
Nogliki 131 Q 5
Nogoya 183 DE 2
Noguera 179 E 4
Nogueira, Serra da 114 B 3
Noguera Pallaresa 114 D 3
Nohar 134 B 2
Noir, Isla 183 B 9
Noirmoutier 114 C 2
Nojane 160 C 4
Nokaneng 160 C 3
Nokia 112 H 3
Nok Kundi 129 G 5
Nokou 157 G 3
Nokra 159 F 1
Nokrek 135 F 2
Nola 158 B 4
Nolinsk 118 J 4
Nomad 144 D 3
Nombre de Dios 172 B 3
Nome 166 D 3
Nomgon 132 D 2
Nomhon 132 C 3
Nomtsas 160 B 4
Nomuka Group 147 D 4
Nomwin 146 B 2
Nonacho Lake 167 Q 3
Nonburg 118 K 2
Nondugl 144 D 3
Nong Khai 135 H 4
Nongoma 161 E 5
Nonoava 170 E 6
Nonouti 146 C 3
Noonkanbah 142 C 2
Noordoewer 160 B 5
Noordzeekanaal 110 D 4
Noorvik 166 E 2
Nóqui 160 A 1
Nora 113 G 4
Nora skog 113 F 4
Norberg 113 G 3
Nordaustlandet 184
Nordborg 113 E 4
Nordby 113 E 4
Nord, Canal du 114 D 1
Norden 111 E 4
Nordenham 111 E 4
Norderstadt 111 E 4
Nordfjord 112 E 3
Nordfjordeid 112 E 3
Nordfold 112 G 2
Nordfriesische Inseln 111 E 4
Nordhausen 111 F 4

Nordkapp 112 J 1
Nordkinn 112 J 1
Nordkinnhalvöya 112 J 1
Nordkjosbotn 112 G 2
Nord-kudløy 112 G 1
Nordland 112 F 2
Nordmaling 112 G 3
Nordostrundingen 184
Nord-Ostsee-Kanal 111 E 4
Nordöyane 112 E 3
Norðoyar 110 A 1
Nordreisa 112 H 2
Nordre Strømfjord 169 R 2
Nordrhein-Westfalen 111 E 4
Nord-Tröndelag 112 F 3
Nordvik 130 K 1
Norefjell 113 E 3
Nore, River 100 B 3
Norfolk (U.K.) 103 E 1
Norfolk Islands 146 C 4
Norfolk Lake 171 H 4
Norfolk (NE, U.S.A.) 170 G 3
Norfolk (VA, U.S.A.) 171 L 4
Norge 112 F 2
Nori 119 O 2
Noril'sk 119 R 2
Normal 171 J 3
Norman 170 G 4
Normanby 145 F 3
Normanby Island 143 J 1
Normandie 114 CD 2
Norman, Lake 171 K 4
Norman River 143 G 2
Normanton 143 G 2
Norquin 183 B 6
Norquinco 183 B 7
Norra Kvarken 112 H 3
Norra Storfjället 112 G 2
Norrbotten 112 G 2
Norresundby 113 E 4
Norris Lake 171 K 4
Norråker 112 G 3
Norrköping 113 G 4
Norrland 112 FG 3
Norrtälje 113 G 4
Norseman 142 C 5
Norsjö (Norway) 113 E 4
Norsjö (Sweden) 112 G 3
Norsk 131 N 5
Norsoup 145 J 5
Nortelândia 180 E 3
Norte, Punta 183 E 6
North Adams 171 M 3
Northallerton 101 E 2
Northam (U.K.) 102 B 2
Northam (Australia) 142 B 5
Northam (South Africa) 160 D 4
Northampton (Australia) 142 A 4
Northampton (U.K.) 103 D 1
Northamptonshire 103 D 1
North Andaman 135 F 5
North Arm 167 P 3
North Aulatsivik Island 169 P 4
North Battleford 167 Q 5
North Bay 171 L 2
North Belcher Islands 169 M 4
North Bend 170 B 3
North Berwick 99 C 3
North Canadian River 170 G 4
North, Cape 169 P 6
North Cape (Norway) 112 J 1
North Cape (New Zealand) 145 Q 7
North Caribou Lake 168 J 5
North Carolina 171 K 4
North Cascades National Park 170 B 2
North Cascades N.P. 170 B 2
North Channel (Canada) 171 K 2
North Channel (U.K.) 100 C 2
North Chicago 171 J 3
Northcliff 142 B 5
North Dakota 170 F 2
North Danger Reef 136 D 1
North Downs 103 E 2
Northeast Cape 166 D 3
Northeast Providence Channel 173 G 2
Northeim 111 F 4
Northern Cook Islands 147 E 3
Northern Dvina River 118 H 3
Northern Indian Lake 167 S 4
Northern Ireland 100 B 2
Northern Mariana Islands 146 B 1
Northern Territory 142 E 2
Northfield 171 H 3
Northfleet 103 C 2
North Foreland 103 E 2
North Fork Pass 166 K 3
North Geomagnetic Pole 184
North Highlands 170 B 4

261

North Horr 159 F 4
North Island 145 Q 8
North Korea 133 J 2
North Lakhimpur 135 F 2
North Las Vegas 170 C 4
North Little Rock 171 H 5
North Loup River 170 F 3
North Magnetic Pole 184
North Minch 98 B 2
North Pacific Basin 193 D 2
North Palisade 170 C 4
North Platte 170 F 3
North Platte River 170 E 3
North Point 144 L 8
North Pole 184
North River 167 T 4
North Rona 98 B 2
North Ronaldsay 98 C 2
North Saskatchewan 167 PQ 5
North Sentinel 135 F 5
North Slope 166 F 2
North Stradbroke Island 143 J 4
North Taranaki Bight 145 Q 8
North Thompson 167 O 5
North Tyne, River 101 D 2
North Uist 98 A 3
Northumberland 101 D 2
Northumberland Islands 143 J 3
Northumberland Strait 169 P 6
North Walsham 103 E 1
Northway Junction 166 J 3
North West Cape 142 A 3
North West Highlands 98 B 3
Northwest Pacific Basin 193 C 2
North West River 169 P 5
Northwest Territories (Canada) 167 N 2
Northwich 101 D 3
Norton (KS, U.S.A.) 170 G 4
Norton (VA, U.S.A.) 171 K 4
Norton (Zimbabwe) 161 E 3
Norton Bay 166 E 3
Norton Sound 166 E 3
Norvegia, Cape 185
Norwalk 171 K 3
Norway 112 F 2
Norway Bay 167 R 1
Norway House 167 S 5
Norway (WI, U.S.A.) 171 J 2
Norwegian Basin 192 A 1
Norwich 103 E 1
Norwich (Airport) 103 E 1
Noshiro 133 M 2
Noshul' 118 J 3
Nosok 119 Q 1
Nosovaya 118 K 2
Nosovka 118 F 5
Nosovshchina 118 G 3
Nosratābād 128 F 5
Nossa Senhora da Glória 178 D 5
Nossob 160 B 4
Nossop 160 C 5
No. 5 Station 154 E 4
No. 10 Station 154 E 5
Nosy Barren 161 G 3
Nosy-Bé 161 H 2
Nosy Boraha 161 HJ 3
Nosy Mitsio 161 H 2
Nosy-Varika 161 H 4
Nota 112 J 2
Noteć 111 G 4
Nótioi Sporádhes 116 C 3
Noto 115 G 4
Notodden 113 E 4
Noto-hantō 133 L 3
Notorskoye 131 O 3
Notre Dame Bay 169 Q 6
Notre Dame, Monts 169 N 6
Nottawasaga Bay 171 K 3
Nottaway 169 M 5
Nottingham (U.K.) 103 D 1
Nottingham (Canada) 169 M 3
Nottinghamshire 103 D 1
Nouadhibou 152 B 4
Nouadhibou, Dakhlet 152 B 4
Nouakchott 152 B 5
Nouamrhar 152 B 5
Nouméa 145 J 6
Noumin He 131 M 6
Nouna 156 D 3
Noupoort 160 CD 6
Nouveau Comptoir 169 M 5
Nouvelle-Calédonie 145 H 6
Nouvelle France, Cap de 169 N 3
Nova 181 H 2
Nova Andradino 181 F 5
Novabad 129 J 3
Nova Caipemba 160 A 1
Nova Cruz 181 J 2
Nova Friburgo 181 H 5
Nova Gorica 115 F 2
Nova Gradiška 115 G 2
Nova Horizonte 181 G 5

Nova Huta 111 H 4
Nova Iguaçu 181 H 5
Nova Lamego 156 B 3
Nova Lima 181 H 5
Nova Mambone 161 F 4
Nova Olinda do Norte 179 G 4
Novara 115 E 2
Nova Scotia 169 P 7
Nova Sento Sé 181 H 2
Nova, Serra 179 F 5
Nova Sofala 161 E 4
Nova Varoš 116 A 2
Nova Venécia 181 H 4
Nova Vida 180 D 3
Novaya Igirma 130 H 4
Novaya Kakhovka 117 D 1
Novaya Kazanka 118 J 6
Novaya Lyalya 119 M 4
Novaya Odessa 116 D 1
Novaya Ushitsa 116 C 1
Novaya Ussuri 131 P 6
Novaya Zemlya 118 L 1
Novaya Zemlya 184
Nova Zagora 116 C 2
Novelda 114 C 4
Nové Zámky 111 G 5
Novgorod 113 K 4
Novgorodka 113 J 4
Novgorodka 117 D 1
Novgorod Severskiy 118 F 5
Novigrad 115 F 2
Novikovo 131 Q 6
Novi Ligure 115 E 3
Novillero 172 A 3
Novi Pazar (Bulgaria) 116 C 2
Novi Pazar (Yugoslavia) 116 B 2
Novi Sad 116 A 1
Novi Vinodolski 115 F 2
Novo Acôrdo 179 H 4
Novoaleksandrovsk 117 F 1
Novoalekseyevka 117 D 1
Novoaltaysk 119 Q 5
Novoanninskiy 118 H 5
Novo Aripuanã 179 F 4
Novo Arkhangelsk 116 D 1
Novoazovsk 117 E 1
Novobiryusinskiy 130 G 4
Novobogatinskoye 128 E 1
Novobogdanovka 116 E 1
Novocherkassk 117 F 1
Novodolinka 119 O 5
Novodolinskiy 119 O 6
Novogeorgiyevka 131 N 5
Novograd-Volynskiy 113 J 5
Novogrudok 113 J 5
Novo Hamburgo 182 F 4
Novokazalinsk 129 G 1
Novokhoperskiy 118 H 5
Novokocherdyk 119 M 5
Novokubansk 117 F 1
Novokuybyshevsk 118 J 5
Novokuznetsk 119 R 5
Novo, Lago 179 H 3
Novolazarevskaya 185
Novoletov'ye 130 H 1
Novoluzino 119 R 2
Novomariinka 130 G 4
Novomariinka Ambarchik 119 T 4
Novomikhaylovskoye 117 E 2
Novomirgorod 116 D 1
Novomoskovsk 117 E 1
Novomoskovsk 118 G 5
Novonikolskoye 119 NO 4
Novonikol'skoye 119 P 4
Novoorsk 119 L 5
Novopavlovskoye 130 K 5
Novopokrovskaya 117 F 1
Novopolotsk 112 J 4
Novo Pskov 118 G 6
Novorossiysk 117 E 2
Novorybnoye 130 J 1
Novo Sagres 137 G 5
Novo-selitsa 116 C 1
Novoselovo 130 F 4
Novo Sergeyevka 118 K 5
Novoshakhtinsk 117 E 1
Novosibirsk 119 Q 4
Novosibirskiye Ostrova → New Siberian Islands 121 QR 2
Novosibirskoye Vodokhranilishche 119 Q 5
Novosokol'niki 113 K 4
Novotroitsk 119 L 5
Novotroitskoye 119 J 2
Novo Troitskoye 117 D 1
Novotsimlyanskiy 117 F 1
Novo Ukrainka 116 D 1
Novo Uzensk 118 J 5
Novoveselyy 117 F 1
Novovolynsk 113 H 5
Novovorontsovka 117 D 1
Novovoskresenovka 131 N 5
Novovvaya Vasyugan 119 P 4

Novo-Vyatsk 118 J 4
Novoyeniseysk 130 F 4
Novoyerudinskiy 130 F 4
Novoye Ust'ye 131 Q 4
Novoyugino 119 Q 4
Novovy Bug 117 D 1
Nový Jičin 111 G 5
Novy Uzen' 128 E 2
Novyy 119 R 4
Novyy 130 J 1
Novyy Afon 117 F 2
Novyy Bor 118 K 2
Novyy Karymkary 119 N 3
Novyy Oskol 118 G 5
Novyy Port 119 O 2
Novyy Tanguy 130 H 4
Nowa Ruda 111 G 4
Nowa Sól 111 G 4
Nowbarān 128 D 3
Nowdesheh 128 D 3
Nowgong 135 F 2
Nowitna 166 G 3
Nowogard 111 G 4
Nowo Korczyn 111 H 4
Nowra 113 J 5
Nowrangapur 134 D 4
Now Shahr 128 E 3
Nowshera 129 K 4
Nowy Dwór 111 H 4
Nowy Sacz 111 H 5
Nowy Targ 111 H 5
Noya 114 B 3
Noyon 132 D 2
Nozay 114 C 2
Nærbö 113 E 4
Närpes (Närpiö) 112 G 3
Närpiö 112 G 3
Nås 113 F 3
Nsa 153 F 2
Nsanje 161 F 3
Nsawam 156 D 4
Näsijärvi 112 H 3
Näsåker 112 G 3
Nsok 157 G 5
Nsombo 160 D 2
Nässjö 113 F 4
Næstved 113 F 5
Nsukka 157 F 4
Nsuta 156 D 4
Ntademele 158 B 5
Ntakat 152 C 5
Ntem 157 G 5
Ntui 157 G 5
Näätämöjoki 112 J 2
Nuaib 152 D 3
Nuanetsi → Mwenezi 160 E 4
Nuatja 156 E 4
Nuba Mountains → Dar Nūbah 154 D 6
Nubia 154 E 5
Nubian Desert → Aş Şaḥrā' an Nūbiyah 154 E 4
Nūbiyah, Aş Şaḥrā' an 154 E 4
Nueces Plains 170 G 6
Nueces River 170 G 6
Nueifed 152 C 4
Nueltin Lake 167 S 3
Nueva Alejandría 178 D 5
Nueva Antioqia 178 E 2
Nueva Esperanza 180 D 4
Nueva Galia 182 C 5–6
Nueva Gerona 172 F 3
Nueva Imperial 183 B 6
Nueva, Isla 183 B 7
Nueva León 172 BC 2
Nueva Lubecka 183 B 7
Nueva Orán 180 D 5
Nueva Rosita 172 B 2
Nueva San Salvador 172 E 5
Nueve de Julio 182 D 6
Nuevitas 173 G 3
Nuevo Berlin 182 E 5
Nuevo 119 Q 2
Nuevo Casas Grandes 170 E 2
Nuevo, Golfo 183 D 7
Nuevo Laredo 172 C 2
Nuevo Mundo, Cerro 180 C 5
Nuevo Rocafuerte 178 C 4
Nugāl 159 H 3
Nuguria Islands 145 G 2
Nui 146 C 3
Nuijamaa 112 J 3
Nuiqsut 166 G 1
Nujiang 132 C 6
Nu Jiang 132 C 6
Nukey Bluff 143 F 5
Nukhayb 155 G 2
Nukhaylak 154 D 5
Nuku'alofa 147 D 4
Nukufetau 146 C 3
Nuku Hiva 147 F 3

Nukuhu 145 E 2
Nukulaelae 146 C 3
Nukumanu Islands 145 G 2
Nukunau 146 C 3
Nukunonu 146 D 3
Nukuoro 146 B 2
Nukus 128 F 2
Nulato 166 F 3
Nullagine 142 C 3
Nullarbor 142 E 5
Nullarbor Plain 142 D 5
Nulloocha 143 G 3
Numan 157 G 4
Numancia 137 G 2
Nu'mānīyah 155 H 2
Numazu 133 L 3
Numbulwar Mission 142 F 1
Numedal 113 E 3
Numfor, Pulau 137 H 4
Numkaub 160 B 3
Num, Pulau 137 J 4
Numto 119 O 3
Numurkah 143 H 6
Nundle 143 J 5
Nundu 158 D 5
Nuneaton 103 D 1
Nungnain Sum 133 G 1
Nungo 161 F 2
Nunivak Island 166 D 3
Nunkun 129 K 4
Nunlygran 166 B 3
Nuntherungie 143 G 5
Nunukan Timur, Pulau 136 E 3
Nunyamo 166 C 2
Nuorajärvi 112 K 3
Nuorgam 112 J 1
Nuoro 115 E 3
Nuqay, Jabal 153 J 4
Nuqrah 155 G 3
Nuquş, Jabal 154 E 4
Nuquí 178 C 2
Nura 119 O 5
Nura 119 O 6
Nurata 129 H 2
Nuratau, Khrebet 129 H 2
Nur Dağları 117 E 3
Nurek 129 H 3
Nuremberg 111 F 5
Nurhak Dağı 117 E 3
Nūrī 154 E 5
Nuristan 129 J 3
Nurlat 118 K 5
Nurmes 112 J 3
Nürnberg 111 F 5
Nurpur 134 C 1
Nurri, Mount 143 H 5
Nusaybin 117 F 3
Nushagak 166 F 4
Nu Shan 132 C 5
Nushki 129 G 5
Nutak 169 P 4
Nutrias 178 E 2
Nuupas 112 J 2
Nuwara Eliya 134 D 6
Nuweveldreeks 160 C 6
Nxai Pan National Park 160 C 3
Nyaake 156 C 5
Nyabéssan 157 G 5
Nyabing 142 B 5
Nyahanga 158 E 5
Nyahua 158 E 6
Nyahururu 159 F 4
Nyainqentanglha Shan 132 B 4
Nyainrong 132 B 4
Nyakakangaga 158 E 5
Nyakanazi 158 E 5
Nyåker 112 G 3
Nyaksimvol' 119 MN 3
Nyala 154 C 6
Nyalam 134 E 2
Nyalikungu 158 E 5
Nyamandhlovu 160 D 3
Nyamboma Rapids 160 C 2
Nyamboyto 119 Q 2
Nyamirembe 158 E 5
Nyamlell 158 D 3
Nyamtumbo 161 F 2
Nyanda Rua 159 F 5
Nyandoma 118 H 3
Nyanga 157 G 6
Nyanga, Lake 142 D 4
Nyangana 160 C 3
Nyanza 145 Q 10
Nyasa, Lake 161 E 2
Nyaungus 135 F 3
Nyayba 131 O 1
Nyazepetrovsk 119 L 4
Nyborg 113 F 5
Nybro 113 G 4
Nyda 119 O 2
Nyêmo 135 F 2
Nyeri 159 F 5

Nyerol 158 E 3
Nyika Plateau 161 E 2
Nyima 134 E 1
Nyimba 161 E 2
Nyingchi 132 B 5
Nyiregyháza 116 B 1
Nyiri Desert 159 F 5
Nyiru, Mount 159 F 4
Nykarleby 112 H 3
Nyköbing (Denmark) 113 E 4
Nyköbing (Denmark) 113 F 5
Nyköbing (Denmark) 113 F 4
Nyköping (Sweden) 113 G 4
Nylstroom 160 D 4
Nymagee 143 H 5
Nynäshamn 113 G 4
Nyngan 143 H 5
Nyon 115 E 2
Nyong 157 G 5
Nyrob 118 L 3
Nysa 111 G 4
Nyslott 112 J 3
Nyssa 170 C 3
Nystad 113 H 3
Nytva 118 L 4
Nyuk, Ozero 112 K 3
Nyuksenitsa 118 H 3
Nyukzha 131 M 5
Nyunzu 158 D 6
Nyurba 130 L 3
Nyurchan 131 S 4
Nyurol'skiy 119 P 4
Nyuya 130 K 3
Nyuya 130 L 3
Nyvrovo 131 Q 5
Nyyiskiy Zaliv 131 Q 5
Nzambi 157 G 6
Nzara 158 D 4
Nzébéla 156 C 4
Nzega 158 E 5
Nzérékoré 156 C 4
N'zeto 160 A 1
Nzi 156 D 4
Nzo 156 C 4

O

Oahe Dam 170 F 3
Oahe, Lake 170 F 2
Oahu 147 E 1
Oakbank 143 G 5
Oakey 143 J 4
Oakham 103 D 1
Oak Hills 143 H 2
Oakland (CA, U.S.A.) 170 B 4
Oakland (MD, U.S.A.) 171 L 4
Oakley 170 F 4
Oakover River 142 C 3
Oak Ridge 171 K 4
Oakridge 170 B 3
Oakville 171 L 3
Oamaru 145 Q 10
Oasis 170 D 3
Oates Coast 185
Oatlands 144 L 9
Olawa 111 G 4
Oaxaca 172 C 4
Oaxaca de Juárez 172 C 4
Ob 119 N 2
Oba 168 L 6
Oban (New Zealand) 144 P 10
Oban (U.K.) 99 B 3
Obanazawa 133 M 3
Obando 178 E 3
Oban Hills 157 F 4
Obbia → Hobyä 159 H 3
Obeh 129 G 4
Obeliai 112 J 4
Oberonovac 116 B 2
Oberpfälzer Wald 111 F 5
Oberpullendorf 115 G 2
Oberstdorf 111 F 5
Obervellach 115 F 2
Óbidos 179 G 4
Obihiro 133 M 2
Obi, Kepulauan 137 G 4
Obil'noye 117 F 1
Obi, Selat 137 G 4
Oblukovino 131 T 4
Obninsk 118 G 4
Obo 132 D 3
Obo 158 D 3
Obock 159 G 2
Obodovka 116 C 1

Obokote 158 D 5
Oborniki 111 G 4
Obouya 157 H 6
Oboyan' 118 G 5
Obozerskiy 118 H 3
Obruk Platosu 117 D 3
Obshchiy Syrt 118 KL 5
Obskaya Guba 119 O 1,2
Obuasi 156 D 4
Obubra 157 F 4
Obudu 157 F 4
Obula 157 G 5
Obzor 116 C 2
Ocala 171 K 6
Ocampo 170 E 6
Ocaña (Spain) 114 C 4
Ocaña (Colombia) 178 D 2
Ocean City 171 L 4
Ocean Falls 167 M 5
Ocean Island 145 J 2
Ochakov 116 D 1
Ochamchire 117 F 2
Ocher 118 K 4
Ochil Hills 99 C 3
Ocho Rios 173 G 4
Ockelbo 113 G 3
Ocmulgee River 171 K 5
Ocoña 180 B 4
Oconee 171 K 5
Oconee River 171 K 5
Ocotlán 172 B 3
Ocotlán de Morelos 172 C 4
Ocreza 114 C 4
Ocumare del Tuy 178 E 1
Oda 156 D 4
Ódáðahraun 112 B 2–3
Oda, Jabal 154 F 4
Ødalen 113 F 3
Ōdate 133 M 2
Odawara 133 L 3
Odda 113 E 3
Odder 113 F 4
Odemiş 114 B 4
Odendaalsrus 160 D 5
Odense 113 F 4
Oder 111 F 4
Ödeshög 113 F 4
Odessa (U.S.S.R.) 116 D 1
Odessa (TX, U.S.A.) 170 F 5
Odiel 114 B 4
Odienné 156 C 4
Ödmården 112 G 3
Odorheiu Secuiesc 116 C 1
Odra 111 F 4
Ødwëyne 159 H 3
Odžak 115 G 2
Odzala National Park 157 GH 5
Oeiras 181 H 2
Oelwein 171 H 3
Oeno 147 G 4
Oenpelli 142 E 1
Of 117 F 2
Ofanto 115 G 3
Ofeigsfjarðarheidi 112 A 2
Offa 157 E 4
Offaly 100 B 3
Offenbach 111 E 4
Offenburg 111 E 5
Offoué 157 G 6
Oficina 179 F 2
Ofotfjorden 112 G 2
Oga 133 L 3
Ogaden 159 GH 3
Og Aguelt Abd el Jebar 152 D 4
Oga-hantō 133 L 3
Ōgaki 133 L 3
Ogallala 170 F 3
Ogan, Air 136 B 4
Ogden 170 D 3
Ogdensburg 171 L 3
Oghroud 153 G 2
Ogilvie Mountains 166 K 2
Oginskiy Kanal 113 J 4
Oglanly 128 E 3
Oglat Beraber 152 E 2
Oglat el Fersig 152 D 4
Oglio 115 F 2
Ogmore 143 H 3
Ognev Yar 119 P 4
Ognon 115 E 2
Ogoamas, Gunung 137 F 3
Ogoja 157 F 4
Ogoki 168 K 5
Ogoki Reservoir 168 K 5
Ogonëk 131 P 4
Ogooué 157 G 5
Ogoron 119 N 5
Ogradžen 116 B 2
Ogre 113 H 4
Ogr → Sharafah 154 D 6
Ogulin 115 G 2
Oguma 157 F 4

Ogun 156 E 4
Ogurchinskiy, Ostrov 128 E 3
Ogwashi Uku 157 F 4
Ohakune 145 R 8
Ohanet 153 G 3
O'Higgins, Cerro 183 B 8
O'Higgins, Lago 183 B 8
Ohio 171 K 3
Ohio River 171 J 4
Ohopoho 160 A 3
Ohře 111 F 4
Ohrid 116 B 2
Ohridskojezero 116 B 2
Oiapoque 179 H 3
Oijärvi 112 J 2
Oise 114 D 2
Ōita 133 K 4
Ōjebyn 112 H 2
Ojinaga 170 F 6
Ojo de Agua 182 D 4
Ojos del Salado, Cerro 182 C 4
Oka 130 H 5
Oka 118 H 4
Okaba 137 J 5
Okahandja 160 B 4
Okahao 160 A 3
Okakarara 160 B 4
Okak Islands 169 P 4
Okanagan Lake 167 O 6
Okanda, Parc National de 157 G 6
Okano 157 G 5
Okanogan River 170 C 2
Okapa 144 E 3
Okaputa 160 B 4
Okara 129 J 4
Okaukuejo 160 B 3
Okavango 160 C 3
Okavango Swamp 160 C 3
Okavarumendu 160 B 4
Okaya 133 L 3
Okayama 133 K 4
Okazaki 133 L 4
Okazize 160 B 4
Okeanskoye 131 T 5
Okeechobee, Lake 171 K 6
Okehamptom 102 B 2
Okene 157 F 4
Okha (India) 134 A 3
Okha (U.S.S.R.) 131 Q 5
Ókhi Oros 116 B 3
Okhota 131 Q 3
Okhotskiy Perevoz 131 P 3
Okhotskoye More 131 R 4,5
Okhotsk, Sea of 131 R 4,5
Okhthonia, Ákra 116 B 3
Okinawa-jima 133 J 5
Okinoerabu-jima 133 J 5
Oki-shotō 133 K 3
Okitipupa 157 EF 4
Oklahoma 170 G 4
Oklahoma City 170 G 4
Oknitsa 116 C 1
Okollo 158 E 4
Okombahe 160 B 4
Okondja 157 G 6
Okorukambe 160 B 4
Okoyo 157 H 6
Öksfjord 112 H 1
Oksino 118 K 2
Okstindan 112 F 2
Oktemberyan 117 F 2
Oktwin 135 G 4
Oktyabr'skiy 119 M 5
Oktyabrskiy 118 K 5
Oktyabr'skiy 130 F 5
Oktyabrskiy 131 N 5
Oktyabr'skiy 131 Q 5
Oktyabr'skiy 117 F 1
Oktyabr'skoye 118 G 5
Oktyabr'skoye 119 N 3
Okurchan 131 S 4
Okushiri-tō 133 L 2
Okuta 156 E 4
Okwa 157 F 4
Ola 131 S 4
Ólafsfjörður 112 B 2
Ólafsvík 112 A 3
Olancha 170 C 4
Öland 113 G 4
Olanga 113 K 2
Olary 143 G 5
Olathe 171 H 4
Olavarria 183 D 6
Olbia 115 E 3
Old Bahama Channel 173 G 3
Old Cherrabun 142 D 2
Old Crow 166 K 2
Oldenburg 111 E 4
Oldenburg 111 F 4

Old Gidgee 142 B 4
Oldham 101 D 3
Old Harbor 166 G 4
Oldmeldrum 98 C 3
Old Mkushi 160 D 2
Olds 167 P 5
Old Wives Lake 167 Q 5
Olekma 130 M 4
Olekminsk 130 M 3
Olekminskiy Stanovik 130 L 5
Olekmo-Charskoye Nagor'ye 130 LM 4
Olema 118 J 3
Olenegorsk 112 K 2
Olenëk 130 K 2
Olenëk 130 M 1
Olenëkskiy Zaliv 130 M 1
Olenevod 131 X 3
Olenevod 131 T 4
Olenitsa 112 L 2
Olen'ya Rechka 130 F 5
Oléron, Ile d' 114 C 2
Oleśnica 111 G 4
Olevsk 113 J 5
Ol'ga 133 K 2
Olga, Mount 142 E 4
Ol'ginka 117 E 1
Ólgiy 130 F 6
Ol'gopol 117 D 1
Ol'gopol 116 C 1
Olhão 114 B 4
Oliana 114 D 3
Olib 115 F 3
Olifants 161 E 4
Olifantshoek 160 C 5
Olimarao 146 A 2
Olimbia 116 B 3
Ólimbos 116 C 3
Olimbos, Kato 116 B 3
Olímpia 181 G 5
Olinda 181 K 2
Olindina 181 J 3
Olite 114 C 3
Oliva (Spain) 114 C 4
Oliva (Argentina) 182 D 5
Oliveira 181 H 5
Olivença 161 F 2
Olkusz 111 G 4
Ollagüe 180 C 5
Ollagüe, Volcán 180 C 5
Olmos 178 C 5
Olochi 130 L 5
Olofström 113 F 4
Olomouc 111 G 5
Olonets 112 K 3
Olongapo 137 H 1
Oloron-Sainte-Marie 114 C 3
Olot 114 D 3
Olovo 115 G 3
Olovyannaya 130 L 5
Olshammar 113 F 4
Olsztyn 111 H 4
Olsztynek 111 H 4
Olt 116 B 2
Olten 115 E 2
Oltenia 116 B 2
Oltenița 116 C 2
Oltu 117 F 2
Olvera 114 B 4
Olympia 170 B 2
Olympia → Olimbia 116 B 3
Olympic National Park 170 B 2
Olympus 116 B 2–3
Olympus, Mount 170 B 2
Olyutorka 131 V 3
Olyutorskiy Gory 131 W 3
Olyutorskiy, Mys 131 VW 4
Olyutorskiy Poluostrov 131 W 3
Olyutorskiy Zaliv 131 V 3
Om' 119 Q 4
Omagh 110 B 4
Omagh 100 B 3
Omaguas 178 D 4
Omaha 171 G 3
Oman 155 K 4–5
Oman, Gulf of 128 F 5–6
Omarama 144 P 9
Omaruru 160 B 4
Omatako 160 B 4
Omatako, Mount 160 B 4
Omate 180 B 4
Omatjete 160 B 4
Ombai, Selat 137 G 5
Ombombo 160 A 3
Omboué 157 F 6
Ombrone 115 F 3
Ombu 134 E 1
Omchali 128 E 2
Omdurman → Umm Durmān 154 E 5
Omeleut 131 W 3
Omeo 143 H 6

Ometepec 172 C 4
Ometepe, Isla de 172 E 5
Omili 117 G 2
Omineca Mountains 167 M 4
Omiš 115 G 3
Omitara 160 B 4
Ōmiya 133 L 3
Ommanney Bay 167 R 1
Ömnödelger 130 J K 6
Ömnögovi 132 D 2
Omo 159 F 3
Omodeo, Lago 115 E 3
Omolon 131 T 2
Omolon 131 U 2
Omoloy 131 O 1
Omoloy 130 J 4
Omsk 119 O 4
Omsukchan 131 T 3
Omsukchanskiy Gory 131 T 3
Ōmulev 111 H 4
Ōmura 133 J 4
Ōmuta 133 K 4
Omutinskiy 119 N 4
Omutninsk 118 K 4
Ona Dikonde 158 C 5
Onamia 171 H 2
Onang 137 E 4
Onawa 171 G 3
Onayena 160 B 3
Onbingwin 135 G 5
Oncócua 160 A 3
Ondangwa 160 B 3
Ondaruza Falls 160 A 3
Ondava 111 H 5
Ondekaremba 160 B 4
Ondjiva 160 B 3
Ondo 157 E 4
Öndörhaan 130 K 6
Öndorkara 129 M 1
Öndörshireet 130 H 6
Ondor Sum 132 F 2
Ondozero, Ozero 112 K 3
Onega 118 G 3
O'Neill 170 G 3
Onekotan, Ostrov 131 S 6
Oneonta 171 L 3
Onesi 161 A 3
Onezhskaya Guba 118 G 3
Onezhskoye, Ozero 118 G 3
Ongiyn Gol 132 D 1
Ongjin 133 J 3
Ongnuid Qi 133 G 2
Ongole 135 M 1
Onguday 119 R 5
Oni 117 F 2
Onilahy 161 G 4
Onitsha 157 F 4
Onk, 153 G 2
Onkuchakh 130 KL 2
Ono-i-Lau Islands 146 D 4
Onomichi 133 K 4
Onon 130 L 5
Onon Gol 130 K 6
Onotoa 146 C 3
Onovgay 131 T 4
Onsala 113 F 4
Onseepkans 160 B 5
Onslow 142 B 3
Onslow Bay 171 L 5
Ontario (Can.) 168 J 5
Ontario (OR, U.S.A.) 170 C 3
Ontario, Lake 171 L 3
Onteniente 114 C 4
Ontojärvi 112 J 3
Ontong Java 145 G 2
Oodnadatta 143 F 4
Ookiep 160 B 5
Ooldea 142 E 5
Oologah Lake 171 G 4
Oorindi 143 G 3
Oostende 110 D 4
Ootacamund 134 C 5
Opala (U.S.S.R.) 131 T 5
Opala (Zaire) 158 C 5
Opanake 134 D 6
Opari 158 E 4
Opasatika 168 L 6
Opatija 115 F 2
Opava 111 G 5
Opelousas 171 H 5
Ophir 166 F 3
Opienge 158 D 4
Opis 155 G 2
Opiscotéo, Lac 169 O 5
Opobo 157 F 5
Opochka 113 J 4
Opoczno Końskie 111 H 4
Opole 111 G 4
Oporto 114 B 3
Oposhnya 118 F 6
Opotiki 145 R 8
Opp 171 J 5
Oppdal 112 E 3

Oppland 112 E 3
Opportunity 170 C 2
Oputo 170 E 5
Oradea 116 B 1
Öræfajökull 112 B 3
Orah 153 J 3
Orahovica 115 G 2
Orai 134 C 2
Oran 152 E 1
Orange (Namibia) 160 B 5
Orange (France) 115 D 3
Orange (TX, U.S.A.) 171 H 5
Orange, Cabo 179 H 3
Orange Free State 160 D 5
Orange Park 171 K 5
Orange Walk 172 E 4
Orango, Ilha de 156 A 3
Orango, Isla de 156 A 3
Oranienburg 111 F 4
Oranje 160 B 5
Oranje Gebergte 179 GH 3
Oranjemund 160 B 5
Oranjestad 178 E 1
Oranzherei 117 G 1
Orapa 160 D 4
Orbetello 115 F 3
Orbigo 114 B 3
Orbost 143 H 6
Orcadas 185
Or, Côte d' 115 D 2
Ordenes 114 B 3
Ord, Mount 142 D 2
Ordoquí 183 D 6
Ordos Plateau 132 E 3
Ord River 142 D 2
Ord River Dam 142 D 2
Ordu 117 E 2
Ordynskoye 119 Q 5
Ordzhonikidze 117 F 2
Ordzhonikidzeabad 129 H 3
Orealla 179 G 2
Orebić 115 G 3
Örebro 113 G 4
Oregon 170 B 3
Oregon Inlet 171 L 4
Öregrund 113 G 3
Orekhov 117 E 1
Orekhovo Zuyevo 118 G 4
Orel 118 G 5
Orel' 117 D 1
Orellana (Peru) 178 C 5
Orellana (Peru) 178 C 4
Orel', Ozero 131 P 5
Orem 170 D 3
Oren 116 C 3
Orenburg 118 K 4
Orense 114 B 3
Orestiás 116 C 2
Öresund 113 F 4
Organá 114 D 3
Organ Peak 170 E 5
Organ Pipe Cactus National Monument 170 D 5
Orgeyev 116 C 1
Órgiva 114 C 4
Orhaneli 116 C 3
Orhangazi 116 C 2
Orhon Gol 130 H 6
Ori 181 J 7
Orick 170 B 3
Oriente 183 D 6
Orihuela 114 C 4
Orillia 171 L 3
Orimattila 112 J 3
Orinduik 179 FG 3
Orinoco 178 E 2–3
Orissa 134 DE 3
Orissaare 113 H 4
Oristano 115 E 4
Orivesi 112 J 3
Oriximiná 179 G 4
Orizaba 172 C 4
Orjahovo 116 B 2
Orjen 116 A 2
Orkadalen 112 E 3
Orkanger 112 E 3
Örkelljunga 113 F 4
Orkla 112 E 3
Orkney (S. Afr.) 160 D 5
Orkney Islands 98 C 2
Orlando 171 K 6
Orléans 114 D 2
Orléansville → El Asnam 153 F 1
Orlik 130 G 5
Orlovskaya 131 V 3
Orlu 157 F 4
Ormara 129 G 5
Ormoc 137 F 1
Örmos Almiroú 116 B 3
Ormskirk 101 D 3
Orne 114 C 2
Örnö 113 G 4
Örnsköldsvik 112 G 3

Oro–Oze

Orobie, Alpi 115 EF 2
Orochen 131 N 4
Orocué 178 D 3
Orodara 156 CD 3
Orofino 170 C 2
Örög Nuur 130 F 5
Orog Nuur 132 D 1
Orogrande 170 E 5
Oroluk 146 B 2
Oromocto 169 O 6
Oro, Monte d' 115 E 3
Oron (U.S.S.R.) 130 L 4
Oron (Nigeria) 157 F 5
Orona 146 D 3
Oropesa 114 D 3
Oropesa 114 B 4
Oroqen Zizhiqi 131 M 5
Oroquieta 137 F 2
Orosei 115 E 3
Óros Ossa 116 B 3
Oroszlány 116 A 1
Orotukan 131 S 3
Oroville (CA, U.S.A.) 170 B 4
Oroville (WA, U.S.A.) 170 C 2
Oroyëk 131 S 3
Orqohan 131 M 6
Orr 171 H 2
Orrefors 113 G 4
Orroroo 143 F 5
Orsa 112 F 3
Orsa Finnmark 112 F 3
Orsasjön 112 F 3
Orsha 113 K 5
Orsk 119 L 5
Orşova 116 B 2
Örsta 112 E 3
Orta 117 D 2
Ortaca 116 C 3
Ortà, Lago d' 115 E 2
Ortegal, Cabo 114 B 3
Orthez 114 C 3
Ortigueira 114 B 3
Ortiz 170 D 6
Ortles 115 F 2
Orto-Ayan 131 N 1
Ortona 115 F 3
Ortonville 171 G 2
Oruhito 160 A 3
Orūmīyeh 128 D 3
Orungo 158 E 4
Oruro 180 C 4
Orust 113 F 4
Orvault 114 C 2
Orvieto 115 F 3
Orzinuovi 115 E 2
Osa 130 H 5
Osa 118 L 4
Ōsaka 133 L 4
Osakarovka 119 O 5
Ōsaka-wan 133 L 4
Osam 116 B 2
Osa, Península de 172 F 6
Osborne 170 G 4
Osby 113 F 4
Osceola 171 H 3
Oschiri 115 E 3
Osen 112 F 3
Osh 129 J 2
Osha 119 O 4
Oshakati 160 B 3
Oshawa 171 L 3
Oshikango 160 B 3
Ō-shima 133 L 2
Oshivelo 160 B 3
Oshkosh 171 J 3
Oshmarino 130 D 1
Oshmyany 113 J 5
Oshnavīyeh 128 D 3
Oshogbo 157 E 4
Oshtorān Kūh 128 D 4
Oshwe 158 B 5
Osijek 115 G 2
Osimo 115 F 3
Osinniki 119 Q 6
Osinovka 119 R 3
Osipovichi 113 J 5
Osire 160 B 4
Oskaloosa 171 H 3
Oskarshamn 113 G 4
Oskarström 113 F 4
Oskino 130 J 3
Öskjuuvatn 112 B 2
Oskoba 130 H 3
Oslo 113 F 4
Oslob 137 F 2
Oslofjorden 113 F 4
Osmanabad 134 C 4
Osmancık 117 D 2
Osmaneli 116 D 2
Osmaniye 117 E 3
Os'mino 113 J 4

Osmyanskaya Vozvyshennost' 113 J 5
Osnabrück 111 E 4
Osor 115 F 3
Osorno 183 B 7
Osoyoos 167 O 6
Osöyra 113 E 3
Ospito 178 E 2
Osprey Reef 143 H 1
Ossa, Mount 144 L 9
Ossa, Óros 116 B 3
Ossau, Pic du Midi d' 114 C 3
Osse 157 F 4
Ossjöen 112 F 3
Ossora 131 U 4
Ostashkov 118 F 4
Østavall 112 G 3
Österdalälven 112 F 3
Österdalen 112 F 3
Östergötland 113 G 4
Österreich 115 F 2
Östersund 112 F 3
Östhammar 113 G 3
Østhavet 112 J K 1
Östmark 113 F 3
Ostroda 111 G 4
Ostroleka 111 H 4
Ostrogozhsk 118 G 5
Ostroshitski Gorodok 113 J 5
Ostrova Chernyye Brat'ya 131 S 6
Ostrova Diomida 166 D 2
Ostrova Medvezh'i 131 U 1
Ostrova Solovetskiye 118 G 2
Ostrova Srednego 131 S 6
Ostrov Atlasova 131 T 5
Ostrov Ayon 131 V 2
Ostrov Barsa-Kel'mes 128 F 1
Ostrov Bol'shoy Begichev 130 K 1
Ostrov Bol'shoy Lyakhovskiy 131 Q 1
Ostrov Bol'shoy Shantar 131 P 4–5
Ostrov Broutona 131 S 6
Ostrov Chirinkotan 131 S 6
Ostrov Dolgiy 119 L 2
Ostrov Ekarma 131 S 6
Ostrov Feklistova 131 P 5
Ostrov Gusmp 131 U 1–2
Ostrov Iony 131 Q 4
Ostrov Iturup 131 R 7
Ostrov Karaginskiy 131 U 4
Ostrov Ketoy 131 S 6
Ostrov Kharimkotan 131 S 6
Ostrov Kil'din 112 K 2
Ostrov Kokaral 128 G 1
Ostrov Kolguyev 118 J 2
Ostrov Konevits 112 K 3
Ostrov Kotel'nyy 131 P 1
Ostrov Krestovskiy 131 U 1
Ostrov Malyy Lyakhovskiy 131 Q 1
Ostrov Matua 131 S 6
Ostrov Men'shikova 131 P 5
Ostrov Mezhdusharskiy 118 K 1
Ostrov Moshchnyy 113 J 4
Ostrov Nansikan 131 PQ 4
Ostrovnoy 131 U 2
Ostrovnoye 131 T 5
Ostrovnoy, Mys 131 T 3
Ostrov Ogurchinskiy 128 E 3
Ostrov Onekotan 131 S 6
Ostrov Paramushir 131 T 5
Ostrov Peschanyy 130 L 1
Ostrov Rasshua 131 S 6
Ostrov Ratmanova 166 D 2
Ostrov Raykoke 131 S 6
Ostrov Semenovskiy 131 O 1
Ostrov Shiashkotan 131 S 6
Ostrov Shumshu 131 T 5
Ostrov Simushir 131 S 6
Ostrov Stolbovoy 131 P 1
Ostrovul Letea 116 C 1
Ostrovul Sfîntu Gheorghe 116 C 1
Ostrov Urup 131 S 6
Ostrov Valaam 112 K 3
Ostrov Vaygach 119 L 1
Ostrov Vozrozhdeniya 128 F 1
Ostrov Zav'yalova 131 S 4
Ostrowiec Świetokrzyski 111 H 4
Ostrów Mazowiecka 111 H 4
Ostrów Wielkopolski 111 G 4
Ostryak, Gora 131 W 3
Ostrzeszów 111 G 4
Ostuni 115 G 3
Ōsumi-shotō 133 K 4
Osuna 114 B 4
Os'van' 118 L 2
Osvejskoje, Ozero 113 J 4
Oswego 171 L 3

Oswestry 102 C 1
Oświęcim 111 G 4
Otago Peninsula 145 Q 10
Otar 129 K 2
Otaru 133 M 2
Otautau 145 P 10
Otava 111 F 5
Otavalo 178 C 3
Otavi 160 B 3
Otchinjau 160 A 3
Otepää Kõrgustik 112 J 4
Otgon 130 G 6
Othonoí 116 A 3
Oti 156 E 4
Oti-daitō-jima 133 K 6
Otish, Monts 169 N 5
Otjiha'vara 160 B 4
Otjikondo 160 B 3
Otjimbingwe 160 B 4
Otjinene 160 B 4
Otjinoko 160 B 4
Otjipatera Mountains 160 B 4
Otjitambi 160 B 3
Otjituuo 160 B 3
Otjiwarongo 160 B 4
Otjovazandu 160 A 3
Otjozondjou 160 B 4
Otkrytyy 131 M 4
Otley 101 E 3
Otoño 183 D 6
Otočac 115 G 3
Otog Qi 132 E 3
Otoskwin 168 J 5
Otra 113 E 4
Otradnaya 117 F 2
Otradnoye 131 T 5
Otranto 115 G 3
Ōtscher 115 G 2
Otshandi 160 A 3
Otshikuku 160 B 3
Ot-Siyen 130 M 1
Otsu 133 L 4
Otta 112 E 3
Ottadalen 112 E 3
Ottagouna 156 E 2
Ottawa (KS, U.S.A.) 171 G 4
Ottawa (Ont., Can.) 169 N 6
Ottawa Islands 169 L 2
Ottawa River 171 L 2
Ottenby 113 G 4
Otterburn 101 D 2
Otter Creek 171 K 6
Ottery St. Mary 102 C 2
Ottumwa 171 H 3
Oturkpo 157 F 4
Otuwe 160 B 4
Otway, Bahía 183 B 9
Otway, Cape 143 G 6
Otwock 111 H 4
Ötz 115 F 2
Ouachita Mountains 171 GH 5
Ouadane 152 C 4
Ouadda 158 C 3
Ouaddaï 157 J 3
Ouad Naga 152 B 5
Ouagadougou 156 D 3
Ouahigouya 156 D 3
Ouahran → Oran 152 E 1
Ouaka 158 C 3
Oualam 156 E 3
Oualata 152 D 5
Oualidia 152 D 2
Ouallene Bordj 153 F 4
Ouanary 179 H 3
Ouanda-Djallé 158 C 3
Ouando 158 D 3
Ouango 158 C 4
Ouangolodougou 156 C 4
Ouani 157 H 2
Ouan Taredert 153 G 3
Ouaqui 179 H 3
Ouarane 152 C 4
Ouargaye 156 E 3
Ouargla 153 G 2
Ouarkziz, Jbel 152 D 3
Ouarou 156 E 3
Ouarra 158 C 3
Ouarsenis, Massif de l' 153 F 1
Ouarzazate 152 D 2
Ouassou 156 B 3
Ouatcha 157 F 3
Oubangi Chari 157 J 4
Oubangui 157 J 4
Oudeïka 156 D 2
Oudje 153 G 2
Oudong 135 H 5
Oudtshoorn 160 C 6
Oued Rhiou 153 F 1
Oued Zem 152 D 2
Oueïta 157 J 2
Ouéllé 156 D 4
Ouémé 156 E 4
Ouessant, Ile de 114 C 2
Ouesso 157 H 5

Ouezzane 152 D 2
Ouham 157 H 4
Ouidah 156 E 4
Ouirigué 172 E 4
Ouistreham 114 C 2
Oujaf 152 D 5
Oujda 152 E 2
Oujeft 152 C 4
Oulad Naïl, Monts des 153 F 2
Oulainen 112 H 3
Oulankajoki 112 J 2
Ould Yenjé 152 C 5
Ouled Djellal 153 G 2
Ouloussébougou 156 C 3
Oulu 112 J 2
Oulujärvi 112 J 3
Oulujoki 112 J 3
Oum Chalouba 157 J 2
Oumé 156 C 4
Oum el Bouaghi 153 G 1
Oum er Rbia 152 D 2
Oum Hadjer 157 H 3
Oumm ed Droûs Gueblî, Sebkhet 152 C 4
Oumm ed Droûs Telli, Sebkha 152 C 4
Ounane, Djebel 153 G 3
Ounasjoki 112 H 2
Oundle 103 D 1
Ou Neua 135 H 3
Ounianga 157 J 2
Ounianga Kebir 157 J 2
Ounianga Serir 157 J 2
Ounissoui Baba 157 G 2
Ouricuri 181 H 2
Ourinhos 181 G 5
Ouro Prêto 181 H 5
Ourthe 115 E 1
Ouse 110 D 4
Ouse, River (Norfolk) 103 E 1
Ouse, River (N. Yorkshire) 101 E 3
Oust 114 C 2
Outagouna 156 E 2
Outaouais 171 L 2
Outapi 160 A 3
Outardes, Rivière aux 169 O 5
Outat Oulad el Haj 152 E 2
Outer Hebrides 98 A 3
Outjo 160 B 4
Outlook 167 Q 5
Outokumpu 112 J 3
Ouvéa 145 J 6
Ouyen 143 G 6
Ovacık 157 G 5
Ovacık 117 D 3
Ovada 115 E 3
Ovalle 182 B 5
Ovamboland 160 B 3
Oveng 157 G 5
Överbygd 112 G 2
Overhalla 112 F 3
Överkalix 112 H 2
Overland Park 171 H 4
Övertorneå 112 H 2
Overuman 112 F G 2
Oviedo (Haiti) 173 H 4
Oviedo (Spain) 114 B 3
Oviksfjällen 112 F 3
Övre Ardal 112 E 3
Övre Fryken 113 F 3
Övre Soppero 112 H 2
Ovruch 113 J 5
Ovsyanka 131 N 5
Ovul 145 F 3
Owando 157 H 6
Owatonna 171 H 3
Owen, Mount 145 Q 9
Owensboro 171 J 4
Owen Sound 171 K 3
Owen Stanley Range 144 E 3
Owerri 157 F 4
Owo 157 F 4
Owosso 171 K 3
Owyhee 170 C 3
Owyhee, Lake 170 C 3
Owyhee River 170 C 3
Oxberg 112 F 3
Oxelösund 113 G 4
Oxford (U.K.) 103 D 2
Oxford (MS, U.S.A.) 171 J 5
Oxford Lake 167 S 5
Oxfordshire 103 D 2
Ox Mountains 110 B 4
Oyapock 179 H 3
Oyash 119 Q 4
Oyem 157 G 5
Oykel, River 98 B 3
Oymyakon 131 Q 3
Oyo (Nigeria) 156 E 4

Oyo (Sudan) 154 F 4
Oyón 179 C 6
Oyonnax 115 E 2
Oyshilik 119 Q 6
Oyster Cliffs 160 A 5
Øystese 113 E 3
Oysurdakh 131 S 2
Oytal 129 J 2
Oyun-Khomoto 131 P 2
Ozamiz 137 F 2
Ozark 171 J 5
Ozark Plateau 171 H 4
Ozarks, Lake of the 171 H 4
Ózd 116 B 1
Ozernaya 131 U 4
Ozernovskiy 131 T 5
Ozernoy, Zaliv 131 U 4
Ozero Agata 130 F 3
Ozero Akzhaykyn 129 H 1–2
Ozero Alakol' 119 Q 6
Ozero Alibey 116 D 1
Ozero Arys 129 H 1
Ozero Aschikol' 129 H 1
Ozero Ayaturku 130 F 2
Ozero Balkhash 119 OP 6
Ozero Baykal 130 J 4 5
Ozero Beringa 121 T 4
Ozero Biylikol' 129 J 2
Ozero Bolon' 131 P 6
Ozero Bol'shoy Yeravnoye 130 K 5
Ozero Bolsjoj Morskoye 131 T 1
Ozero Bustakh 131 Q 1
Ozero Chany 119 P 5
Ozero Chatyrkel' 129 K 2
Ozero Chervonoye 113 J 5
Ozero Chukchagirskoye 131 P 5
Ozero Dadynskoye 117 G 1
Ozero Donuzlav 117 D 1
Ozero El'gygytgyn 131 W 2
Ozero Engozero 112 K 2
Ozero Gimolskoye 112 K 3
Ozero Ilirgytkin 131 T 1
Ozero Il'men 113 K 4
Ozero Imandra 112 K 2
Ozero Issyk-Kul 129 K 2
Ozero Kamennoye 112 K 3
Ozero Kanozero 112 K 2
Ozero Karakoin 129 H 1
Ozero Keke Usun 117 G 1
Ozero Keret' 112 K 2
Ozero Keta 130 F 3
Ozero Khanka 133 K 1
Ozero Khantayskoye 130 F 2
Ozero Khummi 131 P 5
Ozero Kitai 116 C 1
Ozero Kiyeng-Kyuyel' 130 J 1
Ozero Kokora 130 H 1
Ozero Kolozero 112 K 2
Ozero Kolvitskoye 112 K 2
Ozero Kovdozero 112 K 2
Ozero Kozhozero 118 G 3
Ozero Krasnoye 131 W 3
Ozero Kubenskoye 118 G 4
Ozero Kulundinskoye 119 P 5
Ozero Kungasalakh 130 H 2
Ozero Kushmurun 119 M 5
Ozero Labaz 130 G 1
Ozero Lacha 118 G 3
Ozero Lama 130 F 2
Ozero Leksozero 112 K 3
Ozero Lovozero 112 L 2
Ozero Manych Gudilo 117 F 1
Ozero Markakol' 119 R 6
Ozero Mednyy 121 T 4
Ozero Mogotoyevo 131 R 1
Ozero Nerpich'ye 131 T 2
Ozero Nyuk 112 K 3
Ozero Ondozero 112 K 3
Ozero Onezhskoye 118 G 3
Ozero Orel' 131 P 5
Ozero Osvejskoje 112 J 4
Ozero Ozhogino 131 R 2
Ozero Paravani 117 F 2
Ozero Portnyagino 130 J 1
Ozero Purinskoye 130 E 1
Ozero Pyaozero 112 K 2
Ozero Pyasino 119 R 2
Ozero Pyukhyayarvi 112 K 3
Ozero Rovkulskoye 112 K 3
Ozero Sadochye 128 F 2
Ozero Sartlan 119 P 4–5
Ozero Sarykamysh 128 F 2
Ozero Sasyk 116 C 1
Ozero Sasykkol' 119 Q 6
Ozero Segozero 112 K 3
Ozero Seletyteniz 119 O 5
Ozero Sevan 117 G 2
Ozero Sonkel' 129 K 2
Ozero Sovetskoye 119 Q 2
Ozero Sredneye Kuyto 112 K 2
Ozero Sukhodolskoye 112 K 3

Ozero Svetloye 117 G 1
Ozero Syamozero 112 K 3
Ozero Taymyr 130 H 1
Ozero Teletskoye 119 R 5
Ozero Tengiz 119 N 5
Ozero Tikhtoozero 112 K 2
Ozero Tikshozero 112 K 2
Ozero Topozero 112 K 2
Ozero Tulos 112 K 3
Ozero Ubinskoye 119 Q 4
Ozero Udyl' 131 P 5
Ozero Umozero 112 K 2
Ozero Vodlozero 118 G 3
Ozero Vozhe 118 G 3
Ozero Vuoksa 112 J 3
Ozero Vyalozero 112 L 2
Ozero Vygozero 118 F 3
Ozero Yalpukh 116 C 1
Ozero Yambuto 119 P 1
Ozero Yanis'yarvi 112 K 3
Ozero Yessey 130 H 2
Ozero Zaysan 119 Q 6
Ozero Zhamanakkal' 129 G 1
Ozero Zvoron 131 P 5
Ozhogina 131 R 2
Ozhogino 131 R 2
Ozhogino, Ozero 131 R 2
Ozinki 118 J 5
Ozona 170 F 5
Ozorków 111 G 4

P

Pa-an 135 G 4
Paarl 160 B 6
Paavola 112 J 3
Pabbay 98 D 3
Pabianice 111 G 4
Pabna 134 E 3
Pabradė 112 J 4
Pab Range 129 G 5
Pacaás Novos, Serra dos 180 D 3
Pacajá 179 H 4
Pacaraima, Sierra 179 F 3
Pacasmayo 178 BC 5
Pachacamac 180 A 3
Pachakshiri 135 F 2
Pachbhadra 134 B 2
Pachino 115 G 4
Pachitea 178 D 5
Pachiza 178 C 5
Pacho 178 D 2
Pachuca de Soto 172 C 4
Pacific Ocean 186
Pacific Ranges 167 M 5
Pacora 178 C 2
Padam 129 K 4
Padang 136 B 4
Padang 136 C 4
Padang 136 C 3
Padangpanjang 136 B 4
Padang, Pulau 136 B 3
Padangsidempuan 136 A 3
Padany 113 K 3
Padas 136 E 3
Padauari 179 F 3
Paddle Prairie 167 O 4
Paderborn 111 E 4
Padilla 180 D 4
Padova 115 F 2
Padrão, Ponta do 160 A 1
Padrauna 134 D 2
Padre Island 171 G 6
Padstow 102 B 2
Paducah 171 J 4
Padula 115 G 3
Paengnyŏng-do 133 H 3
Paestum 115 G 3
Pafuri 161 E 4
Pag 115 FG 3
Paga Centa 179 H 4
Pagadian 137 F 2
Pagan 146 A 1
Pagasitikós Kólpos 116 B 3
Pagatan 136 E 4
Page 170 D 4
Pago Mission 142 D 1
Pago-Pago 146 D 3
Pagosa Springs 170 E 4
Pagri 134 E 2
Pagwi 144 D 2
Pahang, Sungai 136 B 3
Paharpur 129 J 4
Pahkaing Bum 135 G 2
Pai 157 G 4
Paide 113 J 4
Paiguás 180 E 4
Päijänne 112 J 3

Paíkon Oros 116 B 2
Paikot 134 D 3
Pailin 135 H 5
Paimi 113 H 3
Paimpol 114 C 2
Painan 136 B 4
Paine Medio, Cerro 183 B 9
Painesville (Austr.) 142 B 4
Painesville (USA) 171 K 3
Painted Desert 170 D 4
Paisley 99 B 4
Paita 178 B 5
Paithan 134 C 4
Pajala 112 H 2
Pajares, Puerto de 114 B 3
Pajatén 178 C 5
Pakala 134 C 5
Pakaraima Mountains 179 FG 2
Pak Beng 135 H 4
Pakhacha 131 V 3
Paki 157 F 3
Pakima 158 C 5
Pakin 146 B 2
Pakistan 129 H 5
Pak Lay 135 H 4
Pak Neun 135 H 4
Pakokku 135 G 3
Pakpattan 129 J 4
Pak Phanang 135 H 6
Pakrac 115 G 2
Paks 116 A 1
Pak Sane 135 H 4
Pakse 135 J 4
Pakwach 158 E 4
Pala (Centr. Afr. Rep.) 158 C 3
Pala (Chad) 157 H 4
Palacios 171 G 6
Palafrugell 114 D 3
Palagruža 115 G 3
Palaiokhóra 116 B 3
Palakollu 134 D 4
Palamau 134 D 3
Palamós 114 D 3
Palanan 131 T 4
Palanan Point 137 J 1
Palanga 113 H 4
Palangkaraya 136 D 4
Palanpur 134 B 3
Palapye 160 D 4
Palatka 131 S 3
Palauk 135 G 5
Palau, Kepulauan 137 H 2
Palaw 135 G 5
Palawan 136–137 E 2
Palawan Passage 136–137 E 1–2
Palayankottai 134 C 6
Palazzo, Punta 115 E 3
Palca 180 C 4
Paldiski 113 H 4
Pale 135 F 2
Palel 135 F 3
Paleleh 137 F 3
Palembang 136 B 4
Palencia 114 C 3
Palenque 172 D 4
Palermo 115 F 4
Palestine (TX, U.S.A.) 171 G 5
Paletwa 135 F 3
Palghat 134 C 5
Palgrave Point 160 A 4
Pali 134 B 2
Palimé 156 E 4
Palinura, Capo 115 G 3
Palitana 134 B 3
Paljakka 112 J 3
Paljenik 115 G 3
Pälkäne 112 H 3
Palkonda Range 134 C 5
Palk Strait 134 C 6
Palla Bianca 115 F 2
Pal Lahara 134 E 3
Pallasovka 118 J 5
Pallastunturit 112 H 2
Palliser, Cape 145 R 9
Palliser, Îles 147 F 4
Palma (Spain) 114 D 4
Palma (Mozambique) 161 G 2
Palma del Río 114 B 4
Palmares 181 J 2
Palmares do Sul 182 F 5
Palmarito 178 D 2
Palmarola 115 F 3
Palmar Sur 172 F 6
Palmas Bellas 178 B 2
Palmas, Cape 156 C 5
Palmas, Golfo di 115 E 4
Palma Soriano 173 G 3
Palm Bay 171 K 6
Palmeira 182 F 4
Palmeirais (Piauí, Brazil) 181 H 2

Palmeiras (Goiás, Brazil) 181 G 3
Palmer (AK, U.S.A.) 166 H 3
Palmer (Antarctica) 185
Palmer Archipelago 185
Palmer Land 185
Palmerston 145 Q 10
Palmerston North 145 R 9
Palmi 115 G 4
Palmira 178 C 3
Palmyra (Oceania) 147 E 2
Palmyra (Syria) 154 F 2
Palmyras Point 134 E 3
Palni 134 C 5
Palo Alto 170 B 4
Paloemeu 179 G 3
Paloh (Indonesia) 136 C 3
Paloh (Malaysia) 136 D 3
Paloich 154 E 6
Palomar, Mount 170 C 5
Palopo 137 F 4
Palo Santo 182 E 4
Palos, Cabo de 114 C 4
Palpa 180 A 3
Palpala 180 C 5
Pal-Pal, Gora 131 V 3
Palpetu, Tanjuna 137 G 4
Paltamo 112 J 3
Palwal 134 C 2
Palu (Turkey) 117 E 3
Palu (Indonesia) 137 E 4
Pama 156 E 3
Pamanukan 136 C 5
Pamban Channel 134 C 6
Pamekasan 136 D 5
Pameungpeuk 136 C 5
Pamiers 114 D 3
Pamir 129 J 3
Pamlico Sound 171 L 4
Pampa 170 F 4
Pampa de Huayuri 180 A 3
Pampa de la Matanzilla 183 C 6
Pampa de las Salinas 182 C 5
Pampa del Castillo 183 C 8
Pampa del Tamarugal 180 C 5
Pampa Grande 180 D 4
Pampas (Arg.) 182–183 D 5–6
Pampas (Peru) 180 B 3
Pamplona (Spain) 114 C 3
Pamplona (Col.) 178 D 2
Pamukan, Teluk 136 E 4
Pamukova 116 D 2
Pamyati 130 F 4
Pana 157 G 6
Panagjurište 116 B 2
Panahan 136 D 4
Panaitan, Pulau 136 C 5
Panaitolikón Óros 116 B 3
Panaji 134 B 4
Panakhaikón Óros 116 B 3
Panama 178 C 2
Panama Canal 178 B 2
Panama City (FL, U.S.A.) 171 J 5
Panamá, Golfo de 178 C 2
Panamá, Istmo de 178 C 2
Panarea 115 G 4
Panay 137 F 1
Pančevo 116 B 2
Pančičev vrh 116 B 2
Panda (Mozambique) 161 E 4
Panda (Zaire) 158 B 4
Pandamatenga 160 D 3
Pandan 137 F 1
Pandaria 134 D 3
Pandharpur 134 C 4
Pandivere Kõrgustik 112 J 4
Pando 182 E 5
Pandokrátor 116 A 3
Pandrup 113 E 4
Panevėžys 113 H 4
Panfilov 129 KL 2
Panga 158 D 5
Pangala 157 G 6
Pangani 159 F 6
Panggoe 145 G 4
Panghkam 135 G 3
Pangi 158 D 5
Pangi Range 129 K 4
Pangkajene 137 E 4
Pangkalanbrandan 136 A 2
Pangkalanbuun 136 D 4
Pangkalpinang 136 C 4
Panglang 135 G 3
Pangnirtung 169 O 2
Pango Aluquém 160 A 1
Pangrango, Gunung 136 C 5
Panguruan 136 A 3
Pangutaran Group 137 F 2
Panhandle 170 F 4
Pania Mutombo 158 C 6
Panié, Mont 145 H 6

Panipat 134 C 2
Panjad 129 J 5
Panjang 136 C 5
Panjao 129 H 4
Panjgur 129 G 5
Panjim 134 B 4
Panjshir 129 J 3
Pankshin 157 F 4
P'anmunjŏm 133 J 3
Panna 134 D 3
Panopah 136 D 4
Panorama 181 F 5
Panovo 119 O 4
Panovo 130 H 4
Panshan 133 H 2
Panshi 133 J 2
Pantanal de São Lourenço 180 E 4
Pantanal do Río Negro 180 E 4
Pantar, Pulau 137 F 5
Pantelleria 115 F 4
Pantemakassar 137 F 5
Pantiacolla, Cadena del 180 B 3
Pantoja 178 C 4
Panuco 172 C 3
Panuco, Rio 172 C 3
Pan Xian 132 D 5
Panyam 157 F 4
Panzi 158 B 6
Paola 115 G 4
Paoua 158 B 3
Pap 158 E 3
Pápa 116 A 1
Papagayo, Golfo del 172 E 5
Papantla de Olarte 172 C 3
Papar 136 E 2
Papa Stour 98 D 1
Papa Westray 98 C 2
Papeete 147 F 4
Papenburg 111 E 4
Papey 112 C 3
Paphos 117 E 4
Papikion Óros 116 C 2
Paposo 182 B 4
Papua, Gulf of 144 D–E 3
Papua New Guinea 146 A 3
Papun 135 G 4
Pará (Brazil) 179 H 5
Parabel' 119 Q 4
Pará (Brazil) → Belém 179 J 4
Paraburdoo 142 B 3
Paracel Islands 135 K 4
Paracatu 181 G 4
Paracuru 181 J 1
Paragould 171 H 4
Paragua 179 F 2
Paraguá (Bolivia) 180 D 3
Paraguaçu 181 J 3
Paraguaná, Península de 178 E 1
Paraguarí 182 E 4
Paraguay 180 E 4–5
Paraíba 181 J 2
Paraíba do Sul 181 H 5
Parainen 112 H 3
Paraiso, Serra do 181 F 3–4
Parakhino Poddubye 118 F 4
Parakou 156 E 4
Paramaribo 179 G 2
Paramillo 161 E 4
Paramirim 181 H 3
Paramonga 179 C 6
Paramushir, Ostrov 131 T 5
Paraná (Goiás, Brazil) 181 G 3
Paraná (Argentina) 182 E 5
Paraná (Brazil) 181 F 5
Paranaguá 181 G 6
Paranaguá, Baía de 181 G 6
Paranaíba 181 F 4
Paranam 179 G 2
Paranapanema 181 F 5
Paranapiacaba, Serra do 181 G 5
Paranaval 181 F 5
Paranéstion 116 B 2
Paranhos 181 E 5
Paraoa 179 G 2
Parapetí 180 D 4
Parapol'skiy Dolina 131 V 3
Parara 181 H 5
Parati 181 H 5
Paratinga 181 H 3
Paratunka 131 T 5
Paravani, Ozero 117 F 2
Paray-le-Monial 114 D 2
Parbati 134 C 2
Parbhani 134 C 4
Parbig 119 Q 4
Parc National de la Boucle De Baoule 156 C 3
Parc National de la Kagera 158 E 5

Parc National de la Komoé 156 D 4
Parc National de la Pendjari 156 E 3
Parc National de Okanda 157 G 6
Parc National de Sinianka-Minia 157 H 3
Parc National de Taï 156 C 4
Parc National de Wonga Wongué 157 F 6
Parc National de Zakouma 157 H 3
Parc National du Bamingui-Bangoran 158 BC 3
Parc National du Niokolo Koba 156 B 3
Parcs Nationaux du "W" 156 E 3
Pardo 181 H 4
Pardubice 111 G 4
Parecis 180 E 3
Parecis, Serra dos 180 DE 3
Pareditas 182 C 5
Pare Mountains 159 F 5
Paren' 131 U 3
Parent 171 M 2
Parepare 137 E 4
Parera 182 E 5
Párga 116 B 3
Pargas (Parainen) 113 H 3
Parguaza 178 E 2
Pari 117 F 2
Pariñas, Punta 178 B 4
Paria, Golfo de 179 F 1
Pariaguán 179 F 2
Pariaman 136 B 4
Paria, Península de 179 F 1
Paricatuba 179 F 4
Paricutín, Volcán 172 B 4
Parigi 137 F 4
Parichi 113 J 5
Parika 179 G 2
Parkkala 112 J 3
Parima, Sierra 179 F 3
Parinari 178 D 4
Parintins 179 F 4
Paris (Fr.) 114 D 2
Paris (IL, U.S.A.) 171 J 4
Paris (TN, U.S.A.) 171 J 4
Paris (TX, U.S.A.) 171 G 5
Parismina 172 F 5
Parit Buntar 136 B 2
Pariti 136 F 6
Parkano 112 H 3
Parker 170 D 5
Parkersburg 171 K 4
Parkes 143 H 5
Parkhar 129 H 3
Parkland 170 B 2
Park Range 170 E 3
Park Rapids 171 H 2
Parlakimidi 134 D 4
Parlakote 134 D 4
Parma (OH, U.S.A.) 171 K 3
Parma (Italy) 115 F 3
Parnaguá 181 H 3
Parnaíba 181 H 1
Parnamirim 181 J 2
Parnarama 181 H 2
Parnassós Óros 116 B 3
Parnon Óros 116 B 3
Pärnu 113 H 4
Pärnu Jõgi 113 J 4
Paro 134 E 2
Parola 112 H 3
Paromay 131 Q 5
Paroo River 143 G 4
Paropamisus 129 G 4
Páros 116 C 3
Parpaillon 115 E 3
Parque Arqieologico 178 C 3
Parque Nacional Canaima 179 F 2
Parque Nacional da Cameia 160 C 2
Parque Nacional da Gorongosa 161 E 3
Parque Nacional da Mupa 160 B 3
Parque Nacional da Quiçama 160 A 1
Parque Nacional de Banhine 161 E 4
Parque Nacional de Bazaruto 161 E 4
Parque Nacional de Chaco 182 E 4
Parque Nacional de la Macarena 178 D 3
Parque Nacional de Monte Pascoal 181 J 4
Parque Nacional de Zinave 161 E 4
Parque Nacional do Aragiaoa 179 HJ 6
Parque Nacional do Araguaia 181 FG 3

265

Par–Pet

Parque Nacional do Bicuari 160 B 3
Parque Nacional do Brasília 181 G 4
Parque Nacional do Chapada dos Veadeiros 181 G 3
Parque Nacional do Emas 181 F 4
Parque Nacional do Iguaçu 182 F 4
Parque Nacional do Iona 160 A 3
Parque Nacional el Tuparro 178 E 2
Parque Nacional los Glaciares 183 B 8
Parque Nacional Moreno 183 B 8
Parque Nacional Símon Bolívar 178 D 2
Parral 183 B 6
Parras de la Fuente 172 B 2
Parras, Sierra de 172 B 2
Parrita 172 F 6
Parry Bay 167 V 2
Parry Islands 184
Parry Peninsula 167 N 2
Parseta 111 G 4
Parshino 130 K 4
Partabpur 134 D 3
Pårtetjåkkå 112 G 2
Parthenay 114 C 2
Partille 113 F 4
Partinico 115 F 4
Partizansk 133 K 2
Partizanske 111 G 5
Partizanskoye 130 F 4
Paru 179 H 4
Paru de Oeste 179 G 3
Paruro 180 B 3
Parvatipuram 134 D 4
Paryang 134 D 2
Parys 160 D 5
Pasadena 170 C 5
Pasado, Cabo 178 B 4
Pasaje 178 C 4
Pasangkayu 137 E 4
Pasarwajo 137 F 5
Pasawng 135 G 4
Pascagoula 171 J 5
Pașcani 116 C 1
Pas de Calais 110 D 4
Pasekudah 134 D 6
Pashkovo 131 O 6
Pashskiy-Perevoz 118 F 3
Pashtun Zarghūn 129 G 4
Pasinler 117 F 3
Pasir Mas 136 B 2
Pasirpengarayan 136 B 3
Pasni 129 G 5
Paso de Indios 183 C 7
Paso del Limay 183 B 7
Paso de los Libres 182 E 4
Paso de los Toros 182 E 5
Paso de los Vientos 173 H 4
Paso de Pino Hachado 183 B 6
Paso de San Francisco 182 C 4
Paso Río Mayo 183 B 8
Paso Socompa 180 C 5
Passagem 181 H 3
Passage of Tiree 99 A 3
Passau 111 F 5
Passero, Capo 115 G 4
Passo della Futa 115 F 3
Passo della Spluga 115 E 2
Passo della Stelvio 115 F 2
Passo dello Scalone 115 G 4
Passo di Resia 115 F 2
Pass of Brander 99 B 3
Pass of Drumochter 99 B 3
Pass of Glen Coe 99 B 3
Pass of Killiecrankie 99 C 3
Passo Fundo 182 F 4
Passos 181 G 5
Pastaza 178 C 4
Pasteur 182 D 6
Pasto 178 C 3
Pasto Grande 179 F 5
Pastos Bons 181 H 2
Paštrik 116 B 2
Pasul Mesteçănis 116 C 1
Pasul Predeal 116 C 1
Pasul Turnu Roșu 116 B 1
Pasuruan 136 D 5
Pasvalys 113 H 4
Pasvikelva 112 J 2
Patacamaya 180 C 4
Patagonia 183 BC 7–9
Patan (India) 134 B 3
Patan (Nepal) 134 E 2
Patani 137 G 3
Pate 159 G 5
Pategi 157 F 4
Patensie 160 C 6
Paterno 115 F 4
Paterson 171 M 3
Pathankot 134 C 1

Pathfinder Reservoir 170 E 3
Pathiu 135 G 5
Patía 178 C 3
Patiala 134 C 1
Pativilca 179 C 6
Patkaglik 129 M 3
Pátmos 116 C 3
Patna 134 E 2
Patnagarh 134 D 3
Patnos 117 F 3
Patomskoye Nagor'ye 130 K L 4
Patonga 158 E 4
Patos 181 J 2
Patos, Cachoeira dos 179 F 5
Patos de Minas 181 G 4
Patos, Lagoa dos 182 F 5
Pátrai 116 B 3
Patras 116 B 3
Patricio Lynch 183 A 8
Patříkos Kólpos 116 B 3
Patrington 101 E 3
Patrocínio 181 G 4
Patta Island 159 G 5
Pattani 135 H 6
Pattaya 135 H 5
Patten Escaprment 193 D 2
Pattle 135 K 4
Pattullo, Mount 166 M 4
Patú 181 J 2
Patuakhali 135 F 3
Patuca, Rio 172 F 4
Patvinsuo 112 K 3
Pau 114 C 3
Pau d'Arco 179 J 5
Pauillac 114 C 2
Pauini 178 E 5
Pauksa Taung 135 F 4
Paulatuk 167 N 2
Paulina Peak 170 B 3
Paulistana 181 H 2
Paulo Afonso 181 J 2
Paulo Afonso, Cachoeira de 181 J 2
Pauls Valley 171 G 5
Paungde 135 G 4
Pauri 134 C 1
Pausa 180 B 4
Pauto 178 D 2
Pavia 115 E 2
Pāvilosta 113 H 4
Pavlikeni 116 C 2
Pavlodar 119 P 5
Pavlof Islands 166 E 5
Pavlof Volcano 166 E 4
Pavlograd 117 E 1
Pavlovka 119 O 5
Pavlovo 118 H 4
Pavlovsk 119 Q 5
Pavlovskaya 117 E 1
Pavlysh 118 F 6
Pavón 178 D 3
Pavullo nel Frignano 115 F 3
Pawahku 135 G 2
Pawan, Sungai 136 D 4
Pawut 135 G 5
Paxoí 116 B 3
Paxson 166 H 3
Payakumbuh 136 B 4
Pay-Khoy, Khrebet 119 M 2
Payne, Baie 169 O 4
Payne, Lac 169 N 4
Paynes Find 142 B 4
Paysandú 182 E 5
Payson 170 D 3
Payturma 130 F 1
Payún, Cerro 183 C 6
Pay-Yer, Gora 119 M 2
Pazña 180 C 4
Pāzanān 128 E 4
Pazar 117 F 2
Pazarcık 117 E 3
Pazaryeri 116 C 2–3
Paz de Aripore 178 D 2
Pazova 116 B 2
Peace Point 167 P 4
Peace River 167 P 4
Peach Springs 170 D 4
Peacock Hills 167 Q 2
Peaima Falls 179 F 2
Peak District 101 E 3
Peaked Mountain 171 N 2
Pearsall 170 G 6
Pearsoll Peak 170 B 3
Peary Land 184
Pebane 161 F 3
Pebas 178 D 4
Pebble Island 183 E 6
Peć 116 B 2
Peca 115 F 2
Pech de Bugarach 114 D 3
Pechenga 112 K 2
Pecherakh 119 MN 3

Pechora 118 L 2
Pechora 118 K 2
Pechorskaya Guba 118 K 2
Pechorskoye More 118 K 2
Pechory 113 J 4
Pecos 170 F 5
Pecos Plains 170 F 5
Pecos River 170 F 5
Pécs 116 A 1
Pededze 113 J 4
Pedernales (Ecuador) 178 B 3
Pedernales (Venezuela) 179 F 2
Pedo La 134 D 2
Pedra Lume 156 B 6
Pedras Negras 180 D 3
Pedreiras 181 H 1
Pedriceña 172 B 2
Pedro Afonso 179 J 5
Pedro Cays 173 G 4
Pedro de Valdivia 180 C 5
Pedro Gomes 181 F 4
Pedro Juan Caballero 180 E 5
Pedro Lur 183 D 6
Pedro R. Fernández 182 E 4
Pedroso, Sierra del 114 B 3
Peebles 99 C 4
Peel (U.K.) 100 C 2
Peel (NWT, Canada) 166 L 2
Peel Sound 167 S 1
Peera Peera Poolanna Lake 143 F 4
Pegasus Bay 145 Q 9
Pegu 135 G 4
Pegunungan Barisan 136 B 4
Pegunungan Charles Louis 137 J 4
Pegunungan Gauttier 137 J 4
Pegunungan Iran 136 D 3
Pegunungan Jayawijaya 137 J 4
Pegunungan Kumawa 137 H 4
Pegunungan Maoke 137 J 4
Pegunungan Meratus 136 E 4
Pegunungan Muller 136 D 3
Pegunungan Schwaner 136 D 4
Pegunungan Sudirman 137 J 4
Pegunungan Tamrau 137 H 4
Pegunungan van Rees 137 J 4
Pegunungan Weyland 137 J 4
Pegu Yoma 135 G 4
Pegysh 118 K 3
Pehuajó 183 D 6
Peine 111 F 4
Peipus, Lake 113 J 4
Peixe (Goiás, Brazil) 181 G 3
Peixe (São Paulo, Brazil) 181 F 5
Pei Xian 133 G 4
Pejantan, Pulau 136 C 3
Pekalongan 136 C 5
Pekanbaru 136 B 3
Pekin 171 J 3
Peking 133 G 3
Pekkala 112 J 2
Pekon 135 G 4
Pekornica 116 A 2
Pekul'ney, Khrebet 131 W 2
Pekul'veyem 131 X 3
Pelabuanratu 136 C 5
Pelabuanratu, Teluk 136 C 5
Pelagonija 116 B 2
Pélagos 116 B 3
Pelaihari 136 D 4
Pelat, Mont 115 E 3
Peleaga, Virful 116 B 1
Peleduy 130 K 4
Peleliu 137 H 2
Peleng 136 F 4
Peleng, Selat 137 F 4
Peleniya 134 H 3
Pelican 166 K 4
Pelican Narrows 167 R 4
Pelinaion Óros 116 C 3
Peliny Osipenko, Iméni 131 P 5
Pelješac 115 G 3
Pelkosenniemi 112 J 2
Pellegrini 183 D 6
Pello 112 H 2
Pelly 166 L 3
Pelly Bay 167 T 2
Pelly Crossing 166 K 3
Pelly Mountains 166 L 3
Peloponnese 116 B 3
Pelopónnisos 116 B 3
Pelotas (Brazil) 182 F 4
Pelotas (Rio Grande do Sul, Brazil) 182 F 5
Pelvoux, Massif du 115 E 3
Pelym 119 MN 3
Pemalang 136 C 5
Pemangkat 136 C 3
Pemarung, Pulau 136 E 4
Pematangsiantar 136 A 3
Pemba (Mozambique) 161 G 2
Pemba (Zambia) 160 D 3
Pemba Island (Tanzania) 159 F 6

Pemberton 142 B 5
Pembina 170 G 2
Pembroke (Ont, Canada) 169 M 6
Pembroke (U.K.) 102 B 2
Pembroke, Cape (NWT, Can.) 169 L 3
Pembroke, Cape (Falkland Is.) 183 E 9
Pembuang 136 D 4
Peñafiel 114 C 3
Peñaranda de Bracamonte 114 B 3
Peñarroya Pueblonuevo 114 B 4
Peñas, Cabo de 114 B 3
Peña, Sierra de la 114 C 3
Penarie 143 G 5
Penarth 102 C 2
Penas, Golfo de 183 B 8
Pendembu 156 B 4
Pender 142 C 2
Pendjari, Parc National de la 156 E 3
Pendleton 170 C 2
Pend Oreille 170 C 2
Pend Oreille, Lake 170 C 2
Pendzhikent 129 H 3
Penedo 181 J 3
Pene Mende 158 D 5
Peng'an 132 E 4
Penge 158 C 6
Penglai 133 H 3
Pengshan 132 D 4
Pengshui 132 E 5
Pengze 132 G 5
Penicuik 99 C 4
Penida, Pulau 136 E 5
Península Brecknock 183 B 9
Península de Azuero 178 B 2
Península de Azuero 173 F 6
Península de Brunswick 183 B 9
Península de Guajira 178 D 1
Península de Nicoya 172 E 6
Península de Osa 172 F 6
Península de Paraguaná 178 E 1
Península de Paria 179 F 1
Península de Taitao 183 AB 5
Peninsula de Yucatán → Yucatán Peninsula 172 E 3–4
Península Tres Montes 183 A 8
Península Valdés 183 D 7
Péninsule de Gaspé 169 O 6
Péninsule d'Ungava 169 N 3
Penisola Salentina 115 G 3–4
Penitente, Serra do 179 J 5
Pénjamo 172 B 3
Penmaenmawr 102 C 1
Penne 115 F 3
Penner 134 C 5
Penn Hills 171 L 3
Pennine, Alpi 115 E 2
Pennine Chain 101 D 2
Pennines (U.K.) 110 C 4
Pennsylvania 171 L 3
Penny Ice Cap 169 O 2
Penobscot Bay 171 N 3
Penola 143 G 6
Peñón Blanco 172 B 3
Penong 142 E 5
Penonomé 178 B 2
Penrhyn 147 E 3
Penrith 101 D 2
Penryn 102 B 2
Pensacola 171 J 5
Pensacola Mountains 185
Pensiangan 136 E 3
Pentecôte 145 J 5
Penticton 167 O 6
Pentland 143 H 3
Pentland Firth 98 C 2
Pentland Hills 99 C 4
Penukonda 134 C 5
Penwegon 135 G 4
Penza 118 H 5
Penzance 102 B 2
Penzhino 131 V 3
Penzhinskaya Guba 131 U 3
Penzhinskiy Khrebet 131 U 3–V 3
Peoria 171 J 3
Pepa 158 D 6
Pepel 156 B 4
Pequizeiro 179 J 5
Perabumulih 136 B 4
Perak 136 A 2
Perales, Puerto de 114 B 3
Percé 169 P 6
Perche, Collines du 114 D 2
Percival Lakes 142 C 3
Pereira 178 C 3
Pereira Barreto 181 F 5
Pereira, Cachoeira 179 G 4
Pereirinha 179 G 5
Perekop 117 D 1
Pereshchepino 118 G 6
Pereval Akbaytal 129 J 3

Pemberton 142 B 5
Pereval Dolon 129 K 2
Pereval Kyzylart 129 J 3
Pereval Torugart 129 K 2
Pereval Yablonitse 116 B 1
Perevolotskiy 118 K 5
Pérez 182 C 4
Pergamino 182 D 5
Pergamon 116 C 3
Perge 116 D 3
Perho 112 H 3
Péribonca 169 N 6
Peribonca, Lac 169 N 5
Pericos 170 E 3
Périgueux 114 D 2
Perijá, Sierra de 178 D 1–2
Perim Island → Barīm 155 G 6
Perito Moreno 183 B 8
Peritoró 181 H 1
Perković 115 G 3
Perlas, Laguna de 172 F 5
Perm 118 L 4
Përmeti 116 B 2
Pernambuco 181 J 2
Pernambuco → Recife 181 K 2
Pernik 116 B 2
Pèronne 114 D 2
Perote 172 C 4
Perpignan 114 D 3
Perros-Guirec 114 C 2
Perry 171 K 5
Perry Island 167 R 2
Perryton 170 F 4
Perryville 166 F 4
Persembe 117 E 2
Persepolis 128 E 5
Perseverancia 180 D 3
Persia 128 E 4
Persian Gulf → The Gulf 155 J 3
Pertek 117 E 3
Perth (Aus.) 142 B 5
Perth (U.K.) 110 C 3
Perth (U.K.) 99 C 3
Perth-Andover 169 O 6
Perthus, Col de 114 D 3
Pertuis 115 E 3
Pertuis Breton 114 C 2
Pertuis d'Antioche 114 C 2
Peru 178 C 5
Peru Basin 193 E 4
Peru-Chile Trench 192 A 4–5
Peručko Jezero 115 G 3
Perugia 115 F 3
Peruíbe 181 G 5
Perušić 115 G 3
Pervari 117 F 3
Pervomaysk (Ukrain, S.S.R.) 116 D 1
Pervomaysk (R.S.F.S.R.) 118 H 5
Pervomayskiy (R.S.F.S.R.) 118 H 3
Pervomayskiy (Kazakh S.S.R.) 119 Q 5
Pervoural'sk 119 L 4
Pervoye Pole 131 X 3
Pervyy Kamen' 131 U 2
Pesaro 115 F 3
Pescadores 133 GH 6
Pescara 115 F 3
Peschanokopskoye 117 F 1
Peschanyy, Mys 128 E 2
Peschanyy, Ostrov 130 L 1
Peschici 115 G 3
Pescoraro 115 G 4
Peshawar 129 J 4
Peshkopia 116 B 2
Peski 129 G 3
Peski Karakum 128 E 1
Peski Karakumy 128 F 3–G 3
Peski Karynzharyk 128 E 2
Peski Kyzylkum 129 G 2
Peski Muyunkum 129 J 2
Peski Priaral'skiye Karakumy 129 G 1
Peski Sary Ishikotrau 119 P 6
Peski Taukum 129 K 2
Pesochny 112 K 3
Peso da Régua 114 B 3
Pesqueira 181 J 2
Pessac 114 C 3
Pestovo 118 G 4
Pestravka 118 J 5
Pestraya Dresva 131 T 3
Petacalco, Bahia de 172 B 4
Petäjävesi 112 J 3
Petaluma 170 B 4
Petare 178 E 1
Petatlán 172 B 4
Petauke 161 E 2
Petén 172 D 4
Petenwell Lake 171 J 3
Peterborough (Ont. Canada) 171 L 3
Peterborough (South Aus.) 143 F 5

Pet–Pod

Peterborough (U.K.) 103 D 1
Peterhead 98 D 3
Peter I Island 185
Peter Lake 167 T 3
Peterlee 101 E 2
Petermann Ranges 142 D 4
Peteroa 183 B 6
Peter Pond Lake 167 Q 4
Petersburg (AK, U.S.A.) 166 L 4
Petersburg (VA, U.S.A.) 171 L 4
Petersfield 103 D 2
Petilia Policastro 115 G 4
Petites Pyrénées 114 D 3
Petit-Mécatina, Rivière du 169 P 5
Petitot 167 N 4
Petitsikapau Lake 169 O 5
Petkula 112 J 2
Petlad 134 B 3
Peto 172 E 3
Petorca 182 B 5
Petra 154 F 2
Petra Azul 181 H 4
Petra Velikogo, Zaliv 133 K 2
Petrel 185
Petrela 116 A 2
Petrified Forest National Park 183 C 8
Petrikov 113 J 5
Petrikovka 117 D 1
Petrila 116 B 1
Petrinja 115 G 2
Petrodvorets 113 J 4
Petrolândia 181 J 2
Petrolina 181 H 2
Petronell 115 G 2
Petropavlovka 130 J 5
Petropavlovka 131 N 5
Petropavlovsk 119 N 5
Petropavlovsk-Kamchatskiy 131 T 5
Petropavlovskoye 119 Q 5
Petropavlovskoye 130 J 4
Petropayelovka 119 Q 6
Petrópolis 181 H 5
Petroşani 116 B 1
Petroso 115 F 3
Petrovac 116 A 2
Petrova Gora 115 G 2
Petrovsk 118 J 5
Petrovskaya 117 E 1
Petrovskiy Yam 118 G 3
Petrovsk-Zabaykal'skiy 130 J 5
Petrozavodsk 118 F 3
Petsamo 112 K 2
Petukhovo 119 N 4
Peuetsagu, Gunung 136 A 3
Peureulak 136 A 2
Peza 118 J 2
Pezas 119 R 5
Pézenas 114 D 3
Pfaffenhofen 111 F 5
Pforzheim 111 E 5
Phalaborwa 161 E 4
Phalodi 134 B 2
Phaltan 134 B 4
Phangnga 135 G 6
Phanom Dang Raek 135 H 5
Phan Rang 135 J 5
Phan Thiet 135 J 5
Phatthalung 135 H 6
Phenix City 171 J 5
Phet Buri 135 G 5
Phetchabun 135 H 4
Phiafay 135 J 5
Philadelphia 171 L 4
Philae 154 E 4
Philippeville → Skikda 153 G 1
Philippi 116 B 2
Philippi, Lake 143 F 3
Philippine Basin 193 C 3
Philippines 137 F 1
Philip Smith Mountains 166 H 2
Philipstown 160 C 6
Phillack 102 B 2
Phillipsburg 170 G 4
Phitsanulok 135 H 4
Phnom Aural 135 H 5
Phnom Penh 135 H 5
Phoenix (AZ, U.S.A.) 170 D 5
Phoenix (Kiribati) → Rawaki (Oceania) 146 D 3
Phoenix Islands 146 D 3
Phong Nha 135 J 5
Phong Saly 135 H 3
Phrao 135 G 4
Phuket 135 G 6
Phulbani 134 D 3
Phu Ly 135 J 3
Phumi Kroy 135 J 5
Phum Khvao 135 H 5
Phum Siem 135 H 5
Phu My 135 J 5

Phung Hiep 135 J 6
Phuoc Le 135 J 5
Phu Set 135 J 4
Phu Tho 135 J 3
Phu Vinh 135 J 6
Piñas 182 C 5
Piūf 181 G 5
Piacá 179 J 5
Piacenza 115 E 2
Piana Mwanga 158 D 6
Pianguan 132 F 3
Pianosa 115 G 3
Pianosa 115 F 3
Piara Açu 179 H 5
Piatra Neamţ 116 C 1
Piauí 181 H 2
Piave 115 F 2
Pibor Post 158 E 3
Pica 180 C 5
Picacho del Centinela 172 B 2
Picardie 114 D 2
Pic Baumann 156 E 4
Pic Boby 161 G 4
Pic de la Selle 173 H 4
Pic de Macaya 173 H 4
Pic d'Estats 114 D 3
Pic du Midi de Bigorre 114 D 3
Pic du Midi d'Ossau 114 C 3
Pichanal 180 D 5
Pichilemu 182 B 5
Pichilingue 170 D 7
Pichimá 178 C 3
Pickering 101 E 2
Pickle Lake 168 J 5
Pickwick Lake 171 J 4
Pico 152 A 1
Pico Aitana 114 C 4
Pico Bolívar 178 D 2
Pico Bonito 172 E 4
Pico Colorado 182 C 4
Pico Cristóbal Colón 178 D 1
Pico da Neblina 178 E 3
Pico das Agulhas Negras 181 H 5
Pico de Almanzor 114 B 3
Pico de Aneto 114 D 3
Pico de Aroche 114 B 4
Pico de Itambé 181 H 4
Pico de Santa Isabel 157 F 5
Pico de Teide 152 B 3
Pico de Tio 156 C 4
Pico de Tomé 157 F 5
Pico Rondón 179 F 3
Picos 181 H 2
Pico San Juan 173 F 3
Picos de Europa 114 BC 3
Picos de Mampodre 114 B 3
Picota 178 C 5
Pico Tamacuarí 178 E 3
Pico Truncado 183 C 8
Pictou 169 P 6
Pic Tousside 157 H 1
Picton 183 C 9–7
Picún Leufú 183 C 6
Pidurutalagala 134 D 6
Piedecuesta 178 D 2
Piedmont (MO, U.S.A.) 171 H 4
Piedrabuena 183 G 2
Piedrabuena 114 C 4
Piedra, Cerro 183 B 6
Piedra Sola 182 E 5
Piedrahita 114 B 3
Piedras Negras 172 B 2
Pieksämäki 112 J 3
Pielavesi 112 J 3
Pielinen 112 J 3
Pierre 170 F 3
Pierrelatte 115 D 3
Piesapa 137 J 4
Pieskehaure 112 G 2
Piešťány 111 G 5
Pietarsaari 112 H 3
Pietermaritzburg 160 DE 5
Pietersburg 160 D 4
Piet Retief 161 E 5
Pigawasi 158 E 5
Pigeon Hole 142 E 2
Pigué 183 D 6
Pihlajavesi 112 J 3
Pihtipudas 112 J 3
Pik Aborigen 131 R 3
Pikangikum 168 J 5
Pikelot 146 A 2
Pikes Peak 170 E 4
Piketberg 160 B 6
Pik Grandioznyy 130 G 5
Pikhtovka 119 Q 4
Pik Karla Marksa 129 J 3
Pik Kommunizma 129 J 3
Pikounda 157 H 5
Pik Lenina 129 J 3
Pik Pobedy 129 KL 2
Pik Revolyutsii 129 J 3
Pila (Argentina) 183 E 6

Piła (Poland) 111 G 4
Pilão Arcado 181 H 3
Pilar (Alagoas, Brazil) 181 J 2
Pilar (Argentina) 182 D 5
Pilar (Uruguay) 182 E 4
Pila, Sierra de la 114 C 4
Pilatus 115 E 2
Pilcaniyeu 183 B 7
Pilcomayo 180 E 5
Pilica 111 H 4
Pilion Óros 116 B 3
Piloncillo Mountains 170 E 5
Pilos 116 B 3
Pilot Peak 170 D 3
Pilot Rock 170 C 2
Pil'tun 131 Q 5
Pil'tun, Zaliv 131 Q 5
Pim 119 O 3
Pimenta Bueno 180 D 3
Pimenta, Cachoeira do 179 F 3
Pimental (Brazil) 179 G 4
Pimentel (Peru) 178 B 5
Pinaki 147 F 4
Pinang, Pulau 136 B 2
Pınarbaşı 117 E 3
Pínar del Rio 172 F 3
Pinarello 115 E 3
Pınarhisar 116 C 2
Pincher Creek 167 P 6
Pinchincha 178 C 3–4
Pinçon, Mont 114 C 2
Pindaíba 181 F 3
Pindaré 181 G 1
Pindaré Mirim 181 G 1
Pindi Gheb 129 J 4
Pindobal 179 J 4
Pindorama 181 G 3
Pindhos Óros 116 B 2–3
Pine Bluff 171 H 5
Pine Bluffs 170 F 3
Pine Creek 142 E 1
Pine Falls 167 S 5
Pinega 118 H 3
Pine Island Bay 185
Pine Mountain 171 K 5
Pine Pass 167 N 4
Pine Point 167 P 3
Pine Ridge 170 F 3
Pinerolo 115 E 3
Pinetown 161 E 5
Ping'anyi 132 D 3
Pingbian 132 D 6
Pingchang 132 E 4
Pingdingshan 132 F 4
Pingdu 133 G 3
Pingelap 146 B 2
Pingelly 142 B 5
Pingguo 132 E 6
Pinghu 133 H 4
Pingjiang 132 F 5
Pingle 132 F 6
Pingli 132 E 4
Pingliang 132 E 3
Pinglu 132 F 4
Pingluo 132 E 3
Pingnan 132 F 6
Pingquan 133 G 2
Pingshan 132 F 3
Pingtan 133 G 5
Pingtung 133 H 6
Pingwu 132 D 4
Pingxiang 132 E 6
Pingxiang 132 E 6
Pingyang 133 H 5
Pingyao 132 F 3
Pingyuan 133 G 3
Pinheiro 181 G 1
Pinheiro Machado 182 F 5
Pinhel 114 B 3
Pini, Pulau 136 A 3
Pinjang 137 F 3
Pink Mountain 167 N 4
Pinlebu 135 G 3
Pinnaroo 143 G 6
Pinnes, Akra 116 B 2
Pinos, Mount 170 C 5
Pinos-Puente 114 C 4
Pinrang 137 E 4
Pins, Île des 146 C 4
Pinsk 113 H 5
Pintados 180 C 5
Pinta, Isla 178 B 6
Pinto 182 D 4
Pinyug 118 J 3
Pio 145 H 4
Pio IX 181 H 2
Pioner 119 R 4
Pionki 111 H 4
Piorini, Lago 179 F 4
Piotrków Trybunalski 111 G 4

Pipar 134 B 2
Pipestone 171 G 3
Pipmouacan, Réservoir 169 N 6
Piquiá 178 E 4
Piquiri 181 F 5
Pira 156 E 4
Piracicaba 181 G 5
Piracuruca 181 H 1
Piraeus → Piraiévs 116 B 3
Piraiévs 116 B 3
Pirámide 183 B 8
Pirámide El Triunfo 182 D 4
Piran 115 F 2
Piranhas 181 F 2
Piranhas 181 J 2
Pirapemas 181 H 1
Pirapora 181 H 4
Pires do Río 181 G 4
Pirgos 116 B 3
Piriá 179 H 4
Pirimapuan 137 J 5
Piripiri 181 H 1
Pirin 116 B 2
Pirmasens 111 E 5
Pirna 111 F 4
Pirot 116 B 2
Pirovano 183 D 6
Piru 137 G 4
Piryatin 118 F 5
Pisa 115 F 3
Pisac 180 B 3
Pisagua 180 B 4
Pisan 129 K 3
Pishan 129 K 3
Pishin 129 H 4
Piso Firme 180 D 3
Pissila 156 D 3
Pisticci 115 G 3
Pistoia 115 F 3
Pisté 172 E 3
Pisuerga 114 C 3
Pita 156 B 3
Pitaga 169 O 5
Pitalito 178 C 3
Pitcairn 147 G 4
Piteå 112 H 2
Piteälven 112 H 2
Piterka 112 J 2
Piteşti 116 B 2
Pit-Gorodoko 130 F 4
Pithapuram 134 D 4
Pithara 142 B 5
Pithiviers 114 D 2
Pitibhit 134 C 2
Pitkjaranta 112 K 3
Pitkul' 112 K 2
Pitlochry 99 C 3
Pitlyar 119 N 2
Pitomača 115 G 2
Pitrufquén 183 B 6
Pitsunda, Mys 117 F 2
Pitt 145 S 9
Pitt Banks 166 L 5
Pittsburg (KS, U.S.A.) 171 H 4
Pittsburgh (PA, U.S.A.) 171 L 3
Pittsfield (IL, U.S.A.) 171 H 4
Pittsfield (MA, U.S.A.) 171 M 3
Pituri River 143 F 3
Pium 181 G 3
Piura 178 B 5
Pivan' 131 P 5
Pizacoma 180 C 4
Pizzo Calabro 115 G 4
Placentia 169 R 6
Placentia Bay 169 R 6
Placer 137 F 1
Placetas 173 G 3
Plaine de Garar 157 J 3
Plaine des Flandres 114 D 1
Plaine du Forez 114 D 2
Plaines et Seuil du Poitou 114 D 2
Plains of Deosai 129 K 3
Plainview 170 F 5
Plake 111 E 5
Plakhino 119 R 2
Plameira dos Indios 181 J 2
Plampang 136 E 5
Planalto 181 H 3
Planalto Central 181 G 4
Planalto da Borborema 181 J 2
Planalto de Angónia 161 E 2
Planalto de Chimoio 161 E 3
Planalto de Lichinga 161 F 2
Planalto de Marávia 161 E 2
Planalto do Brasil 181 H 4
Planalto do Mato Grosso 180–181 EF 3–4
Planalto Maracanaquará 179 H 3–4
Planeta Rica 178 C 2
Planicie de la Loma Negra 183 C 6

Plasencia 114 B 3
Plast 119 M 5
Plastun 133 L 2
Plastunka 117 E 2
Platanal 179 F 3
Plateau de Basso 157 J 2
Plateau de Haute-Saône 115 E 2
Plateau de la Manika 158 D 6
Plateau de l'Androna 161 H 3
Plateau de Langres 115 DE 2
Plateau de L'ardenne 110 D E 4
Plateau de Millevaches 114 D 2
Plateau des Achikouya 157 G 6
Plateau du Bemaraha 161 G 3–H 3
Plateau du Djado 157 G 2
Plateau du Kontum 135 J 5
Plateau du Tademaït 153 F 3
Plateau du Tchigai 157 G 1
Plateau Laurentien 169 O 5
Plateau of Tibet 134 DE 1
Plateaux 157 H 6
Plateaux de la Marche 114 D 2
Plati 116 B 2
Plato 178 D 2
Plato Syverma 130 G 3
Plato Ustyurt 128 F 2
Plato Yagtali 130 G 2
Platte 135 K 6
Platte River 170 G 3
Platterville 171 H 3
Plattsburg 171 M 3
Plattsmouth 171 G 3
Plau 111 F 4
Plauen 111 F 4
Pļaviņas 113 J 4
Plavsk 118 G 5
Playa Azul 172 B 4
Playas 178 B 4
Playgreen, Lake 167 S 5
Playitas 178 B 4
Plaza Huincul 183 C 6
Pleasanton 170 G 6
Pleiku 135 J 5
Plenty, Bay of 146 C 5
Plentywood 170 F 2
Plesetsk 118 H 3
Pleshchenitsy 112 J 5
Pleszew 111 G 4
Plétipi, Lac 169 N 5
Pleven 116 B 2
Plibo 156 C 5
Plitvice 115 G 3
Pljevlja 116 A 2
Ploča, Rt 115 G 3
Ploče 115 G 3
Ploieşti 116 C 2
Plomárion 116 C 3
Plomb du Cantal 114 D 2
Plouguerneau 114 C 2
Plovdiv 116 B 2
Plumridge Lake 142 D 4
Plumtree 160 D 4
Plunge 113 H 4
Plymouth (Montserrat) 173 K 4
Plymouth (U.K.) 110 C 4
Plymouth (U.K.) 102 B 2
Plymouth Sound 102 B 2
Plyussa 113 J 4
Plzeň 111 F 5
Plzeňská Pahorkatina 111 F 4–5
Po (Italy) 115 F 3
Pô (Upper Volta) 156 D 4
Pobè (Benin) 156 E 4
Pobé (Upper Volta) 156 D 3
Pobeda, Gora 131 R 2
Pobedino 131 Q 6
Pobedy, Pik 129 KL 2
Pobrežije 116 C 2
Pocatello 170 D 3
Pochala 158 E 3
Pochinok 118 F 5
Pochtovaya 131 R 3
Płock 111 H 4
Pocklington Reef 143 J 1
Poçoes 181 H 3
Pocoma 180 B 4
Poconé 180 E 4
Pocono Mountains 171 L 3
Poços de Caldas 181 G 5
Podgornoye 119 Q 4
Podgornyy 131 R 6
Podkagernoye 131 U 3
Podkamennaya Tunguska 130 F 3
Podlesnoye 119 J 5
Podoľsk 118 G 4
Podosinovets 118 J 3
Podporozh'ye 118 F 3
Podravska Slatina 115 G 2
Podresovo 119 N 4
Podtësovo 130 F 4
Pod'yelanka 130 H 3
Podyuga 118 H 3

Pof–Pra

Pofadder 160 B 5
Poggibonsi 115 F 3
Pogibi 131 Q 5
Pogórze Karpackie 111 G H 5
Pogoso 158 B 6
Pogradeci 116 B 2
Pogranichnoye 131 Q 5
P'ohang 133 J 3
Pohjan lahti 112 GH 3
Pohjanmaa 112 H 3
Pohjois-Karjala 112 J 3
Pohorje 115 G 2
Poi 135 F 2
Poiana Mare 116 B 2
Poie 158 C 5
Poinsett, Cape 185
Point Arena 170 B 4
Point Baker 166 L 4
Point Barrow 166 F 1
Point Calimere 134 C 5
Point Cloates 142 A 3
Point Conception 170 B 5
Point Culver 142 C 5
Point D'Entrecasteaux 142 B 5
Pointe-à-Pitre 173 K 4
Pointe aux E'cueils 169 M 4
Pointe de Barfleur 114 C 2
Pointe de Grave 114 C 2
Pointe de la Coubre 114 C 2
Pointe de l'Est 169 P 6
Pointe de Penmarch 114 C 2
Pointe de Saint-Gildas 114 C 2
Pointe de Saint-Mathieu 114 C 2
Pointe des Monts 169 O 6
Pointe du Croisic 114 C 2
Pointe du Raz 114 C 2
Pointe Louis-XIV 169 M 5
Pointe Noire 157 G 6
Point Hope 166 D 2
Point Kadami 158 E 4
Point Lake 167 P 2
Point Lay 166 E 2
Point of Ayre 100 C 2
Point of Stoer 98 B 2
Point Pleasant 171 M 3
Point Stuart 142 E 1
Poissonnier Point 142 B 2
Poitiers 114 D 2
Poitou 114 CD 2
Poitou, Plaines et seeuil du 114 D 2
Poivre Islands 159 J 6
Pojeierze Pomorskie 111 G 4
Pojezierze Mazurskie 111 H 4
Pokaran 134 B 2
Pokhara 134 D 2
Pokhodsk 131 U 3
Pokhvistnevo 118 K 5
Poko 158 D 4
Pokontopugol 119 Q 3
Pokrovsk 131 N 3
Pokrovskoye 117 E 1
Pola de Siero 114 B 3
Poland 111 H 4
Polar Plateau 185
Polatlı 117 D 3
Polcura 183 B 6
Polei Monu 135 J 5
Pole of Inaccessibility 185
Polese 113 H 5
Polesie Lubelskie 111 H 4
Polessk 113 H 5
Polesskoye 113 J 5
Polesye 113 K 5
Polevskoy 119 M 4
Polewali 137 E 4
Polgovskoye 119 N 4
Pólgyo 133 J 4
Poli 157 G 4
Policastro, Golfo di 115 G 3
Policoro 115 G 3
Poligus 130 F 3
Polillo Islands 137 J 1
Polillo Strait 137 J 1
Pólis 117 D 3
Polist' 113 K 4
Polistena 115 G 4
Poliyiros 116 B 2
Pollachi 134 C 5
Pollensa 114 D 4
Pollock Reef 142 C 5
Polnovat 119 N 3
Pologi 117 E 1
Polonio, Cabo 182 F 5
Polonnaruwa 134 D 6
Polonnoye 113 J 5
Polotsk 113 J 4
Polousnyy, Kryazh 131 PQ 2
Polovniki 118 K 3
Polska 111 H 4
Polson 167 P 6
Poltava 118 F 6
Poltavka 119 O 5

Põltsamaa 113 J 4
Polunochnoye 119 MN 3
Poluostrov Buzachi 128 E 1
Poluostrov Govena 131 V 4
Poluostrov Gusinaya Zemlya 118 K 1
Poluostrov Kamchatka 131 T 4
Poluostrov Kanin 118 H 2
Poluostrov Karchyk 131 V 2
Poluostrov Kol'skiy 118 G 2
Poluostrov Koni 131 S 4
Poluostrov Mamonta 130 C 1
Poluostrov Mangyshlak 128 E 2
Poluostrov Pyagina 131 S 4
Poluostrov Rybachiy 112 K 2
Poluostrov Shirokostan 131 PQ 1
Poluostrov Shmidta 131 Q 5
Poluostrov Taygonos 131 U 3
Poluostrov Taymyr 130 E 1–J 1
Poluostrov Yamal 119 N 1
Poluy 119 N 2
Polvijärvi 112 J 3
Pol'yanovo 119 N 3
Polyarnik 166 B 2
Polyarnyy (Kamchatka U.S.S.R.) 131 R 1
Polyarnyy (Kola Pen. U.S.S.R.) 112 K 2
Polyarnyy Ural 119 MN 2
Poman 182 C 4
Pombal (Portugal) 114 B 4
Pombal (Bahía, Brazil) 181 J 3
Pombal (Paraíba, Brazil) 181 J 2
Pomerania 111 F G 4
Pomio 146 B 3
Pomme de Terre Reservoir 171 H 4
Pommersche Bucht 111 F 4
Pomona 170 C 5
Pomorije 116 C 2
Pomoshnaya 116 D 1
Pomozdino 118 K 3
Pompei 115 E 3
Pompeyevka 131 O 6
Ponape 146 B 2
Ponca City 171 G 4
Ponce 173 J 4
Pondicherry 134 CD 5
Ponente, Rivera di 115 E 3
Ponérihouen 145 J 6
Ponferrada 114 B 3
Pongkolaero 137 F 5
Pongo 158 D 3
Pongola 161 E 5
Pongo Manserichi 178 C 4
Ponnani 134 C 5
Ponnyadaung Range 135 F 3
Ponomarevka 118 K 5
Ponorogo 136 D 5
Ponoy 118 H 2
Ponoy 118 G 2
Pons (France) 114 C 2
Pons (Spain) 114 D 3
Ponta da Baleia 181 J 4
Ponta das Salinas 160 A 2
Ponta Delgada 152 A 1
Ponta de Mutá 181 J 3
Ponta do Manguinho 181 J 3
Ponta do Padrão 160 A 1
Ponta Grossa 182 F 4
Ponta Porã 181 E 5
Pontant 183 D 6
Pontarddulais 102 C 2
Pontarlier 115 E 2
Pontassieve 115 F 3
Pont-Audemer 114 D 2
Pontchartrain, Lake 171 H 5
Pontchâteau 114 C 2
Pont de Suert 114 D 3
Ponte de Pedra 180 E 3
Ponte do Lima 114 B 3
Pontefract 101 E 3
Ponteland 101 E 2
Ponte Nova 181 H 5
Pontes-e-Lacerda 180 E 4
Pontevedra 114 B 3
Pontiac (IL, U.S.A.) 171 J 3
Pontianak 136 C 4
Pontine, Alpi le 115 E 2
Pontine Mountains 117 F 2
Pontino, Agro 115 F 3
Pont-l'Abbé 114 C 2
Pontremoli 115 E 3
Pontypool 102 C 2
Pontypridd 102 C 2
Ponza 115 E 3
Ponzari 118 H 5
Ponziane, Isola 115 F 3
Poochera 142 E 5
Pool 157 H 6
Poole 103 C 2
Pool Maleb 158 B 5
Poona 134 B 4

Poopó 180 C 4
Poopó, Lago de 180 C 4
Poorman 166 F 3
Popar Hill 168 J 5
Popa Taung 135 G 3
Poperechnoye 130 K 5
Popigay 130 J 1
Popigay 130 K 1
Poplar Bluff 171 H 4
Popocatépetl 172 C 4
Popokabaka 158 B 6
Popondetta 144 E 3
Popovo 116 C 2
Popoyán 178 C 3
Poprad 111 H 5
Poptún 172 E 4
Poquis 180 C 5
Porahat 134 E 3
Porangatu 181 G 3
Porbandar 134 A 3
Porco 180 C 4
Porcuna 114 C 4
Porcupine 166 J 2
Porcupine Plain 166 K 2
Pordenone 115 F 2
Poretta 115 E 3
Pórfido, Punta 183 D 7
Porhov 113 J 4
Pori (Björneborg) 112 H 3
Porirua 145 R 9
Porjus 112 G 2
Porkkala 113 H 4
Porlamar 179 F 1
Porma 114 B 3
Pornic 114 C 2
Porog 118 L 3
Porog Bol'shoy 130 H 1
Porog 118 G 3
Poronaysk 131 Q 6
Porosozero 112 K 3
Porpoise Bay 185
Porrentruy 115 E 2
Porsangen 112 J 1
Porsanerhalvöya 112 HJ 1
Porsgrunn 113 E 4
Porsuk 116 D 3
Porsuk Baraji 116 D 3
Portachuelo 180 D 4
Portadown 100 B 2
Portaferry 100 C 2
Portage la-Prairie 167 S 5
Port Alberni 167 N 6
Portalegre 114 B 4
Port Alfred 160 D 6
Port Alice 167 M 5
Port Angeles 170 B 2
Port Antonio 173 G 4
Portarlington 100 B 3
Port Arthur (TX, U.S.A.) 171 H 6
Port Arthur (Tas, Aus.) 144 L 9
Port Arthur (China) → Lüshun 133 H 3
Port Augusta 143 F 5
Port au Prince 173 H 4
Portavogie 100 C 2
Port-Bergé-Vao Vao 161 H 3
Port Blair 135 F 5
Port Blandford 169 R 6
Port-Bou 114 D 3
Port Burwell 169 P 3
Port-Cartier 169 O 5
Port Chalmers 145 Q 10
Port Charlotte 171 K 6
Port Darwin 142 E 1
Port Davey 144 L 9
Port Douglas 143 H 2
Port Edward 160 DE 6
Port Elgin 171 K 3
Port Elizabeth 160 D 6
Port Ellen 100 B 2
Port Erin 100 B 2
Porterville 170 C 4
Portes d'Enfer 158 D 6
Port Étienne → Nouadhibou 152 A 4
Port Fairy 143 G 6
Port Gentil 157 F 6
Port Glasgow 99 B 4
Port Graham 166 G 4
Port Harcourt 157 F 5
Port Hardy 167 M 5
Port Hawkesbury 169 P 6
Port Hedland 142 B 3
Port Heiden 166 F 4
Porthleven 102 B 2
Port Hope Simpson 169 Q 5
Port Huron 171 K 3
Portile de Fier 116 B 2

Portimão 114 B 4
Portishead 102 C 2
Portiţa 116 C 2
Port Jackson 145 R 8
Port Katon 117 E 1
Port Keats 142 D 1
Port Láirge 110 B 4
Portland (New S. Wales, Aus.) 143 H 5
Portland (Victoria, Aus.) 143 G 6
Portland (ME, U.S.A.) 171 M 3
Portland (OR, U.S.A.) 170 B 2
Portland Bill 102 C 2
Portland, Cape 144 L 9
Port-la-Nouvelle 114 D 3
Portlaoise 110 B 3
Port Laoise 100 B 3
Port Lavaca 171 G 6
Port Lincoln 143 F 5
Port Loko 156 B 4
Port-Louis (Mauritius) 161 K 6
Port-Louis (Guadeloupe) 173 K 4
Port Macquarie 143 J 5
Portmadoc 110 C 4
Port Menier 169 P 6
Port Moller 166 E 4
Port Moresby 144 E 3
Portnaguran 98 A 2
Port Nelson 167 T 4
Portnockie 98 C 3
Port Nolloth 160 B 5
Port-Nouveau-Québec 169 O 4
Portnyagino, Ozero 130 J 1
Porto Amboim 160 A 2
Pôrto (Brazil) 181 H 1
Porto (Corse, France) 115 E 3
Porto (Portugal) 114 B 3
Pôrto Acre 178 E 5
Porto Alegre 157 F 5–6
Pôrto Alegre (Amazonas, Brazil) 178 E 5
Pôrto Alegre (Mato Grosso du Sul, Brazil) 181 F 5
Pôrto Alegre (Rio Grande du Sul, Brazil) 182 F 5
Pôrto Artur 181 F 3
Porto Azzurro 115 F 3
Pôrto Barra 181 F 5
Portobello (Spain) 114 B 3
Portobelo (Panama) 178 C 2
Pôrto Camargo 181 F 5
Porto Cervo 115 E 3
Pôrto Conceição 180 E 4
Pôrto da Barca 179 H 4–5
Pôrto de Moz 179 H 4
Pôrto de Pedras 181 J 2
Pôrto dos Gauchos 180 E 3
Pôrto dos Meinacos 181 F 3
Porto Empedocle 115 F 4
Pôrto Esperança 180 E 4
Pôrto Esperidião 180 E 4
Portoferraio 115 F 3
Port of Ness 98 A 2
Port of Spain 179 F 1
Portogruaro 115 F 2
Pôrto Grande 179 H 3
Pôrto Jofre 180 E 4
Pôrto Lucena 182 F 4
Pôrtom 112 H 3
Pôrto Mendes 181 F 5
Pôrto Murtinho 180 E 5
Pôrto Nacional 181 G 3
Porto Novo (Benin) 156 E 4
Porto Novo (India) 134 C 5
Port Ontario 171 L 3
Pôrto São José 181 F 5
Porto Santana 179 H 4
Pôrto Santo 152 B 2
Porto Santo Stefano 115 F 3
Pôrto Seguro 181 J 4
Porto Tolle 115 F 3
Porto Torres 115 E 3
Pôrto União 182 F 4
Pôrto Valter 178 D 5
Pôrto Velho 179 F 5
Porto-Vecchio 115 E 3
Portoviejo 178 B 4
Portpatrick 100 C 2
Port Pegasus 144 P 10
Port Phillip Bay 143 G 6
Port Pirie 143 F 5
Port Radium 165
Portree 98 A 3
Portrush 100 B 2
Port Said 154 E 2
Port Saint Joe 171 J 6
Port Saint Johns 160 D 6
Port Saunders 169 Q 5
Port Shepstone 160 DE 6
Port Simpson 166 L 5
Portsmouth (U.K.) 103 D 2

Portsmouth (N.H., U.S.A.) 171 M 3
Portsmouth (OH, U.S.A.) 171 K 4
Portsmouth (VA, U.S.A.) 171 L 4
Portsoy 98 C 3
Portstewart 100 B 2
Port Sudan → Bûr Sûdân 154 F 5
Port Sulphur 171 J 6
Port Talbot 102 C 2
Porttipahdan tekojärvi 112 J 2
Portugal 114 B 3–4
Portugalete 114 C 3
Port Victoria 158 E 4
Port-Vila 145 J 5
Port Wakefield 143 F 5
Porvenir 183 B 9
Porvoo 113 J 3
Posadas 182 E 4
Poschiavo 115 E 2
Posht-e Badam 128 F 4
Posio 112 J 2
Positos 180 D 5
Poso 137 F 4
Posof 117 F 2
Pospelikha 119 Q 5
Pos Poluy 119 N 2
Posse 181 G 3
Possel 158 B 3
Possesion 160 AB 5
Postavy 113 J 4
Post Bobonazo 178 C 4
Poste-de-la-Baleine 169 M 4
Poste Maurice Cortier 153 F 4
Poste Weygand 152 EF 4
Postmasburg 160 C 5
Pôsto Alto Manissauá 181 F 3
Postojna 115 F 2
Postville 169 Q 5
Potapovo 119 R 2
Potchefstroom 160 D 5
Potenza 115 G 3
Potes 114 C 3
Potgietersrus 160 D 4
Potholes Reservoir 170 C 2
Poti (Georgian S.S.R.) 117 F 2
Poti (Brazil) 181 H 2
Potiskum 157 G 3
Potnarhvin 145 J 5
Potomac River 171 L 4
Potosí (Mexico) 172 B 3
Potosi (Bolivia) 180 C 4
Potrerillos 182 C 4
Potsdam 111 F 4
Potters Bar 103 D 2
Pottstown 171 L 3
Pou Bia 135 H 3
Poulapouca Reservoir 100 B 3
Pou Loi 135 H 3
Pou Miang 135 H 4
Pou San 135 H 4
Pou Sao 135 H 4
Pouso Alegre (Mato Grosso, Brazil) 180 E 3
Pouso Alegre (Minas Gerais, Brazil)181 G 5
Povenets 118 F 3
Póvoa de Varzim 114 B 3
Povungnituk 169 M 3
Powassan 171 L 3
Powder River 170 E 2
Powell Creek 142 E 2
Powell, Lake 170 D 4
Powell River 167 N 6
Powys 102 C 1
Poxoreu 181 F 4
Poya 145 J 6
Poyarkovo 131 N 6
Pozanti 117 D 3
Požarevac 116 B 2
Poza Rica de Hidalgo 172 C 3
Pozdeyevka 131 N 5
Pozega 116 B 2
Poznan 111 G 4
Pozo Almonte 180 C 5
Pozo del Molle 182 D 5
Pozo del Tigre 180 D 5
Pozzuoli 115 F 3
Prabuty 111 G 4
Prachuap Khiri Khan 135 G 5
Praděd 111 G 4
Pradera 178 C 3
Prades 114 D 3
Prado 181 J 4
Praha → Prague 111 F 4
Praia 156 B 7
Praia Albandão 182 F 5
Praia Azul 160 A 3
Prainha 179 H 4
Prainha 179 F 5
Prairie Dog Town Fork 170 F 5
Prairie du Chien 171 H 3

Prakhon Chai 135 H 5
Prapat 136 A 3
Praslin 159 K 5
Prata 181 G 4
Pratapgarh 134 B 3
Prat de Llobregat 114 D 3
Prato 115 F 3
Pratt 170 G 4
Praya 136 E 5
Prechistoye 118 F 4
Predgornoye 117 G 2
Predivinsk 130 F 4
Pregolja 113 H 5
Prek Kak 135 J 5
Premuda 115 F 3
Prenjasi 116 B 2
Prentice 171 H 2
Prenzlau 111 F 4
Preobrazhenka 130 J 3
Prepansko jezero 116 B 2
Preparis Island 135 F 5
Preparis Nourth Channel 135 F 5
Preparis South Channel 135 F 5
Přerov 111 G 5
Presa de la Boquilla 170 E 6
Presa Falcon 172 C 2
Presa Miguel Alemán 172 C 4
Presa Netzahualcyótl 172 D 4
Prescott 170 D 5
Presidencia Roque Sáenz-Reña 182 D 4
Presidente Dutra 181 H 2
Presidente Epitácio 181 F 5
Presidente Murtinho 181 F 4
Presidente Prudente 181 F 5
Preslav 116 C 2
Presnogor'kovka 119 N 5
Presnovka 119 N 5
Prešov 111 H 5
Prespa 116 B 2
Presque Isle 171 N 2
Prestatyn 102 C 1
Prestea 156 D 4
Preston (U.K.) 101 D 3
Preston (MT, U.S.A.) 170 D 3
Prestonburg 171 K 4
Prestonpans 99 C 4
Prestwick 99 B 4
Prestwick (Airport) 99 B 4
Prêto 181 G 4
Prêto do Igapó Açu 179 F 4
Pretoria 160 D 5
Prévesa 116 B 3
Prey Veng 135 J 5
Priangarskoye Plato 130 G 4
Priaral'skiye Karakumy, Peski 129 G 1
Priazovskaya Vozvyshennost' 117 E 1
Pribilof Islands 166 CD 4
Priboj 116 A 2
Příbram 111 F 5
Pribrezhnyy, Khrebet 131 P 4
Price 170 D 4
Prichard 171 J 5
Prichernomorskaya Nizmennost' 117 D 1
Priekule 113 H 4
Priene 116 C 3
Prieska 116 C 5
Prieta, Sierra 170 D 5
Prievidza 111 G 5
Prijedor 115 G 3
Prikaspiyskaya Nizmennost 118 JK 6
Prikubanskaya Nizmennost' 117 E 1
Prilep 116 B 2
Priluki 118 F 5
Priluki 118 H 3
Primavera 185
Primeira Cruz 181 H 1
Primorsk 112 J 3
Primorskiy 117 E 1
Primorskiy Khrebet 130 H J 5
Primorsko-Akhtarsk 117 E 1
Primorskoye 117 E 1
Primošten 115 G 3
Primrose Lake 167 Q 4
Prince Albert (Saskatch, Canada) 167 Q 5
Prince Albert (S. Africa) 160 C 6
Prince Albert Mountains 185
Prince Albert National Park 167 Q 5
Prince Albert Peninsula 167 O 1
Prince Albert Road 160 C 6
Prince Albert Sound 167 P 1
Prince Alfred, Cape 167 O 1
Prince Charles Island 169 M 1
Prince Charles Mountains 185
Prince-de-Galles, Cap 169 N 3

Prince Edward Island (Canada) 169 P 6
Prince Edward Islands (Antarctic 185
Prince George 167 N 5
Prince of Wales 167 S 1
Prince of Wales, Cape 166 D 2
Prince of Wales Island (AK, U.S.A.) 166 L 4
Prince of Wales Island (Aus.) 143 G 1
Prince of Wales Strait 167 O 1
Prince Patrick Island 184
Prince Rupert 166 L 5
Princes Risborough 103 D 2
Princess Astrid Coast 185
Princess Charlotte Bay 143 G 1
Princess Martha Coast 185
Princess Ragnhild Coast 185
Princess Royal Island 166 M 5
Princeton (Br. Col., Can.) 167 N 6
Princeton (IN, U.S.A.) 171 J 4
Princeton (MS, U.S.A.) 171 H 3
Prince William Sound 166 H 3
Príncipe 157 F 5
Príncipe da Beira 180 D 3
Prineville 170 B 3
Prins Christians Sund 169 T 3
Prinzapolka 172 F 5
Priozersk 112 K 3
Pripolyarnyy Ural 119 M 3
Pripyat 113 J 4
Pripyat marshes → Polesye 113 K 5
Pirechnyy 112 K 2
Pristina 116 B 2
Pritzwalk 111 F 4
Privas 115 D 3
Privolzhskaya Vozvyshennost' 118 J 5
Privolzhskiy 128 D 1
Priyutnoye 117 F 1
Priyutovo 118 K 5
Prizren 116 B 2
Probolinggo 136 D 5
Proddatur 134 C 5
Progreso 172 E 3
Prohod Vráška čuka 116 B 2
Prokhladnyy 117 F 2
Prokhorkino 119 P 4
Prokop'yevo 130 H 4
Prokop'yevsk 119 R 5
Prokuplje 116 B 2
Proletariy 113 K 4
Proletarsk 117 F 1
Proletarskiy 118 G 5
Proliv Bussol' 131 S 6
Proliv Dmitriya Lapteva 131 Q 1
Proliv Friza 131 R 6
Proliv Karskiye Vorota 118 L 1
Proliv Krunzenshterna 131 S 6
Proliv Nevel'skogo 131 Q 5
Proliv Sannikova 131 PQ 1
Proliv Yekateriny 131 R 7
Proliv Yugoriskiy Shar 119 M 2
Prome 135 G 4
Promissão, Reprêsa 181 G 5
Promontoire Portland 169 M 4
Promontorio del Gargano 115 G 3
Promyshlennaya 119 R 5
Propria 181 J 3
Propriano 115 E 3
Proserpine 143 H 3
Prosna 111 G 4
Prosperidad 137 G 2
Prospikhino 130 G 4
Prosser 170 C 2
Prostějov 111 G 5
Protochnyye 119 N 3
Provadija 116 C 2
Provence 115 E 3
Providence (U.S.A.) 171 M 3
Providence (Seychelles) 159 J 6
Providence, Cape 144 P 10
Providence Channel 173 G 2
Providencia, Isla de 173 F 5
Providência, Serra da 180 D 3
Provideniya 166 C 2
Provincetown 171 M 3
Provincias Vascongadas 114 C 3
Provins 114 D 2
Provo 170 D 3
Prozor 115 G 3
Prudhoe 101 E 2
Prudhoe Bay 166 H 1
Prudnik 111 G 4
Prussia 111 H 4
Pruszków 111 H 4
Prut 116 C 1
Pruzhany 113 H 5
Pryazha 118 F 3
Prydz Bay 185
Przemyśl 111 H 5

Przeworsk 111 H 4
Prżheval'sk 129 K 2
Psará 116 C 3
Pshada 117 E 2
Pshino 119 Q 4
Pshish 117 E 2
Pshish, Gora 117 F 2
Pskov 113 J 4
Pskovskoye Ozero 113 J 4
Ptich 113 J 5
Ptolemaïs (Greece) 116 B 2
Ptolemaïs → Ṭulmaythah (Libya) 153 K 2
Ptu 115 G 2
Ptuj 115 G 2
Pualu Baso 136 B 4
Pualu Sebanka 136 B 3
Puán 183 D 6
Pubei 132 E 6
Pucallpa 178 D 5
Pucará 180 C 4
Pucheng 133 G 5
Pucheveem 131 W 2
Pucioasa 116 C 1
Pudasjärvi 112 J 2
Pudino 119 P 4
Pudozh 118 G 3
Pudsey 101 E 3
Puduchcheri → Pondicherry 134 CD 5
Pudukkottai 134 C 5
Puebla de Alcocer 114 C 4
Puebla de Zaragoza 172 C 4
Pueblo 170 F 4
Pueblo Hundido 182 C 4
Puelches 183 C 6
Puelén 183 C 6
Puente Alto 182 B 5
Puente-Genil 114 C 4
Pu'er 132 D 6
Puerto Acosta 180 C 4
Puerto Adela 181 F 5
Puerto Aisén 183 B 8
Puerto Alegre 180 D 3
Puerto Angel 172 C 4
Puerto Arista 172 D 4
Puerto Armuelles 178 B 2
Puerto Asis 178 C 3
Puerto Ayacucho 178 E 2
Puerto Baquerizo Moreno 178 B 6
Puerto Barrios 172 E 4
Puerto Bermúdez 180 B 3
Puerto Berrio 178 D 2
Puerto Boyacá 178 D 2
Puerto Caballas 180 A 3
Puerto Cabello 178 E 1
Puerto Cabezas 172 F 5
Puerto Carreño 178 E 2
Puerto Casade 180 E 5
Puerto Chicama 178 BC 5
Puerto Cisnes 183 B 7
Puerto Coig 183 C 9
Puerto Colombia 178 D 1
Puerto Cortés 172 E 4
Puerto Cumarebo 178 E 1
Puerto de Contreras 114 C 4
Puerto del Escudo 114 C 3
Puerto del Madeiro 114 C 3
Puerto del Rosario 152 C 3
Puerto de Mazarrón 114 C 4
Puerto de Miravete 114 B 4
Puerto de Morata 114 C 3
Puerto de Pajares 114 B 3
Puerto de Perales 114 B 3
Puerto Deseado 183 C 8
Puerto de Somport 114 C 3
Puerto de Torre Miró 114 C 3
Puerto de Villatoro 114 B 3
Puerto Escondido 172 C 4
Puerto Esperanza 182 F 4
Puerto Estrella 178 D 1
Puerto Etén 178 BC 5
Puerto Grether 180 D 4
Puerto Guaraní 180 D 5
Puerto Harberton 183 C 9
Puerto Heath 180 C 3
Puerto Huitoto 178 D 3
Puerto Iguazu 182 F 4
Puerto Juárez 172 E 3
Puerto la Concordia 178 D 3
Puerto la Cruz 179 F 1
Puerto la Paz 180 D 5
Puerto Leguizamo 178 D 4
Puerto Leigue 180 D 3
Puerto Lempira 172 F 4
Puerto Libertad 170 D 6
Puerto Limón 178 D 3
Puerto Lobos 183 C 7
Puerto Lomas 180 B 4
Puerto López 178 D 1
Puerto Madero 172 D 5
Puerto Madryn 183 C 7

Puerto Magdalena 170 D 7
Puerto Maldonado 180 C 3
Puerto Miraña 178 D 4
Puerto Montt 183 B 7
Puerto Nariño 178 E 3
Puerto Natales 183 B 9
Puerto Nuevo 178 E 2
Puerto Ocampo 182 E 4
Puerto Ordaz 179 F 2
Puerto Padilla 180 B 3
Puerto Páez 178 E 2
Puerto Patiño 180 C 4
Puerto Patillos 180 B 5
Puerto Pinasco 180 E 5
Puerto Pirámides 183 D 7
Puerto Plata 173 H 4
Puerto Portillo 178 D 5
Puerto Princesa 137 E 2
Puerto Reyes 178 D 4
Puerto Rico (U.S.A.) 173 J 4
Puerto Rico (Arg.) 182 F 4
Puerto Rico (Bolivia) 180 C 3
Puerto Rico (Col.) 178 C 3
Puerto Rico Trench 192 A 3
Puerto Rondón 178 D 2
Puerto Sastre 180 E 5
Puerto Siles 180 C 3
Puerto Suárez 180 E 4
Puerto Tejada 178 C 3
Puerto Umbría 178 C 3
Puerto Vallarta 172 A 3
Puerto Varas 183 B 7
Puerto Verlarde 180 D 4
Puerto Victoria 178 D 5
Puerto Villamizar 178 D 2
Puerto Villazón 180 D 3
Puerto Visser 183 C 8
Puerto Wilches 178 D 2
Puerto Williams 183 C 9
Puerto Ybapobó 180 E 5
Pueyrredón, Lago 183 B 8
Pugachev 118 J 5
Pugal 134 B 2
Pugalu 157 F 6
Puget Sound 170 B 2
Puigcerda 114 D 3
Puigmal 114 D 3
Puisaye, Collines de la 114 D 2
Pujehun 156 B 4
Puka 116 A 2
Pukapuka (Cook Islands) 146 D 3
Pukapuka (French Polynesia) 147 F 3
Pukaruha 147 F 4
Pukaskwa National Park 171 J 2
Pukatawagan 167 R 4
Pukch'ŏng 133 J 2
Puketeraki Range 145 Q 9
Puksoozero 118 H 3
Pula 115 F 3
Pula, Capo di 115 E 4
Pulap 146 A 2
Pulau Adi 137 H 4
Pulau Adonara 137 F 5
Pulau Alor 137 F 5
Pulau Ambon 137 G 4
Pulau Atauro 137 G 5
Pulau Babi 136 A 3
Pulau Bacan 137 G 4
Pulau Bangka 136 B 4
Pulau Bangkaru 136 A 3
Pulau Batam 136 B 3
Pulau Batanta 137 H 4
Pulau Bawean 136 D 5
Pulau Belitung 136 C 4
Pulau Bengkalis 136 B 3
Pulau Besar 137 F 5
Pulau Biak 137 J 4
Pulau Binongko 137 F 5
Pulau Bintan 136 B 3
Pulau Boano 137 G 4
Pulau Breueh 136 A 2
Pulau Butung 137 F 4
Pulau Damar (Moluccas) 137 G 4
Pulau Damar (L. Sunda Is.) 137 G 5
Pulau Enggano 136 B 5
Pulau Gag 137 G 4
Pulau Gebe 137 G 4
Pulau Jatisiri 136 E 4
Pulau Jemaja 136 C 3
Pulau Jos Sodarso 137 J 5
Pulau Kabaena 137 F 5
Pulau Kai Besar 137 H 5
Pulau Kalao 137 F 5
Pulau Kalaotoa 137 F 5
Pulau Kalukalukuang 136 E 5
Pulau Karakelong 137 G 3
Pulau Karimata 136 C 4
Pulau Karimunjawa 136 D 5
Pulau Kasiruta 137 G 4
Pulau Kawalusu 137 F 3

Pulau Kayoa 137 G 3
Pulau Kelang 137 G 4
Pulau Kisar 137 G 5
Pulau Kobroor 137 H 5
Pulau Komodo 137 E 5
Pulau Komoran 144 C 3
Pulau Kundur 136 B 3
Pulau Labengke 137 F 4
Pulau Lasia 136 A 3
Pulau Laut 136 E 4
Pulau Lepar 136 C 4
Pulau Lingga 136 B 4
Pulau Lomblen 137 F 5
Pulau Madura 136 D 5
Pulau Makian 137 G 3
Pulau Mandioli 137 G 4
Pulau Mangole 137 G 4
Pulau Manipa 137 G 4
Pulau Manui 137 F 4
Pulau Masalembo 136 D 5
Pulau Masela 137 G 5
Pulau Maya 136 C 4
Pulau Mega 136 B 4
Pulau Midai 136 C 3
Pulau Misool 137 H 4
Pulau Morotai 137 G 3
Pulau Moyo 136 E 5
Pulau Muna 137 F 5
Pulau Mursala 136 A 3
Pulau Nias 136 A 3
Pulau Nila 137 G 5
Pulau Num 137 J 4
Pulau Numfor 137 H 4
Pulau Nunukan Timur 136 E 3
Pulau Padang 136 B 3
Pulau Pantar 137 F 5
Pulau Pejantan 136 C 3
Pulau Peleng 137 F 4
Pulau Pemarung 136 E 4
Pulau Penida 136 E 5
Pulau Pinang 136 B 2
Pulau Pini 136 A 3
Pulau Rakata 136 C 5
Pulau Rangsang 136 B 3
Pulau Rinja 137 E 5
Pulau Romang 137 G 5
Pulau Roti 137 F 6
Pulau Rupat 136 B 3
Pulau Salawati 137 H 4
Pulau Samosir 136 A 3
Pulau Sanana 137 G 4
Pulau Sanding 136 B 4
Pulau Sangeang 137 E 5
Pulau Sangihe 137 G 3
Pulau Sawu 137 F 6
Pulau Sayang 137 G 3
Pulau Sebatik 136 E 3
Pulau Sebuku 136 E 4
Pulau Selaru 137 H 5
Pulau Selatan 136 B 4
Pulau Selayar 137 F 5
Pulau Semau 137 F 6
Pulau Sepanjang 136 E 5
Pulau Serasan 136 C 3
Pulau Siberut 136 A 4
Pulau Sibutu 137 E 3
Pulau Simeulue 136 A 3
Pulau Simuk 136 A 3
Pulau Singkep 136 B 4
Pulau Sipora 136 A 4
Pulau Solor 137 F 5
Pulau Subi 136 C 3
Pulau, Sungai 137 J 5
Pulau Supiori 137 J 4
Pulau Taliabu 137 F 4
Pulau Tanahbala 136 A 4
Pulau Tanahjampea 137 F 5
Pulau Tanahmasa 136 A 4
Pulau Tebingtinggi 136 B 3
Pulau Terentang 136 E 4
Pulau Trangan 137 H 5
Pulau Tuangku 136 A 3
Pulau Tubelai 137 G 4
Pulau Utara 136 B 4
Pulau Waigeo 137 H 4
Pulau Wangiwangi 137 F 5
Pulau Weh 136 A 2
Pulau Wetar 137 G 5
Pulau Wokam 137 H 5
Pulau Wowoni 137 F 4
Pulau Yamdena 137 H 5
Pulau Yapen 137 J 4
Puławy 111 H 4
Pulicat 134 D 5
Pulkkila 112 J 3
Pullman 170 C 2
Pulo Anna 137 H 3
Pulog, Mount 137 J 1
Pulonga 118 H 2
Pulozero 112 K 2
Pulton-Le-Fylde 101 D 3
Pulusuk 146 A 2
Puluwat 146 A 2

Pum–Rae

Puma Yumco 135 F 2
Puna 178 B 4
Puna de Atacama 180 C 5–6
Punakha 134 E 2
Puncak Jaya 137 J 4
Puncak Trikora 137 J 4
Punch 129 J 4
Punda Milia 161 E 4
Punduga 118 H 3
Pune 134 B 4
Punia 158 D 5
Puning 132 G 6
Punjab 134 BC 1
Punkaharju 112 J 3
Puno 180 B 4
Punta Alegre 171 L 7
Punta Almina 152 D 1
Punta Alta 183 D 6
Punta Angamos 180 B 5
Punta Arenas 183 B 9
Punta Ballenita 182 B 4
Punta Bermeja 183 D 7
Punta Burica 172 F 6
Punta Cachos 182 B 4
Punta Carreta 180 A 3
Punta Catalina 183 C 9
Punta, Cerro de 173 J 4
Punta de Arenas 183 C 9
Punta de Chilca 178 C 6
Punta de Europa 114 B 4
Punta del Diamante 172 C 4
Punta Delgada 183 D 7
Punta dell' Alice 115 C 4
Punta de Mata 179 F 2
Punta Desengaño 183 C 8
Punta Eugenia 170 C 6
Punta Falcone 115 E 3
Punta Fijo 178 D 1
Punta Galera 183 B 6–4
Punta Gallinas 178 D 1
Punta Gorda (Belize) 172 E 4
Punta Gorda (Nicaragua) 172 F 5
Punta Gorda, Bahía de 172 F 5
Punta Granitola 115 F 4
Punta Gruesa 180 B 5
Punta Guascama 178 C 3
Punta Lachay 178 C 6
Punta Lavapié 183 B 6
Punta Lengua de Vaca 182 B 5
Punta Licosa 115 E 5
Punta Magdalena 178 C 3
Punta Maisí 173 H 3
Punta Mala 178 B 2
Punta Mariato 178 B 2
Punta Medanosa 183 C 8
Punta Morro 182 B 4
Punta Negra 178 B 5
Punta, Ninfas 183 D 7
Punta Norte 183 E 6
Punta Palazzo 115 E 3
Punta Pariñas 178 B 4
Punta Pórfido 183 D 7
Punta Poro 182 E 4
Punta Prieta 170 D 6
Punta Rasa 183 D 7
Puntarenas 172 F 6
Punta Rieles 180 E 5
Punta Roja 183 C 7
Punta Rotja 114 D 4
Punta Sarga 152 B 4
Punta Stilo 115 G 4
Punta Sur 183 E 6
Punta Topocalma 182 B 5
Punta Verde 172 F 5
Puolanka 112 J 3
Puper 137 H 4
Puqi 132 F 5
Puquio 180 B 3
Puquios 182 C 4
Pur 119 P 2
Pura 130 E 1
Puracé 178 C 3
Purcell Mountains 167 O 5
Purdy Islands 146 A 3
Puri 160 B 1
Purificación 178 D 3
Purii 134 E 4
Purikari Neem 113 J 4
Purinskoye, Ozero 130 E 1
Purna 134 C 3
Purnea 134 E 2
Pursat 135 H 5
Purtuniq 169 N 3
Purukcahu 136 D 4
Purulia 134 E 3
Purus 179 F 4
Puruvesi 112 J 3
Purwakarta 136 C 5
Purwokerto 136 C 5
Pusan 133 J 3
Puschino 131 T 5
Pushkin 113 K 4
Pushkino 118 J 5

Pusht-i-Rud 129 G 4
Pusteci 116 B 2
Pustoretsk 131 U 3
Pustoshka 113 J 4
Puszcza Notecka 111 G 4
Putao 135 G 2
Putian 133 G 5
Putina 180 C 3
Puting, Tanjung 136 D 4
Putla de Guerrero 172 C 4
Putnok 116 B 1
Putorana, Gory 130 F 2–H 2
Puttalam 134 C 6
Puttgarden 111 F 4
Putumayo 178 D 4
Pułtusk 111 H 4
Putussibau 136 D 3
Puulavesi 112 J 3
Puyang 132 G 3
Puy Crapaud 114 C 2
Puy de Dôme 114 D 2
Puy de Sancy 114 D 2
Puyo 178 C 4
Puzla 118 K 3
Pwani 159 F 6
Pweto 158 D 6
Pwllheli 102 B 1
Pyagina, Poluostrov 131 S 4
Pyakupur 119 P 3
Pyal'ma 118 G 3
Pyandzh 129 H 3
Pyaozero, Ozero 112 K 2
Pyapon 135 G 4
Pyasina 130 E 1
Pyatigorsk 117 F 2
Pyatigory 118 K 3
Pyatikhatki 117 D 1
Pyatistennoy 131 TU 2
Pyat'kovende, Gora 131 T 2
Pyawbwe 135 G 3
Pygmalion Point 135 F 6
Pyhäjärvi 112 J 3
Pyhäjärvi 112 H 3
Pyhäjoki 112 H 3
Pyhäntä 112 J 3
Pyhäselkä 112 J 3
Pyhätunturi 112 J 2
Pyinmana 135 G 4
Pyl'karamo 119 Q 3
Pymta 131 T 5
P'yŏngyang 133 J 3
Pyramid Lake 170 C 3
Pyramids 154 E 3
Pyrénées 114 CD 3
Pyshchug 118 J 4
Pytalovo 112 J 4
Pyu 135 G 4

Q

Qābis 153 H 2
Qābis, Khalīj 153 H 2
Qabr Hūd 155 H 5
Qādir Karam 155 GH 1
Qāḍub 159 J 2
Qā'emshahr 128 E 3
Qafṣah 153 G 2
Qagan (Nei Monggul Zizhiqu, China) 130 L 6
Qagan Nur (Qinghai, China) 132 C 3
Qagan Nur (Nei Monggul Zizhiqu, China) 132 F 2
Qagan Tohoi 132 B 3
Qagcaka 134 D 1
Qahar Youyi Houqi 132 F 2
Qahar Youyi Qianqi 132 F 2
Qahremänshahr 128 D 4
Qaidam He 132 C 2
Qaidam Pendi 132 B 3
Qala'an Nahl 154 EF 6
Qālat 129 H 4
Qal'at al Akhḍar 154 F 3
Qal'at al Mu'aẓam 154 F 3
Qal'at Bīshah 155 G 4
Qal'at Dīzah 155 H 1
Qal'at Ṣāliḥ 155 H 2
Qal'at al Sukkar 155 H 2
Qallābāt 154 F 6
Qamalung 132 C 4
Qamar, Ghubbat al 155 J 5
Qamata 160 D 6
Qamdo 132 C 4
Qamīnis 153 JK 2
Qandala 159 H 2
Qapqal 129 L 2
Qarā Dāgh 128 D 3
Qārah 154 D 3

Qarā', Jabal 155 J 5
Qarānqū 128 D 3
Qar'at al Ashkal 115 E 4
Qara Tarai 129 H 4
Qārat Dalmā' 153 K 3
Qarawah 155 H 3
Qardo 159 H 3
Qareh Sū 128 DE 4
Qarhan 132 B 3
Qarqan He 129 M 3
Qarqannah 153 H 2
Qarqannah, Juzur 153 H 2
Qarqi 129 M 2
Qārūn, Birkat 154 E 3
Qaryat al 'Ulyā 155 H 3
Qar Wagēr 159 H 2
Qasa Murg 129 G 4
Qaṣr Aḥmād 153 J 2
Qaṣr 'Āmij 155 G 2
Qaṣr bū Hādī 153 J 2
Qasr Burqu' 154 F 2
Qasr-e Qand 129 G 5
Qasr-e Shīrīn 128 D 4
Qaṣr Farāfirah 154 D 3
Qaṣr Ḥamām 155 H 4
Qatar 155 J 3
Qatlīsh 128 F 3
Qattara Depression 154 D 3
Qawz Abū Dulu' 154 E 5
Qawz Rajab 154 F 5
Qāyen 128 F 4
Qaysān 154 E 6
Qayyārah 155 G 1–2
Qazvīn 128 E 3
Qeshm 128 F 5
Qezel Owzan 128 D 3
Qian'an 133 H 1
Qian Gorlos 133 H 1–2
Qianjiang 132 E 5
Qianning 132 D 4
Qian Shan 133 H 2
Qianwei 132 D 5
Qianxi 132 E 5
Qianyang 132 F 5
Qiaojia 132 D 5
Qiaowan 132 C 2
Qichun 132 G 4
Qidong 133 H 4
Qiemo 129 M 3
Qijiang 132 E 5
Qijiaojing 132 B 2
Qila Ladgasht 129 G 5
Qila Saifullah 129 H 4
Qilian 132 D 3
Qilian Shan 132 C–D 3
Qimantag 132 B 3
Qimen 133 G 5
Qinā 154 E 3
Qin'an 132 E 4
Qingchuan 132 E 4
Qingdao 133 H 3
Qinggang 133 J 1
Qinghai 132 C 3
Qinghai Hu 132 D 3
Qing He 132 D 3
Qinghe 129 N 1
Qingjiang (Jiangxi, China) 132 G 5
Qingjiang (Jiangsu, China) 133 G 4
Qing Jiang 132 F 4
Qinglong (Guizhou, China) 132 E 5
Qinglong (Beijing Shi, China) 133 G 2
Qingshen 132 D 5
Qingshuihe 132 F 3
Qingxu 132 F 3
Qingyang 132 E 3
Qingyuan 133 H 2
Qing Zang Gaoyuan 134 DE 1
Qinhuangdao 133 G 3
Qinling 132 E 4
Qinliu 132 G 5
Qin Xian 132 F 3
Qinzhou 132 E 6
Qionghai 132 F 7
Qionglai 132 D 4
Qionglai Shan 132 D 5
Qiongshan 132 F 7
Qiongzhou Haixia 132 F 6
Qiqihar 131 M 6
Qira 129 L 3
Qirzah 153 H 2
Qishn 155 J 5
Qishrān 155 FG 4
Qitai 129 M 2
Qitaihe 133 K 1
Qitbīt, Wādī 155 J 5
Qiyang 132 F 5
Qogir Feng 129 K 3
Qog Ul 133 G 2
Qolleh-ye Damāvand 128 E 3
Qoltag 132 A 2
Qom 128 E 4

Qomdo 132 C 4
Qomolangma Feng 134 E 2
Qomsheh 128 E 4
Qonggyai 135 F 2
Qôrnoq 169 R 3
Qotbābād 128 F 5
Qotur 128 C 3
Qorveh 128 D 3
Quairading 142 B 5
Quajará 179 G 5
Quan Dao Nam Du 135 H 6
Quang Ngai 135 J 4
Quang Tri 135 J 4
Quang Yen 135 J 3
Quan Long 135 J 6
Quan Phu Quoc 135 H 5
Quanshuigou 129 K 3
Quanzhou (Guangxi Zhuangzu Zizhiqu, China) 132 F 5
Quanzhou (Fujian, China) 133 G 6
Qu'Appelle 167 R 5
Quaraí 182 E 5
Quartu Sant' Elena 115 E 4
Quartz Lake 169 L 1
Quartz Mountain 170 B 3
Quartzsite 170 D 5
Quatro Ciénegas 172 B 2
Qūchān 128 F 3
Queanbeyan 143 H 6
Qu'aytī 155 H 5
Québec 169 N 6
Québec 169 N 5
Quebracho 182 E 5
Quebracho Coto 182 D 4
Quedal, Cabo 183 B 7
Queen, Cape 169 M 3
Queen Charlotte Islands 166 L 5
Queen Charlotte Sound 167 M 5
Queen Charlotte Strait 167 M 5
Queen Elizabeth Islands 184
Queen Fabiola Mountains 185
Queen Mary Coast 185
Queen Maud Gulf 167 R 2
Queen Maud Land 185
Queen Maud Mountains 185
Queens Channel 142 D 1
Queensferry 99 C 4
Queensland 143 G 3
Queenstown (South Afr.) 160 D 6
Queenstown (New Zealand) 144 P 9
Queenstown (Tasmania) 144 L 9
Quehue 183 D 6
Queimada 181 G 5
Queimadas 181 J 3
Quela 160 B 1
Quelimane 161 F 3
Quellón 183 B 7
Quelpart 133 J 4
Quemado 170 E 4
Quembo 160 B 2
Quemchi 183 B 7
Quemoy 133 G 6
Quemu Quemu 183 D 6
Quen Bess, Mount 167 N 5
Que Que 160 D 3
Quequén 183 E 6
Querétaro 172 B 3
Quesada 172 F 6
Queshan 132 F 4
Quesnel 167 N 5
Quesnel Lake 167 N 5
Quetena 180 C 5
Quetta 129 H 4
Quevedo 178 C 4
Quezaltenango 172 D 5
Quezon City 137 J 1
Quiñones 170 D 7
Quibala 160 A 1
Quibaxe 160 A 1
Quiberon 114 C 2
Quibdó 178 C 2
Quibilī 153 G 2
Quicabo 160 A 1
Quiçama National Park 160 A 1
Quiches 178 C 5
Quiculungo 160 B 1
Quienha 160 B 2
Quiha 159 F 2
Quihita 160 A 3
Quiindy 182 E 4
Quila 170 E 7
Quilán, Cabo 183 B 7
Quilberry 143 H 4
Quilca 180 B 4
Quilco 183 D 6
Quilenda 160 A 2
Quilengues 160 A 2
Quilino 132 F 5
Quillacollo 180 C 4
Quillagua 180 C 5
Quillaicillo 182 B 5
Quillamba 180 B 3

Quillota 182 B 5
Quilon 134 C 6
Quilpie 143 G 4
Quimbele 160 B 1
Quimilí 182 D 4
Quimper 114 C 2
Quince 180 B 3
Quincy 171 H 4
Quines 182 C 5
Quingey 115 E 2
Quinhagak 166 E 4
Qui Nhon 135 J 5
Quintanar de la Orden 114 C 4
Quintana Roo 172 E 4
Quinto 182 D 5
Quionga 161 G 2
Quipapá 181 J 2
Quipungo 160 A 2
Quirima 160 B 2
Quirinópolis 181 F 4
Quissanga 161 G 2
Quissico 161 E 4
Quitasueño, Banco 173 F 5
Quiterajo 161 G 2
Quito 178 C 4
Quivilla 178 C 5
Quixadá 181 J 1
Quixeramobim 181 J 2
Qujing 132 D 5
Qulansiyah 159 J 2
Qulaybiah 153 H 1
Qulbān Layyah 155 H 3
Qumarlêb 132 C 4
Qumarrabdün 132 B 4
Qumbu 160 D 6
Qunayfidhah, Nafūd 155 H 4
Qu'nyido 132 C 4
Quoich 167 T 3
Quorn 143 F 5
Qurdūd 154 D 6
Qūs 154 E 3
Qusaybah 155 G 2
Qushan 167 T 3
Quşayr ad Daffah 153 K 2
Qusum 132 B 5
Qu Xian 133 G 5
Qüxü 135 F 2
Quyang 132 F 3
Quynh Luu 135 J 4
Qyteti Stalin 116 A 2

R

Rañadoiro, Sierra de 114 B 3
Raab 115 G 2
Raahe 112 H 3
Rääkkylä 112 J 3
Ra's-al Kūh 128 F 5
Raasay 98 A 3
Rab 115 F 3
Rába 116 A 1
Rabai 137 H 5
Rabak 154 E 6
Rabakah, Gunung 137 F 5
Rabal 137 E 5
Rabalou 114 D 4
Rabat (Morocco) 152 D 2
Rabat (Malta) 115 F 4
Rabaul 145 E 3
Rābigh 155 F 4
Rabka 111 G 5
Rabocheostrovsk 112 K 3
Rabyānah 153 K 4
Rabyānah, Ramlat 153 JK 4
Racconigi 115 E 3
Race, Cape 169 R 6
Rach Gia 135 HJ 5
Rachid 152 C 5
Racibórz 111 G 4
Racine 171 J 3
Radā' 155 G 6
Rădăuţi 116 C 1
Radebeul 111 F 4
Radeče 115 G 2
Radekhov 113 H 5
Radhanpur 134 B 3
Radisson 169 M 5
Radom 111 H 4
Radom (Sudan) 158 C 3
Radomir 116 C 1
Radomsko 111 G 4
Radöy 112 D 3
Radstadt 115 F 2
Radstock 102 C 2
Radun 113 J 5
Radviliškis 112 H 4
Radville 167 R 6
Raḍwā, Jabal 154 F 4
Radzyń Podlaski 111 H 4
Rae 167 O 3

270

Rae Bareli 134 D 2
Rae Isthmus 167 U 2
Raeside, Lake 142 C 4
Raevavae 147 F 4
Rafaela 182 D 5
Rafael, Cachoeira do 180 D 3
Rafaḥ 154 E 2
Rafaï 158 C 3–4
Raffili Rapids 158 D 3
Rafḥā' 155 G 3
Rāf, Jabal 155 F 3
Rafsanjān 128 F 4
Raga 158 D 3
Ragam 157 F 3
Ragang, Mount 137 F 2
Ragay Gulf 137 F 1
Ragged Island Range 173 G 3
Ragusa 115 F 4
Raha 137 F 4
Rahad al Bardī 154 C 6
Raḥāh, Ḥarrat ar 154 F 3
Rahaṭ, Ḥarrat 155 G 4
Raheita 159 G 2
Rahib, Jabal 154 E 6
Rahimyar Khan 129 J 5
Raia 114 B 4
Raiatea 147 E 4
Raichur 134 C 4
Raiganj 134 E 2
Raigarh 134 D 3
Raimangal 134 E 3
Rainbow Peak 170 C 3
Rainier, Mount 170 B 2
Rainy Lake 168 J 6
Raipur 134 D 3
Raisen 134 C 3
Raisio 113 H 3
Raiwind 129 K 4
Rajabasa 136 B 5
Rajada 181 H 2
Rajahmundry 134 D 4
Rajakoski 112 J 2
Rajang 136 D 3
Rajanpur 129 J 5
Rajapalaiyam 134 C 6
Rajapur 134 B 4
Rajasthan 134 BC 2
Rajasthan Canal 134 B 2
Rajgarh 134 C 2
Rajgarh 134 C 3
Rajinac 115 FG 3
Rajkot 134 B 3
Rajmahal Hills 134 E 3
Raj Nandgam 134 D 3
Rajshahi 134 E 3
Rajura 134 C 4
Raka 134 E 2
Rakahanga 147 E 3
Rakan, Sungai 136 B 3
Rakata, Pulau 136 C 5
Raka Zangbo 134 E 2
Rakhmanoviskoye 119 R 6
Rakhov 116 B 1
Rakitnoye 113 J 5
Rakkestad 113 F 4
Rakoko 160 C 3
Rakops 160 C 4
Rakshan 129 G 5
Rakulka 118 J 3
Råkvåg 112 F 3
Rakvere 112 J 4
Raleigh 171 L 4
Raleigh Bay 171 L 5
Ralik Chain 146 C 2
Rama 172 F 5
Ramādah 153 H 2
Ramalho, Serra do 181 H 3
Ramalio 182 D 5
Ramanathapuram 134 C 6
Ramapo Deep 121 R 6
Ramatlabama 160 D 5
Ramblon 182 C 5
Rambouillet 114 D 2
Rambutyo 144 E 2
Ramea 169 Q 6
Rameswaram 134 C 6
Ramgarh (Bangla Desh) 135 F 3
Ramgarh (India) 134 E 3
Ramgul 129 J 3
Rāmhor moz 128 D 4
Ramkola 134 D 3
Ramlat al Wīgh 153 J 4
Ramlat as Sab'atayn 155 H 5
Ramlat Dahm 155 H 5
Ramlat Rabyānah 153 JK 4
Ramlat Yām 155 H 5
Ramlu 159 G 2
Ramm, Jabal 154 F 3
Ramnagar 134 D 3
Ramo 159 G 3
Ramokgwebana 160 D 4
Ramotswa 160 D 4
Rampart 166 G 2

Rampart of Genghis Khan 130 K L 6
Rampur 134 C 2
Rampur 134 D 3
Ramree 135 F 4
Ramsele 112 G 3
Ramsey (U.K.) 110 C 4
Ramsey (Canada) 171 K 2
Ramsey (Cambridgeshire) 103 D 1
Ramsey (Isle of Man) 100 C 2
Ramsey Bay 100 C 2
Ramsey Island 102 B 2
Ramsgate 103 E 2
Ramsjö 112 G 3
Ramsund 112 G 2
Ramu 159 G 4
Ramu River 144 D 2
Ramvik 112 G 3
Rana 112 F 2
Rancagua 182 B 5
Rance 114 C 2
Rancha de Caça dos Tapiúnas 180 E 3
Rancharia 181 F 5
Ranchi 134 E 3
Rancul 182 D 6
Randa 112 J 2
Randalstown 100 B 2
Randers 113 F 4
Randijaure 112 G 2
Rand Rifles 160 A 4
Randsfjorden 113 F 3
Råneå 112 H 2
Råneälven 112 H 2
Ranérou 156 B 2
Rangamati 135 F 3
Rangantamiang 136 D 4
Ranger 170 G 5
Rangia 135 F 2
Rangiroa 147 F 3
Rangkasbitung 136 C 5
Rangoon 135 G 4
Rangpur 134 E 2
Rangsang, Pulau 136 B 3
Rania 134 B 2
Ranibennur 134 C 5
Ranikhet 134 C 2
Rāniyah 155 G 1
Ranken River 143 F 3
Ranken Store 143 F 2
Rankin Inlet 167 T 3
Rannes 143 J 3
Rannoch, Loch 99 B 3
Rannoch, Moor of 110 BC 3
Rann of Kutch 134 AB 3
Ranohira 161 H 4
Ranon 145 J 5
Ranong 135 G 6
Ranongga 145 G 2
Ransaren 112 G 2
Ransiki 137 H 4
Rantabe 161 H 3
Rantasalmi 112 J 3
Rantauprapat 136 A 3
Rantau 136 E 4
Raohe 131 Q 3
Raoui, Erg er 152 E 3
Raoul 147 D 4
Rapa 147 F 4
Rapadalen 112 G 2
Rapallo 115 E 3
Rapa Nui 147 H 4
Raper, Cabo 183 A 8
Raper, Cape 169 O 2
Rapid City 170 F 3
Rappang 137 E 4
Rapulo 180 C 3
Raraka 147 F 4
Raroïa 147 F 4
Rarotonga 147 E 4
Rarytkin, Khrebet 131 WX 3
Ra's Abū Madd 154 F 4
Ra's Abū Shajarah 154 F 4
Ra's ad Daqm 155 K 5
Ra's Ajdīr 153 H 2
Ra's al Abyad (Saudi Arabia) 154 F 4
Ra's al Abyad (Tunisia) 153 G 1
Ra's 'Alam al Rūm 154 D 2
Ra's al Aswad 154 F 4
Ra's al Ḥadārim 154 F 4
Ra's al Ḥadd 155 K 4
Ra's al Kanā'is 154 D 2
Ra's al Khafjī 155 H 3
Ra's al Khaymah 155 K 3
Ra's al Madrakah 155 K 5
Ra's al Milh 153 L 2
Ra's al Mish'āb 155 H 3

Ra's aṭ Ṭarfā 155 G 5
Ra's aṭ Ṭīb 155 H 1
Ra's at Tin 153 K 2
Ra's az Zawr 155 H 3
Ra's Banās 154 F 4
Ra's Barīdī 154 F 4
Ra's Chiamboni 159 G 5
Ra's Ḍurbat 'Alī 155 J 5
Ra's el Cheil 159 H 3
Ras el Ma 156 D 3
Ra's Fartak 155 J 5
Ra's Ghārib 154 E 3
Rashād 154 E 6
Ra's Ḥāfūn 159 J 2
Ra's Ḥaṭībah 154 F 4
Rashīd 154 E 2
Rasht 128 D 3
Ras Jiwani 129 G 6
Ra's Kabūdiyāh 153 H 1
Ra's Karkūmā 154 F 3
Ra's Kasr 154 F 5
Ra's Khānzīr 159 H 2
Raskoh 129 G 5
Ra's Lānūf 153 J 2
Ra's Miṣrātah 153 J 2
Ras Muari 129 H 6
Ra's Muḥammad 154 E 3
Rasmussen Basin 167 T 2
Ras Ngomeni 159 G 5
Rason, Lake 142 C 4
Ra's Qaṭṭārah 154 D 2
Ras Rawura 161 G 2
Ra's Sharbithāt 155 K 5
Rasshevatskaya 117 F 1
Rasshua, Ostrov 131 S 6
Rasskazovo 118 H 5
Rassokha 131 S 2
Ra's Sura 159 H 2
Rastigaissa 112 J 1
Råstojaure 112 H 2
Rasūl 128 F 5
Ra's Zayt 154 E 3
Rat 166 A 5
Ratak Chain 146 C 2
Ratangarh 134 B 2
Rat Buri 135 G 5
Rath 134 C 2
Rathenow 111 F 4
Rathfriland 100 B 2
Rathkeale 110 B 4
Rathlin Island 100 B 2
Rathmelton 100 B 2
Rathnew 100 B 3
Rat Islands 166 A 5
Ratkal Hills 135 G 2
Ratlam 134 C 3
Ratmanova, Mys 118 L 1
Ratmanova, Ostrov 166 D 2
Ratnagiri 134 B 4
Ratnapura 134 D 6
Ratno 113 H 5
Raton 170 F 4
Rattray Head 98 D 3
Ratta 131 O 3
Rattvik 113 G 3
Ratz, Mount 166 L 4
Raub 136 B 3
Rauch 183 E 6
Rauchua 131 V 2
Raufarhöfn 112 B 2
Raufoss 113 F 3
Raukela 134 D 3
Raúl Leoni, Represa 179 F 2
Rauma (Norway) 112 E 3
Rauma (Raumo) (Finland) 112 H 3
Raumo 112 H 3
Raupelyan 166 C 2
Rava-Russkaya 112 H 5
Ravelsbach 115 G 2
Ravānsar 128 D 3
Ravar 128 F 4
Ravenna 115 F 3
Ravensburg 111 E 5
Ravenshoe 143 H 2
Ravensthorpe 142 C 5
Ravi 129 J 4
Ravnina 129 G 3
Rāwah 155 G 2
Rawaki 146 D 3
Rawalpindi 129 J 4
Rawāndūz 155 G 1
Rawas 137 E 4
Rawicz 111 G 4
Rawlinna 142 D 5
Rawlins 170 E 3
Rawson 183 D 7
Rawtenstall 101 D 3
Rawura, Ras 161 G 2
Raya, Bukit 136 D 4

Rayachoti 134 C 5
Rayadrug 134 C 5
Rayagadai 134 D 4
Ray, Cape 169 Q 6
Raychikhinsk 131 N 6
Raykoke, Ostrov 131 S 6
Rayleigh 103 E 2
Raymond 170 B 2
Raymondville 170 G 6
Rayón 172 C 3
Rayong 135 H 5
Razan 128 D 3
Razdan 117 F 2
Razdel'naya 116 D 1
Razdolinsk 130 F 4
Razdolnoye 131 S 3
Razdol'noye 117 D 1
Razgrad 116 C 2
Razlog 116 B 2
Razmak 129 H 4
Read 167 P 2
Reading 103 D 2
Real, Cordillera 178 C 4
Real del Padre 182 C 5
Realico 182 D 6
Rèalmont 114 D 3
Reao 147 F 4
Reata 172 B 2
Rebbenesöy 112 G 1
Rebecca, Lake 142 C 5
Rebi 137 H 5
Rebiana Oasis → Wāḥāt 153 K 4
Rebiana Sand Sea → Ramlat Rabyānah 153 JK 4
Rebojo, Cachoeira do 179 G 4–5
Reboly 113 K 3
Rebun-tō 133 M 1
Recalde 183 D 6
Recaş 116 B 1
Rechitsa 118 F 5
Rechna Doab 129 J 4
Recife 181 K 2
Récifs Bellona 143 K 3
Récifs de l'Astrolabe 146 C 4
Récifs de L'Astrolabe 145 J 5
Recifs d'Entrecasteaux 145 H 5
Récifs et Iles Chesterfield 143 K 2
Reconquista 182 E 4
Recreio 179 G 4–5
Recreo 182 D 4
Recuay 178 C 5
Red Bank 171 J 4
Red Basin 132 E 4
Red Bay (Canada) 169 Q 5
Red Bay (U.K.) 100 C 2
Red Bluff 170 B 3
Redcar 101 E 2
Redcliffe 143 J 4
Redcliffe, Mount 142 C 4
Red Cloud 170 G 3
Red Deer 167 P 5
Red Deer River (Alb., Can.) 167 P 5
Red Deer River (Sask., Can.) 167 R 5
Red Devil 166 F 3
Redding 170 B 3
Redditch 103 D 1
Redenção da Gurguéia 181 H 2
Redfield 170 G 3
Red Hill (New Zealand) 145 Q 9
Red Hill (Australia) 143 F 5
Red Hills 170 G 4
Red Lake 168 J 5
Redlands 170 C 5
Red Lodge 170 E 2
Red Oak 171 G 3
Redon 114 C 2
Redondo Volcano 166 G 3
Red River (LA, U.S.A.) 171 H 5
Red River (MN, U.S.A.) 171 G 2
Red Rock River 170 D 3
Redruth 102 B 2
Red Sea 154 F 3–4
Red Tower Pass 116 B 1
Red Water 167 P 5
Red Wing 171 H 3
Redwood Empire 170 B 3
Ree, Lough 100 B 3
Refahiye 117 E 2
Refresco 182 C 4
Regar 129 H 3
Regencia 181 J 4
Regensburg 111 F 5
Reggane 152 EF 2
Reggio di Calabria 115 G 4
Reggio nell'Emilia 115 F 3
Reghin 116 B 1
Regina 167 R 5
Regina (Fr. Guiana) 179 H 3
Registan 129 G 4
Regocio 172 A 3

Rehoboth 160 B 4
Reigate 103 D 2
Reims 114 D 2
Reina Adelaida, Archipiélago de la 183 A 9
Reindeer 167 R 4
Reindeer Lake 167 R 4
Reine 112 F 2
Reinoksfjellet 112 G 2
Reinosa 114 C 3
Reisaelva 112 H 2
Reitoru 147 F 4
Reitz 160 D 5
Rekarne 113 G 4
Rekinniki 131 U 3
Reliance 167 Q 3
Relizane 152 F 1
Ré, lle de 114 C 2
Remansão 179 J 4
Remanso 181 H 2
Rembang 136 D 5
Remeshk 128 F 5
Rémire 179 H 3
Remiremont 115 E 2
Remontnoye 117 F 1
Rena 112 F 3
Renascença 178 E 4
Rendova 145 G 2
Rendsburg 111 E 4
Renfrew 171 L 2
Renfrew Heights 99 B 4
Rengat 136 B 4
Rengma Hills 135 F 2
Rengo 182 B 5
Reni 116 D 1
Renmark 143 G 5
Rennell 145 H 4
Rennell, Islas 183 B 9
Rennes 114 C 2
Rennie Lake 167 Q 3
Reno 170 B 4
Reno (Italy) 115 F 3
Renqiu 133 G 3
Renshou 132 D 4
Renton 170 B 2
Ren Xian 132 F 3
Reo 137 F 2
Repartição 179 G 4
Repartimento 179 G 4
Replot 112 H 3
Reprêsa Agua Vermelha 181 FG 4–5
Reprêsa Bariri 181 G 5
Reprêsa Boa Esperança 181 H 2
Reprêsa da Capivara 181 F 5
Reprêsa de Furnas 181 G 5
Reprêsa de Jupi 181 F 5
Reprêsa de Jurumirim 181 G 5
Reprêsa de Xavantes 181 G 5
Reprêsa do Estreito 181 G 4–5
Reprêsa Promissão 181 G 5
Represa Raúl Leoni 179 F 2
Reprêsa Três Marias 181 G 4
Republic 170 C 2
Republican River 170 G 4
Repulse Bay 167 U 2
Repvåg 112 J 1
Requena 114 C 4
Requena 178 D 4–5
Reşadiye 117 E 2
Reşadiyel Yarımadası 116 C 3
Reserva especial do Milando 160 B 1
Reserva natural e integral do Luando 160 B 2
Reserva parcial de Namibe 160 A 3
Réservoir Baskatong 171 L 2
Réservoir Cabonga 171 L 2
Réservoir Decelles 171 L 2
Réservoir Dozois 171 L 2
Réservoir Gouin 171 M 2
Réservoir Manicouagan 169 O 5
Réservoir Pipmouacan 169 N 6
Reservoir Rocklands 143 G 6
Reshteh-ye Esfārāyen 128 F 3
Reshteh-ye Kūhhā-ye Alborz 128 E 3
Resia, Passo di 115 F 2
Resistencia 182 E 4
Reşiţa 116 B 1
Resolution 144 P 10
Resolution Island 169 P 3
Resplendor 181 H 4
Retalhuleu 172 D 5
Rethel 115 D 2
Rethimnon 116 B 3
Retkucha 131 W 2
Retz 115 G 2
Réunion 161 HJ 5
Reus 114 D 3
Reut 116 C 1

Reu – Rom

Reutlingen 111 E 5
Reutte 115 F 2
Revantazón 178 B 5
Revda 112 K 2
Revda 119 L 4
Revelstoke 167 O 5
Revilla Gigedo 166 L 4
Revilla Gigedo Islands 163 G 8
Revin 115 D 2
Revolyutsii, Pik 129 J 3
Revsundssjön 112 G 3
Revue 161 E 3
Rewa 134 D 3
Rewari 134 C 2
Rexburg 170 D 3
Rey 128 E 3
Rey Bouba 157 G 4
Reyes 180 C 3
Reyhanlı 117 E 3
Rey, Isla del 178 C 2
Reykjahlið 112 B 2
Reykjanes 112 A 3
Reykjavik 112 A 3
Reynaldo Cullen 182 D 5
Reynosa 172 C 2
Rezé 112 C 2
Rēzekne 113J 4
Rezovo 116 C 2
Rhallamane 152 CD 4
Rhallamane, Sebkha de 152 D 4
Rharis 153 F 3
Rharsa, Chott el 153 G 2
Rhein 111 E 4
Rheinisches Schiefergebirge 115 E 1
Rheinland 110 E 4
Rheinland-Pfalz 111 E 4 5
Rhemilès 152 E 3
Rhinelander 171 J 2
Rhinmal 134 B 2
Rhino Camp 158 E 4
Rhir, Cap 152 CD 2
Rhode Island 171 M 3
Rhodes 116 C 3
Rhodes Grave 160 D 4
Rhodesia → Zimbabwe 160–161 DE 3
Rhodope Mts 116 B 2
Rhön 111 E 4
Rhondda 102 C 2
Rhône 115 DE2
Rhone au Rhin, Canal de 115 E 2
Rhourde el Baguel 153 G 2
Rhuddlan 101 D 3
Rhuis 114 C 2
Rhum 110 B 3
Rhyl 102 C 1
Rhymney 102 C 2
Riaba 157 F 5
Riachão 179 J 5
Riachão do Jacuípe 181 J 3
Riacho de Santana 181 H 3
Riachos, Islas de los 183 D 6
Ría de Arosa 114 B 3
Ría de Santa Marta 114 B 3
Ría de Vigo 114 B 3
Rianápolis 181 G 4
Riangnom 158 E 3
Rías Altas 114 B 3
Rías Bajas 114 B 3
Riasi 129 J 4
Riau, Kepulauan 136 B 3
Riaza 114 C 3
Ribadeo 114 B 3
Ribamar 181 H 1
Ribas do Río Pardo 181 F 5
Ribáuè 161 F 2
Ribble, River 101 D 3
Ribe 113 E 4
Ribeirão Prêto 181 G 5
Ribeira 181 G 5
Ribeira Brava 156 B 6
Ribeira Grande 156 A 6
Ribeiro Gonçalves 181 G 2
Ribera 115 F 4
Riberalta 180 C 3
Ribnica 115 F 2
Riccione 115 F 3
Rich 152 E 2
Richard Collinson Inlet 167 P 1
Richards 166 K 2
Richard's Bay 161 E 5
Richardson Mountains 166 K 2
Richard Toll 156 A 2
Richfield 170 E 4
Richland 170 C 2
Richmond (U.K.) 101 E 2
Richmond (Australia) 143 G 3
Richmond (CA, U.S.A.) 170 B 4
Richmond (S. Afr.) 160 C 6
Richmond (VA, U.S.A.) 171 L 4
Richmond Hill 171 L 4
Ricklëan 112 H 3

Rickmansworth 103 D 2
Ricobayo, Embalse de 114 B 3
Riding Mountain National Park 167 R 5
Ried im Innkreis 115 F 2
Riesa 111 F 4
Riesco, Isla 183 B 9
Rietavas 113H 4
Rietfontein (Namibia) 160 C 4
Rietfontein (S. Africa) 160 C 5
Rieti 115 F 3
Rifstangi 112 B 2
Riga 112 H 4
Rigachikun 157 F 3
Riga, Gulf of 112 H 4
Riggins 170 C 2
Rigolet 169 Q 5
Rig Rig 157 G 3
Rihand Dam 134 D 3
Riihimäki 113 H 3
Riiser-Larsen Ice Shelf 185
Riiser-Larsen Peninsula 185
Rijau 157 F 3
Rijeka 115 F 2
Riley 170 C 3
Rimatara 147 E 4
Rimavská Sobota 111 H 5
Rimbo 113 G 4
Rimini 115 F 3
Rîmnicu Sărat 116 C 1
Rîmnicu Vîlcea 116 B 1
Rimouski 169 O 6
Rinbung 134 E 2
Rinchinlhümbe 130 G 5
Rinconada 180 C 5
Ringe 113 F 4
Ringerike 113 F 3
Ringgold Isles 147 D 4
Ringhkung 135 G 2
Ringim 157 F 3
Ringkøbing 113 E 4
Ringkøbing Fjord 113 E 4
Ringládes 116 B 3
Ringsted 113 F 4
Ringvassöy 112 G 2
Ringwood 103 D 2
Rinihue 183 B 6
Rinja, Pulau 137 E 5
Rinjani, Gunung 136 E 5
Rinka Neem 112 H 4
Ritchie's Archipelago 135 F 5
Rito 160 B 3
Ritsa 117 F 2
Ritter, Mount 170 C 4
Ritzville 170 C 2
Rivadavia 182 B 4
Rivas 172 E 5
River 117 F 2
Rivera (Arg.) 183 D 6
Rivera (Uruguay) 182 E 5
River Aire 101 E 3
River Avon (Avon) 102 C 2
River Avon (Grampian) 98 C 3
River Avon (Warwickshire) 103 D 1
River Bann 100 B 3
River Barrow 100 B 3
River Blackwater 103 E 2
River Boyne 100 B 3
River Brora 98 B 2
River Bure 101 E 1
River, Cape 143 H 3
River Cess 156 C 4
River Cherwell 103 D 2
River Clyde 100 D 2
River Coquet 101 E 2
River Dee (Clwyd) 102 C 1
River Dee (Grampian) 98 C 3
River Derwent 101 E 2
River Deveron 98 C 3
River Don (Grampian) 98 C 3
River Don (S. Yorkshire) 101 E 3
River Dove 101 E 3
River Eden 101 D 2
River Erne 100 A 2
River Exe 102 C 2
River Farrar 98 B 3
River Findhorn 98 C 3
River Forth 99 B 3
River Foyle 100 B 2
River Humber 101 E 3
River Kennet 103 D 2
River Liffey 100 B 3
River Little Ouse 103 E 1
River Lune 101 D 2
River Medway 103 E 2
River Mersey 101 D 3
River Nene 103 E 1
River Nidd 101 E 3
River Nore 100 B 3
River North Tyne 101 D 2
River Ouse (Norfolk) 103 E 1
River Ouse (N. Yorkshire) 101 E 3

Río Maule 183 B 6
Rio Mezcalapa 172 D 4
Río Muerto 182 D 4
Río Mulatos 180 C 4
Rion 116 B 3
Río Negrinho 181 G 6
Río Negro (Brazil) 179 F 4
Río Negro (Uruguay) 182 EF 2
Rioni 117 F 2
Río Panuco 172 C 3
Río Pardo 182 F 4
Río Patuca 172 F 4
Río Real 181 J 3
Río Sabinas 172 B 2
Rio San Juan 157 F 5
Rio Siquia 172 F 5
Rio Sonora 170 D 6
Ríosucio 178 C 2
Río Tercero 182 D 5
Río Tinto 181 J 2
Río Turbio Mines 183 B 9
Rio Usumacinta 172 D 4
Rioverde (Mexico) 172 C 3
Ríoverde (Ecuador) 178 C 3
Río Verde (Goiás, Brazil) 181 F 4
Rio Verde (Mato Grosso do Sul, Brazil) 181 F 5
Río Verde de Mato Grosso 181 F 4
Rio Viejo 172 E 5
Rio Yaqui 170 D 6
Ríozinho 178 E 4
Ripley (U.K.) 101 E 2
Ripley (N.Y., U.S.A.) 171 L 3
Ripley (W.V., U.S.A.) 171 K 4
Ripoll 114 D 3
Ripon 101 E 2
Riposto 115 G 4
Risan 116 A 2
Risasi 158 D 5
Risbäck 112 G 3
Rishiri-tō 133 M 1
Risør 113 E 4
Risøyhamn 112 G 2
Risti 113H 4
Ristiina 112 J 3
Ristijärvi 112 J 3
Ristna Neem 112 H 4
Ritchie's Archipelago 135 F 5
Rito 160 B 3
Ritsa 117 F 2
Ritter, Mount 170 C 4
Ritzville 170 C 2
Rivadavia 182 B 4
Rivas 172 E 5
River 117 F 2
Rivera (Arg.) 183 D 6
Rivera (Uruguay) 182 E 5
River Aire 101 E 3
River Avon (Avon) 102 C 2
River Avon (Grampian) 98 C 3
River Avon (Warwickshire) 103 D 1
River Bann 100 B 3
River Barrow 100 B 3
River Blackwater 103 E 2
River Boyne 100 B 3
River Brora 98 B 2
River Bure 101 E 1
River, Cape 143 H 3
River Cess 156 C 4
River Cherwell 103 D 2
River Clyde 100 D 2
River Coquet 101 E 2
River Dee (Clwyd) 102 C 1
River Dee (Grampian) 98 C 3
River Derwent 101 E 2
River Deveron 98 C 3
River Don (Grampian) 98 C 3
River Don (S. Yorkshire) 101 E 3
River Dove 101 E 3
River Eden 101 D 2
River Erne 100 A 2
River Exe 102 C 2
River Farrar 98 B 3
River Findhorn 98 C 3
River Forth 99 B 3
River Foyle 100 B 2
River Humber 101 E 3
River Kennet 103 D 2
River Liffey 100 B 3
River Little Ouse 103 E 1
River Lune 101 D 2
River Medway 103 E 2
River Mersey 101 D 3
River Nene 103 E 1
River Nidd 101 E 3
River Nore 100 B 3
River North Tyne 101 D 2
River Ouse (Norfolk) 103 E 1
River Ouse (N. Yorkshire) 101 E 3

River Oykel 98 B 3
River Plate → Río de la Plata 182 E 5
River Ribble 101 D 3
River Severn (Gloucestershire) 102 C 2
River Severn (Powys) 102 C 1
River Shannon 100 B 3
Riverside 170 C 5
Rivers Inlet 167 M 5
River Slaney 100 B 3
River South Tyne 101 D 2
River Stour 103 E 2
River Suir 100 B 3
River Swale 101 E 2
River Tamar 102 B 2
River Taw 102 C 2
River Tay 99 C 3
River Tees 101 E 2
River Teifi 102 B 1
River Teme 102 C 1
River Teviot 99 C 4
River Thames 103 E 2
Riverton (New Zealand) 144 P 10
Riverton (Man., Can.) 167 S 5
Riverton (WY, U.S.A.) 170 E 3
River Torridge 102 B 2
River Towy 102 B 2
River Trent 103 D 1
River Tweed 99 C 4
River Tyne 101 E 2
River Ure 101 E 2
River Usk 102 C 2
River Waveney 103 E 1
River Wear 101 D 2
River Welland 103 D 1
River Wey 103 D 2
River Wharfe 101 E 3
River Witham 103 D 1
River Wye 102 C 1
River Yare 103 E 1
Rivesaltes 114 D 3
Riviera di Levante 115 E 3
Riviera di Ponente 115 E 3
Rivière à la Baleine 169 O 4
Rivière aux Feuilles 169 N 4
Rivière aux Mélèzes 169 N 4
Rivière aux Outardes 169 O 5
Rivière-du-Loup 169 O 6
Rivière du Petit-Mécatina 169 P 5
Rivoli 115 E 2
Rivungo 160 C 3
Riwoqê 132 C 4
Riyadh 155 H 4
Riyān 155 H 6
Rize 117 F 2
Rize Dağları 117 F 2
Rizhao 133 G 3
Rizhskiy Zaliv 113 H 4
Rizokarpásso → Dipkarpas 117 D 3
Rjukan 113 E 4
Rjuven 113 E 4
Rkiz 152 B 5
Ro 135 J 4
Roadtown 173 K 4
Roanne 114 D 2
Roanoke 171 L 4
Roanoke Rapids 171 L 4
Roanoke River 171 L 4
Roan Plateau 170 E 4
Roatán 172 E 4
Robāt-e-Khān 128 F 4
Robbah 153 G 2
Robben Island 160 B 6
Robbins 143 F 6
Robe 143 F 6
Robe, Mount 143 G 5
Robert Butte 185
Robert Lee 170 F 5
Robertsfield 156 B 4
Roberts, Mount 143 J 4
Robertsport 156 B 4
Robi 159 F 3
Robinson Crusoe 183 A 5
Robinson Ranges 142 B 4
Robinson River 143 F 2
Robore 180 E 4
Robstown 170 G 6
Robson, Mount 167 O 5
Rocas 172 H 3
Rocha 183 F 5
Rocha de Galé, Barragem da 114 B 4
Rochdale 101 D 3
Rochefort 114 C 2
Rocher River Fort Resolution 167 P 3
Rocher Thomasset 147 F 3
Rochester (U.K.) 103 E 2
Rochester (MN, U.S.A.) 171 H 3
Rochester (N.H., U.S.A.) 171 M 3

Rochester (N.Y., U.S.A.) 171 L 3
Rochlitzer Berg 111 F 4
Rocigalgo 114 C 4
Rockau Bank 192 A 2
Rockefeller Plateau 185
Rockford 171 J 3
Rockhampton 143 HJ 3
Rockhampton Downs 142 F 2
Rock Hill 171 K 5
Rockingham (U.S.A.) 171 L 5
Rockingham (Australia) 142 B 5
Rock Island 171 H 3
Rocklands Reservoir 143 G 6
Rockport (CA, U.S.A.) 170 B 4
Rockport (TX, U.S.A.) 171 G 6
Rock River 171 J 3
Rock Springs 170 E 3
Rockstone 179 G 2
Rockville 171 L 4
Rocky Mount 171 L 4
Rocky Mountain House 167 O 4
Rocky Mountain National Park 170 E 3
Rocky Mountains 167, 170
Rödby 113 F 5
Rødby Havn 113 F 5
Roddickton 169 Q 5
Rodel 98 A 3
Rodeo (AZ, U.S.A.) 170 E 5
Rodeo (Mexico) 172 B 2
Rodez 114 D 3
Rodholivos 116 B 2
Rodhopi, Dytike 116 B 2
Ródhos 116 C 3
Rodina 130 G 4
Rodionovo 118 L 2
Rodney, Cape (AK, U.S.A.) 166 D 3
Rodney, Cape (Papua New Guinea) 144 E 4
Rodopi 116 BC 2
Rodrigues 178 D 5
Roebourne 142 B 3
Roebuck Bay 142 C 2
Roeselare 110 D 4
Roes Welcome Sound 167 U 2
Rogachev 112 K 5
Rogagua, Lago 180 C 3
Rogaland 113 E 4
Rogaška Slatina 115 G 2
Rogatica 115 G 3
Rogen 112 F 3
Rogers City 171 K 2
Rogers Peak 170 D 4
Roggeveld Berge 160 C 6
Rognan 112 G 2
Rogoaguado, Lago 180 C 3
Rogovskaya 117 E 1
Rogozhina 116 A 2
Rogue River 170 B 3
Rohri 129 H 5
Rohtak 134 C 2
Roi Et 135 H 4
Roi Georges, Îles du 147 F 3
Roine 112 H 3
Roja, Punta 183 C 7
Rojas 182 D 5
Rojo, Cabo 173 J 4
Rokeby 143 G 1
Rokel 156 B 4
Rola Co 129 M 3
Rolândia 181 F 5
Røldal 113 E 4
Rolla (MO, U.S.A.) 171 H 4
Rolla (N.D., U.S.A.) 170 G 2
Rolleston 143 H 3
Rolvsöya 112 H 1
Roma (Queensland, Austr.) 143 H 4
Roma (Rome) 115 F 3
Romaine 169 P 5
Roman 116 C 1
Romanche Fracture Zone 192 A 3
Romang, Pulau 137 G 5
Romania 116 B 1
Roman Kosh 117 D 2
Romanova 130 H 4
Romanovka 118 H 5
Romans-sur-Isère 115 E 2
Romanzof, Cape 166 D 3
Romanzof Mountains 166 J 2
Romblon 137 F 1
Rome (Italy) 115 F 3
Rome (GA, U.S.A.) 171 J 5
Rome (N.Y., U.S.A.) 171 L 3
Rome (OR, U.S.A.) 170 C 3
Romerike 113 F 3
Romilly-sur-Seine 114 D 2
Rommani 152 D 2
Romny 118 F 5
Römö 113 E 4
Romont 115 E 2

Romorantin-Lanthenay 114 D 2
Romsdal 112 E 3
Romsey 103 D 2
Rona 98 B 3
Ronaldsway 100 C 2
Ronas Hill 98 D 1
Ronay 98 A 3
Roncador 145 G 2
Roncador, Cayos de 173 FG 5
Roncador, Serra do 181 F 3
Roncesvalles 114 C 3
Ronda (Spain) 114 B 4
Ronda (China) 129 K 3
Rondane 112 E 3
Rondas das Salinas 180 D 4
Rönde 113 F 4
Rondônia 180 D 3
Rondonópolis 181 F 4
Rondón, Pico 179 F 3
Rongan 132 E 5
Rongcheng 133 H 3
Ronge, Lac la 167 R 4
Rongelap 146 C 2
Rongerik 146 C 2
Rongjiang 132 E 5
Rongklang Range 135 F 3
Rongshui 132 E 5
Rong Xian 132 D 5
Rong Xian 132 F 6
Rönne 113 F 4
Ronneby 113 G 4
Ronnebyån 113 G 4
Ronne Ice Shelf 185
Ronuro 181 F 3
Rooikop 160 A 4
Roorkee 134 C 2
Roosendaal 110 D 4
Roosevelt 180 D 3
Roosevelt Island 185
Roosevelt, Mount 167 M 4
Roper River 142 E 1
Ropi 112 H 2
Roquetas de Mar 114 C 4
Roraima (Brazil) 179 F 3
Roraima (Venezuela) 179 F 2
Rori 134 C 2
Røros 112 F 3
Rørvik 112 F 3
Rosa 161 E 1
Rosa, Lake 173 H 3
Rosamorada 172 A 3
Rosario 172 A 3
Rosario (Arg.) 182 D 5
Rosario (Chile) 180 B 5
Rosário (Maranhão, Brazil) 181 H 1
Rosario (Paraguay) 180 E 5
Rosario, Bahía 170 C 6
Rosario de la Frontera 182 D 4
Rosario de Lerma 182 C 4
Rosario del Tala 182 E 5
Rosário do Sul 182 F 5
Rosário Oeste 180 E 3
Rosarito 170 D 6
Rosas, Golfo de 114 D 3
Roscoff 114 C 2
Roscommon 100 A 3
Roscrea 100 B 3
Roseburg 170 B 3
Rosenberg 171 G 6
Rosenheim 111 F 5
Rosetown 167 Q 5
Rosetta → Rashīd 154 E 2
Rosh Pinah 160 B 5
Rosignol 179 G 2
Roskilde 113 F 4
Roslagen 113 G 4
Roslavl' 118 F 5
Roslyn 170 B 2
Ross (Canada) 166 L 3
Ross (Senegal) 156 A 2
Rossano 115 G 4
Rossan Point 110 B 4
Rossel 145 F 4
Rossel Island 143 J 1
Rossell y Rius 182 E 5
Ross Ice Shelf 185
Rössing 160 A 4
Ross Island 185
Rosslare 102 A 1
Rosso 152 B 5
Rossön 112 G 3
Ross-on-Wye 102 C 2
Rossosh 118 G 5
Ross River 166 L 3
Ross Sea 185
Rössvatn 112 F 2
Röst 112 F 2
Rosta 112 G 2
Rosthern 167 Q 5
Rostock 111 F 4
Rostonsölkä 112 H 2

Rostov 118 G 4
Rostov-na-Donu 117 E 1
Rostrevor 100 B 2
Roswell 170 F 5
Rota 114 B 4
Rota 146 A 2
Rothenburg 111 F 5
Rothera 185
Rotherham 101 E 3
Rothes 98 C 3
Rothesay 99 B 4
Rothwell 101 E 3
Roti, Pulau 137 F 6
Roti, Selat 137 F 6
Rotja, Punta 114 D 4
Roto 143 H 5
Rotorua 145 R 8
Rotterdam 110 D 4
Rottweil 111 E 5
Rotuma 146 C 3
Roubaix 114 D 1
Rouen 114 D 2
Round Mountain 143 J 5
Rousay 110 C 3
Rousay 98 C 2
Rouyn 171 L 2
Rovaniemi 112 J 2
Rovdino 118 H 3
Rovereto 115 F 2
Rovigo 115 F 2
Rovinj 115 F 2
Rovkulskoye, Ozero 112 K 3
Rovno 113 J 5
Rovnoye 118 J 5
Rovuma 161 F 2
Rowley 169 M 1
Rowley Shoals 142 B 2
Roxas (Phil.) 137 F 1
Roxas (Phil.) 137 E 1
Roxburgh 144 P 10
Roxen 113 G 4
Roxo, Cap 156 A 3
Roy 170 F 4
Royal Canal 100 B 3
Royal Leamington Spa 103 D 1
Royal Tunbridge Wells 103 E 2
Royan 114 C 2
Roy Hill 142 B 3
Royston 103 D 1
Rozhdestvenskoye 118 J 4
Rozhkao 117 F 2
Rozovka 117 E 1
Roztocze 111 H 4
Rtanj 116 B 2
Rtishchevo 118 H 5
Rt Kamenjak 115 F 3
Rt Ploča 115 G 3
Ruacana Falls 160 A 3
Ruaha 158 F 6
Ruaha National Park 159 E 6
Ruahine Range 145 R 8–9
Ruapehu 145 R 8
Ruapuke 144 P 10
Ruawai 145 Q 8
Rubeho Mountains 159 F 6
Rubi 158 D 4
Rubiku 116 A 2
Rubinéia 181 F 5
Rubio 178 D 2
Rubondo Island 158 E 5
Rubtsovsk 119 Q 5
Ruby 166 F 3
Ruby Mountains 170 C 3
Rudall River National Park 142 C 3
Rudao 133 H 4
Rudauli 134 D 2
Rudbar 129 G 4
Rudkøbing 113 F 5
Rudnaya Pristan' 133 L 2
Rudnik 116 B 2
Rudnya 118 F 5
Rudnyy 119 M 5
Rudolf, Lake 159 F 4
Rudong 133 H 4
Rüd Sar 128 E 3
Rudyard 170 D 2
Rufā'ah 154 E 6
Ruffec 114 D 2
Rufiji 159 F 6
Rufino 182 D 5
Rufunsa 160 D 3
Rugby (U.S.A.) 170 G 2
Rugby (U.K.) 103 D 1
Rugeley 101 D 3
Rügen 111 F 4
Rugley 103 D 1
Ruhea 134 E 2
Ruhengeri 158 D 5
Ruhnu 113 H 4
Ruhr 111 E 4
Ruhuhu 161 E 2

Rui'an 133 H 5
Rui Barbosa 181 H 3
Ruijin 132 G 5
Ruili 132 C 6
Rujm al Mudhari 155 F 2
Rukumkot 134 D 2
Rukwa, Lake 158 E 6
Rum 99 A 3
Ruma 116 A 1
Rumādah 155 G 6
Rumaylah 154 F 6
Rumbalara 142 E 4
Rumbek 158 D 3
Rum Cay 173 H 3
Rumia 111 G 4
Rum Jungle 142 E 1
Rummah, Wādī ar 155 G 3
Rumoi 133 M 2
Rumphi 161 E 2
Runan 132 F 4
Runanga 145 R 8
Runcorn 101 D 3
Runde 160 E 4
Rundu 160 B 3
Rungu 158 D 4
Rungwa 158 E 6
Rungwa West 158 E 6
Rungwe 158 E 6
Runn 113 G 3
Ruokolahti 112 J 3
Ruo Shui 132 C 2
Ruovesi 112 G 3
Rupanco 183 B 7
Rupara 160 B 3
Rupat, Pulau 136 B 3
Rupert (ID, U.S.A.) 170 D 3
Rupert (Quebec, Can.) 169 M 5
Rupert, Baie de 169 M 5
Rupnagar 134 B 2
Ruponda 161 F 2
Rurrenabaque 180 C 3
Rurutu 147 E 4
Rusakovo 131 U 4
Rusanovo 118 L 1
Rusape 161 E 3
Ruse 116 C 2
Ruşeţu 116 C 2
Rushan (China) 133 H 3
Rushan (U.S.S.R.) 129 J 3
Rushden 103 D 1
Rusinga Island 158 E 5
Russas 181 J 1
Russell (New Zealand) 145 Q 8
Russell (Canada) 167 R 5
Russell Islands 145 G 3
Russell Range 142 C 5
Russellville (AL, U.S.A.) 171 J 5
Russellville (AR, U.S.A.) 171 H 4
Russkaya 133 L 1
Russkaya 185
Rustak 129 H 3
Rustavi 117 G 2
Rustenburg 160 D 5
Ruston 171 H 5
Rutana 158 E 5
Ruteng 137 F 5
Rutenga 160 E 4
Rutherglen 99 B 4
Ruthin 101 D 3
Ruthlin 102 C 1
Rutland Island 135 F 5
Rutog 134 C 1
Rutshuru 158 D 5
Ruvu 159 F 6
Ruvuma 161 F 2
Ruwaybah 154 D 5
Ruwenzori National Park 158 D 5
Ruwenzori Range 158 E 4
Ruzayevka 118 H 5
Ruzayevka 119 N 5
Ruzhnikova 131 T 2
Ruzitgort 119 MN 3
Ružomberok 111 G 5
Rwanda 158 DE 5
Ryan 170 G 5
Ryazan' 118 G 5
Ryazhsk 118 G 5
Rybachiy, Poluostrov 112 K 2
Rybach'ye 129 K 2
Rybinsk → Andropov 118 G 4
Rybinskoye Vodokhranilishche 118 G 4
Rybnik 111 G 4
Rybnitsa 116 C 1
Rybnovsk 131 Q 5
Ryde 103 D 2
Rye 103 E 2
Ryegate 170 E 3
Ryfylke 113 E 4
Ryl'sk 118 F 5
Ryōtsu 133 L 3

Rytterknegten 113 F 4
Ryukyu Islands 133 J 5
Rzepin 111 F 4
Rzeszów 111 H 4
Rzhev 118 F 4

S

São Antônio 179 H 5
São Bente do Norte 181 J 1–2
São Bento (Maranhão, Brazil) 181 H 1
São Bento (Roraima, Brazil) 179 F 3
São Bernardo 181 H 1
São Borja 182 E 4
São Brás, Cabo de 160 A 2
São Carlos (São Paulo, Brazil) 181 G 5
São Carlos (Sta. Catarina, Brazil) 182 F 4
São Christóvão 181 J 3
São Domingos 181 G 3
São Domingos 156 A 3
São Felix 181 F 3
São Felix do Xingu 179 H 5
São Francisco (Brazil) 181 H 4
São Francisco (Brazil) 181 J 2
São Francisco do Sul 181 G 6
São Gabriel 181 F 7
São Gabriel de Goiás 181 G 4
São Geraldo do Araguaia 179 J 5
São Jerônimo, Serra de 181 EF 4
São João da Barra 181 H 5
São João da Boa Vista 181 G 5
São João da Madeira 114 B 3
São João de Aliança 181 G 3
São João del Rei 181 H 5
São João do Araguaia 179 J 5
São João do Paraíso 181 H 4
São João do Patos 181 H 2
São João do Piauí 181 H 2
São João, Ilhas de 179 K 4
São Joaquim (Amazonas, Brazil) 178 E 4
São Joaquim (Sta. Catarina, Brazil) 182 F 4
São Jorge 152 A 1
São José (Amazonas, Brazil) 178 E 4
São José do Anauá 179 F 3
São José do Norte 182 F 5
São José do Peixe 181 H 2
São José do Rio Pardo 181 G 5
São José do Río Prêto 181 G 5
São José dos Campos 181 G 5
São Leopoldo 182 F 4
São Lourenço 180 E 4
São Lourenço do Sul 182 F 5
São Luís (Maranhão, Brazil) 181 H 1
São Luis de Cassianã 178 E 5
São Luis Gonzaga 182 F 4
São Mamede, Serra de 114 B 4
São Manuel → Teles Pires 179 G 5
São Marcelino 178 E 3
São Mateus 181 J 4
São Miguel 152 A 1
São Miguel do Araguaia 181 F 3
São Nicolau 156 B 6
São Paulo 181 G 5
São Paulo de Olivença 178 E 4
São Pedro do Sul 182 F 4
São Pedro do Sul 114 B 3
São Raimundo das Mangabeiras 181 G 2
São Raimundo Nonato 181 H 2
São Romão (Amazonas, Brazil) 178 E 5
São Romão (Minas Gerais, Brazil) 181 G 4
São Roque, Cabo de 181 J 2
São Sebastião (Pará, Brazil) 179 H 5
São Sebastião (São Paulo, Brazil) 181 G 5
São Sebastião do Paraíso 181 G 5
São Sebastião, Ilha de 181 G 5
São Sepé 182 F 5
São Tiago 156 B 6
São Tomé 157 F 5
São Tomé and Principe 157 F 5
São Vicente 156 A 6
São Vicente (Cape Verde) 181 G 5
São Vicente, Cabo de (Brazil) 114 B 4
Sa'ādatābād 128 E 4
Sa'ādatābād 128 F 5

Sääksjärvi 112 H 3
Saale 111 F 4
Saalfeld 111 F 4
Saanen 112 E 2
Saarbrücken 111 E 5
Sääre 112 H 4
Saaremaa 112 H 4
Saarijärvi 112 J 3
Saariselkä 112 J 2
Saarland 110 E 5
Saarlouis 110 E 5
Saas Fee 115 E 2
Saavedra 183 D 6
Šabac 116 A 2
Sabadell 114 D 3
Sabah 136 E 2
Sabak 136 B 3
Sabán 178 E 2
Sabana 178 D 3
Sabanalarga 178 D 1
Sabang 136 A 2
Sabang 137 E 3
Sabanözü 117 D 2
Săbăoani 116 C 1
Sabará 181 H 4
Sabari 134 D 4
Sabaya 180 C 4
Sabderat 158 F 1
Sabhā (Libya) 153 H 3
Şabhā' (Saudi Arabia) 155 G 4
Sabhā, Wāhāt 153 H 3
Sabi 161 E 3
Sabidana, Jabal 154 F 5
Sabinas 172 B 2
Sabinas Hidalgo 172 B 2
Sabina Shoal 136 E 2
Sabine 171 H 6
Sabini, Monti 115 F 3
Şabīr, Jabal 155 G 6
Sabkhat Maṭṭī 155 J 4
Sable, Cape (FL, Can.) 171 K 6
Sable, Cape (Nova Scotia, Can.) 169 O 7
Sable, Île de 146 B 4
Sable Island 169 P 7
Sablinskoye 117 F 2
Sabonkafi 157 F 3
Sábor 114 B 3
Sabou 156 D 3
Sabozo 157 G 1
Sabrātah 153 H 2
Sabres 114 C 3
Sabrina Coast 185
Sabun 119 Q 3
Şabyā' 155 G 5
Sabyndy 119 O 5
Sabzawar → Shindand 129 G 4
Sabzevār 128 F 3
Sacajawea Peak 170 C 2
Sacanana 183 C 7
Sacavém 114 B 4
Sacco 115 F 3
Sacedón 114 C 3
Săcele 116 C 1
Sachkhere 117 F 2
Sachs Harbour 167 N 1
Saco 119 Q 3
Sacramento 170 B 4
Sacramento Mountains 170 E 5
Sacramento Valley 170 B 3–4
Sadabá 114 C 3
Ṣa'dah 155 G 5
Sadani 159 F 6
Sad Bi 'Ar 154 F 2
Saddajaure 112 G 2
Sadd al Aswān 154 E 4
Saddle Peak 135 F 5
Sa Dec 135 J 5
Sadiya 135 G 2
Sadiyah, Hawr as 155 H 2
Sado 114 B 4
Sadochye, Ozero 128 F 2
Sado-shima 133 L 3
Sadon 117 F 2
Sadovoye 117 F 1
Sæböl 112 A 2
Sæby 113 F 4
Safané 156 D 3
Safāqis 153 H 2
Safed Khirs 129 J 3
Safed Koh 129 H 4
Säffle 113 F 4
Safford 170 E 5
Saffron Walden 103 E 1
Safi 152 D 2
Safonovo 118 J 2
Safonovo 118 F 4
Safonovo 131 X 3
Safrā' al Asyāḥ 155 G 3
Safrā' as Sark 155 G 3

Saf–Sam

Safranbolu 117 D 2
Şafwān 155 H 2
Saga (China) 134 E 2
Saga (Japan) 133 K 4
Saga (U.S.S.R.) 119 M 5
Sagaing 135 G 3
Sagala 156 C 3
Sagan 129 K 3
Sagar 134 E 3
Sagar 134 C 3
Sagara, Lake 158 E 6
Sagastyr 131 N 1
Sagavanirktok 166 H 2
Sage 170 D 3
Saginaw 171 K 3
Saginaw Bay 171 K 3
Sagiz 128 E 1
Sagleipie 156 C 4
Saglek Bay 169 P 4
Saglouc 169 M 3
Sagres 114 B 4
Sagu (Romania) 116 B 1
Sagu (Indonesia) 137 F 5
Saguache 170 E 4
Sagua de Tánamo 173 G 3
Sagua la Grande 173 F 3
Saguenay 171 M 2
Saguia el Hamra 152 C 3
Sagunto 114 C 4
Sagwon 166 H 2
Sahagún (Spain) 114 B 3
Sahagún (Colombia) 178 C 2
Sahara 152–153 EFG 4
Saharanpur 134 C 2
Saharsa 134 E 2
Sahibganj 134 E 2
Sahiwal 129 J 4
Sahlābad 128 F 4
Sahl Rakbah 155 G 4
Şahrā' al Ḥajārah 155 G 2–H 3
Şaḥrā' Bayyūdah 154 E 5
Sahuaripa 170 E 6
Sahuayo de Díaz 172 B 3
Sahul Shelf 193 C 4
Sa Huynh 135 J 5
Saiapoun 135 H 4
Saibai 144 D 3
Saïda 152 EF 2
Sa'īdābād 128 F 5
Said Bundas 158 C 3
Saidor 144 E 3
Saidpur 134 E 2
Saigon 135 J 5
Saihan Toroi 132 D 2
Saiki 133 K 4
Saimaa 112 J 3
Saimaan kanava 112 J 3
Sain Alto 172 B 3
Saindak 129 G 5
Sā'īn Dezh 128 D 3
St. Albans (U.K.) 103 D 2
Saint Alban's (Newfoundl., Can.) 169 Q 6
Saint Albans (VT, U.S.A.) 171 M 3
Saint Albert 167 P 5
Saint-Amand-Mont-Rond 114 D 2
Saint-André, Cap 161 G 3
St. Andrews 99 C 3
Saint Ann's Bay 173 G 4
Saint Anthony 169 Q 5
Saint Arnaud 143 G 6
Saint Augustine 171 K 6
Saint Augustin Saguenay 169 Q 5
St. Austell 102 B 2
St. Austell Bay 102 B 2
Saint-Avold 115 E 2
Saint-Barthélemy 173 K 4
St. Blazey 102 B 2
St. Brides Bay 102 B 2
Saint-Brieuc 114 C 2
Saint-Calais 114 D 2
Saint Catharines 171 L 3
Saint Catherine, Monastery of 154 E 3
St. Catherine's Point 103 D 2
Saint-Chamond 115 D 2
Saint Christopher 173 K 4
Saint Clair River 171 K 3
Saint-Claude 115 E 2
St. Clears 102 B 2
Saint Cloud 171 H 2
Saint Croix 173 K 4
Saint-Cyr-sur-Loire 114 D 2
St. David's 102 B 2
St. David's Head 102 B 2
Saint-Denis (France) 114 D 2
Saint-Denis (Réunion) 161 K 6
Saint-Denis-d'Oléron 114 C 2
Saint-Dié 115 E 2
Saint-Dizier 115 D 2
Sainte Genevieve 171 H 4
Saint Elias, Mount 166 J 3

Saint Elias Mountains 166 K 3
Saint-Elie 179 H 3
Sainte Lucie, Canal de 173 K 5
Sainte Marie, Cap 161 H 5
Saintes 114 C 2
Saintes-Maries-de-la Mer 115 D 3
Sainte-Thérèse 171 M 2
Saint-Étienne 114 D 2
Saint Félicien 171 M 2
Saintfield 100 C 2
Saint-Florent, Golfe de 115 E 3
Saint Flores National Park 158 C 3
Saint-Flour 114 D 2
Saint Francis 170 F 4
Saint Francis Bay 160 A 5
Saint Francis, Cape 160 C 6
Saint Francois 159 J 6
Saint Francois Mountains 171 H 4
St. Gallen 115 E 2
Saint-Gaudens 114 D 3
Saint George (Australia) 143 H 4
Saint George (AK, U.S.A.) 166 D 4
Saint George (UT, U.S.A.) 170 D 4
Saint George, Cape (Canada) 169 Q 6
Saint George, Cape (Papua New Guinea) 145 F 2
Saint-Georges 169 N 6
Saint George's 173 K 5
Saint Georges (Fr. Guiana) 179 H 3
Saint George's (Grenada) 179 F 1
Saint George's Bay 169 Q 6
Saint George's Channel 145 F 1–2
Saint George's Channel 110 B 4
St. George's Channel 102 B 1
Saint-Gildas, Pointe de 114 C 2
Saint Helena 148 B 6
Saint Helena Bay 160 B 6
St. Helens 101 D 3
Saint Helens, Mount 170 B 2
St. Helier 103 C 4
Saint Ignace 171 K 2
Saint Ignace Island 168 K 6
St. Ives (Cambridgeshire) 103 D 1
St. Ives (Cornwall) 102 B 2
St. Ives Bay 102 B 2
Saint James, Cape 166 L 5
Saint Jean 171 M 2
Saint-Jean-d'Angély 114 C 2
Saint-Jean-de-Luz 114 C 3
Saint-Jean-de-Monts 114 C 2
Saint-Jean, Lake 169 N 6
Saint Jérôme 171 M 2
Saint-John 171 N 2
Saint John (Liberia) 156 C 4
Saint John River (ME, U.S.A.) 169 O 6
Saint John's (Antigua) 173 K 4
Saint Johns (AZ, U.S.A.) 170 E 5
Saint John's (Newfoundl., Can.) 169 R 6
Saint Johnsbury 171 M 3
Saint Johns River (FL, U.S.A.) 171 K 6
Saint Joseph (Seychelles) 159 J 6
Saint Joseph (MI, U.S.A.) 171 J 3
Saint Joseph (MO, U.S.A.) 171 H 4
Saint Joseph, Lake 168 J 5
Saint-Junien 114 D 2
St. Just 102 B 2
Saint Kilda 110 B 3
Saint Kitts (Saint Christopher) 173 K 4
Saint Laurent 179 H 2
Saint Lawrence 143 H 3
Saint Lawrence, Gulf of 169 P 6
Saint Lawrence Island 166 C 3
Saint Lawrence River 169 O 6
Saint-Lô 114 C 2
Saint-Louis (U.S.A.) 171 H 4
Saint-Louis (Senegal) 156 A 2
Saint Lucia 173 K 5
Saint Lucia, Cape 161 E 5
Saint Lucia, Lake 161 E 5
Saint Magnus Bay 110 C 2
St. Magnus Bay 98 D 1
Saint-Malo 114 C 2
Saint-Marc 173 H 4
St. Margaret's Hope 98 C 3
St. Marks 171 K 5
Saint-Martin 173 K 4
Saint-Martin-Vésubie 115 E 3
Saint Mary Peak 143 F 5
Saint Marys 144 L 9
St. Marys (AK, U.S.A.) 166 E 3
St. Mary's (U.K.) 102 A 3
Saint Mary's Bay 169 R 6
Saint Mary's, Cape 169 R 6
Saint Matthew 166 C 3

Saint Matthias Group 145 E 2
Saint Maurice 171 M 2
St. Mawes 102 B 2
Saint Michael 166 E 3
Saint Michaels 170 E 4
St Moritz 115 E 2
Saint-Nazaire 114 C 2
St. Neots 103 D 1
St. Niklaas 110 D 4
Saint-Omer 114 D 1
Saint-Paul (Réunion) 161 K 6
Saint Paul (Liberia) 156 BC 4
Saint Paul (AK, U.S.A.) 166 CD 4
Saint Paul (Alb., Can.) 167 P 5
Saint Paul (MN, U.S.A.) 171 H 3
Saint-Péray 115 D 3
St. Peter and St. Paul Rocks 175 G 2
St. Peter Port 103 C 3
Saint Petersburg 171 K 6
Saint Pierre (Canada) 169 Q 6
Saint Pierre (Seychelles) 159 J 6
Saint-Pierre (Réunion) 161 K 6
Saint Pierre (Australia) 143 H 6
Saint Pierre et Miquelon 169 Q 6
Saint-Pons 114 D 3
Saint-Quentin 114 D 2
St. Roch Basin 167 T 2
Saint-Savin 114 D 2
Saint-Seine-l'Abbaye 115 D 2
Saint Stephen 169 O 6
Saint-Thomas (Ont., Can) 169 L 7
Saint-Thomas (Puerto Rico) 173 JK 4
Saint-Tropez 115 E 3
Saint Vincent 173 K 5
Saint Vincent HJ 5
Saint Vincent and the Grenadines 179 F 1
Saint Vincent, Gulf 143 F 6
Saint Vincent Passage 173 K 5
St. Walburg 167 Q 5
Saipal 134 D 2
Saipan 146 A 1
Sai Yok 135 G 5
Sajama 180 C 4
Sajama, Nevado 180 C 4
Sajānan 115 E 4
Sajid 155 G 5
Sajó 111 H 5
Saka 159 F 5
Sakabinda 160 D 2
Sakai 133 L 4
Sakākah 155 G 3
Sakala Kõrgustik 113 J 4
Sakami 169 M 5
Sakami, Lac 169 M 5
Sakami River 169 N 5
Sakania 160 D 2
Sakar 116 C 2
Sakaraha 161 G 4
Sakarat Daği 117 E 2
Sakarya 116 D 2
Sakata 133 L 3
Sakçağöz 117 E 3
Sakchu 133 J 4
Saketé 156 F 4
Såkevare 112 G 2
Sakhalin 131 Q 5
Sakhalinskiy Khrebet, Zapadno 131 Q 5
Sakhalinskiy Zaliv 131 Q 5
Sakhandzha 131 N 2
Sakht Sar 128 E 3
Saki 133 L 4
Sakoli 134 D 3
Sakon Nakhon 135 H 4
Sakrivier 160 C 6
Saksaul'skiy 129 G 1
Sakti 134 D 3
Säkylä 112 H 3
Sal (Cape Verde) 156 B 6
Sal (U.S.S.R.) 117 F 1
Sala 113 G 4
Sala Andong Tuk 135 H 5
Salaca 112 H 4
Salacgrīva 113 H 4
Sala Consilina 115 G 3
Salada 170 F 6
Salada, Gran Laguna 183 C 7
Saladillo 183 E 6
Salado 183 C 6
Salado 182 D 4
Salaga 156 D 4
Salagle 159 G 4
Salair 119 R 5
Salairskiy Kryazh 119 R 5
Salal 157 H 3
Salālah (Oman) 155 J 5
Salālah (Sudan) 154 F 4
Salamá 172 D 4
Salamanca (Mexico) 172 B 3
Salamanca (Spain) 114 B 3
Salamat 157 J 3
Salamina 178 C 2

Salamis (Cyprus) 117 D 3
Salamis (Greece) 116 B 3
Salar de Antofalla 182 C 4
Salar de Arizaro 180 C 5
Salar de Atacama 180 C 5
Salar de Coipasa 180 C 4
Salar de Hombre Muerto 182 C 4
Salar de Uyuni 180 C 5
Salas 114 B 3
Salatiga 136 D 5
Salaverry 178 C 5
Salavat 118 L 5
Salawati, Pulau 137 H 4
Sala y Gómes 147 H 4
Salbris 114 D 2
Salcantay, Nevado 180 B 3
Salchininkai 113 J 5
Salcombe 102 C 2
Saldanha 160 B 6
Saldus 113 H 4
Salé (Morocco) 152 D 2
Sale (U.K.) 101 D 3
Sale (Australia) 143 H 6
Saleh, Teluk 136 E 5
Salekhard 119 N 2
Salem (India) 134 C 5
Salem (IL, U.S.A.) 171 J 4
Salem (OR, U.S.A.) 170 B 3
Salemi 115 F 4
Sälen 112 F 3
Salentina, Penisola 115 G 3–4
Salerno 115 E 3
Salerno, Golfo di 115 E 3
Sales 179 HJ 5
Saletekri 134 D 3
Salford 101 D 3
Salgótarján 116 A 1
Salgueiro 181 J 2
Salhus 113 E 3
Sali (Yugoslavia) 115 G 3
Sali (Argentina) 182 C 4
Sali (Algeria) 152 E 3
Salida 170 E 4
Salihli 116 C 3
Salima 161 E 2
Salīmah, Wāḥat 154 D 4
Salin 135 F 3
Salina (Italy) 115 F 4
Salina (KS, U.S.A.) 170 G 4
Salina (UT, U.S.A.) 170 D 4
Salina del Gualicho 183 CD 4
Salina Grande 183 C 6
Salinas (U.S.A.) 170 B 4
Salinas (Ecuador) 178 B 4
Salinas (Minas Gerais, Brazil) 181 H 4
Salinas, Cabo de 114 D 4
Salinas de Hidalgo 172 B 3
Salinas Grandes 182 D 4–5
Salinas Peak 170 E 5
Salinas, Ponta das 160 A 2
Salinitas 180 B 5
Salinópolis 179 J 4
Salisbury (U.K.) 103 D 2
Salisbury (Canada) 169 M 3
Salisbury (MD, U.S.A.) 171 L 4
Salisbury → Harare 161 E 3
Salisbury Plain 103 D 2
Şalkhad 154 F 2
Salla 112 J 2
Salling 113 E 4
Sallūm 154 F 5
Salluyo, Nevado 180 C 3
Sallyana 134 D 2
Salmäs 128 C 3
Salmi 112 K 3
Salmon 170 D 2
Salmon Arm 167 O 5
Salmon Mountains 170 B 3
Salmon River 170 C 2
Salmon River Mountains 170 C 3
Salo (Centr. Afr. Rep.) 158 B 4
Salo (Finland) 113 H 3
Saló (Italy) 115 F 2
Salon-de-Provence 115 E 3
Salonga 158 C 5
Salonga National Park 158 C 5
Salong, Tünel-e- 129 H 3
Salonica 116 B 2
Salonta 116 B 1
Salor 114 B 4
Salou 114 D 3
Saloum 156 A 3
Salpausselkä 112 J 3
Sal-Rei 156 B 6
Salsbruket 112 F 3
Sal'sk 117 F 1
Salso 115 F 4
Salsomaggiore Terme 115 E 3
Salt 114 D 3
Salta 180 C 5

Saltash 102 B 2
Saltburn 101 E 2
Saltcoats 99 B 4
Saltdalselva 112 G 2
Salten 112 G 2
Saltfjellet 112 G 2
Saltfjorden 112 F 2
Saltfleet 101 E 3
Salt Fork Brazos 170 F 5
Saltholm 113 F 4
Saltillo 172 B 2
Salt Lake (Queensland, Austr.) 143 F 3
Salt Lake City 170 D 3
Salt Lakes 142 C 3
Salt Lakes 142 B 4
Salto (Uruguay) 182 E 5
Salto Angel 179 F 2
Salto Angostura 178 D 3
Salto Basaseachic 170 E 6
Salto da Divisa 181 J 4
Salto das Sete Quedas 181 F 5
Salto del Guaira 181 F 5
Salton Sea 170 C 5
Saltos do Iguaçu 182 F 4
Salt Range 129 J 4
Salt River (U.S.A.) 170 D 5
Salt River (S. Africa) 160 C 6
Salue Timpaus, Selat 137 F 4
Salumbar 134 B 3
Salur 134 D 4
Salvador (Libya) 157 G 1
Salvador (Brazil) 181 J 3
Salvatierra 172 B 3
Salvatierra 114 C 3
Salwā 155 J 4
Salwá Baḥrī 154 E 4
Salween 135 G 4
Sal'yany 128 D 3
Salzach 115 F 2
Salzburg 115 F 2
Salzgitter 111 F 4
Salzwedel 111 F 4
Sa Madre 172 D 4
Sa Madre Occiental 172 A, B 2–3
Samagaltay 130 G 5
Samāh (Libya) 153 J 3
Samāh (Saudi Arabia) 155 H 3
Samaipata 180 D 4
Samak, Tanjung 136 C 4
Samales Group 137 F 2
Samalga Pass 166 D 5
Samālūt 154 E 3
Samaná 173 J 4
Samandaği 117 E 3
Samangan 129 H 3
Samani 133 M 2
Samar 137 G 1
Samara 118 K 5
Samara 117 E 1
Samarai 145 F 4
Samarinda 136 E 4
Samarkand 129 H 3
Sāmarrā' 155 G 2
Samar Sea 137 F 1
Samarskoy 119 Q 6
Samastipur 134 E 2
Samate 137 H 4
Samaúma 178 E 5
Samba 158 D 5
Samba 158 C 4
Samba Caju 160 B 1
Sambaliung 136 E 3
Sambalpur 134 D 3
Sambar, Tanjung 136 D 4
Sambas 136 C 3
Sambava 161 J 2
Sambhar 134 C 2
Samboja 136 E 4
Sambor (Kampuchea) 135 J 5
Sambor (U.S.S.R.) 111 H 5
Samborombón, Bahía 183 E 6
Samborondón 178 BC 4
Sambre 114 D 2
Sambu 136 B 3
Sambuan 136 E 4
Samburg 119 P 2
Samch'ŏnp'o 133 J 4
Same (Indonesia) 137 G 5
Same (Tanzania) 159 F 5
Samfya 160 D 2
Sami 116 B 3
Sami Ghar 129 H 4
Samīrah 155 G 3
Samka 135 G 3
Sam Neua 135 H 3
Samnū 153 HJ 3
Samoa Islands 147 D 3
Samo Alto 182 B 5
Samobor 115 G 2
Samokov 116 B 2
Sámos 116 C 3
Samosir, Pulau 136 A 3

Sam – San

Samothraki **116** C 2
Sampaga **137** E 4
Sampit **136** D 4
Sampit, Sungai **136** D 4
Sampit, Teluk **136** D 4
Sampun **145** F 3
Sampwe **158** D 6
Sam Rayburn Reservoir **171** H 5
Samrong **135** H 5
Samsang **134** D 1
Samsö **113** F 4
Samsö Bælt **113** F 4
Sam Son **135** J 4
Samsun **117** E 2
Samthar **134** C 2
Samtredia **117** F 2
Samuel, Mount **142** E 2
Samus' **119** Q 4
Samut Prakan **135** H 5
Samut Songkhram **135** H 5
San (Poland) **111** H 4
San (Mali) **156** D 3
San'ā' **155** G 5
Sana **115** G 2
Sanaba **156** D 3
Sanae **185**
Sanāfīr **154** E 3
Sanaga **157** G 5
Sanagir **134** C 2
San Agustin, Cape **137** G 2
San Agustin de Valle Fértin **182** C 5
Sanain **117** F 2
Sanak Islands **166** E 5
S. Ambrosio Island **175** C 5
Sanana **137** G 4
Sanana, Pulau **137** G 4
Sanandaj **128** D 3
San Andrés **173** F 5
San Andrés del Rabanedo **114** B 3
San Andres Mountains **170** E 5
San Andrés Tuxtla **172** C 4
Sananduva **182** F 4
San Angelo **170** F 5
San Antonia de Cortés **172** E 4
San Antonio (U.S.A.) **170** G 6
San Antonio (Portugal) **152** A 1
San Antonio (Chile) **182** B 5
San Antonio (Urug.) **182** E 5
San Antonio (Ven.) **178** E 3
San Antonio Abad **114** D 4
San Antonio Bay **171** G 6
San Antonio, Cabo (Cuba) **172** F 3
San Antonio, Cabo (Argentina) **183** E 6
San Antonio de Caparo **178** D 2
San Antonio de los Cobres **180** C 5
San Antonio del Tachira **178** D 2
San Antonio Oeste **183** D 7
San Antonio, Sierra de **170** D 5
Sanariapo **178** C 3
Sanāw **155** J 5
San Bernadetto del Tronto **115** F 3
San Bernardino **170** C 5
San Bernardo (Mexico) **170** D 6
San Bernardo (Chile) **182** B 5
San Blas **172** A 3
San Blas **170** E 6
San Blas **172** B 2
San Blas, Cape **171** J 6
San Borja **180** C 3
San Borjas, Sierra de **170** D 6
San Bruno, Serra **115** G 4
San Buenaventura **172** B 2
Sancai **158** F 2
San Carlos (Arg.) **182** C 4
San Carlos (Argentina) **182** C 5
San Carlos (Chile) **183** B 6
San Carlos (Mexico) **172** C 3
San Carlos (Nicaragua) **172** F 5
San Carlos (Phil.) **137** F 1
San Carlos (Uruguay) **182** F 5
San Carlos (Venezuela) **178** E 2
San Carlos de Bariloche **183** B 7
San Carlos del Zulia **178** D 2
San Carlos de Río Negro **178** E 3
San Casme **182** E 4
San Cataldo **115** F 4
Sancerrois, Collines du **114** D 2
Sánchez **173** J 4
Sanchor **134** B 3
San Christóbal (Argentina) **182** D 5
San Clemente **170** C 5
San Clemente Island **170** C 5
San Cristóbal (Dom. Rep.) **173** H 4
San Cristobal (Sol. Is.) **145** H 4
San Cristóbal (Venezuela) **178** D 2
San Cristóbal de las Casas **172** D 4
San Cristóbal, Isla **178** B 6
Sancti Spíritus **173** G 3
San Custodio **178** E 3
Sand **112** E 4
Sandai **136** D 4
Sandakan **136** E 2
Sandanski **116** B 2
Sandaré **156** B 3
Sandarne **112** E 3
Sanday **98** C 2
Sandbach **102** C 1
Sand Cay **134** B 5
Sandefjord **113** F 4
Sanderson **170** F 5
Sandhammaren **113** F 4
Sand Hills **170** F 3
Sandia **180** C 3
San Diego **170** C 5
San Diego, Cabo **183** C 9
Sandıklı **116** D 3
Sandila **134** D 2
Sandiman, Mount **142** B 3
San Dimitri Point **115** F 4
Sanding, Pulau **136** B 4
Sandnes **113** E 4
Sandnessjöen **112** F 2
Sandoa **158** C 6
Sandomierz **111** H 4
San Dona di Piave **115** F 2
Sandoway **135** F 4
Sandown **110** C D 4
Sandoy **110** A 1
Sand Point **166** E 4
Sandray **99** A 3
Sandspit **166** L 5
Sandstone (U.S.A.) **171** H 2
Sandstone (Australia) **142** B 4
Sandur **110** A 1
Sandusky **171** K 3
Sandvig **113** F 4
Sandvika **113** F 4
Sandviken **113** G 3
Sandwich **103** E 2
Sandwich Bay (Canada) **169** Q 5
Sandwich Bay (Namibia) **160** A 4
Sandwip **135** F 3
Sandy **103** D 1
Sandy Cape **143** J 3
Sandy Desert, Great **142** C 3
Sandykachi **129** G 3
Sandy Lake **168** J 5
Sandy Point **135** F 5
San Estanislao **180** E 5
San Esteban de Gormaz **114** C 3
San Felípe (Chile) **182** B 5
San Felípe (Colombia) **178** E 3
San Felipe (Mexico) **172** B 3
San Felipe (Mexico) **170** D 5
San Felipe (Venezuela) **178** E 1
San Felipe, Cerro de **114** C 3
San Felíu de Guixols **114** D 3
San Feliu de Llobregat **114** D 3
S. Félix Island **175** B 5
San Fernando (Spain) **114** B 4
San Fernando (Mexico) **172** C 3
San Fernando (Chile) **182** B 5
San Fernando (Phil.) **137** H 1
San Fernando (Phil.) **137** J 1
San Fernando (Trinidad) **179** F 1
San Fernando de Apure **178** E 2
San Fernando de Atabapo **178** E
Sånfjället **112** F 3
Sanford **171** L 4
Sanford, Mount **166** J 3
Sanford River **142** B 4
San Francisco (U.S.A.) **170** B 4
San Francisco (Arg.) **182** D 5
San Francisco, Cabo de **178** B 3
San Francisco de Arriba **172** B 2
San Francisco del Chanar **182** D 4
San Francisco del Monte de Oro **182** C 5
San Francisco del Oro **170** E 6
San Francisco del Rincón **172** B 3
San Francisco de Macorís **173** HJ 4
San Francisco Javier **114** D 4
San Francisco, Paso de **182** C 4
Sanga **161** F 2
Sanga-Kyuyel' **131** Q 3
Sangamner **134** B 4
Sangar **131** N 3
Sangareddipet **134** C 4
Sangatolon **131** R 3
Sangayán **180** A 3
Sangay, Volcán **178** C 4
Sange **158** D 6
Sangeang, Pulau **137** E 5
Sanger **170** C 4
Sanggan He **132** F 2
Sanggar, Teluk **137** E 5
Sanggau **136** D 3
Sangha **157** H 5
Sangihe, Kepulauan **137** G 3
Sangihe, Pulau **137** G 3
San Gil **178** D 2
Sangilen, Nagor'ye **130** G 5
Sangin **129** G 4
San Giovanni in Fiore **115** G 4
Sangiyn Dalay Nuur **130** G 6
Sangju **133** J 3
Sangkhla Buri **135** G 5
Sangkulirang, Teluk **136** E 3
Sangli **134** B 4
Sangmélima **157** G 5
San Gotthard **115** E 2
Sangre de Cristo Mountains **170** E 4
San Gregorio (Chile) **183** B 9
San Gregorio (Uruguay) **182** E 5
Sangre Grande **179** F 1
Sangri **132** B 5
Sangro **115** F 3
Sangrur **134** C 1
Sangue **180** E 3
Sangüesa **114** C 3
Sangzhi **132** F 5
Sanhala **156** C 3–4
Sanhe **130** M 5
San Hilario **170** D 7
San Ignacio (Argentina) **183** E 6
San Ignacio (Belize) **172** E 4
San Ignacio **180** D 4
San Ignacio (Bolivia) **180** C 3
San Ignacio (Mexico) **170** D 6
San Ignacio (Paraguay) **182** E 4
San Ignacio, Isla de **170** E 6
Sanikiluaq **169** M 4
San Isidro (Costa Rica) **172** F 6
San Isidro (Argentina) **182** E 5
San Isidro (Peru) **178** C 4
San Jacinto **178** C 2
San Javier (Spain) **114** C 4
San Javier (Argentina) **182** D 5
San Javier (Bolivia) **180** D 4
San Javier (Chile) **183** B 6
San Javier (Urug.) **182** E 5
Sanjawi **129** H 4
Sanjiang **132** E 5
Sanjō **133** L 3
San Joaquín **180** D 3
San Joaquin River **170** B 4
San Joaquin Valley **170** BC 4
San Jorge **178** C 2
San Jorge, Bahia de **170** D 5
San Jorge, Golfo **183** C 8
San Jorge, Golfo de **114** D 3
San Jose (CA, U.S.A.) **170** B 4
San José (Costa Rica) **172** F 6
San José (Guatemala) **172** D 5
San Jose (Phil.) **137** F 1
San Jose (Phil.) **137** J 1
San José de Amacuro **179** F 2
San Jose de Buenavista **137** F 1
San José de Chiquitos **180** D 4
San José de Feliciano **182** E 5
San José de Gracia **170** E 6
San José del Cabo **170** E 7
San José del Guaviare **178** D 3
San José de Mayo **182** E 5
San José de Ocuné **178** D 3
San José, Isla **170** D 6
San Juan (Argentina) **182** C 5
San Juan (Peru) **180** A 4
San Juan (Puerto Rico) **173** J 4
San Juan (Rep. Dominicana) **173** H 4
San Juan (Ven.) **178** E 2
San Juan Bautista (Paraguay) **182** E 4
San Juan Bautista (Spain) **114** D 4
San Juan Bautista Tuxtepec **172** C 4
San Juan, Cabo **157** F 5
San Juan de Guadalupe **172** B 3
San Juan del Norte **172** F 5
San Juan de los Cayos **178** E 1
San Juan de los Morros **178** E 2
San Juan del Rio **172** C 3
San Juan de Payara **178** E 2
San Juan Mountains **170** E 4
San Juan, Pico **173** F 3
San Juan, Rio **172** F 5
San Julián **183** C 8
San Justo **182** D 5
Sankarana **156** C 3
Sankosh **134** E 2
Sankt Gotthard-Pass **115** E 2
Sankt Martin **115** G 2
Sankt Michel **112** J 3
Sankt Pölten **115** G 2
Sankt Veit an der Glan **115** F 2
Sankt-Vith **110** E 4
Sankuru **158** C 5
San Lázaro, Sierra de **170** D 7
San Lorenzo (Mexico) **170** E 7
San Lorenzo (Argentina) **182** D 5
San Lorenzo (Ecuador) **178** C 3
San Lorenzo, Cabo **178** B 4
San Lorenzo, Cerro **183** B 8
Sanlúcar de Barrameda **114** B 4
San Lucas (Bolivia) **180** C 5
San Lucas (Mexico) **172** B 3
San Lucas (Mexico) **170** E 7
San Lucas, Cabo **170** E 7
San Luis (Mexico) **170** D 6
San Luis (Arg.) **182** C 5
San Luís (Venezuela) **178** E 1
San Luis de la Paz **172** B 3
San Luis Gonzaga, Bahía **170** D 6
San Luis, Isla **170** D 5
San Luis, Lago de **180** D 3
San Luis Obispo **170** B 4
San Luis Peak **170** E 4
San Luis Rio Colorado **170** D 5
San Marco, Capo **115** E 4
San Marcos (Colombia) **178** C 2
San Marcos (Mexico) **172** C 4
San Marcos (Mexico) **172** B 3
San Marcos (TX, U.S.A.) **170** G 6
San Marcos, Isla **170** D 6
San Marino **115** F 3
San Martín (Spain) **114** C 3
San Martín (Colombia) **178** D 3
San Martín (Bolivia) **180** D 3
San Martín de los Andes **183** B 7
San Martín, Lago **183** B 8
San Mateo **170** B 4
San Matías **180** E 4
San Matías, Golfo **183** D 7
Sanmen **133** H 5
Sanmenxia **132** F 4
San Miguel (El Salvador) **172** E 5
San Miguel (Bolivia) **180** D 3
San Miguel (Peru) **180** B 3
San Miguel de Allende **172** B 3
San Miguel de Horcasitas **170** D 6
San Miguel de Huachi **180** C 4
San Miguel del Padrón **173** F 3
San Miguel de Tucumán **182** C 4
San Miguel Islands **137** E 2
San Miguel Sole de Vega **172** C 4
Sanming **133** G 5
Sannār **154** E 6
San Nicolás (Mexico) **172** B 2
San Nicolás (Peru) **180** A 4
San Nicolás de los Arroyos **182** D 5
Sannikova **184**
Sannikova, Proliv **131** P 1
Sanniquellie **156** C 4
Sanok **111** H 5
San Onofre **178** C 2
San Pablo (Argentina) **183** C 9
San Pablo (Bolivia) **180** C 5
San Pablo (Phil.) **137** F 1
San Pédro (Ivory Coast) **156** C 5
San Pedro (Mexico) **172** B 2
San Pedro (Argentina) **182** E 5
San Pedro (Argentina) **180** D 5
San Pedro (Paraguay) **180** E 5
San Pedro de Arimena **178** D 3
San Pedro de Atacama **180** C 5
San Pedro de las Bôcas **179** F 2
San Pedro de Lloc **178** C 5
San Pedro de Macorís **173** J 4
San Pedro Martir, Sierra de **170** C 5
San Pedro Pochutla **172** C 4
San Pedro, Sierra de **114** B 4
San Pedro Sula **172** E 4
San Pietro **115** E 4
Sanquhar **99** C 4
San Quintín **170** C 5
San Quintin, Bahia de **170** C 5
San Rafael (Mexico) **172** B 2
San Rafael (Argentina) **182** C 5
San Rafael (Bolivia) **180** D 4
San Rafael (Chile) **183** B 6
San Rafael, Cabo **173** J 4
San Rafael Mountains **170** C 5
San Ramón **180** A 3
San Ramón de la Nueva Orán **180** D 5
San Remo **115** E 3
San Roque **114** B 4
San Salvador (El Salvador) **172** E 5
San Salvador (Sp.) **114** D 4
San Salvador (Watling Isl.) **173** H 3
San Salvador de Jujuy **180** C 5
San Salvador, Isla **178** B 6
Sansanding **156** C 3
Sansanné Mango **156** E 3
San Sebastian (Argentina) **183** C 9
San Sebastián (Sp.) **114** C 3
Sansepolero **115** F 3
San Severo **115** G 3
San Silvestre **178** D 2
Santañy **114** D 4
Santa Ana (Solomon Islands) **145** H 4
Santa Ana (Bolivia) **180** C 3
Santa Ana (CA, U.S.A.) **170** C 5
Santa Ana (Ecuador) **178** B 4
Santa Ana (Mex.) **170** D 5
Santa Ana (San Salv.) **172** E 5
Santa Ana, Cuchilla de **183** EF 2
Santa Barbara (CA, U.S.A.) **170** B 5
Santa Barbara (Mexico) **170** E 6
Santa Barbara Channel **170** B 5
Santa Bárbara do Sul **182** F 4
Santa Carolina, Ilha **161** F 4
Santa Catalina (Argentina) **180** C 5
Santa Catalina (Chile) **182** C 4
Santa Catalina Island (CA, U.S.A.) **170** C 5
Santa Catarina (Brazil) **182** F 4
Santa Catarina, Ilha de **181** G 6
Santa Clara (Colombia) **178** E 4
Santa Clara (CA, U.S.A.) **170** B 4
Santa Clara (Cuba) **173** F 3
Santa Clara (Mexico) **170** E 6
Santa Clotilde **178** D 4
Santa Comba **114** B 3
Santa Cruz (Arg.) **183** B 9
Santa Cruz (Bolivia) **180** D 4
Santa Cruz (Brazil) **179** H 4
Santa Cruz (Brazil) **181** H 5
Santa Cruz (Brazil) **178** D 5
Santa Cruz (CA, U.S.A.) **170** B 4
Santa Cruz (Chile) **182** B 5
Santa Cruz (Costa Rica) **172** E 5
Santa Cruz (Peru) **178** C 5
Santa Cruz (Phil.) **137** H 1
Santa Cruz (Phil.) **137** F 1
Santa Cruz de la Palma **152** B 3
Santa Cruz de la Zarza **114** C 4
Santa Cruz del Sur **173** G 3
Santa Cruz de Mudela **114** C 4
Santa Cruz de Tenerife **152** B 3
Santa Cruz do Río Pardo **181** G 5
Santa Cruz do Sul **182** F 4
Santa Cruz, Isla **178** B 6
Santa Cruz Island (U.S.A.) **170** C 5
Santa Cruz Islands (Sol. Is.) **145** J 4
Santa Elena **178** B 4
Santa Elena, Bahía de **172** E 5
Santa Elena, Cabo **172** E 5
Santa Fe **170** E 4
Santafé **114** C 4
Santa Fé (Arg.) **182** D 5
Santa Fé (Brazil) **181** F 4
Santa Filomena **181** G 2
Sant' Agata di Militello **115** F 4
Santa Helena **179** J 4
Santai **132** E 4
Santa Inês **179** J 4
Santa Ines, Bahía **170** D 6
Santa Inés, Isla **183** B 9
Santa Isabel **146** B 3
Santa Isabel (Arg.) **183** C 6
Santa Isabel (Brazil) **179** G 5
Santa Isabel (Brazil) **180** D 3
Santa Isabel (Sol. Is.) **145** G 2
Santa Isabel do Araguaia **179** J 5
Santa Isabel, Pico de **157** F 5
Santa Juana **178** E 2
Santa Júlia **179** G 4–5
Santa Lucía (Uruguay) **182** E 5
Santa Lucia Range **170** B 4
Santa Luzia **156** A 6
Santa Margarita, Isla de **170** D 7
Santa Maria (U.S.A.) **170** B 4
Santa Maria (Portugal) **152** A 1
Santa María (Amazonas, Brazil) **179** G 4
Santa Maria (Amazonas, Brazil) **179** F 4
Santa María (Arg.) **182** C 4
Santa María (Rio Grande do Sul, Brazil) **182** F 4
Santa Maria, Bahia de **170** E 6
Santa Maria, Cabo de **161** E 5
Santa Maria, Cabo de **114** B 4
Santa María de Ipire **178** E 2
Santa María del Oro **172** A 2
Santa Maria del Río **172** B 3
Santa Maria di Leuca, Capo **115** G 4
Santa Maria dos Marmelos **179** F 5
Santa María, Isla **178** B 6
Santa Maria Zacatepec **172** C 4
Santa Marta **178** D 1
Santa Marta, Cabo de **160** A 2
Santa Marta Grande, Cabo de **181** G 6
Santa Marta, Ría de **114** B 3

San–Seg

Santa Monica 170 C 5
Santan 136 E 4
Santana 181 H 3
Santander (Colombia) 178 C 3
Santander (Spain) 114 C 3
Sant' Antioco 115 E 4
Santa Olalla del Cala 114 B 4
Santarém (Portugal) 114 B 4
Santarém (Brazil) 179 H 4
Santaren Channel 173 G 3
Santa Rita (U.S.A.) 170 E 5
Santa Rita (Colombia) 178 D 3
Santa Rita (Venezuela) 178 E 2
Santa Rita do Araguaia 181 F 4
Santa Rosa (Argentina) 183 C 6
Santa Rosa (Argentina) 182 C 5
Santa Rosa (Argentina) 183 D 6
Santa Rosa (Bolivia) 180 C 3
Santa Rosa (CA, U.S.A.) 170 B 4
Santa Rosa (Columbia) 178 E 3
Santa Rosa (N.M., U.S.A.) 170 F 5
Santa Rosa (Peru) 180 B 3
Santa Rosa (Rio Grande de Sul, Brazil) 182 F 4
Santa Rosa de Cabal 178 C 3
Santa Rosa de Copán 172 E 5
Santa Rosa de la Roca 180 D 4
Santa Rosa Island 170 B 5
Santa Rosalia 170 D 6
Santa Sylvina 182 D 4
Santa Teresa (Espírito Santo, Brazil) 181 H 5
Santa Teresa (Goiás, Brazil) 181 G 3
Santa Teresinha 181 F 3
Santa Vitória do Palmar 182 F 5
Santee River 171 L 5
San Telmo 170 C 5
Santiago (Brazil) 182 F 4
Santiago (Chile) 182 B 5
Santiago (Haïti) 173 H 4
Santiago (Panama) 178 B 2
Santiago, Cerro 173 F 6
Santiago da Cacém 114 B 4
Santiago de Compostela 114 B 3
Santiago de Cuba 173 G 3
Santiago del Estero 182 D 4
Santiago de Papasquiaro 172 A 2
Santiago Ixcuintla 172 A 3
Santiago, Rio Grande de 172 A 3
Santiago, Serranía de 180 DE 4
Santoña 114 C 3
Santo Amaro 181 J 3
Santo André 181 G 5
Santo Ângelo 182 F 4
Santo Antão 156 A 6
Santo Antonio (São Tomé) 157 F 5
Santo Antonio (Brazil) 181 F 6
Santo Antônio de Jesus 181 J 3
Santo Antônio do Içá 178 E 4
Santo Domingo (Arg.) 182 D 4
Santo Domingo (Cuba) 173 F 3
Santo Domingo (Domin. Rep.) 173 J 4
Santo Domingo (Mexico) 170 D 6
Santopitar 114 C 4
Santos 181 G 5
Santos Dumont (Amazonas, Brazil) 178 E 5
Santos Dumont (Minas Gerais, Brazil) 181 H 5
Santo Tomás (Peru) 180 B 3
Santo Tomás (Nicaragua) 172 F 5
Santo Tomé (Arg.) 182 E 4
Santo Tomé de Guayana 179 F 2
Santurce-Antiguo 114 C 3
San Valentín, Monte 183 B 8
San Vicente (Mexico) 170 C 5
San Vicente (Phil.) 137 J 1
San Vicente de Cañete 180 A 3
San Vicente de la Barquerq 114 C 3
San Vicente del Raspeig 114 C 4
Sanza Pombo 160 B 1
Sao Hill 158 F 6
Saône 115 D 2
Sa Oui 135 H 5
Saoura 152 E 3
Sápai 116 C 2
Sapanca Gölü 116 D 2
Sape (Indonesia) 137 E 5
Sapé (Brazil) 181 J 2
Sapele 157 F 4
Sape, Selat 137 E 5
Sape, Teluk 137 E 5
Sapiéntza 116 B 3
Saponé 156 D 3
Saposoa 178 C 5
Sapporo 133 M 2
Sapri 115 G 3
Sapulpa 171 G 4
Sapulut 136 E 3

Sapwe 160 D 2
Sāqand 128 F 4
Sāq, Jabal 155 G 3
Saqqez 128 D 3
Sarāb 128 D 3
Sara Buri 135 H 5
Sarafére 156 D 2
Sarafjagär 128 E 4
Saraguro 178 C 4
Sarajevo 115 G 3
Sarakhs 128 G 3
Saraktash 118 L 5
Saralzhin 128 E 1
Saramati 135 FG 2
Saran' 119 O 6
Saranda 116 B 3
Sarandí Grande 182 E 5
Sarangani Bay 137 G 2
Sarangani Islands 137 G 2
Sarangarh 134 D 3
Saran, Gunung 136 D 4
Saranley 159 G 4
Saranpaul' 119 M 3
Saransk 118 J 5
Sarapul 118 K 4
Sarapul'skoye 131 P 6
Sarare 178 E 2
Sarasota 171 K 6
Sarata 116 C 1
Saratok 136 D 3
Saratov 118 J 5
Saravan 135 J 4
Sarawak 136 D 3
Saray 116 C 2
Saraya 156 B 3
Sarayköy 116 C 3
Sarbāz 129 G 5
Sarca 115 F 2
Sarco 182 B 4
Sardalas → Al 'Awaynāt 153 H 3
Sardarshahr 134 B 2
Sar Dasht 128 D 3
Sar Dasht 128 D 4
Sardegna 115 E 3
Sardina 178 D 3
Sardinia 115 E 3
Sarek National Park 112 G 2
Sarektjåkkå 112 G 2
Sarempaka, Gunung 136 E 4
Sarenga 159 F 2
Sarga, Punta 152 B 4
Sargasso Sea 173 JK 2
Sargatskoye 119 O 4
Sargento Lores 178 D 4
Sargento Paixão, Serra do 180 DE 2
Sargodha 129 J 4
Sarh 157 H 4
Sarhro, Jbel 152 D 2
Sārī 128 E 3
Saría 116 C 3
Sarıbuğday 117 E 2
Sarigan 146 A 1
Sarıkamış 117 F 2
Sarıkaya 117 E 3
Sarikei 136 D 3
Sarila 134 C 2
Sarınoğlan 117 E 3
Sar-i-Pul 129 H 3
Sarir 151
Sarīr al Qaṭṭūsah 153 J 3
Sarīr Tibistī 153 J 4
Sariwŏn 133 J 3
Sariyar Barajı 116 D 2–3
Sanyer 116 C 2
Sark 103 C 3
Sarkand 119 P 6
Şarkikaraağaç 116 D 3
Şarkışla 117 E 3
Şarköy 116 C 2
Sark, Safrā' as 155 G 3
Sarlat-la-Canéda 114 D 3
Sarmi 137 J 4
Sarmiento 183 C 8
Sarmiento, Monte 183 B 9
Särna 112 F 3
Sarnen 115 E 2
Sarnia 171 K 3
Sarny 113 J 5
Saroako 137 F 4
Sarobi 129 H 4
Sarolangun 136 B 4
Saronikós Kólpos 116 B 3
Saronno 115 E 2
Saros Körfezi 116 C 2
Saroto 119 N 2
Sarpa 117 G 1
Sarpinskaya Nizmennost' 117 G 1
Sarpsborg 113 F 4
Sarralbe 115 E 2
Sarrebourg 115 E 2
Sarreguemines 115 E 2

Sars 118 L 4
Sartang 131 O 2
Sartène 115 E 3
Sarthe 114 C 2
Sartlan, Ozero 119 P 4–5
Sarto 178 D 3
Sartyn'ya 119 MN 3
Saruhanlı 116 C 3
Sarvestān 128 E 5
Sárvár 116 A 1
Sárviz 116 A 1
Sary 118 L 4
Sarych, Mys 117 D 2
Sary Ishikotrau, Peski 119 P 6
Sarykamysh, Ozero 128 F 2
Saryoba 128 G 1
Sary-Ozek 129 K 2
Sary-Shagan 119 O 6
Sarysu 129 H 1
Sary-Tash 129 J 3
Sasa Baneh 159 G 3
Sasamungga 145 G 3
Sasaram 134 D 3
Sasar, Tanjung 137 E 5
Sasebo 133 J 4
Saskatchewan 167 QR 5
Saskatoon 167 Q 5
Saskylakh 130 K 1
Saslaya 172 F 5
Sason Dağları 117 F 3
Sasovo 118 H 5
Sassandra 156 C 5
Sassandra (River) 156 C 4
Sassari 115 E 3
Sassuolo 115 F 3
Sas-Tobe 129 J 2
Sastre 182 D 5
Sasykkol', Ozero 119 Q 6
Sasyk Ozero (Russia, U.S.S.R.) 117 D 1
Sasyk, Ozero (Ukraina, U.S.S.R.) 116 C 1
Satadougou 156 B 3
Satakunta 112 H 3
Satara (India) 134 B 4
Satara (U.S.S.R.) 131 O 2
Satawal 146 A 2
Satawan 146 B 2
Säter 113 G 3
Satmala Range 134 C 4
Satna 134 D 3
Satoou 157 F 3
Sátoraljaújhely 116 B 1
Satpura Range 134 C 3
Sattahip 135 H 5
Satthwa 135 G 4
Sattur 134 C 6
Satu Mare 116 B 1
Satun 135 H 6
Sauðarkrókur 112 B 1
Sauce 182 E 5
Sauceda Mountains 170 D 5
Saucillo 170 E 6
Sauda 113 E 4
Saudi Arabia 155 GH 3–4
Sauiá 179 G 4
Sauk Centre 171 H 2
Saúl 179 H 3
Saulieu 114 D 2
Sault Sainte Marie 171 K 2
Saumarez Reef 143 J 3
Saumlaki 137 H 5
Saumur 114 C 2
Saundersfoot 102 B 2
Saungai Sesayap 136 E 3
Saßnitz 111 F 4
Saura 128 E 2
Saurimo 160 C 1
Sautar 160 B 2
Sava 116 A 2
Savai'i 147 D 3
Savalou 157 E 4
Savanna 168 J 4
Savannah 171 K 5
Savannah River 171 K 5
Savannakhet 135 H 4
Savanna la Mar 173 G 4
Savant Lake 168 J 5
Savanur 134 C 5
Sävar 112 H 3
Savaştepe 116 C 3
Savé (Benin) 156 E 4
Save (Mozambique) 161 E 4
Sāveh 128 E 3
Savelugu 156 D 4
Saverdun 114 D 3
Saverne 115 E 2
Savigliano 115 E 3
Savino 118 K 2
Sävirşin 116 B 1

Savitaipale 112 J 3
Savo 112 J 3
Savoie 115 E 2
Savona 115 E 3
Savonlinna 112 J 3
Savonselkä 112 J 3
Savoonga 166 C 3
Savukoski 112 J 2
Savur 117 F 3
Sawah 136 E 3
Sawahlunto 136 B 4
Sawai Madhopur 134 C 2
Sawākin 154 F 5
Sawang 136 B 3
Sawankhalok 135 G 4
Sawatch Range 170 E 4
Sawbā 158 E 3
Sawbridgeworth 103 E 2
Sawdirī 154 D 6
Sawek 137 J 4
Sawel 100 B 2
Sawḥāj 154 E 3
Sawmill Bay 167 O 2
Sawno 111 G 4
Şawqirah 155 K 5
Sawtayr 154 E 5
Sawtooth Mountains 171 H 2
Sawu Laut 137 F 5
Sawu, Pulau 137 F 6
Şawwān, Arḍ aş 154 F 2
Saxmundham 103 E 1
Say 156 E 3
Sayaboury 135 H 4
Sayak 119 P 6
Sayakskaya Pristan' 119 P 6
Sayán 179 C 6
Sayang, Pulau 137 G 3
Sayan Vostochnyy 130 F H 5
Sayan, Zapadnyy 130 F 5
Sayat 129 G 3
Saydā 154 F 2
Saydy 131 O 2
Sayḥūt 155 J 5
Saynshand 132 F 2
Sayram Hu 129 L 2
Saywūn 155 H 5
Sázava 111 F 4
Sazdy 128 D 1
Sazin 129 J 3
Sbaa 152 E 3
Scaër 114 C 2
Scafell Pike 101 D 2
Scaife Mountains 185
Scalea 115 G 4
Scalone, Passo dello 115 G 4
Scalpay 98 B 3
Scammon Bay 166 D 3
Scapa Flow 98 C 2
Ščara 111 H 4
Scaramia, Capo 115 F 4
Scarba 99 B 3
Scarborough (U.K.) 101 E 2
Scarborough (Trinidad and Tobago) 179 F 1
Scarp 98 A 2
Schaffhausen 115 E 2
Schärding 115 F 2
Schefferville 169 O 5
Schelde 110 D 4
Schenectady 171 M 3
Schio 115 F 2
Schiltigheim 115 E 2
Schladming 115 F 2
Schleswig 111 E 4
Schleswig-Holstein 111 E 4
Schneeberg 111 F 4
Schönebeck 111 F 4
Schouten Islands 144 D 2
Schuls → Scoul 115 F 2
Schultz Lake 167 S 3
Schurz 170 C 4
Schwabach 111 F 5
Schwäbische Alp 111 E 5
Schwäbisch Hall 111 E 5
Schwaner, Pegunungan 136 D 4
Schwarzwald 111 E 5
Schwatka Mountains 166 F 2
Schwaz 115 F 2
Schwedt 111 F 4
Schweinfurt 111 F 4
Schweiz 115 E 2
Schweizer Reneke 160 D 5
Schwerin 111 F 4
Schwyz 115 E 2
Sciacca 115 F 4
Scicli 115 F 4
Scilly, Isles of 110 B 5
Scioto River 171 K 4
Scoresby Sound 184

Scoresbysund 184
Scotia Ridge 192 A 5
Scotia Sea 185
Scotland 110 C 3
Scotlandville 171 H 5
Scott (Canada) 167 Q 5
Scott (Antarctica) 185
Scottburgh 161 E 6
Scott, Cape (Australia) 142 D 1
Scott, Cape (Canada) 166 M 5
Scott City 170 F 4
Scott Island 185
Scott Reef 142 C 1
Scottsbluff 170 F 3
Scottsdale (U.S.A.) 170 D 5
Scottsdale (Australia) 144 L 9
Scottsville 171 J 4
Scourie 98 B 2
Scranton 171 L 3
Scugog, Lake 171 L 3
Scunthorpe 101 E 3
Scuol 115 F 2
Scutari, Lake → Skardarsko Jezero 116 A 2
Seabra 181 H 3
Seabrook, Lake 142 B 5
Seaford 103 E 2
Seahorse Point 167 V 3
Sea Islands 171 K 5
Seal 167 S 4
Sea of Crete 116 BC 3
Sea of Japan 133 KL 3
Sea of Marmara → Marmara Denizi 116 C 2
Sea of Okhotsk 131 R 4,5
Sea of the Hebrides 98 A 3
Seaside 170 B 2
Seaton 102 C 2
Seaton Delaval 101 E 2
Seattle 170 B 2
Seba 137 F 6
Sebanka, Pulau 136 B 3
Sebastián Vizcaino, Bahía 170 D 6
Sebatik, Pulau 136 E 3
Sebba 156 E 3
Sébé 157 G 6
Sébékoro 156 C 3
Sebeş 116 B 1
Sebewaing 171 K 3
Sebezh 113 J 4
Sebha Oasis → Wāhāt Sabhā 153 H 3
Sebha → Sabhā 153 H 3
Şebinkarahisar 117 E 2
Sebjet Agsumal 152 C 4
Sebjet Aridal 152 C 3
Sebkha Azzel Matti 152 F 3
Sebkha de Ndrhamcha 152 B 5
Sebkha de Rhallamane 152 D 4
Sebkha de Timimoun 152 F 3
Sebkha de Tindouf 152 D 3
Sebkha Iguetti 152 D 3
Sebkha Mekerrhane 153 F 3
Se Sebkha Oumm ed Droûs Telli 152 C 4
Sebkha Tah 152 C 3
Sebkhet Idjil 152 C 4
Sebkhet Oumm ed Droûs Guebli 152 C 4
Sebkra de Timimoun 152 F 3
Sebou 152 D 2
Sebring 171 K 6
Sebuku, Pulau 136 E 4
Sebuku, Teluk 136 E 3
Secchia 115 F 3
Sechura 178 B 5
Sechura, Bahía de 178 B 5
Sechura, Desierto de 178 B 5
Second Baku 108
Secunderabad 134 C 4
Seda 114 B 4
Sedah 137 F 6
Sedalia 171 H 4
Sedan 115 D 2
Sedanka 166 D 5
Sedano 114 C 3
Sedbergh 101 D 2
Seddenga 154 E 4
Sededema 131 S 2
Sedel'nikovo 119 P 4
Sédhiou 156 A 3
Sedona 170 D 5
Seeheim 160 B 5
Sées 114 D 2
Seesen 111 F 4
Şefaatli 117 E 3
Sefadu 156 B 4
Sefrou 152 E 2
Segag 159 G 3
Segamat 136 B 3
Segantur 136 E 3
Sebgana 156 E 3
Segesta 115 F 4

Seget 137 H 4
Segeza 113 K 3
Seghe 145 G 2
Seghnän 129 J 3
Segine I-yy 131 P 3
Segorbe 114 C 4
Ségou 156 C 3
Segovia 114 C 3
Segozero, Ozero 112 K 3
Segré (France) 114 C 2
Segre (Spain) 114 D 3
Seguam 166 C 5
Séguédine 157 G 1
Séguéla 156 C 4
Seguin 170 G 6
Segula 166 A 5
Segura 114 C 4
Segura, Sierra de 114 C 4
Sehithwa 160 C 4
Sehore 134 C 3
Sehwan 129 G 5
Seil 99 B 3
Seiland 112 H 1
Seinäjoki 112 G 3
Seine 114 D 2
Seine, Baie de la 114 C 2
Sejerö 113 F 4
Sekatak, Muara 136 E 3
Sekayu 136 B 4
Seke 158 E 5
Sekenke 158 E 5
Seki 116 C 3
Sekkemo 112 H 2
Sekoma 160 C 4
Sekondi-Takoradi 156 D 5
Sekondya 131 M 2
Se Kong 135 J 4
Selaru, Pulau 137 H 5
Selassi 137 H 4
Selat Alas 136 E 5
Selat Alor 137 F 5
Selatan, Pulau 136 B 4
Selatan, Tanjung 136 D 4
Selat Bangka 136 C 4
Selat Berhala 136 B 4
Selat Dampier 137 H 4
Selat Gaspar 136 C 4
Selat Jailolo 137 G 4
Selat Karimata 136 C 4
Selat Laut 136 E 4
Selat Lombok 136 E 5
Selat Madura 136 D 5
Selat Makassar 136 E 4
Selat Manipa 137 G 4
Selat Mentawai 136 A 4
Selat Morotai 137 G 3
Selat Obi 137 G 4
Selat Ombai 137 G 5
Selat Peleng 137 F 4
Selat Roti 137 F 6
Selat Salue Timpaus 137 F 4
Selat Sape 137 E 5
Selat Selayar 137 F 5
Selat Serasan 136 C 3
Selat Sumba 137 E 5
Selat Sunda 136 B 5
Selat Tiworo 137 F 4
Selat Wetar 137 G 5
Selat Yapen 137 J 4
Selawik 166 E 2
Selawik Lake 166 F 2
Selayar, Pulau 137 F 5
Selayar, Selat 137 F 5
Selbu 112 F 3
Selby (U.S.A.) 170 F 2
Selby (U.K.) 101 E 3
Selçuk 116 C 3
Seldovia 166 G 4
Selebi-Pikwe 160 D 4
Selebir 131 O 5
Selemdzha 131 O 5
Selemdzhinsk 131 O 5
Selendi 116 C 3
Selenduma 130 J 5
Selenge 130 H 6
Selenge (Mongolia) 130 J 6
Selenge (Zaïre) 158 B 5
Selennyakh 131 Q 2
Sélestat 113 E 2
Selety 119 O 5
Seletyteniz, Ozero 119 O 5
Selfoss 112 A 2
Selgon 131 P 6
Sélibaby 152 C 5
Selim 117 F 2
Selima Oasis → Wāḥāt Salīmah 154 D 4
Selinunte 115 F 4
Seliyarovo 119 O 3
Selizharovo 118 F 4
Seljord 113 E 4
Selkirk 99 C 4

Selkirk Mountains 167 O 5
Sella di Conza 115 G 3
Selle, Pic de la 173 H 4
Sellyakhskaya Guba 131 P 1
Selma (AL, U.S.A.) 171 J 5
Selma (CA, U.S.A.) 170 C 4
Selong 136 E 5
Selous Game Reserve 159 F 6
Selsey Bill 103 D 2
Selty 118 K 4
Selukwe → Shurugwi 160 DE 3
Selva 182 D 4
Selvagens, Ilhas 152 B 2
Selvänä 128 C 3
Selvas 178–179 EF 5
Selwyn 143 G 3
Selwyn Lake 167 R 4
Selwyn Mountains 166 L 3
Semani 116 A 2
Semara 152 C 3
Samarang 136 D 5
Sematan 136 C 3
Semau, Pulau 137 F 6
Sembakung, Sungai 136 E 3
Sembé 157 G 5
Şemdinli 117 F 3
Semenovskiy, Ostrov 131 O 1
Semichi Islands 166 A 5
Semidi Islands 166 F 4
Semikarakorskiy 117 F 1
Semiluki 118 G 5
Semiozernoye 119 M 5
Semipalatinsk 119 Q 5
Semirara Islands 137 F 1
Semisopochnoi 166 A 5
Semitau 136 D 3
Semium 136 C 3
Semiyarka 119 P 5
Semiz-Bugu 119 OP 5
Semliki 158 D 4
Semmedaban, Khrebet 131 P 3
Semnän 128 E 3
Semporna 137 E 3
Sem Tripa 179 H 4
Semuda 136 D 4
Sena (Bolivia) 180 C 3
Sena (Mozambique) 161 E 3
Senador Canedo 181 G 4
Senador Pompeu 181 J 2
Senaja 136 E 2
Sena Madureira 178 E 5
Senanga 160 C 3
Sendai 133 K 4
Sendai 133 M 3
Sendai-wan 133 M 3
Sendelingsdrif 160 B 5
Sêndo 132 C 4
Senegal 156 AB 3
Sénégal (River) 156 B 2
Senekal 160 D 5
Seney 171 J 2
Senftenberg 111 F 4
Sênggê Zangbo 134 D 1
Sengiri, Mys 128 E 2
Sengkang 137 F 4
Senhor do Bonfim 181 H 3
Senigallia 115 F 3
Senja 112 G 2
Senjavin Islands 146 B 2
Senjsko Bilo 115 G 3
Senkaku-shotō 133 H 5
Şenkaya 117 F 2
Senkyabasa 130 K 2
Sennaya 117 F 1
Senneterre 171 L 2
Senno 113 J 5
Sennybridge 102 C 2
Seno de Otway 183 B 9
Senorbi 115 E 3
Seno Skyring 183 B 9
Sens 114 D 2
Senta 116 B 1
Sentani 144 D 2
Sentinel Peak 167 N 5
Şenyurt 117 F 3
Seo de Urgel 114 D 3
Seoni 134 C 3
Seoul 133 J 3
Sepanjang, Pulau 136 E 5
Separation Point 169 Q 5
Sepasu 136 E 3
Sepik 146 A 3
Sepik River 144 D 2
Sepone 135 J 4
Sept-Îles 169 O 5
Sequillo 114 B 3
Sequoia National Park 170 C 4
Şerafettin Dağları 117 F 3
Seraing 110 E 4
Serakhs 129 G 3
Seram 137 G 4
Seram, Laut 137 G 4
Seram Laut, Kepulauan 137 H 4

Serang 136 C 5
Serasan, Pulau 136 C 3
Serasan, Selat 136 C 3
Serbia 116 B 2
Serdo 159 G 2
Serdobsk 118 H 5
Serebryansk 119 Q 6
Serebryanskiy 112 L 2
Sered 111 G 5
Seredka 113 J 4
Şereflikoçhisar 117 D 3
Seremban 136 B 3
Serengeti National Park 158 EF 5
Serengeti Plain 158 EF 5
Serenje 161 E 2
Sergach 118 J 4
Sergelen 130 J 6
Sergeyevo 119 R 4
Sergino 119 N 3
Sergipe 181 J 3
Sergiyevka 117 F 2
Seria 136 D 3
Serian 136 D 3
Sérifos 116 B 3
Serifou, Sténon 116 B 3
Serik 116 D 3
Seringapatam Reef 142 C 1
Seringa, Serra da 179 H 5
Serkovo 119 R 2
Sernovodsk 118 K 5
Sernyy-Zavod 128 F 2
Serov 119 M 4
Serowe 160 D 4
Serpa 114 B 4
Serpentine Lakes 142 D 4
Serpiente, Boca de la 179 F 1–2
Serpukhov 118 G 5
Serra Acarai 179 G 3
Serra Bom Jesus da Gurguéia 181 H 2
Serra Bonita 181 G 4
Serra da Bodoquena 180 D 5
Serra da Canastra 181 G 4
Serra da Chela 160 A 3
Serra da Estrela (Brazil) 181 F 4
Serra da Estrêla (Portugal) 114 B 3
Serra da Gorongosa 161 E 3
Serra da Ibiapaba 181 H 1–2
Serra da Mantiqueira 181 H 5
Serra da Neve 160 A 2
Serra da Providência 180 D 3
Serra das Alpercatas 179 JK 5
Serra das Araras 181 F 4
Serra das Cordilheiras 179 J 5
Serra da Seringa 179 H 5
Serra da Tabatinga 181 H 3
Serra de Alvelos 114 B 4
Serra de Caldeirão 114 B 4
Serra de Grândola 114 B 4
Serra de Itiúba 181 HJ 3
Serra de Maracaju 180–181 EF 5
Serra de Nogueira 114 B 3
Serra de São Jerônimo 181 EF 4
Serra de São Mamede 114 B 4
Serra do Aguapeí 180 E 4
Serra do Apiaú 179 F 3
Serra do Cachimbo 179 G 5
Serra do Caiapó 181 F 4
Serra do Caramulo 114 B 3
Serra do Chifre 181 H 4
Serra do Divisor 178 D 5
Serra do Escorial 181 H 3
Serra do Espinhaço 181 H 4
Serra do Estrondo 179 J 5
Serra do Gerás 114 B 3
Serra do Gurupi 179 J 5
Serra do Jibão 181 G 4
Serra do Mar 181 G 6
Serra do Marêo 114 B 3
Serra do Matão 179 H 5
Serra do Mogadouro 114 B 3
Serra do Navio 179 H 3
Serra do Paraiso 181 H 3–4
Serra do Paranapiacaba 181 G 5
Serra do Penitente 179 J 5
Serra do Ramalho 181 H 3
Serra do Roncador 181 F 3
Serra dos Aimorés 181 H 4
Serra dos Apiacás 181 E 2–3
Serra do Sargento Paixão 180 DE 3
Serra dos Caiabis 180 E 3
Serra dos Carajás 179 H 5
Serra dos Gradaús 179 H 5
Serra dos Pacaás Novos 180 D 3
Serra dos Parecis 180 DE 3
Serra dos Xavantes 181 G 3
Serra do Tiracambu 181 G 1
Serra do Tombador 180 E 3

Serra Dourada 181 G 3
Serra do Uruçuí 181 GH 2
Serra Formosa 181 E 3
Serra Geral 182 F 4
Serra Geral de Goiás 181 G 3
Serra Geral do Paraná 181 G 3
Serra Geral ou Grande 181 G 3
Serra Grande 181 H 2
Serrai 116 B 2
Serralbe 115 E 2
Serra Lombarda 179 H 3
Serra Negra 179 J 5
Serrana, Banco de 173 FG 5
Serrana, Banco de 173 FG 5
Serranía de Baudó 178 C 2
Serranía de Huanchaca 180 D 3
Serranía de Imataca 179 F 2
Serranía del Darién 178 C 2
Serranía de Santiago 180 DE 4
Serranía de Tabasara 178 B 2
Serranías Turagua 179 F 2
Serranilla, Banco 173 G 4
Serra Nova 179 F 5
Serra San Bruno 115 G 4
Serra Talhada 181 J 2
Serra Tumucumaque 179 H 3
Serra Urubuquara 179 H 4
Serre-Ponçon Reservoir de 115 E 3
Serres 115 E 3
Serrezuela 182 C 5
Serrinha 181 J 3
Serrota 114 B 3
Sertã 114 B 4
Sêrtar 132 D 4
Sertavul Geçidi 117 D 3
Serui 137 J 4
Serule 160 D 4
Seruyan, Sungai 136 D 4
Servia 116 B 2
Serwaru 137 G 5
Sêrxü 132 C 4
Seryshevo 131 N 5
Sesao 156 E 2
Sesayap 136 E 3
Sesayap, Sungai 136 E 3
Seseganaga Lake 168 J 5
Sese Islands 158 E 4
Sesfontein 160 A 3
Seshachalam Hills 134 C 5
Sesheke 160 C 3
Sesibi 154 E 4
Sesimbra 114 B 4
Seskarö 112 H 2
Sessa Aurunca 115 F 3
Sesto Fiorentino 115 F 3
Sestri Levante 115 E 3
Sestroretsk 112 K 3
Sesupé 113 H 5
Sesvete 115 G 2
Setana 133 L 2
Séte 115 D 3
Sete Lagoas 181 H 4
Sete Quedas, Cachoeira das 179 G 4–5
Sete Quedas, Salto das 181 F 5
Setermoen 112 G 2
Setesdal 113 E 4
Sétif 153 G 1
Seto-naikai 133 K 4
Settat 152 D 2
Setté Cama 157 F 6
Sette Daban, Khrebet 131 P 3,4
Settle 101 D 2
Setúbal 114 B 4
Setúbal, Baía de 114 B 4
Seui 115 E 3
Seumanyam 136 A 3
Sevan 117 F 2
Sevan, Ozero 117 G 2
Sevarujo 180 C 4
Sevastopol' 117 D 2
Sevenoaks 103 E 2
Seven Pagodas → Mahabalipuram 134 D 5
Sever 131 V 3
Severino Ribeiro 182 E 5
Severn 110 C 4
Severnaya 119 R 2
Severnaya Bruingra 131 N 4
Severnaya Sos'va 119 MN 3
Severnaya Zemlya 184
Severnayy 118 J 2
Severn Bridge 102 C 2
Severn Lake 168 J 5
Severnoye 118 K 5
Severnoye 119 P 4
Severn, River (Gloucestershire) 102 C 2
Severn River (Ont., Can.) 168 K 4
Severn, River (Powys) 102 C 1
Severnykh 128 C 2
Severnyy 119 M 2

Severnyy Anyuyskiy Khrebet 131 U 2–W 2
Severnyy Dvina 118 H 3
Severnyy Ural 119 L 3
Severo Baykal'skoye Nagor'ye 130 K 4
Severodvinsk 118 G 3
Severo-Kuril'sk 131 T 5
Severomorsk 113 K 2
Severo-Sibirskaya Nizmennost' 130 E 1–L 3
Severoural'sk 119 L 3
Severo-Yeniseyskiy 130 F 3
Severskiy Donets 118 G 6
Severskiy Donets 117 F 1
Sevier 170 D 4
Sevier Desert 170 D 4
Sevilla 114 B 4
Sevlijevo 116 C 2
Sevola 116 B 1
Sevrey 132 D 2
Sewa 156 B 4
Seward (AK, U.S.A.) 166 H 3
Seward (NE, U.S.A.) 170 G 3
Seward Peninsula 166 E 2
Sewell 182 B 5
Seyah Band Koh 129 G 4
Sëyakha 119 N 1
Sëyakha 119 O 1
Seychelles 159 J 5
Seychelles Bank 192 B 4
Seydişehir 117 D 3
Seyfe Gölü 117 D 3
Seyhan 117 E 3
Seyhan Barajı 117 E 3
Seyðisfjörður 112 C 2
Seyitgazi 116 D 3
Seyla' 159 G 2
Seymchan 131 S 3
Seymour (S. Africa) 160 D 6
Seymour (Australia) 143 H 6
Seymour (U.S.A.) 171 J 4
Seyyedābād 129 H 4
Sežana 115 F 2
Sfax 153 H 2
Sferracavallo, Capo 115 E 4
Sfintu, Gheorghe, Bratul 116 C 1
Sfîntu Gheorghe, Ostruvul 116 C 1
'S-Gravenhage 110 D 4
Shaanxi 132 E 4
Shaartuz 129 H 3
Shaba 158 CD 6
Shabani → Zvishavane 160 DE 4
Shäbelle, Webi 159 G 4
Shabelsk 117 E 1
Shabunda 158 D 5
Shabwah 155 H 5
Shache 129 K 3
Shackleton Ice Shelf 185
Shackleton Range 185
Shaddādī 155 G 1
Shädegän 128 D 4
Shadrinsk 119 M 4
Shadwān 154 E 3
Shadzud 129 J 3
Shaftesbury 103 C 2
Shageluk 166 F 3
Shagonar 130 F 5
Shah Alam 136 B 3
Shahbandar 129 H 6
Shahdol 134 D 3
Shah Fuladi 129 H 4
Shaḥḥāt 153 K 2
Shahjahanpur 134 C 2
Shāh Kūh 128 F 4
Shahmīrzad 128 E 3
Shahpura 134 D 3
Shahpura 134 BC 2
Shahrak 129 G 4
Shahr Kord 128 E 4
Shahtinsk 129 J 1
Shā'ib al Banāt, Jabal 154 E 3
Shaikh Dāgh 128 C 3
Shaim 119 MN 3
Shajapur 134 C 3
Shakawe 160 C 3
Shakhrisyabz 129 H 3
Shakhtersk 131 Q 6
Shakhterskiy 131 X 3
Shakhty 117 F 1
Shakhun'ya 118 J 4
Shaki 156 E 4
Shaksgam 129 K 3
Shaktoolik 166 E 3
Shalakusha 118 H 3
Shala, Lake 159 F 3
Shalamzār 128 E 4
Shalänböd 159 GH 4
Shaler Mountains 167 P 1
Shalgacheva 118 G 3
Shalgiya 119 O 6
Shali 117 F 1
Shalkar 118 K 5

277

Sha–Sig

Shaluli Shan 132 C 4
Shalunti 135 G 2
Shalya 119 L 4
Shalym 119 R 5
Shamattawa 167 T 4
Shambe 158 E 3
Shambo 159 F 3
Shām, Jabal ash (Oman) 155 J 5
Shām, Jabal ash (Oman) 155 K 4
Shammar, Jabal 155 G 3
Shamokin 171 L 3
Shamrock 170 F 4
Shamsī 154 D 5
Shamuhombo 158 B 6
Shamva 161 E 3
Shan 135 G 3
Shandan 132 D 3
Shandī 154 E 5
Shandong 133 G 3
Shandong Bandao 133 H 3
Shangaly 118 H 3
Shangani 160 D 3
Shangcai 132 F 4
Shangcheng 132 G 4
Shangchuan Dao 132 F 6
Shangdu 132 F 2
Shanghai 133 H 4
Shanghang 132 G 5
Shanglin 132 E 6
Shangnan 132 F 4
Shangombo 160 C 3
Shangqiu 132 G 4
Shangrao 133 G 5
Shangsi 132 E 6
Shang Xian 132 E 4
Shangyi 132 F 2
Shangzhi 133 J 1
Shanh 130 H 6
Shani 157 G 3
Shanklin 103 D 2
Shankou 132 B 2
Shannon 110 B 4
Shannon, Mouth of the 110 A 4
Shannon, River 100 B 3
Shano 159 F 3
Shanshan 132 B 2
Shantarskiye Ostrova 131 P 4
Shantou 132 G 6
Shantung Peninsula → Shandong Bandao 133 H 3
Shanxi 132 F 3
Shanyin 132 F 3
Shaodong 132 F 5
Shaoguan 132 F 6
Shaoshan 132 F 5
Shaowu 133 G 5
Shaoxing 133 H 5
Shaoyang 132 F 5
Shapinsay 98 C 2
Shapkina 118 K 2
Shāpūr 128 E 5
Shaqqat al Kharītah 155 H 5
Shaqrā' 155 H 6
Sharāf 155 G 2
Sharafah 154 D 6
Sharāh, Jibāl ash 154 F 2
Sharan 118 K 5
Sharbithāt, Ra's 155 K 5
Sharjah → Ash Shāriqah 155 K 3
Shark Bay 142 A 4
Sharlauk 128 F 3
Sharlyk 118 K 5
Sharm ash Shaykh 154 E 3
Sharqī, Jabal ash 154 F 2
Sharshar, Jabal 154 E 4
Shary 155 G 3
Shar'ya 118 J 4
Sharypovo 119 R 4
Shashamanna 159 F 3
Shashe 160 D 4
Shashi 132 F 4
Shasta Lake 170 B 3
Shasta, Mount 170 B 3
Shatsk 118 H 5
Shatt al 'Arab 155 H 2
Shatt al Fijāj 153 G 2
Shatt al Jarīd 153 G 2
Shaunavon 167 Q 6
Shaviklde 117 G 2
Shawan 129 M 2
Shawāq 154 F 3
Shawinigan 171 M 2
Shawnee 171 G 4
Sha Xian 133 G 5
Shaybārā 154 F 3
Shaykh Sa'd 155 H 2
Shaykh 'Uthmān 155 H 6
Shchara 113 J 4
Shchel'yayur 118 K 2
Shcherbakty 119 P 5
Shchigry 111 G 5
Shchuchin 113 H 5
Shchuchinsk 119 N 5

Shchuch'ya 119 N 2
Shchuch'ye 119 M 4
Shea Ghimirra 158 F 3
Shebalin 117 F 1
Shebalino 119 R 5
Shebekino 118 G 5
Sheboygan 171 J 3
Shebshi Mountains 157 G 4
Shebunino 131 Q 6
Shedin Peak 167 M 4
Shedok 117 F 2
Sheelin, Lough 100 B 3
Sheenjek 166 J 2
Sheerness 103 E 2
Sheet Harbour 169 P 7
Sheffield (U.K.) 101 E 3
Sheffield (AL, U.S.A.) 171 J 5
Shegarka 119 Q 4
Shehong 132 E 4
Sheikh Idris 154 E 6
Shekhawati 134 C 2
Shekhupura 129 J 4
Sheki 128 D 2
Shelburne 169 O 7
Sheldon Point 166 D 3
Shelekhov 130 H 5
Shelekhova 131 T 5
Shelikhova, Zaliv 131 T 3,4
Shelikof Strait 166 G 4
Shellbrook 167 Q 5
Shellharbour 143 J 5
Shell Lakes 142 D 4
Shelopugino 130 L 5
Shemakha 128 D 2
Shemonaikha 119 Q 5
Shenandoah National Park 171 L 4
Shenber 129 H 1
Shenchi 132 F 3
Shendam 157 F 4
Shenge 156 B 4
Shengsi Liedao 133 H 4
Sheng Xian 133 H 5
Shenkursk 118 H 3
Shenmu 132 F 3
Shenqiu 132 G 4
Shenton, Mount 142 C 4
Shenyang 133 H 2
Shenze 132 G 3
Shenzhen 132 F 6
Sheopur 134 C 2
Shepetovka 113 J 5
Shepparton 143 H 6
Shepperd, Lake 142 C 4
Shepton Mallet 102 C 2
Sherborne 102 C 2
Sherbro Island 156 B 4
Sherbrooke 169 N 6
Sherda 157 H 1
Shere Hill 157 F 4
Sheridan 170 E 3
Sheringham 103 E 1
Sherkaly 119 N 3
Sherlovaya Gora 130 L 5
Sherman 171 G 5
Sherman Station 171 N 2
Sherpur 134 E 3
Sherridon 167 R 4
Shetland Islands 98 D 1
Shevchenko 128 E 2
Shevykan 130 J 5
Sheya 130 L 3
Sheyang 133 H 4
Sheyenne River 170 G 2
Shiant Isles 98 A 3
Shiashkotan, Ostrov 131 S 6
Shibām 155 H 5
Shibarghan 129 H 3
Shibazhan 131 N 5
Shibeli, Webbe 159 G 3
Shibīn al Kawm 154 E 2
Shibogama Lake 168 K 5
Shibotsu Jima 131 R 7
Shicheng Dao 133 H 3
Shidao 133 H 3
Shidian 132 C 6
Shiel, Loch 99 B 3
Shifā', Jabal ash 154 F 3
Shihezi 129 M 2
Shijiazhuang 132 F 3
Shikarpur 129 G 5
Shikoku 133 K 4
Shikotan 131 R 7
Shila 130 F 4
Shilabo 159 G 3
Shildon 101 E 2
Shilikarym 119 Q 6
Shilka 130 L 5
Shilkan 131 R 4
Shilla 134 C 1
Shillong 135 F 2

Shilovo 118 H 5
Shimanovsk 131 N 5
Shimian 132 D 5
Shimizu 133 L 3
Shimoga 134 C 5
Shimo la Tewa 159 F 5
Shimoni 159 F 5
Shimonoseki 133 K 4
Shīnak Pass 155 GH 1
Shindand 129 G 4
Shingbwiyang 135 G 2
Shinghar 129 H 4
Shingozha 119 Q 6
Shingshal 129 K 3
Shingū 133 L 4
Shinjō 133 M 3
Shinkafi 157 F 3
Shinyanga 158 E 5
Ship Canal 101 D 3
Shiping 132 D 6
Shipley 101 E 3
Shippegan 169 P 6
Shipston-on-Stour 103 D 1
Shipunovo 119 Q 5
Shipunskiy, Mys 131 U 5
Shiquan 132 E 4
Shiquanhe 134 C 1
Shir 128 E 4
Shirabad 129 H 3
Shirase Glacier 185
Shire 161 F 3
Shirikrabat 129 G 2
Shiriya-zaki 133 M 2
Shirley Mountains 170 E 3
Shirokaya Pad 131 Q 5
Shirokostan, Poluostrov 131 PQ 1
Shirokovo 130 G 4
Shirokoye 117 D 1
Shīrvān 128 F 3
Shīrvān 128 H 4
Shisanzhan 131 N 5
Shishaldin Volcano 166 E 5
Shishmaref 166 D 2
Shishou 132 F 5
Shithāthah 155 G 2
Shiveluch, Sopka 131 U 4
Shivpuri 134 C 2
Shiwan Dashan 132 E 6
Shiwa Ngandu 161 E 2
Shiyan 132 F 4
Shizong 132 D 6
Shizuishan 132 E 3
Shizuoka 133 L 4
Shkodra 116 A 2
Shmidta, Poluostrov 131 Q 5
Shnezhnoye 117 E 1
Shoa 159 F 3
Sholapur 134 C 4
Shoptykul' 119 P 5
Shorapur 134 C 4
Shorawak 129 H 4
Shoreham-by-Sea 103 D 2
Shortandy 119 O 5
Shoshone 170 C 3
Shoshone Peak 170 C 4
Shoshong 160 D 4
Shoshoni 170 E 3
Shostka 118 F 5
Shouguang 133 G 3
Shou Xian 133 G 4
Showa 185
Show Low 170 E 5
Shoyna 118 H 2
Shpakovskoye 117 F 1
Shqiperia 116 AB 2
Shreveport 171 H 5
Shrewsbury 102 C 1
Shuangcheng 133 J 1
Shuangjiang 132 C 6
Shuangliao 133 H 3
Shuangyang 133 J 2
Shuangyashan 133 K 1
Shu'ayt 155 J 5
Shubar-Kuduk 128 F 1
Shucheng 133 G 4
Shufu 129 K 3
Shuga 119 O 2
Shuga 119 P 5
Shugur 119 N 3
Shuguri Falls 159 F 6
Shuicheng 132 D 5
Shūl 128 E 4
Shulan 133 J 2
Shule 129 K 3
Shule He 132 C 2
Shulehe 132 C 2
Shulu 132 G 3
Shumagin Islands 166 F 4
Shumerlya 118 J 4

Shumikha 119 M 4
Shumshu, Ostrov 131 T 5
Shumskiy 130 G 5
Shunak, Gora 129 J 1
Shunchang 133 G 5
Shungnak 166 F 2
Shuolong 132 E 6
Shuo Xian 132 F 3
Shūr 128 F 5
Shūrāb 128 F 4
Shūr Gaz 128 F 5
Shurinda 130 K 4
Shurugwi 160 DE 3
Shushenskoye 130 F 5
Shūshtar 128 D 4
Shuwak 154 F 6
Shuya 118 H 4
Shuya 112 K 3
Shuyak 166 G 4
Shuyang 133 G 4
Shveli 131 O 5
Shwebo 135 G 3
Shwegun 135 G 4
Shwegyin 135 G 4
Shweli 135 G 3
Shyok 129 K 3
Sia 135 H 5
Siahan Range 129 G 5
Siāh-Kūh 128 E 4
Siak Sri Indrapura 136 B 3
Siak, Sungai 136 B 3
Sialkot 129 J 4
Siam 135 H 4
Sian → Xi'an 132 E 4
Siapa 178 E 3
Siargao 137 G 2
Siassi 144 E 3
Šiauliai 113 H 4
Siavonga 160 D 3
Sibā'ī, Jabal as 154 E 3
Sibay 119 L 5
Šibenik 115 G 3
Siberut, Pulau 136 A 4
Sibigo 136 A 3
Sibirskiye Uvaly 119 N 3
Sibirskoye Ploskogorye, Sredne 130 G 2–K 3
Sibiti 157 G 6
Sibiu 116 B 1
Sibolga 136 A 3
Sibsagar 135 F 2
Sibu 136 D 3
Sibuguey Bay 137 F 2
Sibut 158 B 3
Sibutu, Pulau 137 F 1
Sibuyan 137 F 1
Sibuyan Sea 137 F 1
Sibvi 129 G 5
Sicani, Monti 115 F 4
Sicasica 180 C 4
Sichon 135 G 6
Sichuan 132 D 4
Sichuan Pendi 132 E 4
Sicilia 115 F 4
Sicilia, Canale de 115 F 4
Sicily 115 F 4
Sicuani 180 B 3
Sidamo 159 F 4
Sidaouet 157 F 2
Side 116 D 3
Sidéradougou 156 D 3
Siderno 115 G 4
Sidheros, Ákra 116 C 3
Sidhirokastrón 116 B 2
Sidhpur 134 B 3
Sidi Aïch 115 D 4
Sīdī Barrānī 154 D 2
Sidi-bel-Abbès 152 E 1
Sidi Bennour 152 D 2
Sidi Ifni 152 C 3
Sidi Kacem 152 D 2
Sidikalang 136 A 3
Sidi Krelil 153 G 2
Sidlaw Hills 99 C 3
Sidmouth 102 C 2
Sidney (Br.Col., Can.) 167 N 6
Sidney (MT, U.S.A.) 170 F 2
Sidney (NE, U.S.A.) 170 F 3
Sidney (OH, U.S.A.) 171 K 3
Sidon → Saydā 154 F 2
Sidorovsk 119 Q 2
Siedice 111 H 4
Siegburg 111 E 4
Siegen 111 E 4
Siegen-Kyuel' 131 O 3
Siem Reap 135 H 5
Siena 115 F 3
Sieradz 111 G 4
Sierpc 111 G 4
Sierra Añueque 183 C 7
Sierra Alamos 170 E 6
Sierra Auca Mahuida 183 C 6

Sierra Bermeja 114 B 4
Sierra Blanca 170 E 5
Sierra Chauchaiñeu 183 C 7
Sierra Cimaltepec 172 C 4
Sierra Colorada 183 C 7
Sierra de Agalta 172 E 4
Sierra de Alcaraz 114 C 4
Sierra de Alfabia 114 D 4
Sierra de Ancares 114 B 3
Sierra de Ancasti 182 C 4
Sierra de Aracena 114 B 4
Sierra de Coalcoman 172 B 4
Sierra de Córdoba 182 D 5
Sierra de Famatina 182 C 4
Sierra de Gata 114 B 3
Sierra de Gredos 114 BC 3
Sierra de Guadalupe 114 B 4
Sierra de Guadarrama 114 C 3
Sierra de Guampi 178 E 2
Sierra de Gúdar 114 C 3
Sierra de Gurupira 178 F 3
Sierra de Juarez 170 C 5
Sierra de la Almenara 114 C 4
Sierra de la Cabrera 114 B 3
Sierra de la Demanda 114 C 3
Sierra de la Encantada 172 B 2
Sierra de la Giganta 170 D 6
Sierra de la Peña 114 C 3
Sierra de la Pila 114 C 4
Sierra de las Estancias 114 C 4
Sierra de las Minas 172 E 4
Sierra de las Tunas 170 E 6
Sierra del Cadí 114 D 3
Sierra del Castañar 114 C 4
Sierra del Chorito 114 C 4
Sierra del Faro 114 B 3
Sierra del Huesco 170 E 5
Sierra del Moncayo 114 C 3
Sierra del Nevado 183 C 6
Sierra del Nido 170 E 6
Sierra de los Alamitos 172 B 2
Sierra de los Cuchumatanes 172 D 4
Sierra de los Huicholes 172 B 3
Sierra del Pedroso 114 B 4
Sierra de Martés 114 C 4
Sierra de Montsant 114 D 3
Sierra de Montsech 114 D 3
Sierra de Montseny 114 D 3
Sierra de Mulegé 170 D 6
Sierra de Parras 172 B 2
Sierra de Perijá 178 D 1–2
Sierra de Rañadoiro 114 B 3
Sierra de San Antonio 170 D 5
Sierra de San Borjas 170 D 6
Sierra de San Lázaro 170 D 7
Sierra de San Pedro 114 B 4
Sierra de San Pedro Martir 170 C 5
Sierra de San Vicente 114 C 3
Sierra de Segura 114 C 4
Sierra de Tepehuanes 172 A 2
Sierra Espinazo del Diablo 172 A 3
Sierra Gorda 180 C 5
Sierra Grande (Argentina) 183 C 7
Sierra Grande (Mexico) 170 F 6
Sierra Leone 156 B 4
Sierra Madre (Mexico) 172 D 4
Sierra Madre (Phil.) 137 J 1
Sierra Madre del Sur 172 BC 4
Sierra Madre de Oaxaca 172 C 4
Sierra Madre Occidental 170 E 6
Sierra Madre Oriental 172 C 3
Sierra Madrona 114 C 4
Sierra Maestra 173 G 3
Sierra Morena 114 BC 4
Sierra Nayarit 172 B 3
Sierra Nevada (U.S.A.) 170 BC 3–4
Sierra Nevada (Spain) 114 C 4
Sierra Nevada de Cocuy 178 D 2
Sierra Pacaraima 179 F 3
Sierra Parima 179 F 3
Sierra Prieta 170 D 5
Sierra San Pedro Mártir 170 C 5
Sierra Tarahumara 170 E 6
Sierra Tasajera 170 E 6
Sierra Velasco 182 C 4
Sierra Vizcaíno 170 D 6
Sierre 115 E 2
Sifani 159 G 2
Sifié 156 C 4
Sífnos 116 B 3
Sig 112 K 2
Sig 152 EF 1
Siğacık 116 C 3
Sigean, Étang de 114 D 3
Sighetu Marmației 116 B 1
Sighișoara 116 B 1
Sigiriya 134 D 6
Sigli 136 A 2
Siglufjörður 112 B 2

Signakhi 117 G 2
Signal Peak 170 D 5
Signy Island 185
Sigoisoinan 136 A 4
Sigovo 119 R 3
Sigsig 178 C 4
Sigtuna 113 G 4
Siguiri 156 C 3
Sigulda 113 H 4
Sihaung Myauk 135 F 3
Sihui 132 F 6
Siikajoki 112 J 3
Siilinjärvi 112 J 3
Siin 131 P 6
Siirt (Turkey) 117 F 3
Sikanni Chief 167 N 4
Sikar 134 C 2
Sikaram 129 H 4
Sikariman 136 A 4
Sikasso 156 C 3
Sikéa 116 B 3
Sikéa 116 B 2
Sikerin 131 Q 2
Sikeston 171 J 4
Sikfors 112 H 2
Sikhote-Alin 131 P 6
Síkinos 116 C 3
Sikkim 134 E 2
Siklós 116 A 1
Sikonge 158 E 6
Sikosi 160 C 3
Siktemey 131 S 2
Siktyakh 131 N 2
Sil 114 B 3
Silagui 136 A 4
Silba 115 F 3
Silchar 135 F 3
Sildagapet 112 D 3
Sile 116 C 2
Silesia 111 G 4
Silet 153 F 4
Silgarhi-Doti 134 D 2
Silhouette 159 J 5
Sili 156 D 3
Silifke 117 D 3
Siligir 130 K 2
Siliguri 134 E 2
Siling Co 134 E 1
Silip 129 G 5
Silistra 116 C 2
Silivri 116 C 2
Siljan 113 F 3
Silkleborg 113 E 4
Sillajhuay → Cerro Toroni 180 C 4
Sillamäe 112 J 4
Sille 117 D 3
Sillian 115 F 2
Sillil 159 G 2
Silloth 99 C 2
Sillustani 180 B 4
Siloam Springs 171 H 4
Siloana Plains 160 C 3
Silom 145 F 2
Silonga 160 C 3
Silsden 101 E 3
Siltou 157 H 2
Šilutė 113 H 4
Silvan 117 F 3
Silvassa 134 B 3
Silver Bank Passage 173 H 3
Silver City 170 E 5
Silverton (U.S.A.) 170 E 4
Silverton (Australia) 143 G 5
Silves 179 G 4
Silyānah 153 G 1
Sil'yeyaki 131 Q 1
Simaleke Hilir 136 A 4
Simanggang 136 D 3
Simao 132 D 6
Simav 116 C 2
Simba 158 C 4
Simbo 158 D 5
Simcoe, Lake 171 L 3
Simenga 130 J 3
Simeulue, Pulau 136 A 3
Simferopol' 117 D 2
Sími 116 C 3
Simití 178 C 2
Simla 134 C 1
Şimleu Silvanier 116 B 1
Simo 112 H 2
Simojärvi 112 J 2
Simojoki 112 J 2
Simojovel de Allende 172 D 4
Símon Bolivar, Parque Nacional 178 D 2
Simonstown 160 B 6
Simpele 112 J 3
Simpelejärvi 112 J 3
Simplicio Mendes 181 H 2
Simplon 115 E 2
Simpson Desert 143 F 3

Simpson Desert National Park 143 F 4
Simpson Hill 142 D 4
Simpson Peninsula 167 U 2
Simrishamn 113 F 4
Simuk, Pulau 136 A 3
Simushir, Ostrov 131 S 6
Sīnā' 154 E 3
Sinabang 136 A 3
Sinabung, Gunung 136 A 3
Sinadaqo 159 H 3
Sinai 154 E 3
Sinaloa 170 E 6–7
Sinalunga 115 F 3
Sinamaica 178 D 1
Sinan 132 E 5
Sināwan 153 H 2
Sinazongwe 160 D 3
Sinbo 135 G 3
Sincé 178 C 2
Sincelejo 178 C 2
Sinch'am 133 J 2
Sinch'ang-ni 133 J 2
Sinclair Mine 160 B 5
Sinclairs' Bay 98 C 2
Sin Cow 136 D 2
Sind 129 G 5
Sinda 131 P 6
Sindal 113 F 4
Sindangbarang 136 C 5
Sindara 157 G 6
Sindeh, Teluk 137 F 5
Sindèr 156 E 3
Sindgi 134 C 4
Sindhuli 134 E 2
Sindor 118 K 3
Sinegorskiy 117 F 1
Sinelnikovo 117 E 1
Sines, Cabo de 114 B 4
Sinettä 112 J 2
Sinfra 156 C 4
Singako 157 H 4
Singapore 136 B 3
Singapore, Strait of 136 B 3
Singaraja 136 E 5
Sing Buri 135 H 5
Singen 111 E 5
Singida 158 E 5
Singitikós Kólpos 116 B 2
Singkaling Hkamti 135 G 2
Singkawang 136 C 3
Singkep, Pulau 136 B 3
Singkilbaru 136 A 3
Singleton 143 J 5
Singleton, Mount 142 B 4
Singö 113 G 3
Singu 135 G 3
Sinhailien 133 H 4
Si Nho 135 J 4
Sinianka-Minia, Parc National du 157 H 3
Siniscola 115 E 3
Siniy-Shikhan 119 M 5
Sinj 115 G 3
Sinjah 154 E 6
Sinjai 137 F 5
Sinjaja 113 J 4
Sinjär 155 G 1
Sinjār, Jabal 155 G 1
Sink 159 G 2
Sinkan 135 G 3
Sinkāt 154 F 5
Sinkiang Uighur 129 L 3
Sinn al Kadhdhāb 154 E 4
Sinnamary 179 H 2
Sinnar 134 E 3
Sinnicolau Mare 116 B 1
Sinnūris 154 E 3
Sinoia 160 DE 3
Sinop 117 E 2
Sinp'o 133 J 2
Sinskoye 131 N 3
Sīntana 116 B 1
Sintang 136 D 3
Sintra 114 B 4
Sinú 178 C 2
Sinŭiju 133 H 2
Sinujif 159 H 3
Sinyaya 131 M 3
Sinyukha 116 D 1
Siocon 137 F 2
Siófok 116 A 1
Sioma 160 C 3
Sion 115 E 2
Sioux City 171 G 3
Sioux Falls 171 G 3
Sioux Lookout 168 J 5
Sipalay 137 F 2
Siping 133 H 2
Sipiwesk 167 S 4
Sipiwesk Lake 167 S 4
Siple Station 185
Sipolilo → Guruve 161 E 3

Sipora 136 A 3
Sipora, Pulau 136 A 4
Siquia, Rio 172 F 5
Siquijor 137 F 2
Siquisique 178 E 1
Sira (India) 134 C 5
Sira (Norway) 113 E 4
Şīr Abū Nu'ayr 155 J 3
Si Racha 135 H 5
Siracusa 115 G 4
Sirajganj 134 E 3
Sir Alexander, Mount 167 N 5
Sirba 156 E 3
Şīr Banī Yās 155 J 4
Sirdalen 113 E 4
Sirdalsvatn 113 E 4
Sire 159 F 3
Sir Edward Pellew Group 143 F 2
Sireniki 166 C 3
Siret 116 C 1
Sirevåg 113 E 4
Sīrgān 129 G 5
Sirhān, Wādī as 154 F 2
Siri 155 F 3
Sīrīk 128 F 5
Sirino 115 G 3
Siris 134 D 3
Sirja 129 G 5
Sir James MacBrian, Mount 166 M 3
Sirkka 112 H 2
Sirnak 117 F 3
Sirohi 134 B 3
Sironj 134 C 3
Siros 116 B 3
Sirotskiy 117 F 1
Sirpur 134 C 4
Sirr, Nafūd as 155 G 3
Sirsa 134 C 2
Sirt 153 J 2
Sirt, Gulf of 153 J 2
Sir Thomas, Mount 142 D 4
Sir Wilfrid Laurier, Mount 167 O 5
Sisak 115 G 2
Si Sa Ket 135 H 5
Sishen 160 C 5
Sisili 156 D 3
Siskiyou Mountains 170 B 3
Sisophon 135 H 5
Sisseton 170 G 2
Sistema Central 114 BC 3
Sistemas Béticos 114 BC 4
Sistem Iberico 114 C 3–4
Sisteron 115 E 3
Sistig-Khem 130 G 5
Sistranda 112 E 3
Sitalike 158 E 6
Sitamarhi 134 E 2
Sitapur 134 D 2
Sitasjaure 112 G 2
Sitges 114 D 3
Sithonia 116 B 2
Sitipo 180 B 3
Sitka 166 K 4
Sitkalidak 166 G 4
Sitla 116 C 3
Sitoli, Gunung 136 A 3
Sitrah 154 D 3
Sittang 135 G 4
Sittingbourne 103 E 2
Sittona 159 F 2
Sittwe 135 F 3
Situbondo 136 D 5
Siuna 172 F 5
Siuri 134 E 3
Sivaki 131 N 5
Sivas 117 E 3
Sivash 118 E 6
Sivaslı 116 C 3
Sivé 152 C 5
Siverek 117 E 3
Siverskiy 113 K 4
Sivrice 117 E 3
Sivrihisar 116 D 3
Sīwah 154 D 3
Siwalik Range 134 C 1–D 2
Siwan 134 D 2
Siwana 134 B 2
Siwa Oasis → Wāhāt Sīwah 154 D 3
Si Xian 133 G 4
Sixin 132 C 3
Sixth Cataract → Ash Shallāl as Sablūkah 154 E 5
Siya 118 H 3
Siyada 159 H 2
Siziwang 132 F 2
Sjælland 113 F 4
Sjaunja 112 GH 2
Sjövegan 112 G 2

Skadovsk 117 D 1
Skærbæck 113 E 4
Skaftá 112 B 3
Skagatá 112 A 2
Skagen 113 F 4
Skagern 113 F 4
Skagerrak 113 E 4
Skagway 166 K 4
Skaidi 112 H 1
Skakhtersk 117 E 1
Skaland 112 G 2
Skala Podolskaya 116 C 1
Skälderviken 113 F 4
Skaliskaya, Gora 130 D 1
Skanderborg 113 E 4
Skåne 113 F 4
Skanör 113 F 4
Skara 113 F 4
Skara Brae 98 C 2
Skärblacka 113 G 4
Skardu 129 K 3
Skärhamn 113 F 4
Skarnes 113 F 3
Skarsøy 112 E 3
Skarstind 112 E 3
Skarsvåg 112 J 1
Skarżysko-Kamienna 111 H 4
Skattungbyn 112 F 3
Skeena 166 M 5
Skeena Mountains 166 M 4
Skeggöxl 112 A 2
Skegness 103 E 1
Skeiðárarsandur 112 B 3
Skeldon 179 G 2
Skeleton Coast Park 160 A 3
Skellefteå 112 H 3
Skellefteälven 112 G 2
Skelleftehamn 112 H 3
Skelmersdale 101 D 3
Skerries 100 B 3
Ski 113 F 4
Skíathos 116 B 3
Skibbereen 110 B 4
Skibotn 112 H 2
Skiddaw 101 D 2
Skidegate 166 L 5
Skidel' 113 H 5
Skien 113 E 4
Skierniewice 111 H 4
Skiftet 113 H 3
Skikda 153 G 1
Skipton 101 D 3
Skive 113 E 4
Skjærhalden 113 F 4
Skjálfandafljót 112 B 2
Skjálfandi 112 B 1
Skjern 113 E 4
Skjervöy 112 H 1
Skjoldungen 169 T 3
Sklad 130 M 1
Škofja Loka 115 G 2
Skoghall 113 F 4
Skokholm 102 B 2
Skomer 102 B 2
Skópelos 116 B 3
Skopi 116 C 3
Skopje 116 B 2
Skorodum 119 O 4
Skorovatn 112 F 3
Skörping 113 E 4
Skövde 113 F 4
Skovorodino 131 M 5
Skowhegan 171 N 3
Skradin 115 G 3
Skrekken 113 E 4
Skudeneshavn 113 E 4
Skurup 113 F 4
Skutskär 113 G 3
Skvira 118 E 6
Skwentna 166 G 3
Skye 110 B 3
Skye 98 A 3
Slagnäs 112 G 3
Slamet, Gunung 136 C 5
Slaney, River 100 B 3
Slannik 116 C 2
Slano 115 G 3
Slantsy 113 J 4
Slashchevskaya 118 H 6
Slatina 116 B 2
Slautnoye 131 V 3
Slave Coast 156 E 4
Slave Lake 167 O 4
Slave River 167 P 3
Slavgorod 119 P 5
Slavgorod 117 E 1
Slavnoye 131 R 6
Slavonska Požega 115 G 2
Slavonski Brod 115 G 2
Slavuta 113 J 5
Slavyanka 133 K 2
Slavyansk 118 G 6

Slavyansk-na-Kubani 117 E 1
Śląsk 111 G 4
Śleza 111 G 4
Sleaford 103 D 1
Sleat 99 B 3
Sleat, Loch 98 B 3
Sleeper Islands 169 M 4
Slettuheiði 112 B 2
Slieve Bloom Mountains 100 B 3
Slieve Donard 100 C 2
Sligo 110 B 4
Slite 113 G 4
Sliven 116 C 2
Slobodchikovo 118 J 3
Slobodka 116 C 1
Slobodskoy 118 K 4
Slobodzeya 116 C 1
Slobozia 116 C 2
Slochteren 108
Slocum Mountain 170 C 4
Slonim 112 J 4
Slough 103 D 2
Slovakia 111 G 5
Slovechno 113 J 5
Slovenijd 115 FG 2
Slovenske Gorice 115 G 2
Slovensko 111 G 5
Sluch' (Belorussiya, U.S.S.R.) 113 J 5
Sluch' (Ukraina, U.S.S.R.) 113 J 5
Slunj 115 G 2
Słupia 111 G 4
Słupsk 111 G 4
Slutsk 113 J 5
Slyudyanka 130 H J 5
Småland 113 F 4
Smålandsstenar 113 F 4
Smallwood Réservoir 169 P 5
Smedervo 116 B 2
Smedjebacken 113 G 3
Smela 118 F 2
Smidovich 131 O 6
Smidovich 184
Smirnovskiy 119 N 5
Smirnykh 131 Q 6
Smith 167 P 4
Smith Arm 167 N 2
Smith Bay 166 G 1
Smith, Cape 169 M 3
Smithers 167 M 5
Smith Falls 171 L 3
Smithton 144 L 9
Smithtown-Gladstone 143 J 5
Smjörfjöll 112 C 2
Smögen 113 F 4
Smokey Dome 170 D 3
Smoky Cape 143 J 5
Smoky Falls 169 L 5
Smoky Hill River 170 F 4
Smoky Hills 170 G 4
Smoky River 167 O 5
Smöla 112 E 3
Smolensk 118 F 5
Smólikas Óros 116 B 2
Smoljan 116 B 2
Smooth Rock Falls 169 L 6
Smorgon' 113 J 5
Smygehamn 113 F 4
Smygehuk 113 F 4
Smyrna → İzmir 116 C 3
Smythe, Mount 167 N 4
Snæfell 112 B 3
Snaefell 100 C 2
Snæfellsjökull 112 A 3
Snæfellsnes 112 A 3
Snag 166 J 3
Snake Bay 142 E 1
Snake River 170 C 2
Snake River Plain 170 D 3
Snare 167 O 3
Snåsa 112 F 3
Snåsvattnet 112 F 3
Snezhnogorsk 119 R 2
Snezhnoye 131 W 2
Snežnik 115 F 2
Śnieżka 111 G 4
Śnieżnik 111 G 4
Snigirevka 117 D 1
Snizort, Loch 98 A 3
Snøhetta 112 E 3
Snoul 135 J 5
Snowbird Lake 167 R 3
Snowdon 102 B 1
Snowdrift 167 P 3
Snow Lake 167 R 5
Snow Mountain 170 B 4
Snowville 170 D 3
Snowy Mountains 143 H 6
Snowy River 143 H 6
Snyatyn 116 C 1
Snyder 170 F 5
Soacha 178 D 3
Soahanina 161 G 3

Soa–Sta

Soalala 161 H 3
Soanierana-Ivongo 161 H 3
Soasiu 137 G 3
Soavinandriana 161 H 3
Soay 98 A 3
Soba 157 F 3
Sobat → Sawbā 158 E 3
Sobolevo 131 T 5
Sobopol 131 N 2
Sobopol Mayan 131 MN 2
Sobradinho, Barragem de 181 H 3
Sobral 181 H 1
Socaire 180 C 5
Sochaczew 111 H 4
Sochi 117 E 2
Society Islands 147 EF 4
Socorro (Colombia) 178 D 2
Socorro (U.S.A.) 170 E 5
Sócota 178 C 5
Socotra 159 J 2
Sodankylä 112 J 2
Soda Plains 129 K 3
Soddu 159 F 3
Söderhamn 112 G 3
Söderköping 113 G 4
Södermanland 113 G 4
Södertälje 113 G 4
Södra Kvarken 113 G 3
Soe 137 F 5
Soela Väin 113 H 4
Soest 111 E 4
Sofádhes 116 B 3
Sofala 161 E 4
Sofala, Baía de 161 F 4
Sofia (Madagaskar) 161 H 3
Sofia → Sofija 116 B 2
Sofija 116 B 2
Sofiyevka 117 D 1
Sofiysk 131 O 5
Sofiysk 131 P 5
Sofporog 112 K 2
Sōfu-gan 133 LM 5
Sogamoso 178 D 2
Soğanlı 117 D 2
Sogda 131 O 5
Sogeri 144 E 3
Sogndalsfjöra 112 E 3
Sognefjorden 112 E 3
Sognesjöen 112 D 3
Sogn og Fjordane 112 E 3
Sogod 137 F 1
Sogo Hills 159 F 4
Sogolle 157 H 2
Sogom 119 N 3
Sogo Nur 132 D 2
Söğüt 116 D 2
Söğüt Gölü 116 C 3
Sog Xian 132 B 4
Sohag → Sawhāj 154 E 3
Soham 103 E 1
Sohano 145 F 3
Sohm Abyssal Plain 192 A 2
Sohŭksan-do 133 J 4
Soila 132 C 4
Soissons 114 D 2
Sojat 134 B 2
Sŏjosŏn-man 133 H 3
Sokal' 113 H 5
Sokch'o 133 J 3
Söke 116 C 3
Sokele 158 C 6
Sokhondo, Gora 130 K 6–L 5
Sokhor, Gora 130 J 5
Sokna 113 E 3
Sokodé 156 E 4
Sokółka 111 H 4
Sokolo 156 C 3
Sokolov 111 F 4
Sokolozero 112 K 2
Sokol Povlen 116 A 2
Sokone 156 A 3
Sokosti 112 J 2
Sokota 159 F 2
Sokoto 157 F 3
Sŏl 159 H 3
Sola 113 E 4
Sola de Vega 172 C 4
Solai 159 F 4
Solbad Hall 115 F 2
Solberg 112 G 3
Soldatovo 131 V 3
Soldotna 166 G 3
Soledad (Colombia) 178 D 1
Soledad (Venezuela) 179 F 2
Soledade (Amazonas, Brazil) 178 E 5
Soledade (Rio Grande do Sul, Brazil) 182 F 4
Solenoye (Russia, U.S.S.R.) 117 F 1
Solenoye (Ukraina, U.S.S.R.) 117 E 1

Solenzara 115 E 3
Solfau 111 E 4
Solferino 115 F 2
Solhan 117 F 3
Soligorsk 113 J 5
Solikamsk 118 L 4
Sol'-Iletsk 118 L 5
Solimões 178 E 4
Soliman 115 F 4
Solingen 111 E 4
Solita 178 D 2
Solitaire 160 B 4
Sollefteå 112 G 3
Sollerön 113 F 3
Solling 111 E 4
Solna 113 G 4
Sologne Bourbonnais 114 D 2
Solok 136 B 4
Solomon Islands 145 G 2
Solomon Sea 145 F 3
Solon 133 H 1
Solontsovo 130 L 5
Solor, Pulau 137 F 5
Solothurn 115 E 2
Solov'yevsk 130 L 5
Solov'yevsk 131 M 5
Solta 115 G 3
Soltānābād 128 F 3
Soltānābād 128 D 4
Sol'tsy 112 K 4
Sölvesborg 113 F 4
Solway Firth 99 C 4
Solwezi 160 D 2
Solyanka 130 M 3
Soma 116 C 3
Somabula 160 D 3
Somalia 159 G 4–H 3
Somali Basin 192 B 3
Sombang, Gunung 136 E 3
Sombo 160 E 4
Sombor 116 A 1
Sombrerete 172 B 3
Sombrero Channel 135 F 6
Somcuţa Mare 116 B 1
Somero 113 H 3
Somerset (U.S.A.) 171 K 4
Somerset (Australia) 143 G 1
Somerset (U.K.) 102 C 2
Somerset East 160 D 6
Somerton 102 C 2
Someş 116 B 1
Someşu Mare 116 B 1
Somme 114 D 1
Sommen 113 G 4
Somnath 134 B 3
Somnitel'nyy 131 P 5
Somontano 114 CD 3
Somoto 172 E 5
Somport, Puerto de 114 C 3
Somuncurá, Meseta de 183 C 7
Son 134 D 2
Soná 178 B 2
Sonakh 131 P 5
Sonaly 119 O 6
Sŏnch'ŏn 133 H 3
Sønderborg 113 E 5
Sondershausen 111 F 4
Søndre Strømfjord 169 R 2
Sondrio 115 E 2
Sonepur 134 D 3
Sonequera 180 C 5
Song 157 G 4
Song Cau 135 J 5
Song Da 135 H 3
Songea 161 F 2
Song Hong 135 H 3
Songhua Hu 133 J 2
Songhua Jiang 133 J 1
Songjiang 133 H 4
Songkhla 135 H 6
Songling 130 M 6
Song Ma 135 H 3
Songnim 133 J 3
Songo 161 E 3
Songolo 158 A 6
Songpan 132 D 4
Songwe 158 E 6
Songxi 133 G 5
Son Ha 135 J 4
Sonid Youqi 132 F 2
Sonipat 134 C 2
Sonkel', Ozero 129 K 2
Son La 135 H 3
Sonmiani 129 G 5
Sonmiani Bay 129 G 5
Sonneberg 111 F 4
Sono 179 J 5
Sonoita 170 D 5
Sonoma Peak 170 C 3
Sonora (Mexico) 170 D 6
Sonora (TX, U.S.A.) 170 F 5
Sonora, Llanos de 170 D 6

Sonoran Desert 170 D 5
Sonora, Rio 170 D 6
Sonqor 128 D 4
Sonsón 178 C 2
Sonsonate 172 E 5
Sonsorol Islands 137 H 2
Soomaaliya 159 G 4–H 3
Sop Bau 135 H 3
Sopka Anangravnen 131 U 4
Sopka Kizimen 131 U 4
Sopka Shiveluch 131 U 4
Sopochnaya Karga 130 D 1
Sopochnoye 131 T 4
Sopot 111 G 4
Soppero 112 H 2
Sopron 116 A 1
Sopur 129 J 4
Sor 114 B 4
Sora 115 F 3
Soradai 134 D 4
Söråker 112 G 3
Sorata 180 C 4
Sordoginskiy Khrebet 131 O 3
Sorel 169 N 6
Sorell 144 L 9
Sörfold 112 G 2
Sorgues 113 G 4
Sorgun 117 E 3
Soria 114 C 3
Soriano 182 E 5
Sorikmerapi, Gunung 136 A 3
Sor Kaydak 128 E 2
Sorkheh 128 E 3
Sor Mertvyy Kultuk 128 E 1
Sorocaba 181 G 5
Sorochinsk 118 K 5
Sorok 130 H J 5
Soroki 116 C 1
Sorolen 119 P 6
Sorong 137 H 4
Soroti 158 E 4
Söröya 112 H 1
Söröyane 112 E 3
Sorraia 114 B 4
Sörreisa 112 G 2
Sorrento 115 F 3
Sör-Trøndelag 112 F 3
Sorsatunturi 112 J 2
Sorsele 112 G 2
Sorso 115 E 3
Sorsogon 137 F 1
Sort 114 D 3
Sortavala 112 K 3
Sortland 112 G 2
Sör Rondane Mountains 185
Sörvær 112 F 2
Sörvagur 110 A 1
Sŏsan 133 J 3
Sosna 130 J 3
Sosnogorsk 118 K 3
Sosnovka 118 J 4
Sosnovka 118 H 2
Sosnovka 130 J 5
Sosnovo-Ozerskoye 130 K 5
Sosnovy Bor 112 J 4
Sosnovyy Bor 119 J 3
Sosnovyy Mys 119 N 3
Sosnowiec 111 G 4
Sosumav 161 H 2
Sos'va 119 M 4
Sos'va, Malaya 119 MN 3
Sos'va, Severnaya 119 MN 3
Sos'vinskaya Kul'tbaza 119 MN 3
Sosyka 117 E 1
Sotavento, Islas de 178 E 1
Sotik 158 F 5
Sotkamo 112 J 3
Sotnikovskoye 117 F 1
Sotonera, Embalse de la 114 C 3
Sotouboua 156 E 4
Sotra 113 D 3
Sotsial 119 P 6
Souanké 157 G 5
Soubré 156 C 4
Soudan 143 F 3
Souf 153 G 2
Souflion 116 C 2
Soufrière (Guadeloupe) 173 K 4
Soufrière (St. Vincent) 173 K 5
Souillac 114 D 3
Souilly 115 E 2
Souk Ahras 153 G 1
Souk el Arbaa du Rharb 152 D 2
Soukouralla 156 C 4
Sŏul 133 J 3
Sound of Arisaig 99 B 3
Sound of Harris 98 A 3
Sound of Jura 99 B 3
Sound of Mull 99 B 3
Sound of Raasay 98 A 3
Sound of Sleat 99 B 3
Sounfat 156 E 1
Soúnion, Ákra 116 B 3

Sountellane 157 G 2
Soure 179 J 4
Souris (Nova Sc., Can.) 169 P 6
Souris River 167 R 6
Sous 152 D 2
Sousa 181 J 2
Sousel 179 H 4
Sousse → Sūsah (Tunisia) 153 H 1
South Africa 160 CD 5
South Alligator River 142 E 1
Southampton 103 D 2
Southampton (Airport) 103 D 2
Southampton, Cape 167 V 3
Southampton Island 167 V 3
South Andaman 135 F 5
South Aulatsivik 169 P 4
South Australia 142–143 E 4
South Australian Basin 193 C 5
South Bay 167 V 3
South Bend (IN, U.S.A.) 171 J 3
South Bend (WA, U.S.A.) 170 B 2
South Benfleet 103 E 2
South Branch Potomac 171 L 4
South Carolina 171 K 5
South China Sea 136 CD 2
South Dakota 170 F 3
South Downs 103 D 2
South East Cape 144 L 9
Southeast Indian Ridge 192 BC 5
South East Point 143 H 6
Southend 167 R 4
Southend (Airport) 103 E 2
Southend-on-Sea 103 E 2
Southern Alps 146 C 5
Southern Alps 145 Q 9
Southern Cook Islands 147 E 4
Southern Cross 142 B 5
Southern Indian Lake 167 S 4
Southern Uplands 99 B–C 4
South Fork 170 C 3
South Geomagnetic Pole 185
South Georgia 185
South Glamorgan 102 C 2
South Horr 159 F 4
South Indian Lake 167 S 4
South Island 144 P 9
South Korea 133 J 3
South Lake Tahoe 170 B 4
South Magnetic Pole 185
South Molton 102 C 2
South Nahanni 167 N 3
South Ockenden 103 E 2
South Orkney Islands 185
South Pass 170 E 3
South Petherton 102 C 2
South Platte River 170 F 3
South Pole 185
Southport 101 D 3
South Ronaldsay 98 C 2
South Ronaldsay 110 C 3
South Sandwich Islands 185
South Saskatchewan 167 Q 5
South Shetland Islands 185
South Shields 101 E 2
South Sioux City 171 G 3
South Taranaki Bight 145 Q 8
South Tasman Rise 193 C 5
South Tyne, River 101 D 2
South Uist 98 A 3
South Walls 98 C 2
South Wellesley Islands 143 F 2
Southwest Cape 144 P 10
Southwestern Pacific Basin 193 D 5
Southwest Indian Ridge 192 B 5
Southwold 103 E 1
South Yemen 155 H 6–J 5
South Yorkshire 101 E 3
South Yolla Bolly Mts. 170 B 3
Soutpansberg 160 D 5
Soutra Hill 144 P 10
Soven 182 C 5
Soverato 115 G 4
Sovetsk 113 H 4
Sovetsk 118 J 4
Sovetskaya 117 F 2
Sovetskaya Gavan' 131 Q 6
Sovetskaya Rechka 119 Q 2
Sovetskiy 117 D 1
Sovetskoje, Ozero 119 Q 2
Sovetskoye 117 G 2
Soya Strait 121 R 5
Soyatita 170 E 6
Soyo 160 A 5
Sozh 118 F 5
Sozimskiy 118 K 4
Sozopol 116 C 2
Spain 114 BC 3
Spalding 103 D 1
Spanish Fork 170 D 3
Spanish Town 173 G 4
Sparbu 112 F 3
Sparks 170 C 4

Spartanburg 171 K 5
Sparta → Spartí 116 B 3
Spartel, Cap 152 D 1
Spartí 116 B 3
Spartivento, Capo 115 E 4
Spassk Dal'niy 133 K 2
Spátha, Ákra 116 B 3
Spearfish 170 F 3
Speke Gulf 158 E 5
Spenard 166 H 3
Spence Bay 167 T 2
Spencer 171 G 3
Spencer Bay 160 A 5
Spencer, Cape 143 F 6
Spencer Gulf 143 F 5
Spennymoor 101 E 2
Sperrin Mountains 100 B 2
Spétsai 116 B 3
Spey 110 C 3
Speyer 111 E 5
Spey, River 98 C 3
Spicer Islands 169 M 1
Spiez 115 E 2
Spilimbergo 115 F 2
Spilsby 103 E 1
Spirit River 167 O 4
Spišská-Nová Ves 111 H 5
Spitsbergen 184
Spittal an der Drau 115 F 2
Spjelkavik 112 E 3
Split 115 G 3
Split Lake 167 S 4
Spluga, Passo della 115 E 2
Spogi 112 J 4
Spokane 170 C 2
Spoleto 115 F 3
Spong 135 J 5
Spooner 171 H 2
Spratly Island 136 D 2
Spree 111 F 4
Sprengisandur 112 B 3
Springbok 160 B 5
Springdale (U.S.A.) 171 H 4
Springdale (Canada) 169 Q 6
Springer 170 F 4
Springer, Mount 169 N 6
Springfield (CO, U.S.A.) 170 F 4
Springfield (IL, U.S.A.) 171 J 4
Springfield (MA, U.S.A.) 171 M 3
Springfield (MS, U.S.A.) 171 H 4
Springfield (OR, U.S.A.) 170 B 3
Springfield (S.D., U.S.A.) 170 G 3
Springfield (TN, U.S.A.) 171 J 4
Springfontein 160 D 5
Springhill 169 P 6
Springlands 179 G 2
Springs 160 D 5
Springs Junction 145 Q 9
Springsure 143 H 3
Springvale 143 G 2
Spurn Head 101 F 3
Squamish 167 N 6
Square Islands 169 Q 5
Squillace, Golfo di 115 G 4
Squinzano 115 G 3
Squires, Mount 142 D 4
Srbija 116 B 3
Sredinnyy Khrebet 131 T 5–U 4
Sredna Gora 116 B 2
Srednebelaya 131 N 5
Srednego, Ostrova 131 S 6
Sredne-Kamchatsk 131 U 4
Srednekolymsk 131 S 2
Sredne Russkaya Vozvyshennost' 118 F 5
Sredne Sibirskoye Ploskogorye 130 G 2–K 3
Sredne Yegorlyk 117 F 1
Sredneye Kuyto, Ozero 112 K 2
Sredniy 131 S 4
Sredniy Kalar 130 L 4
Sredniy Ural 119 L 4
Sredniy Vasyugan 119 P 4
Srednyaya Itkana 131 U 3
Srednyaya Nyukzha 131 M 4
Srednyaya Olekma 130 M 4
Śrem 111 G 4
Sremska Mitrovica 116 A 2
Sretensk 130 L 5
Sriharikota 134 D 5
Srikakulam 134 D 4
Sri Lanka 134 D 6
Sri Madhopur 134 C 2
Srinagar 129 J 4
Staaten River 143 G 2
Staaten River National Park 143 G 2
Stack Skerry 98 B 2
Stadhavet 112 DE 3
Städjan 112 F 3
Stadlandet 112 DE 3
Staffa 99 A 3
Staffanstorp 113 F 4

Sta–Sun

Stafford 103 C 1
Staffordshire 103 C 1
Stagno di Cabras 115 E 4
Stainach 115 F 2
Staines 103 D 2
Ställdalen 113 F 4
Stalowa Wola 111 H 4
Stalybridge 101 D 3
Stamford (U.K.) 103 D 1
Stamford (CT, U.S.A.) 171 M 3
Stamford (TX, U.S.A.) 170 G 5
Stampriet 160 B 4
Stamsund 112 F 2
Stanchik 131 S 1
Standerton 160 D 5
Stanger 161 E 5
Stanke Dimitrov 116 B 2
Stanley (U.S.A.) 170 F 2
Stanley (U.K.) 101 E 2
Stanley Falls 158 D 4
Stanley Mission 167 R 4
Stanley Reservoir 134 C 5
Stannakh-Khocho 130 M 1
Stanovaya 131 T 2
Stanovka 119 O 4
Stanovoy Khrebet 131 MN 4
Stanovoy Nagor'ye 130 K L 4
Stanovoy Range 131 N 4
Stanraer 110 B 4
Stans 115 E 2
Stansted (Airport) 103 E 2
Stansted Mountfitchet 103 E 2
Stanthorpe 143 J 4
Starachowice 111 H 4
Stara Planina 116 B 2
Staraya Russa 112 K 4
Staraya Vorpavla 119 N 3
Stara Zagora 116 B 2
Starbuck 147 E 3
Stargard Szczecinski 111 G 4
Starichkova 131 V 2
Starigrad 115 G 3
Staritsa 131 Q 6
Starnberg 111 F 5
Starobel'sk 118 G 6
Starodub 118 F 5
Starogard Gdanski 111 G 4
Starokonstantinov 112 J 6
Starominskaya 117 E 1
Staromlinovka 117 E 1
Starovercheskaya 118 J 4
Staroye Linde 130 M 2
Start Bay 102 C 2
Start Point 102 C 2
Staryy Dom 131 Q 1
Staryy Krym 117 E 1
Staryy Oskol 118 G 5
State College 171 L 3
Staten Island → Isla de los Estados 183 D 9
Statesboro 171 K 5
Statesville 171 L 4
Statford-upon-Avon 110 C 4
Statland 112 F 3
Staunton 171 L 4
Stavanger 113 E 4
Staveley 101 E 3
Stavern 113 F 4
Stavropol' 117 F 1
Stavropolka 119 N 5
Stavropol'skaya Vozvyshennost' 117 F 1
Stavrós 116 B 2
Stavroupolis 116 B 2
Stawell 143 G 6
Stawiski 111 H 4
Stebnik 111 H 5
Steelport 160 DE 4
Steenkool 137 H 4
Steen River 167 O 4
Steensby Inlet 169 M 1
Ştefăneşti 116 C 1
Stefanie, Lake 159 F 4
Stefansson Island 167 Q 1
Stege 113 F 4
Stegi 161 E 5
Steilrand Mountains 160 A 3
Steinach 115 F 2
Steinbach 167 S 6
Steinfeld 160 B 4
Steinkjer 112 F 3
Steinkopf 160 B 5
Stekol'nyy 131 S 4
Stella 160 C 5
Stellenbosch 160 B 6
Stello 115 E 3
Stelvio, Passo della 115 F 2
Stenay 115 E 2
Stendal 111 F 4
Stende 113 H 4
Stenfjället 112 F 3
Stenhouse Bay 143 F 6
Stenon 116 C 3

Sténon Serifou 116 B 3
Stenungsund 113 F 4
Stepanakert 128 D 3
Stephens Passage 166 L 4
Stephenville (Newfoundl., Can.) 169 Q 6
Stephenville (TX, U.S.A.) 170 G 5
Stepnoye 117 F 2
Stepnyak 119 O 5
Step' Shaidara 129 H 2
Sterkstroom 160 D 6
Sterling 170 F 3
Sterlitamak 118 L 5
Šternberk 111 G 5
Stettin 111 F 4
Stettiner Haff 111 F 4
Stettler 167 P 5
Steubenville 171 K 3
Stevenage 103 D 2
Stevenson Entrance 166 G 4
Stevens Point 171 H 3
Stevenston 99 B 4
Stewart (New Zealand) 144 P 10
Stewart (Chile) 183 B 9
Stewart (AK, U.S.A.) 166 M 4
Stewart (NWT., Can.) 166 K 3
Stewart Crossing 166 K 3
Stewart Island 146 B 3
Stewart Islands 145 H 3
Stewart River 166 K 3
Stewart Sound 135 F 5
Steynsburg 160 D 6
Steyr 115 F 2
Stikine 166 L 4
Stikine Ranges 166 L 4
Stillwater 171 G 4
Stilo, Punta 115 G 4
Stip 116 B 2
Stirling 99 B 3
Stirling Creek 142 D 2
Stirling Range 142 B 5
Stirling Range National Park 142 B 5
Stjernöya 112 H 1
Stjördal 112 F 3
Stockerau 115 G 2
Stockholm 113 G 4
Stockport 101 D 3
Stocksbridge 101 E 3
Stockton 170 B 4
Stockton Lake 171 H 4
Stockton-on-Tees 101 E 2
Stockton Plateau 170 F 5
Stöde 112 G 3
Stoffberg 160 D 5
Stoke-on-Trent 101 D 3
Stokksnes 112 C 3
Stokmarknes 112 F 2
Stol 116 B 2
Stolbovoy, Ostrov 131 P 1
Stolbtsy 113 J 5
Stolin 113 J 5
Ston 115 G 3
Stone 103 C 1
Stonehaven 99 C 3
Stonehenge 103 D 2
Stonehouse 99 B 4
Stony 166 F 3
Stony Rapids 167 Q 4
Stony River 166 F 3
Stony Stratford 103 D 1
Stony Tunguska River 130 GH 3
Storå 113 E 4
Stora Le 113 F 4
Stora Luvelvatten 112 G 2
Storån 112 G 3
Stora Sjöfallet 112 G 2
Storavan 112 G 2
Stor-Björkvattnet 112 G 2
Stord 113 E 4
Store Bælt 113 F 4
Storfjorden 112 E 3
Storis Passage 167 S 2
Storjön 112 F 3
Storkerson Bay 167 N 1
Storkerson Peninsula 167 Q 1
Storlien 112 F 3
Storm Bay 144 L 9
Stornoway 98 A 2
Stornoway (Airport) 98 A 2
Storozhevsk 118 K 3
Storozhinets 116 C 1
Storsjöen 113 F 3
Storsjöen 112 F 3
Storsjön (Sweden) 112 G 3
Storstenfjellet 112 G 2
Storuman 112 G 2
Storvätteshågna 112 F 3
Storvigelen 112 F 3
Storvindeln 112 G 2
Stöttingfjället 112 G 3
Stourbridge 103 C 1
Stourport 103 C 1

Stour, River 103 E 2
Stövring 113 E 4
Stowmarket 103 E 1
Stow on-the-Wold 103 D 2
Stoyba 131 O 5
Strabane 100 B 2
Strahan 144 L 9
Strait of Belle Isle 169 Q 5
Strait of Bonifacio 115 E 3
Strait of Canso 169 P 6
Strait of Dover 103 E 2
Strait of Gibraltar 114 B 4
Strait of Hormuz 155 K 3
Strait of Juan de Fuca 167 M 6
Strait of Magellan 183 B 9
Strait of Malacca 136 A 2
Strait of Singapore 136 B 3
Straits of Florida 171 K 7
Straits of Mackinac 171 K 2
Strakonice 111 F 5
Stralsund 111 F 4
Strand 160 B 6
Strangford 100 C 2
Strangford Lough 100 C 2
Strängnäs 113 G 4
Stranraer 100 C 2
Strasbourg 115 E 2
Strasswalchen 115 F 2
Stratford (Can) 171 K 3
Stratford (N.Z.) 145 Q 8
Stratford (TX, U.S.A.) 170 F 4
Stratford (Victoria, Australia) 143 H 6
Stratford-upon-Avon 103 D 1
Strathaven 99 B 4
Strathbogie 98 C 3
Strathclyde 99 B 4
Strath Dearn 98 B 3
Strath Earn 99 C 3
Strathmay 143 G 1
Strathmore (Australia) 143 G 2
Strathmore (U.K.) 99 C 3
Strathpeffer 98 B 3
Strath Spey 98 C 3
Strathy Point 98 C 2
Stratton 102 B 2
Straubing 111 F 5
Straumnes 112 A 2
Straumsjöen 112 F 2
Strawberry Mountain 170 C 3
Streaky Bay 142 E 5
Street 102 C 2
Strehaia 116 B 2
Strelka 131 S 3
Strelka 130 F 4
Strelka-Chunya 130 H 3
Strelna 113 K 4
Stretton 142 B 5
Streymoy 110 A 1
Strickland River 144 D 3
Strimón 116 B 2
Strimonikós Kólpos 116 B 2
Strizhovo 119 O 4
Stroeder 183 D 7
Strofádhes, Nísoi 116 B 3
Stromboli 115 G 4
Stromeferry 98 B 3
Strömfjord, Norde 169 R 2
Strömfjord, Söndre 169 R 2
Stromness 98 C 2
Strömsbruk 112 G 3
Strömsnäsbruk 113 F 4
Strömstad 113 F 4
Strömsund 112 G 3
Ströms Vattudal 112 F 3
Stronsay 98 C 2
Stronsay Firth 98 C 2
Stroud 103 C 2
Struer 113 E 4
Struga 116 B 2
Struma 116 B 2
Strumica 116 B 2
Strydenburg 160 C 5
Stryy 111 H 5
Strzeke Opolskie 111 G 4
Strzyzów 111 H 5
Stuart 166 E 3
Stuart, Lake 167 N 5
Stuart, Bukit 142 E 1
Stung Treng 135 J 5
Sturgeon Lake 168 J 6
Sturt Creek 142 D 2
Sturt Desert 143 G 4
Sturt National Park 143 G 4
Sturt Plain 142 E 2
Stutterheim 160 D 6
Stuttgart 111 E 5
Stykkishólmur 112 A 2
Styr' 113 J 5
Suai 137 G 5
Suao 133 H 6
Subansiri 135 F 2

Subayhah 154 F 3
Subay', 'Urūq as 155 G 4
Subei Monggolzu Zizhixian 132 B 3
Subi, Pulau 136 C 3
Sublette 170 F 4
Subotica 116 A 1
Suceava 116 C 1
Suck 110 B 4
Sucre 180 C 4
Sucuaro 178 E 3
Sucuriju 179 J 3
Sudak 117 D 2
Sudan 154 DE 6
Sudbury (Canada) 171 K 2
Sudbury (U.K.) 103 E 1
Sudd 158 E 3
Suddie 179 G 2
Sudety 111 G 4
Sudirman, Pegunungan 137 J 4
Sue 158 D 3
Suez 154 E 3
Suez Canal 154 E 2
Şufaynah 155 G 4
Suffolk 103 E 1
Sufiän 128 D 3
Suğla Gölü 117 D 3
Sugoy 131 T 3
Suguta 159 F 4
Suhai Hu 132 B 3
Sühbaatar 130 J 5
Sühbaatar 132 F 1
Suhl 111 F 4
Suiá-Missu 181 F 3
Suibin 131 O 6
Suichang 133 G 5
Suichuan 132 F 5
Suide 132 F 3
Suifenhe 133 K 2
Suihua 133 J 1
Suijang 132 D 5
Suileng 131 N 6
Suining 132 E 4
Suining 133 G 4
Suipacha 180 C 5
Suir 110 B 4
Suir, River 100 B 3
Suixi 133 F 3
Suixi 133 G 4
Sui Xian 132 F 4
Suizhong 133 H 2
Suizhou 132 F 4
Sujangarh 134 B 2
Sujstamo 112 K 3
Sukabumi 136 C 5
Sukadana 136 C 4
Sukagawa 133 M 3
Sukaraja 136 D 4
Sukau 137 E 2
Sukeva 112 J 3
Sukhana 130 L 2
Sukhodolskoye, Ozero 112 K 3
Sukhona 118 H 4
Sukhothai 135 G 4
Sukhotinskiy 117 F 1
Sukhoy 117 F 1
Sukhumi 117 F 2
Suki 154 E 6
Sukkertoppen 169 R 2
Sukkozero 112 K 3
Sukkur 129 G 5
Sukma 134 D 4
Şuknah 153 J 3
Sukses 160 B 4
Suksukan 131 S 3
Suksun 119 L 4
Sula (U.S.S.R.) 118 JK 2
Sula (Norway) 112 D 3
Sulaimäniya 155 K 1
Sulaiman Range 129 G 5
Sulak 128 D 2
Sula, Kepulauan 137 F 4
Sulakyurt 117 D 2
Sulanheer 132 E 2
Sularya Dağları 116 C 3
Sula Sgeir 98 A 2
Sulat, Bukit 142 E 1
Sulawesi 137 E 4
Sulawesi, Laut 137 F 3
Sulb 154 E 4
Sul, Canal do 179 J 4
Sulechów 111 G 4
Sulen, Mount 144 D 2
Sule Skerry 110 C 3
Sule Skerry 98 B 2
Sulima 156 B 4
Sulina 116 C 1
Sulitjelma 112 G 2
Sulkava 112 J 3
Sullana 178 B 4

Sullom Voe 98 D 1
Sulmona 115 F 3
Sulphur 171 H 5
Sulphur Springs 171 G 5
Sultān 153 K 2
Sultan Dağları 116 D 3
Sultanhanı 117 D 3
Sultanpur 134 D 2
Sultanpur 134 C 1
Sulu Archipelago 137 F 2
Suly 119 N 5
Sulyukta 129 H 3
Sumalata 137 F 3
Sumarokovo 119 R 3
Sumatera 136 A 3
Sumaúma 179 G 5
Šumava 111 F 5
Sumba 137 E 5
Sumba Game Reserve 161 E 1
Sumba, Selat 137 E 5
Sumbawa 136 E 5
Sumbawa Besar 136 E 5
Sumbawanga 158 E 6
Sumbe 160 A 2
Sümber 132 E 1
Sumbu 161 E 1
Sumburgh (Airport) 98 D 2
Sumburgh Head 98 D 2
Sumedang 136 C 5
Šumen 116 C 2
Sumenep 136 D 5
Sumesar Range 134 D 2
Sumgait 128 D 2
Sumisu-jima 133 LM 4
Sumkino 119 N 4
Summer Lake 170 B 3
Summit Lake 167 N 4
Summit Peak 170 E 4
Sumperk 111 G 5
Sumprabum 135 G 2
Sumter 171 K 5
Sumuma 130 G 3
Sumy 118 G 5
Sumzom 132 C 5
Suna 112 K 3
Suna 158 E 6
Sunamganj 135 F 2
Sunan 132 C 3
Sunart, Loch 99 B 3
Sunbury 171 L 3
Suncho Corral 182 D 4
Sunch'ön (N. Korea) 133 J 3
Sunch'ön (S. Korea) 133 J 3
Sundarbans 134 E 3
Sundargarh 134 D 3
Sunda, Selat 136 B 5
Sunday Creek 142 E 2
Sunday Strait 142 C 2
Sundbron 112 G 3
Sunde 113 E 4
Sunderland 101 E 2
Sündiren Dağları 116 D 3
Sundsvall 112 G 3
Sundsvallsbukten 112 G 3
Sunduyka 130 K 6–L 5
Sunflower, Mount 170 F 4
Sungaianyar 136 E 4
Sungai Barito 136 D 4
Sungaidareh 136 B 4
Sungaigerong 136 B 4
Sungaiguntung 136 B 3
Sungai Inderagiri 136 B 4
Sungai Kampar 136 B 3
Sungai Kapuas 136 D 4
Sungai Kapuas 136 C 4
Sungai Karama 137 E 4
Sungai Kayan 136 E 3
Sungai Kutai 136 E 4
Sungailiat 136 C 4
Sungai Mahakam 136 E 3
Sungai Mamberamo 137 J 4
Sungai Melawi 136 D 4
Sungai Mendawai 136 D 4
Sungai Mentarang 136 E 3
Sungai Pahang 136 B 3
Sungai Pawan 136 D 4
Sungaipenuh 136 B 4
Sungai Pulau 137 J 5
Sungai Rokan 136 B 3
Sungai Sampit 136 D 4
Sungai Sembakung 136 E 3
Sungai Seruyan 136 D 4
Sungai Siak 136 B 3
Sungai Tariku 137 J 4
Sungai Taritatu 137 J 4
Sungai Tembesi 136 B 4
Sungai Wama 137 J 4
Sungai Warenai 137 J 4
Sungei Patani 136 B 2
Sungguminasa 137 E 5

Sun – Tal

Sungurlu 117 D 2
Suning 133 G 3
Sunja 115 G 2
Sunjikäy 154 D 6
Sun Kosi 134 E 2
Sunnan 112 F 3
Sunndalen 112 E 3
Sunndalsfjorden 112 E 3
Sunndalsöra 112 E 3
Sunnfjord 112 E 3
Sunnhordland 113 E 4
Sunnmöre 112 E 3
Suntar 130 L 3
Suntar Khayata, Khrebet 131 PQ 3
Sun Valley 170 D 3
Sunwu 131 N 6
Sunyani 156 E 4
Suokonmäki 112 H 3
Suolahti 112 J 3
Suomenselkä 112 J 3
Suomi 112 J 3
Suomussalmi 112 J 3
Suomutunturi 112 J 2
Sũo-nada 133 K 4
Suonenjoki 112 J 3
Suoyarvi 113 K 3
Superior (MT, U.S.A.) 170 D 2
Superior (WI, U.S.A.) 171 H 2
Superior, Lake 171 J 2
Supetar 115 G 3
Suphan Buri 135 H 5
Süphan Daği 117 F 3
Suq ash Shuyūkh 155 H 2
Sūq Suwayq 154 F 4
Suquṭrā 159 J 2
Ṣūr (Lebanon) 154 F 2
Şūr (Oman) 155 K 4
Sura 118 J 4
Surabaya 136 D 5
Surahammar 113 G 4
Sūrak 128 F 5
Surakarta 136 D 5
Surar 159 G 3
Sura, Ra's 159 H 2
Surat (India) 134 B 3
Surat (Australia) 143 H 4
Suratgarh 134 B 2
Surat Thani 135 G 6
Surazh 112 K 4
Surendranagar 134 B 3
Surgut 119 O 3
Surgutikha 119 R 3
Suriapet 134 C 4
Surigao 137 G 2
Surigao Strait 137 G 1
Surin 135 H 5
Surinam 179 G 3
Sūrīyah 154 F 2
Surkhab 129 H 3
Surmän 153 H 2
Sürmene 117 F 2
Surovikino 118 H 6
Sur, Punta 183 E 6
Surrah, Nafūd as 155 G 4
Surrey 103 D 2
Sursee 115 E 2
Surskoye 118 J 5
Surte 113 F 4
Surtsey 112 A 3
Sürüç 117 E 3
Surud Ad 159 H 2
Surulangun 136 B 4
Survey Pass 166 G 2
Susa 128 D 4
Susa 115 E 2
Sušac 115 G 3
Sūsah (Libya) 153 K 2
Sūsah (Tunisia) 153 H 1
Susak 115 F 3
Süsangerd 128 D 4
Susanino 131 Q 5
Susanville 170 B 3
Suşehri 117 E 2
Sušice 111 F 4
Susitna 166 H 3
Susquehanna River 171 L 3
Susques 180 C 5
Sussex (Canada) 169 O 6
Sussundenga 161 E 3
Susuman 131 R 3
Susunu 137 H 4
Susurluk 116 C 3
Sutam 131 N 4
Sutgun 131 S 2
Sutherland 160 C 6
Suðureyri 112 A 2
Suðuroy 110 A 1
Sutlej 129 J 4
Sut Ta 135 G 4
Sutton (AK, U.S.A.) 166 H 3
Sutton (W.V., U.S.A.) 171 K 4
Sutton Coldfield 103 D 1

Sutton in Ashfield 101 E 3
Sutton-on-Sea 103 E 1
Suttor River 143 H 3
Sutun'ya 131 O 2
Sutwik 166 F 4
Suur-Pakri 113 H 4
Suur Väin 113 H 4
Suva 146 C 4
Suva Gora 116 B 2
Suva Planina 116 B 2
Suvasvesi 112 J 3
Suvorov 146 E 3
Suwa 133 L 3
Suwałki 111 H 4
Suwannaphum 135 H 4
Suwannee River 171 K 6
Suwanose-jima 133 J 5
Suwayqīyah, Hawr as 155 H 2
Suwon 133 J 3
Su Xian 133 G 4
Suynsvatn 112 E 3
Suzhou 133 H 4
Suzu 133 L 3
Suzun 119 Q 5
Sværholthalvöya 112 J 1
Svalbard 184
Svalyava 116 B 1
Svantvadi 134 B 4
Svappavaara 112 H 2
Svartisen 112 F 2
Svatay 131 S 2
Svatovo 118 G 5
Svatoy Nos, Mys 131 P 1
Svay Rieng 135 J 5
Svealand 113 FG 4
Sveg 112 F 3
Svegsjön 112 F 3
Svendborg 113 F 4
Svenljunga 113 F 4
Šventoji 113 J 4
Sverdlovsk 119 M 4
Sverige 112 G 3
Svetac 115 F 3
Svetlaya 131 P 6
Svetlogorsk (Belorussiya, U.S.S.R.) 118 B 3
Svetlogorsk (Russia, U.S.S.R.) 113 H 5
Svetlograd 117 F 1
Svetloye, Ozero 117 G 1
Svetly 113 H 5
Svetlyy 119 M 5
Svetlyy 131 N 4
Svetlyy 130 L 4
Svetogorsk 112 J 3
Svetozarevo 116 B 2
Svidnik 111 H 4
Svir' 118 F 3
Sviritsa 113 K 3
Svirsk 130 H 5
Svistov 116 C 2
Svitavy 111 G 5
Svobodnyy 131 N 5
Svobodnyy Port 116 D 1
Svolvær 112 F 2
Svrljig 116 B 2
Svullrya 113 F 3
Swadlincote 103 D 1
Swaffham 103 E 1
Swain Reefs 143 J 3
Swains 147 E 3
Swakop 160 B 4
Swakopmund 160 A 4
Swale 110 C 4
Swaledale 101 E 2
Swale, River 101 E 2
Swallow Reef 136 D 2
Swamp 160 D 2
Swanage 103 C 2
Swan Hill 143 G 6
Swan Islands → Islas del Cisne 172 F 4
Swanlinbar 100 B 2
Swan Range 170 D 2
Swan River 167 R 5
Swansea 102 B 2
Swansea (Airport) 102 B 2
Swansea Bay 102 C 2
Swartberge 160 C 6
Swaziland (Ngwane) 161 E 5
Sweden 112 G 3
Sweet Home 170 B 3
Sweetwater 170 F 5
Sweetwater River 170 E 3
Swellendam 160 C 6
Świdnica 111 G 4
Świdnik 111 H 4
Świdwin 111 G 4
Świebodzin 111 G 4
Świecie 111 G 4
Swift 166 L 4

Swift Current 167 Q 5
Swift River 166 L 3
Swilly, Lough 100 B 2
Swinburne, Cape 167 S 1
Swindon 103 D 2
Swinoujście 111 F 4
Swinton 101 D 3
Switzerland 115 E 2
Swords 100 B 3
Syadaykharvuta 119 O 2
Syagannakh 131 Q 2
Syalakh 131 M 2
Syamozero, Ozero 112 K 3
Syangannakh 131 R 2
Sydney (Australia) 143 J 5
Sydney (Canada) 169 P 6
Sydney (Kiribati) → Manra 147 D 3
Sydney Mines 169 P 6
Sydprøven 169 S 3
Syktyvkar 118 JK 3
Sylacauga 171 J 5
Sylarna 112 F 3
Sylhet 135 F 3
Sylt 111 E 4
Sylvan Pass 170 D 3
Sym 119 R 3
Synegey 131 O 2
Syracuse (KS, U.S.A.) 170 F 4
Syracuse (N.Y., U.S.A.) 171 L 3
Syr-Dar'ya 129 H 2
Syrdar'ya 129 H 2
Syria 154 F 2
Syriam 135 G 4
Syrian Desert 154–155 FG 2
Sysmä 112 J 3
Sysola 118 K 3
Systengnakh 131 P 1
Syöri-Hagangur 112 B 2
Syotomino 119 O 3
Syuge-Khaya, Gora 131 P 2
Syurkum 131 Q 5
Syuryakh-Dzhangy, Vozvyshennost' 130 M 1
Syuryun-Kyuyel' 131 O 2
Syväri 113 J 5
Syverma, Plato 130 G 3
Syzhevka 131 F 4
Syzran 118 J 5
Szamotuły 111 G 4
Szczecin 111 F 4
Szczecinek 111 G 4
Szczytno 111 H 4
Szechwan 132 D 5
Szeged 116 B 1
Székesfehérvár 116 A 1
Szekszárd 116 AB 1
Szentes 116 B 1
Szeskie Wzgórza 111 H 4
Szolnok 116 B 1
Szombathely 116 A 1
Szprotawa 111 G 4

T

Taaga, Khrebet 131 N 4
Ṭa'ām 155 G 5
Taarom 143 H 4
Tabacal 180 D 5
Tabajara 179 F 5
Tabankort 156 E 2
Tabaqah 154 F 1
Tabar Islands 145 F 2
Tabarqah 153 G 1
Tabarsuq 115 E 4
Tabas 128 G 4
Tabas 128 F 4
Tabasara, Serranía de 178 B 2
Tabasco 172 D 4
Tabatinga 178 E 4
Tabatinga, Serra da 181 H 3
Tabelbala 152 E 3
Tabelbala, Kahal de 152 E 3
Tabelbalet 153 G 3
Tabelkoza 152 F 3
Tabeng 135 H 5
Taber 167 P 6
Taberg 113 F 4
Tabernas 114 C 4
Tabernes de Valldigna 114 C 4
Tabiteuea 146 C 3
Tabla 156 E 3
Tablas 137 F 1
Table Mountain 160 B 6
Table Rock Lake 171 H 4
Tabor 131 S 1
Tábor 111 F 5

Tabora 158 E 5–6
Tabou 156 C 5
Tabrīz 128 D 3
Tabuaeran 147 E 2
Tabūk 154 F 3
Tabuleiro 179 G 5
Tabuleiro de Norte 181 J 2
Täby 113 G 4
Tacámbaro 172 B 4
Tacheng 129 L 1
Tachiumet 153 H 3
Tachov 111 F 5
Tacloban 137 F 1
Tacna 180 B 4
Tacoma 170 B 2
Taco Pozo 182 D 4
Tacora 180 C 4
Tacuarembó 182 E 5
Tadcaster 101 E 3
Tademaït, Plateau du 153 F 3
Tadjakant 152 C 5
Tadjemout Bordj 153 F 3
Tadjetaret 153 G 4
Tadjourah 159 G 2
Tadjourah, Golfe de 159 G 2
Tadoule Lake 167 S 4
Tadpatri 134 C 5
Tadzhikistan 129 HJ 3
Taebaek-Sanmaek 133 J 3
Taegu 133 J 3
Taejŏn 133 J 3
Tafahi 147 D 4
Tafalla 114 C 3
Tafassasset 153 G 4
Tafassasset, Ténéré du 157 G 1
Tafermaar 137 H 5
Taffi Viejo 182 C 4
Tafo 156 D 4
Tafraoute 152 D 3
Tagama 157 F 2
Tagan 144 D 3
Taganrog 117 E 1
Taganrogskiy Zaliv 117 E 1
Tagaung 135 G 3
Tagbilaran 137 F 2
Tageru, Jabal 154 D 5
Taggafadi 157 F 2
Taghit 152 E 2
Taghrīfat 153 J 3
Tagish Lake 166 L 4
Tagliamento 115 F 2
Tagounite 152 D 3
Taguá 181 H 3
Taguatinga 181 G 3
Tagudin 137 H 1
Taguenout Haggueret 156 D 1
Taguersimet 152 B 4
Taguienout 153 G 4
Tagula 145 F 4
Tagula Island 143 J 1
Tagum 137 G 2
Tagus 114 B 4
Tahanea 147 F 4
Tahan, Gunung 136 B 3
Tahat, Mont 153 G 4
Tahe 131 M 5
Tahifet 153 G 4
Tahiryuak Lake 167 P 1
Tahiti 147 F 4
Tahkuna Neem 113 H 4
Tahoe, Lake 170 C 4
Tahoua 157 F 3
Tahrūd 128 F 5
Ta Hsai 135 G 3
Taḥtā 154 E 3
Tahtali Dağlari 117 E 3
Tahuamanu 180 C 3
Tahuata 147 F 3
Tahuna 137 G 3
Taï 156 C 4
Tai'an 133 G 3
Tai'an 133 H 2
Taibai Shan 132 E 4
Taibus Qi 132 G 2
Taichung 133 H 6
Taigu 132 F 3
Taihang Shan 132 F 3
Taihe 132 F 5
Taihu 132 G 4
Tai Hu 133 H 4
Taikang 132 F 4
Tailai 133 H 1
Taimani 129 G 4
Taimba 130 G 3
Tainan 133 H 6
Taínaron, Ákra 116 B 3
Taining 133 G 5
Taï, Parc National de 156 C 4
Taipei 133 H 6
Taiping (China) 133 G 4

Taiping (Malaysia) 136 B 3
Taiping Ling 130 M 6
Taipu 181 J 2
Taisetsu-zan 133 M 2
Taishan 132 F 6
Tai Shan 133 G 3
Taishun 133 G 5
Taitao, Península de 183 AB 5
Taitung 133 H 6
Taivalkoski 112 J 2
Taiwan 133 H 6
Taiwan Haixia 133 GH 5
Taiwan Shan 133 H 6
Taiyetos Óros 116 B 3
Taiyuan 132 F 3
Taizhou 133 G 4
Ta'izz 155 G 6
Tajarhī 153 H 5
Tajito 170 D 5
Tajo 114 C 3
Tajrīsh 128 E 3
Tajumulco, Volcán 172 D 4
Tak 135 G 4
Takāb 128 D 3
Takabba 159 G 4
Takalar 137 E 5
Takamatsu 133 K 4
Takaoka 133 L 3
Takara-jima 133 J 5
Takasaki 133 L 3
Takatshwane 160 C 4
Takaungu 159 F 5
Takazze 159 F 2
Takengon 136 A 3
Takeo 135 H 5
Takestan 128 D 3
Taketa 158 B 5
Takhādīd 155 G 3
Takhta 179 F 1
Takhta-Bazar 129 G 3
Takhtabrod 119 N 5
Takhtakupyr 128 GF 2
Takhtamygda 131 M 5
Takhtamysk 131 S 3
Takht-e Soleiman 128 E 3
Takht-i-Sulaiman 129 HJ 4
Taki 145 G 2
Takijuq Lake 167 P 2
Takikawa 133 M 2
Takket → Aïn el Hadjadj 153 G 3
Takla Lake 167 M 4
Takla Landing 167 M 4
Takla Makan 129 L 3
Taklaun, Gora 131 Q 3
Taklimakan Shamo 129 L 3
Takolokouzet, Massif de 157 F 2
Takoradi (Sekondi-) 156 D 5
Takpa Shiri 135 F 2
Takua Pa 135 G 6
Takum 157 F 4
Takume 137 F 4
Takutea 147 E 4
Tala 172 B 3
Talagante 182 B 5
Talagapa 183 C 7
Tälah 153 G 1
Talak 157 F 2
Talakan 131 O 6
Talakmau, Gunung 136 B 3
Talandzha 131 O 6
Talara 178 B 4
Talar-i-Band 129 G 5
Talas 129 J 2
Talasea 145 F 3
Talasskiy Alatau, Khrebet 129 J 2
Talata Mafara 157 F 3
Tala-Tumsa 131 O 2
Talaud, Kepulauan 137 G 3
Talavera de la Reina 114 C 4
Talawdī 154 E 6
Talca 183 B 6
Talcahuano 183 B 6
Talcher 134 E 3
Taldora 143 G 2
Taldy-Kurgan 119 P 6
Taleḥ 159 H 3
Talence 114 C 3
Tälesh 128 D 3
Talgar 129 K 2
Talgath 102 C 1
Taliabu, Pulau 137 F 4
Talima 179 G 3
Talimardzhan 129 H 3
Taliqan 129 H 3
Talitsa 119 M 4
Taliwang 136 E 5
Talkalakh 154 F 2
Talkeetna 166 H 3
Talkeetna Mountains 166 H 3
Tall 'Afar 155 G 1

Tal–Teb

Tallahassee 171 K 5
Tallapoosa River 171 J 5
Tall aṣ Ṣuwār 155 G 1
Tallinn 112 H 4
Tall Kūshik 155 G 1
Tallulah 171 H 5
Tălmaciu 116 B 1
Tal'menka 119 Q 5
Talmine 152 E 3
Talnakh 119 R 2
Tal'nik 131 T 4
Tal'noye 116 D 1
Talo 159 F 2
Taloda 134 B 3
Talok 137 E 3
Talovka 131 UV 3
Talovka 117 G 2
Talsi 113H 4
Talsinnt 152 E 2
Taltal 182 B 4
Taltson 167 P 3
Taltson 167 Q 3
Taluma 131 M 4
Talvik 112 H 1
Tamabo Range 136 E 3
Tamada 153 F 4
Tamaia 157 F 2
Tamala 142 A 4
Tamale 156 D 4
Tama, Mount 160 A 2
Taman 117 E 1
Tamana 146 C 3
Tamanrasset 153 G 4
Tamanrasset 153 F 4
Tamar 134 E 3
Tamara (Yugoslavia) 116 A 2
Támara (Colombia) 178 D 2
Tamar, River 102 B 2
Tamarugal, Pampa del 180 C 5
Tamaské 157 F 3
Tamaulipas 172 C 3
Tamaya 182 B 5
Tamazunchale 172 C 3
Tamba 156 B 3
Tambacounda 156 B 3
Tambalan 136 E 3
Tambara 161 E 3
Tambelan, Kepulauan 136 C 3
Tambisan 137 E 2
Tambo (Peru) 180 B 3
Tambo (Australia) 143 H 3
Tambo de Mora 180 A 3
Tambohorano 161 G 3
Tambor 160 A 3
Tambora, Gunung 137 E 5
Tamboril 181 H 3
Tambov 118 F 5
Tambovka 131 N 5
Tambre 114 B 3
Tambura 158 D 3
Tamburi 181 H 3
Tamch 130 F 6
Tamchaket 152 C 5
Tamdybulak 129 G 2
Tame 178 D 2
Tamel Aike 183 B 8
Tamesguidat 153 F 3
Tamgak, Monts 157 F 2
Tamgué, Massif du 156 B 3
Tamil Nadu 134 C 5
Tamis 116 B 1
Tam Ky 135 J 4
Tammerfors 112 H 3
Tammisaari 113 H 3
Tampa 171 K 6
Tampa Bay 171 K 6
Tampere (Tammerfors) 112 H 3
Tampico 172 C 3
Tamrau, Pegunungan 137 H 4
Tamri 152 CD 2
Tamsagbulag 133 G 1
Tamshiyacu 178 D 4
Tamsu 160 C 3
Tamsweg 115 F 2
Tamu 135 F 3
Tamuin 172 C 3
Tamuin, Rio 172 C 3
Tamworth (Australia) 143 J 5
Tamworth (U.K.) 103 D 1
Tana (Kenya) 159 F 2
Tana (Norway) 112 J 1
Tana bru 112 J 1
Tanacross 166 J 3
Tanafjorden 112 J 1
Tanaga 166 B 5
Tanahbala, Pulau 136 A 4
Tanahgrogot 136 E 4
Tanahjampea, Kepulauan 137 F 5
Tanahmasa, Pulau 136 A 4
Tanah Merah 136 B 2
Tanahmerah 144 D 3
Tanakpur 134 D 2
Tana, Lake 159 F 2

Tanama 119 Q 1
Tanam, Cape 167 T 4
Tanami 142 D 2
Tanami Desert Wildlife Sanctuary 142 E 2–3
Tan An 135 J 5
Tanana 166 G 2
Tanana River 166 H 3
Tanaro 115 E 3
Tanch'ŏn 133 J 2
Tanda 156 D 4
Tandag 137 G 2
Tandaho 159 G 2
Tandaltī 154 E 6
Tăndărei 116 C 2
Tandil 183 E 6
Tandragee 100 B 2
Tandsjöborg 112 F 3
Tanḍubāyah 154 D 5
Tane-ga-shima 133 K 4
Tan Emellel 153 G 3
Tanezrouft 152 E 4
Tanezrouft N-Ahenet 152–153 F 4
Ṭanf, Jabal at 154 F 2
Tang 128 F 5
Tanga 159 F 3
Tangail 134 E 3
Tanga Islands 145 F 2
Tangalla 134 D 6
Tanganyika, Lake 158 DE 6
Tanger 152 D 1
Tangerang 136 C 5
Tanggula Shan 132 B 4
Tanggula Shankou 132 B 4
Tanghe 132 F 4
Tangier → Tanger 152 D 1
Tangmai 132 C 4
Tangra Yumco 134 E 1
Tangshan 133 G 3
Tanguiéta 156 E 3
Tangwanghe 131 N 6
Tangyin 132 F 3
Tangyuan 133 J 1
Tani 135 H 5
Taniantaweng Shan 132 C 4
Tanimbar Islands 144 B 3
Tanimbar, Kepulauan 137 H 5
Tanjore → Thanjavur 134 C 5
Tanjuncu Poliwali 137 E 4
Tanjung 136 E 4
Tanjung Api 136 C 3
Tanjung Aru 136 E 4
Tanjung Arus 137 F 3
Tanjungbalai 136 A 3
Tanjungbatu 136 E 3
Tanjung Blitung 136 C 3
Tanjung Bugel 136 D 5
Tanjung Cangkuang 136 B 5
Tanjung Cina 136 B 5
Tanjung De Jong 137 J 5
Tanjung, Jabung 136 B 4
Tanjung Jambuair 136 A 2
Tanjung Kandi 137 F 3
Tanjung Karossa 137 E 5
Tanjung Kolff 137 H 5
Tanjung Lalereh 137 E 4
Tanjung Layar 136 E 4
Tanjung Libobo 137 G 4
Tanjung Lumut 136 C 4
Tanjung Malatayur 136 D 4
Tanjung Mangkalihat 137 E 3
Tanjung Manimbaya 137 E 4
Tanjung Palpetu 137 G 4
Tanjungpandan 136 C 4
Tanjungpinang 136 B 3
Tanjungpusu 136 D 4
Tanjung Puting 136 D 4
Tanjungredeb 136 E 3
Tanjung Samak 136 C 4
Tanjung Sambar 136 D 4
Tanjung Selatan 136 D 4
Tanjungselor 136 E 3
Tanjung Vals 137 J 5
Tanjung Waka 137 G 4
Tan Kena Bordj 153 G 3
Tankhoy 130 J 5
Tankovo 119 R 3
Tankse 129 K 4
Tanlovo 119 O 2
Tanna 146 C 4
Tanna 145 J 5
Tännäs 112 F 3
Tannu Ola 130 F 5
Tanoucherte 152 C 4
Tanout 157 F 2
Ṭanṭā 154 E 2
Tan Tan 152 C 3
Tanto Adam 129 G 5
Tantoyuca 172 C 3
Tanuku 134 D 4
Tanyurer 131 X 2
Tanzania 158 EF 6

Tao'an 133 H 1
Taoghe 160 C 3
Taolanaro 161 H 4–5
Taongi 146 C 2
Taormina 115 G 4
Taos 170 E 4
Taoudenni 156 C 1
Taoudjafet 152 C 5
Taounate 152 E 2
Taouriri (Algeria) 152 F 3
Taouriri (Morocco) 152 E 2
Taouz 152 E 2
Taoyuan 133 H 5
Tapa 112 J 4
Tapachula 172 D 5
Tapah 136 B 3
Tapaktuan 136 A 3
Tapan 136 B 4
Tapauá 178 E 5
Tapauá 179 F 5
Tapes 182 F 5
Tapeta 156 C 4
Tapini 144 E 3
Tapirapua 180 E 3
Tapoa 156 E 3
Tappahannock 171 L 4
Tapti 134 B 3
Tapul Group 137 F 2
Tapurucuara 178 E 4
Taquara 182 F 4
Taquari 180 E 4
Taquari 181 F 4
Tara (U.S.S.R.) 119 O 4
Tara (Zambia) 160 D 3
Tara (Rep. of Ireland) 110 B 4
Tara (Yugoslavia) 116 A 2
Taraba 156 F 4
Tarābulus (Lebanon) 154 F 2
Tarābulus (Libya) 153 H 2
Taracua 178 E 3
Tarahouahout 153 G 4
Tarahumara, Sierra 170 E 6
Tarai 134 E 2
Tarakan 136 E 3
Tarakki 153 G 3
Tarakliya 116 C 1
Taraku Shima 131 R 7
Taran 119 O 1
Tarancón 114 C 3
Tarangire National Park 159 F 5
Taran, Mys 113 G H 5
Taransay 98 A 3
Taranto 115 G 3
Taranto, Golfo di 115 G 3–4
Tarapacá 178 E 4
Tarapoto 178 C 5
Tararua Range 145 R 9
Tarascon 115 D 3
Tarasovo 118 J 2
Tarat 153 G 3
Tarata (Bolivia) 180 C 4
Tarata (Peru) 180 B 4
Tarauacá 178 D 5
Tarawa 146 C 2
Tarazit 157 F 1
Tarazit, Massif de 157 F 1
Tara Zlatibor 116 A 2
Tarazona 114 C 3
Tarazona de la Mancha 114 C 4
Tarbagatay, Khrebet 119 Q 6
Tarbagatay Shan 129 L 1
Tarbat Ness 98 C 3
Tarbert (Strathclyde) 99 B 4
Tarbert (Western Isles) 98 A 3
Tarbes 114 D 3
Tarbū 153 J 3
Tarcoola (New South Wales, Austr.) 143 G 5
Tarcoola (South Australia) 142 E 5
Tarcutta 143 H 6
Tardoki Yani, Gora 131 P 6
Taree 143 J 5
Tareina 159 G 2
Tärendö 112 H 2
Tareya 130 F 1
Tarfā, Ra's aṭ 155 G 5
Tarfaya 152 C 3
Târgovište 116 C 2
Tarhūnah 153 H 2
Tarīf 155 J 4
Tarifa 114 B 4
Tarija 180 D 5
Tariku, Sungai 137 J 4
Tarim (China) 129 L 2
Tarīm (S. Yemen) 155 H 5
Tarime 158 E 5
Tarim He 128 E 2
Tarim Liuchang 132 A 2
Tarin Kowt 129 H 4
Ṭarīq Masūs 153 K 2
Taritatu, Sungai 137 J 4
Tarka 157 F 3

Tarkhankut, Mys 117 D 1
Tarko-Sale 130 C 3
Tarkwa 156 D 4
Tarlac 137 J 1
Tarma 180 A 3
Tarn 114 D 3
Tärnaby 112 G 2
Tarnobrzeg 111 H 4
Tarnów 111 H 4
Tarnowskie Góry 111 G 4
Taron 145 F 2
Tarou 157 H 1
Tarouadji 157 F 2
Tarouadji, Monts 157 F 2
Taroudant 152 D 2
Tarpon Springs 171 K 6
Tarquí 178 CD 4
Tarquinia 115 F 3
Tarradalen 112 G 2
Tarrafal 156 B 6
Tarragona 114 D 3
Tarrasa 114 D 3
Tárrega 114 D 3
Tarso Taro 157 H 1
Tarso Tiéroko 157 H 1
Tarsū Mūsá 153 J 4
Tarsus 117 D 3
Tart 132 B 3
Tartagal 180 D 5
Tartas 114 C 3
Tartuke 156 C 4
Tartu 113 J 4
Ṭarṭus 154 F 2
Tarumovka 117 G 2
Tarutino 116 C 1
Tarutung 136 A 3
Tarvo 180 D 4
Tasajera, Sierra 170 E 6
Tas-Buget 129 H 2
Tasedjibest 153 G 3
Tashakta 119 R 6
Tashauz 128 F 2
Tashigang 135 F 2
Tashkent 129 H 2
Tashkepri 129 G 3
Tash-Kumyr 129 J 2
Tashkurghan 129 H 3
Tashtagol 119 R 5
Tashtyp 119 R 5
Tasikmalaya 136 C 5
Tåsjön 112 G 3
Taskan 131 S 3
Tasker 157 G 2
Taşköprü 117 D 2
Taskyl, Khrebet 130 G 5
Tas-Kystabys, Khrebet 131 Q 3
Taşlıçay 117 F 3
Tasman Basin 193 C 5
Tasman Bay 145 Q 9
Tasmania 144 L 9
Tasman Peninsula 144 L 9
Tasman Sea 144 NO 8
Tasova 117 E 2
Tassara 157 F 2
Tassiast 152 B 4
Tassialouc, Lac 169 N 4
Tassili N-Ajjer 153 G 3
Tassili Oua-n Ahaggar 153 FG 4
Tas-Tumus 131 N 3
Tas-Tumus 131 O 3
Tastūr 115 E 4
Taşucu 117 D 3
Tasūj 128 D 3
Tas-Yuryakh 130 K 3
Tata 116 C 2
Tatabánya 116 A 1
Tatakoto 147 F 4
Tatarbunary 116 C 1
Tatarsk 119 P 4
Tatarskiy Proliv 131 Q 5–6
Tatau 136 D 3
Tathlina Lake 167 O 3
Tathlīth 155 G 5
Tatos Dağları 117 F 2
Tatry 111 GH 5
Tatta 129 H 6
Tattershall 101 E 3
Tatty 129 J 2
Tatung 125
Tatvan 117 F 3
Tauá 181 H 2
Tauapeçaçu 179 F 4
Tauariã 179 F 5
Taubaté 181 G 5
Tauchik 128 E 2
Tauere 147 F 4
Taufstein 111 E 4
Taukum, Peski 129 K 2
Taumarunui 145 R 8
Taumaturgo 178 D 5

Taung 160 C 5
Taungdwingyi 135 G 3
Taunggon 135 G 3
Taung-gyi 135 G 3
Taunglau 135 G 3
Taungnyo Range 135 G 4
Taungup 135 F 4
Taunton 102 C 2
Taunus 111 E 4
Taupo 145 R 8
Taupo, Lake 145 R 8
Tauragė 113 H 4
Tauranga 145 R 8
Tauria-nova 115 G 4
Taurisano 115 G 4
Taurus Mountains → Toros Dağ-
    lari 117 D 3
Tauu Islands 145 G 2
Tauwsa Barrage 129 J 4
Tauysk 131 R 4
Tauz 117 G 2
Tavas 116 C 3
Tavastehus 112 H 3
Tavatuma 131 T 3
Tavda 119 N 4
Taverner Bay 169 N 1
Taveta 159 F 5
Taviano 115 G 4
Tavistock 102 B 2
Tavolara 115 E 3
Tavoy 135 G 5
Tavşanlı 116 C 3
Tavvaskaite 112 H 2
Tavyskaya Guba 131 RS 4
Tāwarghā' 153 J 2
Tawas City 171 K 3
Tawau 136 E 3
Tawfīqīyah 158 E 3
Tawitawi Group 137 F 2
Tawkar 154 F 3
Taw, River 102 C 2
Tawzar 153 G 2
Taxco de Alarcón 172 C 4
Taxkorgan 129 K 3
Tay 110 C 3
Tayakhtakh 131 N 4
Tayandu 137 H 5
Taybamba 178 C 5
Taybola 112 E 2
Tayègle 159 G 4
Tayga 119 R 4
Taygonos, Mys 131 U 3
Taygonos, Poluostrov 131 U 3
Tay, Loch 99 B 3
Taylor 166 DE 2
Taylorville 171 J 4
Taymā' 154 F 3
Taymura 130 G 3
Taymylyr 130 M 1
Taymyr 130 H 1
Taymyra, Verkhnyaya 130 G 1
Taymyr, Ozero 130 H 1
Taymyr Peninsula 130 FG 1
Taymyr, Poluostrov 130 E 1–J 1
Tay Ninh 135 J 5
Tay, River 99 C 3
Tayshet 130 G 4
Taytay 137 E 1
Tayura 130 J 4
Tayshir 130 G 6
Tayside 99 C 3
Taz 119 Q 2
Taz 119 P 2
Taza 152 E 2
Tāzah Khurmātū 155 G 1–2
Tazdağ 116 C 2
Tazenakht 152 D 2
Tazerbo Oasis → Wāḥāt at Tā-
    zirbū 153 K 3
Tazovskaya Guba 119 P 2
Tazovskij 119 P 2
Tazumal 172 E 5
Tazungdam 135 G 2
Tbilisi 117 F 2
Tbilisskaya 117 F 1
Tchabal Mbabo 157 G 4
Tchad 157 H 3
Tchamba (Cameroon) 157 G 4
Tchamba (Togo) 156 E 4
Tchaourou 156 E 4
Tchibanga 157 G 6
Tchié 157 H 2
Tchien 156 C 4
Tchigai, Plateau du 157 G 1
Tchollíré 157 G 4
Tczew 111 G 4
Te Anau, Lake 144 P 10
Teapa 172 D 4
Tea Tree 142 E 3
Teba 137 J 4
Tebahalet 156 E 2
Teberda 117 F 2
Tébessa 153 G 1

283

Teb – Tid

Tebingtinggi 136 B 4
Tebingtinggi 136 A 3
Tebingtinggi, Pulau 136 B 3
Tebulos Mta 117 G 2
Tecalitlán 172 B 4
Tecate 170 C 5
Tecer Dağlari 117 E 3
Tecka 183 B 7
Tecomán 172 B 4
Tecuala 172 A 3
Tecuci 116 C 1
Tedzhen 128 G 3
Tedzhenstroy 129 G 3
Teesdale 101 D 2
Tees, River 101 E 2
Teesside 101 E 2
Teesside (Airport) 101 E 2
Tefé 178 E 4
Tefé 179 F 4
Tefenni 116 C 3
Tegal 136 C 5
Tegguidda In Tessoum 157 F 2
Tegina 157 F 3
Tegre 159 FG 2
Tegucigalpa 172 E 5
Tegul'det 119 R 4
Tegyul'te-Tërde 131 O 3
Tehamiyam 154 F 5
Te Hapua 145 Q 7
Teheran → Tehrān 128 E 3
Téhini 156 D 4
Tehi-n Isser 153 G 4
Tehoru 137 G 4
Tehrān 128 E 3
Tehuacán 172 C 4
Tehuantepec 172 C 4
Tehuata 147 F 4
Teide, Pico de 152 B 3
Teifi, River 102 B 1
Teiga Plateau → Ḥaḍabat Tayga 154 D 5
Teignmouth 102 C 2
Teixeira Pinto 156 A 3
Téjo 114 B 4
Teju 135 G 2
Tekeli 129 K 2
Tekes 129 L 2
Tekes He 129 L 2
Tekija 116 B 2
Tekin 131 O 6
Tekirdağ 116 C 2
Tekman 117 F 3
Teknaf 135 F 3
Tekouiât 153 F 4
Tekouiat 153 F 4
Tekro 157 J 2
Te Kuiti 145 R 8
Tel 134 D 3
Telavåg 113 D 3
Telavi 117 G 2
Tel Aviv-Yafo 154 E 2
Telč 111 G 5
Tele 158 C 4
Telefomin 144 D 3
Telegraph Creek 166 L 4
Telemaco Borba 181 F 5
Telemark 113 E 4
Telén 183 C 6
Teleneshty 116 C 1
Telerhteba, Djebel 153 G 4
Telescope Peak 170 C 4
Teles Pires 179 G 5
Teletskoye, Ozero 119 R 5
Telfane, Hadjer 157 H 3
Telfel 176 E 2
Telford 101 D 3
Teli 130 F 5
Télimélé 156 B 3
Teljo, Jabal 154 D 6
Tell 154 F 2
Tell al 'Amārna 154 E 3
Teller 166 D 2
Tellicherry 134 C 5
Tello 182 C 5
Telmen Nuur 130 G 6
Telmest 152 D 2
Telok Anson 136 B 3
Teloloapan 172 C 4
Tel'pos-Iz, Gora 119 L 3
Telsen 183 C 7
Telšiai 113 H 4
Teluk Adang 136 E 4
Teluk Balikpapan 136 E 4
Telukbatang 136 C 4
Teluk Berau 137 H 4
Telukbetung → Bandarlampung 136 C 5
Teluk Bima 137 E 5
Teluk Bintuni 137 H 4
Teluk Bone 137 F 4
Teluk Buli 137 G 3
Telukbutun 136 C 3
Teluk Cendrawasih 137 H 4

Telukdalam 136 A 3
Teluk Darvel 137 E 3
Teluk Kau 137 G 3
Teluk Kuantan 136 B 4
Teluk Kumai 136 D 4
Teluk Kupang 137 F 6
Teluk Mandar 137 E 4
Teluk Pamukan 136 E 4
Teluk Pelabuanratu 136 C 5
Teluk Saleh 136 E 5
Teluk Sampit 136 D 4
Teluk Sanggar 137 E 5
Teluk Sangkulirang 136 E 3
Teluk Sape 137 E 5
Teluk Sebuku 136 E 3
Teluk Sindeh 137 F 5
Teluk Tolo 137 F 4
Teluk Tomini 137 F 4
Teluk Weda 137 G 3
Téma 156 DE 4
Témacine 153 G 2
Tematangi 147 F 4
Tembenchi 130 G 3
Tembenchi 130 G 2
Tembesi, Sungai 136 B 4
Tembilahan 136 B 4
Temblador 179 F 2
Tembleque 114 C 4
Tembo 158 B 6
Tembo Falls 158 B 6
Tembo, Mont 157 G 5
Tembué 161 E 2
Temerin 116 A 1
Teme, River 102 C 1
Temerloh 136 B 3
Temir 128 F 1
Temirgoyevskaya 117 F 1
Temirtau 119 O 5
Temiscaming 171 L 2
Temki 157 H 3
Temoe 147 G 4
Temora 143 H 5
Tempa 184
Tempe 170 D 5
Tempio Pausania 115 E 3
Temple 171 G 5
Templemore 100 B 3
Tempué 160 B 2
Temryuk 117 E 1
Temryukskiy Zaliv 117 E 1
Temuco 183 B 6
Tena 178 C 4
Tenali 134 D 4
Tenasserim 135 G 5
Tenby 102 B 2
Tenda, Col di 115 E 3
Ten Degree Channel 135 F 6
Tendel 152 C 5
Tendrara 152 E 2
Tendrovskaya Kosa 117 D 1
Tendürek Dağı 117 F 3
Tenekert 156 E 2
Tenenkou 156 CD 3
Ténéré 157 G 1–2
Ténéré du Tafassasset 157 G 1
Ténéré, Erg de 157 G 2
Tenerife 152 B 3
Ténès 153 F 1
Tengchong 132 C 5
Tenggarong 136 E 4
Tengger Shamo 132 D 3
Tengiz, Ozero 119 N 5
Tengushevo 118 H 5
Teng Xian 132 F 6
Teng Xian 133 G 3
Tenialig 152 C 4
Teniente Marsh 185
Teniente Matienzo 185
Tenkasi 134 C 6
Tenke (U.S.S.R.) 130 L 3
Tenke (Zaire) 160 D 2
Tenkodogo 156 D 3
Tennant Creek 142 E 2
Tennessee 171 J 4
Tennessee River 171 J 4
Teno 182 B 5
Tenojoki 112 J 2
Tenom 136 E 2
Tenosique de Pino Suárez 172 D 4
Tenterden 103 E 2
Tenterfield 143 J 4
Tentolomatinan, Gunung 137 F 3
Tentugal 179 J 4
Teocaltiche 172 B 3
Teófilo Otoni 181 H 4
Teotihuacan 172 C 4
Teouit 153 G 3
Tepa 137 G 5
Tepa 144 A 3
Tepache 170 E 6
Tepatitlán de Morelos 172 B 3
Tepe Gawra → Khorsābād 155 G 1

Tepehuanes, Sierra de 172 A 2
Tepelena 116 B 2
Tepic 172 B 3
Teplice 111 F 4
Teplik 116 C 1
Teplogorka 118 K 3
Tepoca, Bahia de 170 D 5
Tequila 172 B 3
Ter 114 D 3
Tera (Portugal) 114 B 4
Téra (Niger) 156 E 3
Teraina 147 E 2
Terakeka 158 E 3
Teramo 115 F 3
Tercan 117 F 3
Terceira 152 A 1
Terekhovka 118 F 5
Terek 117 F 2
Terek 128 D 2
Terempa 136 C 3
Terenni 152 D 5
Terenos 181 F 5
Terentang, Pulau 136 E 4
Tereraimbu, Cachoeira do 179 H 5
Teresina 181 H 2
Teresinha 179 H 3
Teresita 178 E 3
Terespol 111 H 4
Teressa 135 F 6
Terhir 153 F 2
Teriberka 112 K 2
Teriberka 112 L 2
Terkezi 157 J 2
Terme 117 F 2
Termeli 117 D 3
Termez 129 H 3
Termini Imerese 115 F 4
Termit Kaoboul 157 G 2
Termit, Massif de 157 G 2
Termoli 115 F 3
Ternate 137 G 3
Terneuzen 110 D 4
Terney 133 L 1
Terni 115 F 3
Ternopol' 118 E 6
Terpeniya, Mys 131 Q 6
Terpeniya, Zaliv 131 Q 6
Terpugovo 119 N 4
Terrace 166 M 5
Terracina 115 F 3
Terracy Bay 168 K 6
Terra de Basto 114 B 3
Terra di Bari 115 G 3
Terra Firma 160 C 5
Terråk 112 F 2
Terralba 115 E 4
Terra Prêta 179 G 4–5
Terra Santa 179 G 4
Terrebonne Bay 171 H 6
Terre Haute 171 J 4
Terre Plaine 114 D 2
Tersakan Gölü 117 D 3
Teruel 114 C 3
Tervola 112 H 2
Teshekpuk Lake 166 G 1
Teslin 166 L 3
Teslin Lake 166 L 3
Tesocoma 172 D 3
Tessalit 156 E 1
Tessaoua 157 F 3
Tesseneï 158 F 1
Testa, Capo 115 E 3
Testigos, Islas los 179 F 1
Tetari, Cerro 178 D 2
Tetbury 103 C 2
Tete 161 E 2
Tetepare 145 G 2
Tetere 145 H 3
Teteven 116 B 2
Tetiaroa 147 F 4
Teton Peak 170 D 2
Tétouan 152 D 1
Tetovo 116 B 2
Tetrino 118 G 2
Tetuan → Tétouan 152 D 1
Teuini 178 E 5
Teulada 115 E 4
Tevere 115 F 3
Teverya 154 F 2
Teviot 110 C 3
Teviotdale 99 C 4
Teviot, River 99 C 4
Tevriz 119 O 4
Te Waewae Bay 144 P 10
Tewkesbury 103 C 2
Tēwo 132 D 4
Texarkana 171 H 5
Texas (U.S.A.) 170 F 5
Texas (Australia) 143 J 4
Texas City 171 H 6
Texel 110 D 4

Teya 130 F 3
Teykovo 118 H 4
Teyuareh 129 G 4
Teziutlán 172 C 4
Tezur 135 F 2
Tha-anne 167 S 3
Thabana Ntlenyana 160 D 5
Thabazimbi 160 D 4
Thādiq 155 H 3
Thagyettaw 135 G 5
Thai Binh 135 J 3
Thailand 135 G 4
Thailand, Gulf of 135 H 5
Thai Nguyen 135 J 3
Thakhek 135 H 4
Thalabarivat 135 J 5
Thal Desert 129 J 4
Thale Luang 135 H 6
Thallon 143 H 4
Thamad Bū Ḥashishah 153 J 3
Thamarīd 155 J 5
Thame 103 D 2
Thames (N.Z.) 145 R 8
Thames, River 103 E 2
Thāmir, Jabal 155 H 6
Thamūd 155 H 5
Thana 134 B 4
Thangoo 142 C 2
Thangool 143 J 3
Thanh Hoa 135 J 4
Thaniyah, Jabal 155 H 5
Thanjavur 134 C 5
Thann 115 E 2
Thano Bula Khan 129 G 5
Tha Pla 135 H 4
Thap Sakae 135 G 5
Thapston 103 D 1
Tharad 134 B 3
Thargomindah 143 G 4
Tharrawaddy 135 G 4
Tharrawaw 135 G 4
Tharthār, Baḥr ath 155 G 2
Thásos 116 B 2
Tha Tako 135 H 4
Thateng 135 J 5
Thaton 135 G 4
Tha Tum 135 H 4
Thau, Bassin de 114 D 3
Thaungdut 135 F 3
Thayetchaung 135 G 5
Thayetmyo 135 F 4
Thazi 135 F 4
The Alps 115 EF 2
The Bahamas 173 GH 2
Thebes 154 E 3
The Broads 110 D 4
The Brothers → Al Ikhwān 159 J 2
The Cheviot 99 C 4
The Dalles 170 B 2
Theddlethorpe 103 E 1
Thedford 170 F 3
The Everglades 171 K 6
The Fens 103 E 1
The Gambia 156 A 3
The Granites 142 E 3
The Great Oasis → Wāḥāt al Khārijah 154 E 3
The Gulf 155 J 3
The Hague 110 D 4
Theinkun 135 G 5
The Johnston Lakes 142 C 5
The Lizard 102 B 2
Thelon 167 R 3
The Mearns 99 C 3
The Merse 99 C 4
The Monument 143 G 3
The Needles 103 D 2
The North Sound 98 C 2
Thénia 114 D 4
Theologos 116 B 2
The Pas 167 R 5
Thermaïkos Kólpos 116 B 2
Thermopílai 116 B 3
Thermopolis 170 E 3
Theronsvalley 160 C 4
Thesiger Bay 167 N 1
The Solent 103 D 2
Thessalía 116 B 3
Thessaloníki 116 B 2
The Teeth 137 EF 2
Thetford 103 E 1
Thetford Mines 169 N 6
The Trossachs 99 B 3
The Twins 145 Q 9
The Valley 173 K 4
The Wash 103 E 1
The Weald 103 E 2
Thief River Falls 171 G 2
Thiers 114 D 2

Thiès 156 A 3
Thiesi 115 E 3
Thika 159 F 5
Thiladummathi Atoll 134 B 6
Thimphu 134 E 2
Þingvallavatn 112 A 3
Þingvellir 112 A 3
Thio (Ethiopia) 159 G 2
Thio (New Caledonia) 145 J 6
Thionville 115 E 2
Thiou 156 D 3
Þíra 116 C 3
Third Cataract → Ash Shallāl ath Thālith 154 E 5
Thirsk 101 E 2
Thisted 113 E 4
Thitu Island 136 D 1
Thivai 116 B 3
Thiviers 114 D 2
Þjórsá 112 B 3
Thlewiaza 167 S 3
Thoeng 135 H 4
Thohoyandou 161 E 4
Thomas Shoal 136 E 2
Thomasville (AL, U.S.A.) 171 J 5
Thomasville (GA, U.S.A.) 171 K 5
Thompson 167 S 4
Thompson Falls 170 C 2
Thomson River 143 G 3
Thon Buri 135 H 5
Thongwa 135 G 4
Thonon-les-Bains 115 E 2
Þórisvatn 112 B 3
Þorlákshöfn 112 A 3
Thorne 101 E 3
Thornton Cleveleys 101 D 3
Þórshöfn 112 B 2
Thowa 159 F 5
Thraki 116 C 2
Thrakion Pélagos 116 BC 2
Three Forks 170 D 2
Three Hummock Island 144 L 9
Three Kings Islands 145 Q 7
Three Pagodas Pass 135 G 4
Three Points, Cape 156 D 5
Three Springs 142 B 4
Throssel, Lake 142 C 4
Thuillier, Mount 135 F 6
Thule 184
Thun 115 E 2
Thundelarra 142 B 4
Thunder Bay 171 K 3
Thung Luang 135 G 5
Thung Song 135 G 6
Thung Wa 135 G 6
Thüringen 111 F 4
Thüringer Wald 111 F 4
Thurles 100 B 3
Thurso 98 C 2
Thurston Island 185
Thusis 115 E 2
Thy 113 E 4
Thylungra 143 G 4
Tíago 179 G 4
Tianchang 133 G 4
Tiandong 132 E 6
Tian'e 131 E 1
Tiangua 181 H 1
Tianjin 133 G 3
Tianjin Xingang 133 G 3
Tianjun 132 C 3
Tianlin 132 E 6
Tianmen 132 F 4
Tianmu Shan 133 G 4
Tian Shan 129 M 2
Tianshifu 133 H 2
Tianshui 132 E 4
Tiantai 133 H 5
Tianyang 132 E 6
Tianzhu 132 D 3
Tiaret 152 F 1
Tiassulé 156 D 4
Tibarardine 153 F 3
Tibati 157 G 4
Tiber 115 F 3
Tiberias → Teverya 154 F 2
Tibesti 157 H 1
Tibet, Plateau of 134 DE 1
Tibistī, Sarīr 153 J 4
Tibro 113 F 4
Tiburon, Isla 170 D 6
Ticao 137 F 1
Tichit 152 D 5
Tichla 152 B 4
Ticino 115 E 2
Ticul 172 E 3
Tidaholm 113 F 4
Tidikelt 153 F 3
Tiddim 135 F 3
Tidirhine, Jbel 152 E 2
Tidjettaouine 153 F 4
Tidjkdja 152 C 5

Tidra, Ile 152 B 5
Tiebissou 156 C 4
Tiel 156 A 3
Tieli 131 N 6
Tieling 133 H 2
Tielongtan 129 K 3
Tiéme 156 C 4
Tienba 156 C 4
Tientsin → Tianjin 133 G 3
Tierp 113 G 3
Tierra Blanca 172 C 4
Tierra Colorada 172 C 4
Tierra de Barros 114 B 4
Tierra de Campos 114 BC 3
Tierra del Fuego, Isla Grande de 183 C 9
Tierra del Pan 114 B 3
Tierra del Vino 114 B 3
Tieté 181 F 5
Tifariti 152 C 3
Tiflis → Tbilisi 117 F 2
Tifton 171 K 5
Tifu 137 G 4
Tiga 145 J 6
Tigalda 166 E 5
Tigil' 131 T 4
Tignère 157 G 4
Tigre 178 C 4
Tigres, Baía dos 160 A 3
Tigris 155 G 2
Tiguent 152 B 5
Tiguentourine 153 G 3
Tigui 157 H 2
Tiguidit, Falaise de 157 F 2
Tihāmat 155 G 5
Tījī 153 H 2
Tijuana 170 C 5
Tijucas 181 G 6
Tikal 172 E 4
Tikamgarh 134 C 3
Tikanlik 132 A 2
Tikaré 156 D 3
Tikchik Lakes 166 F 3
Tikhoretsk 117 F 1
Tikhtoozero, Ozero 112 K 2
Tikhvin 118 F 4
Tikkakoski 112 J 3
Tikopia 145 J 4
Tikrīt 155 G 2
Tiksha 112 K 3
Tikshozero, Ozero 112 K 2
Tiksi 131 N 1
Tilaiya Reservoir 134 E 3
Tilbeşar Ovası 117 E 3
Tilbooroo 143 H 4
Tilburg 110 D 4
Tilbury 103 E 2
Tilcara 180 C 5
Tilemsi el Fasi 152 E 3
Tilemsi, Vallée du 156 DE 2
Tilia 152 F 3
Tilichiki 131 V 3
Tilin 135 F 3
Tillabéri 156 E 3
Tillamook 170 B 2
Tillanchong Island 135 F 6
Tillia 157 E 2
Tiloa 156 E 2
Tilogne 156 B 2
Tiflos 115 F 3
Tilpa 143 G 5
Til'tim 119 M 2
Ţimā 154 E 3
Timagami, Lake 171 K 2
Timanskiy Kryazh 118 J 2–K 3
Timar 117 F 3
Timaru 145 Q 9
Timashevsk 117 E 1
Timbákion 116 B 3
Timbauba 181 J 2
Timbédra 152 D 5
Timbio 178 C 3
Timbo 156 C 4
Timbuktu → Tombouctou 156 D 3
Timeiaouine 153 F 4
Timétrina 156 D 2
Timétrine, Monts 156 DE 2
Timfi Óros 116 B 3
Timg'aouine 153 F 4
Timia 157 F 2
Timimoun 152 F 3
Timimoun, Sebkha de 152 F 3
Timir-Atakh-Tas 131 S 2
Timiris, Cap 152 B 5
Timiş 116 B 1
Timiskaming, Lake 171 L 2
Timişoara 116 B 1
Timkapaul' 119 MN 3
Timmins 171 K 2
Ti-m Missao 153 F 4
Timmoudi 152 E 3
Timok 116 B 2
Timon 181 H 2

Timor 137 G 5
Timor, Laut 137 G 5
Timor Sea 137 G 6
Timoshino 118 G 3
Timote 182 D 6
Timpton 131 N 4
Timrå 112 G 3
Timur 129 H 2
Tinaca Point 137 G 2
Tinaco 178 D 2
Tin Asaguid 156 E 2
Tin City 166 D 2
Tindalo 158 E 3
Tindivanam 134 C 5
Tindouf 152 D 3
Tindouf, Hamada de 152 D 3
Tindouf, Sebkha de 152 D 3
Tinef 153 F 4
Tineldjame 153 F 3
Tineo 114 B 3
Tinerhir 152 D 2
Tin Ethisane 156 D 2
Tinfouchy 152 D 3
Tin Fouye 153 G 3
Tingharat, Hamādat 153 H 3
Tingkawk Sakan 135 G 2
Tingmiarmiut 169 T 3
Tingo María 178 C 5
Tingréla 156 C 3
Tingri 134 E 2
Tingsryd 113 G 4
Tinguiririca 182 B 5
Tingvoll 112 E 3
Tinharé 181 J 3
Tinharé, Ilha de 181 J 3
Tinh Gia 135 J 4
Tinian 146 A 2
Tini Wells 154 C 6
Tinkisso 156 B 3
Tinnoset 113 E 4
Tinnsjö 113 E 4
Tinogasta 182 C 4
Tinompo 137 F 3
Tínos 116 C 3
Tinrhert, Hamada de 153 G 3
Tinsukia 135 G 2
Tintagel Head 102 B 2
Tintane 152 C 5
Ti-n Taoundi 153 G 4
Ti-n Tarabine 153 G 4
Tintina 182 D 4
Ti-n-Toumma 157 G 2
Tin Tounannt 156 D 1
Ti-n Zaouâtene 153 F 4
Tioman 136 B 3
Tione di Trento 115 F 2
Tiongui 156 C 3
Tio, Pico de 156 C 4
Tiouardiouine Aguelman 153 G 4
Tiouilit Anagoum 152 B 5
Tipperary 100 B 3
Tipton, Mount 170 D 4
Tiquisate 172 D 5
Tiracambu, Serra do 181 G 1
Tirah 129 J 4
Tīrān 154 E 3
Tirana 116 A 2
Tirano 115 F 2
Tiras Mountains 160 B 5
Tiraspol' 116 C 1
Tire 116 C 3
Tirebolu 117 E 2
Tiree 99 A 3
Tiree (Airport) 99 A 3
Tirekhtyakh 131 R 2
Tirgelir 131 Q 3
Tîrgovişte 116 C 2
Tirgu Bujor 116 C 1
Tîrgu Cărbuneşti 116 B 2
Tîrgu Neamţ 116 C 1
Tirgu Ocna 116 C 1
Tîrgu Secuiesc 116 C 1
Tirich Mir 129 J 3
Tiririne 153 G 4
Tiris 152 C 4
Tirnavos 116 B 3
Tiro 156 B 4
Tirol 115 F 2
Tirso 115 E 3
Tiruchchirappalli 134 C 5
Tiruchendur 134 C 6
Tirunelveli 134 C 6
Tiruntán 178 D 5
Tirupati 134 C 5
Tiruppur 134 C 5
Tiruvannamalai 134 C 5
Tisa 116 B 1
Tisdale 167 R 5
Tisisat Falls 159 F 2
Tissemsilt 153 F 1
Tista 134 E 2

Tisul' 119 R 4
Tisza 116 B 1
Tiszafüred 116 B 1
Tiszántúl 116 B 1
Tit 153 F 3
Tit-Ary 131 N 1
Titaf 152 E 3
Titlagarh 134 D 3
Titicaca, Lago 180 C 4
Titograd 116 A 2
Titova Korenica 115 G 3
Titovo Užice 116 A 2
Titov Veles 116 B 2
Titov vrh 116 B 2
Titran 112 E 3
Titule 158 D 4
Titusville 171 K 6
Tiui 179 GH 3
Tiva 159 F 5
Tivaouane 156 A 3
Tiveden 113 F 4
Tiverton 102 C 2
Tivoli 115 F 3
Tiwī 155 K 4
Tiworo, Selat 137 F 4
Tizatlan 172 C 4
Tizimín 172 E 3
Tizi n'Test 152 D 2
Tizi Ouzou 153 F 1
Tiznit 152 D 3
Tjåhumas 112 G 2
Tjeggelvas 112 G 2
Tjidtjak 112 G 2
Tîrgu Jiu 116 B 1
Tîrgu Mureş 116 B 1
Tîrnava Mica 116 B 1
Tîrnăveni 115 B 1
Tjöme 113 F 4
Tjörn 113 F 4
Tjotta 112 F 2
Tjust 113 G 4
Tkhach 117 F 2
Tkibuli 117 F 2
Tkvarcheli 117 F 2
Tlalnepantla 172 C 4
Tlapa de Comonfort 172 C 4
Tlaxcala 172 C 4
Tlemcen 152 E 2
Tlemcès 157 E 2
Tlētē Ouate Gharbī, Jabal 155 F 1
Tlyarata 117 H 3
Tmassah 153 J 3
Tni Haïa 152 E 4
Toamasina 161 Q 6
Toay 183 D 6
Toba, Danau 136 A 3
Toba & Kakar Ranges 129 H 4
Tobarra 114 C 4
Tobermorey 143 F 3
Tobermory (Canada) 171 K 2
Tobermory (U.K.) 99 A 3
Tobi 137 H 3
Tobin, Lake 142 D 3
Tobo 137 H 4
Toboali 136 C 4
Tobol 119 M 5
Tobol'sk 119 N 4
Tobruk → Ţubruq 153 K 2
Tobseda 118 K 3
Tobysh 118 K 3
Tocantinia 179 J 5
Tocantinópolis 179 J 5
Tocantins 179 J 4
Tocapilla 180 B 4
Töcksfors 113 F 4
Toco 180 C 5
Toconao 180 C 5
Tocorpuri, Cerro de 180 C 5
Todenyang 159 F 4
Todi 115 F 3
Todmorden 101 D 3
Todos os Santos, Baía de 181 J 3
Todos Santos 170 D 7
Tofino 167 M 6
Tofte 113 F 4
Togatax 129 L 3
Togian, Kepulauan 137 F 4
Togni 154 F 5
Togo 156 E 4
Togqén 134 D 1
Togtoh 132 F 2
Toguchin 119 Q 4
Togur 129 G 1
Togwotee Pass 170 D 3
Togyz 129 G 1
Tohen 159 J 2
Tohma 117 E 3
Toibalewe 135 F 5
Toijala 112 H 3
Toisvesi 112 H 3
Tok (Czechoslovakia) 111 F 5

Tok (AK, U.S.A.) 166 J 3
Tokaj 116 B 1
Tokara-kaikyō 133 K 4
Tokara-rettō 133 J 5
Tokat 117 E 2
Tokelau Islands 146 D 3
Tokhtamysh 129 J 3
Tokko 130 L 4
Tokma 130 J 4
Tokmak 129 K 2
Tokmak 117 E 1
Tokomaru Bay 145 R 8
Toksun 132 A 2
Toktamysh 129 J 3
Toktogul 129 J 2
Toku-no-shima 133 J 5
Tokur 131 O 5
Tokushima 133 K 4
Tōkyō 133 L 3
Tolbazy 118 L 5
Tolbuhin 116 C 2
Toledo (Spain) 114 C 4
Toledo (U.S.A.) 171 K 3
Toledo (Chile) 182 B 4
Toledo Bend Reservoir 171 H 5
Toledo, Montes de 114 C 4
Tolga (Norway) 112 F 3
Tolga (Algeria) 153 G 2
Toli 129 L 1
Toliara 161 G 4
Tolima 178 C 3
Tolitoli 137 F 3
Tollarp 113 F 4
Tolmezzo 115 F 2
Tolmin 115 G 2
Tolo 158 B 5
Tolochin 113 J 5
Tolon 131 R 4
Tolon 130 K 4
Tolo, Teluk 137 F 4
Tolstoe 116 C 1
Tolstoy, Mys 131 T 4
Toltén 183 B 6
Tol'yatti 118 J 5
Tolybay 119 M 5
Tom' 119 Q 4
Tomakomai 133 M 2
Toman 119 H 3
Tomar (Brazil) 179 F 4
Tomar (Portugal) 114 B 4
Tomari 131 Q 6
Tómaros 116 B 3
Tomaszów Lubelski 111 H 4
Tomaszów Mazowiecki 111 H 4
Tomatlán 172 A 4
Tombador, Serra do 180 E 3
Tombe 158 E 3
Tombigbee River 171 J 5
Tomboco 160 A 1
Tombouctou 156 D 2
Tômbua 160 A 3
Tomé 183 B 6
Tomé Açu 179 J 4
Tomelilla 113 F 4
Tomelloso 114 C 4
Tomé, Pico de 157 F 5
Tominé 156 B 3
Tominian 156 D 3
Tomini, Teluk 137 F 4
Tomkinson Ranges 142 D 4
Tomma 112 F 2
Tommot 131 N 4
Tomo 178 E 2
Tompa 130 J 4
Tompo (Indonesia) 137 F 3
Tompo (U.S.S.R.) 131 P 3
Tom Price 142 B 3
Tomsa 159 G 3
Tomsk 119 R 4
Tomtor 131 O 2
Tom White, Mount 166 J 3
Tonantins 178 E 4
Tonasket 170 C 2
Tonate 179 H 2–3
Tonbridge 103 E 2
Tondano 137 F 3
Tondela 114 B 3
Tönder 113 E 5
Tondibi 156 D 2
Tondou, Massif du 158 C 3
Tonekābon 128 E 3
Tonga (Sudan) 158 E 3
Tongaat 161 E 5
Tonga Islands 146 D 4
Tongariro National Park 145 R 8
Tongatapu Group 146 D 4
Tonga Trench 193 D 4
Tongbai Shan 132 F 4

Tongcheng 133 G 4
Tongchuan 132 E 3
Tongdao 132 E 5
Tongde 132 D 3
Tonghai 132 D 6
Tonghe 133 J 1
Tonghua 133 H 2
Tongjiang 131 O 6
Tongjoson-man 133 J 3
Tongliao 133 H 2
Tongliong 132 E 5
Tongling 133 G 4
Tonglu 133 G 5
Tongoy 182 B 5
Tongren 132 D 3
Tongren 132 E 5
Tongsa 135 F 2
Tongshan 132 F 5
Tongta 135 G 3
Tongtian He 132 C 4
Tongue 98 B 2
Tongue of the Ocean 173 G 3
Tongulakh 131 M 3
Tongwei 132 E 3
Tong Xian 133 G 3
Tongxin 132 E 3
Tongyu 133 H 2
Tonhil 130 F 6
Tonichi 170 E 6
Tonj 158 D 3
Tonk 134 C 2
Tonkin 135 J 4–5
Tonkou, Mont 156 C 4
Tonle Sap 135 H 5
Tonneins 114 D 3
Tonnerre 114 E 2
Tonopah 170 C 4
Tonosí 178 B 2
Tönsberg 113 F 4
Tonstad 113 E 4
Tonya 117 E 2
Tonzang 135 F 3
Tooday 142 B 5
Tooele 170 D 3
Toompine 143 G 4
Toowoomba 143 J 4
Topchikha 119 Q 5
Topeka 171 G 4
Topiche 178 D 5
Topki 119 R 4
Topko, Gora 131 P 4
Topliţa 116 C 1
Topocalma, Punta 182 B 5
Topoli 128 E 1
Topolinyy 131 P 3
Topolobampo 170 E 6
Topolobampo, Bahía de 170 E 6
Topozero, Ozero 113 K 2
Toppenish 170 B 2
Toprak-Kala 129 G 2
Tora-Khem 130 G 5
Toranggekuduk 129 N 2
Toraya 180 B 3
Torbalı 116 C 3
Torbat-e Heydarīyeh 128 F 3
Torbat-e Jām 128 G 3
Torbay 102 C 2
Torbino 118 F 4
Töreboda 113 F 4
Torekov 113 F 4
Torenberg 110 E 4
Torey 130 H 5
Torez 117 E 1
Torgau 111 F 4
Torgovoye 117 F 1
Tori 158 E 4
Toribulu 137 F 4
Torino 115 E 2
Tori-shima 133 LM 4
Torit 158 E 4
Torkovichi 113 K 4
Törmänen 112 J 2
Tormes 114 B 3
Torneå 112 H 2
Torneälven 112 H 2
Torneträsk 112 G 2
Torngat Mountains 169 P 4
Tornio 112 H 2
Tornionjoki 112 H 2
Tornquist 183 D 6
Toro (Spain) 114 B 3
Toro (Nigeria) 157 F 3
Toro, Cerro del 182 C 4
Torodi 156 E 3
Toro Doum 157 H 2
Toro, Isla del 172 C 3
Torokina 145 G 3
Toro, Lago del 183 B 9
Torom 131 P 5
Toro, Monte 114 D 4

Tor – Tum

Toroni, Cerro 180 C 4
Toronto 169 M 7
Toropets 118 F 4
Tororo 158 E 4
Toros Dağlari 117 D 3
Torpoint 102 B 2
Torquato Severo 182 F 5
Torquay 102 C 2
Torra Bay 160 A 4
Torra Miro, Puerto de 114 C 3
Torre Annunziata 115 E 3
Torre del Greco 115 E 3
Torre de Moncorvo 114 B 3
Torrejón de Ardoz 114 C 3
Torrelavega 114 C 3
Torremolinos 114 C 4
Torrens Creek 143 H 3
Torrens, Lake 143 F 5
Torrens River 143 H 3
Torrente 114 C 4
Torreón 172 B 2
Tôrres 181 G 6
Torrès, Îles 146 C 3
Torres Islands 145 J 4
Torres Strait 143 G 1
Torres Vedras 114 B 4
Torridge, River 102 B 2
Torridon, Loch 98 B 3
Torrijos 114 C 4
Torrington 143 J 4
Torrington 170 F 3
Torröjen 112 F 3
Torsby 113 F 3
Torshälla 113 F 3
Tórshavn 110 A 1
Torsken 112 G 2
Torsö 113 F 4
Tortkuduk 119 O 5
Tortola 173 K 4
Tortona 115 E 3
Tortosa 114 D 3
Tortosa, Cabo de 114 D 3
Tortue, Ile de la 173 H 2
Tortuga, Isla 170 D 6
Tortuguero 172 F 5
Tortum 117 F 2
Torud 128 F 3
Torugart, Pereval 129 K 2
Torul 117 E 2
Toruń 111 G 4
Torup 113 F 4
Torzhok 118 F 4
Tosashimizu 133 K 4
Tosa-wan 133 K 4
Toscana 115 F 3
Toscanini 160 A 4
Tosenfjorden 112 F 2
Tosno 113 K 4
Toson Hu 132 C 3
Tosontsengel 130 G 6
Tossa 114 D 3
Tostado 182 D 4
Tõstamaa 113 H 4
Tostuya 130 K 1
Tosya 117 D 2
Totak 113 E 4
Totana 114 C 4
Toten 113 F 3
Toteng 160 C 4
Tõtias 159 G 4
Totma 118 H 4
Totnes 102 C 2
Totness 179 G 2
Totonicapan 172 D 5
Totoras 182 D 5
Totota 156 BC 4
Totten Glacier 185
Totton 103 D 2
Tottori 133 K 3
Touba (Ivory Coast) 156 C 4
Touba (Senegal) 156 A 3
Toubkal, Jbel 152 D 3
Tougan 156 D 3
Touggourt 153 G 2
Tougué 156 B 3
Touila 152 D 3
Toukoto 156 C 3
Toul 115 E 2
Toulépleu 156 C 4
Toulon 115 E 3
Toulouse 114 D 3
Toummo → Bir al War 157 G 1
Toumodi 156 C 4
Tounassine 152 E 3
Tounassine, Hamada 152 DE 3
Toungo 157 G 4
Toungoo 135 G 4
Touraine 114 D 2
Toura, Monts de 156 C 4
Tourassine 152 C 4
Tourcoing 114 D 1
Touriñán, Cabo 114 B 3
Tourine 152 C 4

Tournai 110 D 4
Tournavista 178 D 5
Tournon 115 D 2
Tournus 115 D 2
Touros 181 J 2
Tours 114 D 2
Toury 114 D 2
Tousside, Pic 157 H 1
Toussoro 158 C 3
Touws River 160 C 6
Towada 133 M 2
Towakaima 179 G 2
Towanda 171 L 3
Tower Hill 143 G 3
Towerhill River 143 G 3
Tow Law 101 E 2
Townsend 170 D 2
Townshend, Cape 143 J 3
Townshend Island 143 J 3
Townsville 143 H 2
Towot 158 E 3
Towson 171 L 4
Towuti, Danau 137 F 4
Towy 110 C 4
Towy, River 102 B 2
Toxkan He 129 K 2
Toyama 133 L 3
Toyohashi 133 L 4
Toyota 133 L 3
Trabzon 117 E 2
Trafalgar, Cabo 114 B 4
Trafshan 129 G 5
Trägha̅n 153 H 3
Traiguén 183 B 6
Trail 167 O 6
Trairi 181 J 1
Tralee 110 B 4
Tralee Bay 110 B 4
Tranås 113 F 4
Trancas 182 C 4
Trancoso 114 B 3
Tranebjerg 113 F 4
Tranemo 113 F 4
Tranent 99 C 4
Trang 135 G 6
Trangan, Pulau 137 H 5
Trani 115 G 3
Transantarctic Mountains 185
Transkei 160 D 6
Transtrand 112 F 3
Transtrandsfjällen 112 F 3
Transvaal 160 D 4
Transylvania 116 B 1
Transylvanian Alps 116 B 1
Trapani 115 F 4
Traralgon 143 H 6
Trarza 152 BC 5
Trasimeno, Lago 115 F 3
Trat 135 H 5
Traunsee 115 F 2
Travemünde 111 F 4
Traverse City 171 J 3
Travers, Mount 145 Q 9
Travesia 172 E 4
Travesia Puntana 182 C 5
Travnik 115 G 3
Trayning 142 B 5
Trbovlje 115 G 2
Třebíc 111 G 5
Trebinje 115 G 3
Trebisacce 115 G 4
Trebišóv 111 H 5
Treblinka 111 H 4
Trebnje 115 G 2
Třebon 111 F 5
Tredegar 102 C 2
Tregosselslets and Reefs 143 J 2
Treinta y Tres 182 F 5
Trélazé 114 C 2
Trelew 183 C 7
Trelleborg 113 F 4
Tremadog Bay 102 B 1
Tremiti, Isole 115 G 3
Tremonton 170 D 3
Tremp 114 D 3
Trenčín 111 G 5
Trenel 183 D 6
Trenque Lauquen 183 D 6
Trento 115 F 2
Trenton (MO, U.S.A.) 171 H 3
Trenton (N.J., U.S.A.) 171 M 3
Trent, River 103 D 1
Trepassey 169 R 6
Tres Arobles 182 E 5
Tres Arroyos 183 D 6
Tres Cerros 183 C 8
Três Corações 181 G 5
Tres Esquinas 178 C 3
Tres Forcas, Cap 152 E 1
Três Lagoas 181 F 5
Tres Lagos 183 B 8
Tres Marías Dam 181 G 4

Tres Montes, Península 183 A 8
Tres Picos 172 D 4
Tres Picos, Cerro 183 D 6
Tres Puentes 182 B 4
Três Ríos 181 H 5
Tres Valles 172 C 4
Tres Zapotes 172 C 4
Treuchtlingen 111 F 5
Treviglio 115 E 2
Treviso 115 F 2
Treze Quedas 179 G 4
Trgovište 116 B 2
Triabunna 144 L 9
Trialetskiy Khrebet 117 F 2
Tríbeč Vtáčnik 111 G 5
Tricase 115 G 4
Trichur 134 C 5
Trident Shoal 136 D 1
Trier 110 E 5
Trieste 115 F 2
Trieste, Golfo di 115 F 2
Triglev 115 G 2
Trikala 116 B 3
Trikhonis Limni 116 B 3
Trikomo 117 D 3
Trikomon → Trikomo 117 D 3
Trikora, Puncak 137 J 4
Trim 100 B 3
Trincomalee 134 D 6
Tring 103 D 2
Trinidad (Bolivia) 180 D 3
Trinidad (Columbia) 178 D 2
Trinidad (CO, U.S.A.) 170 F 4
Trinidad (Cuba) 173 G 3
Trinidad (Trinidad and Tobago) 179 F 1
Trinidad (Uruguay) 182 E 5
Trinidad and Tobago 179 F 1
Trinidade Island 175 G 5
Trinidad, Golfo 183 A 8
Trinidad, Isla (Arg.) 183 D 6
Trinity Bay (Canada) 169 R 6
Trinity Bay (Australia) 143 H 2
Trinity Islands 166 G 4
Trinity River 171 G 5
Trinkitat 154 F 5
Tripoli (Lebanon) 154 F 2
Tripoli (Libya) 153 H 2
Tripolis 116 B 3
Tripolitania 153 HJ 2
Tripura 135 F 3
Tristao, Îles 156 A 3
Triton 135 K 4
Trivandrum 134 C 6
Trjavna 116 C 2
Trobriand Islands 146 B 3
Trobriand or Kiriwina Islands 145 F 3
Trofimov 117 F 1
Trofimovsk 131 N 1
Trofors 112 F 3
Trogir 115 G 3
Troglav 115 G 3
Trois-Pistoles 169 O 6
Trois Rivières 169 N 6
Troitsk 160 C 4
Troitsk 119 M 5
Troitskiy 130 K 5
Troitskiy 118 K 5
Troitskiy 119 O 5
Troitsko-Pechorsk 118 L 3
Troitskoye 119 Q 5
Troitskoye 118 L 5
Troitskoye 116 D 1
Trojan 116 B 2
Trojanski Manastir 116 B 2
Trolla 157 G 6
Trollhättan 113 F 4
Trollheimen 112 E 3
Trollhetta 112 E 3
Trolltindane 112 E 3
Trombetas 179 G 4
Tromelin 149 H 6
Tromöya 113 E 4
Tromso 112 G 2
Trona 170 C 4
Tronador, Monte 183 B 7
Trondheim 112 F 3
Trondheimsfjorden 112 F 3
Troodos 117 D 4
Troon 99 B 4
Tropoja 116 B 2
Trosa 113 G 4
Trosh 118 L 2
Trostan 100 B 2
Trostyanets 116 C 1
Trotternish 98 A 3
Trout Lake (NWT, Can.) 167 N 3
Trout Lake (Ont., Can.) 168 K 5
Trout Lake (Ont., Can.) 168 J 5

Trout Peak 170 D 3
Trout River 169 Q 6
Trowbridge 103 C 2
Troy (AL, U.S.A.) 171 J 5
Troyekurovo 118 G 5
Troyez 114 D 2
Troy Peak 170 C 4
Troys 116 C 3
Trubchevsk 118 F 5
Truc Giang 135 J 5
TrucialCoast 155 J 3–4
Trudovoye 133 K 2
Trujillo (Spain) 114 B 4
Trujillo (Honduras) 172 E 4
Trujillo (Peru) 178 C 5
Trujillo (Venezuela) 178 D 2
Truk Islands 146 B 2
Trumbell, Mount 170 D 4
Truro (Canada) 169 P 6
Truro (U.K.) 102 B 2
Truskavecs 111 H 5
Trusovo 118 K 2
Trust Territory of the Pacific Islands 146 AB 2
Truth or Consequences (Hot Springs) 170 E 5
Trutnov 111 F 5
Truvéra 114 D 3
Truva 116 C 3
Trysilelva 112 F 3
Trysilfjellet 112 F 3
Trzcianka 111 G 4
Tsagaannuur 130 E 6
Tsagaan-Uul 130 G 6
Tsagaan Uür 130 H 5
Tsagan-Nur 117 G 1
Tsageri 117 F 2
Tsaidam Basin → Qaidam Pendi 132 B 3
Tsalka 117 F 2
Tsangpo 132 B 5
Tsapelka 112 J 4
Tsaratanana 161 H 3
Tsaratanana, Massif du 161 H 2
Tsaris Mountains 160 B 4
Tsatsana 160 C 3
Tsau 160 C 4
Tsaukaib 160 B 5
Tsavo 159 F 5
Tsavo National Park 159 F 5
Tsawisis 160 B 5
Tselina 117 F 1
Tselinnoye 119 R 5
Tselinograd 119 O 5
Tsenhermandal 130 J 6
Tsenogora 118 J 3
Tsentral'nyy 119 R 4
Tses 160 B 5
Tsetseg 130 F 6
Tsetserleg 130 H 6
Tsetserleg 130 G 6
Tsévié 156 E 4
Tshabong 160 C 5
Tshabuta 158 C 6
Tshane 160 C 4
Tshangalele, Lac 160 D 2
Tshchikskoye Vodokhranilishche 117 E 1
Tshela 157 G 6
Tshele 158 D 5
Tshesebe 160 D 4
Tshibamba 158 C 6
Tshikapa 158 C 6
Tshilenge 158 C 6
Tshimbalanga 158 C 6
Tshimbulu 158 C 6
Tshkudu 160 C 4
Tshofa 158 D 6
Tshopo 158 D 4
Tshuapa 158 C 5
Tshwane 160 C 4
Tsiafajavona 161 H 3
Tsiazonano 161 H 3
Tsihombe 161 H 5
Tsimlyansk 117 F 1
Tsimlyanskoye Vodokhranilishche 117 F 1
Tsineng 160 C 5
Tsinghai 132 C 4
Tsingtao 133 H 3
Tsintsabis 160 B 3
Tsipa 130 L 4
Tsipanda 131 P 4
Tsipikan 130 K 5
Tsiroanomandidy 161 H 3
Tsitondroina 161 H 3
Tskhaltubo 117 F 2
Tskhinvali 117 F 2
Tsna 113 J 5
Tsna 118 H 5
Tsodilo Hills 160 C 3

Tsomonang → Pangong 129 K 4
Tsu 133 L 4
Tsuchiura 133 M 3
Tsugaru-kaikyō 133 M 2
Tsumeb 160 B 3
Tsumis Park 160 B 4
Tsumkwe 160 C 3
Tsuruga 133 L 3
Tsuruoka 133 L 3
Tsushima 133 J 4
Tsuyama 133 K 3
Tsyurupinsk 117 D 1
Tua (Portugal) 114 B 3
Tua (Zaire) 158 B 5
Tual 137 H 5
Tuamotu Archipelago 147 F 3–4
Tuan 135 H 3
Tuangku, Pulau 136 A 3
Tuapse 117 E 2
Tuaran 136 E 2
Tuba 130 F 5
Tuba City 170 D 4
Tuban 136 D 5
Tubarão 181 G 6
Tubayq, Jabal aţ 154 F 3
Tubbataha Reefs 137 E 2
Tübingen 111 E 5
Ţubruq 153 K 2
Tubuaï 147 F 4
Tubuai Islands 147 EF 4
Tucacas 178 E 1
Tucano 181 J 3
Tucavaca 180 E 4
Tuchola 111 G 4
Tucson 170 D 5
Tucumcari 170 F 4
Tucuparé 179 G 5
Tucupita 179 F 2
Tucuruí 179 J 4
Tudela 114 C 3
Tudmur 154 F 2
Tuensang 135 F 2
Tufi 144 E 3
Tugela 161 E 5
Tuguegarao 137 J 1
Tugur 131 P 5
Tuim 119 R 5
Tukangbesi, Kepulauan 137 F 5
Ţukrah 153 K 2
Tuktoyaktuk 166 L 2
Tukums 112 H 4
Tukuringra, Khrebet 131 N 5
Tukuyu 158 E 6
Tukzar 129 H 3
Tula (U.S.S.R.) 118 G 5
Tula (Mex.) 172 C 3
Tula (Mex.) 172 C 4
Tulai 132 C 3
Tulancingo 172 C 4
Tulangbawang 136 BC 4
Tulare 170 C 4
Tulasi 134 D 4
Tulay-Kiryaka-Tas, Vozvyshennost' 130 J 1
Tulbagh 160 B 6
Tulcán 178 C 3
Tulcea 116 C 1
Tulchin 117 D 1
Tulemalu Lake 167 S 3
Tuli 160 D 4
Tulihe 131 M 5
Tullahoma 171 J 4
Tullamore 100 B 3
Tulle 114 C 3
Tulln 115 G 2
Tullner Becken 115 G 2
Tullow 100 B 3
Tullus 154 C 6
Tully 143 H 2
Tulmaythah 153 K 2
Tuloma 113 K 2
Tulos, Ozero 112 K 3
Tulpan 118 L 3
Tulsa 171 G 4
Tul'skaya 117 F 2
Tuluá 178 C 3
Tuluksak 166 E 3
Tulum 172 E 3
Tulun 130 H 5
Tulungagung 136 D 5
Tumaco 178 C 3
Tumanovo 118 F 4
Tumanskiy 131 X 3
Tumany 131 T 3
Tumat 131 P 1–R 1
Tumatumari 179 G 2
Tumba 113 G 4
Tumba, Lac 158 B 5
Tumbarumba 143 H 6
Tumbes 178 B 4
Tumbling Waters 142 E 1

Tumcha 112 K 2
Tumd Youqi 132 F 2
Tumd Zuoqi 132 F 2
Tumen 133 J 2
Tumen Jiang 133 J 2
Tumeremo 179 F 2
Tumkur 134 C 5
Tumnin 131 PQ 6
Tump 129 G 5
Tumpat 136 B 2
Tumu 156 D 3
Tumuc-Humac, Serra 179 H 3
Tumupasa 180 C 3
Tūmū → Toummo 153 H 5
Tunari, Cerro 180 C 4
Tunas 181 G 5
Tunas, Sierra de las 170 E 6
Tunceli 117 E 3
Tundla 134 C 2
Tunduma 158 E 6
Tunduru 161 F 2
Tundza 116 C 2
Tünel-e-Salong 129 H 3
Tunemouth 101 E 2
Tunga 157 F 4
Tungabhadra 134 C 4
Tungku 117 E 2
Tungnaá 112 B 3
Tungokochen 130 L 5
Tungsten 166 E 3
Tunguska, Nizhnyaya 130 F 2
Tunguska, Podkamennaya 130 F 3
Tungus-Khaya 131 N 3
Tünhel 130 J 6
Tuni 134 D 4
Tūnis 153 GH 1
Tunisia 153 GH 2
Tunja 157 E 2
Tunnhovdfjorden 113 E 3
Tununak 166 D 3
Tunungayualok 169 P 4
Tunuyan 182 C 5
Tunxi 133 G 5
Tuöroyri 110 A 1
Tuostakh 131 P 2
Tuotuo He 132 B 4
Tuotuo Heyan 132 B 4
Tupã 181 F 5
Tupaciguara 181 G 4
Tupanciretã 182 F 4
Tupelo 171 J 5
Tupik 130 L 5
Tupinambaranas, Ilha 179 G 4
Tupirama 179 J 5
Tupirantins 179 J 5
Tupiza 180 C 5
Tuquan 133 H 1
Túquerres 178 C 3
Tura (Tanzania) 158 E 6
Tura (India) 134 E 2
Tura (U.S.S.R.) 130 H 3
Tura (U.S.S.R.) 119 M 4
Turabah 155 G 3
Turabah 155 G 4
Turagua, Serranías 179 F 2
Turakh 130 M 1
Turallin 143 J 4
Turama 130 G 3
Turan 130 F 5
Turana, Khrebet 131 O 5
Turanskaya Nizmennost' 128–129 F 3–G 1,2
Turbaco 178 C 1
Turbat 129 G 5
Turbo 178 C 2
Turda 116 B 1
Tūreh 128 D 4
Tureia 147 F 4
Turek 111 G 4
Turen 178 E 2
Turfan Depression 132 A 2
Turgay 129 G 1
Turgayskaya Dolina 119 M 5,6
Turgayskaya Stolovaya Strana 119 M 5
Türgen Uul 130 F 6
Turgutlu 116 C 3
Turhal 117 E 2
Türi 113 J 4
Turia 114 C 4
Turiaçu 179 J 4
Turin 115 E 2–3
Turinsk 119 M 4
Turiy Rog 133 K 1
Turka 130 J 5
Turkana 158 EF 4
Turkana, Lake 159 F 4
Turkannakh 130 M 1
Turkd 111 H 5
Turkestan 129 H 2
Turkestanskiy Khrebet 129 H 3
Turkey 117 DE 3

Türkiiye 117 DE 3
Turkmeniya 128 F 3
Türkoğlu 117 E 3
Turks and Caicos Islands 173 H 3
Turks Island Passage 173 H 3
Turks Islands 173 H 3
Turku (Åbo) 113 H 3
Turkwe 158 F 4
Turneffe Islands 172 E 4
Turner River 142 D 2
Turnu Măgurele 116 B 2
Turnu Roşu, Pasul 116 B 1
Turobay 119 P 6
Turochak 119 R 5
Turpan 132 A 2
Turpan Pendi 132 A 2
Turpan Zhan 129 M 2
Turriff 98 C 3
Tursha 118 J 4
Turtkul' 129 G 2
Turtle Islands 156 B 4
Turugart Shankou 129 K 2
Turukhan 119 Q 2
Turukhansk 119 R 2
Turukta 130 L 3
Tuscaloosa 171 J 5
Tutak 117 F 3
Tutayev 118 G 4
Tuticorin 134 C 6
Tutóia 181 H 1
Tutonchana 130 F 3
Tutonchana, Vozvyshennost' 130 F 2
Tutonchany 130 F 3
Tutrakan 116 C 2
Tuttle Creek Lake 171 G 4
Tüttlingen 111 E 5
Tutubu 158 E 6
Tutuila 147 D 3
Tutupaca, Volcán 180 B 4
Tutuwang 137 G 5
Tutuwawang 144 A 3
Tuul Gol 130 H 6
Tuvalu 146 C 3
Ṭuwayq, Jabal 155 H 3–4
Tuxpán 172 A 3
Tuxpan de Rodríguez Cano 172 C 3
Tuxpan, Rio 172 C 3
Tuxtla Gutiérrez 172 D 4
Tuy 114 B 3
Tuyen Quang 135 J 3
Tuy Hoa 135 J 5
Tuymazy 118 K 5
Tuz Gölü 117 D 3
Tüz Khurmātū 155 G 2
Tuzla 115 G 3
Tuzluca 117 F 2
Tuzly 116 D 1
Tvedestrand 113 E 4
Tweed, River 99 C 4
Tweedsmuir Hills 101 D 3
Twee Rivieren 160 B 5
Twin Falls (ID, U.S.A.) 170 D 3
Twin Falls (Newfoundl., Can.) 169 P 5
Twin Islands 169 L 5
Twisp 170 B 2
Two Harbors 171 H 2
Tyan'-Shan' 129 J–L 2
Tyatino 131 R 7
Tychkino 119 P 4
Tychy 111 G 4
Tydal 112 F 3
Tygda 131 N 5
Tyk 131 Q 5
Tyler 171 G 5
Tylkhoy 131 U 3
Tylösand 113 F 4
Tyl'skiy Khrebet 131 OP 5
Tym 119 Q 4
Tymovskoye 131 Q 5
Tynda 131 M 4
Tyne and Wear 101 E 2
Tyne, River 101 E 2
Tynset 112 E 3
Tyräjärvi 112 J 2
Tyre → Ṣūr 154 F 2
Tyrifjorden 113 E 4
Tyrma 131 O 5
Tyrrell Lake 167 Q 3
Tyrrhenian Sea 115 F 3–4
Tyry 131 P 3
Tysnesøy 113 E 4
Tysse 113 E 4
Tyssedal 113 E 3
Tyubelyakh 131 Q 2
Tyugene 131 N 3
Tyugyuren 131 Q 2
Tyukalinsk 119 O 4
Tyukhtet 119 R 4

Tyul'-Bannovka 129 J 2
Tyulen'i, Ostrova 128 E 1
Tyul'gan 118 L 5
Tyumen' 119 N 4
Tyumsyu 131 Q 3
Tyung 130 L 2
Tyungulyu 131 O 3
Tyuntyugur 119 N 5
Tywyn 102 B 1
Tzaneen 160 DE 4

U

Uad el Jat 152 C 3
Ua Huka 147 F 3
Ua Pou 147 F 3
Uatumá 179 G 4
Uauá 181 J 2
Uaupés 178 E 4
Uaxactún 172 E 4
Ubá 181 H 5
Ubagan 119 N 5
Ubaitaba 181 J 3
Ubangi 158 B 4
Ubari → Awbārī 153 H 3
Ube 133 K 4
Ubeda 114 C 4
Uberaba 181 G 4
Uberaba, Laguna 180 E 4
Uberlândia 181 G 4
Ubiaja 157 F 4
Ubinskoye, Ozero 119 Q 4
Ubiyenka 131 W 2
Ubolratna Dam 135 H 4
Ubombo 161 E 5
Ubon Ratchathani 135 H 4
Ubort' 113 J 5
Ubundi 158 D 5
Ucayali 178 D 5
Uch 129 J 5
Uchaly 119 L 5
Uchami 130 F 4
Uchami 130 G 3
Uch-Aral 119 Q 6
Uchiura-wan 133 M 2
Uch Kuduk 129 G 2
Uchkulan 117 F 2
Uchur 131 O 4
Učka 115 F 2
Uckfield 103 C 2
Uda 131 O 5
Udachnaya 130 K 2
Udaipur 134 B 3
Udamalpet 134 C 5
Udanna 131 Q 2
Udaquilla 183 E 6
Udayagiri 134 C 5
Udbina 115 G 3
Uddevalla 113 F 4
Uddjaure 112 G 2
Uddjaure 113 G 2
Uddjaure 133 K 2
Udgir 134 C 4
Udialla 142 C 2
Udine 115 F 2
Udipi 134 B 5
Udokan, Khrebet 130 L 4
Udon Thani 135 H 4
Udskaya Guba 131 P 5
Udskoye 131 O 5
Udyl', Ozero 131 P 5
Udzha 130 L 1
Uebi Scebeli → Webi Shābelle 159 G 4
Uebonti 137 F 4
Ueda 133 L 3
Uekali 137 F 4
Uekali 137 F 4
Uele 158 C 4
Uelen 166 D 2
Uelzen 111 E 2
Uengan, Mys 119 N 1
Uere 158 D 4
Ufa 118 L 5
Ufa 118 L 4
Ugab 160 A 4
Ugagli 131 N 5
Ugalla 158 E 6
Ugalla River Game Reserve 159 E 2
Uganda 158 E 4
Ugashik 166 E 4
Ughelli 157 F 4
Uglegorsk 131 Q 6
Uglekamensk 133 K 2
Uglich 118 G 4
Uglovaya 131 N 5
Ugol'naya 131 X 3
Ugoyan 131 N 4
Ugulan 131 T 3
Ugumun 130 L 2

Ugun 131 N 4
Ugut 119 O 3
Uherské Hradiště 111 G 5
Uíñaimarca, Lago 180 C 4
Uig 98 A 3
Uíge 160 B 1
Uil 128 E 1
Uilpata 117 F 2
Uinta Mountains 170 D 3
Uis Mine 160 A 4
Uitenhage 160 D 6
Ujae 146 C 2
Ujar 130 F 4
Ujarrás 172 F 6
Ujelang 146 B 2
Ujiji 158 D 5
Ujjain 134 C 3
Ujung 137 F 5
Ujunglamuru 137 F 4
Ujungpandang 137 E 5
Uk 130 G 4
Uka 131 U 4
Ukara Island 158 E 5
Ukelayat 131 W 3
Ukerewe Island 158 E 5
Ukholovo 118 H 5
Ukhta 118 K 3
Ukiah (CA, U.S.A.) 170 B 4
Ukiah (OR, U.S.A.) 170 C 2
Ukmergė 112 H 4
Ukraina 118 EF 6
Ukrainka 119 P 4
Uktym 118 J 3
Uku 160 A 2
Ukuma 160 B 2
Ukwaa 158 E 3
Ula 116 C 3
Ulaanbaatar 130 J 6
Ulaangom 130 E 6
Ulaanhus 130 E 6
Ulaga 131 O 2
Ulakhan Botuobuya 130 K 3
Ulakhan-Kyugel' 130 L 3
Ulakhan-Cistay, Khrebet 131 R 2,3
Ulakhan-Sis, Kryazh 131 S 2
Ulakhe 133 K 2
Ulamba 158 C 6
Ulan 132 C 3
Ulan Bator 130 J 6
Ulanbel 129 J 2
Ulan-Burgasy, Khrebet 130 J 5
Ulan-Khol 117 G 1
Ulansuhai Nur 132 E 2
Ulan-Ude 130 J 5
Ulan Ul Hu 132 B 4
Ularunda 143 H 4
Ulaş 117 E 3
Ulastay 129 M 2
Ulawa 145 H 3
Ul'ba 119 Q 5
Ul'beya 131 Q 3
Ulbeya 131 Q 4
Ulchin 133 J 3
Ulcinj 116 A 2
Uleåborg 112 J 2
Ulefoss 113 E 4
Ulhasnagar 134 B 4
Uliastay 130 G 6
Uliga 146 C 2
Ulindi 158 D 5
Ullapool 98 B 3
Ullared 113 F 4
Ullatti 112 H 2
Ulldecona 114 D 3
Ullsfjorden 112 G 2
Ullswater 101 D 2
Ullŭng-do 133 K 3
Ulm 111 E 5
Ulmeni 116 C 1
Ulongué 161 E 2
Ulovo 131 S 1
Ulricehamn 113 F 4
Ulsan 133 J 3
Ulsberg 112 E 3
Ulsteinvik 112 E 3
Ulster 110 B 4
Ultevis 112 G 2
Ulu 154 E 6
Ulubat Gölü 116 C 2
Uludağ 116 C 2
Ulugqat 129 J 3
Ulukışla 117 D 3
Ulunga 131 P 6
Ulungur He 129 M 1
Ulungur Hu 129 M 1
Ulunkhan 130 K 5
Ulus 117 D 2
Ulusiau 137 H 3
Ulutau, Gory 129 H 1
Ulva 99 A 3
Ulverston 101 D 2
Ulvön 112 G 3

Ul'ya 131 Q 4
Ul'yankovo 118 J 4
Ul'yanovsk 118 J 5
Ul'yanovskoye 119 O 5
Uma 130 M 5
Uman' 116 D 1
Umanak 184
Ūmánaq 169 T 3
Umari 137 J 4
Umarkot 129 G 5
Umba 113 K 2
Umboi 144 E 3
Umbria 115 F 3
Umeå 112 H 3
Umeälven 112 G 3
Umiat 166 G 2
Umm al 'Abīd 153 J 3
Umm al Arānib 153 H 3
Umm al Birak 155 F 4
Umm al Ḥayt, Wādī 155 J 5
Umm al Qaywayn 155 K 3
Umm as Samīm 155 K 4
Umm az Zumūl 155 K 4
Umm Bāb 155 J 3
Umm Badr 154 D 5
Umm Bel 154 D 6
Umm Buru 154 C 5
Umm Dafok 154 C 6
Umm Dhibbān 154 D 6
Umm Durmān 154 E 5
Umm Hagar 159 F 2
Umm Haraz 154 C 5
Umm Inderaba 154 E 5
Umm Kaddādah 154 D 6
Umm Lahai 154 D 5
Umm Lajj 154 F 4
Umm Qawzayn 154 D 6
Umm Rumaylah 154 E 5
Umm Ruwābah 154 E 6
Umm Sa'īd → Musay'īd 155 J 4
Umm Sayyālah 154 E 6
Umm Urūmul 154 F 3
Umnak 166 D 5
Umnyn Syverma, Khrebet 130 GH 3
Umozero, Ozero 112 K 2
Umpilua 161 F 2
Umpulo 160 B 2
Umraniye 116 D 3
Ums 160 B 4
Umtali → Mutare 161 E 3
Umtata 160 D 6
Umuarama 181 F 5
Umvuma 161 E 3
Una (Brazil) 181 J 4
Una (Yugoslavia) 115 G 2
Unadilla 171 K 5
Unaf 181 G 4
Unai Pass 129 H 4
Unalakleet 166 E 3
Unalaska 166 D 5
Unapoo 98 B 2l
Unari 112 J 2
'Unayzah (Jordan) 154 F 2
'Unayzah (Saudi Arabia) 155 G 3
Uncia 180 C 4
Underberg 160 D 5
Undva Neem 113 H 4
Undyulyung 131 N 2
Unecha 118 F 5
Uneiuxi 178 E 4
Unga 166 E 4
Ungava Bay 169 O 4
Ungava, Peninsule d' 169 N 3
Ung, Jabal al 115 F 3
Ungwatiri 154 F 5
Ungião (Acre, Brazil) 178 D 5
União (Maranhão, Brazil) 181 H 1
União dos Palmares 181 J 2
União do Vitória 182 F 4
Uniabmund 160 A 4
Unije 115 F 3
Unimak 166 E 5
Unimak Pass 166 E 5
Unini 179 F 4
Unión 183 C 6
Union City 171 J 4
Uniondale 160 C 6
United Arab Emirates 155 J 4
United Kingdom 110 C D 3
United States 170–171
Unitsa 118 F 3
Unity 167 Q 5
Universales, Montes 114 C 3
University City 171 H 4
Unkyur 131 O 2
Unnao 134 D 2
Unst 110 C 2
Unst 98 D 1
Unuli Horog 132 B 3
Ünye 117 E 2
Unzba 118 H 4
Uoyan 130 K 4

Upu – Vas

Upanu 131 X 3
Upar Ghat 134 D 3
Upata 179 F 2
Upemba, Lac 158 D 6
Upemba National Park 158 D 6
Upernavik 184
Upi 137 F 2
Upington 160 C 5
Upolu 147 D 3
Upper Arlington 171 K 3
Upper Klamath Lake 170 B 3
Upper Lough Erne 110 B 4
Upper Lough Erne 100 B 2
Upper Red Lake 171 H 2
Upper Volta 156 DE 3
Uppingham 103 D 1
Uppland 113 G 3
Uppsala 113 G 4
Upshi 129 K 4
Upwey 102 C 2
'Uqlat aş Şuqūr 155 G 3
Ur 155 H 2
Uracoa 179 F 2
Urad Qianqi 132 E 2
Urad Zhonghou Lianheqi 132 E 2
Ura Guba 113 K 2
Urak 131 Q 4
Ural 119 L 5
Ural 128 E 1
Ural Mountains 119 L 2–4
Uralovka 131 N 5
Ural'sk 118 K 5
Urambo 158 E 6
Urandangie 143 F 3
Urandi 181 H 3
Urangan 143 J 4
Uranium City 167 Q 4
Uraricoera 179 F 3
Ura-Tyube 129 H 3
'Urayq, Nafūd al 155 G 3–4
Urbandale 171 H 3
Urbano Santos 181 H 1
Urbino 115 F 3
Urco 178 D 4
Urcos 180 B 3
Urdzhar 119 Q 6
Uré 178 C 2
Ureki 117 F 2
Uren 118 J 4
Urengoy 119 P 2
Ure, River 101 E 2
Urewera National Park 145 R 8
Urez 119 P 4
Urfa 117 E 3
Urfa Platosu 117 E 3
Urgamal 130 F 6
Urgel, Llano de 114 D 3
Urgench 128 G 2
Ürgüp 117 D 3
Urgut 129 H 3
Urho 129 M 1
Ūrī 153 J 4
Uribe 178 D 3
Uribia 183 D 1
Urimán 179 F 2
Uritskoye 119 N 5
Uritskoye 131 M 3
Urjala 112 H 3
Urkan 131 N 5
Urla 116 C 3
Urlu Dağ 117 D 2
Urluk 130 J 5
Urmannyy 119 N 3
Urmi 131 O 5
Urmia, Lake → Daryācheh-ye Orūmīyeh 128 D 3
Urninskoye Boloto 119 O 4
Uromi 157 F 4
Uroševac 116 B 2
Urrao 178 C 2
Urshult 113 F 4
Ursus 111 H 4
Uruaçu 181 G 3
Uruana 181 G 4
Uruapan 172 B 4
Urubamba 180 B 3
Urubu 179 G 4
Urubupunga Dam 181 F 5
Urubuquara, Serra 179 H 4
Urucará 179 G 4
Urucu 179 F 4
Uruçuca 181 J 3
Uruçuí 181 H 2
Urucuia 181 G 4
Uruçuí Prêto 181 GH 2
Uruçuí, Serra do 181 GH 2
Urucurituba 179 G 4
Uruguaiana 182 E 4
Uruguay 182 E 5
Urul'ga 130 K 5
Urumchi 129 M 2
Urumkuveem 131 W 2
Ürümqi 129 M 2

Urup 117 F 2
Urup, Ostrov 131 S 6
'Uruq ar Rumaylah 155 H 4
'Urūq as Subay' 155 G 4
Urusha 131 M 5
Urutágua 181 G 3
Uruwira 158 E 6
Uruzgan 129 H 4
Uryung-Khaya 130 K 1
Uryupinsk 118 H 5
Urzhum 118 J 4
Urziceni 116 C 2
Usa 119 M 2
Uşak 116 C 3
Usakos 160 B 4
Usal'gin 131 P 5
Usambara Mountains 159 F 5
Usborne, Mount 183 E 9
Ušče 116 B 2
Usedom 111 F 4
'Usfān 155 F 4
'Ushayrah 155 H 3
'Ushayrah 155 G 4
Ushirombo 158 E 5
Ushkan'iy, Gory 131 X 2
Ushki 131 U 4
Ushki, Zaliv 131 R 4
Ush-Tobe 119 P 6
Ushuaia 183 C 9
Ushumun 131 N 5
Ushurakchan, Gory 131 U 2
Usina 179 H 5
Usinge 158 E 6
Usk 102 C 2
Uska 134 D 2
Usk, River 102 C 2
Üsküdar 116 C 2
Usman 118 G 5
Usmas ezers 113 H 4
Usoke 158 E 6
Usol'ye 118 L 4
Usol'ye-Sibirskoye 130 H 5
Uspenka 119 P 5
Uspenskiy 119 O 6
Uspenskoye 117 F 2
Ussuri 133 K 1
Ussuriysk 133 K 2
Ust 130 K 9
Ust'Allakh 131 O 3
Ust'-Amginskoye 131 O 3
Ust'-Barguzin 130 J 4 5
Ust'-Bokhapcha 131 S 3
Ust'-Bol'sheretsk 131 T 5
Ust'-Charky 131 P 2
Ust'-Chayka 130 J 3
Ust'Chernaya 118 K 3
Ust'-Chona 130 K 3
Ust'-Dzhegutinskaya 117 F 2
Uster 115 F 4
Usti 111 F 4
Ustica 115 F 4
Ust'-Ilimpeya 130 J 3
Ust'-Ilimsk 130 H 4
Ust'-Ilimskiy Vodokhranilishche 130 H 4
Ustinovka 117 D 1
Ust'Ishim 119 O 4
Ustka 111 G 4
Ust-Kada 130 H 5
Ust'-Kamchatsk 131 U 4
Ust-Kamenogorsk 119 Q 6
Ust'-Kamo 130 G 3
Ust'-Kan 130 F 4
Ust'-Karenga 130 L 5
Ust'-Kara 131 K 3
Ust'-Katav 119 L 5
Ust'-Khayryuzovo 131 T 4
Ust'-Koksa 119 R 5
Ust' Kolik'yegan 119 P 3
Ust' Kulom 118 K 3
Ust'-Kut 130 J 4
Ust'-Kuyga 131 P 2
Ust-Labinsk 117 E 1
Ust'Lyzha 118 L 2
Ust'Maya 131 Q 3
Ust'-Mayn 131 W 2
Ust'-Mil' 131 O 4
Ust'Nem 131 K 3
Ust'-Nera 131 Q 3
Ust'-Olenëk 130 L 1
Ust' Omchug 131 R 3
Ust'-Ordynskiy 130 H 5
Ust'-Ozernoye 119 R 4
Ust'Paden'ga 118 H 3
Ust'-Penzhino 131 V 3
Ust'-Pit 130 F 4
Ust'-Port 119 Q 2
Ust Reka 118 J 3
Ustrem 119 O 4
Ust'-Shchugor 118 L 3
Ust'-Sopochnoye 131 T 4
Ust'-Sugoy 131 S 3

Ust'-Tatta 131 O 3
Ust'-Tigil 131 T 4
Ust'Tsil'ma 118 K 2
Ust'-Tym 119 Q 4
Ust'-Ulagan 119 R 5
Ust'Umal'ta 131 O 5
Ust'Un'ya 119 L 3
Ust'Un'ya 131 N 5
Ust' Ura 118 H 3
Ust'-Urgal 131 O 5
Ust'Urov 130 M 5
Ust-urt 128 F 2
Ust Usa 118 J 5
Ust'-Usa 130 F 5
Ust'Usa 118 L 2
Ustuyurt, Plato 128 F 2
Ust'Vaga 118 H 3
Ust'-Voyampolka 131 T 4
Ust'Vym' 118 K 3
Ust' Vyyskaya 118 J 3
Ust'Yuribey 119 N 2
Usu 129 L 2
Usulután 172 E 5
Usumacinta, Rio 172 D 4
Utah 170 D 4
Utah Lake 170 D 3
Utajärvi 112 J 3
Utara, Pulau 136 B 4
Utata 130 H 5
Utena 113 J 4
Utēs 119 P 5
Utesiki 131 W 2
Utete 159 F 6
Uthai Thani 135 H 4
Uthal 129 G 5
Uthumphon Phisai 135 H 5
Utiariti 180 E 3
Utica 171 L 3
Utiel 114 C 4
Utique 115 F 4
Utirik 146 C 2
Utkholok 131 T 4
Utlängan 113 G 4
Utopia 142 E 3
Utorgosh 113 K 4
Utrecht 110 D E 4
Utrera 114 B 4
Utsira 113 D 4
Utsjoki 112 J 2
Utsunomiya 133 L 3
Utta 117 G 1
Uttaradit 135 H 4
Uttar Pradesh 134 CD 2
Uttoxeter 103 D 1
Uttyakh 131 O 2
Utukok 166 E 2
Utulik 130 H J 5
Utupua 146 C 3
Utupua 145 J 4
Uulbayan 132 F 1
Uuldza 130 K 6
Uuldza Gol 130 K 6
Uusikaarlepyy 112 H 3
Uusikaupunki (Nystad) 113 H 3
Uusimaa 113 H 3
Uva (U.S.S.R.) 118 K 4
Uvá (Brazil) 181 F 4
Uvalde 170 G 6
Uvarovo 118 H 5
Uvdal 113 E 3
Uvéa 147 D 3
Uvinza 158 E 6
Uvira 158 D 5
Uvs Nuur 130 F 5
Uwajima 133 K 4
Uwayl 158 D 3
'Uwaynāt, Jabal al 154 D 4
'Uwayrid, Ḥarrat al 154 F 3
Uxin Qi 132 E 2
Uxituba 179 G 4
Uxmal 172 E 3
Uy 119 M 5
Uyaly 129 G 2
Uyandi 131 Q 2
Uyandina 131 R 2
Uyëdey 131 P 1
Uyega 131 Q 3
Uyo 157 F 4
Üyönch 130 F 6
Uyuk 129 J 2
Uyuni 180 C 5
Uyuni, Salar de 180 C 5
Uzbekistan 129 GH 2
Uzbel Shankou 129 J 3
Uzen 128 E 2
Uzerche 114 D 2
Uzh 113 J 5
Uzhgorod 116 B 1
Uzhur 119 R 4
Üzī 153 J 4

Üzū 153 J 4
Uzungwa 159 F 6
Uzunköprü 116 C 2
Uzynkair 129 G 2

V

Vääksy 112 J 3
Vaal 160 C 5
Vaala 112 J 3
Vaal Dam 160 D 5
Vaalwater 160 D 4
Vaasa (Vasa) 112 G 3
Vacaria 182 F 4
Vác 116 A 1
Vadehavet 113 E 4
Vadodara 134 B 3
Vadsö 112 J 1
Vadstena 113 F 4
Vaduz 115 E 2
Vaga 118 H 3
Vågåmo 112 E 3
Vágar 110 A 1
Vågåvatn 112 E 3
Vaggeryd 113 F 4
Vågsöy 112 D 3
Váh 111 G 5
Vahitahi 147 F 4
Vaigai 134 C 6
Vailjapur 134 B 4
Vainikkala 112 J 3
Vairaatea 147 F 4
Vaitupu 146 C 3
Vakarevo 131 W 3
Vakh 119 P 3
Vaknavolok 112 K 3
Valaam 112 K 3
Valaam, Ostrov 112 K 3
Valašské Meziříčí 111 G 5
Valcheta 183 C 7
Valdagno 115 F 2
Valday 118 F 4
Valdayskaya Vozvyshennost' 118 F 4
Valdecañas, Embalse de 114 B 4
Val de Loire 114 D 2
Valdemarsvik 113 G 4
Valdepeñas 114 C 4
Valderaduey 114 B 3
Valdés, Península 183 D 7
Valdez 166 H 3
Val-d'Isère 115 E 2
Valdivia (Chile) 183 B 6
Valdivia (Colombia) 178 C 2
Valdobbiadene 115 F 2
Val-d'Or 171 L 2
Valdosta 171 K 5
Vale 117 F 2
Valea lui Mihai 116 B 1
Valença 181 J 3
Valenca do Piauí 181 H 2
Valence 115 D 2
Valence-d'Apen 114 D 3
Valencia (Spain) 114 C 4
Valencia (Ven.) 178 E 1
Valencia de Alcántara 114 B 4
Valencia, Golfo de 114 CD 4
Valencia Island 110 A 4
Valenciennes 114 D 1
Vălenii de Munte 116 C 1
Valentin 133 K 2
Valentine 170 F 3
Valera 178 D 2
Valga 113 J 4
Valinco, Golfe de 115 E 3
Valjevo 116 A 2
Valkeakoski 112 H 3
Valladolid (Spain) 114 C 3
Valladolid (Mexico) 172 E 3
Vall de Uxó 114 C 4
Valle de la Pascua 178 E 2
Valle de Topia 172 A 2
Valle de Zaragoza 172 E 6
Valledupar 178 D 1
Vallée de l'Azaouak 156 E 2
Valle Edén 182 E 5
Vallée du Tilemsi 156 DE 2
Valle Grande 180 D 4
Valle Hermoso 172 C 2
Valle Longitudinal 183 B 6
Vallenar 182 C 5
Valle Salado 172 B 3
Valletta 115 F 4
Valley City 170 G 2
Valleyfield 169 N 6
Valley Station 171 J 4
Valleyview 167 O 4

Vallgrund 112 H 3
Vallorbe 115 E 2
Valls 114 D 3
Valmiera 112 J 4
Valparaíso (Mexico) 172 B 3
Valparaíso (Chile) 182 B 5
Valpovo 115 G 3
Valsjöbyn 112 F 3
Vals, Tanjung 137 J 5
Valtimo 112 J 3
Valuyevka 117 F 1
Valuyki 118 G 5
Válvi, Limni 116 B 2
Vamizi, Ilha 161 G 2
Vammala 113 H 3
Van 117 F 3
Vanajavesi 112 H 3
Vanavana 147 F 4
Vanavara 130 H 3
Van Blommestein Reservoir 179 G 3
Van Buren 171 H 4
Van Canh 135 J 5
Vancouver 167 N 6
Vancouver Island 167 M 6
Vanda 185
Vanderbijlpark 160 D 5
Vanderhoof 167 N 5
Vanderlin Island 143 F 2
Van Diemen, Cape 142 D 1
Van Diemen Gulf 142 E 1
Vanduzi 161 F 3
Vänern 113 F 4
Vänersborg 113 F 4
Vang 112 E 3
Vangaindrano 161 H 4
Van Gölü 117 F 3
Vangou 133 K 2
Vangunu 145 G 2
Vang Vieng 135 H 4
Van Horn 170 F 5
Vanikolo Islands 145 J 4
Vanillas 180 B 5
Vanimo 144 D 2
Vanino 131 PQ 6
Vankarem 166 B 2
Vännäs 112 G 3
Vannes 114 C 2
Van Ninh 135 J 5
Vanoise, Massif de la 115 E 2
Vanoua Lava 145 J 4
Vansbro 113 F 3
Vansittart 167 V 2
Vanua Levu 146 C 4
Vanuatu 145 J 5
Van Wert 171 K 3
Vanwyksvlei 160 C 6
Vanzevat 119 N 3
Vanzhil'kynak 119 Q 3
Vao Vao-Port-Bergé 161 H 3
Vapnyarka 116 C 1
Var 115 E 3
Varanasi 134 D 2
Varandey 118 L 2
Varangerfjorden 112 K 1
Varangerhalvöya 112 JK 1
Varano, Lago di 115 G 3
Varaždin 115 G 2
Varberg 113 F 4
Vardar 116 B 2
Varde 113 E 4
Vardö 112 K 1
Vardofjällen 112 F G 2
Värend 113 F 4
Varenikovskaya 117 E 1
Varese 115 E 2
Vårgårda 113 F 4
Vargas 182 C 5
Vargashi 119 N 4
Varginha 181 G 5
Varkaus 112 J 3
Värmland 113 F 4
Värmlandsnäs 113 F 4
Varna (Bulgaria) 116 C 2
Varna (U.S.S.R.) 119 M 5
Värnamo 113 F 4
Varnensi zaliv 116 C 2
Varnya 119 O 2
Varsinais Suomi 113 H 3
Varsinaissuomi 113 H 3
Värska 113 J 4
Varto 117 F 3
Värtsilä 112 K 3
Var'yegan 119 P 3
Várzea Grande 180 E 4
Varzi 115 E 3
Varzino 118 G 2
Varzuga 118 G 2
Varzy 114 D 2
Vasa 112 G 3
Vasai 134 B 4

Vascos, Montes 114 C 3
Vashnel 119 N 3
Vasiliká 116 B 2
Vasil'kov 118 F 5
Vasilyevka 117 E 1
Vasiss 119 O 4
Vaslui 116 C 1
Väsman 113 F 3
Vassdalsegga 113 E 4
Vasta 117 G 1
Vasta 128 D 1
Vastenjaure 112 G 2
Västerås 113 G 4
Västerbotten 112 G 3
Västerdalälven 113 F 3
Västergötland 113 F 4
Västervik 113 G 4
Vasto 115 F 3
Västra Granberget 112 H 2
Vasyugan 119 P 4
Vatan 114 D 2
Vaternish 98 A 3
Vatersay 99 A 3
Vaté-Village 145 J 6
Vaticano, Capo 115 G 4
Vaticano, Citta Del 115 F 3
Vatican State 115 F 3
Vatnajökull 112 B 3
Vatneyri 112 A 2
Vatod 147 D 4
Vatomandry 161 H 3
Vatra Dornei 116 C 1
Vättern 113 F 4
Vatyna 131 W 3
Vaudémont, Butte de 115 E 2
Vaughn 170 E 5
Vaupés 178 D 3
Vaux du Loir 114 D 2
Vavatenina 161 H 3
Vava'u Group 146 D 4
Vavoua 156 C 4
Vavuniya 134 D 4
Vaxholm 113 G 4
Växjö 113 F 4
Vayalpad 134 C 5
Vayegi 131 W 3
Vaygach 119 L 1
Vaygach, Ostrov 119 L 1
Vayvida 130 F 3
Vaza Barris 181 J 2–3
Vazhgort 118 J 3
Veadeiras 181 G 3
Veal Renh 135 H 5
Vecht 110 E 4
Vedeno 117 G 2
Vedia 182 D 5
Vefsna 112 F 2
Vega 112 F 2
Vegorritis, Limni 116 B 2
Vegreville 167 P 5
Veijo, Cerro 178 C 4
Veintocinco de Mayo 182 D 6
Veiros 179 H 4
Vejen 113 E 4
Vejle 113 E 4
Velasco, Sierra 182 C 4
Velbǎždski prohod 116 B 2
Velenje 115 G 2
Velestínon 116 B 3
Velež 115 G 3
Vélez-Málaga 114 C 4
Vélez Rubio 114 C 4
Velhas 181 H 4
Velichayevskoye 117 G 2
Velika Plana 116 B 2
Velikaya 113 J 4
Velikaya 131 X 3
Velikaya Kema 133 L 1
Veliki Kanal 116 A 1
Velikiye Luki 113 K 4
Velikiy Ustyug 118 J 3
Velikonda Range 134 C 4–5
Veliko Tǎrnovo 116 C 2
Veli Lošinj 115 F 3
Vélingara 156 B 3
Velingrad 116 B 2
Velino 115 F 3
Vel'kal' 166 B 2
Vella Lavella 145 G 2
Velletri 115 F 3
Vellore 134 C 4
Velsk 118 H 3
Vel't 118 K 2
Vemdalen 112 F 3
Vemor'ye 131 Q 6
Ven 113 F 4
Venado Tuerto 182 D 5
Venafro 115 F 3
Vena Park 143 G 2
Venda 160 DE 4
Venda Nova 181 H 4
Vendas Novas 114 B 4
Vendôme 114 D 2

Vendrell 114 D 3
Vendsyssel 113 F 4
Veneta, Laguna 115 F 2
Venetie 166 H 2
Venezia 115 F 2
Venezuela 178–179 EF 2
Venezuela, Golfo de 178 D 1
Vengerovo 119 P 4
Vengurla 134 B 4
Veniaminof, Mount 166 F 4
Venice 115 F 2
Vénissieux 115 D 2
Venjan 113 F 3
Venkatapuram 134 D 4
Vennesla 113 E 4
Venosa 115 G 3
Venta 113 H 4
Venta de Baños 114 C 3
Ventersdorp 160 D 5
Ventimiglia 115 E 3
Ventor 103 D 2
Ventotene 115 E 3
Ventoux, Mont 115 E 3
Ventselevo 131 O 6
Ventspils 113 H 4
Ventuari 178 E 2
Ventura 170 C 5
Venus Bay 143 H 6
Venustiano Carranza 172 D 4
Vera (Argentina) 182 D 4
Vera (Spain) 114 C 4
Veracruz (Mexico) 172 C 4
Veraval 134 B 3
Verbania 115 E 2
Vercelli 115 E 2
Vercors 115 E 2–3
Verdalsöra 112 F 3
Verde 170 D 5
Verde, Cape (Senegal) 152 B 6
Verde, Costa 114 B 3
Verdun 115 E 2
Vereeniging 160 D 5
Vereshchagino 118 K 4
Verga, Cap 156 B 3
Vergara 182 F 5
Verhnedvinsk 113 J 4
Verkhn'aya Salda 119 M 4
Verkhnearshinskiy 119 L 5
Verkhnebakanskiy 117 E 2
Verkhne Dneprovsk 117 D 1
Verkhneimbatskoye 119 R 3
Verkhne-Ozernaya 131 U 4
Verkhnetulomskiy 112 K 2
Verkhnetulomskoye Vodokhrani-
  lishche 112 K 2
Verkhneural'sk 119 L 5
Verkhnevilyuyskt 130 M 3
Verkhneye Kuyto 112 K 3
Verkhneye Skoblino 119 R 4
Verkhniy Ufaley 119 M 4
Verkhnyaya Amga 131 N 4
Verkhnyaya Angara 130 K 4
Verkhnyaya Baikha 119 Q 2
Verkhnyaya Chunku 130 G 3
Verkhnyaya Pakhacha 131 V 3
Verkhnyaya Taymyra 130 G 1
Verkhnyaya Toyma 118 J 3
Verkhnyaya Vol'dzha 119 P 4
Verkholensk 130 J 5
Verkhoyansk 131 O 2
Verkhoyanskiy Khrebet
  131 N 2–P 3
Verkhoyansk Range 131 OP 3
Verme Falls 159 G 3
Vermilion Bay 171 J 6
Vermion Óros 116 B 2
Vermont 171 M 3
Vernal 170 E 4
Verneuk Pan 160 C 5
Vernon (France) 114 D 2
Vernon (Canada) 167 O 5
Vernon (U.S.A.) 170 G 5
Vernon, Mount 142 B 3
Vero Beach 171 K 6
Véroia 116 B 2
Verona 115 F 2
Versailles 114 D 2
Vershina 119 MN 3
Vershino-Darasunskiy 130 L 5
Vershino-Shakhtaminskiye
  130 L 5
Vert, Cap 156 A 3
Vertiskos Óros 116 B 2
Verviers 110 E 4
Verwood 103 D 2
Vescovato 115 E 3
Veselovskoye Vodokhranilishche
  117 F 1
Veseloye 117 DE 1
Veselyy 117 F 1
Veshenskaya 118 H 6

Vesoul 115 E 2
Vest-Agder 113 E 4
Vestbygd 113 E 4
Vesterålen 112 FG 2
Vesterhavn 113 F 4
Vestfirðir 112 A 2
Vestfjorden 112 FG 2
Vestmannaeyjar 112 A 3
Vestre Jakobselv 112 J 1
Vest Spitsbergen 184
Vestvågöy 112 F 2
Vesuvio 115 F 3
Veszprém 116 A 1
Vet 160 D 5
Vétaounde 145 J 4
Vetlanda 113 G 4
Vetluga 118 J 4
Vetluzhskiy 118 J 4
Vetrenyy 131 R 3
Vettore 115 F 3
Vetvey 131 V 3
Vevey 115 E 2
Vežen 116 B 2
Vezh'yudor 118 K 3
Veziköprü 117 E 2
Viacha 180 C 4
Viamonte 182 D 5
Viamonte 183 C 9
Viana (Angola) 160 A 1
Viana do Castelo 114 B 3
Viar 114 B 4
Viareggio 115 F 3
Vibo Valentia 115 G 4
Vicari 115 F 4
Vicecommodoro Marambio 185
Vicenza 115 F 2
Vichada 178 E 3
Vichuga 118 H 4
Vichy 114 D 2
Vicksburg 171 H 5
Victor Harbour 143 F 6
Victoria (Arg.) 182 D 5
Victoria (Australia) 143 G 6
Victoria (Canada) 167 N 6
Victoria (Chile) 183 B 6
Victoria (Guinea) 156 B 3
Victoria (Hong Kong) 132 F 6
Victoria (Malaysia) 136 E 2
Victoria (Malta) 115 F 4
Victoria (Seychelles) 159 K 5
Victoria (TX, U.S.A.) 171 G 6
Victoria de Durango 172 B 3
Victoria de las Tunas 173 G 3
Victoria Falls 160 D 3
Victoria, Grand Lake 171 L 2
Victoria Island 169 PQ 1
Victoria, Lake 158 E 5
Victoria Land 185
Victoria, Mount (Papua New Guin-
  ea) 144 E 3
Victoria, Mount (Burma) 135 F 3
Victoria Nile 158 E 4
Victoria River 142 E 2
Victoria River Downs 142 E 2
Victoria Strait 167 R 2
Victoria West 160 C 6
Victoriaville 169 N 6
Victorica 183 D 6
Victorino de la Plaza 183 D 6
Victorville 170 C 5
Victory Downs 142 E 4
Vicuña Mackenna 182 D 5
Vidin 116 B 2
Vidisha 134 C 3
Vidra 116 C 2
Vidsel 112 H 2
Viduša 115 G 3
Vidzemes Augstiene 113 J 4
Vidzy 113 J 4
Viedma 183 D 7
Viedma 183 B 8
Viedma, Lago 183 B 8
Viejo, Rio 172 E 5
Vieng Pou Kha 135 H 3
Vienna (Austria) 115 G 2
Vienna (U.S.A.) 171 K 4
Vienne 114 D 2
Vienne 115 D 2
Vientiane 135 H 4
Vientos, Paso de los 173 H 4
Vieques, Isla de 173 J 4
Vierwaldstätter See 115 E 2
Vierzon 114 D 2
Viesca 172 B 2
Vieste 115 G 3
Vietas 112 G 2
Vietnam 135 J 4
Viet Tri 135 J 3
Vieux-Fort 169 Q 5

Vigan 137 J 1
Vigevano 115 E 2
Vignola 115 F 3
Vigo 114 B 3
Vigo, Ría de 114 B 3
Vigra 179 J 4
Vihanti 112 J 3
Vihoflat 111 H 5
Viiala 112 H 3
Viitasaari 112 J 3
Vijayadurg 134 B 4
Vijayawada 134 D 4
Vik 112 B 2
Vikersund 113 E 4
Vikhorevka 130 H 4
Viking 167 P 5
Vikna 112 F 3
Vila Bittencourt 178 E 4
Vila Conceição 179 F 3
Vila do Porto 152 A 1
Vila Franca de Xira 114 B 4
Vila Gamito 161 E 2
Vilaine 114 C 2
Vilanculo 161 F 4
Viļāni 112 J 4
Vila Nova de Gaia 114 B 3
Vila Pouca de Aquiar 114 B 3
Vila Real 114 B 3
Vila Velha (Amapá, Brazil)
  179 H 3
Vila Velha (Espirito Santo, Brazil)
  181 H 5
Vila Velha de Rodão 114 B 4
Vilcabamba 178 D 6
Vileyka 113 J 5
Vilhelmina 112 G 3
Vilhena 180 D 3
Viliga-Kushka 131 T 3
Viliya 113 J 5
Viljandi 113 H 4
Vilkija 113 H 4
Vilkovo 116 C 1
Vil'gort 118 L 3 118 L 3
Villa Abecia 180 C 5
Villa Ahumada 170 E 5
Villa Ángela 182 D 4
Villa Bella 180 C 3
Villablino 114 B 3
Villacarrillo 114 C 4
Villacastin 114 C 3
Villach 115 F 2
Villacidro 115 E 4
Villa Colón 182 C 5
Villa Constitución 182 D 5
Villa Coronado 170 E 6
Villa de Cos 172 B 3
Villa de Guadalupe 172 B 3
Villa del Rosario (Argentina)
  182 D 5
Villa del Rosario (Venezuela)
  178 D 1
Villa de Reyes 172 B 3
Villa Dolores 182 C 5
Villa Federal 182 E 5
Villa Flores 172 D 4
Villafranca del Cid 114 C 3
Villafranca di Verona 115 F 2
Villa Frontera 172 B 2
Villagarcia de Arosa 114 B 3
Villa General Roca 182 C 5
Villaguay 183 E 5
Villa Guillermina 182 E 4
Villa Hayes 182 E 4
Villahermosa 172 D 4
Villa Hidalgo 172 B 2
Villa Huidobro 182 D 5
Villa Ingavi 180 D 5
Villajoyosa 114 C 4
Villalba 114 B 3
Villaldama 172 B 2
Villalón de Campos 114 C 3
Villalonga 183 D 6
Villalpando 114 B 3
Villa María 182 D 5
Villa Martín (Bolivia) 180 C 5
Villamartin (Spain) 114 B 4
Villa Mazán 182 C 4
Villa Mercedes 182 C 5
Villa Minetti 182 D 4
Villa Montes 180 D 5
Villanova y Geltrú 114 D 3
Villanueva 172 B 3
Villanueva de Córdoba 114 C 4
Villanueva de la Serena 114 B 4
Villanueva del Fresno 114 B 4
Villa Ocampo 172 A 2
Villa Oliva 182 E 4
Villa Regina 183 C 6
Villa Rey 180 D 5
Villarreal de los Infantes 114 C 4
Villarrica (Chile) 183 B 6

Vas – Vir

Villarrica (Paraguay) 182 E 4
Villarrobledo 114 C 4
Villa S. Giovanni 115 G 4
Villatoro, Puerto de 114 B 3
Villa Unión (Argentina) 182 C 4
Villa Union (Mexico) 172 A 3
Villavicencio 178 D 3
Villaviciosa 114 B 3
Villazón 180 C 5
Villefranche-sur-Saône 115 D 2
Villena 114 C 4
Villeneuve-sur-Lot 114 D 3
Villmanstrand 112 J 3
Villupuram 134 C 5
Vil'mo 130 F 3
Vilnius 113 J 5
Vilppula 113 J 3
Vilsandi 113 H 4
Vilyuy 130 J 3
Vilyuyskoye Plato 130 J 2
Vilyuyskt 130 M 3
Vilyuyskoye Vodokhranilishche
  130 K 3
Vimmerby 113 G 4
Vina 157 G 4
Vinaroz 114 D 3
Vincennes 171 J 4
Vinces 178 C 4
Vinchina 182 C 4
Vindelälven 112 G 2
Vindeln 112 G 3
Vindhya Range 134 C 3
Vineland 171 L 4
Vingåker 113 G 4
Vinh 135 J 4
Vinh Giat 135 J 5
Vinh Linh 135 J 4
Vinh Loi 135 J 6
Vinh Long 135 J 5
Vinica (Yugoslavia) 115 G 2
Vinica (Yugoslavia) 116 B 2
Vinniki 113 H 6
Vinnitsa 118 E 1
Vino, Tierra del 114 B 3
Vinson Massif 185
Vinstervatn 112 E 3
Vinstra 112 E 3
Viqueque 137 G 5
Virac 137 F 1
Viramgam 134 B 3
Virandozero 118 G 3
Viranşehir 117 D 3
Viranşehir 117 E 3
Virarajendrapet 134 C 5
Virden 167 R 6
Vire 114 C 2
Virei 160 A 3
Virful Balota 116 B 1
Virful Bivolu 116 C 1
Virful Budacu 116 C 1
Virful Cindrelu 116 B 1
Virful Ciucasu 116 C 1
Virful Curcubǎta 116 B 1
Virful Farcǎu 116 B 1
Virful Giumalǎu 116 C 1
Virful Gogu 116 B 1
Virful Goru 116 C 1
Virful Hǎmaşu Mare 116 C 1
Virful Iezerul 116 B 1
Virful Moldoveanu 116 B 1
Virful Negoiu 116 B 1
Virful Nemira 116 C 1
Virful Omu 116 C 1
Virful Peleaga 116 B 1
Virful Pietrii 116 B 1
Virful Pietrosu 116 B 1
Virful Pleşu 116 B 1
Virful Saca 116 C 1
Virful Tarhǎus 116 C 1
Virful Toaca 116 C 1
Virful Vlǎdeasa 116 B 1
Virful Vulcan 116 B 1
Virgem da Lapa 181 H 4
Virgenes, Cabo 183 C 9
Virginia (U.S.A.) 171 L 4
Virginia (MN, U.S.A.) 171 H 2
Virginia (S. Afr.) 160 D 5
Virginia (U.K.) 100 B 3
Virginia Beach 171 L 4
Virginia Falls 167 MN 3
Virgin Islands 173 K 4
Virihaure 112 G 2
Virojoki 113 J 3
Virovitica 115 G 2
Virrat 112 H 3
Virserum 113 G 4
Virsko More 115 FG 3
Virtsu 113 H 4
Virtul Gutii 116 B 1
Virú 178 C 5
Virudunagar 134 C 6

289

Vir – War

Virunga National Park 158 D 4–5
Vis 115 G 3
Visalia 170 C 4
Visayan Sea 137 F 1
Visby 113 G 4
Viscount Melville Sound 167 P 1
Visegrad 116 A 2
Viseu 179 J 4
Vişeu de Sus 116 B 1
Vishakhapatnam 134 D 4
Vishera 118 L 3
Vishnevka 119 O 5
Visingsö 113 F 4
Viskafors 113 F 4
Visoko 115 G 3
Visp 115 E 2
Vista 161 E 5
Vista Alegre (Amazonas, Brazil) 178 E 3
Vista Alegre (Amazonas, Brazil) 178 E 5
Vista Alegre (Roraima, Brazil) 179 F 3
Vistula 111 G 4
Vitarte 180 A 3
Vitebsk 113 K 4
Viterbo 115 F 3
Vitiaz Strait 144 E 3
Viti Levu 146 C 4
Vitim 130 K 4
Vitim 130 L 5
Vitimskiy 130 K 4
Vitimskoye Ploskogor'ye 130 K 5
Vitolište 116 B 2
Vitória (Espiritu Santo, Brazil) 181 H 5
Vitória (Pará, Brazil) 179 H 4
Vitória da Conquista 181 H 3
Vitorra 114 C 3
Vitré 114 C 2
Vitry-le-François 115 D 2
Vittangi 112 H 2
Vittoria 115 F 4
Vittorio d'Africa → Shalānbōd 159 GH 4
Vittorio Veneto 115 F 2
Viver 114 C 4
Vivero 114 B 3
Vivi 130 G 3
Viviers 115 D 3
Vivonne 143 F 6
Vivorata 183 E 6
Vizagapatam → Vishakhapatami 134 D 4
Vizcachas, Meseta de las 183 B 9
Vizcaino, Sierra 170 D 6
Vize 116 C 2
Vizianagaram 134 D 4
Vizinga 118 K 3
Vjartsilja 112 K 3
Vjosa 116 A 2
Vladimir 133 L 2
Vladimir 118 H 4
Vladimirovka 118 K 5
Vladimirovskiy 119 M 5
Vladimir-Volynskiy 113 H 5
Vladislavovka 117 E 1
Vladivostok 133 K 2
Vlahina 116 B 2
Vlasenica 115 G 3
Vlissingen 110 D 4
Vlora 116 A 2
Vlorë 116 A 2
Vltava 111 F 4
Vöcklabruck 115 F 2
Voderrhein 115 E 2
Vodice 115 G 3
Vodla 118 G 3
Vodlozero, Ozero 118 G 3
Vodnjan 115 F 3
Vogan 156 E 4
Vogel Peak 157 G 4
Vogelsberg 111 E 4
Voghera 115 E 2
Vohimarina 161 J 2
Vohipeno 161 H 4
Voi 159 F 5
Voinjama 156 C 4
Voiron 115 E 2
Vojens 113 E 4
Vojmån 112 G 3
Vojmsjön 112 G 2
Vojnić 115 G 2
Vojvodina 116 AB 1
Volcán Antofalla 182 C 4
Volcán Barú 178 B 2
Volcán Ceboruco 172 B 3
Volcán Citlaltépetl 172 C 4
Volcán Corcovado 183 B 7
Volcán Domuyo 183 B 6
Volcán Irazú 178 B 1
Volcán Lanin 183 B 6
Volcán Las Tres Virgenes 170 D 6

Volcán Lliama 183 B 6
Volcán Llullaillaco 180 C 5
Volcán Maipo 182 C 5
Volcán Miravalles 172 E 5
Volcán Misti 180 B 4
Volcán Ollagüe 180 C 5
Volcán Paricutín 172 B 4
Volcán Popocatéptl 172 C 4
Volcán Sangay 178 C 4
Volcán San Juan 172 B 3
Volcán Tajumulco 172 D 4
Volcán Tutupaca 180 B 4
Volcán Wolf 178 B 6
Volchikha 119 Q 5
Volchya 117 E 1
Volda 112 E 3
Voldafjorden 112 E 3
Volga 117 G 1
Volgo-Balt (I.V. Lenin) Kanal 118 G 3
Volgodonsk 117 F 1
Volgograd 118 H 6
Volgogradskoye Vodokhranilishche 118 J 6
Volikovisochnoe 118 K 2
Volkhov 113 K 4
Volkovysk 113 H 5
Volksrust 160 D 5
Volna, Gora 131 T 3
Volnovakha 117 E 1
Volochanka 117 F 1
Volochayevka 131 O 6
Volodarskoye 119 N 5
Volodorsk 118 G 4
Vologda 118 G 4
Volokon 130 J 4
Volokovaya 118 J 2
Volonga 118 J 2
Volos 116 B 3
Volosovo 113 J 4
Volovets 116 B 1
Volozhin 113 J 5
Volsini, Monti 115 F 3
Vol'sk 118 J 5
Volta 156 E 4
Volta Blanche 156 D 3
Volta, Lake 156 DE 4
Volta Noire 156 D 4
Volta Redonda 181 H 5
Volta Rouge 156 D 3
Volterra 115 F 3
Volteva 118 H 3
Voltsberg 115 G 2
Volturino 115 G 3
Volturno 115 F 3
Volupai 145 E 2
Volynskaya Vozvyshennost' 113 H 5
Volynskoje Polesje 113 L 5
Volzhsk 118 J 4
Volzhskiy 118 J 6
Vondrozo 161 H 4
Von Frank Mountain 166 G 3
Vonitsa 116 B 3
Vopnafjörður 112 C 2
Vopnafjörður 112 B 2
Vora 116 A 2
Vorau 115 G 2
Vordingborg 113 F 4
Vórioi Sporádhes 116 B 3
Vórios Evvoikós Kólpos 116 B 3
Vorjing 135 F 2
Vorkuta 119 M 2
Vormsi 113 H 4
Vorob'yevo 130 H 4
Vorob'yevo 119 P 4
Vorogovo 119 R 3
Vóroi Sporádhes 116 B 3
Voronezh 118 G 5
Voronovo 119 Q 4
Vorontsovka 118 H 5
Vorontsovka 130 K 4
Vorontsovo 130 D 1
Voron'ya 112 L 2
Voroshilovgrad 117 E 1
Võrts Järv 113 J 4
Võru 113 J 4
Vor'yapaul' 119 MN 3
Vosges 115 E 2
Voskhod 117 F 1
Voss 113 E 3
Vostochnaya Litsa 118 G 2
Vostochno-Kounradskiy 119 P 6
Vostochno-Sakhalinskiy Khrebet 131 Q 5–6
Vostok Sibirskoye More 131 ST 1
Vostochnyy 131 Q 6
Vostochnyy 131 Q 5
Vostochnyy Sayan 130 F H 5
Vostok (Antarctica) 185
Vostok (Kiribati) 147 E 3
Vostok Manych 117 F 1

Vostykhoy 119 N 3
Votkinsk 118 K 4
Votkinskoye Vodokhranilishche 118 L 4
Vœune Sai 135 J 5
Vourinos Oros 116 B 2
Vouziers 115 D 2
Voxnan 112 F 3
Voyampolka 131 T 4
Voyvozh 118 L 3
Vozhega 118 H 3
Vozhe, Ozero 118 G 3
Vozhgora 118 J 3
Voznesensk 116 D 1
Vozrozhdeniya, Ostrov 128 F 1
Vozvrashcheniye 131 Q 6
Vozvyshennost' Byraya-Tas 130 M 1
Vozvyshennost' Gabrey 130 F 1
Vozvyshennost' Karabil' 129 G 3
Vozvyshennost' Syuryakh-Dzhangy 130 M 1
Vozvyshennost' Tulay-Kiryaka-Tas 130 J 1
Vozvyshennost' Tutonchana 130 F 2
Vozyvshennost' Byraya-Tas 130 M 1
Vraca 116 B 2
Vradiyevka 116 D 1
Vran 115 G 3
Vranje 116 B 2
Vráška čuka, Prohod 116 B 2
Vratnica 116 B 2
Vrbas 115 G 3
Vrbovsko 115 G 2
Vrede 160 D 5
Vreed en Hoop 179 G 2
Vriddhachalam 134 C 5
Vrigstad 113 F 4
Vršac 116 B 1
Vryburg 160 C 5
Vryheid 161 E 5
Vsetin 111 G 5
Vsevidof, Mount 166 D 5
Vsevolozhsk 113 K 3
Vucitrn 116 B 2
Vukovar 115 G 2
Vulcano 115 F 4
Vung Tau 135 J 5
Vuohijärvi 112 J 3
Vuokkijärvi 112 J 3
Vuoksa 112 J 3
Vuollerim 112 H 2
Vuotso 112 J 2
Vyalotsevo 118 H 4
Vyatka 118 K 4
Vyatskiye Polyany 118 K 4
Vyazemskiy 131 O 6
Vyaz'ma 118 F 4
Vyazovka 118 J 5
Vyborg 112 J 3
Vychegda 118 J 3
Vydrino 130 G 4
Vygoda 116 D 1
Vygozero, Ozero 118 F 3
Vyksa 118 H 4
Vym' 118 K 3
Vyngapur 119 P 3
Vyritsa 113 K 4
Vyselki 145 H 4
Vyshniy-Volochek 118 F 4
Vysokaya Parma 119 L 3
Vysokogornyy 131 P 5
Vysokouaiti 145 Q 10
Vysokoye 118 F 4
Vysotsk 113 J 3
Vytegra 118 G 3
V'yuny 119 Q 4
Vyvenka 131 V 3

W

Wa 156 D 3
Waal 110 D E 4
Wabag 144 D 3
Wabana 169 R 6
Wabara 159 G 3
Wabasca 167 P 4
Wabasca River 167 O 4
Wabash River 171 J 4
Wābirī 153 J 3
Wabowden 167 S 5
Wabrah 155 H 3
Wałbrzy 111 G 4
Waco (Quebec, Can.) 169 O 5
Waco (TX, U.S.A.) 171 G 5
Waconda Lake 170 G 4

Wałcz 111 G 4
Wad 129 G 5
Wad al Ḥaddād 154 E 6
Wad Bandah 154 D 6
Waddān 153 J 3
Waddān, Jabal 153 J 3
Waddeneilanden 110 D E 4
Waddenzee 110 E 4
Waddington, Mount 167 M 5
Wadebridge 102 B 2
Wad Ḥāmid 154 E 5
Wādī ad Dawāsir 155 G 4
Wādī al Bāṭin 155 H 3
Wādī al Ḥamḍ 154 F 3
Wādī al Malik 154 D 5
Wādī al Masīlah 155 J 5
Wādī an Natrūn 154 DE 2
Wādī ar Rummah 155 G 3
Wādī ash Shāṭi' 153 H 3
Wādī as Sirḥān 154 F 2
Wādī Bayy al Kabīr 153 H 2
Wadi Drâa 152 D 3
Wādī Fajr 154 F 3
Wādī Fārigh 153 K 2
Wādī Ḥalfa' 154 E 4
Wādī Ḥamīm 153 K 2
Wādī Ibrah 154 C 6
Wādī Īrāwan 153 H 3
Wādī Jabjabah 154 E 4
Wādī Qitbīt 155 J 5
Wādī Sūf Ajjīn 153 H 2
Wādī Umm al Hayt 155 J 5
Wadley 171 K 5
Wad Madanī 154 E 6
Wad Nimr 154 E 6
Wad Rawa 154 E 5
Wadsworth 170 C 4
Wafrah 155 H 3
Wager Bay 167 U 2
Waggabundi 147 F 2
Wagga Wagga 143 H 6
Wagin 142 B 5
Wagoner 171 G 4
Wagon Mound 170 F 4
Wah 129 J 4
Wahai 137 G 4
Wāḥāt ad Dākhilah 154 D 3
Wāḥāt al Baḥarīyah 154 D 3
Wāḥāt al Farāfirah 154 D 3
Wāḥāt al Jufrah 153 J 3
Wāḥāt al Khārijah 154 E 3
Wāḥāt al Kufrah 153 K 4
Wāḥāt al Rabyānah 153 K 4
Wāḥāt al Tāzirbū 153 K 3
Wāḥāt Jālū 153 K 3
Wāḥāt Sabḥā 153 H 3
Wāḥāt Salīmah 154 D 4
Wāḥāt Sīwah 154 D 3
Wāḥāt Zīghan 153 K 3
Wahībah 155 K 4
Waḥidī 155 H 6
Wahni 159 F 2
Wahpeton 171 G 2
Wai 134 B 4
Waibeem 137 H 4
Waigama 137 G 4
Waigeo, Pulau 137 H 4
Waihi 145 R 8
Waikabubak 137 E 5
Waikato 145 R 8
Waikouaiti 145 Q 10
Waimate 145 Q 9
Wainanga 134 C 3
Waingapu 137 F 5
Wainwright (AK, U.S.A.) 166 E 1
Wainwright (Alb., Can.) 167 P 5
Waipara 145 Q 9
Waipukurau 145 R 8
Wairoa 145 R 8
Waisai 137 H 4
Waitaki River 145 Q 9
Waitara 145 Q 8
Wājid 159 G 4
Wajir 159 G 4
Waka (Ethiopia) 159 F 3
Waka (Zaire) 158 C 4
Wakasa-wan 133 KL 3
Waka, Tanjung 137 G 4
Wakatipu, Lake 144 P 10
Wakayama 133 L 4
Wake 146 C 1
Wa Keeney 170 G 4
Wakefield 101 D 3
Wakenaam Island 179 G 2
Wakkanai 133 M 1
Wakre 137 H 3
Wakuach, Lac 169 O 4
Waku Kungo 160 B 2
Wala 158 E 6

Walachia 116 BC 2
Walaga 158 F 3
Walden 170 E 3
Waldia 159 F 2
Waldo 171 K 6
Waldport 170 B 3
Walenzee 115 E 2
Wales (U.K.) 110 C 4
Wales (AK, U.S.A.) 166 D 2
Wales Island (NWT, Can.) 167 U 2
Walewale 156 D 3
Walgett 143 H 5
Walikale 158 D 5
Walinga 144 E 3
Walker Lake 170 C 4
Walkite 159 F 3
Wall 170 F 3
Wallaby Island 143 G 2
Wallaceburg 171 K 3
Wallal Downs 142 C 2
Wallaroo 143 F 5
Wallasey 101 C 3
Walla Walla 170 C 2
Wall Creek 142 E 4
Wallel 158 E 3
Wallendbeen 143 H 5
Wallingford 103 D 2
Wallis 146 D 3
Wallis and Futuna 146 D 3
Walls 98 D 1
Wallsend 143 J 5
Walnut Ridge 171 H 4
Walpole, Ile 145 J 6
Walrus Islands 166 E 4
Walsall 103 D 1
Walsenburg 170 F 4
Walsh 143 G 2
Walsingham, Cape 169 P 2
Walt Disney World 171 K 6
Walterboro 171 K 5
Walton le Dale 101 D 3
Walvis Bay 160 A 4
Walvis Ridge 192 B 5
Wama, Sungai 137 J 4
Wamba (Kenya) 159 F 4
Wamba (Nigeria) 157 F 4
Wamba (Zaire) 158 B 6
Wamba (Zaire) 158 D 4
Wamena 137 J 4
Wami 159 F 6
Wamsisi 137 G 4
Wan 137 J 5
Wana 129 H 4
Wanaaring 143 G 4
Wanaka 144 P 9
Wanaka, Lake 144 P 9
Wanapiri 137 J 4
Wandel Sea 184
Wanganella 143 G 6
Wanganui 145 R 8
Wangaratta 143 H 6
Wangcang 132 E 4
Wanggameti, Gunung 136 F 6
Wangi 159 G 2
Wangiwangi, Pulau 137 F 5
Wangka 135 G 4
Wang Kai 158 D 3
Wangkui 133 J 1
Wangmo 132 E 5
Wangqing 133 J 2
Wan Hsa-la 135 G 3
Wanie Rukula 158 D 4
Wanigela 144 E 3
Wankaner 134 B 3
Wankie 160 D 3
Wankie National Park 160 D 3
Wanle Weyn 159 G 4
Wanning 132 F 7
Wanor 157 G 4
Wanrhynsdorp 160 B 6
Wanshan Qundao 132 F 6
Wantage 103 D 2
Wanxian 132 E 4
Wanyuan 132 E 4
Wanzai 132 F 5
Wapamoiwa 145 F 3
Warangal 134 C 4
Waratah 144 L 9
Waratah Bay 143 H 6
Warbumi 137 H 4
Warburg 111 E 4
Warburton Bay 167 P 3
Warburton Mission 142 D 4
Warburton Range 142 D 4
Warburton River 143 F 4
Warder 159 H 3
Wardha 134 C 3
Ward Hunt Strait 145 EF 3
Ware 167 M 4
Ware 103 D 2
Wareham 103 C 2
Waren 137 J 4

290

Warenai, Sungai 137 J 4
Warenda 143 G 3
Warialda 143 J 4
Warin Chamrap 135 H 4
Warley 103 C 1
Warlingham 103 D 2
Warmbad (Namibia) 160 B 5
Warmbad (S. Africa) 160 D 4
Warmfontein 160 B 5
Warminster 103 C 2
Warm Springs 170 C 4
Warnemünde 111 E 2
Warner Mount 170 B 3
Warner Peak 170 C 3
Warner Robins 171 K 5
Waroona 142 B 5
Warora 134 C 3
Warragul 143 H 6
Warrawagine 142 C 3
Warrego River 143 H 4
Warren (Australia) 143 H 5
Warren (U.S.A.) 171 K 3
Warrenpoint 100 B 2
Warrenton 160 C 5
Warri 157 F 4
Warrington 101 D 3
Warrnambool 143 G 6
Warrow 143 F 5
Warrumbungle Range 143 H 5
Warsaw 111 H 4
Warshīkh 159 H 4
Warsop 101 E 3
Warszawa → Warsaw 111 H 4
Warta 111 G 4
Waru 137 H 4
Warwick (U.K.) 103 D 1
Warwick (Australia) 143 J 4
Warwick Channel 143 F 1
Warwickshire 103 D 1
Wasagu 157 F 3
Wasatch Range 170 D 3
Wasco 170 C 4
Wase 157 F 4
Washburn 170 F 2
Washim 134 C 3
Washington (U.S.A.) 170 B 2
Washington (IN, U.S.A.) 171 J 4
Washington (Kiribati) → Teraina 147 E 2
Washington (D.C., U.S.A.) 171 L 4
Washington (U.K.) 101 E 2
Washington Court House 171 K 4
Washita River 170 G 4
Washuk 129 G 5
Wasian 137 H 4
Wasior 137 H 4
Wāsiṭ 155 H 2
Waspám 172 F 5
Wasserburg 111 F 5
Wasserkuppe 111 E 4
Wasua 144 D 3
Wasum 145 E 3
Watampone 137 F 4
Watan Soppeng 137 E 4
Watchet 102 C 2
Waterberg 160 B 4
Waterbury 171 M 3
Waterford 110 B 4
Waterhouse River 142 E 1
Waterloo (Belgium) 110 D 4
Waterloo (U.S.A.) 171 H 3
Waterloo (Sierra Leone) 156 B 4
Watersmeet 171 J 2
Waterton Lakes National Park 167 P 5
Watertown (N.Y., U.S.A.) 171 L 3
Watertown (S.D., U.S.A.) 170 G 2
Watertown (WI, U.S.A.) 171 J 3
Waterville 171 N 3
Watford 103 D 2
Watford City 170 F 2
Wa'th 158 E 3
Watheroo 142 B 5
Watling Island 173 H 3
Watrous (U.S.A.) 170 F 4
Watrous (Canada) 167 Q 5
Watsa 158 D 4
Watsi Kengo 158 C 5
Watson Lake 166 M 3
Watts Bar Lake 171 K 4
Watubela, Kepulauan 137 H 4
Wauchope 142 E 4
Waukara, Gunung 137 E 4
Waukarlycarly, Lake 142 C 3
Waukegan 171 J 3
Waukesha 171 J 3
Wausau 171 H 2
Wau → Wāw 158 D 3
Wave Hill 142 E 2
Waveney, River 103 E 1
Waverly 171 H 2
Wāw 158 D 3

Wawa (Nigeria) 157 E 4
Wawa (Canada) 171 K 2
Wāw al Kabīr 153 J 3
Wāw an Nāmūs 153 J 4
Wawotobi 137 F 4
Waxxari 129 M 3
Wayabula 137 G 3
Wayamli 137 G 3
Wayao 132 C 5
Waycross 171 K 5
Way, Lake 142 C 4
Wayland 171 K 4
Wayne 171 K 4
Waza (Burma) 135 G 2
Waza (Cameroon) 157 G 3
Waza National Park 157 G 3
Wāzīn 153 H 2
Wazirabad 129 J 4
Wąbrzeźno 111 G 4
Wągrowiec 111 G 4
Wda 111 G 4
Wé 145 J 6
Weagamow Lake 168 J 5
Wear, River 101 D 2
Webbe Gestro 159 G 3
Webbe Shibeli 159 G 4
Webi Shābelle 159 G 4
Webster City 171 H 3
Weda 137 G 3
Weda, Teluk 137 G 3
Weddell Island 183 D 9
Weddell Sea 185
Wedel 111 E 4
Weeki Wachee 171 K 6
Weert 110 D 4
Weet Burra 98 D 1
Weh, Pulau 136 A 2
Wehterby 101 E 3
Weichang 133 G 2
Weiden 111 F 4
Weifang 133 G 3
Weihai 133 H 3
Wei He 132 E 4
Weimar 111 F 4
Weinan 132 E 4
Weipa 143 G 1
Weirton 171 K 3
Weiser 170 C 3
Weishan 133 G 4
Weishan Hu 133 G 4
Weishi 132 F 4
Weissbrünn 160 A 3
Weitra 115 F 2
Weixi 132 C 5
Wei Xian 132 E 3
Weiyuan 132 D 5
Weiyuan 132 D 3
Weizhou Dao 132 E 6
Wejherowo 111 G 4
Welbourn Hill 142 E 4
Welcome Kop 160 B 6
Welkom 160 D 5
Welland, River 103 D 1
Wellesley Island 143 F 2
Wellesley Islands, South 143 F 2
Wellingborough 103 D 1
Wellington (New South Wales, Austr.) 143 H 5
Wellington (KS, U.S.A.) 170 G 4
Wellington (NV, U.S.A.) 170 C 4
Wellington (N.Z.) 145 Q 9
Wellington (U.K.) 102 C 2
Wellington, Isla (Chile) 183 AB 5
Wells (U.K.) 102 C 2
Wells (NV, U.S.A.) 170 D 3
Wells (VT, U.S.A.) 171 M 3
Wellsboro 171 L 3
Wells-next-the-Sea 103 E 1
Wellton 170 D 5
Welo 159 FG 2
Wels 115 F 2
Welshpool 102 C 1
Welwyn Garden City 103 D 2
Wema 158 C 5
Wembere 158 E 5
Wenatchee 170 B 2
Wenchang 132 F 7
Wenchi 156 D 4
Wenchuan 132 D 4
Wendeng 133 H 3
Wendover (U.S.A.) 170 D 3
Wendover (U.K.) 103 D 2
Wengshui 132 C 5
Wengyuan 132 F 6
Wenjiang 132 D 4
Wenling 133 H 5
Wenlock River 143 G 1
Wenquan 132 C 3
Wenshan 132 D 6
Wenshang 133 G 3
Wensley 110 C 4

Wensley 101 E 2
Wensleydale 101 D 2
Wensu 129 L 2
Wentworth 143 G 5
Wen Xian 132 D 4
Wen Xian 132 F 4
Wenzhou 133 H 5
Wepener 160 D 5
Werda 160 C 5
Weri 137 H 4
Werra 111 F 4
Werribee 143 G 6
Werris Creek 143 J 5
Wesel 110 E 4
Weser 111 E 4
Wesiri 137 G 5
Weslaco 170 G 6
Wesleyville 169 R 6
Wessel, Cape 143 F 1
Wessel Islands 143 F 1
Wessington Springs 170 G 3
West Allis 171 J 3
West Antarctica 185
West Bend 171 J 3
West Bengal 134 E 3
West Bridgford 103 D 1
West Bromwich 103 C 1
Westbrook 171 M 3
Westbury 103 C 2
West Cape 146 C 6
West Cape Howe 142 B 6
West Elk Mountains 170 E 4
Westerland 111 E 4
Western Australia 142 B 3
Western Desert → Aṣ Saḥrā' al Gharbīyah 154 D 3
Western Ghats 134 B 4
Western Isles 98 A 3
Western Port 143 H 6
Western Sahara 152 C 4
Western Samoa 147 D 3
Wester Ross 98 B 3
Westfalen 110 E 4
West Falkland 183 DE 6
West Fayu 146 A 2
Westgate 143 H 4
West Glamorgan 102 C 2
West Ice Shelf 185
West Indies 173 G, H, J 4
West Irian 144 C 2
West Kilbride 99 B 4
Westlock 167 P 5
West Memphis 171 H 4
West Mersea 103 E 2
West Midlands 103 D 1
Westmoreland 143 F 2
West Nicholson 160 D 4
Weston 171 K 4
Weston-super-Mare 102 C 2
West Palm Beach 171 K 6
West Plains 171 H 4
West Point 171 J 5
Westport 145 Q 9
Westray 98 C 2
Westray Firth 98 C 2
Westree 171 K 2
West Siberian Plain 119 OP 3
West Sussex 103 D 2
Westwood 170 B 3
West Wyalong 143 H 5
West Yellowstone 170 D 3
West Yorkshire 101 E 3
Wetar, Pulau 137 G 5
Wetar, Selat 137 G 5
Wetaskiwin 167 P 5
Wete 159 F 6
Wetzlar 111 E 4
Wewak 144 D 2
Wexford 102 A 1
Weybridge 103 D 2
Weyburn 167 R 6
Weyland, Pegunungan 137 J 4
Weymouth 102 C 2
Wey, River 103 D 2
Whakataki 145 R 9
Whakatane 145 R 8
Whale Cove 167 T 3
Whaley Bridge 103 D 1
Whalsay 98 D 1
Whangarei 145 Q 8
Wharfe, River 101 E 3
Wharfedale 101 D 3
Wharton Basin 192 D 3
Wharton Lake 167 S 3
Wheatland 170 F 3
Wheat Ridge 170 E 4
Wheeler (OR, U.S.A.) 170 B 2
Wheeler (Quebec, Can.) 169 O 4
Wheeler Peak (N.M., U.S.A.) 170 E 4

Wheeler Peak (NV, U.S.A.) 170 D 4
Wheeling 171 K 3
Whitby 101 E 2
Whitchurch 101 D 3
White Bay 169 Q 5
White Bear Lake 171 H 2
White Butte 167 R 6
White Cliffs 143 G 5
Whitecourt 167 O 5
White Escarpment 160 B 5
Whitefish Bay 171 K 2
Whitefish Point 171 J 2
Whitehaven 101 D 2
Whitehead 100 C 2
Whitehorse 166 K 3
White Island 167 V 2
White, Lake 142 D 3
Whiteman Range 145 F 3
Whitemark 144 L 9
White Mountain (AK, U.S.A.) 166 E 3
White Mountain Peak 170 C 4
White Mountains 166 H 2
White Nile 154 E 6
White Nile Dam → Khazzān Jabal al Awlīyā' 154 E 5
White Pass 166 L 4
White River (IN, U.S.A.) 171 J 4
White River (NWT., Can.) 166 J 3
White River (Ont., Can.) 168 L 6
White River (S.D., U.S.A.) 170 F 3
White Sea 118 G 2
White Sulphur Springs 170 D 2
White Volta 156 D 4
Whitewater Bay 171 K 6
Whitewood 143 G 3
Whithorn 100 C 2
Whitley Bay 101 E 2
Whitmore Mountains 185
Whitney 171 L 2
Whitney, Mount 170 C 4
Whitstable 103 E 2
Whitsunday Island 143 H 3
Whittier 166 H 3
Whittlesea 143 H 6
Whittlesey 103 D 1
Wholdaia Lake 167 R 3
Whyalla 143 F 5
Wiawso 156 D 4
Wiay 98 A 3
Wibaux 170 F 2
Wichita 170 G 4
Wichita Falls 170 G 5
Wick 98 C 2
Wick (Airport) 98 C 2
Wickenburg 170 D 5
Wickepin 142 B 5
Wickham 142 B 3
Wickham, Cape 144 K 8
Wickham Market 103 E 1
Wicklow 100 B 3
Wicklow Mountains 100 B 3
Widefield 170 F 4
Widgiemooltha 142 C 5
Widnes 101 D 3
Wielkopolska 111 G H 4
Wien 115 G 2
Wiener Becken 115 G 2
Wiener Neustadt 115 G 2
Wienerwald 115 G 2
Wierpz 111 H 4
Wiesbaden 111 E 4
Wieżyca 111 G 4
Wieżyca 111 G 4
Wigan 101 D 3
Wigston 103 D 1
Wigton 101 D 2
Wigtown 100 C 2
Wigtown Bay 100 C 2
Wil 115 E 2
Wilbur 170 C 2
Wilcannia 143 G 5
Wildspitze 115 F 2
Wilhelmina Gebergte 179 G 3
Wilhelm, Mount 144 D 3
Wilhelm-Pieck-Stadt 111 F 4
Wilhelmshaven 111 E 4
Wilkes-Barre 171 L 3
Wilkes Land 185
Willamette River 170 B 3
Willapa Bay 170 B 2
Willard 170 E 5
Willcox 170 E 5
Willemstad 178 E 1
Willeroo 142 E 2
Williambury 142 B 3
William Lake (Man., Can.) 167 R 5
Williams (AZ, U.S.A.) 170 D 4

Williamsburg (KY, U.S.A.) 171 K 4
Williamsburg (VA, U.S.A.) 171 L 4
Williams Lake (Br.Col., Can.) 167 N 5
Williamsport 171 L 3
Williston (U.S.A.) 170 F 2
Williston (S. Africa) 160 C 6
Williston Lake 167 N 4
Willoughby, Mount 142 E 4
Willow 166 G 3
Willow Bunch 167 Q 6
Willow Lake 167 O 3
Willows 170 B 4
Willow Springs 171 H 4
Wills Creek 143 F 3
Wills, Lake 142 D 3
Wilmington (DE, U.S.A.) 171 L 4
Wilmington (N.C., U.S.A.) 171 L 5
Wilmslow 101 D 3
Wilowmore 160 C 6
Wilson 171 L 4
Wilson Bluff 142 D 5
Wilson, Cape 167 V 2
Wilson Lake 171 J 5
Wilson, Mount 170 E 4
Wilson River 143 G 4
Wilsons Promontory 143 H 6
Wilson's Promontory National Park 143 H 6
Wilton River 142 E 1
Wiltshire 103 C 2
Wiltz 110 E 5
Wiluna 142 C 4
Wimborne Minster 103 C 2
Winbin 143 G 4
Winburg 160 D 5
Wincanton 102 C 2
Winchester (U.K.) 103 D 2
Winchester (KY, U.S.A.) 171 K 4
Windermere, Lake 110 C 4
Windhoek 160 B 4
Windischgarsten 115 F 2
Windorah 143 G 4
Wind River 170 E 3
Wind River Range 170 E 3
Windsor (Canada) 169 P 7
Windsor (U.K.) 103 D 2
Windsor Forest 171 K 5
Windsor Locks 171 M 3
Windward Islands (Lesser Antilles) 173 H 4
Windward Islands (French Polynesia) 147 F 4
Winfield (AL, U.S.A.) 171 J 5
Winfield (KS, U.S.A.) 171 G 4
Wingen 143 J 5
Winisk 168 K 4
Winisk Lake 168 K 5
Winisk River 168 K 5
Winneba 156 D 4
Winnebago, Lake 171 J 3
Winnemucca 170 C 3
Winnfield 171 H 5
Winnibigoshish, Lake 171 H 2
Winning 142 A 3
Winnipeg 167 S 6
Winnipeg, Lake 167 S 5
Winnipegosis 167 R 5
Winnipegosis, Lake 167 R 5
Winnipesaukee, Lake 171 M 3
Winona 171 H 3
Winsford 101 D 3
Winslow (U.S.A.) 170 D 4
Winslow (Kiribati) 146 D 3
Winston-Salem 171 K 4
Winter Park 171 K 6
Winterthur 115 E 2
Wintinna 142 E 4
Winton (N.Z.) 144 P 10
Winton (Queensland, Austr.) 143 G 3
Wirksworth 103 D 1
Wisbech 103 E 1
Wisconsin 171 H 2
Wiseman 166 G 2
Wishaw 99 C 4
Wismar 111 F 4
Wisła 111 G 4
Wissembourg 115 E 2
Witbank 160 D 5
Witchcliff 142 A 5
Witham 103 E 2
Witham, River 103 D 1
Withernsea 101 F 3
Witney 103 D 2
Witpütz 160 B 5
Wittenberg 111 F 4
Wittenoom 142 B 3

Witti Range 136 E 3
Witu 159 G 5
Witu Islands 144 E 2
Witvlei 160 B 4
Witwatersrand 160 D 5
Wkra 111 H 4
Włocławek 111 G 4
Wodonga 143 H 6
Wodzisław Śląski 111 G 4
Wogr Sheikh 159 H 3
Wokam, Pulau 137 H 5
Woking 103 D 2
Wokingham 103 D 2
Wolds, The 110 CD 4
Woleai 146 A 2
Wolf 178 B 6
Wolf Creek 170 D 2
Wolf Point 170 E 2
Wolfratshausen 111 F 5
Wolf River 171 J 2
Wolfsberg 115 F 2
Wolfsburg 111 F 4
Wolf, Vulcán 178 B 6
Wolgast 111 F 4
Wolin 111 F 4
Wollaston, Islas 183 C 10
Wollaston Lake 167 R 4
Wollaston Peninsula 167 O 2
Wollongong 143 J 5
Wolmaransstad 160 D 5
Wologosi Mountains 156 BC 4
Wołow 111 G 4
Wolseley 167 R 5
Wolstenholme, Cap 169 M 3
Wolverhamton 103 C 1
Wonarah 143 F 2
Wondo 159 F 3
Wondoola 143 G 2
Wonga Wongué, Parc National de 157 F 6
Wonju 133 J 3
Wonotobo Falls 179 G 3
Wŏnsan 133 J 3
Wonthaggi 143 H 6
Woocalla 143 F 5
Woodall Mountain 171 J 5
Woodbridge 103 E 1
Wood Buffalo National Park 167 P 4
Woodburn 143 J 4
Wooden Bridge 100 B 3
Woodhall Spa 103 D 1
Woodland 170 B 4
Woodlark 145 F 3
Wood River Lakes 166 F 4
Woodroffe, Mount 142 E 4
Woods, Lake 142 B 4
Woods, Lake of the 168 J 6
Woodstock (Canada) 169 O 6
Woodstock (Australia) 143 G 2
Woodstock (U.K.) 103 D 2
Woodstock (U.S.A.) 171 M 3
Woodville 171 H 5
Woodward 170 G 4
Woŏi 137 J 4
Wooler 99 C 4
Wooler 110 C 3
Woolgar 143 G 2
Woomera 143 F 5
Wołomin 111 H 4
Wooramel 142 A 4
Wooramel River 142 A 4
Wooton Bassett 103 D 2
Worcester (U.K.) 103 C 1
Worcester (S. Afr.) 160 B 6
Worchester (MA, U.S.A.) 171 M 3
Wörgl 115 F 2
Workington 101 D 2
Worksop 101 E 3
Workworth 145 Q 8
Worland 170 E 3
World's View → Rhodes Grave 160 D 4
Worms 111 E 5
Worms Head 102 B 2
Wörther See 115 F 2
Worthing 103 D 2
Worthington 171 G 3
Wosi 137 G 4
Wotho 146 C 2
Wotje 146 C 2
Wour 157 H 1
Wowenda 137 H 5
Wowoni, Pulau 137 F 4
"W", Parcs Nationaux, du 156 E 3
Wrangell 166 L 4
Wrangell, Cape 166 A 5
Wrangell Mountains 166 J 3
Wrangell–Saint Elias National Park and Preserve 166 J 3
Wreck Reef 143 K 3

Wrexham 102 C 1
Wrexham 110 C 4
Wright Patman Lake 171 H 5
Wrightson, Mount 170 D 5
Wrigley 167 N 3
Wrocław 111 G 4
Wrottesley, Cape 167 N 1
Września 111 G 4
Wuchale 159 F 2
Wuchang 132 F 4
Wuchang 133 J 2
Wuchuan 132 E 5
Wuchuan 132 F 2
Wuchuan 132 F 6
Wuda 132 E 3
Wudang Shan 132 F 4
Wudaoliang 132 B 3
Wudi 133 G 3
Wuding 132 D 5
Wudu 132 D 4
Wufeng 132 F 4
Wugang 132 F 5
Wugong 132 E 4
Wuhai 132 E 3
Wuhan 132 F 4
Wuhe 133 G 4
Wuhu 133 G 4
Wuhua 132 G 6
Wüjang 134 C 1
Wuji 133 G 3
Wu Jiang 132 E 5
Wukari 157 F 4
Wuliang Shan 132 D 6
Wuling Shan 132 E 5
Wulong 132 E 5
Wum 157 G 4
Wumeng Shan 132 D 5
Wunnummin Lake 168 K 5
Wun Rog 158 D 3
Wun Shwai 158 D 3
Wuntho 135 G 3
Wuppertal 111 E 4
Wuqi 132 E 3
Wuqia 129 K 3
Wuqiang 133 G 3
Wuqing 133 G 3
Wurno 157 F 3
Wurung 143 G 2
Würzburg 111 E 5
Wurzen 111 F 4
Wu Shan 132 E 2
Wushan 132 E 4
Wusheng 132 E 4
Wushi 129 K 2
Wusuli Jiang 133 K 1
Wutai Shan 132 F 3
Wutunghliao 132 D 5
Wuvulu 144 D 2
Wuwei 132 D 3
Wuwei 133 G 4
Wuxi 132 E 4
Wuxi 133 H 4
Wuxing 133 H 4
Wuxuan 132 E 6
Wuyang 132 F 3
Wuyiling 131 N 6
Wuyi Shan 132 G 5
Wuyuan 132 E 2
Wuzhai 132 F 3
Wuzhong 132 E 3
Wuzhou 132 F 6
Wye, River 102 C 1
Wylie, Lake 171 K 4
Wymondham 103 E 1
Wynbring 142 E 5
Wyndham 142 D 2
Wynniatt Bay 167 P 1
Wynyard 167 R 5
Wyoming (U.S.A.) 170 E 3
Wyoming (MI, U.S.A.) 171 J 3
Wyoming Peak 170 D 3
Wyperfeld National Park 143 G 6
Wysoczyzna Ciechanowska 111 GH 4
Wyszków 111 H 4
Wyzyna Lubelska 111 H 4

X

Xabyaisamba 132 C 4
Xailongmoin 134 E 2
Xainza 134 E 1
Xai-Xai 161 E 5
Xalapa → Jalapa Enríquez 172 C 4
Xambioá 179 J 5
Xá-Muteba 160 B 1
Xangongo 160 B 3

Xánthi 116 B 2
Xanthos 116 C 3
Xanxerê 182 F 4
Xapecó 182 F 4
Xapuri 180 C 3
Xarag 132 C 3
Xarba La 134 D 2
Xar Moron 132 F 2
Xar Moron He 133 G 2
Xauen → Chechaouen 152 D 1
Xaundo 160 B 1
Xavantes, Reprêsa de 181 G 5
Xavantes, Serra dos 181 G 3
Xavantina 181 F 5
Xayar 129 L 2
Xenia 171 K 4
Xiachuan Dao 132 F 6
Xiaguan 132 D 5
Xiahe 132 D 3
Xiajin 133 G 3
Xiamen 133 G 6
Xi'an 132 E 4
Xianfeng 132 E 5
Xiangfan 132 F 4
Xianghua Ling 132 F 5
Xianghuang 132 F 2
Xiang Jiang 132 F 5
Xiangride 132 C 3
Xiangshan 133 H 5
Xiangtan 132 F 5
Xiangyin 132 F 5
Xianju 133 H 5
Xianning 132 F 5
Xianyang 132 E 4
Xiao'ergou 131 M 6
Xiaogan 132 F 4
Xiao Hinggan Ling 131 N 6
Xiaojin 132 D 4
Xiaowutai Shan 132 G 3
Xiaoyi 132 F 3
Xiapu 133 H 5
Xichang 132 D 5
Xichou 132 D 6
Xicoténcatl 172 C 3
Xieng Khouang 135 H 4
Xifeng 133 H 2
Xifengzhen 132 E 3
Xigazê 134 E 2
Xi He 132 D 2
Xiji 132 E 3
Xi Jiang 132 F 6
Xijir Ulan Hu 132 B 3
Xikouzi 130 M 5
Xiliao He 133 H 2
Xilin 132 E 6
Xilókastron 116 B 3
Ximeng 132 C 6
Ximiao 132 D 2
Xin'anjiang Shuiku 133 G 5
Xin Barag Youqi 130 L 6
Xin Barag Zuoqi 130 L 6
Xincai 132 F 4
Xincheng 133 G 3
Xincheng 132 D 3
Xincheng 132 E 6
Xindu 132 D 4
Xinfeng 132 F 6
Xinfengjiang Shuiku 132 F 6
Xing'an 132 F 5
Xingcheng 133 H 2
Xingdi 132 A 2
Xingguo 132 G 5
Xinghai 132 C 3
Xinghe 132 F 2
Xingkai Hu 133 K 1
Xinglong 133 G 2
Xingning 132 G 6
Xingren 132 E 5
Xingshan 132 F 4
Xingtai 132 F 3
Xingu 179 H 4
Xing Xian 132 F 3
Xingxingxia 132 C 2
Xingyi 132 D 5
Xinhe 129 L 2
Xinhe 132 G 3
Xining 132 D 3
Xinjiang Uygur Zizhiqu 129 L 2–M 2
Xinjin 132 D 4
Xinjin 133 H 3
Xinle 132 F 3
Xinlitun 131 N 5
Xinlong 132 D 4
Xinping 132 D 6
Xinqing 131 N 6
Xintai 133 G 3
Xintian 132 F 5
Xinwen 133 G 3
Xin Xian 132 F 3
Xinxiang 132 F 3

Xinxing 132 F 6
Xinyang 132 F 4
Xinyi 133 G 4
Xinyi 132 F 6
Xinyuan 129 L 2
Xinzheng 132 F 4
Xiong Xian 133 G 3
Xiqing Shan 132 D 4
Xique-Xique 181 H 3
Xishui 132 G 4
Xi Taijnar Hu 132 B 3
Xi Ujimqin Qi 133 G 2
Xiushui 132 F 5
Xiuwu 132 F 3
Xiuyan 133 H 2
Xiwu 132 C 4
Xixabangma Feng 134 E 2
Xi Xian 132 F 3
Xixiang 132 E 4
Xiyang 132 F 3
Xizang Zizhiqu 129 J 4
Xizanq Zizhiqu 134 DE 1
Xochimilco 172 C 4
Xorkol 132 B 3
Xpuhil 172 E 4
Xuan'en 132 E 5
Xuanhan 132 E 4
Xuanhua 132 G 2
Xuanwei 132 D 5
Xuchang 132 F 4
Xue Shan 132 CD 5
Xuguit Qi 130 M 6
Xümatang 132 C 4
Xundian 132 D 5
Xungru 134 D 2
Xun He 131 N 6
Xun Jiang 132 F 6
Xunke 131 N 6
Xunwu 132 G 6
Xupu 132 F 5
Xur 132 C 3
Xuwen 132 F 6
Xuyi 133 G 4
Xuyong 132 E 5
Xuzhou 133 G 4

Y

Ya'an 132 D 4
Yabassi 157 FG 5
Yabelo 159 F 4
Yablochnyy 131 Q 6
Yablon 131 V 2
Yablonitse, Pereval 116 B 1
Yablonovo 130 K 5
Yablonovyy Khrebet 130 J–L 5
Yabrai Yanchang 132 D 3
Yabrei Shan 132 D 3
Yabrīn 155 H 4
Yabrūd 154 F 2
Yabuli 133 J 2
Yacuiba 180 D 5
Yacurai 178 E 3
Yadé, Massif du 158 B 3
Yadgir 134 C 4
Yadong 134 E 2
Yaeyama-rettō 133 H 6
Yagodnaya Polyana 118 J 5
Yagodnoye 131 R 3
Yagoua 157 GH 3
Yagradagze Shan 132 C 3
Yahila 158 C 4
Yahisuli 158 C 5
Yahuma 158 C 4
Yahyalı 117 E 3
Yajiang 132 D 4
Yakacık 117 E 3
Yakima 170 B 2
Yakima River 170 B 2
Yakmach 129 G 5
Yako 156 D 3
Yakoma 158 C 4
Yakovlevka 130 D 1
Yakrik 129 L 2
Yakumo 133 M 2
Yaku-shima 133 K 4
Yakutat 166 K 4
Yakutat Bay 166 J 4
Yakutsk 131 N 3
Yakuttork 131 U 2
Yakuty 119 R 2
Yala (Sri Lanka) 134 D 6
Yala (Thailand) 135 H 6
Yalakköy 117 E 3
Yale Point 170 E 4
Yalgoo 142 B 4
Yali 158 C 4
Yalinga 158 C 3

Yalleroi 143 H 3
Yallourn 143 H 6
Yalnızçam Dağları 117 F 2
Yaloké 158 B 3
Yalong Jiang 132 D 5
Yalova 116 C 2
Yalpukh, Ozero 116 C 1
Yalta 117 D 2
Yalu Jiang 133 H 2
Yalutorovsk 119 N 4
Yalvaç 116 D 3
Yalym 119 N 5
Yamagata 133 M 3
Yamaguchi 133 K 4
Yam-Alin', Khrebet 131 OP 5
Yamal Peninsula 119 NO 1
Yamal, Poluostrov 119 N 1
Yamantau, Gora 119 L 5
Yamarovka 130 K 5
Yamba 158 F 3
Yambering 156 B 3
Yambio 158 D 4
Yamburg 119 P 2
Yambuto, Ozero 119 P 1
Yambuya 158 C 4
Yamdena, Pulau 137 H 5
Yamethin 135 G 3
Yamia 157 G 3
Yaminbot 144 D 2
Yam Kinneret 154 F 2
Yamm 113 J 4
Yamma Yamma, Lake 143 G 4
Yamoussoukro 156 C 4
Yampol' (Ukraina, U.S.S.R.) 116 C 1
Yamsk 131 S 4
Yamuna 134 D 2
Yamunanagar 134 C 1
Yamzho Yumco 135 F 2
Yana 131 P 1
Yanam 134 D 4
Yan'an 132 E 3
Yanaoca 180 B 3
Yanartaş Dağları 116 D 3
Yanbian 132 D 5
Yanbu' 154 F 4
Yanchang 132 F 3
Yancheng 133 H 4
Yanchi 132 E 3
Yan Dağ (Ukraina, U.S.S.R.) 116 C 3
Yandang Shan 133 H 5
Yandja 158 B 5
Yandrakinot 166 C 5
Yanfolia 156 C 3
Yangalia 158 C 3
Yangambi 158 C 4
Yangarey 119 M 2
Yangbajain 135 F 1
Yangbi 132 C 5
Yangchun 132 F 6
Yanggao 132 F 2
Yanggu 132 G 3
Yangikishlak 129 H 2
Yangiyul' 129 H 2
Yangjiang 132 F 6
Yangquan 132 F 3
Yangshan 132 F 6
Yangshuo 132 F 6
Yangtze Kiang → Chang Jiang 133 G 4
Yang Xian 132 E 4
Yangxiu 132 G 5
Yangzhou 133 G 4
Yanhe 132 E 5
Yanhuqu 134 D 1
Yanis'yarvi, Ozero 112 K 3
Yanji 133 J 2
Yanjin 132 D 5
Yankan, Khrebet 130 L 4
Yanking 133 G 2
Yankton 170 G 3
Yano-Indigirskaya Nizmennost 131 P 1–R 1
Yanov Stan 119 Q 2
Yanqi Huizu Zizhixian 129 LM 2
Yanshan 133 G 3
Yanshan 132 D 6
Yan Shan 133 G 2
Yanshi 132 F 4
Yanshiping 132 B 4
Yanshou 133 J 1
Yanskiy 131 O 2
Yanskiy Zaliv 131 OP 1
Yantai 133 H 3
Yanting 132 E 4
Yanwa 132 C 5
Yany-Kurgan 129 H 2
Yanyuan 132 D 5
Yanzhou 133 G 3
Yao 157 H 3
Yaoundé 157 G 5
Yapei 156 D 4

Yapen, Pulau 137 J 4
Yapen, Selat 137 J 4
Yaptiksale 119 O 2
Yapura 178 D 4
Yaqui, Rio 170 D 6
Yaraka 143 G 3
Yaraligöz 117 D 2
Yaransk 118 J 4
Yarda 157 H 2
Yaremcha 116 B 1
Yarensk 118 J 3
Yare, River 103 E 1
Yari 178 D 3
Yarim 155 G 6
Yarishev 118 G 5
Yaritagua 178 E 1
Yarkant 129 K 3
Yarkant He 129 K 3
Yarkant → Shache 129 K 3
Yarkino 130 G 4
Yarlung Zangbo Jiang 132 B 5
Yarmouth (U.K.) 103 D 2
Yarmouth (Canada) 169 O 7
Yarongo 119 N 2
Yaroslavl' 118 G 4
Yarraloola 142 B 3
Yarram 143 H 6
Yarra Yarra Lakes 142 B 4
Yarrie 142 C 3
Yarroto 119 O 2
Yar Sale 119 O 2
Yartsevo 119 S 3
Yartsevo 118 F 4
Yarumal 178 C 2
Yarwa 132 C 4
Yasawa Group 146 C 4
Yasel'da 113 J 5
Yashalta 117 F 1
Yashi 157 F 3
Yashkino 131 P 5
Yashkul' 117 G 1
Yasin 129 J 3
Yasinovataya 117 E 1
Yasinya 116 B 1
Yasnyy 131 N 5
Yass 143 H 5
Yassachnaya 131 S 3
Yasun Burnu 117 E 2
Yata 180 C 3
Yatağan 116 C 3
Yatakala 156 E 3
Yatenga 156 D 3
Yate'-Village 145 J 6
Yathkyed Lake 167 S 3
Yatina 180 D 5
Yatolema 158 C 4
Yatsushiro 133 K 4
Yatta Plateau 159 F 5
Yatton 143 H 3
Yatua 178 E 3
Yauca 180 B 4
Yauna Moloca 178 D 4
Yauyos 180 A 3
Yavarí 178 D 4
Yavatmal 134 C 3
Yavi, Cerro 178 E 2
Yavita 178 E 3
Yawatahama 133 K 4
Yawng-hwe 135 G 3
Yaxchilán 172 E 4
Ya Xian 132 E 7
Yaya 119 R 4
Yay Gölü 117 E 3
Yayladağı 117 E 3
Yayva 118 L 4
Yazd 128 E 4
Yazdān 128 G 4
Yazd-e-Khvāst 128 E 4
Yazılıkaya 116 D 3
Yazılıkaya 117 D 2
Yazoo 171 HJ 5
Yazoo City 171 H 5
Ybbs an der Donau 115 G 2
Yding Skovhöj 113 E 4
Ydre 113 G 4
Ydzhid Parma 119 L 3
Ye 135 G 4
Yebawmi 135 G 2
Yebbi Bou 157 H 1
Yecheng 129 K 3
Yecla 114 C 4
Yedarma 130 H 4
Yedashe 135 G 4
Yedinka 131 P 6
Yedintsy 116 C 1
Yedoma 118 H 3
Yedseram 157 G 3
Yeeda River 142 C 2
Yefira 116 B 2
Yefremov 118 F 5
Yeggueba 157 G 2
Yegorlyk 117 F 1
Yegorlykskaya 117 F 1

Yegor'yevsk 118 G 4
Yegros 182 E 4
Yeha 159 F 2
Yei 158 E 4
Yeji 156 D 4
Yekateriny, Proliv 131 R 7
Yekepa 156 C 4
Yekhegnadzor 117 G 2
Yékiasahal 157 H 2
Yelabuga 118 K 4
Yelan' 118 H 5
Yelanets 116 D 1
Yelantsy 130 J 5
Yele 156 B 4
Yelets 118 G 5
Yeletskiy 119 M 2
Yelgu 158 E 3
Yelia 144 E 3
Yelimané 156 B 2
Yelizavetinka 119 L 5
Yelizovo 131 T 5
Yelizarovo 119 N 3
Yell 98 D 1
Yellandu 134 D 4
Yellowhead Pass 167 O 5
Yellowknife 167 P 3
Yellow River → Huang He 133 G 3
Yellow Sea 133 H 4
Yellowstone 170 E 2
Yellowstone Lake 170 D 3
Yellowstone National Park 170 D 3
Yell Sound 98 D 1
Yel'nya 118 F 5
Yeloguy 119 R 3
Yelovka 131 U 4
Yel'sk 113 J 5
Yelua 152 B 4
Yelvertoft 143 F 3
Yelwa 157 E 3
Yemanzhelinsk 119 M 5
Yematan 117 E 1
Yematan 132 C 3
Yemen 155 G 5
Yemet 131 V 3
Yen 157 G 5
Yena 112 K 2
Yenagoa 157 F 5
Yenakiyevo 117 E 1
Yenanma 135 F 4
Yenashimski Pol'kan, Gora 130 F 4
Yen Bai 135 H 3
Yendi 156 DE 4
Yendondin 130 K 5
Yenge 158 C 5
Yengisar 129 K 3
Yengo 157 H 3
Yengue 157 F 5
Yenice 117 D 3
Yenice 117 D 2
Yenice 117 E 3
Yenişehir 116 C 2
Yenişehir 119 R 2
Yenisey, Bol'shoy 130 G 5
Yenisey, Malyy 130 F 5
Yeniseysk 130 F 4
Yeniseyskiy Kryazh 130 F 3
Yeniseyskiy Zaliv 130 D 1
Yenotayevka 117 G 1
Yeo, Lake 142 C 4
Yeovil 102 C 2
Yepoko 119 O 2
Yeppoon 143 J 3
Yeraliyevo 128 E 2
Yerbogachen 130 J 3
Yercha 131 R 2
Yerema 130 J 3
Yerema, Bol'shaya 130 J 3
Yerementau, Gory 119 O 5
Yergeni 117 F 1
Yerka Inadeypur 119 P 3
Yerköy 117 D 3
Yermak 119 P 5
Yermakovo 119 O 3
Yermakovo 119 R 2
Yermakovskoye 130 F 5
Yermentau 119 O 5
Yermitsa 118 K 2
Yermo 170 F 6
Yerofey-Pavlovich 131 M 5
Yeropol 131 V 2
Yershov 118 J 5
Yertom 118 J 3
Yertsevo 118 H 3
Yerupajá, Nevado 179 C 6
Yerushalayim 154 F 2
Yesa, Embalse de 114 C 3
Yesil 119 N 5
Yeşilhisar 117 DE 3
Yeşilırmak 117 E 2
Yeşilköy 116 C 2

Yessentuki 117 F 2
Yessey 130 H 2
Yessey, Ozero 130 H 2
Yët-Kyuyel' 130 M 3
Yetman 143 J 4
Yetti 152 D 3
Yeu 135 G 3
Yeu, Ile d' 114 C 2
Yevlakh 128 D 2
Yevpatoriya 117 D 1
Yévre 114 D 2
Yevsyavan' 119 M 2
Yeya 117 E 1
Yeysk 117 E 1
Yeyskoye Ukrepleniye 117 E 1
Yezhikha 118 J 4
Ygyatta 130 L 3
Yialousa 117 D 3
Yiannitsá 116 B 2
Yi'an 131 N 6
Yibin 132 D 5
Yibug Caka 134 E 1
Yichang 132 F 5
Yichuan 132 F 4
Yichuan 132 F 3
Yichun 132 F 5
Yichun 131 N 6
Yidu 132 F 4
Yidu 133 H 4
Yidun 132 C 4
Yifeng 132 F 5
Yifran 153 H 2
Yi He 133 G 3
Yilan 133 J 1
Yıldız Dağı 117 E 2
Yıldızeli 117 E 3
Yilehuli Shan 131 M 5
Yiliang 132 D 6
Yinchuan 132 E 3
Yingde 132 F 6
Yingjiang 132 C 6
Yingkou 133 H 2
Yingshan 132 F 4
Yingshan 132 G 4
Yingtan 133 G 5
Yining 129 L 2
Yi'ong Zangbo 132 B 4
Yirga Alem 159 F 3
Yirol 158 E 3
Yirshi 130 L 6
Yishui 133 G 3
Yithion 116 B 3
Yitong 133 J 2
Yitulihe 131 M 5
Yiwu 132 B 2
Yi Xian 133 H 2
Yiyang 132 F 5
Yiyang 133 G 5
Yizhang 132 F 5
Ykhnov 118 G 5
Ylas-Yuryakh 130 J 2
Ylikitka 112 J 2
Yli-li 112 J 2
Ylitornio 112 H 2
Ylivieska 112 H 3
Yllästunturi 112 H 2
Ylöjärvi 112 H 3
Yngaren 113 G 4
Ynykchanskiy 131 P 3
Yoboki 159 G 2
Yogoum 157 H 2
Yogyakarta 136 D 5
Yojoa, Lago de 172 E 5
Yokadouma 157 GH 5
Yoko 157 G 4
Yokoate-jima 133 J 5
Yokohama 133 L 3
Yokosuka 133 L 3
Yokote 133 M 3
Yol 157 G 4a
Yolombo 158 C 5
Yome 137 G 4
Yonago 133 K 3
Yonaguni-jima 133 H 6
Yonezawa 133 M 3
Yŏngan 133 J 2
Yong'an 133 G 5
Yongchang 132 D 3
Yongchuan 132 E 5
Yongchun 133 G 5
Yongde 132 C 6
Yong deng 132 D 3
Yongding 132 G 6
Yonghung 133 J 3
Yongji 133 J 2
Yongjing 133 J 3
Yŏngju 133 J 3
Yongkang 133 H 5
Yongning 132 E 3
Yongping 132 C 5
Yongren 132 D 5
Yongshan 132 D 5

Yongshou 132 E 4
Yongshun 132 E 5
Yongxin 132 F 5
Yongxiu 132 G 5
Yonibana 156 B 4
Yonkers 171 M 3
Yonne 114 D 2
Yopal 178 D 2
Yopurga 129 K 3
York (Australia) 142 B 5
York (U.K.) 101 E 3
York (NE, U.S.A.) 170 G 3
York (PA, U.S.A.) 171 L 4
York, Cape 143 G 1
Yorke Peninsula 143 F 5
Yorkshire Moors 101 E 2
Yorkshire Wolds 101 E 3
York Sound 142 D 1
Yorkton 167 R 5
Yoro 172 E 4
Yoron-jima 133 J 5
Yorosso 156 D 3
Yorubaland Plateau 156–157 E 4
Yosemite National Park 170 C 4
Yoshkar Ola 118 J 4
Yŏsu 133 J 4
Yotala 180 C 4
Yotau 180 D 4
Yotvata 154 F 3
Youanmi 142 B 4
Youdunzi 132 B 3
Youghal 110 B 4
You Jiang 132 E 6
Youllemmedene 156 E 2
Young 143 H 5
Younghusband Peninsula 143 F 6
Youngstown 171 K 3
Youshashan 132 B 3
Youssoufia 152 D 2
Youyang 132 E 5
Youyi Feng 129 M 1
Yozgat 117 D 3
Ypaceraí 182 E 4
Ypeihu 180 E 5
Yreka 170 B 3
Yrieix-la-Perche 114 D 2
Ysabel Channel 145 EF 2
Ystad 113 F 4
Yst'-Yudoma 131 P 4
Ytterhogdal 112 F 3
Ytyk-Kel' 131 O 3
Yuan Jiang 132 F 5
Yuan Jiang 132 D 6
Yuanjiang 132 D 6
Yuanling 132 F 5
Yuanmou 132 D 5
Yuanping 132 F 3
Yuanqu 132 F 3
Yuanshanzi 132 C 3
Yuanshi 132 F 3
Yuanyang 132 D 6
Yūbari 133 M 2
Yuben' 129 J 3
Yucatán Peninsula 172 E 3
Yucheng 133 G 3
Yuci 132 F 3
Yudoma 131 P 4
Yudoma-Krestovskaya 131 P 3
Yudomo Mayskoye Nagor'ye 131 P 4
Yudomskiy Khrebet 131 Q 3
Yudu 132 G 5
Yueqing 133 H 5
Yuexi 132 D 5
Yueyang 132 F 5
Yug 118 J 3
Yugan, Bol'shoy 119 O 3
Yugorskiy Poluostrov 119 M 2
Yugorskiy Shar 119 M 2
Yugorskiy Shar, Proliv 119 M 2
Yugoslavia 115 G 2–3
Yugo-Tala 131 S 2
Yuhang 133 H 4
Yu Jiang Binyang 132 E 6
Yukagirskoye Ploskogor'ye 131 ST 2
Yukhta 130 J 4
Yuki 158 B 5
Yukon 166 E 3
Yukon Flats 166 H 2
Yukon Flats National Monument 166 HJ 3
Yukon, Fort 166 H 2
Yukon Plateau 166 K 3
Yukon-Charley Rivers National Preserve 166 J 2–3
Yukon Territory 166 K 3
Yüksekova 117 F 3
Yuli 157 G 4
Yulin 132 E 3
Yulin 132 F 6

Yulu Rapids 158 C 4
Yuma (U.S.S.R.) 113 K 2
Yuma (AZ, U.S.A.) 170 D 5
Yuma (CO, U.S.A.) 170 F 3
Yumari, Cerro 178 E 3
Yumbe 158 E 4
Yumbi (Zaire) 158 B 5
Yumbi (Zaire) 158 D 5
Yumbo 178 C 3
Yumen 132 C 3
Yumenzhen 132 C 2
Yumin 129 L 1
Yumurchen 130 K 5
Yumurtalık 117 E 3
Yun' 131 P 3
Yunaska 166 C 5
Yuncheng 132 F 3
Yunekit 130 M 3
Yungay 183 B 6
Yunhe 133 G 5
Yunkai Dashan 132 F 6
Yunlin 133 H 6
Yunling Shan 132 C 5
Yunlong 132 C 5
Yunnan 132 D 6
Yun Xian 132 F 4
Yun Xian 132 D 6
Yunxiao 133 G 6
Yunyang 132 E 4
Yuqing 132 E 5
Yur 131 P 4
Yurga 119 Q 4
Yuribey 119 O 2
Yuriby 119 P 1
Yurimaguas 178 C 5
Yuroma 118 J 2
Yurty 131 Q 4
Yurungkax He 129 L 3
Yur'yevka 117 E 1
Yushan (China) 133 G 5
Yushan (Taiwan) 133 H 6
Yu Shan 132 G 5
Yushe 132 F 3
Yushno Muyskiy Khrebet 130 KL 4
Yushnoye 131 Q 6
Yushu 133 J 2
Yushu 132 C 4
Yushu Zangzu Zizhizhou 132 B 4
Yusta 117 G 1
Yusufeli 117 F 2
Yuti 180 D 4
Yutian 129 L 3
Yutian 133 G 3
Yuxi 132 D 6
Yu Xian 133 F 3
Yuyao 133 H 4
Yuzhno Chuyskiy, Khrebet 119 R 6
Yuzhno-Kamyshovyy Khrebet 131 Q 6
Yuzhno-Sakhalinsk 131 Q 6
Yuzhno-Uralsk 119 N 5
Yuzhno-Yeniseyskiy 130 F 4
Yuzhnyy 117 F 1
Yuzhnyy Anyuyskiy Khrebet 131 U 2–V 2
Yuzhnyy Bug 116 D 1
Yuzhnyy, Mys 131 T 4
Yuzhnyy Ural 119 L 5
Yverdon 115 C 2
Yvetot 114 D 2
Ywamun 135 G 3

Z

Zaanstad 110 D 4
Zabarjad 154 F 4
Zabaykal'sk 130 L 6
Zāb-e Kūchek 128 D 3
Zabéré 156 D 3
Zabid 155 G 6
Zabok 115 G 2
Zabol 128 G 4
Zāboli 129 G 5
Zabolotov 116 C 1
Zabřeh 111 G 5
Zabrze 111 G 4
Zaburun'ye 128 E 1
Zabzugu 156 E 4
Zacapa 172 E 5
Zacapu 172 B 4
Zacatecas 172 B 3
Zadar 115 G 3
Zadetkale Kyun 135 G 5
Zadetkyi Kyun 135 G 6
Zadi 135 G 5
Zadoi 132 C 4
Zadran 129 H 4

Zaf – Zyw

Za'faranah 154 E 3
Zafīr 155 J 4
Zafra 114 B 4
Zag 152 D 3
Żagań 111 G 4
Zaggūt 153 J 3
Zaghāwa 154 C 6
Zaghwān 153 H 1
Zagora 152 D 2
Zagorsk 118 G 4
Zagreb 115 G 2
Zagros Mountains 128 E 5
Zagros Mountains → Kūhhā ye-Zagros 128 E 5
Za'gya Zangbo 134 E 1
Zagyva 111 G 5
Zāhedān 129 G 5
Zāhirah 155 K 4
Zahlah 154 F 2
Zahrān 155 G 5
Zahrez Rharbi 153 F 2
Zair 128 F 2
Zaire 158 B 5
Zaire (Angola) 160 A 1
Zaire (River) 157 G 7
Zaječar 116 B 2
Zakak 157 E 2
Zakamensk 130 H J 5
Zakataly 128 D 2
Zakharo 116 B 3
Zakharov 131 O 3
Zakharovka 119 O 6
Zakhmet 129 G 3
Zākhū 155 G 1
Zákinthos 116 B 3
Zakopane 111 G 5
Zakouma 157 H 3
Zakouma, Parc National de 157 H 3
Zakur'ya 130 J 4
Zalābiyah 155 FG 1
Zalaegerszeg 116 A 1
Zalari 130 H 5
Zălau 116 B 1
Zaleshchiki 116 C 1
Zalesskiy 118 G 4
Zalew Szczecinski 111 F 4
Zalew Wislany 111 G 4
Zalim 155 G 4
Zalingei 154 C 6
Zaliv Akademii 131 P 5
Zaliv Aniva 131 Q 6
Zaliv Chayvo 131 Q 5
Zaliv Kara-Bogaz Gol 128 E 2
Zaliv Korfa 131 V 3
Zaliv Kresta 166 B 2
Zaliv Ozernoy 131 U 4
Zaliv Petra Velikogo 133 K 2
Zaliv Pil'tun 131 Q 5
Zaliv Shelikhova 131 T 3,4
Zaliv Terpeniya 131 Q 6
Zaliv Ushki 131 R 4
Zallah 153 J 3
Zalṭan 153 J 3
Zamakh 155 H 5
Zambeze 161 E 3
Zambezi 160 C 2
Zambia 160 D 2
Zamboanga 137 F 2
Zamboanga Peninsula 137 F 2
Zambrów 111 H 4
Zambuè 161 E 3
Zamfara 157 E 3
Zamkowa, Góra 111 H 4
Zamora (Spain) 114 B 3
Zamora (Ecuador) 178 C 4
Zamora de Hidalgo 172 B 3
Zamość 111 H 4
Zamtang 132 D 4
Zanaga 157 G 6
Záncara 114 C 4
Zanda 134 C 1
Zanesville 171 K 4
Zangezurskiy Khrebet 128 D 3
Zangla 129 K 4
Zanjān 128 D 3
Zannone 115 E 3
Zanthus 142 C 5
Zanul'e 118 J 3
Zanzibar 159 F 6
Zanzibar Island 159 F 6
Zaouatallaz 153 G 3
Zaoyang 132 F 4
Zaozernyy 130 F 4
Zaozhuang 133 G 4

Zap 117 F 3
Zapadna Morava 116 B 2
Zapadnaya Dvina 112 J 4
Zapadnaya Lvina 118 F 4
Západne Karpaty 111 G 5
Zapadni Rodopi 116 B 2
Zapadno-Karelskaya Vozvyshennost' 112 K 3
Zapadno-Sakhalinskiy Khrebet 131 Q 5
Zapadno-Sibirskaya Nizmennost' 119 N–Q 3
Zapadnyy Sayan 130 F 5
Zapala 183 B 6
Zapata 170 G 6
Zapolyarnyy 112 K 2
Zaporosh'ye 117 E 1
Zapug 134 D 1
Za Qu 132 C 4
Zara 117 E 3
Zarafshan 129 G 2
Zaragoza (Spain) 114 C 3
Zaragoza (Mexico) 172 B 2
Zaragoza (Col.) 178 D 2
Zarand 128 F 4
Zarand 128 E 3
Zaranj 129 G 4
Zaranou 156 D 4
Zarasai 113 J 4
Zárate 182 E 5
Zarauz 114 C 3
Zaraza 178 E 2
Zard Kūh 128 E 4
Zarechensk 112 K 2
Zarghat 155 G 3
Zarghun 129 H 4
Zarghun Shahr 129 H 4
Zaria 157 F 3
Zarma 156 D 1
Zarrīneh 128 D 3
Zaruma 178 C 4
Zarumilla 178 B 4
Żary 111 G H 4
Zarya Oktyabrya 128 F 1
Zarzaitine 153 G 3
Zarzal 178 C 3
Zasheyek 112 K 2
Zaskar 129 K 3
Zaskar Mountains 129 K 4
Zaslavl 113 J 5
Zastron 160 D 5
Zatishye 116 C 1
Zatish'ye 131 T 2
Zatoka Gdańska 111 G 4
Zatoka Pomorska 111 F 4
Zaunguzskiye Karakumy 128 FG 2
Zavetnoye 117 F 1
Zavitinsk 131 N 5
Zavodoukovsk 119 N 4
Zav'yalova, Ostrov 131 S 4
Zawiercie 111 G 4
Zāwiyat Masūs 153 K 2
Zāwiyat Qirzah 153 H 2
Zāwiyat Shammās 154 D 2
Zawr, Ra's az 155 H 3
Zayarsk 130 H 4
Zaysan 119 Q 6
Zaysan, Ozero 119 Q 6
Zayü 132 C 5
Zayü Qu 132 C 5
Zduńska Wola 111 G 4
Zdvinsk 119 P 5
Zebak 129 J 3
Zeballos, Monte 183 B 8
Zebediela 160 D 4
Zedness, Mont 152 C 4
Zeehan 144 L 9
Zeeland 110 D 4
Zeerust 160 D 5
Zegdou 152 E 3
Zêkog 132 D 3
Zelenoborskiy 112 K 2
Zelenodol'sk 118 J 4
Zelenogorsk 113 J 3
Zelenogradsk 113 H 5
Zelenokumsk 117 F 2
Zeleznodorožny 113 H 5
Zelfana 153 F 2
Zeline 157 F 2
Zell am See 115 F 2
Žemaičiu Aukštuma 113 H 4
Žemaitija 113 H 4
Zemgale 113 H 4
Zemio 158 CD 3

Zemlya Frantsa Iosifa → Franz Josef Land 184
Zémongo 158 C 3
Zenica 115 G 3
Zenza do Itombe 160 A 1
Žepče 115 G 3
Zepu 129 K 3
Zeravshan 129 H 3
Zerav'shanskiy Khrebet 129 H 3
Zerhamra 152 E 3
Zerind 116 B 1
Zermatt 115 E 2
Zernograd 117 F 1
Zestafoni 117 F 2
Zeya 131 N 5
Zeya Vodokhranilishche 131 N 5
Zeysko-Bureinskaya Ravnina 131 NO 5
Zêzere 114 B 4
Zgierz 111 G 4
Zgorzelec 111 G H 4
Zhag'yab 132 C 4
Zhailma 119 M 5
Zhaksylyk 119 O 6
Zhamanakkal', Ozero 129 G 1
Zhamansor 128 E 1
Zhamshi 119 O 6
Zhanabas 129 H 1
Zhanabek 119 P 6
Zhanang 135 F 2
Zhana-Semey 119 Q 5
Zhanatas 129 H 2
Zhangbei 132 F 2
Zhangguangcai Ling 133 J 1
Zhangiz-Tobe 119 Q 6
Zhangjiakou 132 F 2
Zhangling 131 M 5
Zhangping 133 G 5
Zhangpu 133 G 6
Zhangwu 133 H 2
Zhangye 132 D 3
Zhangzhou 133 G 6
Zhangzi 132 F 3
Zhanhua 133 G 3
Zhanjiang 132 F 6
Zhanteketsi 119 Q 6
Zhao'an 132 G 6
Zhaodong 133 J 1
Zhaojue 132 D 5
Zhaoping 132 F 6
Zhaoqing 132 F 6
Zhaosu 129 L 2
Zhaotong 132 D 5
Zhaoyuan 133 J 1
Zhaozhou 133 J 1
Zhari Namco 134 E 1
Zharkamys 128 F 1
Zharkova 119 R 4
Zharlykamys 119 P 6
Zharma 119 Q 6
Zharyk 119 O 6
Zhashkov 118 F 6
Zhatay 131 N 3
Zhaxi Co 134 D 1
Zhaxizê 132 C 4
Zhayma 130 F 5
Zhdanov 117 E 1
Zhecheng 132 G 4
Zhejiang 133 G 5
Zhelaniya, Cape 184
Zhel'dyadyr 129 H 1
Zhelenogorsk-Ilimskiy 130 H 4
Zhelezinka 119 P 5
Zheleznodorozhnyy 118 K 3
Zheleznodorozhnyy 130 H 4
Zheleznodorozhnyy 119 M 2
Zheleznogorsk 118 F 5
Zhen'an 132 E 4
Zhengding 133 G 3
Zhenghe 133 G 5
Zhenglan 133 G 2
Zhengning 132 E 3
Zhengxiangbai 132 F 2
Zhengyang 132 F 4
Zhengzhou 132 F 4
Zhenjiang 133 G 4
Zhenkang 132 C 6
Zhenlai 133 H 1
Zhenning 132 E 5
Zhenxiong 132 D 5
Zhenyuan 132 F 3
Zhenyuan 132 D 6
Zherdevka 118 H 5

Zherebtsovo 131 P 5
Zheshart 118 J 3
Zhetybay 128 E 2
Zhicheng 132 F 4
Zhidan 132 E 3
Zhidoi 132 C 4
Zhigalovo 130 J 5
Zhigansk 131 M 2
Zhigulevsk 118 J 5
Zhijiang 132 E 5
Zhitkovichi 113 J 5
Zhitomir 113 J 5
Zhlatyr 119 P 5
Zhmerinka 118 E 6
Zhob 128 H 4
Zhodino 113 J 5
Zholymbet 119 O 5
Zhongba 134 D 2
Zhongdian 132 C 5
Zhongning 132 E 3
Zhongshan 132 F 6
Zhongwei 132 E 3
Zhongxiang 132 F 4
Zhongye Islands 136 D 1
Zhongye Qundao 136 D 1
Zhosaly 119 P 5
Zhoukouzhen 132 F 4
Zhou Shan Qundao 133 H 4
Zhovnino 118 F 6
Zhovtnevoye 116 D 1
Zhovten 116 D 1
Zhuanghe 133 H 3
Zhuanglang 133 J 1
Zhuantobe 129 H 2
Zhubgyügoin 132 C 4
Zhucheng 133 G 3
Zhugqu 132 D 4
Zhuhai 132 F 6
Zhujiang Kou 132 F 6
Zhukovka 118 F 5
Zhumadian 132 G 2
Zhuolu 132 G 2
Zhuo Xian 133 G 3
Zhuozi 132 F 2
Zhupanovo 131 U 5
Zhupanovskiy 131 T 5
Zhuravlevka 119 NO 5,6
Zhurban 131 N 5
Zhushan 132 F 4
Zhuya 130 L 4
Zhuzagashkiy 119 P 6
Zhuzhou 132 F 5
Ziama Mansuria 115 E 4
Ziarat 129 H 4
Zibā 154 F 3
Zibo 133 G 3
Zicavo 115 E 3
Zichang 132 E 3
Ziel, Mount 142 E 3
Zielona Góra 111 G 4
Zigaing 135 F 2
Zighan, Wāhāt 153 K 3
Zighout Youssef 115 E 4
Zigong 132 D 5
Zigos Métsevon 116 B 3
Ziguey 157 H 3
Zigui 132 F 4
Ziguinchor 156 A 3
Zihuatanejo 172 B 4
Zilair 119 L 5
Zile 117 E 2
Žilina 111 G 5
Zima 130 H 5
Zimatlán de Alvarez 172 C 4
Zimba 160 D 3
Zimbabwe 160–161 DE 3
Zimi 156 B 4
Zimla 152 E 4
Zimnicea 116 C 2
Zimovniki 117 F 1
Zina 157 G 3
Zinave National Park 161 E 4
Zincirli 117 E 3
Zinder 157 F 3
Zinga (Tanzania) 159 F 6
Zinga (Centr. Afr. Rep.) 158 B 4
Zipaquirá 178 D 2
Ziqudukou 132 C 4
Ziri 152 C 4
Žirje 115 G 3
Ziro 135 F 2
Zistonis, Limni 116 C 2
Zittau 111 F 4

Zitunda 161 E 5
Ziwa Magharibi 158 E 5
Ziyanchurino 118 L 5
Ziyang 132 E 4
Ziyang 132 D 4
Ziz 152 E 2
Zizhong 132 D 5
Zlatarsko Jezero 116 A 2
Zlatijata 116 B 2
Zlatoust 119 L 4
Zlatoustovsk 131 O 5
Žlītan 153 H 2
Złotów 111 G 4
Zlynka 116 D 1
Zmeinogorsk 119 Q 5
Znamenka 119 P 5
Znamenka 130 H 5
Znamenka 118 F 5
Znamenka 117 D 1
Znamenskoye 119 O 4
Żnin 111 G 4
Znojmo 111 G 5
Zóbuè 161 E 3
Zoekmekaar 160 D 4
Zoetélé 157 G 5
Zogang 132 C 5
Zogqên 132 C 4
Zohreh 128 E 4
Zoigê 132 D 4
Zolochev 113 H 6
Zolotaya Gora 131 N 5
Zolotinka 131 M 4
Zolotogorskaya 131 U 3
Zolotogorskiy 119 R 5
Zomba 161 F 3
Zongo 158 B 4
Zonguldak 117 D 2
Zoo Baba 157 G 2
Zorritos 178 B 4
Zorzor 156 C 4
Zouar 157 H 1
Zouerate 152 C 4
Zoulabot 157 G 5
Zouping 133 G 3
Zrenjanin 116 B 1
Zruč 111 G 5
Zuara 153 H 2
Zubayr 155 G 5
Zubets, Gora 131 X 3
Zubova-Polyana 118 H 5
Zudanez 180 D 4
Zuénoula 156 C 4
Zuera 114 C 3
Ẓufār 155 J 5
Zug 115 E 2
Zug 152 C 4
Zugdidi 117 F 2
Zugspitze 115 F 2
Zújar 114 B 4
Zula 159 F 1
Zumba 178 C 4
Zumbo 161 E 3
Zungeru 157 F 4
Zunyi 132 E 5
Zuo Jiang 132 E 6
Zuoquan 132 F 3
Zuoyun 132 F 2
Županja 115 G 2
Zurbāṭīyah 155 H 2
Zürich 115 E 2
Zürichsee 115 E 2
Zurmat 129 H 4
Zuru 157 F 3
Zurmi 157 F 3
Zuwārah 153 H 2
Zuwaylah 153 J 3
Zuwe 160 C 4
Zuyevka 118 K 4
Zvezdnyy 184
Zvishavane 160 DE 4
Zvolen 111 G 5
Zvoron, Ozero 131 P 5
Zwai, Lake 159 F 3
Zwettl in Niederösterreich 115 G 2
Zwickau 111 F 4
Zwolle 110 E 4
Zyrardów 111 H 4
Zyryanka 131 S 2
Zyryanovo 119 R 3
Zyryanovsk 119 Q 6
Zyryanskoye 119 R 4
Żywiec 111 G 5

KEY

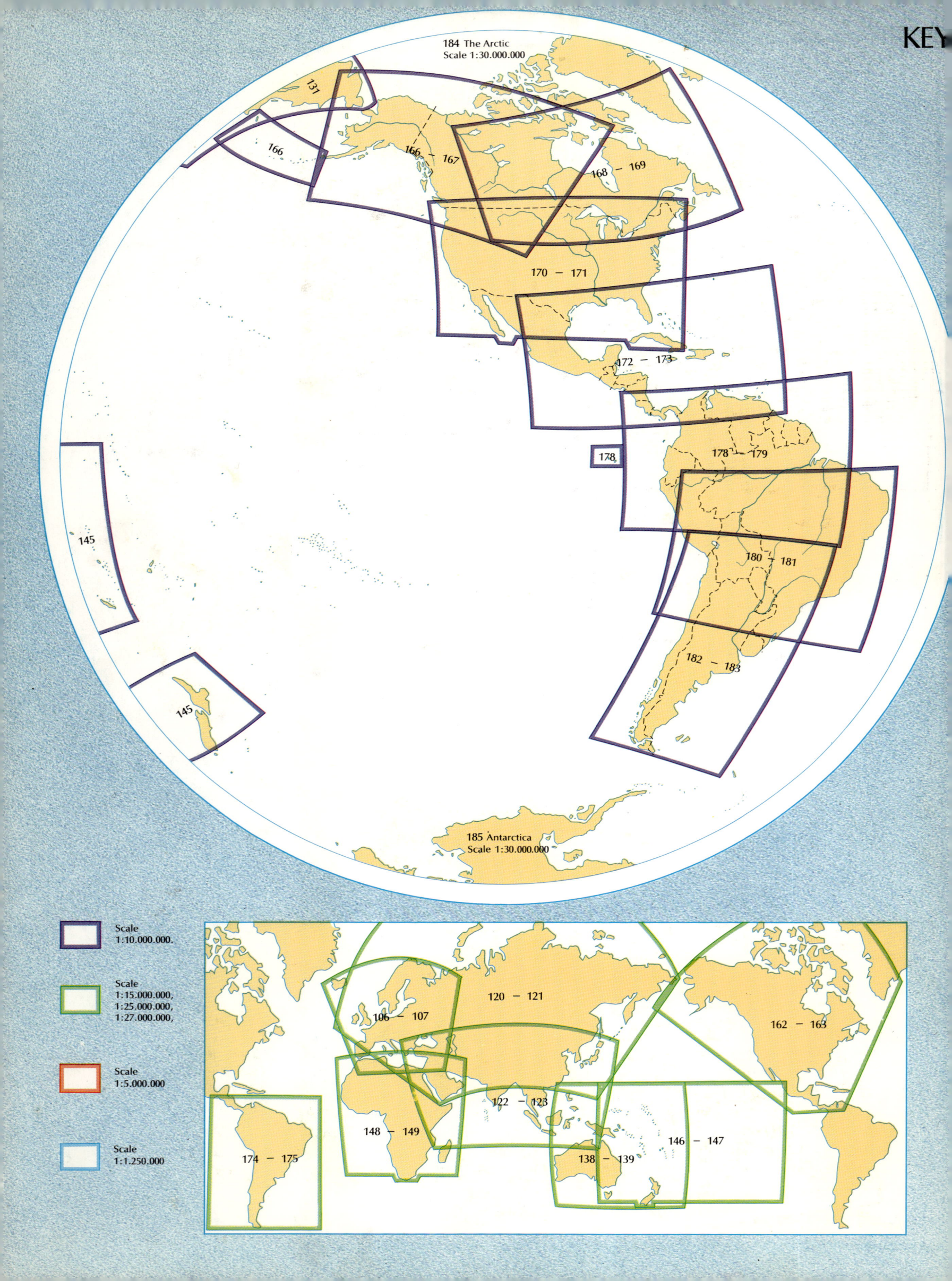

184 The Arctic
Scale 1:30.000.000

131
166
166 167
168 – 169
170 – 171
172 – 173
178
178 – 179
180 – 181
182 – 183
145
145

185 Antarctica
Scale 1:30.000.000

Scale 1:10.000.000

Scale 1:15.000.000, 1:25.000.000, 1:27.000.000,

Scale 1:5.000.000

Scale 1:1.250.000

106 – 107
120 – 121
162 – 163
122 – 123
148 – 149
146 – 147
174 – 175
138 – 139